One golf legend.
One missing sand wedge.
One nervous caddy.

One rush delivery to the 18th fairway.

It's every caddy's worst nightmare: a missing club. Happily, Gary Player's caddy, citizen of the wired world, knew just where to go – the mySAP.com™ Marketplace. With a few clicks he connected three different companies – garyplayer.com, which designs the wedge; the foundry that would custom-build it; and the overnight service that would deliver it – thus saving both Gary's par and his own reputation.

What is mySAP.com? It's a new way for lots of companies, in all their roles – as buyers, sellers, employers, and business partners – to work together as one.

Want to know how your business can get in the game? Visit www.sap.com/mysap and we'll show you.

my**SAP**.com®

you can. it does.™

Five empty seats.
Twenty-five anxious passengers.
One woman with a laptop.

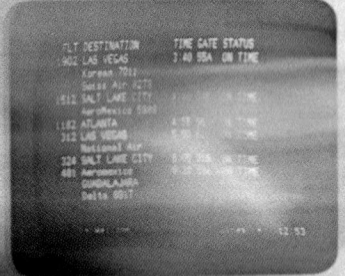

DEPARTURES

Make that four empty seats.

Sara Berg had a problem: a cancelled flight, a strange city, and a strong desire to sleep in her own bed. So she logged on to mySAP.com™. With a few clicks, she went right to a travel booking system and grabbed a seat on the next flight out. And with those same few clicks, her expense report and travel plans were also updated. Instantly. Easily. Automatically.

What is mySAP.com? It's a new way to use the Internet to run your business more intelligently. A way for lots of companies – together with their employees, customers, suppliers, and partners – to work as if they were one extremely well-run company.

Want to find out how every person in your organization can be more powerful? Visit www.sap.com/mysap and we'll show you how.

you can. it does™

Proud Sponsor of Jesper Parnevik.

A Better Return On Information.^{SM}

PRESENTS

The World of Professional Golf
Mark H. McCormack
2000

An IMG PUBLISHING Book

An IMG PUBLISHING Book

All rights reserved
First published 2000
© IMG Operations, Inc. 2000

Designed and produced by Davis Design

ISBN 1-878843-28-1

Printed and bound in the United States of America.

Contents

1. The Year in Retrospect

Greatness in golf is usually measured in major championships and Tiger Woods won one in 1999, the PGA Championship. Two or more major titles in one year have been won by many, including Mark O'Meara just one year ago, but for sheer numbers Woods had a year like none in 50 years or more.

• His 11 worldwide victories was a total not reached since the primes of Byron Nelson, Ben Hogan and Sam Snead in 1945-50.
• His 21 victories by age 23 exceeded the start of Horton Smith, who had 15 career victories in 1931 at age 23. Smith had 10 victories in his first three years as a professional, including eight in 1929.
• He was the first to have eight PGA Tour victories in one year since Johnny Miller in 1974. His total has been exceeded only five times.
• He won his last four PGA Tour events of the year. There have been only two longer winning streaks, Nelson's 11 consecutive victories in 1945 and Hogan's six consecutive in 1948.
• His PGA Tour earnings of $6,616,585 were more than double the previous record. He won an amazing 52 percent of the prize money he could have won. He finished $2,974,679 ahead of runner-up David Duval, with 81.7 percent more than Duval, the highest margin since Nelson in 1945 (87.2 percent) and Hogan in 1946 (85 percent).
• He led the World Money List with $7,681,625, more than double the previous record and more than double Duval's second-place total.
• He achieved the highest points average (20.61) in the history of the Official World Golf Ranking and had the largest margin ever over his closest challenger (7.46 points), leading Duval by that amount on November 7. His 750 points earned were also a record.
• He was chosen as The Associated Press Male Athlete of the Year for the second time in three years and was the seventh man — and second golfer — to win the award twice, following Nelson, Don Budge, Sandy Koufax, Carl Lewis, Joe Montana and Michael Jordan, who won three times.
• His two professional major championships, the other of course being the 1997 Masters Tournament, and his three U.S. Amateur titles brought his total to five major championships, the same total as Jack Nicklaus had at his age. Nicklaus had three professional major victories and two U.S. Amateur titles.

The biggest story of the year, however, was one of the most tragic incidents in the history of golf — a moment when the world watched in helpless horror as a runaway airplane streaked across the skies of the midwestern United States before crashing in a South Dakota field. Five people were killed on Monday, October 25th in an accident the National Transportation Safety Board attributed to "cabin depressurization," the loss of pressure and oxygen as the Learjet 35 ascended. One of the casualties was 1999 U.S. Open champion Payne Stewart.

Stewart had chartered the airplane to travel from his home in Orlando to Dallas, where he was to meet with a land developer about a golf course design project. From there he would proceed to Houston for the Tour Championship, which was to begin on Thursday. On board with Stewart were his agents, Robert Fraley and Van Arden, and Bruce Borland, a golf course architect.

It was a cruel twist of fate that Stewart was making the flight because of his success this year. After only winning once in seven years, and having a second-place finish in the 1998 U.S. Open, Stewart came into 1999 with a strong game and an even stronger resolve. He picked up an early victory at the AT&T Pebble Beach National Pro-Am. It was clear that Stewart was a harder-working competitor who wanted to win more than once after a slump that in 1994 plummeted him to 123rd on the money list. One of his goals was to make the Ryder Cup team.

Then came Pinehurst and one of the most exciting and memorable U.S. Opens. Just as he had in 1998, Stewart led after 54 holes, but Phil Mickelson had a realistic shot at winning, as did Woods and Duval. It had been a decade since Stewart won his first major title, the 1989 PGA Championship at Kemper Lakes, and seven years since he had won more than once in a single year. Stewart's only victory between his 1991 U.S. Open win and his Pebble Beach triumph was the 1995 Shell Houston Open.

Something was different about the Stewart who strolled to the tee on that misty Sunday in the sandhills of eastern North Carolina. When he holed putts at the 16th and 17th holes to gain a one-stroke advantage, the atmosphere was electric. Stewart hadn't blown a three-shot lead as he had done in 1998; he hadn't whined about driving into sand-filled divots, even though he found more than his fair share, and he hadn't missed the crucial putts as he had done in years past.

Clad in navy blue knickers with a matching cap and rain vest, a red-and-blue striped shirt and white socks, Stewart came down the 18th fairway needing one more putt to clinch the title. He stood over the 15-foot par putt, forcing himself to go through his normal routine. He knew the putt was on the left edge, because he had putted it several times through the week, but it looked as if the putt would break more. He had to trust his judgment.

Church bells had been ringing in the background when Stewart walked off the 18th tee, and he felt a sense of fate as he played the hole. Since having become a devout Christian, Stewart had worn a bracelet given to him by his son Aaron that read W.W.J.D. (an acronym for What Would Jesus Do?). People had seen a change in Stewart. He had gone from being a brash, often smug and egocentric player to a man who always found a kind word, and who lit up the locker room with his smile and his Ozarks accent, always a little louder than everyone else.

When Stewart stroked the putt he focused on keeping his head still. Then he looked up and saw that the ball was on the line he wanted, rolling at the speed he wanted. Two inches away, he knew it was in. Stewart thrust his fist forward as the ball fell into the cup and let out a scream.

For many reasons that putt on the 72nd hole at Pinehurst is my choice as the SAP Shot of the Year. Like Mark O'Meara's 18-footer for birdie on the 18th at Augusta to win his first major championship in 1998, Stewart's 15-footer at Pinehurst was the one shot that everyone will remember from the major championships of 1999. It wasn't the longest putt he made that week. It wasn't even the hardest putt he had made on the final nine — that was his par save at the 16th — but it was certainly the defining shot of Stewart's career.

Four months later, Stewart's Learjet took off for Dallas and flew 1,600 miles on autopilot. Neither the pilot, Captain Michael Kling, nor the co-pilot, Stephanie Bellegarrigue, issued a distress call. The last communication was when controllers at the Jacksonville Air Traffic Control Center cleared the aircraft out of an initial height of 17,500 feet to its approved cruising altitude of 39,000 feet. When the airplane continued to climb above 39,000 feet and failed to turn west, controllers tried to raise the pilots with no success.

Joe Hembrite, a manager at the Atlanta Air Traffic Control Center who had come down from his office to the sector control room to work a few hours in order to keep his rating current, tracked the airplane past Gainesville, Florida, and over the Georgia-Alabama border. He contacted the Air Force and two F-15s from Eglan Air Force Base in Destin, Florida, were scrambled to make visual contact. Captain Chris Hamilton of the 46th Test Wing was the first to see the aircraft, and what he saw sent chills down his spine.

"There was ice on the cockpit windshield and the windows in the cabin were frosted over," Hamilton said. "It was a really helpless feeling to know there was nothing you could do for the people onboard."

Controllers knew at once that the crew and all passengers were dead. At 48,000 feet, the altitude the airplane climbed to as it passed near Stewart's hometown of Springfield, Missouri, there is no breathable oxygen, and even if there were, the temperature ranged from 50 to 60 degrees below zero.

The image that remained indelible — the one shown hundreds of times on television networks after Stewart's death — was of the putt on the 72nd hole of the U.S. Open. That the tragedy was covered by the 24-hour news channels and was the lead story in every newscast and on the front pages of newspapers around the world spoke volumes for Stewart's popularity, and it also was an indication of how popular golf had become by the autumn of 1999.

In September golfers and non-golfers were brought together around their televisions. The Ryder Cup at The Country Club in Brookline, Massachusetts, was one of the most thrilling golf events ever. Those who saw the matches were captivated, as were those who participated. "It was the greatest golf event of my life," Hal Sutton said. "I can't recall anything like it."

The United States team came in as favorites, but they had also been favorites in 1995 at Oak Hill and in 1997 at Valderrama. The Americans lost both. Everyone knew that on any given week, in a match-play format, Europe's best could win again.

The Europeans opened a four-point lead and held the margin with only the singles matches remaining. As Europe led 10-6, the grumbling that had permeated this Ryder Cup for months spilled over. An online poll showed that almost 60 percent of Americans watching the matches were pulling for the Europeans. It wasn't just the missed putts and lost opportunities that caused so many fans to change their allegiances. It was a festering controversy that turned many Americans away from their countrymen.

No one knows who coined it "Pay for Play," but the alliteration stuck and became part of the golf vernacular in the summer. It stemmed from comments made by Mark O'Meara after the Valderrama matches. He suggested that players should be compensated for participating in the Ryder Cup. When *Golf World* magazine reported that the PGA of America would gross $63 million at Brookline, commentary resumed on how those funds should be disbursed, with Duval, Woods and Mickelson joining O'Meara in saying players should be entitled to earmark some of the money for charities of their choice.

"No matter which side you come down on, we should all be ashamed of ourselves for bringing this up now," Tom Lehman said of the controversy at the PGA Championship. In a closed-door meeting, players and PGA of America officials voiced their opinions. It became public when U.S. captain Ben Crenshaw said of his team members, "It burns the hell out of me to hear some of their views."

It seemed that most Americans agreed with Crenshaw, even though the players involved simply wanted a say in how the PGA of America spent the money earned off the players' efforts. Duval thought the proceeds could help build soccer fields for children in Jacksonville, Florida, while Woods said he thought the players should be given money for other charities in their communities. Those opinions were lost in a cry of greed from the public. The Ryder Cup players were accused of being unpatriotic, selfish, spoiled and ungrateful. It carried over to the matches, where some in the gallery heckled the players.

When the United States team fell behind, there was an emotional Saturday night meeting, and the embattled team members bonded and shared their feelings. Sutton took the lead, saying, "There isn't a single person on the fifth floor," where the Europeans were housed in the Four Seasons Hotel, "who can beat a single person on the sixth floor," where the Americans stayed. Everyone who attended that meeting believed the Americans were going to win, even if the media and public did not.

The United States did win in the biggest comeback in Ryder Cup history. Justin Leonard made the winning putt, a 45-foot bomb on the 17th green that sealed the victory. When the putt went in, U.S. players, their wives and caddies stormed the green, hoisting Leonard amidst a cacophony of cheers. The celebration was premature. Leonard's opponent, Jose Maria Olazabal, still had a 25-foot putt to tie the hole. Olazabal had to compose himself and try to make the 25-footer. His ball scooted past the hole.

Had it not been for the tragedy that later befell Stewart and the significance his untimely death placed on his U.S. Open victory, Leonard's putt would have been my choice for Shot of the Year. It was a putt for the ages, and even though Leonard lost the 18th hole and halved his match with Olazabal, the putt at the 17th will long be remembered.

The high of the Ryder Cup drama and the low of the Stewart tragedy were two of the three most significant stories of the year. The third rested on the shoulders of the 1999 Player of the Year. Only 23 years old and in his third full year as a professional, Woods had become one of the most celebrated athletes on the planet. But Woods' potential was not realized as quickly as many would have liked, and some suggested that Woods wasn't close to being the dominant force many anticipated when he burst on the scene late in 1996.

Even though he retained his spot atop the World Ranking when the year began, Woods had only one PGA Tour victory in 1998 (BellSouth Classic) and three wins overall (Johnnie Walker Classic and PGA Grand Slam), leading some to speculate that Woods was in a slump. As he acknowledged, Woods spent a portion of 1997 and all of 1998 retooling his swing with the help of coach Butch Harmon in order to develop a game that would last longer and hold better under pressure. "I'm hitting the ball better now," Woods said through the early stages of 1999. Why wasn't Tiger winning if his swing was better? Woods heard the criticism, but ignored it. He knew he and Harmon were on the right track.

After his 1997 Masters victory, Woods and Harmon watched a video of the tournament. "My timing was perfect that week," Woods said, "but I couldn't believe what I saw. I knew I had to make some changes." Woods felt he needed to shallow his swing plane in order to develop a more consistent path through impact. The change wouldn't make him any longer but, as one of the longest hitters in golf, Woods didn't need extra length. It would improve his misses, cutting down on the shot dispersion and providing more distance control with his irons. Woods also began lifting weights, stretching and working on cardiovascular exercises to increase muscle mass and stamina without hindering his flexibility. He added 15 pounds of muscle and his conditioning improved tremendously.

Like most changes in golf, the process was slow, but because of Woods' ability and work ethic he remained competitive and he kept his position as No. 1 on the World Ranking. He had the best 1998 major championship record of any player who did not win, and he qualified for and won the PGA Grand Slam since Mark O'Meara won two majors, opening the fourth spot in the match-play competition. Woods also topped the World Money List with just over $2.9 million, edging out Duval even though Duval won four times on the PGA Tour.

Duval's win in the season-opening Mercedes Championships had many questioning how Woods could maintain his position as the No. 1 player in the world when Duval kept winning tournaments. It was Duval's eighth win in 27 starts. That argument intensified two weeks later when Duval shot a final-round, record-equaling 59 at the Bob Hope Chrysler Classic and came from seven strokes behind to win. How, the critics cried, could Duval not be the best player in the world?

Even when Woods answered with a victory at the Buick Invitational, the sentiment was in Duval's favor. "Ain't a doubt who's the best player," Steve Pate said, "but there wasn't a doubt even before he put up a 59." Fred Couples said, "There's nobody better out here than David Duval, and there's nobody who handles it better either." Frank Lickliter asked a group of players in the locker room at Torrey Pines, venue of the Buick Invitational, "Is there anyone who doesn't think Duval is the No. 1 player in the world?"

Tony Greer, who maintains the World Ranking, came under fire but defended the system, which evaluates the performance of players over a two-year period. Said Greer, "It's obviously a point of contention that David isn't No. 1, but there are a lot of factors to consider. The fact that he's close, that he is on the verge of No. 1, shows that the system is working. I'm comfortable and confident with the way it is."

Six weeks later, with spectacular play under some of the toughest conditions of the year, Duval ascended to the top spot with a two-stroke victory in The Players Championship. The win and the move to the No. 1 position was made sweeter by the fact that it came at the TPC at Sawgrass, less than a mile from Duval's home, with the fans chanting his name as he walked down the 18th fairway. "He deserves it," Woods said. "To win a big one like this, he deserves to be No. 1 in the world."

The next week, Duval gained his fourth victory of the year in Atlanta, capturing the BellSouth Classic with a final-round 67 and a two-stroke margin over former Georgia Tech teammate Stewart Cink. It was Duval's 11th win in 34 starts, and he became the first player since Johnny Miller in 1974 to win four times before the Masters. After Duval tied for sixth at Augusta, he led the PGA Tour with $2,723,500 while Woods was in fourth place with $1,343,448, less than half of Duval's total.

Seven months later, when Woods won the PGA Grand Slam for his 11th title of the year, the golf world stood in amazement at what Tiger had accomplished.

TIGER WOODS

Event	Position
Mercedes Championships	T-5
Phoenix Open	3
AT&T Pebble Beach National Pro-Am	T-53
Buick Invitational	1
Nissan Open	T-2
WGC Andersen Consulting Match Play	T-5
Bay Hill Invitational	T-56
The Players Championship	T-10
Masters Tournament	T-18
MCI Classic	T-18
GTE Byron Nelson Classic	T-7
Deutsche Bank-SAP Open	1
Memorial Tournament	1
U.S. Open Championship	T-3
Motorola Western Open	1
British Open Championship	T-7
PGA Championship	1
Sprint International	T-37
WGC NEC Invitational	1
National Rental Car Classic	1
Tour Championship	1
WGC American Express Championship	1
Johnnie Walker Classic	6
World Cup	1
PGA Grand Slam	1

It was one of the greatest single-year performances in golf history, even though Woods never really felt comfortable with his swing changes until mid-May. Just before departing his Orlando home for the GTE Byron Nelson Classic, Woods stood on the practice range at Isleworth and felt all the parts of the puzzle come together. He called Harmon in Las Vegas. "I've got it," Woods said without preamble. That was all he needed to say.

The next week, at the Deutsche Bank-SAP Open in Germany, Woods made just three bogeys in 72 holes and beat a strong PGA European Tour field, then returned to America and won the Memorial Tournament. He missed six greens during the final round at Muirfield Village, but saved par five times with a deft touch that even Nicklaus called "unbelievable." A bogey on the 71st hole of the U.S. Open cost him a chance at a victory and he tied for third behind Stewart and Mickelson. He then played the par-five holes at Cog Hill in 12 under par while winning the Motorola Western Open. During that summer stretch, Woods finished first-first-third-first in four starts.

A 74-74 weekend at Carnoustie left Woods four strokes out of the playoff at the British Open, but he returned with a vengeance, winning the PGA Championship in a dramatic final-round duel with 19-year-old Sergio Garcia. While his second major championship was not historic, as was his 1997 Masters win, Woods led the field at Medinah in driving distance and made one of the bravest putts of his career to save par at the 17th hole after the momentum had shifted in Garcia's favor.

Woods didn't play well the next week at the Sprint International as he battled a cold. The week after that at the NEC Invitational, against a strong field of Ryder Cup and Presidents Cup players, Woods won with a performance that drew praise from his fellow professionals. "Just awesome," Nick Price said. Woods led the field in driving distance and greens in regulation that week as well, just as he did in his next start at the National Car Rental Classic, where Ernie Els said, "I was in awe." Woods then traveled to Houston for the Tour Championship, where he shot four rounds in the 60s, led the field in greens in regulation, and won his third consecutive event over a field that included the top 29 money winners for the year.

Then came Valderrama, the final installment of the newly created World Golf Championships, which also included the Andersen Consulting Match Play Championship and the NEC Invitational. Woods' final-round 68 on a day when the wind off the Mediterranean left many players wondering why they had made the trip was, according to Price, "one of the all-time best rounds of golf I've witnessed in my career." Even with a triple bogey on the ghastly par-five 17th hole, Woods closed the week with a six-under-par 278 aggregate, tied local favorite Miguel Angel Jimenez, then defeated the Spaniard on the first playoff hole.

Woods was off to Taiwan after that for the Johnnie Walker Classic, where he slipped to sixth place, then he went on to Malaysia for the World Cup. His closing rounds of 63 and 65 won the individual title by nine strokes and the team honors, with O'Meara, by five strokes. His marathon of six consecutive tournaments, and five victories, ended in Hawaii with match-play wins over Paul Lawrie and Davis Love III for the PGA Grand Slam title.

By the numbers, Woods won the Vardon Trophy with an adjusted scoring average of 69.43, a record low. He led the PGA Tour in greens in regulation with an average of 74.1 percent (up from 67.6 percent in 1998), and he led in birdies per round with a 4.46 average. After being ranked 147th in putting in 1998 with 1.805 putts per hole, Woods finished tied for 24th with 1.761 putts. Compare that statistic with the number of greens hit in regulation and it's easy to see how Woods dominated. His accuracy off the tee improved as well. In 1998 he hit 67.9 percent of the fairways, and in 1999 he hit 71.3 percent, although his driving distance was three yards shorter. Still, with an average length of 293.1 yards off the tee, many of those shots coming with fairway woods and irons, the lost yardage was of little consequence. When Woods did miss a green, he was also better than in previous years, saving par from the sand 56.8 percent of the time, compared to 53 percent in 1998.

"I think Tiger has exhibited some exceptional strength in his golf," Arnold Palmer said, "and there is no question about it: He has the ability to get stronger when he needs to be." Nicklaus was equally impressed. "The competition was great and he played great," he said. "Tiger's year stands on its own. He played great in all the significant tournaments. He won four in a row, and nobody's done that in 46 years. That's pretty good. I never did it."

Miller, the last to win eight PGA Tour events in a season, said, "I think it's getting to a point where he's scaring the field, which is where Nicklaus was, where Palmer was, where Watson was. Tiger is moving into that realm. Before, everybody knew his potential was phenomenal. Now they're saying he's unbelievable. You're not supposed to say that when you're competing against somebody. You can think it. But you don't say it — even if it's true."

In Tiger's case it certainly seemed true. For three years, every time he led or shared the lead after 54 holes, he won. In 1999 he came from behind to win (WGC American Express Championship), he rallied on weekends (Buick Invitational), he held on while others charged around him (PGA Championship), he beat people he was expected to beat (Mike Weir and Jimenez), and he beat the stars (Price, Els and Vijay Singh).

COLIN MONTGOMERIE

Event	Position
Dubai Desert Classic	T-5
WGC Andersen Consulting Match Play	T-33
Honda Classic	T-38
Bay Hill Invitational	T-60
The Players Championship	T-23
BellSouth Classic	T-61
Masters Tournament	T-11
MCI Classic	T-60
Benson and Hedges International Open	1
Deutsche Bank-SAP Open	T-20
Volvo PGA Championship	1
Compass Group English Open	T-5
U.S. Open Championship	T-15
Murphy's Irish Open	T-7
Standard Life Loch Lomond	1
British Open Championship	T-15
Smurfit European Open	T-15
Volvo Scandinavian Masters	1
PGA Championship	T-6
BMW International Open	1
WGC NEC Invitational	T-30
Victor Chandler British Masters	2
Trophee Lancome	T-3
Linde German Masters	T-9
Cisco World Match Play	1

Volvo Masters	T-16
WGC American Express Championship	T-20
World Cup	T-24
Holden Australian Open Championship	T-4
Nedbank Million Dollar Challenge	2

While all performances paled in comparison to Woods, another benchmark was set that could stand for a very long time. Colin Montgomerie got off to a slow start, struggling with his putter, experimenting with new equipment at the Callaway Golf Test Center in California, and searching for a rhythm that could propel him to the kind of play that had won six consecutive European Order of Merit titles. Not until May did Montgomerie find the swing keys he needed to be on top of his game. After a three-week layoff where he didn't so much as take a club out of his bag, Montgomerie went on one of the best streaks of his career.

It started at the Benson and Hedges International Open where, if Montgomerie had made half the 15-footers he had for birdies, the result would have been a rout. "While I know that someone who hits as many greens as I do cannot possibly hole as many putts as someone who is chipping a lot, I still feel my putting could be better," Montgomerie said.

Montgomerie held a one-stroke lead after three rounds, but was still the last person on the putting green that Saturday, a sign of the level of determination that would pay off as the year progressed. "It looks like we are just average workers and he's the one who is gifted," Jose Maria Olazabal said. "He doesn't practice much — he doesn't need much practice — and he keeps hitting the ball straight down the fairway and straight onto the green and scoring well. What can you say?"

You could say "Congratulations," which is what Olazabal told Montgomerie that week, and again two weeks later when Montgomerie won the Volvo PGA Championship. He then ventured back to America for the U.S. Open where he finished in a tie for 15th.

The disappointment was mitigated a few miles from his boyhood home in Scotland when Montgomerie captured the Standard Life Loch Lomond for his third European win of the year, moving him well into the lead in the Order of Merit standings a week before the British Open at Carnoustie, a course where Montgomerie held the course record. Opening rounds of 74 and 76 dropped him far down the list, and he finished tied for 15th again.

Following the British Open, Montgomerie's closest challenger for Order of Merit honors, Lee Westwood, won the TNT Dutch Open and the Smurfit European Open in consecutive weeks, moving him close to Montgomerie's lead. A month later Montgomerie hoisted another trophy at the Volvo Scandinavian Masters, and two weeks after that he got his fifth victory at the BMW International Open. The two August wins bracketed another major championship defeat. Montgomerie tied for sixth in the PGA Championship.

His seventh Order of Merit title appeared in jeopardy when Westwood captured the Canon European Masters and Sergio Garcia won his second European title at the Linde German Masters. Because Garcia had finished second to Woods in the PGA Championship (and the prize money counted on the PGA European Tour), both Garcia and Westwood still had a chance of catching Montgomerie.

For that to happen, Westwood or Garcia would have to win the WGC American Express Championship. With its $1 million first prize — a disproportionately large winner's check by European standards — the event in Spain was crucial.

"This is the seventh year in a row I've finished the Volvo Masters as No. 1, and I'm proud of that," Montgomerie said before teeing off at Valderrama. "Whatever happens this week, the Order of Merit this year is a very different one than what we've had in the past. Some big purses have been included. It's all come down to one huge, huge purse at the end of the day."

Westwood tied for fourth and Garcia tied for seventh. Both beat Montgomerie, who tied for 20th, but it didn't matter. He ranked as Europe's best player a record seven years in a row. While his record in the majors was a disappointment, his extended dominance in Europe remained unparalleled.

"Now that the last few months are over, I can relate to what Tiger has achieved," Montgomerie said. "It's getting tougher, and the standard behind me is improving all the time. Whether it's going to happen eight times or not, I'll be trying."

With a sixth victory in the Cisco World Match Play Championship and the seventh Order of Merit title, Montgomerie was No. 3 on the World Ranking and fourth on the World Money List with $2,988,543.

DAVID DUVAL

Event	Position
Mercedes Championships	1
Bob Hope Chrysler Classic	1
Phoenix Open	T-18
AT&T Pebble Beach National Pro-Am	T-15
Nissan Open	T-5
WGC Andersen Consulting Match Play	T-17
The Players Championship	1
BellSouth Classic	1
Masters Tournament	T-6
Shell Houston Open	T-64
Compaq Classic of New Orleans	MC
Memorial Tournament	T-3
U.S. Open Championship	T-7
Buick Classic	T-10
British Open Championship	T-62
Canon Greater Hartford Open	T-11
PGA Championship	T-10
Sprint International	2
Ganter Cup Challenge	4
WGC NEC Invitational	T-27
Michelob Championship	T-8
Tour Championship	T-15
Franklin Templeton Shark Shootout	1

The third most impressive player in 1999 had to be shaking his head and wondering what he needed to do to be first. For the second year in a row,

Duval had a record that under most circumstances would have earned year-end awards. In 1998 Duval won four times, finished second in the Masters, and won the Vardon Trophy with the lowest stroke average. Unfortunately for him, O'Meara won two major championships and, as Jim Furyk said, "You win two majors, you're the Player of the Year, period."

Undaunted, Duval went back to work in 1999, putting up the first-quarter numbers that had many observers writing off the rest of the year. Duval would be Player of the Year, No. 1 in the world, and probably break numerous scoring records. He already had shot 59 in the final round to win a PGA Tour event, the first time that had ever been done. "He knocked down flagsticks all day," Bob Tway, who played with Duval in the Bob Hope Chrysler Classic, said of the momentous effort. "I shot 72, which isn't great, but it is par, and he beat me by 13 shots! What is that?"

Commissioner Tim Finchem joked that he wished Duval would go away and leave some money for the other players. "I offered to write David a $3 million check right now if he'll just go home for the rest of the year," Finchem said. Duval responded, "If he raises it to $4 million we can talk."

"Not to take anything away from Tiger Woods, but if Duval is the No. 2 player in the World Ranking, something's wrong," Jeff Sluman said. "What we need is take up a collection and send David on a nice ski trip, a nice long ski trip. Like about six months."

All this after Duval had won two events. He still had two more victories in two months ahead of him. After he won The Players Championship and the BellSouth Classic in consecutive weeks, almost everyone wrote the year off as Duval's. Except, of course, Tiger Woods.

Butch Harmon would only speculate on the impact Duval's play had on Woods. "Do I think Duval playing so well the last 18 months pumps Tiger up?" he asked. "You bet I do. You know he's not publicly going to say that, but you know that's the case."

Sports psychologist Dr. Richard Coop said, "The greatest golfers — in fact, all the greatest athletes — have always had someone pushing them and someone right ahead of them to look to, to see what could be possible. Duval went and got Tiger, and now Tiger's got to get Duval. It doesn't have to be a head-to-head thing. The standard of excellence has been set."

Woods never named Duval as a motivating force behind his record-setting year, but others believed they played off of each other's successes. Said Love, "I told both of them it was going to be a lot of fun trying to keep up."

While Duval failed to keep up after the first of April, his World Money List total for the year was $3,840,406. He made a final-round run for the U.S. Open title that was spoiled by a misplaced approach shot to the ninth green that found a bunker and resulted in a double bogey and a tie for seventh place, and he finished second at the Sprint International one week after the PGA Championship. While it was a disappointing close to a season that showed so much promise early on, Duval wasn't distressed. He had eight top-10 finishes in addition to his four victories. That meant Duval finished 10th or higher in 59 percent of the PGA Tour events he entered.

In September, Duval was instrumental in the comeback by the Ryder Cup team. He went up against hot-handed Jesper Parnevik in the singles. Parnevik had been one of Europe's stalwarts through the week, playing in all four matches on Friday and Saturday, winning 3½ points along with partner Garcia. In three matches Duval was 0-2-1. Like the rest of his team, Duval was embarrassed, but not without hope.

When Duval stood on the tee at the par-five 14th hole, he held a 4-up lead on Parnevik. After hitting his second shot in the right bunker, Duval blasted out to six feet. When the putt went in for birdie, Duval closed out Parnevik 5 and 4 and the celebration began. With an overhand fist-pump that was out of character, Duval jumped around the 14th green, inciting the crowd to cheer louder and longer, even placing his hand to his ear in an "I can't hear you" taunt.

He called the Ryder Cup, "the most exciting golf experience of my life."

SERGIO GARCIA

Event	Position
Peugeot Open de Espana	T-25
GTE Byron Nelson Classic	T-3
Deutsche Bank-SAP Open	T-20
Volvo PGA Championship	T-19
Memorial Tournament	T-11
Murphy's Irish Open	1
Standard Life Loch Lomond	T-2
British Open Championship	MC
Smurfit European Open	T-49
Buick Open	MC
PGA Championship	2
Sprint International	T-13
WGC NEC Invitational	T-7
Linde German Masters	1
Alfred Dunhill Cup	1
Cisco World Match Play	T-9
Volvo Masters	T-5
WGC American Express Championship	T-7
Sumitomo Visa Taiheiyo Masters	T-55
Dunlop Phoenix Tournament	2
Nedbank Million Dollar Challenge	9

One shot in the final major championship of the year typified the rise of the second young and dynamic star to burst on the golf scene in three years. When the 19-year-old Garcia announced his intention to turn professional after finishing as low amateur in the Masters, many wondered if it was too soon for the Spaniard they called "El Niño." When he won his first professional tournament at the Murphy's Irish Open, those questions were answered. When he closed his eyes and swung a six iron at the base of a tree at the PGA Championship while making a run at Woods' lead, Garcia's stature was secure.

Garcia had made birdie at the par-three 13th hole to pull to within three of Woods, and when Woods made double bogey on the same hole, the lead had dwindled to one. A bogey at the 14th dropped Garcia two behind when he stood on the 16th tee and hit a shot that drifted through the fairway and beneath one of the stately hardwoods surrounding Medinah. His view to the green was obstructed, the tree was precariously close, and the ball had nestled between two roots making any shot questionable.

"Nine out of 10 players on the PGA Tour chip it back to the fairway," Garcia's caddie, Jerry Higginbotham, said. "Nine out of 10 guys don't even think about hitting that shot."

Garcia hadn't been around long enough to know that, and being two shots down with three holes to play, he never considered anything but a miraculous shot around the tree. "I just closed my eyes and swung, then fell back in case the ball hit the tree," he said. The shot curved 20 yards around the tree and into the green, and Garcia ran down the fairway and leapt into the air to see the result. Even though he made pars on the 16th, 17th and 18th holes and lost by one, Garcia became a rising star that afternoon with a charm that reminded golf fans of a young Seve Ballesteros.

His good play continued for the remainder of the year, including another victory at the Linde German Masters. Garcia also captained the victorious Spanish team that included Olazabal and Jimenez in the Alfred Dunhill Cup at St. Andrews. In total, Garcia played in 20 tournaments as a professional in his rookie year (not counting the Alfred Dunhill Cup and the Ryder Cup where he finished with a 3-1-1 record). In those 20 starts, he picked up two victories, three seconds, a third and a fifth, earning a worldwide total of $2,277,314. That was enough for a seventh-place finish on the World Money List.

There were plenty of other outstanding performances in 1999. Els won three times, twice in South Africa at the Alfred Dunhill South African PGA Championship and the Nedbank Million Dollar Challenge, and once in America at the Nissan Open. He finished third on the World Money List behind Woods and Duval with $3,284,079, and ranked No. 5 in the world.

Then there was Love, who was fourth on the World Ranking and who managed to claim third place on the U.S. money list and fifth on the World Money List with $2,756,578 without a victory. Second-place finishes (or ties for second) at the Sony Open in Hawaii, Nissan Open, Masters Tournament and Tour Championship did wonders for Love's bank account, but he was disappointed about not winning. "I'm not content," he said.

Love was credited with hitting one of the most memorable shots of the year. On the par-three 16th at Augusta National, Love was trying to catch eventual winner Olazabal, who led by two strokes. A couple of birdies in the closing holes would apply the pressure and perhaps give Love his first Masters title. His tee shot on the 16th flew long and left, stopping over the green and leaving Love a seemingly impossible chip.

After examining his options, Love played the chip shot away from the hole, skipping it up the ridgeline in the middle of the green. The ball hopped forward, then stopped on top of the hill before slowly rolling back toward the hole. The crowd noise began to grow as the ball came closer and closer. When the ball fell into the left edge of the hole, the crowd erupted and Love sprang forward with his fists in the air.

Had Love gone on to win, his shot would probably have topped the list for 1999. As it was, Olazabal also birdied the 16th, hitting a six iron to three feet, then punch-hooked a five iron onto the 17th green and two-putted for par to secure a two-stroke victory and his second green jacket. Olazabal's performance, after a pinched nerve in his lower back was misdiagnosed as arthritis and had virtually crippled the Spaniard for 18 months, not only earned his second major championship, but also won the Ben Hogan Award for players who have overcome physical adversity to return to the game.

The most impressive full shot by a major championship winner (excluding Stewart's putt) was the four iron to the 18th green at Carnoustie by Paul Lawrie. Holding a one-shot lead in the British Open playoff with Jean Van de Velde and Justin Leonard, Lawrie drove the ball safely into the 18th fairway, then chose to go for the green with his second rather than lay up before the dreaded Barry Burn that guarded the green.

At the time, analyst Curtis Strange questioned Lawrie's choice, but seconds later the point was moot. Lawrie launched the four iron to within three feet. His birdie gave him a three-shot margin in the four-hole playoff. It concluded a fantastic day for Lawrie, whose 67 in regulation play and two birdies in the playoff enabled him to come from 10 strokes behind to win, a record comeback for the championship.

If Lawrie's shot was less celebrated than the others, it was not because of the champion, the playoff format or that Van de Velde and Leonard both bogeyed the final hole. It was because of what Van de Velde had done earlier in the day. Leading by three going to the 72nd hole, Van de Velde shocked everyone by pulling out driver on the 18th tee. An iron to the fairway, an iron to lay up, a pitch onto the green, and he would have had three putts to win. But Van de Velde had trusted his driver all week, and he trusted it on the final hole.

He pushed his tee shot, barely missing the Barry Burn on the right. From there he compounded his mistake by trying to hit a three iron onto the green. The ball bounced off the grandstand and landed in the rough. He chunked his third shot into the Barry Burn, took off his shoes and examined his lie before accepting his fate, taking a penalty drop and hitting his fifth shot into the greenside bunker. From there he made a save for triple bogey and a spot in the playoff, but the damage was done.

Had he handled the situation poorly, Van de Velde could have gone down as the biggest buffoon ever to play major championship golf. The attention he drew to himself and the way in which he handled his collapse shone a new light on Van de Velde. "It is just golf," he said. He earned a great deal of respect.

In addition to Woods, Duval and Stewart, four other players had more than one victory on the U.S. PGA Tour. Two-time winners were Carlos Franco, Notah Begay III, Duffy Waldorf and David Toms. Franco, the international veteran from Paraguay, was chosen Rookie of the Year over Begay, the only Native American on the circuit. Begay and Franco were among nine first-time winners on the PGA Tour, a list that included Mike Weir, who won on home soil in the Air Canada Championship after being a victim twice earlier in victories by Woods. Weir's 266 total, 18 under par, was second only to Duval's 26-under performance on the same total in the Mercedes Championships.

Among other notables, there were victories and over $2 million in earnings each by Vijay Singh, Hal Sutton, Jim Furyk and Jeff Maggert, whose win came in the first World Golf Championships event, the Andersen Consulting Match Play.

Chris Perry had the best year other than Love among the non-winners in America, taking fifth place on the money list. He had 14 top-10 finishes, climbing from No. 92 to No. 23 on the World Ranking and earning $2,234,832 for eighth place on the World Money List.

Others who did not win included Justin Leonard, who still earned over $2 million on the World Money List, and O'Meara, the Player of the Year in 1998 who had only three top-10 finishes while falling from No. 2 to No. 10 on the World Ranking. Also prominent on the list of non-winners were Mickelson, Fred Couples, Tom Lehman and Greg Norman, who was limited to 16 events as he continued to recover from shoulder surgery, although he contended for late-season titles in Australia and Japan. A victory in Japan saved Nick Price from being shut out, and he finished the year above the $2 million mark on the World Money List, one of 17 regular tour players to do so.

On the PGA European Tour, Westwood followed Montgomerie on the Order of Merit, having four victories, and earned $2,167,768 on the World Money List. Garcia, Jimenez and Retief Goosen were also in the top five of the Order of Merit. Jimenez won twice in Europe, as did Jarmo Sandelin, and Goosen had one victory.

The domination of the Japan Tour by Masashi (Jumbo) Ozaki finally ended at age 52, and his successor at the top of the money list was his brother, Naomichi (Joe), who had three victories and $1,414,214 on the World Money List. Rounding out the top five of the Japanese money list were Kazuhiko Hosokawa (two victories), Shigeki Maruyama (one), Toshimitsu Izawa (two) and Tsuyoshi Yoneyama (three). All five were among the top 100 on the World Ranking, not that Jumbo Ozaki disappeared entirely. He had two victories and $714,308 worldwide while falling from No. 13 to No. 36 on the World Ranking, still the highest position by a Japanese player. Korean Kim Jong-duk also won twice in Japan. Thomas Bjorn won the late-season Dunlop Phoenix in addition to one victory in Europe.

Choi Kyung-ju of Korea won twice on the Japan Tour and once on the Asian PGA Davidoff Tour. Fran Quinn, who won once on the Nike Tour in America, came to Asia and won the last two events, including the Omega PGA Championship. Kenny Druce won in Australasia and Asia, and Nico van Rensburg won in South Africa and Asia.

Michael Campbell of New Zealand revived his career in Asia after a skid that began in 1996, winning the Johnnie Walker Classic, a PGA European Tour event played in Taiwan. Jarrod Moseley was the 1998-99 Order of Merit winner in Australasia and won the Heineken Classic. Craig Spence won the Ericsson Masters, Craig Parry won the Ford Open Championship, and two amateurs took all the headlines at the year's end, with Aaron Baddeley winning the Holden Australian Open Championship and Brett Rumford winning the Australasian Players Championship.

Multiple winners were common on the Nike Tour, led by Matt Gogel and his three victories. The two-time winners were Steve Gotsche, Mathew Goggin, Ryan Howison, Carl Paulson, Brad Elder and Bob Heintz. On the Canadian Tour, Kenneth Staton won three times, while Ray Stewart, Arron Oberholser, Ken Duke, Brian Kontak and Scott Petersen won twice each. Europe's Challenge

Tour featured Carl Suneson's three victories and two each by Lucas Parsons and Iain Pyman. David Park won once in addition to winning on the PGA European Tour. Richard Johnson won on the Nike Tour and on the Challenge Tour, while Hennie Otto won twice in South Africa and once on the Challenge Tour. Other two-time winners in Africa were Desvonde Botes and Bobby Lincoln, in addition to Ernie Els' two big victories.

Scott Dunlap won early in the year in South Africa, then twice later in South America. That continent in 2000 will be host to two PGA European Tour events in Brazil and a World Golf Championships event, the EMC World Cup, in Argentina.

In senior golf, rookies Bruce Fleisher and Allen Doyle had 11 victories between them. Fleisher, the 1968 U.S. Amateur champion who only had one PGA Tour win in a 30-year professional career, staved off charges by 1997 and 1998 Player of the Year Hale Irwin, who won five times, to capture the honor for himself with seven wins and $2,629,105 in worldwide earnings. Doyle finished with four wins (including one major title) and enough top-10 finishes to make his presence felt almost every week.

Irwin was second on the Senior World Money List with $2,261,482 and Gil Morgan took third with $1,981,282 on his four victories. Doyle was fourth with $1,961,640. Larry Nelson won three times and earned $1,861,024 worldwide. Christy O'Connor, Jr. took three titles, two in America and the Senior British Open.

The senior major titles in the United States went to Doyle in the PGA Seniors' Championship, Irwin in the Ford Senior Players Championship, Graham Marsh in The Tradition and Dave Eichelberger in the U.S. Senior Open. Marsh also won the Japan Senior Open.

Others winning twice were Eichelberger, Gary McCord, Jack Nicklaus, and newcomer Tom Watson in America; Neil Coles, Tommy Horton, Eddie Polland, Ross Metherell and Bob Shearer in Europe, and Hiroshi Ishii and Fujio Kobayashi in Japan.

Juli Inkster, who began the year with no designs on the LPGA Hall of Fame, won two major championships and played her way into the Hall with three other victories, plus the Diners Club Matches with Dottie Pepper. Even with her storybook season, Inkster didn't capture the money title or Player of the Year honors. Both went to Karrie Webb, who finished with six wins and $1,641,959 worldwide for the year, prompting another debate on how the LPGA selects its Player of the Year.

Inkster won the U.S. Women's Open and McDonald's LPGA Championship, while other major titles were won by Webb in the du Maurier Classic and Pepper in the Nabisco Dinah Shore. Se Ri Pak had four LPGA victories. Pepper won three and Rachel Hetherington, Meg Mallon, Annika Sorenstam, Mi Hyun Kim and Akiko Fukushima won twice each.

Sherri Steinhauer won the Weetabix Women's British Open to go with one LPGA victory, and Laura Davies won three times in Europe, once in Japan and the JCPenney Classic with John Daly. Catrin Nilsmark also won once in America and once in Europe. Sandrine Mendiburu, Sofia Gronberg Whitmore and Trish Johnson had two wins each in Europe. In Japan, Kaori Higo and Fumiko Muraguchi won three times each. Ok-Hee Ku, Hee-Won Han and Junko Yasui all won twice. Maria Hjorth won in America and Japan.

While 1999 will be remembered for many of the spectacular shots that were hit, and for the tragedy the game felt at the loss of one of its own, the longer view of history will no doubt peg this as a year of transformation in professional golf; a year we looked to players such as Nick Faldo, Seve Ballesteros, Ian Woosnam, Sandy Lyle and Bernhard Langer, not for the golf they played, but for the memories they provided. The new breed, players such as Woods, Duval and Garcia, have supplanted the old guard and in the process reshaped the public's perception of golf and of those who play it for a living. While there are still times when Langer's name appears at the top of European leaderboards, and while Faldo shows an occasional flicker, the players who helped define the game in the 1980s, shrinking the golfing planet and elevating European golf to heights it had never seen before, have given way to a new generation. The Spaniard creating the excitement in the future will be Garcia, not Ballesteros (or even Olazabal, even though the 1999 Masters champion still has some golfing life left), and Woosnam is giving way to Westwood and others in their 20s. Golf is now a cool sport to play — a sport as popular among youngsters as it is for their parents. And the new group of professionals is continuing to lead this transition.

2. Masters Tournament

Every professional who has ever made the champion's march up the gently rising slope of the 18th fairway at Augusta National Golf Club will tell you that there is no more majestic walk in golf. Arnold Palmer made that trek as a Masters Tournament winner four times in his career. Jack Nicklaus made it a record six times. Jimmy Demaret, Sam Snead, Nick Faldo and Gary Player did it three times, while Horton Smith, Byron Nelson, Ben Hogan, Tom Watson, Seve Ballesteros, Bernhard Langer and Ben Crenshaw all made it on two occasions.

On a sunny April afternoon in 1999, as the shadows from the stately pines stretched across the green landscape, Jose Maria Olazabal made perhaps the most emotional victory march up that hill since Hogan returned from a near-fatal automobile crash to win in 1951 and 1953. It was Olazabal's second championship walk, the first coming in 1994, but the patrons who cheered him as he crested the hill appreciated this victory more than his first, because they knew how greatly Olazabal had suffered. They knew that the very act of walking was, for the Spaniard, a symbolic triumph.

It had only been two years since many people, including Olazabal himself, wondered if he would ever walk again. His career in golf appeared to be over as he struggled through foot pain so devastating he had to crawl to the bathroom. He couldn't even stand to take a shower. Rheumatoid arthritis forced Olazabal off the tour in 1996, and his condition reached a point where he questioned how he could conduct himself in everyday life. Walking was out of the question, and swinging a golf club was the last thing on his mind. That made his comeback all the more special. After a German doctor recognized that Olazabal's ailments stemmed not from his feet but from his back, a treatment was prescribed that worked miracles, and the 14-year veteran started on the long road to recovery.

He was a hero of the 1997 Ryder Cup Matches in Valderrama after becoming a controversial captain's pick, winning 2½ points in Europe's 14½-to-13½ victory. And if any questions about his health remained after the Ryder Cup, they were answered early in 1998 when Olazabal won the Dubai Desert Classic. Still, many wondered if Olazabal was the player he had been in 1994, when he won the Masters and set a course record at Firestone Country Club while winning the NEC World Series of Golf. All doubt was removed at Augusta, with Olazabal waving to the crowd before rolling in a five-foot putt for an eight-under-par 280 aggregate, two strokes better than second-place finisher Davis Love III.

"When I was at my lowest I never thought about this," Olazabal said. "I thought I would never play golf again. The situation was so bad, everybody in my family was suffering. There is nothing they could say that could cheer me up. I mean, when you're in a situation like that, I don't wish that on anybody. Maybe the most positive thing about my foot problems was that I appreciate things more in life now. I'm not talking about the game itself. I'm talking about the usual things in life. Just being able to wake up in the morning and do whatever you want to do, go out, enjoy the weather, enjoy the scenery, and also just enjoy being on the golf course. I think that was the most positive thing that I learned from that period of time in my life.

"I think it has also helped me in such a way that I'm more patient now on the course. I don't lose control of myself so quickly. I think that is the right way to get the right results. It's very difficult for me to express how I feel at this particular moment, especially after what I went through. I'm very proud of myself. I'm a really happy man at the moment. I feel happy not just for myself, but also for all the people who supported me through the bad times, my family, my friends. To be right here, standing in front of you with a green jacket, it's an achievement I didn't even dream about when I was at my lowest."

It was not something many observers expected, either, not so much because of Olazabal's health, but because of other players who held the attention of golf fans.

There was 27-year-old David Duval, who had put together a spring unlike any in professional golf for over two decades. Duval arrived in Augusta having won four times in 1999 and 11 times in his previous 33 starts. One of the those victories, The Players Championship, had propelled Duval into the No. 1 spot on the Official World Golf Ranking, pushing Tiger Woods to second place for the first time in almost two years. Duval also had shot the only 59 ever recorded in a final round of a PGA Tour event at the Bob Hope Chrysler Classic, which propelled him to victory after starting the day seven strokes off the lead.

The week before the Masters and the week after The Players Championship, Duval made a trip to Atlanta for the BellSouth Classic, a tournament he had played since his college days at nearby Georgia Tech. What was supposed to be a warm-up for Augusta turned into Duval's fourth title of the year when he shot 18-under-par 270 and came from one stroke back after the third round to win by two over former college teammate Stewart Cink.

That prompted the kind of praise from his peers that was once reserved for players like Nicklaus, Palmer and Watson. "A lot of guys go to the range and find a certain type of shot for the day," Phil Mickelson said. "They go with what they find. But David seems to have his swing every day. It's the same shot pattern, day in and day out." His short game and mental approach seemed to match that consistency. "Duval is not a good putter, he's a great putter," said instructor Jim McLean. "He's getting close to the Ben Crenshaw, Brad Faxon and Mark O'Meara level." Snead also thought Duval's putting was the strongest part of his game. "You don't see him missing many six- and eight-footers. He pours in everything." Paul Stankowski added, "He's smart and patient and every part of his game works. He is a mental giant."

What made Duval's ascension so compelling wasn't just the statistics, but the rivalry it seemed to have established between Duval and Woods. "A lot of rivalries over history started when guys were in their 30s, and it's not as interesting when it's that way," said Johnny Miller, who sparked a rivalry with Nicklaus in the 1970s. "Duval and Woods are young. That's what makes this terrific. I like David's attitude better than Tiger's right now, and I used to feel the other way. But Duval is all positive and all business. He never gets angry. Tiger has got a lot of talent, but now it seems as if sometimes he's trying to put a square peg in a round hole. He's mad more often, frustrated more often, a lot more than Duval. I think Duval expects to win this Masters. He might not tell you that, but he expects to win. Tiger probably hopes to win. That's the difference."

If a rivalry didn't exist prior to the Masters, that kind of commentary certainly created one as far as golf fans were concerned. Duval and Woods insisted they did not consider a rivalry as valid because they had yet to meet head-to-head in a major championship. "It's nice and flattering that I might be considered the favorite going into Augusta," Duval said, "but it has no bearing on how I play or how I perform. If I am the favorite and Tiger is the favorite, nobody else in the field cares, so I certainly don't."

Sports psychologist Bob Rotella acknowledged that, "In the seven years I've known David, I've never heard him bring up Tiger's name, and I've never brought it up with him. My guess is it would probably be the same with Tiger."

Woods' instructor, Butch Harmon, confirmed that Tiger, who practiced and rested at home in Orlando before coming to Augusta, didn't talk about the rivalry except to discount it as "a media thing." But Harmon went on to say, "Do I think Duval playing so well the past 18 months pumps Tiger up? You bet I do. You know he's not publicly going to say that, but you know that's the case."

Going into Augusta, the buzz was the rivalry — perceived or real — between Duval and the 23-year-old Woods, the holder of numerous Masters records from his 1997 victory, and the hottest golfer on the planet for the previous 18 months. Palmer summed it up in recounting his duels with Nicklaus in the 1960s. "We had a lot of fun being the center of all that attention," Palmer said. "But most of all, we wanted to beat each other to a pulp. That's the nature of healthy sportsmanship, and the spirit of tournament golf."

As if the anticipated Woods-Duval showdown weren't enough to keep everyone talking, the players arrived in Augusta for the first time to something they had never seen on the 365 acres off Washington Road — rough. The members of Augusta National made the decision to protect the golf course from the kind of assault Woods had inflicted in 1997 by adding rough and changing the configuration of some of the holes. While that might sound minor, those were the most sweeping changes Augusta National had implemented in a single year since changing from rye to bent grass greens in 1981. And just as the new grass had an immediate impact, the alterations changed the complexion of the golf course.

The second hole, a par-five that Woods and others of his length had reached with ease, was lengthened 30 yards, and the bunker that guards the right side of the fairway was moved to the left to tighten the landing area. From the new position, only the longest hitters could reach the green, and no one would ever hit a driver and nine iron into the green again, as Woods had done in 1997. "When I played it the first time, it was a little cool and I certainly couldn't get there," Duval said. "In the past, I could. I could hit it right over that bunker and not have a problem."

While it wasn't moved back very much, a new green at the 11th made all the difference. Rather than hitting short irons to the right of the green, as had been the play in years past for the longer hitters, the new green required a longer approach shot with fewer options in terms of where to miss the second shot. Water still guarded the front and left portions of the green, but with the changes, water also came into play behind the green, and missing the approach to the right was no guaranteed par. The hole played harder in 1999 than it had in any year since 1992.

The trees that were added to the 13th hole in 1998 had matured nicely, making that par-five more difficult from the tee, but the newest changes were to the 15th, the 500-yard par-five that Tiger turned into a pitch-and-putt par-four in 1997 by hitting the green with a pitching wedge on his second shot. The mounds along the right side of the fairway were lowered so that players could no longer expect a sling-shot effect off the hills, but that wouldn't likely matter, because the men in Augusta planted trees along the right side of the 15th fairway, considerably narrowing the driving area. "Fifteen is still reachable in two," defending champion Mark O'Meara said, "but you're going to be forced to think about your tee shot a little more."

Those same trees had a dramatic effect on the 17th hole, which parallels the 15th. The tee at the 17th was also moved back an additional 25 yards and positioned slightly to the left of its original location so that the famed Eisenhower pine, a stately tree guarding the left side of the fairway, would once again be brought into play. Those changes turned the 17th into one of the more demanding par-fours on the course. The trees kept players from bombing tee shots without worry, while the added length caused many to drive their balls into the upslope of the fairway, killing any potential roll. The result was an approach shot that averaged two clubs longer than in previous years, and a hole that averaged 4.306 strokes for the week, making it the third hardest hole on the course. The 17th gave up only 18 birdies throughout the week, the least since 1963, and the stroke average was the highest for the hole since Jackie Burke won in 1956.

If the variations on those holes caused players to reconsider their strategies, the newly added rough around the course threw them into a tailspin. It wasn't USGA-caliber hay by any means, and the rough at Pinehurst (1999 U.S. Open) and Carnoustie (British Open) made the $1\frac{3}{8}$-inch "second cut," as CBS announcers called it, seem like closely mown fairway. But for Augusta National, the rough was a dramatic departure and posed a strategic test. "What it does is change some of the lines you take off the tees," Duval said. "I did that my first practice round. I was in that second cut a couple of times that was fairway in the past."

Love's brother and caddie Mark — a good player in his own right — saw a more subtle problem with the rough. "The new rough is just enough to keep you from spinning the ball, which will make it harder to put it in the right spot on the green, which is so important there," he said. "You can get the club on the ball from the new cut with no problem, but there is just enough grass to create a little doubt about what the ball will do."

Woods thought the rough would only help the longer hitters. "I think the rough gives the longer hitters a huge advantage," he said. "That little bit of rough is enough to take the spin off. Players like myself, John Daly, David Duval, Vijay Singh and some of the other guys, we're in the rough and we've got sand wedges and wedges in our hands. That's a huge advantage."

Love agreed. "I think everything they do to make it harder is better for the longer hitter," he said. "The more difficult, the longer and deeper the rough, whatever it is, that's all an advantage for us."

No one could have guessed that a player who was not particularly long and who, by his own admission, was alarmingly inaccurate off the tee would beat the longest, straightest hitters in the game, but then Olazabal had been underestimated before.

The champions gathered on Wednesday for the annual dinner at the club and defending champion Mark O'Meara surprised everyone with sushi and chicken fajitas as his menu choice, stating, "Hey, I know it's different, but if it was my last meal, that's what I would go with." The talk centered around the rough, the course changes, and the one player who wouldn't be teeing off the next day. Although he attended the champions' dinner, Nicklaus would miss his first Masters in 41 years after undergoing hip replacement surgery. Greg Norman said, "It's like your wife losing the diamond out of her wedding ring. He's got the greatest record here. He really put the Masters on the map as far as I'm concerned, for the modern generation of players, and for Jack not to be playing here is like losing the diamond out of your ring. It will be a sad week, honestly, from a player's perspective."

There was a 90-minute weather delay on Thursday, and the anxiety felt on the first tee was heightened by the fact that the 96-player field was the fifth largest in the tournament's history. As a result of the large field and the threat of rain, officials made the decision to play in threes rather than the traditional twos.

One thing they didn't change was the traditional opening shots by legends Gene Sarazen, Byron Nelson and Sam Snead. At 97 years old, Sarazen had the honor of teeing off first, an event, he said, that was "the hardest day of my life." Asked to elaborate, Sarazen said, "When you don't play golf at all, and you're afraid you're going to miss the ball and become the laughing stock of everybody, it's terrible. These hands are 97 years old. All the meat is gone. They're all skin and bones."

With gloves on both hands and a custom-built grip on a Wilson woman's three wood, Sarazen neither missed nor fell. He split the middle of the fairway for what would turn out to be the last time. Dressed in knickers and a camel cardigan sweater, Sarazen waved to the crowd after his shot, then returned to the clubhouse, where a car waited to take him away. Two months later, at home in Florida, Sarazen died of natural causes. The man who hit the "shot heard round the world" — a four wood for double eagle at the 15th hole in the 1935 Masters to tie Craig Wood — spent a lifetime giving back to the game he loved, and it was appropriate that the tournament he helped make famous with the most famous shot in history would be his last public appearance. The last time Sarazen would ever hit a golf ball would be on April 8, on the first tee at Augusta National.

After Sarazen, Nelson and Snead were escorted from the tee, Doug Ford, Gay Brewer and Billy Casper teed off as the first official group of the day. Although they played badly — Ford shot 88, Casper 86, and Brewer 80 — they did set a good pace, playing in only four hours and 15 minutes. Unfortunately, the group behind them didn't finish until 45 minutes later. Four groups didn't finish before darkness and the average pace of play for the day was five hours. "Just very, very slow out there," said Per-Ulrik Johansson, one of 12 players who had to return early on Friday to complete Thursday's round. "Slow enough to watch grass grow."

Part of the problem was the threes, but a contributing factor was the golf course. As Colin Montgomerie put it, "There is a lot of mental strain when you play this course. As soon as you relax you drop a shot or more." When he won in 1996, Nick Faldo called Augusta National "a seductive layout that lures you into a false sense of comfort," and Raymond Floyd called it "the most strategically laid-out golf course anywhere."

Those axioms proved true on Thursday when players started out strongly only to be seduced into their comfort zones. Woods played the first seven holes in one under par, putting him briefly within a shot of the lead. On the par-five eighth, a hole that should have played into his length off the tee, Woods took a triple bogey. He pulled his tee shot into the pines guarding the left side, then attempted to punch out, only to hit a tree. The ball careened under an azalea bush from which Woods had to take a penalty drop. He punched back into the fairway, and flew his next shot over the green. One chip and two putts later, Woods had gone from one under to two over par.

"It was too warm out there to make a snowman," Woods said, using professional slang for an eight. "The blunder came on the tee shot, but I just had to hang in there and be patient." Woods did exactly that, making three consecutive birdies on the back nine to finish at even-par 72 for the day, three off the first-round lead.

Woods wasn't the only victim. Mickelson played the first 14 holes two under par and found himself atop the leaderboard with the reachable par-five 15th left to play. Instead, he made double-bogey seven at the 15th and followed that with bogeys at the 17th and 18th to finish with 74. Ernie Els was leading at three under par through 17 holes, but a double bogey on the 18th dropped him to 71 for the day.

Even Duval was lulled by Augusta National's design. After taking the lead at three under par through 11 holes and sending murmurs throughout the gallery, Duval had three consecutive bogeys and finished tied with Els and six others at 71. "It wasn't bad swings," Duval said. "It was bad decisions. You have to think out there."

The field averaged 74.5 for the day, which meant there were more bad decisions than good ones when the wind didn't become a factor until late afternoon. Bogeys outnumbered birdies 371 to 242, and while the biggest conversation topic was the rough, most people didn't have trouble with it. The field hit 69.2 percent of the fairways in regulation, but only hit 51.4 percent of the greens. Take an average of 1.60 putts per green, and it became immediately apparent why three under par led after the opening round, and why twice as many players shot 80 or above as those who broke 70. Joe Durant, playing in his first Masters, hit 13 out of 14 fairways to take the lead in that category, but Durant shot 87, while Scott McCarron hit only seven of 14 fairways to be in the bottom quarter of the field in that statistic, but finished with 69 and a share of the first-round lead with Love, Nick Price and Brandel Chamblee.

Chamblee was a Masters rookie who said he gained most of his knowledge of Augusta National from watching the Masters on television. Chamblee joked, "It was the best round I've ever played here." He almost drove past the entrance when he first arrived, then turned onto Magnolia Lane. He held his PGA Tour money clip for the guard on duty, but the attendant said, "I don't need to see that. What's your name?" When Chamblee told him, he was allowed to drive onto the grounds for the first time, an experience he said was "pretty special."

Although he was vying to become the first Masters rookie to win since Fuzzy Zoeller in 1979, Chamblee tried to put his best Texas philosophy on the week. "I've read everything there is to read about Augusta, and you hear how it's a pretty tight ship. Essentially it is. It's a pretty tight club 51 weeks out of the year, and they open it up one week, so that's the intriguing thing about it. Everybody wants to see it, and they can't get in here but one week of the year. I don't know anybody who wouldn't want to be a member of this club. Gosh, I'd love to be a member here. I was playing in the par-three tournament and I had a buddy caddying for me. He said, 'Heck, I'd like to be a member of this course,' and he was just talking about the par-three."

Chamblee birdied the 11th hole, eagled the 13th, and then drew from his years of watching on television when he arrived at the 18th. "I've been watching the tournament since about 1975, so I knew if I hit it to the right of the hole it would kick back. I felt like I had played here before just from watching all those years. I hit a good shot and it did just what I wanted it to do." Chamblee's eight-iron shot ended up 10 feet from the hole and he closed with a birdie.

Love's 69 was the same score that his late father, Davis Jr., shot in the opening round of the 1964 Masters to take the lead. Love didn't play well the rest of that week because his wife was expecting their first child at any moment. One week later, Davis III was born. Now, it was the younger Love's turn to lead. "Obviously, I'm pleased," he said.

He didn't start out pleased, however. After missing a "pretty easy" birdie effort at the second hole, Love bogeyed the third hole, and parred the rest of the first nine, turning in 37. He hit a three wood and a six iron to within a foot for birdie on the 10th, and followed with a driver, nine iron and a 30-foot putt for birdie at the 11th, saying, "The changes don't mean much when you make a 30-footer." He parred both par-fives on the back, meaning that one of the game's longest drivers did not birdie any of the par-fives. He did come home with two more birdies, hitting a seven iron to 10 feet on the 16th and making the putt, then hitting driver and sand wedge to eight feet for birdie on the 17th.

"I don't think anybody is going to tear the golf course up," Love said afterward. "The greens are firm and fast, and there are some really hard pins. With that wind blowing, it's just going to get harder and harder, and dry up more and more." Of his chances, Love said, "I'm the quietest number three player in the world there has ever been. I haven't won since Hilton Head last year on our tour and I've just been quietly hanging in there. So I'm happy where I am. I'm chasing down some guys that are playing good golf."

After one day of play at the Masters, the scoreboard looked like this:

Davis Love III	69	Lee Janzen	70
Brandel Chamblee	69	Justin Leonard	70
Nick Price	69	Jeff Sluman	70
Scott McCarron	69	Mark O'Meara	70
Jose Maria Olazabal	70	Andrew Magee	70
Colin Montgomerie	70		

The course played a little easier on Friday. The field averaged 74.13, clipping Thursday's average by less than half a shot. Birdies outnumbered bogeys with the course surrendering 243 birdies and 11 eagles and only 159 bogeys. Double bogeys were down from 54 to 48.

Those numbers didn't help players like Nick Faldo, who failed to break par for the sixth time since winning the tournament for the third time in 1996. Faldo followed his first-round 80 with 73 and missed the cut by five strokes. He wasn't alone. Stuart Appleby went home early after rounds of 73 and 77, while Jesper Parnevik and Tom Watson matched cards with 74s and 77s to miss the 148 cut score by three. Ben Crenshaw (153) didn't hang around for the weekend, and neither did Hal Sutton (155), Seve Ballesteros (156) or Andersen Consulting Match Play champion Jeff Maggert (154).

Arnold Palmer shot 83-78 and missed the cut to cheers and standing ovations at every turn. When he walked up the 18th fairway to thunderous applause, Palmer just shook his head and said, "I didn't even break 80." Nobody in the gallery cared. Simply by teeing off, Palmer set a record, becoming the first man to compete in 45 consecutive Masters. The fans were overjoyed, earlier in the week cueing up for two hours at a local bookstore for autographed copies of Palmer's autobiography, *A Golfer's Life*.

At least one player, however, suggested it was time for Palmer to consider retirement. Mark Calcavecchia, who also missed the cut at 152, opined that Palmer's insistence on playing into his 70s wasn't good for the game or for Palmer. "I love Arnie to death," Calcavecchia said, "but it's time for him to surrender. I know he still loves to play golf, but there's no point being out there if you shoot 83 or 84. I would love to see him play great. I love him, and he'll probably keep playing until he can't walk anymore. But eventually you have to end it, don't you?"

Palmer disagreed, saying of Calcavecchia's comments, "That's his opinion and he's welcome to it." Most observers said Palmer should play as long as we wants, going out on his own terms at a time he deems appropriate. Calcavecchia later apologized for the comments, saying he meant no disrespect to Palmer. As he has done for over half a century, Palmer graciously accepted the apology.

With so many former Masters winners missing the weekend, it surprised many that four of the six amateurs invited in the field played well enough to have spots in the final two rounds. Led by Spanish sensation and British Amateur champion Sergio Garcia (72-75), the amateurs who made the cut included Tom McKnight (73-74), Trevor Immelman (72-76) and Matt Kuchar (77-71). The noticeable absentee from the list was U.S. Amateur champion Hank Kuehne, who shot 74-78. John Miller also missed the cut, shooting a pair of 81s. Garcia said, "At the amateurs dinner Matt Kuchar said there is a very high level of amateur players, and I think we demonstrated that."

For a while it looked as thought the amateurs might beat the man who set the tournament record and for whom the course modifications were made. Woods chunked an eight iron on the par-three 12th so badly on Friday that the ball landed in the middle of Rae's Creek. The double bogey moved Tiger to three over par for the tournament. At the time that was the projected cut. But Woods, who had only missed one cut in his professional career, rallied again with three late birdies on the second nine to get back to even par, eight shots off the lead.

Olazabal, who did not make a bogey on the windswept second day, held the lead by virtue of a six-under-par 66 for a 136 total, six under par. The birdies started early when a sand wedge at the par-five second hole stopped five feet from the hole. After a difficult downhill, eight-foot par save at the fifth, Olazabal hit a six iron at the downhill, par-three sixth to within six feet. That set up his second birdie of the day. Another great par save on the seventh from 12 feet kept him at two under for the round, and that's where he stayed until the 11th where he hit a driver and four iron to within five feet for his third birdie. At the par-five 13th, he laid up with his second shot, then chipped poorly to 18 feet, but made the putt for birdie. The second par-five on the second nine was a little easier. He hit a driver and one iron just off the edge of the green, and chipped to within tap-in range for another birdie to move to five under for the day. Then at the 18th, he hit a three wood off the tee to the center of the fairway, where he hit a nine-iron approach to within 10 feet. When that putt fell for birdie, Olazabal held a one-shot lead over Scott McCarron.

"The conditions were tough," Olazabal said. "The wind was blowing quite hard. It was swirling, and we all know what happens here when the wind blows. We've always said that experience on this golf course helps you a lot, and that is a fact. Because I won here in 1994, obviously that makes me feel maybe a little bit better than the players who haven't won. It's a special place for me and it will remain like that. Experience is a great factor. The more you know about the course, the more you know what you have to do, where you have to hit the ball, how you have to play the holes. I mean, day after day, you have to play well, obviously. It's a good thing for those who have played here often."

Although he had no major championship victories, McCarron had made enough trips to Augusta to feel confident. His second-round 68 showed it. "It was a great day," McCarron said. "I made some great par saves in the middle of my round to keep things going, and I hit some great par-threes on the back side. With the wind swirling they were difficult to judge."

The first great par-three he played was the fourth, where he hit a four iron into the center of the green and made a 55-foot putt that broke eight feet for the only birdie the fourth hole surrendered all day. It was his second birdie of the day, the first coming when he hit a wedge to within two feet on the first hole. A bogey from the bunker on the 12th dropped him back to one under for the day, but a long drive on the 13th left him with only a seven iron to the green. From there McCarron two-putted for another birdie from 14 feet. His next birdie was at the 14th, where a driver and a wedge left him eight feet away, and on the 18th, McCarron's length paid off again as he hit the par-five in two with a driver and five iron, two-putting for birdie from 45 feet. He bogeyed the 16th from a bunker, then hit a sand wedge into the 18th and made a six-footer.

"I'm one shot back with two days left," McCarron said. "They always say the Masters starts at the back nine on Sunday, so we've still got a lot of golf left, but you had better play well on Thursday and Friday to get to that back nine on Sunday. Handling myself at the Masters down the stretch is going to be a very difficult achievement and accomplishment that I'm looking forward to."

Another player looking forward to the weekend was Norman, the man whose well-chronicled collapse in the 1996 Masters left some wondering if he would ever recover. He did, shooting 68 to move to within three shots of Olazabal's lead at the halfway mark, tied with Lee Janzen at 139. "It's great to be in this position," he said. "It's great when you've worked yourself so hard to get back into it. It's great from the fact that I feel a little less urgency when I approach things on the golf course or approach things off the golf course. I don't reflect on packing my bags and going home. I've never done that. I've always been one for what's done is done and move on with life. Right now I'm feeling extremely relaxed and in control of what I'm doing."

Norman was certainly in control of his golf. After a poor chip on the first hole ended in a bogey, Norman went to work, hitting a driver and three wood to the fringe of the second, then chipping to five feet and making the putt for birdie. On the third, he hit a two iron off the tee and a pitching wedge to 15 feet and made the putt. At the par-four fifth, Norman hit a driver and eight iron to 30 feet and made that putt for his third birdie in five holes. That's when things slowed down. Norman didn't make another birdie until the par-three 12th, where he hit a seven iron to 25 feet. The final birdie came at the 13th where he hit a three wood off the tee, six iron to lay up, and a sand wedge to within six inches of the hole.

"What happened here in 1996 changed my life," Norman said. "There is a huge amount of support out there from people on a global basis. My locker is full of letters this week. So you still get people writing to you from 1996. That's what I mean when I say it changed my life. You can roll it into what happened last year with the surgery, roll it into the fact that you get to see and appreciate other things in life more than just the game of golf. There are other things out there that can touch you, and 1996 did that. If I had won the tournament, would it have changed my life? Who knows? I didn't win. I can only go on what happened. It changed my life and made me appreciate people in a different way because of the support they gave me."

When asked about being the sentimental favorite, Norman quipped, "I don't know. How do you determine that? Is it from 1996, or because I'm getting old?" Whether he understood or not, Norman was clearly the sentimental favorite, garnering cheers and ovations with every step. The gallery was squarely with Norman, and the weekend was shaping up nicely.

With two rounds to go, the leaderboard read like a who's who of golf greats:

Jose Maria Olazabal	66 - 136	Bernhard Langer	66 - 142
Scott McCarron	68 - 137	Colin Montgomerie	72 - 142
Greg Norman	68 - 139	Bill Glasson	70 - 142
Lee Janzen	69 - 139	Brandel Chamblee	73 - 142
Nick Price	72 - 141	Justin Leonard	72 - 142
Davis Love III	72 - 141	Steve Elkington	70 - 142

Eleven players started the third round within six strokes of Olazabal's lead, but rather than Saturday being "moving day," it turned into a day where par was good enough to hold your own. In fact, par moved you up a notch or two. The benchmark score for the day was 73. Anything better and you advanced. Price found that out. After starting with 40 on the first nine, Price rallied to shoot even par in the third round for a 213 total and moved one shot closer to the leader. Els moved four shots closer with 69, while Carlos Franco, Lee Westwood and Bob Estes improved their positions with rounds in the 60s.

The biggest move of all came from Steve Pate, who began the day tied for 29th place at 146 and finished tied for third with Love at 211. That leap came as a result of a record-setting seven birdies in a row starting at the seventh and extending through the 13th. "I really didn't do anything differently than I did the first two days," Pate said. "But instead of two birdies, I made seven in a row. I don't know how I did it really."

Had Norman not birdied the 18th hole, Pate would have played in the final group with Olazabal. The only player who thought he had shot himself out of contention was McCarron, who posted 76. As it turned out, McCarron only fell four shots off the lead. He was still within striking range. Duval moved up, shooting 70, which negated the 74 he shot on Friday. With one round remaining he was only six shots back, and as had been proven so often at Augusta National, anything was possible on Sunday afternoon.

The man who knew that better than anyone also had a good day. Norman inched closer to his goal of winning the Masters when he fired 71 for a 210 total and moved within one shot of Olazabal. The gutsy performance included two bizarre holes, back-to-back in Amen Corner. At the par-three 12th, after moving into a share of the lead, Norman's ball flew over the green and into the brush on the embankment behind. He and Janzen searched frantically for the allotted five minutes, then Norman took the lonely walk back to the tee, having been forced to declare the ball lost.

"As I was walking back I was saying to myself, just accept it," Norman said. "You hit a good shot, that's just run of the mill. Those things happen. I didn't hit a bad shot. That's what I was saying to myself. I knew the yardage, so I put my tee in the ground right next to the divot that I just hit before. I aimed to the right of the same tree, and the ball went exactly on the same line." Only the second time, the ball landed pin high, just left of the hole. He walked back to the green, declining a ride from a passing official. "I wanted to gather my pace and gather my momentum," Norman said. "Then when I got there, I saw the putt all the way. I never doubted I was going to make that putt."

When he did make the putt for bogey, the crowd erupted in cheers that were normally reserved for Sunday. He had become more than the sentimental favorite. He was the spark that charged the patrons, and men and women by the thousands poured themselves into his every shot.

Norman drove the ball into the fairway at the 13th, and decided to lay up short of Rae's Creek for the second time in two days. It had worked on Friday when Norman hit a spinning wedge third shot he rated "a 9½ on a scale of one to 10." This time, he chose the same club, a six iron, and hit the ball into the spot he wanted, just short of the water, but with enough room to spin his third shot close to the flag. When he arrived at his ball, however, he was shocked.

"I walked down there and I was in a sandy little hole," he said. "At the end of the day, I thought where I had to re-gather my composure more was the lay-up on 13 where I laid it up in the divot. That seemed to get to me more than the 12th hole. I found it hard to keep my composure after making six there."

He did keep his composure, however, making a 10-foot birdie putt at the final hole to claw back, one shot off Olazabal's lead. Olazabal shot 73 for a 209 total, seven under par.

"We all want to give ourselves the chance to win the tournament tomorrow," Norman said. "It's great to have the lead. I would have loved to have the lead, but whether you have the lead or not, you always want to give yourself the chance of having the shot at winning. Whether that means going to the 10th tee two or three back or with a two- or three-shot lead, things change dramatically on the back nine at Augusta National."

With one round remaining, the leaderboard at the Masters looked like this:

Jose Maria Olazabal	73 - 209	Lee Janzen	73 - 212
Greg Norman	71 - 210	Ernie Els	69 - 212
Davis Love III	70 - 211	Steve Elkington	71 - 213
Steve Pate	65 - 211	Colin Montgomerie	71 - 213
Bob Estes	69 - 212	Nick Price	72 - 213
Carlos Franco	68 - 212	Scott McCarron	76 - 213

The first part of the tournament to be settled was the low amateur competition, and that went down to the wire. With wind drying the already speedy greens, Garcia showed poise beyond his 19 years by shooting 73 for a 295 total to edge 44-year-old Virginia petroleum dealer Tom McKnight by two strokes. Garcia's composure had many wondering if he would become the next great Spanish golfer. "His composure comes from within," Garcia's father said. "I think some people are born with it. Some people have it. The ones who have it are here."

"I was very impressed with how he hung in there and grinded," Woods said. The two were paired for the first two rounds, and Woods saw a lot of good things. "He never took any chances, which was very impressive," Woods said.

Garcia chalked it up as a learning experience. "I think I learned a lot this week," he said. "I learned to be real patient, to wait for the right time to be aggressive. I think this tournament has been great for my career."

With the amateur honors decided, all attention focused on the leaders and on those who were making early moves. The first name that got everyone's attention was that of Duval, who came roaring back from six shots off the pace to pull to within two before hitting his second shot in the water on the 11th and taking a double bogey.

"I did the thing that I wanted to do, which was get up on the leaderboard quickly, but I failed to keep it going on the back," Duval said. "I figured if I got to five or six under I would have a decent chance. You know, you just try to learn a few things each time you have the chance and don't pull it off and try to apply that to the next year."

Even if Duval had been able to reach six under, it wouldn't have been enough, but in the early going no one could have known that. Olazabal relinquished the lead on the first nine with three consecutive bogeys beginning at the third hole. He missed the green with a nine iron on the third, chipped to nine feet and missed his par effort, then he missed the green on the fourth in the bunker and left his first bunker shot in the sand. A good second bunker shot followed by a four-foot putt kept him from making double bogey at the par-three. Then at the fifth, he missed the green with a six iron, chipped to 12 feet and missed the putt. At that point, five players were tied for the lead and Olazabal was not among them.

One of the players among the five was England's Westwood, a 26-year-old rising star with 13 worldwide victories, including one win in America (1998 Freeport-McDermott Classic in New Orleans). As he made the turn, Westwood glanced at the leaderboard between the 10th tee and the 18th green and was stunned by what he saw. With nine holes to play, he not only had a chance, he was leading the Masters.

Unfortunately, that lead was short-lived. A bogey at the 10th followed by a double bogey at the 11th (the same hole Duval double-bogeyed earlier) dashed Westwood's hopes for his first major championship. Still, Westwood felt good about his performance. Even though he finished tied for sixth at 285 with Franco, Duval, Mickelson and Price, Westwood managed to rally to shoot a final-round 71, one of only six sub-par scores on the day. Finishing one stroke ahead at 284 were Estes and Pate.

Olazabal regained a share of the lead on the par-three sixth when he hit a six iron to nine feet for a birdie. "I was not a very happy camper after five holes," he said. "I bogeyed three, four and five, and I said, 'My God, I think we're giving this tournament away.' Then I said to Brandon (his caddie), 'We still can make a few pars, make a birdie or two, and I think we have a chance to win the tournament. It was a good thing I birdied number six. After that I just tried to keep calm and make as many shots as possible."

He settled down and parred the seventh, eighth and ninth, making the turn tied for the lead. A three wood off the 10th tee found the fairway, and an eight-iron approach stopped 12 feet away. When Olazabal made that putt for birdie, he held the lead once more.

At that time, Norman was one shot back, but a birdie putt at the 11th moved him back into a share of the lead. Once more, in the heart of Amen Corner, the roars of the gallery energized Norman, but he had to be careful. "Sometimes it can work against you," he said. "The emotion was great, no doubt about it, but I still had work to do."

A bogey at the 12th dropped Norman one behind Olazabal. At the par-five 13th Norman knew he had to make something happen. Rather than play conservatively, as he had done all week, the 44-year-old Australian went for broke, driving the ball perfectly and hitting a 198-yard four iron to within 25 feet of the hole. As he was walking to the green, Norman's caddie said, "You know you're going to make that, don't you?" Norman said, "Yes, I do." He had made it before for an eagle in years past. He knew what the putt would do. He aimed at the center of the hole, and the ball broke a little left at the beginning, then back to the right at the end, falling in the center for eagle. For the moment, Norman held a one-shot lead.

"As soon as he hit the putt it looked like it was in all the way," Olazabal said of Norman's putt. "While the ball was rolling, I was saying to myself, 'Just try to make yours.' I didn't want to go one stroke behind at that time."

Olazabal had laid up short of Rae's Creek with a six iron, then hit a wedge to 21 feet, not his best approach shot of the day, but when he hit his putt, he knew it was in. The birdie on top of Norman's eagle left the two tied with five holes to play. As they walked off the 13th green, Norman and Olazabal pointed to each other, acknowledging jobs well done. "That's the relationship we have," Olazabal said. "Every time we play together we are close. When he made that putt and I made mine, I looked at him and we both understood. He pointed at me, I pointed at him, and we were saying to each other that those were great putts."

Unfortunately, as he had done at the 12th, Norman couldn't follow up his critical putt with a par. He three-putted the 14th for a bogey, dropping one shot back. Then at the 15th, after laying up and leaving himself 98 yards to the green, Norman pushed a wedge shot that found the greenside bunker. When he was unable to save par, Olazabal held a two-shot advantage.

One group ahead, Love had clawed his way to even par for the day, five under for the tournament, just two shots off Olazabal's lead with three holes to play. His chances appeared to be dashed at the 16th when, like Duval had done earlier, Love flew the tee shot over the back of the par-three, leaving himself an almost impossible chip. Par would have been a good score, most assumed. Love had different plans. He had played Augusta National enough to know that any ball hit onto the slope that bisects the green will always funnel back to the hole. So rather than play a lob shot at the hole, Love picked a spot on the hill, pitched his ball there, and begged it to come back down. It did, and when the ball slowly trickled into the cup for birdie, Love threw his fists in the air and ran onto the green. He had given himself a chance. With two holes to play, he was only one shot back.

Olazabal watched it all from the 16th tee. He knew he had to hold onto his lead with a good swing at the par-three. He answered with a six iron to within three feet of the hole. Norman hit a good shot as well, his ball stopping six feet away. When Norman was unable to convert his birdie, his hopes of a Masters victory were all but over. Olazabal studied his birdie putt, then made one of the best strokes of the day. "You can't imagine what a three-footer that was," he said. "Downhill and lightening quick with a left-to-right break. I don't know how the hell I made that putt."

The birdie gave Olazabal a two-shot cushion with two holes to play.

Up ahead, Love heard the roar when Olazabal's putt went in. He knew he had to play the last two holes in one under, perhaps two to have a chance. When his birdie effort at the 17th slipped by the hole, his heart sank. His best chance of winning a Masters since his second-place finish in 1995 had just slipped away. He finished with 71 for a 282 total, two behind Olazabal.

Meanwhile, Olazabal's driving inaccuracy finally caught up with him. He hit a low hook off the tee at the 17th, and the ball hit the Eisenhower pine, leaving him with a tough shot under one tree limb and around another 188 yards from the hole. With the wind at his back, he laced a five iron that bounded in the fairway and ran onto the green, 40 feet from the hole. His birdie putt rolled seven feet past, but he made the putt for par. Norman, who shot 73 to finish third at 283, called that seven-footer "the biggest putt he made all day," and Olazabal agreed with him.

"Scrambling for a four at 17, giving myself two shots, was crucial," Olazabal said, after closing with 71 for an eight-under-par 280 effort. "I died for a four on that hole, and when I got it, I knew the jacket should be mine."

3. U.S. Open Championship

It will go down as one of the most memorable U.S. Open Championships in history, in part because of the dramatic play of those involved and a sensational finish at a great venue, and because of the tragedy that befell the champion four months later. Payne Stewart, or William Payne Stewart as his father always insisted he write on his Open application, was within one putt of his second U.S. Open victory in 1998, but his birdie effort on the 72nd hole slipped just below the cup. Stewart, who had led through the first three rounds, was gracious in defeat but the memory stayed with him. When Stewart found himself in the same position — leading after three rounds of the 1999 U.S. Open at Pinehurst, North Carolina — he knew that his time had come, and despite a charge by the world's No. 1 player, Tiger Woods, and good play by his Sunday playing companion, Phil Mickelson, Stewart did what he had to do, making putts on the 70th, 71st and finally a 15-footer on the 72nd hole to capture his second national championship.

In late October, Stewart and his agents Robert Fraley and Van Arden, along with golf course architect Bruce Borland and two pilots, were killed in a bizarre accident aboard a Learjet bound for Dallas, Texas. After departing Orlando International Airport and climbing through 17,500 feet over Gainsville, Florida, controllers at the Jacksonville Air Traffic Control Center cleared the airplane to a cruising altitude of 39,000 feet. When the airplane continued to climb above its specified altitude and failed to change its heading west toward Dallas, controllers knew there was a problem. The Atlanta Air Traffic Control Center attempted radio contact, and when the pilots failed to respond, two F-16 fighters from Panama City Beach, Florida, were scrambled to make a visual inspection. What they found was an airplane flying on autopilot with the windows frosted over from the inside, a sign of depressurization.

At that point, the F-16 pilots and everyone in the control center knew that the passengers were dead. The temperature at 40,000 feet is 60 degrees below zero, but fortunately the passengers never felt that frigid air. Without supplemental oxygen, they were unconscious after five to 10 seconds once the plane passed 20,000 feet. Death from oxygen deprivation soon followed. As the airplane lost fuel, it climbed above 50,000 feet, porpoising between a height of 56,000 and 40,000 feet. The harrowing ride continued for four hours until the Learjet finally ran out of fuel and crashed into a field in Mina, South Dakota.

Everyone in golf was shocked by the tragedy, and the outpouring of support and grief among those who knew Stewart did little to ease the sadness. Through the memorial services and tributes paid to Stewart and the others in the following days and months, the one image that kept coming up was from the 72nd green of the U.S. Open, Stewart dressed in his trademark knickers and touring cap, raising his right fist and thrusting it forward, exhaling a triumphant shout as the final putt fell in. The scene of Stewart in victory, dancing across the green, then picking up his caddie, Mike Hicks, and hugging him like Don Larson held Yogi Berra after pitching a perfect game in the 1956 World Series, was burned into our memory.

No professional major championship had been held on the famed Pinehurst No. 2 course since the 1936 PGA Championship — a match-play event won by Denny Shute — and the classic Donald Ross design lived up to its reputation. Jack Nicklaus said, "Pinehurst is my favorite golf course in the country from a design standpoint." Greg Norman said, "It's the type of golf course I'd play every day of my life." And Raymond Floyd said, "Pinehurst No. 2, in my mind, cannot be out of anybody's top five golf courses in the world. I put it in my top three."

That sort of praise was common when discussing Pinehurst No. 2, unusual when you consider that the golf course has no water to speak of (except for a small pond in front of the 16th tee that does not come into play), no forced carries over marshes or wetlands, no island greens or cross ties, no overhanging trees or sharp doglegs, and no extraordinary vistas of crashing ocean waves or majestic mountains. The hills are small and the pines are neither towering nor stately. But Pinehurst has always been considered one of the best, if not *the* best test of golf in the South.

"Augusta National is good one week out of the year," said Tom Weiskopf when asked to compare Pinehurst No. 2 to other classic courses. "But Augusta doesn't compare to this course. Augusta only shows its teeth and demands when the greens are so fast and with those unbelievably difficult pin positions. I've played Augusta two or three weeks before the Masters and it's a piece of cake. A piece of cake! Pinehurst No. 2 is never a piece of cake!"

Shortly after James W. Tufts, a Boston industrialist who made his fortune in the soda fountain business, developed the village of Pinehurst in 1895, he hired Ross, a young Scottish immigrant, to be his golf professional. Ross, who later became one of the most noted course architects, lived in Pinehurst and devoted much of his life to developing what he saw as his masterpiece design.

"A championship course," Ross wrote, "should call for long and accurate tee shots, accurate iron play (and let me say here that I consider the ability to play the longer irons as the supreme test of a great golfer), precise handling of the short game, and finally consistent putting." By building greens that were crested on the natural sand mounds of eastern North Carolina, Ross was able to test the iron play and short games of the world's best players of the 20th century. In explaining his philosophy of the greens at Pinehurst, Ross wrote, "The contouring around a green makes possible an infinite variety in the requirements for short shots that no other form of hazard can call for."

USGA president Buzz Taylor said before play began that Pinehurst No. 2 had the "potential to be as good a test of golf as we've ever had for our national championship. It demands every shot in the great player's repertoire and some shots that some players don't have. Put it this way: More than a few players will not have the required level of skill around those greens. Play around the greens will be very demanding, and some in a U.S. Open field will have trouble with pace of play and difficulty around the greens."

In trying to describe the difficulty of the convex greens and the subtle mounding, David Duval told a group of baseball players the week after the Open, "It was like trying to stop a six iron on a pitcher's mound." Woods, who arrived early to get extra practice, said, "You have so many options that you can actually get kind of confused. It requires a lot of imagination."

Indeed, the USGA departed from its traditional course set-up procedures to take advantage of Ross' design. Rather than having three- and four-inch rough adjacent to the putting surfaces, the USGA decided to closely mow the areas surrounding the greens so that players would have the option of putting, chipping, pitching or playing bump-and-run shots. Woods used his three wood to great effect, while Mickelson chose to pitch shots with a flat-soled 62-degree sand wedge most of the time. Mickelson called Pinehurst, "the best test of golf I've ever played in a major championship."

Stewart arrived in Pinehurst earlier than he had expected. After missing the 36-hole cut at the FedEx St. Jude Classic in Memphis, he made a week-end trek to Pinehurst where he met his longtime instructor, Chuck Cook. The two took several leisurely strolls around the No. 2 course, but for the first couple of days, Stewart took nothing but his short irons and his putter. He was a student of golf history. He knew that Pinehurst had hosted the oldest continuous tournament in American golf history (the North and South Amateur which had been contested there every year since 1901) as well as having been the site of the 1951 Ryder Cup, 1994 Senior Open and the 1991 and 1992 Tour Championships.

Stewart had competed in the Tour Championships, and while he never contended, he remembered his and other players' impressions at the time. "You could play a U.S. Open here without growing rough, without doing anything," Ian Baker-Finch had said in 1992. "Where has this been all my life? I haven't been this pumped up about playing golf since the British Open!" Now the U.S. Open was being held there, and the USGA had grown rough, although not around the greens, but Stewart knew it was a much different course than what he had seen seven years earlier.

As part of their agreement with the USGA, ClubCorp (owner of the Pinehurst resort) agreed to reconstruct the greens. In doing so they brought in architect Rees Jones, who had restored The Country Club in Brookline, Massachusetts, before the 1989 U.S. Open and Congressional Country Club in Bethesda, Maryland, before its U.S. Open bid. Jones took his duties to heart, remaining true to the original design intentions of Ross while understanding the need for new grasses.

"Most of what we did was just restore certain areas that were once part of the greens, but that had become fringe over the years. The greens started out as Bermuda grass, then they were converted to bent, but because of the heat and other factors the greens had simply lost a lot of their original contour," Jones said. In addition to restoring that original contour, Jones, ClubCorp and the USGA gambled on a new strain of bent grass, Penn G-2, which had been developed by Penn State University to be one of the most heat-tolerant bent grasses ever grown. While the track record for the new grass was good, very few courses had tried Penn G-2 for an extended period, and none had hosted a major championship on it.

"ClubCorp agreed that if the G-2 didn't work, they would replace it in time for the Open," USGA executive director David Fay said. That wasn't necessary. The grass took hold and Jones' restoration was complete. "Pinehurst No. 2 is sacred ground in golf," Jones said. "This is where Donald Ross lived and worked. It is his ultimate design because it is his most hands-on creation."

Unlike many who prepared for the Open, Stewart appreciated the changes because he understood and appreciated the historical significance of the course. Pinehurst truly was, as Fay put it, "the St. Andrews of American golf, and a site worthy of hosting a United States Open Championship."

Fay chose not to make the pairings for the first two days, a task he had taken on every year since assuming the reins as executive director of the USGA after Frank Hannigan's retirement. "I let Tom (Meeks) do it this year." Meeks, the head of competitions, had come under sharp criticism in 1998 when, on Friday, the pin on the 18th green at The Olympic Club was placed on the back portion of the green. As the green dried and hardened throughout the day, one player after another rolled putts up to the hole then watched as their balls rolled back down the hill. By the USGA's own admission, it was ridiculous and embarrassing.

The most lasting image of that Friday belonged to Stewart, who hit his approach shot on the 18th pin high, 10 feet to the right of the hole. Although his first putt almost went in, traveling slowly enough to normally leave a tap-in for par, Stewart's ball, like others before it, continued to roll down the hill. Stewart demonstrated the absurdity of the situation by walking to the bottom of the hill and standing with his arms folded, waiting for the ball to reach him.

"It was one of the worst days I've spent," Meeks said. "After four or five groups, I knew I was a dead duck." Meeks had questioned whether the hole would work on the back portion of the green, because the only other option was to have the hole up front all four days — a situation that could lead to a chewed-up green from all the foot traffic at best, and a dead green from all the compaction at worst. Meeks decided that a lot of water and a change in the mowing of the 18th might do the trick. It didn't, and he spent the day watching ball after ball roll back down the hill. "I've always made it a policy that if I have any doubt about a hole location, I don't use it. But because we had so few options on that green I went against my own rule and against my instincts and I got burned."

Now he was faced with another task that would win him few friends. There was no magic formula to making the pairings, but it was a lot more than just pulling names out of a hat. Television had to be considered, as did personalities. Two players who abhorred each other probably wouldn't be paired together (although that sort of thing was rare in golf), and players who were habitually slow were usually separated and put in time slots that might mask their measured tendencies. All those things went through Meeks' mind as he laboriously penciled in names and times.

Fay didn't completely divorce himself from the process. "I made some suggestions for the marquee players," Fay said, but for the most part, he let Meeks be the guy who would take the heat at Pinehurst. As was normally his nature, Meeks did an admirable job. He paired two of the game's premier players, Duval and Mickelson, neither of whom had ever won a major title, together with Paraguayan Carlos Franco, a likely candidate for PGA Tour Rookie of the Year honors after a top-10 finish at the Masters and a win in New Orleans. That group would go off at 7:30 on Thursday, which was too early for the television coverage. On Friday they were scheduled for 11:50, making them the featured television group for the second round. On the other side of that 11:50-7:30 television coin, Meeks paired Woods with English sensation Lee Westwood. Former U.S. Open winner Corey Pavin, who was in the midst of a comeback after a two-year slump, rounded out that group.

Thursday viewers not only got to see the Woods group, but Meeks also paired Greg Norman, Justin Leonard and Davis Love III in the group just ahead, while the group behind included defending U.S. Open champion Lee Janzen, Mark O'Meara and U.S. Amateur champion Hank Kuehne. It was a USGA tradition to pair the Amateur and Open champions in the first two rounds, and Meeks knew that the long-driving Kuehne would be in good, steady company with O'Meara and Janzen.

Stewart was paired in the 12:10 and 7:50 group right behind Janzen, O'Meara and Kuehne, but rather than having to risk suffering through the travails of an amateur in his first U.S. Open appearance, Stewart was paired with a couple of veterans and good friends. Stuart Appleby had recently bought a home in Orlando near Stewart's and while the two had always been friends, they drew even closer as they spent more time with each other at home. The other member of the group was Jeff Maggert, a quiet 35-year-old professional who was a veteran of two Ryder Cups. Stewart was comfortable with the pairing and comfortable with the times — not so early as to be considered a dew-sweeper, and not so late that the greens would be chewed up from spike marks.

Unlike the rest of the season at most courses around the country where soft-spiked shoes were mandatory, PGA Tour players, including everyone participating in the U.S. Open, were still allowed to wear hard metal spikes in their golf shoes. Many, including Stewart, did. That didn't create much of a problem at 7:30 and it was only a minor annoyance at noon. By 3:00, however, over 120 players had marched around the holes leaving spike marks, footprints and other indentations in the soft surfaces. That was why players like Greg Gregory of Burleson, Texas, and Dennis Zinkon of Haines City, Florida, got the 10:40 and 3:00 times. It might not seem fair, after working as hard as they had to qualify for a spot in the U.S. Open, to be relegated to the last starting time of the day, but somebody had to play there, and given the choice between putting Woods or David Lebeck from Portland in the last group, Meeks made the prudent call.

It also didn't hurt when two of the guys playing together in one of his featured threesomes shot three-under-par 67s to share the lead with two others.

With overnight rains doing little to soften the layout Tom Lehman described as "the hardest golf course I've ever played," Duval and Mickelson, whose combined age was still younger than Nicklaus but who had already amassed 24 PGA Tour titles between them, were considered favorites coming into Pinehurst, but both had to overcome distractions before teeing off.

Duval arrived early in the week with a bandage over his left thumb and index finger. While attempting to make tea on the previous Friday, Duval had scalded himself on the hot kettle, leaving second-degree burns on two critical digits of his left hand. Always cool under pressure, Duval attempted to dismiss it as "no big deal," but that didn't stop the media from speculating that Duval might be out of contention.

Mickelson wasn't injured, but his wife Amy was home in Scottsdale, Arizona, expecting the couple's first child at any moment. She had been in bed since April due to complications with the pregnancy, and Mickelson had vowed that if Amy went into labor, he would be on his jet and heading home. Jim

"Bones" McKay, Mickelson's caddie, carried a beeper, and if it went off with the proper code punched in, they were walking off the course.

"When I was 20 years old I thought that, gosh, the majors would be so important and I didn't really know how I would feel," Mickelson said. "But this baby is something I don't want to miss. I have a once-in-a-lifetime opportunity to be there for the birth of my daughter, whereas the U.S. Open takes place every year. We are expecting it to be at least June 30th, and possibly a little bit later, so things look good. But obviously with labor you just never know. It's been a really exciting time for us."

Mickelson didn't decide to come to Pinehurst until he and Amy visited with Amy's doctor on Tuesday morning, leaving him time for only one practice round before teeing off in a major championship on a golf course that everyone agreed took time to understand. Mickelson took it in stride, saying he might actually be fresher as a result of the late arrival. "I have something to take my mind off a major championship," he said. "I was really excited about this tournament heading in. I'm really excited about the set-up of the golf course, and I think this is the best test of golf that I've played in a major championship. It tests every area of your game. It tests every shot. Past Opens have not really tested you off the tee as well with the driver. Most have required that you hit two, three and four irons, but this week the fairways are as wide at 240 yards as they are at 320, and every player has an opportunity to hit any club he wants off the tee."

Mickelson, one of the longest drivers on the PGA Tour and long acknowledged as a wizard of the short game, found Pinehurst perfectly suited for his combination of skills. "Around the greens, we've seen in years past, the short game be obsolete," he said of the USGA's propensity for high rough around the putting surfaces. "This year there's a lot of emphasis placed on the short game. It's an integral part of the tournament, so I was really excited heading in. I thought this would be a good opportunity for me to play well in a U.S. Open."

He did just that on Thursday, jumping out early with three birdies. The first came at the 447-yard, par-four second hole where Mickelson hit an eight iron to 18 feet and made the putt. He then missed the fairway with his drive on the par-five fourth, but laid up with a six iron to 112 yards. From there he hit a pitching wedge to eight feet. On the fifth, Mickelson showed why he thought Pinehurst No. 2 suited his game when he missed the green on the 482-yard par-four with a five iron, then chipped in for his third birdie in five holes. "That was a very basic chip," Mickelson said. "It was straight uphill and it didn't round off. Every shot on and around these greens is extremely difficult. If you don't hit a chip just right, it races past the hole, but if you hit it too easy, it could come back to you."

Those tough chips caught up to Mickelson on the sixth and eighth holes, where he failed to get up and down after chipping to five and 15 feet, respectively. That dropped him back to one under par for the day, where he remained until he reached the 383-yard, par-four 13th. There, on one of the few par-fours where Mickelson did not hit a driver, his two-iron tee shot left him with 147 yards to the flag. Because of the hole location, Mickelson had to play conservatively, hitting an eight iron 30 feet away. He said he was just trying to trickle the putt down beside the hole when "it caught the corner and went in. That's an example of how the round tends to level out," he said.

"I missed a five-footer on number six, but I was just trying to knock that 30-footer straight downhill somewhere by the hole."

His plans were much different on the next hole. A perfect drive on the 436-yard par-four left Mickelson with a nine iron from 135 yards. He hit it eight feet away from the flag and made the putt for his fifth birdie of the day and 67 total.

"Obviously the course is playing as easy as it can today with the greens being as soft as they are," Mickelson said. "Yet it's a tribute to how difficult the course is in that there aren't any real low scores. For three under to be up there right now at the top of the leaderboard ... I think we're going to be in for a long weekend if the greens dry out."

Duval agreed with that assessment, but said it was typical of some of the Opens he had seen in the past. "It was playing a little bit easier," he said. "But at the same time it seems to me in past Opens I've played in that the golf courses the first day are set up so that if you're playing well you can make birdies and put up a two-, three- or four-under-par score. After that, everybody tends to drift backwards a little bit. I'm obviously very pleased to go out early on a day when there's going to be some scores under par and do that."

Finally putting questions about his burned hand to rest, Duval shot a much different 67 than Mickelson. After hitting a seven iron to eight feet and making birdie on the second hole, Duval made 12 straight pars, missing only three greens and getting up and down easily on those occasions. Then at the par-three 12th he hit a five iron from 202 yards to two feet for his second birdie of the day, and he followed it with another birdie on the 191-yard, par-three 17th, where his seven-iron shot stopped 10 feet from the hole and he made the putt.

When asked about the steadiness of his round, Duval said, "That's how I try to play." Through a wry smile, he said, "I find it to be less stressful." Then turning serious, the man who shot 59 earlier in the year said, "I had no expectations when I started today. Based on how I played the last two days in practice, I would have been looking to get under par. Expectations? I don't like to do that because on a day when you really get things going, it might prevent you from getting even a couple more."

Stewart would have been tied for the lead, but a poor drive in the left rough on the 18th fairway caused him to miss the green with a six iron and he failed to recover for par. That was the only blemish on Stewart's card. His first birdie came at the short par-four third, where Stewart hit a three iron and a pitching wedge to 15 feet. The next birdie came at the 610-yard, par-five 10th where he hit driver, three iron and pitching wedge to two feet. At the 13th Stewart picked up his third birdie when he made another 15-footer, and his last birdie came at the par-three 15th, where he hit a five iron to 20 feet.

Even though he finished the first round only one shot off the lead, Stewart had his share of adversity. Three times he drove the ball into sand-filled divots, the same kind of divot he drove into on the 12th hole of the final round in 1998. That poor break cost Stewart a shot, caused him to be warned for slow play, and was one of the factors in his loss. This time he held himself together and recovered nicely, making birdie on two of the three holes where he drove into divots.

"I'm very, very pleased with how I controlled myself today," he said. "When I was walking around the course on Saturday there wasn't a divot on the golf course. But the areas we're playing from, everybody seems to play from the same areas, so that's going to happen and you've got to deal with it."

Stewart also agreed with Mickelson and Duval that the golf course would undoubtedly get harder as the week progressed. "After the rains the golf course was a little softer," he said. "I think that we took advantage of that today. The golf course is going to continue as the days progress to get harder and firmer and play more like Pinehurst is supposed to play or would have played last week before the rain. To get off to a start like this is very satisfying."

If Stewart was satisfied, John Daly was shocked. Daly was overweight and in need of a haircut when he arrived in Pinehurst. He was also searching for some semblance of the golf game that won two major championships. Daly's last appearance before the Open was the first round of the Memorial Tournament where he six-putted the 18th green before withdrawing. Two weeks later, he bogeyed the 18th hole at Pinehurst to fall out of a share of the lead and tie Stewart and Woods, Kaname Yokoo and David Berganio at two-under-par 68.

"I'm about as much in shock as everybody else right now," Daly said. "I got off to a great start — something I haven't done in quite a long time. I felt like my whole game was gone. I didn't have any confidence or expectations coming in here, but knowing that I could pretty much hit a driver on most of the holes helped an awful lot. My short game sort of came back a little bit and when I missed the green I got up and down most of the time. It just felt good."

Later in the day, two more names joined Duval and Mickelson atop the leaderboard. Billy Mayfair birdied his first two holes and picked up a third birdie on the fourth hole en route to 67. Then Paul Goydos, who once earned a living by substitute teaching while working on his game, made five birdies, two bogeys and had five up-and-down par saves to also finish with 67. With one round completed, the leaderboard was crowded:

David Duval	67	Tiger Woods	68
Phil Mickelson	67	John Daly	68
Billy Mayfair	67	David Berganio	68
Paul Goydos	67	Kaname Yokoo	68
Payne Stewart	68		

The first news on Friday was before the first shot was struck. There would be no Grand Slam in 1999, since the only player with a chance to win the impregnable quadrilateral, Masters champion Jose Maria Olazabal, shot an opening-round 75 then took out his frustrations on a wall in the Carolina Hotel, breaking the fifth metacarpal of his right hand. "The doctor said I would be out three to four weeks," Olazabal said. "It was my fault, but fortunately, it was a clean break."

Adding confusion to the situation was that Olazabal's fuse didn't ignite until long after he had finished his round. After finishing bogey, bogey, par, double bogey and signing for his 75, Olazabal ate lunch, hit a few balls, spoke to a few reporters, then showered at his hotel and went to dinner with his manager, Sergio Gomez, at a local Thai restaurant. The waitresses there had their pictures taken with the Masters champion, and he and Gomez left around 10:30. It was only then that Olazabal decided his 75 was worth taking out a 12-inch concrete and plaster wall.

"That has to fall into that 'one-of-the-stupidest-things-I've-ever-done' category," said Pavin, who only nipped Olazabal by one shot in the opening round. "I've gotten mad enough to do it, but I've done other things. Obviously he feels dumb."

Duval couldn't hide an upturning at the corners of his mouth when asked about the incident, but when someone asked the demure Duval if he had ever thrown a similar fit, he said, "I had a putter about three years ago. I grabbed one end and grabbed the other end and broke it. Maybe that's the angriest thing I've ever done, but it was the putter's fault. It just wasn't working."

Mickelson denied even going that far. "I had to buy my clubs if I broke them," he said. "So I didn't break them."

As Olazabal, his hand in a cast, drove out of the parking lot, Greg Norman offered some words of counsel for the future. "It sounds like he misclubbed," Norman said. "It's always smarter to kick than punch."

Olazabal wasn't the day's last victim, although he was the only one who carried his departure to such extremes. Hale Irwin also withdrew for the first time in his professional career. Shoulder soreness led Irwin to seek expert advice. "They told me in the fitness trailer that it could be the rotator cuff," Irwin said. "Or it may be just some inflammation, but there's no sense in trying to play. I've got a lot of things coming up in my schedule. Still, this is something new for me."

Shooting 78-75 and missing the 36-hole cut by six shots was something new for Nicklaus as well. The still-not-fully-recovered Golden Bear tied amateur Andrew Barnes, Grant Masson, Jeff Freeman, Joe Durant and Chris Riley at 153. He did edge out Masashi (Jumbo) Ozaki by a shot, for what it was worth. At least Nicklaus wasn't among the 17 players who posted an 80 or higher in the first two rounds.

He also wasn't the only big name player to miss the cut. Scott Hoch, Nick Faldo, Fred Couples, Westwood, Appleby, O'Meara and Norman all checked out early. Nicklaus summed it up for all of them when he said in disgust, "It wasn't very good."

Scores on the whole were higher on Friday as the course dried out and the greens hardened, as the leaders had predicted. There were 89 fewer birdies in the second round than there were in the first, and 138 more bogeys. On average the field hit two-thirds of the fairways on Friday but missed over half the greens. The low round was 69, the high was 83 and the average score was 75.44, almost two full shots higher than Thursday's average.

One of those 69s belonged to Stewart, who had a two-birdie, two-bogey first nine, then birdied the par-three 15th with a four iron and a 15-foot putt to get to 69 for the day and 137 for the tournament. He was tied for the lead and confident about his chances.

"I feel good about the way I'm playing," Stewart said. "I'm playing better at the Open this year than I played last year, and I do have 36 holes left to play. I can't worry about what anybody else is doing. I could have crawled away and hid after what happened last year, or I could build on what happened and use it to strengthen myself. That's the avenue I chose to take. I think one of the reasons I do well at the U.S. Opens is that I get a mindset that par is a good score. However I go about making par — whether it's two beautiful golf shots and two putts or two ugly golf shots, a chip and a nice holed putt, whatever it is — I take my par and go. You're never losing to the field on any hole if you're making a par."

Duval and Mickelson didn't hear Stewart when he said that, but they were proving him right. Both first-round leaders shot even-par 70s to be at 137 with Stewart.

Unlike Thursday's even-keel round, Duval's 70 was a roller coaster ride. Two birdies in the first five holes were immediately followed by a double-bogey five on the sixth. That was followed by two birdies on the seventh and eighth, followed by a bogey at the par-three ninth for 34 on the first nine that included only three pars. The second nine was more like Duval usually plays. He missed two greens, the 11th and 16th, and failed to save par both times. For the second day in a row, he hit a seven iron close on the par-three 17th and made birdie to get back to even par for the day. It was the kind of round Duval said, "makes me a little goofy." Still, he held a share of the lead and was pleased.

The other player at the top of the leaderboard had a much more consistent round than on Thursday, with no beepers going off to distract him. Mickelson made two birdies and two bogeys, and saved pars after missing the greens on four occasions. "I felt starting the day that 70 was going to be an exceptional score because the wind was stronger and the greens weren't nearly as soft," Mickelson said. "I would have taken 70 at the start, and I'm very pleased to take 70 at the end."

At the end of the second round, the leaderboard looked like this:

Payne Stewart	69 - 137	Vijay Singh	70 - 139
Phil Mickelson	70 - 137	Billy Mayfair	72 - 139
David Duval	70 - 137	Jeff Maggert	69 - 140
Tiger Woods	71 - 139	John Huston	69 - 140
Hal Sutton	70 - 139		

The wind and heat were never brutal on Friday and Saturday, but they were steady, making hard fast greens even harder and faster. Players had a better chance of throwing a rock onto a beachball and having it stick than they did stopping approach shots on Pinehurst's greens. What once were negotiable but demanding targets were becoming impossible. John Cook, the first player to finish on Saturday, said, "A birdie today is out of the question unless you chip in, hole a bunker shot, or make a 30-foot putt. You're not going to hit it close from anywhere on the fairway. I played it as a par 88." With that as the standard, Cook shot an 11-under-par 77 for the day, which was only 1.03 shots higher than the field average.

It was the second-hardest U.S. Open day of the 1990s, the first coming in a strong wind during the opening around of the 1992 Open at Pebble Beach. When you consider that the wind on Saturday in North Carolina wasn't strong enough to blow a pine cone out of a tree, the condition of the golf course becomes apparent.

"I've been asked many times to name the hardest golf course I've ever played," Janzen said after posting 76. "Now I have the answer."

Golf writer Bob Verdi suggested a new statistical category after the third round: greens visited briefly in regulation. Woods said he might have led that category. "I hit a lot of greens today," Woods said. "The ball didn't stay on, but I hit them."

Only one player, Steve Stricker, broke par. Stricker shot 69 and moved three shots closer to the lead. The next lowest score was 70 by Tim Herron, but without Stricker's and Herron's scores, the benchmark for the day was two-over-par 72, shot by Stewart, Woods and Scott Verplank. Everyone else shot 73 or higher, in some cases much higher. Lehman, who shot 73, called the course "August National on steroids."

"I can't recall a lot of courses that are more difficult," Woods said. "I knew it was going to be a struggle. I just happened to be out early, but I look forward to tomorrow. Everybody is going to back up more. The guy who backs up the smallest amount is probably going to win. The harder it is, the better it is."

Just as was the case in 1998, Stewart was the only player under par after 54 holes. His lead then had been three shots. This time it was only one over Mickelson and two over Woods. Duval shot 75 and dropped four off the lead, but as he and everyone else knew, anything could happen on Sunday at the U.S. Open.

"I would like to think that my knowledge and my maturity and my understanding will all benefit me tomorrow," Stewart said. "Like I told myself today, 'You've won this championship before and you deserve to be out here the way you are performing.'" Stewart's two-over-par day included a birdie from 15 feet on the final green, and his comments foretold his expectation of the final round. "I love this golf tournament," he said. "I enjoy playing where pars get rewards, no matter how you make them. My adrenaline gets flowing more, my concentration is better, and all of those things put me in the position I'm in now, I guess.

"The other people who are not with me, who haven't won the U.S. Open, have a different pressure on them. There's going to be pressure on me, and if I get to the first tee and I'm not nervous, then something is really wrong with me. I'll be sick. But it's a nervous excitement. It's a lot of adrenaline, and in that situation, you have to be able to control all your emotions. That's what the USGA does. It tests everything. They test your mental, your physical ... They test it all!"

With one round remaining, the leaders were:

Payne Stewart	72 - 209	Steve Stricker	69 - 212
Phil Mickelson	73 - 210	David Duval	75 - 212
Tiger Woods	72 - 211	Billy Mayfair	74 - 213
Tim Herron	70 - 211	Jeff Maggert	74 - 214
Vijay Singh	73 - 212		

Even before the leaders teed off, the crowd's enthusiasm had swelled with cheers and shouts. Practice at the nearby putting green stopped when Woods was announced because of the roar from the gallery. Duval received a similar ovation. None of them, however, earned the kind of sustained cheers that Mickelson and Stewart received. As the players walked from the putting green to the first tee, the thunderous greeting left them shocked. Mickelson said something to McKay, his caddie, but he couldn't hear him even though he was only two feet away. Mickelson just smiled and shook his head. He couldn't even hear himself. There was a brief moment of silence as the leaders were introduced, then the roars started again.

Up ahead there were roars as well. Woods birdied the first hole to draw within one shot of the lead, then Duval birdied the second and third holes to pull back within a shot. Tiger went on an up-and-down stretch where he bogeyed the third, but got it back with a birdie at the par-five fourth, then bogeyed the fifth. He moved to the second nine at even par on his round, one over for the tournament and trailing by three. Duval found trouble, bogeying the seventh and eighth holes before hitting his ball into the green-side bunker at the ninth, where he took two shots to get out. A double bogey dropped Duval to two over for his round and out of contention for the championship.

Meanwhile, Stewart had an eventful opening to his round. A three wood and seven iron on the first hole ended up 15 feet from the hole and he made birdie. A pushed three iron on the second hole cost him a bogey and he fell back to one under for the tournament. That changed again at the third, the 335-yard par-four, when Stewart hit a three iron and nine iron to two feet and made the putt for his second birdie in three holes.

Mickelson had no such adventures. Routine pars on the first three holes were followed by more pars on the fourth, fifth and sixth. It wasn't until a 30-foot birdie putt at the seventh caught the edge of the hole and fell in that Mickelson moved back to within one of the lead. Both he and Stewart turned in one-under 34.

Ahead of them Vijay Singh, who started the day three shots off the lead, also turned in 34, but quickly gained one more with a birdie at the par-five 10th to move within one shot of Mickelson and two of Stewart.

The leaderboard changed quickly on the second nine. After driving in the fairway bunker, Stewart hit a poor third shot at the 10th, then a mediocre chip before missing a 10-footer for par. He had committed the cardinal sin of professional golf by making bogey on a par-five. There weren't many birdie opportunities in U.S. Open conditions and the par-fives were usually them. Granted the 10th measured a whopping 610 yards, but it was still a straightforward hole that most players had at least parred. When he needed it most, Stewart hadn't been able to produce. He had let Mickelson gain a share of the lead on an unforced error.

Another poor tee shot at the 12th forced Stewart to chip back out to the fairway. Then he hit a wedge to 15 feet but missed his par effort to give Mickelson the outright lead. It appeared to be a repeat of 1998 with Stewart falling back and allowing anyone who made pars to catch him.

That was what Mickelson kept doing. He parred the 10th, 11th, 12th, 13th, 14th and 15th, and even after Stewart birdied the 13th with a 15-footer to draw even again, he gave it right back with a bogey at the par-three 15th. Mickelson felt he had the crowd with him, the beeper hadn't gone off (even though several gallery members told his caddie they would buy it from him to keep the tournament going), and he held a one-stroke lead with three holes to play.

That's when both members of the last group heard a roar up ahead. Woods, who had bogeyed the 11th when he pushed a two-foot putt, drained a birdie at the 489-yard 16th, the longest par-four in the history of major championship golf. A three on the 16th was always enough to pick up one shot on the field and sometimes enough to pick up two. Stewart and Mickelson knew what had happened. They also knew that the outcome of the Open was in their hands.

Stewart, at 42 years old, was never considered a long driver of the golf ball although he wasn't short either. He was consistently in the top third in total driving, which was fine as long as he didn't have to play 489-yard converted par-fives as par-fours. Then he struggled. This time he hit a good drive in the center of the fairway, which gave him a slight advantage over Mickelson, who found the rough. Stewart's two-iron approach went into the right rough, while Mickelson chipped back to the fairway, then hit a seven iron to eight feet.

"For some reason I felt I needed to chip that ball in," Stewart said. It made perfect sense. Mickelson was more likely to make the eight-footer than miss it, but if Stewart could chip in with birdie and apply a little pressure, anything could happen. "I hit a very poor chip, and I shouldn't have thought that way. As it went 25 feet past the hole I said to myself, 'You didn't need to do that.'"

Not only had he not made the chip, he hadn't even gotten inside Mickelson's ball. It looked as thought that might be the tournament. If Mickelson could have opened a two-shot lead with two to play, the tournament should, by all rights, have been his.

No one knew that better than Stewart. As he prepared to putt his 25-footer, he remembered that he had played that hole all week as if it had been a par-five. This was just another birdie putt in his mind. The card simply read par-four. It was, in his estimation, a good par-five. "So I stood up there and I got my line," he said. "I went though my routine that I've been doing all day with my putter, and I made my stroke. I looked up and it's going in the hole. It's another birdie on 16, and off I went."

The crowd erupted with cheers at Stewart's performance at the 16th. Mickelson, meanwhile, pulled his eight-foot par putt. "It didn't go left," he said. "I pulled it."

They were tied with two holes remaining.

Woods was only one shot back, playing ahead of the leaders. He hit a seven iron to eight feet at the par-three 17th and another Tiger roar went out from the gallery. "Unfortunately, I hit the putt too hard," Woods said. "The line I chose was inside left, and if you look at it, it hit the inside left of the hole and lipped out. At that pace you had to go left center, and I just hit it too hard."

He had one more chance when his approach shot to the 18th stopped 35 feet from the hole. The putt broke two feet, and while he hit the edge of the hole going slowly, the birdie didn't fall. Woods finished with an even-par round of 70 and tied for third place at 281 with Singh, who shot 69.

On the 17th tee, the leaders were preparing to hit their tee shots when McKay, Mickelson's caddie, overheard something that surprised him. As Stewart and Hicks were discussing what club to hit on the downhill 191-yard hole, the debate seemed to be between the six and seven iron. McKay was sure they would choose the seven. In that situation, with adrenaline pumping so hard you could feel it with each heartbeat, you rarely chose the longer club. So when Stewart said to Hicks, "Let's go with the smooth six," McKay tried not to show any sign of surprise. Nobody tried to "smooth" anything under those circumstances. A smooth six was something you hit in practice rounds. The 71st hole of the U.S. Open when you're tied for the lead was a time to grip it and rip it. But Stewart went with the longer club.

"I put a real good swing on that six iron," Stewart said. "All four rounds, my shots at 17 went right at the pin this week." The shot never left the flag, stopping three feet from the hole.

Mickelson followed with a strong seven-iron shot that finished mere inches outside of Stewart's. But Mickelson putted first, and for the second time in two holes he pulled his putt and it caught the edge without going in. Stewart stepped up to his ball and rolled it in for a birdie two and a one-shot lead with one hole to play.

USGA officials warned the final group that they were "on the clock" after they fell behind the group ahead of them at the 16th. It was an annoyance to Stewart, who turned to the official and said, "I didn't realize this was a foot race." He put his annoyance behind him for one last hole. When he struck the tee shot at the 18th, he thought it was in the fairway, but the ball bounded into the right rough and disappeared.

"When I got up there I had no chance to even think about the green," he said. "So I took my medicine and put the ball out there where I at least could give myself a chance to get up and down. That's what I've done all week. When I was in a bad position, I didn't compound the situation by making two mistakes in a row. Once I saw Phil hit his shot (onto the green), I didn't feel like he was going to make that one. That was a very difficult putt. I figured I wanted to be underneath the hole putting back up at it. I would have liked my chip to be a little closer, but I knew my putt was going to go up and to the right. I said to myself, 'It's an inside left putt. Just believe it.' So I stood there and went though my routine and kept my head still. When I looked up it was about two feet from the hole and breaking right in the center. I couldn't believe it. I couldn't believe I had accomplished another dream of mine."

Stewart and Mickelson both finished with 70s, Stewart having a one-under-par 279 total to Mickelson's 280.

After the victory celebration with Hicks, Stewart embraced Mickelson and said, "You're going to be father! There's nothing better in this world. God love you." Then Stewart found his wife Tracey and fell into her outstretched arms, tears of joy streaming down his face. He had captured his second U.S. Open title — a trophy that would turn out to be the last he would ever hoist. But even though Payne Stewart passed too young, he left a great legacy and some great memories, none greater though than the final day at the 99th U.S. Open Championship.

4. British Open Championship

No player until the 128th British Open Championship at Carnoustie had come from more than five strokes back to win. Three champions had overcome a five-stroke deficit to hold the silver claret jug: Jim Barnes at Prestwick in 1925, Tommy Armour in the first Carnoustie Open in 1931 and Justin Leonard at Royal Troon in 1997. As fate would have it, entering the final round, Leonard shared second place with Craig Parry, five strokes behind Jean Van de Velde.

Leonard almost repeated the trick the American had performed at Royal Troon and twice elsewhere, including the 1998 Players Championship. Van de Velde should have become the first Frenchman to win the British Open since Arnaud Massy at Hoylake in 1907. None of this came to pass. It was all far more extraordinary than that.

Paul Lawrie started the final round at Carnoustie 10 strokes behind Van de Velde. Even when the Scot had finished with a closing 67, he thought he had no hope. When Van de Velde teed off at the 72nd hole with a three-stroke lead, he should have had no hope. But the Frenchman incredibly took a seven at the last and there was a three-way, four-hole playoff.

Eventually, in the rain and the gloaming, Sir Michael Bonallack, for the last time as secretary of the Royal and Ancient Golf Club, proclaimed Lawrie as the "champion golfer of the year" and the 30-year-old from Aberdeen held the trophy aloft.

Lawrie was the first qualifier to win the British Open since exemptions for the leading players were introduced in 1963. But more importantly, he was the first Scot to win since Sandy Lyle at Sandwich in 1985 and the first Scottish-born player to win in Scotland since Armour 68 years before, and even then, though the "Silver Scot" was born in Edinburgh, he was a naturalized American. He thus was the first home-based Scot to win in Scotland since Willie Auchterlonie in 1893.

"It is a huge thing to win the Open, no matter where it is," Lawrie said, "but obviously here it is extra special being so close to home. Every kid dreams of winning the Open. There's probably no golfer who doesn't dream of winning the Open."

For many, the British Open was a nightmare. Carnoustie had not played host to the Open for 24 years. In the intervening time the course had fallen into neglect before being restored to its former glory. A new hotel, behind the 18th green and the first tee, was completed just months before. The course superintendent, John Philp, produced an immaculately conditioned links golf course, but many worried that the combination of narrow fairways and high rough with the inevitable wind that buffets the Barry headland might be too daunting even for the world's best players. Some thought the winner would not break 300.

When Rodney Pampling, a 29-year-old Australian, completed his first round shortly before noon on Thursday, he became the first player to match Carnoustie's strict par of 71. Almost 10 hours later, he had become the only player to match par.

"I knew it was a good score, but I didn't realize I would be leading at the end of the day," Pampling said that evening. "It was nice to sit back at home and watch everyone else struggle on television."

Pampling began his round at 7:25, along with Bernhard Langer and Steve Pate. Langer scored 72 to share second place with Scott Dunlap, while Pate had 73, two over par, to tie for fourth in a group that included Leonard and Lawrie. Van de Velde was two worse with 75, dropping four strokes in the final four holes.

Langer, one of the best managers of his game in difficult conditions, described the challenge presented by Carnoustie's 7,361 yards by saying, "It is the longest course I think we've ever played and yet there are so many holes you can't hit driver on because it is just too narrow. It's not percentage golf at all."

The average first-round score was 78.31, or seven over par, and out of the starting field of 156, some 57 failed to break 80. Tom Watson, the 1975 champion at Carnoustie, scored 82, the same as Zane Scotland, an Englishman despite his name who just a few days before his 17th birthday was one of the youngest players ever to come through regional and final qualifying. Mark O'Meara had handled the wind superbly at Royal Birkdale the year before, but now the defending champion, he slipped to 83. "It does hurt your pride to shoot in the 80s," O'Meara said. "I mean, I'm a professional golfer. But I felt I got the score I deserved today."

Sergio Garcia was the center of attention after the 19-year-old Spaniard, who won the amateur honors at Augusta in April, won his first PGA European Tour event, the Murphy's Irish Open, with a stunning final round of 64. But he started with a triple-bogey seven and his 89 was "beaten" only by Tom Gillis' 90 and the 91 from Prayad Marksaeng, the first Thai golfer to qualify to play in the Open.

Such was the clamor that by the end of the day the Royal and Ancient officials were explaining it was not their intent to embarrass the competitors. Nor had fertilizer been put on the rough to make it grow so tangled. "We don't set out to make the players look like idiots," said Bonallack. "Carnoustie has lived up to its reputation as the hardest championship course. We don't like seeing players struggle, but this is a test of character as well as golf."

Pampling went out in 36, mainly thanks to a short game that made sure he had only 10 putts despite only finding the sixth green in regulation figures. Eschewing a driver for much of the round, he played the hole with two driving irons and a six iron. "My driving iron has a loft of 18 degrees and goes about 180 into the wind and 300 downwind," Pampling said.

The Australian parred the first 11 holes but then only two more. His first dropped shot came the 12th, where he drove into the rough, wedged out but missed the green with his third. The damage was repaired with a nine iron to 10 feet at the short 13th and then, at the 515-yard 14th, playing downwind, Pampling hit his driving iron and a six iron to 25 feet and holed the putt for an eagle to go two under par.

Carnoustie's last four holes can destroy many a card and dropped shots at the 15th and 17th was better than most achieved. This was Pampling's first visit to the Open and followed his first victory on the Australasian Tour earlier in the year at the Canon Challenge in Sydney. Having grown up in the Queensland farming town of Caboolture, Pampling had done a three-year greenskeeping apprenticeship to get out of school. "I don't mind the wind," Pampling said. "My ball flight is generally low anyway, so I don't have to worry about keeping it low, and it makes you think a lot harder. The course was playing extremely hard. If you don't hit the fairways you are looking at bogey straightaway, if not worse."

"There are so many things you have to factor into each shot," Leonard said. "After 72 holes here, I think the guys are going to need a few days off." The young American had taken the opportunity over the practice days to savor some of the history of the town, especially that relating to the late Hogan. Leonard represents the equipment company founded by the 1953 champion. "This is a special place and it means a lot that Mr. Hogan did so well here," Leonard said. "I was walking back from dinner two days ago and a gentleman stopped me and talked about Mr. Hogan for 20 minutes. He was so excited, I worried he was going to have heart palpitations."

With a late tee time, Lawrie was able to have a lie-in at home in Aberdeen, an hour by car up the coast north of Carnoustie, and watch some of the golf on television before setting out for work. By the time the 30-year-old had finished, at 8:40 p.m., his card showed only three bogeys and a birdie at the 12th.

As well as the hazards faced by everyone else, Lawrie had the added distractions of a cool evening, plus the noise of various people packing up and the waste collection vans moving in. "That was the draw I was given and you just have to get on with it," he said. "I've no complaints and would take 73 every day around here."

As far as distractions go, Tiger Woods had what turned out to be the most enjoyable. As the world's No. 1 player lined up his putt at the 18th, a scantily clad woman, dressed only in bra and panties, ran onto the green to give Tiger a hug and a kiss. Yvonne Robb, a 20-year-old dancer, then spent the night at the pleasure of the Arbroath Constabulary.

The first hint for Woods that something was happening as he was crouching over the line of his putt came from one of his playing partners, Ian Woosnam. "I looked up and Woosie was laughing," Woods explained. "He was still chuckling and then all of a sudden I saw these feet run by. With my spikes, I didn't want to step on her bare feet. She gave me a hug and a kiss and ran off."

For the record, Tiger's putt came up just short of the hole. His game plan was to steer his way around the course and he only used the driver at the fourth, which cost his first bogey in a 74. "I hit some pretty weird clubs off the tees but I kept the ball in play beautifully and just wasn't able to make the birdie putts," Woods said. "You have to stay away from the high numbers."

These were the first-round leaders:

Rodney Pampling	71	Dudley Hart	73
Bernhard Langer	72	Hal Sutton	73
Scott Dunlap	72	Justin Leonard	73
Mark McNulty	73	Len Mattiace	73
Steve Pate	73	Paul Lawrie	73

Where no one ventured the previous day, under par, seven players made it in the second round. Four players managed rounds in the 60s, led by Van de Velde with 68 that gave him the halfway lead at 143, one over par. There were 69s for David Frost and Costantino Rocca, both of whom had failed to break 80 on Thursday, and for Argentina's Angel Cabrera, who moved into second place at two-over 144.

Three others scored rounds of 70, Mark Brooks, with the day's lowest first nine of 32 thanks to birdies at four of the first six holes, Tim Herron and Greg Norman.

Once again the wind blew hard, but the early morning calm lasted longer than on Thursday. All seven of the sub-par men had early starting times, but Van de Velde was actually the last of them to set off, at 10:25. He therefore played most of his round in similar conditions to the day before, but managed to score seven strokes better.

It helped that for 12 holes Van de Velde did not drop a shot. Better than that, he birdied the sixth, with a putt from 30 feet, and the seventh, with a four iron to 15 feet. He bogeyed the 13th and failed to birdie the par-five 14th, one of the few holes to average under its par. Now he stood on the 15th tee, and his thoughts returned to how he played the last four holes in the first round.

"Playing the 15th yesterday, I was level par," Van de Velde recalled. "But then I put an iron into the bunker on 15 and had to chip out sideways because it hit the face and plugged. Then I hit a seven iron to six feet and missed. So I bogeyed there and I bogeyed 16 because again I missed the green and didn't get up and down. Then on 17, I made a perfect drive but took a wrong decision. I took a two iron, tried to hit it low and ended in the face of a bunker. So that was a six but, you know, 75 was still all right, no disaster, just a poor finish."

This time, leaving the 14th green, Van de Velde turned to his caddie, a compatriot by the name of Christophe Angiolini, and said, "I will try to think well, try to hit the proper shots and let's try to put four pars in the bag."

Through the back of the 15th green, after a four iron and an eight iron, Van de Velde chipped to three feet to get up and down. At the next, the 250-yard 16th, he found the green and holed across the putting surface, fully 50 feet, "a monster," he enthused, for a birdie two. At the 17th, he safely took his par, and then at the 18th, a 487-yard hole playing downwind, he hit a two iron and a wedge to three feet for another birdie. From four over par the previous day, he was two under for the last four holes this time. No one else got close to doing the same.

"Obviously, I am very pleased," Van de Velde said. "It is very, very tough. If you miss a fairway, you are not going to get a break, you just have to go out sideways. And it is very draining to be out there all day. The holes playing downwind are at least as difficult as those into the wind, probably more because you have to allow for the run and the bounce."

Van de Velde was the first Frenchman to lead the British Open since Jean Garaialde tied Christy O'Connor, Sr., after the first round at St. Andrews in 1964.

For Cabrera, known as "El Pato" or the Duck, there was the inspiration of another Argentine, Roberto de Vicenzo, winning the Open in 1967 at Hoylake. When he hit a seven iron to two feet at the 16th, he claimed his fourth birdie of the round. "The big names don't matter to me," he added.

"All I see is the course. I don't know who is behind me."

Almost everyone, actually, but it was Norman who was beginning to look like a potent threat. Starting the day five over par, Norman was still four under for the round on the 17th tee. Now the hardest hole on the course, 459 yards into the wind, the 17th cost the Shark a triple-bogey seven. His drive finished three yards off the fairway, but so thick was the rough he did not move the ball as he attempted to hack out. On his next swing, Norman got the ball over the Barry Burn into the rough on the left. From there he had to chop out again and, from the fairway, was short with his fifth before getting up and down for the triple bogey.

"I got a real dose of the punishment and it doesn't feel good," admitted Norman, a two-time British Open champion. "I don't think my tee shot deserved or warranted having an air swing for my second shot. I was right over the top of it and couldn't see the ball. I had to guesstimate where it was and was only trying to move it six, 12 feet, not 100 yards.

"I don't think that's the way the game should be played. The width of the fairway is fine, but not having rough you cannot move your ball in nine feet off the fairway. I don't like the circumstances I got the seven, but I accept it. Forgetting that hole, I did what I wanted to do today and got myself into position come the weekend."

Woods did the same and still managed to keep a high number off his card. His 72 promised more than it delivered after he rolled in a 30-footer at the first hole and again he had a poor finish, bogeying the 16th and 18th.

"Right now good shots are borderline," Woods said. "You have to hit great shots. But I have always enjoyed playing in terrible conditions. Growing up in southern California, we didn't have too many bad days, but I took advantage of the ones we did have because I enjoyed it. You have to use your repertoire of shots and not be afraid to trust your instincts. I'm in good shape right now. Any time you are moving up spots on the leaderboard, you must be playing well."

The American was suffering from hay fever, but not as severely as Parnevik, whose 71 in the circumstances might have been the most valiant effort of the day. "It could have been 78 or 79, so to shoot a 71 is beyond my dreams, actually," said the Swede. "I was very close to walking in after the fifth. I was sneezing constantly and my nose was dripping all the time, even on the ball. I had to time my putts and shots between the sneezes."

Parnevik stuck a bit of tissue up each nostril and a marshal came to his aid by seeking medical assistance. "He gave me something that he said was going to help but it didn't, actually," Parnevik said. "But then I birdied No. 7, so I decided to carry on."

There, he hit one of his best one irons to 20 feet and holed the putt, while at the next, the 183-yard eighth hole, he hit a seven iron to six feet. Twice a runner-up in the British Open, at Turnberry in 1994 and Royal Troon in 1997, playing in difficult conditions appeals to Parnevik's inquiring mind and sense of the ridiculous. "At the eighth, I was just trying to hook it at the out of bounds on the left and hoping the wind was going to straighten it out sooner or later," he said.

His second nine consisted of a birdie at the 10th and a bogey at the 17th to be two behind Van de Velde. After 36 holes, Leonard and Lawrie were four behind at five over par after both had rounds of 74. If neither man took full advantage of the slightly easier conditions in the morning, both showed the virtue of not giving up.

Never before had the first-round leader in the British Open missed the 36-hole cut. Pampling did so with 86, one of the 31 rounds of 80 or worse during the day. He had 10 bogeys, a double bogey and a triple bogey. "I didn't feel worried being the leader," said the Australian. "I just got off to a slow start with bogeys at the first two holes and you can't pick it up on this course. I didn't play well all day and kept getting bad lies. All of a sudden, you have a lot of score. I will always have the knowledge that I led the Open, but I will always have the bad second round, too."

O'Meara improved from 83 to 74 but became the first defending champion since Mark Calcavecchia in 1990 to miss the cut. Many other former champions failed to qualify, including Nick Faldo, for the first time since his debut in the Open in 1976 at the age of 18. Garcia scored an 83 to finish dead last at 30 over par.

The leaders after the second round were:

Jean Van de Velde	68 - 143	Brian Watts	73 - 147
Angel Cabrera	69 - 144	Bradley Hughes	71 - 147
Jesper Parnevik	71 - 145	Justin Leonard	74 - 147
Patrik Sjoland	72 - 146	Len Mattiace	74 - 147
Greg Norman	70 - 146	Paul Lawrie	74 - 147
Tiger Woods	72 - 146		

Van de Velde started the third day leading by one stroke and, with 70, completed 54 holes with a 213 total and a five-stroke advantage. The previous day, Van de Velde said one of the heroes who inspired him to play the game was Seve Ballesteros. On this Saturday, he played like Seve. He got up and down from everywhere, holed everything, it seemed, on the greens. Just when the rest of the field thought he was heading back towards them, Van de Velde birdied the 14th and the 18th, the latter accompanied with an impassioned fist-pumping display, to lay down a comfortable cushion for the night. He was the only player to stand at even par for the championship with a round to play.

A calm but drizzly start gave way to the strongest gusts of the week around lunchtime and early afternoon, before the wind died again and the sun came out to shepherd the Frenchman home. Out of the 73 who had qualified for the last two rounds, only three men broke par and the low round of the day, compiled in the worst of the weather, was by Parry, whose 67 left the diminutive Australian sharing second place at 218 with Leonard, who had 71.

Parry started in 30th place at nine over and continued to make progress up the leaderboard even after completing his round. "You know, I am actually only five-foot-six, but I felt six-foot out there the way I was playing," he said.

Parry, who finished third in the Scottish Open at Carnoustie in 1995, birdied the third from six feet but felt he might be in for a good day when he holed from 35 feet from off the front of the green at the fourth. At the par-five sixth, he put a one iron into the rough but had a good enough lie to hit a seven iron up the fairway. With 224 yards to the flag, he then hit another one iron to six feet and holed that for his third birdie. The fourth arrived courtesy of a 15-footer at the 10th, but he immediately three-putted at the next hole.

The dropped shot did not affect his momentum. He got up and down from a bunker at the 14th for another birdie and then hit a five iron to 12 feet at the 16th. "I am always happy to hit that green, let alone make birdie," Parry said. He could not save par from a thick patch of rough by the 17th green but was still delighted by his effort.

"A lot of guys are complaining about this course," the 32-year-old said, "but someone is going to walk away with their name on the trophy. There is no use complaining about it. I've done enough of that about our courses in Australia and it is only going to get you into trouble. I really like bouncing the ball into the aprons of these greens. You have to use the banks and things like that. You've got to know links golf. I think I've had a long enough apprenticeship of playing links golf."

Other players had soon taken note of Parry's advance. "I did find myself watching the leaderboard to gauge what was going on," said Leonard. "Craig Parry's 67 is an incredible score, but for the most part, par is a very good score, too. Basically, the way I have tried to play all week is to play fairly conservatively and that didn't change too much today. I've accomplished my primary goal at the beginning of the week of having a chance to win the tournament going into Sunday."

Leonard's round was up and down — three birdies and a bogey on the first nine, three bogeys and a birdie on the second nine — but this was steadiness itself compared to Van de Velde. The Frenchman drove into a bunker at the 10th but got up and down from 95 yards for a par.

Another poor drive at the 11th finished in jungle right of the fairway. With an awful lie, Van de Velde decided his only option, instead of going for the green, was to chip sideways onto the fairway. For this shot, however, there was a television camera tower in his line of sight. "I asked the referee if I could get relief or, if I played it, if I killed the cameraman, what would happen?" Van de Velde explained. "The only shot I had was to come back on the fairway."

The referee with his group, Michael Lunt, granted free relief from the tower, although this was later admitted to be an error. From the fairway, Van de Velde pitched to six feet and holed the putt for another extraordinary par.

Having followed the instructions of the referee, Van de Velde was not liable for the error. But later, David Rickman, the R and A rules secretary, reviewed the television coverage and explained, "It is regrettable that the ruling on the 11th hole with Jean Van de Velde was incorrect. In the circumstances, the player's request was both reasonable and understandable, but, in accordance with the Local Rule for Temporary Immovable Obstructions, relief should not have been granted because no part of the tower intervened between the player's ball and the hole. That having been said, the referee's decision is final (Rule 34-2)."

At the time, Van de Velde had a bigger worry about his driving. He found more bunkers at the 12th, where he bogeyed, and the 14th where his third shot ran onto the adjoining fourth green at the back of the 14th. He was 70 feet away from the correct pin, but, magically, the ball disappeared for a birdie. "A good bonus," he admitted.

Once again, Van de Velde stood on the 15th tee hoping for four pars but knowing that disaster lurked on each. This time his second shot found a bunker to the left of the 15th green but he came out to five feet and saved par. He made a good two-putt at the 16th, and then found the right greenside bunker with his approach at the 17th. Another brilliant escape left him only a tap-in for par. And the 18th he played simply enough, with a two iron and a nine iron to 45 feet, and one putt. "For sure, I didn't play so well today but I was fighting very hard and that's all I can do," he said.

"Definitely, I am surprised to be five ahead," added Van de Velde, who had won the qualifying at Monifieth. "But, no I'm not surprised with myself. If you believe you can make it through, it might happen. If you don't believe, it will never happen. This is the biggest tournament in the world, but perhaps one of the smallest players is going to win.

"But the bottom line is, no matter what, even if I shoot 90 tomorrow, I'm going to enjoy it. Maybe people will say, 'Oh, he blew it,' or whatever. Maybe I'm going to blow it, it's the first time I've ever been there. What do you expect? You know I am not the No. 1 in the world. My knees are going to touch each other on the first tee tomorrow. But, let me tell you, I'm going to enjoy it."

While Van de Velde went off to enjoy his customary red wine over dinner, Woods was recalling how he felt before the final round of the 1997 Masters. "Anyone who has a lead like that has got to sleep on it," Woods said. "You know, that's not easy to do. It wasn't exactly an easy night's sleep before I won the Masters and I had a nine-shot lead."

Woods had made more pars than anyone else on Saturday, 16 of them, but had bogeyed the seventh and had his first double bogey of the week at the 17th, the result of missing the fairway off the tee. He could not remember a round in a major championship as a professional when he had not made a birdie, something he knew he could not afford on the final day. "Myself and a few other players who are right in the hunt need to play a great round of golf," Woods said. "What Craig Parry did today, we are going to have to do tomorrow."

Lawrie, after a disappointing 76, was 10 over par. His third round started bogey, bogey, birdie, bogey, par, bogey, bogey. He then had the day's longest run of pars, from the eighth to the 17th, before another bogey at the last. "I didn't play well today and five over was about right," he said.

"I'd imagine 10 over is a little too much out of the question. Van de Velde looks hard to beat, but the beast might roar again tomorrow. I'll be trying hard and if I could shoot like Parry did today then you can get back into the picture, but realistically you have to think it's too far away."

If Lawrie was not ruling himself out, he was not, like Woods, definitely ruling himself in. For all those chasing Van de Velde, Woods laid the ground rules for the next day. "Anyone who is 10 over par still has a shot at it," Woods declared. "If you can post a number early, you never know what can happen."

The leaderboard looked like this after the third round:

Jean Van de Velde	70 - 213	Angel Cabrera	77 - 221
Craig Parry	67 - 218	Frank Nobilo	70 - 222
Justin Leonard	71 - 218	Miguel Angel Martin	72 - 222
David Frost	71 - 220	Colin Montgomerie	72 - 222
Andrew Coltart	72 - 220	Bernhard Langer	73 - 222
Tiger Woods	74 - 220	Len Mattiace	75 - 222
Greg Norman	75 - 221	Paul Lawrie	76 - 223

Surely someone would make a move on the final day. It turned out to be Lawrie. His 67 equaled Parry's effort from the previous day as the low round of the week and, despite the improved conditions, was two strokes better than anyone else could manage in the round.

Lawrie's start was steady, a shot picked up at the third given away, however, at the fifth. But he holed from 35 feet at the sixth and 25 feet for a two at the eighth to be out in 34. A four iron to three feet at the 12th was not the last brilliant shot he would hit with that club. Now he was seven over and moving up the leaderboard.

A shot went at the short 13th, but he got back to seven over by getting up and down from beside the 14th green for a birdie. Then he got to six over with a 25-footer at the 17th, and he made sure he stayed there at the last. His approach with a five iron from a clumpy lie in the rough skirted over the Barry Burn and rolled into a greenside bunker on the left, but a fine recovery ensured his par.

It was a fine effort, better than Lawrie's last-round 65 to finish sixth in the 1993 Open at Royal St. George's. No one then, with the leaders still 90 minutes from finishing, knew quite how much better. "The way the course is set up, I would have to say that's my best round of golf ever," Lawrie said. "To shoot four under around here, even with no wind, is lovely."

Lawrie was in a relaxed mood as he discussed the top-four finish he would almost certainly achieve to book a debut trip to the Masters, how gaining a place on the European Ryder Cup team might be a possibility, and how pleasing it was to have played four rounds at Carnoustie and not had a double bogey or worse. "That's a big achievement for me because every hole is a potential double bogey, every single one," he said.

He revealed his parents, James, a taxi driver who would chauffeur him to junior events, and Margaret, and his brother, Stephen, were on holiday in Majorca. His wife Marian, who had caddied for him when he first set out on the PGA European Tour, was at home with their sons, Craig, four, and seven-month-old Michael. A week before, he was not even in the championship. He played the second nine of the second round at Downfield in four under par just to qualify. "I was desperate to make it," he said. "I was looking forward to coming to Carnoustie. I've won around this course before in the Daily Express Pro-Am in 1991."

And then someone informed him that four over was now leading on the course. "Does it really?" Lawrie said. "Where are my sticks? This interview is over. No. I still can't see six over winning. I'll probably be second, third or fourth but you never know, six over could play off."

Lawrie chatted away some more before leaving the press room. Few others were making a move. Woods still could not make a birdie and abandoned his safety-first approach from the tee. Pulling out the driver did not help, however, and instead of getting under par for the day, he drove into a bad spot on the 12th, hit his second shot into an even worse place, in a bush by the green for his second double bogey of the week. He limped home with 74 and finished tied with Davis Love III and Frost at 10 over.

Norman managed 72 to be nine over and Cabrera rallied after a poor third day with 70 to get into the clubhouse at seven over. Rather than Leonard, of the pair tied for second overnight, it was Parry who made the first move.

Bogeys from Van de Velde at the second and third, and a birdie by Parry at the latter, put the Australian only two behind. They were tied after a two-shot swing at the short eighth, the Frenchman three-putting from the front edge of the green, Parry holing from 10 feet. Van de Velde then birdied the ninth and Parry the 10th, but a bogey from Van de Velde at the next put the little Aussie into the lead for the first time. He did not hold it for long.

Parry drove into the rough and took three more to get out of it and three to get down from the back of the green. A triple-bogey seven and the Australian challenge was over. He bogeyed the next and took a double bogey at the 17th, eventually tying Cabrera at seven over.

Despite a second successive bogey at the 12th, Van de Velde was now back in the lead. His nearest rival was Leonard, but the American was looking his solid, reliable self. His second birdie of the day came at the 14th and took him into a tie for the lead, but he immediately dropped a shot at the next while Van de Velde, in the group behind, birdied the 14th. Leonard came to the 18th tee two behind. He reached for his three wood, determined to put the ball on the fairway, but saw it leak into the left rough.

Still, it was a good lie. He had 229 yards to the green, 216 to clear the Barry Burn. "I knew Jean was on the green at 17," Leonard said. "I felt I needed to make birdie. It didn't come out the way I hoped and ended up trickling into the burn."

Leonard took his drop and got up and down for a five. "At that point, I really didn't think it meant a lot," he said. "I thought I'd lost." In the scorer's hut, he signed for 72 that left him on the same six over total as Lawrie. By now, the Scot had been persuaded out onto the putting green by his coach, Adam Hunter, a former PGA European Tour player and fellow Scot.

"Adam did a great job of keeping me focused," Lawrie said. "He was the one who believed six over would win, or at worst get into a playoff." The first Leonard or Lawrie knew that they might be required again was when they caught sight, from their separate locations, of Van de Velde chipping into the burn at 18. Leonard hurried from the recorder's hut to the practice range.

Van de Velde had parred the 15th, 16th and 17th and had moved three ahead with Leonard's bogey at the last. "I stood there and there is no easy tee shot, I think," he said. "Even being three ahead, what do you do? Do you hit a five iron down the left or do you hit something down the right or do you try to go as far up as you can? I took that option. I didn't hit a good shot."

The Barry Burn, as well as cutting across in front of the green at the last, horseshoes around the start of the fairway. Van de Velde hit a wild push but his ball finished to the right of the burn on a little peninsula. "I was lucky to miss the creek," he admitted.

But what to do next? While all around were urging, or later claimed they were urging, the Frenchman to lay up onto the fairway, Van de Velde considered the going-for-the-green-option.

"I could not have placed the ball any better and the only thing I had was 189 yards to carry the burn, which wasn't very demanding. The only thing you didn't want to do was hit it left into the out of bounds. So the option was to hit a wedge down the left and pitch on and two-putt or three-putt or whatever, or to try to move forward. The ball was lying so good and I took my two iron and thought, 'You're going to hit it down there. Either you're on the green or just on the right in the bunker or the semi.'"

Again, however, Van de Velde hit a poor shot, pushing the ball to the right. On the plus side, he did clear the burn by some distance. Unfortunately, the ball was heading into the grandstand. Even then, had the ball finished in the stand, he would have got a free drop in the drop zone and would have made no worse than a five. "It was not something absolutely mad I was trying to do, it just came out to be a nightmare," he lamented.

What happened was a freak bounce. The ball hit the railing of the stand and rebounded backwards towards the burn, bounced off the top of the stone wall of the burn and finished in a horrid tangle of hay. "I would have been better off in the burn, because then I would have had somewhere to drop," he said.

"But no, it came back and I had a dramatic lie. I couldn't go backwards, I don't think I could have gone anywhere." With a few days' thought, Van de Velde said this was the shot he would like to take over again, a second time chipping back to the fairway. Instead, he took aim at the green which meant trying to cross the water. He failed to make the carry.

At this point, drama seemed to turn into farce. Van de Velde went to have a look at his ball in the burn, then started to take his shoes and socks off and clambered down into the water. He couldn't possibly be thinking of playing it, could he?

"When I looked at the ball from short of the green, it looked as if the ball was three-quarters outside the water. I knew I had to drop again, but as I started to climb down, I could see the ball sinking. It was two or three inches underneath the water so there was no hope. It was telling me: 'Hey, you, silly man. Not for you.'"

Van de Velde took his drop and had another bad lie, but this time got his pitch over the water and into the right-hand greenside bunker. Parry was in the same bunker and holed from the sand for a birdie. Van de Velde needed to do the same for a six and victory. He came out to 12 feet but holed the putt to get into the playoff.

With a closing 77, Van de Velde was the third player to finish on a total of 290. That meant the winner's score would be the highest for 53 years, but it was only one stroke more than the 289 at which Ian Woosnam won the Scottish Open at Carnoustie in 1996, when the par of the course was 72 instead of 71.

So for the second year running, a four-hole playoff was required, and when the players finally assembled on the 15th tee, Van de Velde told his opponents, "I thought it would be better if we kept the entertainment going, and that is why I have invited you to play a few more holes."

Each of the players hit terrible drives. None of them were in sight of the fairway, but while Leonard and Lawrie managed to scramble fives, Van de Velde, not surprisingly perhaps, had been so wild he ended up in a bush, had to take an unplayable and ended up with a six.

All three bogeyed the 16th. Was this Open ever going to be won? Although Van de Velde birdied the 17th, it was Lawrie who provided the answer. With a four iron to 15 feet, he set up a birdie chance that he gratefully took to give himself a one-stroke lead over Leonard.

The American was the player most expected to triumph from the unlikely threesome, but also with the most to lose. Having taken driver off the 18th tee this time around, amazingly, he put his second into the Barry Burn again. "I had an uphill lie, got a little behind the ball and hit it a hair fat," Leonard said.

Now Lawrie was in command and sent another four iron soaring towards the green, giving himself another close birdie chance. "I was shaking so much, but you don't want to miss a putt to win the Open," Lawrie said. "To birdie the last two holes to win is obviously a fairy story."

Leonard felt a double pang of disappointment. "Basically, I lost the British Open twice in one day, which is maybe twice as hard to take," he said. "But as bad as I feel, Jean must feel worse. If there is something he can learn from that, it's that he got himself into position to win the tournament."

"You know," Van de Velde said, "I made plenty of friends because a Scottish man won. Maybe I was not humble enough. I didn't need to go for glory. Maybe I should have laid up. But there's worse things in life. I read the newspaper like you this morning" — with the reports of the death of John F. Kennedy, Jr., in a plane crash — "and some terrible things are happening to other people. It is a golf tournament, a game, and I gave it my best shot. Next time I hit a wedge, okay, you all forgive me? You say I'm a coward, whatever. Next time I hit a wedge."

Holding the trophy, with a check for £350,000 and knowing his life was going to change, Lawrie acknowledged the Frenchman's part in his triumph. "Jean should have won. He had it in his pocket, no doubt about that," Lawrie said. "All he had to do was chip it down the fairway and make five. I would have chipped it down the fairway. No disrespect, but I'm glad he did what he did.

"On the 15th tee of the playoff, I didn't feel good, but the other two seemed as nervous as I was, Justin probably more because he was the one who was expected to win. But when I birdied the 17th, that was the moment I thought I could win. I knew I couldn't see myself bogeying the last. I had practiced too hard for that moment.

"I can't explain it, but I had a feeling at the start of the week that someone could come through who wasn't supposed to. With the knee-high rough and some of the big names complaining about it, which they are entitled to do, I felt if I kept quiet and did my own thing, I could come through."

5. PGA Championship

In a week filled with distractions and tense dialogue, the 81st PGA Championship came down to two players whose combined age was still almost a decade shy of Senior PGA Tour eligibility, and whose performances on a sunny Sunday outside Chicago in Medinah, Illinois, set the stage for a much-anticipated rivalry of the future. In the final nine holes of the final major championship of the 20th century, golf fans saw a glimpse of the 21st century, and a tournament that risked becoming one of the dullest in a decade sprang to life thanks to the dramatic play by Tiger Woods and Sergio Garcia, the charging teenage Spaniard he beat by one stroke.

There was a certain Jack Nicklaus-Arnold Palmer air to the final holes at Medinah Country Club as Garcia pulled off one shot after another in his attempt to catch Woods. The world's No. 1 player would not be denied his second major title, and when Woods two-putted the 18th green for an even-par 72 and an 11-under-par 277 total, he slumped his shoulders in exhaustion, hugged his mother, his coach and his girlfriend, then embraced the 19-year-old Garcia in a show of sportsmanship that roused an ovation from the enthusiastic gallery.

At that moment all the bickering over money and complaints about heat-stressed greens became secondary. Golf had a new rivalry. As Nicklaus and Gary Player were to Palmer, and Lee Trevino, Johnny Miller and Tom Watson were to Nicklaus, Garcia, with his swashbuckling style, magnetic personality and flair for hitting dramatic golf shots in pressure-packed situations, asserted himself as the challenger, while Woods continued to prove his dominance by picking up his 15th worldwide victory in a three-year professional career. He was the fifth youngest player to win the PGA Championship at 23 years, seven months, 16 days.

Woods' sense of relief was obvious. He had finished in the top 10 in seven of the 12 major championships he had entered and endured near-misses at the 1999 U.S. and British Opens, and he was a more mature person than the kid who shattered numerous Masters records while marching to a 12-stroke victory in 1997. "Getting number two is definitely a relief," Woods said. "I've given myself chances. I've come close. I've been right there. Sometimes you just need a bit of luck to go your way. This week I definitely played well, but I also had a few lucky breaks."

It should have come as no surprise that Woods and Garcia, two of the game's longest hitters, were dueling it out in the final two groups. The No. 3 course at Medinah, a storied layout that played host to U.S. Opens in 1949, 1975 and 1990, had undergone a series of renovations for the PGA Championship. The result was a 7,401-yard monster, one of the longest courses to host a major championship. After the spectacles of the U.S. Open at Pinehurst, where the average score on Saturday was almost five over par, and the British Open at Carnoustie, a course that some thought was unplayable, the prospect of the final major of the year being contested on a 7,401-yard, brick-hard, high-rough course left many pros shaking their heads.

"I object to the disproportionate emphasis placed on length," Nick Faldo said of both Carnoustie and Medinah. "Yes, we are all hitting the ball a little farther nowadays, but shouldn't we also be encouraged to hit it a little straighter? Is length more important than accuracy and control? More to the point, should length be more significant than imagination and judgment? Why is it, I wonder, that the golf holes we tend to remember best are the par-three holes?"

Even at the new length, Medinah's most memorable holes were the par-threes, three of which measured over 200 yards. The 17th provided the most controversial change, with a newly located green. That renovation came as a result of the USGA's decision to use only one pin placement on the 17th during the 1990 Open. "The slope of the green was too severe," USGA executive director David Fay said of the old 17th. In 1999, the slope wasn't a problem, since the new green was much larger and gentler than the original, but instead of a 168-yard tee shot over Lake Kadijah, the new 17th measured 205 yards.

"The change on 17 will make it a different hole," said Hale Irwin, winner of the 1990 Open. "I remember hitting six and seven irons into that hole. Now the water is not a factor. Your focus now goes from precision to length. I've always thought that on the last few holes of a major championship it's good to introduce nerves. Often the pressure comes not from hitting the ball for distance, but with putting the ball in the proper position on the green."

The par-three 13th also underwent renovations that included adding length. For the PGA Championship, the hole would measure 219 yards over Lake Kadijah. The 16th was also lengthened to a whopping 452-yard, dogleg-left par-four with two hundred-year-old hardwood trees overhanging the left side of the fairway and green. Little could the committee members have known that their newly designed 16th would become the focal point for the most talked about shot of the tournament and the most memorable iron shot of the year.

Many, including Irwin, were skeptical of the changes. "If they're going to play Medinah at 7,400 yards, I may be ready for the funny farm," he said.

The concern was well founded. On the eve of the 1990 Open, when Medinah played at 7,185 yards, the USGA's P.J. Boatwright concluded that the greatest golfers in the world would never break 80 on the diabolical layout, so he ordered the rough cut on Wednesday afternoon. To the hue and cry of Medinah members, many of whom were looking forward to seeing Irwin, Faldo and Watson struggle around their treasured No. 3, the USGA softened the course before play began, then rains on Wednesday and Thursday softened it even further.

"The club was furious," said Frank Hannigan, former USGA executive director. "But it wasn't cutting the rough. It was the storm that softened the course which had been rock hard. Without it, par would have been out of the question. The winning score would have been (six-over-par) 290." When Irwin stood victorious after 91 holes, 72 in regulation followed by a 19-hole playoff with Mike Donald, the winning total was seven under par, a far cry from an assault on the course's integrity, but low enough to prompt the changes before big-hitters like Woods, Garcia and David Duval took their turn at No. 3.

With or without rough, it was bound to be a tough test. Three of the par-five holes played over 580 yards, while six of the par-fours were 439 yards or longer. "Medinah has proven itself to be one of our better golf courses,"

Irwin said. "It mandates that you be a good iron player, but if you don't put it in the fairway, your irons aren't going to do you any good. It's a position golf course because of the number of trees that come into play, so it places a premium on accuracy off the tee."

With length, accuracy and putting being put to the ultimate test at Medinah, all that was left to complete the pre-tournament festivities was a controversy. Ben Crenshaw and the PGA of America obliged.

It was a pot that had been threatening to boil over for two years. From the moment in New York when, as the members of 1997 Ryder Cup team were receiving their send-off from President Clinton at a dinner at the Waldorf-Astoria Hotel, Mark O'Meara approached PGA executive director Jim Awtrey and asked why the players were not allowed to share in the profits from the Ryder Cup, the controversy was underway.

O'Meara had a legitimate question, given the time and expense the players were being asked to sacrifice, and given that the Presidents Cup (the PGA Tour's event between the U.S. and an international team) had been donating $100,000 in each player's name to the charity of his choice. If the Tour could do it with the Presidents Cup, why couldn't the PGA of America do the same thing? The Ryder Cup was a much more profitable event than the Presidents Cup and the demands on players and their spouses were much greater. Why, O'Meara wondered, couldn't the PGA of America show some dispensation to the players?

Awtrey looked at him as if he had two heads. The Ryder Cup wasn't about compensation, Awtrey told O'Meara in unambiguous terms. It was about pride, and playing for God and country. It was the closest thing professional golf had to the Olympics, and it shouldn't and wouldn't be tainted by money.

When O'Meara's comments became public, the so-called "pay-for-play" controversy was born. "The Ryder Cup is one of the unique events in all of sports that transcends compensation," Awtrey said at the time. While he was saying those things, the Ryder Cup was becoming one of the most lucrative events in golf, with the 1999 matches having gross income upwards of $63 million.

During the 1997 matches, Phil Mickelson asked Awtrey if the players would have any say in the disbursement of Ryder Cup funds in the future, and Awtrey answered with a blunt and unequivocal "No." Even though Ryder Cup captain Tom Kite warned officials of the pending unrest two years before, nothing was done to satisfy the players' desires to direct some of the profits to the charities of their choice. Duval said he thought it would be "great if some of that money went to building soccer fields for kids in Jacksonville," while Mickelson opening questioned why The Country Club in Brookline, Massachusetts, had been paid $6 million for the privilege of hosting the 1999 Ryder Cup while the players continued to have no say in where the profits were allocated.

When some players began saying things like "there might come a day when players simply chose not to play in the Ryder Cup," things got ugly. Awtrey pointed to the PGA's Ryder Cup Outreach Program, a well-intentioned charitable foundation but with a vague mission statement and no financial disclosure. When the players asked for specifics about that program, none were given and the explanations that were provided did nothing to mediate the players' personal philanthropic concerns.

Then the media chimed in, calling the players "greedy" for bringing up the subject of compensation in an event designed to foster good will and sportsmanship between continents. With the level of dialogue escalating to alarming heights, and players as prominent as Woods referring to the Ryder Cup as an "exhibition," Awtrey realized he had a public relations nightmare on his hands and called a meeting at Medinah on Tuesday before the first round to try and smooth things out. If anything, the meeting only made things worse.

"No matter which side you come down on, we should all be ashamed of ourselves for bringing this up now," Tom Lehman said. "This all could have been handled privately, behind closed doors."

The meeting took place behind closed doors, but it wasn't long before details began to leak out. With PGA Tour commissioner Tim Finchem present as an arbiter for the players, there were still a few heated exchanges. At one point Davis Love III, an ardent PGA of America supporter, faced the most vocal dissenters and said, "This isn't about charity. It's about putting money in your pockets."

Mickelson asked several pointed questions about the financial decisions the PGA of America had made, including the sale of the organization's two merchandise shows for a reported $120 million and the payment of $6 million to The Country Club. Mickelson's logic was simple. If Sherwood Country Club had paid $1 million to host a made-for-television event in 1999 (the Motorola Showdown at Sherwood between Woods and Duval), then there must be plenty of courses out there willing to pay for the Ryder Cup. In fact, the $7 million difference between what Sherwood paid for a one-day, two-man match and what The Country Club was paid was enough for the PGA of America to build its own golf course. "They've got courses beating down the door to host the Ryder Cup, yet they're giving the club all that money," Mickelson said. "Who negotiated that deal?"

That was one of many questions Awtrey failed to answer in the one-hour meeting. Afterward, Awtrey and Finchem held a joint press conference intended to put the issue to rest.

"Basically, where we are is that it is not an issue with the players and the PGA," Awtrey said to the reporters. "We're going to be working together to look at basically how we can continue to grow the game of golf, support the Ryder Cup, and the players would like to look at how we can involve them in the charitable input. That's basically it. There is no issue between us and the players, and we're going to talk, cooperate and work together."

Asked whether the PGA would designate a specific amount to charity in each player's name, Awtrey said, "Well, there's details to work out. What we've agreed to do is sit down and work toward making sure that as we go forward with charitable contributions, that we seek input from the players and that's basically what this was about. We didn't sit down and try to decide any immediate answers, but an agreement on what our objectives were, and that's what we did in the meeting."

Then Awtrey attempted to paint the episode as a media-driven non-event, "No big deal," as he was prone to say. "I really believe that this issue started this summer with the media, and as a result of all the discussions, we're now talking about it and we're finding that we've all got the same objectives; that the players do not want to be paid, but the players are looking at how the

Ryder Cup can be supportive of growth of the game and charities, and that's where we are. Players understand where the money is going. That's not something that's hidden. We've talked about that. We've shared with them where the money is going and what the PGA is all about and they're supportive of that."

This was news to many of the players who walked away from Tuesday's meeting with no idea where the Ryder Cup money was going. But the press conference was designed to soothe tensions, and put forth a unified front on a contentious issue, and Awtrey felt pleased that he had accomplished that task as he left the podium.

Twenty-four hours later, all that good will and we-are-one camaraderie fell to the bottom of Lake Kadijah when Crenshaw stood before the assembled scribes. Crenshaw, one of the game's great ramblers, had a moment of laconic lucidity on Wednesday. After filling the media center with pre-tournament ramblings on everything from captain's picks to the relative merits of a match-play format, Crenshaw was asked about the previous day's meeting with the players. He started his answer by saying, "It was a good meeting, the philosophies that were discussed from some people, they've agreed to — Jim Awtrey has spoken, and so has Tim (Finchem). They have to take it down the road."

Then it happened. Crenshaw's gaze hardened, and his normally jovial mannerisms changed suddenly. He became still and intense, gripping the base of the microphone before speaking again. "I want to say one thing," he said, leaning closer to the table. "I'm personally disappointed in a couple of people in that meeting. I mean that. They know who they are. And whether some players like it or not, there are some people who came before them who mean a hell of a lot to this game. It burns the hell out of me to listen to some of their viewpoints. The meeting was good because it cleared the air. Those players knew how I stood before I went in there, and that's all I'm going to say about that."

But it wasn't all he would say. Afterward Crenshaw named names, singling out Woods, Duval, O'Meara and Mickelson as the players with whom he was "personally disappointed."

"I'm sorry he feels that way," O'Meara said. "I thought when we left that meeting, everybody was on the same page. I'm disappointed because I thought it was a dead issue." O'Meara rhetorically asked, "If I'm so unpatriotic, how come I'm the only player who did a clinic for the U.S. troops?" He was referring to a May trip to Ramstead Air Force Base in Germany, where O'Meara gave a clinic, signed autographs and mingled with U.S. troops.

"I'm disappointed names were leaked," Mickelson said. "The meeting was designed for the players to ask questions."

Mickelson obviously asked the wrong questions, and was branded as a greedy malcontent for daring to ask how an organization grossing $63 million could only be netting $23 million. He was no management expert, but $40 million in expenses for three days of golf seemed out of line. But to ask the question was to be named as a greedy troublemaker, and that didn't sit well with Mickelson.

"I was told he mentioned names and I was one of those names," Woods said. "I don't know what that means, but I've been talking about this since the last Ryder Cup. The Ryder Cup is an enormous moneymaker. Because of that, I think it's our right to give funds to help our communities." Woods remained unrepentant and unwavering in his stance, a position that ruffled some feathers, but earned him respect as a leader among his peers.

Crenshaw called all of the players on Wednesday night to apologize then went on television Thursday afternoon to apologize again. Awtrey also appeared on television later in the week and said, "We'll have a final plan by the end of the year," when asked about the meeting, but the damage was done. Players left more confused than when they arrived, Awtrey had thrown gasoline on a brushfire, and Crenshaw had raised concerns about his diplomatic skills six weeks before he was to lead the U.S. team to try to reclaim the Ryder Cup.

Almost completely lost in the brouhaha of the Ryder Cup controversy was one of the most selfless acts in recent PGA Championship memory by a past champion. Steve Elkington, who won in 1995, withdrew when his caddie, Joe Grillo, collapsed with chest pains and was hospitalized. It would have certainly been easy for Elkington to pick up another caddie, but according to Grillo, "Only somebody like Elk would do that. I know it must have been a tough decision for him. He's a past champion and it's a tournament that is special for him. He's playing good and he could have done well, but he wanted to do what's most important for him. Elk knows there's a lot more in life than golf. He has always lived that way."

With all the off-course hoopla, it was little wonder the first two rounds of the 81st PGA Championship failed to generate as much excitement as usual among players or fans. Even with the strongest field in the history of tournament golf (92 of the top 100 players in the Official World Golf Ranking were there, including 43 international players from 19 countries) and a course-record-tying round by Garcia in the opening round, Medinah lacked the electricity of a major championship. A 45-minute rain delay in the afternoon didn't help the mood, although it did soften the course, which made scoring much easier. Even at 7,401 yards, Medinah gave up nine rounds in the 60s and 34 sub-par scores, led by Garcia's six-under-par 66.

"Today was a great day," Garcia said. "I think I've proved myself today. Probably my best day with my irons was the 62 I shot at Loch Lomond (in the Standard Life Loch Lomond). I don't think I ever played as well as I played that day, but today I really played well. It was close to my best round with my irons."

After arriving from Dublin on Tuesday and fighting jet lag and a bout of queasiness early in the week, Garcia said he felt rested and ready when he teed off in the first round. His first birdie came at the par-three second hole where he hit a five iron over the green, but chipped in for a two. On the par-five fifth, he hit a driver and three wood into the greenside bunker and got up and down to move to two under par, where he remained until the par-four 11th where he almost holed a nine-iron approach for eagle. He had a tap-in for birdie. On the par-five 14th he caught a break after a good tee shot. His three-iron second shot drifted left into the trees, but even though his ball found the rough, Garcia had an open shot. His lob wedge stopped six feet away and he made the putt for his fourth birdie of the day.

The rain delay came after Garcia missed his birdie effort at the 15th, but that didn't seem to stop the 19-year-old's momentum. After having a sandwich and watching television in the locker room while he waited for play to resume, Garcia went back out to the 15th, tapped in for par, then hit a nine-iron approach to the par-four 16th that stopped 30 feet from the hole. When that 30-footer fell, Garcia assumed sole possession of the lead at five under par. He wasn't finished. Another nine-iron approach at the par-four 18th left him with a six-footer for birdie, which he rolled in for the 66 and a two-shot lead over Jay Haas, Mike Weir and J.P. Hayes.

Afterward Garcia went back to his hotel where he ran for an hour before getting a massage, eating dinner with his family, and going to bed — a typical day for a 19-year-old prodigy.

The 45-year-old Haas was a veteran who joined the PGA Tour two months before Woods was born and whose son, Jay Jr. (who caddied for him at Medinah), was only six months younger than Garcia. Armed with a new putter and the same great attitude that had made him one of the most popular guys on tour, Haas posted an early 68 which, at the time, was good enough for the lead.

"I didn't leave many out there," Haas said. "I played well. I had a lot of opportunities, but I don't feel like I gave many away. You know, 68 in a major championship, I don't care if the greens are soft or not on a course that's 7,400 yards long. I'm sure there are a lot of people who would take that."

Haas played early in a steady rain before the delay, which made the course play even longer, but as he said, "It softened the greens up a little. They were a nice speed, so you were able to take a run at a few putts." He started the day off with a birdie at the par-four first hole after his seven-iron approach stopped 12 feet away. Then the rain picked up even more. On the 415-yard, par-four third, Haas hit a driver and six iron to 30 feet, and with water dripping from the bill of his cap, he drained the 30-footer for his second birdie. He gave one back at the 449-yard sixth after missing the green, chipping to seven feet and missing his par putt.

One-under-par 35 on the first nine was respectable, given the conditions, but Haas knew he was playing better than that score indicated, and he needed to take advantage of the soft conditions while he could. A birdie from eight feet at the par-five 10th got Haas back on track, but he gave the advantage back with a poor drive in the trees on the 407-yard 11th. From the left rough he was unable to recover, carding his second bogey of the day. He got it back just as quickly on the 468-yard 12th when his six-iron approach shot almost went in for a two. A tap-in from inside a foot moved Haas to two under par, and another birdie from 12 feet at the par-five 14th gave him the early lead. Haas made one more birdie, a 35-foot breaker that found the hole at the 16th, to move to four under par.

Haas' lead held up for most of the day, even though he was later tied by Hayes and Weir, a left-handed Canadian. It wasn't until Garcia's late birdies after the rain delay that Haas and company fell into a tie for second place. But it was early, and as Haas said, "It's a major championship and you never know what's going to happen."

At the end of round one, the leaderboard looked like this:

Sergio Garcia	66	Corey Pavin	69
Jay Haas	68	Brandt Jobe	69
Mike Weir	68	Jerry Kelly	69
J.P. Hayes	68	Brian Watts	69
Stewart Cink	69		

Although he denied any knowledge or involvement, Awtrey seemed to be the only person who wasn't surprised by O'Meara's tee times in the first two rounds. Just as is done at the U.S. Open, the PGA Championship sets the pairings and times for the first two rounds, considering numerous factors including television, speed of play and where the players stand on the World Ranking and the money list. Woods would not be placed in the final group of the day, since the later groups are forced to contend with spiked greens, sun-baked conditions and slow play. So imagine O'Meara's surprise when he saw that he was in the third-from-the-last group on Friday with Loren Roberts and Naomichi (Joe) Ozaki. It was a slap in the face for the two-time 1998 major champion and Player of the Year, and it didn't go unnoticed.

"I bet 20 guys must have come up to me this week and said, 'Nice tee time,'" O'Meara said. "I was warming up and the club pros (the only players playing behind him) were saying, 'What are you doing here?' I saw some guys in the locker room and they said, 'How'd you do?' I told them, 'I'm just going out.' I was out there picking up flag sticks."

Awtrey denied that O'Meara's tee time had anything to do with the controversy over Ryder Cup funds or because O'Meara was the first to go on record raising the issue of player compensation, but when O'Meara confronted Awtrey about the tee time, O'Meara said that Awtrey averted eye contact and gave O'Meara the kind of non-answer he had been saying the entire week. To O'Meara, the message from the PGA was clear: We take care of guys who are on our side.

"I must be in the penalty box," O'Meara said. It showed. He shot 74 in the second round to move to two-over-par 146 at the halfway point of the tournament.

O'Meara was the exception on Friday, as the course played easier than it did in the rain-soaked first round. Fifteen players shot below 70 and 46 broke par, with the field averaging almost a third of a stroke less than on Thursday.

Even so, more than a few marquee players packed their bags after the second round. Ryder Cup teammates Justin Leonard and Jeff Maggert went home early, Leonard having 148 to miss the 36-hole cut by two, but edging Maggert by one. Three members of the European Ryder Cup team missed the cut. Darren Clarke shot even par the first day, but followed with 75 to be one short, while Jarmo Sandelin opened with 77 and followed with 72 to tie Maggert, Watson and Greg Norman at 149. The worst performance by a Ryder Cupper was also the worst by a 1999 major champion. Jose Maria Olazabal continued his struggles by shooting 79-72 to tie Billy Andrade, Stuart Appleby, Tim Herron and Crenshaw.

Crenshaw was the only player who didn't seem to mind having the weekend off, since it gave him two uninterrupted days to ponder his two captain's picks for the American Ryder Cup team which he would announce the Monday following the PGA Championship. Armed with a notepad and pen, Crenshaw scoured Medinah like a baseball scout looking for his next great pitcher. He had plenty of help. As he returned to clean out his locker on Friday, Crenshaw found a sign taped to the locker door. "Pick Me," the sign read, with an arrow pointing left. Fred Couples had the locker to Crenshaw's immediate left.

Crenshaw's European counterpart, Mark James, shared no such recruiting luxury. James shot 74 on Friday, but his opening 70 was good enough to keep the Englishman playing on the final two days. His 144 total also left James tied with one of the men he would captain. Frenchman Jean Van de Velde of Barry Burn fame recovered from an opening 74 to shoot 70 and was tied for 40th place with 11 others including Mickelson and defending champion Vijay Singh.

"This is a different type of golf in general than what we are accustomed to in Europe," James said. "The greens tend to be harder and it's slightly alien to us. That shouldn't be an excuse. I mean someone from Europe should have won the PGA by now really. I think we have a better chance on this course. There is enough room and it's playing really long. That feels more comfortable. The way I played these two rounds, to make the cut here means it's more a European-style test."

While play was never suspended on Friday, the rain never stopped, leaving the greens soft and receptive but leaving the rest of the course soft and long. Garcia's course-record 66 didn't hold up long. Skip Kendall, a 34-year-old Milwaukee native in his seventh year on tour, came back from 74 to shoot a course record of 65. Kendall called it "one of those rounds you dream about, especially in a major. I held it together pretty well on the back side. I'm very happy to be where I am." Then with a smile he said, "I saw the leaderboard and it looked like three guys from Wisconsin were up there at one point. That's a little bit of a motivator. Wisconsin is not that far away, so we're used to playing in these conditions."

Kendall's round left him at 139, five under par for the tournament, a position he would end up sharing with first-round leader Garcia who said, "I probably played better than yesterday, but my putter didn't work too good. I think I only missed two fairways and three greens and shot 73. I made a couple of bogeys and had one three-putt, and I missed a couple of good chances for birdie. But I'm happy knowing that I still have a chance. My long game was almost perfect. I know you're going to have one of these rounds in every tournament, so let's hope that this will be the worst one."

Stewart Cink wound up tied with Garcia and Kendall at five under, as did the 54-year-old Irwin, who won here in the 1990 U.S. Open and who had returned in what many assumed was a ceremonial role, a senior invitee for the sake of nostalgia. If Irwin's opening 70 didn't prove he came to play, his 69 certainly did. He was the oldest competitor in the field, and he played the first two days with Garcia, the youngest player in the PGA Championship since Gene Sarazen in 1921, prompting Irwin to say, "You know, the PGA has a way of doing things like that." But Irwin was also tied with the youngest player in the field after two rounds, showing that he too was competitive.

"To play as well as I have the last couple of days is a bonus," Irwin said. "I don't want to sit up here and tell anybody that I expected to play like this. In my heart I hoped to and I wanted to, but it's not always the easiest thing to do to step into an environment in which you're not terribly accustomed. To be able to perform at this level, I feel very pleased. But I don't want to go backwards and say I can't continue. Just the opposite is true. I think I can continue playing like this, and I frankly don't feel I've had the best golf out of me the last two days. When I'm comparing my distance with Garcia and Mickelson (his two playing companions for the first two rounds), I can't compete, but my irons are pretty good, I keep the ball in play, and I make a putt every now and again. I control my game and get the most out of it."

Irwin bogeyed the first hole, but got the stroke back with a birdie at the third, followed by another birdie at the par-five fifth. He continued his fairways-and-greens game through the remainder of the first nine, turning in 35. Another birdie at the par-five 10th was followed by a steady line of pars until Irwin reached the 15th, the only par-four on the second nine under 400 yards. Measuring 389 yards, at the 15th Irwin hit a nine-iron approach to five feet and made his fourth birdie of the day to reach five under for the tournament.

By late afternoon, on a golf course where everyone assumed even par would be a fantastic score, five under par was only good enough for a share of fifth place. Four players were ahead of them as the sun set over the towering hardwoods west of Chicago. One stroke ahead of the four at 139 was Lee Westwood, the young Englishman who followed up his first-round 70 with 68 to reach 138.

"Fortunately, I haven't been pushed into the 'best player never to win a major' category yet," Westwood said. "I suppose it's because I'm only 26 years old, and I suppose it's because I haven't come close to winning one yet, so nobody's mentioned me in that group. Having won 16 tournaments now, I suppose the next step is a major championship, so that will be another platform to go on if I were to win."

He would have to beat some pretty good players in order for this to be his first major victory. Westwood would be paired on Saturday with Woods who shot a second-round 67 after an opening 70. Woods, at seven-under-par 137, stood alone in third place at the halfway mark. "I got off to a good start today," Woods said. "I birdied the first three holes, and even though I bogeyed the fourth, I got it right back at five. Basically, it was the start I wanted, and I got myself right back in contention after two rounds. That's right where you want to be. The key is to keep giving yourself chances, and I've done that this year. I'm proud of the way I played with the conditions as difficult as they were with the wind and rain, and this weekend I just need to go out and continue to do the same thing."

The only two players between Woods and the lead after two rounds were Weir, who bogeyed the 16th and 17th en route to his second consecutive 68 for a 136 total, and Haas, who continued his good play with a second-round 67 to reach nine-under-par 135. "The soft greens are the reason that the scores are so low," Haas offered. "The rough is still high, the course is still long, but the greens just don't have the firmness or the speed they would otherwise have."

With two rounds to play, the low-scoring affair looked like this:

Jay Haas	67 - 135	Sergio Garcia	73 - 139
Mike Weir	68 - 136	Hale Irwin	69 - 139
Tiger Woods	67 - 137	Stewart Cink	70 - 139
Lee Westwood	68 - 138	Miguel Angel Jimenez	70 - 140
Skip Kendall	65 - 139	Brian Watts	71 - 140

Temperatures cooled down on Saturday and the rain stopped, which was both good news and bad news. The good news was that the golf course had a chance to dry out. The bad news was that the spotty greens became spottier as conditions improved. One of the first victims among the contenders was Irwin, who started the third round with a three-putt bogey and proceeded downhill from there. "I might as well have had my hat on backwards," said Irwin, who shot 78 to fall 12 strokes behind the leaders. "I didn't know if I was putting with a two iron or a wedge. You have those days sometimes." Irwin dropped from the fifth-place tie into a tie for 34th place. "Anytime you shoot 78 you're disappointed," he said, shaking his head. "This was just disappointing."

The golf course continued to be benign by major championship standards with the field averaging 73.581, a little harder than on Friday, but a fraction easier than on Thursday. Twenty players broke par, and seven shot rounds in the 60s, including Woods and Garcia, who both posted 68s. Garcia's four-under performance left him tied for third with Cink at 207, while Woods moved into a tie for the lead with Weir, who shot 69 to reach 205.

"I feel more comfortable out there now," Woods said of his position atop the leaderboard of a major championship. "I've played major championships at a high level where I've been in contention, and it does make you feel more at ease to have been there before. I've learned from my mistakes as well as my successes, and I've applied those and gotten better.

"I need to go out there and play in my own game and execute my own golf shots. I know I'm tied with Mike and there are two players at nine under par. If those guys get off to a quick start, then they're right in it. But we're basically the four guys who have got a very good shot at winning this championship, and the guys at six under, if they play a great round tomorrow, they've got a chance too. So I just need to go out and take care of my own business first before I can ever start worrying about kicking in the door and winning my second major."

It was the second time in 1999 Woods and Weir had been tied going into the final round. Ironically enough, the first was in Chicago at the Motorola Western Open, a tournament Woods won handily. But Woods had nothing but good things to say about the Canadian. "Mike is a very solid player," Woods said. "I'm going to have to go out there and play a good round of golf in order to beat him as well as the other guys."

With one round to play, these were the leaders:

Tiger Woods	68 - 205	Nick Price	69 - 210
Mike Weir	69 - 205	Jim Furyk	69 - 210
Stewart Cink	68 - 207	Skip Kendall	71 - 210
Sergio Garcia	68 - 207	Jay Haas	75 - 210

As they were standing in the locker room on Sunday morning before heading to the practice range to warm up, Garcia hugged Haas and wished him well. "He is really a special person," Haas said of Garcia. "Not just a golfer. He's got something that a lot of people are missing."

Before the day was complete everyone would know that the 19-year-old who said "Just call me Sergio" had something special as the young Spaniard captured the hearts of millions with his daring play and magnetic personality. "I've always said he is a better person than he is a golfer, and as you can tell he's a great golfer," Garcia's friend Robert Gutterriez said. "He is something special."

Engaging the crowd with a wave and a smile on every hole, Garcia showed his moxie early when he hit his tee shot into the water on the par-three second hole, then hit a tremendous recovery shot and made the putt for bogey four. "I probably hit the wrong club," he said. "I was between a six and seven iron, and I tried to hit a smooth six and pulled it way left. I dropped and hit a nine iron about 12 feet and made it for bogey."

Garcia recovered with a birdie at the fifth to get back to nine under par, and birdied the 10th to reach 10 under, but by then it looked as though the tournament was over. Woods, who had closed out his opponents seven consecutive times when he had led or shared the lead after three rounds, was on a roll. Through 11 holes, Woods was four under on his round, 15 under for the week, and held a five-shot lead with eight holes to play. It appeared to be a runaway, but Woods knew better. "A five-shot lead can evaporate pretty quickly," he said. "If I make a couple of mistakes, they make a couple of birdies, and, boom, we're tied. That's exactly what happened. I made a couple of mistakes."

The first mistake came at the 12th where Woods reached the green in regulation, but three-putted for a bogey to drop one shot. Then, at the 13th tee, Woods watched as Garcia hit a six iron to 18 feet. After examining it from every angle, the 19-year-old nestled the downhill left-to-right putt into the hole for a birdie to reach 11 under. When the ball went in, Garcia looked back at the tee, his fist in the air. "I wanted him to know that I was still there and to show him that he had to finish well to win," Garcia said of his stare back at Woods. "But it wasn't a bad thing. I mean, I did it with good feelings, not hoping he would make a triple bogey or whatever. I was kind of telling him: If you want to win, you have to play well."

If the crowd wasn't with Garcia before, the putt at the 13th certainly swayed them. The Chicago faithful flocked to see Garcia, cheering his every move. And while he might not have wished anything bad on Woods, bad things certainly came calling. A five-iron shot at the 13th flew into the long rough behind the green. From there, Woods had to be careful not to blade the ball over the green and into the water. He hit his shot too firm, and it rolled off the front edge. From there, he hit a poor third shot and two-putted for a double-bogey five. His lead was down to one.

Garcia bogeyed the par-five 15th, which left the door open for Woods. With his length, Garcia felt sure Woods would birdie the 15th to regain his three-shot advantage. Instead Wood made par at the 15th. His lead remained two shots.

Then at the 16th, Garcia drove his ball through the fairway, and it nestled between two roots at the base of a large tree. He was, according to every analyst who saw his predicament, dead. The only option was to punch the ball out to the fairway and try to save par. But Garcia grew up, if you consider a 19-year-old to have grown up, playing countless rounds with Seve Ballesteros, the master of the inventive shot, and he knew that being two down with three holes to play called for drastic measures.

"I had a shot, but I had to hit a big slice," Garcia said. "The problem was that on the downswing I could hit part of the tree. If I aimed right, I might hit the second part of the tree."

Garcia's caddie, Jerry Higginbotham, took issue with the "I had a shot," statement. "Nine out of 10 guys on the PGA Tour chip out sideways," Higginbotham said. "Nine out of 10 don't even think about hitting that shot."

Armed with a six iron, Garcia took a vicious swing, closing his eyes and falling backwards on one foot. The ball shot out from the brush and curved 25 yards toward the green. "I opened the clubface, made a full swing, closed my eyes and hit the ball, and went backwards in case it hit the tree," Garcia said. "Then I opened my eyes and saw the ball was going at the green and I was pretty excited." So excited in fact that he ran down the fairway, leaping into the air to watch the ball come to rest 25 feet from the flag. "I'll put it in my top five shots," Garcia said when asked to rate the shot on his all-time hit list. "I learned a lot playing with Seve."

Crenshaw was impressed. "Unbelievable," he said. "I don't think anybody has ever seen a shot like that."

Garcia almost made the birdie putt, but settled for the year's most memorable par, and when Woods bogeyed the 16th, the lead had dwindled back to one. But that was where it would remain. Garcia parred the 17th and 18th for 71 and a 278 total, and Woods made a clutch eight-footer for par on the 17th, then two-putted for par on the 18th for 72–277 before dropping his eyes, clinching his fist, and exhaling. It wasn't easy, but Woods picked up the second major title of his career in a way that would always be remembered.

Like Ben Hogan and Sam Snead, Nicklaus and Palmer, the duel between Garcia and Woods at Medinah made all the incidental issues surrounding the 1999 PGA Championship seem incidental. In the end, it was the golf and the golfers that mattered most.

6. The Players Championship

On a day when the ocean breeze from Ponte Vedra Beach made kite flying popular and turned golf into a virtual nightmare, a hometown boy from Jacksonville, Florida, who spent many hours of his youth watching the greatest players in the world parade around the Tournament Players Club at Sawgrass in The Players Championship, returned as a 27-year-old man to the thunderous ovations he had heard as a child. Only this time the ovations were for him, and as he marched down the 18th fairway the huge gallery began to chant his name. "Du-val, Du-val, Du-val," the throng of spectators shouted as David Duval walked to his ball nestled in the fringe just right of the 18th green.

"This will never stray out of my top two or three golf memories," Duval said afterward. "The day I won my first PGA Tour event in Williamsburg was one of the greatest days in golf I have ever had. I put all the questions behind me that day. I knew I could do it. I just had to prove to everyone else. I embrace that day still. Today, however, is certainly running right next to it. I didn't know if it would ever happen. I certainly had thought about it, but I don't know if I even dreamed about it as much as I might have dreamed about winning a Masters or a U.S. Open or such, because I knew that the task would be very, very difficult here at home."

Not only did he survive the test of winning at home, Duval defeated a field rated as the third-best assemblage of talent in the 1990s at a course that was described as a cross between the Masters and the U.S. Open. "It was survival of the fittest," second-place finisher Scott Gump said. "No question. It was definitely major championship conditions. It was fun, no question. I stayed aggressive, and that was always my game plan, so I enjoyed it."

So did Duval, even though he did say, "If we had to play in these conditions every week, I don't think a lot of people would be playing golf." His three-under-par 285 total was the highest winning score since The Players Championship moved to the TPC at Sawgrass in 1982. Hal Sutton and Lee Janzen had shared the highest wining score at 283, Sutton's coming in 1983 and Janzen's in 1995. Still, Duval's win came on a day when the field averaged 75.369 strokes and only one, Fred Couples, shot in the 60s the entire weekend. Couples' 68 on Sunday moved him into a tie for fourth place, but the performance still left him at 289 for the week, proving just how difficult the Pete Dye creation played all week. And as had become the case so many times at this tournament, a 132-yard stretch over a shallow pond became the most feared piece of real estate in golf, the 17th hole with its island green.

The first-round lead with 68s was shared by two unlikely candidates. Bob Estes and Brian Watts grew up together in Texas and played against each other from the time they were old enough to carry their clubs. They were born 44 days apart, competed against each other at the junior level, in high school and in college, but when it came time to move to the next level, their careers took varying routes. Estes reported for duty on the PGA Tour in 1988 and never left, finishing in the top 150 money winners every year and carding at least one top-10 finish a season. His only win came at the 1994 Texas

Open, but Estes had proven himself a consistent contender. Watts, on the other hand, failed to qualify for the PGA Tour and spent six years playing overseas before finding success in Japan, then taking Mark O'Meara to a playoff at the 1998 British Open and earning a spot on the 1999 PGA Tour.

"To be honest, Bob could probably tell you every round we played together against each other since we were 10 years old, but I couldn't even begin to tell you," Watts said. "We have played a lot of tournaments against each other, junior golf, AJGA stuff. He went to Texas and I went to Oklahoma State so we played against each other in college, but we took different paths as professionals."

It took Watts three-plus holes to get going in the opening round, but after that he set the Stadium Course on fire. He started on the second nine, where he parred the 424-yard, par-four 10th. Then he triple-bogeyed the par-five 11th without hitting a single ball in the water and without incurring one penalty shot. A great drive left Watts with what appeared to be an easy lay-up shot, but he pulled the four iron into the thick left rough. From there, fearing he might chunk the ball into the hazard, he hit a sand wedge thin and the ball squirted into a plugged lie in the greenside bunker. It took Watts two shots to extricate his ball from the sand, and three more putts to get down for an eight. Then he bogeyed the par-four 12th to be four over par after only three holes.

"I was like, 'Wow, what a great start this is going to be,'" Watts said. "I tried not to get down on myself. The worst thing that could happen is I either shoot in the 80s or miss the cut. I'm still going to live through the day most likely. I really get down on myself a lot of times, especially if I have only missed one shot, but I was swinging so well on the range that I just tried to stay ahead."

After a brief lecture to himself between the 12th green and 13th tee, which Watts said was "unprintable," he hit a high six iron to the par-three 13th that funneled down to 12 feet. He made birdie and was on a roll. On the 14th he hit a good tee shot, but a thin iron shot left him short and right of the green. When he holed his chip for another birdie, Watts began to turn things around in his own mind. "That was probably the shot that really got me believing it could be a bit of a comeback. I never believed it would be this big a comeback, but starting on the 15th tee, I started hitting the ball real well."

A six-iron shot on the 15th ended up 20 feet away and Watts made that putt for another birdie. Then on the 18th he hit a driver and six iron to 20 feet and made that birdie as well. The next birdie came at the third hole, where he hit yet another six iron to four feet, followed by a pitching wedge approach at the fourth hole that also stopped four feet away, setting up his sixth birdie of the day. The final birdie came at the next hole when Watts hit a seven iron to the middle of the fifth green and made a 35-footer.

Estes' round was less eventful. Six birdies and two bogeys gave the other Texan his 68. "I guess this is the kind of tournament where you want to get off to a fast start because you know the golf course can play much tougher as the week goes along," Estes said. "Usually the greens get firmer and faster as time goes by, and especially in the afternoon, the wind may start picking up just like it was as we finished."

Tied for third place with 69s were Duval, Sutton and Naomichi (Joe)

Ozaki, then with 70s came Tiger Woods, Davis Love III, Skip Kendall, Chris Perry, Kirk Triplett, Jeff Sluman and Bradley Hughes.

Duval started on the second nine in conditions he called "perfect," and he began to move. A seven iron on the 13th hole stopped three feet from the pin for an easy birdie, and on the 14th he hit another seven iron to 12 feet and made that putt for his second birdie. On the 15th he hit a seven iron out of a fairway bunker, but the ball flew over the green and into thick rough. A chip to 20 feet away resulted in a bogey, and Duval was back to one under par for the day.

He came right back, though, hitting an eight-iron second shot on the par-five 16th just left of the green. He chipped to three feet and made birdie. On the 17th he hit a nine iron to the center of the green and made par. On the 18th he drove in the middle of the fairway and hit a nine iron to 18 feet where he made his second long putt. The wind picked up as Duval and Sutton, his playing companion, made the turn and Duval felt comfortable with an even-par score on the second nine under those circumstances.

"The wind wasn't really a factor on the first nine holes," he said. "It really picked up later on. The greens dried out rather quickly, and it became a lot more difficult after 10:00 or 10:30 in the morning. I think the weather is going to dictate a lot of how the tournament is going to play. If it rains it could soften the golf course up, but if it doesn't I think the way the golf course has been prepared, this isn't going to be a low scoring affair. I just don't see a lot of low scores happening out there."

Sutton said of his 69, "I played solid. The greens were a little firm, and the wind swirled at the end of the round so you had to pay a lot of attention to what was going on out there, but overall, I felt like I played well. There's plenty of trouble lurking out there, but I'm not complaining. Somebody's going to accept the winner's check at the end of 72 holes every week, and if you get caught up in complaining about the hard greens or wishing it was a different way, it is probably not going to be you accepting the winner's check. We all have to play the same greens."

Sutton played better than most on the first day. He started with a birdie at the 10th after hitting a seven iron to five feet. He quickly gave it back. After driving perfectly on the par-five 11th, he attempted to lay up, only to have his ball hit an overhanging tree limb, which kicked the ball back into the rough. He chunked his third shot into the cross-ties guarding the front of the green and the ball splashed in the water. After a penalty drop, he got what he termed "one heck of a six." He also birdied the 12th with a long putt from outside 60 feet. Then, after turning onto the first nine and contending with the wind, Sutton turned his game up a notch. A six iron at the fifth nestled 12 feet from the hole and he made the putt for another birdie. One more birdie coming in gave Sutton the 69.

It didn't rain on Thursday night or Friday, and even though the skies were overcast and the breeze was slight, the greens got harder and the rough got thicker. Players such as Nick Price, who got out early, had the advantage of minimal wind and greens that hadn't taken the pounding from players and caddies. Price, Fulton Allem and Ernie Els used the early tee times to their advantage, firing tournament-low scores of 67 to move up considerably in the standings. Price and Allem started the day tied for 61st place after opening rounds of 74, but by the second day's end they were tied for seventh, while

Els, who shot an opening 73, moved into a tie for fourth with his five-under-par effort.

Allem and Bernhard Langer, playing in the same group on Friday, both eagled the 384-yard, par-four fourth hole. Langer couldn't do much after that, finishing with a disappointing 72. Allem, on the other hand, was in the midst of the best four-hole stretch in The Players Championship history. Starting at the second hole, his scores were eagle-birdie-eagle-birdie. Allem played the other 14 holes in one over par for his 67.

Those scores were the exception to the rule on Friday, as was Ozaki's 68 to move the Japanese player into first place at 137. The average score was 73.591, which made it the highest second round of the year. Thursday's 74.523 average was the highest first-round average of 1999 as well. The cut was made at four over par, also the highest of the season. Duval was in second place after another 69 for a 138 total, and Bruce Lietzke matched Ozaki's 68 with four early birdies to move into third place at 139. Lietzke expressed concern about the speed and firmness of the greens, saying they were "getting away from them," a common phrase among golfers when they believe course conditions are too difficult.

Love stood out on Friday with one of the more consistent performances, following his opening 70 with another two-under-par round for a 140 total and tie for fourth place with Els and Curtis Strange. "I'm happy with four under because it's a good position with two days to go and it's not going to get any easier out there," Love said, but he too was concerned about how the greens would hold up over the weekend. "They are right on the edge, that's for sure," he said. "It's tough. You hit good shots and make bogeys and hit bad shots and you're struggling to make bogeys. But it's not like this is the first year it has been like this.

"I remember in 1995 you almost couldn't play it was so difficult, so they have got it right where they want it again this year. If they have a 65-degree day tomorrow (as predicted), it will be okay, but if it goes to 75 or 80 again, they could have a problem. They're keeping the greens right on the edge. I think the scores will shake out a lot tomorrow. There are a lot of big names in this tournament, so you expect they are going to be at the top of the leaderboard, but you'll see it spread out tomorrow."

One of those big names Love discussed was Duval, who started slowly. After hitting his opening approach shot to within five feet and missing the putt, Duval hit his third shot short at the second hole and made bogey. He found himself one over par and less than thrilled. He turned things around at the third hole, hitting a seven iron to within four feet and making the putt. At the fourth he hit a sand wedge from a fairway bunker to within two feet and made the putt for another birdie, then he made two critical par saves at the fifth and sixth, the latter coming with a 30-foot putt.

Those pars energized Duval, and on the ninth he hit a sand wedge to within six inches of the hole for a birdie. His next birdie came at the par-five 11th, where he hit a two iron over the green, chipped to four feet and made the putt, but he had a bogey at the 13th. That dropped him back to two under par for the day, five under for the tournament and two behind Ozaki. But Duval had one more birdie in his bag. At the 15th, he hit a sand wedge to 12 feet and made another putt for birdie. Pars on the 16th, 17th and 18th gave him what appeared to be a consistent scoring run with two

69s, but Duval knew better. "I left plenty of putts out there," he said. "You put great golfers under difficult circumstances and you are going to have some crazy things happen, both good and bad."

Course superintendent Fred Klauk watched all the forecasts on Friday night, looked at his weather radar and made what turned out to be a fateful decision. Humidity was supposed to be high on Saturday, which meant the greens would hold their moisture well. Winds were predicted to be out of the east at 10 to 15 miles an hour — breezy but not enough to dry out the greens. Klauk consulted with tournament officials and agronomists, and everyone agreed that a light watering on Friday should do the trick. They wanted to keep the conditions "right on the edge," as Love had put it.

By the time half the field had teed off on Saturday, Klauk realized he had made a terrible mistake. "We had very low humidity," he said. "Because of that, evaporation was at its peak." The winds had also picked up to 25 miles an hour. Fast, hard greens suddenly became impossible, rock-hard targets. By noon a half dozen greens wouldn't hold any shot, and six more were receptive to only the softest lob shots.

"It's laughable," said Strange, after struggling to 78. "If you're going to make the golf course and the greens this hard, that's okay, but you have to give us an alley, like a links golf course. Pete Dye and Deane Beman designed this golf course to be played in the air. This is target golf. Dye never envisioned those greens being what they are. He would come in here and be nauseous. They ruined this tournament for me. They ruined the course. I don't think there is anything they can do to save this tournament."

Even though Duval hung on to shoot 74 to take a one-stroke lead over Kendall and Mickelson at 212, Duval was also whipped after the round. "We just got kicked around," he said. "It probably played as difficult as I have seen, certainly at this golf course and maybe as difficult as any course I have ever seen."

PGA Tour Commissioner Tim Finchem recognized there was little they could do about it. "People might like to watch this, but I'm not comfortable with it," Finchem said.

"It was like playing Augusta and the U.S. Open on the same day," said Colin Montgomerie, who handled the adversity well, shooting 73 for a 215 total, three shots off the lead. "When Phil (Mickelson) and I got to the first green, we were shocked. We could see our own reflections."

Lietzke shot 80, and had harsh words for course conditions as well. "We were putting on 'browns' today," Lietzke said. "Yesterday they looked sickly, but today they looked dead. There's no moisture in them. The golf course turned the best players in the world into knuckleheads. It was unfair. There were at least four or five instances when perfectly struck shots ended up in spots where you literally had no shot."

Els joined Lietzke, Brad Fabel, Bob Estes, Craig Stadler, Tom Byrum and Frank Nobilo in shooting 80s, but they all beat Ozaki, the second-round leader, who shot 81. Even that was not the worst score of the day. Allem and Nick Faldo shared that distinction, shooting rounds of 83. Afterward, Faldo said, "Sometimes I wish there was no tomorrow."

Some players handled it better than others. Kendall, for example, shot 70 to jump into a tie for second place. Scott Gump matched Kendall's score, having 70 after earlier rounds of 72 and 74, which left him four shots off the lead. Steve Stricker also shot 70 for a 216 total.

Mickelson shot his third consecutive 71 to reach 213, a position no one imagined would be a single shot off the lead, especially when seven under par led after the second round. "It was obviously a tough day," Mickelson said. "Everybody had some problems. I had something happen I've never seen happen before. On the first hole, I had a putt that was just trickling up, just going by the hole, and it hit a spike mark and came backwards. That's when I knew it was going to be a long day.

"At first I was thinking that I could go out and shoot three, four or five under par, but as the day wore on, after four or five holes, it became evident to me that everybody was going to have difficulties and that the leaders were going to come back. The pin placements and the firmness of the greens and the wind — combine all those elements together and bogeys are just going to be more prevalent than birdies."

As an example of how difficult the course was playing, Mickelson cited the one par-five where he had a reasonable chance to reach the green. "On the 11th, I had six iron into the hole and couldn't even shoot at the green," he said. "Think about that for a second. I couldn't lay up. If I did that I would have to play over the bunker, and I couldn't stop it on the green. I had to play into the bunker, where I ended up getting up and down for birdie. Now, think about the last time you had a six iron and you didn't try to hit the green. That's the type of shots we were faced with and the strategy we faced."

Finchem took an active role in setting up the course for the final round. After meeting with Klauk on Sunday morning, Finchem said, "You should be able to keep the ball on the green, play aggressively, and try to make birdies. We tried to get the golf course today to the same place it was on Thursday." They failed, in large part because the wind refused to cooperate. With gusts up to 30 miles an hour coming from the Atlantic, scores continued to climb. Tom Kite shot a second straight 79 to finish tied for last place with Allem, who had an 83-82 weekend.

Those further up the leaderboard had problems of their own. Mickelson and Montgomerie, who played together, collapsed early. Mickelson shot 82 to tie for 32nd place at 295, while Montgomerie shot 79 to drop to a tie for 23rd at 294. That left the door open for any challengers who wanted to take on Duval, and an unlikely pair stepped up to the challenge. Kendall, a winless six-year veteran, got off to a fast start, birdieing the second and third holes to reach five under for the tournament and open up a two-shot lead over Duval. Two bogeys in the next three holes dropped him back into a tie with Duval, Steve Stricker and a charging Scott Gump.

Gump, Stricker, Kendall and Duval were tied at three under when Duval made a fateful decision on the ninth. After driving in the left rough and pulling his lay-up shot into a bunker beneath some overhanging trees, Duval faced 101 yards to the flag with two trees directly in his line and a portion of green only six paces wide. Duval turned to his caddie and said, "I've got two plays here. Either I'm coming out sideways or we're going to try this." After a few more seconds, he said, "It's time to play golf. Let's go and see what happens." He hit a great shot, but the ball kicked into a greenside bunker. From there Duval holed his bunker shot for birdie to resume the lead.

"That really settled me down and made me feel as if I'd made the right decision," he said. "To tell myself, 'Let's start playing now,' that was the right thing to do."

After that, Stricker and Kendall fell back, both shooting 41s on the final nine. Stricker finished with 74 and tied for sixth at 290 with Mark O'Meara, Scott Hoch and Lee Westwood, while Kendall had 78 and fell back into a seven-way tie for 10th at 291. Kendall summed up his week saying, "When you start missing fairways out here, you're going to get into trouble. This is the toughest field in golf, and I'm pretty satisfied with my finish. One of these days, I'm going to get one."

That was also how Gump felt, although he thought his "one of these days" might be this one. After falling three behind Duval through 14 holes, Gump made birdies at the 15th and 16th to draw to within one. Gump saw his opportunity before him. He walked to the 17th tee knowing that a par and a birdie might just win it. Two pars might even do it.

Even though Gump didn't know it, things were moving in his favor behind him. Duval bogeyed the 14th and 15th holes after someone in the gallery advised him that his father, Bob, had just won the Emerald Coast Classic on the Senior PGA Tour. While he later claimed it didn't distract him, Duval knew that if he could somehow hold on, he and his dad would become the first father and son to win tournaments on the same day.

Gump, meanwhile, controlled his destiny on the par-three 17th hole. He had 137 yards to the flag on the back portion of the green. Like countless others before him, Gump wrestled with what club to hit. "For me it was a big nine iron," he said. "I went with the extra club, choked down on it, and really smoothed it." It was the same scenario Len Mattiace had faced on the same hole a year earlier. And Gump had made the same mistake. With the pressure of possibly winning The Players Championship on the line, he had chosen the longer club in the hopes that he could throttle it down and coax the shot to the target. Like Mattiace in 1998, the results were disastrous. "I knew, pretty much as soon as I hit it, that it was in the water," Gump said. "I killed it."

His shot flew onto the back quarter of the green, bounced in the air and rolled off the back. "The reason you see so many balls short of the green is because you know you can't land the ball in the middle and stay on," Gump said. "It's definitely nerve-wracking. There are so many train wrecks out there, and I was just one of many. Fair, unfair ... that's golf. That is why we all play it."

After moving to the drop area, Gump hit his third shot within eight feet of the flag and made the putt for bogey. When he birdied the 18th, he realized he had played the last two holes even par, but by then he knew that it was not enough. He finished with 71 for a 287 total, one under par.

Duval reached the 17th tee with a one-shot lead. If he found the green, the tournament was most likely his. If he found the water, his chances were greatly diminished. Duval pulled out a pitching wedge and tried to conjure memories of what he considered one of the best golf swings he had ever seen.

"The most impressive pre-shot routine and golf swing that I have ever seen was when Nick Price won this tournament. He walked up to (the 17th tee), grabbed his club, stood out over the ball, and hit it. He never gave himself enough time to think about anything other than hitting it up there close. That's all I tried to do, grab the club and hit it."

Duval's ball sailed on line toward the center of the green. When it hit, the crowd erupted. The ball took one large hop and rolled six feet from the hole. He made the putt for birdie.

Then the victory march started as the gallery chanted his name and shouted their congratulations. The victory moved Duval into the No. 1 spot on the Official World Golf Ranking for the first time. "You know I'm kind of anxious to watch some tapes of this," Duval said. "It must have been brutal looking, and to see the golf ball doing some of the things that it did just really blows your mind. I just hung in there. I knew that if I could make 18 pars, I would win for sure. Unless they went out there and really soaked the greens, people were going to be backing up again, and three under was a winning score for sure. So I just went out there and tried to put the ball in places I could, make pars, and every now and then, if I had a shot I felt like I could go a little more aggressively, I tried to do that."

Even though he didn't make 18 pars, Duval's 72 was enough for a two-stroke win over Gump, a three-shot margin over Price and a four-shot edge over Sutton and Couples.

7. Ryder Cup

Before leaving his home in Austin, Texas, for the three-hour flight to Boston, some who knew Ben Crenshaw had serious concerns for his mental and physical health. His normally relaxed mannerisms — the slight cock of the head, the toothy smile and the mischievous wink from his always sparkling green eyes — were gone, replaced by deepening lines on his furrowed brow and a twitch in the muscles of his neck as if he were slowly choking on a slab of underdone Texas barbecue. His nicotine intake had doubled to the point where he was lighting a new Marlboro Light before the final plume of smoke from the previous one had dissipated in the thick air that surrounded him.

"Look at this!" he said, pointing at the *Dallas Morning News*. "Now the umpires want to go on strike! They're supposed to be fighting with the baseball players, not the baseball owners. It's a sign of the times. Every morning you pick up the sports section, and it's something new. That's the reason why I feel the way I do about this! The Ryder Cup should remain special."

That sort of diatribe was so anti-Crenshaw that some speculated that if the U.S. Ryder Cup team — a team and an event Crenshaw had devoted himself to like no previous captain — didn't win back the much-coveted cup at The Country Club in Brookline, the captain might well suffer a nervous breakdown.

"Boston, Boston, Boston," Crenshaw chanted as if lost in the trance of some mystic incantation. "That's all our players should be thinking of now. All the other stuff, like talk about money, can wait. What they do there in Boston, starting with Monday's practice rounds, will be paramount. I'll want to see where the guys' games are, where their heads are, whether one hole is giving them fits, that sort of thing. You can book it. They (the Europeans) will be united. More than us? I can't say that. I hope not, but I know in the past you could almost feel that it meant more to them. They want it terribly. That's why I told David Duval to think twice before calling it an exhibition. He hasn't played in one yet. I told him this will be like nothing you've ever seen or heard in golf.

"My first Ryder Cup in 1981 wasn't nearly as big as it is now, but it was over there, and our captain, Dave Marr, did a great job of preparing us for what was going to happen. Our misses would be cheered. That's something completely contrary to the nature of golf, and one reason is the flag. That's why the Ryder Cup has become so huge. It's because of patriotism. Patriotism! The other reason is that golf itself has become so big, so global. And, let's face it, interest in the Ryder Cup grew when we started losing it. Like the America's Cup in yachting. Roll all that together, plus the fact that a close competition is almost guaranteed, and you have what we have now — an unbelievably special occasion.

"Am I tough enough? That's a fair question. Given my reputation, it's understandable. Hopefully it won't have to be a question of my being too hard or too soft. I'd like to be the kind of captain the guys want to play well for. You know, the kind of guy they say in baseball is a 'player's manager.'

These guys know me. I can't transform myself into Woody Hayes or they'll know something is up. I mean, it's an honor and it's a pressure-packed competition. But it is supposed to be fun."

On and on he went, rambling about the history, tradition and impact of the Ryder Cup on all of sports and on all the men who participated in it. Between sentences, Crenshaw would pull the carcinogens from the Marlboro Light into his recessed cheeks and stare into the vacuum of a Ryder Cup-induced hypnosis. He had foregone his own playing career to micro-manage every detail of the 1999 matches. He spent hours at The Country Club, discussing the course set-up, the rough, the pin placements, the subtleties of the greens and the strategies of playing one of America's classic courses.

Of course Crenshaw knew the history: the epic tale of young Francis Ouimet, an American golfer in an age when Americans had yet to master the ancient game, who walked from his home off the 17th fairway to The Country Club in Brookline and defeated Harry Vardon and Ted Ray in a playoff for the 1913 U.S. Open, becoming the first American to win that title. Crenshaw not only knew the history, he lived it, speaking, as historians often do, in the present tense when recounting details of that turning point in American golf. It was as though he was channeling ghosts, from Ouimet to instructor Harvey Penick, whose legend had grown exponentially after Crenshaw won the 1994 Masters the week of Penick's death.

Crenshaw not only picked out the uniforms the team would wear, he designed them, calling in a specialist from Jeff Rose manufacturers to create what he called "a unique and special outfit that would have some special meaning." He also had rings made up for everyone on the team, handing them out at the Tuesday dinner at the Oyster House in Boston. "In the Super Bowl or the World Series you have to wait until you win to get a ring," Crenshaw said. "But I'm so confident that I'm giving out your rings now." After that moment, no one doubted Crenshaw's almost religious commitment.

As the team enjoyed oysters, lobster and an award-winning sea bass special the chef whipped up especially, no one could have predicted the history that awaited Crenshaw and his controversial team. And no one, not even the most romantic fan of sappy fiction, could have foreseen the comeback the U.S. team would make to wrestle the Ryder Cup back from a four-point deficit with only the Sunday singles matches remaining.

As he sat down in the press tent on Saturday night after watching his team fall into what many saw as an insurmountable hole, Crenshaw looked and sounded like a man on the verge of cracking up. There were numerous palpable pauses during his oration when some of the assembled scribes wondered if Crenshaw shouldn't be led away by white-clad caregivers who would pat him on the arm and say, "There, there, Mr. Crenshaw. There, there."

"Well, everyone, I know we've reached a long and exciting day," Crenshaw said as if talking to a group of children on a field trip to Walt Disney World. "I'll just say this right now. I've never been so proud of a bunch of guys in all my life. They played their hearts out, and they'll continue to play their hearts out. I saw a lot of wonderful things today on both sides. I think that the viewing audience will certainly say that the Ryder Cup is the most exciting kind of golf that you can ever see. That atmosphere was palpable today. It's a heck of a contest. It's a contest that … It's a game that we all love and we're proud of. And it was played hard, competitive and fair. That's ... Continuing on that note, that's why both these teams continue to be proud of golf. It's great to be a part of, I can tell you."

The Golf Channel telecast the Ryder Cup press conferences live, and as Crenshaw continued to ramble, Peter Kessler, the network's most recognized anchor, looked at his producer with a mixture of confusion and worry. Was Crenshaw having a breakdown? Did he witness the same contest that the rest of the world saw? The Americans, who started Saturday's second round down 6-2 after a first-day thumping reminiscent of the Saturday massacre at Valderrama in 1997, hadn't managed to close the gap at all.

American stalwarts Hal Sutton and Jeff Maggert, the latter having called the American team "the best golfers in the world," had won again on Saturday morning, and Steve Pate and Tiger Woods had also picked up an early point, but the Europeans had held tough, splitting the morning matches 2-2. Then in the afternoon Phil Mickelson and Tom Lehman beat Darren Clarke and Lee Westwood, 2 and 1, but that was it for U.S. victories. Sutton and Justin Leonard, who were paired in the afternoon in what Crenshaw called "a pure hunch," halved their match with Spaniards Jose Maria Olazabal and Miguel Angel Jimenez, while Paul Lawrie and Colin Montgomerie handed Woods his third defeat of the week, beating him and Pate, 2 and 1. The matches for the day were split 4-4, but it felt much worse for the Americans. No team had ever come back from more than two points down with one day to play. So what was Crenshaw babbling about?

"The matches are tremendously close," Crenshaw said. "Tremendously close. Anyone can speculate whether points can go either way, but it's still ... there it is. The outcome will hinge on tomorrow. It will take a ..." his voice trailed off and the muscles of his face twitched with an almost imperceptible spasm. Those close enough to see it knew he was cracking up. The next words out of his mouth would certainly be nonsensical.

"I think we did a hell of a job of having people on our team and our players and the people ... They felt that. It was wonderful."

No doubt about it, Crenshaw was a shadow of himself, a living testament to the dangers of pouring one's soul into a singular venture. "Maybe golf in America has changed a little bit over the last eight or 10 years," he continued. "There's vast distances to cover. It is ... economics, maybe. There's a lot to play for each week."

He stared into space again, before saying, "Boy, we're just so close. I mean, unbelievably close. I think everyone knows that, and everybody feels it on both sides. There are just some tremendously hard-fought matches out there, some superlative golf. Gosh, we're seeing some unbelievable golf this week. Their side has played very well. The horses we have put in have stayed in, and they've produced. They've done wonderful things."

Then, as if he had been snapped back to the present by a flash of rational perception, his gaze turned serious and he leaned forward — the exact pose he had struck at Medinah when he chastised some members of his team for their views on compensation, saying, "It burns the hell out of me to listen to some of their viewpoints." This time he paused, his back straighter, even straighter than it was at Medinah, and with the microphone firmly grasped in his left hand, he wagged his right index finger at his audience and said, "I'm going to leave ya'll with one thought, and I'm going to leave." Everyone perched on the edge of their seats. This was the moment Crenshaw would define himself. It was his Gettysburg.

"I'm a big believer in fate," he said. Then another pause, as everyone leaned closer hoping to catch the words first. "I have a good feeling about this. That's all I'm going to tell you."

That was it? Kessler cut his eyes back at his producer in a what-the-hell-was-that gaze, and there were even a few audible snickers from the back of the packed room. Yes, yes, many walked out thinking, the Ryder Cup had claimed its first casualty. The event had driven Ben Crenshaw nuts.

Davis Love III saw the interview live on television from the player's lounge at the Four Seasons Hotel where he had grabbed a plate of Chinese food from the buffet table after returning with his wife Robin. He couldn't believe how hungry he was after grinding through an 18-hole match where he and David Duval had let Sergio Garcia and Jesper Parnevik steal a halve. As Love chewed on an egg roll and stirred sweet and sour sauce into his rice, he saw Crenshaw's image fill the screen of the 36-inch television, and he saw the finger being wagged. When he heard the words his captain spoke, he stopped chewing. "Oh my God," he thought to himself, "Ben really believes we're going to win this."

Love knew that Crenshaw hadn't been speaking for the players' benefit, because he may have been the only player who had seen the interview. It wasn't a motivational tactic, or an attempt to play mind games with the other team. Crenshaw really, truly, in all his heart believed that fate would intervene and the U.S. team would make history on Sunday. A shudder ran down Love's spine as he thought about it. History was less than a day away, and he would be a part of it.

As more players began to trickle into the team room, Love sat alone and pondered what had transpired over the previous two days. Friday had been a disaster, with the U.S. team searching but not finding its motivation or spark until it was almost too late. Crenshaw had gone with two of his big guns early, sending Duval and Mickelson out in the first group against Montgomerie and Lawrie. It seemed a strange pairing given that the same twosome had played together in three matches in the Presidents Cup in Australia last year and come back with a 0-2-1 record, and given the fact that Crenshaw had named Duval and Mickelson as culprits in the "pay-for-play" skirmish. Some thought it might have been a conciliatory gesture — a nod of confidence from Crenshaw to the men he had so publicly chastised. Whatever the rationale, the results were not what anyone expected.

Even at the turn after a shaky start by both Duval and Lawrie, the U.S. team began to show cracks in the early moments of the second nine. Mickelson, normally a clutch putter in the alternate-shot format, missed a four-footer for par on the 10th. Then Duval flubbed a chip shot at the 12th leading to another bogey and the Americans were two down. They never recovered, losing 3 and 2. Europe had drawn first blood.

"The players look to Monty for inspiration and leadership," captain Mark James said of Montgomerie. "He sets the tone, no question." Lawrie called Montgomerie "a rock," while Montgomerie chimed in by saying, "The Ryder Cup brings out the best in me, and I'm glad it does."

The second match was the one everyone wanted to see, and the one the Americans desperately wanted to win. When the pairings were announced

Thursday evening and everyone saw that the anticipated match-up of Garcia and Woods would, indeed, come about on the first day, Crenshaw joked at his press conference that, "Mark James and I met down by the skating pond on number three and worked this out for ya'll." After the thrilling final-round duel in the PGA Championship between Woods and Garcia, everyone had speculated about the two young men meeting again in Boston. While it lacked the excitement of a Sunday singles finale, the match-up did indeed happen: Woods paired with Lehman, one of Crenshaw's picks and a man who tried desperately to assume a leadership role, and Garcia paired with Parnevik, who was also playing as a captain's pick. Adding to the drama was the fact that Garcia, the youngest player in Ryder Cup history at 19 years, didn't fear Woods or anyone else, and it showed.

All four players lacked any sort of putting touch through the first 10 holes. Then, with the match all-square through 11, Garcia hit a deft little chip on the long par-four 12th that stopped four feet from the hole. Woods then charged his long birdie effort eight feet by the hole. Lehman missed the comeback par putt, while Parnevik easily made the four-footer for par. The Europeans had the lead.

Two holes later, Parnevik stepped up again, draining a 14-footer to halve the hole and retain a 1-up advantage for Europe. When that putt went in, basketball legend Michael Jordan, an interested spectator in Woods' gallery, puffed his Cohiba cigar and said, "I'm worried." That worry was well founded. Garcia hit his approach shot on the 17th within eight feet, and when Parnevik made the putt for birdie, Woods and Pate were done. Europe led 2-0 in the early going.

American leadership came to the forefront in the fourth match of the day when Sutton and Maggert took on Clarke and Westwood. Even though Maggert was the reigning WGC Anderson Consulting Match Play champion and Sutton had won the Bell Canadian Open two weeks before leaving for Boston, the two were considered underdogs. That soon changed as Sutton provided the fist-pumping excitement the Americans so desperately needed. When Sutton closed out Clarke and Westwood on the par-three 16th, American flags were finally waving.

The excitement died quickly, however, when the third match of the morning — Love and Payne Stewart, two Ryder Cup veterans, against rookies Jimenez and Padraig Harrington — ended in a halve, with Jimenez missing a six-footer at the 18th that would have given the Europeans the win outright.

It was 2½ to 1½ in Europe's favor after the morning, but then things got really ugly for the Americans. Westwood and Clarke resoundingly thumped the two top-ranked players in the world, Woods and Duval, in their afternoon fourball match. The final tally of the match was a 1-up victory for the Europeans, but it never appeared that close. Duval only made one birdie on the second nine, and even though he left the driver in the bag most of the day, he had trouble finding the fairway. When Clarke birdied the 17th to move his team 1 up, both Woods and Duval missed the 18th fairway. Duval then missed the green and chunked his chip, while Woods pulled his approach into the greenside bunker. When Westwood nearly holed a chip for birdie, the Americans never took their putters out of their bags. The match was conceded and American fans were stunned.

Boston fans mercilessly abused Duval, who had been chastised for his use of the world "exhibition" in discussing the Ryder Cup. Throughout Friday's matches, Duval was peppered with comments like "What do you think of this exhibition now?" and "Show us an exhibition shot." He was also hammered in the press for a lack of emotion. Chris Elsberry of the *Connecticut Post* wrote that, "Duval's emotions never seemed to change, and that was the sad thing. He never cracked a smile, furrowed a brow, pounded a club, pumped a fist or issued an expletive." C.W. Nevius of the *San Francisco Chronicle* was equally brutal when he wrote, "This is starting to look less and less like a coincidence and more and more like the wrong guys are doing all the commercials."

Even the gut-it-out team of Sutton and Maggert suffered on Friday afternoon. Olazabal, paired with fellow Spaniard Jimenez, poured in birdie putts at the sixth, eighth and ninth holes to assume a lead that the Americans couldn't overcome, losing 2 and 1.

The most demoralizing loss of the day for the Americans came, again, at the hands of the other Spaniard, 19-year-old Garcia, and his partner Parnevik. The two Europeans made birdies from everywhere, igniting their fans and earning the respect of everyone in attendance. But it was Mickelson's performance with Jim Furyk that deflated the U.S. Despite having made seven birdies, Mickelson missed a five-foot putt on the 18th that would have halved the match and provided a much-needed half point for the Americans.

Behind the 18th green, Mickelson was inconsolable, opening weeping with his head in his hands as his wife, Amy, provided what little comfort she could. The birdies would be forgotten, Mickelson knew. Just as it had been in the U.S. Open when he battled Stewart to the final hole of the final round, the only putts anyone would remember were the ones he missed. None, it seemed, was bigger than that five-footer at the 18th on Friday.

Love and Leonard eked out a halve in their afternoon match against Montgomerie and Lawrie, but the damage was done. The Europeans led 6-2 after the opening day, and many were writing the Americans off. George Willis of the *New York Post* wrote, "You might as well take down the corporate tents and park all the shuttle buses. The overrated, overconfident American team has shockingly played itself out after only one day."

Love remembered how he felt that day, and he remembered what he had said. "I felt a little pressure out there today that I don't normally feel and I kind of let it get away from us," he said. "For some reason the Europeans raise the level of their play for this tournament. Our team seems to come in and not play to its capabilities."

Now they were faced with a do-or-die situation on Sunday, and even though Crenshaw had "a good feeling" and the Saturday matches had indeed been closer, history was not on their side. Love knew the statistics. No team had come back from more than two points down on Sunday. "No matter what we do, they do us one better," Love had said before hopping in his courtesy car for the 20-minute drive back to the Four Seasons.

Crenshaw had gambled in the morning matches, benching Love, Duval, Lehman and Mickelson, sending out Mark O'Meara, who sat out all of Friday, Leonard and Furyk for what he hoped would be some fresh blood and new life. The strategy backfired, and Furyk and O'Meara, paired in alternate-shot match, were trounced 3 and 2 by Clarke and Westwood. Leonard and Stewart suffered a similar fate, losing 3 and 2 to the hottest players the Europeans had to offer, Garcia and Parnevik. Pate and Woods eagled the 14th to go 1 up on Harrington and Jimenez, and they were able to hold onto that lead through 18, while the most heroic twosome the Americans had, Sutton and Maggert, dismissed Montgomerie and Lawrie 1 up.

On paper, splitting the morning matches 2-2 seemed okay for the Americans. Crenshaw had rested his stars without losing any ground, and if he could sweep the afternoon matches, he could tie the Europeans with eight points and gain the momentum for the singles matches on Sunday, a day the Americans had historically dominated.

The best-laid plans didn't work out, however. While Mickelson redeemed himself by pairing with Lehman for a 2-and-1 win over Clarke and Westwood, Duval and Love halved their match with Garcia and Parnevik, and Leonard and Sutton halved Olazabal and Jimenez. Woods lost another match, falling with Pate to Lawrie and Montgomerie 2 and 1.

The biggest question Crenshaw had to answer was why he had split up Maggert and Sutton on Saturday afternoon and played Leonard, who had yet to win a Ryder Cup point at either Valderrama or Brookline. "A pure hunch," Crenshaw has said, to which NBC analyst Johnny Miller responded, "Yeah, I've got a hunch too. My hunch is that Justin should go home and watch it on television."

Love was one of the first to hear of Miller's comments, but he wouldn't tell Leonard. Better to let him read about it in the paper or hear it when he was in better spirits.

Saturday night, as the team members and their wives gathered on the sixth floor team room at the hotel, emotions ran high as Crenshaw played a video showing all the great shots of the year as well as a clip from National Lampoon's movie *Animal House* in which the late John Belushi stood in front of his ravaged fraternity brothers and said, "Over! Nothing's over until we say it is! Was it over when the Germans bombed Pearl Harbor? No! Who's with me?" That brought some lighthearted laughter to the room. Texas Governor George W. Bush, there at Crenshaw's invitation, spoke to the group and read them a passage about the defense of the Alamo. Then each player shared his thoughts on the week.

Duval, criticized for his lack of emotion, had tears streaming down his cheeks as he talked about how much he wanted to win and how important it was for him to be a part of the team. Robin Love invoked the memory of Harvey Penick, quoting one of the instructor's simple edicts: "Go out and take dead aim." Stewart spoke of his late father Bill, and how much it would have meant for him to see this team come together.

The most inspirational speaker of the evening, and the man who energized the team the most, was Sutton, who said, "There isn't one person on the fifth floor (where the Europeans were housed) that can hold a candle to anybody on the sixth floor (the Americans' floor). We can go out tomorrow and win every match, but we've got to jump on them early and we've got to get the crowd into it." By the time Sutton had finished, the 11 other men on that team would have run through a wall if he'd led the charge.

If there was one statistic on the Americans' side going into the final day, it was that since 1985, Europeans who have played in all four team matches before Sunday have gone 10-19-5 on the last day. Mark James had played

Montgomerie, Lawrie, Clarke, Westwood, Garcia and Parnevik in all four matches on Friday and Saturday. He hadn't played Jean Van de Velde, Jarmo Sandelin and one of his captain's picks, Andrew Coltart, at all. The strategy seemed radical, but it had proven effective.

The Europeans held a commanding lead, and even if fatigue played a part, the lead was so commanding that James felt confident he could hold on. The other statistic, which 1997 captain Tom Kite brought to the team's attention, was that players who sat out all four matches until Sunday lost their singles matches 80 percent of the time. That meant Sandelin, Van de Velde and Coltart were on the wrong side of the statistics, as were Montgomerie, Lawrie, Clarke, Westwood, Garcia and Parnevik. That totaled nine matches where the U.S. had a statistical advantage. They only needed 8½ points.

Crenshaw knew he needed to create momentum early, so he sent out his strongest horses first. Lehman started against Westwood, and Sutton was second against Clarke. Then four of the best players in the world, Mickelson, Love, Woods and Duval, were sent out in succession against Sandelin, Van de Velde, Coltart and Parnevik.

In the first six matches the U.S. dominated, winning all six before any one reached the 17th tee. Love provided the largest margin of victory with a 6-and-5 trouncing of Van de Velde, but the most emotional win, and the one that sent the crowd into a frenzy, came when Duval holed a 10-foot birdie putt at the par-five 14th to close out Parnevik. The normally reserved Duval pumped his fists in an overhead gesture, then ran along the gallery ropes and whipped the crowd into a roaring cacophony by holding his hand to his ear in an "I can't hear you!" taunt. It was emotion unlike anything anyone had ever seen from Duval, who later called the Ryder Cup, "the greatest golfing experience of my life."

Lehman also provided an emotional lift, hitting every fairway and every green in his 3-and-2 win over Westwood. "Tom didn't miss a shot today," Westwood said. When Furyk closed out Garcia, 4 and 3, and Pate trounced Jimenez, 2 and 1, the U.S. held the lead for the first time. But Maggert lost his match to Lawrie, 4 and 3, which meant the cup came down to three matches: Leonard against Olazabal, O'Meara versus Harrington, and the duel between U.S. Open champion Stewart and European team leader Montgomerie.

Leonard had been four holes down through the 10th, and the Stewart-Montgomerie match was too close to call, so all attention turned to O'Meara and Harrington. When O'Meara made a deft save at the 17th to keep the match all-square with one to play, it looked as though the cup would be decided by the man who had been largely blamed with instigating the Ryder Cup controversy. When O'Meara hooked his tee shot, then pulled his approach in the bunker at the 18th and failed to get up and down for par, Harrington won the match and the Europeans were within a putt or two of thwarting the comeback.

The U.S. team members and their wives and caddies scurried back to the 17th, where Leonard and Olazabal had just arrived. After the 10th, Olazabal had gone into one of his well-chronicled driving funks, missing the fairway and making bogey on four straight holes from the 11th through the 14th. Leonard was still 1 down at the 15th, but when a 30-footer found the hole, Leonard had squared the match and the crowd was going wild. The match remained tied through the 16th, and when Leonard saw his teammates at the 17th, he knew his match would decide the cup. All he needed was a halve. The U.S. had earned a staggering eight points in 10 matches. They only needed a half point more to complete the greatest comeback in Ryder Cup history and fulfill Crenshaw's prophesy.

Both players drove in the fairway for a change, but when Leonard hit his approach shot, he knew there was a problem. The hole was cut on the top shelf of the two-tiered green and, while his ball hit on the top level, it spun back, running some 50 feet from the hole. Olazabal's approach flew to almost exactly the same spot as Leonard's, but the Spaniard's ball stayed on the top shelf, stopping 20 feet from the hole.

Leonard lined up his improbable putt on the same green where Ouimet had holed two long putts to win 86 years ago, as Crenshaw had told Leonard earlier in the week. He made the best stroke he could, then watched as the ball rolled up the hill and disappeared. Pandemonium erupted. Leonard thrust both arms skyward and raced to the edge of the green, where the first person he found to hug was the standard bearer (or "sign boy" as he was commonly called). The U.S. team, led by Lehman, charged Leonard and hoisted him into the air. Crenshaw kissed the ground.

The celebration was untoward given the fact that Olazabal still had a putt for birdie to halve the hole, but with everything that had transpired throughout the day, the odds against the Spaniard holing that putt were too large to calculate. He made a good stroke, but the ball failed to find the hole, and the U.S. had won back the Ryder Cup in one of the greatest comeback victories in history.

Crenshaw had a feeling, and after his team responded and won, he simply smiled and said, "Darned if we didn't pull it off." Who could argue with fate at that point?

8. Alfred Dunhill Cup

Sergio Garcia's teammates, older, wiser and more experienced, knew what they were doing when handing the captaincy of the Spanish team to a 19-year-old rookie. Jose Maria Olazabal was making his eighth appearance in the Alfred Dunhill Cup and Miguel Angel Jimenez his ninth. A certain Seve Ballesteros played a few times as well, but Spain had never won the championship in 14 previous attempts at attaining glory on the Old Course at St. Andrews, Scotland. "I thought one of the other guys would be in charge," Garcia said, "but they said the rookie was always the captain."

Olazabal knew the real reason. Garcia was on a roll, having dazzled at the Ryder Cup and won the German Masters in the previous fortnight. With El Niño to inspire them, Spain could not lose. "Sergio is amazing," Olazabal said, "and has done everything right so far. Now we want to see if he can do everything right as our captain."

There would be few complaints on a chilly Sunday evening when Garcia, flanked by Olazabal and Jimenez, was holding up the trophy. A year before, when Spain lost in the final, Santiago Luna was the third member of the team and managed a great victory over Tiger Woods in the semi-finals. This time, ironically, Garcia lost both his matches on Sunday but still came out a winner thanks to his teammates' wins as Spain beat defending champion South Africa, 2-1, in the semi-finals and then Australia by the same margin in the final.

Interestingly, Spain won all its five matches by the same score, proving that the key to success in the event is to have two players performing well each day. For the first two days the man to miss out for the Spaniards was Jimenez. You could not get a more stark contrast with Garcia, the latest boy wonder of the game, than the 35-year-old from Malaga. Jimenez, whose nickname of "The Mechanic" shows what he was doing at Garcia's age, is a late-bloomer who was Ballesteros' assistant at the 1997 Ryder Cup but who qualified on merit and performed admirably at Brookline, Massachusetts. After two defeats, he declared he would be there when it mattered and he came good on the promise with three important wins over the weekend.

"Miguel said that 'if you need me, I'll be there,' and he proved that," Garcia said. "He and Jose Maria gave me a lot of confidence, knowing that they were going to be there even if they were one or two shots behind. It is a team event and everybody played their part. We needed two people to play well and that's what we did every single day.

"We made history today," Garcia added. "This is a great day for Spain."

This was Garcia's first-ever appearance at the Home of Golf. "To play here was the one thing I didn't do as an amateur, so I was really looking forward to it," he said. "I've been told about all the things that have happened here, about Seve winning the Open and that all the great players in the game have played here."

Garcia can be added to the list of those who have mastered the links. They say it takes time to get to know and appreciate the venerable layout, but Garcia took to it immediately. In 91 holes, he never found any of those scorecard-wrecking, fairway pot bunkers. His first three scores were 67s and he ended his five rounds 18 under par. It was his first visit to Scotland since a humbling experience in the British Open Championship at Carnoustie, but he will be among the favorites when the Millennium Open is played over the Old Course.

"I'm looking forward to the Open with some confidence, but you know it will be different," said Garcia, who missed the cut at Carnoustie at 30 over par. "You know what happened to me at the Open this year after winning the Irish Open and finishing second at Loch Lomond. It's a totally different tournament, the weather, you don't know what the weather will be. I hope I will win the Open next year. But don't expect me to win. I'll come here and try to win, and that's all I can do."

As the week began, however, it was almost as if the game of golf was on trial, such were the ramifications of the behavior of both the crowd and the American players, at least in the eyes of most European observers, at the Ryder Cup. As expected, the tournament went off without a hitch, but the Americans arrived trying to smooth things out.

"What better place to try to set things straight than St. Andrews?" said Tom Lehman, considered by some as one of the main culprits at Brookline. "We are very much aware of the honor of golf and the courtesy and history of the game.

"It was never our intention to show any lack of respect or lack of courtesy to the European players. We're sorry for running on the green at the 17th, but the excitement of the moment spilled over. I really hope the Europeans all know how much the American side respects them for the effort they put up. There was some phenomenal golf played on both sides. The European side had their foot on our necks and on Sunday we played a remarkable day of golf. I feel there's been a few remarks about me personally that were unfair. I never walked on anybody's line, I'm not a monster, I'm not a rogue, I'm not a hooligan. I am not here to throw any arrows or darts. I definitely don't think it's worth losing friendships over a golf tournament."

It did not prove to be Lehman's week, however, and it started badly when he missed the opening ceremony. The simple flag-raising formality was about to take place when the American captain, Mark O'Meara, phoned Lehman's hotel room to ask where he was. "I'm sleeping, where are you?" Lehman replied. He explained, "I had no idea there was an opening ceremony, which was ignorance on my part. I should have read the information pack. I still felt a bit jet-lagged so I set my alarm for nine o'clock for a 10:50 match."

But Lehman and the American team, the No. 1 seeds, did get off to a winning start, beating New Zealand 2-1. In the other match in group one, Sweden dismissed Italy 3-0. Elsewhere, it was a day of potential shocks which somehow did not quite come about. The most dramatic escape, not least for its implications later in the tournament, was Australia's 2-1 win over Japan.

Stephen Leaney was always in command against Katsuyoshi Tomori, but Peter O'Malley was defeated by the 57-year-old Isao Aoki. And Craig Parry came to the last hole one stroke behind Tsuyoshi Yoneyama, a state of affairs he promptly altered to one in front when he pitched in for eagle from 50 yards. Yoneyama called it "a miracle" and Parry admitted, "I have never done anything like that before. It was like Nick Faldo's shot in the 1990 Open."

The other teams in group one were the hosts Scotland and their old foes Paraguay. In 1993, Colin Montgomerie had stated that if the Scots could not beat Paraguay they should go home. They could not, but now it was Monty who was on his way home, suffering from an infected tooth following routine root canal work earlier in the week. It was Sam Torrance who responded to the message for a replacement the previous evening.

The last time Torrance had played in the event he captained the team to a home victory in 1995 and now he beat Raul Fretes, the man who had defeated Montgomerie six years earlier. "I am glad, because it has taken me a long time to do something Monty couldn't do," Torrance said. Gary Orr could not do much against Carlos Franco's 65, the best score of the week, but Paul Lawrie, the British Open champion, sealed the win by beating Franco's brother, Angel.

Despite being down early on, South Africa, hoping to become the first nation to achieve a hat-trick of victories after their triumphs in 1997 and 1998, beat China 2-1. But Retief Goosen, unbeaten throughout the previous two campaigns, saw his chance to tie Greg Norman's record of 11 straight wins evaporate with a 72-73 defeat by Wu Xiang-bing. "He started very well with three birdies at the first three holes and my putter went cold on me," Goosen said.

"I'm actually glad Retief lost," said Goosen's captain, David Frost. "There is no pressure on him now. He can just relax and play golf."

India's Jeev Milkha Singh beat Lee Westwood, who was trying to shake off a heavy cold, but David Howell and Mark James saw England to a 2-1 win over India. James, Europe's Ryder Cup captain at Brookline, was enjoying playing again rather than watching and came back from three behind with eight to play against Jyoti Randhawa. While his opponent bogeyed the tricky 17th, James holed his par putt from 18 feet to go one ahead.

Westwood, the English captain whose tongue can occasionally reach a fair way up his cheek, was also enjoying having the roles reversed. "I was telling Mark just to focus, don't look at the scoreboards, if you get a few behind, don't worry about it, things can change very quickly. And keep the crowd calm, don't go punching the air and wind up the crowd."

In group four there was a clean sweep for Ireland, none of whose players scored over 71, against the Zimbabweans, none of whom could do better than 72.

While France's Marc Farry beat Jimenez by five with a 68, Garcia won comfortably against Jean Francois Remesy, which left the bottom match to decide the tie. Olazabal was two ahead of Jean Van de Velde until he drove into the hotel, out of bounds, on the right of the 17th and, with his second ball, visited the Road Hole bunker for a triple-bogey seven. Now one behind, Olazabal pitched brilliantly to six inches at the 18th for the tying birdie and then hit another fine approach at the 19th for a winning birdie.

On Friday, matches went as predicted in groups three and four. Goosen was back to winning ways as South Africa beat India 3-0, while England defeated China 2-1. Spain and Ireland had 2-1 wins over Zimbabwe and France, respectively. In the other two groups, the shocks finally arrived to leave anything possible in the last round of qualifying matches.

The United States team had two players from the world's top 10, O'Meara and Payne Stewart, while Lehman was at No. 23. Italy had two players outside the world top 200 and Costantino Rocca, who never contended for a place at Brookline after playing in the three previous Ryder Cups, at No. 121. Rocca's season was marred by an injury the previous Christmas when he sliced off a portion of his thumb while trying to open a bottle of red wine. The Italian captain led by example to beat O'Meara in the top match by two strokes, although the American birdied the 17th to close the gap to one playing the last hole. Lehman also found himself one behind playing the last and when Emanuele Canonica safely made his par, Lehman picked up his marker, failing to realize he had to hole out under the medal-matchplay format, where aggregate scores could still be decisive. Lehman, who was given a one-shot penalty, said, "I wasn't thinking. I'm breaking all the rules this week."

Massimo Scarpa then birdied the last to beat Stewart by a stroke and earn a memorable clean sweep of the No. 1 seeds. Scarpa said, "To beat the USA is a great day for us. Last night this was a dream for us, now it is reality. Costantino said to us at breakfast we could win."

Despite losing to New Zealand 2-1, Sweden was still well-placed in group one, and Australia was in a similar situation even after losing 2-1 to Paraguay. Parry, proving a hard man to beat yet again, tied Carlos Franco with 70 and only lost at the second extra hole. "I really enjoy playing at St. Andrews," Franco said.

There was another famous win for Japan over Scotland. Aoki beat Torrance 71-76, and Orr's 69 gave him a two-stroke win over Yoneyama, so the middle match was decisive. Lawrie was one ahead of Tomori playing the 17th, but after thinking about hitting a seven iron for his second shot, put his six iron over the green and took a double-bogey six to fall one behind. Remarkably, for the second day running, a Japanese player saw his opponent eagle the last hole, Lawrie holing his wedge shot from 77 yards, but Tomori made sure of his three. Then, at the first extra hole, he almost holed his sand-wedge approach shot to put the pressure on Lawrie, who three-putted for a bogey. "He's a hell of a player," Lawrie said, "and even when I made a two at the last, I knew he would make a three."

"I feel great after this win," said Tomori. "Lawrie's eagle at 18 was quite something and all I could do was make a birdie, which I did."

Any of the teams could still qualify on Saturday and Japan did all they could, beating Paraguay 2-1. But because Australia beat Scotland by the same score, and Australia had earlier beaten Japan thanks to Parry's miracle shot at the 18th on Thursday, it was the Aussies who went through. It took more heroics from Parry, however, for the result of the Australia-Scotland match and the whole group depended on his match with Torrance. Tied playing the last, Parry holed from 25 feet for the winning birdie. "We are a bit fortunate to be here, but the 18th has been good to us all week," Parry said.

There were also a number of permutations still to sort out in group one, but with New Zealand beating Italy 2-1, Sweden could afford to drop a match to America. Patrik Sjoland lost to O'Meara, but Gabriel Hjertstedt and Jarmo Sandelin had comfortable wins over Stewart and Lehman. "It's not the same as winning the Ryder Cup, but it is great to beat the Americans," said Sandelin.

The other semi-finalists would be decided by straight shootouts, but while

South Africa was a convincing 3-0 winner over England, the match between Spain and Ireland provided compelling drama. It might have been stretching a point for Paul McGinley, the Irish captain, to describe Spain's comeback as greater than the Americans in the Ryder Cup, but only just.

Conditions were perfect for scoring early on, before the breeze got up, and Darren Clarke was seven under par after 11, McGinley four under at the turn and Padraig Harrington four under after five to be up by four strokes in all three matches. Only McGinley hung on to beat Olazabal 68-70, a two-shot swing at the last to the Spaniard making the result appear closer than it was.

Clarke's problems, after Garcia had birdied the 13th to go four under himself, started when he found Hell bunker with his second shot at the 14th. He had to chip out backwards and took a bogey six. But when Clarke birdied the next and his opponent missed from inside, even Garcia's optimism wavered at three behind with three to play. Yet Clarke found more bunker problems at the 16th to drop a shot and then double-bogeyed the 17th. His right foot slipped on the drive, which ended up way to the left, by the second fairway.

The Irishman's second shot found a tiny pot bunker 70 yards short of the green and again Clarke could only chip out and took three more to get down, while Garcia had played the most delightful approach, a low-runner with a six iron, and just missed the birdie putt to take the lead. But Garcia made no mistake with his birdie chance at the last. Clarke made par on the hole after leaving his second short of the Valley of Sin, and now the attention was on Jimenez, who had been three behind before he birdied the 14th. Jimenez then also birdied the 16th and holed from 12 feet for another at the last to force extra time against Harrington.

Playing against his Ryder Cup foursomes partner, Harrington had done nothing wrong, but saw Jimenez, who beat Montgomerie at the 19th to secure Spanish qualification on the same day a year before, again hole from a similar distance at the first for his fourth birdie in six holes. Jimenez had lost his first two matches but said he would be there when needed. "I promised and I always make my promises," he said. Olazabal added, "He is a warrior."

"I'm stunned that we were beaten," said McGinley, whose team was a combined 11 under par. "Padraig is bitterly disappointed and Darren is 10 times worse. He feels he has let everyone down. We were all under par very early on, but somehow they wriggled free. I'll be surprised if they don't go on to win. It seemed destined for Jimenez to hole that putt at the first."

And once Jimenez had started winning, he would not stop. It was cooler on Sunday morning for the semi-finals and the wind was blowing as it can at St. Andrews. Ernie Els mastered the conditions better than anyone and only three birdies from Garcia in the last five holes brought the Spaniard back to a two-shot deficit, 70-72. But Jimenez beat Frost 73-77 and Olazabal birdied the 17th, after a four iron to 11 feet, for a two-shot swing on Goosen. He would need the advantage as Goosen drove the green and holed the putt from 35 feet for a two, but lost 75-76.

Parry won again for the Australians and even O'Malley's defeat by Sjoland was good news: the Aussies had always won when O'Malley lost. They would do so again, but only after Leaney and Sandelin halved their match with 80s. The Swede had a triple bogey and two doubles in the first 10 holes to be five behind, but the Australian was seven over par on the way home.

Returning to the first, Sandelin was dismayed to see a gust of wind spring up just after hitting his nine-iron approach and the ball fell short of the green in the Swilcan Burn. "We both made a lot of mistakes out there," Leaney said. "I guess I just made one less."

In the final, Garcia chose himself to play against Parry, but it backfired as the Aussie won his 13th match out of 16 in the Alfred Dunhill Cup. For his third successive match, Garcia played a marvelous approach at the notorious 17th, a long, low pitch-and-run catching the contours of the green perfectly. This was by far the best, being played out of the rough with the ball below his feet, but for the third time he missed the birdie putt. Parry got up and down from the path behind the green, holing from 20 feet for par, but then Garcia knocked in an 18-footer himself for a birdie to square the match at the last.

The script went momentarily wrong as Garcia three-putted the first extra hole, but, just as in the morning, the elder statesmen of the team saved their young leader. Olazabal's 72 beat Leaney, who four-putted at the seventh, by six strokes and Jimenez got home two in front of O'Malley. "This is very satisfying, especially because we lost in the final to South Africa last year but beat them in the semi-final," said Olazabal.

One man who was not at St. Andrews was Olazabal's manager, Sergio Gomez, whose brother died just before the tournament. "I want to dedicate this victory to Sergio and his family," said Olazabal. "They're going through tough times, especially his mum."

Garcia added his tribute. "We talked to Sergio and told him, 'Now we have a good reason to win this tournament.' I am so proud of my team. I think Sergio and the whole of his family deserve this trophy."

9. Cisco World Match Play

Not for the first time, Colin Montgomerie did not achieve his first four goals for the season, which refer to the year's four major championships. Yet the 36-year-old Scotsman continues to come up with new ways of demonstrating he is one of the best players in the world.

His performance at the Ryder Cup, gaining 3½ points in the face of some of the foulest abuse anyone has had to suffer on a golf course, was one such occasion and another came with his first victory in the Cisco World Match Play Championship. Montgomerie's win at Wentworth Golf Club near London, his second over the West Course after claiming the Volvo PGA Championship there earlier in the year, was his sixth of the season and equaled the modern European record set by Seve Ballesteros (1986) and Nick Faldo (1992). Norman von Nida in 1947 and Flory van Donck in 1953 are credited with seven, but it was a seventh Order of Merit title Montgomerie would secure a few weeks later.

In six rounds at Wentworth, Montgomerie was 29 under par and his 99 holes included only four bogeys. It was a supreme display of golf as the European No. 1 defeated the defending champion, Mark O'Meara, 3 and 2 in the final. It was enough to convince the American of Montgomerie's credentials for winning the game's highest honors. "There is no doubt in my mind that Colin will win a major and there is no reason why it won't happen within the next year," O'Meara said.

"A lot of things go into winning a major. You are looking at a guy who took 17 or 18 years to win one, so Colin has plenty of time. He is a great competitor. He drives the ball well, he is a great long iron player, he can play all the shots. His technique looks different, but his swing has always stayed the same. He knows what he is capable of and does it. He has great hands and he has great desire.

"I told Colin, I don't think there is one American player, or fan, that doesn't respect his ability to play the game. It is unfortunate there have been some situations, but I told him even Jack Nicklaus had people screaming things like 'Fat Jack' at him when he started to take over from Arnold Palmer. To win the money list on any tour six times in a row with the possibility of winning seven times is phenomenal. The competition in Europe has definitely gotten better over the last decade, yet he keeps bringing his game up to a new level."

Few would disagree with O'Meara's words, and Montgomerie was genuinely appreciative. He did not want to make any rash predictions, however. "You can never say I will win a major," he said. "There are only four. Tiger Woods will win one and I am sure Sergio Garcia will win another, so I'm down to two already. It's not easy. You have got to be there and be fortunate. Hopefully, I will be in contention in a couple of them and the door might open."

As Bill Rogers, Greg Norman, Corey Pavin and Vijay Singh proved, winning the World Match Play is sometimes one of the stepping stones to a major triumph. Montgomerie became the 20th winner in the 36 years of the tournament and only two others, Graham Marsh and Isao Aoki, were not, or did not become, major champions. "You have to go a long way back to see another non-major winner," Monty sighed. "I'd like to change that."

But for Montgomerie, defeated by Ernie Els in the 1994 final, this was a victory to be savored in its own right. "There is a word in the title of this championship which means an awful lot. It's the word 'world' and whenever you are the World Match Play champion or the 'world' anything else it means an awful lot, as does getting my name on this roll of honor. This is a quality championship, a unique tournament and will remain unique as long as it keeps the 36-hole matches. There were a lot of matches this week where a player was down at lunchtime and still won because it is the best player on the day and not just over 18 holes. As long as it remains over 36 holes, it will keep its unique atmosphere and remain a world-class tournament."

Ironically, both finalists had to miss the event's pro-am and might not have been able to tee up without being given a bye through to the second round on Friday thanks to their seedings. O'Meara was No. 1 as the defending champion, and Montgomerie was No. 2 as the highest rated player on the World Ranking. The Scot had to visit the dentist to see about the infected tooth that forced him to withdraw from the Alfred Dunhill Cup. He was due to go back to have the tooth extracted on the Monday morning after the final. "The whole of the left side of my jaw is numb," he said. "It is worst in the cold air, but perhaps concentrating on the golf takes my mind off it."

That might have been the reason for Montgomerie's impressive golf, but O'Meara was truly bewildered after he woke up with a pinched nerve in his back on Wednesday morning. He tried to hit balls on Thursday afternoon, but stopped after hitting just one four-wood shot. For the rest of the week, any time O'Meara was not playing he spent it not on the practice range but in the hands of the PGA European Tour physiotherapist Jonathan Shrewsbury. "The way I felt then, the week I've had has been pretty amazing," O'Meara said.

With the West Course in immaculate condition and all four days blessed with perfect autumn sunshine, it was a record-setting week. The combined score of the field was 165 under par, beating the previous record set in 1989 by three strokes. With Ernie Els and Nick Price also having byes through to the second round, Thursday's first round saw two majors champions, Paul Lawrie and Jose Maria Olazabal, in action along with the irrepressible Sergio Garcia. The 19-year-old was still on a high from leading Spain to victory in the Alfred Dunhill Cup the previous week but found a doughty opponent in Retief Goosen.

When Garcia birdied the first two holes, the 30-year-old South African feared he might be in for a 9-and-8 defeat, but no one goes about their business in a quieter or more unfussy way than Goosen, and he ended the morning round with a one-up lead. "I'm someone who likes to hang at the back of the pack," Goosen said. "At the end of the day, it comes down to the scorecard." And, in the afternoon, the scorecard made breathtaking reading.

On the first nine, Goosen and Garcia combined for a score of 10 under par, with Goosen's 29, six under, equaling the tournament record. The South African hit a nine iron at the 471-yard first hole to 11 feet and holed the putt and then sank a 15-footer for a two at the short second. At the third, Garcia holed from seven feet for a birdie to prevent going four down, and then eagled the fourth and birdied the fifth and sixth to draw level. Goosen immediately stopped the Spaniard's run by winning the next two, but Garcia birdied the ninth from 17 feet.

The brilliance could not last as the tension increased in a match in which, as Garcia said, "No one was giving his arm to break." Goosen went two up when Garcia bogeyed the 11th, but the next three holes were halved. Goosen hit a fine drive down the 15th and Garcia, needing to make something happen quickly, knew he had to match him. But his back foot slipped and the ball hooked into the trees to provoke a rare outburst from the teenager.

Garcia hit a provisional shot, which he hooked even further into the trees, and threw his driver at caddie Jerry Higginbotham. In a match of such sublime golf, it was the player who lost his cool who lost the match. After finding his first ball, Garcia did well to make a five, but birdieing the next only prolonged the game by one hole as Goosen won 2 and 1.

It was a bad day for Spain, as Olazabal lost 4 and 3 to Notah Begay. The Spaniard was suffering from flu and, despite the sunshine, wore a woolly hat throughout a match in which he never led. "At least I'm alive," Olazabal said afterwards, but he never gave up, winning the 12th and 14th after going five down with 10 holes to play. Generously the Masters champion added, "There is nothing you can do when the other guy plays so well."

Begay, 27, was invited under the category of promising newcomer after an impressive rookie season on the U.S. PGA Tour, and he was full of confidence after gaining his second win the previous week. The only Native American on tour, having shot 59 on the Nike Tour in 1998, Begay was playing in Britain for the first time since appearing for the defeated American Walker Cup team at Royal Porthcawl in 1995. He was still switching between putting right- and left-handed — always giving himself a favorable break — to good effect. Although Begay enjoyed telling a new audience he played No. 1 ahead of Tiger Woods and Casey Martin at Stanford University, he added, "Tiger got a little better than me a little quicker."

Padraig Harrington had the day's most convincing victory with a 7-and-6 win over Carlos Franco. Both played superbly in the morning, Harrington winning the 13th, 15th and 17th holes to go two up after an approximate 65 to Franco's 67. It was only in the afternoon that Harrington's relentless success on the greens ground the Paraguayan down and put him six up at the turn. "His putting was wonderful," Franco said. "It was impossible. He saved, saved, saved."

Beating O'Meara in the singles at the Ryder Cup was by no means the 28-year-old Irishman's first experience of match-play success. During a long amateur career, while he completed an accountancy degree, Harrington was considered a strong match player. "I always had a big chip on my shoulder as an amateur that I could never play stroke play like I played match play," he said. "I have certainly never shot 65 around a golf course like this, but I wasn't paying too much attention to the scores. It seemed like a tough draw and I knew I had to play exceptionally well to beat Carlos. For me, today was my final."

Lawrie, the British Open champion, did not complain about not getting a bye to the second round, but might have considered himself unlucky to have been drawn against such a tough opponent as Craig Parry. The Australian is a gritty competitor, as he has shown in the Alfred Dunhill Cup and in winning all three of his Presidents Cup singles, and completed a 4-and-3 win. "I feel I don't give players too many opportunities to win easy holes," said Parry, who only had one bogey.

The match included some classic match-play moments. Lawrie is probably still shaking his head at how Parry, then two up, managed to halve the last three holes of the morning round. The Scot had a chance from 10 feet at the 16th but missed, saw Parry hole from 40 feet at the 17th, and then Lawrie missed from three feet at the 18th. "I don't think I deserved to go in two down, but you don't always get what you deserve," Lawrie said.

The crucial moment came at the 11th in the afternoon, just after Lawrie had birdied the previous two holes to get back to one down. Parry holed from 35 feet, Lawrie missed from eight, and then the Australian birdied the 12th to go three up. Parry could look forward to a match against O'Meara, and Lawrie went home.

No one was more surprised than O'Meara to come out and shoot 63 on Friday morning. Though delighted just to be able to swing the club, he had reason to be disappointed at being only three up at lunch, but then Parry could be forgiven for thinking his luck was out to shoot 66 and be three down. "It is amazing what happens when your expectations aren't very high," said O'Meara. "I just went out to play a few holes and see what happened. The key was realizing I didn't really know where the ball was going and swinging only at 70 percent."

Even when his caddie told him he looked like a pirate the way he was walking, O'Meara found it hurt when he laughed. He was not sure if he could continue, but after more treatment in the interval, he appeared for the afternoon and held his lead over the front nine. Parry leveled the match three times after the turn, but having three-putted the 18th himself, he could not see O'Meara missing from four feet to do likewise and had shaken hands with his caddie and was prepared to walk in when O'Meara missed. "I just misread it," he said.

For the first time since 1981, the match went on to the 39th hole, which necessitated cutting in front of the bottom two matches to play the 17th for a third time. "I heard Mark and Craig had gone into extra holes, but I didn't realize they were ours," noted Montgomerie. The Scot would not have to wait much longer. Parry, on in three and two-putting, parred the hole, while O'Meara looked to be struggling when his pitch from the bank short left of the green flew over the putting surface. But the man who holed a putt from off the green to beat Tiger Woods in the 1998 final proceeded to chip in with an eight iron from 14 feet for a birdie four.

"I was practicing those shots the other day and I thought to myself I could make it," O'Meara said. "It was the same line as the putt I had earlier, so I decided to take dead aim and got a little lucky." Parry was 13 under par for the day, but going back to Australia for two weeks off.

Price was also 13 under par, but only had to play 31 holes in beating Goosen 6 and 5. The Zimbabwean's morning effort of 64 had put him five up and he cruised home in the afternoon, occasionally betraying a hint of embarrassment when he holed another putt. "There's a bit of life in the old dog yet," Price, age 42, said. He had recently returned to a face-balanced putter and his improved form included a victory in Japan.

"That's about as fine as I have putted for a long time," Price continued.

"I've been in the doldrums with my putter since 1994. I can speak from authority on how important putting is because I have played a lot of my career with a balky putter. If I could just putt like this for two more years, I'd then hang up my clubs a very happy camper." The match contained the curiosity of a halve at the first in the afternoon in birdie threes, only the third time that had happened in the 36 years of the event. The second time had been only that morning in the O'Meara-Parry match.

The day's other match to go to extra holes saw a remarkable upset as Els, the three-time champion who had won 11 of his previous 13 matches in the tournament, lost to Harrington at the 38th hole. Both players hit their tee shots at the 155-yard second hole to within 10 feet, but Els missed and Harrington holed. Els, who struggled with his putter all day, was three down at lunch but fought back to go ahead for the first time at the 26th hole, but the Irishman finished strongly. "Ernie was not on his best form, but I hung in well after going one down," Harrington said. He birdied the 16th from seven feet to square the match and forced the South African to match his four at the last from 10 feet to force the playoff.

Harrington knew his next opponent would not get any easier. Before their match, Begay had labeled Montgomerie as the "best match player in the world," but Begay proved a difficult opponent himself, taking Montgomerie to the 35th hole before being defeated 2 and 1. Begay started in fine style, birdieing four of the first seven holes to go three up. Montgomerie responded to the challenge and was one up at lunch after 65 to Begay's 66. "That's where I won the match, the last 11 holes this morning," Montgomerie said.

It was not all plain sailing in the afternoon, and Begay won the 14th and 15th holes with birdies to get back to one down before the Scot's birdie at the 17th concluded proceedings. "Notah gave me a great line for my putt," Montgomerie said. "He thought it would come from the left but it didn't, so I hit it straight. I would have missed but for seeing his putt. Notah is a nice guy and a very good player with a very good future ahead of him. He hit the ball consistently well off the tee and his irons were good."

Harrington could not put up the same fight in the semi-finals the following day and driving out of bounds at the 15th and 17th holes contributed to Montgomerie's five-up lead at lunch after 66. Any hope of the Irishman getting back into the match went when Montgomerie single-putted five greens in a row from the fourth. Only one of those was for a win, the rest for crucial halves. "If I had holed two of those five, which you would expect normally, it would have been a different ball game," Montgomerie said.

"Padraig has proved himself a worldwide player over the last two months and his win against Ernie was a tremendous victory, but I've only played four rounds and he's played six and that is a big difference. I've won two games, he's won two games and he's going home and I'm in the final."

"It's a convenient excuse, but I lost concentration because of the tiredness," Harrington admitted. Without admitting to a defeatist attitude, Harrington conceded that the right man had won. "He is the No. 3 in the world. My best can't beat his best. Monty playing his best is phenomenal. He is great under pressure."

But then so is O'Meara, who recovered from four down after 17 holes to beat Price at the 36th with another spectacular finale. Price, who had 66 in the morning to be three up, slumped to 73 and three-putted three times in the afternoon. "My feel left me," he said. O'Meara woke up feeling his injured neck again, but after treatment it eased up in the afternoon and he holed from 30 feet at the eighth to square the match. After going ahead for the first time at the 14th, he found the trees off the tee at the next two holes and was lucky to find himself level playing the last.

In the semi-rough, 40 yards short and left of the green in two, a spectator told him to chip it in. "I said to myself that sounds easier than it is," O'Meara recalled, "but as soon as I hit it, I knew I had hit an excellent pitch. Any time you hole a pitch like that there is luck involved, but if you are going to get lucky, that was the right time."

Montgomerie began the final in stunning fashion, hitting a six iron to four feet at the first. When O'Meara failed to get up and down for a par, Monty was not required to putt. He would probably have holed it anyway, given that he went on to single-putt the next five greens. Only one of those was a long one, from over 40 feet at the sixth for his fourth birdie. Three up, Montgomerie misjudged the pace of the seventh green, three-putting for only his third bogey of the week. He won the 10th with a par and birdied the next three to go five up.

It was the wobble at the last two holes that gave O'Meara hope. Montgomerie could not match the American's birdie at the 17th and then was unfortunate at the 18th. Both players missed the fairway, but Monty was only just off in thick rough while O'Meara was 20 yards wide but had a good lie. He took advantage by hitting a terrific approach with a four wood to two feet. When Montgomerie, who was credited with an approximate 66, only found the green in four, he conceded the hole. "It was a great finish and I knew I had to come out smoking in the afternoon, but Colin is a tremendous competitor and played smart, composed golf," O'Meara said.

Although the wind got up in the afternoon, Montgomerie, after briefly being pegged back to two up and twice going four up for one hole, maintained his three-up advantage through the turn. O'Meara, however, was always likely to come good on the greens at some point and chose the second nine to do it. He holed from seven feet for a halve on the 10th and from double that to win the 11th, after Monty had hit his bunker shot stiff.

Two holes later Montgomerie made a rare long-game mistake, duffing his five-iron approach well short of the green. "At the top of the backswing I suddenly thought I had too much club," he explained. But he got up and down for a four, as O'Meara did from a bunker. The 14th was halved in pars and then Montgomerie's three-iron second at the next left him a 12-foot birdie putt. Crucially, O'Meara had to putt first from just outside. "Mark gave me a great line. It broke just a little more than he thought," Montgomerie admitted.

Montgomerie missed the green at the 16th, but O'Meara found a bunker and pushed his recovery 14 feet past. Inevitably, he holed the one back to force Montgomerie to hole out from three feet for the victory. "In match play you always have to expect the worst," he said. "I knew I was never far enough ahead against someone who can play and putt like Mark can. I lost in the final to Ernie in 1994, so it was nice to get back into the final and be victorious."

10. American Tours

This was one of the most memorable years of golf in recent history. It also was a year of tragedy, with golf losing one of its most colorful and recognizable ambassadors. The year began with everyone questioning how good one player would be, and ended with all eyes focused on the achievements of another.

Golf certainly became more lucrative in 1999. With a new television contract, the purses for PGA Tour events leapt into the $3 million range with events such as The Players Championship and the three World Golf Championship events reaching the $5 million mark. The new purses impacted players top to bottom. A half-million dollars in earnings in 1998 would have put one on the cusp of breaking into the top 50; in 1999, Scott Dunlap won $504,000 and finished 77th on the money list. Thirty-five players won over $1 million on the PGA Tour in 1999, 13 of whom did not win an event. The top players shattered earnings records, and it took over $326,000 just to keep a PGA Tour card.

Every round of every tournament on the PGA Tour was televised, as the game began appealing to a broader demographic audience. Tiger Woods had become one of the most recognized figures in the world, while second- and third-tier players found rewards they had not known before.

The money and the increased television exposure would have meant less if the play had been boring. Thanks to two of the game's best competitors, golf in 1999 couldn't have been much better.

Starting in Hawaii at the Mercedes Championships, a new venue the PGA Tour established in hope of capitalizing on a prime-time television audience, golf took on a new look. Not that die-hard golfers weren't familiar with the wraparound sunglasses and baggy chinos that had become trademarks for David Duval, but many newcomers got their first glimpse of the game's hottest player when he marched to victory at Kapalua. Two weeks later Duval took the spotlight again when he came back to win from seven strokes behind in the final round of the Bob Hope Chrysler Classic with a record-equaling 59. When the eagle putt fell on the final hole, Duval stepped back and pumped his fists in the air. The season was young, and before it was over, there would be more displays, more intensity and more news out of Duval than he could have imagined.

A debate raged as to who was the best golfer in the world. The Official World Golf Ranking still placed Woods in the No. 1 spot with Duval a close second, but while Woods had continued to post good numbers in 1998, he only had one American victory the previous year. Woods won the Buick Invitational in La Jolla, California and, while it wasn't enough to silence the critics, it did send a statement that Woods wasn't about to relinquish No. 1 without a fight. He knew he was close to breaking out.

With a victory at The Players Championship, Duval ascended to the top spot in the World Ranking. Then he won the next week in Atlanta.

Even though he made a final-round run, Duval didn't win the Masters and neither did Woods. That event turned into a memorable duel between a man who already owned a green jacket, Jose Maria Olazabal, and two men who desperately wanted one, Greg Norman and Davis Love III. Olazabal won the battle, picking up his second Masters title and recognition as the comeback player of the year. Three years before, Olazabal had been confined to his bed with foot pains so debilitating that he couldn't walk through his house.

Glen Day, Jesper Parnevik, Stuart Appleby, Carlos Franco and Rich Beem all won PGA Tour events after the Masters, but it was at the Memorial Tournament that the tone for the rest of the year was set. Woods put on a remarkable short-game display, hitting deft chip shots that even host Jack Nicklaus called "unbelievable." Woods' victory in the Memorial, his second of the year, would propel him to heights in golf not seen in over two decades.

In his next start, Woods finished third after missing two putts in the closing holes. The event was the U.S. Open and the winner, Payne Stewart, had one of the more memorable rounds in Open history, making critical putts on the 70th, 71st and 72nd holes to edge Phil Mickelson by one stroke. When the final putt on the 72nd hole fell for par, Stewart thrust his fist forward and expelled a scream. He then hugged his caddie, Mike Hicks, lifting him off the ground in a bear hug that had Tracey Stewart wincing and wondering if her husband's back could withstand such exertion. But Tracey didn't have to worry. Payne's back was fine, his career was fine, and when he looked Mickelson in the eye and said, "You're going to be a father. That's the most important thing you can imagine," everyone knew that his life and priorities were fine as well.

Four months later, Tracey Stewart received the most devastating telephone call of her life. The Learjet carrying Payne Stewart, two of his agents, a golf course architect and two pilots had lost cabin pressure and was flying on autopilot. All passengers onboard were dead, and all the FAA could do was track the airplane until it crashed in a field in Mina, South Dakota.

The golf world was in shock, and as the 29 top money winners gathered in Houston for the Tour Championship, there was a sense that golf was the last thing on anyone's mind. It became Woods' third consecutive victory, his fourth in five starts, including the PGA Championship, WGC NEC Invitational and National Car Rental Classic, but even that accomplishment couldn't replace the profound shock and sadness that was felt throughout the week.

With a playoff victory in the season-ending WGC American Express Championship, Woods became the first player since Ben Hogan in 1953 to win four events in the row, and the first since Johnny Miller in 1974 to win eight PGA Tour events in a season. He was, truly, in a class by himself. Not only did Woods win $6.6 million for the season, he won more than the next two players on the money list (Duval and Love) combined.

Duval and Woods weren't the only multiple winners of the year. Stewart won the AT&T Pebble Beach National Pro-Am in addition to the U.S. Open, and Franco won twice, locking up Rookie of the Year honors for the Paraguayan. David Toms, Duffy Waldorf and Notah Begay III all had two wins as well.

U.S. PGA Tour

Mercedes Championships—$2,600,000
Winner: David Duval

In one of the most impressive displays of golf in his career, David Duval soaked up the sun and surf at Maui's Kapalua Resort, then proceeded to shoot 26-under-par 266 and run away from an elite field, winning the Mercedes Championships by nine shots. It was Duval's eighth win in 27 starts, and it was the largest margin of victory on the PGA Tour since Tiger Woods' record-setting 12-stroke victory in the 1997 Masters.

"It's really great to do it in an event where everybody knows how to win," Duval said of his performance against 29 of the PGA Tour's best. "You've got to have a lot of things come together for this kind of thing to happen. Steve Jones did it a couple of years ago at the Phoenix Open, and Tiger did it at Augusta."

In Hawaii it was Duval's turn. After opening with 67 and trailing Billy Mayfair, Steve Pate, Joe Durant and Fred Funk by one shot, Duval put some distance between himself and the field by firing a course-record 63 on Friday. He widened the gap on Saturday by shooting 68 for a 21-under-par 198 total, five better than Funk, who followed his opening 66 with 69 and 68.

About the only thing that could have stopped Duval on Sunday was an intervening act of nature. Even some horseplay from Funk didn't distract him. After borrowing Duval's courtesy car Saturday night, Funk made a few alterations before returning the vehicle. "I messed with the seats, the mirrors, turned the wipers on, moved the steering wheel, turned the heat on full-blast … everything. If it had been his own car, I would have flattened the tires."

Even that bit of mischief didn't distract Duval. "On 17 I said to him, 'By the way, how was your car this morning?'" Funk said. "It didn't faze him. He gets into this rhythm, and he never gets out of it. He never hits a shot until he's ready to hit it, never hits a putt until he feels comfortable. He's extremely straight, very long and exceptionally accurate with the long irons. It's fun to watch a guy who has a game I don't have."

Duval had a somewhat different assessment of his Sunday game, however. "When you start out with a big lead, it's weird, kind of unsettling. It wasn't until the fifth hole, where I ran my birdie putt five feet past the hole and made it coming back that I settled down. I did a nice job avoiding the downhill, downwind, down-grain putts. Some greens you can actually see the grass laying sideways," he said.

On the eighth hole Sunday, Duval left himself with a precarious side-hill chip from 70 feet that had almost 40 feet of break. Had he chipped poorly, bogey or even double bogey could have been factored into the equation, leaving the door open for Mayfair and Mark O'Meara. Instead, he hit what Funk called, "one of the greatest chips I've ever seen," to within three feet. Duval made par, retained his five-stroke advantage, and increased the margin to nine with a closing-round 68.

O'Meara also closed with 68 to tie Mayfair for second at 275, while Vijay Singh shot 70-68-69-68 for a total of 275. All were impressed by Duval's play. "He's got all the tools," O'Meara said. "I've seen him when he's playing his best and he's so relaxed, but I also remember last year at the Trophee Lancome, when he had a chance to win and he hit it in the water on 18. He was like, 'I hit a bad shot, it's not the end of the world. I could have won the golf tournament, but I didn't. There will be another time.' He had a great attitude about it."

Sony Open in Hawaii—$2,600,000
Winner: Jeff Sluman

After the 1998 scoring assault during the Sony Open in Hawaii, where John Huston shot a PGA Tour-record, 28-under-par 260, the members of Waialae Country Club in Honolulu took things personally. According to Brandel Chamblee, who led after two rounds in 1999, "We cussed John Huston all week for what he did here last year. Somebody got mad and grew some rough. I don't know what kind of grass that is, but if I had it in my yard, I would kill it."

Not only did the members grow the rough after Huston's pillage of par, they lengthened several holes and reduced par from 72 to 70. As a result, birdies fell from 2,019 in 1998 to 1,181 in 1999 and the winning score jumped from 260 to 271. That allowed steady contenders like Chamblee, Jeff Maggert and eventual winner Jeff Sluman to play off their strengths.

"I don't think I could have won in the same conditions as last year," Sluman said. "The old par-fives were so easy for the longer guys. I like a golf course where par is the same for everybody."

For a while it didn't look as though Sluman would win this year, either. He never held the outright lead until his six-iron tee shot on the 71st hole — a 189-yard par-three — landed three feet from the hole. Before Sluman slammed that three-foot birdie putt into the center of the cup, the lead was up for grabs with third-round leader Tommy Tolles (who came to Hawaii sporting a peroxide-blonde hairstyle he described as "a little extreme"), Davis Love III, Jeff Maggert, Len Mattiace and Chris Perry all bidding for the championship. Mistakes by the leaders and a strong finish by Sluman turned the tide in the 41-year-old's favor.

"I made the turn in good shape," Sluman said. "I felt that if I played a mistake-free second nine and picked up a couple of birdies I had a chance."

He was right on all counts. Tolles, who started the final round at 202 and one stroke ahead of Love, made double bogey and bogey on the front nine from which he could not recover. That allowed Love to grab the lead briefly, but he couldn't recapture the magic that produced a seven-under-par 63 on Saturday and after bogeys at the fifth and 13th, Love never seriously contended again despite finishing tied for second with 70 and 273.

Then Maggert made a charge. He and Sluman started the day in a six-way tie for fifth at 205, but two birdies on the front followed by a third at the 13th moved Maggert to eight under par and in sole possession of the lead. A bogey at 15 slipped Maggert into a tie with Sluman at seven under, but then Maggert bogeyed the par-three 17th while Sluman was making birdie.

On the tricky, par-five 18th, Sluman hit his third shot over the green and into a fluffy lie, briefly giving life to Maggert, Tolles (who finished with a one-over 71), Love (who managed an even-par 70), Perry (who entered the fray with a final-round 66), and Mattiace (who shot 68). All were in the clubhouse at 273 when Sluman addressed his chip, but their hopes faded when he nestled the ball to within two feet of the cup and tapped in for a birdie-birdie finish and a two-stroke victory.

"I had a good idea what was going to happen going up the 18th fairway," Sluman said. "I had it, but you don't know until it's over. Winning is important out here for you as an individual and for your status among your peers. Nobody out here is a loser, but, in this game, there is only one champion each week. A thousand players can run over you. You never know when it might be your last win."

Bob Hope Chrysler Classic—$3,000,000
Winner: David Duval

Before January 24, 1999, the PGA Tour had seen 60 broken on two occasions. The first came in 1977, when Al Geiberger posted a 59 in the second round of the Danny Thomas Memphis Classic, earning Geiberger the title "Mr. 59." The second came in 1991, when Chip Beck brought the relatively easy Sunrise Golf Club in Las Vegas to its knees with 59 in the Las Vegas Invitational. Unlike Geiberger, Beck did not go on to win the Las Vegas Invitational, and before 1999 no one had broken 60 on a weekend. It was the equivalent of the four-minute mile, and 22 years after it was first accomplished, 59 was still golf's magic number.

So when David Duval birdied four of the first five holes in the Bob Hope Chrysler Classic at the PGA West Palmer Course in La Quinta, California, no one could have anticipated what was to come. After all, Duval started the day seven shots off the pace. Duval told his girlfriend, Julie McArthur, that his chances of winning were "slim and none." Fred Funk had led since early in the second round, and his 20-under-par 268 was good enough for a one-shot edge over Steve Pate and a two-shot margin over John Huston and Bob Estes. With a dozen players ahead of him, Duval was being realistic about his chances.

Even when Duval hit an eight iron to eight feet on the par-four ninth hole and made the putt for birdie to turn in 31, no one took much notice. He was creeping up the leaderboard, but Pate was playing well and had wrested the lead from Funk in the first few holes of the final round.

The birdies just kept coming, though. A three wood and sand wedge to four feet on the 10th produced the sixth birdie of the round, and got the crowd murmuring about Duval. That murmur grew louder as Duval made another four-foot birdie putt on the 11th, then hit six iron to two feet on the par-three 12th for his fourth consecutive birdie and his eighth of the day. The first par of the second nine came at the 13th when Duval missed from 12 feet, but he made up for it at the par-five 14th by making a 10-footer for birdie. That would be the longest putt he would make all day.

"He knocked down the flag all day," said Bob Tway, who played in the threesome with Duval. "It was something to watch."

On the par-three 15th Duval hit an eight iron to one foot and tapped in for his 10th birdie. When his approach to the 16th almost went in for eagle, and he tapped in from five inches for birdie, he assumed the lead for the first time and people began uttering the magic number. Was 59 possible in the final round of a PGA Tour event? A par at the 17th from 20 feet seemed to dash a few hopes, but after booming a tee shot on the par-five 18th, Duval hit another five iron to within six feet of the flag.

He knew that history lay before him, but the ever-cool Duval showed no emotion as he walked to the green and spotted his ball. In fact, he and his caddie, Mitch Knox, chatted about the Chrysler luxury car perched on a floating stand in the middle of the water hazard left of the fairway as they marched toward the record books. When he sank the six-footer, assumed the lead, and became a member of the most exclusive club in golf, Duval pumped his fist in the air and gave Knox a high-five, but then the emotion stopped. If Pate birdied the 18th, there would be a playoff. But Pate missed, and Duval had accomplished the unimaginable. He had shot 59 to come from seven shots back to win.

"I don't know what to say," Duval said. "It's like pitching a perfect game. I stole this tournament from Steve Pate."

Pate said, "There's no doubt who's the best golfer in the world, but there wasn't a doubt even before he put up a 59."

Phoenix Open—$3,000,000
Winner: Rocco Mediate

With David Duval on one of the best runs in golf history and Tiger Woods, the reigning No. 1 golfer in the world, playing with more confidence than he had displayed in some time, no one expected Rocco Mediate, ranked No. 111 in the world and winless in six years, to walk away with the Phoenix Open. As the drama unfolded at the event that draws the largest and rowdiest crowds in golf, it was Mediate, 60 pounds lighter after back surgery, that surprised the spectators by hanging on to the lead with the likes of Woods and Justin Leonard nipping at his heels.

"I'm the first to admit I didn't know whether I could do it," Mediate said, after shooting a final-round 71 for a 273 total and a two-shot victory over Leonard, while Woods finished three behind. "It's been a long time since I've been here. I can't do what Tiger and David Duval can do. They're single and I have a wife and three kids, but I couldn't do what they do even if I didn't have a family. They're so good. Me, I didn't know if I could do what I had to do today. I didn't sleep well last night. The demons came."

The demons in Mediate's head weren't as threatening as some that actually found their way onto the golf course. During Sunday's final round, as Mediate and Woods made their way to the sixth tee, an inebriated spectator boisterously showed his support for Woods. When a police officer tried to quiet him an altercation ensued. The incident would have gone unnoticed but for the fact that the spectator was found to be carrying a loaded pistol. He had a permit to carry a concealed weapon, but for a few moments the situation was, as Woods put it, "scary."

After 11 pars, Mediate ran into gallery trouble again when, at the 12th tee, a fan of Woods loudly proclaimed that Woods was one birdie away from causing Mediate to fold under the pressure. "That really ticked me off," Mediate said. "If there hadn't been water there, I would have had to go after him I was so mad. But Tiger told me to shake it off, and I made birdie at the 13th, my first of the day. I should get mad like that every morning when I come out here."

Woods acted as a calming force for Mediate throughout the day, but he provided very few heroics for which he had become famous. The only drama Woods offered came at the same 13th hole on Sunday when his errant tee shot landed behind a large boulder. When Woods asked PGA Tour rules official Orlando Pope if the object was a loose impediment and therefore movable under the Rules of Golf, Pope said that as long as play wasn't disrupted Woods could move the boulder. Twelve gallery members happily obliged by pushing the boulder out of Woods' line, and the world's No. 1 player went on to make birdie.

"He was very lucky to have a number of people in the gallery who were willing to move that rock for him," said PGA Tour tournament director Ben Nelson.

The ruling didn't matter, however. Despite a final-round 68, Woods never make a charge at Mediate. Leonard came the closest, firing a 66 to reach 275, but the former British Open champion couldn't overcome the 75 he posted on Friday. Woods finished alone in third at 276.

AT&T Pebble Beach National Pro-Am—$2,800,000
Winner: Payne Stewart

The AT&T Pebble Beach National Pro-Am was once again hampered and ultimately shortened by rain as the greens, fairways and some tees were covered in water. "In the old days they still played," mused R.J. Harper, the director of golf at Pebble Beach. "If you take a look at the old film, they always found a way to play. Standards have changed. I'm not suggesting it's right or wrong. It's just a fact."

Indeed, back in the days when the event was the Crosby Pro-Am, players slogged their way through virtually unplayable conditions, then warmed their toes at the post-round clambake. But with almost $3 million in prize money at stake, the standards for acceptable playing conditions in 1999 were much different.

The weather proved too much for many of the players, as the scoring average on Pebble Beach for Saturday's third and final round soared to 79.4. Winds whipped in from the Pacific, blowing cold rain sideways. According to Payne Stewart (who played his third round at Spyglass Hill, edged into the lead, and was declared the winner after the rainout), "It was the luck of the draw that I wasn't at Pebble today. It would not have been a fun day to be at Pebble Beach."

Even though Stewart had no idea it would be the final round, the last few holes were not short of dramatics. After opening rounds of 69 and 64 to open a three-shot lead on Frank Lickliter and Vijay Singh, Stewart struggled through the rain to play the first 17 holes at Spyglass in two over par. That allowed

Lickliter to pull even despite his own three-putt bogey on the 17th. That three-putt proved crucial. On the next hole, Stewart hit a five-iron approach to the 18th green that ended up 14 inches from the hole. That birdie finished off a round of 73 for Stewart and a three-day total of 10-under-par 206.

On Sunday, David Duval, coming off his final-round 59 at the Bob Hope Chrysler Classic, started seven shots back, but holed his second shot from the fairway on the first hole for eagle. Then, 20 minutes before the leaders were to tee off, the rain siren sounded, and not long after that the tournament was called off, and Stewart was declared the winner.

"Anybody could have won out there today," Stewart said. "If I went out and shot 78 and David Duval went for 70, boom, he wins." But Stewart couldn't have been happier with his victory. "If you stay out there long enough, what goes around comes around. I wanted the opportunity to play, but I was the leader after 54 holes, and that was good enough. This win is not tainted by any means."

The $504,000 first-place check wasn't tainted either, and, even though the event was shortened by rain, the winner felt he found his game when he changed putters. "I've been swinging at it as good as I have in years," he said. "I rolled it very well. I made so many putts I felt like Mark O'Meara out there. It was great."

Even Lickliter, who finished alone in second at 207, one shot off Stewart's pace and two shots ahead of third-place finisher Craig Stadler, couldn't complain. "This is such a gorgeous place, if you told me it was going to rain for the next 20 years, I'd still come back to play." A $302,400 second-place check might have made that decision a little easier.

Buick Invitational—$2,700,000
Winner: Tiger Woods

Just at the moment when David Duval was capturing attention with his spectacular play, leaving many to question Tiger Woods' position atop the World Ranking, Woods answered the critics by coming from nine strokes back to win the Buick Invitational by two over Billy Ray Brown. In the process, Woods shot a course-record 62 on the storied Torrey Pines layout in La Jolla, California, and played the weekend in 17-under-par 127, putting an exclamation point on the finish with an eagle at the 72nd hole.

"I told you I was close to putting it all together," Woods said. "It's been this way for months, but nothing has ever gelled. Golf is a wave. You're constantly going up and down, and it's a matter of how fast you get out of a lull. Nothing has changed with my outlook. It's a matter of getting the right breaks at the right time and making your own destiny."

The breaks started coming Woods' way on Saturday when, after starting the day at 139, nine shots off of Ted Tryba's lead, Woods made eagle on the par-five sixth hole after his three-wood second shot from the rough hit a sprinkler head. The ball bounced forward and ended up 10 feet from the hole. That's when the roars started.

"We didn't see him, but we heard him," said Brown, who began the third round at 134. "There are birdie roars for Tiger and there are eagle roars for Tiger."

Scorching the seaside course with a 62, Woods made up 10 shots and held a one-stroke advantage at 201 going into the final round. "I was just trying to make it known that I was coming," Woods said of his record-breaking round. "I've always been a good putter — not a great putter — but I've always been able to make them down the stretch. Working with Butch (Harmon), putting in a lot of time, it's coming to fruition. Forty feet or four feet, it doesn't matter. I feel I can make it."

Those feelings carried over into the final round, where Woods opened with three birdies in the first four holes. But Brown, who started the day at 202, didn't back down. His closing round of 66 was only marred by a bogey on the first hole, and a par that felt like a bogey at the last. After pulling even with Woods at 20 under par through 70 holes, Brown tried to reach the par-five 18th with his second shot only to find the water that fronts the green. Woods, after an enormous drive, hit a seven-iron second shot to the par-five that stopped 10 feet from the hole. Brown got his ball up and down for par, but it didn't matter. Woods holed the eagle putt for a 65 and 266 total, and the victory was his.

"I'm glad he made (the eagle putt)," Brown said. "It didn't make me look so bad."

Brown's second-place finish was a dramatic comeback for a player who hadn't won since the 1997 Deposit Guarantee Classic and who only made eight of 24 cuts in 1998, falling to 201st on the money list. His $291,600 second-place check was more money than Brown made in nine of his previous 12 seasons on tour.

As for Tiger, he smiled, raised his arms to the crowd after the victory, and said, "You know you can laugh and have a good time, just concentrate over your shots. If you try to stay focused for five hours every day, you're going to be exhausted. Having fewer shots, I had more time to smell the roses along the way."

Nissan Open—$2,800,000
Winner: Ernie Els

With a win in the Alfred Dunhill South African PGA and a runner-up finish in the Heineken Classic, Ernie Els came to Los Angeles for his PGA Tour debut with his "A" game intact. He knew he would need it. Seven of the world's top-10 players were in the field at Riviera Country Club for the Nissan Open, with all eyes on the rivalry between the No. 1-ranked player, Tiger Woods, and the hottest player in golf, No. 2-ranked David Duval. In the end it was Els who slipped in with consistent play to beat a star-studded field for his second victory of the year.

"With all those great names on the leaderboard, I should have taken a picture," Els said. "When you have players of that caliber in the field and they're all playing well and you're in the middle of it, coming out on top is very satisfying to say the least."

Certainly Woods, Duval, Davis Love III and Nick Price all had their chances even though none of them ever broke into the lead after Duval finished the first round tied with Bob Estes at five-under-par 66. However, none of the top three golfers in the world were ever more than three shots away from the lead. Els, who was within one shot of Estes' 133 lead at the end of the second round and two shots off the pace at the beginning of the final round, seemed genuinely pleased to remain backstage in the Woods-Duval showdown, even after closing with a four-under-par 68 and 270 total to handily defeat both of them.

"I would like to think of myself as maybe No. 3 at the moment," Els said. "I'm still six wins behind David in the last 18 months, and Tiger will always play the leading role in this little tale. But Duval is definitely the best player in the world right now. Phil Mickelson (who tied for 15th at 278) is awfully good too. He has won the most tournaments of anyone in his 20s. I accept the fact that you go by records, and my record hasn't been that good in the last year."

Records didn't seem to matter at the Nissan Open. The first to fall was the course record, which went on Saturday to a 10-year journeyman professional, Ted Tryba. With only one PGA Tour win on his resume, the 1995 Anheuser-Busch Classic, Tryba shocked the field by firing a 61 that could have been a 59. Poised at 11 under par for the day as he strode down the 18th fairway, Tryba was one birdie away from golf's magic number, but his approach shot nestled into the rough behind the green. The resulting bogey forced Tryba to settle for a 61, a 200 total, and a two-shot lead over Els, Woods and Love going into the final round.

"When I heard he had a chance to shoot 59, I thought, 'That's unbelievable,'" Els said of Tryba's spectacular round. "Riviera is one of the classic, tough courses. I don't think you'll ever see 61 here again."

For all his praise of Tryba's round, Els offered a sobering prediction. "The best players in the world are on the leaderboard," he said. "I think Ted Tryba's going to have an uneasy night tonight."

While Tryba said he slept fine on Saturday night, his even-par round on Sunday, capped by another bogey on the 18th, left him tied for second with Woods and Love, both of whom finished with final rounds of 70 for totals of 272. Els finished strong, birdieing the 11th, 12th and 13th to capture the lead by two strokes, a lead he maintained until the 18th where he missed a four-footer for par. But neither Woods nor Tryba could birdie the 18th. In fact, both made bogey and Els could breathe a sigh of relief.

"It's a lot to ask a guy to make birdie in that situation," Els said. "I'm thankful 18 was playing hard. I've given Tiger a chance or two in the past and he has taken it."

WGC Andersen Consulting Match Play—$5,000,000
Winner: Jeff Maggert

The Andersen Consulting Match Play Championship at La Costa Resort in Carlsbad, California, reaffirmed the premise that match play is fun to watch, even in the early going, and secondly, the event confirmed that match play is almost always full of surprises.

"In an 18-hole match-play format with players of this caliber anybody can beat anybody," Tiger Woods said of the unpredictability of this first-ever World Golf Championship event. That proved to be true from the start. On Wednesday, the first day of this single-elimination, five-day format, the lower seeded player won 18 of 32 matches. Early victims included third-seeded Mark O'Meara who was beaten 4 and 2 by 62nd-ranked Michael Bradley, Davis Love III (fourth) who lost 1 up to Steve Pate (64th), Lee Westwood (fifth) who took a 3-and-2 beating at the hands of Eduardo Romero (60th), and Ernie Els (seventh) who was sent packing by Paul Azinger (58th).

Azinger was defeated in the second round by Loren Roberts (ranked 39th) after Roberts had upset 26th-ranked Hal Sutton in the opener. Pate won over Brandt Jobe, who had upset Jeff Sluman in the first round, and Steve Jones upset Scott Verplank, who had upset 19th-ranked Tom Lehman to advance to the second round.

The biggest early-round surprise was Romero, who followed his Westwood upset with an improbable 21-hole victory over Greg Norman after Norman blew a three-up lead with four holes to play, then hit his tee shot out of bounds on the third extra hole. Romero continued his rise by defeating 12th-ranked Phil Mickelson 2 and 1 in the quarterfinals. In the semi-finals, Romero's streak came to an end when he was beaten 3 and 2 by another underdog, Steve Pate (ranked 61st), whose rise to the semi-final match included beating Love, Jobe (36th) and Fred Couples (13th).

"I don't think there's that big a difference between the skill level from top to bottom," Jones said. "The stroke average between the top guy and the bottom guy over the course of an entire year isn't much, and it's pretty meaningless for 18 holes."

He obviously had a point. By the end of the third round, Woods was the only top-10 player left in the field, a development Woods said, "doesn't surprise me."

"We expected maybe two of the top-10 players to make it into the final four," Mickelson said. "The upsets weren't unexpected, but nobody thought the entire top 20 would be out."

The upsets weren't over yet, however. Jeff Maggert, ranked 24th and known more for his 12 runner-up finishes than his one win in the 1993 Walt Disney World Classic, defeated the world's No. 1 player, Woods, 2 and 1 in the quarterfinals. Maggert went on to defeat Pate 1 up in the semi-final match, while, on the other side of the bracket, Andrew Magee (50th) upset John Huston (27th) 3 and 1 to advance to the final.

The final between Maggert and Magee turned out to be anything but dull, even though, between them, the two players hadn't won an event in 218 consecutive starts. It was nip-and-tuck throughout the morning round, with Magee taking a 2-up lead in the first 18, then giving it back when Maggert won holes three, four and five in the afternoon.

When Maggert holed a 25-foot putt at the 10th, the match was all-square again. It remained so at the end of regulation when Maggert missed an eight-foot birdie putt on the 18th that would have clinched the victory in regulation. On the second extra hole of the match, the 38th hole of the day, Maggert pulled an eight iron on the par-three 11th that ended up in the fringe. He had his caddie take out the flag, and as Maggert examined the chip only one thought went through his mind.

"The last thing I wanted to do was run it four or five feet past the hole because I'd been struggling with those all day," he said. "But, lo and behold, I hit the thing too hard."

Fortunately for Maggert, his ball hit the center of the hole, jumped up and fell straight in for a birdie, a 1-up victory, and a $1 million payday. He also ended a six-year winless streak that had many wondering why a player with Maggert's talent couldn't break through.

"The first half-dozen or so times I came up short it bothered me," he said. "Then I came to realize that I wasn't giving golf tournaments away. Other people were playing good golf to beat me. I know there are going to be a lot of doubters, but I don't care what they say. This was a good win for me, myself, and I."

Touchstone Energy Tucson Open—$2,750,000
Winner: Gabriel Hjertstedt

With the top 64 players in the world competing in the Andersen Consulting Match Play Championship, the field at the Touchstone Energy Tucson Open was light in marquee value, but the drama of the finish made up for the absence of the big names. Gabriel Hjertstedt of Sweden sank a 25-foot birdie putt on the first playoff hole to defeat Tommy Armour III and take his first victory since the 1997 B.C. Open and the largest paycheck ($495,000) of his three-year professional career.

Hjertstedt had no one but himself to blame for being in a playoff. He came to the 72nd tee with a two-shot lead and seemed ready to cruise to victory, but an errant tee shot on the 440-yard par-four hole narrowly avoided the water guarding the right side. The ball found the rough some 236 yards from the green. From there Hjertstedt advanced his ball into the greenside bunker. When he blasted out to 16 feet, all he had to do was two-putt for the victory. He misjudged the speed of the downhill putt and left it three feet short. From there his bogey putt hit the lip of the hole and spun out.

"The only time I was nervous all day was over the last two putts in regulation," said Hjertstedt, who shot 68 for his 12-under-par 276 total.

He quickly righted himself in the playoff, finding the center of the fairway on the hole he had, only moments earlier, struggled through in six shots. Hjertstedt's approach landed safely in the center of the green, 25 feet from the hole, and when the putt fell he had cut his previous performance on the same hole by three shots and taken back the championship he felt should have been his in regulation.

The double bogey at the last was Hjertstedt's second in two days, and both times he used the event to his advantage. On Saturday, his second shot on the 663-yard, par-five 15th found the fairway bunker, and it took him four to get down for a seven. That left Hjertstedt two shots off the third-round lead, but it inspired him to play better on Sunday.

"I was bored coming into 15 (on Saturday)," he said. "I didn't care too much. I felt like I was playing great, but the birdies weren't coming. That double bogey got me excited again."

After that costly double bogey, Hjertstedt played the next 20 holes in six under par before getting excited again by the double bogey at the 72nd. Still, his 12-under-par 276 total was Hjertstedt's best performance in two years, even with the two hiccups. "I felt like it was mine. I just needed to take it," he said.

After entering the final round tied for the lead at 206 with Barry Cheesman,

Armour's 70 was marked by accurate drives and consistent iron play, but very few putts falling, including a birdie effort of his own on the playoff hole. Still, the $297,000 second-place check was the largest of Armour's 18-year career, a consolation that didn't seem to please the 39-year-old Texan. "I don't play for the money," Armour said. "I only play for the victories." There has only been one of those to date in Armour's career — the 1990 Phoenix Open — but he wasn't the only wandering soul to find his way to the top of this leaderboard. The low round of the tournament came on Thursday when Nike Tour veteran R.W. Eaks shot a 64, but followed it up with a 75. Cheesman, another Nike Tour veteran, shot a final-round 72 to finish tied for fifth with another winless professional, Brent Geiberger, while Mike Reid and Kirk Triplett tied for third at 277.

Doral-Ryder Open—$3,000,000
Winner: Steve Elkington

After three-putting the final green for bogey in the Doral-Ryder Open, Steve Elkington kicked the scorer's trailer so hard he left spike marks in the aluminum siding. A casual observer would have never suspected that Elkington had just shot a tournament-low score of 64 to take a one-stroke lead into the clubhouse.

"I was just frustrated when I came off because I had done all that work," Elkington said. "I didn't want to leave any crumbs out there. I wanted to send a message. It's a menagerie of emotions, different scenarios and different things that go on in your mind. It's so hard to win. People don't understand how hard it is to execute under that type of pressure."

Elkington's frustrations boiled over after his five-foot par putt lipped out because he was sure that, despite coming from six shots back, his 13-under-par 275 total would be one short of what he needed to force a playoff with Greg Kraft, the third-round leader, or Ernie Els. That prediction turned out to be wrong, but only because Els and Kraft also both made errors on the par-four 18th.

Playing in the penultimate group, Els stood in the middle of the 18th fairway at 13 under par with an eight iron in his hands. The pin was cut back left, guarded by water, but accessible to a player of Els' length. A birdie would certainly clinch the title. A par would force a playoff. But rather than coming away with either of those scores, Els pulled his approach shot into the wiry Bermuda rough. After leaving his third shot in the rough, Els hit his fourth shot long and two-putted for double bogey.

"I tried to hit (the eight iron) too hard and just came over the top like I did all day yesterday," Els said. "The way I played the weekend, I didn't deserve to win."

That could not be said for Kraft, a winless nine-year veteran who played consistent golf from the moment he ascended to the top of the leaderboard with a 135 two-day total. Kraft hit fairways and greens and avoided disaster on Saturday, coming in with a 70 to retain a two-shot lead over Els and Glen Day. When he stood in the middle of the 18th fairway poised at 13 under par for the tournament and looking at a reasonably easy five-iron shot to the pin, Kraft turned to his caddie and said, "Let's end it right here."

He ended it, just not the way he intended. Kraft hit the approach shot less than 100 yards before it plummeted into the water in front of the 18th green. Kraft got up and down for bogey from the drop area in front of the green for 71 and a 276 total, but even the $324,000 second-place check provided little consolation.

"This was tough," Kraft said. "It's going to leave a bad taste in my mouth I probably won't forget for a long time. Everybody wants to win. I mean if you win five times, you want to win six. If you win zero, you want to win one."

Even Elkington, who could finally relax in victory, felt for Kraft. "Greg is a good player and I feel for young guys like him," he said. "But he had control of his own destiny. It's just very hard for fellows to break through."

Elkington's breakthrough this week in Miami came on Sunday's front nine where, beginning on the sixth hole, he reeled off six straight birdies, adding two more on the 16th and 17th before the three-putt bogey at the 18th.

"Elk doesn't back off," his caddie, Joe Grillo, said of Elkington. "When he's healthy, he's hard to beat and when he gets the green light, he goes."

That might have explained the uncharacteristic fit of temper Elkington displayed at the scorer's trailer. After locking up the victory and collecting the $540,000 winner's check, an obviously embarrassed Elkington smiled sheepishly and said, "My foot is fine. What would you have done? Jumped in the lake?"

Honda Classic—$2,600,000
Winner: Vijay Singh

With windy conditions and a brewing Florida storm front that forced the final group to tee off five hours earlier than scheduled, no one was surprised that the Sunday scores at the Honda Classic ballooned to an average 73.53, over two strokes higher than any of the previous three days. Only four players broke 70 in the final round: Dudley Hart, who shot 69 to tie for ninth at 283; Hal Sutton, who shot 69 for a share of seventh at 282; Carlos Franco, who shot 69 to tie for third with Doug Dunakey at 280, and Vijay Singh, who shot 69 for an 11-under-par 277 total and a two-stroke victory over Payne Stewart.

"This was the kind of day that separates the men from the boys," said Singh's caddie, Dave Renwick, of the brutal conditions.

After Sutton was the first-round leader with 64, rookie Eric Booker, a 35-year-old graduate of the Nike Tour, won the battle of the first three days by shooting 65 and 66 in the calm conditions and an even-par 72 when the wind picked up to 25 miles an hour on Saturday. He also entertained the media with Elvis Presley imitations and anecdotes of his days as a teaching pro in Michigan. "I used to give 40 lessons a day at a store called Carl's Golfland," he said. Then there were the karate references. "One of my students was a martial arts expert known as the 'Angel of Death.' I traded out golf lessons for karate lessons," he said.

There was nothing to prepare Booker for the conditions that awaited him on Sunday. The final tee time was moved to 9:45 a.m. from 2:15 p.m., and the storm brewing in the Atlantic whipped 35-knot winds across the TPC at

Heron Bay, making the second nine as tough as any the PGA Tour had seen in some time. Bradley Hughes, who had managed to position himself just two strokes back at the start of the day, shot 80 which included a 43 on the second nine, while Tommy Tolles (who also started two back) could manage no better than 41 in the final nine for 77 on the day, 282 for the week.

In the beginning Booker seemed immune to the conditions, birdieing two of his first three holes. After a bogey at the seventh, Booker still carried a four-shot advantage over Singh, Stewart and Mark O'Meara into the second nine. With conditions worsening, Booker's game fell victim to the wind, rain and pressure. He double-bogeyed the 10th after a hooked tee shot and three putts, then he bogeyed the par-five 14th. On the 16th, still clinging to a one-shot edge, Booker topped a two-iron shot that squirted along the ground for 40 yards before coming to rest in a fairway bunker, from which he made another double bogey. Another bogey on the 17th and a final bogey on the 18th shattered Booker's dreams, but not his spirit.

"I can't be too disappointed," he said afterward. "With nine holes to play I had a chance to win. That's why I'm out here."

Singh, on the other hand, put on an impressive display, turning in 34, then playing the difficult second nine with eight pars and one birdie. The birdie came on the 245-yard, par-three 15th where Singh cut a driver into the gusting wind, then sank a 30-foot putt for a two, a performance that drew great praise from his peers.

"He's so solid from tee to green that he's going to give himself eight or 10 birdie opportunities a round," Tolles said. "On days like this, that's going to be eight or 10 more than some other guys."

Bay Hill Invitational—$2,500,000
Winner: Tim Herron

In a week when nostalgia loomed as large as the $2.5 million purse, it seemed fitting that a throwback professional who refuses to give up cigarettes and who is, by his own admission, 30 pounds overweight, won the Bay Hill Invitational. Tim Herron, who would have fit right in on the PGA Tour in the 1950s and 1960s and who carries the nickname "Lumpy," proved he belongs with his own generation's best players by shooting 14-under-par 274 at the Bay Hill Club then making another birdie to defeat Tom Lehman on the second hole of a playoff.

It was Herron's first victory since the 1997 LaCantera Texas Open, and in beating Lehman and third-place finisher Davis Love III (275), Herron felt good about his game. "I don't think I'm that far behind Tom and Davis," he said. "I'm just going to keep working on my game. But it is just a game. You don't want to get too serious about it or it will drive you crazy."

It almost drove Love crazy. After hitting a poor bunker shot on Friday, Love, in an unusual display of temper, hit a greenside sprinkler head with his sand wedge in disgust. The sprinkler head broke and a stream of water gushed into the bunker, flooding the area and disrupting play. The next morning, Love found a note from host Arnold Palmer in his locker, along with a bill for $175,003.50.

"The parts were about $3.50," Palmer said. "But I had to have two irrigation engineers, an assistant and a leading superintendent get that fixed. That was labor of about $175,000."

"That's expensive labor," Love said. "The nice note from Arnold made me feel better. It shows what a classy guy he is."

Palmer and Love also exchanged words after the final round when Love, who started Sunday's round tied for the lead with Herron at 202, shot a closing 73 to finish alone in third, one shot out of the playoff. "One of these years," Love said to Palmer. "I'm going to give you a putting lesson," Palmer said.

After taking 79 putts in the first three days, Love had 31 putts on Sunday, which included short birdie misses on the first three holes of the day. "There's not much to say except I missed a lot of putts," Love said.

Lehman also missed a few coming down the stretch. Starting the final round one shot off the lead, Lehman passed Love and Herron with a birdie putt on the eighth. Herron had made bogey at the par-five fourth after hitting his tee shot out of bounds, and Love missed a short putt for birdie. Lehman held the lead until the 17th, when his approach shot found the front bunker. He blasted out to within eight feet, but lipped out the par putt.

Meanwhile Herron was making eight consecutive pars including four impressive up-and-downs in the final nine holes. "Lumpy made a lot of putts," Love said. "I kept walking off the side of the green thinking eventually he would miss one. But he just kept pouring them right in."

When Lehman and Herron finished at 274 (Lehman having closed with 71 and Herron shooting 73 on a day when the average score skyrocketed 2.5 strokes higher than the previous three days), it was the first time in anyone's memory that two players from Minnesota had contested in a playoff for a PGA Tour title. Not only were Lehman and Herron virtual neighbors, but Herron's sister worked for Lehman's brother and Lehman himself played a lot of golf over the years with Herron's father.

Family ties and friendships were set aside for two holes. After both players parred the first playoff hole, the 18th, they went back to the 511-yard, par-five 16th. Lehman's drive found the right-side fairway bunker, and Herron split the fairway with a 326-yard tee shot, his longest of the tournament. After Lehman pulled his second shot into the left rough and hit his third shot well over the green, Herron virtually ended the event with a 188-yard five iron to 15 feet. Even though he missed his eagle attempt, Herron tapped in for birdie and the win.

"I am disappointed that I didn't win," Lehman said. Still, his second-place finish was his best since a tie for second in the 1998 Players Championship just days before injuring his shoulder — an injury that would result in surgery in the off season to remove bone spurs. "This was really the first week I played where I have been able to work hard, practice hard, have no pain and play. If you'd have told me before the week started that I'd have been in a playoff, I probably would have been overjoyed."

The Players Championship—$5,000,000
Winner: David Duval

See Chapter 6.

BellSouth Classic—$2,500,000
Winner: David Duval

Sometimes stellar play must be coupled with good fortune in order for a streak to continue. David Duval had both on his side in Duluth, Georgia, when he edged out fellow Georgia Tech alumnus Stewart Cink in the BellSouth Classic. It was Duval's second victory in a row, his 11th win in 34 starts, and his fourth in 1999, making him the first since Johnny Miller in 1974 to win four events prior to the Masters.

"I never envisioned winning four golf tournaments before the Masters, but I don't think any player would out here anymore," Duval said after shooting 18-under-par 270 to win by two shots over Cink. "It is really nice and flattering to be considered the favorite. There again, it has absolutely no bearing on how I play or how I perform."

He performed quite admirably in front of the Atlanta-area crowd, many of whom remembered Duval from his college days. A shot back of third-round leaders Cink and Mike Weir and having never held the lead, Duval's final-round 67 was the lowest of any of the top 15 contenders on Sunday. Still his victory wasn't sealed until the final hole at the TPC at Sugerloaf, when rookie Rory Sabbatini tried to reach the par-five with his second shot and found the water instead.

It had been a wild ride for Sabbatini, who got into the BellSouth Classic as an alternate, assumed the second-round lead with impressive scores of 65 and 65, hung on with 73 on Saturday to remain tied with Duval, one shot back of Cink and Weir, then matched Duval birdie-for-birdie until the 17th hole. There Sabbatini saw his dreams dashed when his second shot found the bunker, his third shot found the trees, scattering gallery members, and before he was finished he had carded a double-bogey six. He finished with 70 and tied for third place at 273 with John Huston.

For a few fleeting moments Sunday there was a four-way tie for the lead at 18 under par. Duval was one shot back when he missed the green on the par-four 15th and found his ball in a depression, five feet below the green. It looked as if he would have difficulty saving par, and even he admitted, "I expected a 15-footer for par." Instead, Duval hit a perfect chip that struck the pin and nestled in the bottom of the hole. The birdie placed him in a tie with Cink, Sabbatini and Huston.

Minutes later the three other competitors had collectively carded two double bogeys and two bogeys and opened the door for Duval. According to Cink, who bogeyed the 16th and the 17th when he mis-clubbed on both holes, said, "I gave the tournament to Duval, and John Huston (who double-bogeyed the 17th) gave it to him. The winner sometimes doesn't go out there and wrestle the trophy from the other guys. A lot of times, he waits around for the gift."

Huston's double bogey came after he hit his tee shot in the fairway bunker, his approach found the greenside bunker, and it took him two more shots to find the green.

Meanwhile, Duval parred the 16th and 17th to quietly take a two-shot lead to the par-five 18th. After a perfect tee shot, Duval confounded many observers when he pulled out a long iron to try to reach the well-protected green with his second shot. Although he made a good swing, the ball landed on a hillside in front of the green and started trickling toward the water. The ball stopped, seemingly defying gravity a few feet from the water. "I hit a pretty good shot, hit it about where I was aiming," Duval said. "I was surprised it didn't bounce up on the green. Then I was surprised it didn't come back into the water. I got a fortunate break. No doubt about it." Despite his play at the 16th and 17th, Cink finished with 70 for a 272 total, good enough for sole second place. Huston and Sabbatini tied for third, while Weir tied Atlanta resident Franklin Langham for fourth at 274.

Masters Tournament—$3,200,000
Winner: Jose Maria Olazabal

See Chapter 2.

MCI Classic—$2,500,000
Winner: Glen Day

No one was more surprised by Glen Day's victory in the MCI Classic at Hilton Head Island, South Carolina, than Day himself. "No way," he said afterward. "No way did I think 10 under (274) would last." In fact, Day had already cleaned out his locker in preparation for a three-hour drive north to Goldsboro, North Carolina, where he was scheduled to play in a Monday pro-am, but with none of the leaders making a move and Day perched in a tie for the lead at 10 under par after finishing with 66, he wisely decided to stay around, hit a few balls, and watch the action on television.

Chris Perry had started the final round at 204 with John Huston and Payne Stewart on his heels at 205. Perry got to 11 under par on three different occasions, but the wind picked up and par became elusive on the 6,916-yard, par-71 Harbour Town Golf Links. As the afternoon wore on, 10 under par began to look as if it would, indeed, last.

Perry had his chances. Standing on the tee at the par-three 17th, he was 11 under par with a one-shot lead over Day, Stewart and a charging Jeff Sluman who shot 67 to move into contention at 10 under. But Perry made bogey at the 17th, pushing him back into a four-way tie for the lead. Then he made bogey at the 18th, blowing any chances he might have had for his second career PGA Tour victory. Stewart parred the 18th to finish at 10 under. So, after waiting for a couple of hours, Day's patience paid off. He was in a playoff with Stewart and Sluman, and after six winless years, he had his best chance yet to capture his first victory.

"I never got to the point where I thought I might not win out here," Day said. "I think I've tried so hard that I've gotten in my own way sometimes." This time, Day felt lucky to be in a position to win. "I was sure I would have to get to 12 under to have a chance, so I was fortunate."

The 18th hole, a treacherous par-four that plays along the edge of Calibogue Sound, was designated as the 73rd hole, and when Day left his approach shot some 30 feet to the right of the hole, the advantage seemed to shift to Stewart. Sluman missed the green, but made a good effort at birdie with his chip shot. It skipped past the hole, however, and Sluman had to settle for par.

Day's right-to-left breaker looked good when he first hit it, but in his words, "the putt rolled for like 30 minutes." When it crept over the front edge of the hole for birdie, Day raised his putter in the air. Sluman had been eliminated and Day could do no worse than play a second extra hole. It was up to Stewart, who had a 20-footer for birdie.

When Stewart's putt slipped by the hole, Day had his first victory on the PGA Tour and his first as a professional since the 1990 Malaysian Open. Stewart graciously stated the obvious. "He played better than anyone out here in some tough conditions," Stewart said. "He deserves it."

Day, who wears a hat pin with a photo of his two daughters, Whitney and Francis, called his family in Little Rock, Arkansas, after the victory and said later, "My only regret is that my family wasn't here to enjoy this with me." His wife Jennifer had been watching every shot on television. "She just cried," Day said. "It really hasn't sunk in with me yet. People have told me that you're going to win when you least expect it, when you are not hitting it your best or not putting it your best. I can assure you I didn't expect this one."

Greater Greensboro Chrysler Classic—$2,600,000
Winner: Jesper Parnevik

One week after being disqualified from the MCI Classic for brushing the line of a putt with his glove, Jesper Parnevik arrived at Forest Oaks Country Club in Greensboro, North Carolina, looking to redeem himself while keeping his good friend Per-Ulrik Johansson company. Parnevik said, "It would be fun for him to not be on his own this week. It was also a good opportunity for me to end on a high note."

Parnevik became the first player since Ernie Els at the 1997 Buick Classic to lead a PGA Tour event from the first hole until the last, and the first since Mike Springer in 1994 to lead the Greater Greensboro Chrysler Classic from start to finish.

Armed with a new putter, new irons and a new caddie (former PGA Tour player Lance Ten Broeck), Parnevik played almost flawless golf the first two rounds, shooting 65 on Thursday in tough winds, and following it up with 63 on Friday after PGA Tour officials softened the greens with a night of watering. The two-day total of 128 was good for a two-shot edge over Jeff Maggert and Jim Furyk and a three-shot margin over Dudley Hart.

His driver started to abandon Parnevik on Saturday. Even though he missed more fairways than he hit in the third round, his iron play continued to shine, and he hit 13 greens in regulation on the way to a 67 and a three-day total of 195. His confidence was so high that Parnevik sent his caddie out to purchase a victory cigar. "You can't believe how much fun it is to play golf when you feel like you can birdie every hole," he said.

By the time the leaders made the turn on Sunday, it was a two-man race with Parnevik holding a five-shot edge over Furyk with 12 holes to play. Still Parnevik struggled with his driver, hitting only seven fairways and blocking his drive on the 14th hole, 70 yards off line. "After that shot I didn't have a clue where the ball was going off the tee," Parnevik said. "Now I know what (Jose Maria) Olazabal means when he says it's pretty nerve-wrecking off the tee when you don't know whether you're going to hit it straight right or straight left."

The tee shot provided little trouble. When Furyk pulled to within one shot at the 11th, Parnevik chipped in for birdie at the 12th to widen the margin. Then at the 15th, Parnevik holed a 15-foot putt for par to keep his margin at two. On the 16th he hit a wedge from 123 yards to within tap-in range for his 27th birdie of the week to go with two eagles.

The cigar was already lit by the time Parnevik tapped in the 12-inch bogey putt on the 18th hole for a final round of 70 and a four-day total of 23-under-par 265, shattering the tournament record by six shots. Furyk finished alone in second after shooting 69 on Sunday, six strokes ahead of third-place finisher Maggert, who shot 68 in the final round.

"The rest of the field had a normal tournament," Maggert said, referencing Parnevik's run-away. "Jesper is a great winner, and a great guy."

Shell Houston Open—$2,500,000
Winner: Stuart Appleby

When he won in Australia at the Schweppes Coolum Classic late in 1998, Stuart Appleby wept and dedicated the victory to his wife Renay, who died in an automobile accident the previous July. Five months later, as Appleby walked into the clubhouse of the TPC at the Woodlands in suburban Houston, Texas, there was the hint of a smile on his face and a quiet determination in his manner. He was three shots back of Hal Sutton with 18 holes to play, but he thought this might be his week.

"I really wanted this thing," Appleby said. "I was not going to back down. I was going to stay there. If I was going to get myself in front, someone else was going to beat me. I just knew it was going to be mine. I wasn't going to let myself down. I was going to be patient. I had a lot of shots in the bag. I put in all the hard work, and I deserved it. That's one thing to winning anything — you have to believe you deserve it. I knew I did."

Even with that amount of confidence, Appleby didn't lead the Shell Houston Open until the next-to-last hole, when he hit seven iron to 12 feet and sank the putt while Sutton three-putted for bogey at the 16th and missed the green at the 17th, making another bogey. "I was having a hard time figuring things out," Sutton said.

Sutton struggled with the wind for most of the day even though he continued to hold the lead until the 17th. "Sooner or later you're supposed to guess right," he said. "It didn't seem like any of these shots were turning out. That doesn't give you a very comfortable feeling, especially when I was hitting it kind of the way I wanted."

Sutton closed with 75 for an eight-under-par 280 total. He had a birdie putt to tie Appleby at the final hole, but it slipped by. "When it's your time to win you can't do anything about it, and when it's not your time to win you can't do anything about it," Sutton said. "It was Stuart's time to win. If someone had to beat me, I'm happy it was Stuart. He's been through a lot, and I certainly can understand how much meaning this has to him. I'm sure there's someone smiling on him right now."

Appleby only shot 71 on Sunday, but that was all he needed. His 279 total edged Sutton and John Cook by one stroke and Mark Wiebe by three. "(Renay) gave me strength," he said after collecting the $450,000 first-place check. "I felt strong today, and I sort of walked like I wanted it. I tried to feel like I had this tournament. I wanted to create the feeling of winning before I had won so I could feel that way all through the day. There was no emotional high, like, 'I'm going to win this now.' It was already there, so when it came to fruition, it was done. And she's going to be there with me forever, no doubt, in anything I do. She'll be there to help me, nothing but that."

There were no tears this time for Appleby, although the lines of grief were still etched on his face. "It's very hard when you lose someone you love so much," he said. "But you've got to turn it around. Time goes on. You have to make sure that if anything happens in your life for good or for bad that you find out that in the end it was ... well, that everything works for the good."

Compaq Classic of New Orleans—$2,600,000
Winner: Carlos Franco

Before this year, no native of Paraguay had ever won a PGA Tour event. Then 33-year-old Carlos Franco broke the Paraguayan drought by shooting a tournament-record 19-under-par 269 in New Orleans to capture the Compaq Classic by two strokes. It was Franco's 30th worldwide victory but his first in the United States.

"This is the greatest time for me, ever," Franco said, in typical first-time-winner fashion. Given Franco's background, the comment seemed more like an understatement than hyperbole. He had been describing his life with six siblings in a one-room dirt-floor house with no indoor plumbing. None of the Francos owned shoes until Carlos won a pair at the local golf course when he was 14. "They felt good, but not as good as this," he said, and he wasn't talking about the money. "I have no idea how many dollars I make here. That's not important because it is not about dollars."

In fact, moments after collecting the $468,000 winner's check, Franco was talking about making donations to golf programs in Paraguay. Before that moment was possible, Franco had needed to make up two shots on the leader, Steve Flesch, and pass such players as Harrison Frazar, Omar Uresti and Eric Booker.

Despite one mistake on the first nine, where Franco chunked a five-iron shot into the water at the sixth that resulted in a bogey, he made few errors after that, adding seven birdies and 10 pars together for a solid final-round 66.

Meanwhile, Flesch could manage no better than 70 for a 271 total and a tie for second place with Frazar. It was the second year in a row that Flesch had finished second in New Orleans, but this time he wasn't surprised by the play of the winner. " It doesn't surprise me a bit," Flesch said. "I played against Franco in Asia, and I knew his day would come."

Frazar, who followed a 65 on Saturday with a closing 68 to catch Flesch, said of Franco, "He's a pure ball striker, and an outstanding gentleman. But he's no rookie."

Franco was, indeed, a member of the Presidents Cup team that trounced the Americans in 1998 and was also a part of Paraguay's 1993 Alfred Dunhill Cup team that upset Scotland. Still, 1999 was his first foray onto the PGA Tour, and a third-place finish at the Honda Classic and a tie for sixth at the Masters along with the win in New Orleans put Franco in the lead for Rookie of the Year honors at the mid-point.

GTE Byron Nelson Classic—$3,000,000
Winner: Loren Roberts

What started as a shootout between two of the most vibrant young players in golf ended on the TPC at Las Colinas in Dallas in a playoff between two of the game's old warhorses. The GTE Byron Nelson Classic marked the U.S. professional debut of 19-year-old Sergio Garcia, the 1998 British Amateur champion and the low amateur at this year's Masters.

When Garcia shot an eight-under-par 62 to trail Woods by one stroke after the first day, the ripples were unmistakable. "It's Dallas, there are 80,000 fans out here, and he's not the least bit intimidated," Nick Price said through an awed smile. "It makes you want to be 19 all over again."

Almost lost in the Woods-Garcia showdown were rounds fired by Steve Pate (63) and Loren Roberts (66). Those weren't bad scores, but this was the Tiger and Sergio show, or so it seemed early in the week. Pate, who finished second at the Bob Hope Chrysler Classic when David Duval shot 59, shot a second-round 65 to gain a share of the lead with Woods at 128 going into the weekend. Roberts carded his second consecutive 66 for a 132 total, four back of the leaders and three back of Garcia and Jeff Gallagher.

Saturday, typically considered moving day on the PGA Tour, lived up to its name. Roberts shot one of the best rounds of the year and one of the best in his 18-year career. In steady 20 to 25 mile-an-hour winds, Roberts had 62 to move into a two-stroke lead over Pate, who shot 68. Those two stood alone going into the final round as the nearest player to them, Lee Janzen, was four behind Pate and six shots off of Roberts' 194 total.

Woods found himself recouping from a quadruple bogey on the 17th and 74 to drop out of the lead. He entered the final round at 202 and unhappy about his performance. "I hit four balls in the water this week," he said. "You can't do that. One thing I do take out of this; I hit a lot of great shots. A lot of low, punchy shots to kick-in range. More than anything, I putted well this week."

Garcia also fell out of the picture, even though he continued to grind his way home with a 71 on Saturday and a 69 on Sunday to finish at 269 and in a tie for third place with Pate, Janzen and Chris DiMarco.

The tournament, however, was a two-man race between veterans. Pate's final-round 66 was the best of the day among the contenders, but it was only good enough for a tie, as Roberts finished with a strong 68 for a 262 total. The two of them were at least six shots ahead of everyone else in the field.

In the playoff, both found greenside bunkers on the 445-yard, par-four 18th. As he had throughout the week, Roberts got up and down for par, while Pate blasted out to 18 feet and missed.

"If I can beat everybody but one guy by six shots, I have to know that eventually one of those will be a win," Pate said.

The win meant a lot to Roberts, who had begun to question his ability. "I was thinking, I'm 43 years old, maybe a little too old now with all these young guys," Roberts said. "I wasn't questioning myself to the point of quitting or anything, but I was having a lot of trouble finding it."

MasterCard Colonial—$2,800,000
Winner: Olin Browne

It seemed appropriate on a cloudy Sunday afternoon at Colonial Country Club in Ft. Worth, Texas, that a late-blooming grinder would win the Master-Card Colonial and accept the trophy under the statue of the late Ben Hogan, the champion grinder of them all. "There's no other sport where you have to embrace failure like you do in golf," 40-year-old Olin Browne said after coming from three strokes back on the final day to win by one. "If you can't handle failure, this game will drive you crazy. There's a lot of depression. I'm a plodder — a late bloomer. To win here, this is great."

Browne didn't earn his PGA Tour card until after his 33rd birthday, and didn't win an event until he was 39 when he captured the 1998 Canon Greater Hartford Open. "I didn't get into golf until I was 19," said the former football and baseball player who studied to be a marine biologist. "Is there any better way to make a living? I mean, how does it get any better than this?"

For Browne, it couldn't get much better. After beginning the week with 73, he looked like anything but a potential winner. Even after clawing his way back to even par with 67 on Friday, Browne still stood seven shots back of second-round leader Corey Pavin, with so many players between Browne and the lead that he felt lucky not to be sweeping the dew off the greens on Saturday morning.

But Saturday proved that back-of-the-pack players still had a chance. Greg Kraft, most noted for his finish at Doral which cost him his first win, came back from an opening-round 75 to shoot a course-record-tying 61, fully 27 twosomes ahead of the final group. As good as the score was, Kraft didn't think his 203 would hold up, and he was partially correct. By the time the sun set on the Texas horizon, Scott Verplank had fired a 66 to reach 203 and Billy Mayfair had carded his second 68 of the week to also reach minus seven.

Browne had another good day, getting out early and posting a respectable 66 before the television cameras came on and after Kraft had scorched the 7,010-yard layout. Still, he was only three back with 18 holes to play, tied with Stuart Appleby and Bob Estes. No one noticed.

It was only when Browne, playing seven groups ahead of the leaders on Sunday, started making birdies that people took notice. Oddly enough, his play had been the model of consistency throughout the week as he found 41 of 56 fairways and hit 70 percent of the greens in regulation, putting him in the top three in both categories. But Browne had been recuperating from left elbow surgery, which limited his practice and forced him to miss the 1999 Mercedes Championships. The injuries had fully healed, but his repu-tation still lagged behind. Even after he finished the final round with an impressive 66, very few people thought it would hold up.

"That just reinforces the quality of Colonial, and how well it can defend itself," Browne concluded.

Indeed, the old course barred its teeth late in the day as one by one the leaders faltered. Vijay Singh, who started the final round two shots off the pace but reached seven under before the leaders teed off, fell back when his second shot found the water on the ninth. Verplank also faded at the ninth when he plunked two balls in the water. Mayfair never got anything going and suffered bogeys at the 10th and 18th to drop back to one over for the day and 274 for the week.

Kraft reached minus 10 early in the day, but he hooked his tee shot on the 12th and never recovered. A double bogey at the 12th and a bogey at the 17th dropped him one shot off of Browne's 272 mark. After hitting his approach shot at the 18th into the greenside bunker, it appeared that, for the second time in the first five months of the 1999 season, Kraft would snatch defeat from the jaws of victory. His effort was gallant at the 18th, but when the bunker shot slipped past the hole, Browne, who had been on the range preparing for a possible playoff, put his clubs away and collected the trophy.

"Like my dad once said," Browne opined, "sometimes you back into a tub of butter. I ended up getting a little bit lucky, but that's what sports are all about."

Kemper Open—$2,500,000
Winner: Rich Beem

After missing the cut in seven of the first 11 tournaments in his rookie year and earning less money than he did as a car stereo salesman in El Paso, Texas, 28-year-old Rich Beem shocked the PGA Tour with the most improbable wire-to-wire win since John Daly's 1991 PGA Championship win. It began when Beem, a former assistant golf pro at El Paso Country Club, earned his card at the 1999 qualifying tournament, then promptly began missing cuts. His earnings before he arrived at the Kemper Open at the TPC· at Avenel in Potomac, Maryland, were less than the $25,000 he made for reaching the qualifying tournament finals, and he was beginning to wonder if he had made the right choice going back into golf after giving it up for a year at age 24.

Then Beem hired a new caddie, Steve Duplantis, who had previously carried for Jim Furyk, and he proceeded to start the relationship by shooting 66 on the 7,005-yard course to take a one-stroke lead over Corey Pavin, Brian Watts and Bill Glasson. Some spectators and more than a few reporters thought some volunteer had simply misspelled Andy Bean's name since Bean was also playing. Rich Beem wasn't even on the radar.

A second-round 67 widened Beem's lead to three over Bradley Hughes, Tommy Armour III and Dave Stockton, Jr. With Glasson four shots back at 137 and Furyk lurking five back going into the weekend, very few gave Beem a chance at being there on Sunday.

Saturday he showed his metal, though. In a wild and woolly round that included five birdies, three bogeys and a double bogey, Beem had an even-par performance to retain a tie for the lead with Armour and remain two ahead of Glasson. It was one of the rounds Beem's father, Larry, described as, "Never a dull moment. He makes a lot of birdies and a lot of bogeys. When he gets going though he can really light it up, but I didn't think he had the interest to make it as a pro. He's a very social person who loves to party and be around people."

Even Beem seemed dismayed by his play. "I'm usually all over the place," he admitted. During Sunday's final round, Beem tightened his game and took charge. With birdies on three of the first five holes, Beem moved away from Armour and extended his lead to three shots, then the eighth hole proved the turning point of the tournament. Having driven into the fairway bunker on the 453-yard par-four, Beem barely advanced his ball out of the bunker, and was faced with a 132-yard third shot to a pin tucked close to another greenside bunker. Meanwhile, Armour hit his approach shot to within 15 feet. If he made the putt and Beem let a double bogey slip in, they would once again be even. But Beem came through, hitting his third shot to within a foot of the hole and tapping for par. "That shot really kept my momentum going," he said.

Having a veteran caddie like Duplantis on the bag also helped Beem. "Without him, this week would not have happened," Beem said. Indeed, as Beem's nerves began to frazzle on the second nine on Sunday, he turned to Duplantis on the 13th and said, "You've got to get me through this. I'm wiped out."

Duplantis obliged. "I was in his ear," he said. "But he hit the shots. He did it for four days. It's not just the fact that he won. It's the way he won. A lot of guys who run into the kind of adversity he did by making some double bogeys would fold their tents, especially a rookie. He just got stronger."

Beem's closing round of 70 and 10-under-par 274 total was good enough for a one-shot edge over Glasson and Hughes and a two-shot margin over David Toms and Hal Sutton. Armour shot a closing-round 73 to tie Stuart Appleby for seventh at 277.

"This helps validate my ability not only to myself, but it helps me gain the respect of my fellow touring pros," Beem said. "That means a lot. I don't have anything deep or emotional to say except I have a job for the next two years, and that makes me really happy. I can't even describe all the fringe benefits, but more than anything I'm happy I won, not just for my father, my family and my friends, but for me too. I can't tell you how awesome this feeling is."

Memorial Tournament—$2,550,000
Winner: Tiger Woods

Coming on the heels of a victory at the Deutsche Bank-SAP Open TPC of Europe, Tiger Woods made his bid to reclaim the world's No. 1 ranking complete when he traveled stateside and shot a closing-round 69 to capture the Memorial Tournament by two strokes over Vijay Singh.

With earlier scores of 68, 66 and 70, Woods relied on a solid short game in the final round to hold onto the lead after entering Sunday with a two-shot edge over Singh. "I was stripping it in Germany, so I didn't need my short game," Woods said. "This week I didn't hit the ball as good as I'd like, and my short game bailed me out."

He missed six of 18 greens in the final round and saved par five of those times. Perhaps the most difficult of those recoveries came at the par-four sixth, where Woods hit a 20-yard flop shot off a hardpan lie and under a tree limb to a green that sloped away from him toward a pond. He executed the shot perfectly to within three feet and made the putt.

The most memorable shot, however, came at the 14th when, after swinging under the ball on his first chip and advancing the ball only a few feet, Woods chipped in for par from the rough just as host Jack Nicklaus opined on television that Woods could easily make double bogey.

"He has the ability to do things no one else can do," Nicklaus said afterward. "And yet has a short game where, if he makes mistakes, he can correct it. That's what's so phenomenal about him."

Singh matched Woods' final-round 69, and most people looked at the chip-in on the 14th as the turning point. Had Nicklaus' prediction been accurate and Woods had walked away with double bogey, he and Singh would have been tied, and Tiger would have risked losing for only the second time in his career after carrying a lead into the final round.

During his second-round 66, Woods brought the 7,163-yard course to its knees, taking advantage of his length and his accuracy. On the 539-yard, par-five 11th, Woods reached the green with a pair of two irons and left himself an 18-inch tap-in for eagle. "You tell me how many people in the game can do that," said Woods' friend Mark O'Meara. "None, that's how many. Not one."

Woods had only 108 putts for the week. That translated to an average of 27 per round as compared to Singh's 116 putts, or 29 per round. "I've tried not to worry about mechanics that much in my putting," Woods said. "Just make sure I'm comfortable and go ahead and be committed, and bury it."

"Tiger is becoming more comfortable with who he is and what's demanded of him," third-place finisher David Duval said. "He's balancing the demand out with the golf and he's obviously doing a good job of it."

Duval, who came to Dublin, Ohio, with four early-season victories and the world's No. 1 ranking, came back from a lackluster opening round of 72 with scores of 68, 69 and 70 to finish at 279, tied for third with Carlos Franco (74-67-70-68) and Olin Browne, who had the low round of the day on Sunday with 65.

But Woods was the one making most of the impressions as players readied themselves for the U.S. Open. "He's enjoying himself more now," Lee Janzen said. "I don't think it has taken away from his focus on what he wants to become, but he has a more relaxed confidence about him. He's really just enjoying himself right now, which could be trouble for the rest of us."

FedEx St. Jude Classic—$2,500,000
Winner: Ted Tryba

It seemed ironic a tournament named after an overnight delivery company would be the first of 1999 to end a day late, but when two inches of rain poured onto the TPC at Southwind course in Memphis, Tennessee, during a 30-minute period in the middle of Sunday's round, officials were left with little choice but to postpone the finish until Monday. This was the first application of a rule the PGA Tour instituted after the 1998 AT&T Pebble Beach National Pro-Am was delayed six months in an effort to complete three rounds.

The rule stated that events should be seen to their 72-hole completion, even if it means returning on Monday. Unfortunately, the Monday of the FedEx St. Jude Classic was the first practice day for the U.S. Open in Pinehurst, North Carolina.

"I would rather have gone on and mucked it out on Sunday," Tom Lehman said, even though Lehman finished tied for second with fellow Minnesotan Tim Herron at 17-under-par 267. But Lehman would never consider taking off the week before the U.S. Open. "We could be playing the Alaskan Open and I would probably play that week," he said. "The Open is the ultimate test of accuracy and competition gets me more target-oriented than hitting balls at home."

An opening 63 tied Lehman for the lead with Hal Sutton and David Frost. Lehman then carded three consecutive rounds of 68 to miss winning his first event of the year by two shots. Sutton also put together sub-par scores until the last round, when he shot 71. He followed his first-round 63 with scores of 67 and 69 to enter the final 18 holes tied for the lead with Lehman, Herron and the man who would persevere to win his second professional event, 32-year-old Ted Tryba, who had scores of 68, 64, 67 and 66 for a 265 total, 19 under par.

None of those players were in the lead when play was halted on Sunday. That honor belonged to Masters winner Jose Maria Olazabal, who started seven shots out of the lead but birdied eight of his first 14 holes to take a one-shot lead. There were 34 players within five strokes of the Spaniard when the rains came. On Monday morning, Olazabal parred in for 62 and a 268 total, a mark that would hold up for most of the day. Olazabal finished tied for fourth with Kevin Wentworth.

Tryba eagled the par-five fifth hole, then added birdies at the seventh, 10th and 12th with one bogey at the eighth to move into a tie for the lead at 16 under par. At the par-five 16th, one ahead of Herron and tied with Olazabal, Tryba hit a four-iron shot from 235 yards to within four feet of the flagstick. Herron, who also reached the green in two, missed from 11 feet, and when Tryba made the four-footer for eagle, the lead was his. Herron finished with 68 after posting 67, 66 and 66 earlier. "I've never gone into the U.S. Open playing this well," Tryba said afterward. "I feel confident I can go in there and compete."

U.S. Open Championship—$3,500,000
Winner: Payne Stewart

See Chapter 3.

Buick Classic—$2,500,000

Winner: Duffy Waldorf

Neither Duffy Waldorf nor Dennis Paulson played in the U.S. Open before journeying to Westchester Country Club in Rye, New York, for the Buick Classic, so neither had suffered any recurring nightmares of undulating greens, closely mown fringes, or USGA rough. All they had on their minds was a victory, something neither had experienced in a while. Waldorf hadn't won since the 1995 LaCantera Texas Open, even though he had consistently finished in the top 100 money winners throughout his 12-year career. Paulson, a journeyman graduate from the 1998 Nike Tour, was looking for redemption after losing his PGA Tour playing privileges in 1995.

At the end of regulation play, they were tied atop the leaderboard at 276, eight under par, although their respective journeys had been much different. Paulson started slowly, opening with rounds of 71 and 70 to find himself five shots off the midway lead of 136 held by Jeff Maggert and Chris Perry and four behind Stephen Ames and Waldorf, who followed his opening 70 with 67. In the third round, Paulson battled his way to 68 for a 209 total. That still wasn't good enough. Waldorf also shot 68 on Saturday to move into a tie for the lead with Jim Carter at 205. Paulson, who played junior golf against Waldorf in California, knew it would be a tough four shots to make up.

That assessment was accurate, but no one could have predicted the finish that would see six players slip in and out of a tie for the lead, and find 12 men within two shots of the lead at one point. Waldorf's round resembled the roller coaster that provides the backdrop to the LaCantera course in southern Texas where he captured his only PGA Tour victory. With six birdies and six bogeys, Waldorf didn't make a par on Sunday until the sixth hole. Still, no one seemed to be making a charge. Perry, who began the final round two shots off the lead, could only manage 70, while Lee Janzen, who also started the day two shots back, temporarily gained a share of the lead but ballooned to 73 with a poor showing on the second nine.

Discouraged, Janzen said afterward, "If I had the money I've lost on the back nine on Sundays this year, I'd have more money than I've made. It's pathetic. I can't believe I can't get one birdie on the final nine. It's not the first time this has happened, but I hope it's the last." Janzen finished tied for 10th at 280.

Meanwhile, Paulson was closing in with a flurry of birdies on the second nine. Playing almost an hour ahead of Waldorf, Paulson birdied three of the last six holes for 67. For a while that looked like it would be good enough to win. When an errant tee shot cost Waldorf a bogey at the 15th, Paulson gained a two-shot lead. A par on the 16th by Waldorf kept Paulson's lead at two with two holes remaining. Waldorf hit a pitching wedge to four feet on the 17th and made the putt for birdie to pull within one. On the 526-yard, par-five 18th Waldorf hit his second shot into a greenside bunker, 90 feet from the hole. He hit a long bunker shot "so good it surprised me," he said, and the ball ended up four feet from the hole. Waldorf made birdie for 71 to tie Paulson and force a playoff.

After waiting in the clubhouse to see if he would win, Paulson hit an errant second shot on the 18th, the first playoff hole, that resulted in a bogey while Waldorf played the hole almost exactly as he had moments earlier. In the greenside bunker in two, Waldorf blasted to 12 feet and made the putt to win.

"When I hit the second bunker shot I felt a lot better and more confident," Waldorf said of the playoff. "I think it was even a harder shot than the first one. Of course, it was a battle right from the start. I expended a lot of energy today making bogeys and coming back with birdies, but it was a battling kind of day."

Motorola Western Open—$2,500,000
Winner: Tiger Woods

The oldest event on the PGA Tour (dating back to 1899, before there was a PGA Tour or a PGA for that matter), the Motorola Western Open seemed the perfect venue for the youngest player ever to earn a No. 1 world ranking, and the youngest to lose it, to regain his No. 1 spot in the world in the heat of a Chicago summer.

Tiger Woods came to the Windy City more comfortable with his golf game than he had ever been. Two of his previous three starts had ended in victories (Memorial Tournament and Deutsche Bank-SAP Open in Germany), and but for a couple of putts by Payne Stewart at Pinehurst, the third (U.S. Open) might have been his. So when Stuart Appleby finished bogey-bogey on Friday to give Woods, who opened with rounds of 68 and 66, a share of the lead going into the weekend, Tiger pounced on the opportunity to show what he had.

"How good is Tiger?" asked second-place finisher Mike Weir. "He's great." Weir should have known. He witnessed Woods' final-round 71 for a 273 total, 15 under par, and a three-shot margin of victory that was never really that close.

A third-round 68 moved Woods into a four-shot lead over Appleby, Weir and Mike Brisky. Woods then finessed his way around the course when he needed to (as he did with his flop shot par save at the 10th) and overpowered it when he had to (as evidenced by the 220-yard three iron on the par-five 15th to within 12 feet for eagle). Woods played the par-five holes in 12 under par for the week, averaging a whopping 315 yards off the tee, 20 yards ahead of his nearest competitor in that category. He also finished second in greens in regulation and he was the only player to shoot in the 60s in each of the first three rounds.

"Being No. 1 in the world is something I had to be told about," Woods said after regaining the title from David Duval with his victory. "It's nice, but not as nice as winning. Being No. 1 and not winning, as I was doing in 1998, that's not great. But I was changing my game then. I knew it was going to take me awhile."

Weir won the battle for second with a closing 70 for a 276 total, one better than Brent Geiberger, who shot a final-round 69 to go with his earlier rounds of 70, 68 and 70. Vijay Singh claimed fourth at 278, while Dicky Pride had his best finish of the year, finishing fifth at 279.

Greater Milwaukee Open—$3,500,000

Winner: Carlos Franco

For most professionals, the road to winning is paved with countless hours on the practice tee, but not Paraguay's Carlos Franco. After finishing sixth in the Masters and returning to his native Asuncion a hero, Franco won his first PGA Tour event in New Orleans, tied for third in the Memorial Tournament, tied for 34th in the U.S. Open, and then came from one stroke back on the final day to defeat Tom Lehman and local favorite Jerry Kelly in the Greater Milwaukee Open, all without so much as breaking a sweat on the practice tee.

"I look at everybody practice and I say, 'Good luck,'" Franco said after shooting a bogeyless 66 in the final round. "I have a natural swing. I need my swing. I don't need to hit 100 or 150 balls. That's over par, no?"

Not only did Franco win in Milwaukee by two shots without striking a single practice ball after the tournament began, he broke the tournament record at the Brown Deer Golf Club by shooting 20-under-par 264. As if that wasn't impressive enough, Franco came to Milwaukee having taken the previous two weeks off, playing only one round between fishing trips and hitting exactly zero practice balls.

"The Masters gave me great confidence in my game," he said. "Before the Masters I wasn't so confident. At the Masters I got big money, almost $260,000. I went home and partied every day. Everybody was happy. Now I'm more relaxed."

For a man who grew up without shoes while living in a mud-floored shack, winning for a second time and collecting $1.3 million in earnings before the British Open will give you reason to relax and celebrate. The victory didn't come without a little work, however. Franco never led until the first nine on Sunday, although he was never far from the top. An opening 65 left him three strokes behind leader Ben Bates. A 66 for a 131 total moved Franco to within one shot of John Maginnes at the halfway mark. On the weekend Franco shot 67 to stay within one of the lead, which was held by Kelly, a native of Madison, only 85 miles from Milwaukee.

Kelly had played well throughout the week, carding 16 birdies and no bogeys in 54 holes. When he teed off in the feature twosome on Sunday with Franco, Kelly was cheered every step of the way, but the home crowd couldn't stop him from coming apart. At the par-five sixth, holding a two-shot lead, Kelly missed the green long with his third shot and failed to save par. Franco birdied and the two were tied. At the par-three seventh, Franco hit a five iron to 10 feet. Kelly played next and missed the green to the right. When he failed to par the hole, Franco rammed in the birdie putt and went from two behind to two ahead in the span of two holes.

From there it was all but over. Kelly made his third bogey in a row at the eighth, but managed to finish with an even-par round of 71 for a 268 total. That was only good enough for third place. Lehman closed with 66 to finish alone in second at 266.

John Deere Classic—$2,000,000
Winner: J.L. Lewis

There was a time when J.L. Lewis wondered if he had made the right choice when he left a club professional's job at Forest Creek Golf Club in Round Rock, Texas, for another try on the PGA Tour.

During an off-again-on-again playing career that began in 1985, Lewis never earned more than $119,000 until 1998 when, after getting another chance at the PGA Tour through finishing seventh in earnings on the Nike Tour, Lewis finished fourth at the Buick Challenge and tied for sixth at the Buick Invitational. Those finishes earned him over $200,000 and a return trip to the PGA Tour by finishing 104th on the 1998 money list.

Then on a hot July afternoon in Coal Valley, Illinois, Lewis outdueled Mike Brisky, another journeyman professional, in a four-hole playoff to capture the newly named John Deere Classic. With rounds of 66, 65, 65 and 65, Lewis came from three shots back in the final 18 holes to finish tied with Brisky at 19-under-par 261. When he made a four-foot birdie putt on the fifth extra hole (his third birdie of the playoff), Lewis not only had a victory, he pocketed a larger check than he had ever earned in any full season on any tour.

After his opening 66 left him two shots off the lead, Lewis put together three of the most consistent rounds of his career. His 65 on Friday placed him three shots behind Brisky, who opened with rounds of 66 and 62, and another 65 on Saturday kept him in the hunt. With one round to play, Lewis stood at 196, tied with Brisky and Robert Damron. The leader was Brian Henninger, who was the only player in the final two groups on Sunday to have ever won a PGA Tour event (1994 Deposit Guarantee Classic). Henninger's final-round 71 dropped him into a tie for third place with Kirk Triplett at 264, while Damron's closing 71 left him all the way back in a tie for 10th with D.A. Weibring.

For a while it looked as if Brisky would win. He made six birdie putts in the first 15 holes — three from outside 20 feet — to reach 20 under par and take a two-shot lead. On the par-three 17th, Brisky three-putted for bogey while Lewis, who had made four birdies on the first nine, rolled in another four-foot birdie putt at the 18th to get into a playoff with Brisky, who finished with 65.

Canon Greater Hartford Open—$2,500,000
Winner: Brent Geiberger

From the 16th tee until he reached the 18th green, Al Geiberger received standing ovations as he made his way around the Park Meadows Country Club in Park City, Utah. Geiberger wasn't leading the Novell Utah Showdown, the Senior PGA Tour event of the week, nor was he even close. The ovations came as the electronic scoreboards flashed the message, "Brent Geiberger wins the Greater Hartford Open ... Congratulations Al."

"It was hard to concentrate out there," Al said of his round in Utah. "I kept having to brush tears out of my eyes."

A father's pride will do that to you. Al had called his son Brent's voice mail on Saturday night after Brent had carried a three-shot lead over Ted Tryba into the final round of the Canon Greater Hartford Open in Cromwell, Connecticut. "Go out there tomorrow and do what you would tell me to do," Al told him. "Be patient and try your best."

After an opening-round 66 left him three shots behind, Geiberger played the best golf of his career on Friday, finishing with 63 which moved him into a tie with Pete Jordan at 129.

In the third round, Geiberger almost let it slip away. Poor driving resulted in a double bogey at the fourth hole, followed by bogeys at the fifth and sixth, a stretch that could have been disastrous. Geiberger dug deep and followed with birdies at three of his next four holes before reaching the 162-yard, par-three 11th. There he hit a nine-iron shot that took one hop and rolled 10 feet into the hole for an ace that gave him the outright lead. He shot 66 for a 195 total.

The momentum carried over to Sunday with Geiberger posting birdies at the second, third, fifth, seventh and ninth holes to open up a six-shot lead with nine to play. His accuracy was stunning, as none of Geiberger's birdie putts were from outside 20 feet. "Every time I looked up he was making another birdie," said Skip Kendall, who played the final round with Geiberger.

"I knew I was playing well coming in," Geiberger said. "It was just a matter of keeping myself calm and not letting any outside things get to me."

Even a double bogey, bogey finish for a closing round of 67 couldn't spoil Geiberger's week. He still finished at 262, 18 under par and three ahead of Kendall.

Buick Open—$2,400,000
Winner: Tom Pernice, Jr.

Par at the 7,101-yard Warwick Hills Golf and Country Club in Grand Blanc, Michigan, is 72, but during the Buick Open anything at or above that number sends you packing early. To win at Warwick Hills, you have to have red numbers on the brain. For example, Brent Geiberger shot an opening 65, a closing 69 and two even-par rounds only to finish tied for 19th.

Ted Tryba shot 29 on the final nine on Thursday, then repeated the feat on Sunday with seven consecutive birdies, but never held the lead. Rocco Mediate shot 69 and 64 in the first two rounds, then played the weekend one under par. He wasn't even close. Even Tom Lehman, who never shot a round over par and only had one round in the 70s, couldn't pull out a victory.

The unlikely winner of the birdie-fest was Tom Pernice, Jr., a veteran of the PGA Tour, PGA European Tour, Asian Tour and Nike Tour. Pernice shot even par one day and he paid the price. After climbing into a share of the halfway lead at 133, Pernice dropped five strokes behind Tom Lehman after failing to break into red numbers.

During the final round Pernice chose not to look at the leaderboard for fear that he might jinx himself. Even after he posted an eagle at the 13th hole and birdies at the 14th, 16th and 17th for a seven-under-par 65 in windy conditions for a 18-under-par total of 270, he didn't call home. "I didn't call because there was nothing to call home about," he said.

For an hour or so he was right. Lehman was still on the course with opportunities to catch and pass Pernice. A bunker shot into the water at the 13th hole followed by missed six-foot birdie opportunities at the 16th and 17th, and a 12-foot putt to tie on the 18th that came up just short, doomed Lehman's chances of picking up his first victory of the year. In so doing, he gave Pernice the first win of his long and arduous professional career.

"Tom deserves it," said Lehman, who shot 71 for a 271 total to tie for second place with Tryba and Bob Tway. "He's been to a lot of the same places I've been. It's good to see him finally break through."

PGA Championship—$3,500,000
Winner: Tiger Woods

See Chapter 5.

Sprint International—$2,600,000
Winner: David Toms

By the time the sun fell against the white-tipped backdrop of the Rockies, an iceman named David had methodically held off all challengers with a crucial up-and-down birdie at the 71st hole at Castle Pines Golf Club to capture the Sprint International. The "David" in question was not four-time 1999 winner David Duval. In fact, Duval, who won 11 out of 35 events including four in 1999 before the Masters, was the victim this week in Colorado. The David who came out on top with his cool demeanor and hot play was 72nd-ranked David Toms, a 32-year-old Louisiana native in his sixth year on tour.

Toms came into the final round of the modified Stableford format event having led from the opening hole on the first day. Duval had pulled within four points of Toms after the second round (29 points to 25 points) and he moved one closer on Saturday by reaching 36 points to Toms' 39. And there was Sergio Garcia, coming off his spectacular duel against Tiger Woods in the PGA Championship, with 32 points through three rounds and clearly in the hunt.

The format, which awards players eight points for a double eagle, five for an eagle, two for a birdie, none for pars, minus one for a bogey and minus three for a double bogey, favored someone who could make birdies by the bushel, and Toms had certainly proven he could do that. Even though he only had one career win (the 1997 Quad City Classic), Toms tied a second-nine record with six consecutive birdies at the 1999 Masters which vaulted him into a tie for sixth place.

Only three players reached double-digit points in the final round and none of those finished in the top seven. Garcia faltered early and often, finishing minus-two for the day to drop all the way back into a tie for 13th place, while Ernie Els, who started tied with Garcia and only seven points behind Toms, earned only three points to tie for fifth with Billy Mayfair.

Midway through the second nine, it was a two-man race with Toms still holding a narrow advantage over Duval. That almost slipped away as Toms found trouble at the 16th hole and picked up after reaching the maximum score of double bogey. Suddenly Duval was back in the picture. The 18th hole was a reachable par-five, one that Vijay Singh had eagled in 1998 en route to winning his second event in a row. Now Toms was faced with having to hold his emotions in check while trying to make birdie or better to regain a comfortable margin. He did both. "It seems as if every emotion you can go through, I went though today," Toms said, although his expression rarely changed during the final few holes.

After the double bogey he split the middle of the 17th fairway with his tee shot, then rifled a four iron through the green and into a precarious lie from which he would have to play a delicate chip onto a green that sloped away from him with the pin cut close to the back edge. At first he considered a chip, then he thought about a bladed wedge shot. Toms' caddie suggested hitting a three wood like a putt. He took the caddie's advice and hit a perfect shot that stopped four feet from the hole. The birdie putt gave Toms 47 points, and a comfortable three-point margin over Duval.

WGC NEC Invitational—$5,000,000
Winner: Tiger Woods

As if the world's No. 1 player needed to prove any more, Tiger Woods put on a clinic for the 40 players from the two previous Ryder Cup and Presidents Cup teams at Firestone Country Club in Akron, Ohio, while picking up his fifth PGA Tour victory and sixth worldwide for the year. His margin might have only been one stroke over Phil Mickelson, and he might have had to two-putt the final green from 60 feet to ensure a win in regulation, but Woods controlled his fate in the NEC Invitational, the second installment of the World Golf Championships. Woods led after the first round, was one back after the second, held a five-stroke lead after the third, then played less-than-perfect golf and still picked up the win.

"You do get the feeling sometimes that the rest of us are all out here playing for second place," Fred Couples observed on Saturday. That was certainly the consensus after Woods' eight-under-par 62 gave him a three-day total of 209. In 11 previous events where Woods had led going into the final round, he came away with the trophy in 10 of them. The exception was the first event when he led as a rookie — the 1996 Quad City Classic that was won by Ed Fiori.

"That 62 could have easily been a 59," said Mark Calcavecchia, who played in the same pairing as Woods on Saturday. "That's as good as I've seen." Woods' round included a first-nine 32, followed by five birdies in the last nine holes. He could have tied the course record, established by Jose Maria Olazabal in 1990, but an eight-foot birdie putt at the 18th skimmed the edge of the hole.

"A couple of holes he blew it 50 yards past me," Calcavecchia added. Ben Crenshaw, who was in the gallery watching his Ryder Cup team, could only say, "My word! You just aren't supposed to be knocking it on some of these par-fours with a driver and a wedge like Tiger is doing here. I don't know that kind of game, but I'm glad to have that kind of game on our side in Boston."

Sunday should have been little more than a victory lap for Tiger, but Mickelson, who started the day at 206, seven shots behind Woods, came on strong. He shot a 30 on the first nine, and when Woods couldn't get anything going, then bogeyed the 14th and 15th holes, it seemed as though Mickelson might pull off the victory. But a two-iron shot at the par-five 16th found the rough and Mickelson made bogey. He came back with a birdie at the 17th, but another bogey at the 18th for 65 and a 271 total forced him to sit in the clubhouse and watch while Woods safely parred the 16th, then increased his lead back to two shots with a birdie at the 17th. On the 18th, however, Woods almost gave it back. After a poor approach that was short of the green, he hit a less-than-stellar chip to the front of the green, leaving himself 60 feet for par. While he didn't make it, he was able to get down in two for a bogey to finish with 71 and a 270 total for a one-stroke victory.

"I'm pleased that I gave myself a shot at winning the tournament," Mickelson said. "It looked like Tiger could have run away with it, but I'm disappointed at the way I finished. That's happened a couple of times this year, and I need to get a little tougher on the last few holes."

"I'm not against playing with a big lead," Woods said. "It means you can make a couple of mistakes, and I did. You're not always going to play your best, and today was an example. I came out with a wonderful round yesterday, and it's always the hardest thing to do to come out the next day and have a good round of golf."

Reno-Tahoe Open—$2,750,000
Winner: Notah Begay III

The last Sunday in August was a good day for Stanford alumni. Not only did Tiger Woods win at the WGC NEC Invitational, but his former Stanford teammate, Notah Begay III, won the inaugural Reno-Tahoe Open at the Montreux Golf and Country Club. The third man in PGA Tour history to shoot 59 when he broke the magic barrier at the Nike Tour's Dominion Open, Begay became the first Native American to win on the regular PGA Tour.

"Golf is not your typical minority sport," Begay said after shooting 14-under-par 274 and beating Chris Perry and David Toms by three strokes. "My main goal my whole life has been to be known as a good golfer. As a Native American, hopefully I can be a role model at the same time."

His play was certainly model at the long (7,552 yards) par-72 course. A first-round 70 left Begay five shots off the lead. He moved up Friday with 69 to get to 139, four strokes behind. It wasn't until Saturday, when Begay got into the same kind of zone he found when he shot the 59, that he broke away from the pack. A course-record 63 and a four-shot lead going into the final round was the result.

"It's weird," Begay said, trying to explain the state he enters when things are going well. "I get very calm. When some players get five or six under, they start to get a little uneasy and begin to guide it instead of just going with it. I have a tendency at times to be too aggressive, but that pays off. Sometimes you can get bitten by it, so I'm learning to find a happy medium.

That's what allows me to shoot so low. On Saturday the putts just went in and I rode the wave."

That wave was too much for the rest of the field to overcome. Perry shot a closing-round 68 to go with his earlier scores of 68, 71 and 70 for a 277 total. Coming off his second career victory at the Sprint International, Toms rolled home with 69 to reach 277 and tie Perry for second place. "If it hadn't been for that 63 he threw at us, we would have had a chance," Toms said.

Begay availed himself of a blackjack table at one of the local casinos for a couple of hours on Saturday night. "I just wanted to seclude myself from everyone," he said. "I've seen deficits like that made up in nine holes. I didn't want anyone to think I'd already won." A final-round 72 did the trick. Begay's total of 274 earned him $495,000, a sum he said would help him pay back his parents for all they had done for him. "They had to sacrifice a lot so I could travel," Begay said. "I'm just glad I can pay them back."

Air Canada Championship—$2,500,000
Winner: Mike Weir

At the Motorola Western Open, Mike Weir was paired with Tiger Woods in the final round and finished second, three shots off Woods' mark. When they returned to Chicago for the PGA Championship, Weir held a two-stroke lead over Woods and found himself in the final pairing again. He shot 80 and finished tied for 10th. But Weir, a native of Brights Grove, Ontario, knew a victory was coming, and when it did it was not only to be special for Weir and his family but for all Canadians who follow golf. Even retired hockey star Wayne Gretzky called after the PGA Championship to offer words of encouragement.

Those memories came flooding back as Weir lagged a 60-foot birdie putt at the 72nd hole of the Air Canada Championship, then tapped in for par to finish with a one-shot advantage over Fred Funk who had yet to play the 18th. If Weir held on, he would be the first Canadian to win a PGA Tour event in Canada since Pat Fletcher in 1954 and the first to win any PGA Tour event since Richard Zokol in 1992.

Funk, the third-round leader, had birdied the 17th to pull within one shot of Weir, but his tee shot on the 18th found the rough. He was forced to chip out, which sent ripples of applause throughout the clearly partisan crowd at the Northview Golf Club in Surrey, British Columbia. "When they saw my ball being chipped out at 18, I knew there would be a roar for that," Funk said. "That's okay. I've got fans at home. I wanted to put on a good show and make the fans sweat a little bit and make Mike sweat a little bit, but I hit it into the rough and that's the end of that story."

The story took twists and turns throughout the final round. Weir started at 202, bolstered by a seven-under-par 64 on Saturday. He entered the weekend five shots off the lead and remained two behind Funk. Weir bogeyed the first hole to drop three back, but birdied three of his next four to pull to within one.

Standing in the 14th fairway with 159 yards to the flag, Weir's caddie said, "We're overdue." Weir agreed. "I almost hit a nine iron, but I thought I would have to fly it all the way back there," he said. "I decided to take an eight iron and hit a bump shot. The ball landed on the green and rolled just like a putt." As the ball rolled closer to the hole, the crowd's roar intensified. It went in for an eagle. "I can't imagine there being a more memorable shot," Weir said. "To do it here, in a tight situation, to leap ahead a little bit, it was an amazing shot."

The crowd noise forced Funk, playing behind Weir, to back away, and even though he birdied the 17th, he could never regain the momentum. Weir finished with another 64 for an 18-under-par 266 total, two ahead of Funk, who closed with 68.

Winning in his home country might not have been the equivalent of a major championship for Weir, but the crowds certainly made it seem that way. "I fed off their energy," he said. "I couldn't have created a better scenario than this. That's the best gallery I've ever heard. It's a great feeling to have that kind of support."

Bell Canadian Open—$2,500,000
Winner: Hal Sutton

Hal Sutton wasn't favored in the Bell Canadian Open, not because he wasn't playing well, but because his focus was elsewhere. "All I know is, we've got to come together (at the Ryder Cup in Boston) and win the cup back," he said. "It's got to be an inside job." That Sutton had made another Ryder Cup team (his first since 1985) was impressive, but there was a golf tournament to be played, and Sutton was still one goal shy for the season.

"My goals for this year were to make our Ryder Cup team at age 41 and finish first somewhere along the way. I've got a daughter, Samantha, who's three, and I didn't want to have to slip a tape in the VCR to show her what daddy used to do, or who daddy used to be," Sutton said. With a three-shot victory over Dennis Paulson at the Glen Abbey Golf Club in Oakville, Ontario, Sutton delivered a stellar final-round performance, shooting 69 for a 275 total, 13 under par, to walk away with his third victory in two years and his 12th top-10 finish of 1999.

A first-round 69 left Sutton three shots behind Lee Janzen and Trevor Dodds, but 67 on Friday moved Sutton atop the leaderboard at 136. That lead would be short-lived. A 70, his worst score of the week, dropped Sutton into second place, one behind Janzen, who came back from 71 to 68.

Janzen ballooned to a final-round 76, clearing the way for Sutton. "I've spent more money than I've made lately," Janzen said. His 281 total dropped him into a tie for third place with Dudley Hart, David Sutherland and Justin Leonard. Sutton continued to split the fairways, and by the time he hit a six-iron approach on the sixth hole to two feet for his third consecutive birdie, he held a six-shot lead over his nearest competitor. "The last time I had a six-shot lead was at Williamsburg in 1983," he said. "Calvin Peete came back to beat me." There would be no such drama in Canada. Sutton's closing 69 left him three clear of Paulson, who also shot 69.

B.C. Open—$1,600,000
Winner: Brad Faxon

Neither Hurricane Floyd, which dropped four inches of rain on Endicott, New York, before the first round of the B.C. Open, nor a broken wrist, nor two years of personal turmoil could stop Brad Faxon from completing his long-awaited comeback. It took 74 holes and one extra day, but Faxon, who suffered through a divorce that became public during the 1997 Ryder Cup and who spent the early part of the year recovering from a broken left wrist, finally won his sixth career PGA Tour event (and his first since 1997) by defeating Fred Funk in a playoff.

Although never out of sight of the leaders, Faxon was far from the favorite as the fog cleared after a 45-minute delay on Sunday and the final groups teed off at the 6,974-yard En-Joie Golf Club. Funk had led through most of the week, taking a five-shot advantage over Faxon and rookie Rory Sabbatini after the second round. That round (which didn't end until Saturday) was marked by Funk's course-record-tying 61, a score that others said could have easily been 59. "It seemed like I was inside of two paces on every green today," Funk said. His longest birdie putt of the day was 15 feet, he hit every fairway, and carded seven consecutive threes.

Sunday's 36-hole final, which became a foot race against darkness after the morning delay, paired Funk with Faxon and Sabbatini although the drama appeared to be all Funk's. After the first 18 holes, he retained a three-shot edge over Sabbatini and five over Faxon. But Faxon had hung in there, following his opening 69 with rounds of 67 and 70 for a 206 total. He was tied with Mike Weir and Craig Spence going into the final round, but Funk had just shot his second 70 for the week and appeared ready to cruise to victory. He began the final round at 201.

The Maryland native hung onto the lead until the 15th hole, when his pitching wedge approach spun off the green and into a pond. The bogey dropped Funk into a tie with Sabbatini. At the 16th, Faxon joined the fray with a birdie to tie the two leaders. The three-way tie remained until the 18th hole, where Funk hit an approach to within three feet while Faxon and Sabbatini looked at 25- and 20-foot birdie putts, respectively. Faxon curled his sidehill 25-footer into the hole for birdie. Sabbatini just missed his effort, and Funk, who had struggled throughout the marathon final day, capped off his round for 72 by making his birdie putt to put him in a tie with Faxon at 273. Sabbatini finished alone in third place at 274.

Darkness prevented the players from finishing, so on Monday morning Faxon and Funk returned to the 10th tee. The first playoff hole ended in a tie, but when they re-teed on the 18th for the third time in three days, Funk pushed his shot into the trees. From there he hit another tree trying to punch a four iron from 155 yards. His third shot with an eight iron caught yet another tree, and Funk had to scramble from a bunker to make bogey. That left the door open for Faxon. His approach shot safely on the green, Faxon rolled his first putt to within four feet and made his par to win.

Westin Texas Open—$2,000,000
Winner: Duffy Waldorf

While 12 of America's finest players were dueling it out with their European counterparts, two guys in San Antonio, Texas, had a match of their own going in the most overlooked PGA Tour event of the 1999 season. Two hours after Justin Leonard clinched the Ryder Cup, Duffy Waldorf sank a 45-footer on the first extra hole at the LaCantera Golf Club to defeat Ted Tryba and win the Westin Texas Open.

Waldorf put together four outstanding rounds in the blustery wind even though he never held the lead until Tryba bogeyed the par-three 17th on Sunday. Neither Tryba nor Waldorf led at the end of three rounds. That honor went to Stephen Ames, who began the week with 64 to take a one-shot lead over Rich Beem. Ames kept that advantage with 69, then extended his lead to two when his 67 gave him a 200 total. Waldorf and Tryba trailed by two, but both had put together some exceptional rounds. Waldorf's 65 moved him to 202, while Tryba added 66 to his previous rounds of 69 and 67. Ames couldn't keep it going, shooting 75 to drop into a tie for eighth place at 275.

Waldorf and Tryba finished with 68s for 270 totals, 18 under par. In the playoff, Tryba hooked his drive into the left rough. Waldorf hit his approach to the center of the green, 45 feet from the hole. Tryba found the greenside bunker with his approach. He blasted out, leaving himself 20 feet for par. It didn't matter. Waldorf drained his birdie putt and won his second event of the year.

"I had one guy beat me," Tryba said. "Duffy made a great putt. That's what exciting tournaments are made of. I've got no qualms losing to a guy like that." Waldorf was thankful that his instincts proved correct. "I always felt I could shoot a low score out here," he said. "I always thought this course suited my game well. That's a positive if you can go to a course where you feel you can go low."

Buick Challenge—$1,800,000
Winner: David Toms

Even players who have never gotten closer to a Ryder Cup match than their televisions couldn't stop talking about it. As late as Sunday afternoon, after David Toms had taken a three-shot lead into the final round of the Buick Challenge and Sergio Garcia had won a playoff in the Linde German Masters, there was only one topic of conversation. They talked about it on the range, in the locker room, out on the course and at the cookouts and parties afterward.

"The Ryder Cup is all anyone's talking about, which is fine with me," said Davis Love III, as he took a week-long victory lap.

Even Toms, the eventual winner, got into the act by calling Hal Sutton at home to congratulate him. "He was exhausted, but he was still excited," Toms said of his fellow Louisianan. "When a guy like that, who has had the successes he has, calls it the greatest golfing experience of his life, there's got to be something to it. Hal was the first person to call me after I won the Sprint, and that meant a lot, so I wanted to call and congratulate him." It didn't seem to bother Toms that his three-stroke victory over Stuart Appleby was overshadowed by a week-old event, but maybe he was used to it. Toms' first victory of the year came one week after the PGA Championship when the Tiger and Sergio duel was still in the minds and mouths of the golfing world, and his only second-place finish of the year came to Notah Begay III at the Reno-Tahoe Open, which ran opposite the WGC NEC Invitational. With the exception of Duffy Waldorf, whose second victory came at the Westin Texas Open the same week as the Ryder Cup, there hasn't been a more ignored multiple winner in recent tour history.

"Maybe I'm sneaking in the back door a little bit," Toms said. He pulled out of the pro-am and spent three hours in the fitness trailer being treated for back and neck pains, then proceeded to shoot rounds of 68, 66, 66 and 71 for a 271 total, 17 under par, to win going away. The final margin was three, but his lead throughout most of the final round was five and sometimes six shots. Toms made one bad swing with a six iron on the 12th hole that resulted in a double bogey, but by that time no one was close enough to matter.

The only thing that could have kept Toms from becoming the PGA Tour's sixth multiple winner of the year was his back. "I definitely had more Advil than birdies," he said. "When I wake up in the morning I feel like if I had to jump out of bed real quick to get the door I couldn't get there. It just sometimes feels like my head weighs 50 pounds. I don't know what's in my future, really. I'll just continue to do some stretching and strengthening exercises. It's getting better every day, but I'm still having to take medication."

Michelob Championship—$2,500,000
Winner: Notah Begay III

Even Notah Begay III was surprised when he walked away with the crystal trophy and the $450,000 winner's check in the Michelob Championship at Kingsmill for his second victory of the season. "I was definitely surprised," Begay said, after coming from behind to overtake Mike Weir, then eliminating Tom Byrum in a two-hole playoff. "I just had to make something happen."

That's what Begay did during the closing holes of the final round. Having never fallen more than one shot behind the leaders, Begay began the day tied with Byrum at 206, but they were one behind Weir. After a two-week hiatus, Weir had come back from an opening 74 with 63 and 68. As the three teed off together on Sunday, it appeared that Weir had the upper hand. His iron play was magnificent, and he made two early birdies to gain a two-shot edge over Byrum and a three-shot margin over Begay. Then Weir's putter abandoned him. He missed four short birdie putts down the stretch. Begay pulled to within two with a chip-in birdie at the 15th, but it still appeared to be a two-man race between Byrum and Weir, after Byrum pulled even with a birdie at the 16th.

That's when Begay knew he had to make his move. At the par-three 17th he fired at a well-guarded flag and watched as his ball stopped 15 feet from the hole. Another birdie pulled Begay to within one. On the 18th, he reached the green safely in two, but had a difficult putt. When the sidehill 25-footer went in for birdie, Begay electrified the crowd and reached 10 under par with his 68 and 274 total.

Weir missed birdie chances at the 16th and 17th, then hit his worst tee shot of the day on the 18th. From the rough he missed the green with his approach, then failed to save par, losing the lead for the first time on the final hole. He placed third at 70–275. The playoff would be between Byrum, who shot a closing 68, and Begay.

The playoff was not pretty. Begay hooked his tee shot into the left rough on the first hole, taking a bogey that should have lost it, but Byrum three-putted from 25 feet for another bogey. Then it was Byrum's turn to hook a tee shot. He was unable to reach the green with his approach, leaving himself 12 feet for par after a weak third shot. Begay wasn't much better. After reaching the fairway with his tee shot, the only Native American ever to play full time on the PGA Tour chunked an eight iron short of the green. His chip stopped four feet from the hole. When Byrum missed his 12-footer, Begay rolled in the four-footer.

Las Vegas Invitational—$2,500,000
Winner: Jim Furyk

There's little question that when it comes to hitting the jackpot, Jim Furyk has Las Vegas' number. For the third time in five years, Furyk came out a winner. Not even a four-shot lead by Harrison Frazar after the second round or an earthquake that rumbled through the Mojave Desert on Saturday morning could dissuade Furyk from winning where he seems most comfortable.

"A lot of winning is believing in yourself," Furyk said. "It's believing that you're going to win the event." Certainly he believes in the Las Vegas Invitational. Three of his four career victories came amidst the glittery lights in Nevada, with the 1999 rendition coming when Furyk shot a final-round 66 and threatened a 90-hole PGA Tour scoring record by finishing with a 29-under-par 331 total, one stroke better than Jonathan Kaye.

It was a week for record-setting scores when the wind was calm, but when the wind kicked up, as it did during Saturday's fourth round, even par was a good number. On Thursday, Tommy Armour III shot a course-record 60 that could have easily been 57 as Armour missed putts of five, six and three feet. The 54-hole cut was 11 under par, a PGA Tour record, and after three rounds Furyk, Frazar and Bob May shared the lead at 22 under par.

Unshaken by the events of Saturday morning, Furyk (who was awakened by the earthquake but went back to sleep) put some distance between himself and the field by shooting 71 for a 265 total. Kaye, who rejoined the tour in 1999 after finishing second at the qualifying tournament, was Furyk's closest challenger. Kaye had followed an opening 63 with two 66s before Saturday's wind. His fourth-round 73 left him three shots off the lead.

Furyk won with a closing 66 while Kaye shot 64. Kaye birdied the first three holes to move to within one of Furyk, who managed to birdie two of the first three. With another birdie at the 11th Kaye pulled even with Furyk, but then at the 12th Kaye pushed his tee shot behind a tree and was forced to chip back to the fairway. The bogey proved the difference. "I hit one bad shot behind a tree and that pretty much cost me," he said. "Jim just doesn't make mistakes, but when he does he always recovers and he's probably the best putter on tour. I played about as good as I can play and still got beat. Sometimes your best isn't good enough."

National Car Rental Classic—$2,500,000
Winner: Tiger Woods

When Tiger Woods completed his third round at Walt Disney World in Orlando, he was tied for the lead with Bob Tway at 18-under-par 198. Guess who won? In a brief career filled with awe-inspiring statistics, perhaps the best was Woods' winning percentage when he held a third-round lead: 10 out of 11 after the National Car Rental Classic for a .909 average. Even a final-round 73 couldn't spoil Woods' sixth PGA Tour victory and seventh overall in 1999. His 271 total edged Ernie Els by one stroke, and cleared Tway and Franklin Langham by three.

"Nobody can touch this guy at the moment," said Els, who played with Woods on Saturday when the winner fired his third straight 66. "He has gone to another level that I don't think the rest of us can find right now. I was totally in awe."

Even Woods' 73 final round was impressive. He lowered the trajectory of his shots when the fairways became wet so that his ball wouldn't collect mud. When he found his shots were still collecting unwanted debris, he chose a slower, arm-punch swing in order to control his approaches into the greens. But Woods had three three-putt greens and a handful of missed opportunities from 10 feet or less. A missed six-footer at the 15th that would have given him sole possession of the lead over Els didn't fall, but in the end it didn't matter. Els three-putted the 17th for bogey, Woods two-putted the 18th from 35 feet for par.

"When I was playing in junior golf, I thought I could never love the game as much as I did then, until I got out here and started playing more," Woods said. "I love it more than ever. I love to play. I love to practice, and I love to compete. I can honestly say I love it more now."

Southern Farm Bureau Classic—$1,500,000
Winner: Brian Henninger

It took five days to finish 54 holes in the Southern Farm Bureau Classic, but after the rain settled and the tributes had been paid, Brian Henninger, who surprised the world by holding a share of the final-round lead with Ben Crenshaw in the 1995 Masters, walked away with his second career victory on the same golf course in Madison, Mississippi. The two wins came under similar circumstances. In 1994 when Henninger won the then-named Deposit Guarantee Classic, the tournament only went 36 holes, with rain soaking the Annandale Golf Club. Henninger won in a one-hole playoff over Mike Sullivan. In 1999, rain once again delayed play, although the event wasn't shorted due to weather. It was reduced from 72 to 54 holes for the players to attend the memorial service on Friday in Orlando for Payne Stewart.

"My thoughts, first and foremost, go out to Payne and his family," Henninger said at the awards ceremony. "It's been a tough week. It's not that Payne Stewart and I were real close, but I just felt like he was such an integral part of this tour and kind of paved the way for young guys like me."

Play resumed on Saturday with Chris DiMarco moving into a tie for the lead with Henninger at 133. Henninger got there with rounds of 67 and 66 while DiMarco shot 65 and 68. While Henninger hadn't won since 1994 and had finished no better than 71st on the money list since 1995, DiMarco had never finished better than third in four years on tour.

Sunday came and went with no winner. Three inches of rain fell in a 24-hour period from mid-morning Sunday though the early hours of Monday, and play was delayed for more than an hour on Monday morning as crews tried to prepare the golf course. After a slow start, Henninger got his putter moving and his 69 was good enough for a 202 total, 14 under par, and a three-shot win over DiMarco.

"My game has improved a lot," Henninger said. "It's been a lot more consistent since 1994. I've been close to winning a few times this year but struggled on Sunday. Today I started poorly and just waited for my putter to show up. My putter won the golf tournament this week."

DiMarco's solo second was the best finish of his career, while Paul Stankowski staged something of a comeback with a 206 total and tie for third with Glen Day and Perry Moss.

Tour Championship—$5,000,000
Winner: Tiger Woods

The primary reason the 29 top money winners from the 1999 season stayed in Houston and played in the Tour Championship is because that is the way Payne Stewart would have wanted it. Only a handful of players had arrived at the Champions Club on Monday when the news of Stewart's airplane crash was broadcast, and many of them were too shocked to believe what was happening.

David Duval got the news as he was checking in at the registration table, but he thought it wasn't accurate. Stewart was in the same jet ownership program as Duval, so when Duval heard that the airplane was a Learjet 35 he knew it wasn't Stewart's. Even though Stewart was part owner of his own jet, he was flying in a leased jet the day of the tragedy. Like everyone, Duval was shocked when he learned the truth — learned that Stewart, two of his agents, a golf course architect and two pilots died in the air when their Learjet depressurized. The most shocking aspect of the tragedy was that the airplane continued to fly on autopilot for over two hours, a cold coffin soaring at between 35,000 and 55,000 feet.

After the decision was made to continue the golf tournament, some unprecedented arrangements were made. The pro-am became optional. A memorial service was held at 7:30 Thursday morning on the first tee of the Champions Club before the field played 27 holes (Stewart's spot in the select group of top 30 money winners was left unfilled). Then on Friday the players boarded a hastily assembled fleet of private jets and flew to Orlando for the memorial service. Afterward they returned to Houston where, according to Tom Lehman, "Payne would be saying, 'Boys, you've got to play.'"

Saturday was another 27-hole day where the applause was minimal and the players' minds and emotions elsewhere. It seemed almost anticlimactic on Sunday when Tiger Woods walked away with his seventh PGA Tour victory of the season and his eighth win overall. Woods' four-shot victory over Davis Love III was the least important of his career in a week when golf took second place to the memory of a champion.

"I was in second place in the golf tournament standing over a birdie putt and having to back away to wipe tears from my eyes," Love said. "You shouldn't be having to do that on the golf course."

Woods had 67 at the end of the official first round, and by the time he played his last hole on Thursday (the 27th of the day) Woods shared the lead, and would never leave the top spot again. Rounds of 66, 67 and 69 followed, the last coming as 25 of the 29 players wore knickers in honor of Stewart. Love finished alone in second at 273, four back of Woods' winning 269 total, 15 under par, while Brent Geiberger had four rounds in the 60s for a 274 total and sole possession of third place.

"I'm not sure how much better I can get," Woods said in a quiet, determined voice. Love echoed those sentiments when he said, "Tiger is not going to play every week and he can't win every week he does play, so there's still a lot out there for us."

Those observations seemed secondary, however. "If we didn't have this tournament, his (Stewart's) absence wouldn't have been felt like it is," said Lehman, who spoke at the Thursday memorial service. "You think back on the history of the game and try to compare Payne to somebody — he was a very unique figure in sports and in golf. I think of Walter Hagan, a player who had this bigness, this presence about him, who dressed for the game, who brought an excitement to it. Payne is, in many ways, irreplaceable from that perspective."

Special Events

CVS/pharmacy Charity Classic—$1,000,000

Winners: Jeff Sluman and Stuart Appleby

Thanks to the efforts of New England natives Billy Andrade and Brad Faxon, Rhode Island was host to a team event called the CVS/pharmacy Charity Classic. It was a two-day, no-pressure, best-ball event, but the golf was no less spectacular and the charities of New England no less thankful to PGA Tour stars such as Stuart Appleby, Tom Kite, Davis Love III, and Jack and Gary Nicklaus, who made the event a special occasion for all.

Appleby and Jeff Sluman opened a two-shot lead in the first round with a 12-under-par 59 at the Rhode Island Country Club in Barrington. The Quigleys, Dana and Brett, were in second place with 61, while the teams of Tim Herron and Scott McCarron and P.H. Horgan III and Jay Sigel were tied for third with 63s.

The scores weren't as low in the second round, but 63s are not considered normal in an average week on tour. It was still enough for Sluman and Appleby to carve out a victory over the Quigleys. The 122 total earned the winners $100,000 each, while the Quigleys took home $75,000 each for their 124 effort. The Quigleys also shot 63 but missed three birdies coming down the stretch. Herron and McCarron finished third by shooting 65 for a 128 total, while tournament organizers Andrade and Faxon came back from an opening 65 to shoot 64 and tie Mark Calcavecchia and Peter Jacobsen for fourth at 129.

Fred Meyer Challenge—$925,000

Winners: Brad Faxon and Billy Andrade

What happens when two friends from Rhode Island travel to Oregon for a two-day, two-man team event? They win, of course.

Well, it might not have been a foregone conclusion that Brad Faxon and Billy Andrade would play some of the best partner golf of their careers at the Reserve Vineyards and Golf Club in Aloha, Oregon, to win the Fred Meyer Challenge by two shots over Jim Furyk and John Huston, and Steve Elkington and Craig Stadler. Their 122 total beat a stellar field that included Arnold Palmer, making his annual trek to the affair, playing again with host Peter Jacobsen. Palmer and Jacobsen didn't fare was well as they had in previous outings, finishing with a 134 total, 12 shots off the lead, but they drew the biggest crowds and loudest ovations.

With an 11-under-par 61, Faxon and Andrade shared the first-round lead with Phil Mickelson and Jay Haas. Stadler and Elkington stood one shot back, along with Billy Mayfair and Steve Pate, Brian Henninger and Tim Herron.

The first team to make a move in the second round was Tom Lehman and Duffy Waldorf, who opened with 64 and followed with 10 birdies for 62.

That tied Lehman and Waldorf with Mayfair and Pate (62-64), Henninger and Herron (62-64) and Haas and Mickelson (61-65). Stadler and Elkington matched their opening 62 with another 10-under-par performance. That turned out to only be enough for the tie for second place.

Furyk and Huston, both known for their precise iron play, ran out of holes before they could catch the leaders. Their 60 ended with a flurry of birdies. Faxon and Andrade followed their 61 with a command performance. Another 61 gave them their first Fred Meyer Challenge title.

Ganter Cup Challenge—$140,000
Winners: Matt Gogel

In one of the more unusual events of the year, four of the top players from the Nike Tour, still vying for their shot at fame on the PGA Tour, took on four of the world's best players in a one-day, four-match exhibition. With $140,000 at stake, Craig Stadler, John Cook, Fred Couples and David Duval teed off against the Nike Tour's Matt Gogel, Ryan Howison, Mathew Goggin and Carl Paulson in the Ganter Cup Challenge on the 7,104-yard Willow Creek Country Club in Sandy, Utah.

The matches were close and the golf exciting. In the first pairing, Gogel had the low round of the day, shooting seven-under-par 65 to beat Stadler by four shots and get the Nike Tour off to a great start. Right behind them, Howison proved he belonged, beating Cook by one shot, 70 to 71. That left the pride of the PGA Tour up to Couples and Duval, a Nike Tour graduate and the No. 2 player in the world. They came through, Couples defeating Goggin by 68 to 76, while Duval shot 73, but hung on to beat Paulson, who had 74.

Ryder Cup
Winner: United States

See Chapter 7.

Franklin Templeton Shark Shootout—$1,500,000
Winners: Fred Couples and David Duval

It seemed appropriate that golf's most laid-back winner would win one of the year's most laid-back events in record-setting style. But then, November, the month of unofficial events with different formats and lots of laughs, was always Fred Couples' favorite month. In addition to two Skins Game titles, two Kapalua International titles and four World Cup of Golf wins, Couples and partner David Duval added another trophy with a six-stroke victory in the Franklin Templeton Shark Shootout.

"We had a great time," Couples said. "I don't know how to say this properly, but the way the format was set up we pretty much knew we were going to win."

So did many of the other competitors in the team competition. "When I heard the teams, I knew Greg (Norman) had stacked the deck," Scott Hoch said. Hoch was paired with Scott McCarron and the two finished second, but had no chance of catching Couples and Duval. Their lead was five after an opening 61 in the alternate-shot format, and when Couples and Duval shot a best-ball 62 on Saturday for a 123 total, the lead going into the final round was six. With Sunday's play being a scramble, Hoch and the rest of the field knew they stood little or no chance. "They're two of the best drivers in the game," Hoch said. "When you're hitting two of them, they're going to be chipping shots all day."

The 61 that Couples and Duval shot in Sunday's scramble wasn't as impressive as the one they fired in alternate-shot play, but it was good enough to lap the field. Hoch and McCarron also shot 61 on Sunday for a 190 total, while Peter Jacobsen and John Cook also shot 61 to finish third at 191.

World Cup of Golf—$1,500,000
Winners: United States/Tiger Woods

Tiger Woods opened the World Cup of Golf — the last of the original — with fireworks and closed it the same way. He was welcomed with a pyrotechnic display at a lavish banquet before the tournament, and four days later he put on his own fireworks show that gave him and fellow American Mark O'Meara the championship by a deceptive five strokes over Spain, 545 to 550, at the Mines Resort and Golf Club in Malaysia.

Woods, shooting 67-68-63-65–263, 21 under par, also won the individual championship. It was his 10th title of a sensational 1999.

Miguel Angel Martin and Santiago Luna, trailing by seven strokes at the start of the final round, wiped out that deficit and even took the lead by one stroke over the first nine. Luna shot 31, Martin 33. Meanwhile, O'Meara was struggling. Then Luna blew up. He started the second nine with a double bogey and two bogeys, a fatal error because now Woods was running off birdies. And soon the Americans were comfortably home with their 22nd World Cup title out of 45 played. Woods shot 65, offsetting 77 by O'Meara, who had 73, 65 and 67 the first three days.

"We had played the front nine not as good as we'd like," Woods said.

"Oh, you played all right," O'Meara cracked. "It was a struggle for me. It was a lack of confidence."

Japan took the first-round lead with 135, with Mamoru Osanai shooting 65 and Mitsuo Harada 70. They led by four over Wales (Phillip Price and David Park). Woods and O'Meara were five behind at 140. Spain led the second round by one stroke over the Americans. Woods shot 63 and O'Meara 67 for a blistering 130 in the third round, and a seven-stroke lead. It seemed to be all over, but then came O'Meara's collapse in the final round, then Luna's collapse on the last nine.

It was good drama for the final playing of the World Cup as the world had known it. Industrialist John Jay Hopkins started it in 1953 as the Canada Cup, to promote international good will through golf. Starting in 2000, in Argentina, it will be part of the World Golf Championships, totally revamped. The purse will go from $1.5 million to $3 million, and the field will shrink from 32 to 24 two-man teams. The format also will change, from four days of individual and team stroke play to alternate shot and better ball.

Callaway Pebble Beach Invitational—$300,000
Winner: Rocco Mediate

No one would argue that there are few prettier venues for golf than the Monterey Peninsula in Northern California, but almost everyone would agree that February, the month of the AT&T Pebble Beach National Pro-Am, is a poor time to play there. From gale force winds to driving rains to temperatures that range from freezing to balmy, the conditions at Pebble Beach in the winter are a battle of the elements.

That was one of the reasons Ely Callaway, chairman and founder of Callaway Golf, decided to host his tournament at Pebble Beach in November. Not only were conditions for the Callaway Pebble Beach Invitational ideal, the field, consisting of the finest players from all three major U.S. professional tours, was strong and diverse.

On the first day former PGA Tour player Brian Henninger was tied for the lead with Bob Ford after both fired rounds of 67. Scores were higher in the second round as only five players broke par. Brian Mogg shot 70 for the day's low score, but his first-round 79 all but eliminated him from contention. Henninger and Ford both had their worst days with 76s. Tom Lehman and Loren Roberts jumped into a tie for the lead, Lehman following his 68 with 72 and Roberts firing 71 to go with his 69.

Lehman and Roberts still led after the third round, but a pair of 73s dwindled their margin to a single stroke. That lead evaporated early in the final round. It became a duel between Rocco Mediate and Annika Sorenstam, and in the end it was Sorenstam's putter — the bane of her season on the LPGA Tour — that cost her the chance for a victory. Although Sorenstam shot her third 69 of the week, crucial putts in the final few holes wouldn't fall. Mediate took advantage by shooting 68 for a 282 total and one-shot victory. Lehman and Roberts tied for third after both shot 71s for 284 totals.

PGA Grand Slam—$1,000,000
Winner: Tiger Woods

Tiger Woods picked up his 10th win in 14 starts — and his 11th of the year — at Poipu Bay, Hawaii, trouncing the No. 3-ranked player in the world, Davis Love III, in the PGA Grand Slam. Woods led Love 5 up at the turn and closed out the former PGA champion, 3 and 2, on the final nine.

Both players birdied the first hole, but Woods eagled the 524-yard, par-five second to go 1 up. Two more birdies by Woods and two bogeys by Love on the first nine virtually sealed the match. Love, who was invited to play after Payne Stewart's death, cut Woods' lead to 3 up by birdieing the 12th and 13th holes, but was unable to regain the momentum. Woods closed him out with a halve at the 16th. "I didn't get off to a great start," Love said. "He got 1 up on an eagle and when he gets off like that, he's hard to beat. You can feel the door closing."

That's the kind of start Love had in the first round when he also eagled the second hole and went on to beat Masters winner Jose Maria Olazabal, 6 and 5.

"I felt it was going to be a tough match because Davis played so well yesterday," said Woods, who defeated British Open champion Paul Lawrie, 3 and 2, in the first round. "After birdieing the first hole, I knew if I could somehow answer, I could stop his momentum." That's what Woods did with the eagle at No. 2, and the $400,000 check pushed Woods' winnings over $7.68 million.

The third-place match between Lawrie and Olazabal ended when Lawrie conceded after twisting his ankle on a rock between the ninth green and the 10th tee. Olazabal was 1 up at the time. Lawrie was taken to a hospital where doctors determined several ligaments had been sprained.

JCPenney Classic—$2,000,000
Winners: Laura Davies and John Daly

When John Daly hoisted the trophy along with partner Laura Davies at the JCPenney Classic, you would have thought he had won another major championship. "This is unbelievable," Daly said. "This being the last year of the JCPenney, to win with Laura is to me one of the greatest wins I could have. It was fun. We went out and whether we played good or bad, we were smiling and laughing. What a way to end this drought I've had for the last four years. Hopefully, I can build some confidence on it and go out next year and start playing a lot better golf than I have been."

They began the last day four shots behind leaders Paul Azinger and Se Ri Pak, and in the history of the event no team had ever lost after taking as much as a three-shot lead into the final round. Earlier rounds of 65 and 64 gave Azinger and Pak a share of the lead with Daly and Davies, then a third-round 62 put Azinger and Pak up by four. They didn't make a bogey in the three days.

On Sunday, however, Azinger and Pak got off to a shaky start. An early bogey and some missed birdie opportunities caused their lead to evaporate. Then they made five birdies to regain a three-shot advantage with three holes to play. That is when Daly and Davies caught fire. It started when Daly dropped a 35-foot birdie putt on the par-four 16th. Moments later, Azinger and Pak picked up only their second bogey of the tournament at the same hole, and the lead was cut to one stroke.

Pars followed at the 17th, and when Davies rolled in a six-footer for birdie at the 18th for a 64, she and Daly had moved into a tie with Pak and Azinger, who shot 69, at 24-under-par 260. Davies continued putting well, draining an eight-footer for par on the second playoff hole to keep her team alive. On the 17th, the third playoff hole, she drained a breaking 30-footer for birdie. Pak missed her birdie try from 25 feet.

"I think that was the longest putt I've holed all year, and it was my last one of the year," Davies said. "This was one of the most enjoyable wins I've ever had. I mean, it's fun to win with someone else. To actually have somebody hitting the shots with you, to enjoy it with them. I was cheering his putts as much as anytime I made a putt. It was just a lot of fun."

Office Depot Father-Son Challenge—$860,000
Winners: Jack and Gary Nicklaus

Just when it looked as if Jack Nicklaus had finally reached the twilight of the most magnificent career in professional golf history, the 60-year-old began lifting weights, working on his new hip, hitting balls, and talking about how well he was playing. "What surprises me most is how long I'm hitting the ball," Nicklaus said. "I was practicing with Jim Flick, and he said, 'Jack, you can't be hitting the ball that far,' but there it was."

It was certainly there on a beautiful December weekend in Naples, Florida, when Jack and his son Gary (who had just earned his 2000 PGA Tour card) fired a 119 total on the Twin Eagles Golf and Country Club, then held off Raymond and Robert Floyd in three playoff holes to win the Office Depot Father-Son Challenge, with the elder Nicklaus sinking the winning birdie putt.

Hale Irwin and son Steve, who caddied for Hale through most of the 1999 season, opened with a 13-under-par 59 for a one-shot lead over the Nicklauses and Floyds. As if one 59 and two 60s weren't enough, four teams were only three shots back after the first round. Craig and Kevin Stadler, Tom and David Kite, Jerry and Wesley Pate, and Dave and Ron Stockton all shot rounds of 62, while Al and John Geiberger shot 63 and were tied for eighth place with Lee and Rick Trevino, and Hubert and Myatt Green.

Sunday's round was all Nicklaus and Floyd, with the elder statesmen teaching their offspring a thing or two about competition. With birdies that seemed to go on forever, the Nicklauses rallied in the final holes of regulation, with Jack hitting a six iron to within two feet on the final hole for birdie and 59 for a 119 total. The Floyds matched them shot for shot, having 59 of their own to take the event to extra holes.

There it stayed for three trips down the 18th. The third time, after Gary Nicklaus hit an approach six feet above the hole, Jack crouched in that familiar style that won 20 major championships, eyed the putt with the same steely gaze that seemed to defy defeat for four decades, and confidently stroked in the winning birdie.

Sprint Puerto Rico Golf Challenge—$250,000
Winner: Robin Freeman

It was only fitting that Robin Freeman would win the $50,000 first prize at the Sprint Puerto Rico Golf Challenge. Freeman, a 40-year-old journeyman who finished second on the Nike Tour money list in 1998, followed his opening 71 with a course-record-tying 64 at the Wyndham El Conquistador Resort in Los Croabos. That gave Freeman a three-shot lead over Wilfredo Morales, Nolan Henke and Jim McGovern going into the final round.

Bobby Wadkins, the brother of former Ryder Cup captain Lanny Wadkins and a man with the dubious distinction of having the highest career earnings of any player who had never won on the PGA Tour, stood four back after rounds of 68 and 71.

Freeman's putter went cold in the final round. He missed birdie opportunities on the second nine that could have put the tournament out of reach, finishing with an even-par 72. That was only good enough to tie Wadkins, who had finished with 68 for a 207 total. The two marched out for a playoff, and after opening pars, Freeman found the missing putting touch, draining a 20-foot birdie on the second extra hole for the win.

Diners Club Matches—$1,200,000

Winners: Fred Couples and Mark Calcavecchia
Jack Nicklaus and Tom Watson
Juli Inkster and Dottie Pepper

The Diners Club Matches are three match-play tournaments rolled into one, and proved to be one of the most impressive displays of golf of the 1999 season, with Jack Nicklaus setting the tone by making seven birdies in 14 holes. Nicklaus and partner Tom Watson trounced Allen Doyle and Dana Quigley, 5 and 4, in the most lopsided match of the day. "I've seen him play that well in lots of instances, but never better," Watson said. Nicklaus agreed, adding, "I'd love to find another event like this next week. That's the best score I've had in 25 years."

The next day in the Senior PGA Tour finals, Nicklaus and Watson defeated Bruce Fleisher and David Graham, 1 up, with Watson coming through with the crucial birdies. Three birdies on the first five holes of the second nine put the two ahead to stay, and even though Fleisher made putts at the 16th and 17th to pull close, he and Graham never got back to even. When Fleisher's 12-foot birdie putt at the 18th slipped by the hole, the title belonged to Nicklaus and Watson

In the other matches of the day, Fred Couples and Mark Calcavecchia, who had advanced to the finals by defeating Skip Kendall and Chris Perry, 2 and 1, went on to win the PGA Tour portion when they beat Steve Elkington and Jeff Maggert, 1 up. In the final match, Couples moved his team ahead with a 20-foot birdie putt on the 10th hole, and Calcavecchia widened the lead by hitting his approach to within tap-in range on the 11th.

The LPGA matches were equally exciting. Two-time defending champions Dottie Pepper and Juli Inkster won a hard-fought match against Kelli Kuehne and Laura Davies, 1 up, to advance to the finals against Karrie Webb and Kelly Robbins, who beat Annika Sorenstam and Lorie Kane, 2 and 1. On Sunday, Inkster and Pepper made it three in a row, drumming Webb and Robbins, 4 and 3, in the most one-sided match of the day.

Nike Tour

The biggest news from the Nike Tour in 1999 came from a man who didn't win a single event. Casey Martin, the man with the golf cart whom the PGA Tour continues to battle through the courts, qualified for the Tour by virtue of finishing 14th on the Nike Tour money list. When he finished his final round at the Nike Tour Championship, Martin nestled in the clubhouse with a bowl of soup and baked potato, wondering if the 77 and 78 he had over the weekend would drop him out of the top 15 on the money list who would advance to the PGA Tour. "It's a struggle," Martin said. "But every week is a struggle. My life definitely can be a struggle, but it's a fairy tale too."

Martin, who was born with Klippel-Trenauney-Weber Syndrome, a circulatory disorder that rendered his right leg withered and almost completely debilitated, sued the PGA Tour under the Americans With Disabilities Act and won the right to use a cart. The Tour appealed and a decision is expected in 2000, but not before Martin is eligible to play in several events. The disease left Martin unable to walk 18 holes and x-rays showed it was getting worse throughout the year. "A radiologist saw the film and said he couldn't imagine getting more than a year on that leg," Martin's mother, Melinda, said. "But other doctors have said it could be five years."

Whether it's a month, a year or five years before Martin takes a wrong step and snaps his tibia, the moment Commissioner Tim Finchem handed him a PGA Tour card, shook his hand and said, "Congratulations, good job," was one Martin had dreamed about for years. "This stuff is fleeting for a lot of reasons, and it could be gone in a minute," Martin said. "I wish I could box how I feel right now. It's a treasure."

One of Martin's college teammates at Stanford summed up the feelings of most tour professionals on the situation. "I think everybody has a lot of respect for the fact that he earned his Tour card through the Nike Tour," Tiger Woods said. "I don't think he's going to get any hard feelings at all. Only congratulations."

Congratulations were also due to Carl Paulson, who won the Utah Classic and Boise Open and finished first in earnings on the Nike Tour with $223,051, and to Joel Edwards, who earned a repeat visit to the PGA Tour after losing his card earlier in his career. There were several former PGA Tour players who earned a second chance through the Nike Tour. Among them were Shaun Micheel, who played the PGA Tour in 1994 and 1995 and won the 1998 Singapore Open; Joel Edwards, who tied for second in the 1992 B.C. Open; Marco Dawson, and Kelly Gibson.

Mathew Goggin, a native of Hobert, Australia, who played the PGA European Tour in 1998, won two Nike events in 1999 and gained his PGA Tour card easily. Steve Gotsche won two events as well, but qualified by the skin of his teeth, finishing in the 15th spot on the money list with $118,638.

The youngest player to qualify was 24-year-old Brad Elder, a former University of Texas All-American who won two events, and the oldest was Gotsche at 38. Martin was the only player to advance who didn't win a tournament, although he had five top-10 finishes, while nine players who did win Nike Tour events failed to make it into the top 15 and will be forced to return to the newly-named Buy.Com Tour in 2000.

Canadian Tour

The Canadian Tour had a decidedly foreign flavor to it in 1999, as most of the winners were migrants from such far-away places as Ormond Beach, Florida, and Tempe, Arizona. It wasn't until the sixth event of the season that a Canadian won, leaving many to wonder if it had become little more than a northern version of the Nike Tour.

If not for Canadian stalwart Ray Stewart, who picked up two victories and led the victorious Canadian team in the Dundee International, the year might well have been a shutout. Certainly the first five events were as red, white and blue as anything the U.S. PGA Tour put together. Kenneth Staton of Ormond Beach, Florida, won the inaugural Crown Isle Open with a 273 total, four better than British Columbia native Darren Griff. Then Ken Duke of Little Rock, Arkansas, made it two in a row when he won the Shell Payless Open by five shots over Ontario's Ian Leggatt.

Staton won again in early June, edging fellow American Steve Wood by two shots in the BC Tel Open. Duke made it a one-two-three U.S. finish in the event, while Rob McMillan of Winnipeg finished as low Canadian in a tie for fourth place with three other Americans.

Brain Kontak of Tempe, Arizona, made it four in a row for the Yanks, as he shot 266 to edge Duke by one stroke in the Telus/Henry Singer Alberta Open, while Manny Zerman of San Diego finished tied for third with New Zealander Matthew Lane. The low Canadian was Stuart Hendley of Lacombe, Alberta, who finished tied for fifth with China's Zhang Lian-wei.

The last week of June the Canadian Tour moved to Calgary, but the results were much the same. Jaime Omar Gomez, Chris Anderson and J.J. West, all U.S. residents, started the final round in the first, second and third spots at the Telus Calgary Open. Although they played 36 holes on Sunday, the only change in the Gomez, Anderson, West finish was that Jim Rutledge of Victoria fired 68 to move into a tie for third place with West.

Finally, on July 7, Stewart came though with a 71 in the final round of the Telus Edmonton Open to hang onto a one-shot lead over South African Alan McLean. It was the 45-year-old Stewart's first Canadian Tour win, and he summed up his drought by saying, "It's been the story of my career. When the heat comes on, the putter melts."

With the U.S. stranglehold finally broken, Aaron Oberholser returned the Americans to victory with a win in the Ontario Open Heritage Classic, but Stewart came back with another win in the Canadian Masters.

Things got back to normal in August as Americans Scott Peterson, Jeff Bloom and Derek Gilchrist finished one, two, three in the Samsung Canadian PGA Championship, while Oberholser won again in the Eagle Creek Classic. Duke won again as well, picking up his second win at the Bayer Championship for what turned out to be a complete romp of the Canadian Tour by U.S. players. Only Mike Weir's play in the U.S. PGA Championship and the Air Canada Championship gave golf fans from Canada something to cheer about.

South American Tour

It is with no small sense of irony that the 1999 Rookie of the Year on the U.S. PGA Tour, Carlos Franco, was one of the best players ever to come out of South America, and certainly the best golfer ever born in Paraguay. But it was equally ironic that the Player of the Year on the South American Tour, a man who posted two wins, one second and one eighth-place finish in five events, was an American who lived in Atlanta, Georgia.

Even though Scott Dunlap finished 77th on the PGA Tour money list for 1999, he failed to break through in his homeland. But Dunlap was known in other regions of the world. He had posted at least one win in South America and South Africa in the two seasons leading up to 1999. Even though he played 23 weeks on the PGA Tour and moved his permanent residence to Atlanta, he found time to return to his old stomping grounds where he won the Dimension Data Pro-Am in South Africa and the Peru Open and Argentina Open on the South American Tour.

It wasn't as if Dunlap played only a group of South Americans. In Buenos Aires he beat Ian Woosnam by one stroke, Franco and Eduardo Romero by five, Craig Stadler by eight, and Padraig Harrington by 12. In Peru Dunlap shot 64 in the opening round and lapped the field, closing with a 273 total. In the Torneo de Maestros Telefonica, Dunlap tied for second with Ryder Cup veteran Costantino Rocca of Italy and Fabian Montovia, but Dunlap's 67-67 weekend was the best in the field, coming only four shots shy of catching Angel Cabrera, who won with a 271 total.

In his only other South American start, Dunlap overcame an opening 75 in the Litoral Open to shoot three consecutive 69s for a share of ninth place. Cesar Monasterio won the Litoral Open, played at the Rosario Golf Club in Argentina, with a 275 total, and in the only other South American event Dunlap missed, Carlos Larrain won in the TPG Open de Venezuela.

It was because of these strong finishes and quality play that Dunlap finished 77th on the World Money List, ahead of such notables as Bernhard Langer, Jean Van de Velde, Brad Faxon, Masashi Ozaki and Paul Azinger.

11. European Tours

When Colin Montgomerie won the PGA European Tour's Order of Merit three times in a row, it was considered outstanding, and when he won it a fourth consecutive time, it was heralded as a magnificent achievement. The fifth and sixth times exhausted all superlatives, and when Montgomerie locked up his seventh consecutive Order of Merit title in the shadow of Gibraltar on the Mediterranean Coast, a record was set that could go unchallenged for decades.

"Now that the last few months are over, I can relate to what Tiger Woods has achieved," Montgomerie said to the media at the WGC American Express Championship at Valderrama after his seventh title became official. "It's getting tougher, and the standard is improving all the time. And whether or not it's going to happen eight times or not, I'll be trying."

After starting the season in Dubai with a tie for fifth place, Montgomerie headed to the United States where he had an abysmal stretch, losing to Craig Stadler in the first round of the WGC Andersen Consulting Match Play Championship. He finished tied for 38th in the Honda Classic, tied for 60th in the Bay Hill Invitational, tied for 23rd in The Players Championship, tied for 61st in the BellSouth Classic, tied for 11th at the Masters and tied for 60th in the MCI Classic.

While Montgomerie was struggling, journeymen were leaving their marks on the European circuit. David Howell won in Dubai, and Paul Lawrie won the following week at the Qatar Masters. Van Phillips picked up the win in the Algarve Portuguese Open, and Miguel Angel Jimenez won the Turespana Masters near his home in the Andalusia region of Spain. Jean Francois Remesy, Jarmo Sandelin, Dean Robertson and Retief Goosen all won in Europe before Montgomerie returned to form.

Once Montgomerie started winning, there was no stopping him. He walked away with the Benson and Hedges International Open, a victory that prompted Jose Maria Olazabal to say, "It looks like we are just average workers and he's the one who is gifted. He doesn't practice much — he doesn't need much practice — and he keeps hitting the ball straight down the fairway and straight onto the green and scoring well. What can you say?"

Even though Montgomerie put on a ball-striking clinic that week in England, he was still not satisfied with his putting, so much so that he remained on the practice green well after dark. "While I know that someone who hits as many greens as I do cannot possibly hole as many putts as someone who is chipping a lot, I still feel my putting could be better," he said.

Throughout the rest of the year, his putting did get better. Two weeks after winning his first event of the year, Montgomerie won again in the Volvo PGA Championship, becoming Europe's first multiple winner of the year.

That distinction was short-lived. As Montgomerie was once again traveling to America in preparation for the U.S. Open, Sandelin picked up his second win of the year at the German Open. Then upstart rookie Sergio Garcia made his presence known with a victory in the Murphy's Irish Open. After finishing as low amateur in the Masters and making his American professional debut with a tie for third place in the GTE Byron Nelson Classic,

Garcia had assumed most of the spotlight, which suited Montgomerie just fine. The veteran had nothing but praise for the young Spaniard, saying, "He would have been on my Ryder Cup team from the beginning."

One week after Garcia captured the headlines, Montgomerie was back to his winning ways, picking up his third win at the Standard Life Loch Lomond only a few miles from his boyhood home. "This is very special for me," Montgomerie said, after coming from three strokes back on the final day to pass six players. "The support I had today was unbelievable. I couldn't be going into an Open feeling better about my golf."

Indeed, Montgomerie held the course record at Carnoustie, site of the British Open Championship, and he was a favorite to capture his first major title. Unfortunately, John Philp, the course superintendent, created a test unlike any other major championship. "Golf has gone soft," Philp said, but there was no softness under the sun in Angus, Scotland, as Montgomerie shot 12-over-par 296 in the Open to finish tied for 15th.

Six-over-par 290 won the British Open. Three players carded that total: Lawrie, Justin Leonard and Jean Van de Velde. Lawrie won the playoff with a deft four-iron shot to the 18th green that set up a birdie, but it was Van de Velde who made history during the final round — a history he would likely prefer to erase. Leading by three standing on the 72nd tee, Van de Velde seemed so certain to win the championship that the engraver was ready to stencil his name on the claret jug.

Van de Velde proceeded to engage in one of the most profound brain lapses in golf history. He blew his tee shot on the 18th to the right, barely avoiding the Barry Burn. ABC announcer Curtis Strange said Van de Velde needed to thank his lucky stars, pitch back to the fairway, chip onto the green, take a bogey and hoist the Open trophy. Van de Velde wasn't listening. From his position on the right side of the 18th fairway he took out a three iron and went for the green. The ball bounced off the grandstands and into the rough. From there Van de Velde chunked a pitch into the burn, prompting an image of the Frenchman that will be etched in the memories of golf fans. With the championship slipping away, Van de Velde took off his shoes, rolled up his pants and waded into the Barry Burn to have a look at his ball as rain drops began to pelt the area. He took a penalty drop and made a triple bogey on the 18th to tie Lawrie and Leonard.

After the British Open, things settled back to normal on the PGA European Tour with Lee Westwood, who had given Montgomerie a run for Order of Merit honors in 1998, winning two in a row at the TNT Dutch Open and the Smurfit European Open to challenge again. Montgomerie answered with victories at the Volvo Scandinavian Masters and BMW International Open to all but lock up the Order of Merit.

Not so fast, Westwood said. A win at the Canon European Masters moved Westwood within striking distance as players entered the final stretch of the year. Garcia also joined the fray, winning for a second time at the Linde German Masters, one week after returning from the Ryder Cup. That moved Garcia within mathematical range of Montgomerie.

The possibility continued until the final week of the year at Valderrama. If either Garcia or Westwood had won the big purse, Montgomerie would have been toppled, but Woods won and Montgomerie had his seventh title.

PGA European Tour

Alfred Dunhill South African PGA—R3,816,000
Winner: Ernie Els
See African Tours chapter.

Mercedes-Benz - Vodacom South African Open—R5,500,000
Winner: David Frost
See African Tours chapter.

Heineken Classic—A$1,500,000
Winner: Jarrod Moseley
See Australasian Tour chapter.

Benson and Hedges Malaysian Open—US$750,000
Winner: Gerry Norquist
See Asia/Japan Tours chapter.

Dubai Desert Classic—€1,190,000
Winner: David Howell

Although only 22 years old, Englishman David Howell entered the 1999 PGA European Tour season with one goal. "I'd like to break into the top 15 on the Order of Merit this season so I can play in next year's majors," he said. "That's a realistic goal the way I've been improving since I joined the tour (three seasons ago). If any wins come along, great."

Howell had indeed improved since joining the tour at age 19, finishing 52nd in his first year as a professional, and steadily moving up to 47th his second season and 32nd in his third. A victory in November of 1998 at the MasterCard PGA Championship in Australia proved to the young Howell that he was ready to move to the next level. But nothing could prepare him for the four-stoke victory he would capture over Lee Westwood in the Dubai Desert Classic in the United Arab Emirates.

"It feels wonderful," Howell said after cruising in with a final round of 67 to complete a 13-under-par 275 performance. "I got a bit lucky at the start. Three times in the first four holes I found the light rough rather than the really heavy stuff. That saved me at least three shots, but from then on I really felt good."

Howell began the final day tied with Wayne Riley at 208, and even though Riley made three consecutive birdies starting at the fifth, he could not dislodge Howell atop the leaderboard. Howell birdied the first and fourth holes, then eagled the fifth to move ahead to stay. Riley dropped from contention as the day progressed, finishing with 74 to tie for fifth place with Colin Montgomerie and Edward Fryatt at 282.

Over the final nine, the only player Howell needed to watch was fellow Englishman Westwood, who returned to form after seven worldwide victories in 1998. Westwood started the day four strokes off Howell's lead, but he matched the winner's final-round 67 to jump past Riley, Montgomerie, Fryatt, Miguel Angel Jimenez and Ryder Cup captain Mark James to finish alone in second place at 279.

"I never looked at a board until the 14th," Howell said. "At that point I was five clear of Lee so I told myself not to mess up now. To be honest, though, I wasn't too worried. All I had to do was keep playing the way I had to that point." When the final putt fell on the 18th, Howell's margin had dropped to four shots, but the victory was his.

Westwood found Howell's performance anything but surprising. "It was a fantastic performance," Westwood said. "I could see it coming, too. When you watch him on the range you can see he has that little bit extra. Last November he went to Japan for the first time and did well. That gave him a clue that he could compete at the highest level. Then, of course, he won the next week in Australia. This could be the first of many."

James and Paul McGinley finished tied for third at 280 with McGinley equaling Howell and Westwood with a final-round 67, while James followed an opening 73 with three consecutive rounds of 69.

Qatar Masters—€870,000
Winner: Paul Lawrie

For Scotland's Paul Lawrie, the first 72-hole win on the PGA European Tour was tougher than his seven-shot margin of victory would seem. It started with a sleepless night of watching cricket and bad movies on television after carrying a five-stroke lead back to his hotel on Saturday evening. Then he started the final round with two scrambling pars and a bogey on the third hole.

No one made a move on Lawrie, however, and when his pitch shot at the par-five fourth stopped two feet from the hole, setting up a birdie, Lawrie found he could breathe a little easier. His only other win came at the rain-shortened 1996 Catalan Open, and Lawrie thought he had something to prove.

"I'd known that a lot of people didn't really consider me a winner because my Catalan Open title was won over two rounds," he said. "I considered it a win, but I did have to prove something to the others."

Four consecutive birdies starting at the eighth hole and a closing round of 68 propelled Lawrie to a 20-under-par 268 and a seven-shot margin over Denmark's Soren Kjeldsen and Phillip Price of Wales. While Kjeldsen and Price both matched Lawrie's final-round 68, they started the final day at 207. Frenchman Jean Van de Velde was Lawrie's closest contender when Sunday's round began, but a one-over-par 73 dropped Van de Velde to 10-under-par 278 and into a tie for fifth place with Christopher Hanell and Raymond Russell. Russell had maneuvered himself into second place with one hole to play, but a triple-bogey eight on the final hole cost Russell over €44,000 and kept Scotsmen from finishing first and second.

For Lawrie, the victory erased any doubts about his ability. "This is obviously better than winning over 36 holes," he said. "I was in the zone as far as my attitude was concerned and I was determined not to let it go. The four birdies around the turn left me feeling it was all done and dusted then. I had a very scrappy start and remembered that only six weeks ago I'd taken a 10 on the ninth hole of a Scottish Alliance tournament. I knew it could happen again."

Lawrie's 268 was his best four-round score as a professional and his €143,196 was the largest check he had ever made. "I've proven I can win," he said. "That is special."

Algarve Portuguese Open—€560,000
Winner: Van Phillips

With some of Europe's top players competing in Florida, many lesser-known talents seized the opportunity by traveling to Penina, Portugal, for the Algarve Portuguese Open. By the early moments of the final round it became clear that one of two Englishmen would have his first PGA European Tour victory.

Tied for the lead at eight-under-par 208 with 18 holes to play, the tournament became a two-man race between Van Phillips and ironman John Bickerton, who was playing in his 29th consecutive event. Neither had ever won and neither seemed ready to back off as the final day progressed.

The 29-year-old Bickerton took an early lead and held a two-shot advantage over 26-year-old Phillips through 14 holes. Phillips came back with a birdie at the 15th, and Bickerton's lead remained only one shot with two holes to play.

The 17th hole, a 459-yard par-four, hadn't set up well for Bickerton all week and he had bogeyed the hole every time. Sunday was no exception. An errant tee shot followed by an even more wayward approach led Bickerton to another bogey, and when Phillips saved par, the two were tied.

On the 18th, Bickerton regained the advantage, splitting the middle of the fairway with his tee shot while Phillips' ball landed in an awkward lie in the left rough, impeded by a cart path and behind a large tree. When Bickerton found the middle of the green with his second shot, Phillips had no choice but to try to curve his ball around the tree. In improbable fashion, he did just that. Phillips' four-iron shot jumped from the rough and spun 30 yards to the right around the tree, stopping on the green just outside of Bickerton's ball. Both players made birdies and ended regulation tied at 12-under-par 276.

The advantage swung to Phillips after his miraculous recovery shot, in part because he was able to force a playoff, and secondly because the first playoff hole was the 17th, the dreaded par-four that had given Bickerton so much trouble throughout the week. This time, however, both players found the center of the fairway, but only Phillips hit the green. Bickerton found a bunker with his approach and, once again, he bogeyed the hole.

"So near and yet so far," Bickerton said. "I thought I had done all that work on the last, but then Van pulled out that great shot. Going back to 17 was tough. It's disappointing to be beaten after my last two rounds, but if I go on playing like this, hopefully I'll go one better soon."

Phillips, who was once known more for his attire (he wore a tie on the course as part of a contract) than for his play, was overcome with emotion after his win. "I always felt I had the temperament to win, but I thought it was never going to happen," he said. "Now I just feel relieved that I've finally done it."

While Phillips and Bickerton were the only two players contending for the title on the final nine, Robert Karlsson, Alexander Cejka and Santiago Luna all had good final rounds to finish in a tie for third at 279. Karlsson's 67 equaled the low round of the day. Massimo Scarpa, who started the final round tied for the lead at eight-under 208 with Phillips and Bickerton, closed with 74 to finish in a seven-way tie for ninth at 282.

Turespana Masters - Open Andalucia—€500,000
Winner: Miguel Angel Jimenez

Miguel Angel Jimenez would certainly agree with the adage that there's no place like home. For the second year in a row, the 35-year-old Spaniard made the 10-minute drive from his home in Malaga to Parador Malaga del Golf and captured the Turespana Masters - Open Andalucia in decisive fashion. This year the win was doubly sweet. While shooting 62 in the third round to open a five-stroke lead, Jimenez received an invitation in the mail from Augusta National Golf Club. While in the process of picking up his fifth career title, Jimenez couldn't have been more pleased at the opportunity to travel to Augusta for the Masters Tournament.

"My game is in great shape for the Masters and for the rest of the year," he said after shooting 264 for a four-stroke victory over Englishman Steve Webster. Frenchman Raphael Jacquelin finished third at 269.

"It was great to win here in front of my friends and family," said Jimenez. "It's been a great week with a lot of good things happening. This was my week."

After a slow start, it certainly seemed to be Jimenez's week. His opening 69 followed by a 66 left him two shots back of Fredrik Lindgren at the halfway mark, but the 10-under-par 62 on Saturday gave Jimenez a commanding five-shot lead over Webster, Marc Ferry, Ignacio Garrido and Per-Ulrik Johansson.

That lead almost evaporated, however. After extending his advantage to seven shots in the first six holes, Jimenez had his fade double-cross him at the seventh tee, and his drive landed out of bounds. A double bogey dropped the lead to five, and a pulled approach shot at the ninth led to a bogey and a whittling away of the lead to four. Meanwhile Webster was in the process of making seven birdies through 14 holes in the final round, thus cutting Jimenez's lead to only one shot.

But fortune smiled on Malaga's native son. In a greenside bunker on the 422-yard, par-four 10th, Jimenez blasted out and his ball found the hole for an unlikely birdie. He missed the 11th green and made a good save for par to retain his advantage, then sealed his fate with another chip-in — this time for eagle — at the par-five 14th. With a four-shot edge regained, Jimenez cruised home to victory.

Ferry finished alone in fourth place after closing with 69 for a total of 271, while second-round leader Lindgren made up for an abysmal 75 on Saturday by shooting the day's low score (64) on Sunday to tie Alexander Cejka and Per-Ulrik Johansson for fifth at 272.

Madeira Island Open—€490,000
Winner: Pedro Linhart

Despite thick fog and persistent rain that softened and lengthened the Santo de Serra Golf Club in Mochiko, Portugal, 36-year-old Pedro Linhart held on by birdieing the 17th hole and parring the 18th to capture his first victory by one shot in the Madeira Island Open. Linhart, who struggled through the qualifying tournament after spending several seasons bouncing through Florida mini-tours and supporting his family as an assistant professional at a private club in New Jersey, took the lead in the second round with 64 to get to 134 and held on, despite a spectacular final-round charge by Ryder Cup captain Mark James, who shot 67 for an 11-under-par 277 total, one more than Linhart's total.

"I have to keep playing well every week if I want to get an exemption into the British Open — and I can't afford to retire," James said after his second-place finish. "I'm just pleased to have done well as a player. I'm a full-time player, not just a Ryder Cup captain. I know some have said the captain's game can be affected by the captaincy, but I think of other things when I am on the golf course. My concentration has been very good."

In fact, of all the contenders, James had the best weekend, shooting 69 and 67 in the final two days to come from five shots back at the midway point to within a single stroke of victory. But Linhart held on with consistent weekend rounds of 71-71, including a solid par from the fairway on the last hole. "It was a struggle, but I came through at the end," the winner said.

After giving up his assistant pro job and taking another stab at a playing career, Linhart had a number of close calls, including a second-place finish in the 1998 French Open. But each of the previous times Linhart edged to the top of the leaderboard he made untimely mistakes that kept him away from victory.

Not on the Portuguese coast, however. After a shaky start of three birdies and three bogeys in the first nine holes, Linhart settled down and found all the fairways and greens in the final nine.

"My aim now is to qualify for the Volvo Masters at the end of the season," Linhart said.

A few other contenders had different goals, not the least of which was qualifying for James' 1999 Ryder Cup team that would travel to Brookline, Massachusetts, in September. David Howell finished with 69 for a 279 total and third place. Howell moved into seventh place in the Ryder Cup standings, one spot ahead of Scotland's Andrew Coltart who slipped into eighth in the standings with a tie for fourth. "It means a great deal, of course," Coltart said of his Ryder Cup standing. "But there are a lot of tournaments left."

Estoril Open—€560,000
Winner: Jean Francois Remesy

Players arriving at the 6,879-yard Penha Longa Golf Club course outside Lisbon, Portugal, for the Estoril Open were greeted by winds so strong they blew the roofs and windshields off golf carts. Before the first tee shot was struck it became apparent that a grinder would win this test. The 36-hole cut fell at five-over-par 149, the highest of the year on the PGA European Tour.

When Frenchman Jean Francois Remesy fought his way into the lead after two rounds by shooting 72 and 69, no one seemed surprised even though Remesy had not only never won on the tour, he had never managed to finish high enough on the Order of Merit to keep his card. Every year of his 12-year career, Remesy had returned to the qualifying tournament where he played his way back onto the circuit for another season. He had only played in one event in 1999 before arriving in Portugal, and his 178th place on the Order of Merit was typical of the way Remesy's career had gone.

But Remesy was a grinder, and after appearing to fail the test on Saturday when he shot a third-round 77 to fall four strokes behind Jose Rivero, he knew he had a victory in him. He also felt no pressure in the final round, as he had everything to gain and nothing to lose. After playing the first 16 holes in six under par, Remesy found himself tied for the lead with Andrew Coltart, a strong player who was contending for a Ryder Cup berth. In years past Remesy might have folded under the two-hole pressure of a possible win and the prospect of an exemption through the 2001 season. Not this time, however. One week prior to arriving in Lisbon, Remesy had won the French PGA Championship at Chantilly, an unofficial event at one of Europe's best courses, so his confidence was high and his resolve hardened.

It didn't hurt that Coltart hit his tee shot on the 204-yard, par-three 17th into an impossible lie in the greenside bunker from where he took four shots to get down for a double bogey. Remesy had the breathing room he needed to cruise home with a 68, a two-shot margin of victory and the first exempt classification of his career.

Coltart's closing 69 left him tied for second at 288 with David Carter, who followed a horrendous 79 on Saturday with a final round of 67, and Massimo Florioli, who never had a round in the 60s, but played the weekend three under par.

Peugeot Open de Espana—€840,000
Winner: Jarmo Sandelin

If there is one Swedish golfer who can make Jesper Parnevik look like a conservative fashion plate, it's 31-year-old Jarmo Sandelin, who regularly wears Italian designer belts and crocodile cowboy boots with spikes in the soles. As for his golf game, Sandelin's consistency and maturity were at their peak when he teed off at the El Prat Golf Club in Barcelona, Spain.

"Four years ago I was a jungle man," Sandelin said. "I was like 'go for it' all the time. Now I try to control myself and stay focused. I've always been a slow learner, but I'm starting to feel like I'm getting to where I want to be in the game."

That maturation, while still not evident in Sandelin's attire, was clearly evident in the numbers he posted. Three consecutive rounds of 66 moved Sandelin up from being one shot out of the lead after the first day to being tied for the lead after the second, to carrying a three-stroke lead into the final round. A fourth 66 would have given Sandelin a seven-shot margin of victory. His 69, however, worked just fine, and Sandelin walked away with a 21-under-par 267 total and a four-shot victory over Miguel Angel Jimenez.

The Peugeot Open de Espana was Sandelin's third PGA European Tour victory, and he dedicated the win to his mother, Sinikka, who passed away two months earlier. "I want to dedicate this one, and the next one, and the one after that," Sandelin said. Then he returned his focus to golf, saying, "The Ryder Cup is my next target. If I keep my golf on this level, I will be there."

For the first few rounds Sandelin's name seemed lost on a crowded leaderboard. His opening 66 left him just one shot back, but there were five players ahead of him including Ignacio Garrido, Anthony Wall and Jamie Spence, all experienced winners.

Sandelin jumped to the top of the pack on Friday with his second 66, but he wasn't alone. Scotland's Paul Lawrie also carded two rounds of 66 for a 132 total and a tie for the lead with Sandelin. Spence lurked one shot back after shooting 68 on Friday, and Paul McGinley shot 68 to go with his opening 67 to stay within striking distance at 135.

By the time Sandelin signed his card for a third straight 66 for a three-day total of 198, his lead was three strokes. McGinley kept improving, adding 66 of his own to move to 201.

Sandelin was on his way to shooting another 66 on Sunday, but some loose play on the final holes, including a missed three-foot putt on the 18th, forced the Swede to settle for 69 and the four-shot victory over McGinley, who could manage no better than a final-round 70, and the Spaniards, Jimenez and Garrido, all of whom finished at 271.

Spence made something of a charge Sunday, but a hooked tee shot on the par-five 12th led to a double bogey after the ball rolled under a car that wasn't supposed to be parked near the course. Even though he couldn't find his ball, Spence believed he was entitled to a free drop. Referee John Paramore disagreed and Spence had to return to the tee. His final-round 69 left him tied for fifth at 272 with Juan Carlos Aguero.

Fiat and Fila Italian Open—€1,000,000
Winner: Dean Robertson

A week before arriving at Circolo Golf Club in Turin for the Fiat and Fila Italian Open, four-year winless Scot Dean Robertson told a friend he was ready to win as a professional. "It's coming," Robertson said. "I can feel it. Just you watch me." This was a remarkable prediction considering Robertson's track record. The closest he had come to victory was in the 1998 Volvo PGA Championship, where he led with five holes to play, but fell back to Colin Montgomerie's charge and ended up tied for fifth. Robertson's 1999 season had gone little better. In 11 starts before arriving in Italy he missed eight cuts. Still, Robertson felt his game was on track and winning was only a matter of time and patience.

"I told some friends that despite my record this year, I'd never hit the ball as well. I said at the odds, which were over 100 to 1, I was worth a bet. I hope they did it."

Anyone fortunate to take Robertson would have been handsomely rewarded as the 28-year-old from Paisley came from eight strokes behind after the first round to shoot consistently stellar rounds of 65, 68 and 68 for a 17-under-par 271 total to win by one shot over Padraig Harrington.

It was nip-and-tuck throughout the round with Harrington, who led Robertson by one stroke after the third round, fell back in the final round with a bogey at the 405-yard, par-four fourth, then regained a share of the lead before bogeying the 16th and 17th, leaving the door open for Robertson. Unfortunately, Robertson had difficulty closing. While Harrington was making his second consecutive bogey, Robertson three-putted the 17th for bogey, blowing his chance to take a three-shot lead into the final hole. He quickly rectified that situation by hitting the 18th green in regulation and lagging his first putt to within 18 inches.

Harrington wasn't finished putting on the pressure. He rammed home a 15-foot birdie putt, moving to within one and forcing Robertson to make the short putt. Up to the task, Robertson told his caddie, "My legs have gone, but my mind's on the job."

"My legs were shaky the last few holes, but I held my nerve," Robertson said. "It's difficult to control adrenaline, but today I went with it and told myself not to get stage fright and that it was natural." Then he joked about his record, saying, "Missing so many cuts this year did at least give me more time for practice."

"Dean played great and thoroughly deserved to win," Harrington said. "Apart from the 17th, he didn't put a foot wrong all day."

The final day's best performance went to Phillip Price who started the day eight shots off the pace before blistering the 6,954-yard layout in 63 strokes to finish tied for third with Russell Claydon and Gary Evans. The day's biggest surprise came when Seve Ballesteros temporarily moved onto the leaderboard after a first-nine 31 on Sunday put him in fifth place. It would have taken a second-nine 30 for Ballesteros to have contended, but his 67 still gave him his best finish of the year, sole possession of 17th place.

Novotel Perrier Open de France—€850,000
Winner: Retief Goosen

Despite three PGA European Tour titles and a game that many would love to possess, 30-year-old South African Retief Goosen felt his career had gone through its share of ups and downs, with the lowest point coming in January, when Goosen broke his arm in a skiing accident.

"My confidence was very low after the broken arm, and I felt my game needed a lot of work on the mental side," Goosen said. He consulted sports psychologist Joss Vantisphout, and began a program of mental exercises that improved his outlook on the game. "He has got me thinking in a much more positive way and getting my mind back on track. I owe him a lot," Goosen said.

That positive outlook was certainly on display in Bordeaux, France, when Goosen defeated Greg Turner in a two-hole playoff to capture his second Novotel Perrier Open de France title in three years. The victory did not come easily. Tied at 202 with Turner and Marc Farry as they entered the final round, Goosen got off to a fast start while Ferry faltered en route to a closing 75. Goosen's birdie at the 12th, while Turner was in the process of bogeying the 13th, gave Goosen what appeared to be a comfortable three-shot margin with six holes to play.

Then Turner made a charge. He birdied the 14th, 15th and 16th holes while Goosen made a string of pars on the 13th through 15th. When Goosen made bogey at the 16th, his lead had evaporated. He and Turner were tied.

"That bogey at 16 was a costly two-shot swing," Goosen said. "When I got ahead with four holes to play I thought I could play even par and win, but I kept my composure."

Despite a see-saw performance, Goosen and Turner both finished the day with scores of 70 for 12-under-par 272 totals. In the playoff, Goosen found the mental toughness he and Dr. Vantisphout had been working on. He saved par from bunkers on both extra holes. The second sand-save was good enough for the win, as Turner hit a poor chip shot and missed his 10-foot par effort.

"With two people in the playoff, unfortunately someone has to come in second," Turner said. "I was out of the tournament with six holes to play but got back into it with three birdies. Then in the playoff I got a little too aggressive and came up one putt short."

Goosen saw the victory as a career milestone. "This victory means a lot more to me than the first (French title)," he said. "In 1997 I was five shots ahead playing the last hole, so there wasn't much pressure. This time I had to hold myself together and stay focused. I feel more confident now that I know I can perform under pressure. I feel I've turned the corner."

Santiago Luna and Jose Coceres finished tied for third at 275, while Ian Woosnam had his best finish of the season, carding 276 to tie Eamonn Darcy and Jorge Berendt for fifth place.

Benson and Hedges International Open—€1,120,000
Winner: Colin Montgomerie

Even though he held a one-stroke lead at 205 after three rounds of the Benson and Hedges International Open, Colin Montgomerie was the last person seen on the practice putting green that afternoon. Had Monty made half the 15-foot putts he missed in the first three rounds, the tournament would have been a rout. He hit all but three fairways in the first three rounds, and missed only three out of 54 greens. Still, Montgomerie had only managed scores of 68, 66 and a particularly frustrating 71 for a one-shot edge over Jose Maria Olazabal.

"While I know that someone who hits as many greens as I do cannot possibly hole as many putts as someone who is chipping a lot, I still feel my putting could be better," Montgomerie said. "I'm going to have to work on that before the U.S. Open."

Twelve players started the final round within three shots of Montgomerie's lead including Per-Ulrik Johansson and Bernhard Langer. Nick Faldo also made a brief appearance on the leaderboard, but none seemed to be able to mount a charge. That is not to say the leaders weren't threatened. England's Jeremy Robinson, a 33-year-old former Walker Cup player who was a late entry into the event, took advantage of morning conditions and fired a course-record 64 to get to 277 before the leaders teed off.

Half an hour later, it didn't matter. Montgomerie continued on Sunday as he had throughout the week. His consistent game had Olazabal saying, "It looks like we are just average workers and he's the one who is gifted. He doesn't practice much — he doesn't need much practice — and he keeps hitting the ball straight down the fairway and straight onto the green and scoring well. What can you say?"

You could say "Congratulations," which is exactly what Olazabal and everyone else in the field eventually said to Montgomerie as the Scot played bogey-free golf en route to his second 68 of the week, a 15-under-par 273 total, and a three-stroke victory over Angel Cabrera. Olazabal missed almost as many fairways as Monty hit, but, as usual, his iron play was stellar. This time, however, his usually deft short game abandoned him, and the Spaniard didn't make a birdie until the 17th hole while taking on three bogeys for a final-round 74. His 280 total left him tied for 16th with Ian Woosnam, Padraig Harrington and Jonathan Lomas.

The only one who made a contest of it was Cabrera, who got to 13 under par before finishing with a bogey. Meanwhile, Montgomerie two-putted for birdie at the 17th.

"The second shot into 17 was the clincher," Monty said. "I had 252 yards over the water off a downhill lie and had to hit it solid to get it over. I did, too. To be honest, it was a gutsy shot in the conditions and given the situation I was in. I didn't want to have to make a four at the last to win."

Deutsche Bank-SAP Open TPC of Europe—€1,680,000
Winner: Tiger Woods

Tiger Woods showed the world that his game was "better than it was in 1997" while winning the Deutsche Bank-SAP Open TPC of Europe.

"My swing is better than it ever has been," Woods said. "The only thing I can say about 1997 is that I made more putts from 30 to 40 feet. I wasn't as good a ball-striker as I am now. I couldn't control my ball trajectory as well as I can now."

There wasn't much Woods couldn't control at the 7,236-yard St. Leon Rot course in Heidelberg, Germany. After an opening 69 that placed him three shots off the first-round lead set by Ernie Els and Gary Orr, Woods played some of the most consistent golf of his career. His second-round 68 moved him into a two-shot lead at 137 over Els, Jesper Parnevik and Jarmo Sandelin. A 30-foot birdie putt on the 18th hole in the third round for another 68 gave Woods a three-shot margin over a charging Peter Baker and Brian Davis, both of whom shot 66s. It was as close as anyone would come.

After the first hole of the final round, Woods had a four-shot lead, after four holes the lead was five, and at the turn, despite good play from Retief Goosen and Nick Price, Woods led by four. A bogey-free third consecutive 68 for a four-day total of 273, 15 under par, was good for a three-stroke victory over Goosen, and a four-shot margin over Price. Baker closed with 71 for a 279 and sole possession of fourth place.

Fifth place was shared by Davis and Els, who had a 70-71 finish after a final-round 80 at the Masters and a five-week respite in which he spent 10 days in Orlando, 10 days in Bermuda and 20 days in his new home at the Wentworth Club near London. "If Montgomerie can take three weeks off and win (at the Benson and Hedges International), why can't I do the same after five weeks," Els asked.

Els didn't win, but neither did Montgomerie, who shot 285 and finished tied for 20th with Marc Ferry and Sergio Garcia. Garcia continued his good play, taking 211 into the final round, then having a closing 74 as his only blemish.

In the end it didn't matter. Woods' victory was as impressive as any since his 1997 Masters win. Goosen finished fast and furious, ending with four birdies in the last six holes, while Price, who barely made the cut after opening rounds of 71 and 76, shot course-record 65s in the last two rounds. Price simply ran out of holes, and ran into a new, and obviously improved, Tiger Woods.

Volvo PGA Championship—€1,820,000
Winner: Colin Montgomerie

Even though Colin Montgomerie was five strokes out of the lead after the second round of the Volvo PGA Championship, the rest of the field saw something unsettling about Montgomerie's play and his position on the leaderboard. Perhaps it was the noticeable absence of bogeys or the radar-like precision with which Monty attacked the Wentworth Club's West Course outside London, but whatever they saw, they were understandably concerned. Montgomerie had posted 139 for the two days, and trailed Darren Clarke by five strokes and Ernie Els by four.

"Faldo used to be the man you would least like to see in your rearview mirror," Montgomerie said. "Now I'd like to think I'm that man, at least in Europe."

Few doubted that the six-time Order of Merit winner was, indeed, the most watched and most feared presence on the PGA European Tour, but with names like Clarke, Els, Bernhard Langer, Jose Maria Olazabal and Mark James all ahead of Montgomerie after the second round, and up-and-coming winners like Retief Goosen and Stephen Leaney tied with or within one shot of Monty going into the weekend, Europe's most prestigious event seemed to be headed toward a showdown that might or might not include its best player.

But the prognosticators were right. In a bogey-free performance that included two eagles and one birdie, Montgomerie picked the 7,006-yard layout apart en route to 67 and a 206 total. He vaulted to the top of the leaderboard, sharing the perch with Goosen, who followed rounds of 67 and 69 with a third-round 70, and two clear of Langer and Mark McNulty.

"Monty is a great player," Mark James said. "He's very long, very straight and he putts better than he thinks."

Montgomerie proved all the accolades true during Monday's final round when he played another round without a bogey. This time, he added six birdies and an eagle to his card, leaving him with a round of 64 and a tournament-record-equaling 270 total, 18 under par.

"I knew I was striking the ball well and that gave me a lot of confidence," Montgomerie said. "Today has to be the best ball-striking round of my career. I'm very proud of what I've just achieved. It's very satisfying."

James pulled out an impressive final round of his own, finishing with 66 to capture second place at 275, one shot better than third-place finisher Paul Eales, but not even within shouting distance of Montgomerie.

"Colin is just great at the moment," said Els, who finished tied for fourth at 277. "He just lapped the field. The way he is playing now he will probably win a major."

Compass Group English Open—€1,000,000
Winner: Darren Clarke

With five consecutive birdies in both the second and third rounds and a commanding five-shot lead with 18 holes to play, Darren Clarke appeared unstoppable at Hanbury Manor as he teed off in the final pairing of the Compass Group English Open. Even Colin Montgomerie, who had dominated the PGA European Tour throughout the summer, was impressed by Clarke's play. Monty started the final round tied for second with Andrew Coltart. The two men would remain tied after shooting final rounds of 70, but they would drop from second to fifth place as Clarke made the victory look much easier than the two-shot margin over England's John Bickerton would indicate.

"I knew that if I kept playing the way I was, then it didn't matter who else was on the leaderboard," Clarke said. "I was only concerned with my own game."

Clarke opened with 68 and immediately fielded questions about the three missed cuts he had accumulated in the 1999 season, the seven-week vacation he took in the winter ("too long in retrospect," he admitted), and his new coach, Butch Harmon. The only thing Clarke wasn't questioned about was that he had given up smoking and lost weight in the previous weeks.

He gave Harmon much of the credit for his good play, which included rounds of 65 and 67 on Friday and Saturday, with a final round of 68 bringing the total to 20-under-par 268. "He said I'd lost my rhythm," Clarke said of Harmon's message. "He suggested I slow my swing down a bit and focus on a smooth takeaway."

The suggestions obviously worked. Only Bickerton, who closed with an impressive 65 after a 90-minute rain delay on Sunday, mounted anything resembling a charge. But even he ran out of holes, as Clarke picked up his fifth European title. David Carter and Stephen Leaney finished tied for third at 274 after both shot final rounds of 69.

German Open—€1,000,000
Winner: Jarmo Sandelin

Sweden's eccentric Jarmo Sandelin, who raised more than a few eyebrows when he wore a see-through mesh golf shirt, arrived at the Berlin Sporting Club with only one thing on his mind: a top-five finish and a secure spot on the European Ryder Cup team. His win in April in Spain and some quality finishes through the early summer had left Sandelin perched near the top 10, and a good finish at the German Open would certainly push him over the top. A victory would simply be added insurance that the 32-year-old would be seated on the Boston-bound Concorde in September.

Win is precisely what Sandelin did in 73 holes on the 7,082-yard, Nick Price-designed course. After an opening 67, which was overshadowed only by the stunning 62 fired by Gary Evans, Sandelin came back with 71 to inch close to the halfway lead of 138 held by Retief Goosen, who shot 69 and 64. On Saturday, Sandelin tied Goosen after Goosen shot 73 to move to 206 while Sandelin shot 68.

On Sunday, Sandelin jumped out with birdies on four of his first six holes. Goosen wouldn't go away, coming back with four birdies of his own to remain in a tie for the lead. Then on the 18th, Goosen had a chance to take his first solo lead of the day with a three-foot birdie putt, but when the ball slipped below the hole, Sandelin and Goosen found themselves tied at 14-under-par 274. Both had finished with 68s.

Sandelin made short work of the playoff with a four on the first extra hole to Goosen's five. The €166,660 first-place check moved him to third on the European Tour Order of Merit, but more important to Sandelin was the security of a lock on the Ryder Cup team. "I feel very lucky," Sandelin said. "The best part of this is the fact that all the hard work I have put into my golf is at last paying off."

Moroccan Open—€490,000
Winner: Miguel Angel Martin

With Colin Montgomerie, Lee Westwood and some other of Europe's best players away at the U.S. Open, it seemed the perfect week at the Moroccan Open for David Park, the leading money winner on the Challenge Tour, to make history by becoming the first player to ever win in his debut on the PGA European Tour. After a second-round 69 moved Park two shots ahead of Carlos Larrain, Park liked his chances. His third-round 68 kept Park atop the leaderboard, and when he held a two-shot lead over Miguel Angel Martin with three holes to play, Park began to rehearse his victory speech.

Unfortunately for Park, there were still lessons to be learned, and golf to be played, more golf, in fact, than anyone imagined. Park birdied the 16th but bogeyed the last two holes for an even-par 72 final round for a 12-under-par 276 total. Meanwhile, Martin birdied the last two holes for 68 to tie Park and force a playoff.

The two played the 457-yard, par-four 18th six times in an exhaustive playoff that Park lost by not winning when he had a five-foot putt on the fifth extra hole. On the sixth playoff hole, Park couldn't save par from a greenside bunker while Martin two-putted for his first victory since 1997. The playoff wasn't pretty. Both started with bogeys the first time through, then pars the second time, followed by bogeys the next three times.

Since winning in 1997, Martin had undergone two surgeries on an injured wrist that plagued him during the final months of that year and cost him a spot on the Ryder Cup team. "It has been tough to come back," he said. "But I'm beginning to see progress. This is a big boost for my confidence."

Park tried to put a good face on what could be described as a sad situation. "I had my chances," the Welshman said. "I didn't have any luck with the putter, but it has been fun. I've learned a lot. I'll be ready the next time I'm in that situation."

Klas Eriksson clawed his way back from an opening-round 75 to shoot three rounds in the 60s and finish alone in third place at 279, while Jorge Berendt shot 69 to finish tied for fourth with Eric Carlberg, who could only manage 75.

Compaq European Grand Prix—€910,000
Winner: David Park

One week after losing a six-hole playoff, David Park succeeded by winning in his second European professional start in the Compaq European Grand Prix at Slaley Hall in Newcastle, England. Once again, Park seemed in command from the early going. An opening 67 placed him two shots behind David Carter, then Park came back with 65 to take a two-shot lead. On Saturday, Park shot 70 and was tied for the lead with Carter, who followed his opening 65 with 69 and 68.

The final day didn't start out well for Park. He bogeyed four holes on the first nine and made only one birdie, handing the lead to Carter, who continued to make pars. On the second nine, Park came back with three more birdies to pull back to even par on the day, 14 under for the tournament, and tied with Carter coming to the final hole, the same position he had been in the previous week with Miguel Angel Martin.

This time the outcome would be different. Carter pulled his drive into the heavy rough on the lengthy 18th and was unable to reach the green with his second shot. From the middle of the fairway, Park showed maturity beyond his 25 years when he hit a long iron to the middle of the green, 35 feet from the hole. A two-putt par for 72 and a 274 total sealed the victory, and put Park in the history books, a week later than expected. Carter shot 73 for his 275 total and tied for second place with Retief Goosen, who finished well with 66.

Murphy's Irish Open—€1,400,000
Winner: Sergio Garcia

It came sooner than most imagined it would, but almost no one was surprised when Spanish sensation Sergio Garcia, the reigning British Amateur champion and low amateur at the 1999 Masters Tournament, fired a final-round, seven-under-par 64 in the Murphy's Irish Open to win his first PGA

European Tour event just 10 weeks into his professional career.

From the moment his name appeared on the leaderboard on Thursday, when he shot 69 to trail leader Craig Hainline by four strokes, the buzz at Druids Glen, one of Ireland's best parkland courses, was swirling around Garcia. Even after 68 on Friday left him five behind Hainline and Phillip Price, Garcia was still considered the man to watch.

Angel Cabrera moved into the lead with his second consecutive round of 66 to reach an 11-under-par 202 total, but that was only two better than Jarrod Moseley, who shot 66, 69 and 69, and Garcia, who kept getting progressively better with a round of 67. Lurking at 206 and looking to regain his spot atop the European Order of Merit was Colin Montgomerie, who followed rounds of 68 and 67 with an even-par 71.

After a bogey at the fifth hole on Sunday, Garcia quickly righted the ship and followed with six birdies that moved him ahead for good at the eighth hole. When Cabrera, who after a slow start came on strong to finish second, pulled to within one, Garcia answered with putts from 15 and 20 feet. On the par-three 17th, a treacherous water-guarded hole, Garcia played a perfect shot to the middle of the green, where he two-putted for par. Then on the equally well-guarded, par-four 18th, Garcia hit a six iron to within six feet for a final birdie to reach 64 for the day and 16-under-par 268 for the week.

Lee Westwood made a brief charge on Sunday, pulling to within one shot of the lead through 15 holes, but a three-putt bogey on the 16th, followed by a water-bound tee shot and double bogey on the 17th, then another three-putt on the 18th dropped him into a tie for seventh place with Montgomerie, who shot another 71, and two others. Miguel Angel Martin, who won the Moroccan Open two weeks earlier, fired a course-record-tying 62 on Sunday, but he started the day at one over par, too far back to make up much ground.

Standard Life Loch Lomond—€1,400,000
Winner: Colin Montgomerie

The temperatures were unseasonably warm for Glasgow in July. "Sweltering" some called it, nothing like the conditions to which European golfers were accustomed during the Standard Life Loch Lomond. They were, however, again competing against one of the strongest fields of the year in an event that has become one of the most popular on the PGA European Tour calendar. It was fitting that Europe's best player would choose the Loch Lomond event to reassert himself atop the Order of Merit with an impressive final-round 64. It was also touching that he should win only a few miles from his birthplace.

"This is very special for me," Colin Montgomerie said after coming from three shots behind on the final day to pass six players including Lee Westwood, Sergio Garcia and Jesper Parnevik. "The support I had today was unbelievable. I couldn't be going into an Open feeling better about my golf."

Final-round 64s will do that for you. But it wasn't simply the win that bolstered Montgomerie's confidence, it was the quality of the field he defeated in the process and the caliber of shotmaking that led him to victory. He made nine birdies in a 12-hole stretch on Sunday to move past Westwood, who held the third-round lead. Montgomerie had a 268 total, 16 under par, to finish three strokes ahead of Garcia, Michael Jonzon and Mats Lanner. Westwood and Parnevik tied for fifth place at 272.

For the 19-year-old Garcia, coming off a win at the Murphy's Irish Open, the attention of an opening 62 and a two-shot lead proved a little daunting. When asked whether he felt he could have broken 60, Garcia answered with an unabashed "yes."

When Montgomerie shot a second-round 65, he took the opportunity to teach the youngster a lesson in diplomatic relations. "I'm not here to say I'm going to break 60," Monty said. "That was an odd thing to say. I've had opportunities to shoot 59 as well, but I don't say I can break 60. Every round could be better, should be better."

British Open Championship—€2,841,930
Winner: Paul Lawrie

See Chapter 4.

TNT Dutch Open—€1,120,000
Winner: Lee Westwood

After a seven-win year in 1998, 26-year-old Lee Westwood said that he wanted to win 100 tournaments in his career. That goal hit a rough spot in 1999 as Westwood, nursing a sore shoulder and an erratic putting stroke, spent the first half of the year without a victory.

Before arriving for the TNT Dutch Open, Westwood had spent 10 winless months on the PGA European Tour, and fallen out of the top 12 in the Order of Merit. That was rectified in the final round at the Hilversumsche Golf Club when Westwood fired a course-record-tying 63 to make up three strokes on the leader and walk away with a one-shot victory over Gary Orr with a 269 total, 15 under par.

"This is a big win for me in terms of building some momentum and it's always good to win to give you confidence with a lot of big tournaments coming up," Westwood said. "It's nice to be back in the chase for Europe's number one."

Westwood began the week with an uninspiring 72 to fall five shots behind first-round leaders Eduardo Romero, Ignacio Garrido, Angel Cabrera, Rolf Muntz, Emanuele Canonica and Katsuyoshi Tomori. From there, Westwood improved his position slightly with 68. Still, a win seemed like a long shot. Romero and Philip Walton were tied at 135 after two rounds.

Saturday saw a shifting in the tides as Orr came though with 65 to take a two-shot lead over Muntz and a three-shot advantage over Westwood, who had 66. Despite a final round of 69, Orr could do nothing but watch as Westwood carded eight birdies. With a late birdie at the 16th, Orr pulled back to within one with the par-five 18th still to play, but a three-putt bogey at the 17th made the task of catching Westwood almost impossible. Even though he birdied the 18th, Orr was relegated to runner-up with 69 and a 270 total.

"I can't complain," Orr said. "I made a couple of silly errors at the wrong times. I made wrong club selections on two holes and bogeyed them both. But if someone beats you fair and square, then good luck to him."

Smurfit European Open—€1,900,000
Winner: Lee Westwood

Victories often come when you least expect them, and after Darren Clarke followed his record-setting round of 60 on Friday with 66 on Saturday, including his first hole-in-one as a professional, no one expected Lee Westwood to come from seven strokes behind to win the Smurfit European Open.

It looked as if Clarke would play little more than a ceremonial round on Sunday. He started the day at 17-under-par 199, fully six shots ahead of his nearest competitor, Peter O'Malley, and seven clear of Westwood and the rest of the field.

While Clarke struggled with pars on the first five holes of the final round, followed by a three-putt bogey at the sixth and a struggling bogey at the seventh after his tee shot found the water, Westwood was making five birdies through eight holes. By the time Clarke finished the eighth with a par, both Westwood and O'Malley had drawn even. When Clarke hooked his tee shot on the ninth and made another bogey, he found himself two shots down to Westwood, who had birdied six of the first 10 holes.

Clarke never got closer than two shots back the rest of the round, capping off a forgettable day with a missed three-footer at the 18th that would have given him sole possession of second place. He finished with 75 and a 273 total to tie with O'Malley for second, two strokes behind Westwood.

O'Malley kept applying pressure to Westwood on the second nine. Having gone on a birdie barrage himself, making five in the first 15 holes, O'Malley was within two shots of Westwood after Westwood made his eighth birdie at the 15th. "When I made the birdie putt at 15, I started to think it was my day," Westwood said. "Then I hit it in the lake at the next hole and I had to think again."

A double bogey by Westwood at the 16th briefly opened the door for O'Malley, but he could not take advantage. Instead, O'Malley hit his tee shot at the 16th behind a tree, then punched out long and into the same lake Westwood had visited only moments before. O'Malley also made double bogey and the lead remained at two.

A two-putt birdie at the 538-yard, par-five 18th, his ninth of the day, sealed the two-shot victory for Westwood, who finished with 65 and a four-day total of 271, 17 under par.

Volvo Scandinavian Masters—€1,400,000
Winner: Colin Montgomerie

It was only at the end of the first round, when Paul Broadhurst finished with a strong second nine to shoot 65, that Colin Montgomerie didn't hold the lead in the Volvo Scandinavian Masters in Malmo, Sweden. Europe's best player shot a respectable 67 to stand two behind Broadhurst and tied with

Dean Robertson, a situation Montgomerie quickly rectified on Friday by shooting another 67 and taking the lead for good.

Geoff Ogilvy moved into second place after Friday's round with a tournament-low score of 62 under perfect scoring conditions at the 7,318-yard Barseback Golf and Country Club. Still, two shots behind Montgomerie, Ogilvy and the rest of the field had an uphill battle ahead.

On Saturday, Montgomerie widened the gap further with an almost flawless ball-striking round in which he hit every fairway and every green en route to 65. Montgomerie was six shots ahead of Broadhurst and seven ahead of David Carter and Jesper Parnevik. Under most circumstances, such a lead would have seemed insurmountable, but with the recent collapses of Jean Van de Velde in the British Open and Darren Clarke at the Smurfit European Open fresh in the minds of everyone, no lead seemed large enough.

"I have to admit (Van de Velde and Clarke) were on my mind," Montgomerie said afterward. "I had everything to lose, because I was expected to win, and that put some pressure on me."

Montgomerie handled that pressure beautifully, putting together another ball-striking clinic. Hitting his approaches pin high in windy conditions and making par after par while protecting his lead, Monty extended his lead to seven shots with a birdie at the par-four ninth. His 69 for a 20-under-par 268 total gave Monty a six-shot victory over Parnevik, who continues to call Sweden home even though he and his family live in Florida. Parnevik put together a strong four days of play, following rounds of 69, 68 and 69 with a closing 71 to edge Ogilvy and Bob May for second place by one shot.

West of Ireland Golf Classic—€350,000
Winner: Costantino Rocca

Costantino Rocca arrived in Galway, Ireland, with one goal in mind: win the West of Ireland Classic. Only a victory would give Rocca a chance at qualifying for the European Ryder Cup team, and even that might not be enough. He would have to win in Ireland and perhaps in Munich at the BMW International if he were to have a chance of moving up from his 24th spot in the standings and be considered for his fourth Ryder Cup team.

Rocca realized the first part of his goal with a two-stroke victory over Padraig Harrington at the Galway Bay Golf Club. It didn't come easily. A 70 in the first round left Rocca four shots off the lead, but he edged himself closer with a second-round 68. Eric Carlberg of Sweden held the halfway lead at 135, while Rocca and Harrington were tied at 138.

Carlberg shot 74 on Saturday and dropped from contention, but Rocca and Harrington remained closely knotted. Both shot 68s in the third round to tie for the lead at 206, and both knew the importance of a victory. Harrington came to Ireland ranked 16th in Ryder Cup points. A victory would move him into the top 10 where he would automatically qualify.

On Sunday, Rocca got off to a rousing start, birdieing three of the first seven holes to open up a three-shot lead, but he dropped two shots in the early going on the second nine to allow Harrington back into a share of the lead. They were still tied at the 16th tee, but with one swing, Harrington handed Rocca the tournament. "I was 99 percent sure I hit it out of bounds on the 16th," Harrington said. "When I couldn't find the ball, that was the end. I was hanging in all day, but I don't think I was destined to be in the winner's chair."

Rocca made a 30-foot birdie putt on the 18th to shoot 70 and reach 12-under-par 276 for the week. "I did what I came here to do, but I can't relax," the 42-year-old Rocca said. "I have to win in Munich now. Even that might not be enough, but I'm feeling good and my mind is very concentrated. If I keep playing well, but don't qualify and Mark James feels I can help the team, I'm here and ready to play."

BMW International Open—€1,190,000
Winner: Colin Montgomerie

In a week when Europe's attention was focused on who would make the 1999 Ryder Cup team, Colin Montgomerie put some distance between himself and his closest rival for Order of Merit honors by winning the BMW International Open in Munich by three strokes. The Ryder Cup situation took such precedence over the week's events that when Padraig Harrington holed a 10-footer for par on the 18th hole to finish second, the roar from the gallery was much larger than the applause Montgomerie received when he tapped in a two-footer to win the tournament. That was because Montgomerie's victory, his fifth of the year, put him a staggering €650,000 ahead of his nearest rival, Lee Westwood. Harrington was battling for the 10th and last automatic spot on the team, which he won by virtue of two second-place finishes in two weeks.

"This is a great feeling," Harrington said after shooting even-par 72 for a 271 total, edging Jarrod Moseley for second by one stroke despite Moseley's final-round 66. "I'm especially pleased after having a bad start today. My trouble came from being too defensive. I was good when I had to be and terrible when I didn't want to be."

After rounds of 66, 67 and 66, Harrington trailed Montgomerie by one stroke going into the final round with the rest of the field no closer than five shots back. But Harrington had a rough start, dropping from 17 under par at the beginning of the day to 13 under after four holes. By the time the par putt fell at the 18th, Harrington had clawed his way back to even par for the day and the biggest thrill of his career. "This hasn't sunk in yet, and it probably won't for a while," he said.

Meanwhile, Montgomerie won in dominating style, coming from seven strokes back after an opening 69, shooting 64 in the second round to tie Harrington for the lead at 133. A 65 on Saturday put Montgomerie ahead for good. His lead was as many as five strokes during the final round, and a closing 70 gave Montgomerie his second week of minus-20 (268) scoring, and a three-stroke victory.

"I'm obviously playing very well," Montgomerie said. "Twenty under par in my last two European Tour events means I'm not doing much wrong. It's a bit of a contrast with last year, when I missed the cut here and played Sunday morning as a marker just to try and get some confidence back. That's something I'm not short of right now."

Scottish PGA Championship—€350,000
Winner: Warren Bennett

Only one year removed from the Challenge Tour, where he won five times in 1998, Warren Bennett proved he not only belonged on the PGA European Tour, he established himself as a contender by defeating Rolf Muntz on the first hole of a playoff to capture the Scottish PGA Championship at Gleneagles.

Muntz led through the first two rounds, opening with a six-under-par 66 to take a one-shot edge over Paul Nilbrink and following it with a 71 to lead Klas Eriksson by a single shot at the halfway mark. Bennett was never far behind. Through two rounds he was at 139, only two shots off the lead.

The third round proved more difficult as scores soared into the 70s. Bennett shot 74 while Muntz also dropped a shot to par, shooting 73. Eriksson was one of the few who managed to break par, shooting 71 for a 209 total and a one-shot lead over Muntz. Bennett was four back with 18 to play.

Bennett saved the best for last, playing the final round in 69, while Eriksson ballooned to 74 for a 283 total, one behind Bennett and Muntz, who shot 72. Muntz needed to par the 533-yard, par-five 18th to force a playoff. It wasn't easy. His third shot found the greenside bunker, but a deft sand shot followed by a solid par putt sent the tournament to extra holes.

Bennett made quick work of the playoff, hitting his third shot to the 18th within four feet of the pin and ramming the putt home for the win. Muntz gave it a valiant try, hitting his third shot to 15 feet and just missing his birdie effort. "I played well all day," Muntz said afterward. "It was just not meant to be."

For Bennett, his first PGA European Tour victory was meant to be. "Definitely the highlight of my career," he said. "It's been a year since I last won, but I contended so many times. It all helps. You get your mind focused on what you did last year and it is pretty much automatic. You know you can't make any mistakes coming in because you will lose the tournament."

Canon European Masters—€1,260,000
Winner: Lee Westwood

Lee Westwood arrived in Crans-sur-Sierre, Switzerland, with one goal in mind: closing in on Colin Montgomerie's lead in the European Order of Merit. Although he started the week a half million euros down, Westwood told the media not to count him out just yet. He proved his point by winning €210,000 with a two-shot victory over Thomas Bjorn in the Canon European Masters for his third title of the year.

Even though it was down to a two-man race by the middle of the third round, the tournament was a dogfight until the last few holes. Bjorn and Westwood tied for the lead at 138 after Friday's second round, then Westwood moved ahead by one on Saturday with 67 to Bjorn's 68. In the early holes of the final round, Westwood thought he might break away. He made four birdies in the first nine holes to clear himself from everyone in the field except Bjorn, who matched him birdie for birdie.

By the 11th hole, after a rare Westwood bogey, Bjorn had assumed a one-shot lead. He maintained that lead with pars on the 12th and 13th, but at the 14th Westwood made another move. The Englishman birdied the 14th, then eagled the par-five 15th while Bjorn could manage no better than par and birdie on the two holes. Westwood then cruised home with three pars while Bjorn made one more bogey coming in. The final round finished with Westwood shooting 65 for a 14-under-par 270 total to Bjorn's 66 for 272. Next was Alex Cejka, who also shot 66 to finish at 276, six shots behind Westwood and four behind Bjorn.

"Thomas had me worried for a long time," Westwood said. "We both played really well. For two guys to shoot 66 and 65 in the final round is a great achievement. Thomas showed a lot of guts when he followed my long putts on the sixth and 15th by holding his. He pushed me all the way and he should be proud."

Victor Chandler British Masters—€1,000,000
Winner: Bob May

With a three-shot lead over American Bob May and a five-shot advantage over Eduardo Romero going into the final round of the Victor Chandler British Masters at Woburn, Colin Montgomerie appeared to be in line for his sixth victory of the season. But Montgomerie got off to a slow start on Sunday, after jumping ahead with a second-round 64 and remaining the front-runner with 68 for a 199 total. His bogeys on the first three holes opened the door, and May, a Las Vegas native playing the PGA European Tour full time, took advantage.

After finishing tied for third at the Scandinavian Masters three weeks earlier, May played his best golf of the season, carding rounds of 69, 67 and 66 for a 202 total in the first three days with a double-eagle two on the par-five 10th hole on Friday. When Montgomerie dropped three shots while May continued to make birdies, an improbable victory seemed more and more likely. A first-nine 30 allowed May to open up a five-shot lead and, while his second nine wasn't as impressive, his 67 for a 19-under-par 269 total was just enough. Montgomerie made one final charge, birdieing two of the last three holes to shoot 71 and claw his way back to 18 under par, but it was too little, too late.

"I didn't putt well enough all week, believe it or not," Montgomerie said. "My second-round 64 didn't include a putt of more than eight feet, and I didn't play to my potential today."

May was simply happy to have realized his potential. "Hopefully this will be the stepping stone to get me up to where my expectations are," he said. "It feels incredible. A dream come true. To beat Colin, one of the world's best players, I couldn't imagine my first victory being like that. I was fortunate that Colin wasn't on his game today, because that would have made the task much tougher."

Trophee Lancome—€1,120,000
Winner: Pierre Fulke

For three rounds it appeared that Ryder Cup rookie Miguel Angel Jimenez would get his game in shape for Boston by winning the Trophee Lancome in Paris. Jimenez shot rounds of 68, 64 and 70 and seemed to have command of every aspect of his game. His 202 total gave him a one-shot edge over Sweden's Pierre Fulke and a two-shot margin over Colin Montgomerie.

For whatever reason, Jimenez lost his focus and his game on Sunday, shooting 74 to finish tied for 10th place at 276. Montgomerie couldn't make a move either, although he finished as low Ryder Cupper in the event. His 68 (the second three-under-par score he posted in as many days) gave Montgomerie a 272 total for the week, two shots shy of what he needed to win. His €57,843 prize money gave him a substantial lead in the Order of Merit standings, but the Scot was none too happy about the way he putted in that final round.

"I hit every green, but had 35 putts," Montgomerie said. "I hit the ball fantastic, and it wasn't as though I was leaving myself 35-footers either. They were all inside 10 feet. It's sad really. I should have had this tournament sewn up by the fifth hole."

With the door left open, Ignacio Garrido and Santiago Luna tried to move ahead. Garrido shot 66 to go with previous scores of 67, 70 and 68 for a 271 total, while Luna also shot 66 but fell one short of Garrido's mark. The only player left on the course with any chance was Fulke, a 28-year-old who had spent seven fruitless years on tour. Fulke had been consistent even as those around him fell away. In his three rounds of 69, 69 and 65, Fulke had missed only two fairways and four greens.

Spurred on by the Parisian gallery who enjoyed the fact that this young Swede had such a French name, Fulke continued to hit fairways and greens, making three birdies in the first 17 holes to pull even with Garrido at 13 under par. Then on the 18th, with a 25-footer for birdie, Fulke knew that his time had finally come. He confidently rolled the birdie putt into the hole to win by one over Garrido with his 67 and 270 total, 14 under par.

Linde German Masters—€1,750,000
Winner: Sergio Garcia

One week after competing in an emotionally charged and ultimately disappointing Ryder Cup, Sergio Garcia rebounded to come from two shots behind in the final 18 holes to tie for the lead in the Linde German Masters, then grind his way through two playoff holes, finally sinking a 15-footer in a driving rain to defeat Ryder Cup teammate Padraig Harrington.

Garcia never led until late, and never held the outright lead until the final putt fell, but he was never that far behind either. An opening 68 put Garcia two off the lead held by Miguel Angel Jimenez and Alex Cejka. Jimenez, who was a stalwart of Captain Mark James' European team in Boston, couldn't keep the momentum. His second-round 73, followed by 72 and 69, left him tied for 12th place.

Jose Rivero assumed the second-round lead with rounds of 68 and 66, but

Garcia was still only three shots back after following his opening 68 with 69. Rivero couldn't keep up either. A third-round 75 in wind-swept conditions at the Gut Larchenhof Golf Club in Cologne dropped Rivero out of the running, even though his final-round 69 moved him back up to within a shot of the leaders. He finished tied for fourth with Peter Baker.

Baker also held the lead. A third-round 69 got him to 207 and gave him a one-shot edge over Ian Woosnam and a two-shot margin over Garcia. Baker let it slip away in the final round, shooting only 71 to finish one short of the playoff.

Saturday's even-par 72 represented Garcia's worst round of the week, but even that kept him close. With the weather proving more brutal on Sunday than any of the previous days, it was anybody's tournament and Garcia liked his chances. A 68 just as the worst of the weather was setting in moved Garcia to 11-under-par 277 and into a tie for the lead with Harrington and Woosnam. The advantage on the last two holes went to Woosnam, who hit deft iron shots inside six feet on the 71st and 72nd holes only to miss the short putts that would have won the tournament.

A playoff ensued between the three Ryder Cup veterans, two with one week and one Ryder Cup under their belts and one with a distinguished career representing Europe. None of that mattered as they walked back down the 18th fairway in the driving rain. The only thing that mattered was the 25-foot par putt Garcia made on the first playoff hole after Harrington had chipped in for par and Woosnam missed a short par putt on the same hole to be eliminated from the playoff.

"I felt very confident with that putt," Garcia said after salvaging par. "I think the Ryder Cup helped me deal with pressure. It showed in the playoff today."

On the second extra hole, Garcia hit his approach to within 15 feet and, when Harrington missed his birdie effort, Garcia calmly stroked his putt into the hole for his second PGA European Tour win of the year. "Now I've won two," he said. "I'll have to go for more. I want to win the majors but they're over until next year."

Alfred Dunhill Cup—€1,400,000
Winner: Spain

See Chapter 8.

Cisco World Match Play—€896,000
Winner: Colin Montgomerie

See Chapter 9.

Sarazen World Open—€560,000
Winner: Thomas Bjorn

Spain was an appropriate place for Thomas Bjorn to make his long anticipated comeback. It was in Spain in April of 1998 that the lanky Dane had
last won, picking up the Peugeot Open de Espana title before embarking on
an 18-month slump where he dropped out of the top 50 in the World Ranking and out of contention for his second Ryder Cup berth. In Barcelona, the
new home of the Sarazen World Open, Bjorn completed his comeback with
a two-stroke victory over Paolo Quirici of Switzerland and Katsuyoshi Tomori
of Japan.

"It's been a long time since I've felt like this," Bjorn said. "You start
doubting yourself a little bit, doubting if you can win again. It was very
enjoyable to do that, and I'm glad it happened this week."

It also didn't hurt his confidence when Bjorn won with Quirici and Tomori
nipping at his heels. The lead see-sawed through the final 18 holes with all
three deadlocked early in the final nine. That's when Bjorn came through.
He made birdies at the 12th and 13th holes while Tomori, bidding to become
the first Japanese golfer since Isao Aoki to win on the PGA European Tour,
bogeyed the 13th and 16th. Meanwhile Quirici matched Bjorn shot-for-shot,
but two closing bogeys left him with a round of 68. Bjorn also shot 68 to
go with earlier rounds of 66, 69 and 70 for a 15-under-par 273 aggregate.
The two-shot lead he held over Quirici going into Sunday's final ended up
being the margin of victory.

"The most important thing was to get into the top 20 on the Volvo Order
of Merit," Bjorn said. "I wanted to make it to Valderrama (for the WGC
American Express Championship) and I've done that. Now I want to move
back into the top 50 in the World Ranking so I can be involved in the majors
and the other big money tournaments."

Belgacom Open—€750,000
Winner: Robert Karlsson

When Robert Karlsson saw his pairing for the first two rounds of the Belgacom
Open, his blood ran cold. The two-time winner found out he would be
playing with Mark James, who had passed Karlsson over as a Ryder Cup
player even though the Swede was 11th in the standings. Instead James
picked Andrew Coltart, who was 12th in the standings, and Jesper Parnevik,
who played most of the year on the U.S. PGA Tour. Parnevik proved to be
a good choice, but Tiger Woods drilled Coltart, who sat out the first two
days of Ryder Cup play, in his only appearance in singles.

"It was a bit tense," Karlsson said. "Mark told me he thought I hadn't
played as well as Andrew after the U.S. Open. It was a difficult decision for
him, and I was obviously disappointed. Actually, if I had been captain, I
would have picked Bernhard Langer because it was such an inexperienced
team."

By Sunday afternoon Karlsson had made a point to James and everyone
else in Europe. With rounds of 69, 68, 69 and 66 for a 272 total, Karlsson
edged out Jamie Spence and Retief Goosen by a single shot for his third

victory of the year. He was the only player to break 70 every day, but he only led for the final two holes. Karlsson's five-under-par final round included three twos, but the birdie that mattered most came at the long par-four 17th, where he finally moved ahead with a 20-footer.

Before that putt, the tournament seemed to belong to Goosen, who led after Thursday with 65, then opened a two-shot margin by reaching 10-under 203 on Saturday. That appeared to be enough after Goosen made one more birdie to reach 11 under. But the cold, windy conditions caught up with Goosen on the final nine and he could manage no better than 70 for a 273 total. That tied him with Spence, who came off an opening 70 to shoot rounds of 68, 68 and 67 for the rest of the week.

Volvo Masters—€1,400,000
Winner: Miguel Angel Jimenez

There was a hushed reverence among Europe's best players as they assembled at the Montecastillo Hotel and Resort in Jerez, Spain, for the Volvo Masters. All of them knew Payne Stewart, and all were shocked by his untimely death. Then there was the rain, as eight inches fell on the sloping course in a week. That was five times as much precipitation as the region normally experiences in the entire month of October, and the course was saturated. The fairways hadn't been mowed in a week when the first round began.

Crowds were also small, even though admission was free and three Spaniards were vying for the title as late as the final nine holes. Everyone, it seemed, was either preoccupied with Rugby World Cup action, the sad news about Stewart coming out of America, or looking forward to the season-ending event at Valderrama. The only drama that could have made the Volvo Masters compelling would have been if Colin Montgomerie had won. The Scot held a substantial lead in the Order of Merit before arriving in Spain, but a win at Jerez would have put the title out of reach no matter what happened at the WGC American Express Championship.

Montgomerie would never seriously contend. His 70-65-71-70–276 performance left him tied for 16th place. That left the door open for Spanish sensation Sergio Garcia, who charged into second place on the Order of Merit. Garcia had a chance to win as late as the final nine holes, but a closing 69 for a 273 total left him tied for fifth, four shots away from the winning total.

That winning total, 19-under-par 269, belonged to another Spaniard and Garcia's Ryder Cup teammate, Miguel Angel Jimenez, the 35-year-old Malaga native. Jimenez began the week with a respectable 68, a good showing under the soggy conditions. He trailed Retief Goosen by six shots.

Goosen, who had jumped into the top four on the Order of Merit, was making his own bid to catch Montgomerie. He got off to a good start with a course-record 62 to open a three-shot lead over Phillip Price. Goosen retained his lead on Friday with 68 for a 130 total. Padraig Harrington moved into second at 131, and Jimenez lost even more ground, shooting 67 to fall seven back.

Goosen continued his good play through Saturday. A 70 moved him to

200, two shots clear of Michael Campbell and four shots ahead of Jimenez, but Goosen's scores were showing a disturbing trend. Each day he had played a little worse than the day before, allowing more players back into the tournament. One good round from one of the nearest contenders and the tournament could turn around.

That's what happened on Sunday when Bernhard Langer, who started the day five shots off Goosen's lead, came on strong with a closing 66 for a 271 total. That total was tied by Goosen, who shot 71, and Harrington, who followed a 73 with 67 on Sunday. Garcia and Clarke also had chances. Clarke closed with 66 to tie Garcia at 273, but missed three critical birdie chances in the final round, while Garcia made three quick birdies but could manage no more.

Jimenez' 65, his lowest score of the week, for a 269 total, propelled him to his second victory of the season on Spanish soil.

WGC American Express Championship—$5,000,000
Winner: Tiger Woods

On a blustery Sunday in Sotogrande, Spain, Tiger Woods played 17 holes of what Nick Price described as "the best round of golf I've ever seen in my life," and one hole that will be remembered for its pure folly. In the end, Woods leapt out to a four-shot lead in pursuit of his eighth PGA Tour victory and his ninth worldwide of the year, then made triple bogey on the much maligned par-five 17th at Valderrama, parred the 18th, lost the lead to Miguel Angel Jimenez, ended regulation play tied for the lead, then won with a birdie on the first playoff hole. Just another day at the office for the greatest golfer in the world.

"I was hoping to catch Greg Norman (on the PGA Tour career money list) before Tiger caught me," Davis Love III said as he watched Woods' Sunday exhibition. "It doesn't look like that's going to happen." That was before Woods played the 536-yard 17th hole. "It's the worst hole we play all year," Montgomerie had said. "Just a bad hole," Stuart Appleby said. "Unbelievable," according to Tom Lehman. "Rubbish," said Lee Westwood.

All those sentiments were magnified when Woods played the hole as good as it could be played and ended up making triple bogey. His drive found the center of the fairway, his second shot laid up about 100 yards from the hole. From there Woods hit a knock-down, spin-free nine iron just beyond the hole. "I went up a club so that I could hit a little chip shot and not have it spin too much," Woods said. "That way I thought I could take the pond out of play."

Everything worked out perfectly. The ball few 15 feet beyond the hole, checked perfectly and stopped. But then, as Woods was repairing his divot and handing the nine iron back to his caddie, the ball began to trickle back toward the water. It gained speed as it rolled off the front edge of the green and didn't stop until it had found the water. Woods bowed his head in disbelief. After his penalty drop, he chipped beyond the hole to ensure that another shot didn't roll back into the water, then he gingerly rolled his first putt beyond the hole, and missed the five-footer coming back. The lead was squandered after he had played the hole the only way he could.

"When you hit three perfect golf shots and end up making eight, something's wrong with the hole," said Lehman, who played in the group with Woods. "It's a shame that a hole like that could ultimately effect the outcome of the tournament," said Price, who was watching the debacle from the fairway. He turned to his caddie and said, "I don't know how to play this hole. What do you do? Where can you hit it?" Price ended up hitting his approach 30 feet away from the hole and making par.

"I could understand if I had hit a hard, spinning sand wedge, but the ball didn't spin back, it just kind of rolled," Woods said. "In fact, it seemed to pick up speed at the hole. Sergio (Garcia) told me afterward that they triple-cut the green today. Combined with the pin position and the wind, that meant there was almost nowhere to hit it."

Even with the triple bogey, Woods shot 68 on a day when the field averaged 75.16, and he finished five shots ahead of everyone in the field except Jimenez, who entered the final round tied for the lead with Chris Perry and bogeyed the last hole to shoot 69 for a 278 total, six under par, and fall into a playoff with Woods. It was a memorable performance by Jimenez, especially given the pressure of playing only 50 miles from his home in front of an openly partisan crowd. Jimenez played in four events in 1999 in Spain and finished first, second, first and second. When Jimenez and Woods played the 18th again in the playoff, Jimenez hooked his drive behind one of the many cork trees that guard the golf course. From there he punched out in front of the green, chipped to within 12 feet, and missed his par effort. Woods found the center of the fairway with a three wood, hit a nine iron to within six feet, and drained the birdie putt.

Johnnie Walker Classic—$1,280,000
Winner: Michael Campbell

See Asia/Japan Tours chapter.

Challenge Tour

Extending over 28 tournaments in 17 countries, the European Challenge Tour began in Kenya in March and ended in Cuba in October. The First Cuba Grand Final proved to be just that, a dramatic conclusion to the season. Stephen Scahill, a 30-year-old from New Zealand, birdied the last two holes at Varadero to win the tournament and secured his PGA European Tour card for 2000.

Scahill moved up from 16th place on the Order of Merit into the top 15 to receive cards. He holed from 25 feet at the short 17th and then from 15 feet for a three at the last. "That was the whole year's golf rolled into two putts," Scahill said. "The one at 17 had a six-foot swing, while the one at the last was a bonus because I knew I could bogey and still get my card. It's great to be back on tour after losing my card two years ago."

Scahill won the tournament by two strokes over Jose Manuel Lara and Henrik Stenson. For Spain's Lara, the disappointment was doubled by the fact he had to finish alone in second place to secure his card. Instead, he was 19th on the Order of Merit, £1,500 short of 15th place. Only £115 separated the four players from 15th to 18th place, with Scotland's Greig Hutcheon securing the last card with £22,162 after tying for 22nd place in Cuba.

Denmark's Knud Storgaard finished with two rounds of 68 and his tie for sixth place took him from 17th to 12th on the Order of Merit, while Sweden's Johan Skold scored the best round of the final day, 66, to finish eighth and move from 18th to 14th.

Carl Suneson avoided the fraught nature of the Grand Final by having already won three times. The 32-year-old from Gran Canaria finished as the No. 1 on the Order of Merit with £49,744. Suneson has a strange background. His father is Swedish and his mother English. He was born in Las Palmas but grew up in Britain, playing international amateur golf for England. After four years at Oklahoma State University, Suneson played on the PGA European Tour but lost his card after discovering he was diabetic. Now living in Las Palmas and married to a Spaniard, he is a naturalized Spaniard. He won the Comunidad Valenciana Challenge de Espana at El Saler in May, Rolex Trophy in Geneva in July and the Beazer Homes Challenge Tour Championship at Bowood in England in August.

Former Walker Cup player Iain Pyman won twice to finish second on the Order of Merit, while the others to earn their cards were Markus Brier, Gustavo Rojas, Hennie Otto, Maarten Lafeber, Bradley Dredge, Benoit Teilleria, Lucas Parsons, Didier De Vooght and Phil Golding.

12. Asia/Japan Tours

The inevitable changing of the guard finally came about in Japan. Although Masashi (Jumbo) Ozaki seemed to go on forever as the dominant player, age had to catch up to him some time. It did — in 1999. In his 52nd year, the remarkable Ozaki yielded the No. 1 position on the money list to his brother, Naomichi (Joe), ending a run of five consecutive championships. Naomichi, who was the leader in 1991, had his hands full securing the 1999 crown. In fact, were it not for a decision to include money won in the four major championships and new World Golf Championship events in the total, he probably would have lost out to the surprising Kazuhiko Hosokawa, a 28-year-old who had won only four times during his previous six years. Nonetheless, the performance of Ozaki, 42, was impressive. He played in just 17 tournaments after returning from an early-season stretch on the U.S. PGA Tour, won both the Japan Open and PGA, as well as the Tsuruya Open, and earned ¥137,641,796. Hosokawa finished with ¥129,058,283.

Shigeki Maruyama, though limited to a single victory in 1999, came on strongly in the late season to place third with ¥114,958,525. Toshimitsu Izawa, a double winner, was fourth with ¥110,927,044, and the late-blooming Tsuyoshi Yoneyama had ¥106,872,033 with three victories, and was the only other player in nine figures. Masashi Ozaki, whose 12 money titles date back to the early 1970s, certainly didn't disappear in 1999. He was one of five with two wins for the season and placed sixth in the standings. South Korean pros Kim Jong-duk and Choi Kyung-ju had pairs of victories during the first half of the season. Yoneyama and Choi were among the six first-time winners on the circuit in 1999.

The victory list of 1999 had more of a Japanese look. Other than the four wins by Choi and Kim, the only victories by overseas players came when Nick Price won the Suntory Open, Thomas Bjorn of Denmark took the Dunlop Phoenix and Eduardo Herrera of Colombia finished on top in the Mizuno Open. Particularly evident was the absence of Americans, both as winners and as regulars on the circuit. For the first time since 1973, no U.S. player triumphed in Japan and even that year, when the Japan PGA Tour was in its infancy, Al Geiberger was low individual in a U.S.-vs-Japan team event. Brian Watts and Brandt Jobe, standouts in Japan in recent seasons, played on the U.S. PGA Tour, as did Carlos Franco of Paraguay, and competed sparingly in Japan.

In a change quite similar to the establishment of the U.S. PGA Tour as a separate entity from the PGA of America in the late 1960s, the Japanese players took over the existing circuit, creating the Japan Tour organization that began operations in 1999 without much of a noticeable difference. In what could probably be blamed on the economy, though, the season included just 32 tournaments, down four from the previous season. The overall prize money remained stable.

The Asian PGA Davidoff Tour ended the year on a high note when Michael Campbell, the New Zealander who faded away after a bright rookie season in 1995, won the Johnnie Walker Classic in Taiwan. Then American Fran Quinn, who narrowly missed earning his playing card on the U.S. PGA Tour, took out his frustrations by winning the last two events, the Mittweida Thailand Open and the Omega PGA Championship. That didn't keep Myanmar's Kyi Hla Han from winning the Davidoff Order of Merit with more than $200,000. The crowning moment of Han's year was his seven-stroke victory in the Volvo China Open.

In other items of note from 1999, Korea's Choi Kyung-ju won twice, taking the Kirin Open in a playoff and the Kolon Korean Open with a late charge. American Gerry Norquist, with his victory in the Benson and Hedges Malaysian Open, became the first player on the tour to win five titles. And the tour didn't lack for its curious moments. In the Sabah Masters, America Robert Huxtable won even though his caddie accidentally kicked his ball, costing him a penalty stroke. That cut Huxtable's winning margin to six strokes. In the Singapore Open, Australian Kenny Druce, trailing by one stroke coming to the final hole, lofted an exquisite flop shot that trickled into the cup to force a tie, and he went on to win the playoff.

The rise of young amateurs in the world was reflected in Asia. India's Ashok Kumar, 17, was in the chase in the Hero Honda Masters before slumping in the final round to finish 18th. Korean whiz Kim Sung-yoon, 17, runner-up in the U.S. Amateur, tied for third in the Kolon Korean Open, and China's Liang Wen-chong, 20, finished fourth in the Volvo China Open.

Asian PGA Davidoff Tour

London Myanmar Open—US$200,000
Winner: Wang Ter-chang

Taiwan's Wang Ter-chang was the very personification of confidence at the London Myanmar Open. "When I eagled the 11th," he said, "I knew I was going to win." That was the 11th hole he was talking about — and he had seven holes to play. In golf, you usually wait until the 18th tee with a comfortable lead before you let yourself even dream of winning.

Nonetheless, that was Wang, taking the 1999 season opener on the Asian PGA Tour. He played the Yangon City Golf Resort course in rounds of 69, 69, 65 and 68 for a 271 total, a robust 17 under par, for a three-stroke victory over Japan's Koichi Nogami and the veteran Frankie Minoza of the Philippines. Nogami closed with 71, Minoza, 70. Wang's 65 in the third round matched the tournament low on the leaderboard.

Wang took a grip on the tournament at the 11th, holing a sand-wedge shot from 92 yards for an eagle two. It gave him a three-stroke lead on Nogami, who birdied the hole, and a six-stroke lead on Minoza. It was Wang's second victory on the tour. It also came as a surprise to him.

"It's very cold and wet in Taiwan at the moment," Wang said, "so I have not been playing very much. I did not expect to win this week."

Benson and Hedges Malaysian Open—US$750,000
Winner: Gerry Norquist

American Gerry Norquist turned in a landmark performance at the Benson and Hedges Malaysian Open — the first player to win five titles on the Asian PGA Tour. For further history, the tournament was the first jointly sanctioned by the PGA European Tour, so Norquist also was the first to win such an event. At the time, he didn't know what the winner's check was (it was US$121,125, the largest of his career), and there was another benefit — a three-year exemption on the PGA European Tour. It was, of course, the biggest title of his 11-year career.

"I hadn't looked at the leaderboard until I got to the 16th tee — after Shaun had hit into the water," said Norquist, who led from the second round. Shaun Micheel, a fellow American, got the closest of anyone during the final round, closing to within two strokes of Norquist with five holes to play. But Micheel, playing with Norquist, took himself out of the running at the 15th when he put his second shot into the water and double-bogeyed.

"I saw I was four ahead," Norquist said, "and I felt that if I parred the last three, it would be miraculous for anyone to tie. I was very calm all day."

Norquist posted scores of 67, 67, 75 and 71, for an eight-under-par total of 280 at the Saujana Club. Micheel finished with 74 and dropped to a tie for fourth. Alexander Cejka of Germany closed with 71 and Bob May of the United States with 72 and they tied for second at 283.

Wills Indian Open—US$300,000
Winner: Arjun Atwal

Arjun Atwal of Calcutta, India, was fast developing a reputation as a fourth-round failure. In his four years on the Asian PGA Tour, he led three times going into the final round. He came away without the win all three times.

"It was getting a bit frustrating to play well for three days and yet finish second," said Atwal, 25. But he came to the Wills Indian Open in March in the perfect frame of mind and game to break through. Which is to say, he wasn't playing worth a darn. Still, he played splendidly for three rounds, playing the par-72 Royal Calcutta course in scores of 72, 68 and 66. Next, he came to the fourth round, previously such a crippling experience for him. But this time he was flawless. He turned in a bogey-free, two-under-par 70 for a 12-under 276 total and a four-stroke victory. Finally, success, and he had an odd explanation for it.

"I think what really clicked for me during this tournament," Atwal said, "was that I came into it playing very bad golf. I missed all four cuts in Australia and nobody thought I would do well here. That helped. There was a lot less pressure this year. I have always maintained that I will be a different player after I win my first title. I think I have proved to myself that I have the ability to win."

And that he did. The pursuit was hot, but Atwal proved too hard to catch, leaving in his wake a three-way tie for second at eight-under 280 — India's Shiv Shankar Prasad Chowrasia (69), Korea's Kang Wook-soon (71) and Thailand's Prayad Marksaeng (68).

Macau Open—US$200,000
Winner: Lee Westwood

Not that the number 13 was unlucky for Lee Westwood — there's nothing unlucky about that many wins — but it was becoming irritating. "People ask me how many tournaments I've won," the young Englishman was saying. It seemed the answer was 13 forever. "And now it's 14," he said. "I've got off 13 at last."

Westwood, 25, made it made it 14 victories with the Macau Open at the Macau Golf and Country Club in April. More than that, he also ran his playoff record to a phenomenal 6-1 with the overtime victory over American Andrew Pitts. Westwood led by one stroke with one hole to play in regulation, but Pitts tied him with a spectacular birdie at the par-five 18th after almost holing his third shot from out of the rough from 135 yards.

Westwood had scores of 66, 69, 70 and 70, and Pitts 67, 71, 68 and 69, tying at nine-under-par 275, two strokes ahead of the field. South Africa's James Kingston and Japan's Satoshi Oide tied for third at 277.

Westwood's never-say-die experience would see him through in the playoff. At the first extra hole, Westwood drove into the heavy rough, pitched back into the fairway, then reached the green with a three iron from 215 yards that finished 12 feet from the pin. He holed the putt for the birdie, matching Pitts' birdie. Westwood also drove into the rough the second time around, again chipped out, and reached with a two iron from 225 yards. Pitts lay three, 40 feet from the flag, only to suffer his only three-putt of the tournament for a losing bogey.

Maekyung Daks Open—US$275,000
Winner: James Kingston

One man's misfortune is another man's reprieve. So it was that South African James Kingston, granted two reprieves by the cruel gods of the game, won the Maekyung Daks Open at the Lakeside Golf Club in Korea. It was the misfortune — actually two misfortunes — of Myanmar's Kyi Hla Han that did it for him.

Han, with a final-round 68 that included an eagle at the 14th, caught Kingston at 11-under-par 277. Han's first chance to win came at the second playoff hole. His 12-foot birdie putt appeared to be good, but lipped out. He had an even better chance at the next hole. Kingston missed from 20 feet, and Han faced a mere four-footer for the win. But he pulled it to the left with his broomhandle putter. Kingston waited no longer. He dropped a 12-foot birdie putt on the fourth extra hole, making the Maekyung Daks his second Asian Tour victory.

"I really thought Kyi Hla was going to make that four-footer," said Kingston, who led from the first round, playing the Lakeside course in scores of 67, 66, 74 and 70. "I felt very confident on the back nine, but Kyi Hla came back with that eagle. I really feel for the guy. We both tried so hard, but unfortunately one of us had to come out as the winner." Kingston's first victory, the 1998 Thailand Open, also came in a playoff, that over India's Jeev Milkha Singh.

Volvo China Open—US$400,000
Winner: Kyi Hla Han

Myanmar's Kyi Hla Han didn't take long to shake off the disappointment of that playoff loss in the Maekyung Daks Open. He went out and won the very next stop on the Asian Tour three weeks later, the Volvo China Open at the Shanghai Silport Golf Club. And he did it with a vengeance, winning by seven strokes over American Christian Pena. It was the first tour victory for the 38-year-old Han.

"My target was to go out and shoot a couple under," said Han, "but everything simply clicked over the opening holes." Translation: He opened the final round with five straight birdies. The outburst gave him an eight-stroke lead. He birdied the first from 20 feet, and followed that one up from three, 20, 15 and six feet. "The key was driving the ball well and setting myself up perfectly in the fairway," said Han after posting a 15-under-par 273 on rounds of 68, 70, 67 and 68. "I have shot five birdies in a row a couple of times before, but never in such a pressure situation."

Han left the rest of the field playing for second place, and Pena staked his claim to second by holing a 147-yard third shot for an eagle at the par-five 18th for a closing 70 and a 280 total, nudging out Dean Wilson, another American, by one stroke. The local favorite was Chinese amateur Liang Wen-chong, age 20. He started the final round with a triple-bogey eight, but bounced back to finish with 71 and tie for fourth at 282.

Casino Filipino Philippine Open—US$200,000
Winner: Anthony Kang

Anthony Kang, an obscure South Korean based in Las Vegas and a resident of the United States for 10 years, couldn't have put it better, and he was speaking for all the baffled people around him. "It's like I'm feeling delusions of grandeur — I can't believe this has happened," said Kang. "It's especially amazing when you consider that I've had such a terrible year." The reason for this confusion of feelings: Kang, who had made only one cut in five Asian Tour starts, won the Casino Filipino Philippine Open.

Kang holed a four-foot knee-knocker for a birdie on the final hole for a six-under-par 66 and a one-stroke victory over Japan's Kazuyoshi Yonekura and South Africa's James Kingston. Kang toured Manila Southwoods in scores of 68, 72, 67 and 66 for a 15-under total of 273. Yonekura and Kingston both closed with 69s for 274 totals.

Kang trailed overnight leader Felix Casas by three strokes going into the final round. And when Casas hit a shot into the water at No. 5 and double-bogeyed, the chase was on. Kang, much to his surprise, found himself deep in that chase. He played the back nine in four under par with birdies at the 12th, 13th, 15th and, finally, the 18th. The last was dramatic.

The 18th is a 541-yard par-five. Kang reached the green with a three-wood second from 230 yards. It finished 20 feet from the hole. His eagle putt narrowly missed, but stopped four feet away. Then he dropped that for a birdie. At that instant, he had the outright lead for the first time. And the last, it turned out.

"I had a poor lie for my second shot," Kang said, "but I just had to go for it. I naturally fade the ball, so the shot is made for me."

Then came the tough part. "On the last putt," Kang said, "my mind was racing and my hands were numb."

Tianjin Teda Open—US$200,000
Winner: Thammanoon Sriroj

Thailand's Thammanoon Sriroj, 30, became the fourth player to win four times on the Asian Tour, taking the Tianjin Teda Open, and he did it with a sigh of relief. "I was scared I would play Park in a playoff," he said. He was spared that problem when Korea's Park No-seok got too hungry at the final hole.

Thammanoon and Park started the final round at 10 under par at the par-70 Tianjin Warner International Golf Club in Tianjin, China. Thammanoon was in the final pairing with overnight leader Rodrigo Cuello of the Philippines. While Cuello was struggling to a closing 75, Park took the lead and held it much of the way, and led by two with five holes to play. But he bogeyed the 16th, and when Thammanoon birdied the 14th behind him, they were tied coming to the 562-yard, par-five 18th. That's where Park, one of the tour's biggest hitters, made his fatal mistake with his second shot.

He was in semi-rough 265 yards from the green and elected to go for it with his three wood. The shot drew into the water to the left near the green. "I did not have a great lie, but I still feel I made the right decision at the time," Park said. "I was playing well, and feel I could have easily made it." Instead, he bogeyed, and Thammanoon parred for 67, a 13-under-par 267 total, and a one-stroke victory over Park. Thammanoon didn't exactly back into the title. He shot rounds of 65, 70, 65 and 67 for his 267 to join countryman Boonchu Ruangkit, Korean Kang Wook-soon and American Gerry Norquist as a four-time winner.

Volvo Masters of Malaysia—US$200,000
Winner: Nico van Rensburg

Most places, they give a car for a hole-in-one. In the Volvo Masters of Malaysia, at the Kota Permai Golf and Country Club, they went far better. They gave a condo for the victory. "This is unbelievable," said Nico van Rensburg, after a four-stroke win that masked a tough fight and an exciting finish. "I've recently been considering basing myself in Kuala Lumpur, and now this week I have won a house here. I am totally shocked."

So was Scotland's Simon Yates, who was giving the South African a stiff battle until he crashed to a triple bogey at the 16th. "It was all over after that hole," Yates said. Van Rensburg took the lead in the third round with an eight-under-par 64, and led Yates by two going into the final round.

Their duel started immediately, at the par-five No. 1. Yates eagled, but the best van Rensburg could do for an answer was a birdie. He was still in the lead, but now only by a stroke. He wasn't alarmed. "I'm a big rugby fan, and in rugby they say that whoever scores first loses," he said. "So when

Simon eagled the first, I wasn't too concerned."

Van Rensburg finally inched ahead and held a two-stroke lead until the par-four 16th. There, Yates challenged the lake. "I hit a great tee shot on the 15th, and I thought I would hit another on 16," Yates said, "but I took it too fine to the water." His drive hit the fairway, but then trickled down into the water, and he made seven. Thus, van Rensburg led by five strokes with two holes to play, which meant his third victory on the Asian Tour. His scores were 69, 69, 64 and 68 for an 18-under-par total of 270. Japan's Toshikazu Sugihara and Singapore's Poh Eing-chong, at 10 under par, tied for third behind Yates.

ERA Taiwan Open—US$300,000
Winner: Kang Wook-soon

Winning was becoming a habit for Korea's Kang Wook-soon. After winning the previous two weeks in domestic events, he made it three in a row at the ERA Taiwan Open on the Asian Tour. Kang wrapped up the victory with an eight-foot putt for a birdie at the par-five 18th to edge Myanmar's Kyi Hla Han by one stroke. The putt gave Kang a final-round, three-under-par 69. After his first three rounds of 68, 70 and 67, he had a 274 total, 14 under par at the Sunrise Golf and Country Club. Han also birdied the 18th for 68 and a 275 total.

The tournament looked far different from the outset. India's Amandeep Johl jolted the field with a course-record 64 in the first round for a three-stroke lead. He stumbled to 74 in the second round and eventually tied for 18th place.

When it came to suspense, Kang had to share the stage with Australian Craig Parry and South African Nico van Rensburg. Both needed a birdie at the last hole to match Johl's course-record 64. Van Rensburg, who won the Volvo Masters of Malaysia the week before, made his four for 64, but alas — he was too late. Parry holed his bunker shot for an eagle three, lowering the course record to 63, and won the $6,000 bonus for the record. Parry finished tied for sixth and van Rensburg tied for ninth.

Kolon Korean Open—US$300,000
Winner: Choi Kyung-ju

"I knew I had to get going on the back nine," Korea's Choi Kyung-ju, 29, was saying. "I was just trying to enjoy myself and not think about winning." Bearing down or having fun, whichever it was, it paid off for Choi in a charge to the Kolon Korean Open championship, his first victory on the Asian Tour. Choi trailed Myanmar's Kyi Hla Han by one stroke at the turn in the final round, then burst into the lead with three consecutive birdies from the 14th. But it wasn't over yet.

Han birdied the 17th from 30 feet to close within one stroke. At the 18th, he missed a birdie from 18 feet and Choi dropped his four-footer for par and his third victory of the year, after two in Japan. He shot rounds of 71, 71, 67 and 69 for a 10-under-par 278 total at Seoul Hanyang Country Club. Han, who won the Volvo China Open in May, also shot 69 and finished second for the third time this season. Korean amateur Kim Sung-yoon, age 17, the runner-up in the U.S. Amateur, tied for third.

In an inspiring effort that fell just short, Korea's Choi Gwang-soo finished fifth after leading the middle rounds. Choi, whose mother died in 1998, lost his father on Tuesday of tournament week, and attended the funeral on Thursday morning. He took the third-round lead with 70 in the rain. "I felt that today's raindrops were the tears of my parents," he said. Then he faded to 75 in the final round. Han wasn't all that unhappy with second place. "I didn't lose it, he won it," Han said. "I didn't miss a fairway or a green today, but Choi deserved to win after making three birdies in a row."

Lexus International—US$220,000
Winner: Jeev Milkha Singh

India's Jeev Milkha Singh, who was making a name for himself on the PGA European Tour, was also carving a place for himself on the Asian Tour. An error cost him victory in regulation play, but he finished dramatically, winning the Lexus International on the third hole of a three-way playoff at Windmill Park in Bangkok in mid-October. It was his fourth Asian victory and his first in three years, and his first playoff victory after three losses.

"It was good to get that monkey off my back," said Singh, who came to the Lexus International ranked 48th on the European money list. Probably more impressive was the fact that he had defeated England's Lee Westwood, ranked No. 5 in the world, in the Alfred Dunhill Cup at St. Andrews the week before. Singh blew an opportunity for the Lexus International victory in regulation play when he three-putted the final hole from 45 feet for a bogey. It gave him a par 72, and left him tied at 13-under-par 275 with Myanmar's Zaw Moe, who finished with 73, and Pakistan's Taimur Hussain, who shot 68.

Hussain was knocked out on the first extra hole by a bogey off a bad drive. Singh and Moe parred the first two holes, and at the decisive third, it was a combination of good and bad. Singh holed a 14-foot putt for a birdie while Moe was flailing around, hooking his tee shot, then hitting his fourth shot over the green. So Singh's playoff problems had ended, but Moe's continued. It was his third playoff loss.

The Lexus International was a putting carnival from the start. South African Hendrik Buhrmann led the first round with 66, and noted, "I didn't hit the ball well, but I putted brilliantly." Hussain credited his putting for 67 and the halfway lead. Then Moe took the third-round lead with 65, making seven birdies, with no putt longer than six feet.

Nokia Singapore Open—US$400,000
Winner: Kenny Druce

It's called a "flop shot," but "flop" in this case doesn't mean failure. This kind is the high, lazy, delicate pitch from just off the green, designed to land softly and settle near the pin. Australian Kenny Druce, who stumbled in the final round after leading the first three, needed a great flop shot on the last hole, and that's just what he hit. South African Desvonde Botes was looking at a 10-foot par putt on the 18th to win the Nokia Singapore Open, one of the Asian Tour's majors. Druce came to the final hole trailing by one stroke, and he seemed out of contention when he hit his third shot over the back of the green. Then, while Botes waited, Druce hit the flop shot. As if in slow motion, the ball lifted high, peaked, then dropped slowly. It hit about six feet from the flag and trickled into the cup for a sensational par. Botes left his putt short, and they went into extra holes.

They tied on the first playoff hole. On the second, Botes, with a bad lie, hit a poor chip shot that left him a 25-foot putt for his par. He missed, and Druce dropped a 12-footer for a par and the victory. It was a great come-back. Druce, playing Orchid Country Club in rounds of 64, 68, 70 and 74 for a 12-under-par 276 total, led through the first three rounds, and led by three strokes going into the final round. He lost the lead with a shaky 40 on the first nine.

"I really struggled on the front nine, but turned things around with two great birdies on 10 and 11," Druce said. He bogeyed the 16th and trailed Botes by one going to the 18th.

"I never thought I was out of it until I went over the green on the last," Druce said. Then came the flop shot. "I said to myself, this has to go in," Druce said, "and amazingly, it did."

Hero Honda Masters—US$200,000
Winner: Jyoti Randhawa

India's Jyoti Randhawa ran away from the field — with one notable excep-tion — in becoming only the second player to successfully defend a title on the Asian Tour. Randhawa took his second successive Hero Honda Masters, and he might have sleepwalked his way home if it hadn't been for South African Sammy Daniels.

Randhawa, who shared the lead after the second round and held it alone after the third, shot a two-under-par 70 in the final round. That was good for an 11-under total of 277 at the Delhi Golf Club in New Delhi, India. Daniels was the only player with a shot at Randhawa. Daniels gave it a run and closed with 68, but fell one stroke short of tying Randhawa. The rest of the field was along for the ride. England's Chris Williams, on a closing 71, and Ecuador's Rafael Ponce, with 68, tied for third — a distant six strokes off the lead.

Randhawa and Daniels, in making a shambles of the tournament, raised the question of whether a new rivalry was sprouting here. The two had tied for third at the Nokia Singapore Open the week before, and here they were again, dueling it out.

Apart from Randhawa's victory, the talk of the tournament was the rally by India's Jeev Milkha Singh. Singh, who won the Lexus International three weeks earlier, made the halfway cut by just two strokes, then closed with 69 and 66 to rocket to a tie for sixth place. Eyes were also on Indian amateur Ashok Kumar, age 17. He was tied for second through the third round, but closed with 79 and finished 18th.

Sabah Masters—US$150,000
Winner: Robert Huxtable

When your caddie kicks the ball and you can laugh off the penalty, you're in the lap of luxury. That was the case of American Robert Huxtable at the Sabah Masters the first week of November. His caddie accidentally kicked his ball during the final round. The penalty stroke held his winning margin to a mere six strokes.

"I walked past my ball on the 16th and turned back to see my caddie walk up behind me and then kick it about a foot forward," Huxtable said. "I couldn't believe it. I really didn't need that." The caddie couldn't apologize enough. "But I told him not to worry," Huxtable said. "We had to get on with it." Huxtable was leading by five strokes at the time — not totally safe, but quite comfortable.

Huxtable, who won the 1998 Fila Open in a playoff, this time opened with a nine-under-par 63 and led wire-to-wire, shooting 65, 67 and 72 the rest of the way for a 267 total, 21 under par at Sutera Harbour, Malaysia. It was the second-lowest winning total on the Asian Tour, but it didn't stand as such because preferred lies were permitted in the first two rounds. His total surpassed Tiger Woods' 20-under total in the 1997 Asian Honda Classic in Thailand. For the record, Thai rookie Thongchai Jaidee finished second, edging out Taiwan's Lin Wen-tang with a birdie on the final hole for a par 72 and a 15-under 273 total.

Big leads are great, but they don't come without problems, Huxtable said. "I'm glad it's over," he said. "Leading by six at the start of the day, people seemed to think it was all over. Your mind does weird things when you're leading by so much. I thought about my wife and six-month-old baby to relax me and take me through it. I really did not play well today. I had to do some damage control."

Huxtable dedicated the win to his friend Payne Stewart, the American star who was killed in a plane crash in the United States the week before.

Johnnie Walker Classic—US$1,280,000
Winner: Michael Campbell

Held at the Westin Resort Ta Shee in Taiwan, the Johnnie Walker Classic was the first tournament to be co-sanctioned by three different organizations — the PGA European Tour, Asian PGA Tour and Australasian PGA Tour. To add to the complexities, consider this time warp: The tournament kicked off the 2000 PGA European Tour. But this was the second week of November, just a week after the 1999 season ended.

So there was no more fitting time for the return of a budding star who had all but disappeared — New Zealand's Michael Campbell. Much had been expected of him after 1995, a year capped by a near-miss at the British Open. Campbell was the third-round leader, then tailed off, but still finished in third place. Then came the wrist injury that all but ended his career.

"It's unbelievable. It has been a long, frustrating last four years," said Campbell after winning. He shot 66, 71, 69 and 70 for a 12-under-par total of 276 and a one-stroke victory over Australia's Geoff Ogilvy.

Tiger Woods, the defending champion, was going for his fifth victory in a row, but the quest fell to a pair of sevens on the first nine of the final round. The first was a double bogey at No. 6, after an errant drive, and the second a triple bogey at No. 8, where he put his second shot into the water. He finished alone in sixth place.

Campbell started the final round three strokes ahead of Ogilvy, and went up by four with three birdies in the first six holes against Ogilvy's eagle at No. 3. Then he double-bogeyed No. 7, needing three to get out of a bunker. With four holes to play, Campbell was tied with Ogilvy and Ernie Els. Els, playing four holes ahead, fell out with bogeys at the 15th and 16th and finished third.

Campbell took the lead with a birdie from 12 feet at the 15th. When Ogilvy bogeyed the 17th, Campbell had a two-stroke lead with one hole to play. Ogilvy could make up only one stroke, with a birdie at the last, and Campbell had erased four years of frustration.

Hong Kong Open—US$300,000
Winner: Patrick Sjoland

Figures don't always lie, but they can deceive. Example: In the final round of the Hong Kong Open, Sweden's Patrik Sjoland blew to 10 strokes over his third-round score and still won by one. Explanation: Sjoland had 62 in the third round.

"After the seventh hole, everything went wrong," Sjoland said. "My putting was not at all positive. I just had to put everything into it to try to win. I am elated." Sjoland, who had had a disappointing year on the PGA European Tour, dropping to 43rd on the Order of Merit, played the Hong Kong Golf Club in 70-65-62-72–269, 11 under par, to beat Ian Woosnam by a stroke.

American Mike Cunning, who led the first round with 65, slipped to a tie for 16th. And American Gary Rusnak, the halfway leader, shot all four rounds in the 60s and was third, three strokes behind Sjoland.

Sjoland looked like a runaway winner early in the final round. Woosnam bogeyed the first two holes. When Sjoland birdied No. 2, he had a hefty seven-stroke lead. The tournament seemed to be over. Then Sjoland's troubles started. Coming home, he bogeyed the 11th, 13th and 16th holes. "There was a lot of wind, and I wasn't comfortable on the back nine," he said. Woosnam birdied the 12th and 14th to close to within a stroke.

But Sjoland held on for the one-stroke win. "I was one ahead at the 17th and 18th," he said. "I thought I would need a birdie to win, but thankfully pars were enough."

Woosnam, himself a struggler of late, was not crushed by falling just short, not after posting 66-69-66-69–270. "I was seven behind at one point," Woosnam said. "So it's better to lose by one than seven."

Mittweida Thailand Open—US$200,000
Winner: Fran Quinn

It was more of a mad dash than a golf tournament, with seven players tied for the lead at one point in the last nine. Fran Quinn, an American working off a deep disappointment, finally broke the jam on the second nine for a one-stroke victory in the Mittweida Thailand Open. It was his first victory after four runner-up finishes in Asia over the years.

Quinn had come to Bangkok fresh from missing his bid for a playing card on the U.S. PGA Tour. He double-bogeyed twice on the second nine and missed the card by two strokes. Things were far different this time.

"It was a lot of fun out there," said Quinn. "This is certainly some consolation. I played really well for the first three days here, but I didn't play as well today. My back nine was solid, though."

Quinn, trailing by five after the first round and by one through the next two, played the Navatanee Golf Course in a 13-under 275 on a card of 71-66-67-71. A tight race? How about a four-way tie for second — Scotland's Simon Yates, Hong Kong's Scott Rowe, Canada's Jim Rutledge and America's Christian Pena, all at 276.

Quinn, who started the final round a stroke off the lead, hit the turn tied with six others at 12 under. He broke out with birdies at the 13th and 14th to take the lead at 14 under. He bogeyed the par-three 16th, three-putting from 65 feet, but his challengers couldn't take advantage of the lapse, and he parred the 17th and 18th for the win.

Omega PGA Championship—US$500,000
Winner: Fran Quinn

If American Fran Quinn was still smarting from missing his U.S. PGA Tour card, he eased the sting further by winning his second consecutive Asian tournament and the season-ending Omega PGA Championship in mid-December. He was only the second player, after Korea's Kang Wook-soon, ever to win back-to-back events on the tour. Quinn, who had won the Mittweida Thailand Open the week before, swept from behind in this one with a closing seven-under-par 65 for a three-stroke victory over Scotland's Simon Yates at Mission Hills in Shenzhen, China.

"If I had got my Tour card, I would not have come here," Quinn said. "It was really tough after the qualifying school. It was extremely disappointing."

Quinn, never more than three behind during the tournament, started the final round a stroke behind the Philippines' Felix Casas, who led or was tied for the lead through the first three rounds, and South Africa's Nico van Rensburg. Quinn broke into a three-stroke lead at the turn with a six-under-par 30 on the first nine. But his lead slipped to one when he double-bogeyed the par-three 13th, which he had aced in the second round. Then Quinn took command with a burst of three straight birdies — a 35-foot putt at the 15th, two putts at the par-five 16th, and a 30-footer at the 17th.

"I played really well last week, and I was playing with an awful lot of confidence when I came here," said Quinn, who scrambled to victory the week before. "I am absolutely delighted." Myanmar's Kyi Hla Han also had a big week, wrapping up the Order of Merit. He actually locked it up when American Gerry Norquist, the only man with a chance to catch him, missed the halfway cut. Han finished 14th here, winning $7,650 and boosting his season total to $204,210, the first in Asian history to top $200,000 in a single season.

Japan Tour

Token Corporation Cup—¥100,000,000
Winner: Masashi Ozaki

Although under a new administration established by the players, the start of the 1999 Japan Tour season had a most familiar ring to it. Masashi (Jumbo) Ozaki, Japan's enduring great, welcomed the new order with the 110th victory of his remarkable career. Ozaki, now 52 but understandably disdaining senior golf, roared from five strokes off the pace with a 67 in the final round of the Token Corporation Cup and posted a one-stroke victory with his 15-under-par 273 total. It was the second time in three years that Ozaki won the season-opening Token Cup.

Until the last day, it appeared that Tsuneyuki (Tommy) Nakajima, another of Japan's top stars in the modern era, might end his four-season victory drought. After starting the tournament with 68, just one stroke off the first-round lead, held jointly by Yoshinori Kaneko, Toru Taniguchi and Shusaku Sugimoto, the 44-year-old Nakajima followed with 66 Friday and joined Taniguchi in first place at 134. They had two strokes on Tsukasa Watanabe and Kaname Yokoo, and Ozaki was in a four-way tie for fifth at 137 after a 65. Nakajima and Taniguchi remained on top after 54 holes at 201 and they then had three strokes on Hirofumi Miyase. Ozaki shot 69 for 206.

Nakajima's quest for his 57th tour victory went by the boards as he managed just a 76 Sunday and dropped into a tie for seventh place. Taniguchi, seeking his second, also had trouble, shooting 73–274, not quite good enough to handle Ozaki's closing 67 at Kedoin Golf Club in Kagoshima Prefecture but good enough to clinch second place.

Daido Drinko Shizuoka Open—¥100,000,000
Winner: Kim Jong-duk

It took 30 holes on a water-logged course on the final day, but Kim Jong-duk of South Korea wound up with the title in the Daido Drinko Shizuoka Open, his first victory since his triumph in the 1997 Kirin Open that gave him the championship of the Asian Tour and its reward of playing privileges on the Japan Tour. Heavy rains plagued the middle stages of the year's second tournament at Shizuoka Country Club, making it impossible for play to be completed on schedule Friday and Saturday and forcing the leaders to spend a long day to finish the tournament Sunday.

Kim led through it all as he became just the second South Korean pro to hold two titles on the Japan circuit. Hahn Chang Sang won twice back in the early 1970s. Before the rains came, the 37-year-old Kim fired a sizzling 65 that included eight birdies and stepped off one stroke ahead of Hidemichi Tanaka and Seiki Okuda, both former Japan Open winners, and Australian Richard Backwell. The South Korean got in only four holes amid downpours Friday, finishing the round Saturday morning with 68. That pushed his lead to two strokes over Okuda, who posted a 69, and three over David Ishii (67-69). Kim played just six holes of the third round that day, holding his own at 11 under par. He led by four when play was suspended for the day.

On Sunday, as rain fell intermittently and winds swirled, Kim finished the third round with 72 for 205 and led Hawaii's favorite son, Ishii, by two. Then, scrambling for pars while chalking up pairs of birdies and bogeys, he nailed down the victory with another 72 for 277, barely enough as Shusaku Sugimoto came from nowhere with 10 birdies, two bogeys and a 64, taking second place, one stroke behind Kim. Ishii, winless in Japan since 1995, matched Kim's par round and finished third.

Georgia KSB Open—¥70,000,000
Winner: Yoshinori Kaneko

A different player — Yoshinori Kaneko — was in front, but, for the second week in a row, the first-round leader held his position from start to finish. This time, it was in the Georgia KSB Open at Tojigaoka Marine Hills Golf Club in Tamano and again weather interfered with play, this time fog that prevented nearly a third of the field from completing the second round on schedule.

Kaneko, who has been working on his game under Masashi Ozaki, redis-covered the touch that had been missing since his big 1996 season when he won three times and finished second to Ozaki on the year's money list. The 38-year-old veteran claimed the first-day lead with a solid, seven-birdie 65, one shot ahead of Masahiro Takahashi and Taiwan's Hsieh Chin-sheng. Kaneko remained bogey-free Friday, shot 67 and moved two strokes in front of Hsieh (68) and Nozomi Kawahara (67-67) as fog twice delayed play and left 35 men on the course at dark.

Saturday came up windy and Kaneko encountered trouble off the tee on the front nine. At one point he trailed Kawahara, but straightened things out on the incoming nine, shot 71–203 and widened his margin to three strokes, then over Frankie Minoza of the Philippines (68-70-68). Kawahara shot 73 for 207. Kaneko overcame several miscues on the way in Sunday, taking bogeys at the 11th and 14th and a double bogey at the 13th to drop into a deadlock with Minoza. But he bounced back with a birdie at the 16th and preserved the one-shot margin when he holed a seven-foot par putt on the final green for 72 and 275. It was his sixth career victory. Minoza shot 70 for 276 and Masahiro Kuramoto was next at 277.

Descente Classic Munsingwear Cup—¥67,500,000
Winner: Masayuki Kawamura

One week heavy rains, the next week fog, then the third week powerful winds disrupted the early season. The winds, blowing at close to 70 miles per hour, forced cancellation of the second round of the Descente Classic Munsingwear Cup in early April. Masayuki Kawamura was the beneficiary as he came from three strokes off the pace over the final 18 holes, joined a three-way tie at 205 and won the subsequent playoff for his third career victory.

Kazumasa Sakaitani, a winless second-season pro, fired a six-under-par 66 Thursday, overcoming a bogey and a double bogey with an eagle and seven birdies to take a one-stroke lead over Toru Suzuki, Yasunori Ida and Kim-pachi Yoshimura. Ida, who has gone 10 years without a victory, had his chance when, after the gales calmed and play resumed Saturday, he shot 68 for 135 and a one-stroke lead over Yasuharu Imano.

Ida still led by one stroke after 71 holes, but disaster struck when he put two shots into the water at the par-four 18th and took an eight. That opened the door for Kawamura (67), Tsuyoshi Yoneyama (67) and Kazuhiko Hoso-kawa (68) to post matching 205s and head into a playoff on that 18th hole. Yoneyama, who had taken a 38 on the back nine after a 29 on the outgoing nine, bogeyed the 18th the first time around in the overtime and Kawamura nabbed the title when he rolled in a six-foot birdie putt the next time as Hosokawa made par.

Tsuruya Open—¥100,000,000
Winner: Naomichi Ozaki

Back home after a nondescript three-month stretch on the PGA Tour in America, Naomichi (Joe) Ozaki discovered a welcome mat awaited him in his first appearance of the year at the Tsuruya Open. Ozaki rolled to a two-stroke win at Kawanishi in the young season's third wire-to-wire victory performance. The 42-year-old's win, the 26th of his career, came after he had gone without one in 1998, a rarity.

Ozaki got things started strongly on Thursday with birdies on the first three holes. He had nine in all in shooting 65 and taking a one-stroke lead over Hajime Meshiai and Toru Suzuki on Sports Shinko Country Club's Yamanohara course. Things remained pretty much the same after Friday's round. All three men shot 70s as Ozaki held his one-stroke lead. Taichi Teshima joined Meshiai and Suzuki in second place, posting a 69 for his 136. Ozaki built a four-stroke cushion Saturday with 66, powered by an eagle and five birdies. Toshiaki Odate replaced the runner-up trio in second place with a 67 as Teshima shot 71, Suzuki 72 and Meshiai 75.

Suzuki bounced back Sunday with 67 and gave Ozaki a run for his money. Ozaki managed just a par 72 with three birdies and three bogeys, but that was good enough for the two-stroke win over Suzuki. Two of the birdies came when he needed them — at the 15th and 17th holes. Teshima also rallied Sunday, shooting 69 and finishing third at 276.

Kirin Open—¥75,000,000
Winner: Choi Kyung-ju

Choi Kyung-ju was speechless after his playoff victory in the Kirin Open. "I can't find words to describe what I just accomplished," said the South Korean, who had played in only his second tournament in Japan. What he accomplished, besides the win, was clinch the money winning title of the Asian Tour (one tournament remaining), earn a spot in the upcoming British Open and, most importantly, acquire a two-year exemption on the Japan Tour.

Remarkably, for the fourth time in 1999, the champion led from the start. Choi, who was the No. 1 money winner on the domestic circuit in his homeland in 1996 and 1997, ran off six birdies on the par 71 West course of Ibaraki Golf Club for 65 and a one-stroke lead over Kazuhiko Hosokawa and Yasuharu Imano with Naomichi Ozaki, the Tsuruya Open winner the previous Sunday, just two back. The 28-year-old South Korean jumped four shots in front in windy, drizzly conditions Friday with 68 for 133. Jeev Milkha Singh of India entered the picture with 67 that put him in a five-way tie for second with China's Zhang Lian-wei, Tsuyoshi Yoneyama, Yasuharu Imano and Hideki Kase.

The weather worsened Saturday and, for the third time in four weeks, a tournament had to be cut to 54 holes. The delay affected Choi, who stuttered early and was fortunate to manage a par 71 Sunday. Singh was much more solid, and produced a 67 that forged a tie with the South Korean at 204. The playoff ended quickly as Singh missed the green in heavy rough on the first extra hole, two-putted for bogey and lost when Choi holed out for par there.

Chunichi Crowns—¥110,000,000
Winner: Yasuharu Imano

Yasuharu Imano found himself in fast company as he sought his first victory in the late stages of the rich Chunichi Crowns in late April, but he didn't let it faze him. Up against two of the Ozaki brothers in the final round, Imano calmly shot his second consecutive 65 on the Wago course of Nagoya Golf Club and gathered a one-stroke victory with his nine-under-par 271. "I didn't put any pressure on myself to win," said the 25-year-old Imano. "I just played relaxed golf, thinking I had nothing to lose."

First, Tateo (Jet) Ozaki, the 45-year-old holder of 14 titles, then Naomichi (Joe) Ozaki, 42, who had won his 26th tournament two weeks earlier, dominated the Chunichi Crowns for three days before bowing to Imano, a fourth-season pro. Battling strong winds Thursday, Tateo managed a 69 and took a one-stroke lead over Naomichi and Kenichi Kuboya. Then the younger brother took over, firing a 66 for 136 and going two strokes up on Kuboya (68) and Masanobu Kimura (67) as Tateo had a 70 for 139.

Naomichi Ozaki retained his two-shot lead with a two-under 68 Saturday as Imano moved into contention with the first 65 for 206 and Tateo Ozaki took sole possession of third place with 68–207. It all came down to the final hole Sunday. Imano, who had birdied the first two holes, made his sixth and final one at the 18th for the 65 that provided the victory when Naomichi

Ozaki missed a par putt there and had to settle for 68–272 and second place. Tateo also had a 68 and placed third at 275. Masashi Ozaki, who had won the tournament four times since 1992, tied for 30th at 282.

Fuji Sankei Classic—¥110,000,000
Winner: Shigemasa Higaki

The Japan Tour crowned its second consecutive first-time winner at the Fuji Sankei Classic when Shigemasa Higaki staked out a three-stroke lead in the third round and rode it home Sunday at the Kawana Hotel's Fuji course with a par 71 for a two-shot triumph. He was 11 under par at 273.

Hisayuki Sasaki, who suffered through a feeble 1998 season with a bad wrist, reappeared as a contender when he shot a six-under-par 65 and took the first-round lead in search of his fourth victory. He had one stroke on Australian Steve Conran and two on six other Japanese pros, including Higaki. Mitsuo Harada and Chen Tze-ming, the veteran Taiwanese star, unseated Sasaki Friday, shooting 66s to lead at 134. Akihito Yokoyama (64) jumped to 135, Sasaki (71) shared fourth place with Toshimitsu Izawa, and Higaki (70) was in sixth place with Conran (71).

The eventual winner ripped off an eagle and five birdies Saturday in taking the three-stroke lead at 202. Conran shot 68 and joined Chen (71) in the runner-up slot. Six years of winless golf ended for the 27-year-old Osaka native Sunday with the two-stroke victory. Conran, who finished second with 70–275, never got closer than two. That it was Higaki's tournament was apparent when an errant three-wood shot at the par-five 16th ricocheted off a tree back into the fairway and he scored a decisive birdie en route to the victory. American Brandt Jobe had 67 Sunday and took third place.

Japan PGA Championship—¥110,000,000
Winner: Naomichi Ozaki

Talk about rarities. The Ozaki brothers sent researchers around the world to the record books when Naomichi (Joe) won the Japan PGA Championship, because brother Masashi (Jumbo) finished second and brother Tateo (Jet) wound up third in the Japan Tour season's first major championship, played in 1999 at Twin Fields Golf Club, Komatsu. It had never happened before in Japan and the only parallel unearthed to our knowledge was in the 1956 Tasmanian Open in Australia, where brothers Peter and John Toogood finished first and third and their father, Alf, placed second.

It appeared that Tateo rather than Naomichi would be the winner at Twin Fields. He took a four-stroke lead into the final round as he went for his third PGA Championship, but was badly off form Sunday. He wound up with a 76. Meanwhile, Naomichi, one of the three players who entered the final round four back, was putting together an up-and-down 69 for 283 that gave him his first PGA Championship. Masashi, who has six PGAs on his gaudy record, shot 70 for 285 to grab second place, one shot in front of Tateo.

Hidemichi Tanaka was the first-round leader with 69 and retained a share of the top spot when he shot 72–141 Friday. Naomichi Ozaki and Toshimitsu Izawa joined him at 141, two strokes in front of Kim Jong-duk, the Shizuoka winner, and three Japanese pros. Masashi Ozaki, who was 49th after an opening 76, vaulted to 12th with a 69 Friday. Tateo Ozaki was one stroke better after two 72s, then roared to his big lead with a 66 for 210 Saturday that included an eagle and five birdies. Naomichi shot 73 and joined Katsunari Takahashi and Kazuhiko Hosokawa at 214. Masashi was at 215 with Izawa after a 70. Naomichi took the lead early Sunday when he racked up an eagle and three birdies on the first five holes and had enough of a cushion to survive three bogeys on the last five and pick up his second win in three weeks and the 27th of his career.

Ube Kosan Open—¥100,000,000
Winner: Choi Kyung-ju

Choi Kyung-ju continued one of the finest rookie seasons, capturing his second victory of 1999, this one a three-stroke win in the rain at the Ube Kosan Open to go with his Kirin Open victory a month earlier that gave him his Japan Tour passport for two years. Choi had only one bogey during the first three rounds as he established a four-stroke lead, then took the decisive victory with a par-72 round for 272 despite bogeys on two of the last three holes.

Hikaru Emoto, who has played for 17 years without a win, had a moment in the sun on Ube Country Club's Mannenike East course Thursday, finishing a wild round — an eagle, six birdies and four bogeys — with 68 and the lead. Choi, fellow South Korean Kim Jong-duk and four Japanese pros trailed by one stroke. When Emoto plummeted from contention with 75 Friday, Choi grabbed the top spot with 65 for 134, one shot ahead of Shingo Katayama (69-66). The 28-year-old Asian champion spread the gap to four when he followed with a 66–200 Saturday, avoiding bogeys for the second round in a row. Kazuhiko Hosokawa, in contention virtually every week, shot 67 for 204.

Choi didn't need a playoff to win as he did at the Kirin Open. The 72, fashioned in a heavy rain, left him unchallenged as Hosokawa trimmed just one stroke off his lead and took the runner-up slot at 275.

Mitsubishi Motors Tournament—¥100,000,000
Winner: Tsuyoshi Yoneyama

The long wait ended for Tsuyoshi Yoneyama at the Mitsubishi Motors Tournament. Dramatically. After 13 years of trying, Yoneyama finally won, but it took five playoff holes before he claimed the title at Lake Green Golf Club at Mitake. "I've said 'congratulations' to other players countless times, but I continued playing, thinking my turn would come," the 34-year-old Yoneyama beamed afterward. His victim was Kazuhiko Hosokawa, who finished as runner-up for the second week in a row and earlier in the season lost in the playoff that decided the Descente Classic.

The lead changed hands in each of the first three rounds and neither

Yoneyama nor Hosokawa was involved. Hawaiian David Ishii, the leading money winner in 1987 but winless since 1995, opened with six birdies on his front nine en route to a 65 and a one-stroke advantage over Masashi (Jumbo) Ozaki and Satoshi Higashi on a rainy Thursday that had a two-hour delay. Australian Richard Backwell did Ishii two better Friday, firing a course-record 63 and breezing into a one-stroke lead over Ozaki (69), Ishii (70) and five others at 135.

The 52-year-old Ozaki took over Saturday. He shot 68 and inched one stroke ahead of Ishii and four others, who had 204s. Among them were Yoneyama, who climbed up with a 65, and Hosokawa, who mustered a 64. Those two remained hot Sunday, shooting nearly identical 64s for 268, two strokes better than Mitsuo Harada's 65 could do, and going on to the playoff. Yoneyama prevailed at the fifth extra hole with a tap-in par after Hosokawa missed his par putt from nine feet.

JCB Classic Sendai—¥100,000,000
Winner: Shingo Katayama

At the JCB Classic Sendai the next week, it was pretty much the same story, different winner. Just as in the Mitsubishi Motors, two players ended in a deadlock at 268. The playoff only lasted three, instead of five, holes, but it was settled the same way. Shingo Katayama made a routine par to win when Shigemasa Higaki, the Fuji Sankei winner in May, missed the green and the subsequent 20-foot par putt. It was Katayama's second win, the earlier one coming in the defunct Sanko Grand Summer in 1998.

Low scores were commonplace, starting with the seven-under 64 of Kazumasa Sakaitani. Still, he led by just one stroke as Hiroyuki Fujita, aided by a hole-in-one, posted 65. Katayama got into the low-scoring act Friday, having a 63 for 132, where he was joined by Mitsuo Harada, who had 65. They led Sakaitani, Fujita, Taichi Teshima and Daisuke Serizawa by one shot. It was Teshima's turn Saturday. Seeking his first win in six years, Teshima produced 65 for a 198 total, and slipped into a one-stroke lead over Higaki, three over Katayama (69) and four over Hideki Kase, who moved up with a 64.

A one-over-par 72 ruined Teshima's victory hopes. Katayama shot 67 and Higaki 69 for their 72-hole 268s. Teshima finished at 270 with Kase (68).

Super Mario Yomiuri Open—¥90,000,000
Winner: Kim Jong-duk

South Korea's successful golf invasion of Japan continued at the Super Mario Yomiuri Open in mid-June. Kim Jong-duk captured his second event of the season and the fourth by a South Korean when he sprinted to a three-stroke victory at Yomiuri Country Club at Nishinomiya. Choi Kyung-ju picked up the other two victories. The Yomiuri win, following the Shizuoka Open at the start of the season and the Kirin Open in 1997, also made Kim the first player from his country ever to land three titles in Japan.

Overseas players dominated the top of the leaderboard all week. Taiwan's

Lin Keng-chi birdied the last three holes for 65 and the first-round lead, one shot ahead of Australian Stewart Ginn. Kim moved into the picture Friday when he shot a bogey-free 65 himself and climbed into a first-place tie with Ginn (68) at 134. They were two shots in front of Toru Taniguchi (65), Hajime Meshiai (67) and Seiki Okuda (69). Kim, who won in rainy weather at Shizuoka, proved a good mudder again at Yomiuri as he shot 68 in showers Saturday and opened a three-stroke lead over Taniguchi and Okuda, who had 69s. The veteran Ginn took 73.

Kim polished off the victory with a comfortable 68 for 270, 18 under par. Hidemichi Tanaka had the galleries buzzing as he was racking up 11 birdies and a bogey, but his sterling 62 didn't faze Kim. It did bring Tanaka from nowhere into a tie for second at 273 with Meshiai (67), the tour's leading money winner in 1993. Choi Kyung-ju took fourth place with 68–275.

Mizuno Open—¥90,000,000
Winner: Eduardo Herrera

Although never clear of other contenders, Eduardo Herrera and Tsukasa Watanabe staged a tournament-long duel for the championship of the Mizuno Open. One or the other held the lead at the Setonaikai Golf Club course throughout, the Colombian eventually prevailing to claim his fifth victory in Japan.

Watanabe, who last won in the 1994 Yomiuri Open, got off to a fast start at Setonaikai, shooting a seven-under-par 65 on a rainy Thursday. Herrera had 66 and Nobuhito Sato was next with 68, all three of whom completed their rounds before play was suspended until Friday morning. Herrera added 69 that inched him one stroke in front of Watanabe (71) and Keiichiro Fukabori (66). He stayed ahead with another 69 Saturday for 204 and Watanabe matched the 69 to remain just one stroke off the pace and join Herrera in the final group Sunday.

The South American had a bit of a shaky round Sunday, absorbing a bogey and a double bogey, but his five birdies factored out to 70, good enough for a two-stroke victory at 274. The final birdie at the 17th hole provided the final margin. Watanabe shot 71 for 275 to edge Tsuyoshi Yoneyama for the runner-up slot by one shot. The victory gave Herrera an invitation to the British Open.

Yonex Open Hiroshima—¥90,000,000
Winner: Masashi Ozaki

Masashi (Jumbo) Ozaki displayed some of the brilliance that made him Japan's most successful player ever when he surged from far off the pace in the final round of the Yonex Open and handed Shigemasa Higaki his second playoff defeat in a month. The remarkable Ozaki scored his awesome 111th career victory, 92 of them official titles, with his birdie on the first hole of the playoff on Hiroshima Country Club's Hachihommatsu course. He was the fourth double winner of the season.

Ozaki's earlier 1999 victory came in the season-opening Token Corporation Cup and he had not been in serious contention since then other than in the memorable blanket finish with his brothers at the PGA Championship. It didn't appear things were going to change for him in the Yonex, a tournament he had won three times in the previous five years and nine times in all. He began with a one-over-par 73 that left him six strokes off the pace of lightly regarded Taisuke Kitajima and Kazunari Matsunaga. Higaki, who had won the Fuji Sankei before losing the JCB Classic Sendai playoff to Shingo Katayama the first week of June, soared into a two-stroke lead Friday with a seven-under-par 65 for 136, one shot in front of David Ishii, Katsunori Kuwabara and Toshimitsu Izawa. Ozaki shot 69 but still trailed by six.

At the end of the third round, all signs indicated a forthcoming victory for either Higaki or Taichi Teshima, since they shared the lead at 203, six strokes ahead of the next contenders, Ozaki and Kaname Yokoo. Teshima ignited his chances with a 64 in overhauling Higaki, who had a 67. Instead, Ozaki duplicated Teshima's 64 Sunday and caught Higaki, who shot 70 for his 273. A 72 dropped Teshima into third place at 275. Ozaki picked up most of the strokes of his rally on the front nine, carding an eagle and three birdies. Then, in the playoff on the 18th hole, Ozaki dropped a six-foot birdie putt for the victory.

Aiful Cup—¥90,000,000
Winner: Toshimitsu Izawa

Toshimitsu Izawa emerged from the pack in the final round and won the Aiful Cup tournament at the end of July, one of just two events in five weeks during the usual lull in the Japan Tour season. Entering the final round at the Ajigasawa Kogen Golf Club, three players shared the lead at 206 and six others, among them Izawa, were just one shot behind. Izawa gained the third victory of his 20-year career when he produced the day's best round, 67, to nip Toru Taniguchi by one stroke with his 274.

Izawa recovered from a weak second round. Tied for second at 67, three strokes behind first-round leader Kazuhiro Takami, Izawa managed only a par 72 Friday and fell four strokes off the pace and behind eight players in the standings. American Todd Hamilton and Taniguchi were the pace-setters at 135. Despite a double bogey by Hamilton and a triple bogey by Taniguchi, the two men followed with 71s Saturday and were joined in first place by Katsunori Kuwabara, who shot 66. Izawa rebounded with 68 and joined the other five at 207. He started fast Sunday when he chipped in for an eagle at the first hole and followed with three birdies, including another chip-in at the 13th hole, for the winning 67.

NST Niigata Open—¥50,000,000
Winner: Toshimitsu Izawa

Toshimitsu Izawa never slowed down when he moved on from Ajigasawa to Toyoura for the NST Niigata Open. Izawa grabbed the first-round lead with a blazing, eight-under-par 64 and was never seriously threatened as he took his second win in eight days. He won by six strokes, the biggest victory margin of the season, and was the first to score back-to-back wins in 1999, although four others had two wins for the season.

The opening 64 gave Izawa just a one-stroke lead, though, as Masanori Kobayashi eagled the final hole for 65. It was a different story Friday. The 31-year-old Kanagawa pro jumped five strokes into the lead with a 67, as Kobayashi faded with 72 and Satoshi Higashi moved into second place at 136 with 69. Nobuhito Sato joined Kobayashi at 137. Izawa had an uncertain round Saturday, but eagled the 18th for 68 to add a stroke to his margin.

It was a breeze Sunday for the 1995 Japan Open champion. No challenges emerged as he knocked off birdies at the seventh and ninth holes, sailed home, avoiding serious trouble with a 15-foot bogey putt at the 12th, and posted 70 for 269 to complete the wire-to-wire victory. Kazuhiko Hosokawa came from far back with 66 to latch onto second place at 275.

Hisamitsu-KBC Augusta—¥90,000,000
Winner: Tsuyoshi Yoneyama

Once the dam breaks ... Tsuyoshi Yoneyama had gone 13 years without a victory on the Japan Tour before breaking through with his playoff victory in the Mitsubishi Motors in May. A second victory then followed much more quickly as the 34-year-old pro picked off the title in the rain-shortened Hisamitsu-KBC Augusta when action resumed after a three-week lapse. Yoneyama edged local favorite Takao Nogami by one stroke in the 54-hole event at Keya Golf Club at Shima, Fukuoka Prefecture, the last weekend of August.

Rainstorms, which had bedeviled the Japan Tour throughout the early season, hit again at Shima and washed out the Thursday round. When play finally got underway Friday, Takashi Kanemoto took the lead with a five-under-par 67, one shot in front of Tateo (Jet) Ozaki and Nobuo Serizawa. Nogami then thrilled the hometown fans Saturday, shooting his career-best round of 64 to slip one stroke in front with 135. He had eight birdies, including a run of four starting at the second hole. Yoneyama produced a 66 and took second place at 136. Masashi (Jumbo) Ozaki, who had won the KBC Augusta the previous three years and four times in all, remained a threat at 139.

Yoneyama scored four birdies and a bogey for 69–205 Sunday, just enough to nip Nogami, who could muster just 71. Richard Backwell of Australia was third at 207. "I didn't expect that a second triumph would come so soon," remarked Yoneyama afterward.

Japan PGA Match Play—¥80,000,000
Winner: Mamoru Osanai

Mamoru Osanai reached the last hole just twice as he marched to the Japan PGA Match Play at the Nidom Classic course at Tomakomai, Hokkaido, polishing off Toru Taniguchi, 4 and 3, in the 36-hole final. It was the second victory for the 29-year-old Osanai and continued the pattern of new winners of the 32-player event. Tsuneyuki Nakajima was the last repeat winner in 1992.

All eight of the seeded players were gone after the first two rounds as Osanai advanced to the third round after a 4-and-3 victory over Shigemasa Higaki and a 1-up win over Eduardo Herrera. Taniguchi advanced with tight triumphs over Satoshi Higashi and Tsuyoshi Yoneyama.

Then, in the third round Saturday morning, Osanai ousted Yasuharu Imano, 3 and 2, and Taniguchi took out Nobumitsu Yuhara, 1 up. In the afternoon semi-finals, Osanai had his other tough match, going the distance to beat Tsukasa Watanabe, 1 up, while Taniguchi took out the 1988 winner, David Ishii, 2 up.

Osanai built a five-hole advantage over Taniguchi in the morning round of the championship match, winning four consecutive holes on the front nine. Osanai was a bit shaky in the afternoon, but held onto his lead to close out the duel at the 33rd hole. Ishii defeated Watanabe on the sixth extra hole for third place.

Suntory Open—¥90,000,000
Winner: Nick Price

Nick Price had put victories on his record wherever tournament golf is played throughout the world — with one exception. He had always left Japan empty-handed. He made up for that omission in September when he added the Suntory Open title to his collection of 39 victories that includes the 1994 British Open and two U.S. PGA Championships. The Zimbabwe pro, who spends most of the year in America, birdied the 72nd hole at Sobu Country Club to edge Japanese star Shigeki Maruyama by one stroke for the title.

Price was in the picture from the start, but never led until nailing the birdie on the final hole Sunday. He and four others were one stroke off the opening-round pace, set by Tateo (Jet) Ozaki and Taiwan's Lin Keng-chi with 66s. Kaname Yokoo made the big noise Friday, shooting a five-under-par 66 for 134 to leap three strokes in front of Maruyama and Eiji Mizoguchi, four ahead of Price.

Scores rose with the winds Saturday and Maruyama found that his two-under-par 69 was worth a two-stroke lead at 206 over Price (70) and Kazu-hiko Hosokawa (69), once again making a strong bid for a 1999 victory. The final-hole birdie the 42-year-old Price made Sunday afternoon gave him a final score of 276, eight under par for the distance. Maruyama, frustrated once again in his victory quest, took a 71 to finish at 277, one stroke behind the winner, while Hosokawa skied to 79 and dropped to 14th place in the final standings.

ANA Open—¥100,000,000
Winner: Kazuhiko Hosokawa

Kazuhiko Hosokawa had done everything but win through the first six and a half months of the season when the Japan Tour arrived in Kitahiroshima for the ANA Open. He had four second-place finishes, including two playoff losses, and quite a few other high finishes. He broke through with a victory that week and, with the ¥20 million prize purse, took over first place in the money standings, skipping over four players to reach the No. 1 slot for the first time in his seven-year career. It wasn't easy. The 28-year-old Ibaraki native carried a one-stroke lead into the final round and won by that margin, closing with a par 72 at the Sapporo Golf Club for 277.

Hosokawa began the tournament with a flourish. He birdied the first two holes en route to 66 and a two-stroke lead over American Todd Hamilton, a seven-time winner in Japan but without a victory in 1999. Hamilton traded places with Hosokawa Friday. He shot 67 while Hosokawa took 70 and dropped one stroke off the pace. Naomichi (Joe) Ozaki, Katsunari Kuwabara and Keiichiro Fukabori were two shots farther back at 138.

Hosokawa regained first place with 69 Saturday in his run for his fifth tour victory. His one-stroke margin was over Fukabori, as Hamilton shot himself out of contention with 75, and Masashi (Jumbo) Ozaki, his bid for a sixth consecutive money title fading despite two victories, withdrew during the round with an ailing back. Two back-nine bogeys nearly derailed Hosokawa Sunday. They dropped him back to just a one-stroke lead over Katsuyoshi Tomori, back from a season on the PGA European Tour, who closed with 66. Naomichi Ozaki, who had spent the early season on the U.S. PGA Tour and was bidding for his 28th title, joined Tomori at 278 when he eagled the 12th and birdied the last two holes.

Gene Sarazen Jun Classic—¥100,000,000
Winner: Hajime Meshiai

It required an extra hole to do it, but Hajime Meshiai, the leading money winner in 1993, finally put another victory on his record. Meshiai's playoff triumph over Hirofumi Miyase in the Gene Sarazen Jun Classic was his 14th, but his first since the opening tournament of the 1998 season.

Masashi (Jumbo) Ozaki was a third party to the victory battle at the Jun Classic Country Club course at Ogawa. Forced out of the previous week's ANA Open in the second round with back trouble, Ozaki had to rein back on his power but utilized his other talents to contend against Meshiai in particular in the first playing of the tournament since its namesake's passing in America at age 97. Ozaki fired a second-round 65 to supplant Kazumasa Sakaitani, the first-day leader (67). Meshiai, who had a 66 that Friday, moved into second place at 137.

Then, the two veterans — Ozaki, 52, and Meshiai, 45 — deadlocked on top at the end of the third round as Meshiai shot 70 to catch Ozaki (72) at 207. Miyase was in a third-place tie at 209 with Shigemasa Higaki and Yeh Chang-ting of Taiwan and forced the playoff when he followed with 68 Sunday to catch Meshiai (70). Ozaki finished one back with 71. Miyase made things easy for Meshiai on the first extra hole when he put his tee shot in the water. Hajime then needed just his par to win.

Japan Open—¥120,000,000
Winner: Naomichi Ozaki

Naomichi (Joe) Ozaki scored the most important victory of his career when he won the Japan Open, but, if par and high scores are the criteria, the Otaru Country Club course was the real winner. With foul weather a contributing factor, par at the Otaru course in Hokkaido was barely attainable on a single-round basis and was unreachable in the overall scoring as Ozaki won the tournament with a 298 total, the only score under 300. The 42-year-old Ozaki, whose career has been overshadowed by the exploits of his older brother, Masashi, had 27 victories on his record, including his first Japan PGA Championship and another win earlier in the year after returning from a spring in America, but not the national championship.

Only three players shot sub-par rounds all week and Naomichi Ozaki had the best of them when he began the tournament with a four-under-par 68, four birdies and a bogey, and took a four-stroke lead over Toru Suzuki and Shusaku Sugimoto. How tough was the course? Naomichi shot 76 Friday and only lost a stroke of his lead. Nobumitsu Yuhara, another tour veteran, managed 73 and was second at 147, one shot ahead of Suzuki (76). Mamoru Osanai had the second sub-par round, but the 70 was little help since he opened with 82.

Heavy rains made things even worse for the players Saturday. Ozaki repeated the 76 in the slosh and Yuhara cut another stroke off Naomichi's lead with 75 for 222. The other Ozakis and money-leader Kazuhiko Hosokawa got into the act. Tateo (Jet) Ozaki had 74 for 223 and Masashi had the third sub-par round of the week, 69, to jump from 43rd place into a tie for fourth with Hosokawa (73) at 224.

Sunday was a wild adventure for Naomichi Ozaki. On the front nine of the rain-drenched course, he absorbed six bogeys and shot 42. Yuhara roared past him into a three-stroke lead with 37, but Ozaki fought back gamely, catching Yuhara at the 15th hole. Yuhara bogeyed the 16th and Naomichi stretched his lead to two with a 20-foot birdie putt at the 17th and a par out of a bunker at the 18th for 78 and a two-stroke victory over Yuhara and Hosokawa, who closed with 76 for his 300. Masashi (77) tied for fourth with Kazuhiro Takami (75) at 301 and Tateo (79) for sixth with Kaname Yokoo (76).

Tokai Classic—¥100,000,000
Winner: Kaname Yokoo

What a difference playing conditions and course set-up can make. Just days after the players endured the trying demands of the Japan Open, 21 broke par in the opening round of the Tokai Classic at Miyoshi Country Club, and at week's end, Kaname Yokoo had scored the second victory of his young career with a 72-hole score of 274, 14 under par and 24 strokes lower than it took for Naomichi (Joe) Ozaki to win the Open the previous Sunday.

Shingo Katayama, the JCB Classic Sendai winner in June, Masanori Kobayashi and faded star Masahiro Kuramoto led the par onslaught Thursday with 65s. Katayama separated himself from the others Friday when he added a 67 for 132. Yokoo also shot 67 and trailed the leader by one as Kuramoto had 70 and Kobayashi 74. Stewart Cink, a regular on the U.S. PGA Tour, made his presence known when he fired 68 and climbed into second place at 204, just one stroke behind Katayama, who retained his one-stroke lead with 71–203.

Another visitor mustered the strongest challenge to the winner Sunday. Vijay Singh put a good score up early when he shot 68 for 275. Yokoo, 27, one of the many Nihon University golf stars on the circuit, had birdied the 13th and 15th holes to take the lead, but almost gave it away at the final hole, when his approach nearly went into the water in front of the green. However, he wedged to three feet and made the putt for his winning 69–274. Cink (72) tied for third with Katayama (73) and Toshimitsu Izawa (71).

Bridgestone Open—¥110,000,000
Winner: Shigeki Maruyama

It had been a fruitless season for Shigeki Maruyama, who had made an international name for himself with his performance and presence in the 1998 Presidents Cup Matches in December in Australia. In fact, Maruyama had gone 15 months without a victory. Perhaps the setting helped. Playing on the Sodegaura Country Club course on which he won the Bridgestone Open in 1995 and 1996, the 30-year-old pro never was out of first place with four rounds in the 60s and put the title away comfortably with a five-stroke victory at 268, 20 under par.

The score of 66 was the number Thursday as Maruyama shared the first-round lead with Masashi (Jumbo) Ozaki and Ikuo Shirahama, who both also were former Bridgestone winners. Both Maruyama and Ozaki had eagles in their rounds. Toshimitsu Izawa, seeking his third 1999 win, joined Maruyama at the top Friday when he shot his second 67 and Maruyama 68 for 134s. Ozaki had 69.

Maruyama broke things open in the latter stages of his third round Saturday. He ran off four birdies on the final six holes for another 66 after he and Izawa had both turned with 34s. Izawa finished with 69, second by three strokes and two ahead of Ozaki (70), young Australian up-and-comer Craig Spence (67) and Toru Taniguchi (69).

Maruyama took any doubt out of things Sunday when he birdied the last three holes for 68 after an uncertain front nine. Both Izawa and Spence shot 70s to hold their positions, while Ozaki and Taniguchi had 71s to tie for fourth.

Philip Morris Championship—¥200,000,000
Winner: Ryoken Kawagishi

Ryoken (Ricky) Kawagishi had arrived in 1990 with great amateur credentials, including two victories in important amateur tournaments in America, and promptly lived up to his advance notices by scoring three victories in one of the best rookie seasons ever.

But his game has never been that productive since then. He scored single victories in 1991 and 1995 and was only an infrequent contender over the next four years. The victory drought ended at a lucrative time for the 32-year-old pro at the end of October when he captured the Philip Morris Championship, the co-richest event on the 1999 Japan Tour. It was another case of affinity for courses. Kawagishi had scored one of those first-season victories in the predecessor Lark Cup on the same ABC Golf Club course.

Kawagishi trailed the leaders for two days. Dinesh Chand of Fiji and veteran Nobumitsu Yuhara opened in front with 67s as Kawagishi began with 71. Chand and Yuhara yielded the top position to Katsunori Kuwabara (68-66) and Zaw Moe of Myanmar (69-65) Friday with Chand one shot back. Kawagishi made a big move with 65, capped by an eagle at the final hole. He slipped into fourth place at 136, two off the lead.

When Kawagishi followed Saturday with 66, running off four straight birdies in fashioning a front-nine 31, he took the lead for good at 202, as Kuwabara had 69 for 203. Both players shot 68s Sunday to finish one-two. Kawagishi had a four-stroke lead at one point, but Kuwabara made it close when he birdied the 15th and 18th around Kawagishi's three-putt bogey at the 16th. Kawagishi had five birdies with the bogey to finish with a 270 total, 18 under par.

Acom International—¥110,000,000
Winner: Hidemichi Tanaka

Another player made a late-season recovery of sorts at the Acom International. Hidemichi Tanaka, who enjoyed the finest of his eight seasons in 1998 with a prestigious victory in the Japan Open and two other wins, had not fared very well in 1999, his best finish a tie for second in the Yomiuri Open. The 28-year-old Tanaka got his game going full blast at Ishioka Golf Club in early November and raced to a five-stroke victory, the sixth of his career.

Tanaka took charge the second day, tacking 69 onto his opening 66, after trailing Toru Suzuki and Mamoru Osanai by one stroke Thursday. His 135 total Friday gave him a two-stroke lead over Nozomi Kawahara (71-66), Taichi Teshima (70-67), Satoshi Higashi (69-68) and Keiichiro Fukabori (66-71). A second 66 Saturday stretched Tanaka's margin to three strokes over Fukabori, who shot 67, and a closing 68 gave him a 19-under-par 269 total and the five-shot margin over Fukabori, who had 70 in the final round.

Sumitomo Visa Taiheiyo Masters—¥140,000,000
Winner: Hirofumi Miyase

While attention was focused on the prominent overseas visitors and the race for the season's money title, lightly regarded Hirofumi Miyase went about the business of winning the Sumitomo Visa Taiheiyo Masters and its healthy first-place purse. European Ryder Cuppers Lee Westwood, Darren Clarke and young Spanish sensation Sergio Garcia came to Japan for the tournament along with American ace Mark O'Meara, but only Clarke and Westwood, who had won the tournament the previous three years, got into the heat of battle at the Taiheiyo Club's Gotemba course. The Irishman, in fact, wound up in a three-way playoff with Miyase and Ryoken (Ricky) Kawagishi that Miyase won on the second extra hole.

Clarke posted his first of two 66s in Thursday's first round and shared the lead with Naomichi (Joe) Ozaki, the money list leader, Hideki Kase, Hajime Meshiai and Miyase. Westwood was just one back with Kawagishi, Tateo (Jet) Ozaki and Toru Suzuki. Rain fell Friday, but Katsuyoshi Tomori still shot 66 and grabbed a one-stroke lead at 135, one shot ahead of Naomichi Ozaki and Miyase and two in front of Clarke, Westwood and Kawagishi.

It was Kawagishi's turn for a 66 Saturday. It gave him a 203. Miyase remained close with 69–205 and Shigeki Maruyama climbed into contention himself with 66–206. Clarke shot a second 71 for 208, but refused to give up, bouncing back Sunday with 66 to overtake Kawagishi, who slipped to 71 for his 274. Miyase shot a solid 69 to create the three-way playoff. Kawagishi went out on the first extra hole when he put his approach in the water in front of the green. Clarke nearly did the same thing on the next hole, was barely able to move the ball from the water's edge and missed a seven-footer for a bogey. Miyase, who had lost in his only two tour playoffs, including the Jun Classic to Meshiai earlier in the season, made par and picked up just the second victory of his 11-year pro career. American Brandt Jobe just missed the playoff when he closed with 65, the week's best score.

Dunlop Phoenix Tournament—¥200,000,000
Winner: Thomas Bjorn

The international cast of champions of the rich Dunlop Phoenix Tournament acquired a new nation in 1999 when Denmark's Thomas Bjorn prevailed in a playoff against young Sergio Garcia, who bounced back from a lukewarm showing the previous week in the Taiheiyo Masters. Players from seven countries now have claimed a Dunlop Phoenix title. Most of the visitors in 1999 came from Europe with the U.S. stars notably absent.

Kaname Yokoo, the Tokai Classic winner, was the first-round leader, shooting a seven-under-par 65 at Phoenix Country Club for a two-stroke lead over Greg Norman, Hidemichi Tanaka, Mathew Goggin and Hiroyuki Fujita. The eventual playoff combatants shared the lead at 135 after 36 holes, Bjorn with 69-66 and Garcia with 68-67. They were two strokes in front of Yokoo and Shusaku Sugimoto.

Nothing changed at the top Saturday as Bjorn and Garcia both fired 68s for 203. That put them three shots up on the field, with Sugimoto, Tanaka and Shigeki Maruyama, who shot a course-record 61, at 206. Garcia built a three-stroke lead on the early holes Sunday, but he slipped back into the final tie as the Dane made birdies on the last two holes for his 67–270 and Garcia missed a 14-footer for a birdie of his own at the 18th. The playoff went four holes before Bjorn put his third shot at the par-five 18th three feet from the hole and Garcia couldn't match the birdie. They needed their 67s in regulation as Maruyama followed his 61 with 65 and finished at 271. Norman came back Sunday with 63 but finished far back in a tie for fourth at 276 with Lee Westwood and Naomichi Ozaki.

Casio World Open—¥140,000,000
Winner: Tsuyoshi Yoneyama

Talk about your late bloomers. Not content just to finally get on the board with a victory after 13 years on the Japan Tour, Tsuyoshi Yoneyama became one of the most successful players in 1999 when he followed his first two career wins earlier in the year with a third triumph in late November in the Casio World Open, one of the most important events, thus becoming one of the year's biggest money winners with more than ¥100 million. He and Naomichi Ozaki were the only three-time winners of the season.

American Hank Kuehne, who has just embarked on a professional career, got off to a good start at Ibusuki Golf Club in his first visit to Japan. He shot 67 and shared the first-round lead with Taichi Teshima, but was no factor after that. Ozaki, seeking to solidify his hold on the money leadership, roared into first place Friday when he recorded a blistering eight-under-par 64 for 135. Tatsuhiko Takahashi joined him there with 69-66. Both players eagled the 18th. For the third straight day, the lead changed hands by twos. Shingo Katayama and Hidemichi Tanaka shot 68s for 207 as Ozaki took a 73 and dropped to 208, sharing that spot with Toshimitsu Izawa.

Yoneyama launched his final-round surge from 209 after shooting a 68 Saturday. Brandishing a splendid short game, Yoneyama one-putted 12 greens, didn't make a bogey and carded a seven-under-par 65 that gave him a one-stroke victory with 274. Teshima had a chance to force a playoff, but he missed a six-foot birdie putt at the 18th, took 66 and placed second.

Japan Series JT Cup—¥90,000,000
Winner: Kazuhiko Hosokawa

Kazuhiko Hosokawa strengthened his bid for the money title by winning the Japan Series JT Cup in which only 25 players, the year's winners and top money winners, competed. Hosokawa started and finished on top in the tournament at Tokyo's par-70 Yomiuri Country Club to score his second win of the season and sixth of his career. The ¥30 million prize temporarily inched him just ahead of Ozaki before Ozaki's international earnings in major events shifted the balance in his favor at the end.

Hosokawa had two brilliant rounds in the Japan Series. He blazed a seven-under-par 63 Thursday to start the tournament with a two-stroke lead over Toshimitsu Izawa, another enjoying his best season in Japan. Izawa, seeking his third win of 1999, seemed well on his way toward it after the next two days. On Friday, he added 70 to his opening 65 and jumped two strokes ahead of Hosokawa, who stumbled to a 74 for 207. Then, on Saturday, Izawa doubled the margin to four over Hosokawa (69) with a 67–202, but couldn't keep it going Sunday, when Hosokawa produced his other sparkling round. Hosokawa shot 64 for 270 and whizzed past Izawa, who had to settle for a par 70 and the runner-up slot. Nobody else threatened, Shingo Katayama placing third at 274.

Fancl Okinawa Open—¥70,000,000
Winner: Taichi Teshima

Taichi Teshima, another Japanese who honed his skills as a collegiate golfer in America, barely averted a seventh straight winless season when he took a playoff victory in the Fancl Okinawa Open, the season's finale. Teshima, who had made several title bids during the year, and Seiki Okuda, the 1993 Japan Open champion and a five-time winner, finished their 72 holes at Daikyo Country Club with 13-under-par 271s to bring on the overtime work.

Most of the attention the first two days was on Naomichi (Joe) Ozaki and Kazuhiro Hosokawa and their duel for the money title, but that fizzled out when Hosokawa shot 143 and missed the cut by one stroke. With the No. 1 spot secure, Ozaki withdrew the next day, citing illness. He was 10 strokes off the lead after 36 holes.

Faring much better in the early going were Eiji Mizoguchi and Nozomi Kawahara, who led with 66s, one shot in front of Toru Taniguchi, Keiichiro Fukabori and Hisayuki Sasaki. Even more so, Satoshi Higashi raced into first place Friday with a nine-under-par 62 for 140, establishing a five-stroke margin on the field. He had an eagle and seven birdies in the near-flawless round. At that point, Teshima and Okuda were seven back at 137. Higashi slipped to 72 Saturday, but still led by four over Hideki Kase, who had 63 that day, five over Okuda and six over Teshima and two others.

Two birdies brought the title to Teshima Sunday. The first was at the 18th. It gave him 66 and a tie with Okuda, who bogeyed the 17th and parred the 18th for 67. The second, on the same 18th hole in the playoff, was a seven-footer that paid off when Okuda missed his from four feet.

13. Australasian Tour

This was the Year of the Amateur on the Australasian Tour with two of the most important titles going to youngsters who were barely old enough to drink celebratory champagne toasts. Aaron Baddeley, an 18-year-old with a game that Ian Baker-Finch called "complete in every way," outplayed Greg Norman and Colin Montgomerie to win the Holden Australian Open Championship. The next week, 22-year-old Brett Rumford birdied the last two holes to tie Craig Spence, then out-dueled Spence in a four-hole playoff that wasn't decided until Rumford made a 25-foot birdie putt. "He spurred me on," Rumford said of Baddeley's victory. "It was like breaking the four-minute-mile barrier. You should see more amateurs winning tournaments now."

Baddeley also spoke of future aspirations. "Tiger Woods definitely motivates me because he sets the level of golf at the moment," Baddeley said. "He is playing great. My goal is to be better than Tiger. If Tiger is the best player in the world and I want to be the best player in the world, I have to be better than Tiger. Tiger is the benchmark, and I want to be better than the benchmark. Hopefully when I turn professional, I won't have to worry about money. As long as I am holding this trophy, money doesn't count."

There were plenty of other winners in Australasia in 1999. Kenny Druce survived a final-round 74 and opened the season with a three-stroke win over Lucas Parsons in the Victorian Open, while Jarrod Moseley won a joint European-Australasian Tour event at the Heineken Classic in Perth. Peter Lonard, Bernhard Langer and Ernie Els tied for second in the Heineken Classic, one shot behind Moseley.

Langer made a bid the next week at the Greg Norman Holden International, but a triple bogey on the last hole, which included a penalty stroke for picking up his marker on the green without first replacing his ball, resulted in a final-round 80 for Langer and a third-place finish behind Michael Long and Michael Campbell.

Craig Spence finished tied for 15th at Norman's event, but came back the next week at the Ericsson Masters and beat Norman head-to-head with a birdie on the final hole. The week after that, Spence finished third behind winner Rodney Pampling and Geoff Ogilvy in the Canon Challenge.

Spence and Pampling had the best overall records going into the Australasian Tour Championship. Pampling made a good run, but not enough to catch Marcus Cain, who shot a final-round 65 to win by four shots over Paul Gow and by five over Pampling, Robin Byrd, Peter Senior, Scott Laycock and Stephen Leaney. Spence tied for ninth, seven shots behind.

Even though Pampling and Spence posted good numbers at the Tour Championship, they were unable to oust Moseley from the top spot in the 1998-99 Australasian Order of Merit. Moseley finished tied for 11th, but his A$9,300 check gave him a total of A$330,798, ahead of Pampling (A$287,907) and Spence (A$277,160). Geoff Ogilvy was named Rookie of the Year, and Pampling was awarded with the Most Consistent Player title.

Victorian Open—A$225,000
Winner: Kenny Druce

With a six-stroke lead going into the final round, Queenslander Kenny Druce knew he would have to struggle to keep from becoming complacent in the final 18 holes of the Victorian Open, and he was right. Druce's margin over Robert Allenby was trimmed to one on the second nine, but birdies by Druce on the 16th and 18th secured his first win by three strokes over Lucas Parsons.

Parsons began the day nine shots back, but when Druce made double bogey after an errant tee shot at the 13th, Parsons and Allenby pulled to within one. Allenby fell away on the 16th when he needed three chips to reach the green and finished with a double bogey, while Parsons finished birdie-birdie-eagle-birdie for 68 to be alone in second place at 278. Druce's 275 total, 13 under par, resulted from rounds of 67, 68, 66 and 74.

"It was a funny day," Parsons said. "I got frustrated, but suddenly it all happened. Nothing was further from my mind than a playoff when I doubled the 12th, but when I birdied 16 I thought I might have a sniff if I finished eagle-eagle. I eagled 17 and made a birdie on the last. I was pretty happy with that. Kenny deserved to win. It would have been a disaster if he hadn't after he got to 15 under in the first three days. Allenby put some pressure on Kenny early, but 16 killed him. It could bring anyone undone. I think it is one of the best par-threes in golf. He went along and three chips later it was over."

The week was not without controversy. Two Melbourne newspapers took exception with several players' decisions to smoke on the golf course with the Victorian Open's major sponsor being SmokeFree Victoria, a government agency charged with encouraging Australians to kick the habit. The main object of the newspapers' wrath was Bradley King, who was photographed smoking in the first round. The picture ran as a front-page item beneath the headline "Sponsor Gruff as Golf Champs Puff."

King was furious and issued a statement saying, "I am deeply offended and upset by the newspaper articles published on Friday which carried the implication that I and my fellow professionals have disregarded our obligations to the tournament sponsor. The facts are very different. I certainly believe all of us have conscientiously observed the no smoking areas designated by the sponsors and the Victorian Golf Association. In addition I, and my fellow players, have also made every effort to avoid smoking in circumstances where that activity might be captured by television cameras. I believe these actions on my part fulfill my obligations as a professional sportsman to SmokeFree Victoria."

When the cloud from the smoking controversy cleared, all attention turned to Druce, who was both relieved and ecstatic with his win. "I had a couple of heart attacks along the way, but it is my first victory and I'm rapt," he said. "When I dropped two shots at 13, I decided I just had to hang in there, although the doubts were creeping in. We had three tough holes ahead and I managed to finish square on the back nine. One of the hardest things was knowing what to do. Having a big lead at the start was new to me. Usually I am five or six shots behind on the last day and just go out with all guns blazing. It was quite a different feeling being in front. I was pretty nervous and excited. Instead of trying to birdie every hole, I just tried to hit the greens and not make too many mistakes."

Heineken Classic—A$1,500,000
Winner: Jarrod Moseley

For a man who grew up watching famous golfers such as Bernhard Langer on television, playing in the Heineken Classic on a sponsor's exemption was the thrill of a lifetime. Coming from five shots back in the final round to defeat Langer, Ernie Els and former club professional Peter Lonard was more than Melbourne's Jarrod Moseley could have dreamed. The 26-year-old, who wasn't exempt on the Australasian Tour and played in the event on a sponsor's invitation, turned in a gritty performance in Perth, firing a final-round 69 on the par-72 Vines Resort course for a 274 total and a one-stroke victory.

"This is unbelievable," Moseley said. "I came here as a spectator six years ago. Today I played with Bernhard Langer. He's won the Masters! I was playing with guys I had seen on television and looked up to for years."

Not only was Moseley playing with legends, he was soundly beating them with consistently good play. He started the week with two 68s and finished with two 69s. "It was a dream come true," he said. "I don't know what I will do with the money. My family has never had money and I've never been around people with money."

Because the Heineken Classic was a joint event on the Australasian and PGA European Tours, Moseley earned an exemption on the European circuit through 2001.

Those thoughts never entered Moseley's mind as he marched through his final round. The only signs of doubt in an otherwise flawless performance came on the last two holes. A pushed approach shot on the 17th led to a bogey, and a similarly leaky drive on the 18th found the fairway bunker and led to a par on a relatively easy par-five.

Even with Moseley's solid performance, the tournament could have belonged to Els. With opening rounds of 65 and 66, Els jumped to a commanding four-stroke lead over Langer and Jarmo Sandelin, with Moseley five shots back. Els shot 69 on Saturday and saw his lead trimmed to three over Sandelin, but Sandelin had trouble early in the final round, and Els seemed to have things under control. With 12 holes to play the big South African had a six-shot lead over a former club professional and sponsor's invitee. This one should have been easy.

Then, on the 413-yard, par-four seventh, Els hit a poor drive into the rough, then hooked his approach shot into an unplayable lie. After slapping around a few more shots, Els took a triple-bogey seven and went on to shoot 75. "One hole killed me," Els said. "I hung in there and had a chance until the end."

Els reached the par-five finishing hole with his second shot and had a chance to tie Moseley with an eagle putt of 25 feet. When the putt slipped below the hole, Moseley had his victory. "I had my eyes closed for that (last putt)," Moseley admitted. Then he smiled as the magnitude of his victory sunk in. "I'll remember this week forever."

As for Els, he waved to the crowd after his final birdie and his third top-10 finish in three weeks, but the dejection was obvious. "I'll be disappointed tomorrow," he said.

Greg Norman Holden International—A$1,000,000
Winner: Michael Long

While New Zealander Michael Long birdied three of the last 10 holes and made an eight-foot putt for bogey at the 18th to win the Greg Norman Holden International in Sydney, the biggest story of the tournament was the remarkable collapse of Bernhard Langer, who led by five with nine holes to play. Despite a run by Long that tied the lead after the 16th, Langer still held a one-shot lead with one hole to play.

Then catastrophe struck. In gusty winds, Langer thought he hit a perfect three iron on the 225-yard, par-three final hole, but the ball drifted right and plugged in a bunker. From there Langer blasted over the green, then chipped well short, the ball stopping nine feet from the hole. He would need to make the uphill putt to tie Long. Langer broke from his normal routine and picked up his ball marker on the green before replacing the ball. After calling a rules official to confirm his suspicions, Langer penalized himself one shot, then three-putted for triple bogey and a score of 80.

"I don't know why. I just picked the marker up," Langer said. "It's never happened before, and it happened today. Don't ask me why I did it. I didn't do it on purpose. It just happened. I was probably focused too much on what I was trying to do."

Long was stunned by Langer's mistake. After pulling even with a chip-in birdie at the 16th, Long thought he had blown his chance when he also found the bunker at the par-three 18th. Like Langer, Long blasted through the green. He then hit a poor chip, not too dissimilar to the one Langer would hit a half hour later, but Long made his eight-footer for bogey.

The one-under-par 71 gave Long a nine-under 283 total, one better than fellow New Zealander Michael Campbell, who closed with 74. Langer placed third at 285.

Ericsson Masters—A$750,000
Winner: Craig Spence

Even though Craig Spence led the Ericsson Masters after every round for the first three days and throughout the day on Sunday, many people watching didn't expect him to win. The man chasing Spence was none other than Greg Norman, who was searching for his seventh Masters title. Norman recovered from an opening 74 to shoot 68 and 66 in the second and third rounds. That was enough to pull within two shots of Spence and put Norman in the final pairing of the day.

Norman also made some provocative comments on Saturday evening about Spence's putting. The youngster used a long putter, something Norman thought showed a weakness in his short game. "I would say his putting is the weakest part of his game," Norman said. "He has hit the ball close enough not to put a lot of pressure on his short game."

Norman drew even with Spence at 15 under par through 17 holes, and it seemed the more experienced and more intimidating Norman would prevail. But Spence came through, hitting a six iron from 185 yards to three feet on the 18th. Norman was unable to match the shot, leaving his approach 30 feet from the hole. When Norman missed his birdie effort and tapped in for par and a score of 69, he could do nothing but watch as Spence rolled in the birdie putt to win. Spence finished with a bogey-free 70 for a 276 total, 16 under par, and the one-stroke victory.

"Norman was definitely on my mind," Spence said. "But my coach, Dale Lynch, and I came up with some keys that helped me settle down. I told myself, 'Everybody expects Greg to win because you've never won and you are playing with the Shark; you've led all week and you've got to be getting tired.' That took the pressure off. I knew I had held in there strong, had done all the hard work. I thought that even if I hit a bad shot, people were going to admire me for hanging in there. Greg Norman is not a bad person to lose to. That is how I kept my emotions down today."

Norman had nothing but praise of the 24-year-old champion, saying, "Craig was very impressive. I thought he played exceptionally well today. He was in control of his game. He never showed any signs of hesitation. Whatever club he hit, he picked it out and hit it with a lot of conviction. I think now he has to go on with it. He has to use this as a stepping stone. I said to him at the presentation, 'Go back, think about this stuff for the next couple of days, the shots you played, the shots you didn't play well and use it.' Once you do it the way he did it for the first time, you know you can keep doing it. He did not show any sign of buckling out there."

Canon Challenge—A$550,000
Winner: Rodney Pampling

After opening a five-stroke lead through three rounds, Rodney Pampling held off several final-round charges to capture his first Australasian Tour victory in Sydney at the Canon Challenge. Pampling's final-round 69 for an 18-under-par 270 total was good enough for a three-shot win over hard-charging Geoff Ogilvy.

Ogilvy shot a final 67 and closed Pampling's lead to two before Pampling made a late birdie. Also mounting a charge was Ericsson Masters champion Craig Spence, who shot 64 to finish alone in third at 274.

"I was a bit worried there for a while," Pampling said. "I didn't think I would make another birdie, but I did and it was nice."

Australasian Tour Championship—A$500,000
Winner: Marcus Cain

If he had to pick an event for his first win as a professional, Marcus Cain said the Australasian Tour Championship was a pretty good choice. The 26-year-old Cain came from behind in the final round with a seven-under-par 65 to finish at 12-under-par 276 for the week, four strokes ahead of second-place Paul Gow, who shot a closing 68.

Third-round leader Peter O'Malley gave up the lead early, but retained a share of second place until the 18th hole on Sunday, when the former Scottish Open winner made a 10 on the par-five to drop into a five-way tie for 11th place. O'Malley finished with 78.

Jarrod Moseley also tied for 11th place, and it was enough to secure his spot atop the Australasian Order of Merit for the 1998-99 season, guaranteeing him invitations to the British Open and U.S. PGA Championship.

Ford Open Championship—A$600,000
Winner: Craig Parry

When the Australasian Tour resumed in November at the Kooyonga Golf Club in Adelaide, the most consistent player for three rounds was Craig Parry, who carded three consecutive 70s to trail Scotland's Raymond Russell by one stroke. Parry broke his two-under-par streak with eight birdies and no bogeys in a final-round 64 that propelled him to a five-stroke victory over Russell in the Ford Open Championship.

"It gives me a great feeling of relief," said Parry, who had a 274 total, 14 under par. "I've been coming here for a long time and had quite a few near-misses. Today I played well for the first time this week. I made a good, fast start with birdies on the first two holes like I wanted. I did some work on the practice green last night and noticed that my shoulders were open, so I fixed that. And I've added a couple of shots to my game. I can now hit a low drive into the wind and that was a big help today."

Russell played well, finishing with 70 to go with his earlier rounds of 68, 72 and 69 for a 279 total. While disappointed, Russell said that few people could have beaten Parry. "When you go into the final round with a one-shot lead, you are looking to win," Russell said. "But Craig played very well and kept the momentum going. He did not make a bogey, and it was a great score. I can't complain. The way I've been playing lately, second is pretty good. I can take some confidence from the fact that I beat 144 guys bar one. I'm looking forward to next week."

Only one other player made a run at Parry. Peter O'Malley started three strokes behind Parry, and four off the lead. When O'Malley reached four under par for his round through 11 holes on Sunday, he had visions of the run he made in the 1992 Scottish Open, when he finished eagle-birdie-birdie-birdie-eagle to edge Colin Montgomerie for the title. Another seven-under run in the final eight holes would have allowed O'Malley to pass Parry, but that was not to be.

"Every time I made a birdie, Craig seemed to make two," O'Malley said. "I'm not too unhappy. I wanted to play well going into the Open next week, and I have done that. Apart from winning a major, that is the title I want to win most. This week I changed to an old putter. The last time I used it I shot 64 in the Volvo Masters. Now I wonder why I changed."

Holden Australian Open Championship—A$1,000,000
Winner: Aaron Baddeley

Sergio Garcia wasn't the only teenage sensation to make his mark on the game during 1999. In one of the most improbable victories of the year, amateur Aaron Baddeley, who entered the final round of the Holden Australian Open Championship with a one-stroke lead, held off challenges by such players as Greg Norman and Colin Montgomerie to win the title by two shots. Baddeley, eight months and 11 days past his 18th birthday, became the youngest winner in the tournament's storied history, and he became the first amateur to take the title since Bruce Devlin won in 1960.

No one expected Baddeley to hold onto the lead with Norman and Montgomerie so close, but Baddeley not only answered them shot-for-shot, he beat them handily. Playing with Montgomerie, Baddeley shot three-under-par 69 to Montgomerie's 71. It was Baddeley's third round in the 60s for the week (67-68-70-69), and his two-shot margin held despite late birdies by Norman and Nick O'Hern, who tied for second place. Montgomerie tied for fourth with Paul McGinley and Michael Long at 277.

Norman, who was hoping to match Jack Nicklaus' record of six Australian Opens, got into contention in the third round with 64 to pull within two strokes of Baddeley, but he would get no closer, finishing with 69. Because Baddeley was an amateur, Norman and O'Hern, who shot 70, split the first and second prizes. "I didn't really get anything going," Norman said. "Aaron put in a great performance, and this should be a slingshot for his career."

Former British Open winner Ian Baker-Finch had nothing but praise for Baddeley, saying, "I've never seen an 18-year-old who is so level-headed and well balanced. To use the old cliché, he has an old head on young shoulders. He says the right things. He walks the walk. He has all the ingredients to be an Australian Tiger Woods. When I was 18, I'd just finished my apprenticeship as a golf pro at Caloundra. I wasn't a patch on this kid, that's for sure.

"I definitely think he will get to the top. My prediction is that he will go a long way. His parents, Jo Ann and Ron, are really looking after his interests. They want him to go out as a teenager and enjoy himself. That's what he is doing. He has the ability to play at a very high level, but still stay in a relaxed state. He is similar in that regard to Sergio Garcia. He has a great time without the Spanish exuberance. He has it all — the mental aspect and technique."

Baddeley took such praise well, saying, "I've been dreaming about this for the last couple of months. It is great to actually do it. The course suited my game, and I was very confident coming here this week because I knew my game was ready."

Australasian Players Championship—A$800,000
Winner: Brett Rumford

For the second week in a row, an amateur beat a field of professionals to win an Australasian Tour title. This time it was 22-year-old West Australian Brett Rumford, who birdied the last two holes of regulation for 68 to reach

12-under-par 280 and tie Ericsson Masters champion Craig Spence for the lead. Then Rumford made gusty up-and-downs on two playoff holes, barely missed a birdie putt on the third, and made a 25-foot birdie for the victory on the fourth extra hole.

Rumford said that Aaron Baddeley was an inspiration to him through the week. "He spurred me on," Rumford said. "It was like breaking the four-minute-mile barrier. You should see a lot more amateurs winning now. I want to give something back to the Australian Golf Union, and I want to represent Australia in the Eisenhower Cup." Baddeley also expressed his desire to play on the Australian team, which would make the Australians the only team with two players who hold titles in professional events.

While Rumford didn't have Greg Norman breathing down his neck, as Baddeley did the previous week, 12 players were within two strokes of the lead in the early stages of the final round. Bradley King led by one going into the final 18 holes, but 73 and a missed birdie opportunity on the last hole left King one stroke out of the playoff and in a tie for third at 281 with Craig Parry, Raymond Russell and Brett Partridge.

"This is what it's all about," Rumford said after hoisting the trophy and watching while Spence collected the A$144,000 first-place check. "That is what practicing eight hours a day is for. I don't miss the money at all. I owe a lot of my experience to the Australian Golf Union. They have given me the opportunity to play in events like this."

Asked how it felt to win as an amateur, Rumford said, "It really hasn't hit me yet. Those four playoff holes were very draining. I am physically and mentally tired. I thought walking down the 18th fairway for the fifth time today that this had to be it. I could feel myself tiring and loose shots come from that. I'm so glad the ball went in."

Spence had nothing but praise for Rumford. "It was a tremendous performance by Brett," he said. "How old is he? That's incredible. I could not play like that when I was 22."

Australian PGA Championship—A$300,000
Winner: Greg Turner

With strong winds sending scores skyward, third-round leader Greg Turner almost gave the Australian PGA Championship to Craig Parry. Turner then had the title handed to him when Parry made double bogey on the 17th. Turner shot even-par 72 for a 278 total to edge Queenslander Shane Tait by two strokes, while Parry, who held a share of the lead on two occasions in the final round, also shot 72 and finished tied for third with Robert Allenby and Nick O'Hern at 281.

Turner's third-round lead disappeared quickly when Parry made a birdie on the fifth hole and Turner carded two early bogeys. Turner regained the lead with birdies at the sixth, seventh and eighth holes, opening a three-shot margin with nine holes to play. At that point, it looked as though Turner had the championship in hand.

Parry had other ideas. Birdies at the 11th, 13th and 14th holes moved Parry back into a share of the lead, but he handed the title back to Turner with loose play on the final four holes. It started on the 15th when Parry attempted to reach the green with a five iron from a fairway bunker. When he didn't get the ball out in his first attempt, Parry made bogey and lost the lead. Then on the 17th he took four shots to reach the green and two putts for a double bogey, allowing Turner to cruise in with the victory.

"I feel like a rank amateur," Parry said of his play down the stretch. I feel like an 18-year-old who has just thrown away a title." Asked what he was thinking in the final few holes, Parry said, "I've got manure for brains."

Turner knew he had been fortunate to take the title, but he couldn't have been happier to have his name on the trophy. "I did not play well today," Turner said. "Sometimes fortune plays a role. I was struggling with my swing. I played well on the first two days, but it was hard after that. Fortunately, I was able to play well over the closing holes and fashion a winning score. From a professional standpoint that was very pleasing.

"At the end of the day, no one will remember how much prize money there was, but they will be awarding this trophy for a long, long time, and my name is on it along with the greats of the game. In years to come when I have my feet up, talking to my grandchildren, it will be a prized possession, along with my (1997) British Masters win. They will be playing it 100 years from now, as long as golf is being played, and it is nice to be on there."

Schweppes Coolum Classic—A$300,000
Winner: Nick O'Hern

After a series of near-misses, including a runner-up finish at the Holden Australian Open and a tie for third at the Australian PGA Championship, Nick O'Hern shot a final-round 69 to capture the rain-shortened Schweppes Coolum Classic by two strokes over fellow Western Australian Wayne Smith. With Saturday's round canceled after a deluge made the course unplayable, the 28-year-old, left-handed O'Hern birdied the 15th and 17th holes to overtake pre-tournament favorite Craig Parry. Parry led with six holes to play but stumbled for the second week in a row, missing short putts on the last three holes to shoot 72 and finish in a five-way tie for third, three strokes behind.

O'Hern showed no signs of stumbling. With 14 birdies in 54 holes and no bogeys in his last 36 holes, O'Hern shot 10-under-par 206 on scores of 71, 66 and 69, and earned A$54,000 for the victory. "I made my first cut here as a professional and won about A$400," O'Hern said. "Because of that I have a soft spot for this event."

14. African Tours

While there were plenty of winners throughout the year on the African Tours, including two-time winners Hennie Otto, Desvonde Botes and Bobby Lincoln, the season started with Ernie Els and ended with him, as Els won two of South Africa's most prestigious events, the Alfred Dunhill South African PGA (a joint event with the PGA European Tour) and the Nedbank Million Dollar Challenge. The latter tournament, played in December when Els was back home with his wife, Leisl, and their new daughter, Samantha, was special because it was his first win in the Sun City event in seven attempts. Els said, "This is not a major, but I had goose bumps from head to toe as I walked up to the 18th green."

It was the perfect end to the season, followed by Nic Henning's victory in the Vodacom Players Championship, which was fitting because of Henning's rich family golf heritage. Henning's father was one of the most respected professionals in the country and two of his uncles, Harold and Allen, were former South African Open champions. The younger Henning had played well throughout the year, finishing second to Chris Davison in the Players Championship earlier in the year, but holding on to win the year-end affair by defeating Darren Clarke in a playoff. "It was unbelievable," Henning said. "The hairs on my back stood up as the final putt went around."

No single player dominated in 1999 and several newcomers left their marks. David Frost, a member of the old guard, won the Mercedes Benz-Vodacom South African Open, and Scott Dunlap, an American who resides in Atlanta, but is a veteran of the Vodacom Tour, picked up a win in the Dimension Data Pro-Am. After that the field was wide open.

Botes shot a final-round 64 to earn his first professional win in the South African Masters and he had some plans for the R158,000 first-place check. "I may have a bit of a party tonight," Botes said. "The first one is very hard. Hopefully this is the start of something. I was pretty nervous out there, but I just tried to concentrate on playing my game. This has been a long time coming."

Otto felt the same way when he gained his first professional victory at the Pietersburg Classic. A double-eagle two on the second hole helped propel Otto to the win. "Making that two was just the cherry on the cake," Otto said. "The crowd went wild and I was able to cruise home." Two weeks later Otto got his second win in the Vodacom Series: KwaZulu-Natal event.

Three weeks after that, Botes won for a second time at the Vodacom Series: Free State, setting a trend for first-time winners. David Toms, winner of two events on the U.S. PGA Tour and a top-10 finisher on the money list, posted his third victory of the year at the Hassan II Trophy, and Jean Hugo took first place in the Zimbabwe Open.

But the year belonged to Els, who finished third in 1999 on the World Money List with $3,284,079, having three wins and a secure spot as the fifth best player in the world according to the Official World Golf Ranking.

Alfred Dunhill South African PGA—R3,816,000
Winner: Ernie Els

He's known as Big Easy, primarily because of his milky swing and easy-going temperament, but Ernie Els made winning look easy in the Alfred Dunhill South African PGA at Houghton Golf Club in Johannesburg. The only time Els didn't lead was the first round, when Nico van Rensburg shot 65. Van Rensburg ballooned to rounds of 74 and 76, recovering with a closing 68 to finish at 283, 10 strokes shy of Els' winning total.

Els breezed to his 25th victory in nine years as a professional. An opening 67 left him two back, but he moved atop the leaderboard by midday on Friday, a spot which he never left. With closing rounds of 69, 69 and 68 and only three bogeys all week, Els made his 15-under-par 273 total and four-shot victory look as easy as his big, sweet swing.

Another South African, Richard Kaplan, was two strokes behind entering the last round, but it became clear that Kaplan didn't have the game to catch Els. "I wasn't intimidated," Kaplan said. "But I missed a lot of putts. We read them correctly, but I just couldn't get them on line." He shot 70 for a 277 total, finishing second alone.

As for Els' stellar play, Kaplan called it, "Fantastic. To watch the ease and grace when Ernie hits the ball is a privilege. He makes it look so easy. It's great to see a player of his class in action up close."

South African veteran David Frost's final 66 moved him into a tie for third place at 280 with Stephen Leaney, Steve Webster and Jeev Milkha Singh. Two of the worst rounds belonged to Nick Faldo, who arrived in Johannesburg full of positive comments about the coming season, but shot 77 and 76 to miss the cut. Mark McNulty, who finished tied for seventh at 281, played with Faldo the first two days and called it "the worst display of ball-striking I've ever seen. He was like a 24-handicapper out there."

Mercedes-Benz - Vodacom South African Open—R5,500,000
Winner: David Frost

It seemed fitting that David Frost, who grew up playing golf at the Stellenbosch Golf Club in Cape Province, would be the winner of the first Mercedes-Benz - Vodacom South African Open ever held at the club. "I played hundreds of rounds here with my dad, and with two holes to play in the final round, those memories came back," Frost said afterward. "My dad used to say that when I broke 80 he would buy me a new set of clubs. I remember one round together when I needed pars on the last two holes to break 80. Dad said, 'Don't worry if you don't do it today,' and I went double bogey, double bogey. With that in mind, I kept telling myself to finish birdie, birdie today."

Frost sank a 25-footer for birdie at the 17th to put him into the lead over Germany's Sven Struver, then managed to save par at the difficult 18th. His final-round 68 on a day when only 12 of the 75 participants broke par was good enough to overcome the four-shot deficit against Struver that Frost faced at the start of the round.

Sitting in the clubhouse with a five-under-par 279 total, Frost watched as

Struver, who bogeyed the 11th and 12th holes before birdieing the 15th to regain a share of the lead, strode up the 18th fairway needing a birdie to win and a par to force a playoff. Struver had hit his tee shot perfectly. He was in the middle of the fairway of the difficult 435-yard par-four, leaving himself with what appeared to be an easy nine iron to the well-protected green.

When Struver arrived at his ball, he found that he had driven into a divot and could barely see the top of his ball. Knowing he needed birdie, Struver tried to dig out a nine-iron shot in the hope that he could find some portion of the putting surface. The ball flew left into the water hazard, and Struver, who held at least a share of the lead after each of the previous three days, made double-bogey six and fell into fourth place behind India's Jeev Milkha Singh and America's Scott Dunlap, who finished tied at 280, one stroke behind Frost.

"I really had no shot," Struver said. "The ball was lying so badly I knew it could come out in any direction. I had no choice and just had to hope. If I had the same shot over, I wouldn't change anything. Sometimes you just need luck in a situation like that."

Whether it came as a result of Struver's misfortune or his own stellar play, Frost was emotional about a victory in his hometown. "I had a vision from the start of the final day that the crowd would be sitting in the stands on the 18th green watching me win this tournament," he said.

Dunlap and Singh both had putts to tie Frost on the 72nd hole, but neither came close. In the end it seemed like Frost's event all the way.

Vodacom Players Championship—R1,000,000
Winner: Chris Davison

Only three years before arriving at Royal Durban for the Vodacom Players Championship, Chris Davison wasn't sure he would ever play golf again. A drunk driver crashed into Davison's car in Johannesburg as the golfer was returning from a cricket match. Compounding the problem was a botched surgery on his shoulder that almost ended Davison's career. He was out of the game for 10 months.

That made Davison's 13-under 275 total for a three-stroke victory all the more special. "That was the worst time of my life," Davison said. "If I see the surgeon who did that first operation, I'll kill him because he absolutely butchered me. But that's why this win is far more special than my win in the South African Masters in 1994, because it's been such a long road. I was so calm and confident out there."

Davison began the final round with a one-shot lead, but got a boost of confidence on the par-three second hole. "I was in the bunker with my tee shot and I managed to get up and down. After that I was off. I just played solidly from there on," Davison said.

He birdied the fifth and ninth holes, then picked up one more birdie on the second nine. His bogey-free 69 was enough to open a three-shot lead over Nic Henning. That held as Henning shot 68 for a 278 total, while Andre Cruse finished third at 279.

Dimension Data Pro-Am—R2,000,000
Winner: Scott Dunlap

Atlanta native Scott Dunlap, the 1995 South African Masters champion, was never seriously challenged in the final round of the Dimension Data Pro-Am, where Dunlap shot 72 for a 273 total and a five-stroke victory. Even a two-shot penalty on the 18th hole that was later rescinded couldn't stop him.

The penalty came after Dunlap hit his approach shot into a greenside bunker, then failed to get the ball out of the hazard. When Dunlap's caddie raked the bunker before Dunlap made his next shot, a rules official assessed the penalty. A quick call to the Royal and Ancient Golf Club in St. Andrews, Scotland, resolved the issue and the penalty was removed.

"I explained to the official that it was not a two-shot penalty because the ball was 10 yards away from where my caddie had raked the sand, but I don't think he understood me," Dunlap said. "At the end of the day, whether you win by three shots or five shots makes no difference, so I let it go. If it would have meant the difference between winning and losing I might not have been so forgiving."

At one point in the final round Dunlap's lead was eight, even though he started the day with only a one-shot lead and never made any spectacular runs. Pars on the first eight holes were enough to open a huge lead as his closest competitor, Bruce Vaughan, shot 77. That opened the door for Steve van Vuuren, who began the day five strokes off the pace, but a closing 67 moved him into second place at 278.

Defending champion Nick Price, who won the 1998 Nedbank Million Dollar Challenge on the same Sun City course, finished tied for eighth with 280, a score that surprised Dunlap. "Nick owns this course," Dunlap said. "But he was not tearing it up. I felt good the whole round. I made a good save at the first, getting up and down out of the bunker for par. As far as I'm concerned that's better than starting your round with a birdie, because you test yourself early on. The wind was brutal out there. My caddie and I were just shaking our heads because we couldn't believe it."

South African Masters—R600,000
Winner: Desvonde Botes

In a barn-burner of a final round, where 15 players had a chance at victory, 24-year-old Desvonde Botes, who won the South African Amateur at age 16, finally realized his potential with his first professional victory in the South African Masters. Botes played the last 12 holes in eight under par for 64, including a birdie on the last hole that turned out to be the difference as he beat Dean van Staden by a single shot.

Botes started the final day two shots behind leader Ashley Roestoff, but the lead changed six times, with the outcome not decided until Botes' 10-footer on the 18th fell for birdie. The first charge came from Marco Gortana, who started the final round five shots back. Seven birdies and an eagle got him into the clubhouse with 64 and a 272 total for a two-shot lead with Botes, Roestoff, van Staden and South African Amateur champion Warren

Abery still on the golf course.

Botes took the lead on the second nine with a birdie on the 16th but van Staden, in the group ahead, answered with a birdie on the 17th to tie him. "I heard a big cheer when I was teeing off and I knew it was Dean," Botes said. "That's when I knew I had to birdie 18."

He did just that, hitting his tee shot in the middle of the fairway, then stopping a pitching-wedge approach 10 feet below the hole. When the putt went in, Botes had a 269 total, 19 under par, for a one-shot victory over van Staden and a two-shot edge over Abery. "The first one is very hard," Botes said. "Hopefully this is the start of something. I was pretty nervous out there, but I just tried to concentrate on playing my game. I think I may have a bit of a party tonight. This has been a long time coming."

Stenham Royal Swazi Sun Open—R1,000,000
Winner: Marc Cayeux

After enduring years of criticism and second-guessing after his decision to drop out of school at age 14 to pursue a career in professional golf, nothing could have made Marc Cayeux's 21st birthday any better than a win in Swaziland at the Stenham Royal Swazi Sun Open. Not only did he walk away with a three-stroke victory over four-time Swazi winner Mark McNulty, Cayeux bested his age by a shot, finishing with 66 to reach 22-under-par 266. It was the Zimbabwean's second career victory, but this one was more special than his 1998 Zambia Open title. Not only did it come on his birthday, but he beat his boyhood idols, McNulty and Nick Price, to achieve it.

"You can't leave McNulty out because he will always be up there," Cayeux said. "Both McNulty and Price are great ambassadors for Zimbabwe."

Cayeux stared the final round tied for the lead with Andre Cruse, but a birdie on the first hole, followed by a bogey on the second by Cruse gave Cayeux a cushion he would never give up. The only blemishes on Cayeux's eight-birdie round were a bogey at the 11th after what he called "a shocking tee shot" and a bogey on the 17th when an on-course television announcer said that the tournament might be over and temporarily distracted Cayeux. "He hinted that I had already won and I lost my concentration because of that," Cayeux said. "After I hit it in the water I looked at my caddie and said, 'How could I do that? It's only 98 meters to the hole.'"

Lombard Tyres Classic—R125,000
Winner: Brett Liddle

With a final-round 69, Brett Liddle ended a two-year victory drought when he captured the Lombard Tyres Classic at the Krugersdorp Golf Club in Johannesburg. Liddle's 19-under-par 269 total was one shot better than Hennie Otto, who closed with 67.

With a three-shot overnight lead, Liddle felt comfortable that the drought, which began after he won the 1996 Kalahari Classic in Sishen, was about to end. The feeling became stronger after he rolled in a 30-foot eagle putt on the par-five first hole. Roger Wessels moved to within two shots of the lead with a birdie on the par-four ninth, but a bogey on the 11th dropped him to three back. He would never get closer.

Otto picked up the mantle of challenger when he birdied the par-four 13th while Liddle was making one of his few bogeys of the day. They were temporarily tied at 17 under par, but Liddle quickly regained the lead.

Liddle made a terrible swing on the par-four 17th, hooking his drive into the trees. From there he hit a miraculous recovery and scrambled for par. "I wasn't driving the ball well, but my second shot out of the trees on 17 was the key shot of the tournament for me," Liddle said. "There wasn't much room to work with, and I just hit a low two iron short of the green, chipped, and two-putted for par."

A par on the 18th secured the one-shot margin over Otto. "I really wanted to win a tournament," Liddle said. "I've watched David Duval win so many tournaments on the U.S. tour, and we don't seem to believe that we can do the same here. I believe I can win two in a row."

Vodacom Series: Gauteng—R200,000
Winner: Nico van Rensburg

With a sensational closing-round 65, his second consecutive seven-under-par score, Nico van Rensburg came from four strokes back to reach 15-under-par 201 and win the Vodacom Series: Gauteng by two over second-round leader Don Gammon, who shot a final-round 71.

"I had a solid first-round 71 and then, with a little help from my mate Des Terblanche, who told me to move the ball two inches in my stance, I was able to come out and shoot back-to-back 65s," van Rensburg said. "It's always great to win in South Africa and it is nice to be among friends again. Des has been staying with me, and I really enjoy the competition on the Vodacom Tour. There are so many new young players out there and some of the names on the leaderboard I don't even know."

He knew Gammon, and he knew that it would take a great final-round effort to catch him. Van Rensburg's other concern was the weather. Lightening delayed the final round for an hour and a half, and van Rensburg was concerned. "I thought they were going to cancel the final round and I needed to put some pressure on the leaders," he said.

Birdies on the first and fourth holes got van Rensburg off to the start he wanted. Meanwhile Gammon was unable to get anything going, and he watched his four-shot lead evaporate.

Pietersburg Classic—R100,000
Winner: Hennie Otto

After a series of near-misses, 22-year-old Johannesburg native Hennie Otto picked up his first win at the Pietersburg Classic with a rare double-eagle two on the par-five second hole. "I knew when I hit it that it was good," Otto said of his eight-iron second shot. "When it went in the crowd went wild."

That gave Otto a five-shot cushion over Ashley Roestoff and Sammy Daniels, and the lead would only get larger. With another birdie on the third hole, Otto reached 18 under par and opened a seven-shot margin. By the time he reached the sixth tee, his lead was nine. That's when Otto lost his concentration and made a few loose swings. Otto bogeyed the sixth, then shanked his second shot on the seventh before scrambling for par. Another bogey on the 11th and a birdie at the 12th was all the excitement Otto could muster for the day. He finished the 54-hole event at 17-under-par 199 on scores of 65, 65 and 69 for a four-shot victory over Roestoff and Des Terblanche.

Vodacom Series: Eastern Cape—R200,000
Winner: Ashley Roestoff

One week after finishing tied for second, Ashley Roestoff picked up his first victory of 1999 in a close one at the Vodacom Series: Eastern Cape event at Humewood Golf Club. He started the third and final round tied for the lead at 136 with Justin Hobday. Bogeys on the second and third holes dropped Roestoff out of the lead before five birdies and a closing 69 for an 11-under-par 205 total gave him a one-shot edge over Hobday and Alan McLean.

"Two and three were two bad holes," Roestoff said. "I landed my approaches too far from the pin and was putting straight into the grain." He recovered on the second nine with five birdies, and he needed every one of them. McLean, who started the day four strokes back, birdied two of his last three holes to shoot 66 and temporarily take the lead at 206.

"I was shocked to see Alan right up there," Roestoff said. "He was nowhere, and then a few birdies later and he's challenging. It was a bit nerve-wracking standing on the 17th. I just said to myself 'fairway, green.' I knew I needed that birdie."

The birdie at the 17th wouldn't have been so important if Roestoff hadn't made a 30-footer for birdie at the 16th to pull even with McLean. "That was a big putt to make, because I knew I had to sink it to be in with a chance of winning," Roestoff said. The putt on the 17th fell as well, and Roestoff cruised in with a one-shot win.

While he made a gallant run that came up one short, McLean wasn't too disappointed about the way his game had come around. "I didn't have a great summer, so I've put a lot of work into my game," McLean said. "I've also been going to the gym to improve myself physically."

Vodacom Series: KwaZulu-Natal—R200,000
Winner: Hennie Otto

With a six-shot lead standing on the 18th tee of the Selborne Country Club, Hennie Otto knew there was no way he could lose the Vodacom Series: KwaZulu-Natal, so it didn't bother him too badly when he made a double bogey on the final hole. A final-round 69 gave the 22-year-old Otto an 11-under-par 202 total for his second victory in three starts. His rounds were 69, 64 and 69.

Otto began the final round in a tie for the lead with Neil Homann at 133, but Homann double-bogeyed the fifth hole and never recovered. When Otto made a superb par at the 12th hole, he knew the title was his. "My hand slipped on the club and I pulled my tee shot into the bushes on the left," Otto said in describing his play on the par-five 12th. "We found the ball and I just chipped out. Then I hit a great three wood to be just short of the green and made sure I got up and down for five. That really strengthened my mind. I was a little bit nervous out there, but after my birdie at the seventh, which took me to 10 under, I just told myself to play my own game and it started coming together from there on. I think the ice was broken with my first win and now it seems to be getting easier."

Ashley Roestoff, who led after a first-round 64, finished second at 206, while Nico van Rensburg and Marc Cayeux tied for third at 207.

Vodacom Series: Mpumalanga—R200,000
Winner: Andre Cruse

With a 10-under-par, final-round 62 at the Hans Merensky Golf Club in Phalaborwa, Andre Cruse came from five strokes back to vault past Justin Hobday and win the Vodacom Series: Mpumalanga by three over Nico van Rensburg. The 62 gave Cruse a total of 14-under-par 202.

Van Rensburg closed with rounds of 67 and 68 to be alone in second at 205, while Brett Little and Richard Kaplan put together 67s in the final round to tie at 207 with Hobday, who closed with 72.

Bearing Man Highveld Classic—R100,000
Winner: Bobby Lincoln

It was nip and tuck to the finish and then some at the Bearing Man Highveld Classic in Witbank as Bobby Lincoln, Darren Fichardt and Lyall McNeill moved in and out of the lead through 54 holes at the Witbank Golf Club. Never did more than two shots separate the three, and when regulation play was completed, they were tied at seven-under-par 209.

Lincoln made quick work of the playoff with a birdie to take the title. He had scores of 67, 73 and 69 while Fichardt (68-72-69) and McNeill (66-73-70) shared second place. Six players tied for fourth at 211: Sammy Daniels (69-73-69), John Nelson (70-72-69), Bradford Vaughan (69-71-71), Sean Ludgater (70-69-72), Steve van Vuuren (66-73-72) and first-round leader Wallie Coetsee (65-73-73).

Vodacom Series: Free State—R200,000
Winner: Desvonde Botes

Despite hard charges in the final 18 holes by Titch Moore and Hennie Otto, Desvonde Botes was able to hang onto his overnight lead in the Vodacom Series: Free State with 71 for a 206 total and one-stroke victory. Entering the final round with a four-shot lead, Botes struggled but was able to put together a gutsy one-under-par 71 performance while watching Moore shoot

66 to reach 207 ahead of him. Otto had his second 69 of the week, good enough for third place, two shy of the winning score.

Darren Fichardt and Callie Swart shared fourth place at 210, while three more players settled one shot back at 211.

Royal Swazi Sun Classic—R200,000
Winner: Bradford Vaughan

With three rounds in the 60s, Bradford Vaughan's three-stroke victory in the Royal Swazi Sun Classic was never as close as it appeared. Vaughan was in command of his game with rounds of 68, 65 and 67 for a 200 total, 16 under par on the Royal Swazi Sun Golf Club in Mbabane. If not for first-round leader Nic Henning's scores of 66, 70 and 67, Vaughan's margin might have been as much as five. As it was, the three-shot margin over Henning was as close as anyone got.

Patrick O'Brien, Justin Hobday and Ulrich van den Berg finished tied for third at 205, while Damian Dunford and Keith Horne shared sixth place at 206.

Vodacom Series: Western Cape—R200,000
Winner: Sean Ludgater

Sean Ludgater led from the start in the Vodacom Series: Western Cape when he fired a 65 at Rondebosch Golf Club in Cape Town, and he remained in the lead until the end, following with scores of 68 and 71 for 204 total, 12 under par, and a two-stroke victory over Des Terblanche. Terblanche attempted a charge in the final round, but a 70 was all he could mount. His 206 total gave him second place, two clear of Bradley Davison, Robbie Stewart and Hennie Walters.

Platinum Classic—R200,000
Winner: Bobby Lincoln

For the second time in 1999, Bobby Lincoln had to go to extra holes to win in South Africa. This time Lincoln defeated Callie Swart, after Swart fired a 65 in the final round to finish regulation play tied with Lincoln at 201, 15 under par. It took Lincoln two extra holes to finish off Swart, who came to the final round four shots off the pace.

Lincoln's lead was due in large measure to his tournament-low 63 in the second round that opened up a four-shot advantage over Swart and Roger Wessels. Lincoln shot 69s in the first and third rounds. While Swart was able to close the gap in the final round, Wessels settled for a tie for third with Neil Homann at 202.

Hassan II Trophy—US$438,000
Winner: David Toms

Chris Perry, son of baseball legend Jim Perry and nephew of Cy Young Award-winning pitcher Gaylord Perry, had to be wondering if his time would ever come. With only one victory to his credit, the 1998 B.C. Open, Perry was one of the best players to have only one career victory. He thought that might change when he shot a closing 65 at the Hassan II Trophy in Rabat, Morocco, but it was not to be.

This time the blow was delivered by David Toms, another under-appreciated player who was perhaps the most unrecognized multiple winner of 1999. Toms won the Sprint International, going head-to-head with David Duval one week after the PGA Championship when Tiger and Sergio were still on everyone's mind, and he won the Buick Challenge in October, one week after the Ryder Cup. This time Toms won in Morocco, taking Perry to a playoff after shooting a final-round 69 and beating him with a birdie on the first extra hole.

Both had 275 totals, 17 under par, with Toms posting scores of 68, 70, 68 and 69. Before his closing 65, Perry shot 69, 71 and 70.

Zimbabwe Open—R400,000
Winner: Jean Hugo

With a four-under-par 68, Jean Hugo surged ahead of co-leader Ulrich van den Berg to win the Zimbabwe Open by two strokes. Hugo, who followed his opening 72 with rounds of 66 and 65, closed out the tournament at Chapman Golf Club in Harare in the closing holes, pulling ahead of van den Berg on the second nine and holding the lead. Van den Berg finished with 70 for a 273 total, two shy of Hugo, while Hennie Otto shot 67 to finish alone in third place at 274.

Nedbank Million Dollar Challenge—US$2,570,000
Winner: Ernie Els

Seven turned out to be Ernie Els' lucky number. Six previous times he had ventured in search of a win at the Nedbank Million Dollar Challenge and six times he had come away disappointed. The seventh time not only turned out to be a charm for Els, he won the event in record fashion, having a record 25-under-par 263 total on scores of 67, 66, 64 and 66.

"If I hadn't won this time, there might have been an attempt on my life," Els cracked after collecting the trophy and kissing his wife, Leisl, and their baby daughter, Samantha. "This is not a major, but I had goose bumps from head to toe as I walked up to the 18th green."

Colin Montgomerie shot 65 to finish alone in second place at 268, but even he conceded defeat to Els, offering his congratulations before they teed off on the 18th. "I don't have sleepless nights about playing with him," Els said of the seven-time European Order of Merit champion. "We certainly

Masters Tournament

After a crippling ailment that almost ended his career, Jose Maria Olazabal won the Masters Tournament for the second time, holding the lead after his 66 in the second round.

His putt on the 16th was the week's best, but Davis Love III finished two strokes back.

Greg Norman made a spirited bid before finishing third.

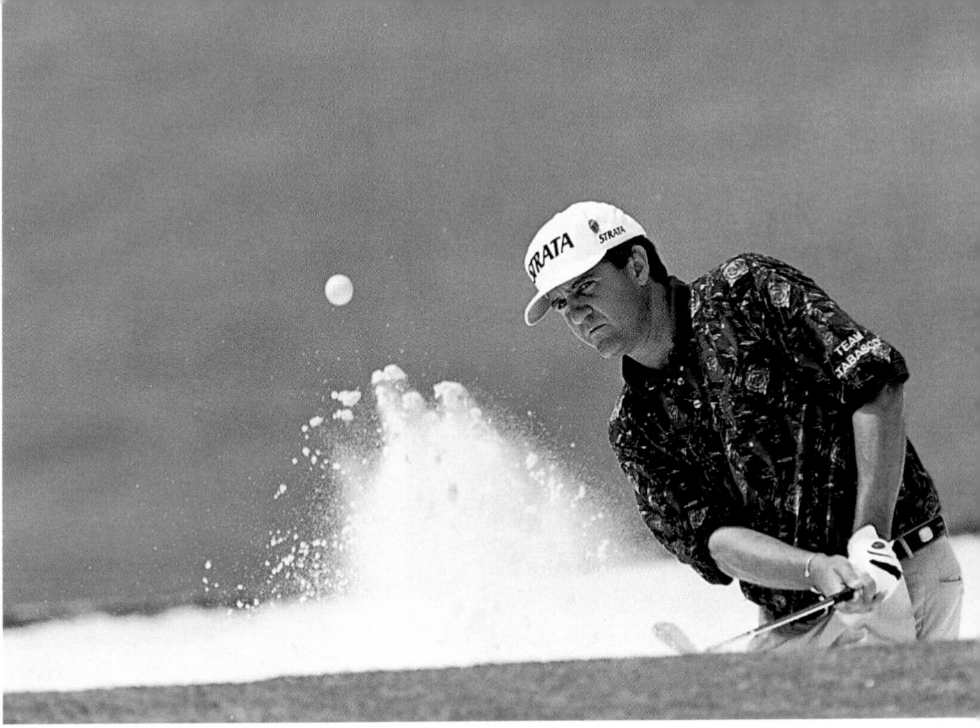

Allsport/Craig Jones

With 65 in the third round, Steve Pate tied for fourth place, four strokes behind.

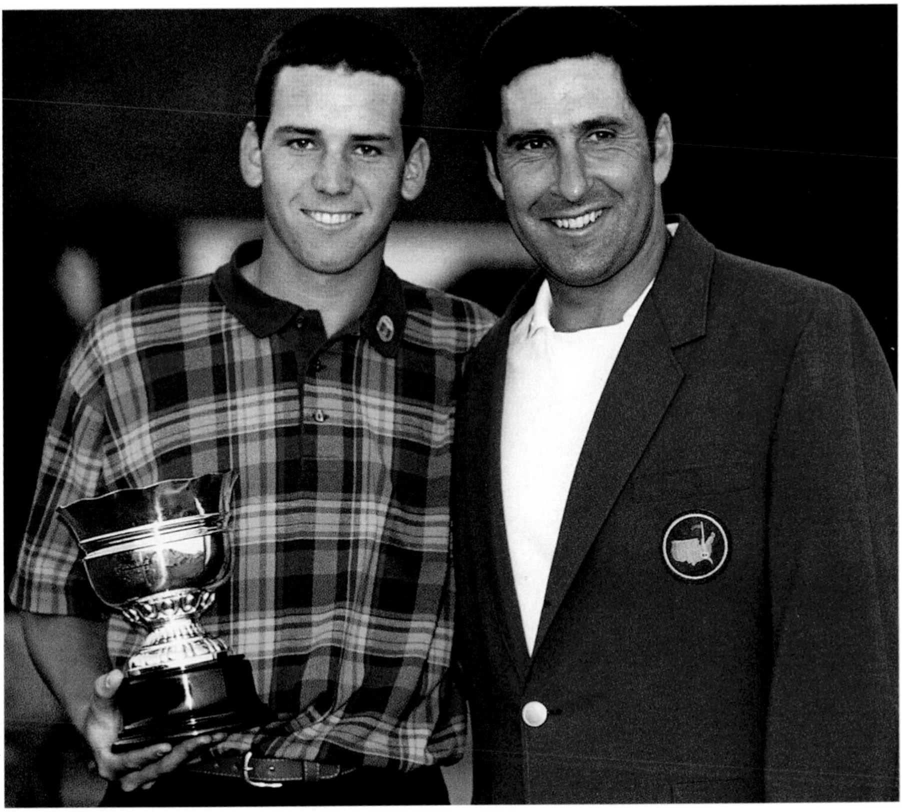

Allsport/David Cannon

Sergio Garcia took low-amateur honors to join countryman Olazabal at the presentation.

U.S. Open

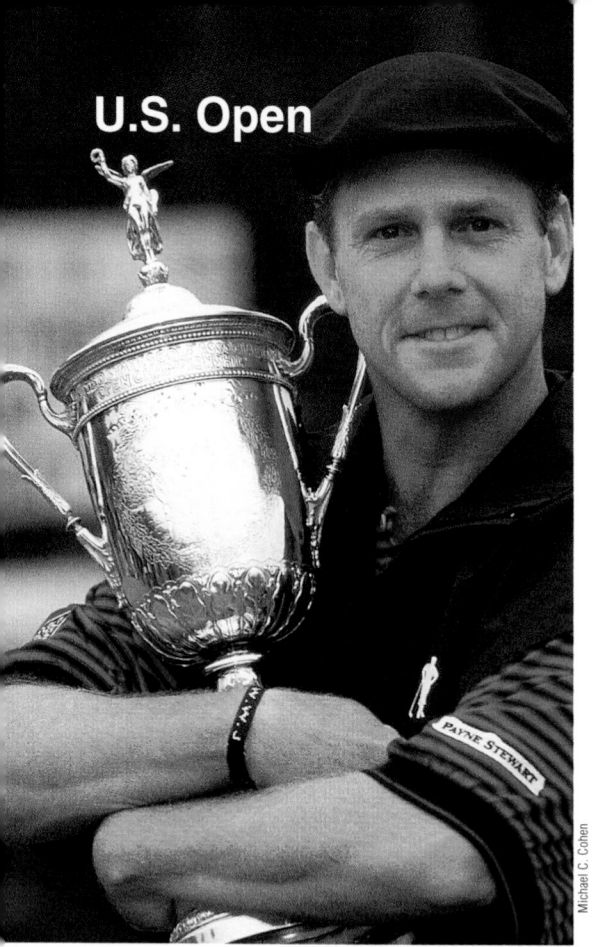

Payne Stewart secured his second U.S. Open title.

Phil Mickelson was one short.

Battling tough Pinehurst No. 2, Steve Stricker finished with 73 for fifth place.

Vijay Singh (left) and Tiger Woods tied for third place, two strokes behind.

Tim Herron faltered but was sixth.

David Duval shared seventh place.

British Open

Allsport/Ross Kinnaird

With a final-round 67, Paul Lawrie came from 10 strokes back to win in a playoff.

Fred Vuich

In a disastrous but comical scene, Jean Van de Velde considered playing from the water while his three-shot lead was evaporating on the 72nd hole.

Justin Leonard shared second place.

Craig Parry finished one behind.

Tiger Woods had a 74-74 finish.

Greg Norman took sixth place.

PGA Championship

Tiger Woods had a hard-earned PGA victory.

Sergio Garcia excited the gallery with his final-day heroics.

Nick Price was alone in fifth place.

Michael C. Cohen

Stewart Cink tied for third place.

Mike Weir faded to a share of 10th.

Michael C. Cohen

Jay Haas led after 36 holes and finished three strokes back.

Ryder Cup

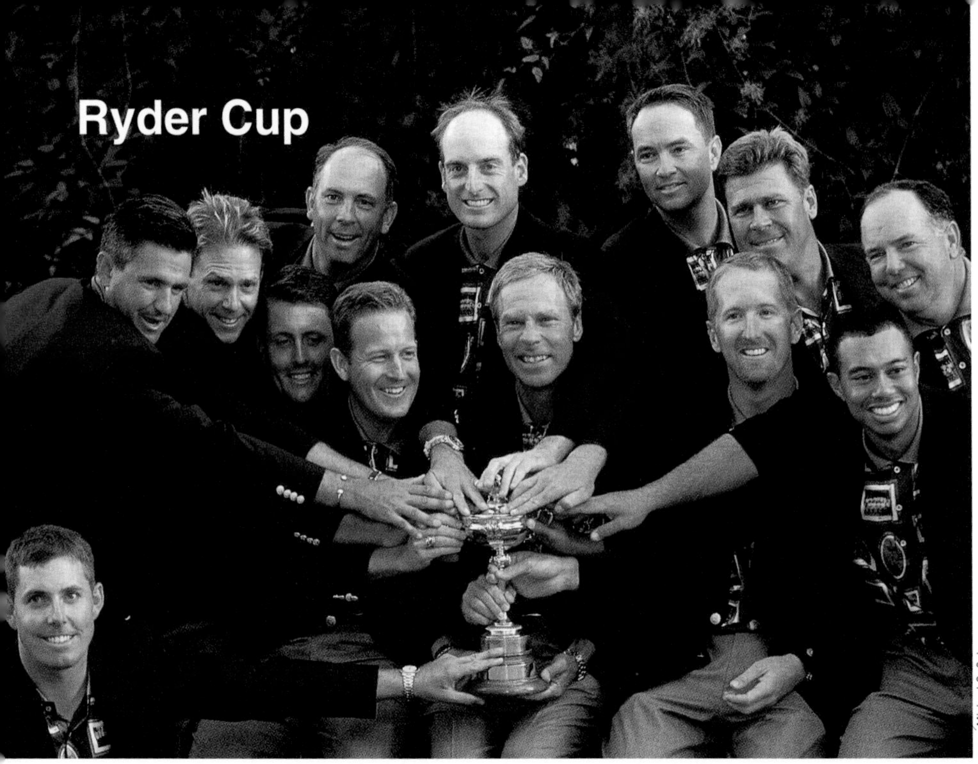

Michael C. Cohen

Ben Crenshaw's U.S. Ryder Cup team celebrated a record comeback on the last day.

Michael C. Cohen

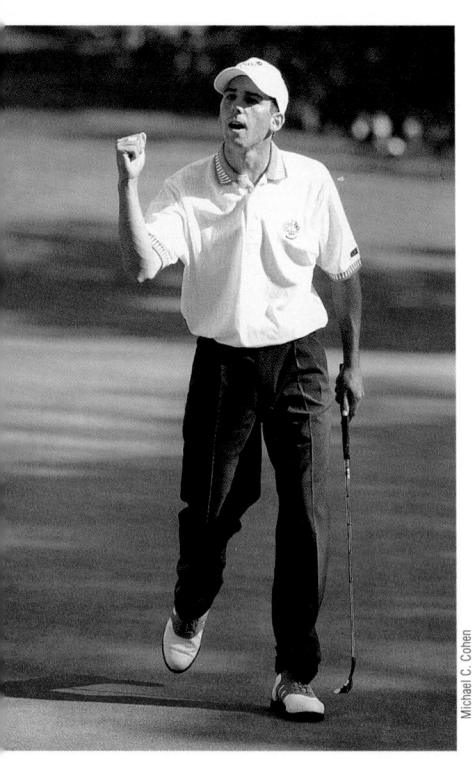

Sergio Garcia, with teammate Jesper Parnevik, led Europe's start.

Michael C. Cohen

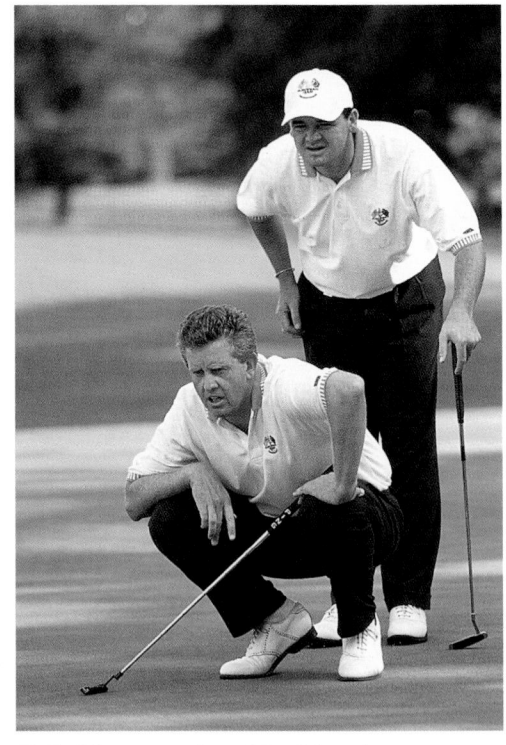

Colin Montgomerie and Paul Lawrie were a formidable pair for the Europeans.

Michael C. Cohen

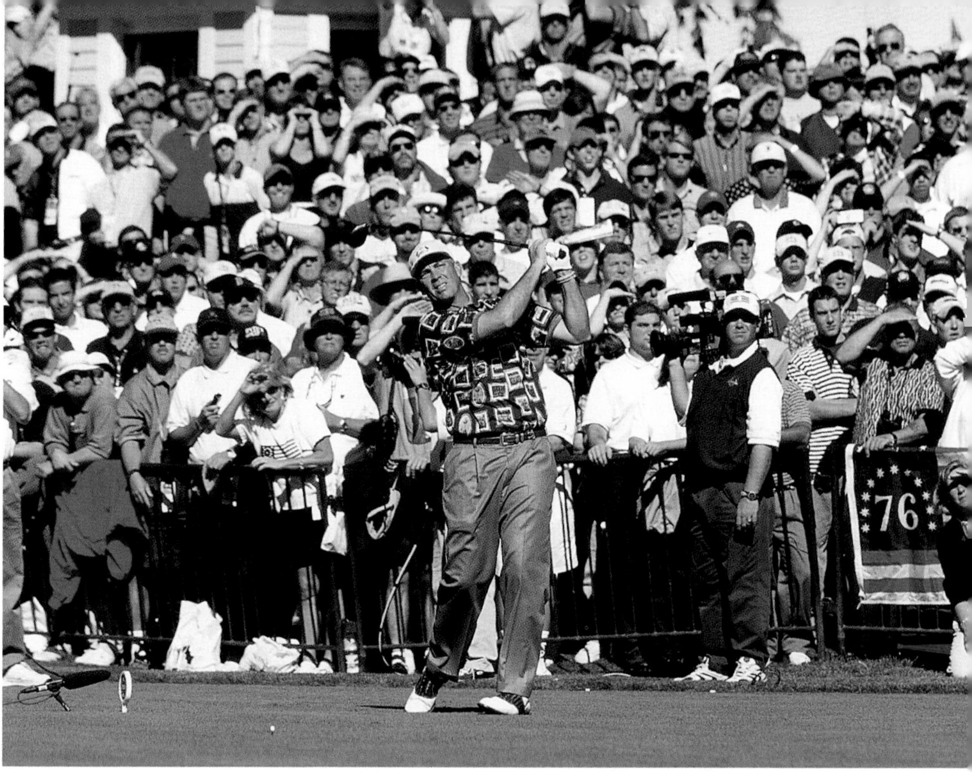

Tom Lehman was first off as the Americans rallied in the singles matches.

Michael C. Cohen

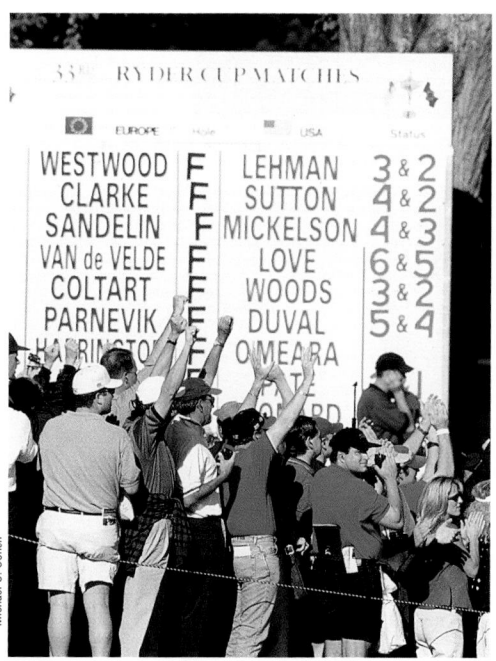

The crowd cheered each result.

Michael C. Cohen

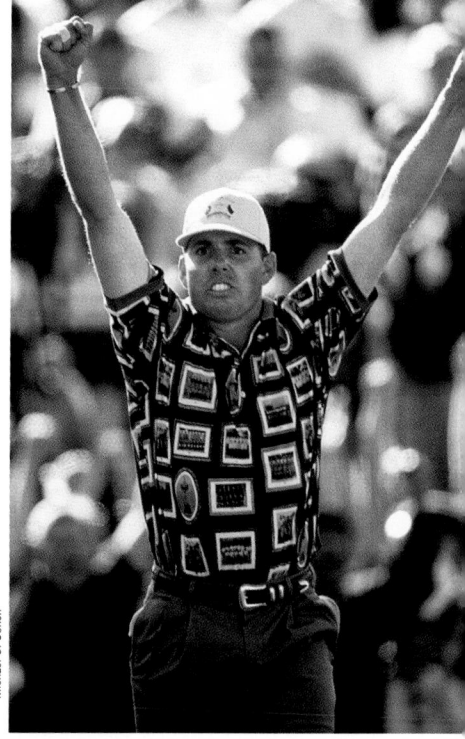

Justin Leonard delivered the clincher.

Cisco World Match Play

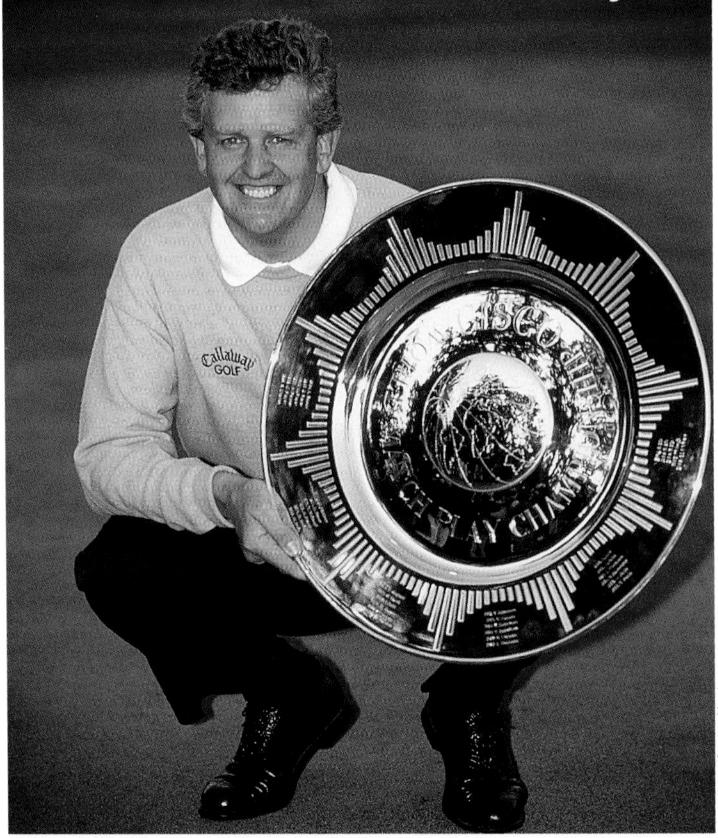

Allsport/Stephen Munday

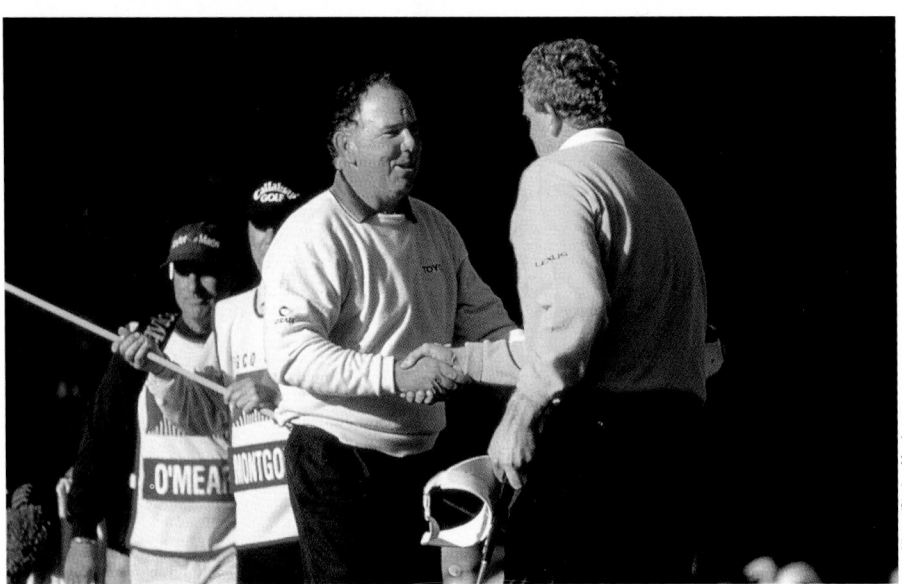

Colin Montgomerie took his sixth title in the Cisco World Match Play.

Allsport/Stephen Munday

Defending champion Mark O'Meara fell 3 and 2 in the final.

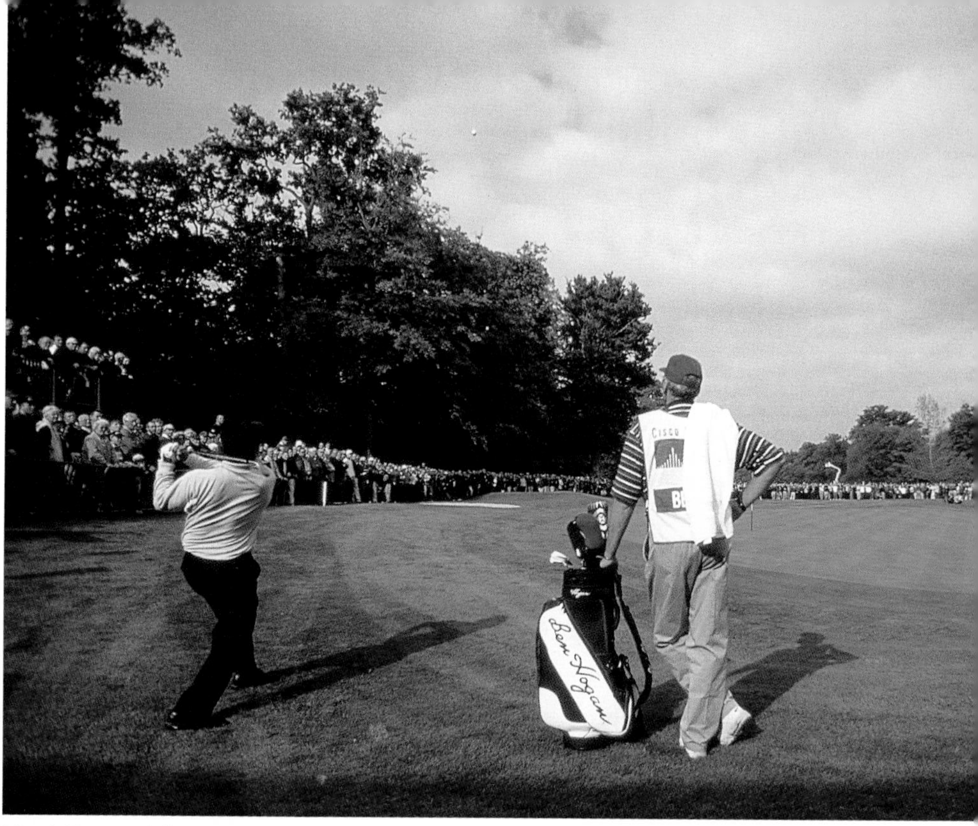

Allsport/Stephen Munday

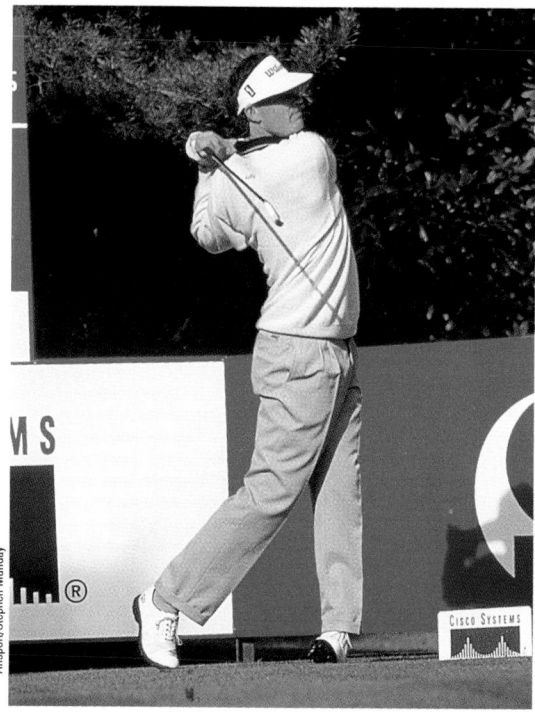

Notah Begay defeated Jose Maria Olazabal before losing to Montgomerie.

Allsport/Stephen Munday

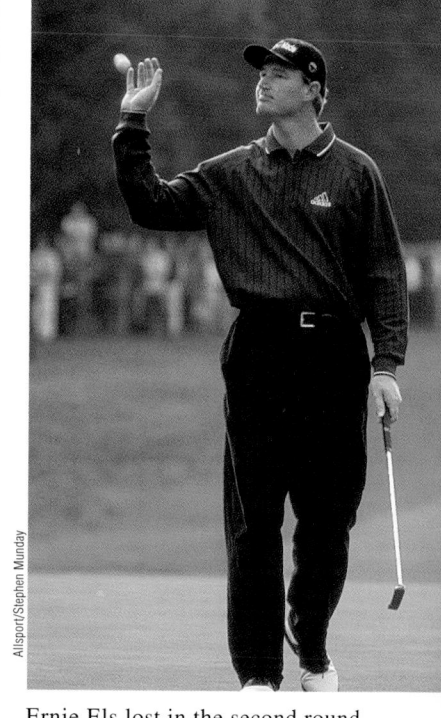

Padraig Harrington was a semi-finalist.

Allsport/Stephen Munday

Ernie Els lost in the second round.

Alfred Dunhill Cup

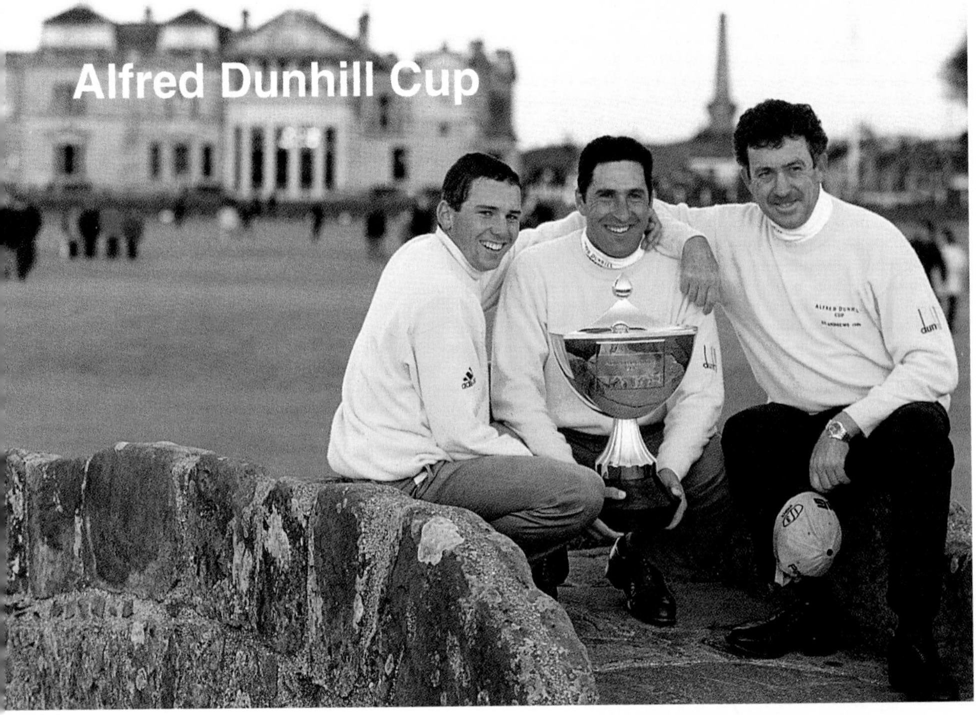

Allsport/Paul Severn

The victorious Spanish team in the Alfred Dunhill Cup consisted of captain Sergio Garcia, Jose Maria Olazabal and Miguel Angel Jimenez.

Allsport/Paul Severn

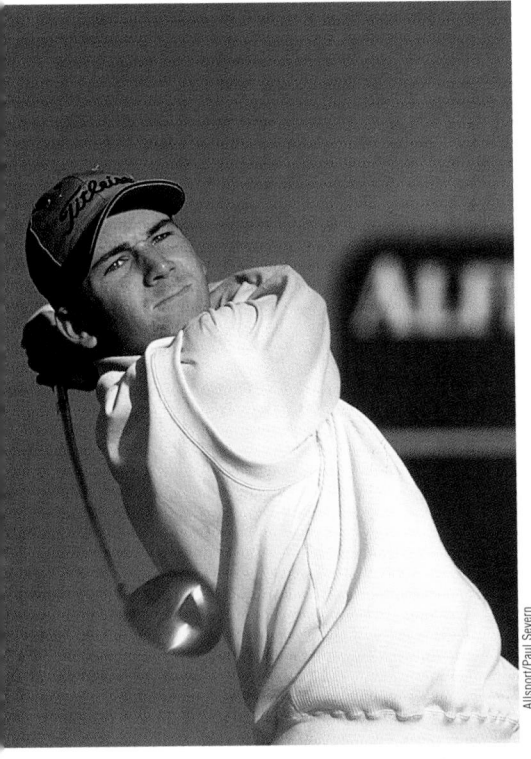

Garcia led Spain for the first three days.

Allsport/Stephen Munday

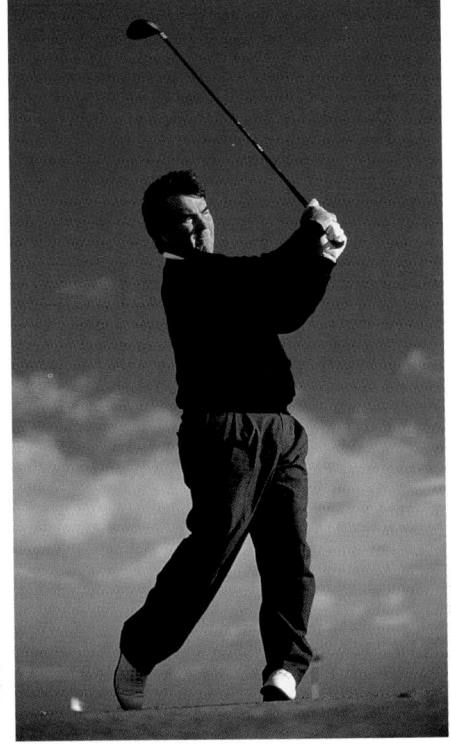

Craig Parry led Australia.

Allsport/David Cannon

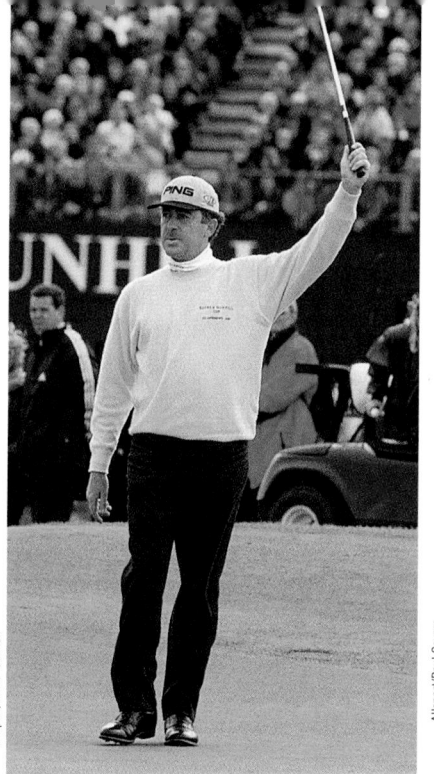

Jimenez won twice on the last day.

Allsport/Paul Severn

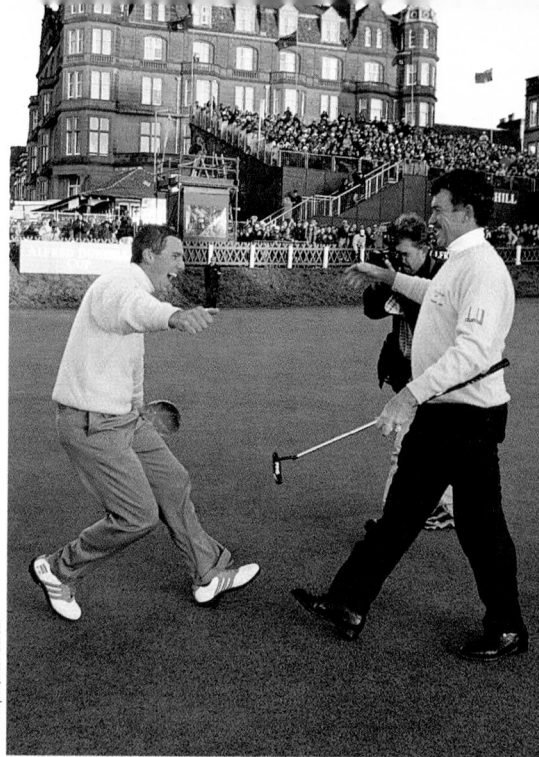

Jimenez was congratulated by Garcia after clinching the Alfred Dunhill Cup.

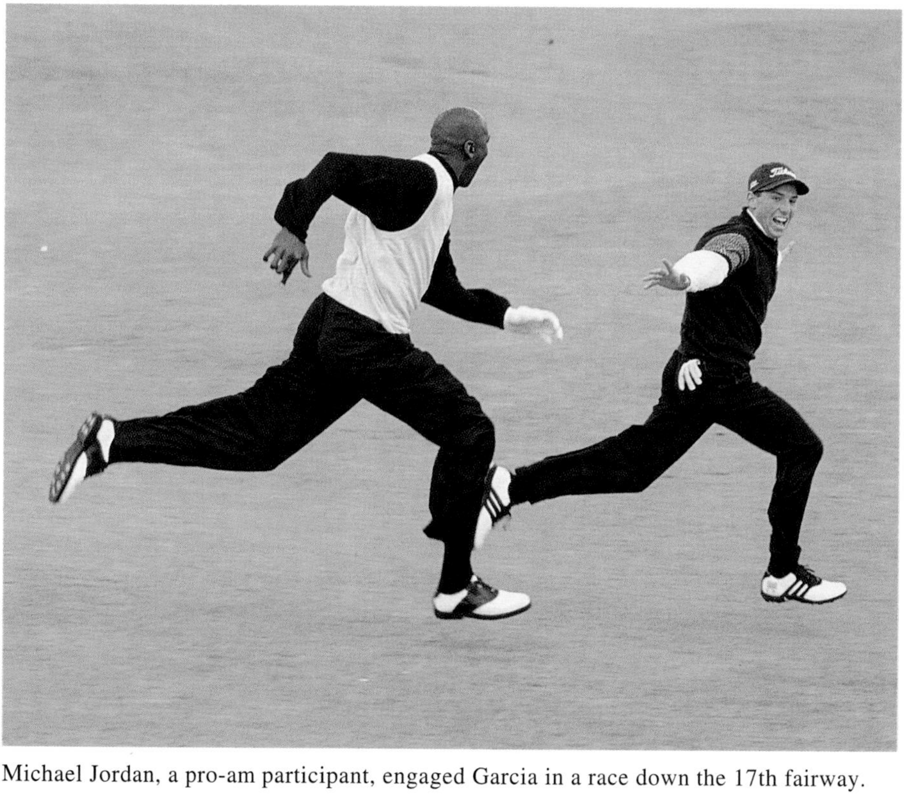

Allsport/David Cannon

Michael Jordan, a pro-am participant, engaged Garcia in a race down the 17th fairway.

Players Championship

Scott Gump took second place.

David Duval was a popular hometown winner.

Nick Price rode a second-round 67 to third place.

Hal Sutton tied for fourth.

feed off each other. I enjoy Monty's company. Today, though, I can't think of a birdie opportunity I missed."

Darren Clarke, who finished third at 270 after a closing 65, had nothing but praise for Els' play. "He was simply unbelievable," Clarke said. "On this course, 25 under par is incredible." Clarke went on a run in the last round with five birdies in the first nine holes, then hit the par-five 10th in two, leaving himself seven feet for an eagle. "When I missed that eagle putt, I was stopped in my tracks," he said.

Lee Westwood finished fourth at 274 when he shot 66 to overtake Jim Furyk by one stroke, while defending champion Nick Price finished seventh at 280.

Vodacom Players Championship—R1,999,999
Winner: Nic Henning

There are few better tournaments in which to pick up your first victory than your tour's Players Championship. That was what Nic Henning did, defeating Ryder Cup veteran Darren Clarke on the second playoff hole in the Vodacom Players Championship. Entering the final round with a one-shot lead over Ernie Els, Henning struggled a bit in the early going, but an up-and-down for par on the 12th hole seemed to calm him down.

Els bogeyed the 14th and 16th holes to finish with 71 and tied for fourth at 278, two strokes out of the playoff and one stroke behind Alan McLean. Clarke blew the best chance at the title. With Henning in trouble off the tee on the 17th, Clarke stood on the 18th green with a 15-foot birdie putt to take the lead. He missed and finished with 68 and a 12-under-par 276 total. Henning parred in to finish with 70, then the playoff began.

It was nerve-wracking stuff for the 30-year-old Henning, but after he watched Clarke miss another 15-foot birdie putt on the first playoff hole, he knew this was his title to win. On the second playoff hole Clarke missed another birdie putt, then Henning sank his 13-footer for birdie, watching as the ball swirled around the hole before falling in.

"It was unbelievable," Henning said. "The hairs on my back stood up as the putt went around."

15. Senior Tours

For two years the U.S. Senior PGA Tour was dominated by the play of three-time U.S. Open champion Hale Irwin. His primary competition for Player of the Year honors had come from Gil Morgan, but that challenge had not been close. Irwin had dominated every statistical category the Senior PGA Tour kept. How things changed in 1999. Not only was Irwin's $2 million mark eclipsed by two seniors and 10 players on the PGA Tour, but also a new class of rookies burst onto the scene and infused fresh blood and new excitement.

In the first seven events of 1999, six different players won and not one of them was Irwin. Morgan was among the winners, but his title came at the Senior Slam, an unofficial event pitting the winners of the previous year's majors championships. Bruce Fleisher, the 1968 U.S. Amateur champion who struggled to only one victory in a 30-year professional career, the 1991 New England Classic, joined the Senior PGA Tour by finishing second to Allen Doyle at the qualifying tournament, then went out and won his first two events. "Honest to God, I had no expectations of this," Fleisher said. "I tried to prepare, but I had no idea. It's terrific. This is just a wonderful time in my life."

Two weeks later life got a lot more wonderful for another senior rookie. Doyle, a driving range operator from La Grange, Georgia, who turned professional at age 48, won the ACE Group Classic in late February, making him the second rookie in four weeks to win. Suddenly there was excitement among the seasoned golfers. "There's a lot of great players and lot of good players out here," Irwin said. "Allen and Bruce are evidence of that."

At the Toshiba Senior Classic, two weeks after Doyle's breakout victory, two of the more colorful personalities dueled it out in a five-hole playoff that provided humor, drama and a healthy dose of excitement. Gary McCord, better known as a humorous announcer in the CBS television booth on Sunday afternoons, outputted John Jacobs in a playoff that wasn't completed until the sun disappeared in Newport Beach, California. "I've won everywhere except high school, college and the pros," McCord said after the victory. It was his second win as a senior and he sounded more like a 20-year-old rookie than a man heading towards his 52nd birthday. "I don't want to be static. I want to have my foot on something," he said. "My wife keeps saying, 'Slow down.' She's the brake and I'm the accelerator. Dawdle and I'll pass you."

That seemed to be the mantra for all the newcomers. Dawdle for a month or two (as Irwin did from January through May) and Doyle, Fleisher, McCord, Bob Duval and Larry Nelson were going to pass you. Nelson picked up two victories in the first quarter, the first coming at the GTE Classic in Tampa, and the second at the Bruno's Memorial Classic in Birmingham. Fleisher won a third event in Charlotte at the Home Depot Invitational (the third oldest event in senior golf behind the U.S. Senior Open and PGA Seniors' Championship), while Doyle added a second title and his first major win in Palm Beach at the PGA Seniors'.

In May Irwin awoke like a hibernating bear who hadn't eaten in five months. With one of the most memorable shots of the year, a 98-yard sand wedge into the cup on the 54th hole, Irwin picked up his first victory of the year at the Nationwide Championship in Atlanta. He offered some explanation as to why it had taken him so long to break out. "All the hype and stuff that happened the last couple of years hasn't been there this year," Irwin said. "In a lot of respects that has been good. I didn't want to get off this year with that heavy hype. It can be all encompassing. I needed a break. I took it, and now I'm ready."

Irwin won again three weeks later at the Boone Valley Classic, then he picked up another victory at the Ford Senior Players Championship. Suddenly a year that had started out looking much different became very similar to previous seasons on the Senior PGA Tour. Irwin vaulted up the money list, challenging Fleisher and Doyle for the top spot.

The rookies answered. Doyle won his third event of the year at the Cadillac NFL Classic, while Fleisher picked up his fourth title in Nashville at the BellSouth Senior Classic. Irwin responded with wins four and five at the Ameritech Senior Open and the Coldwell Banker Burnet Classic in back-to-back weeks. Suddenly Irwin was in a familiar position atop the Senior PGA Tour money list. He led in victories and was closing in on the $2 million mark again. Then, just as he had in the first five months of the year, Irwin stopped winning. The putts didn't fall and the shots that had come in the critical moments through the last two years weren't there. He lost a heartbreaker in Park City, Utah, at the Novell Utah Showdown to Dave Eichelberger and he couldn't get his putter working in Long Island at the Lightpath Classic, an event Fleisher won to tie Irwin with five victories and move back to the top of the money list.

Fleisher won two more times at The Transamerica and the EMC² Kaanapali Classic. Also in the final months a new face emerged on the Senior PGA Tour that sparked a great deal of interest and enthusiasm for the future. Tom Watson turned 50 in early September and proceeded to win the second event he entered, the Bank One Championship. He later teamed with Jack Nicklaus to dominate the Diners Club Matches, and the fact that Watson was now a regular created a real sense of excitement. "It's good for the game and great for this tour," Jim Colbert said of Watson's arrival.

Fleisher ran away with the money title, Player of the Year honors and Rookie of the Year, but Doyle also made his mark with four victories. Irwin had five victories and another $2 million season, finishing second on the money list behind Fleisher. Nelson was fourth on the money list with three wins, matching Gil Morgan and Ireland's Christy O'Connor, Jr. in victories. Eichelberger ended the year with two wins, including the U.S. Senior Open, and McCord also picked up a second victory at the season-ending Ingersoll-Rand Senior Tour Championship.

One of O'Connor's victories was unofficial on the Senior PGA Tour, but very significant — the Senior British Open. In addition, the European circuit, with 17 events, produced five two-time winners in Bob Shearer, Neil Coles, Ross Metherell, Tommy Horton and Eddie Polland.

Hiroshi Ishii and Fujio Kobayashi each won twice in the nine senior events played in Japan, while Australian Graham Marsh, winner of The Tradition in America, took the Japan Senior Open title.

U.S. Senior PGA Tour

MasterCard Championship—$1,100,000
Winner: John Jacobs

After 30 years without a professional victory in America, John Jacobs, one of the longest hitters on the Senior PGA Tour and one of the premier personalities, won his second event in seven months when he captured the MasterCard Championship in Kailua-Kona, Hawaii, with a wire-to-wire performance. From his first birdie on the first nine of the first day, Jacobs held the lead and never let go. His opening-round, eight-under-par 64 led Raymond Floyd and Isao Aoki by three strokes.

Floyd, who took an early-week lesson from his father and corrected a flaw in his swing, saying "I'm looking forward to playing golf again," challenged Jacobs on the second day with 69 to go with his 67, but he never got closer than within three shots. "I didn't get the job done on the greens," Floyd said. "Nobody made a run at (Jacobs), so he got comfortable. It's a tribute to him. It's hard to hold a lead, but he handled it well."

Jacobs, who closed with 70 for a 54-hole total of 203, 13 under par, wasn't so sure how well he handled his lead. "I had never been in this position against this caliber of players before," the 53-year-old said. "I had to protect the lead on every hole. I played so safe the last few holes it was embarrassing."

Floyd matched Jacobs' final-round 70, but had to share second place with a surging Jim Colbert, who bettered his scores each day, shooting 71, 68 and 67 for a 206 total. Neither Hale Irwin nor Gil Morgan were factors in this season-opener. Morgan tied Joe Inman for Sunday's low score with 66, but he could manage no better than a tie for sixth at 208. Irwin shot 214 for the week.

Making a rare appearance, Tom Weiskopf, who hadn't played since early in 1997, tied for 17th at 212 with rounds of 71, 73 and 68.

Royal Caribbean Classic—$1,000,000
Winner: Bruce Fleisher

It isn't every day that you win in your rookie debut, but it's an even rarer event when you win because your nearest competitor whiffs a shot down the stretch. That's what happened to Senior PGA Tour rookie Bruce Fleisher at the Crandon Park Golf Club in Key Biscayne, Florida, when he made his debut at the Royal Caribbean Classic.

In the final round, with the pressure of his first professional victory since the 1991 New England Classic on the line, Fleisher pushed his drive on the 18th hole into a cluster of tangled mangrove trees. Recovery seemed a bleak possibility. Just as it appeared Fleisher might be giving the tournament away, his closest competitor, Isao Aoki, slapped his tee shot on the final hole even further into the same trees. Fleisher found his ball, and after determining that an unplayable lie drop wouldn't put him in any better position, he punched a seven-iron shot about 40 yards back into the fairway, from where he was able to hit the green and close out the victory.

"It was one of those shots I could have whiffed," Fleisher said.

Aoki wasn't so lucky. He did whiff his second shot after the club hit a tree root on his downswing. Then he took an unplayable lie, and finally advanced his ball onto the green, too late to wrestle the lead away. In winning his Senior Tour debut, Fleisher joined such notables as Jack Nicklaus and Gary Player. Fleisher became the first among that elite group to capture the victory in wire-to-wire fashion, despite his near-disaster at the last.

An opening round of five-under-par 66 set the tone and gave the 1968 U.S. Amateur champion a one-stroke lead over Bob Duval and Walter Morgan. Fleisher had a second-round 69 to carry a two-shot advantage over Aoki and Jose Maria Canizares into the final day. It looked as if Fleisher would match his second-round score until the wayward 18th. A 70 on Sunday for a 54-hole total of 205 was good enough. Aoki walked away with rounds of 69, 68 and 70 for a 207 and second place, while Dana Quigley (69-71-68) and Leonard Thompson (70-72-66) jumped past Duval (67-71-71) to share third at 208. Duval finished tied for fourth with Jim Thorpe at 209.

Afterward Fleisher couldn't hold back his emotions. "I can't express what I'm feeling right now," he said. "It's hard to believe a 50-year-old man can sit here and cry, but this is something I've dreamed about for the last four or five years." After he gathered himself, Fleisher went on to say, "I think I'm going to feel comfortable out here. The next time I get in this position, it will be easier."

American Express Invitational—$1,200,000
Winner: Bruce Fleisher

In the 19-year history of the Senior PGA Tour no player had ever won his first two starts after turning 50. That changed in Sarasota, Florida, when Bruce Fleisher shot rounds of 67, 67 and 69 for a 203 total, 13 under par, at the TPC at Prestancia to win the American Express Invitational by three strokes over Larry Nelson.

In over 400 starts on the PGA Tour Fleisher had only one victory, the 1991 New England Classic. Then, after turning 50 in October and capturing medalist honors in the qualifying tournament, Fleisher won the Royal Caribbean Classic and followed that with an impressive victory in Sarasota, taking a three-shot lead in the second round at 134, and holding that margin through the finish.

"I knew (Fleisher) would do well," Hale Irwin said. "He's a guy who has continued his play from the regular tour. It's just a step over. His game is ready for this tour, and his performance is obviously showing it."

Even Fleisher seemed surprised by his start. "Honest to God, I had no expectations of this," he said. "I tried to prepare, but I had no idea. It's terrific. This is just a wonderful thing in my life."

The only thing missing from Fleisher's performance was a wire-to-wire win in Florida, and that was spoiled in the opening round when Bruce Summerhays shot 65 to take a two-shot lead over Fleisher, Hugh Baiocchi and Jim Albus. Early in the second round, Fleisher took the lead with steady play while Summerhays fell back with 75. Baiocchi also fell back with two final rounds of 73 and 74, while Albus slipped away with 74 and 75.

Nelson and Walter Hall both made late charges, Nelson shooting a final-round 67 to close to within three shots of Fleisher and take second place alone at 206, while Hall shot 66 to capture third place at 207.

GTE Classic—$1,200,000
Winner: Larry Nelson

Larry Nelson felt a twinge in his neck as he teed off in the final group of the GTE Classic at the TPC of Tampa Bay in Lutz, Florida, which was cause for concern. A neck injury sidelined Nelson for six weeks in 1998 and hampered his ability to make a run at either Hale Irwin or Gil Morgan for Player of the Year honors. Still, Nelson finished the season with three victories and entered 1999 with a fresh outlook. When he teed off on the cool, cloudy afternoon, however, he didn't feel confident, because of the neck.

"I was really concerned because it felt tight," he said. "But it didn't bother me too much. The cold weather might have helped."

What did bother Nelson was the play of rookie sensation Bruce Fleisher, who, after winning his first two starts as a senior, made three quick birdies on the first nine to catch and then pass Nelson atop the leaderboard.

"I was thinking about winning my third in a row," Fleisher said. He had certainly played well enough. After opening with two rounds of 70, Fleisher started the day two shots back of Nelson's 138 lead. He made up the difference by playing the first nine on Sunday in 33. For a while it looked as if Fleisher would become the first in Senior PGA Tour history to win his first three starts.

Nelson had other plans. After playing conservatively on the first nine and losing his lead, the 51-year-old Nelson knew he would have to pull out all the stops for his first victory of the year. "I was really happy to be pushed by Bruce," he said. "I think it got me out of my shell."

Nelson parred the 10th and 11th holes and continued to trail by one until he birdied the par-four 12th to draw even. Then, at the 528-yard, par-five 14th, Nelson hit a five-wood second shot to within 25 feet and made the putt for eagle. Fleisher parred the 14th, and called that two-shot swing, "the turning point of the tournament. I knew Larry would be a little hard to catch after that."

Adding another birdie at the par-four 15th, Nelson stretched his lead to three shots with three to play before bogeying the 16th and parring in for the win. His closing 67 matched Fleisher's final-round score, but his 11-under-par 205 total was good enough for a two-shot victory and a $180,000 paycheck, pushing Nelson's career Senior PGA Tour earnings over the $2 million mark.

"His bank account is a lot bigger than mine," Fleisher said. "Look, here's a guy who has won the PGA Championship and the U.S. Open, as well as numerous PGA Tour events. He's a seasoned player, so I'm very pleased, trust me. There were a number of guys who could have pushed Larry and didn't. I was the only one."

Graham Marsh made a run, shooting the low round of the day, 66 on Sunday, to finish alone in third at 208. Marsh's 69-66 weekend equaled Nelson's play the final two rounds, but an opening 73 left Marsh too far back to contend. Hale Irwin couldn't make a run at the lead either, even though the 1997 and 1998 Player of the Year started the final round only one shot back at 139. A closing round of 70 left Irwin tied for fourth with Jim Dent at 209.

ACE Group Classic—$1,200,000
Winner: Allen Doyle

With Hale Irwin languishing in 24th place on the money list, Senior PGA Tour rookies walked away with three of the first four titles on the 1999 schedule. Bruce Fleisher took the first two events of the year and finished second to Larry Nelson in the third. Then, on a sunny and mild Sunday afternoon at the Bay Colony Golf Club in Naples, Florida, 50-year-old rookie Allen Doyle waltzed to a five-shot victory in his second start. Doyle's final-round 69 for a 13-under-par 203 total looked easy for the 1998 qualifying tournament medalist. After he made birdie on the par-five 12th, Doyle played a conservative fairways-and-greens game that proved effective. "After the birdie at 12, it was guide city," Doyle said.

The victory cruise started early on Friday when Doyle shot a course-record, eight-under-par 64 to take a one-shot lead over Vicente Fernandez. That lead was extended in the second round when Doyle shot 70 to take a two-shot advantage over Fernandez, Hugh Baiocchi and Graham Marsh. By the time he reached the 13th tee on Sunday, the lead was five and Doyle knew his first victory as a senior was in his sights.

"I feel as though I'm playing up to my potential, now," Doyle said. "I'm swinging real good, and I had hoped to get off to a good start."

Doyle didn't turn professional until 1995 when he qualified for the Nike Tour at age 46 as a tune-up for a potential Senior PGA Tour run. To everyone's surprise, Doyle won three times on the Nike Tour and became the oldest rookie in PGA Tour history at age 47. In two seasons he won more than $200,000 on the tour, but failed to break into the win column and didn't reach the goals he had set for himself.

"I was disappointed," Doyle said. "I maybe put a little too much pressure on myself to play well. I didn't work on my game the way I should have."

For Doyle, who has what many regard as the shortest, flattest swing in the history of professional golf, working on his game consisted of installing a gym in his La Grange, Georgia, home and developing a center-of-the-fairway consistency. He led the field in driving accuracy and greens hit in regulation for the week, a pattern Doyle hopes to continue.

"I'd like to see if I can become one of the top players," he said. "We've all just come out of the gate real well. Maybe we're a little less afraid of the big boys."

For the second week in a row Graham Marsh had a chance, but a final-round 73 left him tied for third at 209 with George Archer, Larry Nelson and Bruce Summerhays.

Senior Slam—$600,000
Winner: Gil Morgan

The Senior Slam was a 36-hole encapsulation of the 1998 season. Larry Nelson and Jay Sigel were part of the show, but the Cabo San Lucas tournament ended up being a two-man race between Hale Irwin and Gil Morgan, just as most of 1998 had been. This time Morgan got the best of it, firing a final-round 65 for a two-stroke win over Irwin.

The tournament was designed for the winners of all four senior major championships from 1998, but since Morgan and Irwin the split the 1998 majors between them, Nelson and Sigel were added as the third- and fourth-place money winners. The two alternates were pretty well out of it after the first day. Nelson shot 68 in the first round, behind Irwin by three, while Sigel shot 73. Sigel rallied in the second round with 66 to tie Nelson, who shot 71 for a 139 total. Neither contended for the lead, however.

Morgan shot 67 in the opener, two shots more than Irwin, who went on a late birdie tear. Within the first few holes of the second round, Morgan had tied for the lead. It remained close throughout the first nine with Irwin regaining the lead, but Morgan came back. He pulled away with four birdies on the final nine holes for 65 and a 132 total and a two-shot victory. Irwin shot 69 for a 134 total, five ahead of Sigel and Nelson.

Toshiba Senior Classic—$1,200,000
Winner: Gary McCord

Television commentator Gary McCord had an explanation for why he missed a four-foot birdie putt that extended his first professional playoff for two more holes. "A couple of the putts in the playoff I didn't want to make," McCord said. "Television was on and people were following us. The more you go into prime time the better the ratings are. And I'm a bit of a ham. Finally it was getting dark, so I had to put (John Jacobs) away."

McCord finally did put Jacobs away with another four-foot birdie putt on the fifth playoff hole of the Toshiba Senior Classic. When it went in, McCord had his first victory as a senior and only his second win as a professional (the first coming in the 1991 Gateway Open, a Hogan Tour event). "I've won everywhere except high school, college and the pros," McCord said in his typical manner. "I don't want to be static. I want to have my foot on something. My wife keeps saying, 'Slow down.' She's the brake and I'm the accelerator. Dawdle and I'll pass you."

That's exactly what McCord did in the waning moments of Sunday afternoon in Newport Beach, California. After sharing the first-round lead at 67 with Tom Jenkins, Jacobs and Bruce Summerhays, McCord put together two respectable rounds of 68 and 69, but assumed it was too little, too late. Jacobs held the second-round lead at 134, but it was Al Geiberger, who shot 69 and 66 the first two days, who came to the par-five 18th hole needing only a par to win by one shot. Geiberger couldn't deliver, however, hitting his second shot into the rough behind a bunker. From there, he hit his third shot over the green and failed to save par. That let McCord and Jacobs into a three-way playoff with Geiberger at nine-under-par 204.

"Al gave it away with one shot on the last hole," Jacobs said. "It was a shame."

On the first playoff hole, it looked as though Jacobs would be the one to capitalize on Geiberger's mistake. After hitting his second shot to the fringe, Jacobs chipped in for an eagle-three which eliminated Geiberger. McCord was left with an 18-footer for eagle that, according to Jacobs, "Gary doesn't make for a $100 Nassau, much less for $180,000." This time McCord made the putt for eagle and extended the playoff.

After two pars on the following playoff holes, the two returned to the 18th where McCord had a four-footer for birdie to win. "It was an easy putt," he said. "Left to right, but there was a lot of waffling on the line. I figured I'd tumble it down there like a staggering drunk trying to get home. But I was down there shaking. The club looked like a figure eight going back." He missed, and the two returned to the 16th for the second time where McCord made a four-footer to win.

"Maybe somebody channeled my body," he joked afterward. "Maybe Tiger was channeled in. I'll blame it on something extraterrestrial."

Liberty Mutual Legends of Golf—$1,610,000
Winners: Hubert Green and Gil Morgan

From the first birdie on the first hole during the first day of the Liberty Mutual Legends of Golf on The Squire and The Slammer course at the World Golf Village in St. Augustine, Florida, there was little doubt as to the outcome. Hubert Green and Gil Morgan were the perfect team, complimenting each other en route to a 22-under-par 194 total and a three-stroke victory over John Mahaffey and Tom Wargo.

"We're pretty good together," Morgan said. "I might hit it longer off the tee than Hubert, but he's got great touch around the greens."

That touch worked wonders in the best-ball format as Green and Morgan got off to a fast start on Friday, combining for an opening-round 61. That was only one shot better than the team of David Graham and Jay Sigel, but they couldn't keep the pace, shooting 69 on Saturday and closing with the same score on Sunday to share third place at 200 with Gibby Gilbert and J.C. Snead.

George Archer and Simon Hobday also had a chance after the second day. Four strokes back at 132, Archer and Hobday couldn't get any putts to fall and settled for a 71 final round and a tie for seventh with John Bland and Graham Marsh at 203.

Mahaffey and Wargo made a charge the final day, shooting a weekend-low 64 for a 197 total, but, according to Wargo, "We just ran out of holes."

In a rare competitive appearance, Sam Snead competed in the Demaret (over 70) Division, and at age 86, he still showed his frustration when the putts didn't drop the way he thought they should. Chi Chi Rodriguez also made a return to the competitive stage after suffering a heart attack in the off season.

The Demaret Division was won for the second straight year by the team of Joe Jimenez and Charlie Sifford. After the victory, Sifford dedicated the win to his wife, Rose, who died in July of 1998. "She was with me when we won this tournament last year," he said. "This means more because she's gone now and I wanted to win it for her."

Emerald Coast Classic—$1,100,000
Winner: Bob Duval

Sitting on a 36-hole total of 11-under-par 129 and a three-shot lead going into the final round of the Emerald Coast Classic, Bob Duval called his son David, the world's No. 1 player at the time, who also held a one-shot lead in The Players Championship going into the final day.

"He said, 'You're going to think about what a win would mean for you,'" Duval said of the conversation with his son. "But he said, 'That's okay. Do it. Embrace it. Then think about your next shot. Just take it one shot at a time.' I was really good at that today."

The elder Duval took all 71 of his final shots one at a time, and as a result he edged a charging Bruce Fleisher by two strokes, capturing his first win on the Senior PGA Tour the same weekend his son won The Players Championship. In addition to being the elder Duval's first win, it was the first time in history that a father and son won PGA Tour and Senior PGA Tour events on the same weekend.

"David is as proud of me as I am of him," Duval said. "For both of us to win is wonderful."

"This is great for golf," Fleisher said. "It makes for a wonderful story. This is a very big win for Bob, and I look at it as a stepping stone for him. Watch out for Duval."

Having spent his career as a club pro in Jacksonville, Florida, Duval's rebirth on the Senior PGA Tour came at the 1997 Emerald Coast Classic, where a third-place finish pushed him into the top 31 on the money list, earning Duval an automatic exemption for 1998. He finished 17th on the money list in 1998 with five straight finishes in the top 10 to start the season, but victory continued to elude him.

An opening-round 61 at 6,843-yard, par-70 Moors Golf Club, one stroke more than the all-time Senior PGA Tour single-round record of 60 held by Isao Aoki, put Duval in the driver's seat with a four-shot lead over Buzz Thomas and a seven-shot advantage over Fleisher. "I wanted to get to 60 so I could tell David he only beat me by one shot," Duval said in reference to his son's 59 earlier in the year. "I came in here feeling real good because I played every day last week with David."

The good play continued on Saturday as Duval shot 68 to move to 129, three clear of Thomas and six ahead of Fleisher. Even though he slipped to 71 on Sunday, it was good enough for a win, and a place in history alongside his son.

"I can't express how happy I am," Duval said.

The Tradition—$1,500,000
Winner: Graham Marsh

An unpredicted turn of events left Graham Marsh the winner of The Tradition for his first senior major victory since the 1997 U.S. Senior Open. The event was shortened because the Senior PGA Tour has a rule prohibiting a full field from playing on a Monday, and snow — that's right, snow in Scottsdale, Arizona — forced officials to cancel the Friday and Sunday rounds. As a result, Marsh, who shot 67 in the sleet on Thursday and 67 when the sun finally peaked through on Saturday, was declared the winner.

"We all played 36 holes and we all had equal chances," Marsh said. "A problem with Mondays is the logistics of getting volunteers, of keeping television, and keeping those things together to give the tournament the atmosphere that is necessary."

With three inches of snow making the Cochise course at Desert Mountain look more like a ski resort than a golf course, tour officials had few options but plenty of critics. It was the fourth time in 11 years that inclement weather has canceled or postponed one or more rounds at The Tradition. Tournament founder Lyle Anderson said he was thinking about moving the event to South Florida where April skies are never dampened by snow clouds. "This year was the worst of all," he said.

Adding to the frustration was the fact that temperatures before play were in the 80s with sunshine. Overnight on Wednesday things changed, and by the time the first group teed off on Thursday, the temperature hovered around freezing, with intermittent snow and sleet mixing with a steady cold rain. "It was the first time in my career I had ice in my mustache," local resident Gary McCord said of the conditions.

Larry Laoretti, Walter Zembriski and Jim Colbert all withdrew because of the conditions on Thursday, and Hubert Green followed by withdrawing on Friday after shooting 81 in the snow. Even veteran cold-weather players such as Brian Barnes from Scotland found the conditions a little much. "If I had been in Europe I would have walked off," Barnes said. "I stayed because I couldn't have flown home on that short notice."

Barnes' decision to stay paid off. He followed his opening 74 with a 69 on Saturday and a tie for ninth place at 143 with John Bland, Terry Dill and Howard Twitty. Rookie Jim Thorpe also shot 69 on Saturday to go with his 73 on Thursday. His 142 total left him tied for seventh with John Morgan, six shots off of Marsh's winning score.

To underscore the brutality of the conditions, the field of 80 players carded only nine rounds in the 60s and Marsh was responsible for two of them.

PGA Seniors' Championship—$1,750,000
Winner: Allen Doyle

For 59 years no one had ever shot as low as a final-round 64 to win the PGA Seniors' Championship. It wasn't until former driving range pro and collegiate hockey player Allen Doyle carded six straight threes in the final round at PGA National Golf Club that a golfer carded a 64 in the final round to win this storied championship.

"It's kind of mind-boggling," Doyle said after coming from four strokes back to capture his first major title in his rookie year as a senior. "I'm just thrilled beyond words."

He deserved to be thrilled. After starting Thursday and Friday with two 71s to trail Vicente Fernandez by seven going into the weekend, no one gave Doyle much of a chance.

He shot a third-round 68 to pull within four shots of Fernandez and co-leader Bruce Fleisher. Still, there were three players ahead of Doyle (Fleisher and Fernandez at 206 and Jose Maria Canizares at 207) and two more (Dana Quigley and Bruce Summerhays) tied with him at 210 as play began.

A birdie-birdie start on Sunday got Doyle off to a quick start, but a careless double bogey at the fourth quickly dropped him back to six under par, where he began the day. Then Doyle caught fire, birdieing the fifth, seventh and ninth holes to make the turn at 33. At the par-five 10th, Doyle hit a delicate little chip shot that found the cup for eagle and he was on a roll.

"That chip was as big a shot as I hit all day," Doyle said. He was right. Up until that point the tournament was still considered a two-man race between Fernandez and Fleisher, who had won his first two tournaments as a senior.

"This guy Doyle has proven himself," Fleisher said. "I saw it at the qualifying school (where Doyle was medalist). I tell you what, he doesn't move. He's tough. He's a rock."

Doyle gave another shot back on the 11th with a bogey, but beginning at the 12th his string of threes started. By the time he hit a 186-yard three iron to within one foot at the par-four 16th, setting up another birdie, he was alone in the lead. Fernandez and Fleisher had made double bogeys at the 15th, and when Doyle reached the 18th, all he had to do was finish, which he did with a routine par to be two strokes ahead of Fernandez.

The PGA Seniors' was Doyle's second win in seven weeks, the first coming in Naples, but his final round was one for the ages. "I kind of blew it today," he said afterward. "I was telling some of the guys that in Naples there were some headlines saying 'He shoots, he scores!' (a reference to Doyle's slapshot swing and hockey background). I said to them, 'I should have brought a hockey helmet and put it on coming down the 18th hole.' Then I'd really be known for something."

Home Depot Invitational—$1,200,000
Winner: Bruce Fleisher

Bruce Fleisher could never have dreamed how his rookie season on the Senior PGA Tour would start. "A friend of mine handed me a note before the season that said, 'Three wins, top five on the money list,'" Fleisher said. "I told him, 'You know, that sounds great, but let's be realistic.'"

Four months into the 1999 season Fleisher hit a wedge to within one foot on the par-five 18th at the TPC at Piper Glen in Charlotte, North Carolina, for a birdie and his third victory in seven starts. He also recorded two seconds and one third.

The man who finished third at the Home Depot Invitational, Allen Doyle, who began the final day tied for the lead with Fleisher, fell two strokes short in Charlotte, but was on track for an equally impressive rookie senior season. Doyle's two wins, including one major (PGA Seniors' Championship) moved him just behind Fleisher on the early-season money list and turned the first four months of the Senior PGA Tour into a two-man show: Doyle, a former driving range owner who played only two uneventful seasons on the PGA Tour, and Fleisher, who won the 1968 U.S. Amateur and the 1991 New England Classic, but little else of note.

"I never dreamed I'd be doing what I'm doing," Fleisher said. "Well, I dreamed I'd do it. But I never dreamed it would happen like this. It's a wonderful place to be."

Playing with Doyle in the final group on Sunday after the two started the day tied with Terry Dill at 136, Fleisher and his rookie buddy spent a little time talking about how lucky they both were. "Walking down No. 1 today, we were reminiscing about the qualifying school. We were talking about what a wonderful opportunity this has been for us," Fleisher said.

Doyle had a chance to take even greater advantage of the opportunity. He led by three shots at the turn, but failed to make a birdie on the second nine, and he made a critical bogey at the par-three 17th. "I felt like I was in control at that point," Doyle said. "It was just a matter of wrong club selection. I used a nine iron instead of the wedge and it was too strong." The ball bounced over the green and found the water, and the resulting bogey dropped Doyle to 71 for the day, 207 for the week, and a tie for fourth with Christy O'Connor, Jr., and DeWitt Weaver.

Dill shot a final-round 70 for 206, which tied him for second place with Jim Holtgrieve, who finished with 69. That would have been good enough for a playoff had Fleisher not hit his wedge to within 12 inches on the final hole. He finished with 69 for a 205 total. "I was really shaky over that last putt," Fleisher said. "You'd think you'd get over that, but you don't."

Fleisher's $180,000 check solidified his position atop the early season money list, but Doyle's $59,200 earnings kept things close. Still, Doyle was anything but upset or greedy over not winning in Charlotte.

"There's a lot of money and a lot of glory to go around," Doyle said. "One guy isn't going to corner it out here. Two aren't likely to."

Bruno's Memorial Classic—$1,200,000
Winner: Larry Nelson

Just when you thought the Senior PGA Tour had taken on a new look with rookies Bruce Fleisher and Allen Doyle replacing the old guard, along came Larry Nelson, who birdied three of the last seven holes during the final round of the Bruno's Memorial Classic to win his second event of the season and produce his sixth top-three finish in 10 events. Nelson posted scores of 70, 67 and 68 for a 205 total, 11 under par, to win by one stroke over Dana Quigley, and by two over Gil Morgan.

"Larry Nelson is unbelievable," said second-round co-leader Joe Inman, who is also Nelson's neighbor and fellow member at the Atlanta Country Club. "Here's a guy who has won three major championships, and he can walk around the mall all day without a soul recognizing him. That's just the way he is."

And that's the way Nelson wants to remain. No one was more comfortable than Nelson when the Senior PGA Tour hoopla shifted to the new crop of rookies. All he wanted was to slip out of town unnoticed with a victory. "I think my newness has worn off," Nelson said. "There was a lot of hype last year everywhere I went because I was a rookie. Now, everybody is used to me, and that's died down. I just want to be low-key and enjoy it."

Despite his best efforts to remain an unnoticed winner, Nelson found himself in a duel in the final round in Birmingham, Alabama, with Morgan. Morgan started the final round two shots off Nelson's 137 lead, but birdied five of the first nine holes to build a two-shot lead of his own with nine holes to play. Morgan's charge faded when he bogeyed two of the three par-five holes on the second nine, the last coming on a three-putt at the 18th.

"I had a chance," Morgan said. "Probably if I'd played safer or a little more aggressive it might have been different. You never know, though."

Indeed, you never know. Despite his one victory, two seconds, two thirds and solid third-place position on the money list behind Fleisher and Doyle, Nelson didn't feel very confident with his swing coming into Birmingham, and he wasn't one of the pre-tournament favorites. A tip from his son on the practice tee got Nelson swinging well enough to shoot a final-round 68 and fend off challenges from Morgan and a charging Quigley.

"I wasn't turning behind the ball in my backswing," Nelson said. "I had a little reverse pivot that was causing me to hit some really ugly shots. I'm still not hitting it the way I would like. I'm putting well, so if my ball-striking catches up to my putting, things could be good."

He struck it well enough to make only one bogey and five birdies, the last coming at the 526-yard, par-five 15th after Nelson reached the green in two strokes with a three wood. "You never like to have to play the last six holes in two under," Nelson said. "I knew it was going to be a fight."

Joining the fight was Quigley, the third-year former club pro who, in his words, is "making up for all those years I was sitting in the shop while these guys were playing." Quigley started Sunday three shots back, but six birdies in the first 15 holes moved him into a tie with Nelson. A missed 10-foot birdie putt on the 18th doused Quigley's chances for his third career victory.

"It was definitely more exciting than I would have liked," Nelson said. "But there's a lot of excitement in senior golf."

Nationwide Championship—$1,400,000
Winner: Hale Irwin

Hale Irwin hadn't performed up to his standards in the first four months of 1999, but that was, in large part, due to the incredible run he had the previous year. "I needed a breather after the campaign of 1998," Irwin said. "After the season I had last year, how do you resurrect that same enthusiasm? I mean, I won't compare myself with (St. Louis Cardinals' slugger) Mark McGwire, but you're seeing the same thing with McGwire, and you see it in other sports all the time. It's hard to come back after a great year and a bit of a layoff and pick back up without missing a beat."

When he finally decided to come back and refocus his efforts, Irwin shot 10-under-par 206 at The Golf Club of Georgia and capped off a two-shot victory over Bob Murphy in the Nationwide Championship by holing a 74-yard wedge shot for eagle on the final hole.

"I've never done anything like that before," Irwin said. "I knocked a long putt in to get into a playoff in the 1990 U.S. Open, but I've never holed a shot like that and 'boom' been handed a trophy."

With a one-birdie, no-bogey round underway, Irwin stood on the par-five 18th assuming he needed a birdie, but he had no idea how Murphy stood. "I heard a roar or something on 18, so I guessed somebody made birdie. I thought it was Bob," he said.

It wasn't. Murphy left his birdie putt hanging on the lip, but in the end it didn't matter. Irwin hit three wood into the center of the fairway, laid up short of the water guarding the green with a five iron, then hit sand wedge onto the front edge of the green and watched as it hopped forward and spun into the cup for an eagle, a closing 69 and a two-stroke victory.

Irwin conjured more memories of his 1990 U.S. Open victory by trotting to the green slapping the hands of zealous gallery members. He also silenced those who prematurely reported his demise. "All the hype and stuff that happened the last couple of years hasn't been there this year," Irwin said. "In a lot of respects that has been good. I didn't want to get off this year with that heavy hype. It can be all-encompassing. I needed a break. I took it, and now I'm ready."

Even Murphy was glad to see Irwin back, although he would have preferred the comeback occur at someone else's expense. "It's not much fun to lose," he said. "But when you lose that way ... Hey, I'm glad to see Hale back. Having him win is good for the game and great for senior golf."

If Irwin's return to glory has any glitches, it could be on the greens where he has struggled through one of his worst putting years since joining the Senior PGA Tour. Irwin arrived in Atlanta ranked 55th in putting, and his performance in the Nationwide Championship did little to boost his numbers. Had he made half of the 10-footers he left himself for birdie during the final round, the tournament wouldn't have been close.

"I know in my soul that my putting is not what it should be," Irwin said.

He has tried three different putters in eight starts in 1999, but nothing clicked. Even after the eagle went in on 18, Irwin's only comment was, "Well, it beats putting. That's all I can say."

But the newly focused Irwin also says he knows the putting will come. "It's good to see and hear the ball going into the hole again," he said. "That's a big part of this comeback I'm trying to make. It's going to be a catch-up year, but I'm ready to get this campaign going."

Las Vegas Senior Classic—$1,400,000
Winner: Vicente Fernandez

Tied for the lead with Dave Eichelberger with three holes to play in the Las Vegas Senior Classic, and looking to capture his third Senior PGA Tour victory, but his first in over two years, Vicente Fernandez took stock of the fact that he was playing in Las Vegas and he did what you're supposed to do — he took a gamble. On the par-five 16th, Fernandez never considered laying up. He pulled out a two iron and, with all the poise he could muster under the circumstances, Fernandez hit his second shot over the water and onto the green. The ball stopped 30 feet away, and the eagle putt went right into the middle of the hole.

"I hadn't won for almost two years, and it made me feel different," Fernandez said. "My first win (the 1996 Burnet Senior Classic, which he won as a Monday qualifier) was unbelievable. The second one (the 1997 Bank One Classic) was good, but his one ... there was more pressure. I knew going into the last round there was more pressure because I knew I could win and I wanted to win very badly."

He never held the outright lead until the eagle putt at the 16th on the last day, but Fernandez was never far from the top of the leaderboard. On Thursday of the four-round event, he shot 69 to trail Isao Aoki by four shots, but by the close of play on Friday, Fernandez, after his 71, and four others stood two shots off the pace.

Lee Trevino held the halfway lead at 138, while Frank Conner, the former professional tennis player who found a second professional sports career in golf, was one stroke back. Aoki followed his opening-round 65 with an uninspiring 75 to tie with Fernandez at 140.

While all the other names around him changed on Saturday, Fernandez continued to play consistently well, carding 67 for a three-day total of 207, one stroke off the lead. The leader turned out to be Fred Gibson, a second-year senior whose best finish was a tie for seventh, and whose only career win came in the 1996 Tobago Open. Gibson did manage to shoot the day's low score on Saturday, adding 66 to his earlier rounds of 69 and 71, but his one-shot margin seemed tenuous. In addition to Fernandez, at one stroke back, Aoki, Conner and Eichelberger were only two off the pace.

"I felt very confident all the way," Fernandez said. "I was close because I was doing well, and it was a matter of time for me to get a win."

If not for a closing 64 by Allen Doyle, Fernandez might have won the PGA Seniors' just five weeks earlier, and he had played well enough in 1998 to make an 18-hole playoff with Hale Irwin at the U.S. Senior Open, which Irwin won by birdieing the final hole.

Things finally came together for Fernandez in Las Vegas, however, and his gamble paid off. The eagle at the 16th gave him a two-shot edge on Eichelberger. Pars at the 17th and 18th sealed the victory as Fernandez finished the week with two 67s and a 14-under-par 274 total, two ahead of Eichelberger, and three ahead of a charging John Mahaffey. Conner shot a closing 70 to finish tied for fourth with Tom Wargo at 278, while Hale Irwin continued his comeback in sixth place. Third-round leader Gibson had trouble finding the fairways on Sunday, closing the week with 75 for a 281 total and seventh place.

Bell Atlantic Classic—$1,100,000
Winner: Tom Jenkins

Through a light drizzling rain that never delayed play, the Senior PGA Tour saw one of its most exciting weekends of the season in Avondale, Pennsylvania, as Jack Nicklaus returned to competition in the Bell Atlantic Classic for the first time since undergoing hip replacement surgery in March. Jim

Thorpe shot a final-round 65 in his first appearance as a senior, and Gil Morgan made a late charge at the lead. In the end neither Nicklaus nor Thorpe nor Morgan would walk away with the title.

The winner was Tom Jenkins, a 51-year-old Texan who had never won as a senior before arriving at Hartefeld National Golf Club, and whose only career PGA Tour victory had come back in 1975 when he captured the IVB Philadelphia Classic. Jenkins, a quiet player with a calm demeanor, didn't mind taking a back seat to the latest version of "Jack Is Back." In fact, he liked it. "He's great for this tour and great for the game," Jenkins said of Nicklaus' presence. When Jenkins shot 70 and 67 in the first two rounds to take a one-shot lead over Morgan, Thorpe and Jesse Patino into the final round, he wasn't surprised that the majority of the spectators followed Nicklaus, even though Jack shot 74 and 70 and never contended for the lead.

"You could just tell that without much of a field here this week, we got great crowds," Dana Quigley said of Nicklaus' fan support. Even though he finished with a third round of 70 and finished eight shots behind the leaders, Nicklaus received standing ovations on every hole and the praise from his fellow competitors. "I told people that Jack didn't come here just to play," Thorpe said. "He came here with his game tight."

Thorpe also came prepared to play. An opening-round 68 in his first 18 holes as a senior put the three-time PGA Tour winner two shots off the lead held by Frank Conner. A second-round 73 seemingly dropped Thorpe from contention. Jenkins had made a move on Saturday, taking the lead at 137, four ahead of Thorpe.

Morgan appeared to be the biggest threat going into the final round. After an opening 71, where his putter seemed to abandon him, Morgan found his touch on Saturday en route to a 67 and a two-day total of 138, good enough for a tie with Patino and Rocky Thompson, one back of Jenkins' lead.

Jenkins held tough on Sunday, birdieing the par-fives when the opportunities arose and making none of the mistakes that one might have expected, given the rainy weather and the pressures of a one-stroke margin. It wasn't until the final hole that Jenkins showed the first signs of pressure. Still clinging to a one-shot edge, he missed the green with his approach, then stood over an eight-foot par putt as Thorpe, who had birdied the 18th to shoot 65, openly rooted against him in the press room. "One for Thorpey," Thorpe said in the presence of a group of reporters.

Thorpe got his wish. Jenkins missed his par effort, finished with 69, and the two were tied at 206. Morgan played well again on Sunday, but couldn't make the putts he needed coming down the stretch. His closing 69 left him one stroke out of the playoff. He tied with Thompson for third at 207. Jim Colbert and John Mahaffey also had good weeks, finishing with rounds of 69 and 68 respectively and tied for fifth at 208.

Jenkins didn't know about Thorpe's negative cheerleading when the two ventured back to the 18th tee for the playoff, but he later said he didn't hold it against him, nor was he offended by the comments. All Jenkins did was go about his business, birdieing the hole he had bogeyed just moments before, and capturing his first win as a senior.

As for Thorpe's choice of words in the press room, the rookie was unapologetic. He said, "I don't root against players, but then I don't root for them either."

Boone Valley Classic—$1,400,000
Winner: Hale Irwin

After taking what he termed "a break to recharge my batteries," Hale Irwin seemed to pick up right where he left off in 1998 when he captured seven titles including two majors and set a single season earnings record. In 1999, after deferring the first few months to rookies Bruce Fleisher and Allen Doyle, who picked up five wins between them before the first of June, Irwin announced his comeback by holing a 74-yard wedge shot to capture the Nationwide Championship in Atlanta, then reaffirmed himself two starts later by calmly shooting a final-round 66 at the Boone Valley Golf Club in Augusta, Missouri, to beat Al Geiberger by two shots in the Boone Valley Classic.

There weren't any theatrics in this victory, just pure ball-striking magic from a master of the art. "I'm hitting the ball so extraordinarily well that it seemed like on every hole I had a birdie opportunity," Irwin said. "I didn't want to get into a position where I was trying to scramble for pars."

Irwin never missed a fairway and hit 17 greens in regulation on Sunday as he came from two shots back to finish at 13-under-par 203. "It's hard to regenerate some of the momentum I had last season," Irwin said. "I wasn't pleased with the elongated slump, and I felt I needed to play better again. I needed to step off and let the waters settle a little, but I'm fine now."

"You could see it coming," said second-round leader Bruce Summerhays, who shot 67 and 68 the first two days and carried a one-shot lead over Frank Conner into Sunday's final round. "All the elements were there for Hale. I knew if I could shoot 68 the way I was playing, Hale could shoot something lower the way he was playing."

Irwin started Sunday at 137, two shots behind Summerhays. Summerhays faded early in the final round, finishing with a 73 for a 208 total and a tie for fifth with Jose Maria Canizares, Jim Dent and Dana Quigley. Meanwhile, the final round became a birdie race between Irwin and Geiberger — a race Irwin won with his 66. Geiberger shot 68 for a 205 total while Kermit Zarley finished third with 206.

This was the closest Irwin might come to a hometown victory, since his house was only 40 miles from Boone Valley. "It's not that easy to come back to your home town," he said. "Other than two years ago (when Irwin won the Boone Valley Classic by two shots over Gil Morgan), I really haven't played well in areas where I've lived or that I'm familiar with. Last year I came into this tournament all psyched up and I played terribly."

Cadillac NFL Classic—$1,100,000
Winner: Allen Doyle

Just when it looked as though Hale Irwin was reasserting himself as the player to watch on the 1999 Senior PGA Tour, rookie Allen Doyle, a two-time winner in the first five months of the year and reigning PGA Seniors' champion, added to his bid for Player of the Year with a gritty playoff victory over Joe Inman in the Cadillac NFL Classic.

"At the beginning of the year, my goal was to win one tournament and finish in the top 30 on the money list," Doyle said. "After I won one, my goal was to win two and finish in the top 15. Now that I've won three, I'm entertaining thoughts of finishing in the top five."

His victory on the fourth playoff hole, despite a weekend plagued by back spasms, moved Doyle to the No. 1 spot on the money list. "This is unbelievable," Doyle said. "If anyone had told me, with the way I felt the last few days, that I would have a chance to win this week, I would have told them they were nuts. I just hung in there though, and somehow it happened."

How it happened was that Doyle shot an opening-round 67 for a six-way tie for the lead along with Inman, Lee Trevino, Bob Charles, DeWitt Weaver and Tom McGinnis. The other contenders faded on Saturday, as Doyle continued to defy the odds and his pain with 66 for a 133 total and a four-shot lead over Trevino. Inman could manage no better than 71 and stood tied for third with Charles and John Bland at 138.

Still, with his back bothering him on every swing, some questioned whether Doyle could even finish, much less win. "I'll crawl in on Sunday if I have to," Doyle answered. "I might shoot 80, but I'll finish."

He shot 71 in the final round despite flinching on every swing because of the pain. "I was really concerned at the turn," said Doyle's daughter and caddie, Erin. "He was really hurting. At impact he was just bracing himself. He didn't even get a chance to practice, but he didn't complain."

The three-day total of 12-under-par 204 was better than everyone in the field except Inman, who shot 66 to force a playoff. Everyone gave Inman the edge in the playoff. He had just come off a six-under-par final round, and his opponent couldn't take a step without his back hurting. But after halving the first three playoff holes, it became apparent that Doyle wasn't going away.

On the fourth playoff hole Inman lipped out a birdie putt from eight feet, giving Doyle a chance at victory, then Doyle's four-footer for birdie went into the center of the hole. "I thought I hit the putt perfectly," Inman said. "I have no regrets. I would hit it the same way if I could do it again."

Trevino finished alone in third after shooting 69 for a 206 total, while Raymond Floyd closed with 67 to tie Mike McCullough for fourth at 208. Charles shot 71-71 for the weekend and finished at 209, six strokes back of Doyle and alone in sixth.

BellSouth Senior Classic—$1,400,000
Winner: Bruce Fleisher

Bruce Fleisher obviously decided he liked the view from the top. Only one week after being bumped from his perch atop the Senior PGA Tour money list, Fleisher remedied the situation with a one-shot win over Al Geiberger at the BellSouth Senior Classic at Opryland in Nashville, Tennessee.

"You have goals and some of them come true, but I'll have to reevaluate mine. I've already passed most of them," Fleisher said after his final-round 66 secured his fourth victory of the year. This victory had a home flair to it. Not only was Fleisher born and raised in Union City, Tennessee, but also the man he edged out, Geiberger, is legendary in the state. It was in 1977 during the second round of the Danny Thomas Memphis Classic that a then

39-year-old Geiberger became the first man in PGA Tour history to shoot 59.

But this was a different era, and while the narrow 6,783-yard Springhouse Golf Club didn't give up any scores under 60, Fleisher's weekend rounds of 63 and 66, coupled with an opening 71, were good enough for a 200 total, 16 under par, and a one-stroke margin.

"He made no mistakes," said Jim Thorpe, who played on Sunday with Fleisher. "He capitalized on every putt. God bless him. He deserved to win."

The two key putts where Fleisher capitalized came on the final nine, the first a 20-footer for eagle at the 10th to take a two-shot lead and the second a 12-foot birdie putt at the 17th to hold the lead for good. "I had the same line as Jim Thorpe, who had a longer putt," Fleisher said of the clincher. "All I had to do was get the ball on line."

Geiberger, who at 61 was a sentimental favorite in Nashville, picked up his third second-place finish of the season. He matched Fleisher's final-round 66, but his opening rounds of 67 and 68 put him one off the lead at the beginning of the final round, a position he maintained to the end.

"A victory is obviously what I need, but three seconds let me know I can do it," Geiberger said. "If I can stay healthy and motivated, I can play. We look at age 50 now like we used to look at 40. Now, we're trying to move that barrier up to 60."

Southwestern Bell Dominion—$1,100,000
Winner: John Mahaffey

With Gil Morgan, Bruce Fleisher and Larry Nelson around the top of the leaderboard, the only big names not prominently displayed at the Southwestern Bell Dominion in San Antonio, Texas, were Allen Doyle, who took the week off, and Hale Irwin, who attempted to play in the U.S. Open in Pinehurst, but had to withdraw after the first round because of shoulder problems. One who had yet to break into the category of big names was 51-year-old John Mahaffey, who recorded only two top-10 finishes in his rookie season on the Senior PGA Tour, finishing 49th on the money list after having high expectations.

"I can sympathize and empathize with the guys in the 40-to-50 age group out on tour," Mahaffey said. He was speaking from first-hand experience. In his last seven seasons on the PGA Tour, Mahaffey never finished better than 120th on the money list. "You get down on yourself. You're disappointed in the way you are playing, but the Senior Tour is the best thing in the world."

The world got even better for Mahaffey in his native Texas where, despite stifling heat and two rain delays, he came from behind to tie Fleisher and Jose Maria Canizares, then went on to birdie the first two holes of the playoff for his first senior win. "To win the Texas Open in 1985 and now win here is something special," Mahaffey told the crowd at the Dominion Country Club. "I am really excited. This is something special."

After shooting a two-day total of 134 and taking a one-shot lead over Fleisher, Gil Morgan and Hugh Baiocchi, Mahaffey fell behind Fleisher and Canizares in the early holes on the last day. On the second nine, after working hard all season to improve his putting, Mahaffey started to see the results. "I made some good putts at the right times," he said. Mahaffey finished with 70 for a 204 total, 12 under par, while Canizares closed with 67 and Fleisher, 69.

He made three crucial putts in a span of four holes: a 20-footer for birdie on the 17th in regulation to regain a share of the lead, and birdie putts of 10 and 30 feet on the two playoff holes. Canizares had a chance to win outright on the 18th, but he missed a six-footer for birdie to force the three-way playoff. Fleisher parred the first playoff hole to be eliminated after both Canizares and Mahaffey made birdies. Then Mahaffey sealed the victory with the 30-footer one hole later.

Ford Senior Players Championship—$2,000,000
Winner: Hale Irwin

Just when it looked as though the old guard on the Senior PGA Tour had bowed out to make room for the newer generation of players, 54-year-old Hale Irwin said, "Not so fast," with a 64-65 weekend and a seven-shot victory in the Ford Senior Players Championship. The 21-under-par 267 total gave notice that the man who dominated in 1997 and 1998 was back after a lackluster spring in which he had only one top-10 finish in his first seven starts and didn't win until the first week of May.

"What Bruce Fleisher and Allen Doyle have done this year is extraordinary, but Hale still has the edge," said Bob Dickson of the tour's most dominant players in 1999. "We always knew he'd be back. They are not the player Hale is."

That point was proven at the TPC of Michigan in Dearborn when, after falling one behind to Graham Marsh and Larry Nelson in the first round, and lagging Marsh by two shots at the midway point, Irwin played almost flawless golf, combining his normally crisp iron play with a total of 51 putts, a superior putting display that had been missing from his early-season performances. His 64 in the third round moved Irwin to 202, four ahead of Marsh and five clear of Nelson and Jose Maria Canizares. Of the tandem of Fleisher and Doyle, only Fleisher remained in striking distance at 208. Doyle stood at 212 after three days, good enough to remain in the top 20.

Jack Nicklaus withdrew on Saturday for only the third time in his professional career. Citing pain from recent hip replacement surgery, Nicklaus called it quits after rounds of 71 and 74 and a first-nine 38 on Saturday. "It got to the point where I could not get onto my left side hitting golf balls the last three or four holes," Nicklaus said. "I was just hoping to get through today and keep on going, but I didn't make it. I played 20 out of 22 days and I hit balls before and after every round. I practiced as though I were 25 years old, and I just started to pay for it."

Irwin slammed the door with seven birdies and no bogeys in his final-round 65. Marsh continued his good play, finishing alone in second after a 68 moved him to 274, one ahead of John Jacobs. Nelson closed the weekend with a pair of 69s for fourth place, while Hubert Green came within one shot of matching Irwin's final round. Green jumped to a tie for fifth with Canizares at 277.

State Farm Senior Classic—$1,300,000
Winner: Christy O'Connor, Jr.

A wire-to-wire victory after relying on a sponsor's exemption to get into the State Farm Senior Classic in Columbia, Maryland, was just what Christy O'Connor, Jr., needed. But after losing his son in an automobile accident only nine months before, the victory seemed less important to the 51-year-old Irishman. After tapping in for par to defeat Bruce Fleisher by one shot, O'Connor broke down in tears. As he accepted the crystal trophy and the $195,000 winner's check, he looked to the sky and said, "This was for you, Daren," his 17-year-old son.

"I won today for my son," he said. "I know he helped me. It's a very sad day and a very happy day all at once. I miss him terribly. I talk to him all the time. I know it sounds stupid, but on the 13th hole I just felt dreadful walking from the tee to my ball. Thinking of my son really got me there."

O'Connor opened a two-shot lead over Fleisher, Bob Duval, Isao Aoki, Hubert Green and Allen Doyle the first day when he fired 65. Despite the star quality of the leaderboard, O'Connor continued to play well on Saturday, carding 66 for a three-shot lead over Fleisher. Green was five back going into the final round, while Doyle, Jim Albus, Fred Gibson and Hugh Baiocchi were seven behind.

Throughout the 97-degree heat on Sunday, O'Connor held his composure and his game together, extending the lead to five shots through five holes with two early birdies. Fleisher came back with four birdies in a six-hole stretch to cut the lead to one. O'Connor birdied the 12th to regain a two-shot advantage, which is where things stood until the final hole.

O'Connor played the par-five final hole conservatively, laying up then hitting his third shot to the center of the green, where two putts for par should assure him a win. Fleisher never gave up. His second shot landed 20 feet from the hole in the fringe, and his eagle chip to tie O'Connor stopped inches from going in the cup. He shot 65 for a 199 total. O'Connor lagged his first putt to within a few inches, then tapped in for 67 and a 198 total, 18 under par, in the emotional win.

"It's the toughest game I've ever had," O'Connor said afterward. "I kept waiting for Bruce to make a blunder, but he never did."

U.S. Senior Open—$1,750,000
Winner: Dave Eichelberger

The most astonishing thing about the U.S. Senior Open, other than that an underdog fended off challenges from the likes of Hale Irwin and Gil Morgan in an impressive Sunday showdown, was the size and vigor of the gallery. An estimated 252,800 people found their way to the Des Moines Golf and Country Club in the Iowa heartland to watch the world's best senior golfers duel it out for this national championship. Sunday's crowd, estimated at over 85,000, was bigger than Iowa's third largest city. "They probably had more people here in seven days than we've drawn in the last month," Allen Doyle said.

Former Senior Open champion Dave Stockton said, "I've never seen this many people smile at one time in my life. You can hit the worst shots in the world and they're clapping." Dana Quigley, who applauded the gallery as he walked up the final fairway, said, "All four days from the first tee on they have been clapping for everything. How can you get this many people out to watch us old guys?"

The best way is to play the kind of golf that 55-year-old Texan Dave Eichelberger did for four days. Eichelberger capped off the most impressive victory of his 33-year professional career with seven birdies in a final-round 68 for a 281 total, seven under par, and a three-shot win over Ed Dougherty. For Eichelberger, who only had three senior victories and whose biggest PGA Tour win came in 1980 at Bay Hill, to win a U.S. Senior Open was more than he could have imagined.

"After I finished I was kind of in a state of shock," Eichelberger said. "I started to shake a little bit, but I recovered after a while. The gist of my career for 35 years has been three weeks of great play followed by two years of mediocrity. Fortunately, the good weeks have been good enough to keep me in there."

It wasn't until early in 1999 that Eichelberger found the key that had eluded him for decades. A student of the late Ben Hogan, Eichelberger believed that Hogan had found the secret to great golf. "I don't know what Hogan's secret was, but I think I found part of it," he said. "It's in the grip. There's a way to put your hands on the golf club where all you can do is fade the ball. For the longest time I couldn't fade the ball if you gave me a million dollars."

That fade, along with crisp iron play and precise putting, allowed Eichelberger to come from three shots behind after the first and second rounds to pass third-round leader Dougherty. The key, however, was accuracy. "For most of my career I was long and wild off the tee," he said. "The last couple of years I've been short and wild. This week I was hitting it close enough to where I had no long lag putt trying to make par."

Dougherty, who opened the tournament with 68 to take a two-shot lead, came to Des Moines with even less impressive credentials than Eichelberger. With one victory on the PGA Tour, Dougherty's best finish as a senior was a tie for third in the 1998 Bell Atlantic Classic. Still, for three and a half rounds it looked as though Dougherty would take home the most coveted title in senior golf. Even a third-round 75 couldn't stop him. Despite the three-over-par performance on Saturday, Dougherty held a one-shot lead over Eichelberger, Irwin and Bruce Summerhays.

On Sunday, Dougherty did what he should have done with a one-shot lead in the U.S. Open. He made pars. That was more than Irwin could accomplish. After three missed birdie opportunities inside of 10 feet on the first nine, the defending champion faded from contention with 73. Irwin finished tied for third at 286 with Joe Inman and Gil Morgan. Dougherty closed out his impressive run with 72 for a 284 total — a great score in any Open, but not good enough this time.

Ameritech Senior Open—$1,300,000
Winner: Hale Irwin

With his dominance over the last four years on the Senior PGA Tour, Hale Irwin had already shown plenty of creativity. In a season when Bruce Fleisher and Allen Doyle were reshaping the look of the tour, Irwin's victory at the Ameritech Senior Open in suburban Chicago, after an opening-round 73 put him six shots off the lead, brought a sense of normalcy back to an otherwise profoundly different season.

"On Friday, all facets of my game were off," Irwin said. "But instead of beating myself up on the driving range, I beat myself up in the fitness trailer. I had a good workout, then I called my son, Steve, who had caddied for me and knows my game. He gave me a putting tip I hadn't thought about." Whatever Steve told his dad, it obviously worked. Irwin had only 52 putts in 36 holes over the weekend at Kemper Lakes. His rounds of 66 and 67 for a 206 total, 10 under par, were good enough to catch and then pass Fleisher (68-72-67), Raymond Floyd (70-67-70) and Gary McCord (73-69-65), who all tied for second at 207.

Floyd shared the second-round lead at 137 with Fred Gibson, who also shot 70 and 67. But Irwin's presence was being felt. His 139 placed him within sight of the leaders, a spot Irwin hadn't frequented many times in 1999. "I had three or four months of indifferent play," Irwin said. "I never got into that mode I was in all of last year. I had sort of this loose plan, but it wasn't really a goal and that's what I think was part of the problem."

Irwin's plan on Sunday was simple: Catch and pass the leaders without letting anyone catch and pass him. He pulled off the first part with 67, and he had some help with the second part from his competitors. Fleisher took the lead with a birdie at the 15th, but one hole later his ball hit a rock and ricocheted into the water. A penalty stroke and a missed putt later, Fleisher walked away with double bogey.

Floyd put together a two-under-par round through 17 holes only to see his lead disappear. Still, the 56-year-old had a chance. His 20-foot birdie putt at the 18th would have tied Irwin and forced a playoff, but the putt stopped a foot short of the hole, prompting Floyd to lament, "I had some opportunities, but I just didn't get the job done."

Coldwell Banker Burnet Classic—$1,500,000
Winner: Hale Irwin

Just when it looked as if Hale Irwin would fade away to the second tier of the Senior PGA Tour, after having dominated for the previous two years, yielding the top spot to rookie Bruce Fleisher, the 54-year-old Irwin put all doubters in their place by winning his fifth event in eight starts with a 15-under-par 201 performance in Coon Rapids, Minnesota.

While several of Irwin's previous wins had been come-from-behind affairs, the victory at the Bunker Hills Golf Club was wire-to-wire. Even when senior rookie Jim Dent stood over a 15-foot birdie putt at the 18th that would have tied him for the lead, the odds were that Irwin would walk away with the Coldwell Banker Burnet Classic trophy.

They were right. After a course-record first round of 64 which opened a one-shot lead over David Graham and Jim Colbert, Irwin methodically picked apart the 7,030-yard, par-72 layout, shooting 68 on Saturday to stay one ahead of Graham. He then added four birdies in the first 14 holes on Sunday to put some distance between him and rest of the field. He made uncharacteristic bogeys at the 15th and 17th, but when Dent missed his birdie effort at the 18th, Irwin clinched the win with an aggressive birdie of his own at the last for a final-round 69, a 201 total and a two-shot margin of victory.

"I think Hale pretty much had things in control all day," said Dale Douglass, who closed with an impressive final-round 65 to tie Dent for second at 203. "Every time he needed a birdie he made one."

Even when he didn't need to make birdie, Irwin came though. After being told that Dent had parred the final hole, Irwin chose to play aggressively at the 18th. Rather than protect his one-shot lead, Irwin hit two drivers on the 535-yard par-five leaving him an easy up-and-down for birdie and a two-shot win. "It was into the wind, and I knew a driver would keep it low," Irwin said. "I didn't change my approach. Trying to play it safe can be the worst thing you can do."

Novell Utah Showdown—$1,350,000
Winner: Dave Eichelberger

In 32 years of professional golf, Dave Eichelberger had never won two events in one year. So, even though he was 15 under par after two days and held a three-shot lead going into the final round of the Novell Utah Showdown, only three weeks after winning the U.S. Senior Open, Eichelberger wasn't at all surprised to be considered the underdog.

Hale Irwin and Gil Morgan were tied with John Mahaffey only three shots back, and Dana Quigley stood four back after shooting a course-record 62. Birdies and eagles were flying all over Park City, so even after finishing Saturday with two eagles and a birdie in his last four holes, Eichelberger didn't mind being a back-burner. In fact, he kind of liked it.

"There's too much other stuff that comes with that herald business," Eichelberger said. "I just want to get in and out and have nobody know I'm here until I win the tournament. Guys like Hale are out here taking the heat of the spotlight. That means I don't have to deal with it."

Eichelberger not only won by beating Quigley with a par on the first playoff hole, he did so by launching a full-scale assault on par. A testy double bogey at the 15th on Sunday was Eichelberger's only over-par hole the entire tournament. He finished with 68, and his 19-under-par 197 total included a second-round 63 when he hit all 14 fairways.

"That was a first for me," Eichelberger said. He came into the week ranked 73rd in driving accuracy and 59th in greens hit in regulation. His only saving grace had been his putter. Things changed three weeks ago when, according to the Eichelberger, he found the secret.

"All of a sudden I had my fade," Eichelberger said. "I had it in 1971. Then I lost it for 28 years. I played really awful before the start of the Open. I think I shot 80 in a practice round. Then I started hitting that pretty little fade again. I found the fairways and played good."

Lightpath Long Island Classic—$1,200,000
Winner: Bruce Fleisher

Bruce Fleisher hadn't planned on playing in the Lightpath Long Island Classic, which fell in the middle of a multi-week vacation the Senior PGA Tour's leading money winner was taking after a four-victory start to his first season. After sitting at home and fielding what he termed "way too many phone calls," Fleisher returned to competition earlier than expected and left with another victory. He won by two strokes over Allen Doyle, although Fleisher admitted to sleepwalking through much of the event at Meadow Brook Club in Jericho, New York.

It started after Fleisher shot a course-record-tying 64 to take a one-stroke, first-round lead over Mark Hayes. Fleisher misread his Saturday starting time. He thought he had a 12:40 start, when it actually was 11:40. Luckily for Fleisher, he arrived at the course eight minutes before his starting time. His caddie rushed him from the parking lot to the first tee without the benefit of a single practice shot or putt. "The worst part about it was putting," Fleisher said. "That was the only thing that bothered me."

Fleisher had 69 to widen his lead over Hayes to three shots. He widened the gap even further during the early going on Sunday, reaching 13 under par by the time he walked off the 12th tee, and seemingly cruising home with a five-stroke lead. A double bogey at the 13th followed by an approach that found the greenside bunker at the 14th, resulting in a bogey, brought Fleisher back to the field.

No one was able to take advantage. Hayes was in the process of shooting 75 to drop into a tie for 13th place, while Tom Shaw, who began the day five strokes back, could manage no better than 71 to finish tied for third place with Jose Maria Canizares, Raymond Floyd, Joe Inman and Jim Thorpe.

Doyle shot the low round of the day. His 67 moved him into second place at 208, but he almost walked away with the victory, even though Fleisher had things well in hand on the 18th. With a four-shot lead, Fleisher moved his ball marker out of Hayes' line on the green. He forgot to replace the marker. Before signing an incorrect scorecard, which would have resulted in disqualification, a spectator told Fleisher about the error, a two-shot penalty was assessed, and Fleisher finished with 73 for a 206 total, 10 under par.

Foremost Insurance Championship—$1,000,000
Winner: Christy O'Connor, Jr.

With Hale Irwin at the PGA Championship and leading money winner Bruce Fleisher having an uncharacteristically poor final round, the door was left open for Senior PGA Tour newcomer Christy O'Connor, Jr., to win his third event in six weeks at the Foremost Insurance Championship in Grand Rapids, Michigan. O'Connor had been forced to rely on sponsor's invitations until his victory at the State Farm Senior Classic earned him an exemption. Three weeks later he captured the Senior British Open in his native Ireland before returning to America, where another victory awaited him in Michigan.

O'Connor's first-round 69 left him two behind Tom Wargo and Dick Lotz, but a second-round 68 gave O'Connor a share of the lead with John Bland who, like O'Connor, had been forced to deal with a mountain of recent personal tragedy. O'Connor lost his 17-year-old son in an automobile accident in Dublin in September of 1998, and Bland came to Michigan having recently lost his brother (who was also his caddie) to kidney failure, the same ailment that had taken Bland's wife the year before. It would have been fitting if the two had finished one-two, but Bland's final-round 76 dropped him into a tie for eighth place.

O'Connor never flinched, even with Fleisher only one shot off the lead going into the final round. He played smart golf, finding the right sides of the greens and shooting his second consecutive 68 for an 11-under-par 205 total and a four-shot victory over Jim Thorpe, George Archer and John Jacobs. O'Connor's strongest asset during the week was his putter. He took only 77 putts for the week. "I gave myself birdie chances," he said. "There were a few sucker pins out there, but I kept away. That really worked for me. I concentrated on hitting the ball to the proper side of the pin so that I would be putting uphill."

BankBoston Classic—$1,200,000
Winner: Tom McGinnis

The Senior PGA Tour has been affectionately referred to as golf's ultimate "mulligan," but for someone like 1999 senior rookie Tom McGinnis the expression couldn't have been truer. "I qualified three times for the PGA Tour and lost my card three times," McGinnis said after his stunning playoff victory over Hale Irwin at the BankBoston Classic. "I always sponsored myself and I went broke every time."

The largest check McGinnis made on the PGA Tour was $4,100 for a fifth-place finish. In the first seven months after finishing eighth at the 1998 Senior Tour qualifying tournament, McGinnis had earned more than his total winnings on the PGA Tour. Winning the BankBoston Classic brought McGinnis $180,000, which pushed his first-year senior earnings to $394,615. "The money is nice," McGinnis admitted, "but the exemption to play out here is great."

McGinnis opened with a three-under-par 69 to be two behind leader Jay Sigel. After a second round of 69, McGinnis found himself one off the pace with 18 holes left to play. Hale Irwin, George Archer and Sigel were all poised at 137, one shot better than McGinnis, so few gave the 51-year-old Tennessean good odds of winning. The three leaders had 50 senior wins between them. McGinnis hadn't won anything since the 1986 New York State Open.

Those who knew McGinnis best knew there was more to him than his record indicated. "He has got a lot of intestinal fortitude," said McGinnis' caddie, Wayne Gilmore. "He is a scrambling player who has had to play for his life."

That's exactly how McGinnis played on Sunday. His 67, capped off by a 15-foot birdie at the 18th, put him in a tie with Irwin at 11-under-par 205 at the end of regulation play. Irwin shot 68 after earlier rounds of 69 and 68. He tied a senior record with his 11th consecutive round in the 60s, and missed a 20-footer for birdie that would have won the event outright. On second playoff hole, Irwin hit his approach shot to within 10 feet, but missed that putt as well.

McGinnis' six-iron approach on the second playoff hole landed inside Irwin's shot, and after Irwin missed, McGinnis knew the tournament was his. "I was grinning," he said. "I knew I was not going to miss mine. There was no way I was going to miss."

AT&T Canada Senior Open—$1,350,000
Winner: Jim Ahern

Hale Irwin couldn't recall if he had ever before lost playoffs in two consecutive weeks, but he won't likely forget the two he suffered in the latter half of August. The first at the hands of Tom McGinnis at the BankBoston Classic was a surprise, but the second to a Monday qualifier from Phoenix named Jim Ahern at the AT&T Canada Senior Open was a shocker. "It's tough to take two playoff losses in two weeks," Irwin said after bogeying the second playoff hole for his second loss in as many weeks. "I'm not sure if I'm ebbing and flowing at the moment. Right now, it seems that if you want to enhance your career on the Senior PGA Tour, you have to play me in a playoff."

Ahern drew strength from recent history. "I knew Tom McGinnis had beaten Hale the week before," he said, "so I knew it could happen again."

After both had routine pars on the first playoff hole, Irwin missed the green on the second, then failed to convert his par. That gave Ahern an uphill, five-foot par putt for the victory. "This has never happened to me at this level," Ahern said after making the par and collecting the $202,500 first-place check. In four years on the PGA Tour, Ahern played 60 events and never finished better than tied for ninth.

"There just aren't words now that can explain this," Ahern said. "When I played the PGA Tour years ago, I wasn't very good. I didn't know where the ball was going. The only place for me was off the tour. I didn't belong there. Now, to best Hale Irwin, to beat the best, is pretty special. You dream about days like this."

For Irwin the dream was a recurring nightmare. After shooting 67 and 65 for a 132 total in the first two rounds and taking a one-shot lead over Larry Nelson into the weekend, Irwin looked to add another trophy to his expanding collection. Even after 71 on Saturday, Irwin retained a one-shot advantage over Ahern. But Irwin's putting woes continued on Sunday, and when Ahern birdied the last two holes — the last one coming with a dramatic 30-footer — the two were tied and the playoff ensued. Irwin finished with 69 for a 272 total, 16 under par, while Ahern had scores of 67, 68, 69 and 68.

"He put on a display of putting the like of which I haven't seen in a long time," Irwin said of Ahern. "I didn't putt too well the last two days, only five birdies the last two rounds. That's not enough."

Other than the five-footer for par in the playoff, the biggest putt of the week was Ahern's birdie at the 72nd hole to send the tournament to extra holes. As he was standing over the downhill slider, he said he was thinking of an inspirational passage he had recently read. "Tom Jenkins told me to read this book by Rick Patino," Ahern said. "One of the quotes is, 'Let the magic happen.' When I got over that putt, I said, 'There's still some magic here.' Can you believe it went in?"

TD Waterhouse Championship—$1,200,000
Winner: Allen Doyle

Just when it appeared the Senior PGA Tour season would be defined by the play of Hale Irwin and Bruce Fleisher, Allen Doyle joined the battle by adding a fourth victory to his impressive rookie resume at the TD Waterhouse Classic in Kansas City, Missouri. His 18-under-par 198 total was not only good enough to edge Ed Dougherty by two shots, it also gave Doyle over $1.5 million in earnings for the year with three productive months left on the schedule.

Doyle made one bogey the entire tournament while shooting rounds of 63, 70 and 65 for a 198 total, 18 under par. The 63 gave him a one-shot lead over Gil Morgan and a three-shot margin over Dougherty, but the 70 dropped Doyle back into a tie with Morgan at 133 while Dougherty surged ahead with his second consecutive round of 66 to reach 132.

The final round was nip-and-tuck all day with Morgan, Dougherty and Doyle playing together. Dougherty played the first nine holes in four under par, but his hot hand soon cooled, and he finished with nine straight pars for 68. Doyle, who fell two behind in the early going, charged into a tie with Dougherty through 15 holes. Another birdie on the 16th gave Doyle a one-shot lead. On the 395-yard 17th, Doyle's drive left him the longest approach to the small green.

"You had to believe one of the three of us was going to knock it close," Doyle said. "Under the circumstances I don't mind being the first one to hit. It's nothing new. People have been outdriving me my whole career."

Doyle hit his shot to within two feet, the closest approach of the three. When he tapped in for his second birdie in a row, the tournament was his. He finished with a par for a bogey-free 65, a 198 total and a two-shot margin over Dougherty. "Allen played great," Dougherty said. "I tried my heart out, but I wasn't good enough. I'm proud of the way I hung in there."

Had Dougherty been able to match his two earlier rounds of 66, he would have tied Doyle, but he could only manage 68 for his second runner-up finish of the season, the first coming to Dave Eichelberger in the U.S. Senior Open. Morgan also shot a final-round 68 to finish alone in third at 201.

Comfort Classic—$1,200,000
Winner: Gil Morgan

For a while during the first round in Indianapolis at the Comfort Classic it looked as though the newest generation of Senior PGA Tour graduates had come to make a statement. In his first round as a senior, Tom Watson shot 66 to share the lead with Jim Dent, Gary McCord, Bob Eastwood and Bobby Stroble. By Sunday, it was a more familiar face among the seniors, Gil Morgan, who won 12 times in two years from early 1997 through 1999.

Morgan picked up his first victory of the year by shooting a closing 69 for a 201 total and a two-stroke win over Ed Dougherty.

"I finally putted at a higher level," Morgan said. "In the other tournaments, I've made a few mistakes."

There weren't many mistakes for Morgan at the 6,798-yard Brickyard Crossing course. After an opening 67 left him one shot behind, Morgan came back with 65. Still, he wasn't in the lead going into the final round. That went to Morgan's best friend on tour, Mike McCullough, who followed his opening 69 with a tournament-record, 10-under-par 62.

McCullough would be paired with Morgan for a final-round showdown. That didn't stop them from going to dinner Saturday night, although the conversation never turned to Sunday's pairing. Morgan knew he was looking for his first win of the season, but he also knew McCullough was looking for his first win in 531 starts on the PGA and Senior PGA Tours.

It was only a contest for about an hour. McCullough lost his putting stroke and ballooned to 74 while Morgan found the confidence with his putter he had been lacking throughout most of the year. His three-birdie, no bogey 69 was good enough. The only drama was over who would finish second, and for the third time in 1999 that honor fell to Dougherty, who also shot 69 for a 203 total, one better than Tom Jenkins and two clear of McCullough and Walter Hall.

As for Watson and his much-anticipated debut, the Senior PGA Tour's newest rookie followed his opening 66 with 69, but closed with 75 which included a three-putt triple bogey on the final hole.

Bank One Championship—$1,300,000
Winner: Tom Watson

The final-round leaderboard at the inaugural Bank One Championship in Dallas was just what the advocates of the Senior PGA Tour wanted to see. Six players named Hale Irwin, Gil Morgan, David Graham, Jim Colbert, Alberto Giannone and Tom Watson (playing in only his second event as a senior) were knotted at the top with totals of 134. The group represented 13 major championship titles and 66 Senior PGA Tour victories.

The advantage had to go to Irwin, who blistered the 6,831-yard Bent Tree Country Club with 63 on Saturday after an opening round of 71 and seemed ready to pull away from the field. Morgan also had a hot hand, following his first-round 70 with 64. He had gone head-to-head with Irwin many times before, so Morgan knew what he needed to do. Everyone was happy to see Watson in the fray, but the memories of his collapse in his senior debut two weeks before were still fresh.

That embarrassment soon vanished, however. Watson wasted no time in shooting a course-record 62 in the final round to rocket past all challengers and win his first senior event by five strokes over Bruce Summerhays. His 20-under-par 196 total established a tournament record that will be hard to break, and the 62 was Watson's lowest round ever in a PGA Tour or Senior Tour event. "I putted great this week and I'm driving the ball well," he said. "A lot of it was unexpected. I felt pressure to win last week, and I was anxious. I wasn't prepared and wasn't tournament ready. I hadn't played that much and had the wedding (Watson married wife Hillary the week before), but when I played in the practice round on Thursday I felt I could shoot a low score."

Watson didn't miss a fairway or a green in the final round and, unlike the week before, he was confident with his putter. "It must the Mexican food," Watson joked. He spent Saturday evening at the home of his mentor, Byron Nelson, and the two shared a Mexican casserole.

Summerhays closed with 66 for 201 to jump past the other five players who started the final round tied with Watson, while Morgan closed with 68 for 202 and sole possession of third place. Irwin could only match his first-round 71 and finished tied for eighth place at 205, but he wasn't ready to concede his senior crown to the newcomer. "Tom Watson is a great player," he said, "but he has done nothing to change my perspective. My congratulations to him, but he's not the only player on the senior tour. Let's see what Tom does. Certainly, if today's an indication of how he's going to play, we've all got to kick it up five notches. Sixty-two is a great round, but I'm not going to jump on the wagon where we're all playing for second place."

Kroger Senior Classic—$1,400,000
Winner: Gil Morgan

For the first eight months of 1999 the biggest surprises on the Senior PGA Tour were the emergence of rookies Bruce Fleisher and Allen Doyle and the noticeable absence of Gil Morgan. All that changed in September as Morgan went on a three-week tear, finishing first-third-first in 20 days, the second victory coming at the Kroger Senior Classic in Mason, Ohio. If there was any question about Morgan's ability to compete, it was erased at the Kings Island Golf Club when he shot a seven-under-par 63 in the final round to leap past Ed Dougherty and win by two shots.

"It was kind of a funny year early on," Morgan said. "The last few weeks I've turned it around. I've been working a lot harder on my game, and all of a sudden my putting is back."

Putting was the key to Morgan's victory. After opening with 67 to trail Jim Colbert and Jimmy Powell by one, Morgan shot 68 in which he made four birdies. Still, he found himself trailing Dougherty by two going to the final day. Dougherty, who began his streak of good play at the U.S. Senior Open, had posted rounds of 68 and 65. Jim Dent, still looking for his first win as a senior, was tied for second at 134 with Powell and Dana Quigley. Morgan and Lee Trevino were tied at 135, while Hale Irwin was at 136, only three back.

On Sunday it looked as though Dougherty, who had three second-place finishes in 1999 but no victories, was finally going to break through. Playing the first nine in two under par, his lead was two and he appeared to be in command of his game. Then Morgan put on a charge. Needing only 25 putts for the round, Morgan strung together five birdies between the sixth and 13th holes, a streak that put him in the lead. Meanwhile Dougherty couldn't find the birdies on the second nine. He made eight straight pars, finally picking up one more birdie at the 18th, but by then it was too late. Morgan had lapped the field with his 63.

"Whatever he needed to call on today when he called, it was there," Doyle said. "He did everything right."

Vantage Championship—$1,500,000
Winner: Fred Gibson

The highlight of Maryland club professional Fred Gibson's career had been a win in the 1996 Tobago Open where his winner's check promptly bounced. The 52-year-old never played the PGA Tour, although he did participate as a Monday qualifier in 17 events over the years, earning $704 for his efforts. Once he turned 50, however, things changed, and in the Vantage Championship on a balmy October Sunday at Tanglewood Park in Clemmons, North Carolina, Gibson went from being an obscure senior rookie to being the fourth 1998 qualifying tournament graduate to win in 1999.

It wasn't easy. An opening 69 left Gibson six shots off the pace set by Jim Dent, who was also looking for his first win as a senior. But Dent's hot hand soon cooled as he could manage no better than even-par rounds of 70 on Saturday and Sunday to finish tied for ninth.

Meanwhile Gibson was finding all the bounces he had missed on Friday. He holed two shots from the fairway on Saturday — a wedge from 100 yards for a birdie at the fourth and a five iron from 175 yards for an eagle at the 12th — en route to 62, but he still didn't have the lead. Tom Jenkins shot a second straight 65 for a 130 total and a one-shot margin over Gibson and Bob Duval.

"In the first round I knew I played better than my score," Gibson said. "Saturday things started happening out there and the runoff from that was Sunday. In Zen, they say the art of archery is to become the arrow. On Sunday, I became the ball."

Jenkins couldn't get things going on Sunday, finishing with 71 for a 201 total and a tie for sixth place. It looked as though a charging Bruce Fleisher, who shot a first-nine 30, would march to his sixth victory of the year. But Gibson, one shot back with nine holes to play, became the ball on the back nine with birdies on four of the last five holes to catch and pass Fleisher who ran into trouble with bogeys at the 10th and 11th holes.

"Coming out of the box, I really felt like it was going to be my day, but Freddie Gibson said, 'Nope,'" Fleisher deadpanned. "He deserved to win."

A final-round 64 for a 195 total gave Gibson a three-shot margin over Fleisher, who shot 65, and a four-shot cushion over Jay Sigel. Duval and David Graham finished tied for fourth at 200, while Jenkins tied Vicente Fernandez for sixth at 201. "I learned three things this week," Gibson said of his first win. "Stay out of your own way, stay out of your own way, and stay out of your own way."

The Transamerica—$1,100,000
Winner: Bruce Fleisher

Just when it looked as if the 1999 Senior PGA Tour would end up looking like the 1997 and 1998 seasons with Hale Irwin topping the money list and

Gil Morgan close behind, rookie Bruce Fleisher distinguished himself again with a wire-to-wire victory in The Transamerica in Napa, California. It was Fleisher's sixth victory of the year, and the $165,000 first-place check moved him back to the top spot on the money list.

Opening the week with two consecutive rounds of 66, Fleisher never played a hole when he wasn't leading or tied for the lead. By the close of business on Friday, he was tied with Hubert Green, Howard Twitty and Walter Hall, but after Saturday, Fleisher's lead was two strokes over Allen Doyle. The only players with a reasonable chance to catch Fleisher were Doyle at 134 and Hall at 135.

The three played together on Sunday and, while Doyle and Hall tried to make runs at various times throughout the day, Fleisher was in command from the beginning. He birdied four of the first six holes to extend his lead to four. Hall eagled the par-five ninth to draw within two shots, and Doyle made a birdie at the 13th to also pull within two of Fleisher, but Fleisher birdied the 14th to regain a three-shot lead.

Doyle made another charge with a 30-foot birdie putt on the 15th and a birdie chip-in on the 16th. He had momentum in his favor as he addressed his birdie putt on the 17th. The stroke looked good, but the ball stopped just short. Doyle couldn't believe it. He waited the obligatory 10 seconds, hoping the ball would fall in, before tapping in for his par.

Doyle had one more chance on the par-five 18th, but after finding the fairway with his drive, he pushed his second shot behind a scoreboard. After a drop he hit the only shot he had, onto the green, but 20 feet away. That putt also came up short, and Fleisher, who continued to make pars, had 67 for a 199 total and one-shot victory over Doyle. Hall finished third at 202, while Green closed with 66 to capture fourth at 203.

Raley's Gold Rush Classic—$1,100,000
Winner: David Graham

After a year-long dry spell, David Graham found his winning swing again in the Raley's Gold Rush Classic. "I play my best golf on courses where I don't feel inhibited," Graham said after shooting a final-round 65 for a 17-under-par 199 total and a four-stroke victory over Larry Mowry at the relatively open Serrano Country Club in El Dorado Hills, California. With five par-fives and generous landing areas, the course was perfectly suited for Graham's driver-oriented game. "That's when I swing my best," he said.

He took advantage of those good feelings with an opening 63 and a three-shot lead over Allen Doyle and J.C. Snead. A second-round 71 in which Graham's putter cooled off dropped him two shots behind Doyle. Looking for his fifth win in his rookie season, Doyle seemed unflappable, shooting rounds of 66 and 66. In Sunday's round Graham's putter got hot as Doyle's cooled down. "David putted very, very well," Doyle said. "If I could have made a couple of the putts on the front nine, those putts David had would have been a little tougher. I gave him too much breathing room."

Graham took advantage, birdieing the par-fives as he had done throughout most of the week, and putting himself out of reach with a birdie on the par-three 15th. Pars coming in ensured that Graham would pick up his fifth career senior win with ease. "It was nice to play the last three or four holes with less stress than that 10-hole playoff," Graham said, referring to his Royal Caribbean Classic win in 1998. "I'm very pleased. This was a good week for me."

The surprise of the week came from Mowry, the second-place finisher. After missing most of 1998 because of sinus and hernia surgery, Mowry announced that 1999 would be his last season as a touring professional. He was playing the year on a special medical exemption, and his 73.66 stroke average for the year confirmed that his decision was probably a good one. The week proved profitable for the 62-year-old Californian. After opening with 67, Mowry finished with rounds of 69 and 67.

EMC² Kaanapali Classic—$1,000,000
Winner: Bruce Fleisher

When Bruce Fleisher roared onto the Senior PGA Tour with two victories in his first two starts, everyone thought it was a nice beginning for a nice man who never achieved the success he had wanted on the regular PGA Tour. Then he won again at the Home Depot Invitational in April and at the BellSouth Senior Classic in June. Suddenly Fleisher, whose only PGA Tour win came at the 1991 New England Classic, was a contender for not just Senior PGA Tour Rookie of the Year, but for Player of the Year, a position occupied by Hale Irwin for the previous two years.

Irwin made a charge in the middle of the year, but Fleisher came back, picking up victories at the Lightpath Long Island Classic and The Transamerica. Irwin had five titles and Allen Doyle had four, so Player of the Year honors and the money title came down to the last three events of the season. The first of those three, the EMC² Kaanapali Classic, ended all debate.

"This year has been one I'll remember for many years to come," Fleisher said after shooting 14-under-par 199 at the Kaanapali Country Club in Hawaii for a wire-to-wire victory and his seventh title of the year. "The venues here suit me and certainly anybody who is 50 or 51 has an advantage."

With an opening 65, Fleisher held a one-shot lead over Irwin and Jim Ahern. Fleisher retained his lead after the second round with 67, but Tom Jenkins took over second place. The second day's low round belonged to Doyle, who came back after a lackluster 70 to shoot 64 and move to within two strokes of the lead. Irwin shot 71 to drop five behind.

Irwin made a run on Sunday, shooting his second 66 of the week for a 203 total and a tie for third place with Ahern, Jenkins and Steven Veriato. That would be four shots too many. By the time the leaders made the turn it was a two-man race, with Fleisher and Doyle battling to stay atop the leaderboard. Tied at 13 under par through 15 holes, Fleisher made the critical putt of the tournament, a 12-foot birdie to take the lead. Doyle had two more chances to tie, but missed an eight-footer at the 17th and a 20-footer at the 18th. "The putt at 17 is one I would like to have over," said Doyle, who shot 66 for a 200 total and lost by one. "I tried to be aggressive, tried to play it straight and hit it good and firm, but pulled it a little."

Fleisher, who finished with 69 and a 199 total, agreed that Doyle's miss at the 17th was the difference. "Allen probably lost the tournament on 17," he said. "He makes that and 18 is real interesting. Still, I have so much respect for this man. I think he's the toughest one out there. Hale's in a different league, but Allen Doyle, shot-for-shot, is as tough as they get."

Pacific Bell Senior Classic—$1,200,000
Winner: Joe Inman

They didn't want to tee off on Friday. Former Ryder Cup captain Dave Stockton openly wept and said, "They can disqualify me if they want, but I'm not teeing off until this is over." He was referring to the televised memorial service for Payne Stewart. The PGA Tour events in Houston and Madison, Mississippi, were postponed, but the Senior PGA Tour event went ahead because, said commissioner Tim Finchem, "the logistics of everyone traveling back from California made it unfeasible," for the seniors to attend the service in Orlando, Florida. The seniors observed the services in the locker room at the Wilshire Country Club in Los Angeles.

Stockton opened the Pacific Bell Senior Classic with rounds of 67 and 64 for a 131 total and held a two-shot lead. John Mahaffey was second at 133, while defending champion Joe Inman was tied with Gary Player and Bob Murphy at 134.

What could have been an easy time for Stockton turned into a nightmare. He three-putted the sixth hole from eight feet for bogey, then three-putted the ninth hole from seven feet for double bogey, dropping out of the lead. Inman and Bruce Summerhays stepped up to the challenge. Summerhays shot a final-round 66, his second of the week, for a 201 total. That was enough to tie Stockton, who recovered enough from his putting debacle to shoot 70, but wasn't enough to catch Inman.

By the time Inman made a 12-foot eagle putt on the par-five 13th, it was his tournament to win or lose. He almost found a way to lose it on the 17th when he pulled his second shot in the water. "Right in my backswing some kid yelled and my brain exploded," Inman said. "I pulled it and starting going, 'Oh my God.' You're leading by three shots and the last hole is no piece of cake. My world was crashing around me, but I got over the chip and before I hit it, I said, 'Joe, be a man. Look at what happened to Payne this week. This is just not that important. It's not life and death.'"

He chipped to within three feet and salvaged a bogey on the 17th. A par on the 18th and Inman had his second career senior victory, both wins coming at this event. His 65 for a 199 total was two better than Stockton and Summerhays and three ahead of Mahaffey and John Bland.

"I have so much more peace," Inman said afterward. "I realized that after watching everything on Friday, it was so emotional, I realized your legacy is your children, your friends, not the trophies you have in your trophy case. I don't want to be the richest guy in the cemetery. It doesn't matter who has the most toys. As you get older you can still gain wisdom."

Ingersoll-Rand Senior Tour Championship—$2,000,000
Winner: Gary McCord

The script was set, the speeches written. All the Senior PGA Tour needed was for Gary McCord to cooperate. It was great that he had played well on the weekend, wonderful that he had managed to reach five under par on his round Sunday at the Dunes Club in Myrtle Beach, South Carolina. It was also great that he had tied for the lead, but McCord hadn't won since April, and he certainly wasn't supposed to win the season-ending Ingersoll-Rand Senior Tour Championship. That role was scripted for Player of the Year favorite Bruce Fleisher, who began the final round tied for the lead and seemed poised to capture his eighth victory of the year on the same day Tiger Woods won his eighth PGA Tour event in Spain.

McCord, however, wasn't reading from the same script. With one clutch par after another, the television commentator kept the pressure on. When he capped a second-nine rally with a 20-footer for birdie and a tie for the lead, it seemed that the perfect ending would have to wait. Fleisher was in the process of missing a three-foot par putt on the 16th hole, then missing another par putt from six feet on the 17th to lose the lead. A par on the 18th left him with 71 and a 277 total, one behind McCord, who strolled to his second victory of the season. Fleisher and Larry Nelson tied for second place.

"It doesn't get any better than this," McCord said. Not only did he top the field on the weekend with his 64-67 finish for a 276 total, McCord beat the top 31 money winners in the process. The only noticeably absent name from the field was Tom Watson who hadn't played enough since turning 50 to make it. McCord, a part-timer himself, couldn't have been happier. "The books I've written are doing unbelievable. The movie we made was fun, but this is your own little canvas right here. There is nobody else."

There were certainly plenty of others earlier in the week while McCord was opening with rounds of 71 and 74. Fleisher and Bruce Summerhays took the early lead with 67s. They had their share of troubles in the second round. Fleisher shot 73 to drop five shots off the lead, while Summerhays shot 71 to fall to three back. George Archer held the lead at the halfway mark with rounds of 68 and 67 for a 135 total.

Saturday, Fleisher came to life again with 66 to move into a tie with Summerhays at 206. The biggest move of the day belonged to McCord, whose 64 beat his second-round score by 10 strokes. He credited his new-found game to television. He saw the highlights of Tiger Woods' performance in Spain and he began thinking, "Tiger's got this saying, 'Wide, tight and rip it,'" McCord said. "So I tried that with my golf swing. I don't know if I was doing it, but I tried it. It got me steady."

Chrysler Senior Match Play Challenge—$720,000
Winner: Larry Nelson

It started as a way to eliminate pressure on his neck after an injury, but once he tried putting cross-handed in Myrtle Beach, South Carolina, Larry Nelson knew he was on to something. "All of a sudden you don't have to be so precise with your irons," Nelson said after defeating Tom Jenkins, 3 and 2, in the Chrysler Senior Match Play Challenge in Puerto Rico. "Putting better makes the rest of your game better. When you're putting badly, you get to the point where it doesn't matter how well you hit it, you're not going to make birdie anyway."

Nelson putted well throughout the week and the results were obvious. He opened the 16-player event by defeating Raymond Floyd on the first extra hole. He then beat Dana Quigley to advance to the semi-finals against Bruce Fleisher. Throughout Sunday morning's match, Nelson continued to make putts from everywhere against Fleisher, carding five birdies and an eagle to win 1 up.

The other semi-final match between Jenkins and Bruce Summerhays was equally close with neither player holding more than a 1-up advantage throughout the day. When they came to the 18th all square, it looked as if the match would be extended to extra holes. An uncharacteristic bogey by Summerhays moved Jenkins into the finals.

Sunday afternoon, Nelson picked up where he left off in the morning, making birdie at the first hole, but then he bogeyed the 230-yard, par-three second to bring the match back to all square. Jenkins bogeyed the third, and Nelson eagled the fourth, his second eagle on that hole in the same day, to move ahead for good. Jenkins never got close again, and Nelson closed out the match on the 16th.

European Seniors Tour

Beko Classic—€250,000
Winner: Tommy Horton

The Beko Classic was launching a new season for the European Seniors Tour in Turkey in early May, so it stood to reason that Tommy Horton would leave with the title. The most successful player had opened the two previous seasons with victories. His third opening-week win in a row came by one stroke over American Alan Tapie, one of the nine 1999 qualifiers playing in his first European event after turning 50 in March. It was the 21st seniors victory for the 58-year-old Horton as he began his eighth season on the tour, admittedly with some trepidation. "At the start of any new season you wonder if you still have it in you to win, especially in my case as I'm not getting any younger," Horton said. "But it was there today ... a lovely feeling."

Experience paid off for Horton in the final going at Klassis Golf and Country Club. He jumped on a mistake by Tapie at the 71st hole to overcome a one-stroke deficit and take the title. Horton played the par-five with a solid birdie after the American, who had eagled the hole in each of the first two rounds, went with his driver for just the second time all day, lost the ball with a wild shot and took six. Horton parred the 18th for 69 and a five-under-par 211 total. Tapie, a Californian who played the U.S. PGA Tour for seven years in the late 1970s and early 1980s, also shot 69, finishing second at 212, two strokes ahead of another qualifier, Ray Carrasco, his friend and fellow Californian, who finished fast with 65 to finish one shot in front of Bernard Gallacher, the former Ryder Cup captain who was making his European Seniors Tour debut.

Horton, the money leader the previous three seasons, opened the tournament with 72, trailing Tapie and Scotland's Norman Wood by three strokes the first day. Horton then forged ahead Saturday with 70 for 142 as Tapie and Wood took 74s and Gallacher surged into contention with 65 after opening with 78, but only Tapie was able to challenge Horton Sunday.

AIB Irish Seniors Open—€250,000
Winner: John Morgan

John Morgan programmed his early 1999 schedule perfectly. The Englishman, who has campaigned full-time in America since 1997 after three brilliant seasons on the European Seniors Tour, decided one of his occasional returns home would be for the AIB Irish Seniors Open. Morgan had won in Ireland the last time he crossed the Atlantic in August of 1998 and he made it two for two with a narrow victory at Mount Juliet Golf Club at Kilkenny.

It was the eighth European Seniors Tour title for the 56-year-old Morgan, who credited his time on the American circuit for the solid state of his game. "I have improved enormously as an all-around player while playing in America the past three years. It has made me a much tougher competitor and it helped me today when things got tight out there," Morgan observed after edging Brian Barnes and Noel Ratcliffe by one stroke with his final-round 72 for a 209 total, seven under par.

Morgan had entered the final round tied for the lead with Craig Defoy at 137 after rounds of 70 and 67 as club professional Jim Rhodes, the first-round leader with 67, faded from contention. Two back-nine bogeys Sunday took Defoy out of the title picture, but Morgan, though playing steadily, was not home free at that point. Barnes, who also now plays primarily in America where the use of golf carts enables him to get along with his arthritic left foot, made an exciting run nonetheless with five birdies in a six-hole stretch on the second nine. His 70 left him a stroke short at 210 with Ratcliffe, who began the day one back and could only match Morgan's par round. Christy O'Connor, Jr., and Eddie Polland each reached six under par with strong first nines, but faltered coming home. Polland, who lost two playoffs to Brian Huggett in 1998, shot 71 and tied for fifth with J.R. Delich and Rhodes, while O'Connor, who also had already played with some success earlier in the season in America, absorbed three straight bogeys on the back nine and took 74.

MDIS & Partners Festival of Golf—€110,000
Winner: David Oakley

David Oakley has found success in golf the second time around. The American, who left the game for other pursuits after giving tournament golf an unproductive try in the 1970s on the U.S. and Asian circuits, turned professional again when he became 50 in 1995 and qualified for the European Seniors Tour in 1996. He made his mark quickly when he finished second to Brian Barnes in the Senior British Open at Royal Portrush, but had to wait until the 1999 season's third event — the MDIS & Partners Festival of Golf — to score his first victory. Oakley never trailed at Mill Ride Golf Club in Ascot, England, and finished six strokes in front of runners-up David Huish of Scotland and fellow American Jerry Bruner.

The 54-year-old Floridian shared the first-round lead with the ever-present Tommy Horton at four-under-par 68, one shot ahead of Terry Gale and two in front of Bruner. Oakley followed with 71 to move two strokes ahead of Horton (73), Bruner (71) and Eddie Polland (71-70), then polished it off with 69 for a 208 total and the six-shot margin. Birdies at the seventh and eighth holes created a comfort zone and, after a bogey at the ninth, he moved out of reach with birdies at the 12th, 13th and 15th. Huish's 70 lifted him into the second-place tie with Bruner, who closed with 73, as Horton, seeking his second win of the season, skied to 77 and a sixth-place tie at 218.

"I've been close before a few times, so it's good to finally break that duck," remarked Oakley, comfortable with the decision he made four years earlier that he belonged on the golf course instead of managing a furniture store in Orlando, Florida.

Philips PFA Golf Classic—€150,000
Winner: Bob Shearer

Bob Shearer took it as a sign of things to come when he holed a 40-yard pitch shot for an eagle in the second round of the Philips PFA Golf Classic, a unique Saturday-to-Monday event on the European Seniors Tour. "I knew it was going to be my week," said the Australian. "I had a strange feeling that I was going to win." Win he did, by one stroke with a closing 67 for a 204 total, 12 under par at the Marriott Meon Valley Hotel and Country Club at Southampton. It was the second seniors victory in Europe for the 51-year-old former Australian Open champion, who carried a 23-victory record from earlier campaigning around the world.

Another Aussie, Terry Gale, started and finished fast, coming up one shot short to tie for second place with American J.R. Delich. Gale opened with 67 and shared the lead with yet another Australian, Ian Stanley, and English club professional Mike Slater, who rattled off eight birdies after hitting his first tee shot of the tournament out of bounds.

Shearer began with 70 and still trailed by two after 36 holes as Northern Ireland's David Jones came up with a duplicate of his 36-hole performance in the Philips PFA in 1998. Again he led by one stroke with 135, this time on the strength of a second-round 66. Spain's Antonio Garrido and Scotland's David Huish were at 136 and Delich shared the 137 spot with Shearer.

Shearer shot a solid five-birdie 67 Monday that held off the threats of eight players who at one time or another were within a stroke of the lead, Gale the most spectacular with 65. Jones, who lost the tournament in a playoff in 1998, fell back to eighth place with 73. Garrido, Huish and Tommy Horton tied for fourth at 206.

Jersey Seniors Open—€140,000
Winner: David Jones

David Jones rid himself of the final-round blahs at the Jersey Seniors Open. Four times in just over two years Jones took a lead into a final round and came away without a title. Three times he finished second and two weeks earlier he faded to eighth. At La Moye Golf Club in Jersey, he did things differently, coming from two strokes off the 36-hole pace and scoring a two-shot victory with his eight-under-par 208 to put his first seniors title onto his record alongside 15 previous wins.

Jones went to the final round in an all-Irish threesome with Paul Leonard, the leader at 137, and Liam Higgins, the runner-up at 138. Leonard had wrested the lead from Bob Lendzion, the American who won the 1998 Beko Classic. Lendzion had opened the Channel Island event with six birdies and a five-under-par 67 to lead Higgins by one, Leonard and Jones by two. Leonard had 68 Saturday, inching ahead of the long-hitting Higgins, who had already shot 70 and converted only one of four short-range eagle putts. Jones also shot 70 after three early birdies, while Lendzion dropped into fourth place at 140, canceling an eagle with three bogeys. Tommy Horton, the local favorite who won the tournament in 1997, shot himself out of contention with 76–146.

The issue came down to Jones and Leonard Sunday. A 25-foot birdie putt by Jones at the 13th leveled the duel. Leonard fell back with bogeys at the 14th and 16th, kept his chances alive with a birdie at the 17th, but missed from 15 feet at the last hole before Jones clinched "a very sweet win" over Leonard and England's Jim Rhodes with a five-foot birdie putt. "It's been hard not to get disheartened when you are so often the 'nearly' man," observed the delighted winner.

Lawrence Batley Seniors—€140,000
Winner: Eddie Polland

The scenario barely changed as the European Seniors Tour resumed after a week's break with the Lawrence Batley Seniors at Huddersfield Golf Club's Fixby Hall. Like David Jones at La Moye, Eddie Polland had been very close but winless as a senior when he arrived in West Yorkshire. When the week ended, the former Ryder Cupper had the sought-after victory and achieved it despite knee surgery that nearly kept him on the shelf. Polland, who had three runner-up finishes during his first two seasons on the tour, including two playoff losses, led all the way at Fixby Hall in posting his two-stroke victory with nine-under-par 204 total.

The Spanish-based Ulsterman had missed the Jersey Open two weeks earlier after undergoing the knee operation and teed it up in the Lawrence Batley Seniors against medical advice. He promptly bogeyed the first hole, then followed with six birdies for 66 and a two-shot lead over Mike Slater, David Huish and Jones, seeking two in a row after the ice-breaker at Jersey. Slater, who also bogeyed the opening hole, played with the 88-year-old Batley, a long-time supporter of golf in Britain.

Polland opened his margin to five strokes Saturday when he repeated the 66. Huish and Slater remained in second place with 69s for 137 and Tommy Horton (69-69) and Jones (70) were another shot back. On Sunday no one seriously threatened Polland, who needed only a one-over-par 72 to nail down the victory, making his third birdie on the final green to establish the two-stroke margin over Antonio Garrido. The Spaniard closed with 68. "I was delighted to win this tournament, especially since I've played golf with Lawrence all over the world," said Polland at the presentation. "Any win is welcome, but this is extra special because of all he has done for me and the other professionals over many years."

Elf Seniors Open—€150,000
Winner: Alan Tapie

Victory came quickly on the European Seniors Tour for Alan Tapie. The 50-year-old American from California finished second in the opening event in Turkey and did well enough in his other starts that the winner's check in the Elf Seniors Open boosted him into first place on the money list. Tapie slipped past Tommy Horton, who was playing in America in the U.S. Senior Open. He was the third straight first-time winner on the European circuit and fourth in the season's first seven tournaments.

A brilliant start set Tapie off toward the victory at Golf de Chantaco in southwest France, the second tournament in a row in which the winner never trailed. Tapie matched six-under-par 64s Friday with Scotland's John McTear, also a first-year player. Tapie had an incoming 29 to equal McTear's seven birdies as the two men led defending champion Brian Waites by one stroke.

Tapie inched a shot ahead with a six-birdie 66–130 Saturday. Fellow American qualifier Jerry Bruner fired a 64 for 131 and McTear birdied the last two holes for 68–132. Tapie prevailed Sunday with 70 for a 10-under-par 200, finishing three strokes ahead of McTear (71) and Liam Higgins (66). Bruner shot 73 and slipped into a fourth-place tie at 204 with redoubtable 65-year-old Neil Coles (66) and injury-plagued Eddie Polland (67), who had won two weeks earlier shortly after undergoing knee surgery and who played in pain at Chantaco with a broken toe he suffered at home after the victory.

"It's the first time I've competed regularly since I quit the U.S. Tour in 1982," explained Tapie, whose wife Marlene ("a calming influence") caddied for him for the first time. "I had chances to win three tournaments during the seven years I played our tour in America and blew them all. Now I've achieved my goal."

Senior British Open—€560,000
Winner: Christy O'Connor, Jr.

Only one member of his immediate family was not there, but Christy O'Connor, Jr., drew spiritual strength from that tragically-absent son as he won the Senior British Open to the delight of his Irish compatriots. "Part of this championship is his," said O'Connor of son Darren, who had died in a traffic accident less than a year before. "I don't believe I would have had the strength to win … without him. I've used up all of Darren's good luck," he said, referring to that prestigious victory at Royal Portrush and his initial win three weeks earlier in America in his first senior season. With wife Ann and his two other children looking on, the 50-year-old O'Connor surged in front for the first time Sunday and went on a three-stroke victory, becoming the first Irishman to win the 13-year-old tournament.

Two Americans attracted the headlines during the first two rounds at the noted course in Northern Ireland. David Oakley, who won his first event two months earlier in England, and Ray Carrasco, the eldest of 15 children of a Southern California family, stole the thunder from the better-known stars on the wind-ruffled Dunluce links with two-under-par 70s. Only three others — John Morgan, Guy Hunt and Antonio Garrido — broke par.

Carrasco disappeared from contention Friday, but Oakley remained on top with 71–141, two in front of Australia's Stewart Ginn and three ahead of South Africa's John Bland. O'Connor, one of four men sitting at one-over 145, signaled what was coming with 69, but he had to defer to another 145-shooter Saturday, two-time former champion Bob Charles. The New Zealander fashioned 67 and moved into first place with 212. O'Connor shot 68–213 and Oakley 73–214.

Oakley fell back Sunday, leaving the title up for grabs between the 63-year-old Charles and O'Connor, 13 years his junior. The big swing came on the front nine. After O'Connor birdied the fifth, Charles absorbed a triple-bogey eight at the sixth as the Irishman birdied to make it a four-stroke swing. Charles fought back with a birdie at the ninth and eagle at the 10th, but gained only a stroke as O'Connor birdied both holes. Another birdie at the 17th gave O'Connor a three-stroke lead and Charles made things easy for him when he butchered the 18th with a quadruple-bogey eight. O'Connor parred the 18th for a 69 and a 282 total. Only three other players broke par for the distance. Bland had 70–285; Gary Player, the three-time champion who had 66 Saturday, finished with 72–286, and Morgan closed with 72–287.

Energis Senior Masters—€210,000
Winner: Neil Coles

Neil Coles, one of the game's most enduring winners, took the victory stand once again a month shy of his 65th birthday, denying one final triumph to Tony Jacklin, another of England's all-time golfing greats, who had decided he would call it a career with his appearance in the Energis Senior Masters at the end of July. Jacklin, who cited tournament golf tensions and time needed to handle business interests in America for his retirement, was in contention throughout but finished four strokes behind the remarkable Coles. Coles was the oldest winner on any of the world's senior circuits, just as he was the oldest victor on the regular PGA European Tour, at age 48, in the 1982 Sanyo Open. It was the 12th European Seniors Tour victory for Britain's active elder statesman and the 43rd since he began his career in 1954. Furthermore, it avenged a playoff defeat a year earlier at Wentworth to Brian Huggett.

Both Coles and Jacklin bogeyed the 18th hole on Wentworth's Edinburgh course Friday, shot 68s nonetheless and, along with American invitee John Grace, trailed the leader, Italy's Alberto Croce, by one stroke. Croce widened his lead to three over Coles with another 67 Saturday, although, in retrospect, Croce may have cost himself the title when he drove into a ditch at the 18th and took a triple bogey on the heels of a five-birdie run earlier on the second nine. Coles shot 69 and Jacklin 70 for 138, where he was joined by Huggett and David Huish, who moved into contention yet another time with 66.

Croce apparently felt after-effects from the Saturday finish on Sunday, yielding his lead and fading to a third-place slot with a 74 for 208. Coles stepped up with a solid 68, heading off the challenge of Huish, who matched the 68 and came up one stroke short when Coles parred the last hole with a slick 25-foot putt on the final green. Coles, whose 205 total was 11 under par, credited his work on the greens for the victory, noting, "I adopted a new putting stroke and it worked all week."

Bad Ragaz PGA Seniors Open—€140,000
Winner: Bob Shearer

When Bob Shearer captured the title in the Bad Ragaz PGA Seniors Open in Switzerland in early August, his second victory of the European Seniors Tour season, he had to rethink his future plans. A successful course designer in his native Australia, Shearer had intended to rejoin his partners in that business after three more events and really wasn't thinking much about 2000. However, Shearer now was thinking about playing the U.S. Senior PGA Tour.

A brilliant second round set up Shearer's victory at Bad Ragaz Golf Club near Zurich. Trailing Northern Ireland's Paul Leonard (64) by three after the opening round, Shearer raced into the lead Saturday with a dazzling 63, the product of nine birdies and a pair of bogeys. His 10-under-par 130 gave him a three-stroke lead over American Bob Menne, who gave up a Massachusetts club position and qualified for the European Seniors Tour in 1997. Like Menne, South Africa's Bob Verwey, the defending champion, shot 65 and stood third at 134.

Shearer jeopardized his position in the early going Sunday, three-putting twice on the first four holes. That opened the door for David Oakley, the MDIS & Partners Festival of Golf winner back in May, who trailed by just one stroke after an outgoing 31 as Shearer fought back to even par on the first nine. Oakley could not advance any further and Shearer wrapped up his third senior victory in Europe with birdies at the 15th and 17th holes to shoot 68 and set a tournament record with his 12-under 198 total. Oakley's

66 gave him the runner-up spot at 201, while Menne had a 69 and placed third at 202. "It was a bit hairy out there at the start," remarked Shearer. "But I managed to grind it out, thanks to those two late birdies."

De Vere Hotels Seniors Classic—€140,000
Winner: Ross Metherell

Ross Metherell practiced what he had been preaching and it paid off in the De Vere Hotels Seniors Classic. Metherell, a 50-year-old Australian from Perth who had coached three young countrymen — Stephen Leaney, Greg Chalmers and Jarrod Moseley — to victory on the regular PGA European Tour, achieved that goal himself, even though he had not played tournament golf for 20 years. "It's been a long time since I was in this position myself. I'm more used to teaching than playing," said Metherell before he shot 69 in the final round and scored a one-stroke victory at Ferndown Golf Club in England. He was the sixth first-time winner this year.

The decision came down to the final hole Sunday. Metherell had taken a two-stroke lead in the second round with a seven-birdie 65, going 11 under par at 131, starting the tournament Friday one stroke off the opening pace of David Huish and fellow Aussie Terry Gale, who fired 65s themselves that day. Huish and Gale had 68s Saturday for 133, joined at that position by American Bill Brask, with Tommy Horton just another shot back.

Brask, Horton and Mike Slater all took runs at the top Sunday, but Metherell stood up to the pressure. He clicked off three birdies and 13 pars through 16 holes, then staggered just a touch with a bogey at the 17th and a bunkered approach at the 18th. He calmly saved par from the sand for 69 and a 200 total and the one-stroke victory over Brask (68). Slater posted 64, the week's best round, and took third place at 202.

The Dalmahoy Scottish Seniors Open—€140,000
Winner: Neil Coles

No wonder Neil Coles stressed after he won his 12th seniors title three weeks earlier that he had no intention of retiring, as Tony Jacklin, 10 years his junior, did that day. He knew that the victory was no fluke, that he may have more of the same in his future. He wasted little time, seizing the title in The Dalmahoy Scottish Seniors Open on Dalmahoy's East Course by one stroke over two American journeymen and becoming the season's second double winner.

Spanish club professional Jose Cabo jumped in front of a big pack of contenders Friday at Dalmahoy. In a round that consisted of eight birdies, eight pars, one bogey and one double bogey, Cabo shot 67 to lead six players by one stroke and five others, including Coles, by two. Jay Dolan III, who gained a modicum of fame when he made eight birdies in a nine-hole stretch in the Senior British Open, attracted attention again Saturday when he shot a second straight 68 and moved one stroke in front of Coles, David Oakley and Michael Hooper, all scoring 69-68 over the first two rounds.

A closing 69 gave Coles a final 10-under-par 206 total and the narrow victory over Dolan, who finished with 71, and Jerry Bruner, who had 68.

The Belfry PGA Seniors Championship—€252,000
Winner: Ross Metherell

Ross Metherell added a second 1999 title to his collection at The Belfry in the PGA Seniors Championship. Again the victory came at the expense of American Bill Brask, who failed to save par at the 72nd hole and finished second in the season's second and last four-day tournament.

Metherell, a frequent winner in his younger days Down Under, had taken the third-round lead Saturday with a fiery 66 for a 205 total, giving him a one-shot advantage over fellow Australian Terry Gale (68-70-68) and England's Mike Slater (72-65-69). Slater had led the field with his 137 Friday, taking first place from Geoff Parslow, who had opened with 66 and a two-stroke lead but fell from contention after that. Gale was at 138 and Metherell at 139 at the end of Friday's round.

With the lead in hand Sunday, Metherell hung tough all day. "It was close out there but I knew what I had to do," Metherell commented. What he had to do was shoot 71–276, which he did. That was enough to win over the fast-closing Brask, who had four birdies in a six-hole stretch on the second nine, but missed the green at the last hole, chipped eight feet long and missed coming back for 69–277. Gale managed only a par 72 and placed third at 278.

Monte Carlo Invitational—€175,000
Winner: Tommy Horton

A cast of international celebrities including actors Kevin Costner and Robert Wagner attracted much of the attention of the galleries through most of the Monte Carlo Invitational with its pro-amateur format, but Tommy Horton brought the focus back to superior golf at the end. Horton, the No. 1 player on the European Seniors Tour through most of the years since he joined in 1992, shook off the distractions of the event with a closing spate of birdies and scored his second 1999 victory. His 22nd seniors victory came four months after he won the season opener in Turkey, linked him with other two-time winners Neil Coles, Ross Metherell and Bob Shearer, and moved him to the top of the money list where he had finished the previous three seasons.

Horton opened the tournament with a par 69 on the scenic Mont Agel course that overlooks Monte Carlo, keeping his cool amid the bedlam of five-and-a-half-hour rounds. "We're definitely second billing this week. You've got to be very patient out there," he noted. Ireland's Denis O'Sullivan was the leader with 67, England's Jim Rhodes had 68 and six others besides Horton matched par.

Horton fell four strokes off the pace Saturday as David Oakley, the MDIS & Partners Festival of Golf winner in May, shot 65 and took the lead at 135, blazing with four consecutive birdies at the start. David Creamer was out in 30 and his 66–136 boosted him into the runner-up slot. Horton shot 70 for 139 and was lethargic in the early going Sunday. "It was tough on the front nine with so much going on in the pro-am, but I got the putter going at the 13th," Horton said. He birdied five of the last six holes, driving the 297-yard 15th, for 68–207, then watched as Bill Brask, needing a par to tie, three-putted and Oakley, needing a birdie to force a playoff, put his approach in the water and took a double bogey. Brask joined Ray Carrasco and Jerry Bruner in second place.

Ordina Legends in Golf—€112,000
Winner: Mike Slater

Twice during the previous five weeks Mike Slater had posted course records, but it wasn't until he did it again at the start of the Ordina Legends in Golf tournament in The Netherlands that he converted such a round into a victory. The four-stroke win Slater scored at Prise d'Eau Golf Club was his first in his two seasons on the circuit and made him the year's fifth first-time winner.

Slater shot the course-record round on opening day at Prise d'Eau — a six-under-par 66 — sharing that accomplishment with Irishman Arnold O'Connor and Australian Terry Gale. (His earlier course-record efforts were 64 in the De Vere Classic and 65 in the PGA Seniors at The Belfry.) American Jerry Bruner, who already had three runner-up finishes on his record, was just one stroke off the pace at 67, then edged one shot ahead of Slater, a long-hitting 210-pounder who is the golf professional at the Portal Club in England, with 66 of his own Saturday for a 133 total. Slater, "Big Red" to his members, had 68 for 134, staying close with a birdie three at the 18th on the heels of a pair of bogeys. Jim Rhodes, another English club pro, was next in line at 136.

Once again Bruner was unable to come up with a strong final round to match the 69 Slater produced Sunday. The Englishman capped the winning round with a 14-foot birdie putt on the final green to stretch his victorious margin to four and post a 13-under-par 203 total. Bruner took 74 for a 207 total and had to share second place when Scot David Huish came from 10 strokes off the second-round pace with 64, breaking the two-day-old course record by two shots and recording his third runner-up finish of the season.

Te Mes Greek Seniors Open—€175,000
Winner: Alberto Croce

It took more than four years and a bit of extra work for Italy's 55-year-old Alberto Croce to win his second title on the European Seniors Tour. He had to go four extra holes. His victory in the season's first and only playoff came at the expense of Spaniard Antonio Garrido, himself a two-time winner on the tour.

Croce began his play in the Te Mes Greek Seniors Open with a two-under-par 70 at Glyfada Golf Club in the shadow of the Athens international airport. It is the country's best course and was the site of the 1979 World Cup. The 70 left Croce just two shots off the pace of Geoff Parslow, the first-round leader for the second time during the season. As happened when he led after the first day in the PGA Seniors, Parslow faded in blustery weather Saturday, giving way to Garrido, who shot 71 for 140 and a one-stroke margin over Bernard Gallacher (69-72), the former Ryder Cup player and captain who was winless at that point of his rookie season. Parslow (74) shared third place with Alan Tapie and Barry Sandry at 142 and Croce (73) finished three behind with Norman Wood (73) and Brian Huggett, who gave back three strokes on his final two holes for 72.

Croce put his 68 and 211 total on the scoreboard first on Sunday and was thrust into a playoff when Garrido parred the 18th for 71 and his 211. Gallacher missed joining them when he bunkered his approach at the last hole, drew a tough lie and failed to salvage a par, finishing at 212. Both players missed winning chances on the first three holes of the playoff before Croce dropped a four-footer for a birdie and the victory.

Senior Tournament of Champions—€168,000
Winner: Eddie Polland

Buckinghamshire Golf Club seems to bring out the best in Eddie Polland and Tommy Horton. The setting for the Senior Tournament of Champions since 1996, Buckinghamshire yielded two victories to Horton in the 1996 and 1997 finales and saw Polland come within one stroke of his first triumph in 1998. In the fourth event there in 1999, Polland got his second win of the season, while Horton finished second with Liam Higgins and clinched his fourth straight and overall fifth season as the leading money winner.

Determined to add another John Jacobs Trophy to his collection, Horton came out flying in the opening round with a seven-under-par 65 Friday, jumping off to a three-stroke lead with Brian Waites and David Huish at 68, Polland and four others at 69. Then, unexpectedly, Horton's game became disjointed and, when he shot 78 Saturday, Polland took advantage. He scored 71 for 140 and took a one-stroke lead over Antonio Garrido (71-70), Craig Defoy (70-71) and Waites (68-73). Huish had 77 and Jerry Bruner, the only player in the field with a chance to catch Horton in the money race, took 74 and entered the final round tied with Tommy. Christy O'Connor, Jr., second on the money list, did not come back from America for the tournament.

The weather came up raw Sunday and only one player — American Fritz Gambetta — broke 70 in the wind and driving rain. Polland, who struggled with injuries through much of the season, wrapped up the title with two long birdie putts on the second nine to get in with a very respectable par-72 round and 212 total. Eddie, who had knee surgery during the season and was hobbled by a broken toe in the later months, ran in putts from 20 feet on the 15th and 60 feet on the 16th to finish two strokes in front of Horton and Higgins, who closed with 71 and 72 respectively. "After all that has happened to me this year with the injuries, this is fantastic," said Polland, who was the season's fifth two-time winner.

Japan Senior Tour

ANA Ishigaki-jima Senior Pro-Am—¥5,000,000
Winner: Hiroshi Ishii

Hiroshi Ishii launched the Japan Senior Tour season at the end of January with a come-from-behind victory in the new ANA Ishigaki-jima Senior Pro-Am. It was his third senior win and first since 1994.

Tetsuhiro Ueda, who also had not won since 1994, fired a sensational 10-under-par 62 in the opening round of the limited-field (30 players) event, but led by just two strokes over Shozo Miyamoto and three over Seiji Ogawa. However, Ueda tumbled all the way to 75 in the second and final round and Ishii moved into the breach. Sitting in a fourth-place tie the first day at 66, Ishii produced 64 the next day to pick up a two-stroke win. Miyamoto and Ogawa shot 68s to finish in second and third place at Ishigaki Golf Club.

Asahi Ryokken Cup—¥10,000,000
Winner: Hiroshi Ishii

Although six weeks passed before the Asahi Ryokken Cup at the Classic Golf Club, Hiroshi Ishii retained his winning touch. Ishii won his fourth senior title with a six-under-par 138 for a one-stroke victory. Akira Kawamata, a non-winner on the circuit, grabbed the first-round lead with 67, one shot ahead of Ishii and Katsuji Hasegawa, who won the Japan Media System tournament in 1997. Ishii came up with 70 the second day to edge Kawamata, who shot 72. Hasegawa (73) and Tadao Nakamura (69-72) placed third in the full-field but unofficial tournament.

Castle Hill Open—¥30,000,000
Winner: Fujio Kobayashi

More than a month passed before the final event of the spring and Hiroshi Ishii's spell was broken by Fujio Kobayashi in the Castle Hill Open on the par-72 Castle Hill Country Club course. Kobayashi, who had single victories in the 1995 and 1996 seasons, led from start to finish in the 54-hole tournament that was played in the rain the first two days. He ended with a one-over-par total of 217, one stroke ahead of Seiji Ebihara and Mitoshi Tomita.

Kobayashi opened with 71 and led by a shot over Koichi Uehara, the defending champion. He managed only 74 in the second round, but clung to the one-shot margin, then over Ebihara and Norihiko Matsumoto, who had matching 74-72s. Kobayashi's final-round 72 for the 217 secured the victory as Ebihara also shot 72 and Tomita came up with the week's lowest round, 68.

Old Man Par Senior Open—¥5,840,000
Winner: Masaji Kusakabe

When action resumed after a four-month hiatus, Masaji Kusakabe scored his second victory, prevailing in a three-man playoff at the end of the 36-hole Old Man Par Senior Open on the Minakami Kogen golf course.

Kusakabe had begun with a six-under-par 66 and a one-stroke lead over Kikuo Arai, but when he shot 70 the second day, he was overhauled by Arai (69) and Koji Nakajima (69-67), forcing the playoff. It went two holes before Kusakabe ousted Arai and Nakajima.

HTB Senior Classic—¥8,000,000
Winner: Fujio Kobayashi

Fujio Kobayashi won the HTB Senior Classic for the second time, capturing the title in the 36-hole event on the second hole of a playoff against Koichi Uehara. Both players had six-under-par 138s. Uehara and Masaru Amano shot 69s the first day, leading Kobayashi, Seiichi Kanai and Hiroshi Ishii by a stroke. Uehara repeated the 69 in the final round and Kobayashi caught him with 68 for his 138. Amano tumbled to 77, while Kanai, the Japan Senior Tour's most successful player with 10 victories on his record, shot 72 for 142 and tied for third place with Tadao Nakamura and Toru Nakayama. Ishii, who won twice in the spring, had a 73 and tied for sixth with Hisao Inoue. The win was Kobayashi's fourth on the circuit. He won the earlier HTB in 1996.

Japan PGA Senior Championship—¥50,000,000
Winner: Tadami Ueno

Tadami Ueno turned 50 just in time. The first-year player won the Japan PGA Senior Championship, the first of the circuit's two major tournaments, as, for the third event in a row, a playoff decided the winner. Ueno, who had seven titles on his record from his regular tour days, birdied the first extra hole at Shimoakima Country Club in Gunma Prefecture to defeat Mitsuo Iwata.

Another rookie, Shigeru Kawamata, was in front after 18 holes, shooting a three-under-par 69. Things bunched up the second day with the quartet of Katsuji Hasegawa, Seiichi Kanai, Ichiro Teramoto and Koji Nakajima showing the way at 141, the first three carding 71s and Nakajima 68. Kanai and Hasegawa retained a share of the lead Saturday with 73s and Yasuhiro Miyamoto joined them at 214 with 71. Ueno and Iwata edged past Kanai and Hasegawa Sunday, Ueno with 71 and Iwata with 72 as the other two had 74s.

Japan Senior Open—¥50,000,000
Winner: Graham Marsh

Even though it required an arduous trip from the United States and back, Graham Marsh fulfilled his obligation to defend the Japan Senior Open championship in mid-October. The journey was certainly worthwhile. The Australian, who has had great success playing in Japan over the years, made a shambles of the Senior Open field at Rokkou Kokusai Golf Club in Kobe, cruising to a nine-stroke victory to make it two in a row. He then returned to America to complete his million-dollar season on the Senior PGA Tour.

Marsh had things in hand from the start at Rokkou Kokusai. He opened with a six-under-par 66 for a two-stroke lead over Haruo Yasuda and Masaru Amano, doubled the margin with 69–139 Friday, went seven up with 67 Saturday for 202, and finished things off Sunday with 70 for his final 16-under-par 272 total. Not only were runners-up Seiji Ebihara and Mitoshi Tomita nine back at 281, but Yasuda, next in line, was 12 back at 284.

Tokyo Tower Senior—¥10,110,000
Winner: Mitoshi Tomita

Mitoshi Tomita turned a futile effort to catch Graham Marsh two weeks earlier at the Japan Senior Open into a victory in a new 36-hole, 36-player event late in the season. Tomita, who finished a distant second in the Senior Open and had another second-place finish earlier in the year, eked out a one-stroke triumph in the Tokyo Tower Senior tournament at the Japan PGA Golf Club for his first senior title.

Unlike Marsh, Katsuji Hasegawa proved catchable in the Tokyo Tower. Hasegawa opened the latter tournament with a seven-under-par 65, two strokes in front of Fujio Kobayashi and Toru Nakayama. Tomita was in a seventh-place tie at 70. But Tomita came up with a 65 of his own the second day and grabbed the victory with the 135 total when Hasegawa managed only 71 in the second round. Kobayashi shot 70 for 137.

TPC Senior—¥5,000,000
Winner: Koichi Uehara

Frustrated as a playoff loser in a victory bid in the Old Man Par Senior Open earlier in the year, Koichi Uehara acquired that triumph at season's end in the same setting, capturing the unofficial TPC Senior on the fourth-hole of a playoff against Seiji Ebihara. The two had completed the 36-hole event with matching four-over-par 148s.

Tatsuo Fujima led the first day with 71, one shot ahead of Mamoru Kondo. Ebihara opened with 73 and Uehara with 74. Fujima slumped to 78 in the second round, dropping into a five-way tie for third place with Takao Kase, Koji Nakajima, Yoshiaki Namiki and Wataru Horiguchi at 149, a shot behind Uehara (74) and Ebihara (75). The victory was Uehara's second. He won the 1998 Castle Hill.

16. Women's Tours

For a second year, the U.S. LPGA Tour was dominated by two players who slugged it out to the end, and as if it were a prerequisite in women's golf, the year finished with a debate over how Player of the Year honors are decided. In 1998 Se Ri Pak won two major championships and four times overall and captured The Associated Press Female Athlete of the Year honors, but lost the LPGA Player of the Year title to Annika Sorenstam. Similarly, in 1999 Juli Inkster won two major championships, six titles overall and qualified for the LPGA Hall of Fame, but to the chagrin of some observers, Inkster wasn't the LPGA Player of the Year. That title went to Karrie Webb, who also won six titles including one major and finished with the lowest scoring average in history (69.43). Webb posted 22 top-10 finishes in 25 events and crushed the single-season earnings record with $1,591,959 in official U.S. earnings and $1,641,959 worldwide.

Inkster, who hadn't won a full-field event since 1992, earned $1,446,378 for the year, the U.S. Women's Open and McDonald's LPGA Championship titles and picked up a fifth victory in late September to qualify for the LPGA Hall of Fame. Not only did the 39-year-old Inkster have her best year ever, she won the LPGA title with an eagle-birdie-birdie finish after being tied with three holes to play. She made the best recovery of the year on the seventh hole in the final round of the U.S. Women's Open, when she gouged her ball from a buried lie in a bunker and almost holed the shot, preserving a two-stroke lead.

The LPGA doesn't vote on Player of the Year, but relies on a mathematical formula that takes victories, scoring average and winning percentage into account. Not that Webb didn't deserve every bit of praise and recognition she received, but the players weren't given a choice, and that was the source of the controversy.

Webb might still have won in a vote of her peers. After losing to her best friend, Kelly Robbins, at the season-opening HealthSouth Inaugural, Webb went on a tear, winning the Office Depot event before returning to her native Australia where she won the Australian Ladies Masters. Two weeks later, she won again at the Standard Register Ping, making Webb a favorite at the Nabisco Dinah Shore. Her major championship disappointments continued as Dottie Pepper ran away with the first major title of the year.

While Pepper's victory, her first major title in seven seasons, should have been the news of the week, newly-named LPGA commissioner Ty Votaw took the headlines with his announcement that the Tour would drop Dinah Shore's name in deference to tournament sponsor Nabisco. Shore was the first and most vocal celebrity endorser of women's golf, and she was the first non-player inducted into the LPGA Hall of Fame, so the announcement was met with disbelief by many in women's golf. Votaw said this was a way "to honor Dinah" while securing Nabisco's sponsorship for the future. "Not bloody likely," Laura Davies said.

One week after Votaw's announcement and Pepper's win, Inkster struck with her second victory of the year at the Longs Drugs Challenge, following her triumph in the Welch's/Circle K Championship, but few thought Inkster had a shot at the Hall of Fame in 1999. The LPGA had revised its qualifying criteria for admission (a move that retroactively qualified Amy Alcott), but Inkster started the year seven points shy of the new guidelines. Even with two victories by the first week of April, she was still five points short. As she said, "That could take a year, or a decade, you never know."

Inkster's win kept April from being an all-Australian month. Queenslander Rachel Hetherington won back-to-back events and Webb picked up her fourth win. Then Kelli Kuehne, the highly touted Texan who won two U.S. Amateur titles before turning professional in 1996, broke out with her first victory at the Corning Classic and made a superb run in the U.S. Women's Open, finishing second. But Inkster's win in the U.S. Women's Open, a major that gave her two more points toward Hall of Fame eligibility, caught everyone's attention.

Webb won again the week after the Open, pushing her total to five before the midway point in the year. Pak reemerged as a winner, after enduring criticism in the later part of 1998 and 1999. With a fresh attitude and more relaxed demeanor, Pak made it two out of three by winning the Jamie Farr Kroger Classic for the second year in a row, proving she was still a force to be counted.

Sandwiched between Pak's two wins, Inkster picked up her fourth victory of the year and her second major title of the season in the McDonald's LPGA Championship. In addition to moving into second place on the money list behind Webb, Inkster came two points closer to Hall of Fame eligibility, and the improbable seemed much more likely. One more victory and she was in.

That win came in September on the same Sunday afternoon that the U.S. Ryder Cup team launched the biggest comeback in the 68-year history of the matches. While the Ryder Cup took the spotlight from Inkster, it didn't dampen her enthusiasm or the mood of the spectators in Portland, Oregon, who chanted "Hall of Fame, Hall of Fame," as Inkster walked up the 18th fairway. "It's a dream come true," she said.

In between Inkster's fourth and fifth wins of the year, Webb picked up her sixth victory at the du Maurier Classic for her first career major title. Webb also had more top-five and top-10 finishes than any other player, making her a contender for Player of the Year honors, if it had come up for a vote. But we'll never know.

What we do know is that Korean Mi Hyun Kim was the overwhelming winner of Rookie of the Year with two victories and a second place, while Pak finished the season strong with two more wins, for a total of four, including the season-ending PageNet Tour Championship. Sorenstam also had two wins, while Pepper picked up a second victory, then paired with Inkster to win the LPGA portion of the Diners Club Matches in December.

Davies had the most victories, three, on the Ladies European Tour, but Sherri Steinhauer won the showcase event, the Weetabix Women's British Open. Sandrine Mendiburu, Sofia Gronberg Whitmore and Trish Johnson each won twice in Europe.

Although Davies took a fourth worldwide victory in Japan (then a fifth with John Daly in the JCPenney Classic), the stars of the Japan LPGA Tour were Fumiko Muraguchi and Kaori Higo, with three victories each. The two-time winners were Yoko Inoue, Junko Yasui, Ok-Hee Ku and Hee-Won Han.

U.S. LPGA Tour

HealthSouth Inaugural—$550,000
Winner: Kelly Robbins

To paraphrase baseball legend Yogi Berra, it looked like déjà vu all over again. For the second year in a row, the LPGA season kicked off with Kelly Robbins shooting a course-record score in the final round at the Grand Cypress Resort in Orlando, Florida, to win the HealthSouth Inaugural. In 1998, the number was 66. The 1999 closing score was 64 which included nine birdies, five in the final nine holes, and one bogey to come from six shots behind and overtake Karrie Webb and Tina Barrett.

"She's such a great player she is capable of shooting scores like that on Sundays," said Webb, who missed an opportunity to tie Robbins when her 25-foot birdie putt at the last hole hung on the lip. "I knew I had to play awesome to beat her."

Robbins' play could be described as awesome, even though her father and swing coach didn't believe her game was ready. "Today was unexpected," Steve Robbins said. "Her swing is close but not where we want it. She told me she didn't feel quite right. Being that far back, you don't expect to win."

There were other surprises from the 54-hole season opener, not the least of which was the opening-day leaderboard. With conditions hard, dry and unseasonably warm, two players tied Robbins' record of 66. Scotland's Catriona Matthew, winless in her four years on the LPGA Tour, shot her lowest round in two years to tie for the lead, but few people paid attention. The co-leader was 42-year-old Hall of Famer Nancy Lopez. The 66 equaled Lopez's low round of 1998 when she tied for second in the Sara Lee Classic, and it was the first time Lopez had been atop a leaderboard in eight months.

Alas, Lopez's moment was fleeting. A second-round 74 opened the door for Matthew (who followed her 66 with 69 to stay in a tie for the lead), Tina Barrett (67-68), and another Hall of Famer, Patty Sheehan, who followed her opening 70 with 66 to move to within one shot of the lead. Meanwhile, Robbins seemed out of the picture, opening with rounds of 70 and 71, behind 16 players with 18 holes to play.

Nine players fired rounds in the 60s on Sunday, with Helen Alfredsson carding 65 to move into eighth place at 210, but none were as good as Robbins, whose 205 total, 11 under par, was one better than Webb and Barrett. After collecting the $82,500 winner's check, Robbins shook Webb's hand and smiled. "I was the lucky one this week," she said.

Naples LPGA Memorial—$750,000
Winner: Meg Mallon

There was a great deal of anxiety among LPGA players and staff before the Naples LPGA Memorial. It was the first year of the event at a new golf course (The Club at Pelican Strand), in a city (Naples, Florida) that had been bereft of women's golf for many years. When the final round of this second LPGA event of the year turned into a showdown between the greatest names in women's golf, with the outcome not being decided until the 72nd hole, the squeals of glee were palpable.

Ten players hovered within three shots of the lead throughout most of the third and fourth rounds, with names like Karrie Webb, Juli Inkster, Kelly Robbins, Helen Alfredsson, Annika Sorenstam, Liselotte Neumann, Hollis Stacy, Laura Davies and Meg Mallon vying for the title. Webb stayed atop the leaderboard for three rounds, opening with a nine-under-par 63 and following it with rounds of 69 and 72 for a 204 total, tied with Inkster.

Mallon, who started the final round tied with four others at 205, was glad to see that the scoreboards had been taken down because of the high winds. "I usually try to put blinders on. I knew I had to make some birdies out there," she said.

She did just that, catching some good breaks early and taking advantage of some mistakes by the leaders. After pulling her tee shot on the par-four fourth hole, Mallon had to stand with her heels inside a water hazard in an awkward lie. But she was able to hook her six-iron approach to within 15 feet, and when she made the putt for birdie it was like getting two shots back.

Three holes later Mallon hit an errant approach shot that appeared destined for trouble until the ball struck a spectator and ended up pin high. After giving the spectator a golf ball and a hug, Mallon played the remaining 11 holes in four under par, capping her run with a nine-foot birdie putt on the 17th to take the lead.

It wasn't over yet. Robbins, who assumed the lead after shooting 33 on the first nine while Webb faltered with a double bogey at the third, failed to save par at the 13th to drop one stroke behind Mallon. Alfredsson joined the fray when a four-foot birdie putt at the 15th briefly put her name at the top until Mallon made birdie at the 17th. Both Robbins and Alfredsson had chances to tie at the 18th, but their long birdie putts missed the mark and Mallon had the 10th victory of her career with her 67 and 272 total, 16 under par.

"It was a race down the stretch," Alfredsson said. "Meg played great. She deserved it."

Despite faltering on the last hole, Robbins was the model of consistency as she attempted to become the first LPGA player since Louise Suggs in 1961 to win the first two events of the year. Her 273 total included an opening 69 followed by three rounds of 68, one shy of what she needed to tie Mallon. Alfredsson shared second place with identical scores.

Sorenstam topped the list of three players tied at 275. Her final-round 66 was the best of the day in extreme conditions, while Neumann shot 69 and Hollis Stacy, 70, to tie for fourth with Sorenstam.

Office Depot—$675,000
Winner: Karrie Webb

At the Office Depot tournament Australian Karrie Webb held off charges from Dottie Pepper and Kris Tschetter to pick up her first win of the season.

When Webb reached the 501-yard, par-five 17th in two shots and two-putted from 20 feet for birdie, she broke a three-way tie and cruised in with a 10-under-par total of 278 and a one-shot victory.

"The spotlight wasn't on me anymore," Webb said of her relegation behind Annika Sorenstam, Se Ri Pak and her best friend, Kelly Robbins. "I wanted it back."

She certainly got it back at the Ibis Golf and Country Club in West Palm Beach, Florida. With a round of 67, Webb tied for the first-day lead with Juli Inkster. Webb seemed determined to make this her week. A second-round 69 kept her tied atop the leaderboard, this time with Hall of Famer Betsy King, who followed her opening 70 with 66. Inkster, Robbins and Nancy Scranton were one back at 137.

Even par was good enough for Webb to retain her lead after Saturday, but she found herself tied once again. This time it was Inkster and Pepper who shared Webb's spotlight at 208. Robbins remained one shot back at 209.

The tide would change temporarily on Sunday. Robbins wrestled the lead away with a birdie on the 11th hole, and it looked as though Webb might come up shy again. "I usually call her 'Horseshoe,' because she's so lucky," Webb said of Robbins. But this time things would be different.

A birdie on the 16th put Webb back into a share of the lead with Pepper and a charging Tschetter, who hadn't won since 1992 but who was having the best round of the day (66). Then on the 17th, after threading the fairway with her tee shot, Webb ripped a three-wood second shot that ran into the green and stopped 20 feet from the flag. It was the kind of pressure shot that proved this was to be her week. Two putts and one birdie later, she was in the lead again. A par at the 18th was all Webb needed for 69 to win. After an emotional trophy presentation, Webb could only say, "I feel happy, but I'm exhausted."

Robbins closed with 71 for a 280 total and a share of fourth place with Inkster and Gail Graham.

Valley of the Stars Championship—$650,000
Winner: Catrin Nilsmark

When Annika Sorenstam walked to the tee of the first playoff hole tied with another Swede, Catrin Nilsmark, at 204 after 54 holes at Oakmont Country Club in Glendale, California, most watchers expected the 1998 LPGA Player of the Year to win. After all, Sorenstam entered the playoff in the Valley of the Stars Championship with a 4-1 playoff record and 16 career victories. When Sorenstam three-putted from four feet to lose to Nilsmark on the first playoff hole, even the winner was stunned.

"I'm still in shock because of the way it ended," Nilsmark said. "That's a once-in-a-lifetime thing for Annika."

Nilsmark arrived in California having never won in her five seasons on the U.S. LPGA Tour. When Sorenstam, who started the final round four shots off Nilsmark's 133 lead, birdied the par-five 18th hole to shoot a final-round 67 and join Nilsmark in a tie for the lead at 204 at the end of regulation, the momentum seemed clearly in Sorenstam's favor. Nilsmark hadn't finished particularly strong, hitting a poor second shot to the 16th but chipping in from 40 feet, then bogeying the 17th for her 71.

As the two made their way back to the par-five 18th for the playoff, Nilsmark wondered if this was another squandered opportunity. Her best finish on tour had been a tie for third, and she felt as if she was playing in the shadow of other Swedish players such as Sorenstam, Liselotte Neumann and Helen Alfredsson. "Maybe I used to wish I was from Norway," she joked.

This looked like Nilsmark's week to add her name to the Swedish winner's list. On Saturday she holed out a difficult bunker shot on the 18th for eagle to shoot a course-record 65 and a two-stroke lead over Stephanie Lowe, and when her chip found the cup on the 17th hole on Sunday, Nilsmark held a two-shot lead with two holes to play. She still had a chance to win with a birdie at the final hole of regulation, but when her birdie putt slipped by and Sorenstam make birdie to tie, Nilsmark realized her best chance might have slipped away. "My caddie said, 'Well, we still had a good tournament,'" Nilsmark said.

Things looked even bleaker when Sorenstam hit her approach shot to within four feet on the 18th. Her first putt slipped past the right edge and rolled three feet past. Nilsmark's caddie changed his tune as Sorenstam lined up her second putt. "She could miss that," he said. When Sorenstam missed the second putt, Nilsmark finally had her victory.

"Many times I wondered if I could win," she said. "Now, I know I have what it takes."

In addition to Nilsmark and Sorenstam, it was a good week for many of the other Swedes on the LPGA Tour. Neumann followed her opening-round 71 with a 70-67 weekend to finish alone in third at 208, while Alfredsson finished tied for sixth at 213. Lowe stumbled on Sunday with 76, but took third, tied with Jane Geddes at 211.

Sunrise Hawaiian Ladies Open—$650,000
Winner: Alison Nicholas

Although she hadn't won since her 1997 U.S. Open victory over Nancy Lopez, 36-year-old Alison Nicholas felt confident after assuming the second-round lead in the Sunrise Hawaiian Ladies Open in Kapolei. After all, Nicholas had struggled to overcome two bouts of pneumonia in 1998, limiting her starts and dropping her from 18th to 84th in LPGA earnings.

"It was frustrating," she said. "I felt like a part-timer. Now, I'm excited to be playing again and to be competitive. I'm finally healthy, although I'm cautious if it rains or gets cold."

It was neither rainy nor cold in Hawaii, but the wind gusted upwards of 25 knots. That suited Nicholas just fine. After opening with 70, Nicholas trailed Mardi Lunn by four shots. That deficit increased early in Friday's round when Nicholas made two bogeys in the first four holes, but she rallied for eight birdies and a tournament-low round of 66. That put her in a share of the lead with Michelle McGann, who followed her opening 67 with 69.

On Saturday (the final day of this 54-hole event) the winds picked up even more, blowing so hard at times that players had to brace themselves to keep from falling over. "If you put any sort of side spin on the ball, you were in trouble," said Annette DeLuca, who started the final day four shots off the lead.

Nicholas knew the conditions would be tough, but she had a game plan that proved effective. "I thought par or one over par (73) would be good," she said. "To get that, I had to hit the middle of the greens and two-putt."

It wasn't the best round of the day, but Nicholas' 73 and 209 total, seven under par, was enough to win by one over DeLuca, who finished with 70, and Moira Dunn, who reeled off a string of late birdies to shoot 68.

"With all that wind going on out there, it was an entertaining day," Nicholas said. "I'm delighted to be back in the winner's circle. This is a great change."

McGann wasn't so fortunate. After four bogeys and four double bogeys, McGann managed an eagle on the 526-yard, par-five 16th and a birdie coming in to shoot 81 for a 217 total. "I started bad and finished bad," McGann said. "It was a tough day."

The only other player to seriously challenge Nicholas was Jan Stephenson, who was searching for her first win since 1987 and who got to six under par early in the final round, but couldn't maintain the pace. Stephenson finished with 71 for a 211 total and sole possession of fourth place. "It's nice to be back in contention again," Stephenson said. "I really thought I had a chance to win the tournament."

Australian Ladies Masters—$750,000
Winner: Karrie Webb

Even before Karrie Webb made four birdies and 14 pars for a final-round 68, the outcome of the Australian Ladies Masters was a foregone conclusion. The only thing that remained to be seen as the leaders teed off at the Royal Pines Resort on the Gold Coast was how many records Webb, the defending champion, would break before the day was done.

She had already established a course record with an opening-round 63 which produced a two-stroke lead over A.J. Eathorne, and her 14-under-par 130 total for 36 holes increased the lead to four over Jane Crafter and Janice Moodie. The records continued to fall. Webb shot 64 in the third round for a 194 total, breaking an LPGA scoring record. By then, Webb had a seven-stroke lead over Moodie and the only record left for the Queensland native was the 72-hole scoring mark of 23 under par shared by Wendy Ward, Se Ri Pak and Lisa Walters.

"The record was the only thing that kept my concentration," Webb said. "I just wanted to get in and start the celebration. My mind kept wandering. I was thinking about what I would say in my speech over the closing few holes. On the front nine I knew I would have to play some good golf to really close it out. I still wanted to play well and did not want to make bogeys. You don't play 72 holes without a bogey very often, and I definitely did not want to make bogey at the last. I dropped a shot there last year (on her way to a five-shot victory) and in other titles I have won by big margins I have finished with a bogey, so I really wanted to make par."

She made par at the last and shattered the old 72-hole scoring record by three strokes. Webb's 26-under-par 262 total was only two shy of the PGA

Tour scoring record of 28 under par set by John Huston at the 1998 Hawaiian Open.

"Karrie was incredible," said Janice Moodie who found herself playing exceptional golf but losing ground to Webb. "She missed only one fairway and that was because she ran out of room and hit through it. She was great to play with, but she was running away with it. There was nothing we could do. It was some consolation that my score would have won here last year. I only had one bogey all week (on the 62nd hole), so I'm very happy."

Moodie finished alone in second at 272, two shots ahead of third-place finisher Becky Iverson but 10 shy of Webb's phenomenal performance. Alison Nicholas made a brief appearance on Saturday's leaderboard after playing the first three holes in five under par. Birdies on the first and second were followed by a double-eagle two on the 470-yard, par-five third. "It was amazing," Nicholas said. It was also short-lived. Nicholas shot 77 on Sunday to drop into a tie for 11th.

Nothing topped Webb's story, however. In front of 50 of her hometown fans, as well as members of her family who rarely get to see her play, an emotional Webb tried to put the win in perspective. "Last year was my first win in front of my home crowd and that was very special," she said. "This week was unbelievable. I think it's going to take some time to fully realize what I've done."

Welch's/Circle K Championship—$625,000
Winner: Juli Inkster

It's a rare occurrence when the fiery Dottie Pepper, hero of the 1998 U.S. Solheim Cup team, doesn't close out a victory when she is given the opportunity. No one was more surprised than Juli Inkster, the winner of the Welch's/ Circle K Championship, when Pepper left a 12-foot birdie putt on the 72nd hole one inch short.

"If there's one person I would want to make a putt for me in a critical situation, it's Dottie," Inkster said. "She doesn't miss many of them."

In this instance, however, Pepper missed the putt that would have tied Inkster at 15-under-par 273 and forced a playoff. It was Pepper's sixth runner-up finish since winning the 1996 Safeway Golf Championship. She led after the first day with 67 and was never more than one shot out of the lead at the Randolph North Golf Club in Tucson, Arizona, but when Inkster fired a tournament-low score of 65 in the final round, Pepper, once again, came up one stroke (and, in this case, one inch) short.

"I thought I had hit a good putt," Pepper said. "Hollis (Stacy, who was playing with Pepper) said it hit a bump. It was half a revolution from going in, if that — a perfect read."

From Inkster's vantage point, it looked good all the way, but instead Inkster had her 18th career victory, courtesy of a come-from-behind finish that included five birdies, one eagle and no bogeys.

"I played the par-fives well and I didn't throw any shots away," Inkster said. "I know I didn't hit the ball that well this week, but one good round and I managed to sneak out with a win." She was the only player in the top 10 who didn't make a bogey in the final 18, and she attributed her domination of the par-fives to the addition of a new seven wood into her arsenal. "It really helped me," she said. "It gave me some height and allowed the ball to sit down on those hard greens. I'm kind of a traditionalist, and I've always thought a seven wood as kind of a cheater's club. But I guess I cheated all the way to the bank."

Her final putt aside, Pepper played consistent golf all week. After the opening 67, she reeled off three consecutive rounds of 69, and her second-place finish moved her to sixth on the LPGA money list after only four starts.

Catriona Matthew finished alone in third after an impressive weekend where she shot 65-68 for a 275 total, one better than fourth-place finishers Ashli Price-Bunch, Tammie Green, Hollis Stacy and Nancy Scranton. Karrie Webb continued her good play after stumbling with an opening-round 74. Webb closed out the week with rounds of 69, 66 and 68 for a 277 total to finish tied for eighth with Helen Alfredsson and remain atop the money list after five starts.

Standard Register Ping—$850,000
Winner: Karrie Webb

Not since her 1996 rookie season, when she won four times, had Karrie Webb experienced the kind of success she found during the first three months of 1999. During a six-week stretch from late January to mid-March, Webb captured three out of six titles including the Standard Register Ping in Phoenix, Arizona, shot better than even par in 19 of 23 rounds for a 68.42 scoring average, set new LPGA 52- and 72-hole scoring records, and picked up her 12th career victory before her 25th birthday. All these accomplishments prompted Judy Rankin to call Webb "the best ball-striker I have seen in women's golf behind Beth Daniel and Mickey Wright."

Many of Webb's victories have been runaways, including the Standard Register Ping, where she climbed to a two-shot lead over Lorie Kane on Saturday by shooting 69 after opening with two 68s, then extended her margin to four shots with a closing 69 and a 274 total, 14 under par.

"She's a rock," said Wendy Ward, who started the final round four strokes behind and finished fifth at 281. "Once she gets ahead, she's hard to catch." Second-place finisher Kane agreed. "She plays with no fear. She's going to win a lot more this year, and a major is just around the corner," Kane said.

With Kane the only player within striking distance at the start of Sunday's round, Webb lengthened her lead to three strokes with a birdie at the first hole. Another birdie at the fourth and another at the eighth extended her lead to four, where it would remain until the finish.

"I worked hard and everything is falling into place," Webb said. "But you never really think that you're going to win three out of six starts. I mean you try to win every week, but this is pretty amazing."

Janice Moodie and Jane Geddes both fired course-record-tying 65s on Sunday to tie for third at 280. After Ward alone in fifth at 281, Eva Dahllof shot 67 to tie Kelly Robbins and Juli Inkster for sixth at 282. Defending champion Liselotte Neumann missed the cut by shooting 82 and 72, her worst opening scores of the year.

Webb attributed her early season success to a change in putting. After visiting with Titleist putting guru Scotty Cameron at the company's facilities in Carlsbad, California, Webb changed her grip to a cross-handed method which prompted her to start lining up putts without her caddie's assistance for the first time in three years.

"It means the world to her to be playing as well as she is" caddie Evan Minster said. "All the top players would love to win their first few like this. She's oozing with confidence."

The soft spoken Webb could only smile when presented with the prospects of the future. "My frame of mind is probably the best it has ever been," she said.

So was her golf game.

Nabisco Dinah Shore—$1,000,000
Winner: Dottie Pepper

The close calls had almost become too much for her. Despite 14 career victories, Dottie Pepper came into the 1999 Nabisco Dinah Shore, the first major championship of the year, having gone winless since 1996. She had 25 top-10 finishes since, with second-place finishes coming at least once a year. But the winless streak was beginning to take its toll. "You begin to wonder what you have to do," Pepper said.

The answer came the last weekend of March as Pepper pummeled the field and the record book at Mission Hills Country Club in Rancho Mirage, California, winning her second Nabisco Dinah Shore title by six strokes with a tournament-record 269 total, 19 under par. "The writing was on the wall because I had been playing so well," Pepper said. "But not winning really tests your patience."

It's no wonder that Pepper found herself staring at the ceiling of her hotel room early Sunday morning wondering if the three-shot lead she held over Meg Mallon would hold up.

"I woke up awfully early and got to stew on it for a while," she said. After staring at the darkness for what seemed an eternity, Pepper woke her husband, Ralph Scarinzi, and they began to talk about the day to come. "There was kind of a calming sense after talking it out a little bit. He told me that all I could do was give it my best shot, and let the chips fall where they may."

Not only did the chips fall in Pepper's favor, she played the best major championship golf in LPGA history. Her 269 total broke the tournament record by four shots, and broke the 72-hole LPGA major championship record (set by Brandie Burton at the 1998 du Maurier Classic) by one stroke. Pepper's scores were 70, 66, 67 and 66.

Pepper never considered the records. All she wanted was the victory. A bogey at the 13th allowed an opening for Mallon, who moved within two strokes, but on the next hole Pepper chipped in from 45 feet for a birdie while Mallon made a bogey. Her lead was four and it would only get larger from there.

On the 390-yard, par-four 16th, Pepper, whose demonstrative play earned her criticism over the years, hit a seven-iron approach from 144 yards and immediately shouted, "Be right, baby!" It was. The ball took three hops on the green and landed in the hole for eagle. The lead was six, and Pepper was on her way to victory.

"I just tried to stay out of my own way," she said. "I'm still amazed at how well it went." Pepper had played in the group with Amy Alcott in 1991 when Alcott posted the previous record of 273. "When Amy shot 15 under, I thought that was so far out of reach," she said. "I guess I had ladybugs following me around this week."

As impressive as the chip at the 14th hole and the holed seven iron at the 16th were, the two turning points in the tournament came on Saturday when Pepper and Mallon were jockeying for position atop the leaderboard. On the ninth, Pepper holed a sand wedge third shot from the fairway for a three that ignited the crowd and energized Pepper. "I think it was the loudest sand wedge I've ever hit," she said. "As the ball got closer and closer to the hole, the sound decibel from the crowd got louder."

The second turning point came at the 18th when Mallon hit what she described as a "ballistic" nine iron over the green that led to a double bogey for a 71 to Pepper's 67, giving Pepper a three-shot lead with 18 to play.

"When (the nine-iron shot) was in the air it was right at the flag," Mallon said. "I thought, 'That's going to be perfect.' The only explanation I can imagine is that it was adrenaline."

When Pepper extended her lead on Sunday with the eagle at the 16th, Mallon pulled out a white towel and waved it in mock surrender. "I saw Dottie hole two eagles and a chip and make about 12 up-and-downs in the last two days," Mallon said. "That is incredible golf at a major. I played pretty well and lost by what, six shots?"

Mallon's six-shot deficit was the only score in the same hemisphere as Pepper's 269. Karrie Webb equaled Pepper's final-round 66 to finish alone in third at 280, a whopping 11 shots behind, while Kelly Robbins finished with an even-par 72 to capture fourth at 281.

Longs Drugs Challenge—$600,000
Winner: Juli Inkster

Three weeks after picking up her first victory of 1999, Juli Inkster ran away from the field, winning the Longs Drugs Challenge by four strokes over Sherri Steinhauer in a contest that was never as close as the final scores might indicate. Inkster led for three of the four rounds, and the only time she wasn't on top of the leaderboard, after the first round, she was only one shot behind.

"This is a pretty good stretch," Inkster said. "I played really well last year at the end of the year and well the year before at the end of the year. I'm doing little things better: making putts, keeping my momentum going. It's a weird game. You just have to ride it while you can."

Inkster rode her momentum well at Twelve Bridges Golf Club in Lincoln, California, following an opening 69 with scores of 67, 74 and 70. She trailed Michelle McGann, Hiromi Kobayashi and Cindy Figg-Currier after the first round, but took a four-shot lead on Friday. No one seemed ready to challenge Inkster over the weekend.

The windy, cold conditions on Saturday kept anyone from making a serious move, although Inkster shot a lackluster 74. Steinhauer, a master at playing in inclement weather, climbed to within three of the lead with 69, but that was as close as anyone would get. Inkster hit fairways and greens and made no mistakes in a final-round 70 for a 280 total and the four-shot victory. In so doing, she became only the fourth player in LPGA history to surpass the $4 million career earnings mark.

"I think I'll play for two and a half more years and then retire," the 39-year-old mother of two said. "My kids don't get to see me much. They were here this week and we spent Saturday night coloring Easter eggs. It's more nerve-wracking playing in front of them. I don't want to let them down."

Chick-fil-A Charity Championship—$800,000
Winner: Rachel Hetherington

After Lorie Kane tapped in for par on the 54th hole at the Eagles Landing Country Club in Stockbridge, Georgia, to finish at 12-under-par 204 and take a two-stroke lead in the clubhouse at the Chick-fil-A Charity Championship, she finally said it. "I think I'm ready to win," Kane said. "I've never said that before, but I think it's time."

Unfortunately for Kane, it wasn't. This time it was Australian Rachel Hetherington who administered the deciding blow, birdieing two of the last three holes to tie Kane before snatching the victory with another birdie on the first playoff hole.

"When Rachel birdied the 16th I told my caddie we needed to get ready to go back to the 18th for a playoff," Kane said. "Last year in the Betsy King Classic, Rachel birdied the last hole to force a playoff with Annika Sorenstam, then she went back and birdied the 18th hole again to win. I knew this kid was tough, and she wasn't going to back down."

Indeed, Hetherington had every opportunity to back down but simply refused. After starting the week by shooting 67 on her 27th birthday, Hetherington followed up with a second 67 on Saturday for a 134 total and a tie for the lead with Barb Mucha, Leslie Spalding, Maria Hjorth and rookie Mi Hyun Kim.

At the midway point on Sunday, Hetherington reached 13 under par but a double bogey at the 10th seemed to drop her from contention. She didn't check the leaderboard again until she reached the 18th tee. There she asked her caddie if she needed a birdie or eagle on the reachable par-five. "Birdie will be fine," he said.

Hetherington dutifully complied, blasting out of a greenside bunker to within 12 feet and making what she would later describe as "my best putt of the week" to force the playoff. Hetherington finished with 70 and Kane, 69.

Both found the fairway on the playoff hole, but Kane figured it would take a birdie or better to win. She decided to go for the green with a five wood, and after hitting the shot she said, "It looked like it was going in the hole." But the ball hit a downslope and shot across the green, nestling precariously against the back rough.

"It would have been better if it had jumped into the high stuff," Kane said.

"As it was, I hit the best shot I could." That shot rolled four feet past the hole, leaving Kane an uphill putt for birdie.

Hetherington also missed the green with her second shot. Then, from an odd lie in the greenside left rough, she called on a shot her husband, Deane Heske, learned from Jose Maria Olazabal. "It's a stance for awkward lies like the one I had," Hetherington said. "By pulling my right foot back, it gives me room to make a swing."

The chip nestled to within two feet of the hole, and Hetherington assumed that another extra hole was ahead. To her surprise, Kane missed her four-footer. "It was the worst putt of the week," Kane said of the putt that never touched the hole.

A stunned Hetherington had to compose herself before tapping in for victory. "On the one hand I felt sorry for Lorie, but I knew I had to put that aside and make my putt," she said. "Then I realized that the two-footer was for the win, but I had to put that out of my mind as well. I just had to concentrate and make that putt."

City of Hope Myrtle Beach Classic—$675,000
Winner: Rachel Hetherington

It took Rachel Hetherington two years to get her first victory on the LPGA Tour. She got another win in her third year at the 1999 Chick-fil-A Charity Championship when she defeated Lorie Kane in a playoff. Even Hetherington was surprised when, one week after winning in Atlanta, she repeated the feat by holding off the likes of Karrie Webb, Helen Alfredsson and Leta Lindley to capture her second title in two weeks at the rain-shortened City of Hope Myrtle Beach Classic in South Carolina.

"I've sort of come out of the blue with these wins," Hetherington said after staying in the clubhouse for an hour and a half to see if her seven-under-par 137 total would hold up. "I've always been a fairly solid putter, but the last few weeks I've been making them from 15, 20 and 30 feet. When you do that, it really makes a difference."

With seven inches of rain falling in a five-day stretch, players never teed off on Friday or Saturday, but by Sunday the Wachesaw East Golf Club was soggy but ready for play in the second and final round.

All eyes turned to a Queenslander, but it wasn't Hetherington they were watching at first. Two-time defending champion Karrie Webb also started the day one stroke off the lead and, with three wins coming into Myrtle Beach, it was no wonder everyone looked to see if Webb would make another move on the field.

She did in the early going, but like Alfredsson, Webb played the last five holes even par, coming up one shy of what she needed to force a playoff with her compatriot. Lindley was tied with Hetherington, but bogeyed the 18th and fell one back of what she needed. Donna Andrews also made a charge, moving to five under par before finishing with a double bogey, and Emily Klein also reached five under but finished with a bogey.

Hetherington got off to a slow start, bogeying the first hole, but she atoned by making birdies on five of the next eight holes. A birdie at the 16th and two pars coming in, and Hetherington posted her 68 and 137 total and sat in front of the clubhouse television to see if anyone could catch her. "It was a nightmare sitting in there watching," she said. "I watched TV and read the paper." Hetherington broke into an infectious smile as she collected the $101,250 winner's check. "I was hoping it would happen like this one day." And of playing with Webb, whom Hetherington has known since both were juniors, the new champion said, "She plays so well all of the time that it lifts your game just to be paired with her."

This time it was Hetherington's turn to win. Webb followed her opening 69 with another 69, but like Alfredsson, who closed with 68, and Lindley, who also shot 68, it was one too many. Nancy Scranton and Akiko Fukushima also shot closing 68s to finish tied for fifth with Cristie Kerr and Juli Inkster at 139, while Scotland's Janice Moodie and Mayumi Hirase tied Klein for ninth at 140.

Mercury Titleholders Championship—$900,000
Winner: Karrie Webb

There was a total of eight hours and 47 minutes of delays, but when the Mercury Titleholders Championship ended on a soggy Monday in Daytona Beach, Florida, the best player of 1999 was once again hoisting the trophy. Karrie Webb capped one of the most impressive springs in LPGA history with another outstanding performance, coming from five strokes back at the start of the fourth round to win by three over Annika Sorenstam.

"Things are just going right for me," Webb said. "It's been a really long week, and it isn't a typical atmosphere out here, but a win is a win, and I'll definitely take it. I'm going to keep riding it for as long as it goes."

In her first 36 rounds of the year, Webb was under par 31 times. Four of those rounds came in Daytona Beach, where Webb shot 69, 66, 70 and 66 on the LPGA International course for a 271 total, 17 under par, culminating in her fourth win of the year. In nine starts her worst finish was a tie for eighth, and her position on the money list for the first four months was so dominant that her earnings exceeded the combined winnings of numbers two and three on the list.

Despite closing with an impressive 66, Webb had some help in Daytona Beach. Becky Iverson, who led at 134 after the second day and extended that lead to four shots on Saturday when she shot a second consecutive 66 for a 200 total, lost her advantage in the first nine holes of the final round. A birdie at the 11th, where she hit her approach shot to within a foot, briefly moved Iverson back into the lead at 15 under par, but back-to-back bogeys on the 12th and 13th holes dropped her out of contention. Iverson's closing 76, which became agonizingly long after rain suspended play on Sunday and forced the leaders to finish on Monday, dropped her into a tie for third place at 276 with Laura Davies (72-66-69-69), Meg Mallon (69-70-67-70) and Chris Johnson (75-63-67-71).

Johnson took the lead with four holes to play when she reached 16 under par, but a bogey at the 15th, a three-putt at the 17th and an approach shot that found the water on the 18th, resulting in a double bogey, dropped her from contention.

Sorenstam, who started the final round one shot ahead of Webb at 204 and four behind Iverson, briefly held the lead as well. Her 70 wasn't enough, as she placed second at 274. When Webb made an eight-foot birdie on the 16th, then reached the par-five 18th with her second shot, it was all over. Webb two-putted for birdie on the last.

Sorenstam felt as if she had let one get away. "I knew what I had to do," Sorenstam said. "I just didn't hit my irons as good as I needed to. When you have someone like Karrie playing so well, it's tough."

Sara Lee Classic—$750,000
Winner: Meg Mallon

The 12th and final Sara Lee Classic could be characterized as the most exciting LPGA tournament you never had an opportunity to see. The event was not televised, so only the local spectators saw Michelle McGann, Annika Sorenstam, Kris Tschetter and Meg Mallon jump in and out of the lead.

An LPGA 18-hole scoring record and a 36-hole scoring record were set by players who did not win the tournament, and the player who did win — Mallon — never held the outright lead until her nine-foot birdie putt on the last hole fell over the front edge of the cup. If that weren't enough, the top four players had a combined 79 birdies in three days, an average of 6.59 per round per player, and the lead changed seven times in the final 18 holes.

Mallon, who characterized her final round as "my 'C' game that I was able to manage like my 'A' game," couldn't believe she had won. "I was like a spectator out there," Mallon said. "I was just hanging around watching Kris Tschetter play some pretty awesome golf, and I had no idea I was in the tournament until I got to 18, turned around and saw the board. All of a sudden, I realized I had a nine-footer to win. I guess that's the way you want it to be, because I didn't have a chance to be nervous."

Nor could Mallon have anticipated the exciting series of events that would lead to her second victory of the year and her fifth top-10 finish in nine starts.

Sorenstam jumped to an early lead with a record-setting, 11-under-par 61 on Friday, the lowest score in LPGA history on a par-72 course, but only two strokes better than McGann that day. Another record fell on Saturday when McGann followed her 63 with 65. Even though her 16-under-par 128 total broke a 14-year-old record held by Judy Dickenson, McGann dismissed it as "something nice, but it won't hold up long. Records are made to be broken."

Everyone including the leaders predicted more records to fall on Sunday. "It's a record-breaking week," Sorenstam said. "The conditions are perfect. You can hit it at the pins. I think it could take as much as 20 under par. I know I'll have to shoot another round on Sunday in the 60s to have a chance."

Sorenstam was right on one count and wrong on another. None of the leaders ever made it to 20 under par, but Sorenstam did need another round in the 60s to have a chance. She seemed on her way with birdies on two of the first four holes, but then Sorenstam's putting abandoned her and she played the next 14 holes one over par, three-putting the par-five 16th for bogey at the worst possible moment.

It gave Tschetter, who started the day two shots back but who had rallied to three under through 17 holes on Sunday, the outright lead at 17 under par. She too needed a round in the 60s to gain her first win since 1992. An errant tee shot on the 18th left Tschetter with a very difficult shot. She punched out into the high rough behind the green but chipped long, leaving herself 16 feet for par.

"I had a terrible lie for that chip," Tschetter said. "Then I thought I had hit a good putt. I'm disappointed, but I've never played well here so I guess I'm pleased that I had such a good tournament."

Tschetter's putt didn't go in, but it did give Mallon a line for her nine-footer. "I looked at the board and asked my caddie, 'What happened? Did the others bogey 17?' He said, 'No, they bogeyed 16.'" McGann, who also struggled with her putter on Sunday, also three-putted the 16th for bogey to drop two shots back.

Mallon finished with 68 for a 17-under-par 199 total, one stroke better than Tschetter, who finished with 70, and Sorenstam, who had 71. McGann was fourth with 73 and a 201 total.

"Amazing, isn't it?" Mallon said through a big smile. "You're out there jockeying for position and all of a sudden it's right there in front of you. It was just so surprising to see it all turn around like that on the last couple of holes."

Philips Invitational Honoring Harvey Penick—$800,000
Winner: Akiko Fukushima

Before arriving at Onion Creek Club in Austin, Texas, for the inaugural Philips Invitational Honoring Harvey Penick, LPGA rookie sensation Akiko Fukushima was already a legend in her homeland of Japan. Having 27 amateur titles and 13 professional wins, Fukushima was one of Japan's most recognized golf figures.

After three top-10 finishes in her first 11 starts in America, Fukushima was just becoming known in LPGA circles. That changed as the 25-year-old played almost flawless golf for three rounds, playing 54 holes without a bogey and posting rounds of 64, 67 and 65 to carry a four-stroke lead into the final round.

Even Beth Daniel's record-setting nine consecutive birdies in route to 62 on Friday was overshadowed by the smiling, young Japanese player. Fellow rookie Mi Hyun Kim of Korea made a charge with 65 on Saturday to reach 200 and take a share of second place with Daniel.

Despite a shaky closing 71, Fukushima sealed the victory with a nine-foot par putt on the 16th, which gave her the confidence to cruise home with her first LPGA victory and a 13-under-par 267 total. Charlotta Sorenstam jumped past Kim and Daniel with 67 to finish alone in second at 269, while Kim and Daniel both shot 71s and shared third.

It was Daniel's best finish in over a year, prompting her to call it "A breakthrough for me. I'm on my way back." To make it back fully, however, Daniel will have to contend with a growing group of international players who are still learning how to order a pizza in English, but who need no help when it comes to golf.

Corning Classic—$750,000
Winner: Kelli Kuehne

Kelli Kuehne never led the Corning Classic until the final round. Then she looked as if she would run away with her first victory, leading by six strokes with four holes to play. But after a double bogey, a three-putt and an errant drive at the last hole, Kuehne avoided a disastrous collapse to edge Rosie Jones by one stroke.

The victory was a big relief for Kuehne, who did not live up to expectations in her rookie season and was forced to return to the LPGA qualifying tournament in 1998. "I had so many expectations last year that I set myself up for failure," she said. "It was a year of real growing pains."

One week after carding her first top-10 finish (a tie for seventh), Kuehne shot 69, 69 and 70 to trail Jones by one going into the final round. It was a good showing, and Kuehne would have been happy with a second-place finish, given the way her season had started. Jones, a former Corning Classic winner, was playing consistent and aggressive golf, shooting 71, 68 and 68.

Kuehne came out with all the tenacity that had been expected of her when she burst onto the professional scene. Seven one-putt greens in the first nine holes gave Kuehne a commanding lead. When her fifth birdie putt of the day fell in on the 14th, she had a six-shot margin. "When I missed my putt at 14 and she made hers, I thought this was a done deal," Jones said. "Her composure was awesome. She was on cruise control."

On the 16th Kuehne found the greenside bunker with her approach, then blasted over the green into another bunker. Her double bogey cut into the lead, and when she three-putted the 17th for bogey, the lead was down to two. When she hooked her tee shot beneath an evergreen on the 18th, it appeared as though Kuehne would blow her best chance in two years to pick up a victory. But a pitch to the fairway, a third shot that found the center of the green and two solid putts for bogey were good enough for 70 and a 278 total.

Jones' final round of 72, her worst score of the week, gave her a 279 total, while Joan Pitcock and Cindy McCurdy both shot 67s to tie Tammie Green for third place at 281.

U.S. Women's Open—$1,750,000
Winner: Juli Inkster

It was a week of record temperatures and record scoring as the U.S. Women's Open moved to June for the first time in 30 years and to Mississippi for the first time ever. Enthusiastic fans who lined the fairways of Old Waverly Golf Club in West Point were accustomed to 95 degree temperatures and 90 percent humidity, but even they were astonished by the caliber of play displayed by the best women golfers in the world.

Before the final putt fell and Juli Inkster hoisted her fourth major championship trophy, the spectators saw the second-lowest opening round in Open history (64 by Kelli Kuehne), the lowest second-round score (64s by Lorie Kane and Becky Iverson), the most sub-par rounds in one day (62 in the second round), and the most after 36 holes (105 rounds), producing the lowest cut in Open history (even-par 144).

It wasn't the kind of Open players had come to expect, and the conditions at Old Waverly were not what fans had come to expect from USGA courses. The weather, more than any decisions from USGA officials, attributed to the low scores. A cooler than normal spring in Mississippi stunted the growth of the normally penal Bermuda rough. Tom Moraghan, director of Agronomy for the USGA, said of the conditions, "The best way to describe the weather's influence is what a guy from Mississippi State University said to me. Until you can kick the covers off at night, Bermuda grass won't grow."

You could certainly kick the covers off by the opening round. Temperatures soared to the upper 90s by Thursday, but that only shortened the 6,433-yard course, and with three inches of rain softening the greens a few days before play began, conditions were ripe for records, and the players obliged.

Inkster's 65 was the best first round by a winner in Open history, and more records would fall to her before the week was over. When Inkster finished Saturday's third round she held the record for the lowest 54-hole score in an Open (15-under-par 201), and the lowest 72-hole record in relation to par (16-under-par 272).

Despite those impressive numbers, the tournament was not a cake-walk for Inkster. Her 65 left her one shot back of the precocious second-year player Kuehne, who was coming off a victory the week before in the Corning Classic. After playing 36 holes in 10 under par, the lowest 36-hole total of any U.S. Open (men's, women's or seniors') in history, Inkster only gained a share of the lead with Kane. It wasn't until the third round, when Inkster added a five-under-par 67 to shatter the 54-hole Open scoring record, that she broke away from the pack, moving four ahead of Kuehne and Kane.

Kuehne did her best to put pressure on Inkster in Sunday's final twosome by playing the first four holes in one under par, but the veteran's steady play proved too much for all contenders. The only mistake in Inkster's final round came on the par-three 17th when her tee shot plugged in the front of a greenside bunker. When Inkster blasted out of the bunker to within six inches, even Kuehne applauded. She knew at that moment she was playing for second place.

To everyone's surprise, Kuehne would lose that battle for second. Sherri Turner, who began the final round one shot behind Kuehne and Kane and five behind Inkster, rallied in the final hole to shoot a closing 71 and leap past both into second place at 277.

But Sunday was Inkster's show. After safely hitting her approach shot to the center of the 18th green, she let her emotions show, waving her fists in the air and acknowledging the cheers. "Wasn't it great seeing all those birdies," Inkster said. "I thought a lot of us played really well. But you play to win majors." And Inkster played her heart out in winning this one.

Wegmans Rochester International—$1,000,000
Winner: Karrie Webb

It isn't often that a player goes from worrying about missing the cut to rallying in the final round to win the golf tournament, but then not many players are as talented and determined as Karrie Webb. In what has become an all-too-familiar scenario, Webb clawed her way into the lead after an opening-round 75 left her tied for 74th in the Wegmans Rochester International in Rochester, New York.

"I know that you're going to have a bad round every once in a while," Webb said. "You just have to put it behind you and move on."

Webb moved on quite well, coming back in the second round with 67 to leap into a tie for fifth with Kristi Albers and Gail Graham. On Saturday, Webb completed the improbable comeback, firing 68 for a 210 total and a two-shot lead over Nancy Scranton, Rosie Jones and Leigh Ann Mills. Three shots back at 213 was Cindy McCurdy, who was looking for her first win since the 1993 Sun-Times Challenge, but with Webb in the lead after such a charge, the Rochester columnist said it didn't seem likely anyone would catch her.

McCurdy obviously forgot to read her newspaper on Sunday morning. Birdies on the first three holes put McCurdy in a tie with Webb at six under par. Another birdie at the ninth hole put McCurdy, playing one group ahead of Webb, in the lead by one.

Webb came back again with a five-foot birdie putt at the 12th to regain a share of the lead. Then McCurdy showed signs of cracking, bogeying the 13th and 14th to allow Webb to reclaim the advantage. McCurdy refused to go down without a fight. She rolled in a 30-foot birdie putt at the 15th, then hit a sand wedge to within three feet and made the putt for another birdie at the 16th. When Webb three-putted the 15th, McCurdy's lead was two shots with three holes left.

With solid pars on the last two holes, McCurdy posted a final-round 68 and a 281 total. She then had to watch and wait to see if it would be good enough.

Webb began her final rally by hitting a sand wedge to four feet on the 16th and making the putt for birdie. She chipped to within tap-in range for birdie at the par-five 17th to close the gap and regain a share of the lead. On the 18th Webb crushed a drive down the middle, leaving herself a pitching wedge approach from 116 yards, which she lofted to within six feet of the hole. When the putt curled into the right side of the cup for 70 and a 280 total, Webb had her 14th victory in the fourth year of her career.

ShopRite Classic—$1,000,000
Winner: Se Ri Pak

Although it took five and a half months, Se Ri Pak silenced any critics in Atlantic City, New Jersey, with an impressive wire-to-wire victory at the ShopRite Classic. "I'm happy I finally got one," Pak said. "Before this win the Korean media asked why I haven't won. They say I don't practice enough or I lack focus because I have a boyfriend. I can't make everybody happy right now, but I tell them to be patient. I want to be around a long time."

The press might not have been patient, but Pak was both a pillar of patience and the perfect model of maturity as she opened with an eight-under-par 63 for a one-shot lead over Trish Johnson. She extended that lead to two shots with a second-round 69, and closed the victory with a six-birdie, one-bogey 66 for a 198 total, 15 under par, to edge Johnson by two strokes.

The lead was three strokes as Pak made the turn on Sunday, thanks to two consecutive birdie putts of six feet. Then Pak saved par from four feet on the 11th and seven feet on the 12th to retain the lead. Johnson wouldn't go quietly. She tied Rosie Jones for the low round on Sunday with 65, but it wasn't enough to catch Pak who played the Seaview Marriott Resort's three par-five holes in nine under par for three rounds.

Johnson, who finished three groups ahead of Pak with a 200 total, waited to see if there would be a playoff, while Pak stood in the middle of the 18th fairway for 10 minutes waiting on a ruling in the group ahead. It would have been the perfect time for the young Korean to feel the pressure. Her lead at the time was one, but instead of being nervous, she turned to her caddie and said, "We have to get ready for next week."

"If she was nervous I never could tell," caddie Jeff Cable said. "She said, 'Let's hit the green and make the putt.'" She did exactly that, finishing the final round with a birdie.

McDonald's LPGA Championship—$1,400,000
Winner: Juli Inkster

Juli Inkster said she never spent a lot of time contemplating her place in the history of women's golf, even after winning the U.S. Open at age 39 and moving within sight of the LPGA Hall of Fame. She knew she was a good player, but with two children and a husband at home to keep her grounded, Inkster never thought of herself as a legendary figure. She was just a mother, wife and golfer with 20 career victories including four major titles.

So when she fired a closing-round 65 to pull away from the pack at the McDonald's LPGA Championship and join Mickey Wright, Louise Suggs and Pat Bradley as only the fourth player in LPGA history to complete the modern career Grand Slam, no one was more surprised than Inkster. "Winner, winner, chicken dinner," she said. "That's all I can think of right now. I can't comprehend this. I don't even know what I was doing out there."

What she was doing as she made her way around the 6,376-yard, par-71 DuPont Country Club with a 16-under-par 268 total was putting together one of the most dramatic finishes in LPGA Championship history. Twenty-three players, including defending champion Se Ri Pak, Meg Mallon and Liselotte Neumann, began the final round within five shots of the lead. Inkster couldn't believe she had played herself into a tie for the lead with Nancy Scranton and Cristie Kerr at 201. On Sunday, Inkster proceeded to make four birdies and an eagle, playing the last three holes in four under par for 65 to win her 21st career event and her fifth major by four shots over Neumann.

"It was her destiny to win," said Meg Mallon who was paired with Inkster. "I mean, who else plays four under on the last three holes to win a major championship? After she made the eagle putt on 16, I had chills. This is an important day for women's golf."

As impressive as the last three holes were, Inkster's putting throughout the final round was unmatched. After missing a five-foot birdie putt at the second hole and an eight-foot birdie try at the sixth, she got things going with a nine-foot par-saving putt at the seventh which led to a run on only 15 putts in the last 12 holes.

Birdies at the eighth and ninth gave Inkster the lead, but Neumann was putting together an impressive round of 68 on her own. The Swede had shared the lead with Inkster, Kerr and Jenny Lidback at 134 after the second round, but 70 on Saturday dropped her one shot back. As they turned onto the last nine on Sunday, it still appeared to be anyone's golf tournament, even though Inkster held a one-shot lead.

Inkster saved par with a 10-footer on the 13th, and then made another eight-footer for par on the 14th to gain the confidence she needed to close out the victory. "Those par saves at seven, 13 and 14 won the tournament," she said. Inkster hit a 232-yard five wood to within 18 feet on the 16th. When the putt for eagle found the cup, Inkster pumped her fist and gave her caddie a high-five as the crowd erupted. The momentum continued onto the par-three 17th where she hit an eight iron to five feet and made that putt for birdie to move three shots ahead of Neumann. At the 18th, Inkster hit a seven iron to 20 feet and capped off her run with another birdie that brought the house down.

Right after the final putt fell, Inkster found her family in the gallery and gave the kids a hug. "Can you believe this?" she asked them. Then, after introducing her children to the spectators gathered around the 18th green, she said, "These guys are my Hall of Fame."

Jamie Farr Kroger Classic—$900,000
Winner: Se Ri Pak

When Carin Koch reached the tee at the 72nd hole of the Jamie Farr Kroger Classic outside Toledo, Ohio, with a two-shot lead, it appeared as though all the jostling for position throughout the week by players like Kelli Kuehne, Sherri Steinhauer, Karrie Webb, Mardi Lunn and Se Ri Pak had been for naught. Koch had played brilliantly, climbing to four under par on the day and 10 under for the tournament through 71 holes for a seemingly secure two-stroke margin. Then the unthinkable happened. There was an errant tee shot and a mediocre recovery, and Koch had made double bogey to squander her lead and fall back into a tie with the other five contenders at 276, eight under par.

The ensuing six-person playoff, the largest in LPGA history, looked like a Tuesday shootout, and on the Fourth of July, the fireworks were spectacular. Five players made par on the par-five 18th, the first playoff hole, but Pak, who shot a final-round 71, the worst score of the six, remembered the 12-foot putt she had in winning the year before. "I knew this was the last putt and I could get the trophy or not," Pak said. "I really want to win here because I love this city and these people. Both old people and young people are very nice to me. They make food for me and give me things for luck. A woman gave me a shiny rock for luck that I carried in my pocket all week to win."

And win she did. When the 12-footer found the center of the cup, Pak had her most improbable victory of the year, and Toledo, a city that named a street after Pak when she won in 1998, crowned its favorite champion once again.

Michelob Light Classic—$800,000
Winner: Annika Sorenstam

When Annika Sorenstam teed off in the final round of the Michelob Light Classic, she was wondering if this would be the day, or if another disappointment awaited her. The three-time Player of the Year had hit a dry spot, going winless through the first six months of 1999, changing caddies, changing putting styles, and doing whatever she could to take that last step to victory.

It wasn't that Sorenstam was playing badly, but after a 1998 season when she became the first LPGA player in history to average below 70 for the entire year (her stroke average was 69.99) anything less than a multiple win season was considered by many to be a slump. She came to St. Louis with three second-place finishes, including a playoff loss to Catrin Nilsmark at the Valley of the Stars Championship, where Sorenstam three-putted from four feet.

After rounds of 68, 72 and 68, Sorenstam found herself trailing Tina Barrett by two strokes, while Lorie Kane and Nancy Scranton, who had experienced a resurgence after a strong finish at the U.S. Women's Open, were tied for second. Sorenstam hadn't been rolling the ball with the same confidence that led her to four wins in 1998, but the beginning of that year had been slow as well. Sorenstam's first win of 1998 came at the Michelob Light Classic on the same course she had just played in eight-under-par 208 for three days.

Then on Sunday things began to turn around. Barrett, who had shot 64, 72 and 70, parred 17 consecutive holes, but that, as it turned out, was not enough. Sorenstam played the first 17 holes in three under par, which gave her a one-shot lead going to the par-five 18th, a hole she had birdied in two of her three previous rounds. Another birdie and the tournament was hers. A par and the pressure would be on Barrett to make a birdie to tie.

Sorenstam did neither. As had been the case too often in 1999, she three-putted the 18th for bogey and 70, dropping to 10-under-par 278. All she could do was watch Barrett, who was also at 10 under, playing behind her. If Barrett birdied the 18th, Sorenstam would have blown another opportunity. If she parred, there would be a playoff.

Barrett pulled a nine-iron approach that left her a 20-footer for birdie. She missed, and the two players headed back to the 18th for the playoff. They would make the trip two more times, as each played the 18th in pars. The third time around, Sorenstam's caddie, Jason Hamilton, said, "It doesn't matter what Barrett does, just think of making yours." When Barrett's 20-foot birdie putt caught the edge of the hole but failed to go in, Sorenstam found the confidence she needed and rolled in a seven-footer to win. She became only the fifth player in LPGA history to win the same event in three consecutive years.

JAL Big Apple Classic—$850,000
Winner: Sherri Steinhauer

After 76 holes in temperatures that hovered around the triple-digit mark and humidity that gave the New York air more buoyancy than the East River, it looked as though Lorie Kane was going to pick up her first victory after four seasons when her second-place total had climbed to seven. She had already come in second twice in 1999, once losing to Rachel Hetherington in a playoff in Atlanta. Now she was in a playoff again, this time with Sherri Steinhauer.

As the two players made their way down the 18th fairway for the fifth time, and the haze from the New Rochelle sunset cast a fading orange glow on the green, Se Ri Pak quietly shook a bottle of champagne in the hopes of celebrating her friend Kane's first win. A moment later, Pak offered Kane a towel, which the Canadian used to hide her tears of disappointment.

After four pars in the playoff, Steinhauer, who had missed three putts inside four feet on the final nine of regulation, drained a 35-foot birdie putt to clinch her fourth career victory, adding a little redemption to what had started out as a questionable day. Steinhauer had clawed her way into a two-shot lead after three rounds, after Pak, who opened with rounds of 66 and 69 to take a one-shot lead into the weekend, had an uncharacteristic 77 on Saturday. Steinhauer, on the other hand, had played consistently well. Her 202 total had included two 68s and a 66, and while Kane was only two back after three rounds, Steinhauer held a four-shot edge over the rest of the field.

Sunday was different. A three-putt from 35 feet on the fourth hole allowed Kane to draw even, then Steinhauer missed three consecutive putts of less than three feet on the 10th, 11th and 12th holes. Kane went ahead by one at the 12th and widened the margin to two with a birdie at the 13th, but Steinhauer steadied herself.

"I think because I missed them, I knew how to deal with it," she said. "I also knew everybody was pulling for Lorie to win, but I'm a competitor. It's taken me a long time to develop some fight, and I wasn't afraid. I told myself, 'There is no failure.' I never gave up."

Kane had some missed opportunities of her own. She could have closed the door on the 16th, but instead three-putted from 20 feet for bogey to allow Steinhauer to draw even again. Then Steinhauer rolled in a 10-footer at the 72nd hole for 71 and a 273 total to force the playoff. Five holes later, she had her first win of the year after two runner-up finishes of her own in 1999.

"I played my heart out and that's all I can ask," said Kane, who finished with 69, after racking up her eighth career second place and her third of the year. "I've shed my tears, and I will remember this feeling because I don't want to be here again. Sherri's an excellent putter and you just can't leave the door open for her."

Giant Eagle Classic—$1,000,000
Winner: Jackie Gallagher-Smith

Growing up and playing golf in Indiana was tough for the youngest of the three Gallagher siblings, even though PGA Tour player Neal Lancaster said that of the three Gallaghers (Jim Jr., a PGA Tour player, Jeff, who has played on both the PGA and Nike Tours, and Jackie) the best golf swing belonged to the sister. "Neal told me that there was no reason I shouldn't win on the LPGA Tour," Jackie Gallagher-Smith said after posting a tournament-record, 17-under-par 199 total in the Giant Eagle Classic in Warren, Ohio.

"I think that's when things turned around for me. People have said to just go out and play golf and trust my ability, so I knew I was due one of these times. I've been hitting the ball well all year, hitting maybe 15 greens per round, but putting has been my nemesis. I wasn't getting anything out of my rounds on the greens."

Gallagher-Smith capped off a bogey-free week with 26 putts in the final round that included three birdie putts on the first nine along with a holed eight iron from 132 yards for an eagle at the seventh. She had a 65, seven under par, to win by three strokes over Marnie McGuire.

McGuire, a New Zealander looking for her first LPGA win, led after the second round on the strength of an impressive 11-under-par 133 performance, but could do nothing more than watch as Gallagher-Smith caught, then passed her on Sunday. McGuire shot 69 in the final round, which included a double bogey at the 14th and birdies on the final two holes. Her 202 total was enough for sole possession of second place, two ahead of Karrie Webb, Leigh Ann Mills and Lorie Kane.

The final round was Gallagher-Smith's show all the way. When she birdied the 15th and 17th holes, she had no idea she had a five-shot lead with one hole to play. "I had no clue," she said of her tactic of not looking at any scoreboards throughout the round.

du Maurier Classic—$1,200,000
Winner: Karrie Webb

Before the first ball was struck in Calgary at Priddis Greens Golf and Country Club, most predicted that a long-hitter would have the advantage in the du Maurier Classic, and at the end of three days of play, it looked as though they were right.

Despite an opening-round 72, which left her five shots off the lead, long-hitting Laura Davies had steadily climbed up the leaderboard and into a two-shot lead. Dawn Coe-Jones, the first-round leader, was Davies' closest competitor.

The name Davies kept looking for on the leaderboard — the one she knew was bound to appear — was that of Karrie Webb, the LPGA's best player through the first half of 1999, and the player with the most to prove. Even though she had won 15 times in three and half years, Webb arrived in Canada without a victory in a major championship.

Early in the week it looked as if this would be another disappointment for Webb. An opening 73 was followed by 72, but Webb came charging back with 66 to move within four strokes of Davies' lead. "I must admit I watched the board all day for Webb to make her move," Davies said. "Sure enough, she birdied four of the last five holes."

In the final round, a par-saving 20-foot putt on the 13th hole got Webb on a roll that didn't stop until she had made four birdies in five holes, including a clutch downhill five-footer at the 18th hole, to finish with 66 and reach 11-under-par 277, sealing the victory. When she was standing over the putt, Webb assumed her birdie effort wouldn't be enough. Davies had birdied the 16th hole to be 11 under, and the 18th was a reachable par-five for someone of her length. However, Davies three-putted the 17th for bogey and failed to birdie the last, shooting 72 and handing Webb a two-stroke victory. "I think adrenaline was carrying me down the fairways," Webb said. "For the last six holes it was like I was watching someone else play. When I sit and think about it, I can't believe I can do those things, but when I'm out there, I know I can."

Webb's play brought praise from the winner of the year's previous two majors, Juli Inkster, who was paired with Webb and witnessed her finish. "Karrie is by far the best player out here right now," she said. "She knocked them close and made the putts when she needed to."

Inkster finished third at 280, having blown any real chance at victory on Saturday with 74. A 69 moved her one behind Davies (72, 66, 69 and 72) and three ahead of Coe-Jones (72, 65, 72 and 74). Catriona Matthew finished alone in fifth at 284, one ahead of Korean rookie sensation Mi Hyun Kim, Maggie Will and Canadian favorite Lorie Kane.

areaWEB.COM Challenge—$800,000
Winner: Mardi Lunn

When three Australians finish in the top three positions and a fourth finishes tied for fifth at an LPGA event, it stands to reason that Karrie Webb would be among them. Not so at the Pleasant Valley Country Club in Sutton, Massachusetts, where players from Down Under did just that in the areaWEB.COM Challenge. Webb wasn't even in the field. The victorious Aussie was 31-year-old Mardi Lunn, who brought an internationally-flavored record with her to New England, but who had become known as one of the most talented underachievers.

"She's always had a lot of talent, but she has just started to believe in herself," said fifth-place finisher and fellow Aussie Jane Crafter. The criticism of Lunn had been that while she had talent and length, her casual approach kept her from winning. While Webb was spending hours on the practice tee, Lunn was usually enjoying herself in the clubhouse.

Her recent successes — including a tie for third at the McDonald's LPGA Championship and a tie for second after being in a six-way playoff at the Jamie Farr Kroger Classic — gave Lunn the confidence and determination she needed to go the extra mile. After opening with 66 to take the lead, Lunn dropped back with two rounds of 71 and trailed Sherri Steinhauer by three strokes. Canadian Lorie Kane was alone in second, two strokes behind, while Beth Daniel stood tied with Lunn going into the final day.

Lunn birdied three of the first five holes in the final round while Steinhauer and Kane struggled. Steinhauer lost her lead on the second hole when she made double bogey, and Kane bogeyed her first two holes, leaving the door open for Lunn, who took full advantage. A closing 67 and a 13-under-par 275 total gave the Aussie her first victory by one shot over a charging 47-year-old Jan Stephenson.

Stephenson, an Australian legend who was Lunn's idol as a teenager, birdied the 13th, 14th, 15th and 18th holes in a 67 of her own for sole possession of second place. She was one shot ahead of Rachel Hetherington who also shot 67 to round out the Australian trifecta.

Firstar Classic—$650,000
Winner: Rosie Jones

When Rosie Jones arrived in Beavercreek, Ohio, for the Firstar Classic, having just flown in from the Weetabix Women's British Open and a few days of vacation in Paris, she had no idea how her body would respond to the travel, the time difference, and the fact that her connecting flight out of Chicago was late and she didn't get to her hotel until 1:00 a.m. on Thursday. Then, Jones found out when she arrived that there was no room for her. She spent her first night on a couch in Liselotte Neumann's room, getting only four hours of sleep before her pro-am time.

The travel and lack of sleep caught up with her on Friday when, in the first nine holes of the tournament, Jones made two bogeys and no birdies. At that point, Jones decided this would be a grinding week. Her goal as she made the turn on Friday was to play the next 27 holes in four under par. She reached the first half of that goal in the final nine on Friday, shooting two-under-par 34 at the 6,331-yard Country Club of the North layout for an even-par 72 opening round. That placed her five shots behind leaders Nancy Scranton, Tracy Hanson and Akiko Fukushima.

Jones exceeded her goal on Saturday, shooting 67 to move within two shots of the lead held by Scranton and Fukushima, who followed up their 67s with 70s. Tied with Jones was a resurgent Jan Stephenson, whose last victory came in 1987 but who came to Ohio having more top-10 finishes in 1999 than at any time in the last five years. Also at four under par was Becky Iverson, who was searching for her first win of the year after several near-misses.

On Sunday a rested Jones continued her good play, firing 68 to move to 207, nine under par for the week, and into a share of the lead with Stephenson (68-71-68) and Iverson (74-66-67). Scranton could only manage 71 in the final round that dropped her into a tie for fourth place at 208 with Korean rookie sensation Mi Hyun Kim, Jill McGill, Leta Lindley and Hollis Stacey. Fukushima shot 75 to finish at 212.

Jones and Iverson both parred the 18th, the first playoff hole, but Stephenson failed to save par after missing the green and was eliminated. The remaining two players both made pars on the 10th (the second playoff hole) and the 18th (the third). The next time they played the 10th (the fourth), Iverson pulled her approach shot into a greenside bunker, blasted out to 12 feet and failed to make the putt for par. Jones also missed the green, but a deft chip left her with an uphill three-footer to win.

Oldsmobile Classic—$700,000
Winner: Dottie Pepper

Before teeing off at the Oldsmobile Classic in East Lansing, Michigan, Dottie Pepper and her husband, Ralph Scarinzi, attended a baseball game at Tiger Stadium in Detroit, where Pepper's father, Don, played in the 1960s. She left with souvenirs of the ballpark, which was razed after the 1999 season, and a sense of nostalgia. Four days later she would slam the door on her nearest competitor, Kelli Kuehne, with a 45-foot birdie putt on the 18th green to win her second event of 1999. "I was stubbornly patient for two days," she said, "but I was shaking pretty good when that putt rolled in. I was just trying to get it close, and it went in."

Close might have been good enough, but given the charge that Kuehne was mounting, Pepper didn't want to take any chances. After opening the week with rounds of 67 and 63 (the latter a course record), Pepper had set a 36-hole tournament record of 14-under-par 130 and opened up a five-stroke lead over Laura Philo. On Saturday, Philo stumbled to 79 and fell back into the pack. Three bogeys in the early going dropped Pepper back, but she recovered and finished the day with 70 for a 200 total and a five-shot lead over Kuehne.

Kuehne entered the final round with good thoughts. She shot 68 and 70 in the first two rounds, and her third-round 67 included an eagle, four birdies and one bogey. She kept those good scores going on Sunday with birdies on four of the first eight holes. Pepper matched her birdie for birdie. On the ninth, Pepper made a bogey and Kuehne inched one shot closer. Another bogey by Pepper at the 10th, and her lead was down to three strokes. At the 13th Kuehne took advantage by rolling in an 18-foot putt for eagle to cut the lead to one.

Pepper had opportunities to widen the margin at the 14th and 16th holes, but her birdie putts spun out of the hole. Kuehne also parred the 14th through 17th, bringing the duel to the 72nd hole. After a good drive and an approach that landed beyond the hole, Pepper had a downhill, right-to-left breaking putt for birdie. When the ball rattled the flag and fell in for birdie three, a final round of 70 and a 270 total, the intense Pepper sprang into the arms of her caddie, a smile beaming all over her face.

"I felt like something good would happen," she said. "I had to gut it out, but to slam the door on number 18 was pretty awesome."

Kuehne, who closed with 67 and a 272 total for second place, stated the obvious when she said, "That was a huge putt considering the circumstances."

State Farm Rail Classic—$775,000
Winner: Mi Hyun Kim

It was a shame that the first LPGA Tour win for Korean rookie sensation Mi Hyun Kim at the State Farm Rail Classic in Springfield, Missouri, would be clouded by one of the great controversies of the year. Kim certainly played well enough — a 12-under-par 204 total to edge Pearl Sinn and Janice Moodie by one stroke, but it was Moodie who was at the center of the controversy.

After an opening 65, which left her two shots off the lead, Moodie moved atop the leaderboard with 67 for a 132 total, two ahead of Kim (66-68), Marisa Baena (67-67), Tina Barrett and Karen Stupples (both 64-70). Stupples, a British rookie unaccustomed to the limelight, led after the opening round but was so nervous the second day she topped her first two shots before settling down for a two-under-par round. Moodie, a second-year player with seven top-10 finishes but no wins, seemed in control. "I've been knocking on the door all year," she said.

But Kim, the diminutive youngster known for wearing long shorts that drooped below her knees and turning her cap around backwards, had also been knocking on the door all season. She came to Springfield in the 22nd spot on the money list, and by the time she made the turn on Labor Day in the final round, she had caught Moodie.

When Moodie stood on the 13th tee, Kim held a one-shot lead, but the Scot wasn't panicked. There were plenty of birdie opportunities left. A birdie was not in the cards at the 13th, however. After hitting her approach shot into the greenside bunker, Moodie marched into the sand and prepared to play her shot. The lie was good, and she felt confident. Just as Moodie prepared to play a butterfly lit on her ball. Distracted, Moodie backed away and waved her hand over the butterfly until it flew away. That is when the controversy began.

Moodie saved par out of the bunker, then parred the 14th and approached the 15th ready to make her move. Then an LPGA rules official informed her that the butterfly she had waved away was considered a loose impediment in a hazard and her actions constituted a breach of the rule against removing such impediments. A two-shot penalty was assessed, and Moodie proceeded to make another bogey. After the bogey, the same official came back to Moodie and informed her that an error had been made, the USGA had been contacted, and the penalty was rescinded. Now, instead of three shots behind and out of the running, Moodie was one shot back and would have been tied for the lead had she played more conservatively and made par on the 16th.

Moodie tried to recover, leaving herself a 12-footer for birdie that would have tied Kim and forced a playoff. When the putt skirted past the hole on the low side, Kim, who shot a final-round 70 to Moodie's 73, had her first LPGA title. Afterward Moodie didn't hold in her contempt for how the ruling was handled. "I'm annoyed," she said. "I think it was handled poorly, and I would hope that such things wouldn't happen again from an organization like the LPGA."

Samsung World Championship—$700,000
Winner: Se Ri Pak

It was not unexpected when Karrie Webb moved into the lead at the elite, 20-player Samsung World Championship in Maple Grove, Minnesota. She had proven that she was the year's best player and most consistent closer. So when Webb, who entered the final 18 holes with a one-shot lead over Se Ri Pak and Laura Davies, came to the 18th tee needed only a par to win, everyone assumed it was over. But it wasn't.

For the first time in her career, Webb double-bogeyed the last hole to hand the victory to Pak, who had finished with an even-par 72 for a 280 total, eight under par, and was sitting in the scorer's tent assuming she had finished second. "People were screaming," Pak said. "But it was a strange sound." Only moments before, Pak had told her caddie that she thought it wise to stay at the course. "I think I still have a small chance," she said. "The tournament is not finished yet."

Pak held the lead through the first two rounds, shooting 67 and 71 for a 138 total and a two-stroke margin. Davies was the nearest pursuer, having shot 69 and 71 for a 140 total, while Webb and Rachel Hetherington were tied for third at 142. Webb made her move on Saturday, shooting 65 to jump to the top of the leaderboard at 207, while Pak shot 70 to stay one back along with Davies, who shot 68.

Pak tried to make a run on Sunday with a birdie on the 17th, but as she walked down the 18th fairway she saw Webb drain a tricky four-footer on the same hole for par to retain a one-shot lead. The 18th was a par-five, yielding birdies under most conditions and certainly easy pars. Pak remembered 1998, when Dottie Pepper needed to make a short birdie putt to tie. Pepper missed and Pak won by one shot.

Webb played the 18th conservatively, splitting the middle of the fairway with her tee shot using a fairway wood. Her attempt to lay up short of the green with an iron failed. She left the ball in the rough 133 yards from the hole. With a flier lie, she expected the ball to jump out of the rough, but she was fooled again and her third shot found the bunker. Webb hit the bunker shot through the green and into the back fringe. The crowd began to murmur at that point, and Pak could hear the groans from her position in the scorer's tent. Webb needed to save par to force a playoff. Her chip ran six feet past, and her uphill putt for bogey never touched the hole.

"Just like a year ago," said Pak, who never saw Webb hit a shot on the 18th but followed the action by listening to the crowd. "I heard sounds like I heard today and I knew I won."

Webb was visibly shaken as she tapped in for double bogey, a final 74 and a total of 281. Afterward, like everyone else, she couldn't believe she had let this one get away. "Obviously, I'm bitter right now," she said. "I'm not going to have many chances to make double bogey to lose a tournament. That's something I never expected."

Safeco Classic—$650,000
Winner: Maria Hjorth

Even though the scores were some of the lowest of the LPGA season, no player seemed ready to break away and capture the Safeco Classic in Kent, Washington, until Swedish sensation Maria Hjorth shot a career-low 64 for a 271 total, 17 under par, to edge Catriona Matthew by two strokes. It was Hjorth's first victory as a professional, and she had to come from behind and beat a group of veterans to do it.

"I had a great amateur career and I always believed that if you can do it there you can do it here," the 25-year-old Hjorth said. "This shows me that I have the capability to win."

Hjorth didn't have much time to ponder her position as she never held the lead until the 71st hole. Chris Johnson led after shooting 64 in the opening round which included eight birdies from outside 18 feet, one 45-footer and two 30-footers. The putter didn't stay hot for long. Johnson shot 75 in the second round and never recovered. She finished the week in sixth place.

Helen Alfredsson picked up where Johnson left off, shooting 65 to reach 133 and take a two-shot lead over Catriona Matthew. Alfredsson's reign would also be short. A 73-73 weekend for a 280 total left her tied for 12th. Even though Hjorth continued to play well, shooting 69, 68 and 70, she wasn't even the low Swede going into the final round. Matthew entered the final round at 204, but that put her one back of Rachel Hetherington, who jumped to the top with 65 to go with earlier rounds of 70 and 68 for a 203 total. Johnson rebounded on Saturday with 66 to move two back, while Hjorth's 207 left her in a tie for fifth.

Hjorth moved quickly in the final round, making six birdies in her first seven holes. After pars at the eighth and ninth, she tied the course record (30), but still trailed Matthew (who had wrestled the lead back from Hetherington) by two. A birdie at the 13th drew Hjorth to within one. Matthew three-putted the 12th for bogey and Hjorth was tied for the lead. Birdie putts by Hjorth at the 14th, 15th and 16th skirted past the hole, but on the 17th she found the cup with her birdie effort and the lead was hers. Moments later Matthew made another bogey at the 15th, finished with 69 for a 273 total, and Hjorth cruised in with the victory.

Safeway LPGA Championship—$800,000
Winner: Juli Inkster

From the moment her name appeared atop the leaderboard during the first round, the murmurs started circulating around the Columbia Edgewater Country Club in Portland, Oregon. Was this to be the week Juli Inkster broke though? Was the Safeway LPGA Championship going to be it? Would Inkster obtain the one victory she needed for the Hall of Fame? "I don't talk about it because I don't like to look ahead," Inkster said. "That can put extra pressure on you."

When Inkster shot 67 to tie Rosie Jones for the first-round lead, she couldn't help but talk about the Hall of Fame because that was all the media wanted to discuss. "About the only time she talked about the Hall of Fame is when she started a tournament well and the media brought it up," Inkster's husband, Brian, said.

"Even early in the year when the criteria was changed, I felt I was still a thousand miles away," she said. "Seven points seemed like an awful lot." The LPGA criteria had been adjusted early in the season so that rather than requiring a player to win 30 events, 27 points (with major championship victories counting two points) qualified someone for the Hall. Inkster entered the year with 20 points, but two major championship wins and two other victories left her only one point shy.

A second-round 70 almost secured that point. Inkster held a three-shot lead over Michele Redman. A decent final round and Inkster's best year in her 16-year career would be complete. As if scripted, Inkster got off to a fast start on Sunday, reaching two under par for the day, nine under for the week, and opening a six-shot lead over Tina Barrett and Grace Park. The last few holes were a victory lap with fans chanting "Hall of Fame" after every shot and an appreciative Inkster waving to everyone she passed.

When she tapped in for par at the last hole for 70 and a 207 total for a six-stroke victory over Barrett and Park, a shower of champagne awaited. "Not in my wildest dreams did I think this would happen to me," she said. "It's hard to believe I got seven points in one year. I'm just glad it's over. This is what you play for, the respect of your peers."

Among those waiting on the 18th hole were fellow Hall of Famers Nancy

Lopez and Beth Daniel, along with Karrie Webb, who missed the cut but stayed for the celebration. "I stayed for this because it is so special," Webb said. "It is awesome what she had accomplished."

New Albany Classic—$1,000,000
Winner: Annika Sorenstam

With only one victory through the first nine months, Annika Sorenstam had critics wondering when she would break out of her slump. In New Albany, Ohio, Sorenstam took the lead in the second round and put on a weekend clinic, shooting 68, 66, 69 and 66 for a 269 total, 19 under par, to win the inaugural New Albany Classic by three strokes over Mardi Lunn.

If Sorenstam had made any putts outside 15 feet, she would have run away with it. Her 134 total after two days provided a two-shot lead over Liselotte Neumann, and she maintained that margin over Lunn on Saturday. She never gave up the lead, but Lunn gained a share of the top spot on Sunday with three birdies on the last four holes of the first nine.

Sorenstam missed two fairways and four greens in the final round but never by more than a few feet and never came close to making a bogey. She broke away on the 12th hole with a birdie putt from three feet. That came after she missed four birdie putts in a row from inside 12 feet. Rather than let her putting woes get the best of her, Sorenstam just started hitting it closer. She birdied the 14th, 15th and 16th holes with putts ranging from four to 10 feet. Lunn could only manage one birdie in the final nine holes for 67 and a 272 total.

"The way I played today is as good as I can play," Sorenstam said. "It has been a long year, but sitting here right now, looking at the way I played today, it has been worth it. I learned a lot this year. I've had a lot of changes this year, but I also learned a lot about my game and about myself and about what is important. I felt like I was in control this week. Every shot I hit and every move I made, I knew what I was doing. I know I can play. I just haven't been able to perform this year. I still feel like I know how, and that makes me feel stronger inside."

First Union Betsy King Classic—$725,000
Winner: Mi Hyun Kim

Korean rookie Mi Hyun Kim couldn't have been happier when she recovered from a poorly played three-wood shot and subsequent bogey on the 71st hole to par the 72nd and capture her second victory of the year at the First Union Betsy King Classic. Her eight-under-par 280 total included rounds of 68, 72, 70 and a final-round 70 that she didn't complete until the sun had already set behind the Pennsylvania pines.

"I am more happy than surprised," Kim said. "At the beginning of the year I wanted to be the top rookie and finish in the top 10 on the money list. I also wanted one win. To win for a second time is a bonus."

It was also something of a marathon, with rain and two days of frost delays. Kim opened with 68 to trail Amy Benz and Lisa Kiggens by one.

Marisa Baena and Jenny Lidback were atop the leaderboard at 138 after Friday's round, with Kim two shots back. On Saturday, battling frost, cold temperatures and windy afternoon conditions, Kim shot 70 to put herself in a threesome tied for second at 210, one stroke behind Beth Daniel.

After Daniel made an early bogey in the final round, the Korean seized the lead with a birdie at the seventh. She increased the lead on the ninth with another birdie. Daniel, a member of the LPGA Hall of Fame, hadn't won since 1995. King, her college teammate, had played herself into contention with two early birdies to tie Daniel for second place, two shots behind the leader. For a while, it looked as though Kim would give the veterans a chance. She missed birdie putts at the 11th, 14th and 15th, then hit her three-wood second shot on the par-five 17th into a water hazard that guarded the front of the green. "I thought I had blown the tournament," she said.

But Daniel bogeyed the 13th and 15th holes and King bogeyed the 13th and 17th. With a par on the 18th at dusk, Kim watched as Daniel attempted a 20-foot birdie putt that would have tied her for the lead. The putt came up short, and Kim had her second victory of the season, this one without a shred of controversy.

AFLAC Tournament of Champions—$750,000
Winner: Akiko Fukushima

The 44 players invited to the AFLAC Tournament of Champions could have called the 1998 Nike Tour graduates to get a preview of the Magnolia Grove Crossing course in Mobile, Alabama, but if they had some of them might have chosen to stay home. "Perhaps they should add a couple of windmills and a dinosaur," Laura Davies said of the severely undulating greens. "Robert Trent Jones was in a bad mood when he designed this one."

Those comments were mild compared to what the Nike Tour players expressed during their championship at the end of the 1998 season, but the feelings were much the same. "Impossible," is how Karrie Webb described the greens. "If you start out struggling, the targets start to look smaller than they really are." According to Davies, the targets were small enough to begin with. "You have to land it in a tea cup," she said.

It isn't surprising that the AFLAC Tournament of Champions was decided by a three-putt from 80 feet across a ridge line in the 72nd green. Sweden's Maria Hjorth led when her 64 in the second round for a 135 total gave her a three-shot advantage over Cindy Figg-Currier. That lead remained intact throughout the third round, when Hjorth shot 72. Webb joined Figg-Currier, Davies and Chris Johnson in second place, while Akiko Fukushima was four shots off the lead.

For a while on Sunday it looked as if Kelly Robbins, who began the week with rounds of 74 and 75, would charge into the lead. After shooting 66 in the third round, Robbins made six birdies in the first 16 holes to pull within one of the lead. A bogey on the 18th dashed Robbins' hopes. She finished with 67 and settled for a tie for fifth place. Webb also appeared to be making a move, but she could only manage 70 for a 280 total, one more than she needed.

The player who managed to escape unscathed was Fukushima, who followed her Saturday 69 with 68 for a 279 total. She had tied Hjorth, who still had the par-four 18th to play. After a good tee shot, Hjorth tried to play a conservative approach, but the ball hit on the wrong side of one of the many slopes and rolled some 80 feet away. She needed two putts to take the event to extra holes. Her first putt came up five feet short, but her second putt dove right and missed, giving Fukushima a one-shot margin of victory.

PageNet Tour Championship—$1,000,000
Winner: Se Ri Pak

With the 30 top money winners in Las Vegas for the PageNet Tour Championship, the odds-makers were betting on a showdown between leading money winner Karrie Webb, the winner of six events in 1999, and new Hall of Famer Juli Inkster, who had five victories including two majors. Then there was Se Ri Pak, who had three victories under her belt.

Pak, who arrived eight days early to practice, opened with a bogey-free 66 to take a one-shot lead over Janice Moodie and a two-shot edge over Webb, Lorie Kane and Kelly Robbins. If that didn't get everyone's attention, the 66 Pak shot next to set a tournament record of 12-under-par 132 certainly did. The South Korean opened a five-shot lead over Laura Davies (71-66) going into the weekend. Suddenly the odds shifted, and Pak became the best bet.

Those who rushed to the casinos suffered anxiety pangs on Saturday, however. Pak never felt comfortable with her swing, and after hitting one tee shot out of bounds and carding four bogeys she rallied with two birdies on the second nine to shoot 74. That dropped Pak into a tie for the lead with Kane. The two would be paired on Sunday, knotted at 206, one ahead of Inkster and two clear of Davies and Webb.

Kane appeared tentative, even a little jumpy on Sunday as she backed away from several shots in the opening holes and continued to make pars throughout the day. The deciding moment for Kane came at the 15th when, after driving the ball into an area marked as ground under repair, she chose not to take a drop from what she considered a good lie, and instead pushed a four wood into a water hazard. The resulting bogey, coupled with another bogey at the 18th, dropped Kane to 74 for the day, 280 for the tournament and alone in fifth place.

"This has never been about money," she said, fighting back tears. "It's about trying to do your best. I'll find a way to win somehow."

That's exactly the same attitude Pak took into the final round, even as she watched Davies make birdies at the 11th, 12th and 13th holes to wrestle away the lead. Pak remained steady, coming in with two birdies for 70 and a 276 total, good enough to tie Webb, who had finished with 68, and Davies, who shot 68 and barely missed winning in regulation when her chip at the 18th lipped out.

In the playoff, Pak drove in the middle of the fairway, hit an eight-iron approach to within five feet, and rolled in a birdie to clinch her fourth win of the year and her second playoff victory against Webb. "She's got my number right now," Webb said. "Se Ri had four wins this year and in three of them I finished second, including two playoffs."

Pak was all smiles, thanking her friends and saying, "I am happy now that everything in my game is fine. I feel really lucky because there are so many good people out there to help me."

Ladies European Tour

Royal Marie-Claire Open-£50,000
Winner: Silvia Cavalleri

This may have been an unofficial event in terms of the Order of Merit on the newly renamed Ladies European Tour, but that did not concern Italy's Silvia Cavalleri. The U.S. and European Amateur champion of 1997 earned her first professional title by one stroke over Federica Dassu, her experienced compatriot, and Spain's Ana Belen Sanchez.

Cavalleri, a 26-year-old from Milan who was 55th on the money list in her rookie season in 1998, scored rounds of 71, 73 and 71 for a one-under-par total of 215. She earned a winner's prize of £7,500 and entry to the first official event of the season, the Evian Masters over the same Royal Evian course.

"I played steady over all three days and apart from a couple of careless moments I was very pleased with my round," said Cavalleri. "My aim this year is to get into the top 30 on the Order of Merit and having a place now in the Evian Masters gives me a good chance of that."

Evian Masters—€1,021,408
Winner: Catrin Nilsmark

Most of the continent's top players returned home from America for the start of the new season and to play in the Evian Masters, the richest event in the history of women's golf in Europe. Having already won the Los Angeles Open, Catrin Nilsmark made it a transatlantic double by taking the £100,800 first prize. The Swede won by two strokes over Laura Davies, with Alison Nicholas a shot further back.

Davies led with a round to play but Nilsmark made light of her two-stroke deficit with seven birdies in the first 13 holes. Three ahead with two to play, the 32-year-old dropped a shot at the 17th and then saw Davies hit her second at the par-five 18th to five feet. Nilsmark was just off the green and her chip came up six feet short and she had settled for a par by the time Davies attempted her eagle putt. But the Englishwoman missed, as she had the previous day, and, just when everyone assumed a playoff would follow, took two more putts to hole out. Nilsmark's rounds of 69, 70, 72 and 68 gave her a nine-under-par total of 279.

"Laura is always a factor," Nilsmark said. "My mental game has improved a lot since the birth of my daughter, although I was a little nervous on the final hole."

Chrysler Open—€223,950
Winner: Laura Davies

The same players were in the top three at the Halmstad course in Sweden, but the order was different as Laura Davies retained her Chrysler Open title. Nor was it quite so close. Davies won by eight strokes over Alison Nicholas, with Catrin Nilsmark two shots further behind. Helen Alfredsson, another local, tied for fourth with Ana Belen Sanchez, while Liselotte Neumann took sixth place.

It was the 55th win of Davies' career but her first for nine months. Davies moved into the lead at halfway after rounds of 71 and 69, then added a 66 which took her five in front and closed the week with 67 for a 15-under-par score of 273.

"I was a little nervous at the start of the day, but after birdies at the first two holes I relaxed and enjoyed the remainder of the round," said Davies, who has won at least once every season since turning professional in 1985. "I can't remember having only four bogeys over four days, especially on a course as good as this one. I joked earlier in the week that I would retire if anybody shot 16 under par on this course because it really is a tough layout. Thankfully, it was me who got close to that number. I have been playing well recently but couldn't sink the putts, but I had only 25 yesterday and 28 today which is very satisfying."

Ladies' French Open—€149,300
Winner: Trish Johnson

Alison Nicholas suffered another near-miss in the Ladies' French Open. The former U.S. Open winner finished second for the second week running but was outdone by Trish Johnson, who was determined not to add to her run of three runner-up finishes in the last year. Johnson and Nicholas both closed with five-under-par rounds of 67 at the Paris International course but Johnson won by one stroke. Fiona Pike, Anne-Marie Knight and Mette Hageman tied for third, three behind the winners, with Patricia Meunier Lebouc a further shot back.

Meunier, a 27-year-old from Paris and one of the third-round leaders, was cheered to the turn as she went out in 34. But there was to be no home winner as Meunier bogeyed the 13th, 14th and 15th holes on the way back in 39.

Instead, Johnson came to the last even with Nicholas, who had failed to birdie the par-five 18th despite her drive receiving a favorable kick off a cart path. Nicholas had only 155 yards to the green but found herself in an awkward lie and decided to lay up. When Johnson, amazingly, also hit the path, she needed no second invitation to go for the green in two with a nine iron and secured the winning birdie.

Her scores of 70, 70, 75 and 67 gave her a total of 282, six under par, and the 11th win of her European tour career but first for three years. "I'd been aiming for that path all week and thankfully hit it today, you need a bit of luck sometimes," Johnson said.

Ladies' Austrian Open—€149,300
Winner: Marina Arruti

While Dale Reid, the 2000 European Solheim Cup captain, and Germany's Elisabeth Esterl thought they were in a private battle to decide the winner of the Ladies' Austria Open, Spain's Marina Arruti birdied the last three holes to beat the pair by one stroke. Arruti, after two rounds of 68, closed with 67 for a 13-under-par total of 203 in the 54-hole event at Steiermarkischer in Graz.

Arruti, who won for the first time five years after turning professional, is the younger sister of Amaia, who won as a rookie in 1993. Their father Jose and uncle Jesus are the pros at Real San Sebastian, where Jose Maria Olazabal learned his golf.

While Reid three-putted the 16th and 17th holes, Arruti needed only a tap-in for her birdie at the 16th and then holed eight-footers at the last two. "I knew I had to birdie the last three just to have a chance of a playoff," she said. "I don't think I have ever had a finish like that in a tournament and I was surprisingly relaxed on the 18th tee because I knew I was playing so well. I think Dale and Elisabeth were concentrating on each other and forgot about me."

stilwerk Ladies' German Open—€149,300
Winner: Anne-Marie Knight

Anne-Marie Knight found the perfect moment to produce the lowest round of her four-year professional career. Her final-round 64, with two halves of 32, was not only a new course record for the Treudelberg Club but gave her victory in the stilwerk Ladies' German Open by one stroke over Laura Davies and Sophie Gustafson, both of whom closed with 65s. With earlier rounds of 74, 69 and 71, Knight, who had not won before on the European tour, finished at 278, 10 under par.

Gustafson, who had collected four birdies in a row earlier in her round, would have got into a playoff with the Australian had she claimed her third consecutive birdie at the 18th, but the Swede missed from 18 inches. Davies holed from 30 feet for an eagle to share second place.

"I've had three second places on the Ladies European Tour so I am thrilled to have won at last," said Knight, who only got a late release from the LPGA to play in the event. "That was the best round of my life. I was certainly in the 'zone'. Everything I looked at I knew was going to go in. I think we all fed off each other today as we played marvelous golf."

McDonald's WPGA Championship of Europe—€447,900
Winner: Laura Davies

Laura Davies won for the second time in Europe, having been runner-up in her other two events, after beating Maria Hjorth at the second extra hole in the McDonald's WPGA Championship of Europe. Both players finished at eight under par, Davies after a closing 72, and Hjorth with 69, the best score on a day of strongly gusting winds at Gleneagles.

Among those blown away was Catrin Nilsmark, who lost the leadership of the Order of Merit to Davies after letting slip a five-stroke lead. Nilsmark, the leader for the first three days, came home in 42 on the way to 80.

"That was my worst day ever on a golf course," Nilsmark said. She finished sixth, while Janice Moodie and Alison Nicholas shared third place and Trish Johnson took fifth.

Davies, who looked out of the event for much of the day, finished in typically dramatic fashion with birdies at the last two holes before securing victory with a par at the second playoff hole. Davies won €67,185 while Hjorth, who gained a degree in English from nearby Stirling University, equaled her best-ever result on tour.

"This is a title I've always wanted to win, and as this could be the last year of the event, I'm thrilled to have finally won it," Davies said after collecting her 30th European victory. "I went out thinking I was playing for second place because Catrin had such a good lead. After a horrible start with a double bogey on the third, I just told myself not to fall too far behind second spot."

Moodie, who earlier in the event had called a one-shot penalty on herself when her ball moved on a green, narrowly missed out on the playoff when her 30-footer at the last shaved the hole. The 26-year-old Scot had spent the previous evening in the hospital with her father who became ill during the tournament.

Weetabix Women's British Open—€858,475
Winner: Sherri Steinhauer

After winning the previous year at Royal Lytham, Sherri Steinhauer became the first player to retain the Weetabix Women's British Open since Donna Massey in 1981. Having made a surprising comeback from an opening 81 the year before, Steinhauer held on to her third-round lead to win by one over Annika Sorenstam. Helen Dobson, Cindy Flom and Fiona Pike all shared third place one stroke further back.

While the 36-year-old from Wisconsin had birdied the last hole at Lytham to set a target which no one else could beat in 1998, Steinhauer came to the par-five 18th at Woburn even with Sorenstam, who had already finished at eight under. Her third shot with a nine iron took a kind kick off a bank on the right of the green and left her with an eight-foot birdie putt which she duly holed.

"This is an incredible feeling and different from any other win I've ever had," said Steinhauer, who had won the JAL Big Apple Classic on the LPGA Tour a month earlier. The American opened with two rounds of 71 and took the lead with 68 on Saturday. Her final round of 73, even par, contained four birdies but also two bogeys and a double bogey.

"Last week in Boston I had a three-shot lead and doubled the third and didn't win," Steinhauer added. "This week I had a one-shot lead and doubled the first and thought, 'Oh, no, here we go again.' It really shook me. But I am pleased with the way I handled it and in many ways this win is more satisfying than last year when I came from behind. This one I will never forget.

"I don't really watch the leaderboard when I'm out there, but I had a feeling I needed a birdie on 18. Whenever I made a mistake today I was penalized for it, but I got a break with my nine iron."

Steinhauer won €149,300 and Sorenstam, who saw her own birdie effort on the final green slide past the hole, €89,580. "It was as if there was a lid on the hole today," Sorenstam said. "The only one that dropped was at the 16th, but I played some really good golf over the last 12 holes and that is all you can do sometimes."

Compaq Open—€447,900
Winner: Laura Davies

After a disappointing week at Woburn, a course she has rarely enjoyed, Laura Davies returned to winning with her second victory of the season in Sweden. Davies won the Compaq Open at Osterakers on the outskirts of Stockholm by beating Sweden's Helen Alfredsson by four strokes, while Alison Nicholas collected a fifth top-three finish of the season a further shot back.

Davies and Alfredsson took the first-day lead with rounds of 67, but Davies went ahead on her own with rounds of 69 and 71. Trish Johnson, two behind after three rounds, closed with a 76 to fall to fourth place, while both Davies and Alfredsson finished with 70s. Davies' total of 277 was 15 under par.

"I didn't want to give any hint of making a mistake today," Davies said, "because there were so many good players behind me who could have taken advantage of that. But I didn't drop any shots and didn't give them any chances of catching me."

Cantor Fitzgerald Laura Davies' Invitational—€447,900
Winner: Sofia Gronberg Whitmore

Laura Davies played the dutiful host at the tournament set up in her honor at Brocket Hall, just north of London, and that included letting others steal the limelight. Davies finished tied for 13th, 12 strokes out of a playoff that saw Sofia Gronberg Whitmore defeat Trish Johnson at the second extra hole. Spain's Raquel Carriedo finished third, six strokes back.

Johnson had earlier equaled the tour record for nine holes by taking only 29 strokes to the turn to move into contention with Gronberg, the overnight leader. The Swede, who has two children with her English husband, made a great save at the 16th and then birdied the 17th to draw even with Johnson, who went in the water at the par-five 18th for the third time in the tournament and bogeyed the hole. Johnson closed with a 65, a new course record, and Gronberg, 69 to be 13 under.

Both parred the 18th the first time around in extra holes but, playing the hole again, Gronberg hit her six-iron second shot to six feet while Johnson went over the back of the green. Johnson played a good chip but missed the five-footer for par while Gronberg two-putted for the winning birdie.

"Surprisingly I felt very calm on the tee each time, but I felt like being sick over that putt," said Gronberg. "Trish played an unbelievable chip and I must admit I was very relieved when she missed the putt. I was quite glad I had two to get down."

globalgolf.com Donegal Irish Ladies' Open—€149,300
Winner: Sandrine Mendiburu

Another playoff was needed to decide the globalgolf.com Donegal Irish Open as France's Sandrine Mendiburu won on the second extra hole at Letterkenny. It was her second tour victory, the first having come in Portugal in 1994. Laura Davies, Spain's Raquel Carriedo and Elisabeth Esterl of Germany shared second place after all four finished at 286, two over par.

Mendiburu, a 26-year-old from Bayonne, might have won in regulation had her six-foot birdie putt at the last hole not hit the cup and stayed out. Mendiburu and Esterl had closing rounds of 72, while Davies had 69 and Carriedo moved up from 16th place with 67, the day's lowest score.

Esterl made a six at the par-five 18th to drop out of the playoff at the first extra hole, where Davies was just short of the green in two but failed to get up and down. Playing the hole again, Davies topped her second shot into a ditch and, though a brilliant recovery left her beside the green in three, she again failed to get down in two. Mendiburu was left with two putts from six feet for the victory. "I am very happy and, to be honest, a little surprised because my mental game has been very poor and I wasn't expecting to win this year," Mendiburu said.

Ladies' Hannover Expo 2000 Open—€149,300
Winner: Sandrine Mendiburu

If she was not expecting to win once this year, winning two weeks later at the Hannover Expo 2000 Open at the Rethmar Golf Links was an even bigger surprise for Sandrine Mendiburu. The Frenchwoman, who scored 64 in the second round, won the 54-hole event by two strokes over Lora Fairclough with an eight-under-par 208. Fairclough finished with 67 to Mendiburu's 71, but the early challenger in the final round, Sweden's Anna Berg, slumped on the back nine and ended up sixth.

No one had won back-to-back on the Ladies European Tour since Liselotte Neumann in 1994. "It's great to win again," Mendiburu said. "This gives me the energy and incentive to practice hard throughout the winter. My aim now is to make the team for the European Cup against the seniors and, although it's still a long way away now, I'd love to qualify for next year's Solheim Cup."

Ladies' Italian Open—€149,300
Winner: Samantha Head

Though her identical twin sister Johanna won in Asia at the start of the year, Samantha Head won the race to a first Ladies European Tour victory, four years after they turned professional, with a one-stroke win in the Italian Open at Poggio dei Medici in Tuscany. Head finished at five-under-par 214 after a final round of 71 in which she had four birdies. A three-putt bogey at the 18th meant she had to endure a nervous few minutes. Finland's Riikka Hakkarainen had a 12-footer at the 18th to tie but missed, while Trish Johnson three-putted to fall into a tie for second with Hakkarainen, Marina Arruti, Patricia Meunier Lebouc and Mette Hageman.

"I thought I had blown it at the last and I didn't expect Trish to three-putt. I kept asking James, my husband, to pinch me because I couldn't believe I'd won," said the 26-year-old Head, whose sister finished tied for 12th. "Jo has been playing better than me for most of the season, which put extra pressure on me. But for some reason we both knew I'd win before she did." Head took most of the 1998 season off to nurse her husband through a life-threatening illness. "This time last year James was recovering from an operation and I didn't know if he would come through it. An experience like that puts everything else into perspective."

Air France Madame Biarritz Open—€149,300
Winner: Sofia Gronberg Whitmore

Sofia Gronberg Whitmore became the third player to win two titles in the season and she beat one of the others, local favorite Sandrine Mendiburu, to secure a three-stroke victory in the Air France Madame Open at Golf de Biarritz Le Phare. After both players scored two rounds of 66, Gronberg closed with 68 in the final round, three better than Mendiburu, to finish at 200, 10 under par. Australian Nicola Munt finished third after a five-under 65 on the final day.

While Mendiburu began with seven straight pars, Gronberg got off to a terrible start with a triple bogey at the first, where she lost a ball up a tree and had to go back to the tee, and a bogey at the next. Six birdies between the ninth and the 15th put her into the lead.

"At the first I was absolutely gutted when my ball disappeared up a tree and I got even more upset when I made a silly mistake at the second," Gronberg said. "But I think my start might have worked in my favor. It gave me strength and helped me to focus more. It was the same at Brocket Hall when I won. I learned from my poor start there."

Marrakesh Palmeraie Open—€149,300
Winner: Trish Johnson

Trish Johnson made it a quartet of double winners by adding the season's final event, the Marrakesh Palmeraie Open, to her earlier French Open crown. The 32-year-old certainly made sure the tour ended in a blaze of brilliant golf. Johnson began her final round with seven consecutive birdies, equaling the tour record, on the way to 67 and a 12-under-par total of 204.

Although Johnson secured a five-stroke victory, she did not provide all the dramatics herself as Belgium's Valerie Van Ryckeghem took second place by a shot from Spain's Raquel Carriedo with a closing 66. Van Ryckeghem holed a seven iron for an eagle two at the second hole and then used the same club to make a hole in one at the 153-yard third. "I didn't see the eagle go in but I did see the hole in one," said the 24-year-old Van Ryckeghem. "I was shaking and very nervous for a couple of holes after that."

Johnson could have won a number of times and she ended the season with 10 top-10 finishes in 12 events. "It's a great feeling to finish with a win," Johnson said. "It goes some way to making up for a few chances this season." Her run of birdies ended at the eighth where she missed from 15 feet but was not too worried as she had a six-shot lead. "I suppose if I had putted a little better these past few months it would have been a remarkable season. I'm still a little gutted about not winning the Laura Davies' Invitational as I played some of my best golf ever that week. But I've got a lot to build on for next year and will certainly enjoy the party tonight."

Johnson finished fifth on the Order of Merit, which was won for the fifth time by Laura Davies.

Princess Lalla Meriem Cup—US$70,000
Winner: Lora Fairclough

England's Lora Fairclough became the first player to win the Princess Lalla Meriem Cup twice at the Royal Dar-es-Salam course in Rabat, Morocco. The tournament, an unofficial event alongside the Hassan II Trophy, became the 29-year-old Fairclough's first win of the season.

Fairclough, who earned $13,000, had previously won the event in 1996. She came to the third and final round tied for the lead with Sweden's Sofia Gronberg Whitmore. Fairclough bogeyed the first two holes, but rallied to be the only player to match the par of 73 in the closing round. With two earlier rounds of 72, Fairclough finished at 217, two under par, and won by two over Samantha Head.

The challenges of Gronberg, Head and Spain's Amaia Arruti all faltered with double bogeys in the last 10 holes. Gronberg finished third, four behind Fairclough, with Arruti, two strokes further back, tying for fourth with Head's twin sister, Johanna.

Praia D'el Rey Rover European Cup—€210,000
Winners: Ladies European Tour

After a victory in the inaugural match in 1997 by the team from the European Seniors Tour was followed by a halved match the next year, the Ladies European Tour won for the first time in the third European Cup at Praia D'el Rey in Portugal. The winning margin of 11-9 was made possible after a 6-4 win in the singles.

Going into the final day, the match was even. The Seniors won the foursomes on the first day 3-2, Laura Davies and Alison Nicholas with the only win for the women over Alan Tapie and Bill Brask. But the women fought back to take the fourballs by the same margin, Tommy Horton and John Morgan gaining the Seniors' only win over Davies and Trish Johnson.

In a tightly contested final series, six of the 10 matches were decided on the final green, from which the women won four points. Johnson and Davies were both four-up at the turn but went the full distance before securing wins over Ross Metherell and Jerry Bruner, respectively. John Morgan was the only player on either side with a maximum three points after beating Nicholas, 2 and 1, and Alan Tapie and David Jones added two more wins for the Seniors.

The women secured their victory when Sofia Gustafson beat Neil Coles 5 and 3, Marie-Laure de Lorenzi defeated Eddie Polland 4 and 3, and Lora Fairclough beat Antonio Garrido at the 18th.

"This was a great result for women's golf in Europe," said captain de Lorenzi. "It was a tough match and I am delighted and very proud of my team that we have won for the first time. This was a great way to end the season. We had a real mixture of players and I was very happy with the way they blended together and played to such a high standard."

Seniors captain Horton said, "The ladies were stronger than in the past and a bit more buoyant with Laura Davies around. The women's tour is in a much better position than it has been in the past and the Seniors Tour is getting better all the time. I definitely think there is a place for this match in the calendar."

Japan LPGA Tour

Daikin Orchid—¥60,000,000
Winner: Yoko Inoue

Yoko Inoue parlayed a course-record-tying round into victory in the season-opening Daikin Orchid tournament at Shimajiri. Inoue, capturing her third victory in six years, blistered the Ryukyu Golf Club with an eight-under-par 64 in the second round to take a three-stroke lead and she rode that margin to victory that Sunday in early March despite a 73 finish. She wound up at 206, 10 under par, three ahead of runner-up Ok-Hee Ku, the highly successful South Korean golfer, and Kasumi Fujii.

Rookie Midori Yoneyama, 22, had also tied the course record Friday when she jumped off to a three-stroke lead over Mayumi Murai. Ku and Michiko Hattori, 1998's top money winner, were among six players at 68 and Inoue began with 69. Like Yoneyama, Inoue ran off nine birdies (the tour record) and took a bogey in shooting her 64 Saturday for 133. Ku moved up to second place with 68–136 as Yoneyama took a 73 and dropped into a third-place tie at 137 with Fujii. Determined to "keep concentration until the end of play," Inoue struggled with two bogeys, only able to offset one with her lone birdie in difficult, windy weather Sunday that plagued the field. Ku could do no better than 73 and Fujii 72 Sunday.

It was the first time in five years that a Japanese player won the season-opening Daikin Orchid. Inoue had not won on tour in almost three years.

Saishunkan Ladies—¥60,000,000
Winner: Nahoko Hirao

Sometimes familiarity breeds not contempt but victory, as was the case when Nahoko Hirao landed her first win in the Saishunkan Ladies tournament. The third-season pro had trained at Kumamoto Kuukou Country Club at Kikuyo for two years before joining the tour. That didn't help her much on her first two visits back home for the tournament, but the third time panned out superbly for the 25-year-old as she led from the start, dropped back into a closing tie with Michie Ohba, then won on the first hole of the event's second straight playoff. Michiko Hattori launched her money-leading season with a third-hole playoff win in 1998.

Hirao, who had overhauled her swing at the end of 1998, jumped off to a four-stroke lead at Kumamoto Kuukou Friday with a career-best, six-under-par 66. The 70-shooters were South Korea's Young-Me Lee and Lee Oh-Soon, Taiwan's Yu-Chuan Tai, Aki Takamura and Kaori Harada, the second-place finisher on the 1998 money list. Although she shot 75 Saturday, Hirao retained her four-stroke lead as the blustery, wet weather took a toll on nearly everybody. Rookie Tomo Sakakibara was the exception, mustering a 71 that elevated her into a second-place tie at 145 with Takamura, who matched the leader's 75.

A 74 Sunday cost Hirao her big margin as Ohba entered the picture with 69 for a 215 that tied her for the lead. The overtime play ended quickly as Hirao rolled in a 13-foot birdie putt when the two replayed the par-five 18th again. Harumi Sakagami and Hee-Won Han missed the playoff by one stroke with 216s.

Nasu Ogawa Ladies—¥37,500,000
Winner: Ok-Hee Ku

Ok-Hee Ku will take the victories any way she can get them. The veteran South Korean star picked up her 15th win on the Japan LPGA Tour in an unusual fashion. The Nasu Ogawa tournament was shortened to 36 holes and she needed only a one-over-par 73 to rally from a one-stroke deficit to win by that margin on the Nasu Ogawa Golf Club course. With her 143, Ku finished one stroke in front of her young compatriot, Hee-Won Han, and Yukiko Ishiguro.

Han, the 1998 LPGA rookie of the year, led the way the first day in her quest for her first victory with an opening, three-under-par 69. The 20-year-old rang up three birdies as she finished one stroke ahead of Ku, Ishiguro and Fumiko Muraguchi. Heavy weather moved in Saturday and washed out the scheduled round. The field was reduced by one-third to 71 players for Sunday's finale and they had to battle severe winds that ballooned the scores. Ku, 42, made the best of the situation, managing three birdies to not quite offset the four bogeys on her card. But the 73–143 carried her to the title as Han took a 75 and Ishiguro a 74 to tie for second at 144.

Katokichi Queens—¥50,000,000
Winner: Ayako Okamoto

A year earlier, it appeared that the Japan LPGA Tour might have seen the last of Ayako Okamoto, one of its greatest champions. Severe back pains put Okamoto on the shelf in June and, at age 48, it seemed possible that she not only might not regain the form that had brought 61 victories in her brilliant international career but that she might not be able to overcome the ailment and get back in action at all. Okamoto refused to quit. With her back problems solved, she returned for the new season and in her fourth outing snatched a one-stroke victory, her 44th on the Japan LPGA Tour, in the Katokichi Queens tournament at Sakaide in Kagawa Prefecture in early May.

That the Okamoto victory was forthcoming was not evident after the Friday round. She shot 73 and trailed co-leaders Kyoko Ono and Hisako Ohgane and a batch of other players. Ono, seeking her second tour victory, and winless Ohgane shot two-under-par 70s. The lead shuffled Saturday as the scoring improved. Aki Takamura, an 18-tournament winner, made the best move, jumping in front with a 67 for 140 and a two-stroke lead over Taiwan's Yueh-Chyn Huang and Akemi Kuwashima.

Okamoto shot her first sub-par round in a year and moved into the picture at 143, then put away the victory Sunday with a 69. She overcame an early bogey with four birdies to slip past Takamura and finish at 212, one shot ahead of Aki (73) and Fumiko Muraguchi (70). It was the first win in Japan since the Open in June of 1997 for Okamoto, Japan's most successful international woman pro who played and won in America for 10 years until 1993.

Gunze Cup World Ladies—¥60,000,000
Winner: Yoko Inoue

With the unintended help of her closest rival, Yoko Inoue landed her second title of the young Japan LPGA Tour season, scoring a one-stroke victory in the Gunze Cup World Ladies tournament at Tokyo's Yomiuri Golf Club in early May. Yuri Fudoh bogeyed the 72nd hole for a 70 and 283, losing her chance for a playoff against the 27-year-old Inoue, who parred the final hole for 71 and the winning 282, six under par, in the year's first 72-hole event. It was the fourth victory in her six years on the circuit.

Early attention at Yomiuri focused on Se Ri Pak, the South Korean sensation of the 1998 LPGA season in America, who was playing in her first Japanese event and Pak didn't disappoint the crowds the first day. She shot 70 to place herself in a three-way tie for second place with little-known Kotomi Akiyama and Kaori Kono, one stroke behind 22-year-old rookie

Midori Yoneyama. But a second-round 76 spoiled her title bid and she eventually tied for sixth at 290.

Fudoh seized the lead Friday with 68 for 139, running off four birdies to go two strokes in front of Yoneyama, who had a 72–141. Inoue moved into third place with 69 after opening with 73, then grabbed the top spot Saturday when she repeated the 69 — four birdies and a bogey — for 211. Fudoh, winless in her four seasons on the tour, shot 74, slipping to second place. In the head-to-head duel Sunday, Fudoh inched into a tie with Inoue as they came down the stretch, only to take that fatal bogey at the final hole.

Yakult Ladies—¥60,000,000
Winner: Fumiko Muraguchi

Fumiko Muraguchi redeemed a 1998 disappointment and ended a two-season dry spell when she scored a two-stroke victory in the Yakult Ladies tournament at Munakata in mid-May. Her strongest bid for victory during the 1998 campaign came in the Yakult, where, after shooting herself into a playoff with a good finish, she lost to Aiko Takasu in overtime. The 32-year-old Muraguchi strung together three rounds in the 60s for an 11-under-par 205 and the fifth victory of her 10-year career.

Muraguchi began the week at Fukuoka Kokusai Country Club just one stroke off the lead as South Korea's Lee Oh-Soon opened with a 67 that included seven birdies in an eight-hole stretch. Ok-Hee Ku and Akemi Yamaoka shared the 68 slot with Muraguchi. Then, those three players produced matching 69s Saturday and took over first place with 137s, one shot ahead of four players, including Yuri Fudoh, who had eight birdies and shot 65.

Muraguchi, a one-time office worker, put the title away Sunday with a solid 68, as Fudoh posted 69 and Yamaoka 70 to tie for the runner-up spot at 207.

Chukyo TV Bridgestone Ladies—¥50,000,000
Winner: Fumiko Muraguchi

No long victory vigils this time. Fumiko Muraguchi, who had gone almost two years between wins when she captured the Yakult Ladies tournament the previous Sunday, marched to a three-stroke victory in the Chukyo TV Bridgestone at Kasugai Country Club in Aichi Prefecture. Just as she did the week before, Muraguchi staged a dominating finish with a five-under-par 67 for the winning 207 total. Her sixth career victory moved Fumiko to the top of the Japan LPGA Tour money list.

As was the case in the Yakult, the first day belonged to South Korea. Two members of that country's contingent — Hee-Won Han and Young-Me Lee — shared first place Friday with 68s, Han with a back-nine 31. Kaori Higo was at 69 and Muraguchi opened with 70. When Muraguchi duplicated that score Saturday, she moved into a tie for the lead with Han, who shot 72 for her 140. Lee slipped one stroke off the lead with 73 and Higo (73) remained in contention at 142 with Masaki Maeda and Mineko Nasu.

Muraguchi jumped ahead quickly Sunday with birdies on the first two holes and was never seriously threatened. She finished three strokes in front of Higo (68). Shin Sora had 68 for 211 and Yuki Fudoh closed with a 65 rush to grab fourth place at 212.

Kosaido Ladies Golf Cup—¥60,000,000
Winner: Junko Yasui

Two veterans battled through a four-hole playoff in the Kosaido Ladies Golf Cup tournament, Junko Yasui finally prevailing to land her first victory in nearly four years. Yasui sank a 27-foot birdie putt on the par-five 18th hole to defeat 39-year-old Miyuki Shimabukuro, who hadn't won since 1993. It was Yasui's 11th career victory and first since the Fujisankei in 1995.

For the second time this season, rookie Midori Yoneyama seized the first-round lead, this time with birdies on the last two holes for a three-under-par 69 and a one-stroke margin over Mineko Nasu and South Korea's Jae-Sook Won. Shimabukuro was in a four-woman group at 71 and Yasui began with 73. They both still trailed after 36 holes as Nasu, 27, winless in four years on the tour, inched into a one-stroke lead with 71 for 141. Yoneyama slipped to 73 and into a second-place tie with Orie Fujino. Shimabukuro (72) and Yasui (70) were among four players at 143.

Nasu crumbled with 79 Sunday, opening the door for the two seasoned pros. Playing in different groups, both shot 72s to forge the tie at 215, one under par at the Chiba Kosaido Country Club course. Yoneyama's bid for her first tour win faded with a 75–217.

Resort Trust Ladies—¥50,000,000
Winner: Hiromi Takamura

Five years beyond her last victory and nearly a decade past her finest season, Hiromi Takamura had been entertaining thoughts of retirement. "I haven't been playing well for so long," she observed after finding her old touch in the opening round of the Resort Trust tournament at Asukecho. Takamura had just shot a seven-under-par 65 at St. Creek Golf Club, a score that gave her a three-stroke lead. Her game remained intact for the rest of the week and the 45-year-old player rolled to a four-stroke victory with an eight-under-par 208 total.

Takamura's start Friday gave no sign of what was coming. She bogeyed the second hole, but then rang up eight birdies the rest of the way for the course-record 68 and the three-shot edge over Harumi Sakagami, Natsuko Noro and Midori Yoneyama, the talented rookie and former collegiate star at nearby Aichi University who had made several sound showings earlier in the campaign. Although shooting just 71 Saturday, Takamura widened her margin to five strokes on the windy day. Sakagami shot 73 and shared the runner-up slot with Young-Me Lee, Kasumi Adachi and Mikino Kubo.

Takamura shook off a tentative start Sunday, carded 72 for the 208, which gave her the four-shot victory over Lee. Nobody else was closer than seven as Takamura, the leading money winner in 1990, posted her eighth career

victory and first since the 1994 Toyo Suisan Ladies Hokkaido. As for retirement? "I don't have to now, at least not for another season."

Suntory Ladies Open—¥50,000,000
Winner: Kaori Higo

For two days, Kaori Higo had the upper hand in the Suntory Ladies Open,
but in the final round she had her hands full, eventually coming from three
strokes off the lead to force a playoff and win on the fourth extra hole. It
was her eighth career victory and first in almost a year.

Higo charged into the lead with a seven-under-par 65. The bogey-free
round gave her a two-stroke advantage over Mikino Kubo and South Korea's
Hee-Won Han and Shin Sora. Higo shot 69 Saturday with birdies on all four
par-fives and remained on top, though joined there by Sora, who duplicated
her opening 67, as she chased her second career victory.

However, Higo's challenge Sunday came from Yuka Irie, who entered the
final round two shots off the pace with 69-67. In fact, Irie moved three
strokes in front of Higo before she bogeyed two of the last three holes. Higo
birdied the 18th for 72 and a 206 total to match Irie's 70 and force the
playoff. At the fourth overtime hole, Higo tapped in a second putt for the
victory after Irie missed for par from six feet. Sora shot 73 for 207, joined
in that slot by Fuki Kido and Ikuyo Shiotani, 36, who won her 18th title in
the 1997 Suntory and hasn't won since.

Apita Circle K Sankus Ladies—¥50,000,000
Winner: Kaori Higo

The Japan LPGA Tour put its second back-to-back victory performance of
the 1999 season into the record books in mid-June when Kaori Higo captured the new Apita Circle K Sankus Ladies tournament at Nakatsugawa.
The follow-up victory came a bit more easily. A playoff winner the previous
Sunday in the Suntory Ladies Open, Higo scored a two-stroke triumph over
three overseas players at New Green Golf Club, the ninth of her 10-year
career. Fumiko Muraguchi won on consecutive Sundays in May.

Carrying momentum from her Suntory triumph, Higo jumped off to a one-
stroke lead Friday at Nakatsugawa with a bogey-free, four-under-par 68.
Rookie Kaori Suzuki opened with 69 and veteran star Ayako Okamoto shared
third place with three others. Fuki Kido shot a mixed-bag 69 that included
a bogey and double bogey and slipped into a one-stroke lead at 140 over
Higo (73) and Yuko Motoyama (71-70).

Kido's game came apart Sunday. As she was soaring to an ultimate 77,
Higo regained the lead and went on to a 71–212 and the two-shot victory.
Deadlocked at 214 were Taiwan's Huang Yu-Chen (68) and Mei-Chi Cheng
(71) and South Korean ace Ok-Hee Ku, the Nasu Ogawa winner in April,
who shot 72.

Japan Women's Open—¥70,000,000
Winner: Mayumi Murai

Long recognized as one of Japan's best women players through the seven victories she had posted during her 11-season career, Mayumi Murai added prestige to her record when she won her first major championship with a record performance at Kasumigaseki Country Club in the Japan Women's Open. Murai never trailed in the year's second 72-hole event, fending off a late charge Sunday by Taiwan's Huang Yu-Chen to record a one-stroke victory. Her 281 total and seven-under-par status were both new records in the Women's Open since it went to the four-round format in 1982.

Murai took a huge step toward the victory Thursday when she shot 66 in an all-day drizzle, her card showing an eagle, six birdies and a double bogey. The 66 gave her a four-stroke lead over the defending champion, Natsuko Noro, and Yuri Kawanami. The rain continued Friday and Murai's 71 stretched her lead to five over amateur Shiho Ohyama, the 1997 Japan Amateur Match Play champion.

Murai gave that stroke back when she shot 72 under overcast skies Saturday, her 209 giving her a four-stroke margin over Midori Yoneyama. Huang was five back after a 69. With four birdies and two bogeys, Murai seemed to have matters well in hand as she played the last hole, even though the Taiwanese pro was posting a 68. Then, the jitters got her. She muffed her approach and three-putted for a double bogey and 72, just enough for the victory. Only one other player, Hee-Won Han, broke par (287).

Toyo Suisan Ladies Hokkaido—¥50,000,000
Winner: Toshimi Kimura

Coming off a near miss the previous Sunday, Taiwan's Huang Yu-Chen maintained a hot hand through the first two rounds of the Toyo Suisan Ladies Hokkaido tournament, but she couldn't sustain the pace and yielded the title to Toshimi Kimura, a 30-year-old Tokyo native who hadn't won in three years. Kimura, who lingered just off the lead the first two days at the Kosaido Sapporo Country Club, closed with a 69 for 210 total and a one-stroke victory, the sixth of her career.

Huang, who had closed with 68 in the Open, falling just one stroke behind winner Mayumi Murai, shot 70 Friday at Sapporo and shared the first-round lead with Taiwanese compatriot Hsiu-Feng Tseng, one stroke in front of Kimura, Aki Nakano, Fusako Nagata and South Korean Jae-Sook Won. A four-under-par 68 Saturday jumped Huang three strokes ahead of Kimura and Yukiko Ishiguro as she sought a second victory in Japan to go with her triumph in the 1998 Dunlop Ladies.

It was not to be. Despite two bogeys in the middle of the round, Kimura mustered the 69 that enabled her to edge Huang when the Taiwan pro took her third bogey of the day at the 18th hole. Huang wound up with 73–211.

Sumitomo Visa Taiheiyo Club Ladies—¥60,000,000
Winner: Junko Yasui

What better way to spend one's birthday than winning a golf tournament. That's what Junko Yasui did in the Sumitomo Visa Taiheiyo Club Ladies tournament at Chonan. Yasui jokingly admonished reporters not to print her age, which they did — 39 — after she scored the come-from-behind victory, her second of the season and 12th of her career. She won the Kosaido Golf Cup two months earlier in late May.

For two days the focus was on Harumi Sakagami, the leader after each of the first two rounds, and Sweden's Annika Sorenstam. Sakagami, who scored her first Japan LPGA Tour victory in the 1998 Goya Kensetsu Cup, fired a six-under-par 66, her career best, in the opening round at the La Vista Golf Resort. Yet she led by just one stroke over Aki Takamura. Sorenstam managed only 71.

Although she clung to the one-stroke lead Saturday, Sakagami lost her touch on the greens at the end of the round, absorbing a three-putt bogey at the 17th and a four-putt double bogey at the 18th for 74 and 140. Sorenstam shot 70 and joined Takamura (74), Chieko Nishida and Ayako Shibata (73s) at 141. The Swedish star seemed poised for a win in Japan, but could manage just 74 Sunday and tied for eighth at 215. Sakagami couldn't shake off the terrible finish and soared to an 81 Sunday. Yasui, on the other hand, was superb on the windy day, ringing up an eagle and three birdies against a single bogey for 68 and the winning 210. Takamura came back with 71 to take second place at 212.

Golf 5 Ladies—¥50,000,000
Winner: Aki Nakano

Another veteran player came to the fore in the Golf 5 Ladies tournament at Mizunami as 36-year-old Aki Nakano registered a two-stroke victory, her first in almost exactly a year and her seventh in her 13-year career. Although she built a three-shot advantage before taking a bogey at the 71st hole, Nakano insisted, "Believe me, it wasn't an easy victory. The pressure was nerve-wracking."

Michiko Hattori, the leading money winner in 1998 who had been conspicuously absent from the leaderboards through most of the season's first five months, was first-round co-leader, shooting a two-under-par 70 to share the top spot with Kumiko Hiyoshi and Michie Ohba. Nakano, who opened with 72, edged in front Saturday at Mizunami Country Club with 69–141, one stroke ahead of Hiyoshi (72), Mikiyo Nishizuka (73-69) and Yuko Moriguchi (71-71).

A par round was all Nakano needed Sunday as things turned out. She took an early bogey at the par-three fourth hole, came back with birdies at the seventh and 10th to build the three-shot lead, then took the final bogey at the 17th when she missed the green. The 72 gave her a three-under-par 213 total and the two-shot victory over little-known Kasumi Fujii, who had six birdies and five bogeys for 71–215. Hattori and Ok-Hee Ku tied for third at 216.

NEC Karuizawa 72—¥45,000,000
Winner: Hee-Won Han

The South Korean contingent on the Japan LPGA Tour had its second 1999 winner in mid-September when Hee-Won Han, one of the youngest, joined veteran compatriot Ok-Hee Ku, the Nasu Ogawa victor in late April, with her triumph in the rain-shortened NEC Karuizawa tournament on Karuizawa 72 Golf Club's North course. Ku, 42, has 17 wins on her record; Han, 21, now has her first.

Keiko Arai fired a six-under-par 66 and took a two-stroke lead in the opening round. Han and four others — Harumi Sakagami, Rie Murata, Ae-Sook Kim and Ku — were second at 68. Then the rains came, leaving the course unplayable and forcing cancellation of the Saturday round. Han broke open a tight finish when she birdied the last two holes to win by two strokes over Arai. She shot 67 for 135; Arai shot 71 for 137. Akiko Fukushima, just back in Japan after spending the season in America, where she picked up two victories and won more than $300,000, tied for 10th place with a 141 score in the NEC event.

Shin Caterpillar Mitsubishi Ladies—¥60,000,000
Winner: Fumiko Muraguchi

Fumiko Muraguchi strengthened her hold on the money lead of the Japan LPGA Tour when she scored her third victory of the season in the Shin Caterpillar Mitsubishi Ladies tournament. Improving by two strokes each day on the par-73 Daihakone Country Club course at Hakone, Muraguchi snatched a one-stroke victory, her career seventh, with a three-under-par 216 total. It followed her back-to-back wins in the Yakult and Chukyo TV Bridgestone tournaments in May.

For the second week in a row, Ae-Sook Kim was a first-round front-runner. Kim shot 70 and led four others — Michiko Hattori, Ok-Hee Ku, Jae-Sook Won and Rie Mitsuhashi — by one stroke. Strong winds came up Saturday and new leaders appeared on the scoreboards. Keiko Arai shot 70 and Yuka Irie, a playoff loser in June at the Suntory Open, had 71 for 143 totals to take over first place, one stroke in front of veteran star Ikuyo Shiotani. Muraguchi trailed by three after rounds of 74 and 72.

With the scoring generally high Sunday, Muraguchi's 70 was all she needed for the victory. She birdied the par-five 18th to beat Arai by one stroke. Six others tied for third at even-par 219, while Irie shot herself out of big money with 81.

Yonex Ladies—¥50,000,000
Winner: Natsuko Noro

Whether she intended the Yonex Ladies to be her final tournament before the birth of her baby, Natsuko Noro made that last appearance of the 1999 Japan LPGA Tour season a memorable and lucrative one. The 33-year-old Noro, six months pregnant, ignited a final-round charge and roared to a one-stroke victory at Yonex Country Club in Niigata. It was the third career win for the 1998 Japan Women's Open champion.

Noro began the final round four strokes off the lead, held then by Yoko Inoue, who had won twice in the early stages of the season and looked solid with a three-stroke lead with 70–141. Inoue had wrested first place away from three-time winner Fumiko Muraguchi, Aiko Takasu and rookie Kaori Suzuki in Saturday's second round, adding 70 to the opening 71 that had placed her just one stroke behind that trio of 70 shooters.

Noro had managed only 72-73 during those two rain-plagued rounds, but on Sunday she was brilliant. She mustered seven birdies over the first 14 holes, including three in a row starting at the 10th, to surge into the lead. She secured a final birdie at the 18th for 65 and a 210 total to forge a one-stroke victory over Michiko Hattori, who also jumped up the leaderboard with 67 for 211.

Fujisankei Ladies Classic—¥60,000,000
Winner: Midori Yoneyama

Breakthroughs were few and far between in 1999. In fact, when Midori Yoneyama won the Fujisankei Ladies Classic in early September, she was not only the first rookie victor of the season but just the third first-time winner. The 22-year-old Yoneyama, who had been making waves much of the year with strong individual rounds, put it together in the Fujisankei and sailed to a three-stroke triumph on the Fujizakura Country Club course.

The tournament started out with the familiar figure of Fumiko Muraguchi sharing the lead with Mikino Kubo at 68 as she launched a bid for her fourth title of the season. Yoneyama trailed by one stroke, tied for third with Shin Sora and Rie Mitsuhashi. When Yoneyama followed with 70 for 139 Saturday, she moved into a two-stroke lead as Muraguchi uncharacteristically faltered with 73 and Kubo took a 75. Harumi Sakagami, Takayo Bandoh and Nobuko Kizawa were at 141.

Although admitting to some jitters late in the round, Yoneyama put up a strong 68 Sunday for her winning 207. Ayako Okamoto made a belated charge with a 66, but it only netted her a fourth-place finish behind Bandoh (69) and Aki Takamura (68) and their 210s. The victory came almost a year to the day after Yoneyama joined the circuit.

Japan LPGA Championship Konika Cup—¥70,000,000
Winner: Fuki Kido

Fuki Kido put a crown jewel — the Japan LPGA Championship — on her 15-season record and did so in decisive fashion. Kido seized the lead in the second round of the year's second major championship and blazed to a six-stroke victory. Mayumi Murai, another veteran (11 seasons), took the Japan Women's Open earlier in the summer.

Aki Nakano, who won the Golf 5 Ladies tournament in early August, made a run at the LPGA title. She shot an erratic 68 — seven birdies, two bogeys and a double bogey — in the opening round and led Ikuyo Shiotani, a two-time leading money winner earlier in the decade, Michie Ohba and Rie Murata by one stroke; four others by two, including Kido and Midori Yoneyama, coming off her first career victory in the Fujisankei Classic the previous Sunday. Kido climbed on top in beastly heat Friday with the day's only sub-70 score. Her 69–140 total gave Kido a two-stroke lead over Nakano, who shot 73, as the other contenders fell back.

Kido put herself just about out of reach Saturday, her 71–211 establishing a five-stroke lead over Nakano, her nearest pursuer, who took a 74. Kido then was the only player under par on the Biwako Country Club course at Ritto. She fashioned a solid 70 Sunday with three birdies and a bogey to build her victory margin to six and run her total to 281. It was her fifth and biggest career title. Yoneyama also shot 70 and pushed into second place with the only other sub-par score of 287. Little-known Yukiyo Haga was third at 289.

Yukijirushi Ladies Tokai Classic—¥60,000,000
Winner: Young-Me Lee

It was more just a matter of when Young-Me Lee would pick up another victory on the Japan LPGA Tour. The South Korean player, who had seven wins in Japan coming into the season, including four in the previous three seasons, grabbed No. 8 the hard way, coming from four strokes off the pace in the final round and, in convincing fashion, ending with a three-stroke margin.

Lee's major victim was Harumi Sakagami, who had gone into Sunday's round at Ryosen Golf Club at Inabe with a three-stroke lead on the strength of a pair of 67s. The first one had put Sakagami in a five-way tie for first place with Masaki Maeda, Hsiu-Feng Tseng, Michiko Hattori and Fuki Kido, fresh from her Japan LPGA Championship win. At 134, Sakagami had the three-stroke lead over Yuri Fudoh and Tseng. Lee and Kido were at 138.

The South Korean star launched her victory move Sunday with birdies on the first two holes. She had seven in all in the day's best round, 67, catching Sakagami at the 15th hole. Sakagami three-putted the 16th and Lee capped her 67 with a birdie on the final hole. She finished with 205, 11 under par. Fudoh and Tseng shot 71s and took second place at 208. Sakagami slipped to 75 and tied for fourth with Michie Ohba.

Miyagi TV Cup Dunlop Ladies Open—¥60,000,000
Winner: Ok-Hee Ku

When things get tough and scores soar, experience pays off in tournament golf. The Miyagi TV Cup Dunlop Ladies Open offered a perfect example of this as veteran South Korean Ok-Hee Ku parlayed a par 72 in the final round into a come-from-behind victory. On a day when a lone 71 was the best score posted at Rainbow Hills Golf Club, Ku overcame a two-stroke deficit and claimed a two-shot victory, her second of the season and 16th of her career in Japan. Interestingly, she scored her early season victory in the rain-shortened Nasu Ogawa tournament with a closing 73.

Overall scoring was much better during the first two rounds of the Dunlop Open tournament. Chikayo Yamazaki took the lead Friday with 68, one shot better than Michiko Hattori and Kayo Yamada with four others at 70 and Ku among eight players at 71. Aki Nakano, a strong contender two weeks earlier in the LPGA Championship and winner of the Golf 5 Ladies event in August, made another bid at Rainbow Hills. She shot the week's best round, 67, and took the second-round lead with 138, one shot ahead of Yamada (69-70) and two in front of Ku (71-69). But again Nakano suffered a final-round collapse and tumbled to 79 amid a host of high scores among the contenders. With 73, Harumi Sakagami took the runner-up slot at 214, two behind the winner.

Osaka Ladies Open—¥60,000,000
Winner: Hee-Won Han

Hee-Won Han wasn't about to let another South Korean get ahead of her. On the heels of Ok-Hee Ku's second victory of the season in the Dunlop Ladies Open, Han put her second 1999 win in the books at the Osaka Ladies Open in a tournament dominated by players from South Korea. In fact, Akane Ohshiro was the lone Japanese pro among the top eight in the final standings.

Ae-Sook Kim began the South Korean influence in the opening round, shooting 68 to lead Man-Soo Kim and 54-year-old Michiko Okada of Japan by one stroke. Han was among six 70 scorers. Then, on Saturday, the 21-year-old produced six birdies, posted 68 and went two strokes in front of Kim (72) and Shiho Katano (71-69). She was rolling smoothly toward victory Sunday until she double-bogeyed the par-three 15th. That opened the door for yet another South Korean, Woo-Soon Ko, who charged from far back with a 66 Sunday. But Han bounced back with a birdie at the 17th, shot 73 and edged Ko by one stroke with her five-under-par 211 at Hanna Country Club in Daito, for the second victory of her young career.

Three other South Koreans — Jae-Sook Won, Chae-Eun Song and Young-Me Lee — tied for third place with Ohshiro and Taiwan's Hsiu-Feng Tseng and Kim placed eighth.

TaKaRa World Invitational—¥80,000,000
Winner: Laura Davies

Laura Davies rarely visits Japan and leaves the country empty-handed and 1999 was no exception. The powerful international star, who numbered five titles in Japan among her many victories around the world, had shot an embarrassing 157 in 1998 in the TaKaRa World Invitational and was eager to make amends when she returned to the Caledonian Golf Club near Tokyo's Narita International Airport. She did, leading from start to finish to win by four strokes with a three-under-par 285 total.

The victory route went like this:

First round — Davies shot 68 and shared the lead with Akane Ohshiro and Fuki Kido, the recently crowned Japan LPGA champion.

Second round — Davies moved two strokes in front of Midori Yoneyama and Yuka Shiroto with 69 for 137.

Third round — Strong, gusty winds plagued the field and Davies struggled to 76 for 213, yet widened her lead to three strokes. She had two birdies, four bogeys and a double bogey in the tough round. Janice Moodie joined Kido, Yoneyama, Mitsuko Kawasaki and Man-Soo Kim of South Korea at 216.

Fourth round — Davies was never threatened. At one point she led by six strokes before taking two late bogeys and finishing with 72 for the 285. Moodie shot 73 and placed second at 289, one stroke ahead of Kido, Kim and the 1998 TaKaRa champion, Aki Takamura.

Fujitsu Ladies—¥60,000,000
Winner: Michiko Hattori

It was a long time in coming, but when it did, it came with a vengeance. Michiko Hattori, who had won five tournaments and the money title in 1998, was still winless when she teed off in the Fujitsu Ladies tournament at the Tokyu Seven Hundred Club. When play ended that Sunday afternoon, Hattori had broken that string with the most decisive win of the season and had her 13th career victory.

Hattori, who had gained international attention when she won the 1985 U.S. Amateur Championship at age 16, followed Laura Davies' lead of the previous week and was in front from the start. She shot a four-under-par 68 Friday and shared first place with Chieko Nishida, one stroke ahead of Akane Ohshiro, two in front of Ok-Hee Ku and Aki Nakano. Hattori spurted to a five-stroke lead Saturday when she shot 67 for a 135 total. Nishida had a 72 and held second place at 140, one stroke ahead of four players, including Ku.

A solid 69 — three birdies, no bogeys — led Hattori to 204 and a seven-stroke victory Sunday, the margin one shot better than Fuki Kido's season-high spread in winning the Japan LPGA Championship in September. "The victory means a lot to me," said Hattori, who had struggled with some swing changes earlier in the season. "I now have confidence again." Ku with 70 and Nishida with 71 shared second place at 211.

Hisako Higuchi Kibun Classic—¥70,000,000
Winner: Fumiko Hiyoshi

Michiko Hattori misplayed one hole over the 54-hole distance of the Hisako Higuchi Kibun Classic in her quest for two consecutive victories and Fumiko Hiyoshi was the beneficiary of her unintended largess. Hiyoshi beat Hattori by one stroke for the title and Hattori had to look back with regret to the first round and the 14th hole of the Kinojo Golf Club course at Soja, Okinawa.

Still on top of her game after her seven-stroke victory in the Fujitsu Ladies, Hattori rang up seven birdies on the first 13 holes at Kinojo. However, she drove out of bounds at the 14th, then three-putted for a triple-bogey seven and had to settle for a 68, the same score shot by Hiyoshi. They trailed leader Fuki Kido by one stroke. Hiyoshi holed two long birdie putts Saturday, shot 70–138 and went two strokes in front of Hattori (72), Kido (73) and Ae-Sook Kim (70-70).

Hiyoshi staggered at the end but held on for 73 and the one-stroke victory over Hattori. She bogeyed the last two holes. Hattori, who won the tournament in 1998, shot 72 for 212. It was the first victory for the 35-year-old Hiyoshi since she captured the 1994 Japan LPGA Championship. She has won five times during her 17 seasons.

Nichirei International—US$702,000
Winner: United States

Even a rather watered-down team was strong enough to extend the dominance of the U.S. LPGA Tour in its annual meeting with the best from the Japan LPGA Tour in the Nichirei International tournament at Sose Country Club in Chiba. Teams from the United States have not lost in the matches since 1984 and have taken 19 of the 21 competitions.

The top four money winners in America — Karrie Webb, Juli Inkster, Annika Sorenstam and Se Ri Pak — passed up the event.

Nonetheless, with a squad made up of players from as far down its money list at 26th place, the U.S. team jumped off to a 4-2 lead in the first day's four-ball, stroke-play matches. The American team won three, tied two and dropped its lone duel when Akiko Fukushima, who played most of the year in the U.S., and Aki Takamura beat Liselotte Neumann and Mi Hyun Kim. The U.S. group widened its margin to 9-3 Saturday, winning all of its four-ball matches except one, Fumiko Muraguchi and Hiromi Kobayashi defeating Rosie Jones and Sherri Steinhauer, 68-71.

The Japan LPGA made its best showing in Sunday's singles, winning five of the 12 matches and halving another, but the U.S. still posted a convincing 15½-8½ victory. Tina Barrett, who was undefeated in her three outings, was named the most valuable player in the competition.

Mizuno Classic—¥84,960,000
Winner: Maria Hjorth

Talk about playing — and winning — under duress. Maria Hjorth spent most of the week of the Mizuno Classic on the telephone with airline personnel trying to find her luggage. By Friday, her clubs, located once, still hadn't arrived and she had to play with a borrowed set. She shot 70, five shots off the first-round lead of Cindy McCurdy, and was comfortable enough with her equipment that, when her bag finally arrived that night, she decided to continue with all of the loaners except the fairway woods and wedges.

Great decision. Hjorth carved out a scintillating 64 Saturday, surged into the lead and went on to a five-stroke victory in the tournament that is an official event on both the U.S. and Japan LPGA Tours and had 46 players from the American circuit and 38 from Japan in the field. It was the second title in seven weeks for the previously winless, 25-year-old Swedish pro.

Hjorth, who explained her handling of the luggage chaos as a decision that "you have to do the best you can with what you have," found clubs similar to her own. "I didn't let myself get down," she said. The 64 with the mixed bag Saturday was the product of eight birdies on the Seta Golf Course and jumped her into the lead by two shots over Japan's Aki Nakano and Fumiko Muraguchi, three ahead of McCurdy (72) and Rachel Hetherington. Hjorth had also shot a final-round 64 when she won the Safeco Classic in mid-September. She quickly widened her lead Sunday with a birdie at the second hole and an eagle at the sixth, closing with a 67 for a 201 total, 15 under par, and the five-stroke victory over Muraguchi, Nakano, Ok-Hee Ku and Laura Davies, who finished with 66.

Itoen Ladies—¥60,000,000
Winner: Yuri Fudoh

Yuri Fudoh capped her finest season when she joined rookie Midori Yoneyama, Hee-Won Han and Nahoko Hirao as a first-time winner in 1999. She came from behind to capture the Itoen Ladies tournament at Chonan. In her fourth season after turning pro in August of 1996, Fudoh posted a nine-under-par 207 total at the Great Island Club for the one-stroke victory.

Aki Nakano, a one-time winner and frequent contender in the latter months of the Japan season, was the second-round leader and victim of Fudoh's strong finish. The two women had shared the first-round lead at 68 with Jae-Sook Won, then Nakano went two strokes up on Fudoh with a 69 for 137 Saturday. Fudoh had 71.

Fudoh turned things around Sunday when she came up with a 68 and Nakano could manage only a 71–208. Mitsuko Kawasaki and Kumiko Hiyoshi, the Kibun Classic winner in October, finished third at 211. Fudoh was to finish fourth on the tour's final 1999 money list with earnings of more than ¥56 million.

Daio Seishi Elleair Ladies Open—¥75,000,000
Winner: Mayumi Hirase

Mayumi Hirase brought back memories of her glory years on the Japan LPGA Tour with a one-stroke victory in the Daio Seishi Elleair Ladies Open at Matsuyama. The veteran Hirase has 18 titles to her credit, but the bulk of those were acquired in the early part of the decade when she twice was the leading money winner (1993 and 1994) and finished second the next season. In fact, Hirase hadn't won since the Toray Queens Cup late in the 1996 campaign when she beat Laura Davies in a playoff.

Hirase put together three rounds in the 60s to gain the narrow victory. She shot 69 in the first round at Elleair Golf Club and was tied with four others one stroke off the pace. Aki Nakano, again a contender, and Chikako Matsuzawa had 68s. Hirase birdied two of the last three holes Saturday for 68 and a share of first place with Matsuzawa (69) and Michie Ohba (69-68). Hirase had a wild ride Sunday en route to the victory. She carded eight birdies, five bogeys and just five pars for 69 and a final 206. Ohba shot 70 for 207, Matsuzawa 71 for 208, where she was joined by Nakano and Kaori Higo.

Japan LPGA Meiji Nyugyo Cup—¥60,000,000

Winner: Kaori Higo

Kaori Higo completed the finest season of her 10-year career by winning the Japan LPGA Meiji Nyugyo Cup, the third major tournament that traditionally closes out the year. Higo not only joined Fumiko Muraguchi as the season's only three-time winners, but she also gave Muraguchi an incidental assist in clinching the year's money winning title. With her four-stroke victory at Hibiscus Golf Club in Sadowara, she held off the challenge of Ok-Hee Ku, who closed with 68 and took second place. As things turned out, Ku had to win the tournament to catch Muraguchi in the race for the No. 1 spot. Muraguchi finished well down the standings at 293, but earned enough to wind up the season just ¥533,312 ahead of her South Korean challenger.

Higo started and finished with 70s, doing the bulk of her scoring in the middle rounds of the 72-hole event, one of just five four-day tournaments on the schedule. Kasumi Fujii, winless in four seasons on the circuit, opened with a career-best 66 that gave her a three-stroke lead at the end of the Thursday round, but she was not a factor after that. Higo shot a five-birdie 67 Friday and moved into first place with Mineko Nasu (69-68), then vaulted to a six-stroke lead with a 68 Saturday as Nasu shot 74 for 211. Ok-Hee Ku tied her for second with a 69 to keep her hopes alive, but she couldn't conjure up the really hot round she needed Sunday to overtake Higo and her 70–275. Higo's three wins in 1999 ran her career victory total to 10.

APPENDIXES

Official World Golf Ranking
(As of December 31, 1999)

Pos.		Player	Country	Points Average	Total Points	No. of Events	97/98 Total	97/98 Minus	1999 Plus
1	(1)	Tiger Woods	USA	19.98	939	47	566	-377	750
2	(3)	David Duval	USA	13.15	605	46	532	-335	408
3	(7)	Colin Montgomerie	Sco	10.36	580	56	508	-334	406
4	(4)	Davis Love III	USA	9.48	436	46	481	-327	282
5	(5)	Ernie Els	SAf	8.64	484	56	505	-351	330
6	(8)	Lee Westwood	Eng	7.85	463	59	536	-335	262
7	(9)	Vijay Singh	Fiji	7.82	485	62	502	-319	302
8	(6)	Nick Price	Zim	7.20	367	51	458	-319	228
9	(10)	Phil Mickelson	USA	6.58	329	50	396	-261	194
10	(2)	Mark O'Meara	USA	6.52	326	50	532	-328	122
11	(12)	Jim Furyk	USA	6.36	356	56	412	-270	214
12	(399T)	Sergio Garcia	Spn	6.20	273	44	10	-5	268
13	(15)	Justin Leonard	USA	6.14	356	58	385	-273	244
14	(33)	Hal Sutton	USA	6.11	336	55	236	-138	238
15	(14)	Jesper Parnevik	Swe	5.43	266	49	330	-222	158
16	(28)	John Huston	USA	5.36	284	53	251	-131	164
17	(30)	Jeff Maggert	USA	5.34	251	47	217	-146	180
18	(38)	Carlos Franco	Par	5.30	249	47	148	-95	196
19	(17)	Darren Clarke	NIr	5.29	296	56	326	-204	174
20	(11)	Fred Couples	USA	5.18	207	40	306	-181	82
21	(53)	Miguel A. Jimenez	Spn	4.91	270	55	155	-89	204
22	(22)	Tom Lehman	USA	4.83	232	48	264	-192	160
23	(92)	Chris Perry	USA	4.42	274	62	116	-76	234
24	(70)	David Toms	USA	4.40	255	58	124	-81	212
25	(16)	Steve Elkington	Aus	4.29	176	41	247	-177	106
26	(25)	Jose Maria Olazabal	Spn	4.24	246	58	245	-159	160
27	(75)	Steve Pate	USA	4.15	224	54	119	-69	174
28	(37)	Jeff Sluman	USA	4.03	254	63	213	-135	176
29	(26)	Steve Stricker	USA	3.95	174	44	198	-104	80
30	(44)	Bob Estes	USA	3.86	228	59	161	-93	160
31	(83)	Tim Herron	USA	3.83	222	58	123	-87	186
32	(45)	Stewart Cink	USA	3.81	221	58	192	-129	158
33	(82)	Retief Goosen	SAf	3.76	233	62	126	-97	204
34	(58)	Dudley Hart	USA	3.75	199	53	144	-89	144
35	(29)	Stuart Appleby	Aus	3.71	219	59	253	-176	142
36	(13)	Masashi (Jumbo) Ozaki	Jpn	3.68	173	47	318	-217	72
37	(43)	Glen Day	USA	3.67	209	57	185	-102	126
38	(40)	Thomas Bjorn	Den	3.63	189	52	163	-102	128
39	(23)	Lee Janzen	USA	3.63	196	54	276	-178	98
40	(19)	Brian Watts	USA	3.61	184	51	251	-157	90
41	(20)	Scott Hoch	USA	3.54	202	57	287	-209	124
42	(52)	Craig Parry	Aus	3.46	194	56	165	-123	152
43	(18)	Greg Norman	Aus	3.45	138	40	243	-217	112
44	(240)	Paul Lawrie	Sco	3.38	169	50	33	-22	158
45	(32)	Bob Tway	USA	3.36	195	58	225	-136	106
46	(55)	Naomichi (Joe) Ozaki	Jpn	3.36	215	64	178	-127	164
47	(90T)	Brent Geiberger	USA	3.32	186	56	104	-68	150
48	(54)	Fred Funk	USA	3.28	223	68	192	-119	150
49	(46)	Loren Roberts	USA	3.27	157	48	148	-117	126
50	(105)	Padraig Harrington	Ire	3.07	169	55	94	-67	142

( ) Figures in brackets indicate 97/98 positions

Pos.		Player	Country	Points Average	Total Points	No. of Events	97/98 Total	97/98 Minus	1999 Plus
51	(27)	Bernhard Langer	Ger	3.08	165	54	227	-168	106
52	(41)	Billy Mayfair	USA	3.05	183	60	198	-111	96
53	(215T)	Bob May	USA	2.96	133	45	30	-17	120
54	(172)	Ted Tryba	USA	2.95	186	63	72	-48	162
55	(115)	Rocco Mediate	USA	2.92	143	49	71	-44	116
56	(47)	Andrew Magee	USA	2.82	161	57	180	-115	96
57	(306)	Mike Weir	Can	2.80	157	56	21	-12	148
58	(21)	Mark Calcavecchia	USA	2.79	162	58	301	-201	62
59	(48)	Bill Glasson	USA	2.77	122	44	122	-94	94
60	(154T)	Angel Cabrera	Arg	2.77	119	43	48	-33	104
61	(35)	Brandt Jobe	USA	2.75	121	44	162	-101	60
62	(42)	Shigeki Maruyama	Jpn	2.73	164	60	196	-144	112
63	(101)	Olin Browne	USA	2.71	138	51	99	-63	102
64	(130)	Duffy Waldorf	USA	2.69	140	52	70	-54	124
65	(617T)	Dennis Paulson	USA	2.67	128	48	0	0	128
66	(31)	John Cook	USA	2.50	135	54	238	-155	52
67	(66)	Robert Karlsson	Swe	2.43	124	51	112	-76	88
68	(112)	Jarmo Sandelin	Swe	2.38	124	52	82	-54	96
69	(71)	Jay Haas	USA	2.37	116	49	112	-78	82
70	(88)	Skip Kendall	USA	2.36	144	61	117	-69	96
71	(61)	Paul Azinger	USA	2.36	106	45	106	-64	64
72	(36)	Ian Woosnam	Wal	2.29	117	51	172	-127	72
73	(49)	Scott Verplank	USA	2.27	125	55	150	-77	52
74	(69)	Greg Turner	NZl	2.24	103	46	110	-73	66
75	(106)	Toshimitsu Izawa	Jpn	2.21	135	61	82	-49	102
76	(208)	Scott Dunlap	USA	2.18	109	50	41	-24	92
77	(65)	Peter O'Malley	Aus	2.18	124	57	140	-92	76
78	(111)	Frank Lickliter	USA	2.17	137	63	96	-55	96
79	(60)	Eduardo Romero	Arg	2.17	89	41	105	-76	60
80	(80)	Kirk Triplett	USA	2.12	108	51	106	-76	78
81	(131)	Mark James	Eng	2.09	94	45	63	-51	82
82	(68)	Andrew Coltart	Sco	2.08	125	60	151	-92	66
83	(136)	Kazuhiko Hosokawa	Jpn	2.06	146	71	94	-58	110
84	(93)	David Frost	SAf	2.04	112	55	103	-83	92
85	(79)	Hidemichi Tanaka	Jpn	1.97	116	59	134	-74	56
86	(50)	Patrik Sjoland	Swe	1.97	114	58	159	-93	48
87	(617T)	Notah Begay III	USA	1.96	98	50	0	0	98
88	(81)	Stephen Ames	T&T	1.95	82	42	87	-57	52
89	(57)	Stephen Leaney	Aus	1.95	113	58	131	-76	58
90	(215T)	Tsuyoshi Yoneyama	Jpn	1.94	120	62	48	-30	102
91	(170)	Jean Van de Velde	Frn	1.92	115	60	61	-36	90
92	(200)	Greg Kraft	USA	1.91	101	53	50	-29	80
93	(64)	Craig Stadler	USA	1.90	76	40	105	-79	50
94	(124)	Alex Cejka	Ger	1.85	100	54	63	-37	74
95	(78)	Brandel Chamblee	USA	1.84	90	49	108	-66	48
96	(39)	Brad Faxon	USA	1.82	89	49	178	-145	56
97	(73)	Steve Flesch	USA	1.80	108	60	109	-55	54
98	(24)	Tom Watson	USA	1.77	71	40	190	-129	10
99	(34)	Steve Jones	USA	1.77	76	43	184	-140	32
100	(51)	Frankie Minoza	Phi	1.77	83	47	133	-84	34

( ) Figures in brackets indicate 97/98 positions

Pos.		Player	Country	Points Average	Total Points	No. of Events	97/98 Total	97/98 Minus	1999 Plus
101	(129)	Shingo Katayama	Jpn	1.73	78	45	53	-31	56
102	(133)	Tommy Armour III	USA	1.73	97	56	76	-43	64
103	(174)	Tom Pernice, Jr.	USA	1.71	99	58	60	-35	74
104	(109)	Phillip Price	Wal	1.70	85	50	81	-48	52
105	(204)	Pierre Fulke	Swe	1.70	78	46	35	-21	64
106	(96)	Peter Baker	Eng	1.69	88	52	95	-57	50
107	(617T)	Jarrod Moseley	Aus	1.69	86	51	0	0	86
108	(359)	Michael Campbell	NZl	1.66	93	56	17	-10	86
109	(299T)	Craig Spence	Aus	1.65	71	43	19	-12	64
110	(138)	Kaname Yokoo	Jpn	1.63	114	70	88	-50	76
111	(205)	Scott Gump	USA	1.62	99	61	52	-33	80
112	(119)	David Carter	Eng	1.59	89	56	78	-49	60
113	(161)	David Howell	Eng	1.58	101	64	73	-44	72
114	(63)	Per-Ulrik Johansson	Swe	1.57	74	47	105	-79	48
115	(233T)	Corey Pavin	USA	1.57	80	51	35	-21	66
116	(132)	Paul Goydos	USA	1.57	94	60	80	-60	74
117	(97)	Larry Mize	USA	1.56	70	45	84	-54	40
118	(617T)	Jonathan Kaye	USA	1.55	82	53	0	0	82
119	(114)	Kevin Sutherland	USA	1.54	91	59	88	-63	66
120	(123)	J.P. Hayes	USA	1.54	77	50	70	-39	46
121	(100)	Hajime Meshiai	Jpn	1.51	89	59	103	-64	50
122	(143T)	Toru Taniguchi	Jpn	1.49	79	53	55	-32	56
123	(417T)	John Bickerton	Eng	1.49	76	51	9	-5	72
124	(156)	Gary Orr	Sco	1.48	80	54	59	-33	54
125	(617T)	Rich Beem	USA	1.48	62	42	0	0	62
126	(90T)	Costantino Rocca	Ity	1.46	86	59	117	-85	54
127	(146)	Paul McGinley	Ire	1.43	76	53	65	-45	56
128	(134)	Harrison Frazar	USA	1.42	78	55	60	-30	48
129	(611T)	Choi Kyung-ju	Kor	1.40	56	40	1	-1	56
130	(121)	Peter Senior	Aus	1.33	64	48	74	-46	36
131	(72)	Mark McNulty	Zim	1.32	58	44	91	-67	34
132	(180)	Santiago Luna	Spn	1.31	63	48	46	-25	42
133	(171)	Steve Webster	Eng	1.30	70	54	50	-32	52
134	(135)	Joey Sindelar	USA	1.29	66	51	75	-45	36
135	(237)	Gabriel Hjertstedt	Swe	1.29	76	59	33	-23	66
136	(117)	Bradley Hughes	Aus	1.29	85	66	86	-47	46
137	(110)	Kenny Perry	USA	1.27	65	51	79	-50	36
138	(99)	Peter Lonard	Aus	1.26	72	57	103	-75	44
139	(151)	Miguel Angel Martin	Spn	1.26	58	46	46	-36	48
140	(267T)	Taichi Teshima	Jpn	1.26	83	66	37	-26	72
141	(361T)	Nick O'Hern	Aus	1.26	59	47	13	-10	56
142	(67)	Greg Chalmers	Aus	1.25	84	67	119	-69	34
143	(86T)	Sam Torrance	Sco	1.24	57	46	102	-63	18
144T	(186)	Nobumitsu Yuhara	Jpn	1.22	61	50	57	-32	36
144T	(98)	Eduardo Herrera	Col	1.22	61	50	91	-60	30
146	(62)	Michael Bradley	USA	1.21	58	48	123	-81	16
147	(77)	Billy Andrade	USA	1.20	71	59	127	-90	34
148	(84)	Robert Allenby	Aus	1.18	77	65	117	-80	40
149	(258)	Hirofumi Miyase	Jpn	1.18	73	62	37	-32	68
150	(125)	Sven Struver	Ger	1.18	67	57	79	-50	38

( ) Figures in brackets indicate 97/98 positions

Pos.		Player	Country	Points Average	Total Points	No. of Events	97/98 Total	97/98 Minus	1999 Plus
151T	(196)	Brian Henninger	USA	1.16	66	57	47	-37	56
151T	(327)	Dean Robertson	Sco	1.16	66	57	21	-13	58
153	(178)	Katsunori Kuwabara	Jpn	1.16	67	58	66	-43	44
154	(617T)	David Park	Wal	1.15	46	40	0	0	46
155	(126)	Ignacio Garrido	Spn	1.15	62	54	72	-56	46
156	(108)	Russell Claydon	Eng	1.14	49	43	67	-42	24
157	(113)	Mathias Gronberg	Swe	1.14	58	51	77	-41	22
158	(202)	Yasuharu Imano	Jpn	1.13	59	52	36	-21	44
159	(103)	Tateo (Jet) Ozaki	Jpn	1.13	61	54	99	-74	36
160	(194)	Kim Jong-duk	Kor	1.13	53	47	37	-26	42
161T	(301)	Chris DiMarco	USA	1.13	72	64	24	-12	60
161T	(321T)	Nic Henning	SAf	1.13	45	40	17	-10	38
161T	(213)	Rodney Pampling	Aus	1.13	45	40	31	-18	32
164	(128)	Robert Damron	USA	1.12	66	59	87	-63	42
165	(95)	Tommy Tolles	USA	1.11	62	56	101	-85	46
166	(173)	Mike Reid	USA	1.10	53	48	54	-39	38
167	(85)	Joe Durant	USA	1.10	54	49	104	-60	10
168	(89)	Trevor Dodds	Nam	1.10	67	61	93	-48	22
169	(319)	Jeev Milkha Singh	Ind	1.10	56	51	18	-12	50
170	(104)	Jay Don Blake	USA	1.09	59	54	86	-59	32
171	(153)	Jim Carter	USA	1.08	65	60	70	-45	40
172	(74)	Scott McCarron	USA	1.07	59	55	122	-97	34
173	(165)	Paul Broadhurst	Eng	1.07	61	57	63	-46	44
174	(497T)	Geoff Ogilvy	Aus	1.06	51	48	4	-3	50
175	(56)	Nick Faldo	Eng	1.06	55	52	119	-98	34
176	(150)	Mark Wiebe	USA	1.06	56	53	59	-43	40
177	(184)	Jose Coceres	Arg	1.05	45	43	41	-32	36
178	(254)	Mark Brooks	USA	1.05	68	65	40	-26	54
179	(118)	Dan Forsman	USA	1.04	51	49	71	-54	34
180	(140T)	Tom Byrum	USA	1.04	58	56	72	-58	44
181	(347)	Franklin Langham	USA	1.03	61	59	18	-9	52
182	(209)	Katsuyoshi Tomori	Jpn	1.02	62	61	53	-35	44
183T	(181)	Jamie Spence	Eng	1.00	49	49	45	-34	38
183T	(145)	Nolan Henke	USA	1.00	53	53	61	-38	30
185T	(116)	Keiichiro Fukabori	Jpn	0.98	63	64	90	-59	32
185T	(191)	Jerry Kelly	USA	0.98	63	64	57	-38	44
187	(193)	Satoshi Higashi	Jpn	0.98	62	63	58	-38	42
188	(94)	Katsumasa Miyamoto	Jpn	0.98	56	57	94	-52	14
189	(176)	Len Mattiace	USA	0.97	60	62	69	-47	38
190	(76)	Paul Stankowski	USA	0.96	54	56	122	-100	32
191	(167T)	Peter Mitchell	Eng	0.96	48	50	56	-36	28
192	(210T)	Mats Lanner	Swe	0.95	42	44	32	-16	26
193	(127)	Toru Suzuki	Jpn	0.95	62	65	90	-58	30
194	(617T)	Aaron Baddeley(Am)	Aus	0.95	38	40	0	0	38
195	(203)	Kevin Wentworth	USA	0.95	53	56	40	-27	40
196	(360)	Jay Delsing	USA	0.94	48	51	17	-11	42
197	(249)	Ryoken Kawagishi	Jpn	0.94	60	64	40	-24	44
198	(230)	J.L. Lewis	USA	0.94	58	62	36	-18	40
199	(617T)	Warren Bennett	Eng	0.93	38	41	0	0	38
200	(190)	Tsukasa Watanabe	Jpn	0.90	57	63	58	-41	40

( ) Figures in brackets indicate 97/98 positions

Age Groups of Current Top 100 World Ranked Players

Under 25	25-27	28-30	31-33	34-36	37-39	40-42	43-45	Over 45
		Duval						
		Els						
		Mickelson						
		Furyk		Montgomerie				
		Herron		Love				
		Goosen	Clarke	Singh				
		Appleby	Toms	Parnevik				
		Bjorn	Olazabal	Maggert	Huston	N. Price		
		Lawrie	Stricker	Franco	C.Perry	O'Meara		
		Harrington	B.Estes	Jimenez	Elkington	Sutton		
		Weir	D.Hart	Day	S.Pate	Couples		
		Maruyama	Watts	Janzen	Mediate	Lehman		
		Cabrera	Parry	Jobe	Magee	Sluman		
		R.Karlsson	Geiberger	Kendall	Calcavecchia	Tway		
		Lickliter	Mayfair	Verplank	Glasson	Langer		
		Coltart	May	Turner	Waldorf	Browne	Hoch	
		Hosokawa	Tryba	Dunlap	D.Paulson	Cook	Norman	M.Ozaki
	Westwood	Tanaka	Sandelin	O'Malley	Azinger	Woosnam	N.Ozaki	Haas
	Leonard	Sjoland	Izawa	Ames	Triplett	Frost	Funk	James
Woods	Cink	Leaney	Van de Velde	Yoneyama	Chamblee	S.Jones	Roberts	Stadler
Garcia	Begay	Cejka	Flesch	Kraft	Faxon	Minoza	Romero	Watson

Highest-Rated Events of 1999

Event	No. of World Ranked Players Participating					World Rating Points
	Top 5	Top 15	Top 30	Top 50	Top 100	
1 PGA Championship	5	14	28	48	92	787
2 Masters Tournament	5	15	30	49	70	738
3 U.S. Open Championship	5	15	30	46	71	719
4 British Open Championship	5	14	26	43	72	694
5 The Players Championship	5	14	29	49	79	751
6 WGC Anderson Match Play	5	14	29	49	64	722
7 WGC American Express Ch.	4	12	24	42	58	596
8 Memorial Tournament	4	10	21	35	61	565
9 Bay Hill Invitational	4	11	21	32	59	547
10 WGC NEC Invitational	5	14	24	34	40	531
11 Nissan Open	3	10	17	28	54	487
12 Sprint International	4	9	14	27	49	471
13 Volvo PGA Championship	1	3	6	8	25	168
14 MCI Classic	2	8	15	28	51	426
15 AT&T Pebble Beach Pro-Am	4	10	15	22	45	415
16 Tour Championship	3	10	17	22	29	386
17 MasterCard Colonial	2	6	14	28	50	402
18 Phoenix Open	2	6	12	24	42	375
19 National Car Rental Classic	1	7	13	24	46	387
20 Mercedes Championships	4	10	16	20	28	361

1999 World Ranking Review

Major Movements Within Top 50

Upward				**Downward**			
	Net Points	Position			Net Points	Position	
Name	Gained	1998	1999	Name	Lost	1998	1999
Tiger Woods	373	1	1	Mark O'Meara	206	2	10
Carlos Franco	101	38	18	Masashi (Jumbo) Ozaki	145	13	36
Hal Sutton	100	33	14	Greg Norman	105	18	43
David Duval	73	3	2	Fred Couples	99	11	20
Colin Montgomerie	72	7	3	Nick Price	91	6	8
Bob Estes	67	44	30	Scott Hoch	85	20	41
Jeff Sluman	41	37	28	Lee Janzen	80	23	39
Jeff Maggert	34	30	17	Lee Westwood	73	8	6
John Huston	33	28	16	Steve Elkington	71	16	25
Stewart Cink	29	45	32	Brian Watts	67	19	40
Thomas Bjorn	26	40	38	Phil Mickelson	67	10	9
Glen Day	24	43	37	Jesper Parnevik	64	14	15

Major Movements Into Top 50   Major Movements Out of Top 50

Name	Net Points Gained	Position 1998	1999	Name	Net Points Lost	Position 1998	1999
Sergio Garcia	263	399	12	Mark Calcavecchia	139	21	58
Chris Perry	158	92	23	Tom Watson	119	24	98
Paul Lawrie	136	240	44	Steve Jones	108	34	99
David Toms	131	70	24	John Cook	103	31	66
Miguel A. Jimenez	115	53	21	Brad Faxon	89	39	96
Retief Goosen	107	82	33	Bernhard Langer	62	27	51
Steve Pate	105	75	27	Ian Woosnam	55	36	72
Tim Herron	99	83	31	Patrik Sjoland	45	50	86
Brent Geiberger	82	90	47	Brandt Jobe	41	35	61
Padraig Harrington	75	105	50	Shigeki Maruyama	32	42	62
Dudley Hart	55	58	34	Scott Verplank	25	49	73
Naomichi (Joe) Ozaki	37	55	46	Andrew Magee	19	47	56

Other Major Movements

Upward				**Downward**			
	Net Points	Position			Net Points	Position	
Name	Gained	1998	1999	Name	Lost	1998	1999
Mike Weir	136	306	57	Frank Nobilo	83	59	207
Dennis Paulson	128	–	65	Paul Stankowski	68	76	190
Ted Tryba	114	172	54	Tom Kite	67	86	324
Bob May	103	215	53	Michael Bradley	65	62	146
Notah Begay III	98	–	87	Nick Faldo	64	56	175
Jarrod Moseley	86	–	107	Scott McCarron	63	74	172
Jonathan Kaye	82	–	118	David Ogrin	57	140	359
Michael Campbell	76	359	108	Billy Andrade	56	77	147
Tsuyoshi Yoneyama	72	215	90	Frankie Minoza	50	51	100
Rocco Mediate	72	115	55	Joe Durant	50	85	167
Angel Cabrera	71	154	60				
Duffy Waldorf	70	130	64				
Scott Dunlap	68	208	76				

World Golf Rankings 1968-1999

Year	No. 1	No. 2	No. 3	No. 4	No. 5
1968	Nicklaus	Palmer	Casper	Player	Charles
1969	Nicklaus	Player	Casper	Palmer	Charles
1970	Nicklaus	Player	Casper	Trevino	Charles
1971	Nicklaus	Trevino	Player	Palmer	Casper
1972	Nicklaus	Player	Trevino	Crampton	Palmer
1973	Nicklaus	Weiskopf	Trevino	Player	Crampton
1974	Nicklaus	Miller	Player	Weiskopf	Trevino
1975	Nicklaus	Miller	Weiskopf	Irwin	Player
1976	Nicklaus	Irwin	Miller	Player	Green
1977	Nicklaus	Watson	Green	Irwin	Crenshaw
1978	Watson	Nicklaus	Irwin	Green	Player
1979	Watson	Nicklaus	Irwin	Trevino	Player
1980	Watson	Trevino	Aoki	Crenshaw	Nicklaus
1981	Watson	Rogers	Aoki	Pate	Trevino
1982	Watson	Floyd	Ballesteros	Kite	Stadler
1983	Ballesteros	Watson	Floyd	Norman	Kite
1984	Ballesteros	Watson	Norman	Wadkins	Langer
1985	Ballesteros	Langer	Norman	Watson	Nakajima
1986	Norman	Langer	Ballesteros	Nakajima	Bean
1987	Norman	Ballesteros	Langer	Lyle	Strange
1988	Ballesteros	Norman	Lyle	Faldo	Strange
1989	Norman	Faldo	Ballesteros	Strange	Stewart
1990	Norman	Faldo	Olazabal	Woosnam	Stewart
1991	Woosnam	Faldo	Olazabal	Ballesteros	Norman
1992	Faldo	Couples	Woosnam	Olazabal	Norman
1993	Faldo	Norman	Langer	Price	Couples
1994	Price	Norman	Faldo	Langer	Olazabal
1995	Norman	Price	Langer	Els	Montgomerie
1996	Norman	Lehman	Montgomerie	Els	Couples
1997	Norman	Woods	Price	Els	Love
1998	Woods	O'Meara	Duval	Love	Els
1999	Woods	Duval	Montgomerie	Love	Els

(*The World of Professional Golf* 1968-1985; World Ranking 1986-1999)

Year	No. 6	No. 7	No. 8	No. 9	No. 10
1968	Boros	Coles	Thomson	Beard	Nagle
1969	Beard	Archer	Trevino	Barber	Sikes
1970	Devlin	Coles	Jacklin	Beard	Huggett
1971	Barber	Crampton	Charles	Devlin	Weiskopf
1972	Jacklin	Weiskopf	Oosterhuis	Heard	Devlin
1973	Miller	Oosterhuis	Wadkins	Heard	Brewer
1974	M. Ozaki	Crampton	Irwin	Green	Heard
1975	Green	Trevino	Casper	Crampton	Watson
1976	Watson	Weiskopf	Marsh	Crenshaw	Geiberger
1977	Marsh	Player	Weiskopf	Floyd	Ballesteros
1978	Crenshaw	Marsh	Ballesteros	Trevino	Aoki
1979	Aoki	Green	Crenshaw	Ballesteros	Wadkins
1980	Pate	Ballesteros	Bean	Irwin	Player
1981	Ballesteros	Graham	Crenshaw	Floyd	Lietzke
1982	Pate	Nicklaus	Rogers	Aoki	Strange
1983	Nicklaus	Nakajima	Stadler	Aoki	Wadkins
1984	Faldo	Nakajima	Stadler	Kite	Peete
1985	Wadkins	O'Meara	Strange	Pavin	Sutton
1986	Tway	Sutton	Strange	Stewart	O'Meara
1987	Woosnam	Stewart	Wadkins	McNulty	Crenshaw
1988	Crenshaw	Woosnam	Frost	Azinger	Calcavecchia
1989	Kite	Olazabal	Calcavecchia	Woosnam	Azinger
1990	Azinger	Ballesteros	Kite	McNulty	Calcavecchia
1991	Couples	Langer	Stewart	Azinger	Davis
1992	Langer	Cook	Price	Azinger	Love
1993	Azinger	Woosnam	Kite	Love	Pavin
1994	Els	Couples	Montgomerie	M. Ozaki	Pavin
1995	Pavin	Faldo	Couples	M. Ozaki	Elkington
1996	Faldo	Mickelson	M. Ozaki	Love	O'Meara
1997	Mickelson	Montgomerie	M. Ozaki	Lehman	O'Meara
1998	Price	Montgomerie	Westwood	Singh	Mickelson
1999	Westwood	Singh	Price	Mickelson	O'Meara

World's Winners of 1999

U.S. PGA TOUR

Mercedes Championships	David Duval
Sony Open in Hawaii	Jeff Sluman
Bob Hope Chrysler Classic	David Duval (2)
Phoenix Open	Rocco Mediate
AT&T Pebble Beach National Pro-Am	Payne Stewart
Buick Invitational	Tiger Woods
Nissan Open	Ernie Els (2)
WGC Andersen Consulting Match Play	Jeff Maggert
Touchstone Energy Tucson Open	Gabriel Hjertstedt
Doral-Ryder Open	Steve Elkington
Honda Classic	Vijay Singh
Bay Hill Invitational	Tim Herron
The Players Championship	David Duval (3)
BellSouth Classic	David Duval (4)
Masters Tournament	Jose Maria Olazabal
MCI Classic	Glen Day
Greater Greensboro Chrysler Classic	Jesper Parnevik
Shell Houston Open	Stuart Appleby
Compaq Classic of New Orleans	Carlos Franco
GTE Byron Nelson Classic	Loren Roberts
MasterCard Colonial	Olin Browne
Kemper Open	Rich Beem
Memorial Tournament	Tiger Woods (2)
FedEx St. Jude Classic	Ted Tryba
U.S. Open Championship	Payne Stewart (2)
Buick Classic	Duffy Waldorf
Motorola Western Open	Tiger Woods (4)
Greater Milwaukee Open	Carlos Franco (2)
John Deere Classic	J.L. Lewis
Canon Greater Hartford Open	Brent Geiberger
Buick Open	Tom Pernice, Jr.
PGA Championship	Tiger Woods (5)
Sprint International	David Toms
WGC NEC Invitational	Tiger Woods (6)
Reno-Tahoe Open	Notah Begay III
Air Canada Championship	Mike Weir
Bell Canadian Open	Hal Sutton
B.C. Open	Brad Faxon (2)
Westin Texas Open	Duffy Waldorf (2)
Buick Challenge	David Toms (2)
Michelob Championship	Notah Begay III (2)
Las Vegas Invitational	Jim Furyk
National Car Rental Classic	Tiger Woods (7)
Southern Farm Bureau Classic	Brian Henninger
Tour Championship	Tiger Woods (8)

SPECIAL EVENTS

CVS/pharmacy Charity Classic	Jeff Sluman (2)/Stuart Appleby (2)
Fred Meyer Challenge	Brad Faxon/Billy Andrade
Ganter Cup Challenge	Matt Gogel (3)
Ryder Cup	United States

Franklin Templeton Shark Shootout	Fred Couples/David Duval (5)
World Cup of Golf	United States/Tiger Woods (10)
Callaway Pebble Beach Invitational	Rocco Mediate (2)
PGA Grand Slam	Tiger Woods (11)
JCPenney Classic	Laura Davies (5)/John Daly
Office Depot Father-Son Challenge	Jack Nicklaus/Gary Nicklaus
Sprint Puerto Rico Golf Challenge	Robin Freeman
Diners Club Matches	Fred Couples (2)/Mark Calcavecchia

NIKE TOUR

South Florida Classic	Curt Byrum
Lakeland Classic	Ryan Howison
Florida Classic	Richard Johnson
Mississippi Gulf Coast Open	Joel Edwards
Monterrey Open	Steve Gotsche
Louisiana Open	Matt Gogel
Shreveport Open	Bob Heintz
South Carolina Classic	Kevin Johnson
Upstate Classic	Steve Gotsche (2)
Carolina Classic	Vance Veazey
Dominion Open	Darron Stiles
Knoxville Open	Jeff Gove
Cleveland Open	Matt Gogel (2)
Dayton Open	John Wilson
Lehigh Valley Open	Mathew Goggin
Hershey Open	Edward Fryatt
Greensboro Open	Shaun Micheel
Wichita Open	Brad Elder
Dakota Dunes Open	Fran Quinn
Omaha Classic	Mathew Goggin (2)
Ozarks Open	Ryan Howison (2)
Fort Smith Classic	Gary Webb
Permian Basin Open	David Berganio, Jr.
Utah Classic	Carl Paulson
Tri-Cities Open	Glen Hnatiuk
Boise Open	Carl Paulson (2)
Oregon Classic	Kelly Gibson
Inland Empire Open	Brad Elder (2)
New Mexico Classic	Dick Mast
Nike Tour Championship	Bob Heintz (2)

CANADIAN TOUR

Crown Isle Open	Kenneth Staton
Shell Payless Open	Ken Duke
BC Tel Open	Kenneth Staton (2)
Telus/Henry Singer Alberta Open	Brian Kontak
Dundee International	Canadian Team
Telus Calgary Open	Jaime Omar Gomez
Telus Edmonton Open	Ray Stewart
MTS Classic	Neale Smith
Ontario Open Heritage Classic	Arron Oberholser
Canadian Masters	Ray Stewart (2)
Samsung Canadian PGA Championship	Scott Petersen
Eagle Creek Classic	Aaron Oberholser (2)
Benefit Partners/NRCS Classic	Kenneth Staton (3)
McDonald's PEI Challenge	David Morland
Bell Bay Matches	Stuart Hendley/Scott Petersen (2)

NewTel Atlantic Cup   Brian Kontak (2)/Philip Jonas
Bayer Championship   Ken Duke (2)
Niagara Classic   Arden Knoll

SOUTH AMERICAN TOUR

TPG Open de Venezuela   Carlos Larrain
Peru Open   Scott Dunlap (2)
Torneo de Maestros Telefonica   Angel Cabrera
Litoral Open   Cesar Monasterio
Argentina Open   Scott Dunlap (3)

PGA EUROPEAN TOUR

Dubai Desert Classic   David Howell
Qatar Masters   Paul Lawrie
Algarve Portuguese Open   Van Phillips
Turespana Masters - Open Andalucia   Miguel Angel Jimenez
Madeira Island Open   Pedro Linhart
Estoril Open   Jean Francois Remesy
Peugeot Open de Espana   Jarmo Sandelin
Fiat and Fila Italian Open   Dean Robertson
Novotel Perrier Open de France   Retief Goosen
Benson and Hedges International Open   Colin Montgomerie
Deutsche Bank-SAP Open TPC of Europe   Tiger Woods (3)
Volvo PGA Championship   Colin Montgomerie (2)
Compass Group English Open   Darren Clarke
German Open   Jarmo Sandelin (2)
Moroccan Open   Miguel Angel Martin
Compaq European Grand Prix   David Park (2)
Murphy's Irish Open   Sergio Garcia
Standard Life Loch Lomond   Colin Montgomerie (3)
British Open Championship   Paul Lawrie
TNT Dutch Open   Lee Westwood (2)
Smurfit European Open   Lee Westwood (3)
Volvo Scandinavian Masters   Colin Montgomerie (4)
West of Ireland Golf Classic   Costantino Rocca
BMW International Open   Colin Montgomerie (5)
Scottish PGA Championship   Warren Bennett
Canon European Masters   Lee Westwood (4)
Victor Chandler British Masters   Bob May
Trophee Lancome   Pierre Fulke
Linde German Masters   Sergio Garcia (2)
Alfred Dunhill Cup   Spain
Cisco World Match Play   Colin Montgomerie (6)
Sarazen World Open   Thomas Bjorn
Belgacom Open   Robert Karlsson
Volvo Masters   Miguel Angel Jimenez (2)
WGC American Express Championship   Tiger Woods (9)

CHALLENGE TOUR

Tusker Kenya Open   Maarten Lafeber
OKI Telepizza Challenge   David Park
Open de Cote D'Ivoire   Ian Poulter
Comunidad Valenciana Challenge de Espana   Carl Suneson
BIL Luxembourg Open   Kevin Carissimi
Open dei Tessali   Gustavo Rojas
Challenge de Sable   Lucas Parsons
NCC Open   Per Nyman
Diners Club Austrian Open   Juan Ciola

Is Molas Challenge — Bradley Dredge
Open des Volcans — Philip Golding
Neuchatel Open Golf Trophy — Richard Johnson (2)
Volvo Finnish Open — Paul Nilbrink
BTC Slovenian Open — Grant Dodd
Rolex Trophy — Carl Suneson (2)
Finnish Masters — Lucas Parsons (2)
Beazer Homes Challenge Tour Championship — Carl Suneson (3)
BMW Russian Open — Iain Pyman
Norwegian Open — Pehr Magnebrant
Formby Hall Challenge — Greig Hutcheon
Ohrlings Swedish Match Play — Kalle Brink
Daewoo Warsaw Golf Open — Niclas Fasth
Gula Sidorna Grand Prix — Raimo Sjoberg
San Paolo Vita Open — Alberto Binaghi
Philips Challenge Xacabeo 99 — Hennie Otto (3)
Challenge de France Bayer — Iain Pyman (2)
First Cuba Grand Final — Stephen Scahill

ASIAN PGA DAVIDOFF TOUR

London Myanmar Open — Wang Ter-chang
Benson and Hedges Malaysian Open — Gerry Norquist
Wills Indian Open — Arjun Atwal
Macau Open — Lee Westwood
Maekyung Daks Open — James Kingston
Volvo China Open — Kyi Hla Han
Casino Filipino Philippine Open — Anthony Kang
Tianjin Teda Open — Thammanoon Sriroj
Volvo Masters of Malaysia — Nico van Rensburg (2)
ERA Taiwan Open — Kang Wook-soon
Kolon Korean Open — Choi Kyung-ju (3)
Lexus International — Jeev Milkha Singh
Nokia Singapore Open — Kenny Druce (2)
Hero Honda Masters — Jyoti Randhawa
Sabah Masters — Robert Huxtable
Johnnie Walker Classic — Michael Campbell
Hong Kong Open — Patrik Sjoland
Mittweida Thailand Open — Fran Quinn (2)
Omega PGA Championship — Fran Quinn (3)

JAPAN TOUR

Token Corporation Cup — Masashi Ozaki
Daido Drinko Shizuoka Open — Kim Jong-duk
Georgia KSB Open — Yoshinori Kaneko
Descente Classic Munsingwear Cup — Masayuki Kawamura
Tsuruya Open — Naomichi Ozaki
Kirin Open — Choi Kyung-ju
Chunichi Crowns — Yasuharu Imano
Fuji Sankei Classic — Shigemasa Higaki
Japan PGA Championship — Naomichi Ozaki (2)
Ube Kosan Open — Choi Kyung-ju (2)
Mitsubishi Motors Tournament — Tsuyoshi Yoneyama
JCB Classic Sendai — Shingo Katayama
Super Mario Yomiuri Open — Kim Jong-duk (2)
Mizuno Open — Eduardo Herrera
Yonex Open Hiroshima — Masashi Ozaki (2)
Aiful Cup — Toshimitsu Izawa
NST Niigata Open — Toshimitsu Izawa (2)

Hisamitsu-KBC Augusta	Tsuyoshi Yoneyama (2)
Japan PGA Match Play	Mamoru Osanai
Suntory Open	Nick Price
ANA Open	Kazuhiko Hosokawa
Gene Sarazen Jun Classic	Hajime Meshiai
Japan Open	Naomichi Ozaki (3)
Tokai Classic	Kaname Yokoo
Bridgestone Open	Shigeki Maruyama
Philip Morris Championship	Ryoken Kawagishi
Acom International	Hidemichi Tanaka
Sumitomo Visa Taiheiyo Masters	Hirofumi Miyase
Dunlop Phoenix Tournament	Thomas Bjorn (2)
Casio World Open	Tsuyoshi Yoneyama (3)
Japan Series JT Cup	Kazuhiko Hosokawa (2)
Fancl Okinawa Open	Taichi Teshima

AUSTRALASIAN TOUR

Victorian Open	Kenny Druce
Heineken Classic	Jarrod Moseley
Greg Norman Holden International	Michael Long
Ericsson Masters	Craig Spence
Canon Challenge	Rodney Pampling
Australasian Tour Championship	Marcus Cain
Ford Open Championship	Craig Parry
Holden Australian Open Championship	*Aaron Baddeley
Australasian Players Championship	*Brett Rumford
Australian PGA Championship	Greg Turner
Schweppes Coolum Classic	Nick O'Hern

AFRICAN TOURS

Alfred Dunhill South African PGA	Ernie Els
Mercedes-Benz - Vodacom S.A. Open	David Frost
Vodacom Players Championship	Chris Davison
Dimension Data Pro-Am	Scott Dunlap
South African Masters	Desvonde Botes
Stenham Royal Swazi Sun Open	Marc Cayeux
Lombard Tyres Classic	Brett Liddle
Vodacom Series: Gauteng	Nico van Rensburg
Pietersburg Classic	Hennie Otto
Vodacom Series: Eastern Cape	Ashley Roestoff
Vodacom Series: KwaZulu-Natal	Hennie Otto (2)
Vodacom Series: Mpumalanga	Andre Cruse
Bearing Man Highveld Classic	Bobby Lincoln
Vodacom Series: Free State	Desvonde Botes (2)
Royal Swazi Sun Classic	Bradford Vaughan
Vodacom Series: Western Cape	Sean Ludgater
Platinum Classic	Bobby Lincoln (2)
Hassan II Trophy	David Toms (3)
Zimbabwe Open	Jean Hugo
Nedbank Million Dollar Challenge	Ernie Els (3)
Vodacom Players Championship	Nic Henning

U.S. SENIOR PGA TOUR

MasterCard Championship	John Jacobs
Royal Caribbean Classic	Bruce Fleisher
American Express Invitational	Bruce Fleisher (2)
GTE Classic	Larry Nelson
ACE Group Classic	Allen Doyle

Senior Slam	Gil Morgan
Toshiba Senior Classic	Gary McCord
Liberty Mutual Legends of Golf	Hubert Green/Gil Morgan (2)
Emerald Coast Classic	Bob Duval
The Tradition	Graham Marsh
PGA Seniors' Championship	Allen Doyle (2)
Home Depot Invitational	Bruce Fleisher (3)
Bruno's Memorial Classic	Larry Nelson (2)
Nationwide Championship	Hale Irwin
Las Vegas Senior Classic	Vicente Fernandez
Bell Atlantic Classic	Tom Jenkins
Boone Valley Classic	Hale Irwin (2)
Cadillac NFL Classic	Allen Doyle (3)
BellSouth Senior Classic	Bruce Fleisher (4)
Southwestern Bell Dominion	John Mahaffey
Ford Senior Players Championship	Hale Irwin (3)
State Farm Senior Classic	Christy O'Connor, Jr.
U.S. Senior Open	Dave Eichelberger
Ameritech Senior Open	Hale Irwin (4)
Coldwell Banker Burnet Classic	Hale Irwin (5)
Novell Utah Showdown	Dave Eichelberger (2)
Lightpath Long Island Classic	Bruce Fleisher (5)
Foremost Insurance Championship	Christy O'Connor, Jr. (3)
BankBoston Classic	Tom McGinnis
AT&T Canada Senior Open	Jim Ahern
TD Waterhouse Championship	Allen Doyle (4)
Comfort Classic	Gil Morgan (3)
Bank One Championship	Tom Watson
Kroger Senior Classic	Gil Morgan (4)
Vantage Championship	Fred Gibson
The Transamerica	Bruce Fleisher (6)
Raley's Gold Rush Classic	David Graham
EMC² Kaanapali Classic	Bruce Fleisher (7)
Pacific Bell Senior Classic	Joe Inman
Ingersoll-Rand Senior Tour Championship	Gary McCord (2)
Chrysler Senior Match Play Challenge	Larry Nelson (3)
Diners Club Matches	Jack Nicklaus (2)/Tom Watson (2)

EUROPEAN SENIORS TOUR

Beko Classic	Tommy Horton
AIB Irish Seniors Open	John Morgan
MDIS & Partners Festival of Golf	David Oakley
Philips PFA Golf Classic	Bob Shearer
Jersey Seniors Open	David Jones
Lawrence Batley Seniors	Eddie Polland
Elf Seniors Open	Alan Tapie
Senior British Open	Christy O'Connor, Jr. (2)
Energis Senior Masters	Neil Coles
Bad Ragaz PGA Seniors Open	Bob Shearer (2)
De Vere Hotels Seniors Classic	Ross Metherell
The Dalmahoy Scottish Seniors Open	Neil Coles (2)
The Belfry PGA Seniors Championship	Ross Metherell (2)
Monte Carlo Invitational	Tommy Horton (2)
Ordina Legends in Golf	Michael Slater
Te Mes Greek Seniors Open	Alberto Croce
Senior Tournament of Champions	Eddie Polland (2)

JAPAN SENIOR TOUR

ANA Ishigaki-jima Senior Pro-Am	Hiroshi Ishii
Asahi Ryokken Cup	Hiroshi Ishii (2)
Castle Hill Open	Fujio Kobayashi
Old Man Par Senior Open	Masaji Kusakabe
HTB Senior Classic	Fujio Kobayashi (2)
Japan PGA Senior Championship	Tadami Ueno
Japan Senior Open	Graham Marsh (2)
Tokyo Tower Senior Open	Mitoshi Tomita
TPC Senior	Koichi Uehara

U.S. LPGA TOUR

HealthSouth Inaugural	Kelly Robbins
Naples LPGA Memorial	Meg Mallon
Office Depot	Karrie Webb
Valley of the Stars Championship	Catrin Nilsmark
Sunrise Hawaiian Ladies Open	Alison Nicholas
Australian Ladies Masters	Karrie Webb (2)
Welch's/Circle K Championship	Juli Inkster
Standard Register Ping	Karrie Webb (3)
Nabisco Dinah Shore	Dottie Pepper
Longs Drugs Challenge	Juli Inkster (2)
Chick-fil-A Charity Championship	Rachel Hetherington
City of Hope Myrtle Beach Classic	Rachel Hetherington (2)
Mercury Titleholders Championship	Karrie Webb (4)
Sara Lee Classic	Meg Mallon (2)
Philips Invitational Honoring Harvey Penick	Akiko Fukushima
Corning Classic	Kelli Kuehne
U.S. Women's Open	Juli Inkster (3)
Wegmans Rochester International	Karrie Webb (5)
ShopRite Classic	Se Ri Pak
McDonald's LPGA Championship	Juli Inkster (4)
Jamie Farr Kroger Classic	Se Ri Pak (2)
Michelob Light Classic	Annika Sorenstam
JAL Big Apple Classic	Sherri Steinhauer
Giant Eagle Classic	Jackie Gallagher-Smith
du Maurier Classic	Karrie Webb (6)
areaWEB.COM Challenge	Mardi Lunn
Firstar Classic	Rosie Jones
Oldsmobile Classic	Dottie Pepper (2)
State Farm Rail Classic	Mi Hyun Kim
Samsung World Championship	Se Ri Pak (3)
Safeco Classic	Maria Hjorth
Safeway LPGA Championship	Juli Inkster (5)
New Albany Classic	Annika Sorenstam (2)
First Union Betsy King Classic	Mi Hyun Kim (2)
AFLAC Tournament of Champions	Akiko Fukushima (2)
PageNet Tour Championship	Se Ri Pak (4)
Diners Club Matches	Juli Inkster (6)/Dottie Pepper (3)

LADIES EUROPEAN TOUR

Royal Marie-Claire Open	Silvia Cavalleri
Evian Masters	Catrin Nilsmark (2)
Chrysler Open	Laura Davies
Ladies' French Open	Trish Johnson
Ladies' Austrian Open	Marina Arruti
stilwerk Ladies' German Open	Anne-Marie Knight
McDonald's WPGA Championship	Laura Davies (2)

Weetabix Women's British Open	Sherri Steinhauer (2)
Compaq Open	Laura Davies (3)
Cantor Fitzgerald Laura Davies' Invitational	Sofia Gronberg Whitmore
globalgolf.com Donegal Irish Ladies' Open	Sandrine Mendiburu
Ladies' Hannover Expo 2000 Open	Sandrine Mendiburu (2)
Ladies' Italian Open	Samantha Head
Air France Madame Biarritz Open	Sofia Gronberg Whitmore (2)
Marrakesh Palmeraie Open	Trish Johnson (2)
Princess Lalla Meriem Cup	Laura Fairclough
Praia D'el Rey Rover European Cup	Ladies European Tour

JAPAN LPGA TOUR

Daikin Orchid Ladies	Yoko Inoue
Saishunkan Ladies	Nahoko Hirao
Nasu Ogawa Ladies	Ok-Hee Ku
Katokichi Queens	Ayako Okamoto
Gunze Cup World Ladies	Yoko Inoue (2)
Yakult Ladies	Fumiko Muraguchi
Cyukyo TV Bridgestone Ladies	Fumiko Muraguchi (2)
Kosaido Ladies Golf Cup	Junko Yasui
Resort Trust Ladies	Hiromi Takamura
Suntory Ladies Open	Kaori Higo
Apita Circle K Sankus Ladies	Kaori Higo (2)
Japan Women's Open	Mayumi Murai
Toyo Suisan Ladies Hokkaido	Toshimi Kimura
Sumitomo Visa Taiheiyo Club Ladies	Junko Yasui (2)
Golf 5 Ladies	Aki Nakano
NEC Karuizawa 72	Hee-Won Han
Shin Caterpillar Mitsubishi Ladies	Fumiko Muraguchi (3)
Yonex Ladies	Natsuko Noro
Fujisankei Ladies Classic	Midori Yoneyama
Japan LPGA Championship Konika Cup	Fuki Kido
Yukijirushi Ladies Tokai Classic	Young-Me Lee
Miyagi TV Cup Dunlop Ladies Open	Ok-Hee Ku (2)
Osaka Ladies Open	Hee-Won Han (2)
TaKaRa World Invitational	Laura Davies (4)
Fujitsu Ladies	Michiko Hattori
Hisako Higuchi Kibun Classic	Kumiko Hiyoshi
Nichirei International	United States
Mizuno Classic	Maria Hjorth (2)
Itoen Ladies	Yuri Fudoh
Daio Seishi Elleair Ladies Open	Mayumi Hirase
Japan LPGA Meiji Nyugyo Cup	Kaori Higo (3)

Multiple Winners of 1999

PLAYER	WINS	PLAYER	WINS
Tiger Woods	11	Bob Heintz	2
Bruce Fleisher	7	Rachel Hetherington	2
Juli Inkster	6	Maria Hjorth	2
Colin Montgomerie	6	Tommy Horton	2
Karrie Webb	6	Kazuhiko Hosokawa	2
Laura Davies	5	Ryan Howison	2
David Duval	5	Yoko Inoue	2
Hale Irwin	5	Hiroshi Ishii	2
Allen Doyle	4	Toshimitsu Izawa	2
Gil Morgan	4	Miguel Angel Jimenez	2
Se Ri Pak	4	Richard Johnson	2
Lee Westwood	4	Trish Johnson	2
Choi Kyung-ju	3	Kim Jong-duk	2
Scott Dunlap	3	Mi Hyun Kim	2
Ernie Els	3	Fujio Kobayashi	2
Matt Gogel	3	Brian Kontak	2
Kaori Higo	3	Ok-Hee Ku	2
Fumiko Muraguchi	3	Bobby Lincoln	2
Larry Nelson	3	Meg Mallon	2
Christy O'Connor, Jr.	3	Graham Marsh	2
Hennie Otto	3	Gary McCord	2
Naomichi Ozaki	3	Rocco Mediate	2
Dottie Pepper	3	Sandrine Mendiburu	2
Fran Quinn	3	Ross Metherell	2
Kenneth Staton	3	Jack Nicklaus	2
Carl Suneson	3	Catrin Nilsmark	2
David Toms	3	Aaron Oberholser	2
Tsuyoshi Yoneyama	3	Masashi Ozaki	2
Stuart Appleby	2	David Park	2
Notah Begay III	2	Lucas Parsons	2
Thomas Bjorn	2	Carl Paulson	2
Desvonde Botes	2	Scott Petersen	2
Neil Coles	2	Eddie Polland	2
Fred Couples	2	Iain Pyman	2
Kenny Druce	2	Jarmo Sandelin	2
Ken Duke	2	Bob Shearer	2
Dave Eichelberger	2	Jeff Sluman	2
Brad Elder	2	Annika Sorenstam	2
Brad Faxon	2	Sherri Steinhauer	2
Carlos Franco	2	Payne Stewart	2
Akiko Fukushima	2	Ray Stewart	2
Sergio Garcia	2	Nico van Rensburg	2
Mathew Goggin	2	Duffy Waldorf	2
Steve Gotsche	2	Tom Watson	2
Sofia Gronberg Whitmore	2	Junko Yasui	2
Hee-Won Han	2		

World Money List

This list of the 400 leading money winners in the world of professional golf in 1999 was compiled from the results of men's (excluding seniors) tournaments carried in the Appendixes of this edition. This list includes tournaments with a minimum of 36 holes and four contestants and does not include such competitions as skins games, pro-ams and shootouts.

In the 34 years during which World Money Lists have been compiled, the earnings of the player in the 200th position have risen from a total of $3,326 in 1966 to $320,753 in 1999. The top-200 players in 1966 earned a total of $4,680,287. In 1999, the comparable total was $178,573,378.

The world money list of the International Federation of PGA Tours was used for the official money list events of the U.S. PGA Tour, PGA European Tour, PGA Tour of Japan, Southern Africa PGA Tour and PGA Tour of Australasia. The conversion rates used in 1999 for other events and other tours were: British pound = US$1.625; Japanese yen = US$0.00872; South African rand = US$0.17; Australian dollar = US$0.64; Canadian dollar = US$0.67.

POS.	PLAYER, COUNTRY	TOTAL MONEY
1	Tiger Woods, USA	$7,681,625
2	David Duval, USA	3,840,406
3	Ernie Els, South Africa	3,284,079
4	Colin Montgomerie, Scotland	2,988,543
5	Davis Love III, USA	2,756,578
6	Vijay Singh, Fiji	2,473,070
7	Sergio Garcia, Spain	2,277,314
8	Chris Perry, USA	2,234,832
9	Carlos, Franco, Paraguay	2,181,347
10	Lee Westwood, England	2,167,768
11	Hal Sutton, USA	2,127,578
12	Nick Price, Zimbabwe	2,100,272
13	Payne Stewart, USA	2,088,805
14	Jim Furyk, USA	2,072,283
15	Jeff Maggert, USA	2,066,469
16	David Toms, USA	2,064,397
17	Justin Leonard, USA	2,030,116
18	Steve Pate, USA	1,871,460
19	Jeff Sluman, USA	1,808,491
20	Miguel Angel Jimenez, Spain	1,800,732
21	Jose Maria Olazabal, Spain	1,791,788
22	Phil Mickelson, USA	1,757,681
23	John Huston, USA	1,721,858
24	Fred Funk, USA	1,658,381
25	Tim Herron, USA	1,623,202
26	Brent Geiberger, USA	1,541,409
27	Ted Tryba, USA	1,538,636
28	Mike Weir, Canada	1,496,914
29	Tom Lehman, USA	1,494,919
30	Stuart Appleby, Australia	1,469,388

POS.	PLAYER, COUNTRY	TOTAL MONEY
31	Retief Goosen, South Africa	1,449,217
32	Naomichi Ozaki, Japan	1,414,214
33	Duffy Waldorf, USA	1,378,784
34	Bob Estes, USA	1,357,618
35	Jesper Parnevik, Sweden	1,349,476
36	Paul Lawrie, Scotland	1,347,515
37	Stewart Cink, USA	1,339,873
38	Craig Parry, Australia	1,323,617
39	Notah Begay III, USA	1,322,114
40	Dennis Paulson, USA	1,321,189
41	Scott Hoch, USA	1,280,067
42	Darren Clarke, N. Ireland	1,279,518
43	Dudley Hart, USA	1,277,119
44	Mark O'Meara, USA	1,274,509
45	Loren Roberts, USA	1,272,245
46	Steve Elkington, Australia	1,234,626
47	Padraig Harrington, Ireland	1,203,589
48	Glen Day, USA	1,190,109
49	Kazuhiko Hosokawa, Japan	1,135,608
50	Fred Couples, USA	1,112,776
51	Shigeki Maruyama, Japan	1,090,373
52	Rocco Mediate, USA	1,028,275
53	Scott Gump, USA	1,025,082
54	Skip Kendall, USA	1,001,767
55	Andrew Magee, USA	997,565
56	Gabriel Hjertstedt, Sweden	990,565
57	Thomas Bjorn, Denmark	988,864
58	Toshimitsu Izawa, Japan	966,613
59	Tsuyoshi Yoneyama, Japan	928,053
60	Bob Tway, USA	899,484
61	Frank Lickliter, USA	887,797
62	Lee Janzen, USA	886,709
63	Mark Calcavecchia, USA	886,471
64	Olin Browne, USA	883,281
65	Kirk Triplett, USA	867,849
66	Bill Glasson, USA	854,263
67	Jonathan Kaye, USA	851,676
68	Greg Norman, Australia	838,350
69	Angel Cabrera, Argentina	832,814
70	Jay Haas, USA	825,611
71	Jarmo Sandelin, Sweden	816,927
72	Greg Kraft, USA	816,127
73	Brian Henninger, USA	815,736
74	Tommy Armour III, USA	791,310
75	Brian Watts, USA	789,632
76	Billy Mayfair, USA	787,430
77	Scott Dunlap, USA	775,478
78	Bernhard Langer, Germany	773,423
79	Kaname Yokoo, Japan	767,607
80	Brad Faxon, USA	754,691
81	Bob May, USA	752,944
82	Masashi Ozaki, Japan	714,308
83	John Cook, USA	714,193
84	Taichi Teshima, Japan	708,801

POS.	PLAYER, COUNTRY	TOTAL MONEY
85	Paul Goydos, USA	695,052
86	Jean Van de Velde, France	694,724
87	Chris DiMarco, USA	679,128
88	Paul Azinger, USA	677,053
89	Ryoken Kawagishi, Japan	672,630
90	Mark James, England	671,446
91	David Frost, South Africa	670,402
92	Tom Pernice, Jr., USA	665,265
93	Shingo Katayama, Japan	665,148
94	Kevin Sutherland, USA	663,891
95	Steve Stricker, USA	662,461
96	J.L. Lewis, USA	659,133
97	Craig Stadler, USA	657,230
98	Michael Campbell, New Zealand	648,033
99	Peter O'Malley, Australia	639,960
100	Robert Karlsson, Sweden	631,647
101	Jarrod Moseley, Australia	618,834
102	Hidemichi Tanaka, Japan	617,671
103	Rich Beem, USA	616,330
104	Toru Taniguchi, Japan	614,599
105	Corey Pavin, USA	610,045
106	Scott McCarron, USA	587,178
107	Ian Woosnam, Wales	582,155
108	Hirofumi Miyase, Japan	578,819
109	Alexander Cejka, Germany	578,420
110	Mark Brooks, USA	578,037
111	Steve Flesch, USA	559,721
112	Eduardo Romero, Argentina	558,784
113	Franklin Langham, USA	540,252
114	Jerry Kelly, USA	538,252
115	Brandt Jobe, USA	538,068
116	Katsunori Kuwabara, Japan	534,985
117	Craig Spence, Australia	531,042
118	Harrison Frazar, USA	530,971
119	David Howell, England	525,790
120	Shigemasa Higaki, Japan	521,556
121	Greg Turner, New Zealand	516,354
122	Choi Kyung-ju, Korea	513,694
123	Patrik Sjoland, Sweden	511,668
124	Hajime Meshiai, Japan	503,258
125	Tom Byrum, USA	495,319
126	John Daly, USA	494,367
127	John Bickerton, England	493,010
128	Bradley Hughes, Australia	492,272
129	Kim Jong-duk, Korea	490,677
130	Gary Orr, Scotland	488,825
131	Mike Reid, USA	487,317
132	Stephen Leaney, Australia	484,217
133	J.P. Hayes, USA	481,302
134	Mamoru Osanai, Japan	480,361
135	Miguel Angel Martin, Spain	477,810
136	Scott Verplank, USA	474,260
137	Tommy Tolles, USA	469,266
138	Billy Andrade, USA	468,301

POS.	PLAYER, COUNTRY	TOTAL MONEY
139	Jim Carter, USA	466,776
140	Andrew Coltart, Scotland	464,259
141	Paul McGinley, Ireland	461,802
142	Stephen Ames, Trinidad & Tobago	460,760
143	Robert Damron, USA	453,657
144	Dan Forsman, USA	452,071
145	Kenny Perry, USA	446,959
146	Dean Robertson, Scotland	443,162
147	Jay Delsing, USA	442,454
148	Jeev Milkha Singh, India	438,109
149	Tom Scherrer, USA	436,974
150	Barry Cheesman, USA	432,340
151	Peter Jacobsen, USA	431,461
152	David Carter, England	430,285
153	Pierre Fulke, Sweden	428,619
154	John Maginnes, USA	426,666
155	Omar Uresti, USA	416,201
156	Brandel Chamblee, USA	414,994
157	Tsukasa Watanabe, Japan	414,719
158	Joey Sindelar, USA	413,993
159	Kevin Wentworth, USA	413,601
160	Ignacio Garrido, Spain	410,677
161	Peter Baker, England	410,241
162	Katsuyoshi Tomori, Japan	410,226
163	Yasuharu Imano, Japan	409,139
164	Geoff Ogilvy, Australia	408,258
165	Mark Wiebe, USA	407,858
166	Seiki Okuda, Japan	403,217
167	Len Mattiace, USA	403,115
168	Santiago Luna, Spain	402,535
169	Satoshi Higashi, Japan	401,832
170	Rory Sabbatini, South Africa	400,822
171	Costantino Rocca, Italy	399,763
172	Jay Don Blake, USA	398,890
173	Steve Lowery, USA	398,437
174	Phillip Price, Wales	398,370
175	Greg Chalmers, Australia	397,035
176	Keiichiro Fukabori, Japan	393,670
177	Esteban Toledo, Mexico	393,046
178	Dicky Pride, USA	390,165
179	Larry Mize, USA	386,554
180	Robert Allenby, Australia	385,072
181	Brad Fabel, USA	380,441
182	David Ishii, USA	378,867
183	Chris Riley, USA	367,805
184	Steve Jones, USA	366,606
185	Mitsuo Harada, Japan	365,478
186	Paul Stankowski, USA	362,889
187	Mike Brisky, USA	361,084
188	Per-Ulrik Johansson, Sweden	356,038
189	Nick Faldo, England	353,751
190	Woody Austin, USA	346,295
191	Nolan Henke, USA	345,691
192	David Sutherland, USA	338,129

POS.	PLAYER, COUNTRY	TOTAL MONEY
193	Hideki Kase, Japan	335,743
194	Doug Barron, USA	334,995
195	Toru Suzuki, Japan	331,383
196	Charles Raulerson, USA	327,658
197	Craig Barlow, USA	327,393
198	David Park, Wales	326,902
199	Jamie Spence, England	325,512
200	Eric Booker, USA	320,753
201	Eduardo Herrera, Colombia	319,508
202	Trevor Dodds, Nambia	317,754
203	P.H. Horgan III, USA	317,206
204	Steve Webster, England	315,746
205	Russ Cochran, USA	314,423
206	Tateo Ozaki, Japan	313,838
207	Ronnie Black, USA	312,005
208	Nobumitsu Yuhara, Japan	311,030
209	Masayuki Kawamura, Japan	304,288
210	Nick O'Hern, Australia	301,801
211	Billy Ray Brown, USA	301,472
212	Joe Ogilvie, USA	300,796
213	Doug Dunakey, USA	298,069
214	Gary Evans, England	297,819
215	Blaine McCallister, USA	295,932
216	Pete Jordan, USA	295,419
217	Brett Quigley, USA	295,005
218	Mark McNulty, Zimbabwe	294,753
219	Emlyn Aubrey, USA	290,806
220	Frank Nobilo, New Zealand	288,934
221	Marc Farry, France	286,737
222	Paul Broadhurst, England	284,600
223	Neal Lancaster, USA	283,140
224	Sven Struver, Germany	281,811
225	Rick Fehr, USA	275,865
226	Frankie Minoza, Philippines	275,580
227	Mike Hulbert, USA	275,524
228	Edward Fryatt, England	273,622
229	David Smail, New Zealand	273,058
230	Jose Coceres, Argentina	266,217
231	Jay Williamson, USA	263,618
232	Peter Lonard, Australia	262,564
233	Phil Blackmar, USA	261,853
234	Richard Backwell, Australia	257,714
235	Michael Bradley, USA	257,525
236	Michael Long, New Zealand	257,213
237	Mike Sposa, USA	255,408
238	Ian Garbutt, England	255,077
239	Peter Mitchell, England	253,486
240	Grant Waite, New Zealand	253,209
241	Peter Senior, Australia	251,335
242	Anthony Wall, England	250,454
243	Russell Claydon, England	247,253
244	Jean Francois Remesy, France	247,206
245	Paul Eales, England	244,437
246	Soren Kjeldsen, Denmark	242,024

POS.	PLAYER, COUNTRY	TOTAL MONEY
247	Fran Quinn, USA	241,818
248	Hiroyuki Fujita, Japan	240,747
249	Perry Moss, USA	240,735
250	Kyi Hla Han, Myanmar	239,881
251	Francisco Cea, Spain	239,813
252	Yeh Chang-ting, Taiwan	238,079
253	Carl Paulson, USA	238,050
254	Yoshinori Kaneko, Japan	237,965
255	Eiji Mizoguchi, Japan	236,817
256	Mike Springer, USA	236,025
257	Matt Gogel, USA	235,173
258	Mathew Goggin, Australia	234,032
259	Phil Tataurangi, New Zealand	232,078
260	Hisayuki Sasaki, Japan	231,270
261	Raymond Russell, Scotland	228,943
262	Tom Kite, USA	228,380
263	Shaun Micheel, USA	225,364
264	Vanslow Phillips, England	224,961
265	Shusaku Sugimoto, Japan	224,814
266	Roger Wessels, South Africa	222,983
267	Ricardo Gonzalez, Argentina	220,591
268	Kazuhiro Takami, Japan	219,122
269	Emanuele Canonica, Italy	216,166
270	Joel Edwards, USA	213,937
271	Christopher Hanell, Sweden	211,671
272	John Senden, Australia	210,806
273	Steen Tinning, Denmark	208,601
274	Chen Tze-chung, Taiwan	206,765
275	Katsumasa Miyamoto, Japan	205,805
276	Zaw Moe, Myanmar	203,668
277	Greg Owen, England	203,276
278	Nobuhito Sato, Japan	201,878
279	Marco Dawson, USA	201,219
280	Todd Hamilton, USA	199,939
281	Dave Stockton, Jr., USA	197,127
282	Lin Keng-chi, Taiwan	193,184
283	Mats Lanner, Sweden	192,512
284	Jeff Gallagher, USA	189,847
285	Mathias Gronberg, Sweden	188,405
286	Michael Jonzon, Sweden	188,231
287	Toshiaki Odate, Japan	187,379
288	Joe Durant, USA	187,062
289	Diego Borrego, Spain	186,613
290	Rodney Pampling, Australia	186,551
291	Sean Murphy, USA	185,299
292	Ryan Howison, USA	184,815
293	Chip Beck, USA	184,423
294	Brian Davis, England	182,912
295	D.A. Weibring, USA	182,713
296	Paolo Quirici, Switzerland	182,294
297	Danny Briggs, USA	182,245
298	Clark Dennis, USA	180,843
299	Eamonn Darcy, Ireland	180,661
300	Bob Heintz, USA	180,222

POS.	PLAYER, COUNTRY	TOTAL MONEY
301	Doug Martin, USA	179,610
302	Masahiro Kuramoto, Japan	179,216
303	Scott Simpson, USA	179,006
304	Jose Rivero, Spain	177,543
305	Ben Bates, USA	176,919
306	Steven Conran, Australia	176,508
307	Glen Hnatiuk, Canada	176,085
308	Shinichi Yokota, Japan	175,302
309	Andrew McLardy, South Africa	173,372
310	Jimmy Green, USA	171,752
311	Bob Friend, USA	170,982
312	Dick Mast, USA	170,363
313	Takao Nogami, Japan	169,982
314	Gerry Norquist, USA	169,013
315	Kelly Gibson, USA	166,239
316	Roger Winchester, England	165,758
317	Warren Bennett, England	165,210
318	Thomas Levet, France	162,202
319	Barry Lane, England	158,021
320	Sam Torrance, Scotland	154,653
321	Steve Allan, Australia	154,438
322	Wayne Riley, Australia	154,272
323	Kang Wook-soon, Korea	153,412
324	Ikuo Shirahama, Japan	152,504
325	Per Nyman, Sweden	152,368
326	Des Smyth, Ireland	150,314
327	Pedro Linhart, Spain	148,569
328	Thomas Gogele, Germany	147,124
329	Cameron Beckman, USA	147,036
330	Craig Hainline, USA	146,933
331	David Peoples, USA	146,580
332	Brad Elder, USA	146,263
333	David Gilford, England	145,836
334	Lee Rinker, USA	145,678
335	Kiyoshi Maita, Japan	145,533
336	Simon Yates, Scotland	144,904
337	Nobuo Serizawa, Japan	144,568
338	Gary Nicklaus, USA	143,950
339	Massimo Scarpa, Italy	142,095
340	Sandy Lyle, Scotland	141,779
341	Dinesh Chand, Japan	141,255
342	David Ogrin, USA	141,082
343	Jyoti Randhawa, India	140,833
344	Kenny Druce, Australia	138,834
345	Bob Burns, USA	138,118
346	Tony Johnstone, Zimbabwe	137,606
347	Mark Roe, England	135,804
348	James Kingston, South Africa	134,574
349	Richard Kaplan, South Africa	132,486
350	Raphael Jacquelin, France	132,201
351	Jim Gallagher, Jr., USA	131,758
352	Jeff Gove, USA	129,692
353	Richard Green, Australia	129,444
354	Gary Emerson, England	129,395

POS.	PLAYER, COUNTRY	TOTAL MONEY
355	Nico van Rensburg, South Africa	128,500
356	David Berganio, Jr., USA	128,414
357	Paul Gow, Australia	128,075
358	Hennie Otto, South Africa	128,068
359	Anders Hansen, Denmark	126,890
360	Jeff Brehaut, USA	126,353
361	Stephen Gallacher, Scotland	125,179
362	Willie Wood, USA	124,171
363	Rolf Muntz, Holland	123,331
364	Casey Martin, USA	122,742
365	Robin Freeman, USA	122,634
366	Jonathan Lomas, England	122,132
367	Chris Couch, USA	121,752
368	John Elliott, USA	121,096
369	Jorge Berendt, Argentina	121,013
370	John Mellor, England	121,009
371	Fulton Allem, South Africa	120,365
372	Kiyoshi Murota, Japan	118,947
373	Steve Gotsche, USA	118,638
374	Deane Pappas, South Africa	118,168
375	Curtis Strange, USA	118,138
376	Stephen Scahill, New Zealand	117,384
377	Hsieh Chin-sheng, Taiwan	117,180
378	Desvonde Botes, South Africa	117,059
379	Jeremy Robinson, England	117,023
380	Chris Smith, USA	116,794
381	Yasunori Ida, Japan	116,647
382	Andrew Oldcorn, Scotland	115,517
383	Briny Baird, USA	115,357
384	Kevin Johnson, USA	115,247
385	Larry Rinker, USA	114,890
386	Jim McGovern, USA	113,828
387	Fredrik Lindgren, Sweden	113,126
388	Takashi Kanemoto, Japan	112,921
389	Lucas Parsons, Australia	111,968
390	Zhang Lian-wei, China	110,875
391	Scott Rowe, Canada	110,727
392	Marco Gortana, Italy	110,396
393	Lee Porter, USA	110,247
394	Peter McWhinney, Australia	110,165
395	Soren Hansen, Denmark	109,354
396	Todd Demsey, USA	109,112
397	Domingo Hospital, Spain	108,272
398	Paul Affleck, Wales	106,927
399	Nic Henning, South Africa	106,350
400	Marcus Cain, Australia	104,954

World Money List Leaders

YEAR	PLAYER, COUNTRY	TOTAL MONEY
1966	Jack Nicklaus, USA	$168,088
1967	Jack Nicklaus, USA	276,166
1968	Billy Casper, USA	222,436
1969	Frank Beard, USA	186,993
1970	Jack Nicklaus, USA	222,583
1971	Jack Nicklaus, USA	285,897
1972	Jack Nicklaus, USA	341,792
1973	Tom Weiskopf, USA	349,645
1974	Johnny Miller, USA	400,255
1975	Jack Nicklaus, USA	332,610
1976	Jack Nicklaus, USA	316,086
1977	Tom Watson, USA	358,034
1978	Tom Watson, USA	384,388
1979	Tom Watson, USA	506,912
1980	Tom Watson, USA	651,921
1981	Johnny Miller, USA	704,204
1982	Raymond Floyd, USA	738,699
1983	Seve Ballesteros, Spain	686,088
1984	Seve Ballesteros, Spain	688,047
1985	Bernhard Langer, Germany	860,262
1986	Greg Norman, Australia	1,146,584
1987	Ian Woosnam, Wales	1,793,268
1988	Seve Ballesteros, Spain	1,261,275
1989	David Frost, South Africa	1,650,230
1990	Jose Maria Olazabal, Spain	1,633,640
1991	Bernhard Langer, Germany	2,186,700
1992	Nick Faldo, England	2,748,248
1993	Nick Faldo, England	2,825,280
1994	Ernie Els, South Africa	2,862,854
1995	Corey Pavin, USA	2,746,340
1996	Colin Montgomerie, Scotland	3,071,442
1997	Colin Montgomerie, Scotland	3,366,900
1998	Tiger Woods, USA	2,927,946
1999	Tiger Woods, USA	7,681,625

Career World Money List

The following is a listing of the 50 leading money winners for their careers through the 1999 season. It includes players active on both the regular and senior tours of the world. The World Money List from this and the 33 previous editions of this annual and a table prepared for a companion book, *The Wonderful World of Professional Golf* (Atheneum, 1973), form the basis for this compilation. Additional figures were taken from official records of major golf associations, although the shortcomings in records-keeping in professional golf outside the United States in the 1950s and 1960s and exclusions from U.S. records in a few cases during those years prevent these figures from being completely accurate. Conversions of foreign currency figures to U.S. dollars are based on average values during the particular years involved.

POS.	PLAYER, COUNTRY	TOTAL MONEY
1	Greg Norman, Australia	$21,814,116
2	Nick Price, Zimbabwe	19,831,966
3	Colin Montgomerie, Scotland	19,317,113
4	Masashi Ozaki, Japan	19,192,561
5	Fred Couples, USA	19,025,004
6	Hale Irwin, USA	18,318,805
7	Bernhard Langer, Germany	18,083,209
8	Davis Love III, USA	17,137,410
9	Nick Faldo, England	16,725,596
10	Ernie Els, South Africa	16,692,410
11	Raymond Floyd, USA	16,187,969
12	Lee Trevino, USA	15,138,657
13	Mark O'Meara, USA	14,947,024
14	*Payne Stewart, USA	14,617,674
15	Isao Aoki, Japan	14,393,739
16	David Frost, South Africa	14,124,043
17	Ian Woosnam, Wales	14,012,266
18	Vijay Singh, Fiji	13,990,692
19	Tiger Woods, USA	13,884,462
20	Scott Hoch, USA	13,752,214
21	Tom Kite, USA	13,579,287
22	Mark Calcavecchia, USA	13,216,674
23	Gil Morgan, USA	12,739,563
24	Jose Maria Olazabal, Spain	12,496,033
25	Corey Pavin, USA	12,273,951
26	Naomichi Ozaki, Japan	11,979,127
27	Jim Colbert, USA	11,892,010
28	Tom Watson, USA	11,826,554
29	Severiano Ballesteros, Spain	11,670,974
30	Tom Lehman, USA	11,279,068
31	Steve Elkington, Australia	11,206,554
32	David Duval, USA	11,189,297
33	Bob Murphy, USA	11,118,654
34	Bob Charles, New Zealand	10,992,664
35	Graham Marsh, Australia	10,917,746
36	Dave Stockton, USA	10,787,845
37	Tsuneyuki Nakajima, Japan	10,646,698
38	Paul Azinger, USA	10,467,475

POS.	PLAYER, COUNTRY	TOTAL MONEY
39	Craig Stadler, USA	10,353,848
40	Jack Nicklaus, USA	10,349,760
41	Phil Mickelson, USA	10,296,791
42	George Archer, USA	10,094,658
43	Curtis Strange, USA	10,085,427
44	Gary Player, South Africa	9,900,861
45	John Cook, USA	9,716,854
46	Hal Sutton, USA	9,535,357
47	Jeff Sluman, USA	9,438,521
48	Ben Crenshaw, USA	9,360,555
49	Larry Nelson, USA	9,181,837
50	Lee Janzen, USA	9,035,848

*Died October 25, 1999

These 50 players have won $658,817,421 in their careers as professional golfers.

Senior World Money List

This list includes official earnings on the U.S. PGA Tour, U.S. Senior PGA Tour, European Seniors Tour and Japan Senior Tour, along with other winnings in established unofficial events when reliable figures could be obtained.

POS.	PLAYER, COUNTRY	TOTAL MONEY
1	Bruce Fleisher, USA	$2,629,105
2	Hale Irwin, USA	2,261,482
3	Gil Morgan, USA	1,981,282
4	Allen Doyle, USA	1,961,640
5	Larry Nelson, USA	1,861,024
6	Dana Quigley, USA	1,452,658
7	Tom Jenkins, USA	1,287,176
8	Bruce Summerhays, USA	1,181,377
9	Graham Marsh, Australia	1,153,144
10	Vicente Fernandez, Argentina	1,152,125
11	Jose Maria Canizares, Spain	1,102,284
12	John Mahaffey, USA	1,094,778
13	Joe Inman, USA	1,066,357
14	David Graham, Australia	1,023,839
15	John Jacobs, USA	1,012,318
16	Gary McCord, USA	993,291
17	Ed Dougherty, USA	951,072
18	Dave Eichelberger, USA	885,932
19	Jim Thorpe, USA	866,246
20	Christy O'Connor, Jr., Ireland	828,588
21	Hubert Green, USA	823,046
22	Raymond Floyd, USA	820,794
23	Walter Hall, USA	816,342

POS.	PLAYER, COUNTRY	TOTAL MONEY
24	J.C. Snead, USA	797,341
25	Hugh Baiocchi, South Africa	767,646
26	George Archer, USA	757,360
27	Jay Sigel, USA	746,311
28	Bob Duval, USA	726,674
29	Jim Dent, USA	725,702
30	Jim Colbert, USA	638,621
31	Leonard Thompson, USA	635,095
32	Fred Gibson, USA	627,839
33	Al Geiberger, USA	627,562
34	Mike McCullough, USA	595,054
35	John Bland, South Africa	593,633
36	Tom Wargo, USA	589,621
37	Terry Dill, USA	583,637
38	Lee Trevino, USA	566,103
39	Kermit Zarley, USA	536,146
40	David Lundstrom, USA	501,491
41	Dave Stockton, USA	494,154
42	Jim Ahern, USA	478,963
43	Tom McGinnis, USA	477,216
44	Bob Murphy, USA	472,956
45	Tom Watson, USA	449,650
46	Jim Albus, USA	443,426
47	Bob Charles, New Zealand	423,728
48	Bob Dickson, USA	421,000
49	Frank Conner, USA	419,631
50	Isao Aoki, Japan	359,573
51	Brian Barnes, Scotland	350,126
52	Dale Douglass, USA	330,439
53	Gibby Gilbert, USA	323,984
54	Walter Morgan, USA	309,068
55	Howard Twitty, USA	308,655
56	Rocky Thompson, USA	305,275
57	John Morgan, England	298,906
58	Tom Shaw, USA	292,836
59	Bob Eastwood, USA	288,789
60	Gary Player, South Africa	287,714
61	Simon Hobday, South Africa	280,087
62	DeWitt Weaver, USA	253,408
63	Jim Holtgrieve, USA	250,854
64	Jack Nicklaus, USA	245,998
65	Stewart Ginn, Australia	226,593
66	Larry Ziegler, USA	209,071
67	Mike Hill, USA	203,664
68	Buzz Thomas, USA	202,908
69	Alberto Giannone, Argentina	195,604
70	Bobby Stroble, USA	191,926
71	Tommy Horton, England	187,094
72	Charles Coody, USA	173,893
73	Barney Thompson, USA	168,293
74	Larry Mowry, USA	165,826
75	Chi Chi Rodriguez, Puerto Rico	163,907
76	Bud Allin, USA	162,959
77	Noel Ratcliffe, Australia	158,426

POS.	PLAYER, COUNTRY	TOTAL MONEY
78	Butch Baird, USA	158,358
79	Jesse Patino, USA	154,570
80	Tommy Aaron, USA	136,848
81	Eddie Polland, N. Ireland	136,564
82	Orville Moody, USA	134,617
83	Jimmy Powell, USA	134,614
84	Harold Henning, South Africa	131,237
85	Jerry Bruner, USA	129,882
86	Steven Veriato, USA	126,474
87	Doug Tewell, USA	124,314
88	Neil Coles, England	121,900
89	Bill Brask, USA	118,561
90	Alan Tapie, USA	114,150
91	Antonio Garrido, Spain	111,250
92	Ross Metherell, Australia	107,403
93	David Jones, N. Ireland	105,702
94	Mike Malone, USA	104,958
95	David Oakley, USA	100,666
96	Tom Weiskopf, USA	100,070
97	Bob Shearer, Australia	95,299
98	David Huish, Scotland	91,643
99	Ray Carrasco, USA	89,881
100	Bernard Gallacher, Scotland	86,694

Women's World Money List

This list includes official earnings on the U.S. LPGA Tour, Ladies European Tour and Japan LPGA Tour, along with other winnings in established unofficial events when reliable figures could be obtained.

POS.	PLAYER, COUNTRY	TOTAL MONEY
1	Karrie Webb, Australia	$1,641,959
2	Juli Inkster, USA	1,446,378
3	Laura Davies, England	1,247,289
4	Se Ri Pak, Korea	1,087,622
5	Annika Sorenstam, Sweden	952,141
6	Lorie Kane, Canada	831,119
7	Maria Hjorth, Sweden	734,945
8	Sherri Steinhauer, USA	719,664
9	Dottie Pepper, USA	715,375
10	Meg Mallon, USA	699,429
11	Fumiko Muraguchi, Japan	642,656
12	Janice Moodie, Scotland	640,305
13	Mi Hyun Kim, Korea	621,746
14	Rosie Jones, USA	621,296
15	Ok-Hee Ku, Korea	599,645
16	Rachel Hetherington, Australia	580,534
17	Mardi Lunn, Australia	576,942

POS.	PLAYER, COUNTRY	TOTAL MONEY
18	Akiko Fukushima, Japan	539,588
19	Kaori Higo, Japan	536,335
20	Yuri Fudoh, Japan	521,593
21	Kelli Kuehne, USA	504,759
22	Kelly Robbins, USA	490,498
23	Hee-Won Han, Korea	487,247
24	Liselotte Neumann, Sweden	472,075
25	Tina Barrett, USA	467,973
26	Helen Alfredsson, Sweden	448,063
27	Aki Nakano, Japan	445,153
28	Catrin Nilsmark, Sweden	431,737
29	Midori Yoneyama, Japan	407,094
30	Catriona Matthew, Scotland	403,845
31	Michiko Hattori, Japan	400,730
32	Aki Takamura, Japan	396,699
33	Cindy McCurdy, USA	396,231
34	Alison Nicholas, England	379,238
35	Emilee Klein, USA	372,608
36	Nancy Scranton, USA	366,433
37	Fuki Kido, Japan	365,724
38	Junko Yasui, Japan	362,861
39	Beth Daniel, USA	355,989
40	Trish Johnson, England	344,502
41	Michie Ohba, Japan	330,799
42	Helen Dobson, England	328,404
43	Mayumi Hirase, Japan	318,007
44	Carin Koch, Sweden	310,343
45	Jan Stephenson, Australia	305,472
46	Sherri Turner, USA	301,086
47	Harumi Sakagami, Japan	298,709
48	Becky Iverson, USA	297,973
49	Charlotta Sorenstam, Sweden	290,333
50	Toshimi Kimura, Japan	288,066
51	Jenny Lidback, Peru	282,966
52	Michele Redman, USA	282,508
53	Huang Yu-Chen, Taiwan	272,144
54	Kumiko Hiyoshi, Japan	271,387
55	Jill McGill, USA	268,734
56	Yoko Inoue, Japan	259,900
57	Kris Tschetter, USA	257,907
58	Young-Me Lee, Korea	257,323
59	Mayumi Murai, Japan	244,403
60	Kristi Albers, USA	242,821
61	Hiromi Kobayashi, Japan	237,886
62	Leta Lindley, USA	235,706
63	Pearl Sinn, Korea	233,063
64	Man-Soo Kim, Korea	227,984
65	Cindy Figg-Currier, USA	227,114
66	Wendy Doolan, Australia	209,896
67	Jackie Gallagher-Smith, USA	199,606
68	Lisa Kiggens, USA	199,128
69	Miyuki Shimabukuro, Japan	199,005
70	Chris Johnson, USA	198,665
71	Jane Geddes, USA	185,642

POS.	PLAYER, COUNTRY	TOTAL MONEY
72	Yuka Irie, Japan	185,391
73	Tammie Green, USA	184,644
74	Jane Crafter, Australia	182,365
75	Marnie McGuire, New Zealand	180,284
76	Cindy Flom, USA	178,705
77	Cristie Kerr, USA	177,978
78	Ayako Okamoto, Japan	177,699
79	Tseng Hsiu-Feng, Taiwan	176,915
80	Kim Saiki, USA	174,886
81	Hollis Stacy, USA	173,127
82	Eva Dahllof, Sweden	169,052
83	Laura Philo, USA	167,602
84	Natsuko Noro, Japan	160,434
85	Ikuyo Shiotani, Japan	159,474
86	Dale Eggeling, USA	158,406
87	Sofia Gronberg Whitmore, Sweden	158,277
88	Dawn Coe-Jones, USA	157,420
89	Sophie Gustafson, Sweden	156,984
90	Nahoko Hirao, Japan	156,894
91	Susie Redman, USA	155,664
92	Donna Andrews, USA	151,440
93	A.J. Eathorne, Canada	150,937
94	Hiromi Takamura, Japan	148,086
95	Kyoko Ono, Japan	147,628
96	Yuko Moriguchi, Japan	147,134
97	Chieko Nishida, Japan	143,285
98	Jae-Sook Won, Korea	142,491
99	Gail Graham, Canada	142,373
100	Lora Fairclough, England	141,736
101	Woo-Soon Ko, Korea	141,019
102	Kasumi Fujii, Japan	140,502
103	Betsy King, USA	138,817
104	Raquel Carriedo, Spain	136,852
105	Joanne Morley, England	130,338
106	Kathryn Marshall, Scotland	129,462
107	Maggie Will, USA	129,286
108	Moira Dunn, USA	129,139
109	Mineko Nasu, Japan	125,671
110	Keiko Arai, Japan	125,555
111	Melissa McNamara, USA	125,042
112	Suzanne Strudwick, England	124,928
113	Yuri Kawanami, Japan	124,770
114	Akane Ohshiro, Japan	122,115
115	Michelle McGann, USA	120,404
116	Tracy Hanson, USA	119,988
117	Wendy Ward, USA	118,799
118	Ae-Sook Kim, Korea	118,003
119	Jean Bartholomew, USA	117,694
120	Denise Killeen, USA	116,475
121	Barb Mucha, USA	112,470
122	Pat Hurst, USA	111,403
123	Sandrine Mendiburu, France	111,254
124	Hisako Takeda, Japan	110,614
125	Joan Pitcock, USA	108,993

American Tours

Mercedes Championships

Plantation Course at Kapalua, Lahaina, Maui, Hawaii
Par 36-37–73; 7,263 yards

January 7-10
purse, $2,600,000

	SCORES				TOTAL	MONEY
David Duval	67	63	68	68	266	$468,000
Billy Mayfair	66	69	69	71	275	228,800
Mark O'Meara	70	68	69	68	275	228,800
Vijay Singh	70	65	70	71	276	124,800
Fred Funk	66	69	68	74	277	94,900
Justin Leonard	68	72	68	69	277	94,900
Tiger Woods	69	69	67	72	277	94,900
Davis Love III	69	68	71	70	278	81,900
Jim Furyk	68	69	68	75	280	76,700
Fred Couples	69	68	73	71	281	72,800
Billy Andrade	67	70	74	71	282	69,550
J.P. Hayes	70	71	70	72	283	66,950
Lee Janzen	69	72	74	69	284	63,050
Jeff Sluman	73	67	72	72	284	63,050
Steve Pate	66	70	73	76	285	59,150
Stuart Appleby	70	71	72	73	286	55,250
Brandel Chamblee	70	71	69	76	286	55,250
Joe Durant	66	70	77	74	287	51,025
John Huston	71	71	73	72	287	51,025
Mark Calcavecchia	70	71	70	77	288	47,125
Chris Perry	69	73	74	72	288	47,125
John Cook	68	69	80	73	290	43,550
Steve Jones	75	69	73	73	290	43,550
Phil Mickelson	72	70	70	78	290	43,550
Scott Simpson	71	71	74	76	292	40,950
Steve Elkington	74	73	73	73	293	39,975
Jesper Parnevik	69	74	73	77	293	39,975
Trevor Dodds	72	73	75	75	295	39,130
Tom Watson	74	71	75	76	296	38,610
Michael Bradley	71	78	76	76	301	38,090

Sony Open in Hawaii

Waialae Country Club, Honolulu, Hawaii
Par 35-35–70; 7,114 yards

January 14-17
purse, $2,600,000

	SCORES				TOTAL	MONEY
Jeff Sluman	69	70	66	66	271	$468,000
Davis Love III	71	69	63	70	273	156,000
Jeff Maggert	69	70	66	68	273	156,000
Len Mattiace	70	66	69	68	273	156,000
Chris Perry	69	69	69	66	273	156,000
Tommy Tolles	63	72	67	71	273	156,000
Chris Couch	69	70	68	67	274	75,660
Paul Goydos	72	68	67	67	274	75,660

	SCORES			TOTAL	MONEY
Jimmy Green	70	70	68	66	274	75,660
Chris Riley	67	71	68	68	274	75,660
Loren Roberts	69	69	69	67	274	75,660
Fred Funk	66	71	73	65	275	52,650
John Huston	68	68	68	71	275	52,650
Larry Mize	69	68	69	69	275	52,650
Mark O'Meara	66	71	67	71	275	52,650
Stuart Appleby	69	68	70	69	276	41,600
Esteban Toledo	65	72	68	71	276	41,600
Tom Watson	71	68	71	66	276	41,600
Jim Furyk	70	72	66	69	277	31,512
Nolan Henke	70	67	68	72	277	31,512
Tim Herron	69	70	70	68	277	31,512
Mike Sposa	71	66	70	70	277	31,512
Duffy Waldorf	69	69	69	70	277	31,512
Cameron Beckman	67	72	71	68	278	21,580
Dan Forsman	67	71	75	65	278	21,580
Mike Hulbert	69	66	70	73	278	21,580
Peter Jacobsen	66	73	70	69	278	21,580
Steve Jones	70	70	70	68	278	21,580
Mike Brisky	72	68	70	69	279	17,290
John Maginnes	67	72	69	71	279	17,290
Jesper Parnevik	71	68	70	70	279	17,290
Craig Stadler	70	66	72	71	279	17,290
Billy Andrade	68	74	70	68	280	14,040
Scott Gump	68	72	71	69	280	14,040
Steve Jurgensen	67	71	72	70	280	14,040
Lee Porter	71	71	69	69	280	14,040
Kaname Yokoo	72	67	72	69	280	14,040
Jay Don Blake	69	70	70	72	281	10,400
Danny Briggs	72	68	71	70	281	10,400
John Cook	68	71	71	71	281	10,400
Joe Durant	66	73	73	69	281	10,400
Keiichiro Fukabori	74	67	71	69	281	10,400
Jonathan Kaye	69	71	72	69	281	10,400
Dicky Pride	72	68	69	72	281	10,400
Vijay Singh	67	75	68	71	281	10,400
Ty Armstrong	66	71	73	72	282	7,800
Naomichi Ozaki	67	72	69	74	282	7,800
Emlyn Aubrey	70	72	68	73	283	6,614.40
Craig Barlow	66	76	71	70	283	6,614.40
Brandel Chamblee	68	66	74	75	283	6,614.40
David Ishii	72	68	73	70	283	6,614.40
Mike Reid	68	71	75	69	283	6,614.40
Rich Beem	71	68	74	71	284	6,084
John Daly	69	69	72	74	284	6,084
Tommy Armour III	68	70	76	71	285	5,850
Ben Bates	68	71	76	70	285	5,850
Carlos Franco	69	69	73	74	285	5,850
Robert Gamez	71	70	75	69	285	5,850
Jerry Kelly	70	71	74	70	285	5,850
Greg Meyer	69	71	73	72	285	5,850
Notah Begay III	65	77	70	74	286	5,616
Bradley Hughes	72	69	71	74	286	5,616
Lee Rinker	71	70	71	74	286	5,616
Fulton Allem	72	68	72	75	287	5,460
Scott Simpson	71	69	76	71	287	5,460
Omar Uresti	71	69	74	73	287	5,460
Franklin Langham	71	70	74	73	288	5,356
Bob Burns	66	74	74	75	289	5,304

		SCORES			TOTAL	MONEY
Jay Williamson	69	73	74	74	290	5,252
Dennis Paulson	73	69	74	77	293	5,200
Robert Damron	70	71	76	82	299	5,148

Bob Hope Chrysler Classic

La Quinta, California   January 20-24
PGA West, Palmer Course: Par 36-36–72; 6,950 yards   purse, $3,000,000
Bermuda Dunes CC: Par 36-36–72; 6,927 yards
Indian Wells CC: Par 36-36–72; 6,478 yards
Tamarisk CC: Par 36-36–72; 6,881 yards

			SCORES			TOTAL	MONEY
David Duval	70	71	64	70	59	334	$540,000
Steve Pate	66	70	64	69	66	335	324,000
John Huston	63	73	71	63	66	336	204,000
Bob Estes	68	71	65	67	68	339	132,000
Fred Funk	65	68	66	69	71	339	132,000
Skip Kendall	67	73	66	64	70	340	108,000
Jeff Maggert	69	72	66	68	66	341	100,500
Paul Goydos	67	72	69	70	64	342	87,000
Jeff Sluman	68	68	70	68	68	342	87,000
Kevin Sutherland	69	72	66	67	68	342	87,000
Robert Allenby	70	70	67	70	66	343	72,000
Scott Verplank	67	71	67	67	71	343	72,000
Gabriel Hjertstedt	67	74	65	67	71	344	54,600
Peter Jacobsen	66	72	70	70	66	344	54,600
John Maginnes	70	70	70	68	66	344	54,600
Tom Pernice, Jr.	63	72	66	74	69	344	54,600
Ted Tryba	69	72	68	69	66	344	54,600
Russ Cochran	69	70	67	72	67	345	42,000
Payne Stewart	71	70	66	71	67	345	42,000
Kirk Triplett	70	70	67	70	68	345	42,000
John Daly	69	66	66	73	72	346	33,600
Loren Roberts	68	69	70	67	72	346	33,600
Steve Stricker	69	75	67	71	64	346	33,600
Stewart Cink	70	71	67	73	66	347	25,575
Len Mattiace	68	70	69	67	73	347	25,575
David Toms	71	76	69	63	68	347	25,575
Bob Tway	66	76	64	69	72	347	25,575
J.P. Hayes	68	72	68	71	69	348	20,850
Billy Mayfair	72	74	67	70	65	348	20,850
Rocco Mediate	65	74	70	68	71	348	20,850
Esteban Toledo	71	73	69	67	68	348	20,850
Ben Bates	63	74	74	70	68	349	16,980
Greg Chalmers	70	69	72	68	70	349	16,980
Nolan Henke	71	72	71	68	67	349	16,980
Scott McCarron	67	72	73	69	68	349	16,980
Mike Weir	67	71	74	66	71	349	16,980
Glen Day	69	72	72	68	69	350	14,100
Bob Friend	69	71	71	72	67	350	14,100
Scott Hoch	69	70	72	70	69	350	14,100
Jay Don Blake	70	73	70	68	70	351	12,300
Jerry Kelly	71	73	66	71	70	351	12,300
Lee Porter	69	77	69	66	70	351	12,300
Fulton Allem	66	73	69	71	73	352	8,766
Stuart Appleby	72	74	67	71	68	352	8,766

	SCORES	TOTAL	MONEY
Mark Brooks	68 76 71 67 70	352	8,766
Robert Gamez	71 71 68 70 72	352	8,766
Jay Haas	74 69 71 68 70	352	8,766
Brian Henninger	71 71 71 68 71	352	8,766
Jonathan Kaye	64 83 62 69 74	352	8,766
Dennis Paulson	67 71 73 70 71	352	8,766
Chris Perry	67 75 69 69 72	352	8,766
Mike Reid	70 76 68 69 69	352	8,766
Barry Cheesman	73 69 70 71 70	353	6,817.50
Keith Fergus	71 71 68 70 73	353	6,817.50
Robin Freeman	71 75 66 71 70	353	6,817.50
Donnie Hammond	68 78 69 65 73	353	6,817.50
Deane Pappas	70 74 69 70 70	353	6,817.50
Kenny Perry	68 70 73 70 72	353	6,817.50
Joey Sindelar	69 74 72 68 70	353	6,817.50
Omar Uresti	70 69 69 74 71	353	6,817.50
Jim Carter	66 72 76 68 72	354	6,450
Frank Lickliter	68 75 71 70 70	354	6,450
Dave Stockton, Jr.	67 74 73 69 71	354	6,450
Grant Waite	71 74 69 70 70	354	6,450
Jeff Freeman	64 74 70 73 74	355	6,270
Corey Pavin	73 71 68 70 73	355	6,270
Phil Blackmar	71 71 70 71 73	356	6,150
Bo Van Pelt	65 70 74 74 73	356	6,150
Chris DiMarco	70 73 75 65 75	358	6,060
Jesper Parnevik	71 70 74 69 76	360	6,000
Bradley Hughes	75 76 66 65 79	361	5,940

Phoenix Open

TPC of Scottsdale, Scottsdale, Arizona
Par 35-36–71; 7,059 yards

January 28-31
purse, $3,000,000

	SCORES	TOTAL	MONEY
Rocco Mediate	69 67 66 71	273	$540,000
Justin Leonard	67 75 67 66	275	324,000
Tiger Woods	71 67 70 68	276	204,000
Hal Sutton	69 70 71 69	279	144,000
Bill Glasson	69 71 70 70	280	120,000
Harrison Frazar	74 69 66 73	282	97,125
Jim Furyk	72 69 70 71	282	97,125
Kenny Perry	72 70 68 72	282	97,125
Kevin Wentworth	72 72 71 67	282	97,125
Stewart Cink	74 69 71 69	283	72,000
Dudley Hart	75 70 70 68	283	72,000
J.P. Hayes	70 71 69 73	283	72,000
Lee Janzen	69 71 69 74	283	72,000
Paul Azinger	68 73 72 71	284	52,500
John Daly	77 70 70 67	284	52,500
Jesper Parnevik	71 71 73 69	284	52,500
Steve Stricker	70 72 71 71	284	52,500
Stuart Appleby	72 70 70 73	285	40,500
David Duval	74 71 66 74	285	40,500
Payne Stewart	69 73 75 68	285	40,500
Willie Wood	72 74 66 73	285	40,500
Fred Funk	71 71 73 71	286	30,000
Scott Hoch	77 66 75 68	286	30,000

		SCORES			TOTAL	MONEY
Scott McCarron	74	73	70	69	286	30,000
Mike Weir	73	72	68	73	286	30,000
Mark Calcavecchia	74	72	68	73	287	21,300
Bob Estes	75	71	68	73	287	21,300
Andrew Magee	72	69	76	70	287	21,300
Dennis Paulson	76	70	66	75	287	21,300
Doug Tewell	74	72	70	71	287	21,300
David Toms	75	69	70	73	287	21,300
Duffy Waldorf	73	70	74	70	287	21,300
Tommy Armour III	77	67	73	71	288	15,514.29
Jonathan Kaye	72	67	76	73	288	15,514.29
Blaine McCallister	69	74	72	73	288	15,514.29
Scott Verplank	70	74	72	72	288	15,514.29
Russ Cochran	73	74	73	68	288	15,514.28
Nolan Henke	74	70	71	73	288	15,514.28
Gabriel Hjertstedt	69	73	69	77	288	15,514.28
Phil Blackmar	72	73	74	70	289	12,000
Jay Don Blake	75	68	78	68	289	12,000
Steve Lowery	72	70	74	73	289	12,000
Tommy Tolles	73	71	71	74	289	12,000
Glen Day	70	73	77	70	290	9,324
Bob Friend	72	69	70	79	290	9,324
Skip Kendall	70	76	71	73	290	9,324
Larry Rinker	76	70	72	72	290	9,324
Kevin Sutherland	71	74	72	73	290	9,324
Robert Damron	73	70	74	74	291	7,580
Tom Purtzer	75	70	73	73	291	7,580
Scott Simpson	74	73	69	75	291	7,580
J.L. Lewis	74	71	71	76	292	7,140
Chris Riley	73	71	73	75	292	7,140
Clark Dennis	78	68	74	73	293	6,870
Chris DiMarco	72	72	75	74	293	6,870
Franklin Langham	70	71	72	80	293	6,870
Steve Pate	74	72	74	73	293	6,870
Tom Byrum	75	71	74	74	294	6,660
Naomichi Ozaki	72	71	76	75	294	6,660
Charles Raulerson	75	72	74	73	294	6,660
Phil Mickelson	74	71	70	80	295	6,540
Brian Henninger	74	71	76	75	296	6,450
Ted Tryba	70	74	79	73	296	6,450
Ben Bates	72	73	73	79	297	6,270
Ronnie Black	75	72	72	78	297	6,270
Scott Gump	75	72	78	72	297	6,270
Ted Purdy	75	68	78	76	297	6,270
Paul Goydos	75	72	71	80	298	6,120
Mike Springer	72	73	77	77	299	6,030
Kirk Triplett	71	75	70	83	299	6,030
Deane Pappas	74	73	82	73	302	5,940

AT&T Pebble Beach National Pro-Am

Pebble Beach, California
Pebble Beach GL: Par 36-36–72; 6,840 yards
Spyglass Hill GC: Par 36-36–72; 6,859 yards
Poppy Hills GC: Par 36-36–72; 6,861 yards
(Fourth round cancelled — rain.)

February 4-7
purse, $2,800,000

	SCORES			TOTAL	MONEY
Payne Stewart	69	64	73	206	$504,000
Frank Lickliter	68	68	71	207	302,400
Craig Stadler	70	67	72	209	190,400
Ronnie Black	71	69	70	210	110,250
Fred Couples	72	65	73	210	110,250
Justin Leonard	70	72	68	210	110,250
Jay Williamson	69	70	71	210	110,250
Neal Lancaster	73	70	68	211	84,000
Tommy Tolles	71	70	70	211	84,000
Paul Azinger	69	71	72	212	64,400
Tim Herron	72	68	72	212	64,400
Davis Love III	73	65	74	212	64,400
Brett Quigley	66	73	73	212	64,400
Vijay Singh	69	67	76	212	64,400
David Duval	72	65	76	213	43,400
Steve Elkington	70	69	74	213	43,400
Skip Kendall	72	73	68	213	43,400
Naomichi Ozaki	69	70	74	213	43,400
Paul Stankowski	71	70	72	213	43,400
Kevin Sutherland	68	71	74	213	43,400
Mark Calcavecchia	73	67	74	214	30,240
Brad Faxon	73	70	71	214	30,240
Phil Mickelson	72	67	75	214	30,240
Mike Reid	73	73	68	214	30,240
Alan Bratton	70	72	73	215	20,920
Steve Flesch	69	73	73	215	20,920
Doug Martin	69	74	72	215	20,920
Chris Riley	76	68	71	215	20,920
Joey Sindelar	71	72	72	215	20,920
Dave Stockton, Jr.	70	70	75	215	20,920
Charles Raulerson	68	71	76	215	20,920
Paul Goydos	70	72	74	216	15,160
P.H. Horgan III	71	73	72	216	15,160
Peter Jacobsen	67	75	74	216	15,160
Dennis Paulson	73	69	74	216	15,160
Mike Sposa	70	72	74	216	15,160
Kevin Wentworth	75	69	72	216	15,160
Willie Wood	73	68	75	216	15,160
Robert Allenby	72	73	72	217	11,480
Brian Claar	69	71	77	217	11,480
Dudley Hart	69	72	76	217	11,480
Jeff Maggert	77	69	71	217	11,480
Greg Kraft	66	72	79	217	11,480
Emlyn Aubrey	72	72	74	218	7,939.56
Craig Barlow	69	75	74	218	7,939.56
Kelly Gibson	72	69	77	218	7,939.56
Jim McGovern	70	73	75	218	7,939.56
Kirk Triplett	68	70	80	218	7,939.56
Jeff Brehaut	74	69	75	218	7,939.55
Scott McCarron	75	67	76	218	7,939.55
Spike McRoy	72	72	74	218	7,939.55

	SCORES			TOTAL	MONEY
Corey Pavin	69	76	73	218	7,939.55
Stuart Appleby	72	74	73	219	6,220.31
Notah Begay III	74	74	71	219	6,220.31
Glen Day	74	73	72	219	6,220.31
Robert Gamez	73	73	73	219	6,220.31
Donnie Hammond	75	72	72	219	6,220.31
Jerry Kelly	70	72	77	219	6,220.31
Jeff Sluman	69	75	75	219	6,220.31
Grant Waite	74	74	71	219	6,220.31
Tom Watson	72	73	74	219	6,220.31
Brian Watts	72	71	76	219	6,220.31
John Maginnes	74	73	72	219	6,220.30
Mark O'Meara	71	72	76	219	6,220.30
Tiger Woods	72	69	78	219	6,220.30
Billy Andrade	76	71	73	220	5,712
Jimmy Green	71	74	75	220	5,712
Jay Haas	68	74	78	220	5,712
Frank Nobilo	73	70	77	220	5,712
Tom Scherrer	71	72	77	220	5,712

Buick Invitational

Torrey Pines Golf Club, San Diego, California
South Course: Par 36-36–72; 7,022 yards
North Course: Par 36-36–72; 6,862 yards

February 11-14
purse, $2,700,000

	SCORES				TOTAL	MONEY
Tiger Woods	68	71	62	65	266	$486,000
Billy Ray Brown	69	65	68	66	268	291,600
Bill Glasson	68	67	68	67	270	183,600
Chris Perry	66	69	72	66	273	111,600
Kevin Sutherland	68	68	67	70	273	111,600
Omar Uresti	71	66	69	67	273	111,600
Dennis Paulson	67	64	74	70	275	81,337.50
Chris Riley	72	65	68	70	275	81,337.50
Loren Roberts	70	70	68	67	275	81,337.50
Scott Simpson	71	68	66	70	275	81,337.50
Billy Andrade	69	67	72	68	276	53,614.29
Bob Estes	71	66	69	70	276	53,614.29
Katsumasa Miyamoto	66	74	66	70	276	53,614.29
David Toms	71	70	64	71	276	53,614.29
Scott Hoch	69	66	69	72	276	53,614.28
Frank Lickliter	67	66	70	73	276	53,614.28
Brian Watts	70	67	68	71	276	53,614.28
Bob Burns	66	71	71	69	277	37,800
Jonathan Kaye	69	67	70	71	277	37,800
Jeff Sluman	69	69	71	68	277	37,800
Woody Austin	68	72	69	69	278	28,080
Michael Bradley	72	65	72	69	278	28,080
Jeff Maggert	70	67	69	72	278	28,080
Charles Raulerson	71	69	68	70	278	28,080
Ted Tryba	65	65	74	74	278	28,080
Stewart Cink	69	69	70	71	279	20,385
Chris Couch	70	70	68	71	279	20,385
Jason Gore	68	68	70	73	279	20,385
Craig Stadler	71	65	70	73	279	20,385
Robert Allenby	68	67	72	73	280	16,767

	SCORES				TOTAL	MONEY
Barry Cheesman	71	69	71	69	280	16,767
Brad Faxon	70	68	73	69	280	16,767
Skip Kendall	72	65	70	73	280	16,767
Frank Nobilo	71	70	70	69	280	16,767
David Berganio, Jr.	69	67	74	71	281	11,920.50
Eric Booker	67	70	70	74	281	11,920.50
Dan Forsman	69	68	71	73	281	11,920.50
Bob Friend	70	70	71	70	281	11,920.50
Bradley Hughes	70	71	72	68	281	11,920.50
Neal Lancaster	69	69	73	70	281	11,920.50
Scott McCarron	69	69	71	72	281	11,920.50
Ted Purdy	72	68	67	74	281	11,920.50
Duffy Waldorf	73	66	70	72	281	11,920.50
Michael Walton	71	68	69	73	281	11,920.50
Steve Elkington	68	70	72	72	282	7,567.72
John Maginnes	72	69	69	72	282	7,567.72
Mike Sposa	74	65	72	71	282	7,567.72
Rich Beem	72	69	70	71	282	7,567.71
John Elliott	68	73	70	71	282	7,567.71
P.H. Horgan III	71	67	74	70	282	7,567.71
Blaine McCallister	67	71	69	75	282	7,567.71
Jim Carter	70	68	75	70	283	6,203.25
Brian Henninger	72	69	72	70	283	6,203.25
Pete Jordan	71	69	72	71	283	6,203.25
Jerry Kelly	74	66	71	72	283	6,203.25
Sean Murphy	70	70	70	73	283	6,203.25
Steve Pate	68	68	74	73	283	6,203.25
Rory Sabbatini	69	72	70	72	283	6,203.25
Tom Scherrer	71	70	74	68	283	6,203.25
Alan Bratton	68	71	71	74	284	5,886
Peter Jacobsen	70	71	71	72	284	5,886
Jay Williamson	68	72	72	72	284	5,886
Mike Hulbert	71	68	73	73	285	5,751
Larry Mize	69	72	73	71	285	5,751
Tommy Armour III	70	70	70	76	286	5,670
Craig Barlow	70	71	73	73	287	5,562
Danny Briggs	73	67	70	77	287	5,562
Robin Freeman	69	71	74	73	287	5,562
Kaname Yokoo	70	68	77	73	288	5,454
Kevin Wentworth	73	67	76	73	289	5,400
Lee Porter	72	69	74	75	290	5,346
David Sutherland	71	70	74	76	291	5,292
Wayne Levi	66	74	78	77	295	5,238

Nissan Open

Riviera Country Club, Pacific Palisades, California
Par 35-36–71; 6,946 yards

February 18-21
purse, $2,800,000

	SCORES				TOTAL	MONEY
Ernie Els	68	66	68	68	270	$504,000
Ted Tryba	70	69	61	72	272	209,066.67
Tiger Woods	69	68	65	70	272	209,066.67
Davis Love III	69	65	68	70	272	209,066.66
David Duval	66	71	67	69	273	106,400
Nick Price	67	71	67	68	273	106,400
Bob Estes	66	67	72	69	274	90,300

		SCORES			TOTAL	MONEY
Scott Hoch	71	69	68	66	274	90,300
Mark Brooks	68	71	70	66	275	72,800
Robert Karlsson	71	66	70	68	275	72,800
Jerry Kelly	68	69	67	71	275	72,800
Frank Lickliter	71	68	66	70	275	72,800
Brent Geiberger	68	70	69	69	276	58,800
Brad Fabel	73	64	71	69	277	53,200
Alan Bratton	67	67	74	70	278	40,670
Brandel Chamblee	74	68	69	67	278	40,670
Carlos Franco	71	67	69	71	278	40,670
Tim Herron	72	68	67	71	278	40,670
Bradley Hughes	70	68	69	71	278	40,670
Justin Leonard	70	70	70	68	278	40,670
Rocco Mediate	69	70	66	73	278	40,670
Phil Mickelson	68	72	68	70	278	40,670
Billy Andrade	68	69	70	72	279	23,600
Phil Blackmar	70	67	69	73	279	23,600
Rick Fehr	68	66	73	72	279	23,600
Steve Flesch	72	70	71	66	279	23,600
Billy Mayfair	69	67	69	74	279	23,600
Scott McCarron	72	67	69	71	279	23,600
Jeff Sluman	70	70	67	72	279	23,600
Greg Chalmers	69	67	71	73	280	17,388
Craig Stadler	73	69	68	70	280	17,388
Kevin Sutherland	67	70	68	75	280	17,388
Kirk Triplett	67	69	71	73	280	17,388
Grant Waite	71	70	70	69	280	17,388
Fred Couples	68	71	72	70	281	12,646.67
J.P. Hayes	70	70	69	72	281	12,646.67
Steve Jones	68	71	72	70	281	12,646.67
Andrew Magee	72	68	71	70	281	12,646.67
Jose Maria Olazabal	70	70	68	73	281	12,646.67
Bob Tway	68	71	71	71	281	12,646.67
Bob Burns	70	69	69	73	281	12,646.66
Chris Perry	70	72	69	70	281	12,646.66
Kenny Perry	72	66	68	75	281	12,646.66
Corey Pavin	72	69	69	72	282	8,465.34
Loren Roberts	67	70	71	74	282	8,465.34
Ben Bates	70	69	67	76	282	8,465.33
Peter Jacobsen	69	73	70	70	282	8,465.33
Larry Mize	75	66	70	71	282	8,465.33
Mike Reid	70	67	71	74	282	8,465.33
Len Mattiace	71	68	71	73	283	6,701.34
Duffy Waldorf	70	71	68	74	283	6,701.34
John Cook	72	68	71	72	283	6,701.33
David Frost	71	69	72	71	283	6,701.33
Vijay Singh	72	68	67	76	283	6,701.33
Geoffrey Sisk	69	69	73	72	283	6,701.33
Tommy Armour III	70	72	71	71	284	6,244
Robert Damron	69	68	74	73	284	6,244
Robin Freeman	74	66	71	73	284	6,244
Scott Gump	70	71	70	73	284	6,244
Neal Lancaster	68	70	76	70	284	6,244
Steve Lowery	71	69	71	73	284	6,244
Stewart Cink	71	71	73	70	285	5,880
Clark Dennis	68	72	72	73	285	5,880
Bob Friend	73	68	72	72	285	5,880
Jim Furyk	71	71	71	72	285	5,880
Bill Glasson	70	68	73	74	285	5,880
Steve Pate	72	70	72	71	285	5,880

	SCORES				TOTAL	MONEY
Tom Pernice, Jr.	69	72	72	72	285	5,880
Skip Kendall	72	69	70	75	286	5,656
Woody Austin	69	72	71	75	287	5,516
Eric Booker	73	69	72	73	287	5,516
Brett Quigley	68	71	74	74	287	5,516
Larry Rinker	72	70	70	75	287	5,516
Trevor Dodds	70	71	70	77	288	5,348
Scott Simpson	71	71	72	74	288	5,348
Mark Calcavecchia	68	74	74	74	290	5,264
Rich Beem	70	70	75	77	292	5,208

WGC Andersen Consulting Match Play

La Costa Resort & Spa, Carlsbad, California

February 24-28

Par 36-36–72; 7,022 yards

purse, $5,000,000

FIRST ROUND

Michael Bradley defeated Mark O'Meara, 4 and 2.
Steve Pate defeated Davis Love III, 1 up.
Eduardo Romero defeated Lee Westwood, 3 and 2.
Craig Stadler defeated Colin Montgomerie, 5 and 3.
Paul Azinger defeated Ernie Els, 1 up.
Patrik Sjoland defeated Jim Furyk, 5 and 3.
Steve Jones defeated Steve Elkington, 2 and 1.
Andrew Magee defeated Darren Clarke, 1 up.
Craig Parry defeated Jesper Parnevik, 1 up.
Stewart Cink defeated Payne Stewart, 3 and 2.
Thomas Bjorn defeated Brian Watts, 1 up.
Scott Verplank defeated Tom Lehman, 3 and 1.
Carlos Franco defeated Mark Calcavecchia, 2 and 1.
Shigeki Maruyama defeated Steve Stricker, 3 and 2.
Loren Roberts defeated Hal Sutton, 5 and 4.
Brandt Jobe defeated Jeff Sluman, 3 and 2.
Bill Glasson defeated Stuart Appleby, 2 and 1.
Bob Tway defeated Tom Watson, 6 and 4.
Jose Maria Olazabal defeated Billy Mayfair, 5 and 3.
Greg Norman defeated John Cook, 3 and 2.
John Huston defeated Bob Estes, 3 and 2.
Bernhard Langer defeated Brad Faxon, 4 and 2.
Jeff Maggert defeated Fred Funk, 2 up.
Lee Janzen defeated Glen Day, 3 and 2.
Scott Hoch defeated Ian Woosnam, 3 and 2.
Fred Couples defeated Dudley Hart, 2 up.
Phil Mickelson defeated Naomichi Ozaki, 3 and 2.
Justin Leonard defeated Miguel Angel Jimenez, 4 and 3.
Nick Price defeated Frankie Minoza, 4 and 3.
Vijay Singh defeated Rocco Mediate, 5 and 3.
David Duval defeated Stephen Leaney, 2 and 1.
Tiger Woods defeated Nick Faldo, 4 and 3.

(Each losing player received $25,000.)

SECOND ROUND

Glasson defeated Duval, 2 and 1.
Langer defeated Singh, 2 and 1.
Maggert defeated Price, 1 up.

Maruyama defeated Leonard, 4 and 2.
Couples defeated Hoch, 1 up.
Mickelson defeated Janzen, 2 and 1.
Romero defeated Norman, 1 up, 21st hole.
Woods defeated Tway, 1 up.
Pate defeated Jobe, 1 up.
Sjoland defeated Franco, 1 up.
Jones defeated Verplank, 5 and 4.
Magee defeated Bjorn, 2 and 1.
Cink defeated Parry, 3 and 2.
Roberts defeated Azinger, 2 and 1.
Huston defeated Stadler, 2 and 1.
Olazabal defeated Bradley, 2 and 1.

(Each losing player received $50,000.)

THIRD ROUND

Romero defeated Mickelson, 2 and 1.
Pate defeated Couples, 1 up.
Maggert defeated Langer, 1 up.
Magee defeated Glasson, 1 up.
Maruyama defeated Roberts, 2 and 1.
Woods defeated Cink, 2 and 1.
Olazabal defeated Jones, 1 up.
Huston defeated Sjoland, 1 up.

(Each losing player received $75,000.)

QUARTER-FINALS

Maggert defeated Woods, 2 and 1.
Huston defeated Olazabal, 2 and 1.
Magee defeated Maruyama, 1 up.
Pate defeated Romero, 3 and 2.

(Each losing player received $150,000.)

SEMI-FINALS

Maggert defeated Pate, 1 up.
Magee defeated Huston, 3 and 1.

THIRD-PLACE MATCH

Huston defeated Pate, 5 and 4.

(Huston received $400,000; Pate received $300,000.)

FINAL

Maggert defeated Magee, 1 up, 38th hole.

(Maggert received $1,000,000; Magee received $500,000.)

Touchstone Energy Tucson Open

Omni Tucson National Resort, Tucson, Arizona
Par 36-36–72; 7,148 yards

February 25-28
purse, $2,750,000

	SCORES				TOTAL	MONEY
Gabriel Hjertstedt	67	68	73	68	276	$495,000
Tommy Armour III	70	69	67	70	276	297,000
(Hjertstedt defeated Armour on first extra hole.)						
Mike Reid	71	67	71	68	277	159,500
Kirk Triplett	69	69	70	69	277	159,500
Barry Cheesman	71	66	69	72	278	104,500
Brent Geiberger	72	68	68	70	278	104,500
Scott Gump	68	67	74	70	279	77,229.17
Nolan Henke	71	70	71	67	279	77,229.17
Franklin Langham	70	68	71	70	279	77,229.17
Corey Pavin	71	68	71	69	279	77,229.17
Eric Rustand	70	69	70	70	279	77,229.16
David Toms	68	69	71	71	279	77,229.16
Jim Carter	69	69	71	71	280	47,142.86
Doug Dunakey	66	70	73	71	280	47,142.86
Steve Flesch	67	72	72	69	280	47,142.86
Sandy Lyle	68	70	74	68	280	47,142.86
Paul Stankowski	71	71	69	69	280	47,142.86
Kenny Perry	69	68	71	72	280	47,142.85
Mike Weir	68	72	67	73	280	47,142.85
R.W. Eaks	64	75	72	70	281	27,740.63
John Elliott	73	69	70	69	281	27,740.63
Scott Simpson	69	74	69	69	281	27,740.63
Kevin Wentworth	69	72	73	67	281	27,740.63
John Daly	69	70	71	71	281	27,740.62
Tim Herron	66	72	71	72	281	27,740.62
Steve Lowery	72	68	71	70	281	27,740.62
Grant Waite	70	69	69	73	281	27,740.62
Briny Baird	71	70	71	70	282	19,112.50
Paul Goydos	68	75	70	69	282	19,112.50
Tom Scherrer	65	73	75	69	282	19,112.50
Bobby Wadkins	74	71	68	69	282	19,112.50
Robert Allenby	67	69	74	73	283	15,565
Emlyn Aubrey	70	68	75	70	283	15,565
Jim Gallagher, Jr.	68	71	73	71	283	15,565
John Maginnes	71	70	73	69	283	15,565
Katsumasa Miyamoto	68	73	70	72	283	15,565
Greg Kraft	70	70	72	72	284	13,200
Don Pooley	69	74	71	70	284	13,200
Bob Burns	70	71	74	70	285	11,000
Brad Fabel	71	72	72	70	285	11,000
P.H. Horgan III	68	74	72	71	285	11,000
Scott McCarron	71	68	72	74	285	11,000
Doug Tewell	71	71	72	71	285	11,000
Tommy Tolles	66	70	71	78	285	11,000
Brandel Chamblee	72	70	71	73	286	7,449.45
Dennis Paulson	67	76	70	73	286	7,449.45
Kevin Sutherland	73	69	73	71	286	7,449.45
Fuzzy Zoeller	75	66	73	72	286	7,449.45
Harrison Frazar	74	71	72	69	286	7,449.44
David Frost	70	72	73	71	286	7,449.44
Jerry Kelly	66	70	72	78	286	7,449.44
Bruce Lietzke	76	68	73	69	286	7,449.44
Perry Moss	70	72	74	70	286	7,449.44

	SCORES				TOTAL	MONEY
Notah Begay III	74	71	71	71	287	6,242.50
Per-Ulrik Johansson	68	70	73	76	287	6,242.50
Joe Ogilvie	71	72	74	70	287	6,242.50
Mike Standly	71	70	70	76	287	6,242.50
Esteban Toledo	72	73	70	72	287	6,242.50
Kaname Yokoo	69	72	70	76	287	6,242.50
Jay Don Blake	69	74	72	73	288	5,940
Robert Gamez	71	70	72	75	288	5,940
Peter Jacobsen	71	74	75	68	288	5,940
Doug Martin	70	70	76	72	288	5,940
Mike Sposa	73	71	70	74	288	5,940
Olin Browne	72	72	72	73	289	5,637.50
Kelly Gibson	77	68	72	72	289	5,637.50
Kent Jones	71	71	72	75	289	5,637.50
Tim Loustalot	72	73	74	70	289	5,637.50
Blaine McCallister	73	69	75	72	289	5,637.50
Lanny Wadkins	72	71	74	72	289	5,637.50
Sean Murphy	70	69	79	72	290	5,390
Omar Uresti	73	72	72	73	290	5,390
Jay Williamson	72	73	73	72	290	5,390
Charles Raulerson	71	69	77	74	291	5,280
Michael Burke, Jr.	72	73	73	74	292	5,197.50
Ted Tryba	76	69	71	76	292	5,197.50
Jeff Brehaut	72	73	73	75	293	5,032.50
Chris DiMarco	71	71	76	75	293	5,032.50
Brian Hull	73	69	72	79	293	5,032.50
David Ogrin	74	69	75	75	293	5,032.50
Mike Brisky	68	76	75	77	296	4,895

Doral-Ryder Open

Doral Golf Resort & Spa, Blue Course, Miami, Florida
Par 36-36–72; 7,125 yards

March 4-7
purse, $3,000,000

	SCORES				TOTAL	MONEY
Steve Elkington	72	70	69	64	275	$540,000
Greg Kraft	68	67	70	71	276	324,000
Tommy Armour III	67	71	71	68	277	135,300
Scott Dunlap	67	72	69	69	277	135,300
Ernie Els	71	66	70	70	277	135,300
Jay Haas	70	69	70	68	277	135,300
David Toms	70	73	67	67	277	135,300
Danny Briggs	71	72	68	67	278	90,000
P.H. Horgan III	69	70	71	68	278	90,000
Greg Chalmers	71	66	72	70	279	69,000
Glen Day	69	71	67	72	279	69,000
Guy Hill	71	69	70	69	279	69,000
Gabriel Hjertstedt	69	72	71	67	279	69,000
Nick Price	72	69	70	68	279	69,000
Neal Lancaster	71	72	72	65	280	49,500
Justin Leonard	72	69	68	71	280	49,500
Jesper Parnevik	71	70	70	69	280	49,500
Bob Tway	72	71	68	69	280	49,500
Billy Andrade	72	70	68	71	281	29,000
Andy Bean	70	69	69	73	281	29,000
Kent Jones	70	68	71	72	281	29,000
Billy Mayfair	72	71	68	70	281	29,000

	SCORES				TOTAL	MONEY
Greg Norman	71	73	68	69	281	29,000
Joe Ogilvie	71	69	71	70	281	29,000
Chris Riley	68	72	69	72	281	29,000
Tom Scherrer	70	72	70	69	281	29,000
Joey Sindelar	69	73	70	69	281	29,000
Geoffrey Sisk	68	72	72	69	281	29,000
Patrik Sjoland	72	71	69	69	281	29,000
Craig Stadler	72	71	67	71	281	29,000
Doug Barron	68	71	72	71	282	18,600
David Frost	72	71	71	68	282	18,600
Franklin Langham	67	76	72	67	282	18,600
Ty Armstrong	71	69	71	72	283	13,890
Briny Baird	70	74	69	70	283	13,890
Craig Barlow	70	73	71	69	283	13,890
Russ Cochran	70	72	73	68	283	13,890
Doug Dunakey	71	70	73	69	283	13,890
Fred Funk	68	71	73	71	283	13,890
Scott Hoch	74	70	72	67	283	13,890
Pete Jordan	70	70	70	73	283	13,890
Esteban Toledo	68	70	71	74	283	13,890
Tommy Tolles	71	70	74	68	283	13,890
Eric Booker	69	73	71	71	284	8,670
Olin Browne	68	71	73	72	284	8,670
Robert Damron	72	72	71	69	284	8,670
Jim Gallagher, Jr.	71	71	70	72	284	8,670
Chris Perry	73	71	73	67	284	8,670
Chris Smith	72	72	71	69	284	8,670
Mike Weir	71	71	68	74	284	8,670
Jay Williamson	70	71	75	68	284	8,670
Robert Gamez	70	73	72	70	285	6,996
Scott Gump	72	72	70	71	285	6,996
Jonathan Kaye	69	75	72	69	285	6,996
Bruce Lietzke	71	73	69	72	285	6,996
Scott Verplank	70	69	72	74	285	6,996
Emlyn Aubrey	69	71	72	74	286	6,660
Stewart Cink	72	72	71	71	286	6,660
Nolan Henke	71	70	74	71	286	6,660
Jerry Kelly	71	70	74	71	286	6,660
Skip Kendall	71	73	72	70	286	6,660
Michael Bradley	74	68	74	71	287	6,330
Bob Burns	67	72	71	77	287	6,330
Mike Hulbert	73	71	72	71	287	6,330
Bernhard Langer	71	73	71	72	287	6,330
Sean Murphy	68	74	73	72	287	6,330
Ted Purdy	72	70	75	70	287	6,330
Jim Carter	72	72	74	70	288	6,090
Lee Rinker	72	71	74	71	288	6,090
Jay Don Blake	69	73	76	71	289	5,910
Chris DiMarco	69	72	77	71	289	5,910
Harrison Frazar	70	74	73	72	289	5,910
Rory Sabbatini	73	71	76	69	289	5,910
Rich Beem	70	74	75	71	290	5,730
Oscar Serna	73	69	79	69	290	5,730
Chip Beck	71	73	75	72	291	5,610
Ed Fiori	71	72	74	74	291	5,610
Woody Austin	73	71	72	76	292	5,460
Thomas Bjorn	72	71	75	74	292	5,460
Mark Calcavecchia	68	73	75	76	292	5,460
John Elliott	72	72	73	76	293	5,340
Raymond Floyd	73	71	78	74	296	5,280

Honda Classic

TPC at Heron Bay, Coral Springs, Florida
Par 36-36–72; 7,268 yards

March 11-14
purse, $2,600,000

	SCORES				TOTAL	MONEY
Vijay Singh	71	69	68	69	277	$468,000
Payne Stewart	70	67	72	70	279	280,800
Eric Booker	65	66	72	77	280	124,800
Doug Dunakey	70	65	75	70	280	124,800
Carlos Franco	72	68	71	69	280	124,800
Mark O'Meara	68	70	69	73	280	124,800
Hal Sutton	64	73	76	69	282	83,850
Tommy Tolles	70	66	69	77	282	83,850
Stuart Appleby	69	70	69	75	283	70,200
Dudley Hart	70	72	72	69	283	70,200
Chris Riley	69	71	72	71	283	70,200
Mark Brooks	70	73	70	71	284	54,600
Chris DiMarco	75	68	70	71	284	54,600
David Sutherland	70	72	70	72	284	54,600
John Cook	70	69	74	72	285	33,150
Bob Estes	72	68	70	75	285	33,150
Harrison Frazar	69	72	66	78	285	33,150
Jim Gallagher, Jr.	72	67	72	74	285	33,150
Brent Geiberger	72	66	71	76	285	33,150
Bradley Hughes	67	68	70	80	285	33,150
Jonathan Kaye	70	72	72	71	285	33,150
Joe Ogilvie	72	71	65	77	285	33,150
Steve Pate	69	70	73	73	285	33,150
Dicky Pride	67	68	75	75	285	33,150
Craig Stadler	69	69	71	76	285	33,150
Paul Stankowski	69	67	76	73	285	33,150
Ty Armstrong	71	71	71	73	286	16,238.19
Perry Moss	73	69	71	73	286	16,238.19
Phil Blackmar	70	70	72	74	286	16,238.18
Michael Bradley	72	66	72	76	286	16,238.18
John Daly	71	67	76	72	286	16,238.18
Robert Damron	72	69	69	76	286	16,238.18
Craig Parry	69	69	71	77	286	16,238.18
Charles Raulerson	71	72	72	71	286	16,238.18
Tom Scherrer	68	73	71	74	286	16,238.18
Mike Sposa	72	71	73	70	286	16,238.18
Brian Watts	68	68	74	76	286	16,238.18
Woody Austin	72	70	73	72	287	10,400
Doug Barron	66	74	68	79	287	10,400
Ben Bates	72	71	72	72	287	10,400
Tom Byrum	72	71	69	75	287	10,400
Barry Cheesman	69	69	75	74	287	10,400
Brian Gay	70	72	73	72	287	10,400
Mike Hulbert	68	71	73	75	287	10,400
Colin Montgomerie	72	70	72	73	287	10,400
Robert Allenby	72	71	72	73	288	6,851
Emlyn Aubrey	72	71	73	72	288	6,851
Briny Baird	72	68	74	74	288	6,851
Greg Chalmers	70	70	72	76	288	6,851
Ernie Els	70	73	71	74	288	6,851
P.H. Horgan III	69	69	76	74	288	6,851
Franklin Langham	68	70	75	75	288	6,851
Blaine McCallister	68	70	72	78	288	6,851
Craig Barlow	71	69	77	72	289	5,902

	SCORES	TOTAL	MONEY
Mike Brisky	70 70 75 74	289	5,902
Brad Bryant	70 72 72 75	289	5,902
Clark Dennis	73 69 75 72	289	5,902
Brad Fabel	70 72 72 75	289	5,902
John Huston	70 72 75 72	289	5,902
Notah Begay III	73 69 74 74	290	5,616
Tim Herron	69 70 73 78	290	5,616
Guy Hill	71 71 74 74	290	5,616
Grant Waite	68 71 74 77	290	5,616
D.A. Weibring	74 67 78 71	290	5,616
Mike Malizia	70 68 75 78	291	5,434
Mark McCumber	74 68 72 77	291	5,434
Danny Briggs	72 70 75 75	292	5,304
Bob Friend	72 69 73 78	292	5,304
Mike Springer	71 71 74 76	292	5,304
Billy Ray Brown	70 72 75 76	293	5,122
Sandy Lyle	72 71 76 74	293	5,122
John Maginnes	70 71 75 77	293	5,122
Geoffrey Sisk	69 71 78 75	293	5,122
Cameron Beckman	69 70 79 77	295	4,940
Mark Calcavecchia	71 70 75 79	295	4,940
Dan Forsman	69 73 76 77	295	4,940
Scott Dunlap	72 69 79 76	296	4,836
Rory Sabbatini	73 69 79 76	297	4,758
Chris Smith	72 71 81 73	297	4,758
Tom Lehman	71 72 76 79	298	4,654
Dave Stockton, Jr.	71 71 77 79	298	4,654
Bo Van Pelt	69 71 82 79	301	4,576

Bay Hill Invitational

Bay Hill Club & Lodge, Orlando, Florida
Par 36-36–72; 7,196 yards

March 18-21
purse, $2,500,000

	SCORES	TOTAL	MONEY
Tim Herron	66 69 67 72	274	$450,000
Tom Lehman	69 68 66 71	274	270,000
(Herron defeated Lehman on second extra hole.)			
Davis Love III	69 66 67 73	275	170,000
Robert Damron	70 71 68 67	276	120,000
Brandel Chamblee	70 69 67 74	280	81,875
Bob Estes	70 70 68 72	280	81,875
Scott Hoch	71 70 70 69	280	81,875
Phil Mickelson	74 67 68 71	280	81,875
Craig Parry	72 67 72 69	280	81,875
Dicky Pride	68 71 70 71	280	81,875
Steve Pate	69 69 71 72	281	60,000
Vijay Singh	69 70 70 72	281	60,000
Kirk Triplett	70 71 70 71	282	48,333.34
Robert Allenby	72 66 71 73	282	48,333.33
Payne Stewart	75 65 68 74	282	48,333.33
David Frost	75 68 75 65	283	40,000
Justin Leonard	69 71 69 74	283	40,000
Hal Sutton	74 69 72 68	283	40,000
Frank Lickliter	71 70 72 71	284	31,375
Andrew Magee	69 67 77 71	284	31,375
Corey Pavin	73 69 69 73	284	31,375

	SCORES				TOTAL	MONEY
David Toms	71	71	68	74	284	31,375
Jim Furyk	70	71	73	71	285	19,625
Bill Glasson	73	71	70	71	285	19,625
Dudley Hart	75	66	72	72	285	19,625
Steve Jones	71	71	67	76	285	19,625
Frank Nobilo	70	73	72	70	285	19,625
Chris Perry	70	72	71	72	285	19,625
Joey Sindelar	71	67	72	75	285	19,625
Grant Waite	72	73	70	70	285	19,625
Jay Williamson	69	69	70	77	285	19,625
Fuzzy Zoeller	72	71	68	74	285	19,625
Paul Azinger	72	68	73	73	286	13,812.50
J.P. Hayes	70	70	70	76	286	13,812.50
Greg Kraft	69	70	73	74	286	13,812.50
Curtis Strange	74	71	69	72	286	13,812.50
Scott Dunlap	70	74	69	74	287	10,750
Steve Lowery	67	75	72	73	287	10,750
Jeff Maggert	71	72	73	71	287	10,750
Billy Mayfair	73	72	69	73	287	10,750
Scott McCarron	72	69	73	73	287	10,750
Steve Stricker	71	70	72	74	287	10,750
Kevin Sutherland	73	71	72	71	287	10,750
Ernie Els	74	67	73	74	288	7,225
Fred Funk	69	69	74	76	288	7,225
Brent Geiberger	73	70	72	73	288	7,225
Neal Lancaster	71	71	71	75	288	7,225
Rocco Mediate	73	67	69	79	288	7,225
Mike Nicolette	73	71	72	72	288	7,225
Naomichi Ozaki	74	68	72	74	288	7,225
Jeff Sluman	73	71	69	75	288	7,225
Bob Friend	73	71	72	73	289	5,862.50
Robert Gamez	70	74	70	75	289	5,862.50
Kenny Perry	70	69	73	77	289	5,862.50
Don Pooley	74	67	74	74	289	5,862.50
Mike Hulbert	73	73	72	72	290	5,625
Dennis Paulson	73	69	70	78	290	5,625
Mike Weir	69	74	69	78	290	5,625
Tiger Woods	74	72	72	72	290	5,625
Colin Montgomerie	71	69	72	79	291	5,475
Lee Westwood	71	68	73	79	291	5,475
*Matt Kuchar	73	69	75	74	291	
P.H. Horgan III	71	74	71	76	292	5,400
Mark Brooks	70	73	76	74	293	5,250
Barry Cheesman	70	75	66	82	293	5,250
Dan Forsman	71	72	73	77	293	5,250
Gary Koch	70	76	75	72	293	5,250
Omar Uresti	73	72	74	74	293	5,250
Fulton Allem	70	68	74	82	294	5,050
Michael Bradley	69	73	74	78	294	5,050
Trevor Dodds	72	74	76	72	294	5,050
Bernhard Langer	74	69	73	79	295	4,925
Ian Woosnam	73	70	73	79	295	4,925
Olin Browne	72	74	74	77	297	4,825
Brad Faxon	74	72	74	77	297	4,825
Billy Ray Brown	72	73	76	78	299	4,750
Jay Haas	71	75	72	82	300	4,700

The Players Championship

TPC at Sawgrass, Stadium Course,
Ponte Vedra Beach, Florida
Par 36-36–72; 6,896 yards

March 25-28
purse, $5,000,000

	SCORES				TOTAL	MONEY
David Duval	69	69	74	73	285	$900,000
Scott Gump	72	74	70	71	287	540,000
Nick Price	74	67	74	73	288	340,000
Fred Couples	77	71	73	68	289	220,000
Hal Sutton	69	74	73	73	289	220,000
Scott Hoch	72	70	73	75	290	161,875
Mark O'Meara	72	73	71	74	290	161,875
Steve Stricker	73	73	70	74	290	161,875
Lee Westwood	73	69	75	73	290	161,875
Mark Brooks	71	77	71	72	291	107,142.86
Mark Calcavecchia	76	70	72	73	291	107,142.86
Davis Love III	70	70	78	73	291	107,142.86
Naomichi Ozaki	69	68	81	73	291	107,142.86
Joey Sindelar	72	71	74	74	291	107,142.86
Skip Kendall	70	73	70	78	291	107,142.85
Tiger Woods	70	71	75	75	291	107,142.85
Ernie Els	73	67	80	72	292	75,000
Jim Furyk	71	76	73	72	292	75,000
Duffy Waldorf	71	71	75	75	292	75,000
David Toms	73	75	74	71	293	60,333.34
John Huston	75	72	73	73	293	60,333.33
Vijay Singh	77	70	74	72	293	60,333.33
Brad Fabel	73	70	80	71	294	40,166.67
Justin Leonard	72	72	75	75	294	40,166.67
Frank Lickliter	71	70	76	77	294	40,166.67
Jesper Parnevik	71	73	74	76	294	40,166.67
Curtis Strange	71	69	78	76	294	40,166.67
Esteban Toledo	73	75	72	74	294	40,166.67
Larry Mize	73	71	73	77	294	40,166.66
Colin Montgomerie	72	70	73	79	294	40,166.66
Payne Stewart	72	70	74	78	294	40,166.66
Gabriel Hjertstedt	73	72	74	76	295	27,666.67
Franklin Langham	71	75	75	74	295	27,666.67
Bruce Lietzke	71	68	80	76	295	27,666.67
Scott Verplank	76	71	73	75	295	27,666.67
Phil Mickelson	71	71	71	82	295	27,666.66
Chris Perry	70	74	73	78	295	27,666.66
Steve Elkington	71	73	78	74	296	20,000
Fred Funk	72	69	76	79	296	20,000
Paul Goydos	71	74	76	75	296	20,000
Dudley Hart	70	74	76	76	296	20,000
Miguel Angel Jimenez	76	69	79	72	296	20,000
Bernhard Langer	73	72	77	74	296	20,000
Kirk Triplett	70	75	76	75	296	20,000
Brian Watts	68	74	78	76	296	20,000
Chris DiMarco	74	72	76	75	297	13,600
Brad Faxon	72	75	79	71	297	13,600
Brent Geiberger	74	71	78	74	297	13,600
Jeff Maggert	73	71	76	77	297	13,600
Jeff Sluman	70	72	79	76	297	13,600
Tommy Tolles	72	73	76	76	297	13,600
Doug Barron	72	73	77	76	298	11,600
Robert Damron	74	72	76	76	298	11,600

	SCORES				TOTAL	MONEY
Dan Forsman	76	70	78	74	298	11,600
David Frost	74	72	74	78	298	11,600
Jeff Gallagher	71	73	77	77	298	11,600
Jose Maria Olazabal	78	70	76	74	298	11,600
Jay Don Blake	77	71	79	72	299	11,050
Barry Cheesman	73	74	73	79	299	11,050
John Cook	78	69	78	74	299	11,050
Steve Pate	74	74	72	79	299	11,050
Billy Andrade	73	74	81	72	300	10,500
Bob Estes	68	74	80	78	300	10,500
Bob Friend	74	69	87	70	300	10,500
Bradley Hughes	70	74	78	78	300	10,500
Greg Kraft	71	74	82	73	300	10,500
Craig Stadler	72	70	80	78	300	10,500
Tom Watson	75	71	79	75	300	10,500
Craig Parry	75	73	73	80	301	10,100
Tom Byrum	76	72	80	74	302	10,000
Jim Carter	76	72	76	80	304	9,700
Darren Clarke	77	70	79	78	304	9,700
Russ Cochran	76	70	79	79	304	9,700
Frank Nobilo	72	71	80	81	304	9,700
Corey Pavin	74	74	82	74	304	9,700
Joe Durant	74	74	78	79	305	9,400
Fulton Allem	74	67	83	82	306	9,250
Tom Kite	76	72	79	79	306	9,250

BellSouth Classic

TPC at Sugarloaf, Duluth, Georgia   April 1-4
Par 36-36–72; 7,216 yards   purse, $2,500,000

	SCORES				TOTAL	MONEY
David Duval	66	69	68	67	270	$450,000
Stewart Cink	71	65	66	70	272	270,000
John Huston	71	65	67	70	273	145,000
Rory Sabbatini	65	65	73	70	273	145,000
Franklin Langham	69	67	68	70	274	95,000
Mike Weir	69	65	68	72	274	95,000
Glen Day	68	67	72	68	275	77,916.67
Davis Love III	69	69	69	68	275	77,916.67
Phil Mickelson	69	71	64	71	275	77,916.66
Chris DiMarco	71	69	68	69	277	55,416.67
Brent Geiberger	70	71	68	68	277	55,416.67
David Toms	71	70	68	68	277	55,416.67
Grant Waite	64	72	73	68	277	55,416.67
Stuart Appleby	74	66	66	71	277	55,416.66
Shigeki Maruyama	66	72	68	71	277	55,416.66
Jay Don Blake	70	66	72	70	278	40,000
Skip Kendall	68	67	73	70	278	40,000
Dennis Paulson	71	72	69	66	278	40,000
Brian Henninger	69	70	69	71	279	35,000
Tom Scherrer	73	70	66	71	280	30,166.67
Mike Sposa	72	68	69	71	280	30,166.67
Jesper Parnevik	66	72	68	74	280	30,166.66
Billy Andrade	68	73	69	71	281	21,071.43
Scott Dunlap	69	68	71	73	281	21,071.43
Brad Fabel	68	68	71	74	281	21,071.43

	SCORES	TOTAL	MONEY
David Frost	66 72 71 72	281	21,071.43
Jeff Gallagher	73 66 69 73	281	21,071.43
Jonathan Kaye	68 69 71 73	281	21,071.43
Paul Stankowski	73 65 68 75	281	21,071.42
J.P. Hayes	72 71 68 71	282	15,187.50
P.H. Horgan III	74 69 67 72	282	15,187.50
Len Mattiace	70 73 70 69	282	15,187.50
Chris Smith	71 71 68 72	282	15,187.50
Kevin Sutherland	68 73 68 73	282	15,187.50
Bo Van Pelt	70 69 69 74	282	15,187.50
Steve Flesch	69 73 70 71	283	11,015.63
Bradley Hughes	69 71 70 73	283	11,015.63
Miguel Angel Jimenez	73 67 72 71	283	11,015.63
Kenny Perry	70 70 70 73	283	11,015.63
Craig Barlow	73 70 69 71	283	11,015.62
Trevor Dodds	70 73 70 70	283	11,015.62
Gabriel Hjertstedt	72 69 67 75	283	11,015.62
Neal Lancaster	72 71 70 70	283	11,015.62
Scott Gump	70 71 73 70	284	8,500
Duffy Waldorf	63 73 75 73	284	8,500
Dicky Pride	72 67 73 73	285	7,283.34
Phil Tataurangi	68 71 74 72	285	7,283.33
Kirk Triplett	70 68 75 72	285	7,283.33
Notah Begay III	70 69 71 76	286	6,108.34
Rick Fehr	71 70 72 73	286	6,108.34
Phil Blackmar	69 72 74 71	286	6,108.33
Bob Friend	70 72 75 69	286	6,108.33
Pete Jordan	71 66 71 78	286	6,108.33
Joe Ogilvie	69 73 75 69	286	6,108.33
Nick Faldo	69 73 73 72	287	5,650
J.L. Lewis	69 70 74 74	287	5,650
Tommy Tolles	67 76 69 75	287	5,650
Scott Verplank	70 70 71 76	287	5,650
Ian Woosnam	70 69 73 75	287	5,650
Charles Warren	70 68 76 74	288	5,550
Dave Barr	71 70 72 76	289	5,375
Jim Gallagher, Jr.	68 74 72 75	289	5,375
Steve Jones	68 73 71 77	289	5,375
Colin Montgomerie	72 68 73 76	289	5,375
Jeff Brehaut	73 70 75 72	290	5,225
Kevin Wentworth	69 73 74 74	290	5,225
Ty Armstrong	70 73 75 73	291	5,075
Barry Cheesman	74 69 75 73	291	5,075
Mike Reid	70 72 70 79	291	5,075
Esteban Toledo	70 73 74 74	291	5,075
Chris Patton	67 72 76 79	294	4,950
David Seawell	72 71 79 76	298	4,900

Masters Tournament

Augusta National Golf Club, Augusta, Georgia
Par 36-36–72; 6,985 yards

April 8-11
purse, $3,200,000

	SCORES	TOTAL	MONEY
Jose Maria Olazabal	70 66 73 71	280	$720,000
Davis Love III	69 72 70 71	282	432,000
Greg Norman	71 68 71 73	283	272,000

	SCORES				TOTAL	MONEY
Bob Estes	71	72	69	72	284	176,000
Steve Pate	71	75	65	73	284	176,000
David Duval	71	74	70	70	285	125,200
Carlos Franco	72	72	68	73	285	125,200
Phil Mickelson	74	69	71	71	285	125,200
Nick Price	69	72	72	72	285	125,200
Lee Westwood	75	71	68	71	285	125,200
Steve Elkington	72	70	71	74	287	92,000
Bernhard Langer	76	66	72	73	287	92,000
Colin Montgomerie	70	72	71	74	287	92,000
Jim Furyk	72	73	70	73	288	70,000
Lee Janzen	70	69	73	76	288	70,000
Brandt Jobe	72	71	74	71	288	70,000
Ian Woosnam	71	74	71	72	288	70,000
Brandel Chamblee	69	73	75	72	289	52,160
Bill Glasson	72	70	73	74	289	52,160
Justin Leonard	70	72	73	74	289	52,160
Scott McCarron	69	68	76	76	289	52,160
Tiger Woods	72	72	70	75	289	52,160
Larry Mize	76	70	72	72	290	41,600
Brad Faxon	74	73	68	76	291	35,200
Per-Ulrik Johansson	75	72	71	73	291	35,200
Vijay Singh	72	76	71	72	291	35,200
Stewart Cink	74	70	71	77	292	29,000
Fred Couples	74	71	76	71	292	29,000
Ernie Els	71	72	69	80	292	29,000
Rocco Mediate	73	74	69	76	292	29,000
Tom Lehman	73	72	73	75	293	23,720
Shigeki Maruyama	78	70	71	74	293	23,720
Mark O'Meara	70	76	69	78	293	23,720
Jeff Sluman	70	75	70	78	293	23,720
Brian Watts	73	73	70	77	293	23,720
John Huston	74	72	71	77	294	20,100
Andrew Magee	70	77	72	75	294	20,100
Billy Andrade	76	72	72	75	295	17,200
Mark Brooks	76	72	75	72	295	17,200
Raymond Floyd	74	73	72	76	295	17,200
Craig Stadler	72	76	70	77	295	17,200
Steve Stricker	75	72	69	79	295	17,200
*Sergio Garcia	72	75	75	73	295	
Jay Haas	74	69	79	75	297	14,000
Tim Herron	75	69	74	79	297	14,000
Scott Hoch	75	73	70	79	297	14,000
*Tom McKnight	73	74	73	77	297	
Sandy Lyle	71	77	70	80	298	12,000
Craig Parry	75	73	73	77	298	12,000
Chris Perry	73	72	74	80	299	10,960
*Matt Kuchar	77	71	73	78	299	
Olin Browne	74	74	72	80	300	9,980
John Daly	72	76	71	81	300	9,980
Payne Stewart	73	75	77	75	300	9,980
Bob Tway	75	73	78	74	300	9,980
*Trevor Immelman	72	76	78	79	305	

Out of Final 36 Holes

Thomas Bjorn	76	73			149	
Fred Funk	76	73			149	
Miguel Angel Jimenez	72	77			149	
Frank Lickliter	72	77			149	

	SCORES		TOTAL
Fuzzy Zoeller	72	77	149
Stuart Appleby	73	77	150
John Cook	76	74	150
J.P. Hayes	76	74	150
Masashi Ozaki	71	79	150
Charles Coody	77	74	151
Jesper Parnevik	74	77	151
Patrik Sjoland	76	75	151
Tom Watson	74	77	151
Willie Wood	79	72	151
Paul Azinger	74	78	152
Mark Calcavecchia	75	77	152
Gabriel Hjertstedt	74	78	152
Hank Kuehne	74	78	152
Loren Roberts	76	76	152
Darren Clarke	75	78	153
Ben Crenshaw	74	79	153
Nick Faldo	80	73	153
Billy Mayfair	78	75	153
Corey Pavin	75	78	153
Jeff Maggert	78	76	154
David Toms	78	76	154
Scott Verplank	78	76	154
Glen Day	78	77	155
Trevor Dodds	78	77	155
Hal Sutton	79	76	155
Seve Ballesteros	78	78	156
Steve Jones	77	79	156
Gary Player	79	79	158
Tommy Aaron	77	82	159
Arnold Palmer	83	78	161
John Miller	81	81	162
Joe Durant	87	79	166
Gay Brewer	80		WD
Billy Casper	86		WD
Doug Ford	88		WD

(Professionals who did not complete 72 holes received $5,000.)

MCI Classic

Harbour Town Golf Links, Hilton Head Island, South Carolina   April 15-18
Par 36-35–71; 6,916 yards   purse, $2,500,000

	SCORES				TOTAL	MONEY
Glen Day	70	68	70	66	274	$450,000
Jeff Sluman	72	67	68	67	274	220,000
Payne Stewart	68	64	72	70	274	220,000
(Day defeated Sluman and Stewart on first extra hole.)						
Chris Perry	69	66	68	72	275	120,000
Nolan Henke	71	70	65	70	276	91,250
John Huston	68	67	69	72	276	91,250
Corey Pavin	70	69	68	69	276	91,250
Lee Janzen	67	70	68	72	277	75,000
Bob Tway	69	73	68	67	277	75,000
Scott Gump	72	69	65	72	278	65,000
Mike Weir	71	69	70	68	278	65,000
Scott Hoch	66	70	71	72	279	47,500

	SCORES				TOTAL	MONEY
Peter Jacobsen	71	70	67	71	279	47,500
Skip Kendall	69	72	65	73	279	47,500
Rocco Mediate	69	70	70	70	279	47,500
Patrik Sjoland	71	71	65	72	279	47,500
Craig Stadler	69	70	71	69	279	47,500
Steve Pate	66	72	73	69	280	28,333.34
Vijay Singh	69	72	68	71	280	28,333.34
Tiger Woods	70	70	69	71	280	28,333.34
Jay Don Blake	69	73	66	72	280	28,333.33
David Frost	72	70	64	74	280	28,333.33
Fred Funk	69	67	72	72	280	28,333.33
Mike Hulbert	68	69	70	73	280	28,333.33
Jerry Kelly	71	68	67	74	280	28,333.33
Mark Wiebe	71	67	70	72	280	28,333.33
Tim Herron	70	73	69	69	281	17,750
Jeff Maggert	65	73	70	73	281	17,750
Larry Mize	67	70	70	74	281	17,750
Lee Porter	70	72	69	70	281	17,750
Willie Wood	70	71	70	70	281	17,750
Scott Dunlap	68	69	73	72	282	14,468.75
Bob Estes	69	69	71	73	282	14,468.75
Dennis Paulson	73	67	71	71	282	14,468.75
Grant Waite	72	69	73	68	282	14,468.75
Jim Carter	69	71	71	72	283	11,267.86
Dudley Hart	68	74	70	71	283	11,267.86
Phil Mickelson	74	67	71	71	283	11,267.86
Craig Parry	71	71	69	72	283	11,267.86
Mike Reid	69	69	73	72	283	11,267.86
Tom Lehman	68	71	69	75	283	11,267.85
Doug Tewell	71	72	66	74	283	11,267.85
Mark Brooks	68	73	69	74	284	8,016.67
Clark Dennis	70	70	74	70	284	8,016.67
Per-Ulrik Johansson	66	68	77	73	284	8,016.67
Len Mattiace	68	71	73	72	284	8,016.67
John Cook	66	67	74	77	284	8,016.66
Donnie Hammond	67	74	68	75	284	8,016.66
Chris Riley	71	71	72	71	285	6,057.15
David Sutherland	71	68	74	72	285	6,057.15
Nick Faldo	69	73	67	76	285	6,057.14
Steve Flesch	65	71	74	75	285	6,057.14
Frank Lickliter	71	69	71	74	285	6,057.14
Loren Roberts	71	71	69	74	285	6,057.14
Esteban Toledo	73	68	72	72	285	6,057.14
Billy Andrade	68	72	72	74	286	5,625
Brent Geiberger	73	69	73	71	286	5,625
Wayne Grady	73	67	75	71	286	5,625
Scott McCarron	71	70	70	75	286	5,625
Brad Fabel	72	71	70	74	287	5,400
Paul Goydos	70	73	67	77	287	5,400
Colin Montgomerie	71	67	76	73	287	5,400
Nick Price	70	67	73	77	287	5,400
Larry Rinker	70	72	70	75	287	5,400
Fulton Allem	70	73	70	75	288	5,225
Chip Sullivan	68	73	76	71	288	5,225
Brian Henninger	69	71	75	74	289	5,150
Greg Norman	74	69	73	74	290	5,150
Frank Nobilo	71	71	75	74	291	5,050
Robert Damron	75	68	72	77	292	4,975
Trevor Dodds	69	72	77	74	292	4,975
Jay Haas	71	71	74	78	294	4,900

Greater Greensboro Chrysler Classic

Forest Oaks Country Club, Greensboro, North Carolina
Par 36-36–72; 7,062 yards

April 22-25
purse, $2,600,000

	SCORES				TOTAL	MONEY
Jesper Parnevik	65	63	67	70	265	$468,000
Jim Furyk	67	63	68	69	267	280,800
Jeff Maggert	68	62	75	68	273	176,800
Dudley Hart	66	65	71	72	274	124,800
Tom Lehman	69	68	69	69	275	104,000
Paul Stankowski	70	69	71	66	276	90,350
Kirk Triplett	69	68	71	68	276	90,350
Trevor Dodds	71	65	72	69	277	80,600
Phil Blackmar	71	69	70	68	278	70,200
J.L. Lewis	70	65	74	69	278	70,200
Vijay Singh	70	70	70	68	278	70,200
Neal Lancaster	69	70	69	71	279	59,800
Jim Carter	72	66	73	69	280	48,750
Brad Faxon	71	70	70	69	280	48,750
Greg Kraft	75	66	69	70	280	48,750
Sean Murphy	68	71	70	71	280	48,750
Brad Fabel	73	69	70	69	281	35,186.67
Donnie Hammond	70	70	70	71	281	35,186.67
Rocco Mediate	68	70	73	70	281	35,186.67
Hal Sutton	70	70	70	71	281	35,186.67
Bill Glasson	74	67	68	72	281	35,186.66
Skip Kendall	72	67	70	72	281	35,186.66
Steve Lowery	66	68	73	75	282	26,000
Jeff Sluman	73	68	71	70	282	26,000
David Frost	71	68	72	72	283	19,846.67
Chris Perry	69	71	73	70	283	19,846.67
Omar Uresti	69	71	73	70	283	19,846.67
Mike Weir	70	68	74	71	283	19,846.67
Frank Nobilo	71	68	72	72	283	19,846.66
Chris Riley	71	69	71	72	283	19,846.66
Woody Austin	70	73	69	72	284	15,080
Fred Funk	68	72	72	72	284	15,080
Jeff Gallagher	70	71	71	72	284	15,080
Mike Hulbert	71	66	74	73	284	15,080
Per-Ulrik Johansson	72	67	71	74	284	15,080
Kenny Perry	72	71	69	72	284	15,080
Tim Herron	69	69	77	70	285	12,220
Jerry Kelly	69	69	76	71	285	12,220
Dennis Paulson	69	69	75	72	285	12,220
Ben Bates	73	69	74	70	286	10,400
Danny Briggs	70	72	71	73	286	10,400
Stewart Cink	72	70	68	76	286	10,400
Wayne Grady	74	64	76	72	286	10,400
Emlyn Aubrey	69	69	74	75	287	8,320
Eric Booker	72	71	71	73	287	8,320
Steve Elkington	71	68	75	73	287	8,320
Lee Porter	75	68	71	73	287	8,320
Paul Goydos	72	69	74	73	288	6,534.67
Kent Jones	71	72	75	70	288	6,534.67
Wayne Levi	70	69	76	73	288	6,534.67
Scott Verplank	73	70	70	75	288	6,534.67
Robert Damron	71	71	69	77	288	6,534.66
Robin Freeman	67	68	74	79	288	6,534.66
Notah Begay III	72	70	77	70	289	5,980

	SCORES				TOTAL	MONEY
Bob Burns	73	70	75	71	289	5,980
Charles Raulerson	76	66	70	77	289	5,980
Barry Cheesman	71	72	73	74	290	5,746
Chris DiMarco	70	72	76	72	290	5,746
Len Mattiace	71	69	77	73	290	5,746
Deane Pappas	72	71	75	72	290	5,746
Lee Rinker	71	70	74	75	290	5,746
Mark Wiebe	70	70	72	78	290	5,746
Briny Baird	73	70	73	75	291	5,460
Cameron Beckman	68	74	75	74	291	5,460
Jimmy Green	73	70	70	78	291	5,460
Jonathan Kaye	71	70	78	72	291	5,460
Ted Tryba	72	70	72	77	291	5,460
Rick Fehr	73	70	74	76	293	5,252
Brian Henninger	71	71	77	74	293	5,252
Lanny Wadkins	72	69	78	74	293	5,252
Charles Warren	69	72	80	73	294	5,148

Shell Houston Open

TPC at The Woodlands, The Woodlands, Texas
Par 36-36—72; 7,045 yards

April 29-May 2
purse, $2,500,000

	SCORES				TOTAL	MONEY
Stuart Appleby	70	68	70	71	279	$450,000
John Cook	68	74	68	70	280	220,000
Hal Sutton	68	68	69	75	280	220,000
Mark Wiebe	69	69	71	73	282	120,000
Clark Dennis	72	69	71	71	283	84,750
J.P. Hayes	72	69	69	73	283	84,750
Jonathan Kaye	74	70	67	72	283	84,750
Loren Roberts	72	69	67	75	283	84,750
Vijay Singh	71	69	70	73	283	84,750
Scott Hoch	73	70	67	74	284	53,571.43
Bradley Hughes	72	72	71	69	284	53,571.43
Frank Lickliter	71	68	69	76	284	53,571.43
Larry Mize	70	70	71	73	284	53,571.43
Esteban Toledo	69	71	73	71	284	53,571.43
Brian Watts	70	70	69	75	284	53,571.43
Joey Sindelar	68	68	71	77	284	53,571.42
Bob Friend	72	70	72	71	285	36,250
Jerry Kelly	71	68	72	74	285	36,250
Greg Kraft	71	71	75	68	285	36,250
Justin Leonard	71	69	75	70	285	36,250
Tom Byrum	70	72	72	72	286	25,000
Chris DiMarco	71	72	72	71	286	25,000
Jimmy Green	73	71	68	74	286	25,000
John Maginnes	71	72	70	73	286	25,000
Craig Parry	70	70	73	73	286	25,000
Omar Uresti	67	71	72	76	286	25,000
Fred Funk	68	77	72	70	287	17,375
Dan Forsman	71	72	72	72	287	17,375
Jeff Gallagher	68	69	76	74	287	17,375
Nolan Henke	70	70	78	69	287	17,375
Bruce Lietzke	69	73	75	70	287	17,375
Clarence Rose	70	74	64	79	287	17,375
David Sutherland	68	75	79	66	288	12,928.58

	SCORES				TOTAL	MONEY
Robert Allenby	69	72	72	75	288	12,928.57
Barry Cheesman	71	72	72	73	288	12,928.57
Tim Loustalot	74	70	75	69	288	12,928.57
Jeff Maggert	69	73	75	71	288	12,928.57
Chris Smith	69	72	73	74	288	12,928.57
Phil Tataurangi	71	72	71	74	288	12,928.57
Notah Begay III	73	71	70	75	289	9,750
Brian Claar	70	73	70	76	289	9,750
Robert Gamez	71	69	77	72	289	9,750
Rory Sabbatini	73	72	70	74	289	9,750
Kevin Sutherland	71	71	76	71	289	9,750
Cameron Beckman	68	74	74	74	290	7,150
Doug Dunakey	72	70	71	77	290	7,150
Tom Pernice, Jr.	72	70	75	73	290	7,150
Lee Porter	71	72	71	76	290	7,150
Steve Stricker	72	72	75	71	290	7,150
Jay Williamson	70	74	69	77	290	7,150
Eric Booker	66	74	75	76	291	5,788.89
Mike Brisky	70	73	75	73	291	5,788.89
Olin Browne	72	73	72	74	291	5,788.89
John Daly	69	74	71	77	291	5,788.89
Peter Jacobsen	70	74	72	75	291	5,788.89
Tom Kite	77	68	72	74	291	5,788.89
Franklin Langham	74	71	72	74	291	5,788.89
Mike Standly	72	73	72	74	291	5,788.89
Scott Gump	69	75	70	77	291	5,788.88
Phil Blackmar	70	72	79	71	292	5,425
Pete Jordan	70	73	75	74	292	5,425
Payne Stewart	74	70	72	76	292	5,425
D.A. Weibring	69	76	73	74	292	5,425
David Duval	69	70	78	76	293	5,250
Skip Kendall	74	68	75	76	293	5,250
Len Mattiace	72	69	78	74	293	5,250
Perry Moss	69	74	76	75	294	5,150
Joe Ogilvie	72	73	73	77	295	5,075
David Ogrin	70	75	78	72	295	5,075
Kelly Gibson	70	69	81	76	296	4,950
Craig Spence	71	73	73	79	296	4,950
Dave Stockton, Jr.	70	73	75	78	296	4,950
Bob Estes	69	72	78	78	297	4,825
Steve Lowery	73	71	77	76	297	4,825

Compaq Classic of New Orleans

English Turn Golf & Country Club, May 6-9
New Orleans, Louisiana purse, $2,600,000
Par 36-36–72; 7,106 yards

	SCORES				TOTAL	MONEY
Carlos Franco	66	69	68	66	269	$468,000
Steve Flesch	66	67	68	70	271	228,800
Harrison Frazar	68	70	65	68	271	228,800
Craig Barlow	66	70	70	67	273	107,466.67
Dennis Paulson	69	69	68	67	273	107,466.67
Eric Booker	68	63	71	71	273	107,466.66
Hal Sutton	68	71	69	66	274	81,033.34
Glen Day	67	69	71	67	274	81,033.33

	SCORES				TOTAL	MONEY
Craig Parry	69	66	72	67	274	81,033.33
Jay Don Blake	72	69	65	69	275	67,600
Dudley Hart	68	70	65	72	275	67,600
Doug Dunakey	70	72	64	70	276	46,475
Brad Fabel	71	66	67	72	276	46,475
Scott Gump	71	70	65	70	276	46,475
Scott Hoch	68	68	72	68	276	46,475
Jerry Kelly	67	70	71	68	276	46,475
Scott McCarron	69	71	66	70	276	46,475
Chris Perry	65	74	66	71	276	46,475
Kirk Triplett	75	65	66	70	276	46,475
Woody Austin	67	72	67	71	277	26,227.50
Jim Carter	68	70	66	73	277	26,227.50
Skip Kendall	71	68	69	69	277	26,227.50
Andrew Magee	70	68	70	69	277	26,227.50
Blaine McCallister	65	69	71	72	277	26,227.50
Chris Smith	69	68	67	73	277	26,227.50
Steve Stricker	67	73	66	71	277	26,227.50
Mark Wiebe	68	71	66	72	277	26,227.50
Robert Allenby	69	72	73	64	278	16,918.58
Phil Blackmar	72	67	68	71	278	16,918.57
Neal Lancaster	67	74	68	69	278	16,918.57
Frank Lickliter	65	70	71	72	278	16,918.57
David Sutherland	67	70	72	69	278	16,918.57
Ted Tryba	71	71	64	72	278	16,918.57
Omar Uresti	66	65	71	76	278	16,918.57
Briny Baird	67	71	72	69	279	11,479
Chip Beck	69	70	70	70	279	11,479
Mark Calcavecchia	71	67	69	72	279	11,479
Mike Hulbert	71	71	68	69	279	11,479
Sean Murphy	68	72	69	70	279	11,479
Mike Reid	74	68	68	69	279	11,479
Tom Scherrer	69	70	72	68	279	11,479
Bob Tway	70	69	70	70	279	11,479
Duffy Waldorf	71	70	70	68	279	11,479
Brian Watts	70	71	69	69	279	11,479
Brian Gay	70	68	71	71	280	8,320
Steve Lowery	68	70	68	74	280	8,320
Ben Bates	69	70	72	70	281	6,994
Chris DiMarco	69	70	71	71	281	6,994
Donnie Hammond	72	70	69	70	281	6,994
Brett Quigley	69	72	72	68	281	6,994
Mathias Gronberg	73	67	74	68	282	5,961.10
Michael Bradley	70	66	70	76	282	5,961.09
Tom Byrum	69	71	71	71	282	5,961.09
Robert Damron	68	73	72	69	282	5,961.09
Scott Dunlap	71	70	67	74	282	5,961.09
Dan Forsman	69	70	68	75	282	5,961.09
Kelly Gibson	70	70	72	70	282	5,961.09
Pete Jordan	67	71	73	71	282	5,961.09
Franklin Langham	69	73	68	72	282	5,961.09
Nick Price	69	71	70	72	282	5,961.09
Phil Tataurangi	67	74	70	71	282	5,961.09
Jeff Brehaut	72	69	71	71	283	5,460
Mark Brooks	71	69	71	72	283	5,460
Trevor Dodds	73	69	68	73	283	5,460
Joe Durant	70	72	75	66	283	5,460
P.H. Horgan III	72	69	68	74	283	5,460
Ted Purdy	70	72	69	72	283	5,460
Mike Standly	71	69	71	72	283	5,460

		SCORES			TOTAL	MONEY
Clark Dennis	68	72	71	73	284	5,174
Doug Martin	65	73	70	76	284	5,174
D.A. Weibring	71	71	70	72	284	5,174
Jay Williamson	69	70	75	70	284	5,174
Ronnie Black	68	74	71	72	285	4,992
Greg Chalmers	73	66	71	75	285	4,992
David Ogrin	71	71	71	72	285	4,992
Russ Cochran	65	73	77	71	286	4,810
Jimmy Green	70	72	76	68	286	4,810
Gary Hallberg	70	72	70	74	286	4,810
Mike Springer	69	72	74	71	286	4,810
Steve Jurgensen	71	70	70	76	287	4,654
Charles Raulerson	73	68	74	72	287	4,654
Mike Sposa	71	71	69	78	289	4,576

GTE Byron Nelson Classic

TPC Four Seasons Resort Las Colinas:
Par 35-35–70; 6,924 yards
Cottonwood Valley Golf Club:
Par 34-36–70; 6,846 yards
Irving, Texas

May 13-16
purse, $3,000,000

		SCORES			TOTAL	MONEY
Loren Roberts	66	66	62	68	262	$540,000
Steve Pate	63	65	68	66	262	324,000
(Roberts defeated Pate on first extra hole.)						
Chris DiMarco	64	69	68	68	269	144,000
Sergio Garcia	62	67	71	69	269	144,000
Lee Janzen	68	64	68	69	269	144,000
Brian Watts	65	71	65	68	269	144,000
Emlyn Aubrey	64	69	69	69	271	96,750
Tiger Woods	61	67	74	69	271	96,750
Barry Cheesman	63	70	69	70	272	81,000
Paul Goydos	62	76	66	68	272	81,000
Chris Perry	67	68	71	66	272	81,000
Greg Kraft	69	68	72	64	273	57,000
Justin Leonard	63	70	69	71	273	57,000
Andrew Magee	67	65	69	72	273	57,000
Blaine McCallister	69	65	67	72	273	57,000
Nick Price	63	71	71	68	273	57,000
Mark Wiebe	69	68	69	67	273	57,000
Doug Barron	69	66	69	70	274	37,800
Brad Faxon	67	66	68	73	274	37,800
Jeff Gallagher	67	62	74	71	274	37,800
Jim Gallagher, Jr.	71	64	73	66	274	37,800
David Ogrin	70	64	70	70	274	37,800
Corey Pavin	63	70	69	72	274	37,800
Robert Allenby	67	69	67	72	275	24,300
Olin Browne	65	70	68	72	275	24,300
Brandel Chamblee	69	69	70	67	275	24,300
Mike Reid	69	68	70	68	275	24,300
Esteban Toledo	65	71	70	69	275	24,300
Kirk Triplett	64	70	71	70	275	24,300
Mark O'Meara	68	65	74	69	276	18,630
Craig Parry	69	65	72	70	276	18,630
Jeff Sluman	69	66	68	73	276	18,630

	SCORES				TOTAL	MONEY
Chris Smith	68	69	69	70	276	18,630
D.A. Weibring	68	68	70	70	276	18,630
Woody Austin	68	69	70	70	277	14,475
Doug Dunakey	67	70	69	71	277	14,475
Dan Forsman	67	70	67	73	277	14,475
Dudley Hart	70	67	70	70	277	14,475
David Sutherland	66	72	71	68	277	14,475
Hal Sutton	67	69	71	70	277	14,475
Notah Begay III	69	69	72	68	278	11,100
Jim Carter	66	70	71	71	278	11,100
Brad Fabel	68	69	71	70	278	11,100
Steve Lowery	62	70	69	77	278	11,100
Tom Scherrer	67	69	69	73	278	11,100
Ben Bates	67	69	73	70	279	8,316
Mike Brisky	70	68	69	72	279	8,316
Brent Geiberger	66	71	66	76	279	8,316
Mike Sposa	67	69	72	71	279	8,316
Ted Tryba	66	70	68	75	279	8,316
Michael Bradley	65	67	76	72	280	6,946.67
Tom Byrum	65	73	70	72	280	6,946.67
Mark Calcavecchia	72	66	73	69	280	6,946.67
Greg Chalmers	71	67	72	70	280	6,946.67
P.H. Horgan III	70	68	71	71	280	6,946.67
Chris Riley	66	71	73	70	280	6,946.67
Fred Couples	69	69	67	75	280	6,946.66
Harrison Frazar	65	72	69	74	280	6,946.66
Brian Henninger	67	69	70	74	280	6,946.66
Russ Cochran	68	70	69	74	281	6,510
Robert Damron	66	69	72	74	281	6,510
Scott Dunlap	64	69	71	77	281	6,510
Frank Lickliter	68	69	73	71	281	6,510
Phil Blackmar	68	70	70	74	282	6,300
Larry Rinker	69	68	70	75	282	6,300
Dave Stockton, Jr.	67	70	74	71	282	6,300
John Daly	66	71	73	73	283	6,090
Glen Day	66	71	70	76	283	6,090
Kent Jones	68	69	74	72	283	6,090
Charles Raulerson	65	69	74	75	283	6,090
Danny Briggs	69	69	69	78	285	5,940
Wayne Levi	68	70	72	76	286	5,880
J.L. Lewis	66	72	74	78	290	5,820

MasterCard Colonial

Colonial Country Club, Ft. Worth, Texas
Par 35-35–70; 7,010 yards

May 20-23
purse, $2,800,000

	SCORES				TOTAL	MONEY
Olin Browne	73	67	66	66	272	$504,000
Fred Funk	68	68	69	68	273	168,000
Paul Goydos	70	68	69	66	273	168,000
Tim Herron	68	69	69	67	273	168,000
Greg Kraft	75	67	61	70	273	168,000
Jeff Sluman	67	71	69	66	273	168,000
Bob Estes	70	68	68	68	274	84,350
John Huston	72	65	71	66	274	84,350
Billy Mayfair	68	67	68	71	274	84,350

	SCORES				TOTAL	MONEY
Craig Parry	72	68	68	66	274	84,350
Stuart Appleby	71	67	68	69	275	50,680
Jim Carter	71	70	68	66	275	50,680
John Cook	68	66	70	71	275	50,680
Davis Love III	72	66	68	69	275	50,680
Len Mattiace	70	69	67	69	275	50,680
Phil Mickelson	72	63	70	70	275	50,680
Corey Pavin	69	64	74	68	275	50,680
Vijay Singh	67	72	66	70	275	50,680
Duffy Waldorf	73	67	68	67	275	50,680
Brian Watts	71	66	70	68	275	50,680
Stewart Cink	70	72	70	64	276	29,120
Dan Forsman	69	72	66	69	276	29,120
Lee Janzen	71	69	65	71	276	29,120
Kirk Triplett	72	66	70	68	276	29,120
Scott Verplank	72	65	66	73	276	29,120
Billy Andrade	73	68	69	67	277	21,140
Mark Calcavecchia	69	67	72	69	277	21,140
Scott Hoch	69	66	70	72	277	21,140
Tom Lehman	71	71	64	71	277	21,140
Tommy Armour III	73	70	67	68	278	18,200
Joe Durant	69	66	70	73	278	18,200
Skip Kendall	71	67	72	68	278	18,200
Chris Perry	70	73	70	66	279	14,793.34
Kenny Perry	73	66	73	67	279	14,793.34
Brandel Chamblee	73	69	70	67	279	14,793.33
Franklin Langham	68	72	67	72	279	14,793.33
Tom Pernice, Jr.	73	71	66	69	279	14,793.33
Mark Wiebe	70	66	74	69	279	14,793.33
Fred Couples	72	71	68	69	280	10,640
Robert Damron	73	66	73	68	280	10,640
Clark Dennis	72	67	69	72	280	10,640
Steve Elkington	68	68	75	69	280	10,640
Brent Geiberger	71	70	68	71	280	10,640
Justin Leonard	73	66	69	72	280	10,640
Andrew Magee	74	70	66	70	280	10,640
Tom Watson	74	70	66	70	280	10,640
Steve Flesch	66	74	66	75	281	7,532
Tom Kite	73	68	71	69	281	7,532
Scott McCarron	72	69	72	68	281	7,532
Kevin Sutherland	73	70	68	70	281	7,532
Glen Day	74	69	73	66	282	6,678
Bob Friend	70	70	69	73	282	6,678
Jim Gallagher, Jr.	71	72	66	73	282	6,678
Loren Roberts	74	69	66	73	282	6,678
Mike Brisky	72	72	74	65	283	6,272
Jim Furyk	74	69	70	70	283	6,272
Mike Hulbert	70	70	73	70	283	6,272
Steve Lowery	72	66	75	70	283	6,272
Frank Nobilo	72	70	72	69	283	6,272
Steve Pate	72	69	68	74	283	6,272
Dennis Paulson	74	68	69	72	283	6,272
Jonathan Kaye	75	69	69	71	284	5,992
Rocco Mediate	71	71	70	72	284	5,992
Dan Pohl	70	69	77	68	284	5,992
Mark Brooks	71	71	70	73	285	5,768
Harrison Frazar	73	68	72	72	285	5,768
Brian Henninger	78	66	72	69	285	5,768
Bradley Hughes	73	71	71	70	285	5,768
D.A. Weibring	72	69	72	72	285	5,768

		SCORES			TOTAL	MONEY
Jay Haas	70	71	73	72	286	5,572
Willie Wood	69	71	75	71	286	5,572
Omar Uresti	72	68	71	76	287	5,460
Mike Weir	71	69	78	69	287	5,460
David Frost	73	71	72	72	288	5,376
Fulton Allem	72	72	73	72	289	5,292
Dave Stockton, Jr.	71	71	73	74	289	5,292
Eric Booker	71	71	75	73	290	5,152
Bill Glasson	71	73	73	73	290	5,152
Fuzzy Zoeller	71	70	73	76	290	5,152

Kemper Open

TPC at Avenel, Potomac, Maryland
Par 36-35–71; 7,005 yards

May 27-30
purse, $2,500,000

		SCORES			TOTAL	MONEY
Rich Beem	66	67	71	70	274	$450,000
Bill Glasson	67	70	69	69	275	220,000
Bradley Hughes	68	68	72	67	275	220,000
Hal Sutton	73	72	66	65	276	110,000
David Toms	72	68	70	66	276	110,000
Stuart Appleby	74	66	69	68	277	86,875
Tommy Armour III	68	68	68	73	277	86,875
Emlyn Aubrey	71	70	66	71	278	75,000
Dennis Paulson	72	67	71	68	278	75,000
Dan Forsman	71	67	73	68	279	60,000
Mike Sposa	73	66	71	69	279	60,000
Steve Stricker	71	67	73	68	279	60,000
Tommy Tolles	68	70	70	71	279	60,000
Jim Furyk	70	70	71	69	280	43,750
Dicky Pride	73	70	67	70	280	43,750
Dave Stockton, Jr.	70	66	73	71	280	43,750
Brian Watts	67	76	69	68	280	43,750
Brent Geiberger	71	67	72	71	281	33,750
Scott Hoch	74	69	71	67	281	33,750
P.H. Horgan III	71	69	71	70	281	33,750
Vijay Singh	71	72	68	70	281	33,750
Kenny Perry	73	69	73	67	282	23,208.34
Jeff Sluman	71	68	74	69	282	23,208.34
Michael Bradley	74	70	70	68	282	23,208.33
Jim Carter	68	69	71	74	282	23,208.33
Stewart Cink	73	70	67	72	282	23,208.33
Justin Leonard	69	75	66	72	282	23,208.33
Mark Carnevale	75	66	73	69	283	16,625
Trevor Dodds	70	72	70	71	283	16,625
Scott Dunlap	68	71	70	74	283	16,625
Jonathan Kaye	73	71	72	67	283	16,625
Mark O'Meara	70	72	72	69	283	16,625
Joey Sindelar	72	73	70	68	283	16,625
Craig Barlow	76	68	72	68	284	12,357.15
John Maginnes	74	70	72	68	284	12,357.15
Doug Barron	71	74	66	73	284	12,357.14
Fred Funk	72	72	68	72	284	12,357.14
Brian Henninger	69	73	69	73	284	12,357.14
Franklin Langham	72	71	72	69	284	12,357.14
Phil Tataurangi	73	69	71	71	284	12,357.14

	SCORES				TOTAL	MONEY
Lee Janzen	75	69	69	72	285	9,750
Doug Martin	73	70	69	73	285	9,750
Tom Scherrer	73	69	72	71	285	9,750
Stephen Ames	76	69	73	68	286	7,225
R.W. Eaks	73	71	73	69	286	7,225
Jeff Gallagher	69	71	73	73	286	7,225
Greg Kraft	75	70	71	70	286	7,225
Jeff Maggert	74	69	72	71	286	7,225
Corey Pavin	67	72	71	76	286	7,225
Larry Rinker	73	69	71	73	286	7,225
Lee Rinker	70	74	70	72	286	7,225
Brian Claar	71	74	71	71	287	5,716.67
John Cook	75	70	71	71	287	5,716.67
Doug Dunakey	71	72	72	72	287	5,716.67
Harrison Frazar	73	72	72	70	287	5,716.67
Brian Gay	73	71	72	71	287	5,716.67
Grant Waite	71	73	70	73	287	5,716.67
Jeff Brehaut	73	72	68	74	287	5,716.66
Chris Couch	70	69	72	76	287	5,716.66
Donnie Hammond	72	71	68	76	287	5,716.66
Cameron Beckman	71	72	70	75	288	5,375
Tom Byrum	70	72	73	73	288	5,375
Naomichi Ozaki	72	73	73	70	288	5,375
Geoffrey Sisk	76	69	73	70	288	5,375
Greg Chalmers	72	73	70	74	289	5,200
Clark Dennis	70	75	70	74	289	5,200
Clarence Rose	74	70	73	72	289	5,200
Rod Butcher	71	72	68	79	290	5,000
Barry Cheesman	71	72	73	74	290	5,000
Jay Delsing	74	66	73	77	290	5,000
Gabriel Hjertstedt	75	66	77	72	290	5,000
Esteban Toledo	72	71	74	73	290	5,000
Ronnie Black	72	70	75	74	291	4,850
Danny Briggs	72	71	71	78	292	4,800
Sean Murphy	72	73	72	77	294	4,750

Memorial Tournament

Muirfield Village Golf Club, Dublin, Ohio
Par 36-36–72; 7,163 yards

June 3-6
purse, $2,550,000

	SCORES				TOTAL	MONEY
Tiger Woods	68	66	70	69	273	$459,000
Vijay Singh	68	67	71	69	275	275,400
Olin Browne	72	70	72	65	279	132,600
David Duval	72	68	69	70	279	132,600
Carlos Franco	74	67	70	68	279	132,600
Dennis Paulson	68	71	69	72	280	91,800
Ernie Els	69	72	70	70	281	76,818.75
Bill Glasson	70	68	71	72	281	76,818.75
Justin Leonard	68	69	74	70	281	76,818.75
Kaname Yokoo	73	70	67	71	281	76,818.75
Sergio Garcia	67	70	74	71	282	58,650
Phil Mickelson	69	73	69	71	282	58,650
Kenny Perry	73	66	71	72	282	58,650
J.P. Hayes	71	68	73	71	283	43,350
Frank Lickliter	73	65	73	72	283	43,350

	SCORES				TOTAL	MONEY
Andrew Magee	71	74	70	68	283	43,350
Corey Pavin	73	69	72	69	283	43,350
Brian Watts	70	74	66	73	283	43,350
Paul Azinger	76	69	66	73	284	30,906
Chris DiMarco	71	72	70	71	284	30,906
Tom Lehman	70	73	73	68	284	30,906
Larry Mize	71	68	76	69	284	30,906
Naomichi Ozaki	70	70	71	73	284	30,906
Choi Kyung-ju	69	72	76	68	285	20,181.43
Stewart Cink	69	71	73	72	285	20,181.43
Chris Perry	67	73	71	74	285	20,181.43
Payne Stewart	75	65	73	72	285	20,181.43
Steve Stricker	69	70	73	73	285	20,181.43
Mike Weir	73	72	74	66	285	20,181.43
Mark Calcavecchia	71	67	71	76	285	20,181.42
Stuart Appleby	69	72	72	73	286	15,459.25
Lee Janzen	65	70	78	73	286	15,459.25
Frank Nobilo	67	75	73	71	286	15,459.25
Curtis Strange	70	70	72	74	286	15,459.25
Joe Durant	71	71	74	71	287	11,777.38
Fred Funk	72	73	72	70	287	11,777.38
Dudley Hart	73	72	72	70	287	11,777.38
Bob Tway	72	75	71	69	287	11,777.38
Greg Chalmers	76	68	71	72	287	11,777.37
John Cook	70	71	72	74	287	11,777.37
Jay Haas	72	69	72	74	287	11,777.37
Tim Herron	71	73	72	71	287	11,777.37
Billy Andrade	69	72	72	75	288	8,415
Glen Day	71	75	71	71	288	8,415
Jim Furyk	71	67	76	74	288	8,415
Jesper Parnevik	72	71	71	74	288	8,415
Tom Pernice, Jr.	72	74	70	72	288	8,415
Bob Estes	72	73	71	73	289	6,579
Skip Kendall	72	67	75	75	289	6,579
Billy Mayfair	72	75	72	70	289	6,579
Scott Verplank	71	73	70	75	289	6,579
Robert Allenby	71	70	74	75	290	6,069
Harrison Frazar	72	76	72	70	290	6,069
David Edwards	72	69	77	73	291	5,840
Steve Flesch	70	78	72	71	291	5,840
Brent Geiberger	72	75	70	74	291	5,840
Scott Simpson	75	70	76	70	291	5,840
Wayne Grady	71	74	73	74	292	5,712
Fred Couples	71	74	76	72	293	5,533.84
Per-Ulrik Johansson	74	69	79	71	293	5,533.84
Mark Brooks	72	71	75	75	293	5,533.83
Trevor Dodds	73	72	75	73	293	5,533.83
Jarrod Moseley	73	74	73	73	293	5,533.83
Mark O'Meara	70	71	76	76	293	5,533.83
Eric Booker	75	73	72	74	294	5,329.50
Len Mattiace	70	77	73	74	294	5,329.50
David Frost	74	74	73	74	295	5,227.50
Doug Tewell	75	71	73	76	295	5,227.50
Greg Norman	76	71	75	74	296	5,151
Jack Nicklaus	74	74	76	73	297	5,074.50
Hidemichi Tanaka	74	71	72	80	297	5,074.50
Bob Friend	74	74	79	72	299	4,972.50
Kevin Sutherland	73	74	78	74	299	4,972.50
Ted Tryba	73	74	78	75	300	4,896
Fuzzy Zoeller	73	72	82	74	301	4,845

FedEx St. Jude Classic

TPC at Southwind, Memphis, Tennessee
Par 36-35–71; 7,006 yards

June 10-13
purse, $2,500,000

	SCORES				TOTAL	MONEY
Ted Tryba	68	64	67	66	265	$450,000
Tim Herron	67	66	66	68	267	220,000
Tom Lehman	63	68	68	68	267	220,000
Jose Maria Olazabal	68	68	70	62	268	110,000
Kevin Wentworth	69	69	63	67	268	110,000
Paul Azinger	66	70	69	65	270	80,937.50
Rick Fehr	66	69	66	69	270	80,937.50
Kevin Sutherland	69	65	66	70	270	80,937.50
Hal Sutton	63	67	69	71	270	80,937.50
Miguel Angel Jimenez	68	67	71	65	271	57,500
Frank Lickliter	65	71	66	69	271	57,500
Davis Love III	67	68	68	68	271	57,500
Brett Quigley	70	65	66	70	271	57,500
Omar Uresti	65	67	68	71	271	57,500
David Frost	63	63	74	72	272	42,500
Sean Murphy	69	69	68	66	272	42,500
Kirk Triplett	68	67	69	68	272	42,500
Pete Jordan	69	69	72	63	273	30,428.58
Ronnie Black	68	70	66	69	273	30,428.57
Phil Blackmar	64	70	69	70	273	30,428.57
Clark Dennis	66	70	65	72	273	30,428.57
Jonathan Kaye	71	65	67	70	273	30,428.57
Tim Loustalot	70	67	71	65	273	30,428.57
Scott Verplank	70	67	70	66	273	30,428.57
Rich Beem	68	69	69	68	274	17,147.73
Danny Briggs	69	64	74	67	274	17,147.73
Paul Goydos	69	68	73	64	274	17,147.73
Billy Mayfair	68	70	67	69	274	17,147.73
Perry Moss	69	68	70	67	274	17,147.73
Tom Scherrer	66	67	74	67	274	17,147.73
Curtis Strange	65	71	70	68	274	17,147.73
Grant Waite	67	68	71	68	274	17,147.73
Glen Day	67	68	68	71	274	17,147.72
Bradley Hughes	70	65	67	72	274	17,147.72
Jerry Kelly	65	66	71	72	274	17,147.72
Trevor Dodds	65	72	70	68	275	11,520.84
P.H. Horgan III	67	64	75	69	275	11,520.84
Notah Begay III	68	68	67	72	275	11,520.84
Jim Carter	67	67	71	70	275	11,520.83
Fred Funk	70	65	69	71	275	11,520.83
Jeff Maggert	70	64	71	70	275	11,520.83
Ben Bates	67	68	68	73	276	8,043.75
Brad Bryant	66	71	69	70	276	8,043.75
Brian Gay	66	68	73	69	276	8,043.75
Jay Haas	66	70	67	73	276	8,043.75
David Ogrin	68	69	69	70	276	8,043.75
Nick Price	64	71	70	71	276	8,043.75
David Sutherland	65	70	67	74	276	8,043.75
Charles Warren	70	68	68	70	276	8,043.75
Jay Don Blake	69	68	72	68	277	6,030
Jay Delsing	68	70	68	71	277	6,030
John Huston	67	69	71	70	277	6,030
Rocco Mediate	69	69	69	70	277	6,030
Frank Nobilo	69	69	70	69	277	6,030

	SCORES				TOTAL	MONEY
Fulton Allem	65	72	69	72	278	5,575
Robert Allenby	67	66	72	73	278	5,575
Stephen Ames	68	68	69	73	278	5,575
Emlyn Aubrey	68	64	74	72	278	5,575
Loren Roberts	69	66	73	70	278	5,575
Mike Sposa	69	69	70	70	278	5,575
Esteban Toledo	69	69	69	71	278	5,575
David Toms	72	65	72	69	278	5,575
Stuart Appleby	69	69	72	69	279	5,325
Franklin Langham	71	67	73	68	279	5,325
Mike Brisky	69	68	70	73	280	5,150
Tom Byrum	69	67	74	70	280	5,150
Doug Martin	69	69	72	70	280	5,150
Lee Rinker	68	68	72	72	280	5,150
Doug Tewell	69	69	74	68	280	5,150
Bob Burns	69	66	68	78	281	5,000
Paul Stankowski	70	68	69	75	282	4,950
Brad Fabel	69	67	76	71	283	4,875
Scott McCarron	70	67	76	70	283	4,875
Woody Austin	72	66	73	74	285	4,750
Scott Simpson	68	70	71	76	285	4,750
Mike Springer	67	70	75	73	285	4,750

U.S. Open Championship

Pinehurst Resort and Country Club, No. 2,
Pinehurst, North Carolina
Par 35-35–70; 7,175 yards

June 17-20
purse, $3,500,000

	SCORES				TOTAL	MONEY
Payne Stewart	68	69	72	70	279	$625,000
Phil Mickelson	67	70	73	70	280	370,000
Vijay Singh	69	70	73	69	281	196,791.50
Tiger Woods	68	71	72	70	281	196,791.50
Steve Stricker	70	73	69	73	285	130,655
Tim Herron	69	72	70	75	286	116,935
Hal Sutton	69	70	76	72	287	96,260.34
David Duval	67	70	75	75	287	96,260.33
Jeff Maggert	71	69	74	73	287	96,260.33
Darren Clarke	73	70	74	71	288	78,862.50
Billy Mayfair	67	72	74	75	288	78,862.50
Paul Azinger	72	72	75	70	289	67,347
Paul Goydos	67	74	74	74	289	67,347
Davis Love III	70	73	74	72	289	67,347
Justin Leonard	69	75	73	73	290	58,214.50
Colin Montgomerie	72	72	74	72	290	58,214.50
Jim Furyk	69	73	77	72	291	46,756.17
Jay Haas	74	72	73	72	291	46,756.17
Dudley Hart	73	73	76	69	291	46,756.17
Jesper Parnevik	71	71	76	73	291	46,756.17
John Huston	71	69	75	76	291	46,756.16
Scott Verplank	72	73	72	74	291	46,756.16
Miguel Angel Jimenez	73	70	72	77	292	33,505.40
Nick Price	71	74	74	73	292	33,505.40
Tom Scherrer	72	72	74	74	292	33,505.40
Brian Watts	69	73	77	73	292	33,505.40
D.A. Weibring	69	74	74	75	292	33,505.40

	SCORES			TOTAL	MONEY
David Berganio, Jr.	68 77 76 72			293	26,185.50
Tom Lehman	73 74 73 73			293	26,185.50
Bob Estes	70 71 77 76			294	23,804.50
Geoffrey Sisk	71 72 76 75			294	23,804.50
Stewart Cink	72 74 78 71			295	22,448.50
Sven Struver	70 76 75 74			295	22,448.50
Brad Fabel	69 75 78 74			296	19,083.75
Carlos Franco	69 77 73 77			296	19,083.75
Gabriel Hjertstedt	75 72 79 70			296	19,083.75
Rocco Mediate	69 72 76 79			296	19,083.75
Craig Parry	69 73 79 75			296	19,083.75
Steve Pate	70 75 75 76			296	19,083.75
Corey Pavin	74 71 78 73			296	19,083.75
Esteban Toledo	70 72 76 78			296	19,083.75
Stephan Allan	71 74 77 75			297	15,067.50
Gary Hallberg	74 72 75 76			297	15,067.50
Len Mattiace	72 75 75 75			297	15,067.50
Chris Perry	72 74 75 76			297	15,067.50
Robert Allenby	74 72 76 76			298	12,060.40
Jim Carter	73 70 78 77			298	12,060.40
Brandel Chamblee	73 74 74 77			298	12,060.40
Lee Janzen	74 73 76 75			298	12,060.40
David Lebeck	74 70 78 76			298	12,060.40
Steve Elkington	71 72 79 77			299	10,305
Chris Tidland	71 75 75 78			299	10,305
Greg Kraft	70 73 82 75			300	9,561.50
Spike McRoy	70 74 76 80			300	9,561.50
Phillip Price	71 73 75 81			300	9,561.50
Jason Tyska	72 74 75 79			300	9,561.50
Jerry Kelly	73 74 79 75			301	8,840
Tom Watson	75 70 77 79			301	8,840
Kaname Yokoo	68 74 78 81			301	8,840
John Cook	74 73 77 78			302	8,459.50
Tom Kite	74 72 80 76			302	8,459.50
Chris Smith	69 77 77 80			303	8,177.50
Bob Tway	69 77 79 78			303	8,177.50
Larry Mize	69 75 84 76			304	7,966
*Hank Kuehne	72 75 81 78			306	
Bob Burns	71 76 84 77			308	7,754.50
Ted Tryba	72 75 82 79			308	7,754.50
John Daly	68 77 81 83			309	7,543

Out of Final 36 Holes

Thomas Bjorn	70 78		148
Ben Crenshaw	74 74		148
Ernie Els	72 76		148
Nick Faldo	74 74		148
Steve Flesch	75 73		148
Mathias Gronberg	70 78		148
Scott Hoch	71 77		148
Stephen Leaney	76 72		148
Andrew Magee	73 75		148
Jim McGovern	71 77		148
Michael Muehr	74 74		148
Bobby Wadkins	75 73		148
Chris Zambri	73 75		148
Stuart Appleby	73 76		149
Peter Baker	75 74		149
Keith Clearwater	73 76		149

	SCORES		TOTAL
Glen Day	70	79	149
Fred Funk	71	78	149
Scott Gump	74	75	149
Steve Lowery	74	75	149
Jeff Sluman	74	75	149
Sam Torrance	75	74	149
Omar Uresti	72	77	149
Mike Weir	73	76	149
Lee Westwood	73	76	149
Dennis Zinkon	71	78	149
Richard Zokol	73	76	149
Notah Begay III	74	76	150
Mark Brooks	74	76	150
Olin Browne	73	77	150
Fred Couples	73	77	150
Robin Freeman	73	77	150
Bob Heintz	73	77	150
Shaun Micheel	73	77	150
Mark O'Meara	71	79	150
Mark Slawter	72	78	150
Barry Cheesman	72	79	151
*Erik Ciotti	72	79	151
Bob Friend	74	77	151
Bob Gilder	74	77	151
Greg Gregory	73	78	151
Bradley Hughes	71	80	151
Gary March	72	79	151
*Bryce Molder	73	78	151
Greg Norman	73	78	151
Joey Sindelar	73	78	151
Jeff Street	76	75	151
Jay Williamson	73	78	151
Garrett Willis	77	74	151
Fuzzy Zoeller	74	77	151
Per-Ulrik Johansson	75	77	152
Keith Kulzer	75	77	152
Alberto Ochoa	77	75	152
Patrik Sjoland	75	77	152
Curtis Strange	78	74	152
Kirk Triplett	71	81	152
*Andrew Barnes	74	79	153
Mark Calcavecchia	79	74	153
Joe Durant	74	79	153
Jeff Freeman	72	81	153
Grant Masson	74	79	153
Jack Nicklaus	78	75	153
Chris Riley	74	79	153
Doug Barron	77	77	154
Steve Jones	72	82	154
Masashi Ozaki	80	74	154
Craig Bowden	75	80	155
Bill Glasson	77	78	155
*Matt Kuchar	76	79	155
*Tom McKnight	72	83	155
Jeb Stuart	77	78	155
Chad Campbell	74	82	156
E.J. Pfister	79	77	156
Ron Philo, Jr.	77	79	156
David Toms	74	82	156
Jeff Gallagher	77	80	157

	SCORES		TOTAL
Retief Goosen	75	82	157
Tim Loustalot	79	78	157
Mike Stone	77	80	157
John DiMarco	79	79	158
Scott Fawcett	79	79	158
Jim White	76	83	159
Mark Mielke	78	81	159
Robert Russell	77	82	159
*Matt Call	81	79	160
Ryan Welborn	82	78	160
Hale Irwin	76		WD
Jose Maria Olazabal	75		WD

(Professionals who did not complete 72 holes received $5,000.)

Buick Classic

Westchester Country Club, Rye, New York
Par 36-35–71; 6,779 yards
June 24-27
purse, $2,500,000

	SCORES				TOTAL	MONEY
Duffy Waldorf	70	67	68	71	276	$450,000
Dennis Paulson	71	70	68	67	276	270,000
(Waldorf defeated Paulson on first extra hole.)					
Chris Perry	70	66	71	70	277	170,000
Scott Hoch	73	70	66	69	278	120,000
Doug Barron	74	68	69	68	279	84,750
Jim Carter	67	72	66	74	279	84,750
Gabriel Hjertstedt	69	70	69	71	279	84,750
Loren Roberts	71	71	68	69	279	84,750
Vijay Singh	75	69	67	68	279	84,750
Tom Byrum	68	70	70	72	280	51,875
Fred Couples	69	69	72	70	280	51,875
David Duval	70	75	68	67	280	51,875
Bob Estes	70	71	69	70	280	51,875
Steve Flesch	72	69	66	73	280	51,875
Lee Janzen	71	67	69	73	280	51,875
David Sutherland	73	66	68	73	280	51,875
Bob Tway	73	68	75	64	280	51,875
Fred Funk	72	67	70	72	281	33,750
Jeff Maggert	70	66	77	68	281	33,750
Corey Pavin	72	73	65	71	281	33,750
Kevin Sutherland	71	70	74	66	281	33,750
Greg Chalmers	68	75	69	70	282	23,208.34
Jim Furyk	70	74	70	68	282	23,208.34
Ernie Els	69	70	70	73	282	23,208.33
Brent Geiberger	70	72	67	73	282	23,208.33
Justin Leonard	71	70	66	75	282	23,208.33
Omar Uresti	71	68	69	74	282	23,208.33
Rich Beem	73	71	68	71	283	16,267.86
Scott Dunlap	69	72	71	71	283	16,267.86
Steve Elkington	76	69	70	68	283	16,267.86
Scott Gump	72	73	68	70	283	16,267.86
J.P. Hayes	73	70	68	72	283	16,267.86
Len Mattiace	69	71	68	75	283	16,267.85
Craig Parry	73	71	66	73	283	16,267.85
Billy Andrade	70	71	70	73	284	12,062.50

	SCORES				TOTAL	MONEY
Paul Azinger	70	71	74	69	284	12,062.50
Jay Haas	68	73	73	70	284	12,062.50
Tom Lehman	75	66	72	71	284	12,062.50
Mike Reid	71	72	68	73	284	12,062.50
Tom Scherrer	74	71	68	71	284	12,062.50
Mike Brisky	74	69	73	69	285	9,250
John Cook	73	71	69	72	285	9,250
Neal Lancaster	70	70	71	74	285	9,250
Dicky Pride	73	69	74	69	285	9,250
Esteban Toledo	71	69	74	71	285	9,250
Brad Bryant	71	73	76	66	286	6,587.50
Doug Dunakey	72	73	69	72	286	6,587.50
Harrison Frazar	73	70	68	75	286	6,587.50
Bradley Hughes	76	68	69	73	286	6,587.50
J.L. Lewis	75	65	73	73	286	6,587.50
Rocco Mediate	75	69	73	69	286	6,587.50
Steve Pate	68	71	72	75	286	6,587.50
Chris Smith	73	70	70	73	286	6,587.50
Notah Begay III	74	70	73	70	287	5,625
John Elliott	73	68	72	74	287	5,625
Rick Fehr	76	69	70	72	287	5,625
Dudley Hart	71	70	75	71	287	5,625
Doug Martin	71	70	71	75	287	5,625
Blaine McCallister	72	70	68	77	287	5,625
Brett Quigley	74	70	72	71	287	5,625
Ted Tryba	74	69	69	75	287	5,625
David Berganio, Jr.	72	73	69	74	288	5,325
Jim Gallagher, Jr.	75	69	72	72	288	5,325
Peter Jacobsen	73	72	72	71	288	5,325
Frank Nobilo	66	72	74	76	288	5,325
Stephen Ames	65	72	75	77	289	5,100
Eric Booker	73	72	68	76	289	5,100
Brad Fabel	73	71	71	74	289	5,100
Steve Lowery	72	73	73	71	289	5,100
Grant Waite	71	74	73	71	289	5,100
Joey Sindelar	71	72	72	75	290	4,950
Mark Brooks	74	70	73	74	291	4,850
Mark Calcavecchia	74	70	71	76	291	4,850
Sean Murphy	69	74	75	73	291	4,850
Willie Wood	73	71	72	76	292	4,750
Chris Couch	72	73	74	74	293	4,650
Charles Raulerson	71	73	71	78	293	4,650
Bo Van Pelt	75	69	71	78	293	4,650
Tom Pernice, Jr.	73	72	73	76	294	4,550
Robert Damron	73	69	71	82	295	4,450
Jimmy Green	71	73	72	79	295	4,450
Lee Rinker	73	72	74	76	295	4,450

Motorola Western Open

Cog Hill Golf & Country Club, Dubsdread Course,
Lemont, Illinois
Par 36-36–72; 7,073 yards

July 1-4
purse, $2,500,000

	SCORES				TOTAL	MONEY
Tiger Woods	68	66	68	71	273	$450,000
Mike Weir	72	67	67	70	276	270,000
Brent Geiberger	70	68	70	69	277	170,000

	SCORES				TOTAL	MONEY
Vijay Singh	67	70	71	70	278	120,000
Dicky Pride	71	68	70	70	279	100,000
John Maginnes	69	70	71	70	280	90,000
Chris Perry	71	70	69	71	281	80,625
Mike Reid	70	70	73	68	281	80,625
Glen Day	69	73	68	72	282	65,000
Brian Henninger	74	67	67	74	282	65,000
Joe Ogilvie	74	66	72	70	282	65,000
Hal Sutton	67	70	73	72	282	65,000
Stuart Appleby	68	66	72	77	283	46,875
Tommy Armour III	71	67	70	75	283	46,875
Mike Brisky	66	69	71	77	283	46,875
D.A. Weibring	69	73	71	70	283	46,875
Greg Chalmers	73	70	69	72	284	37,500
Franklin Langham	70	70	70	74	284	37,500
Frank Lickliter	70	70	73	71	284	37,500
Doug Barron	74	69	71	71	285	26,071.43
Rick Fehr	72	68	70	75	285	26,071.43
Mike Hulbert	70	68	74	73	285	26,071.43
Justin Leonard	74	69	70	72	285	26,071.43
Nick Price	73	69	70	73	285	26,071.43
Lee Rinker	68	72	69	76	285	26,071.43
David Toms	71	68	72	74	285	26,071.42
Phil Blackmar	70	71	71	74	286	17,000
Mark Brooks	72	71	73	70	286	17,000
Scott Dunlap	69	72	72	73	286	17,000
John Elliott	68	71	70	77	286	17,000
Scott Gump	72	69	71	74	286	17,000
J.L. Lewis	70	73	70	73	286	17,000
Jeff Sluman	73	66	74	73	286	17,000
Ty Armstrong	72	68	76	71	287	12,093.75
Woody Austin	73	69	72	73	287	12,093.75
Ben Bates	69	72	75	71	287	12,093.75
Jay Don Blake	71	66	72	78	287	12,093.75
Jim Carter	69	73	74	71	287	12,093.75
Jim Furyk	71	70	69	77	287	12,093.75
Dudley Hart	71	67	76	73	287	12,093.75
Esteban Toledo	70	69	73	75	287	12,093.75
Briny Baird	67	73	74	74	288	8,264.29
Michael Bradley	70	69	79	70	288	8,264.29
Dan Forsman	69	72	75	72	288	8,264.29
Blaine McCallister	72	70	72	74	288	8,264.29
Tom Byrum	70	69	73	76	288	8,264.28
Neal Lancaster	69	74	71	74	288	8,264.28
Loren Roberts	69	68	72	79	288	8,264.28
Harrison Frazar	74	68	77	70	289	6,108.34
Mike Springer	73	70	77	69	289	6,108.34
Craig Barlow	71	72	73	73	289	6,108.33
Robert Damron	73	70	75	71	289	6,108.33
Len Mattiace	69	72	75	73	289	6,108.33
Ted Purdy	74	66	71	78	289	6,108.33
Clark Dennis	70	72	76	72	290	5,625
Skip Kendall	73	70	75	72	290	5,625
Frank Nobilo	73	70	71	76	290	5,625
Dennis Paulson	71	72	73	74	290	5,625
Steve Stricker	71	72	71	76	290	5,625
Scott Verplank	72	70	74	74	290	5,625
Pete Jordan	70	71	76	74	291	5,325
Steve Lowery	73	67	76	75	291	5,325
Andrew Magee	73	70	73	75	291	5,325

	SCORES				TOTAL	MONEY
Paul Stankowski	72	69	74	76	291	5,325
Curtis Strange	69	74	72	76	291	5,325
Omar Uresti	71	69	77	74	291	5,325
Kent Jones	73	70	72	77	292	5,150
Olin Browne	71	70	73	79	293	5,000
Brandel Chamblee	73	67	78	75	293	5,000
Bob Estes	74	69	77	73	293	5,000
Nolan Henke	71	72	76	74	293	5,000
Joey Sindelar	72	67	78	76	293	5,000
Peter Jacobsen	73	69	76	76	294	4,850
Brian Gay	73	69	75	78	295	4,800
David Frost	69	73	72	82	296	4,725
Katsumasa Miyamoto	72	71	72	81	296	4,725

Greater Milwaukee Open

Brown Deer Park Golf Club, Milwaukee, Wisconsin   July 8-11
Par 35-36–71; 6,739 yards   purse, $3,500,000

	SCORES				TOTAL	MONEY
Carlos Franco	65	66	67	66	264	$414,000
Tom Lehman	68	67	65	66	266	248,400
Jerry Kelly	66	65	66	71	268	156,400
Dan Forsman	67	68	66	68	269	101,200
Steve Lowery	70	70	68	61	269	101,200
Skip Kendall	67	70	68	65	270	79,925
Chris Perry	65	68	67	70	270	79,925
Mark Calcavecchia	64	70	69	68	271	69,000
Joey Sindelar	65	68	68	70	271	69,000
Ben Bates	62	73	70	67	272	49,285.72
Michael Bradley	70	67	69	66	272	49,285.72
Steve Stricker	69	67	69	67	272	49,285.72
Jay Delsing	68	70	66	68	272	49,285.71
Jay Haas	69	68	66	69	272	49,285.71
John Maginnes	66	64	74	68	272	49,285.71
Mark Wiebe	68	68	68	68	272	49,285.71
Doug Barron	69	70	65	69	273	32,200
Blaine McCallister	72	68	65	68	273	32,200
Spike McRoy	68	68	70	67	273	32,200
Larry Mize	65	72	67	69	273	32,200
David Ogrin	65	72	67	69	273	32,200
Brandel Chamblee	65	72	69	68	274	21,351.67
Doug Martin	66	70	70	68	274	21,351.67
Rory Sabbatini	67	65	74	68	274	21,351.67
Curtis Strange	69	68	68	69	274	21,351.67
Mike Hulbert	69	69	67	69	274	21,351.66
Jeff Sluman	71	64	69	70	274	21,351.66
Greg Chalmers	71	67	67	70	275	16,330
R.W. Eaks	68	68	68	71	275	16,330
Lee Rinker	69	69	69	68	275	16,330
Jeff Brehaut	70	69	67	70	276	12,765
Mike Brisky	68	70	67	71	276	12,765
Jim Carter	70	71	66	69	276	12,765
Steve Flesch	68	73	66	69	276	12,765
Jeff Gallagher	70	67	69	70	276	12,765
Dicky Pride	70	71	65	70	276	12,765
Mike Sullivan	67	72	67	70	276	12,765

	SCORES				TOTAL	MONEY
Mark Wilson	68	73	67	68	276	12,765
Brad Fabel	71	70	69	67	277	8,970
Robin Freeman	67	72	69	69	277	8,970
Robert Gamez	71	67	68	71	277	8,970
Kelly Gibson	71	70	63	73	277	8,970
David Peoples	69	71	66	71	277	8,970
Tom Pernice, Jr.	64	73	70	70	277	8,970
Willie Wood	70	66	71	70	277	8,970
Brian Claar	68	71	71	68	278	5,980
Chris Couch	71	70	71	66	278	5,980
John Elliott	66	73	69	70	278	5,980
P.H. Horgan III	70	68	71	69	278	5,980
J.L. Lewis	70	70	66	72	278	5,980
Deane Pappas	68	72	66	72	278	5,980
Brett Quigley	67	71	71	69	278	5,980
Loren Roberts	68	72	69	69	278	5,980
Ted Schulz	69	71	69	69	278	5,980
Joe Durant	67	69	70	73	279	5,152
Bob Gilder	66	75	68	70	279	5,152
Nolan Henke	71	69	73	66	279	5,152
Perry Moss	69	70	71	69	279	5,152
Charles Raulerson	70	70	70	69	279	5,152
Chris Smith	66	72	70	71	279	5,152
Grant Waite	68	72	67	72	279	5,152
Cliff Kresge	68	73	68	71	280	4,876
Frank Lickliter	69	70	69	72	280	4,876
Dan Pohl	69	68	69	74	280	4,876
Lee Porter	68	70	70	72	280	4,876
Doug Tewell	71	68	70	71	280	4,876
Tommy Armour III	70	70	66	75	281	4,692
Jimmy Green	69	72	69	71	281	4,692
Joel Kribel	69	70	69	73	281	4,692
Mark Carnevale	74	67	70	71	282	4,554
Rick Fehr	65	70	73	74	282	4,554
Harrison Frazar	71	69	72	70	282	4,554
Robert Damron	69	71	71	72	283	4,416
Mike Donald	67	73	71	72	283	4,416
Neal Lancaster	70	71	73	69	283	4,416
Phil Blackmar	71	70	70	73	284	4,232
Alan Bratton	70	71	70	73	284	4,232
Gary Hallberg	67	73	75	69	284	4,232
J.P. Hayes	73	68	68	75	284	4,232
Omar Uresti	68	73	72	71	284	4,232
Ronnie Black	66	75	70	74	285	4,094
Tom Purtzer	70	69	73	74	286	4,025
Charles Warren	69	72	71	74	286	4,025
Scott Hoch	68	73	70	76	287	3,933
Sean Murphy	67	72	75	73	287	3,933
Mark Hayes	68	72	71	79	290	3,841
Andy North	70	70	75	75	290	3,841

John Deere Classic

Oakwood Country Club, Coal Valley, Illinois
Par 35-35–70; 6,796 yards

July 22-25
purse, $2,000,000

		SCORES			TOTAL	MONEY
J.L. Lewis	66	65	65	65	261	$360,000
Mike Brisky	66	62	68	65	261	216,000
(Lewis defeated Brisky on fifth extra hole.)						
Brian Henninger	66	63	64	71	264	116,000
Kirk Triplett	68	68	64	64	264	116,000
Steve Jones	68	66	68	63	265	73,000
Pete Jordan	68	67	64	66	265	73,000
Chris Perry	71	67	63	64	265	73,000
Dick Mast	69	67	64	66	266	60,000
Scott Verplank	66	67	66	67	266	60,000
Robert Damron	64	67	65	71	267	52,000
D.A. Weibring	67	67	65	68	267	52,000
Joe Durant	69	68	66	65	268	40,500
David Peoples	65	67	66	70	268	40,500
Dicky Pride	68	65	67	68	268	40,500
David Toms	66	69	67	66	268	40,500
Doug Barron	68	70	65	66	269	30,000
Dan Forsman	68	66	70	65	269	30,000
Joe Ogilvie	64	69	69	67	269	30,000
Tom Pernice, Jr.	66	67	66	70	269	30,000
Bob Tway	67	67	67	68	269	30,000
Chip Beck	67	69	68	66	270	18,266.67
Phil Blackmar	67	67	67	69	270	18,266.67
Harrison Frazar	66	71	66	67	270	18,266.67
Scott McCarron	69	64	71	66	270	18,266.67
Rory Sabbatini	68	66	69	67	270	18,266.67
Joey Sindelar	69	67	67	67	270	18,266.67
Notah Begay III	70	63	66	71	270	18,266.66
Kenny Perry	64	70	64	72	270	18,266.66
Mike Standly	69	66	64	71	270	18,266.66
Perry Moss	69	69	69	64	271	10,909.10
Fulton Allem	69	65	66	71	271	10,909.09
Stephen Ames	70	66	68	67	271	10,909.09
Briny Baird	65	73	64	69	271	10,909.09
Jim Carter	69	67	70	65	271	10,909.09
R.W. Eaks	66	67	68	70	271	10,909.09
Jerry Kelly	67	71	68	65	271	10,909.09
Frank Lickliter	71	66	67	67	271	10,909.09
Jack Renner	68	70	66	67	271	10,909.09
Lee Rinker	71	66	67	67	271	10,909.09
Ted Schulz	66	70	69	66	271	10,909.09
Greg Chalmers	69	68	67	68	272	6,330.91
David Frost	67	66	71	68	272	6,330.91
J.P. Hayes	68	67	68	69	272	6,330.91
Mike Hulbert	70	68	67	67	272	6,330.91
Jonathan Kaye	67	68	68	69	272	6,330.91
Greg Kraft	71	65	67	69	272	6,330.91
John Maginnes	69	66	68	69	272	6,330.91
David Sutherland	67	66	69	70	272	6,330.91
Doug Tewell	67	70	69	66	272	6,330.91
Esteban Toledo	69	66	69	68	272	6,330.91
David Edwards	70	64	65	73	272	6,330.90
Steve Jurgensen	68	69	70	66	273	4,617.15
Doug Martin	66	71	73	63	273	4,617.15

	SCORES				TOTAL	MONEY
Woody Austin	69	67	69	68	273	4,617.14
Cameron Beckman	68	68	71	66	273	4,617.14
Charles Raulerson	70	67	69	67	273	4,617.14
Jeff Sluman	69	68	70	66	273	4,617.14
Fuzzy Zoeller	68	70	68	67	273	4,617.14
John Elliott	68	69	71	66	274	4,340
Robin Freeman	67	69	69	69	274	4,340
Deane Pappas	68	69	70	67	274	4,340
Brett Quigley	65	66	72	71	274	4,340
Larry Rinker	68	69	68	69	274	4,340
Mike Sullivan	69	68	66	71	274	4,340
Barry Cheesman	67	67	70	71	275	4,140
Russ Cochran	68	67	71	69	275	4,140
Jim Gallagher, Jr.	67	70	72	66	275	4,140
Dan Pohl	67	70	68	70	275	4,140
Ben Bates	67	69	73	67	276	3,980
Mark Carnevale	68	69	72	67	276	3,980
Bob Friend	70	67	72	67	276	3,980
Paul Stankowski	67	71	66	72	276	3,980
Alan Bratton	72	66	71	68	277	3,840
Curt Byrum	69	67	72	69	277	3,840
Tim Loustalot	69	69	71	68	277	3,840
Geoffrey Sisk	70	68	69	71	278	3,760
Steve Lowery	69	67	70	73	279	3,660
Katsumasa Miyamoto	65	73	69	72	279	3,660
Mike Springer	69	69	69	72	279	3,660
Mark Wiebe	67	71	71	70	279	3,660
Ronnie Black	70	67	69	74	280	3,560
Mac O'Grady	65	73	74	75	287	3,520

Canon Greater Hartford Open

TPC at River Highlands, Cromwell, Connecticut
Par 35-35–70; 6,820 yards

July 29-August 1
purse, $2,500,000

	SCORES				TOTAL	MONEY
Brent Geiberger	66	63	66	67	262	$450,000
Skip Kendall	63	68	68	66	265	270,000
Mark Calcavecchia	67	67	68	64	266	130,000
Justin Leonard	64	67	68	67	266	130,000
Ted Tryba	72	64	62	68	266	130,000
Pete Jordan	64	65	71	67	267	86,875
Dave Stockton, Jr.	68	68	64	67	267	86,875
Stewart Cink	64	68	68	68	268	72,500
Tim Herron	66	73	67	62	268	72,500
Mike Springer	63	73	65	67	268	72,500
David Duval	68	66	72	63	269	57,500
Mark O'Meara	66	64	71	68	269	57,500
Kirk Triplett	65	66	69	69	269	57,500
Notah Begay III	69	68	69	64	270	45,000
Jay Delsing	64	68	67	71	270	45,000
Davis Love III	67	70	66	67	270	45,000
Tom Kite	67	69	65	70	271	37,500
Frank Lickliter	65	70	67	69	271	37,500
Kevin Sutherland	63	71	71	66	271	37,500
Fred Funk	67	68	69	68	272	27,083.34
Tom Pernice, Jr.	68	68	69	67	272	27,083.34

		SCORES			TOTAL	MONEY
Paul Azinger	72	67	65	68	272	27,083.33
Jay Don Blake	67	68	67	70	272	27,083.33
Bob Burns	67	69	66	70	272	27,083.33
Chris DiMarco	68	70	65	69	272	27,083.33
Olin Browne	71	66	69	67	273	17,375
Tom Byrum	69	69	69	66	273	17,375
Harrison Frazar	68	70	69	66	273	17,375
Gabriel Hjertstedt	67	70	69	67	273	17,375
Jonathan Kaye	69	66	66	72	273	17,375
Franklin Langham	71	68	67	67	273	17,375
Tom Scherrer	63	70	68	72	273	17,375
Grant Waite	69	65	70	69	273	17,375
Clark Dennis	70	66	70	68	274	12,357.15
Charles Raulerson	64	68	73	69	274	12,357.15
Joe Durant	68	67	69	70	274	12,357.14
Doug Martin	67	69	69	69	274	12,357.14
Lee Porter	71	67	69	67	274	12,357.14
Mike Reid	69	68	68	69	274	12,357.14
Fuzzy Zoeller	68	68	68	70	274	12,357.14
Ty Armstrong	69	69	67	70	275	9,250
Woody Austin	70	69	69	67	275	9,250
Russ Cochran	70	69	66	70	275	9,250
Brad Fabel	69	67	71	68	275	9,250
Omar Uresti	66	69	71	69	275	9,250
Fulton Allem	69	69	70	68	276	6,587.50
Mark Brooks	68	69	68	71	276	6,587.50
Dan Forsman	69	68	68	71	276	6,587.50
John Maginnes	68	68	72	68	276	6,587.50
Scott McCarron	70	67	69	70	276	6,587.50
Larry Mize	69	69	67	71	276	6,587.50
Chris Riley	68	70	69	69	276	6,587.50
Geoffrey Sisk	64	72	71	69	276	6,587.50
Ben Bates	69	70	66	72	277	5,750
David Frost	70	69	68	70	277	5,750
Blaine McCallister	68	70	69	70	277	5,750
Mike Sposa	69	70	70	69	278	5,650
Tommy Armour III	67	67	75	70	279	5,550
Bob Estes	69	69	70	71	279	5,550
Paul Goydos	68	67	71	73	279	5,550
Alan Bratton	64	72	74	70	280	5,450
Robert Allenby	69	70	69	73	281	5,275
Billy Andrade	68	71	69	73	281	5,275
Cameron Beckman	71	67	73	70	281	5,275
Danny Briggs	70	69	70	72	281	5,275
Tom Lehman	67	69	71	74	281	5,275
Willie Wood	67	71	71	72	281	5,275
Duffy Waldorf	67	72	71	72	282	5,100
Perry Moss	68	71	73	71	283	5,050
Doug Dunakey	66	69	73	77	285	4,975
Deane Pappas	68	69	75	73	285	4,975
Jimmy Green	70	68	73	76	287	4,900
Robert Friend	68	71	77	72	288	4,850

Buick Open

Warwick Hills Golf & Country Club,
Grand Blanc, Michigan
Par 36-36–72; 7,105 yards

August 5-8
purse, $2,400,000

	SCORES				TOTAL	MONEY
Tom Pernice, Jr.	67	66	72	65	270	$432,000
Tom Lehman	67	69	64	71	271	179,200
Ted Tryba	66	70	69	66	271	179,200
Bob Tway	67	69	70	65	271	179,200
Bob Estes	70	65	73	64	272	96,000
Ernie Els	68	65	71	69	273	86,400
Esteban Toledo	66	72	67	69	274	80,400
Hal Sutton	69	70	70	66	275	74,400
Tommy Armour III	70	67	69	70	276	57,600
Jim Furyk	70	67	71	68	276	57,600
Rocco Mediate	69	64	72	71	276	57,600
Loren Roberts	68	71	66	71	276	57,600
Joey Sindelar	70	72	64	70	276	57,600
Brian Watts	70	70	67	69	276	57,600
Fulton Allem	67	72	66	72	277	39,600
Woody Austin	68	69	73	67	277	39,600
Mark Brooks	72	66	69	70	277	39,600
Chris Perry	69	69	67	72	277	39,600
Tom Byrum	71	69	70	68	278	28,080
Glen Day	71	69	69	69	278	28,080
Fred Funk	68	70	67	73	278	28,080
Brent Geiberger	65	70	74	69	278	28,080
Lee Janzen	70	70	67	71	278	28,080
Skip Kendall	71	69	67	71	278	28,080
Stuart Appleby	71	64	71	73	279	17,550
Steve Elkington	73	69	67	70	279	17,550
Dudley Hart	69	68	70	72	279	17,550
Scott Hoch	71	68	66	74	279	17,550
Justin Leonard	68	71	71	69	279	17,550
Larry Mize	67	70	74	68	279	17,550
Larry Rinker	70	72	68	69	279	17,550
Omar Uresti	66	70	75	68	279	17,550
Briny Baird	69	70	69	72	280	12,411.43
Jeff Maggert	70	69	69	72	280	12,411.43
Blaine McCallister	74	65	69	72	280	12,411.43
Perry Moss	70	72	66	72	280	12,411.43
Jeff Roth	71	68	72	69	280	12,411.43
Steve Stricker	71	68	70	71	280	12,411.43
Jeff Sluman	69	71	67	73	280	12,411.42
Chris Couch	70	70	69	72	281	9,360
Gabriel Hjertstedt	72	67	70	72	281	9,360
P.H. Horgan III	70	70	72	69	281	9,360
Tom Kite	66	68	72	75	281	9,360
Andrew Magee	68	72	67	74	281	9,360
Robert Allenby	68	72	73	69	282	6,501.34
Phil Blackmar	67	72	73	70	282	6,501.34
Mike Hulbert	72	70	70	70	282	6,501.34
Notah Begay III	70	72	69	71	282	6,501.33
Jay Don Blake	73	67	71	71	282	6,501.33
Eric Booker	68	69	70	75	282	6,501.33
Brian Henninger	70	72	67	73	282	6,501.33
Greg Kraft	67	69	74	72	282	6,501.33
Naomichi Ozaki	70	71	70	71	282	6,501.33

		SCORES			TOTAL	MONEY
Doug Barron	70	69	72	72	283	5,376
Cameron Beckman	70	71	73	69	283	5,376
Steve Flesch	71	69	73	70	283	5,376
Tim Herron	72	68	70	73	283	5,376
Peter Jacobsen	71	70	69	73	283	5,376
Jonathan Kaye	70	71	71	71	283	5,376
Rodney Pampling	72	69	72	70	283	5,376
Tommy Tolles	68	71	70	74	283	5,376
Lanny Wadkins	68	72	70	73	283	5,376
Stephen Ames	68	69	73	74	284	5,016
Paul Goydos	71	71	71	71	284	5,016
J.P. Hayes	71	70	71	72	284	5,016
J.L. Lewis	69	73	69	73	284	5,016
Deane Pappas	71	66	76	71	284	5,016
Dave Stockton, Jr.	70	72	70	72	284	5,016
Ty Armstrong	72	70	70	73	285	4,800
Trevor Dodds	70	70	72	73	285	4,800
Wayne Levi	70	70	72	73	285	4,800
Carlos Franco	72	68	73	73	286	4,680
Vijay Singh	68	66	76	76	286	4,680
David Berganio, Jr.	69	70	72	76	287	4,584
Bob Friend	72	70	75	70	287	4,584
Craig Barlow	71	70	74	75	290	4,512
Mamoru Osanai	70	72	75	75	292	4,440
Charles Raulerson	66	71	79	76	292	4,440

PGA Championship

Medinah Country Club, Medinah, Illinois
Par 36-36–72; 7,401 yards

August 12-15
purse, $3,500,000

		SCORES			TOTAL	MONEY
Tiger Woods	70	67	68	72	277	$630,000
Sergio Garcia	66	73	68	71	278	378,000
Stewart Cink	69	70	68	73	280	203,000
Jay Haas	68	67	75	70	280	203,000
Nick Price	70	71	69	71	281	129,000
Bob Estes	71	70	72	69	282	112,000
Colin Montgomerie	72	70	70	70	282	112,000
Jim Furyk	71	70	69	74	284	96,500
Steve Pate	72	70	73	69	284	96,500
Miguel Angel Jimenez	70	70	75	70	285	72,166.67
Jesper Parnevik	72	70	73	70	285	72,166.67
Corey Pavin	69	74	71	71	285	72,166.67
Chris Perry	70	73	71	71	285	72,166.67
David Duval	70	71	72	72	285	72,166.66
Mike Weir	68	68	69	80	285	72,166.66
Mark Brooks	70	73	70	74	287	48,600
Gabriel Hjertstedt	72	70	73	72	287	48,600
Brandt Jobe	69	74	69	75	287	48,600
Greg Turner	73	69	70	75	287	48,600
Lee Westwood	70	68	74	75	287	48,600
David Frost	75	68	74	71	288	33,200
Scott Hoch	71	71	75	71	288	33,200
J.L. Lewis	73	70	74	71	288	33,200
Kevin Wentworth	72	70	72	74	288	33,200
Skip Kendall	74	65	71	78	288	33,200

	SCORES				TOTAL	MONEY
Fred Couples	73	69	75	72	289	24,000
Carlos Franco	72	71	71	75	289	24,000
Jerry Kelly	69	74	71	75	289	24,000
Hal Sutton	72	73	73	71	289	24,000
Jean Van de Velde	74	70	75	70	289	24,000
Paul Goydos	73	70	71	76	290	20,000
Mark James	70	74	79	67	290	20,000
Ted Tryba	70	72	76	72	290	20,000
Tom Lehman	70	74	76	71	291	15,428.58
Paul Lawrie	73	72	72	74	291	15,428.57
Billy Mayfair	75	69	75	72	291	15,428.57
Kenny Perry	74	69	72	76	291	15,428.57
Scott Verplank	73	72	73	73	291	15,428.57
Lanny Wadkins	72	69	74	76	291	15,428.57
Steve Flesch	73	71	72	75	291	15,428.57
Paul Azinger	77	69	71	75	292	11,250
Angel Cabrera	73	73	74	72	292	11,250
Chris DiMarco	74	71	74	73	292	11,250
Nick Faldo	71	71	75	75	292	11,250
Hale Irwin	70	69	78	75	292	11,250
Robert Karlsson	70	76	73	73	292	11,250
Duffy Waldorf	74	71	70	77	292	11,250
Brian Watts	69	71	72	80	292	11,250
Olin Browne	73	72	74	74	293	8,180
Davis Love III	71	72	75	75	293	8,180
Rocco Mediate	71	72	78	72	293	8,180
Vijay Singh	74	70	77	72	293	8,180
Kirk Triplett	73	70	70	80	293	8,180
J.P. Hayes	68	76	76	74	294	7,400
Andrew Magee	72	72	77	73	294	7,400
Jeff Sluman	72	73	73	76	294	7,400
Phil Mickelson	72	72	74	77	295	7,175
Payne Stewart	75	71	75	74	295	7,175
Bob Tway	73	71	80	71	295	7,175
Mark O'Meara	72	74	73	76	295	7,175
Mark Calcavecchia	71	75	76	74	296	6,975
Brad Faxon	72	73	77	74	296	6,975
Greg Kraft	74	70	75	77	295	6,975
Bernhard Langer	71	75	74	76	296	6,975
Alex Cejka	71	73	75	78	297	6,800
Andrew Coltart	72	74	80	71	297	6,800
Mike Reid	72	74	76	75	297	6,800
Scott Dunlap	74	72	71	81	298	6,675
Bruce Zabriski	70	75	77	76	298	6,675
Rich Beem	72	73	78	76	299	6,550
Thomas Bjorn	73	73	78	75	299	6,550
Naomichi Ozaki	73	73	78	75	299	6,550
Fred Funk	75	69	76	80	300	6,450
Joey Sindelar	73	70	75		WD	

Out of Final 36 Holes

Darren Clarke	72	75	147
Retief Goosen	74	73	147
Shigeki Maruyama	77	70	147
Craig Parry	75	72	147
Dennis Paulson	77	70	147
Loren Roberts	70	77	147
Sven Struver	71	76	147
Tommy Tolles	78	69	147

	SCORES		TOTAL
Ian Woosnam	73	74	147
Ernie Els	72	76	148
Bob Ford	74	74	148
Harrison Frazar	75	73	148
Brent Geiberger	72	76	148
Dudley Hart	75	73	148
Nolan Henke	73	75	148
Toshimitsu Izawa	72	76	148
Lee Janzen	73	75	148
Steve Jones	75	73	148
Justin Leonard	73	75	148
Peter O'Malley	75	73	148
Eduardo Romero	71	77	148
Steve Schneiter	74	74	148
Steve Stricker	72	76	148
Kevin Sutherland	74	74	148
Bob Boyd	74	75	149
Brandel Chamblee	78	71	149
Bob Friend	71	78	149
Per-Ulrik Johansson	76	73	149
Jeffrey Lankford	78	71	149
Jeff Maggert	73	76	149
Greg Norman	75	74	149
Tom Pernice, Jr.	74	75	149
Jarmo Sandelin	77	72	149
Chris Tucker	75	74	149
Tom Watson	75	74	149
Jim Carter	76	74	150
John Cook	74	76	150
Glen Day	74	76	150
Mike Gilmore	74	76	150
Frank Lickliter	73	77	150
Jay Overton	75	75	150
Ken Schall	75	75	150
Robert Allenby	76	75	151
Billy Andrade	75	76	151
Stuart Appleby	77	74	151
Ben Crenshaw	77	74	151
Tim Herron	74	77	151
Shawn Kelly	74	77	151
Stephen Keppler	73	78	151
Brent Murray	76	75	151
Jose Maria Olazabal	79	72	151
John Huston	72	80	152
Stephen Leaney	76	76	152
David Toms	76	76	152
George Bryan	76	77	153
Scott Davis	81	72	153
Jeff Freeman	73	80	153
Scott Gump	77	76	153
Wayne Defrancesco	78	76	154
Bradley Hughes	80	74	154
Tom Kite	77	77	154
Craig Stadler	77	77	154
Hidemichi Tanaka	78	76	154
Tommy Armour III	74	81	155
Mike Baker	80	75	155
Darrell Kestner	75	80	155
Patrik Sjoland	78	77	155
Tim Thelen	78	77	155

	SCORES		TOTAL
Kim Thompson	78	77	155
Larry Nelson	79	77	156
Ronald Stelten	77	79	156
Christopher Toulson	79	78	157
Brett Upper	79	78	157
Scott Spence	80	79	159
Milan Swilor	80	80	160
Bill Glasson			WD

(Professionals who did not complete 72 holes received $1,750.)

Sprint International

Castle Pines Golf Club, Castle Rock, Colorado
Par 36-36–72; 7,559 yards

August 19-22
purse, $2,600,000

	POINTS				TOTAL	MONEY
David Toms	16	13	10	8	47	$468,000
David Duval	10	15	11	8	44	280,800
Stephen Ames	11	12	13	7	43	176,800
Chris Perry	10	15	3	9	37	124,800
Billy Mayfair	10	13	7	5	35	98,800
Ernie Els	10	14	8	3	35	98,800
Steve Elkington	13	10	4	7	34	87,100
Olin Browne	7	14	7	4	32	78,000
Jay Haas	10	5	5	12	32	78,000
Steve Flesch	8	16	4	3	31	65,000
Eduardo Romero	5	8	11	7	31	65,000
Kirk Triplett	7	8	5	11	31	65,000
Greg Norman	0	14	11	5	30	50,266.67
Sergio Garcia	5	16	11	-2	30	50,266.67
Mark O'Meara	11	9	0	10	30	50,266.66
Phil Mickelson	15	4	2	8	29	41,600
Rory Sabbatini	9	6	6	8	29	41,600
Bob Tway	4	13	3	9	29	41,600
Vijay Singh	11	9	4	4	28	36,400
Darren Clarke	5	9	6	7	27	32,500
Andrew Magee	11	13	-5	8	27	32,500
Rocco Mediate	5	10	4	7	26	28,080
Jesper Parnevik	10	4	5	7	26	28,080
Billy Andrade	9	3	9	4	25	22,880
Skip Kendall	11	8	8	-2	25	22,880
Mark Wiebe	13	3	4	5	25	22,880
Doug Martin	6	6	7	5	24	19,630
David Sutherland	12	9	2	1	24	19,630
Jonathan Kaye	7	4	8	4	23	18,460
Brett Quigley	6	7	8	1	22	17,680
Paul Goydos	8	18	-5	0	21	16,510
Mike Reid	9	9	9	-6	21	16,510
Brandt Jobe	3	8	8	1	20	15,015
Frank Lickliter	9	10	4	-3	20	15,015
Kevin Sutherland	9	6	5	-2	18	14,040
Rick Fehr	12	8	2	-8	14	13,390

IN THE MONEY

Davis Love III	14	5	-1		18	12,480
Tiger Woods	7	9	2		18	12,480

	POINTS			TOTAL	MONEY
Mark Calcavecchia	14	3	0	17	10,920
Jose Maria Olazabal	4	12	1	17	10,920
Dennis Paulson	-1	11	7	17	10,920
Lee Westwood	4	9	4	17	10,920
Robert Allenby	-1	11	6	16	9,360
Harrison Frazar	1	15	0	16	9,360
Jay Don Blake	0	11	4	15	8,060
Scott Gump	4	5	6	15	8,060
J.L. Lewis	3	11	1	15	8,060
Dudley Hart	1	15	-2	14	6,812
J.P. Hayes	2	7	5	14	6,812
Nick Price	7	5	2	14	6,812
Doug Barron	0	9	4	13	6,156.80
Notah Begay III	3	8	2	13	6,156.80
Greg Chalmers	5	6	2	13	6,156.80
Tim Herron	4	10	-1	13	6,156.80
Willie Wood	4	5	4	13	6,156.80
Mark Brooks	8	4	0	12	5,876
Steve Pate	5	7	0	12	5,876
Clarence Rose	2	7	3	12	5,876
Tom Pernice, Jr.	3	7	1	11	5,746
Dicky Pride	-1	12	0	11	5,746
Chris DiMarco	5	4	1	10	5,616
Jerry Kelly	1	9	0	10	5,616
Mike Sposa	7	6	-3	10	5,616
Woody Austin	7	4	-2	9	5,486
Brad Faxon	8	2	-1	9	5,486
Stuart Appleby	2	7	-1	8	5,382
Geoffrey Sisk	2	7	-1	8	5,382
Ken Green	6	4	-3	7	5,252
Steve Jones	7	3	-3	7	5,252
Corey Pavin	8	1	-2	7	5,252
Tom Scherrer	9	4	-7	6	5,148
Patrik Sjoland	8	4	-7	5	5,096
Ted Purdy	4	5	-6	3	5,044
Tom Purtzer	3	6	-8	1	4,992
Barry Cheesman	8	1	-13	-4	4,940

WGC NEC Invitational

Firestone Country Club, South Course, Akron, Ohio   August 26-29
Par 35-35–70; 7,139 yards   purse, $5,000,000

	SCORES				TOTAL	MONEY
Tiger Woods	66	71	62	71	270	$1,000,000
Phil Mickelson	69	67	70	65	271	510,000
Craig Parry	71	66	69	69	275	327,500
Nick Price	67	69	68	71	275	327,500
Ernie Els	71	69	67	69	276	234,000
Shigeki Maruyama	72	67	70	68	277	179,000
Carlos Franco	68	67	70	73	278	154,000
Sergio Garcia	67	70	69	72	278	154,000
Jeff Maggert	71	67	69	71	278	154,000
Jim Furyk	67	72	69	71	279	129,000
Davis Love III	68	69	70	72	279	129,000
Mark Calcavecchia	68	69	73	70	280	109,000
Padraig Harrington	72	67	70	71	280	109,000

	SCORES				TOTAL	MONEY
Steve Pate	69	71	68	72	280	109,000
Fred Couples	71	70	63	77	281	88,000
Tom Lehman	67	72	67	75	281	88,000
Vijay Singh	71	67	72	71	281	88,000
Payne Stewart	70	67	69	75	281	88,000
Hal Sutton	69	67	72	73	281	88,000
Justin Leonard	73	68	69	72	282	73,000
Paul Lawrie	67	68	74	74	283	66,000
Greg Turner	70	71	68	74	283	66,000
Stuart Appleby	72	70	72	70	284	58,000
Scott Hoch	68	73	71	72	284	58,000
Greg Norman	70	75	66	74	285	50,000
Mark O'Meara	73	70	71	71	285	50,000
Miguel Angel Jimenez	72	70	70	74	286	41,333.34
David Duval	67	72	71	76	286	41,333.33
Jesper Parnevik	75	69	66	76	286	41,333.33
Lee Janzen	71	70	72	74	287	37,000
Colin Montgomerie	69	75	67	76	287	37,000
Jarmo Sandelin	71	71	73	72	287	37,000
Andrew Coltart	71	71	69	77	288	34,000
John Huston	69	71	70	78	288	34,000
Lee Westwood	74	72	70	72	288	34,000
Darren Clarke	73	72	69	75	289	31,500
Jean Van de Velde	75	71	68	75	289	31,500
Frank Nobilo	73	69	75	73	290	30,000
Steve Elkington	70	74	71	76	291	29,000
Jose Maria Olazabal	70	80	69	73	292	28,000
Naomichi Ozaki	75	74	75	72	296	27,000

Reno-Tahoe Open

Montreux Golf & Country Club, Reno, Nevada   August 26-29
Par 36-36–72; 7,552 yards   purse, $2,750,000

	SCORES				TOTAL	MONEY
Notah Begay III	70	69	63	72	274	$495,000
Chris Perry	68	71	70	68	277	242,000
David Toms	68	70	70	69	277	242,000
John Cook	68	70	73	69	280	113,666.67
Fred Funk	69	71	73	67	280	113,666.67
Brandt Jobe	69	69	69	73	280	113,666.66
Dennis Paulson	71	72	67	71	281	88,687.50
Bob Tway	69	69	70	73	281	88,687.50
Emlyn Aubrey	69	71	73	69	282	61,531.25
Woody Austin	68	70	73	71	282	61,531.25
Mark Brooks	71	73	70	68	282	61,531.25
Stewart Cink	68	70	73	71	282	61,531.25
Russ Cochran	72	70	73	67	282	61,531.25
Steve Jones	70	72	69	71	282	61,531.25
Jonathan Kaye	71	66	71	74	282	61,531.25
Tom Scherrer	67	70	69	76	282	61,531.25
Paul Goydos	72	72	71	68	283	35,985.72
Dudley Hart	68	71	75	69	283	35,985.72
Kenny Perry	68	75	69	71	283	35,985.72
Cameron Beckman	66	74	69	74	283	35,985.71
Brad Fabel	69	72	69	73	283	35,985.71
Jay Haas	71	68	69	75	283	35,985.71

	SCORES				TOTAL	MONEY
Kevin Sutherland	69	69	72	73	283	35,985.71
Brian Gay	69	73	72	70	284	21,278.13
Mike Springer	73	71	74	66	284	21,278.13
Phil Tataurangi	71	74	69	70	284	21,278.13
Duffy Waldorf	73	71	72	68	284	21,278.13
Billy Andrade	68	72	70	74	284	21,278.12
J.L. Lewis	67	72	72	73	284	21,278.12
Craig Stadler	72	70	65	77	284	21,278.12
Charles Warren	73	72	69	70	284	21,278.12
Tommy Armour III	70	72	68	75	285	15,565
Robert Damron	71	71	71	72	285	15,565
J.P. Hayes	73	70	69	73	285	15,565
Bradley Hughes	72	68	70	75	285	15,565
Esteban Toledo	69	76	68	72	285	15,565
Ben Bates	69	66	75	76	286	12,100
Greg Chalmers	72	71	70	73	286	12,100
Frank Lickliter	71	69	72	74	286	12,100
Joe Ogilvie	72	69	74	71	286	12,100
Rodney Pampling	72	68	71	75	286	12,100
Grant Waite	69	74	68	75	286	12,100
Danny Briggs	70	66	76	75	287	8,580
Scott Dunlap	74	70	71	72	287	8,580
Brian Henninger	69	72	71	75	287	8,580
Franklin Langham	65	73	77	72	287	8,580
Mike Reid	72	71	73	71	287	8,580
Victor Schwamkrug	73	70	72	72	287	8,580
Dave Stockton, Jr.	70	74	65	78	287	8,580
Trevor Dodds	72	73	70	73	288	6,581.67
Joe Durant	71	70	74	73	288	6,581.67
Steve Flesch	72	69	72	75	288	6,581.67
Dan Forsman	73	70	71	74	288	6,581.67
P.H. Horgan III	72	70	71	75	288	6,581.66
Scott Verplank	71	73	68	76	288	6,581.66
Doug Barron	74	70	70	75	289	6,105
Tom Byrum	70	75	73	71	289	6,105
Jay Delsing	71	73	65	80	289	6,105
Jeff Gallagher	72	69	72	76	289	6,105
Kent Jones	75	69	72	73	289	6,105
Tom Purtzer	73	72	71	73	289	6,105
Ted Tryba	73	69	73	74	289	6,105
Olin Browne	71	71	72	76	290	5,802.50
Harrison Frazar	72	73	74	71	290	5,802.50
Perry Moss	71	74	72	73	290	5,802.50
Rory Sabbatini	73	70	74	73	290	5,802.50
Ty Armstrong	69	74	72	76	291	5,527.50
Brad Faxon	74	69	72	76	291	5,527.50
Ted Purdy	66	77	71	77	291	5,527.50
Geoffrey Sisk	75	69	75	72	291	5,527.50
David Sutherland	70	74	74	73	291	5,527.50
Brian Watts	73	72	72	74	291	5,527.50
Mike Brisky	71	73	75	73	292	5,280
Bob Burns	72	72	75	73	292	5,280
Jim Gallagher, Jr.	73	72	68	79	292	5,280
David Peoples	71	74	74	74	293	5,142.50
Omar Uresti	71	73	73	76	293	5,142.50
Tim Loustalot	73	71	73	79	296	5,060

Air Canada Championship

Northview Golf & Country Club, Surrey,
British Columbia, Canada
Par 36-35–71; 6,817 yards

September 2-5
purse, $2,500,000

	SCORES				TOTAL	MONEY
Mike Weir	68	70	64	64	266	$450,000
Fred Funk	71	64	65	68	268	270,000
Carlos Franco	67	67	67	69	270	170,000
Scott McCarron	72	67	72	61	272	103,333.34
Payne Stewart	68	67	69	68	272	103,333.33
Phil Tataurangi	66	70	65	71	272	103,333.33
Charles Raulerson	65	68	69	71	273	83,750
Jay Delsing	70	68	72	64	274	75,000
Kevin Wentworth	69	70	68	67	274	75,000
Bob Estes	73	67	67	68	275	62,500
Brad Fabel	71	66	68	70	275	62,500
Steve Lowery	68	69	69	69	275	62,500
Gabriel Hjertstedt	69	69	69	69	276	41,562.50
Mike Hulbert	70	72	67	67	276	41,562.50
Blaine McCallister	68	70	70	68	276	41,562.50
Katsumasa Miyamoto	70	67	70	69	276	41,562.50
Tom Pernice, Jr.	68	70	71	67	276	41,562.50
Ted Tryba	70	66	70	70	276	41,562.50
Omar Uresti	70	66	72	68	276	41,562.50
Jay Williamson	69	69	67	71	276	41,562.50
Mark Calcavecchia	67	69	70	71	277	25,000
Greg Chalmers	68	71	65	73	277	25,000
Trevor Dodds	67	70	71	69	277	25,000
Mike Springer	72	70	67	68	277	25,000
David Toms	69	69	69	70	277	25,000
Mark Wiebe	70	68	69	70	277	25,000
Scott Gump	71	70	66	71	278	18,125
Scott Hoch	72	69	67	70	278	18,125
Greg Kraft	69	68	70	71	278	18,125
Kevin Sutherland	69	67	73	69	278	18,125
Chip Beck	68	74	67	70	279	15,156.25
Nolan Henke	71	70	67	71	279	15,156.25
Brian Henninger	69	73	67	70	279	15,156.25
Mike Sposa	72	70	69	68	279	15,156.25
P.H. Horgan III	70	70	70	70	280	11,803.58
Phil Blackmar	71	70	70	69	280	11,803.57
Franklin Langham	71	68	72	69	280	11,803.57
Doug Martin	68	72	70	70	280	11,803.57
Larry Rinker	68	70	71	71	280	11,803.57
Dave Stockton, Jr.	71	71	70	68	280	11,803.57
Richard Zokol	67	68	74	71	280	11,803.57
Notah Begay III	70	69	70	72	281	8,500
Scott Dunlap	68	68	70	75	281	8,500
Peter Jacobsen	64	72	73	72	281	8,500
Pete Jordan	71	67	71	72	281	8,500
Dicky Pride	70	72	70	69	281	8,500
Chris Riley	71	69	70	71	281	8,500
Chris DiMarco	68	67	75	72	282	6,360
Joe Durant	72	66	74	70	282	6,360
Bob Friend	69	68	72	73	282	6,360
Brandt Jobe	63	70	72	77	282	6,360
Len Mattiace	69	69	69	75	282	6,360
Eric Booker	69	72	71	71	283	5,816.67

		SCORES			TOTAL	MONEY
Kevin PomArleau	65	70	73	75	283	5,816.67
John Maginnes	71	70	71	71	283	5,816.66
Kent Jones	66	70	77	71	284	5,700
Stuart Appleby	73	68	72	72	285	5,475
Craig Barlow	73	68	73	71	285	5,475
Tom Byrum	70	70	71	74	285	5,475
Barry Cheesman	72	70	70	73	285	5,475
Rick Fehr	68	71	76	70	285	5,475
Jonathan Kaye	68	74	70	73	285	5,475
Esteban Toledo	71	71	70	73	285	5,475
Grant Waite	73	67	74	71	285	5,475
Fulton Allem	70	69	73	74	286	5,125
Ty Armstrong	67	73	71	75	286	5,125
Brent Geiberger	70	68	77	71	286	5,125
Bill Glasson	73	69	74	70	286	5,125
Skip Kendall	70	71	74	71	286	5,125
Ray Stewart	75	67	73	71	286	5,125
Danny Briggs	67	71	75	74	287	4,900
Wes Martin	70	69	73	75	287	4,900
Lee Porter	70	71	73	73	287	4,900
Robert Damron	69	71	77	71	288	4,800
Jeff Brehaut	70	67	74	78	289	4,750
Robert Gamez	72	69	73	76	290	4,650
Hank Kuehne	70	69	72	79	290	4,650
Lanny Wadkins	73	69	73	75	290	4,650
Jimmy Green	72	69	76	76	293	4,550
Guy Boros	69	70	83	77	299	4,500

Bell Canadian Open

Glen Abbey Golf Club, Oakville, Ontario, Canada
Par 36-36–72; 7,112 yards

September 9-12
purse, $2,500,000

		SCORES			TOTAL	MONEY
Hal Sutton	69	67	70	69	275	$450,000
Dennis Paulson	70	68	71	69	278	270,000
Dudley Hart	72	69	70	70	281	120,000
Lee Janzen	66	71	68	76	281	120,000
Justin Leonard	72	67	72	70	281	120,000
David Sutherland	73	65	72	71	281	120,000
Scott Dunlap	72	74	66	70	282	83,750
Nick Faldo	73	72	67	71	283	77,500
Paul Azinger	71	66	70	77	284	65,000
Jesper Parnevik	68	73	73	70	284	65,000
Charles Raulerson	67	74	70	73	284	65,000
Phil Tataurangi	74	72	69	69	284	65,000
Steve Stricker	67	70	72	76	285	50,000
Bob Tway	71	73	68	73	285	50,000
Chip Beck	69	72	74	71	286	40,000
Greg Chalmers	71	72	75	68	286	40,000
Bob Estes	71	70	72	73	286	40,000
Mark O'Meara	71	73	69	73	286	40,000
Jeff Sluman	72	73	71	70	286	40,000
Jay Don Blake	70	70	77	70	287	28,100
Steve Lowery	69	73	74	71	287	28,100
Billy Mayfair	71	72	71	73	287	28,100
Brett Quigley	73	70	71	73	287	28,100

	SCORES				TOTAL	MONEY
Bo Van Pelt	73	73	68	73	287	28,100
Mark Calcavecchia	70	68	79	71	288	19,937.50
Brad Faxon	70	70	79	69	288	19,937.50
Steve Jones	67	75	74	72	288	19,937.50
Doug Martin	70	71	74	73	288	19,937.50
Woody Austin	69	70	74	76	289	15,218.75
Mark Brooks	71	70	75	73	289	15,218.75
Glen Day	72	73	72	72	289	15,218.75
Hank Kuehne	74	71	72	72	289	15,218.75
Kevin Sutherland	73	72	69	75	289	15,218.75
Charles Warren	71	71	74	73	289	15,218.75
Jay Williamson	71	71	75	72	289	15,218.75
Richard Zokol	73	72	72	72	289	15,218.75
Jim Furyk	68	72	77	73	290	10,750
Ken Green	72	74	74	70	290	10,750
Jonathan Kaye	69	74	75	72	290	10,750
Scott McCarron	73	71	77	69	290	10,750
David Morland	70	74	78	68	290	10,750
Joe Ogilvie	74	69	77	70	290	10,750
Tom Scherrer	73	71	75	71	290	10,750
Chris DiMarco	70	74	72	75	291	7,770
Rick Fehr	71	72	71	77	291	7,770
Keith Fergus	72	74	74	71	291	7,770
Bill Glasson	73	72	71	75	291	7,770
Bradley Hughes	68	74	77	72	291	7,770
Jeff Brehaut	70	75	76	71	292	6,108.34
Bob Burns	70	72	79	71	292	6,108.34
Brandt Jobe	72	71	73	76	292	6,108.33
Tim Loustalot	74	71	75	72	292	6,108.33
Andrew Magee	67	72	74	79	292	6,108.33
Len Mattiace	70	70	79	73	292	6,108.33
Michael Bradley	70	76	68	79	293	5,700
Trevor Dodds	66	73	78	76	293	5,700
Franklin Langham	71	73	72	77	293	5,700
Jim Gallagher, Jr.	76	70	78	70	294	5,475
P.H. Horgan III	72	73	73	76	294	5,475
Craig Matthew	69	74	75	76	294	5,475
Rory Sabbatini	68	72	72	82	294	5,475
Joey Sindelar	72	72	74	76	294	5,475
Mike Sposa	71	75	71	77	294	5,475
Briny Baird	71	68	77	79	295	5,175
Robert Damron	70	72	81	72	295	5,175
Brad Fabel	71	74	71	79	295	5,175
Bob Friend	70	74	79	72	295	5,175
Sandy Lyle	70	75	77	73	295	5,175
Tommy Tolles	78	67	78	72	295	5,175
Robert Karlsson	77	69	75	75	296	4,975
Dave Stockton, Jr.	67	77	73	79	296	4,975
Bob Gilder	73	71	75	78	297	4,900
Steve Jurgensen	74	72	76	77	299	4,825
David Ogrin	70	73	78	78	299	4,825
Ian Leggatt	71	75	81	73	300	4,725
Deane Pappas	70	75	77	78	300	4,725
David Seawell	77	68	76	80	301	4,650

B.C. Open

En-Joie Golf Club, Endicott, New York
Par 37-35–72; 6,974 yards

September 16-20
purse, $1,600,000

		SCORES			TOTAL	MONEY
Brad Faxon	69	67	70	67	273	$288,000
Fred Funk	70	61	70	72	273	172,800
(Faxon defeated Funk on second extra hole.)						
Rory Sabbatini	69	67	68	70	274	108,800
Stephen Ames	68	71	67	70	276	60,320
Ronnie Black	71	67	68	70	276	60,320
Mark Carnevale	69	70	70	67	276	60,320
Jonathan Kaye	72	71	67	66	276	60,320
Craig Spence	74	69	68	65	276	60,320
Peter Jacobsen	67	71	71	68	277	46,400
Trevor Dodds	71	66	72	69	278	41,600
Mike Weir	69	68	69	72	278	41,600
Chip Beck	68	71	69	71	279	30,400
Padraig Harrington	72	69	67	71	279	30,400
Skip Kendall	71	72	70	66	279	30,400
Phil Mickelson	68	76	71	64	279	30,400
Katsumasa Miyamoto	69	71	70	69	279	30,400
Deane Pappas	71	71	67	70	279	30,400
Doug Barron	72	69	69	70	280	20,864
David Edwards	71	67	68	74	280	20,864
David Ogrin	70	72	72	66	280	20,864
David Peoples	73	70	71	66	280	20,864
Mike Sposa	72	71	69	68	280	20,864
Russ Cochran	70	69	70	72	281	13,840
John Elliott	72	69	66	74	281	13,840
Gabriel Hjertstedt	72	66	73	70	281	13,840
Pete Jordan	73	69	69	70	281	13,840
Robert Karlsson	70	71	71	69	281	13,840
Frank Lickliter	70	69	72	70	281	13,840
Mike Springer	70	71	70	71	282	11,360
Brandel Chamblee	72	72	69	70	283	9,720
Chris DiMarco	73	68	72	70	283	9,720
Frank Nobilo	72	72	71	68	283	9,720
Gene Sauers	70	74	71	68	283	9,720
Tom Scherrer	71	72	70	70	283	9,720
D.A. Weibring	74	70	70	69	283	9,720
Woody Austin	74	69	72	69	284	7,866.67
Joe Ogilvie	70	73	70	71	284	7,866.67
Ted Tryba	71	73	70	70	284	7,866.66
Greg Chalmers	71	69	76	69	285	6,560
Steve Lowery	74	70	69	72	285	6,560
Chris Perry	70	69	73	73	285	6,560
Bobby Wadkins	68	73	69	75	285	6,560
Grant Waite	75	69	72	69	285	6,560
Billy Andrade	74	69	74	69	286	4,837.34
Nick Faldo	70	72	68	76	286	4,837.34
Robin Freeman	72	72	73	69	286	4,837.33
Brian Henninger	69	71	73	73	286	4,837.33
Bradley Hughes	67	70	75	74	286	4,837.33
John Maginnes	76	67	74	69	286	4,837.33
Jerry Kelly	72	68	73	74	287	4,032
Phil Tataurangi	72	72	74	70	288	3,936
Tim Conley	72	72	75	70	289	3,676
Jeff Gallagher	73	70	74	72	289	3,676

	SCORES				TOTAL	MONEY
Bill Glasson	75	69	72	73	289	3,676
Wayne Grady	73	70	74	72	289	3,676
Tim Loustalot	73	70	73	73	289	3,676
Blaine McCallister	71	73	71	74	289	3,676
Bo Van Pelt	74	68	73	74	289	3,676
Duffy Waldorf	71	71	75	72	289	3,676
P.H. Horgan III	74	70	74	72	290	3,488
Ted Schulz	73	69	74	74	290	3,488
Tim Straub	74	68	74	74	290	3,488
R.W. Eaks	76	68	73	74	291	3,408
Tom Sieckmann	73	68	76	74	291	3,408
Wayne Levi	72	72	73	77	294	3,360
Brandt Jobe	71	71	75	78	295	3,328

Westin Texas Open

LaCantera Golf Club, San Antonio, Texas
Par 36-36–72; 6,889 yards

September 23-26
purse, $2,000,000

	SCORES				TOTAL	MONEY
Duffy Waldorf	68	69	65	68	270	$360,000
Ted Tryba	69	67	66	68	270	216,000
(Waldorf defeated Tryba on first extra hole.)						
Brent Geiberger	66	70	68	67	271	136,000
Rich Beem	65	70	68	69	272	96,000
Jay Haas	69	70	69	65	273	73,000
Brian Henninger	68	66	70	69	273	73,000
Mike Reid	69	67	69	68	273	73,000
Stephen Ames	64	69	67	75	275	60,000
Jeff Brehaut	67	67	71	70	275	60,000
Steve Elkington	68	71	70	67	276	52,000
Larry Mize	71	70	68	67	276	52,000
Jay Delsing	68	72	68	69	277	32,581.82
Scott Dunlap	68	72	68	69	277	32,581.82
Scott Gump	70	71	71	65	277	32,581.82
J.L. Lewis	72	68	67	70	277	32,581.82
Corey Pavin	70	70	68	69	277	32,581.82
Lee Rinker	67	72	71	67	277	32,581.82
David Toms	68	72	67	70	277	32,581.82
Omar Uresti	69	70	70	68	277	32,581.82
Mark Wiebe	69	68	72	68	277	32,581.82
Rick Fehr	69	69	68	71	277	32,581.81
Charles Raulerson	65	72	69	71	277	32,581.81
Mike Brisky	74	68	70	66	278	17,300
Dan Forsman	68	71	70	69	278	17,300
Bob Friend	73	69	68	68	278	17,300
Sandy Lyle	66	68	73	71	278	17,300
Scott McCarron	73	68	69	68	278	17,300
David Ogrin	69	68	69	72	278	17,300
Jonathan Kaye	74	67	72	66	279	11,911.12
Jay Don Blake	69	69	70	71	279	11,911.11
R.W. Eaks	69	72	67	71	279	11,911.11
Bob Estes	71	71	70	67	279	11,911.11
Fred Funk	69	69	73	68	279	11,911.11
Tim Herron	69	72	69	69	279	11,911.11
Len Mattiace	68	70	70	71	279	11,911.11
Kenny Perry	71	67	71	70	279	11,911.11

	SCORES				TOTAL	MONEY
Bob Tway	70	70	71	68	279	11,911.11
Tommy Armour III	68	69	70	73	280	8,000
Cameron Beckman	70	68	74	68	280	8,000
Mark Brooks	67	70	70	73	280	8,000
Russ Cochran	69	68	69	74	280	8,000
Robin Freeman	74	67	69	70	280	8,000
Brian Gay	73	69	72	66	280	8,000
Andrew Magee	69	73	68	70	280	8,000
Clarence Rose	68	72	70	70	280	8,000
Bradley Hughes	74	65	70	72	281	5,826.67
Brett Quigley	71	70	73	67	281	5,826.67
Joel Kribel	71	68	69	73	281	5,826.66
Danny Briggs	69	73	66	74	282	4,936
Pete Jordan	71	68	69	74	282	4,936
Neal Lancaster	67	74	72	69	282	4,936
Rocco Mediate	72	70	69	71	282	4,936
Chris Riley	69	72	68	73	282	4,936
Stewart Cink	72	69	68	74	283	4,500
Robert Damron	70	72	70	71	283	4,500
David Edwards	67	68	69	79	283	4,500
John Elliott	71	70	71	71	283	4,500
Steve Flesch	72	68	75	68	283	4,500
Harrison Frazar	72	68	72	71	283	4,500
Paul Goydos	71	69	72	71	283	4,500
Perry Moss	66	69	76	72	283	4,500
Larry Rinker	69	72	74	69	284	4,300
Loren Roberts	69	73	71	71	284	4,300
Andy Bean	68	71	76	70	285	4,200
Scott Hoch	67	72	76	70	285	4,200
Esteban Toledo	73	69	69	74	285	4,200
Doug Martin	68	72	70	76	286	4,120
Notah Begay III	68	72	75	72	287	4,040
Gabriel Hjertstedt	70	68	73	76	287	4,040
Sean Murphy	73	69	73	72	287	4,040
Briny Baird	69	73	72	76	290	3,960
Ken Green	69	72	74	76	291	3,920
Tom Purtzer	71	69	77	75	292	3,880

Buick Challenge

Callaway Gardens Resort, Mountain View Course,
Pine Mountain, Georgia
Par 36-36–72; 7,057 yards

September 30-October 3
purse, $1,800,000

	SCORES				TOTAL	MONEY
David Toms	68	66	66	71	271	$324,000
Stuart Appleby	70	64	69	71	274	194,400
Craig Barlow	71	65	70	70	276	93,600
Jay Delsing	70	68	71	67	276	93,600
Davis Love III	70	68	68	70	276	93,600
Paul Azinger	70	70	70	67	277	52,585.72
Stewart Cink	73	68	69	67	277	52,585.72
Scott Gump	67	71	70	69	277	52,585.72
Dan Forsman	69	68	69	71	277	52,585.71
Greg Kraft	71	66	69	71	277	52,585.71
John Maginnes	70	71	64	72	277	52,585.71
Rocco Mediate	70	70	68	69	277	52,585.71

		SCORES			TOTAL	MONEY
Justin Leonard	67	72	73	66	278	30,857.15
Chris Perry	74	67	69	68	278	30,857.15
Cameron Beckman	67	70	69	72	278	30,857.14
Mark Brooks	71	69	66	72	278	30,857.14
Jeff Maggert	73	63	71	71	278	30,857.14
David Peoples	68	70	70	70	278	30,857.14
Loren Roberts	70	66	73	69	278	30,857.14
Tom Byrum	72	70	70	67	279	20,232
Harrison Frazar	67	67	70	75	279	20,232
Andrew Magee	69	69	73	68	279	20,232
Perry Moss	71	69	70	69	279	20,232
Grant Waite	69	68	71	71	279	20,232
Eric Booker	70	68	68	74	280	13,740
Bob Estes	71	68	72	69	280	13,740
Jerry Kelly	68	71	67	74	280	13,740
Doug Martin	70	71	71	68	280	13,740
Larry Mize	68	69	73	70	280	13,740
Tom Scherrer	70	72	72	66	280	13,740
Stephen Ames	67	69	74	71	281	10,440
Paul Goydos	73	69	72	67	281	10,440
Deane Pappas	71	68	71	71	281	10,440
Tom Pernice, Jr.	68	70	70	73	281	10,440
Dicky Pride	72	69	72	68	281	10,440
Jay Williamson	72	69	72	68	281	10,440
Ben Bates	69	70	72	71	282	7,740
Ronnie Black	68	73	75	66	282	7,740
Michael Bradley	70	70	69	73	282	7,740
Fred Funk	69	70	73	70	282	7,740
Tom Kite	71	65	73	73	282	7,740
Joe Ogilvie	71	68	76	67	282	7,740
Bo Van Pelt	69	72	71	70	282	7,740
Jay Don Blake	69	68	74	72	283	5,202
Robert Damron	70	68	75	70	283	5,202
Glen Day	73	67	73	70	283	5,202
Joe Durant	69	70	73	71	283	5,202
Steve Flesch	71	69	69	74	283	5,202
Bob Friend	65	73	71	74	283	5,202
P.H. Horgan III	70	69	72	72	283	5,202
Sean Murphy	70	71	73	69	283	5,202
Tim Herron	69	69	73	73	284	4,248
Steve Pate	68	73	75	68	284	4,248
Charles Raulerson	72	70	73	69	284	4,248
Phil Blackmar	70	71	71	73	285	4,050
Danny Briggs	70	72	74	69	285	4,050
Nolan Henke	68	74	73	70	285	4,050
Mike Hulbert	69	72	70	74	285	4,050
Dennis Paulson	69	71	73	72	285	4,050
Omar Uresti	74	67	69	75	285	4,050
Notah Begay III	73	69	75	69	286	3,870
Robin Freeman	72	68	72	74	286	3,870
Blaine McCallister	71	70	73	72	286	3,870
Charles Warren	70	71	73	72	286	3,870
Rory Sabbatini	72	70	72	73	287	3,780
Skip Kendall	70	69	77	72	288	3,744
Steve Lowery	72	69	73	75	289	3,690
Paul Stankowski	71	71	76	71	289	3,690
Chip Beck	70	72	73	77	292	3,636
Frank Lickliter	67	73	73	80	293	3,600

Michelob Championship

Kingsmill Golf Club, Williamsburg, Virginia
Par 36-35–71; 6,853 yards

October 7-10
purse, $2,500,000

	SCORES				TOTAL	MONEY
Notah Begay III	67	70	69	68	274	$450,000
Tom Byrum	69	67	70	68	274	270,000
(Begay defeated Byrum on second extra hole.)						
Mike Weir	74	63	68	70	275	170,000
Barry Cheesman	73	68	68	67	276	120,000
Jay Don Blake	73	68	70	66	277	91,250
Nick Faldo	70	70	70	67	277	91,250
Tom Scherrer	72	70	66	69	277	91,250
Ronnie Black	72	70	68	68	278	67,500
Jay Delsing	73	70	65	70	278	67,500
David Duval	70	70	69	69	278	67,500
John Maginnes	70	70	71	67	278	67,500
Brian Watts	75	68	67	68	278	67,500
Robert Allenby	68	75	67	69	279	46,875
Stephen Ames	72	70	69	68	279	46,875
Lee Janzen	70	72	65	72	279	46,875
Kenny Perry	71	70	67	71	279	46,875
Scott Dunlap	71	71	71	67	280	32,714.29
David Edwards	74	70	69	67	280	32,714.29
J.P. Hayes	71	72	67	70	280	32,714.29
Lanny Wadkins	71	74	71	64	280	32,714.29
Doug Barron	73	67	69	71	280	32,714.28
Robert Damron	71	70	68	71	280	32,714.28
Peter Jacobsen	75	65	69	71	280	32,714.28
Greg Chalmers	72	68	71	70	281	19,343.75
Trevor Dodds	72	69	72	68	281	19,343.75
Scott Gump	69	68	72	72	281	19,343.75
Scott Hoch	70	69	71	71	281	19,343.75
Pete Jordan	75	69	70	67	281	19,343.75
Frank Lickliter	70	68	74	69	281	19,343.75
Perry Moss	72	72	69	68	281	19,343.75
Corey Pavin	67	74	69	71	281	19,343.75
Fred Funk	73	70	71	68	282	14,791.67
Dudley Hart	74	69	71	68	282	14,791.67
Scott Verplank	73	67	68	74	282	14,791.66
Chad Campbell	75	68	70	70	283	11,037.50
Steve Flesch	71	72	72	68	283	11,037.50
Jim Furyk	72	71	70	70	283	11,037.50
Franklin Langham	74	68	69	72	283	11,037.50
J.L. Lewis	72	71	73	67	283	11,037.50
Doug Martin	72	70	71	70	283	11,037.50
Dennis Paulson	70	73	66	74	283	11,037.50
Larry Rinker	72	73	67	71	283	11,037.50
Loren Roberts	72	69	71	71	283	11,037.50
Ted Tryba	68	74	71	70	283	11,037.50
Mark Calcavecchia	71	70	72	71	284	7,320
Mark Carnevale	71	72	67	74	284	7,320
Robin Freeman	67	74	71	72	284	7,320
Chris Riley	69	69	75	71	284	7,320
Esteban Toledo	73	71	69	71	284	7,320
Mark Brooks	78	66	69	72	285	5,983.34
Lee Rinker	70	71	72	72	285	5,983.34
Ty Armstrong	72	69	69	75	285	5,983.33
Woody Austin	70	70	73	72	285	5,983.33

	SCORES				TOTAL	MONEY
Joe Ogilvie	70	70	75	70	285	5,983.33
Hal Sutton	71	70	70	74	285	5,983.33
Chip Beck	75	70	71	70	286	5,650
Larry Mize	74	71	72	69	286	5,650
Charles Raulerson	71	70	74	71	286	5,650
Briny Baird	74	70	72	71	287	5,425
Jeff Brehaut	73	71	71	72	287	5,425
Mike Standly	70	74	74	69	287	5,425
Dave Stockton, Jr.	71	73	71	72	287	5,425
David Toms	74	71	72	70	287	5,425
Grant Waite	71	74	69	73	287	5,425
John Cook	74	70	69	75	288	5,175
Jeff Gallagher	75	69	67	77	288	5,175
Nolan Henke	73	72	72	71	288	5,175
Mike Sposa	75	70	75	68	288	5,175
Danny Briggs	75	69	73	72	289	4,950
John Elliott	69	76	74	70	289	4,950
Wayne Levi	76	68	70	75	289	4,950
David Ogrin	73	70	73	73	289	4,950
Tom Pernice, Jr.	77	67	73	72	289	4,950
Craig Barlow	72	73	73	72	290	4,775
Bob Burns	72	72	72	74	290	4,775
Charles Warren	69	74	78	70	291	4,700
Doug Dunakey	74	71	77	70	292	4,625
Rory Sabbatini	72	71	77	72	292	4,625
Glen Day	72	73	72	76	293	4,525
Willie Wood	74	71	73	75	293	4,525

Las Vegas Invitational

Las Vegas, Nevada
TPC at Summerlin: Par 36-36–72; 7,243 yards
Las Vegas Country Club: Par 36-36–72; 7,164 yards
Desert Inn Country Club: Par 36-36–72; 7,111 yards

October 13-17
purse, $2,500,000

	SCORES					TOTAL	MONEY
Jim Furyk	67	64	63	71	66	331	$450,000
Jonathan Kaye	63	66	66	73	64	332	270,000
Dudley Hart	65	68	67	74	64	338	170,000
Chris Perry	67	63	67	74	68	339	120,000
Andrew Magee	63	67	70	72	68	340	100,000
Brandel Chamblee	66	68	67	73	67	341	83,750
Robert Damron	65	67	67	75	67	341	83,750
Kevin Sutherland	67	69	63	73	69	341	83,750
Stephen Ames	69	66	67	73	67	342	72,500
Tommy Armour III	70	60	67	77	69	343	62,500
Fred Couples	63	65	70	79	66	343	62,500
Joe Ogilvie	63	70	66	79	65	343	62,500
Bob May	63	68	63	78	72	344	50,000
Brian Watts	63	70	68	75	68	344	50,000
Glen Day	69	69	67	70	70	345	41,250
Harrison Frazar	65	62	67	76	75	345	41,250
Jerry Kelly	67	66	69	75	68	345	41,250
Billy Mayfair	63	69	66	77	70	345	41,250
Craig Barlow	61	68	68	77	72	346	32,500
Justin Leonard	65	64	73	78	66	346	32,500
Mike Weir	66	67	68	76	69	346	32,500

	SCORES					TOTAL	MONEY
Stewart Cink	66	69	65	78	69	347	23,208.34
Jay Delsing	68	67	65	78	69	347	23,208.34
Steve Jones	69	69	66	72	71	347	23,208.33
Sandy Lyle	68	69	66	72	72	347	23,208.33
Lee Porter	65	65	69	77	71	347	23,208.33
Larry Rinker	70	65	67	76	69	347	23,208.33
Edward Fryatt	70	67	66	76	69	348	17,375
Peter Jacobsen	71	66	68	75	68	348	17,375
Frank Lickliter	64	67	70	76	71	348	17,375
Dennis Paulson	69	64	67	81	67	348	17,375
Olin Browne	66	71	67	76	69	349	14,150
Steve Flesch	67	68	69	78	67	349	14,150
Blaine McCallister	68	69	67	75	70	349	14,150
Lee Rinker	64	68	67	79	71	349	14,150
Vijay Singh	65	63	67	80	74	349	14,150
Woody Austin	71	68	64	76	71	350	11,000
John Daly	67	69	68	75	71	350	11,000
Bob Estes	69	65	69	82	65	350	11,000
Bill Glasson	66	64	69	81	70	350	11,000
Phil Mickelson	69	63	69	79	70	350	11,000
Kirk Triplett	67	69	67	74	73	350	11,000
J.L. Lewis	70	66	66	78	71	351	9,250
Greg Chalmers	71	68	66	78	69	352	7,770
Brian Gay	68	68	69	74	73	352	7,770
J.P. Hayes	67	68	68	83	66	352	7,770
Skip Kendall	68	69	64	80	71	352	7,770
Chris Riley	71	67	67	79	68	352	7,770
Trevor Dodds	68	70	65	81	69	353	6,170
Charles Raulerson	68	66	71	78	70	353	6,170
Jeff Sluman	69	70	65	78	71	353	6,170
David Sutherland	68	66	71	76	72	353	6,170
Duffy Waldorf	68	67	69	80	69	353	6,170
Steve Pate	66	64	72	78	74	354	5,775
Tommy Tolles	70	66	68	81	69	354	5,775
Paul Azinger	69	67	67	82	71	356	5,600
Lee Janzen	70	67	67	79	73	356	5,600
Perry Moss	68	68	68	79	73	356	5,600
Sean Murphy	68	66	71	80	71	356	5,600
Chris Smith	70	66	66	84	70	356	5,600
Doug Martin	68	68	65	83	73	357	5,400
Bob Tway	67	71	66	79	74	357	5,400
Scott Verplank	65	67	70	81	74	357	5,400
Steve Lowery	66	69	67	77	79	358	5,300
Mark Brooks	69	70	65	75	80	359	5,250
Russ Cochran	68	70	67	81	74	360	5,175
Robert Gamez	68	68	67	83	74	360	5,175
Gabriel Hjertstedt	68	68	68	85	72	361	5,100
Brent Geiberger	68	71	66	77	80	362	5,050
Greg Kraft	67	65	70	82	79	363	5,000
Brian Henninger	63	72	69	85	77	366	4,950

National Car Rental Classic

Lake Buena Vista, Florida
Magnolia Course: Par 36-36–72; 7,190 yards
Palm Course: Par 36-36–72; 6,957 yards

October 21-24
purse, $2,500,000

	SCORES				TOTAL	MONEY
Tiger Woods	66	66	66	73	271	$450,000
Ernie Els	68	65	68	71	272	270,000
Franklin Langham	67	67	68	72	274	145,000
Bob Tway	67	65	66	76	274	145,000
John Huston	67	69	72	67	275	95,000
Vijay Singh	66	71	69	69	275	95,000
Russ Cochran	68	69	68	72	277	75,312.50
Glen Day	71	68	72	66	277	75,312.50
Dudley Hart	70	67	67	73	277	75,312.50
Jeff Sluman	70	65	70	72	277	75,312.50
Woody Austin	65	72	73	69	279	51,250
Jim Carter	67	65	71	76	279	51,250
Stewart Cink	69	70	70	70	279	51,250
Steve Elkington	66	69	71	73	279	51,250
Scott Hoch	67	71	67	74	279	51,250
Steve Lowery	70	68	70	71	279	51,250
Brian Henninger	70	67	76	67	280	28,568.19
Sean Murphy	73	68	71	68	280	28,568.19
Paul Azinger	70	69	69	72	280	28,568.18
Jay Delsing	69	65	69	77	280	28,568.18
Chris DiMarco	69	69	69	73	280	28,568.18
Scott Dunlap	72	69	69	70	280	28,568.18
Paul Goydos	69	70	68	73	280	28,568.18
Jonathan Kaye	67	69	72	72	280	28,568.18
Billy Mayfair	68	68	72	72	280	28,568.18
Rocco Mediate	65	68	76	71	280	28,568.18
Scott Verplank	67	71	72	70	280	28,568.18
Pete Jordan	71	68	71	71	281	15,583.34
Chris Riley	70	70	69	72	281	15,583.34
Kevin Sutherland	70	70	70	71	281	15,583.34
Barry Cheesman	67	68	73	73	281	15,583.33
Brad Faxon	65	73	64	79	281	15,583.33
Brent Geiberger	68	69	71	73	281	15,583.33
Scott McCarron	73	64	71	73	281	15,583.33
Corey Pavin	71	70	67	73	281	15,583.33
Loren Roberts	67	68	68	78	281	15,583.33
Tommy Armour III	72	69	70	71	282	10,750
Notah Begay III	70	67	71	74	282	10,750
Lee Janzen	67	71	70	74	282	10,750
Jesper Parnevik	69	72	68	73	282	10,750
Chris Perry	70	69	73	70	282	10,750
Dicky Pride	69	70	72	71	282	10,750
Hal Sutton	68	66	77	71	282	10,750
Chip Beck	68	69	73	73	283	7,225
Mark Brooks	70	71	69	73	283	7,225
Jeff Gallagher	71	67	74	71	283	7,225
Gabriel Hjertstedt	69	65	72	77	283	7,225
J.L. Lewis	70	68	71	74	283	7,225
Mike Reid	71	70	71	71	283	7,225
David Sutherland	69	67	72	75	283	7,225
Willie Wood	71	67	72	73	283	7,225
Dan Forsman	69	69	71	75	284	5,830
Greg Kraft	73	65	70	76	284	5,830

	SCORES				TOTAL	MONEY
Joe Ogilvie	69	72	73	70	284	5,830
Larry Rinker	71	66	69	78	284	5,830
Paul Stankowski	71	67	75	71	284	5,830
Fulton Allem	73	66	70	76	285	5,375
Craig Barlow	71	68	72	74	285	5,375
Olin Browne	71	68	72	74	285	5,375
Robert Damron	67	67	75	76	285	5,375
Doug Dunakey	70	69	70	76	285	5,375
Bill Glasson	68	73	73	71	285	5,375
Tom Lehman	71	70	73	71	285	5,375
Wayne Levi	68	71	72	74	285	5,375
Kenny Perry	69	69	72	75	285	5,375
Lee Rinker	70	66	74	75	285	5,375
David Toms	72	66	72	75	285	5,375
Mike Weir	67	70	73	75	285	5,375
Jeff Brehaut	69	69	73	75	286	4,875
Steve Flesch	71	69	72	74	286	4,875
Blaine McCallister	72	69	73	72	286	4,875
Katsumasa Miyamoto	69	72	70	75	286	4,875
Chris Smith	72	69	72	73	286	4,875
Mike Springer	67	70	71	78	286	4,875
Curtis Strange	71	69	73	73	286	4,875
Duffy Waldorf	71	68	72	75	286	4,875
John Cook	68	72	70	77	287	4,575
Scott Gump	67	73	75	72	287	4,575
P.H. Horgan III	69	70	75	73	287	4,575
Frank Nobilo	71	70	72	74	287	4,575
Brandt Jobe	68	73	73	74	288	4,375
Jerry Kelly	71	70	72	75	288	4,375
Charles Raulerson	69	69	73	77	288	4,375
Lanny Wadkins	70	71	72	75	288	4,375
Ben Bates	71	69	75	75	290	4,250
Tom Purtzer	72	69	76	74	291	4,200

Southern Farm Bureau Classic

Annandale Golf Club, Madison, Mississippi
Par 36-36–72; 7,157 yards
(Reduced to 54 holes due to memorial service for Payne Stewart.)

October 29-31
purse, $1,500,000

	SCORES			TOTAL	MONEY
Brian Henninger	67	66	69	202	$360,000
Chris DiMarco	65	68	72	205	216,000
Glen Day	69	71	66	206	104,000
Perry Moss	67	69	70	206	104,000
Paul Stankowski	70	69	67	206	104,000
Jonathan Kaye	71	68	68	207	72,000
Rick Fehr	72	70	66	208	64,500
Kirk Triplett	69	70	69	208	64,500
Mark Calcavecchia	72	69	68	209	44,750
Russ Cochran	64	72	73	209	44,750
Jeff Gallagher	69	72	68	209	44,750
Nolan Henke	66	73	70	209	44,750
Mike Hulbert	70	68	71	209	44,750
Len Mattiace	69	72	68	209	44,750
Blaine McCallister	72	67	70	209	44,750
Kevin Wentworth	69	71	69	209	44,750

	SCORES			TOTAL	MONEY
Brad Faxon	69	74	67	210	29,000
Dan Forsman	71	67	72	210	29,000
Deane Pappas	68	75	67	210	29,000
Jay Williamson	71	73	66	210	29,000
Greg Chalmers	72	69	70	211	23,200
John Elliott	68	77	66	211	23,200
Doug Dunakey	69	75	68	212	16,857.15
Franklin Langham	70	72	70	212	16,857.15
Jim Carter	71	70	71	212	16,857.14
Trevor Dodds	71	69	72	212	16,857.14
Jimmy Green	74	68	70	212	16,857.14
J.L. Lewis	73	69	70	212	16,857.14
Tom Scherrer	71	71	70	212	16,857.14
*David Gossett	68	74	70	212	
Briny Baird	73	71	69	213	12,420
Cameron Beckman	71	71	71	213	12,420
Tom Byrum	68	72	73	213	12,420
Bill Glasson	72	69	72	213	12,420
Mike Sposa	70	74	69	213	12,420
Brad Bryant	65	76	73	214	9,650
John Daly	68	70	76	214	9,650
Scott Gump	70	74	70	214	9,650
Greg Kraft	68	75	71	214	9,650
Neal Lancaster	71	73	70	214	9,650
Frank Lickliter	72	70	72	214	9,650
Jerry Kelly	71	74	70	215	6,631.12
Ronnie Black	72	69	74	215	6,631.11
Phil Blackmar	73	68	74	215	6,631.11
Eric Booker	69	75	71	215	6,631.11
Michael Bradley	71	69	75	215	6,631.11
Bob Friend	71	73	71	215	6,631.11
David Peoples	72	72	71	215	6,631.11
Dicky Pride	67	72	76	215	6,631.11
Mike Standly	72	72	71	215	6,631.11
Robert Allenby	72	73	71	216	4,647.28
Brandt Jobe	71	74	71	216	4,647.28
Billy Mayfair	71	74	71	216	4,647.28
Olin Browne	71	71	74	216	4,647.27
Joe Durant	71	73	72	216	4,647.27
Steve Flesch	72	72	72	216	4,647.27
Kelly Gibson	72	72	72	216	4,647.27
J.P. Hayes	70	73	73	216	4,647.27
P.H. Horgan III	74	71	71	216	4,647.27
Sean Murphy	70	72	74	216	4,647.27
Kevin Sutherland	73	71	72	216	4,647.27
Craig Barlow	70	75	72	217	4,300
Jim Gallagher, Jr.	69	71	77	217	4,300
Gabriel Hjertstedt	71	71	75	217	4,300
Brett Quigley	71	72	74	217	4,300
Woody Austin	74	71	73	218	4,160
Bradley Hughes	71	74	73	218	4,160
Jeff Street	68	77	73	218	4,160

Tour Championship

Champions Golf Club, Cypress Course, Houston, Texas   October 28-31
Par 36-35–71; 7,202 yards   purse, $5,000,000

	SCORES				TOTAL	MONEY
Tiger Woods	67	66	67	69	269	$900,000
Davis Love III	64	69	73	67	273	540,000
Brent Geiberger	68	69	68	69	274	345,000
Chris Perry	70	64	69	72	275	240,000
Fred Funk	66	70	71	69	276	177,500
John Huston	68	71	69	68	276	177,500
Jeff Sluman	69	70	69	68	276	177,500
Duffy Waldorf	66	74	66	70	276	177,500
Vijay Singh	74	68	70	65	277	142,333.34
Tim Herron	66	72	71	68	277	142,333.33
Hal Sutton	72	70	64	71	277	142,333.33
Justin Leonard	67	73	69	70	279	122,000
Steve Pate	67	69	69	74	279	122,000
David Toms	73	68	67	71	279	122,000
Notah Begay III	70	69	71	70	280	103,200
David Duval	70	71	67	72	280	103,200
Carlos Franco	65	72	71	72	280	103,200
Jim Furyk	69	72	72	67	280	103,200
Tom Lehman	72	67	68	73	280	103,200
Jeff Maggert	73	72	64	72	281	96,000
Phil Mickelson	73	68	70	71	282	91,000
Nick Price	70	66	72	74	282	91,000
Loren Roberts	73	72	68	69	282	91,000
Ted Tryba	70	70	69	73	282	91,000
Bob Estes	70	70	75	68	283	86,000
Stuart Appleby	72	69	70	74	285	83,000
Ernie Els	68	71	75	71	285	83,000
Mike Weir	76	73	68	68	285	83,000
Dennis Paulson	72	70	69	76	287	81,000

Special Events

CVS/pharmacy Charity Classic

Rhode Island Country Club, Barrington, Rhode Island
Par 36-35–71; 6,688 yards

August 2-3
purse, $1,000,000

	SCORES		TOTAL	MONEY (Team)
Jeff Sluman/Stuart Appleby	59	63	122	$200,000
Brett Quigley/Dana Quigley	61	63	124	150,000
Tim Herron/Scott McCarron	63	65	128	110,000
Billy Andrade/Brad Faxon	65	64	129	95,000
Mark Calcavecchia/Peter Jacobsen	64	65	129	95,000
Tom Kite/Jay Haas	66	64	130	77,500
P.H. Horgan III/Jay Sigel	63	67	130	77,500
Jim Furyk/Lee Janzen	65	66	131	70,000
John Cook/Davis Love III	66	66	132	62,500
Jack Nicklaus/Gary Nicklaus	67	65	132	62,500

Fred Meyer Challenge

Reserve Vineyards and Golf Club, Fought Course,
Aloha, Oregon
Par 36-36–72; 7,037 yards

August 23-24
purse, $925,000

	SCORES		TOTAL	MONEY (Team)
Brad Faxon/Billy Andrade	61	61	122	$150,000
Jim Furyk/John Huston	64	60	124	92,500
Craig Stadler/Steve Elkington	62	62	124	92,500
Tom Lehman/Duffy Waldorf	64	62	126	70,000
Billy Mayfair/Steve Pate	62	64	126	70,000
Brian Henninger/Tim Herron	62	64	126	70,000
Jay Haas/Phil Mickelson	61	65	126	70,000
David Frost/Glen Day	63	64	127	64,000
John Cook/Scott McCarron	66	62	128	63,000
Andrew Magee/Stewart Cink	67	62	129	62,000
Fuzzy Zoeller/John Daly	66	64	130	61,000
Arnold Palmer/Peter Jacobsen	68	66	134	60,000

Ganter Cup Challenge

Willow Creek Country Club, Sandy, Utah
Par 36-36–72; 7,104 yards

September 6
purse, $140,000

Matt Gogel ($55,000), Nike Tour, defeated Craig Stadler ($22,500), PGA Tour, 65-69.
Ryan Howison ($30,000), Nike Tour, defeated John Cook ($10,000), PGA Tour, 70-71.
Fred Couples ($45,000), PGA Tour, defeated Mathew Goggin ($6,500), Nike Tour, 68-76.
David Duval ($23,500), PGA Tour, defeated Carl Paulson ($7,500), Nike Tour, 73-74.

Ryder Cup

The Country Club, Brookline, Massachusetts September 24-26
Par 434 444 345–35, 444 454 344–36–71; 7,033 yards

FIRST DAY
Morning Foursomes

Colin Montgomerie and Paul Lawrie (Europe) defeated David Duval and Phil
Mickelson (USA), 3 and 2

Montgomerie/Lawrie	4 3 4	3 4 4	3 3 5	4 4 4	4 4 4	3
Duval/Mickelson	4 3 4	3 4 3	4 4 4	5 4 5	4 5 4	3

Sergio Garcia and Jesper Parnevik (Europe) defeated Tom Lehman and Tiger
Woods (USA), 2 and 1

Garcia/Parnevik	4 3 4	4 5 4	2 4 5	4 4 4	4 4 4	3 3
Lehman/Woods	3 3 4	4 4 5	3 4 5	4 4 5	4 4 4	3 4

Miguel Angel Jimenez and Padraig Harrington (Europe) halved with Davis Love
III and Payne Stewart (USA)

Jimenez/Harrington	4 3 4	4 5 3	3 4 5	3 4 4	4 4 4	3 5 4
Love/Stewart	4 3 3	3 5 4	3 4 5	4 4 5	4 4 4	3 4 4

Jeff Maggert and Hal Sutton (USA) defeated Lee Westwood and Darren Clarke
(Europe), 3 and 2

Westwood/Clarke	4 3 4	3 4 4	3 4 5	4 4 4	4 5 4	3
Maggert/Sutton	5 3 4	4 4 3	2 3 5	4 4 4	4 4 4	2

POINTS: Europe 2½, United States 1½

Afternoon Fourball

Jesper Parnevik and Sergio Garcia (Europe) defeated Phil Mickelson and Jim
Furyk (USA), 1 up

Parnevik	3 3 4	3 4 3	3 2 4	3 4 4	4 4 5	3 4 4
Garcia	4 3 3	4 5 4	3 3 4	4 4 5	4 3 4	3 4 4
Mickelson	3 2 4	4 3 3	3 3 4	4 3 4	4 4 4	3 4 4
Furyk	3 3 4	4 3 3	3 3 5	4 4 4	3 4 4	3 4 4

Colin Montgomerie and Paul Lawrie (Europe) halved with Davis Love III and
Justin Leonard (USA)

Montgomerie	4 3 4	4 4 4	4 4 5	4 4 4	3 3 4	4 3 4
Lawrie	4 3 4	4 4 3	3 4 5	5 4 4	4 3 4	3 4 4
Love	4 3 4	4 4 3	3 4 5	4 4 4	4 3 4	3 4 3
Leonard	4 3 4	4 4 3	3 4 4	4 4 4	4 4 4	3 4 4

Miguel Angel Jimenez and Jose Maria Olazabal (Europe) defeated Hal Sutton and
Jeff Maggert (USA), 2 and 1

Jimenez	3 3 4	3 4 3	3 4 5	4 5 4	5 5 4	3 4
Olazabal	4 3 4	4 4 3	3 3 4	4 5 4	4 4 4	3 4
Sutton	4 3 4	4 4 3	4 3 4	4 4 5	4 4 4	3 4
Maggert	4 3 5	4 6 3	3 5 6	4 4 5	4 4 4	3 4

Lee Westwood and Darren Clarke (Europe) defeated David Duval and Tiger
Woods (USA), 1 up

Westwood	4 3 4	5 4 5	3 4 4	4 4 3	4 4 4	3 4 4
Clarke	4 3 3	5 3 4	3 3 4	4 3 4	5 4 4	3 3 4
Duval	4 3 4	4 4 3	3 3 4	4 5 4	4 4 4	3 4 5
Woods	4 3 4	4 5 3	3 3 5	3 5 3	4 4 4	3 4 4

POINTS: Europe 6, United States 2

SECOND DAY
Morning Foursomes

Hal Sutton and Jeff Maggert (USA) defeated Colin Montgomerie and Paul Lawrie (Europe), 1 up

Montgomerie/Lawrie	4 2 4	4 4 3	3 4 5	4 5 4	4 5 3	3 4 3
Sutton/Maggert	4 3 4	4 4 3	3 4 4	4 4 5	4 5 3	3 3 3

Darren Clarke and Lee Westwood (Europe) defeated Jim Furyk and Mark O'Meara (USA), 3 and 2

Clarke/Westwood	4 3 5	4 4 3	3 4 4	4 4 4	4 4 4	3
Furyk/O'Meara	4 3 4	4 4 4	3 4 5	4 4 5	4 5 4	3

Tiger Woods and Steve Pate (USA) defeated Miguel Angel Jimenez and Padraig Harrington (Europe), 1 up

Jimenez/Harrington	4 3 5	3 5 3	3 3 5	4 4 5	4 4 4	3 5 4
Woods/Pate	3 2 3	3 5 4	3 4 5	4 5 5	4 3 4	3 5 4

Jesper Parnevik and Sergio Garcia (Europe) defeated Payne Stewart and Justin Leonard (USA), 3 and 2

Parnevik/Garcia	4 4 4	4 4 3	3 4 4	3 4 5	4 4 4	3
Stewart/Leonard	5 3 4	4 4 5	3 4 6	4 5 5	3 4 4	3

POINTS: Europe 8, United States 4

Afternoon Fourball

Phil Mickelson and Tom Lehman (USA) defeated Darren Clarke and Lee Westwood (Europe), 2 and 1

Clarke	4 3 4	4 4 4	3 4 4	4 4 5	4 4 4	3 4
Westwood	4 3 4	4 4 4	3 5 5	5 4 4	5 4 4	2 4
Mickelson	4 4 3	4 4 4	3 3 4	3 4 4	4 4 4	3 4
Lehman	4 3 4	4 4 4	3 3 4	3 4 4	4 5 4	3 4

Jesper Parnevik and Sergio Garcia (Europe) halved with Davis Love III and David Duval (USA)

Parnevik	4 3 4	4 4 3	3 4 5	4 3 4	4 4 4	3 4 4
Garcia	4 3 4	4 3 4	3 3 5	4 4 4	4 5 4	3 4 3
Love	3 4 4	4 4 4	3 4 3	4 4 4	4 5 4	2 4 4
Duval	3 3 4	3 4 4	3 4 5	3 4 4	3 5 4	2 5 4

Miguel Angel Jimenez and Jose Maria Olazabal (Europe) halved with Justin Leonard and Hal Sutton (USA)

Jimenez	4 4 4	3 3 3	3 4 5	4 4 4	4 5 4	3 4 4
Olazabal	4 4 5	4 4	3 4 5	4 4 4	4 6 4	3 5 5
Leonard	4 4 4	4 4 4	3 4 4	4 5 4	4 5 4	3 4 4
Sutton	4 3 4	4 4 4	4 5	4 4 4	4 5 5	2 4 4

Colin Montgomerie and Paul Lawrie (Europe) defeated Steve Pate and Tiger Woods (USA), 2 and 1

Montgomerie	5 3 3	3 4 4	3 3 5	3 5 5	4 4 3	3 4
Lawrie	4 3 4	4 4 4	3 4 5	4 4 5	4 5 4	2 4
Pate	3 3 4	4 4 3	2 4 5	4 4 3	4 5 4	3 4
Woods	3 3 4	4 4 3	3 4 5	4 4 3	4 4 4	3 4

POINTS: Europe 10, United States 6

THIRD DAY
Singles

Tom Lehman (USA) defeated Lee Westwood (Europe), 3 and 2
Westwood	4 3 4	4 4 3	2 4 6	5 4 4	4 4 4	3
Lehman	4 3 4	3 3 3	3 4 5	4 4 4	3 5 4	3

Hal Sutton (USA) defeated Darren Clarke (Europe), 4 and 2
Clarke	3 3 5	5 4 4	3 4 5	4 4 5	5 4 4	4
Sutton	4 2 4	4 4 3	3 4 5	4 4 4	5 5 4	3

Phil Mickelson (USA) defeated Jarmo Sandelin (Europe), 4 and 3
Sandelin	4 3 5	4 4 3	3 4 4	6 5 5	3 5 4
Mickelson	4 3 4	3 4 4	3 4 4	5 4 4	4 4 4

Davis Love III (USA) defeated Jean Van de Velde (Europe), 6 and 5
Van de Velde	5 3 3	4 4 3	4 4 5	4 4 5	5
Love	4 3 4	4 3 3	3 4 5	3 3 4	4

Tiger Woods (USA) defeated Andrew Coltart (Europe), 3 and 2
Coltart	5 3 4	3 4 3	4 4 6	4 4 4	4 4 4	3
Woods	5 3 4	3 4 3	3 3 4	4 4 4	4 4 4	3

David Duval (USA) defeated Jesper Parnevik (Europe), 5 and 4
Parnevik	4 3 5	4 4 5	4 5 4	4 4 4	3 4
Duval	4 2 4	3 4 4	3 4 5	4 3 4	4 4

Padraig Harrington (Europe) defeated Mark O'Meara (USA), 1 up
Harrington	3 4 4	3 3 4	3 4 3	4 4 4	5 6 4	3 4 4
O'Meara	4 3 3	4 4 4	3 3 5	4 4 4	4 6 4	3 4 5

Steve Pate (USA) defeated Miguel Angel Jimenez (Europe), 2 and 1
Jimenez	4 3 4	5 4 3	2 5 4	5 4 5	4 6 4	3 4
Pate	4 3 4	4 4 4	2 4 4	5 4 4	4 4 4	4 4

Jose Maria Olazabal (Europe) halved with Justin Leonard (USA)
Olazabal	4 3 4	4 4 3	3 4 4	4 5 5	5 5 4	3 4 3
Leonard	5 2 4	5 4 4	3 4 6	5 5 4	4 4 3	3 3 4

Colin Montgomerie (Europe) defeated Payne Stewart (USA), 1 up
Montgomerie	5 3 3	4 3 3	3 4 5	4 4 4	4 5 5	3 4 3
Stewart	5 3 3	4 4 4	4 3 4	4 4 5	4 4 4	3 4 4

Jim Furyk (USA) defeated Sergio Garcia (Europe), 4 and 3
Garcia	4 3 4	4 4 3	3 4 5	5 5 4	4 5 4
Furyk	4 3 4	3 4 4	3 3 4	5 4 3	4 5 4

Paul Lawrie (Europe) defeated Jeff Maggert (USA), 4 and 3
Lawrie	5 2 4	3 4 4	3 3 4	5 4 5	5 4 4
Maggert	5 3 4	4 4 4	3 4 5	5 4 5	4 C 4

TOTAL POINTS: United States 14½, Europe 13½

LEGEND: C—conceded hole to opponent; W—won hole by concession without holing out.

Franklin Templeton Shark Shootout

Sherwood Country Club, Thousand Oaks, California
Par 36-36–72; 7,025 yards

November 12-14
purse, $1,500,000

	SCORES			TOTAL	MONEY (Team)
Fred Couples/David Duval	61	62	61	184	$350,000
Scott McCarron/Scott Hoch	66	63	61	190	200,000
Peter Jacobsen/John Cook	66	64	61	191	137,000
Andrew Magee/Jay Haas	66	64	62	192	110,000
Greg Norman/Steve Elkington	69	64	60	193	104,000
Brad Faxon/Jeff Sluman	67	64	63	194	99,000
Chip Beck/John Daly	71	65	59	195	94,000
Carlos Franco/Olin Browne	72	64	60	196	89,000
Duffy Waldorf/Glen Day	70	69	58	197	82,000
Corey Pavin/Steve Pate	71	66	60	197	82,000
Craig Stadler/Tom Kite	74	69	63	206	78,000
Ben Crenshaw/Bruce Lietzke	75	70	64	209	75,000

World Cup of Golf

Mines Resort and Golf Club, Kuala Lumpur, Malaysia
Par 35-36–71; 6,808 yards

November 18-21
purse, $1,500,000

	INDIVIDUAL SCORES				TOTAL
UNITED STATES (545)—$400,000					
Tiger Woods	67	68	63	65	263
Mark O'Meara	73	65	67	77	282
SPAIN (550)—$200,000					
Santiago Luna	71	66	68	72	277
Miguel Angel Martin	69	66	70	68	273
IRELAND (554)—$125,000					
Padraig Harrington	71	68	70	67	276
Paul McGinley	70	71	69	68	278
ARGENTINA (555)—$100,000					
Eduardo Romero	72	68	70	72	282
Angel Cabrera	69	69	68	67	273
SWEDEN (556)—$80,000					
Jarmo Sandelin	74	65	71	69	279
Patrik Sjoland	72	66	69	70	277
ENGLAND (558)—$60,000					
Mark James	71	67	71	68	277
Peter Baker	71	70	70	70	281
JAPAN (562)—$38,500					
Mamoru Osanai	65	76	67	65	273
Mitsuo Harada	70	73	74	72	289
ZIMBABWE (562)—$38,500					
Mark McNulty	73	73	71	69	286
Tony Johnstone	68	70	68	70	276

	INDIVIDUAL SCORES	TOTAL

WALES (563)—$28,000

Phil Price	68 67 68 73	276
David Park	71 72 75 69	287

NEW ZEALAND (564)—$24,000

Frank Nobilo	69 68 68 67	272
Stephen Scahill	77 70 76 69	292

SOUTH AFRICA (566)—$20,000

David Frost	71 69 68 69	277
Richard Kaplan	74 71 70 74	289

REP. OF KOREA (567)—$17,000

Kim Wan-tae	81 69 74 68	292
Kang Wook-soon	69 70 68 68	275

DENMARK (568)—$14,000

Anders Hansen	73 75 70 69	287
Soren Kjeldsen	68 73 72 68	281

MEXICO (568)—$14,000

Rafael Alarcon	72 69 71 72	284
Jose Gonzalez	72 75 68 69	284

SCOTLAND (571)—$11,000

Colin Montgomerie	70 73 70 72	285
Dean Robertson	75 69 70 72	286

AUSTRALIA (573)—$10,000

Terry Price	75 74 70 68	287
Paul Gow	72 72 71 71	286

MYANMAR (574)—$9,000

Kyi Hla Han	75 68 67 71	281
Soe Kyaw Naing	74 73 75 71	293

PHILIPPINES (575)—$8,800

Marciano Pucay	72 77 73 68	290
Felix Casas	72 69 73 71	285

NETHERLANDS (576)—$8,500

Joost Steenkamer	80 73 69 69	291
Maarten Lafeber	75 70 69 71	285

COLOMBIA (576)—$8,500

Jesus Amaya	73 73 73 66	285
Gustavo Mendoza	74 73 75 69	291

FRANCE (582)—$8,200

Jean Francois Remesy	72 76 69 72	289
Marc Farry	75 70 77 71	293

CANADA (583)—$8,000

Ray Stewart	76 74 70 76	296
Arden Knoll	72 72 70 73	287

PARAGUAY (584)—$7,800

Raul Fretes	76 76 71 71	294
Pedro Rodolfo Martinez	72 74 74 70	290

	INDIVIDUAL SCORES				TOTAL
SWITZERLAND (585)—$7,500					
Steve Rey	77	73	74	74	298
Carlos Duran	72	71	71	73	287
GERMANY (585)—$7,500					
Sven Struver	71	72	71	70	284
Heinz Peter Thul	72	79	75	75	301
ITALY (586)—$7,100					
Emanuele Canonica	77	75	71	74	297
Costantino Rocca	73	71	76	69	289
MALAYSIA (586)—$7,100					
Marimuthu Raymayah	70	76	74	68	288
Periasamy Gunasagaran	76	75	73	74	298
FINLAND (592)—$6,800					
Mika Lehtinen	70	78	72	67	287
Kim Wiik	76	72	81	76	305
PUERTO RICO (593)—$6,600					
Rafael Castrillo	74	74	72	78	298
Wilfredo Morales	74	76	71	74	295
CHINESE TAIPEI (594)—$6,400					
Tsai Chi-huang	76	73	69	76	294
Chen Liang-hsi	79	69	72	80	300
CHILE (595)—$6,200					
Guillermo Encina	79	72	73	74	298
Roy Mackenzie	77	71	73	76	297
JAMAICA (615)—$6,000					
Peter Horrobin	74	68	74	72	288
Ralph Campbell	74	87	82	84	327

INTERNATIONAL TROPHY

WINNER: Woods - 263 - $100,000. RUNNER-UP: Nobilo - 272 - $50,000. ORDER OF FINISH: Osanai, Cabrera, Martin - 273 - $16,667 each.

Callaway Pebble Beach Invitational

Pebble Beach, California
Pebble Beach GL: Par 36-36–72; 6,840 yards
Spyglass Hills GC: Par 36-36–72; 6,859 yards
Del Monte GC: Par 36-36–72; 6,278 yards

November 18-21
purse, $300,000

	SCORES				TOTAL	MONEY
Rocco Mediate	70	76	68	68	282	$60,000
Annika Sorenstam	69	76	69	69	283	32,500
Tom Lehman	68	72	73	71	284	13,500
Loren Roberts	69	71	73	71	284	13,500
Jim Thorpe	69	77	65	74	285	8,500
Mark Brooks	68	75	70	72	285	8,500
Brian Henninger	67	76	70	74	287	6,250
J.L. Lewis	71	71	72	73	287	6,250

	SCORES				TOTAL	MONEY
Frank Lickliter	71	74	71	71	287	6,250
Brian Mogg	79	70	69	69	287	6,250
Barry Lane	69	72	73	74	288	4,450
Ed Fryatt	69	73	73	73	288	4,450
Olin Browne	70	78	67	73	288	4,450
Kirk Triplett	73	73	70	72	288	4,450
Mike Reid	70	81	65	72	288	4,450
Bob Ford	67	76	74	71	288	4,450
Bruce Fleisher	71	74	74	71	290	3,400
Dave Eichelberger	73	74	73	70	290	3,400
Helen Alfredsson	70	71	77	73	291	3,000
Bruce Summerhays	73	71	74	73	291	3,000
Rick Hartman	70	76	71	75	292	2,750
Jim Carter	73	72	73	74	292	2,750
Mark Pfeil	69	73	78	73	293	2,600
Darryl Kestner	74	72	75	73	294	2,500
Shawn McEntee	72	78	70	75	295	2,350
Mark Wiebe	71	80	73	71	295	2,350

PGA Grand Slam

Poipu Bay Resort, Kauai, Hawaii
Par 36-36–72; 6,957 yards

November 23-24
purse, $1,000,000

FIRST-ROUND MATCHES

Tiger Woods defeated Paul Lawrie, 3 and 2
Davis Love III defeated Jose Maria Olazabal, 6 and 5

CHAMPIONSHIP MATCH

Woods defeated Love, 3 and 2
(Woods received $400,000; Love received $250,000.)

THIRD-PLACE MATCH

Olazabal defeated Lawrie, after Lawrie conceded due to injury.
(Olazabal received $200,000; Lawrie received $150,000.)

JCPenney Classic

Westin Innisbrook Resort, Copperhead Course,
Palm Harbor, Florida
Par 36-35–71; 7,054 yards (men), 6,330 yards (women)

December 2-5
purse, $2,000,000

	SCORES				TOTAL	MONEY
						(Team)
Laura Davies/John Daly	63	66	67	64	260	$220,000
Se Ri Pak/Paul Azinger	65	64	62	69	260	115,000
(Davies/Daly defeated Pak/Azinger on third extra hole.)						
Melissa McNamara/Mike Springer	67	66	65	64	262	70,350
Maria Hjorth/Scott Gump	65	65	65	67	262	70,350
Kristi Albers/J.P. Hayes	67	67	63	66	263	45,000
Marta Figueras-Dotti/Brad Bryant	66	68	65	65	264	37,500
Dottie Pepper/Jeff Sluman	69	65	65	65	264	37,500
Jill McGill/J.L. Lewis	65	70	64	66	265	30,000

	SCORES				TOTAL	MONEY (Team)
Pat Hurst/Rory Sabbatini	63	72	67	64	266	19,500
Charlotta Sorenstam/Robert Damron	66	66	67	67	266	19,500
Tina Barrett/Fred Funk	68	66	65	67	266	19,500
Meg Mallon/Steve Pate	63	70	64	69	266	19,500
Catriona Matthew/Dan Forsman	68	68	65	66	267	12,500
Wendy Ward/Mark Brooks	68	70	63	66	267	12,500
Chris Johnson/Steve Lowery	68	69	63	67	267	12,500
Donna Andrews/Mike Hulbert	65	68	67	68	268	11,000
Dina Ammaccapane/Omar Uresti	67	67	65	69	268	11,000
Wendy Doolan/Esteban Toledo	66	68	63	71	268	11,000
Michelle Estill/Tom Pernice, Jr.	64	69	68	68	269	9,125
Jan Stephenson/Frank Lickliter	64	72	65	68	269	9,125
Dawn Coe-Jones/Dudley Hart	67	66	67	69	269	9,125
Leslie Spalding/Dicky Pride	67	69	66	67	269	9,125
Michele Redman/Skip Kendall	67	70	65	67	269	9,125
Cindy Figg-Currier/Tommy Armour III	67	68	65	69	269	9,125
Barb Mucha/Tom Scherrer	64	69	69	67	269	9,125
Carin Koch/Jay Don Blake	71	67	65	66	269	9,125
Catrin Nilsmark/Chris Perry	68	67	63	71	269	9,125
Juli Inkster/Justin Leonard	65	66	66	72	269	9,125
Kim Saiki/Dennis Paulson	66	69	66	69	270	7,375
Janice Moodie/Steve Flesch	68	65	67	70	270	7,375
Annika Sorenstam/Scott Hoch	68	72	65	65	270	7,375
Joan Pitcock/Bill Glasson	68	67	62	73	270	7,375
Lisa Hackney/Chris DiMarco	66	69	67	69	271	6,625
Nancy Scranton/Jonathan Kaye	69	69	67	66	271	6,625
Kris Tschetter/John Cook	66	69	67	70	272	5,775
A.J. Eathorne/Rich Beem	68	67	67	70	272	5,775
Lorie Kane/Mike Weir	67	67	66	72	272	5,775
Jane Crafter/Kenny Perry	72	68	64	68	272	5,775
Michelle McGann/Greg Kraft	64	69	69	71	273	5,350
Emilee Klein/Stewart Cink	69	68	66	70	273	5,350
Rachel Hetherington/Rocco Mediate	67	71	63	73	274	5,200
Cindy Flom/Ted Tryba	67	73	66	69	275	5,000
Gloria Park/Jim Carter	67	70	70	68	275	5,000
Marisa Baena/Mark Calcavecchia	66	74	68	67	275	5,000
Leta Lindley/Tommy Tolles	67	72	67	70	276	4,825
Dale Eggeling/Carl Paulson	68	71	68	69	276	4,825
Maggie Will/Barry Cheesman	70	69	66	72	277	4,725
Jackie Gallagher-Smith/David Toms	69	69	69	70	277	4,725
Laura Philo/Gabriel Hjertstedt	72	68	65	73	278	4,650
Cindy McCurdy/Franklin Langham	70	69	70	70	279	4,600
Annette DeLuca/Jerry Kelly	68	70	70	72	280	4,550
Amy Fruhwirth/Clarence Rose	72	67	71	72	282	4,500

Office Depot Father-Son Challenge

Twin Eagles Golf & Country Club, Naples, Florida
Par 36-36–72; 7,214 yards

December 4-5
purse, $860,000

	SCORES		TOTAL	MONEY (Won by professional)
Jack/Gary Nicklaus	60	59	119	$150,000
Raymond/Robert Floyd	60	59	119	100,000
(Jack and Gary Nicklaus defeated Raymond and Robert Floyd on third extra hole.)				
Craig/Kevin Stadler	62	62	124	80,000
Tom/David Kite	62	63	125	65,000

	SCORES		TOTAL	MONEY
				(Won by professional)
Jerry/Wesley Pate	62	64	126	55,000
Bob/David Charles	64	63	127	45,000
Dave/Ron Stockton	62	65	127	45,000
Hale/Steve Irwin	59	68	127	45,000
Billy/Bobby Casper	67	61	128	37,500
Al/John Geiberger	63	65	128	37,500
David/Andrew Graham	65	64	129	35,500
Lee/Rick Trevino	63	66	129	35,500
Hubert/Myatt Green	63	67	130	34,000
Larry/Josh Nelson	65	67	132	32,500
Charles/Kyle Coody	67	65	132	32,500
Tom/Eric Weiskopf	69	64	133	30,000

Sprint Puerto Rico Golf Challenge

Wyndham El Conquistador Golf & Country Club,
Farjardo, Puerto Rico
Par 36-36–72

December 9-11
purse, $250,000

	SCORES			TOTAL	MONEY
Robin Freeman	71	64	72	207	$50,000
Bobby Wadkins	68	71	68	207	30,000
(Freeman defeated Wadkins on second extra hole.)					
Wilfredo Morales	69	68	71	208	15,000
P.H. Horgan III	70	70	69	209	12,500
Nolan Henke	67	71	72	210	9,887
Barry Cheesman	69	70	71	210	9,887
Jim McGovern	67	70	74	211	8,750
Miguel Suarez	70	71	70	211	8,750
Tom Purtzer	69	72	71	212	8,325
John Daly	70	72	71	213	8,287
Willie Wood	71	71	71	213	8,287
Brett Quigley	76	68	70	214	8,187
Damon Green	70	75	69	214	8,187
Fulton Allem	70	70	76	216	8,150
Tommy Tolles	75	68	77	220	8,125
Bill Glasson	76	72	73	221	8,100
Lon Hinkle	75	78	69	222	8,075
Bill Britton	74	72	78	224	8,050
Keith Clearwater	82	70	73	225	8,025
Rafael Castrillo	77	78	83	238	8,000

Diners Club Matches

Pelican Hill Golf Club, Corona del Mar, California
Par 35-36–71; 6,914 yards

December 11-12
purse, $1,200,000

FIRST-ROUND MATCHES

Fred Couples and Mark Calcavecchia defeated Chris Perry and Skip Kendall, 2 and 1
Steve Elkington and Jeff Maggert defeated Steve Pate and Mark Wiebe, 3 and 1

THIRD-PLACE MATCH

Perry and Kendall defeated Pate and Wiebe, 1 up, 19th hole

(Perry and Kendall received $30,000 each; Pate and Wiebe received $20,000 each.)

CHAMPIONSHIP MATCH

Couples and Calcavecchia defeated Elkington and Maggert, 1 up
(Couples and Calcavecchia received $100,000 each; Elkington and Maggert received
$50,000 each.)

Nike Tour

South Florida Classic

Palm-Aire Country Club, Pompano Beach, Florida
Par 36-36–72; 6,932 yards

January 7-10
purse, $225,000

	SCORES				TOTAL	MONEY
Curt Byrum	73	66	69	67	275	$40,500
Stan Utley	68	66	71	70	275	25,537.50
(Byrum defeated Utley on first extra hole.)						
Gibby Gilbert, Jr.	72	69	67	71	279	18,562.50
Brian Tennyson	69	72	68	71	280	14,062.50
Michael Allen	72	71	69	69	281	8,531.25
Guy Boros	74	70	71	66	281	8,531.25
Michael Clark	69	72	70	70	281	8,531.25
Brad Elder	72	70	71	68	281	8,531.25
Matt Gogel	72	70	72	67	281	8,531.25
Ed Humenik	69	73	70	69	281	8,531.25
Pat Bates	71	70	71	70	282	3,909.38
David Peoples	72	71	70	69	282	3,909.38
Jeff Gove	70	70	69	73	282	3,909.37
Gene Sauers	74	71	67	70	282	3,909.37
Shane Bertsch	70	73	73	67	283	3,031.88
Todd Demsey	73	73	69	68	283	3,031.88
Ronnie Black	72	73	71	67	283	3,031.87
Paul Claxton	70	70	72	71	283	3,031.87
Eric Brito	74	71	68	71	284	2,306.25
Joel Edwards	68	74	72	70	284	2,306.25
Patrick Frasca	71	68	74	71	284	2,306.25
Jeff Hart	68	70	74	72	284	2,306.25
Richard Johnson	75	71	69	69	284	2,306.25
Greg Lesher	73	73	71	67	284	2,306.25
Michael Muehr	69	72	72	71	284	2,306.25
Fred Wadsworth	74	68	74	68	284	2,306.25
Edward Fryatt	67	71	76	71	285	1,636.88
Glen Hnatiuk	69	67	78	71	285	1,636.88
Mike Heinen	72	71	70	72	285	1,636.87
Jerry Smith	71	72	71	71	285	1,636.87

Lakeland Classic

Grasslands Golf & Country Club, Lakeland, Florida
Par 36-36–72; 7,040 yards

January 14-17
purse, $225,000

	SCORES				TOTAL	MONEY
Ryan Howison	68	71	68	68	275	$40,500
Glen Hnatiuk	67	70	72	67	276	19,387.50
Jim McGovern	68	71	66	71	276	19,387.50
Shaun Micheel	69	70	66	71	276	19,387.50
Craig Bowden	70	73	64	70	277	11,812.50
Edward Fryatt	75	68	66	69	278	9,562.50
Mike Heinen	68	71	69	70	278	9,562.50
Todd Demsey	69	69	71	70	279	6,187.50
Steve Lamontagne	69	68	74	68	279	6,187.50
Dick Mast	72	70	69	68	279	6,187.50
Vance Veazey	68	71	68	72	279	6,187.50
Tripp Isenhour	72	69	69	70	280	3,600
Greg Lesher	72	64	71	73	280	3,600
Spike McRoy	70	68	70	72	280	3,600
David Peoples	68	72	69	71	280	3,600
Joel Edwards	70	70	66	75	281	2,655
Jerry Foltz	69	70	71	71	281	2,655
Matt Gogel	71	71	67	72	281	2,655
Bob Heintz	73	70	71	67	281	2,655
Jeff Julian	72	70	68	71	281	2,655
David Kirkpatrick	73	69	69	70	281	2,655
Wes Short	67	74	70	70	281	2,655
Richard Zokol	70	68	69	74	281	2,655
Chad Ginn	70	68	73	71	282	1,803.22
Pat Nanney, Jr.	70	71	70	71	282	1,803.22
Jeff Street	72	69	72	69	282	1,803.22
Marco Dawson	70	71	69	72	282	1,803.21
Michael Muehr	66	74	70	72	282	1,803.21
Matt Peterson	70	73	67	72	282	1,803.21
Don Walsworth	72	70	68	72	282	1,803.21

Florida Classic

Gainesville Country Club, Gainesville, Florida
Par 35-35–70; 6,842 yards

February 4-7
purse, $225,000

	SCORES				TOTAL	MONEY
Richard Johnson	68	65	68	69	270	$40,500
Bobby Wadkins	69	68	67	68	272	25,537.50
Ashley Chinner	69	67	67	70	273	16,312.50
Joel Edwards	67	65	70	71	273	16,312.50
Greg Lesher	69	68	65	72	274	10,968.75
Don Reese	69	70	70	65	274	10,968.75
Paul Claxton	70	71	65	69	275	7,875
Matt Gogel	69	70	67	69	275	7,875
Roger Rowland	66	69	74	66	275	7,875
Kris Cox	69	69	70	68	276	4,443.75
Joe Daley	67	69	69	71	276	4,443.75
Steve Ford	70	71	68	67	276	4,443.75
Joey Snyder	70	69	68	69	276	4,443.75
Brian Bateman	69	66	72	70	277	2,799
Pat Bates	69	69	68	71	277	2,799

	SCORES				TOTAL	MONEY
Brad Elder	69	72	65	71	277	2,799
Brian Fogt	67	70	71	69	277	2,799
Jim Johnson	71	67	67	72	277	2,799
Casey Martin	67	69	73	68	277	2,799
Mark Mielke	70	66	68	73	277	2,799
Darron Stiles	71	68	70	68	277	2,799
Dicky Thompson	67	71	67	72	277	2,799
Richard Zokol	69	68	69	71	277	2,799
Peter Dyson	72	67	68	71	278	2,025
Jim Estes	68	67	73	70	278	2,025
David Kirkpatrick	68	71	68	71	278	2,025
Bob Gaus	70	71	70	68	279	1,636.88
Jeff Gove	69	68	73	69	279	1,636.88
Craig Bowden	68	70	70	71	279	1,636.87
Greg Twiggs	72	69	68	70	279	1,636.87

Mississippi Gulf Coast Open

The Oaks Golf Club, Pass Christian, Mississippi — February 18-21
Par 36-36–72; 6,885 yards — purse, $250,000

	SCORES				TOTAL	MONEY
Joel Edwards	68	70	73	69	280	$45,000
John Riegger	69	75	69	68	281	28,375
Kevin Johnson	70	69	70	74	283	20,625
Joe Daley	70	73	71	71	285	11,750
Brad Elder	72	70	68	75	285	11,750
Kelly Gibson	72	71	70	72	285	11,750
Mike Heinen	70	73	72	70	285	11,750
Shane Supple	70	72	74	69	285	11,750
Mike Grob	70	75	70	71	286	6,250
Glen Hnatiuk	73	73	72	68	286	6,250
Ryan Howison	70	71	71	74	286	6,250
Craig Bowden	69	73	72	73	287	4,125
David Edwards	75	68	72	72	287	4,125
Matt Peterson	72	71	74	70	287	4,125
Jeff Gove	71	74	71	72	288	3,090.63
Steve Haskins	72	74	71	71	288	3,090.63
David Kirkpatrick	71	70	74	73	288	3,090.63
Jim McGovern	73	70	74	71	288	3,090.63
Kris Cox	67	77	69	75	288	3,090.62
Tripp Isenhour	69	70	76	73	288	3,090.62
Eric Johnson	73	70	71	74	288	3,090.62
Keith Nolan	67	76	71	74	288	3,090.62
Steve Ford	68	70	75	76	289	2,375
Greg Lesher	71	70	74	74	289	2,375
Brian Tennyson	72	72	72	73	289	2,375
Peter Dyson	70	72	79	69	290	2,000
Steve Lamontagne	74	71	70	75	290	2,000
Chris Tidland	74	70	67	79	290	2,000
Matt Gogel	71	75	73	72	291	1,650
Craig Kanada	73	72	70	76	291	1,650
Terry Mauney	72	74	71	74	291	1,650

Monterrey Open

Club Campestre, Garcia Garza, N.L., Mexico
Par 36-36–72; 7,070 yards

March 18-21
purse, $275,000

	SCORES				TOTAL	MONEY
Steve Gotsche	67	67	70	66	270	$49,500
Kelly Gibson	67	68	68	69	272	31,212.50
David Berganio, Jr.	69	71	68	65	273	18,104.17
Mathew Goggin	68	67	68	70	273	18,104.17
Todd Demsey	66	67	68	72	273	18,104.16
Ben Ferguson	70	69	67	68	274	12,375
Brad Elder	65	69	67	74	275	8,937.50
Carl Paulson	71	67	69	68	275	8,937.50
Mike Small	70	68	69	68	275	8,937.50
Jason Tyska	70	67	69	69	275	8,937.50
R.W. Eaks	64	72	67	73	276	4,620
Kevin Johnson	70	69	68	69	276	4,620
Richard Johnson	67	69	70	70	276	4,620
Chris Zambri	70	68	69	69	276	4,620
Richard Zokol	71	66	66	73	276	4,620
Greg Bruckner	67	72	67	71	277	3,245
Mike Heinen	67	69	71	70	277	3,245
J.J. Henry	72	63	70	72	277	3,245
Casey Martin	72	65	69	71	277	3,245
Fran Quinn	68	69	68	72	277	3,245
Kevin Riley	68	70	68	71	277	3,245
Oscar Serna	66	72	67	72	277	3,245
Tom Silva	69	71	69	68	277	3,245
Ron Ewing	68	69	70	71	278	2,612.50
Bill Britton	68	72	71	68	279	1,973.89
Ashley Chinner	70	68	71	70	279	1,973.89
Michael Clark	68	67	73	71	279	1,973.89
Keith Fergus	69	70	68	72	279	1,973.89
Edward Fryatt	71	68	69	71	279	1,973.89
Ryan Hietala	69	67	71	72	279	1,973.89
Randy Leen	68	71	69	71	279	1,973.89
Shaun Micheel	68	71	72	68	279	1,973.89
Jeff Julian	66	72	67	74	279	1,973.88

Louisiana Open

Le Triomphe Country Club, Broussard, Louisiana
Par 36-36–72; 6,954 yards

March 25-28
purse, $300,000

	SCORES				TOTAL	MONEY
Matt Gogel	69	71	68	69	277	$54,000
Kris Cox	69	73	68	68	278	34,050
Tim Clark	70	70	69	71	280	21,750
Richard Zokol	67	69	74	70	280	21,750
Jerry Smith	70	67	72	72	281	15,750
Gary Rusnak	66	72	72	72	282	13,500
Chad Ginn	71	68	70	74	283	11,250
Casey Martin	76	68	68	71	283	11,250
Woody Austin	72	73	69	70	284	8,250
Ashley Chinner	72	73	70	69	284	8,250
Ren Budde	74	71	69	71	285	5,400
Joel Edwards	74	69	72	70	285	5,400

	SCORES				TOTAL	MONEY
Fran Quinn	72	70	70	73	285	5,400
R.W. Eaks	70	72	70	74	286	3,732
Steve Ford	71	67	71	77	286	3,732
Donnie Hammond	69	75	69	73	286	3,732
Stan Utley	73	71	66	76	286	3,732
Glen Hnatiuk	77	67	71	71	286	3,732
Jeff Julian	72	70	72	72	286	3,732
Shaun Micheel	72	70	75	69	286	3,732
Brian Tennyson	69	73	71	73	286	3,732
Charlie Wi	72	73	70	71	286	3,732
John Wilson	73	71	71	71	286	3,732
David Berganio, Jr.	72	73	72	70	287	2,475
Richard Johnson	69	72	69	77	287	2,475
Craig Kanada	73	71	73	70	287	2,475
David Peoples	73	71	69	74	287	2,475
Oscar Serna	74	71	70	72	287	2,475
Don Walsworth	67	75	72	73	287	2,475
Joe Daley	73	70	73	72	288	1,748.58
Michael Allen	69	75	70	74	288	1,748.57
Paul Claxton	70	72	71	75	288	1,748.57
Brad Elder	73	71	72	72	288	1,748.57
J.J. Henry	68	73	73	74	288	1,748.57
Perry Moss	72	72	72	72	288	1,748.57
Dave Schreyer	72	69	74	73	288	1,748.57

Shreveport Open

Southern Trace Country Club, Shreveport, Louisiana   April 15-18
Par 36-36–72; 6,916 yards   purse, $225,000

	SCORES				TOTAL	MONEY
Bob Heintz	72	67	72	72	283	$40,500
Craig Bowden	72	72	73	67	284	22,050
Joel Edwards	72	70	75	67	284	22,050
Jay Delsing	76	65	75	69	285	10,575
Marco Gortana	70	70	77	68	285	10,575
Jim McGovern	71	70	73	71	285	10,575
Sam Randolph	75	71	69	70	285	10,575
Vance Veazey	69	71	73	72	285	10,575
Edward Fryatt	75	68	74	70	287	5,203.13
Jerry Smith	71	69	74	73	287	5,203.13
Kelly Gibson	68	75	70	74	287	5,203.12
Mark Hensby	73	71	70	73	287	5,203.12
*Trevor Immelman	74	72	71	70	287	
Ren Budde	71	69	70	78	288	3,303
Paul Claxton	70	72	73	73	288	3,303
Joe Daley	72	73	72	71	288	3,303
Kevin Johnson	71	75	71	71	288	3,303
John Riegger	74	71	73	70	288	3,303
Michael Allen	70	73	76	70	289	2,587.50
Jim Johnson	71	71	76	71	289	2,587.50
Tim Petrovic	74	68	74	73	289	2,587.50
Darron Stiles	72	74	72	71	289	2,587.50
Chris Zambri	74	71	71	73	289	2,587.50
Spike McRoy	71	72	79	68	290	2,025
Shaun Micheel	72	69	74	75	290	2,025
Anthony Painter	75	71	72	72	290	2,025

	SCORES				TOTAL	MONEY
Fran Quinn	69	75	74	72	290	2,025
Dave Schreyer	69	72	77	72	290	2,025
Jim Estes	75	70	74	72	291	1,466.25
Steve Gotsche	70	74	78	69	291	1,466.25
Steve Haskins	75	70	76	70	291	1,466.25
Mike Heinen	73	72	73	73	291	1,466.25
Dick Mast	70	73	74	74	291	1,466.25
Carl Paulson	73	73	73	72	291	1,466.25

South Carolina Classic

Country Club of South Carolina, Florence, South Carolina
Par 36-36–72; 7,150 yards

April 22-25
purse, $225,000

	SCORES				TOTAL	MONEY
Kevin Johnson	71	71	66	71	279	$40,500
Bob Heintz	70	70	68	72	280	25,537.50
Edward Fryatt	70	71	69	71	281	14,812.50
Brian Kamm	72	69	68	72	281	14,812.50
Darron Stiles	76	68	66	71	281	14,812.50
Jim Estes	71	70	70	72	283	8,437.50
Mathew Goggin	69	76	67	71	283	8,437.50
Joey Gullion	75	66	69	73	283	8,437.50
Brian Tennyson	70	70	71	72	283	8,437.50
Gibby Gilbert, Jr.	69	74	69	72	284	5,625
Todd Demsey	70	71	72	72	285	4,218.75
Matt Gogel	72	74	71	68	285	4,218.75
Jim Johnson	70	75	71	70	286	3,487.50
Anthony Painter	72	69	68	77	286	3,487.50
Carl Paulson	70	75	69	72	286	3,487.50
Steve Haskins	71	71	72	73	287	2,891.25
Jim McGovern	71	73	75	68	287	2,891.25
Oscar Serna	67	74	74	72	287	2,891.25
Fred Wadsworth	73	73	69	72	287	2,891.25
Mark Carnevale	73	70	73	72	288	2,418.75
Tripp Isenhour	74	72	66	76	288	2,418.75
Chris Tidland	68	72	73	75	288	2,418.75
Stan Utley	72	71	72	73	288	2,418.75
Tim Conley	71	74	71	73	289	1,912.50
Jerry Foltz	72	74	70	73	289	1,912.50
Steve Gotsche	70	74	72	73	289	1,912.50
Dick Mast	74	70	74	71	289	1,912.50
Shane Supple	73	73	68	75	289	1,912.50
David Berganio, Jr.	70	76	72	72	290	1,451.25
Glen Hnatiuk	71	75	71	73	290	1,451.25
Craig Merrell	74	69	74	73	290	1,451.25
Don Reese	76	68	72	74	290	1,451.25

Upstate Classic

Verdae Greens Golf Club, Greenville, South Carolina
Par 36-36–72; 6,773 yards
(Fourth round cancelled — rain.)

April 29-May 2
purse, $225,000

	SCORES			TOTAL	MONEY
Steve Gotsche	71	68	69	208	$40,500
Jeff Gove	70	70	70	210	19,387.50
Jim Johnson	71	68	71	210	19,387.50
Sam Randolph	71	69	70	210	19,387.50
Marco Dawson	71	70	70	211	10,968.75
Jim Estes	72	70	69	211	10,968.75
Brian Fogt	71	74	67	212	7,312.50
Tim Petrovic	72	72	68	212	7,312.50
Don Reese	69	73	70	212	7,312.50
Wes Tuck	76	70	66	212	7,312.50
Jerry Smith	73	69	71	213	3,909.38
Shane Supple	76	69	68	213	3,909.38
Guy Boros	75	67	71	213	3,909.37
Chris Zambri	72	68	73	213	3,909.37
Matt Gogel	74	70	70	214	2,781.57
Dennis Zinkon	77	67	70	214	2,781.57
Michael Allen	72	71	71	214	2,781.56
Mathew Goggin	71	67	76	214	2,781.56
Vance Heafner	73	72	69	214	2,781.56
Glen Hnatiuk	74	71	69	214	2,781.56
Fran Quinn	71	71	72	214	2,781.56
Gene Sauers	71	71	72	214	2,781.56
Bob Boyd	72	71	72	215	1,807.50
Jason Gore	75	68	72	215	1,807.50
Joey Gullion	70	71	74	215	1,807.50
Bob Heintz	72	71	72	215	1,807.50
Richard Johnson	71	72	72	215	1,807.50
Greg Lesher	71	68	76	215	1,807.50
Keith Nolan	72	72	71	215	1,807.50
John Rollins	76	65	74	215	1,807.50
Tom Silva	74	68	73	215	1,807.50

Carolina Classic

Raleigh Country Club, Raleigh, North Carolina
Par 36-35–71; 6,724 yards

May 6-9
purse, $225,000

	SCORES				TOTAL	MONEY
Vance Veazey	68	67	67	67	269	$40,500
Steve Haskins	67	71	65	67	270	22,050
Glen Hnatiuk	66	70	68	66	270	22,050
Jeffrey Lankford	68	65	74	64	271	12,937.50
David Peoples	72	65	68	66	271	12,937.50
Jim McGovern	68	68	70	67	273	10,125
Ren Budde	65	70	69	70	274	8,437.50
Carl Paulson	65	69	70	70	274	8,437.50
Mike Grob	71	68	71	65	275	6,187.50
Kevin Johnson	70	67	68	70	275	6,187.50
Jim Estes	70	69	69	68	276	4,218.75
Steve Gotsche	66	71	69	70	276	4,218.75
Tim Clark	69	72	71	65	277	3,391.88

	SCORES	TOTAL	MONEY
Richard Johnson	66 70 74 67	277	3,391.88
Curt Byrum	68 72 70 67	277	3,391.87
Don Reese	70 69 70 68	277	3,391.87
Bob Heintz	71 69 70 68	278	2,947.50
Todd Demsey	71 69 69 70	279	2,306.25
Marco Gortana	68 72 68 71	279	2,306.25
Ryan Hietala	70 68 72 69	279	2,306.25
Craig Matthew	71 69 72 67	279	2,306.25
Shaun Micheel	72 68 71 68	279	2,306.25
Dave Schreyer	72 68 69 70	279	2,306.25
Shane Supple	66 71 69 73	279	2,306.25
Charlie Wi	72 69 68 70	279	2,306.25
Chris Winchip	69 72 69 69	279	2,306.25
Dennis Zinkon	69 69 70 71	279	2,306.25
Rich Barcelo	69 67 70 74	280	1,498.50
Guy Boros	68 72 72 68	280	1,498.50
Jeff Julian	73 68 68 71	280	1,498.50
Michael Muehr	68 72 72 68	280	1,498.50
Gene Sauers	70 70 70 70	280	1,498.50

Dominion Open

The Dominion Club, Richmond, Virginia
Par 36-36–72; 7,020 yards

May 13-16
purse, $250,000

	SCORES	TOTAL	MONEY
Darron Stiles	67 71 74 67	279	$45,000
Mathew Goggin	66 76 68 70	280	24,500
Dick Mast	70 70 68 72	280	24,500
Greg Lesher	72 69 72 68	281	12,500
Jim McGovern	72 70 72 67	281	12,500
Brian Tennyson	64 72 73 72	281	12,500
Steven Young	66 73 72 70	281	12,500
J.J. Henry	71 66 75 70	282	8,125
Chris Zambri	69 74 71 68	282	8,125
Tim Clark	67 72 69 75	283	5,625
Chad Ginn	71 73 69 70	283	5,625
Marco Dawson	68 73 72 71	284	3,787.50
Edward Fryatt	72 70 72 70	284	3,787.50
Marco Gortana	71 72 71 70	284	3,787.50
Shaun Micheel	68 72 73 71	284	3,787.50
Pat Nanney, Jr.	71 73 71 69	284	3,787.50
Greg Twiggs	71 70 72 71	284	3,787.50
Rich Barcelo	70 73 71 71	285	2,500
Brian Bateman	69 74 70 72	285	2,500
Craig Bowden	71 71 72 71	285	2,500
Ben Ferguson	70 73 73 69	285	2,500
Kelly Gibson	71 71 75 68	285	2,500
Glen Hnatiuk	69 71 70 75	285	2,500
Richard Johnson	71 70 74 70	285	2,500
Brian Kamm	71 71 70 73	285	2,500
Steve Lamontagne	69 73 71 72	285	2,500
Brett Quigley	69 71 74 71	285	2,500
Richard Zokol	71 72 70 72	285	2,500
Robin Freeman	69 73 76 68	286	1,413.64
Joey Gullion	70 72 74 70	286	1,413.64
Tripp Isenhour	71 72 71 72	286	1,413.64

	SCORES				TOTAL	MONEY
Carl Paulson	70	72	72	72	286	1,413.64
Matt Peterson	69	73	72	72	286	1,413.64
Fran Quinn	70	73	71	72	286	1,413.64
Vance Veazey	69	72	75	70	286	1,413.64
Curt Byrum	71	73	70	72	286	1,413.63
Gary Christian	69	70	72	75	286	1,413.63
David Peoples	71	71	69	75	286	1,413.63
Jason Tyska	69	69	75	73	286	1,413.63

Knoxville Open

Three Ridges Golf Club, Knoxville, Tennessee
Par 36-36–72; 7,142 yards

May 20-23
purse, $250,000

	SCORES				TOTAL	MONEY
Jeff Gove	69	69	68	71	277	$45,000
Marco Dawson	70	71	69	68	278	21,541.67
Carl Paulson	72	71	70	65	278	21,541.67
Glen Hnatiuk	71	66	70	71	278	21,541.66
Jason Tyska	70	71	72	66	279	11,458.34
Guy Boros	68	70	69	72	279	11,458.33
Patrick Lee	70	69	70	70	279	11,458.33
Kris Cox	72	71	68	69	280	8,125
Craig Kanada	68	75	69	68	280	8,125
Jim Estes	70	68	71	72	281	5,625
Richard Zokol	69	73	69	70	281	5,625
Paul Claxton	71	72	69	70	282	3,606.25
Mike Heinen	66	75	70	71	282	3,606.25
Casey Martin	71	70	70	71	282	3,606.25
Pat Nanney, Jr.	67	73	69	73	282	3,606.25
Matt Peterson	70	71	72	69	282	3,606.25
Andrew Price	70	70	71	71	282	3,606.25
Don Reese	71	70	70	71	282	3,606.25
Dennis Zinkon	70	69	69	74	282	3,606.25
David Berganio, Jr.	69	73	69	72	283	2,500
Craig Bowden	73	71	70	69	283	2,500
Michael Clark	73	70	70	70	283	2,500
Steve Ford	72	68	71	72	283	2,500
Mike Grob	71	71	71	70	283	2,500
Steve Lamontagne	70	74	70	69	283	2,500
Brian Tennyson	69	72	73	69	283	2,500
Ryan Howison	70	72	72	70	284	1,682.15
David Peoples	69	75	71	69	284	1,682.15
Joe Daley	70	69	70	75	284	1,682.14
Todd Demsey	72	70	69	73	284	1,682.14
Jay Hobby	69	75	70	70	284	1,682.14
John Riegger	70	71	67	76	284	1,682.14
Chris Starkjohann	72	71	71	70	284	1,682.14

Cleveland Open

Quail Hollow Resort, Devlin Course, Concord, Ohio
Par 36-36–72; 6,712 yards

June 10-13
purse, $225,000

	SCORES				TOTAL	MONEY
Matt Gogel	68	69	68	68	273	$40,500
Casey Martin	73	63	67	70	273	25,537.50
(Gogel defeated Martin on second playoff hole.)						
Jerry Smith	69	71	69	66	275	18,562.50
Carl Paulson	69	68	68	71	276	14,062.50
Paul Claxton	72	65	67	74	278	11,812.50
Steve Haskins	74	66	68	72	280	9,562.50
Kevin Johnson	68	72	68	72	280	9,562.50
Edward Fryatt	73	69	68	71	281	7,312.50
Jim Johnson	69	65	73	74	281	7,312.50
David Berganio, Jr.	75	69	70	68	282	4,252.50
Jason Gore	69	71	70	72	282	4,252.50
Rob Moss	70	70	70	72	282	4,252.50
Chris Zambri	73	68	71	70	282	4,252.50
Dennis Zinkon	69	75	71	67	282	4,252.50
Jim Estes	73	68	69	73	283	3,105
Gary Nicklaus	71	71	69	72	283	3,105
Gary Rusnak	69	73	69	72	283	3,105
Gary Christian	69	69	73	73	284	2,475
Tim Conley	70	69	72	73	284	2,475
Marco Dawson	68	75	67	74	284	2,475
Joel Edwards	72	71	68	73	284	2,475
Robert Gamez	74	70	73	67	284	2,475
Sam Randolph	72	70	70	72	284	2,475
Steve Woods	66	77	71	70	284	2,475
Roy Biancalana	69	75	67	74	285	1,747.50
Jeff Gove	70	70	73	72	285	1,747.50
Craig Kanada	68	72	70	75	285	1,747.50
Fran Quinn	71	72	69	73	285	1,747.50
Shane Supple	72	70	67	76	285	1,747.50
Mark Wurtz	71	68	70	76	285	1,747.50

Dayton Open

Golf Club at Yankee Trace, Centerville, Ohio
Par 36-36–72; 6,904 yards

June 17-20
purse, $250,000

	SCORES				TOTAL	MONEY
John Wilson	68	66	66	68	268	$45,000
Brian Tennyson	66	70	68	65	269	28,375
Marco Dawson	68	68	66	69	271	20,625
Mike Grob	70	67	67	69	273	14,375
Craig Spence	68	67	71	67	273	14,375
Steve Ford	71	67	64	72	274	11,250
Michael Clark	72	70	62	71	275	8,125
Mathew Goggin	72	69	65	69	275	8,125
Craig Kanada	72	70	65	68	275	8,125
Rob Moss	66	68	68	73	275	8,125
Brad Elder	69	71	65	71	276	4,500
Ryan Howison	71	70	68	67	276	4,500
Mark Wurtz	67	71	69	69	276	4,500
Jim Estes	70	69	68	70	277	3,875

	SCORES				TOTAL	MONEY
David Peoples	67	70	69	72	278	3,537.50
Conrad Ray	70	68	70	70	278	3,537.50
Jim Johnson	70	72	68	69	279	3,068.75
Matt Peterson	70	72	72	65	279	3,068.75
Mike Standly	73	69	69	68	279	3,068.75
Bo Van Pelt	69	70	68	72	279	3,068.75
Bill Britton	74	67	71	68	280	2,687.50
Gene Sauers	73	67	71	69	280	2,687.50
Brian Fogt	73	68	68	72	281	2,250
Jeff Gove	67	73	70	71	281	2,250
J.J. Henry	72	70	67	72	281	2,250
Jay Hobby	72	70	68	71	281	2,250
Chris Starkjohann	68	73	70	70	281	2,250
Shane Bertsch	70	69	68	75	282	1,665
Christian Chernock	71	70	69	72	282	1,665
Dick Mast	66	72	69	75	282	1,665
Gary Rusnak	70	70	69	73	282	1,665
Karl Zoller	70	72	70	70	282	1,665

Lehigh Valley Open

Center Valley Club, Center Valley, Pennsylvania　　　　　June 24-27
Par 36-36–72; 6,904 yards　　　　　　　　　　　　　　purse, $225,000

	SCORES				TOTAL	MONEY
Mathew Goggin	67	65	66	72	270	$40,500
Matt Gogel	67	68	69	68	272	25,537.50
Mark Hensby	67	72	63	71	273	18,562.50
Marco Dawson	69	64	68	73	274	11,250
Fran Quinn	67	68	68	71	274	11,250
Jerry Smith	69	69	67	69	274	11,250
Dennis Zinkon	67	67	68	72	274	11,250
Edward Fryatt	69	70	68	68	275	7,312.50
Craig Kanada	70	67	66	72	275	7,312.50
Kris Cox	67	69	67	73	276	4,687.50
Todd Demsey	70	68	69	69	276	4,687.50
Brian Fogt	69	68	72	67	276	4,687.50
Spike McRoy	69	68	67	73	277	3,600
Don Walsworth	70	69	69	69	277	3,600
Christian Chernock	71	70	70	67	278	3,031.88
Keith Nolan	73	68	71	66	278	3,031.88
Ashley Chinner	65	69	70	74	278	3,031.87
David Edwards	69	70	69	70	278	3,031.87
Brad Elder	67	71	70	71	279	2,475
Kelly Gibson	68	70	69	72	279	2,475
David Peoples	69	70	69	71	279	2,475
Larry Silveira	71	70	71	67	279	2,475
Richard Zokol	69	71	70	69	279	2,475
Brian Claar	71	70	67	72	280	1,856.25
Ben Ferguson	66	74	69	71	280	1,856.25
Jim Johnson	72	70	68	70	280	1,856.25
Ted Oh	69	70	70	71	280	1,856.25
Carl Paulson	70	69	71	70	280	1,856.25
Craig Spence	67	73	68	72	280	1,856.25
Mike Grob	73	66	70	72	281	1,383.75
Kevin Johnson	67	70	71	73	281	1,383.75
Steve Pope	68	73	67	73	281	1,383.75
Rocky Walcher	67	71	71	72	281	1,383.75

Hershey Open

Country Club of Hershey, East Course,
Hershey, Pennsylvania
Par 36-35–71; 7,061 yards

July 1-4
purse, $225,000

	SCORES				TOTAL	MONEY
Edward Fryatt	69	67	69	70	275	$40,500
Brett Wayment	72	66	67	73	278	25,537.50
John Rollins	73	70	69	67	279	18,562.50
Michael Clark	70	70	69	71	280	11,250
Marco Dawson	66	73	73	68	280	11,250
John Wilson	73	68	71	68	280	11,250
Dennis Zinkon	67	71	70	72	280	11,250
Robin Freeman	69	69	73	70	281	7,875
Ken Green	72	71	68	71	282	6,750
Steve Ford	72	69	69	73	283	4,687.50
Dicky Thompson	69	70	72	72	283	4,687.50
Jason Tyska	71	72	72	68	283	4,687.50
Shane Bertsch	71	72	70	71	284	3,391.88
Matt Gogel	71	74	73	66	284	3,391.88
Paul Claxton	73	68	68	75	284	3,391.87
Marco Gortana	72	70	68	74	284	3,391.87
Jim McGovern	72	68	72	73	285	2,761.88
Mark Wurtz	71	71	72	71	285	2,761.88
Joel Edwards	69	70	70	76	285	2,761.87
Shane Supple	67	73	70	75	285	2,761.87
Brad Elder	73	65	75	73	286	2,306.25
Greg Lesher	71	70	71	74	286	2,306.25
Gary Nicklaus	72	64	73	77	286	2,306.25
Fred Wadsworth	73	72	69	72	286	2,306.25
Tim Conley	72	69	73	73	287	1,653.75
Joe Daley	72	70	71	74	287	1,653.75
Mathew Goggin	71	71	70	75	287	1,653.75
Mike Grob	69	70	71	77	287	1,653.75
Richard Johnson	74	69	73	71	287	1,653.75
Craig Kanada	71	71	74	71	287	1,653.75
Spike McRoy	69	72	71	75	287	1,653.75
Jerry Smith	69	74	69	75	287	1,653.75

Greensboro Open

Sedgefield Country Club, Greensboro, North Carolina
Par 35-35–70; 6,737 yards

July 8-11
purse, $225,000

	SCORES				TOTAL	MONEY
Shaun Micheel	67	66	67	69	269	$40,500
Garrett Willis	65	64	70	71	270	25,537.50
Mike Small	71	65	66	69	271	18,562.50
J.J. Henry	69	65	69	69	272	10,575
Jay Hobby	67	69	69	67	272	10,575
Kevin Johnson	68	68	65	71	272	10,575
Richard Johnson	70	68	66	68	272	10,575
Brian Tennyson	70	67	64	71	272	10,575
Steve Haskins	66	67	72	69	274	5,203.13
Carl Paulson	70	67	68	69	274	5,203.13
Ted Oh	66	70	68	70	274	5,203.12
Dicky Thompson	68	69	64	73	274	5,203.12

	SCORES				TOTAL	MONEY
Jeffrey Lankford	66	70	68	71	275	3,600
Greg Lesher	66	70	67	72	275	3,600
Michael Clark	68	69	70	69	276	2,965.50
Joe Daley	68	69	71	68	276	2,965.50
Joel Edwards	67	70	67	72	276	2,965.50
Steve Ford	65	69	71	71	276	2,965.50
Joey Gullion	67	70	73	66	276	2,965.50
Christian Chernock	67	72	68	70	277	2,250
Edward Fryatt	64	69	71	73	277	2,250
Gibby Gilbert, Jr.	70	68	67	72	277	2,250
Bob Heintz	67	71	70	69	277	2,250
Sam Randolph	69	66	69	73	277	2,250
Hugh Royer III	66	72	74	65	277	2,250
Stan Utley	69	70	68	70	277	2,250
Craig Bowden	70	64	75	69	278	1,548.75
Greg Bruckner	67	70	70	71	278	1,548.75
Mathew Goggin	68	69	72	69	278	1,548.75
Pat Nanney, Jr.	69	66	73	70	278	1,548.75
Dick Mast	68	69	69	72	278	1,548.75
Darron Stiles	69	70	72	67	278	1,548.75

Wichita Open

Willowbend Country Club, Wichita, Kansas
Par 36-36–72; 7,000 yards

July 22-25
purse, $225,000

	SCORES				TOTAL	MONEY
Brad Elder	66	65	66	71	268	$40,500
Mark Wurtz	67	66	68	69	270	25,537.50
Mike Grob	66	64	73	68	271	14,812.50
Gary Nicklaus	67	68	68	68	271	14,812.50
Garrett Willis	67	68	67	69	271	14,812.50
Craig Kanada	67	69	69	67	272	10,125
Edward Fryatt	66	70	68	69	273	9,000
Ahmad Bateman	73	67	70	64	274	6,187.50
Michael Clark	67	68	68	71	274	6,187.50
Matt Gogel	68	70	69	67	274	6,187.50
Kevin Johnson	71	67	64	72	274	6,187.50
Robin Byrd	68	69	67	71	275	3,712.50
Kevin Dillen	68	68	69	70	275	3,712.50
Jim McGovern	69	65	70	71	275	3,712.50
Brian Bateman	72	66	67	71	276	2,841.43
Todd Demsey	70	69	67	70	276	2,841.43
Shaun Micheel	67	71	70	68	276	2,841.43
Carl Paulson	67	68	74	67	276	2,841.43
Tim Petrovic	68	70	67	71	276	2,841.43
John Riegger	69	68	68	71	276	2,841.43
Michael Muehr	65	70	68	73	276	2,841.42
Greg Bruckner	69	71	67	70	277	2,193.75
Mathew Goggin	70	69	71	67	277	2,193.75
Steve Gotsche	72	67	66	72	277	2,193.75
Chad Magee	71	64	71	71	277	2,193.75
Joel Edwards	66	71	71	70	278	1,642.50
J.J. Henry	67	70	70	71	278	1,642.50
Mike Meehan	67	73	70	68	278	1,642.50
Keith Nolan	72	68	65	73	278	1,642.50
Bobby Wadkins	70	70	68	70	278	1,642.50
Gary Webb	68	69	71	70	278	1,642.50

Dakota Dunes Open

Dakota Dunes Country Club, Dakota Dunes, South Dakota
Par 36-36–72; 7,165 yards

July 29-August 1
purse, $350,000

	SCORES				TOTAL	MONEY
Fran Quinn	65	69	68	68	270	$63,000
Ryan Howison	67	65	65	73	270	34,300
Craig Kanada	66	67	67	70	270	34,300
(Quinn defeated Howison and Kanada on first extra hole.)						
Rich Barcelo	71	68	67	66	272	20,125
Shaun Micheel	69	66	72	65	272	20,125
Tim Clark	67	68	68	70	273	14,000
Tripp Isenhour	69	68	69	67	273	14,000
Casey Martin	70	67	67	69	273	14,000
Michael Clark	67	68	66	73	274	8,750
Dicky Thompson	68	67	69	70	274	8,750
Bobby Wadkins	65	68	67	74	274	8,750
Craig Bowden	70	65	71	69	275	5,446
Brian Claar	69	63	70	73	275	5,446
Eric Johnson	72	66	68	69	275	5,446
Carl Paulson	67	65	71	72	275	5,446
Vance Veazey	69	66	67	73	275	5,446
Ted Oh	70	67	68	71	276	4,207
Tim Petrovic	63	72	70	71	276	4,207
Don Reese	66	73	67	70	276	4,207
Darron Stiles	70	66	71	69	276	4,207
Mark Wurtz	70	67	68	71	276	4,207
Marco Dawson	67	69	69	72	277	3,237.50
Joel Edwards	68	70	68	71	277	3,237.50
Chad Ginn	73	67	66	71	277	3,237.50
Michael Muehr	69	69	68	71	277	3,237.50
Garrett Willis	71	67	69	70	277	3,237.50
Dennis Zinkon	65	71	69	72	277	3,237.50
Mike Grob	69	70	68	71	278	2,280.84
Brian Tennyson	67	69	71	71	278	2,280.84
Edward Fryatt	72	67	70	69	278	2,280.83
Mathew Goggin	71	69	71	67	278	2,280.83
Paul Gow	65	73	71	69	278	2,280.83
Keith Nolan	68	70	69	71	278	2,280.83

Omaha Classic

The Champions Club, Omaha, Nebraska
Par 36-36–72; 7,034 yards

August 5-8
purse, $300,000

	SCORES				TOTAL	MONEY
Mathew Goggin	66	67	66	65	264	$54,000
Casey Martin	66	71	66	65	268	34,050
Marco Dawson	70	68	66	65	269	24,750
Michael Clark	65	68	69	69	271	16,000
Joey Gullion	66	67	70	68	271	16,000
Craig Kanada	64	67	72	68	271	16,000
Joe Daley	65	72	67	68	272	9,750
Glen Hnatiuk	65	71	68	68	272	9,750
Craig Matthew	70	69	64	69	272	9,750
Gary Nicklaus	65	70	67	70	272	9,750
Todd Demsey	68	68	67	70	273	5,040

	SCORES				TOTAL	MONEY
Bob Heintz	67	66	66	74	273	5,040
Tripp Isenhour	66	70	69	68	273	5,040
Don Reese	67	68	67	71	273	5,040
Joey Snyder III	66	67	72	68	273	5,040
Christian Chernock	68	67	69	70	274	3,774
Jeff Gove	69	70	68	67	274	3,774
Mark Hensby	70	65	67	72	274	3,774
Ted Oh	66	69	71	68	274	3,774
Carl Paulson	70	67	71	66	274	3,774
Mike Grob	69	70	72	64	275	3,075
Craig Perks	67	71	71	66	275	3,075
John Riegger	70	65	69	71	275	3,075
Brian Tennyson	67	68	71	69	275	3,075
Edward Fryatt	70	66	72	68	276	2,475
Dave Schreyer	72	67	72	65	276	2,475
Chris Tidland	68	69	72	67	276	2,475
Vance Veazey	67	67	70	72	276	2,475
Steve Ford	68	72	67	70	277	1,935
Ryan Howison	67	71	68	71	277	1,935
Matt Peterson	69	71	72	65	277	1,935
Stan Utley	68	69	70	70	277	1,935

Ozarks Open

Highland Springs Country Club, Springfield, Missouri
Par 36-36–72; 7,058 yards

August 12-15
purse, $250,000

	SCORES				TOTAL	MONEY
Ryan Howison	67	68	69	66	270	$45,000
Edward Fryatt	66	63	73	68	270	28,375
(Howison defeated Fryatt on first extra hole.)						
Gibby Gilbert, Jr.	69	66	73	64	272	18,125
Spike McRoy	68	70	65	69	272	18,125
Mathew Goggin	68	71	67	69	275	13,125
Todd Demsey	71	70	67	68	276	10,000
Mike Small	71	65	72	68	276	10,000
Darron Stiles	74	67	69	66	276	10,000
Christian Chernock	71	69	70	67	277	5,450
Marco Dawson	71	68	72	66	277	5,450
Mike Heinen	68	69	70	70	277	5,450
John Kernohan	69	70	68	70	277	5,450
Michael Muehr	71	68	70	68	277	5,450
David Berganio, Jr.	69	71	65	73	278	3,177.78
Gary Christian	74	65	72	67	278	3,177.78
Joel Edwards	67	69	71	71	278	3,177.78
Mike Grob	73	68	72	65	278	3,177.78
Bob Heintz	70	69	70	69	278	3,177.78
Matt Peterson	71	69	69	69	278	3,177.78
Mike Sullivan	69	69	70	70	278	3,177.78
Steve Haskins	69	66	69	74	278	3,177.77
Jay Hobby	65	72	68	73	278	3,177.77
Brian Fogt	72	70	69	68	279	2,250
J.J. Henry	74	68	65	72	279	2,250
Jeff Julian	68	66	73	72	279	2,250
Shane Supple	66	72	71	70	279	2,250
Mark Wurtz	68	71	67	73	279	2,250
Brad Elder	69	71	68	72	280	1,706.25

	SCORES				TOTAL	MONEY
Ben Ferguson	72	67	73	68	280	1,706.25
Marco Gortana	70	70	69	71	280	1,706.25
Steve Gotsche	69	68	70	73	280	1,706.25

Fort Smith Classic

Hardscrabble Country Club, Fort Smith, Arkansas
Par 35-35–70; 6,620 yards

August 19-22
purse, $250,000

	SCORES				TOTAL	MONEY
Gary Webb	65	66	65	68	264	$45,000
Matt Peterson	65	71	64	65	265	28,375
Patrick Lee	66	68	63	70	267	15,156.25
Shaun Micheel	69	69	63	66	267	15,156.25
Carl Paulson	67	68	63	69	267	15,156.25
Dave Schreyer	69	67	67	74	267	15,156.25
Joey Gullion	65	65	70	68	268	9,375
Fran Quinn	67	66	66	69	268	9,375
Brad Elder	70	67	66	67	270	7,500
Glen Hnatiuk	70	69	66	66	271	5,208.34
Chris Starkjohann	66	69	66	70	271	5,208.33
Chris Zambri	66	71	63	71	271	5,208.33
Todd Demsey	67	67	71	67	272	3,670
Jeff Gove	70	67	67	68	272	3,670
Mike Grob	67	69	71	65	272	3,670
Mark Hensby	67	65	72	68	272	3,670
Dicky Thompson	70	67	66	69	272	3,670
Jay Hobby	69	64	70	70	273	3,062.50
Anthony Painter	69	67	68	69	273	3,062.50
Gary Christian	64	71	69	70	274	2,750
Gary Nicklaus	70	67	68	69	274	2,750
Stan Utley	73	66	67	68	274	2,750
Brian Fogt	68	70	64	73	275	2,312.50
Marco Gortana	70	68	68	69	275	2,312.50
Ryan Howison	70	70	69	66	275	2,312.50
Grant Masson	72	66	68	69	275	2,312.50
Casey Brown	69	69	70	68	276	1,818.75
Joe Daley	70	70	71	65	276	1,818.75
Kelly Gibson	73	67	67	69	276	1,818.75
J.J. Henry	71	68	69	68	276	1,818.75

Permian Basin Open

The Club at Mission Dorado, Odessa, Texas
Par 36-36–72; 7,034 yards

August 26-29
purse, $225,000

	SCORES				TOTAL	MONEY
David Berganio, Jr.	64	67	68	70	269	$40,500
Paul Gow	68	69	65	69	271	22,050
Dicky Thompson	62	68	68	73	271	22,050
Ryan Hietala	67	70	69	68	274	14,062.50
Joel Edwards	65	70	70	70	275	10,968.75
Ben Ferguson	65	71	71	68	275	10,968.75
Steve Ford	68	70	67	71	276	6,750
Bob Gaus	72	67	68	69	276	6,750

	SCORES	TOTAL	MONEY
Craig Matthew	69 71 66 70	276	6,750
Mike Meehan	70 68 71 67	276	6,750
Chris Zambri	68 69 70 69	276	6,750
Mark Hensby	66 70 71 70	277	3,712.50
Mike Sullivan	72 68 69 68	277	3,712.50
Dean Wilson	69 70 70 68	277	3,712.50
Rich Barcelo	70 71 65 72	278	2,841.43
Ron Ewing	68 72 71 67	278	2,841.43
Edward Fryatt	68 70 69 71	278	2,841.43
Keith Nolan	68 71 67 72	278	2,841.43
Tim Petrovic	68 69 71 70	278	2,841.43
Vance Veazey	69 72 70 67	278	2,841.43
Tim Conley	66 70 67 75	278	2,841.42
Paul Claxton	68 67 69 75	279	2,081.25
Kris Cox	69 71 71 68	279	2,081.25
Marco Gortana	67 68 73 71	279	2,081.25
J.J. Henry	70 66 72 71	279	2,081.25
Ryan Howison	72 67 72 68	279	2,081.25
John Rollins	66 68 72 73	279	2,081.25
Roy Biancalana	67 73 71 69	280	1,436.79
Greg Bruckner	67 68 75 70	280	1,436.79
Jim McGovern	64 75 73 68	280	1,436.79
Jason Schultz	71 69 72 68	280	1,436.79
Ronnie Black	70 69 70 71	280	1,436.78
Brian Claar	67 67 72 74	280	1,436.78
Mike Small	65 73 71 71	280	1,436.78

Utah Classic

Willow Creek Country Club, Sandy, Utah
Par 36-36–72; 7,124 yards

September 2-5
purse, $375,000

	SCORES	TOTAL	MONEY
Carl Paulson	68 64 65 69	266	$67,500
Craig Bowden	68 67 69 68	272	36,750
Marco Gortana	66 69 67 70	272	36,750
Edward Fryatt	72 64 68 69	273	21,562.50
Shaun Micheel	69 66 69 69	273	21,562.50
Marco Dawson	69 67 67 71	274	13,125
Todd Demsey	68 67 70 69	274	13,125
Tripp Isenhour	71 68 69 66	274	13,125
Michael Muehr	70 66 70 68	274	13,125
Jason Tyska	69 70 68 67	274	13,125
Robin Byrd	73 64 67 71	275	6,515.63
Dean Wilson	68 71 66 70	275	6,515.63
Tom Kalinowski	67 68 70 70	275	6,515.62
Dave Schreyer	70 67 69 69	275	6,515.62
Tim Conley	70 68 68 70	276	4,837.50
Joel Edwards	67 69 71 69	276	4,837.50
Steve Ford	67 72 66 71	276	4,837.50
Matt Gogel	71 66 70 69	276	4,837.50
Glen Hnatiuk	68 72 68 68	276	4,837.50
Steve Schneiter	68 69 67 72	276	4,837.50
Kevin Dillen	66 70 69 72	277	3,843.75
Mike Heinen	69 72 68 68	277	3,843.75
Sam Randolph	69 69 68 71	277	3,843.75
Don Walsworth	71 68 68 70	277	3,843.75

	SCORES				TOTAL	MONEY
Don Reese	67	71	69	71	278	2,828.58
Rich Barcelo	71	70	67	70	278	2,828.57
Mark Hensby	71	70	66	71	278	2,828.57
Kevin Johnson	69	69	69	71	278	2,828.57
Tim Petrovic	74	66	69	69	278	2,828.57
John Riegger	69	69	71	69	278	2,828.57
Darron Stiles	72	69	68	69	278	2,828.57

Tri-Cities Open

Meadow Springs Country Club, Richland, Washington
Par 36-36–72; 6,926 yards

September 9-12
purse, $225,000

	SCORES				TOTAL	MONEY
Glen Hnatiuk	68	72	69	69	278	$40,500
J.J. Henry	71	73	66	69	279	22,050
Larry Silveira	72	70	69	68	279	22,050
Jim McGovern	69	67	72	72	280	12,937.50
Tim Petrovic	70	73	67	70	280	12,937.50
Kelly Gibson	70	69	69	73	281	9,000
Steve Haskins	71	71	68	71	281	9,000
Shane Supple	66	71	74	70	281	9,000
Michael Combs	70	69	75	68	282	5,203.13
Jim Johnson	69	69	73	71	282	5,203.13
Ren Budde	71	67	72	72	282	5,203.12
Casey Martin	66	72	71	73	282	5,203.12
Shane Bertsch	70	70	72	71	283	3,600
Robin Byrd	71	70	71	71	283	3,600
Mike Grob	72	71	69	72	284	3,031.88
Brian Kamm	73	69	73	69	284	3,031.88
Jerry Foltz	67	71	72	74	284	3,031.87
Don Reese	69	69	73	73	284	3,031.87
Justin Bolli	69	75	68	73	285	2,475
Michael Clark	73	70	70	72	285	2,475
Bob Heintz	77	67	69	72	285	2,475
Craig Perks	72	71	70	72	285	2,475
Matt Peterson	69	71	74	71	285	2,475
Kevin Burton	72	72	72	70	286	1,912.50
Todd Demsey	69	73	72	72	286	1,912.50
John Kernohan	69	72	72	73	286	1,912.50
Garrett Willis	69	71	68	78	286	1,912.50
Steve Woods	68	72	75	71	286	1,912.50
Mike Barnett	68	71	72	76	287	1,395
Tim Conley	73	68	70	76	287	1,395
Joe Daley	72	71	73	71	287	1,395
Matt Gogel	70	73	72	72	287	1,395
Jeff Gove	71	72	72	72	287	1,395
Tripp Isenhour	68	71	72	76	287	1,395

Boise Open

Hillcrest Country Club, Boise, Idaho
Par 36-35–71; 6,698 yards

September 16-19
purse, $325,000

	SCORES				TOTAL	MONEY
Carl Paulson	69	66	65	66	266	$58,500
Joel Edwards	67	69	62	72	270	31,850
Michael Muehr	68	67	68	67	270	31,850
Anthony Painter	67	69	70	65	271	17,333.34
Paul Claxton	68	69	68	66	271	17,333.33
Glen Hnatiuk	65	69	67	70	271	17,333.33
Kelly Gibson	69	68	68	67	272	13,000
Marco Dawson	65	68	71	69	273	8,937.50
Jeff Gove	67	69	68	69	273	8,937.50
Keith Nolan	67	70	67	69	273	8,937.50
Dicky Thompson	69	66	64	74	273	8,937.50
Craig Kanada	68	68	68	70	274	4,688.13
Shaun Micheel	70	69	67	68	274	4,688.13
John Rollins	67	69	71	67	274	4,688.13
Jerry Smith	68	71	66	69	274	4,688.13
Curt Byrum	68	65	68	73	274	4,688.12
Paul Gow	65	66	72	71	274	4,688.12
Craig Perks	70	66	68	70	274	4,688.12
Garrett Willis	66	72	64	72	274	4,688.12
Rich Barcelo	68	69	67	71	275	3,575
Edward Fryatt	70	66	67	72	275	3,575
Sam Randolph	67	69	71	68	275	3,575
Matt Peterson	72	65	71	68	276	3,168.75
Dave Schreyer	68	69	71	68	276	3,168.75
Steve Ford	70	67	67	73	277	2,600
Kevin Johnson	68	70	68	71	277	2,600
Brian Kamm	70	67	72	68	277	2,600
Stiles Mitchell	69	69	67	72	277	2,600
Stan Utley	70	66	70	71	277	2,600
Michael Clark	66	72	69	71	278	1,894.29
J.J. Henry	66	73	68	71	278	1,894.29
Richard Johnson	71	68	70	69	278	1,894.29
John Riegger	68	67	72	71	278	1,894.29
David Berganio, Jr.	70	69	67	72	278	1,894.28
Steve Schneiter	65	72	69	72	278	1,894.28
Rocky Walcher	70	68	66	74	278	1,894.28

Oregon Classic

Shadow Hills Country Club, Junction City, Oregon
Par 36-36–72; 7,007 yards

September 23-26
purse, $225,000

	SCORES				TOTAL	MONEY
Kelly Gibson	65	68	71	75	279	$40,500
Craig Perks	68	71	67	74	280	25,537.50
Jim Johnson	70	65	73	73	281	18,562.50
Bob Heintz	72	68	73	69	282	14,062.50
Marco Dawson	70	69	71	73	283	10,312.50
Keith Nolan	73	70	71	69	283	10,312.50
Richard Zokol	74	70	70	69	283	10,312.50
Glen Hnatiuk	71	69	69	75	284	7,312.50
Steve Lamontagne	73	71	70	70	284	7,312.50

	SCORES				TOTAL	MONEY
Paul Claxton	70	72	73	70	285	3,947.15
Ryan Hietala	72	71	74	68	285	3,947.15
Tim Conley	73	72	67	73	285	3,947.14
Joel Edwards	72	73	69	71	285	3,947.14
Ron Ewing	69	71	72	73	285	3,947.14
Jim McGovern	68	74	71	72	285	3,947.14
Don Reese	75	67	68	75	285	3,947.14
Gibby Gilbert, Jr.	72	72	72	70	286	2,761.88
Eric Johnson	70	75	69	72	286	2,761.88
Mathew Goggin	70	69	74	73	286	2,761.87
Dennis Zinkon	69	74	70	73	286	2,761.87
Kevin Johnson	70	71	70	76	287	2,250
Mike Meehan	72	72	71	72	287	2,250
Bill Porter	69	76	70	72	287	2,250
John Riegger	71	73	70	73	287	2,250
Vance Veazey	70	71	72	74	287	2,250
Shane Bertsch	70	70	73	75	288	1,692
Curt Byrum	72	70	73	73	288	1,692
Brian Fogt	71	73	75	69	288	1,692
Jason Tyska	73	72	72	71	288	1,692
Mark Wurtz	69	73	71	75	288	1,692

Inland Empire Open

Moreno Valley Ranch Golf Club,
Moreno Valley, California
Par 36-36–72; 6,880 yards

September 30-October 3
purse, $225,000

	SCORES				TOTAL	MONEY
Brad Elder	70	64	67	66	267	$40,500
Dick Mast	68	67	65	70	270	25,537.50
Todd Demsey	66	69	67	69	271	16,312.50
Patrick Lee	67	64	66	74	271	16,312.50
Michael Clark	67	65	73	67	272	10,968.75
Craig Perks	64	72	67	69	272	10,968.75
Joel Edwards	69	65	68	71	273	7,312.50
Chad Ginn	68	68	69	68	273	7,312.50
Michael Muehr	67	71	66	69	273	7,312.50
Matt Peterson	70	67	65	71	273	7,312.50
R.W. Eaks	68	71	66	69	274	4,218.75
Joey Snyder III	70	71	68	65	274	4,218.75
Gary Christian	70	68	68	69	275	3,391.88
Marco Dawson	66	71	71	67	275	3,391.88
Stan Utley	66	66	74	69	275	3,391.87
Chris Zambri	70	67	67	71	275	3,391.87
Kelly Gibson	68	72	69	67	276	2,590.72
Bob Heintz	68	70	67	71	276	2,590.72
Sam Randolph	64	73	68	71	276	2,590.72
Mathew Goggin	69	70	65	72	276	2,590.71
Rick Price	67	72	65	72	276	2,590.71
Steve Sear	67	74	64	71	276	2,590.71
Dicky Thompson	71	68	66	71	276	2,590.71
Tripp Isenhour	70	70	68	69	277	1,968.75
Eric Johnson	69	70	66	72	277	1,968.75
Jim McGovern	72	68	67	70	277	1,968.75
Keith Nolan	68	68	72	69	277	1,968.75
Greg Bruckner	67	72	69	70	278	1,631.25

	SCORES				TOTAL	MONEY
Jeff Gove	69	71	65	73	278	1,631.25
Edward Fryatt	69	68	72	70	279	1,335
Gibby Gilbert, Jr.	67	71	71	70	279	1,335
Steve Haskins	70	70	69	70	279	1,335
Pat Nanney, Jr.	72	68	71	68	279	1,335
Don Reese	72	68	67	72	279	1,335
Dean Wilson	70	68	69	72	279	1,335

New Mexico Classic

Santa Ana Golf Club, Santa Ana Pueblo, New Mexico   October 7-10
Par 36-36–72; 7,407 yards   purse, $225,000

	SCORES				TOTAL	MONEY
Dick Mast	73	64	67	63	267	$40,500
Joel Edwards	71	66	67	66	270	25,537.50
Casey Martin	70	67	68	66	271	18,562.50
Matt Gogel	72	64	69	67	272	12,937.50
Darron Stiles	69	66	70	67	272	12,937.50
Ashley Chinner	72	69	68	67	276	9,562.50
Mark Hensby	74	67	68	67	276	9,562.50
Steve Gotsche	72	67	69	69	277	7,312.50
Tripp Isenhour	74	67	66	70	277	7,312.50
Matt Peterson	71	70	67	70	278	4,687.50
Jerry Smith	76	68	68	66	278	4,687.50
Brad Sutterfield	73	68	66	71	278	4,687.50
Jeff Julian	71	66	71	71	279	3,487.50
Jim McGovern	72	72	69	66	279	3,487.50
John Riegger	71	71	69	68	279	3,487.50
David Berganio, Jr.	74	68	71	67	280	2,830.50
Tim Clark	71	71	69	69	280	2,830.50
Joe Daley	73	67	68	72	280	2,830.50
Todd Demsey	72	70	70	68	280	2,830.50
Dicky Thompson	71	65	73	71	280	2,830.50
Jim Estes	75	67	71	68	281	2,250
Keith Fergus	71	69	70	71	281	2,250
Kelly Gibson	76	64	70	71	281	2,250
Keith Nolan	77	66	65	73	281	2,250
Rocky Walcher	76	68	70	67	281	2,250
Brad Elder	70	70	72	70	282	1,800
Craig Kanada	74	70	70	68	282	1,800
Don Walsworth	72	72	71	67	282	1,800
Brian Kamm	69	69	75	70	283	1,530
Michael Muehr	70	69	75	69	283	1,530

Nike Tour Championship

Highland Oaks, Dothan, Alabama   October 21-24
Par 36-36–72; 7,407 yards   purse, $400,000

	SCORES				TOTAL	MONEY
Bob Heintz	68	68	75	72	283	$72,000
Marco Dawson	72	68	74	69	283	45,400
(Heintz defeated Dawson on first extra hole.)						
Jeff Gove	68	68	76	73	285	30,000

	SCORES				TOTAL	MONEY
Shaun Micheel	70	72	73	70	285	30,000
Jim Johnson	71	70	72	73	286	22,000
Joel Edwards	70	73	74	70	287	17,000
Edward Fryatt	70	69	77	71	287	17,000
Michael Clark	71	74	68	75	288	13,000
John Riegger	74	72	70	72	288	13,000
Brian Tennyson	73	68	76	72	289	8,466.67
Richard Zokol	69	74	70	76	289	8,466.67
Ryan Howison	72	70	69	78	289	8,466.66
Brad Elder	73	70	73	74	290	6,266.67
Tripp Isenhour	75	73	72	70	290	6,266.67
Craig Bowden	72	72	70	76	290	6,266.66
Marco Gortana	69	72	80	70	291	5,253.34
Todd Demsey	74	70	76	71	291	5,253.33
Fran Quinn	70	73	73	75	291	5,253.33
Glen Hnatiuk	73	76	73	70	292	4,600
Jim McGovern	72	72	73	75	292	4,600
Don Reese	72	72	76	72	292	4,600
Jerry Smith	71	72	76	74	293	4,200
Tim Clark	77	72	75	70	294	3,800
Mathew Goggin	73	76	73	72	294	3,800
J.J. Henry	75	70	73	76	294	3,800
Dicky Thompson	70	79	76	70	295	3,213.34
David Berganio, Jr.	74	70	77	74	295	3,213.33
Vance Veazey	76	72	75	72	295	3,213.33
Paul Claxton	76	75	73	72	296	2,720
Kelly Gibson	69	77	77	73	296	2,720
John Wilson	71	74	76	75	296	2,720

Canadian Tour

Crown Isle Open

Crown Isle Golf Club, Courtenay, British Columbia
Par 36-36–72; 7,024 yards

May 20-23
purse, C$150,000

	SCORES				TOTAL	MONEY
Kenneth Staton	69	67	68	69	273	C$27,000
Darren Griff	72	69	66	70	277	15,000
Dirk Ayers	71	68	69	70	278	6,900
Ian Leggatt	70	68	73	67	278	6,900
Arron Oberholser	69	68	74	67	278	6,900
Scott Wearne	70	71	69	68	278	6,900
Bobby Kalinowski	69	71	70	69	279	4,519
David Morland	69	69	70	71	279	4,519
Neale Smith	71	70	70	68	279	4,519
Chad Wright	70	69	71	69	279	4,519
Joe Acosta, Jr.	68	73	72	67	280	3,450

With 11 victories and over $7.6 million worldwide, Tiger Woods posted numbers unmatched in half a century as he dominated from May onwards.

David Duval briefly reached No. 1 in the world after four early victories.

Davis Love III was second four times.

Vijay Singh won the Honda Classic.

Allsport/Harry How

Allsport/David Cannon

Allsport/Andy Lyons

Chris Perry had 14 top-10 finishes.

Hal Sutton took the Canadian title.

Jeff Maggert won the Match Play.

Justin Leonard did not win.

David Toms triumphed in Colorado.

Jim Furyk won over $2 million.

Carlos Franco was the top rookie.

Ernie Els took three world titles.

Jeff Sluman won in Hawaii.

Tom Lehman was second twice.

Nick Price had a Japanese win.

Tim Herron took the Bay Hill title.

Ted Tryba was the Memphis champion.

Brent Geiberger won in Hartford.

Rocco Mediate won in Phoenix.

Notah Begay claimed two victories.

European Tour

Lee Westwood posted four wins.

Colin Montgomerie led Europe again.

Sergio Garcia emerged as a new star.

Miguel Angel Jimenez won twice.

Retief Goosen won in France.

Paul Lawrie won the Qatar Masters.

Darren Clarke took one victory.

Padraig Harrington was second five times.

Jarmo Sandelin had two titles.

Angel Cabrera rose to the No. 60 ranking.

Thomas Bjorn had a victory in the Sarazen World Open.

Van Phillips won in Portugal.

Ian Woosnam slipped to No. 72.   Miguel Angel Martin won once.

Pedro Linhart won at Madeira.

David Park had two wins.

Bernhard Langer went from No. 27 to No. 51.

David Howell was the winner in Dubai.

Jean Francois Remesy held the Estoril trophy.

Other Men's Tours

Craig Spence took the Ericsson Masters.

Jarrod Moseley won the Heineken Classic.

Ernie Els had two African victories.

Desvonde Botes won twice.

Allsport/Paul Severn

David Frost won the South African Open.

Allsport/Stephen Munday

Jumbo Ozaki yielded the top spot.

Allsport/Harry How

Michael Campbell was back in form.

Allsport/Stephen Munday

Kazuhiko Hosokawa had two wins.

Allsport/Jamie Squire

Joe Ozaki was No. 1 in Japan.

Senior Tours

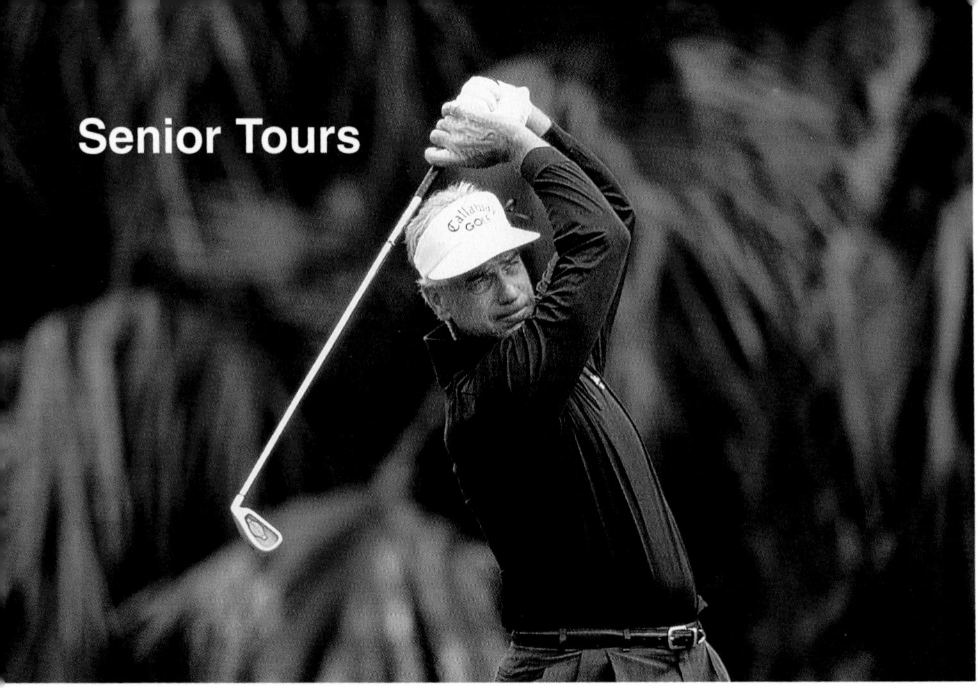

Allsport/Andy Lyons

Bruce Fleisher was Player of the Year with seven victories.

Michael C. Cohen

Hale Irwin had a strong second half.

Michael C. Cohen

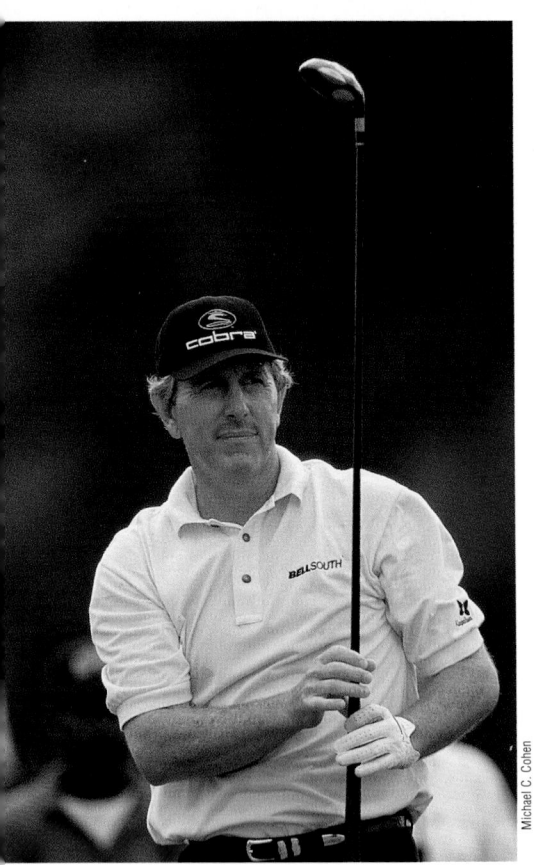

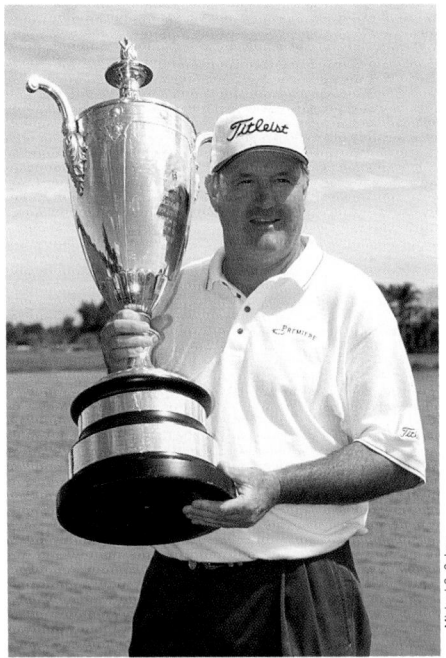

Allen Doyle was the PGA Seniors' champ.

Gary McCord posted two wins.

Dave Eichelberger won the Senior Open.

Gil Morgan won four titles.

Larry Nelson had three wins.

Tom Watson won on his second try.

Christy O'Connor took the British title.

Women's Tours

Allsport/Harry How

Karrie Webb won six titles, one major.

Allsport/Harry How

Juli Inkster got in the Hall of Fame.

Allsport/Andrew Redington

Annika Sorenstam posted two wins.

Michael C. Cohen

Se Ri Pak had four victories.

Allsport/Andrew Redington

Meg Mallon had two early wins.

Allsport/Harry How

Lorie Kane was fifth on the money list.

Allsport/Stephen Munday

Sherri Steinhauer was British champion.

Allsport/Donald Miralle

Mi Hyun Kim won twice.

Allsport/Andrew Redington

Dottie Pepper won the Nabisco Dinah Shore.

Laura Davies claimed three in Europe.

Rosie Jones won once.

Maria Hjorth had two victories.

Rachel Hetherington won back-to-back.

Fumiko Muraguchi took three titles.

	SCORES				TOTAL	MONEY
Paul Devenport	71	71	68	70	280	3,450
Ken Duke	71	72	68	69	280	3,450
Grant Masson	73	70	67	71	281	2,775
Roger Tambellini	70	70	70	71	281	2,775
Chris Anderson	72	71	71	68	282	1,950
Tim Balmer	73	68	70	71	282	1,950
John Douma	73	70	71	68	282	1,950
Mike Fergin	70	71	68	73	282	1,950
Ray Freeman	70	67	72	73	282	1,950
Bruce Heuchan	68	70	73	71	282	1,950
Matthew Lane	72	71	67	72	282	1,950
Rob McMillan	72	72	72	66	282	1,950
Anthony Musgrave	69	71	74	68	282	1,950
Todd Pence	72	72	68	70	282	1,950
Jason Bohn	69	68	75	71	283	1,322
Tony Carolan	70	73	70	70	283	1,322
Davidson Matyczuk	69	71	74	69	283	1,322
Ray Stewart	70	70	72	71	283	1,322
Marcus Cain	69	71	72	72	284	1,106
Scott Ford	70	73	69	72	284	1,106
Shaun Haberstroh	67	72	73	72	284	1,106
Mark James	68	72	71	73	284	1,106
Arden Knoll	73	71	74	66	284	1,106
Brett Liddle	73	71	71	69	284	1,106

Shell Payless Open

Uplands Golf Club, Victoria, British Columbia
Par 35-35–70; 6,315 yards

May 27-30
purse, C$125,000

	SCORES				TOTAL	MONEY
Ken Duke	64	65	66	69	264	C$27,000
Ray Freeman	69	70	65	65	269	15,000
Ian Leggatt	64	66	70	70	270	9,000
Tim Balmer	67	70	64	71	272	5,655
Shaun Haberstroh	68	70	66	68	272	5,655
Rob Johnson	64	67	71	70	272	5,655
Jim Rutledge	71	66	68	67	272	5,655
Ray Stewart	67	69	67	69	272	5,655
Dave Barr	68	66	72	67	273	4,200
Stuart Wallace	68	69	69	67	273	4,200
Marcus Cain	72	66	68	68	274	3,075
Matthew Lane	68	68	69	69	274	3,075
Perry Parker	71	69	70	64	274	3,075
Todd Pence	68	67	73	66	274	3,075
Rick Todd	68	67	72	67	274	3,075
Manny Zerman	71	66	71	66	274	3,075
Jason Bohn	69	71	68	67	275	2,250
Arden Knoll	70	68	70	67	275	2,250
Doug LaBelle	72	68	68	67	275	2,250
Rob McMillan	69	68	72	67	276	1,875
Dave Pashko	65	69	74	68	276	1,875
Matt Daniel	73	67	69	68	277	1,467
Jaime Omar Gomez	70	68	69	70	277	1,467
Stuart Hendley	69	70	72	66	277	1,467
Allan MacDonald	68	72	70	67	277	1,467
Grant Moorhead	69	65	71	72	277	1,467

	SCORES				TOTAL	MONEY
Blair Piercy	68	72	70	67	277	1,467
Tyler Shelton	68	68	70	71	277	1,467
Roger Tambellini	68	72	68	69	277	1,467
Aaron Barber	71	67	69	71	278	1,069
Mark Brown	69	71	66	72	278	1,069
Nathan Green	68	70	75	65	278	1,069
Chris Kamin	67	70	71	70	278	1,069
Rich Massey	68	70	71	69	278	1,069
Grant Masson	71	69	69	69	278	1,069
Marty Schiene	70	69	71	68	278	1,069
Stephane Talbot	69	66	70	73	278	1,069

BC Tel Open

Mayfair Lakes Golf & Country Club,
Richmond, British Columbia
Par 36-35–71; 6,641 yards

June 3-6
purse, C$150,000

	SCORES				TOTAL	MONEY
Kenneth Staton	66	67	70	66	269	C$27,000
Steve Woods	66	68	70	67	271	15,000
Ken Duke	66	69	70	68	273	9,000
Chris Anderson	69	69	69	68	275	5,906.25
Rob McMillan	71	69	66	69	275	5,906.25
Paul Parlane	67	68	71	69	275	5,906.25
Scott Petersen	67	71	70	67	275	5,906.25
Tony Carolan	67	67	73	69	276	4,650
Ray Freeman	71	70	68	68	277	3,900
Brian Kontak	65	69	74	69	277	3,900
Neale Smith	70	69	71	67	277	3,900
Ray Stewart	68	70	68	71	277	3,900
Ian Leggatt	68	71	69	70	278	2,812.50
Davidson Matyczuk	68	71	67	72	278	2,812.50
Manny Zerman	67	71	69	71	278	2,812.50
Richard Zokol	68	71	68	71	278	2,812.50
Darren Fichardt	70	63	72	74	279	2,100
Shaun Haberstroh	69	72	68	70	279	2,100
Mark Johnson	71	67	70	71	279	2,100
Dave Pashko	66	72	71	70	279	2,100
Jim Rutledge	71	69	69	70	279	2,100
Aaron Barber	72	69	70	69	280	1,650
Jace Bugg	68	69	68	75	280	1,650
Chad Wright	70	67	69	74	280	1,650
John Bizik	70	69	73	69	281	1,262.50
Duane Bock	70	69	70	72	281	1,262.50
Marcus Cain	68	72	68	73	281	1,262.50
Todd Fanning	69	70	74	68	281	1,262.50
Chris Ferguson	67	69	71	74	281	1,262.50
Mark James	68	71	71	71	281	1,262.50
David Kureluk	70	71	72	68	281	1,262.50
Rich Massey	69	71	72	69	281	1,262.50
Kent Wiese	68	71	72	70	281	1,262.50

Telus/Henry Singer Alberta Open

Wolf Creek Golf Resort, Ponoka, Alberta
Par 35-35–70; 6,516 yards

June 10-13
purse, C$150,000

		SCORES			TOTAL	MONEY
Brian Kontak	62	65	67	72	266	C$27,000
Ken Duke	68	63	67	71	269	15,000
Matthew Lane	72	62	69	67	270	8,100
Manny Zerman	67	65	69	69	270	8,100
Stuart Hendley	68	62	70	71	271	5,700
Zhang Lian-wei	67	71	68	65	271	5,700
Davidson Matyczuk	65	66	69	72	272	5,025
Darren Griff	67	69	68	69	273	4,350
Rob McMillan	66	66	71	70	273	4,350
David Morland	68	69	68	68	273	4,350
Rob Johnson	71	68	65	70	274	3,600
David McKenzie	68	66	70	70	274	3,600
Tony Carolan	71	68	68	68	275	2,650
Alan McLean	72	65	71	67	275	2,650
Scott Rowe	68	66	71	70	275	2,650
Warren Schutte	67	73	68	67	275	2,650
Ray Stewart	69	69	65	72	275	2,650
Stephen Woodard	71	69	65	70	275	2,650
Ian Leggatt	68	69	64	75	276	1,800
Wes Martin	69	69	72	66	276	1,800
Jim Rutledge	67	69	71	69	276	1,800
Brad Sutterfield	70	68	67	71	276	1,800
Roger Tambellini	69	67	65	75	276	1,800
J.J. West	71	68	65	72	276	1,800
Tim Balmer	69	68	67	73	277	1,387.50
Paul Fitzgibbon	69	71	70	67	277	1,387.50
Tyler Shelton	75	63	68	71	277	1,387.50
Rick Todd	68	71	69	69	277	1,387.50
Chris Anderson	69	67	71	71	278	1,200
Arron Oberholser	68	68	71	71	278	1,200
Dave Pashko	68	73	64	73	278	1,200

Dundee International

Willows Golf and Country Club, Saskatoon, Saskatchewan
Par 36-36–72; 6,621 yards

June 19-20
purse, C$50,000

FIRST DAY
Foursomes

Arden Knoll and Rick Todd (Canada) halved with Paul Devenport and Brian Kontak.
Todd Fanning and Ian Leggatt (Canada) defeated Manny Zerman and Scott Petersen, 3 and 1.
Darren Griff and Rob McMillan (Canada) defeated Rob Johnson and Perry Parker, 3 and 2.
Stuart Hendley and Wes Martin (Canada) halved with Derek Gilchrist and Ben Walter.
Jim Rutledge and Philip Jonas (Canada) defeated David McKenzie and Scott Wearne, 3 and 2.
Ken Duke and Ray Freeman (International) defeated Davidson Matyczuk and Dave Pashko, 2 and 1.

POINTS: Canada 4, International Team 2

Fourball

Zerman and Petersen (International) defeated Rutledge and Jonas, 1 up.
Fanning and Leggatt (Canada) halved with Devenport and Kontak.
Johnson and Parker (International) defeated Griff and McMillan, 5 and 4.
McKenzie and Wearne (International) defeated Matyczuk and Pashko, 5 and 4.
Gilchrist and Walter (International) defeated Hendley and Martin, 2 and 1.
Knoll and Todd (Canada) defeated Duke and Freeman, 2 and 1.

POINTS: Canada 1½, International Team 4½

SECOND DAY
Singles

Knoll (Canada) defeated Kontak, 3 and 2.
Leggatt (Canada) defeated Walter, 2 up.
Johnson (International) defeated Jonas, 5 and 4.
Todd (Canada) defeated Wearne, 2 up.
Pashko (Canada) defeated Freeman, 1 up.
Gilchrist (International) defeated Martin, 2 and 1.
Fanning (Canada) defeated Devenport, 1 up.
Parker (International) defeated McMillan, 1 up.
Griff (Canada) defeated McKenzie, 3 and 2.
Matyczuk (Canada) defeated Petersen, 1 up.
Rutledge (Canada) defeated Zerman, 2 and 1.
Duke (International) defeated Hendley, 2 and 1.

POINTS: Canada 8, International 4

TOTAL POINTS: Canada 13½, International 10½

(Each member of Canada team received C$2,666; each member of International team received C$1,500.)

Telus Calgary Open

Heritage Pointe Golf and Country Club, Calgary, Alberta
Par 36-36–72; 7,119 yards

June 24-27
purse, C$150,000

		SCORES			TOTAL	MONEY
Jaime Omar Gomez	70	65	64	69	268	C$27,000
Chris Anderson	68	66	67	68	269	15,000
Jim Rutledge	66	68	69	68	271	8,100
J.J. West	73	64	64	70	271	8,100
Tim Balmer	70	70	69	65	274	5,475
Ken Duke	69	68	66	71	274	5,475
Will Yanagisawa	67	71	69	67	274	5,475
Arden Knoll	71	66	69	69	275	4,500
Ian Leggatt	68	67	70	70	275	4,500
Andrew Smeeth	67	70	69	70	276	3,750
Mario Tiziani	72	67	69	68	276	3,750
Rick Todd	69	72	66	69	276	3,750
Marcus Cain	70	68	69	70	277	2,650
Nathan Green	68	66	71	72	277	2,650
Shaun Haberstroh	66	72	70	69	277	2,650
Rob McMillan	69	70	70	68	277	2,650
Ray Stewart	73	65	68	71	277	2,650
Brad Wilson	70	72	68	67	277	2,650
Aaron Barber	69	68	69	72	278	1,845

	SCORES				TOTAL	MONEY
Tony Carolan	74	67	67	70	278	1,845
Bob Conrad	69	69	69	71	278	1,845
Philip Jonas	65	70	72	71	278	1,845
Arron Oberholser	72	69	70	67	278	1,845
Mike Fergin	70	68	74	67	279	1,462.50
David McKenzie	68	71	71	69	279	1,462.50
Todd Pence	74	67	70	68	279	1,462.50
Vic Wilk	71	69	69	70	279	1,462.50
Mark James	73	66	71	70	280	1,237.50
Norm Jarvis	69	70	71	70	280	1,237.50
Martin Price	71	71	67	71	280	1,237.50

Telus Edmonton Open

Mayfair Golf and Country Club, Edmonton, Alberta — July 1-4
Par 71; 6,744 yards — purse, C$150,000

	SCORES				TOTAL	MONEY
Ray Stewart	63	67	65	72	267	C$27,000
Alan McLean	67	67	68	66	268	15,000
Zhang Lian-wei	67	69	68	65	269	9,000
Duane Bock	64	69	71	67	271	5,655
Matthew Lane	69	66	71	65	271	5,655
David McKenzie	66	70	70	65	271	5,655
Kent Wiese	69	66	69	67	271	5,655
Manny Zerman	65	69	71	66	271	5,655
Ken Duke	65	65	73	69	272	4,200
Arden Knoll	72	66	68	66	272	4,200
Todd Fanning	69	68	65	71	273	3,450
Ian Leggatt	67	70	68	68	273	3,450
David Morland	69	71	69	64	273	3,450
Tony Carolan	71	67	66	70	274	2,625
Justin Cooper	65	72	69	68	274	2,625
Brian Kontak	68	66	72	68	274	2,625
Jim Rutledge	69	70	67	68	274	2,625
Aaron Barber	68	71	67	69	275	2,100
Doug LaBelle	65	71	74	65	275	2,100
Kenneth Staton	68	71	68	68	275	2,100
Dirk Ayers	70	67	72	67	276	1,762.50
Darren Fichardt	70	70	70	66	276	1,762.50
Jason Bohn	69	67	69	72	277	1,500
Bob Conrad	66	66	76	69	277	1,500
Chris Ferguson	67	69	71	70	277	1,500
Jaime Omar Gomez	71	70	68	68	277	1,500
Martin Price	71	69	68	69	277	1,500
Paul Devenport	68	68	70	72	278	1,200
Stuart Hendley	73	68	71	66	278	1,200
Allan MacDonald	68	70	70	70	278	1,200
Grant Moorhead	68	73	69	68	278	1,200
Mario Tiziani	66	72	72	68	278	1,200

MTS Classic

Elmhurst Golf and Country Club, Winnipeg, Manitoba
Par 35-36–71; 6,690 yards

July 8-11
purse, C$125,000

		SCORES			TOTAL	MONEY
Neale Smith	65	68	67	68	268	C$22,500
Arden Knoll	69	67	70	65	271	12,500
Marcus Cain	69	67	68	68	272	7,500
Aaron Barber	65	70	69	72	276	5,500
Mark Johnson	70	69	68	69	276	5,500
Doug LaBelle	71	71	66	69	277	4,343.75
Blair Piercy	72	67	66	72	277	4,343.75
Dirk Ayers	71	68	71	69	279	3,875
Justin Cooper	71	69	70	70	280	2,625
Ken Duke	68	76	68	68	280	2,625
Mike Fergin	68	72	71	69	280	2,625
Matthew Lane	69	71	73	67	280	2,625
Perry Parker	71	65	71	73	280	2,625
Scott Petersen	70	72	70	68	280	2,625
Scott Rowe	72	71	69	68	280	2,625
Vic Wilk	69	71	70	70	280	2,625
Brad Wilson	69	71	71	69	280	2,625
Zhang Lian-wei	68	72	71	69	280	2,625
Duane Bock	72	70	70	69	281	1,537.50
Philip Jonas	71	69	68	73	281	1,537.50
Brian Mogg	73	66	74	68	281	1,537.50
Arron Oberholser	68	74	69	70	281	1,537.50
Todd Tanner	64	72	72	73	281	1,537.50
Mike Pero	70	72	70	70	282	1,281.25
Rick Todd	67	73	73	69	282	1,281.25
Dean Kennedy	73	70	69	71	283	1,062.50
Rob McMillan	67	73	76	67	283	1,062.50
Marcus Meloan	71	71	70	71	283	1,062.50
Dave Pashko	72	71	71	69	283	1,062.50
Todd Pence	72	70	69	72	283	1,062.50
Warren Schutte	75	69	70	69	283	1,062.50

Ontario Open Heritage Classic

Sault Ste. Marie Golf Club, Sault Ste. Marie, Ontario
Par 36-36–72; 6,746 yards

July 15-18
purse, C$125,000

		SCORES			TOTAL	MONEY
Arron Oberholser	66	66	65	67	264	C$22,500
Tony Carolan	68	67	72	68	275	10,000
Ian Leggatt	70	68	67	70	275	10,000
Zhang Lian-wei	72	67	67	70	276	6,000
Martin Price	71	70	69	67	277	5,000
Perry Parker	68	70	70	70	278	4,343.75
Chad Wright	67	71	70	70	278	4,343.75
Dirk Ayers	71	66	70	72	279	3,500
Doug LaBelle	74	71	66	68	279	3,500
Scott Petersen	71	68	70	70	279	3,500
Warren Schutte	71	68	68	72	279	3,500
Kip Byrne	73	71	67	69	280	2,450
Justin Cooper	71	66	72	71	280	2,450
Mark Johnson	71	69	70	70	280	2,450
Rich Massey	71	69	72	68	280	2,450

	SCORES				TOTAL	MONEY
J.J. West	69	67	74	70	280	2,450
Darren Fichardt	70	70	71	70	281	1,812.50
Don Martone	73	69	72	67	281	1,812.50
Danny Mijovic	71	69	70	71	281	1,812.50
Jason Samuelian	71	71	71	68	281	1,812.50
Marcus Cain	71	75	68	68	282	1,343.75
Ken Duke	69	72	71	70	282	1,343.75
Todd Fanning	73	67	73	69	282	1,343.75
Scott Rowe	69	72	69	72	282	1,343.75
Brad Wilson	69	70	74	69	282	1,343.75
Stephen Woodard	68	71	70	73	282	1,343.75
Mark Brown	72	72	68	71	283	1,020.83
Gordon Burns	70	72	68	73	283	1,020.83
Ray Freeman	69	69	72	73	283	1,020.83
Shaun Haberstroh	70	71	72	70	283	1,020.83
Kari Kekki	72	73	70	68	283	1,020.83
Brian Kontak	69	68	73	73	283	1,020.83

Canadian Masters

Heron Point Golf Links, Ancaster, Ontario
Par 35-36–71; 6,841 yards

July 22-25
purse, C$200,000

	SCORES				TOTAL	MONEY
Ray Stewart	70	64	65	70	269	C$36,000
Darren Griff	65	70	68	68	271	20,000
Bob Conrad	66	67	68	72	273	8,700
Todd Fanning	65	68	70	70	273	8,700
Alan McLean	66	73	67	67	273	8,700
David Morland	70	69	66	68	273	8,700
Manny Zerman	66	71	66	70	273	8,700
Dirk Ayers	69	69	69	67	274	5,600
Tony Carolan	64	71	70	69	274	5,600
Ken Duke	73	67	67	67	274	5,600
Marty Schiene	66	70	64	74	274	5,600
David Faught	68	70	66	71	275	4,200
Arden Knoll	70	70	65	70	275	4,200
Martin Price	67	72	69	67	275	4,200
Jason Samuelian	70	69	71	66	276	3,500
Kenneth Staton	68	67	67	74	276	3,500
Chris Anderson	69	70	68	70	277	2,643
Aaron Barber	67	73	64	73	277	2,643
Jesse Collinson	70	71	66	70	277	2,643
*Michael Hospodar	66	74	69	68	277	
Pat Perez	70	64	73	70	277	2,643
Jim Rutledge	67	71	69	70	277	2,643
Warren Schutte	68	70	69	70	277	2,643
Vic Wilk	69	66	70	72	277	2,643
Justin Cooper	65	70	70	73	278	1,900
Darren Fichardt	71	66	71	70	278	1,900
Ray Freeman	66	75	66	71	278	1,900
Brian Kontak	67	66	74	71	278	1,900
David McKenzie	70	68	69	71	278	1,900
Matthew Lane	71	70	67	71	279	1,550
Rich Massey	70	68	72	69	279	1,550
Tom Stankowski	71	69	67	72	279	1,550
Stephane Talbot	72	69	62	76	279	1,550
Chad Wright	69	71	72	67	279	1,550

Samsung Canadian PGA Championship

DiamondBack Golf Club, Richmond Hill, Ontario
Par 36-36–72; 7,079 yards

July 30-August 1
purse, C$125,000

	SCORES			TOTAL	MONEY
Scott Petersen	68	66	69	203	C$22,500
Jeff Bloom	70	65	70	205	10,000
Derek Gilchrist	65	72	68	205	10,000
Bruce Heuchan	67	70	69	206	6,000
Chris Greenwood	72	69	66	207	4,562.50
David McKenzie	70	66	71	207	4,562.50
Ray Stewart	70	71	66	207	4,562.50
Jason Bohn	72	68	68	208	3,625
Shaun Haberstroh	70	67	71	208	3,625
Stephen Woodard	70	67	71	208	3,625
Grant Masson	65	71	73	209	3,000
Scott Rowe	68	69	72	209	3,000
Jace Bugg	69	72	69	210	2,275
Perry Parker	71	70	69	210	2,275
Pat Perez	66	69	75	210	2,275
John Robertson	66	71	73	210	2,275
Vic Wilk	67	69	74	210	2,275
John Douma	70	70	71	211	1,812.50
Ian Leggatt	72	71	68	211	1,812.50
Jack Abney	72	68	72	212	1,416.67
Chris Anderson	68	71	73	212	1,416.67
Rob McMillan	68	73	71	212	1,416.67
David Morland	68	68	76	212	1,416.67
Jim Rutledge	72	71	69	212	1,416.67
Manny Zerman	71	69	72	212	1,416.67
Tony Carolan	70	67	76	213	1,027.34
Stuart Hendley	70	71	72	213	1,027.34
Brian Kontak	69	68	76	213	1,027.34
Danny Mijovic	67	74	72	213	1,027.34
Mike Pero	71	69	73	213	1,027.34
Tino Rugerio	70	73	70	213	1,027.34
Neale Smith	69	70	74	213	1,027.34
Brad Sutterfield	73	70	70	213	1,027.34

Eagle Creek Classic

Eagle Creek Golf Club, Ottawa, Ontario
Par 36-36–72; 7,067 yards

August 5-8
purse, C$125,000

	SCORES				TOTAL	MONEY
Aaron Oberholser	69	64	70	67	270	C$22,500
Scott Rowe	72	69	69	63	273	12,500
Manny Zerman	70	68	72	64	274	7,500
Norm Jarvis	72	65	70	69	276	4,921.88
Doug LaBelle	71	67	70	68	276	4,921.88
Ian Leggatt	68	65	75	68	276	4,921.88
Stephane Talbot	71	68	70	67	276	4,921.88
Chad Wright	68	70	70	69	277	3,875
Jeff Bloom	66	71	73	68	278	3,375
John Douma	68	72	70	68	278	3,375
Will Yanagisawa	68	70	69	71	278	3,375
Nathan Green	72	70	66	71	279	2,625

	SCORES				TOTAL	MONEY
Shaun Haberstroh	71	67	69	72	279	2,625
Dave Pashko	71	71	69	68	279	2,625
Ken Duke	73	68	70	69	280	2,125
Todd Fanning	69	70	68	73	280	2,125
Jaime Omar Gomez	71	71	73	65	280	2,125
Jack Abney	74	67	69	71	281	1,687.50
Chris Greenwood	73	70	69	69	281	1,687.50
Roger Tambellini	70	69	72	70	281	1,687.50
Vic Wilk	70	71	69	71	281	1,687.50
Dave Branshaw	75	70	69	68	282	1,312.50
Philip Jonas	70	71	70	71	282	1,312.50
David McKenzie	71	70	68	73	282	1,312.50
Rob McMillan	68	73	70	71	282	1,312.50
Scott Petersen	69	67	76	70	282	1,312.50
David Kureluk	71	66	71	75	283	1,093.75
Craig Marseilles	71	72	69	71	283	1,093.75
Matt Filipowicz	70	73	71	70	284	1,015.63
Stuart Hendley	74	70	67	73	284	1,015.63

Benefit Partners/NRCS Classic

Timberwolf Golf Club, Sudbury, Ontario
Par 36-36–72; 7,126 yards

August 19-20
purse, C$75,000

	SCORES		TOTAL	MONEY
Kenneth Staton	69	64	133	C$13,500
Scott Petersen	70	67	137	7,875
Manny Zerman	67	70	137	7,875
Ken Duke	70	68	138	3,975
Darren Griff	68	70	138	3,975
Tim Balmer	71	68	139	2,700
Stuart Hendley	70	69	139	2,700
Alan McLean	69	70	139	2,700
Todd Fanning	70	70	140	2,250
Craig Marseilles	72	68	140	2,250
Davidson Matyczuk	69	71	140	2,250
Aaron Barber	70	71	141	1,950
Bruce Heuchan	69	73	142	1,762.50
Doug LaBelle	70	72	142	1,762.50
David McKenzie	69	73	142	1,762.50
Chad Wright	73	69	142	1,762.50
Neale Smith	72	71	143	1,575
John Hastie	75	69	144	1,462.50
Don Martone	72	72	144	1,462.50
Danny Mijovic	74	71	145	1,350
Chris Anderson	70	78	148	1,200
Brian Kontak	74	74	148	1,200
Ian Leggatt	74	74	148	1,200
Ryan Cooney	76	74	150	1,050
Dirk Ayers	74	78	152	975
Ray Freeman	76	77	153	900
Russ DaSilva	82	74	156	825
George Lasko	77	81	158	750

McDonald's PEI Challenge

Brudenell River Resort, Montague, Prince Edward Island
Par 36-36–72; 6,542 yards

August 26-29
purse, C$125,000

		SCORES			TOTAL	MONEY
David Morland	68	68	67	71	274	C$22,500
Ken Duke	72	68	69	67	276	10,000
Manny Zerman	68	74	69	65	276	10,000
Darren Griff	69	66	72	70	277	5,166.67
Danny Mijovic	68	70	69	70	277	5,166.67
Chad Wright	74	67	70	66	277	5,166.67
Ian Leggatt	73	67	70	69	279	4,031.25
Alan McLean	73	68	71	67	279	4,031.25
Brian Kontak	72	69	69	70	280	3,250
Davidson Matyczuk	70	69	71	70	280	3,250
Scott Petersen	71	67	72	70	280	3,250
Kenneth Staton	69	72	73	66	280	3,250
Duane Bock	72	72	69	68	281	2,275
Dave Branshaw	72	69	69	71	281	2,275
Todd Fanning	70	73	72	66	281	2,275
David McKenzie	67	71	68	75	281	2,275
Rob McMillan	67	71	73	70	281	2,275
Trent Norcross	75	67	70	70	282	1,750
Neale Smith	69	70	73	70	282	1,750
Brett Taylor	74	69	70	69	282	1,750
Kari Kekki	76	70	69	68	283	1,500
Rob Johnson	74	70	74	66	284	1,406.25
Grant Moorhead	73	69	71	71	284	1,406.25
Jeff Bloom	75	71	69	70	285	1,138.39
Stuart Hendley	71	69	77	68	285	1,138.39
Craig Marseilles	69	67	77	72	285	1,138.39
Rich Massey	72	68	75	70	285	1,138.39
Stephane Talbot	74	72	68	71	285	1,138.39
Roger Tambellini	73	69	71	72	285	1,138.39
Keith Whitecotton	70	74	70	71	285	1,138.39

Bell Bay Matches

Bell Bay Golf Club, Baddeck, Nova Scotia
Par 36-36–72; 7,037 yards

September 4-5
purse, C$50,000

	SCORES			TOTAL	MONEY (Each)
Stuart Hendley/Scott Petersen	70	66	136	272	C$5,000
Tim Balmer/Chad Wright	72	64	138	274	2,500
Dirk Ayers/Aaron Barber	74	65	136	275	2,300
Duane Bock/Brian Kontak	71	67	143	281	2,025
Todd Fanning/David McKenzie	73	67	141	281	2,025
Chris Anderson/J.J. West	71	65	147	283	1,750
Alan McLean/Perry Parker	72	70	141	283	1,750
Davidson Matyczuk/Neale Smith	78	68	138	284	1,600
Martin Price/Manny Zerman	70	67	150	287	1,550
Kip Byrne/Paul Devenport	75	67	146	288	1,500
Jeff Bloom/Ray Freeman	78	69	144	291	1,500
Brian McDonald/Stuart Musgrave	77	70	144	291	1,500

NewTel Atlantic Cup

Clovelly Golf Course, St. John's, Newfoundland
Par 36-36–72; 6,521 yards

September 11-12
purse, C$50,000

	SCORES			TOTAL	MONEY (Team)
Brian Kontak/Philip Jonas	69	65	149	283	C$10,000
Chad Wright/Paul Devenport	74	64	146	284	4,800
Tim Balmer/Jason Bohn	70	63	151	284	4,800
Neale Smith/Grant Masson	71	65	149	285	4,050
Doug LaBelle/Rob Johnson	75	68	142	285	4,050
Dave Pashko/David McKenzie	72	67	151	290	3,600
Jeff Bloom/Duane Bock	72	65	155	292	3,300
J.J. West/Perry Parker	69	69	154	292	3,300
Aaron Barber/Brad Wilson	74	66	155	295	3,100
Davidson Matyczuk/Walter Keating, Jr.	80	63	153	296	3,000
Alan McLean/Stephen Woodard	74	68	159	301	3,000
Chris Anderson/Rich Massey	81	70	153	304	3,000

Bayer Championship

Huron Oaks Golf Course, Sarnia, Ontario
Par 35-35–70; 6,322 yards

September 16-19
purse, C$200,000

	SCORES				TOTAL	MONEY
Ken Duke	69	66	69	67	271	C$36,000
Arron Oberholser	70	68	65	69	272	20,000
Aaron Barber	67	69	72	65	273	8,283.33
Chris Greenwood	69	73	65	66	273	8,283.33
Doug LaBelle	67	71	68	67	273	8,283.33
Rob McMillan	69	65	68	71	273	8,283.33
David Morland	66	69	68	70	273	8,283.33
Manny Zerman	68	68	68	69	273	8,283.33
David McKenzie	67	71	65	72	275	5,600
Scott Petersen	73	68	68	66	275	5,600
Jason Bohn	74	66	68	68	276	4,400
Bob Conrad	67	74	70	65	276	4,400
Shaun Haberstroh	71	65	67	73	276	4,400
Chad Wright	69	73	67	67	276	4,400
Jace Bugg	71	70	67	69	277	3,200
Paul Devenport	70	70	68	69	277	3,200
Chris Ferguson	70	72	66	69	277	3,200
Scott Rowe	70	73	64	70	277	3,200
Warren Schutte	69	73	66	69	277	3,200
Rob Johnson	68	64	76	70	278	2,375
Rich Massey	70	69	66	73	278	2,375
Mario Tiziani	70	70	70	68	278	2,375
Stephen Woodard	72	65	71	70	278	2,375
Derek Gilchrist	69	69	68	73	279	2,000
Davidson Matyczuk	72	71	68	68	279	2,000
James Watt	68	72	71	68	279	2,000
Brett Bingham	71	72	66	71	280	1,716.67
Derek Ingram	68	68	72	72	280	1,716.67
Roger Tambellini	70	69	68	73	280	1,716.67
Jack Abney	70	68	70	73	281	1,425
David Banks	73	69	66	73	281	1,425
John Douma	75	67	70	69	281	1,425

	SCORES				TOTAL	MONEY
Todd Fanning	70	65	76	70	281	1,425
Mark Johnson	71	72	69	69	281	1,425
Arden Knoll	72	70	71	68	281	1,425
Stuart Wallace	68	70	68	75	281	1,425
Kent Wiese	75	67	68	71	281	1,425

Niagara Classic

Whirlpool Golf Club, Niagara Falls, Ontario
Par 36-36–72; 7,217 yards

September 25-26
purse, C$75,000

	SCORES		TOTAL	MONEY
Arden Knoll	71	65	136	C$13,500
Jason Bohn	74	62	136	9,000
(Knoll defeated Bohn on first extra hole.)				
Todd Fanning	68	71	139	5,775
Roger Tambellini	70	69	139	5,775
Paul Devenport	70	70	140	2,812.50
Darren Griff	67	73	140	2,812.50
Scott Petersen	69	71	140	2,812.50
Manny Zerman	73	67	140	2,812.50
Derek Gilchrist	70	71	141	2,250
Doug LaBelle	70	71	141	2,250
Chad Wright	69	72	141	2,250
Chris Greenwood	69	74	143	1,800
Arron Oberholser	70	73	143	1,800
Perry Parker	73	70	143	1,800
Dirk Ayers	70	74	144	1,425
Aaron Barber	72	72	144	1,425
Duane Bock	72	72	144	1,425
Danny Mijovic	74	70	144	1,425
Vic Wilk	74	70	144	1,425
Alan McLean	75	70	145	1,162.50
Brad Wilson	71	74	145	1,162.50
Davidson Matyczuk	69	77	146	1,050
Kenneth Staton	72	75	147	993.75
Kent Wiese	73	74	147	993.75
Shaun Haberstroh	74	74	148	937.50
Martin Price	72	77	149	881.25
Warren Schutte	74	75	149	881.25
Dave Pashko	74	80	154	825
Rob Johnson	81	75	156	768.75
J.J. West	78	78	156	768.75

South American Tour

TPG Open de Venezuela

Valle Arriba Golf Club, Venezuela
Par 35-35–70; 6,372 yards

November 11-14
purse, US$51,000

	SCORES				TOTAL	MONEY
Carlos Larrain	68	65	69	64	266	US$10,000
Henrique Lavie	65	68	66	70	269	5,700
Angel Romero	68	70	65	67	270	3,600
Miguel Martinez	64	70	67	69	270	3,600
Rob Corcoran	68	68	68	67	271	2,600
Rigoberto Velasquez	70	67	67	68	272	1,900
Scott Ford	65	66	68	73	272	1,900
Eduardo Pesenti	69	69	70	65	273	1,300
Hampus Von Post	68	71	65	69	273	1,300
Rafael Barcellos	68	68	67	70	273	1,300
Damaso Galban	72	72	66	64	274	1,050
Ramon Munoz	65	73	70	66	274	1,050
Christoph Gunther	70	72	68	65	275	875
Maury Beasley	69	71	67	68	275	875
Claudio Muskus	68	66	72	69	275	875
Eric Bogar	68	64	71	72	275	875
Ruberlei Felizardo	66	69	72	69	276	725
Juan Echeverri	68	64	73	71	276	725
Renaud Guillard	70	71	70	66	277	625
Frederik Eskelid	68	69	68	72	277	625
Allen MacDonald	68	71	74	65	278	513
Ramon Franco	69	75	67	67	278	513
Steve Schriver	68	69	70	71	278	513
Mark Monroe	67	72	72	68	279	450
Teunis Stolk	68	65	74	72	279	450
Eduardo Caballero	71	71	70	68	280	400
David Montesi	74	69	68	69	280	400
Brett Bingham	74	65	71	70	280	400
Peter Hansson	73	71	73	64	281	370
Fernando Posada	69	70	76	68	283	345
Carlos Maestre	76	66	70	71	283	345
Glenn Preciado	73	68	70	72	283	345
Dennis Tymosko	69	72	69	73	283	345

Peru Open

Los Inkas Golf Club, Lima, Peru
Par 36-36–72; 6,943 yards

November 18-21
purse, US$100,000

	SCORES				TOTAL	MONEY
Scott Dunlap	64	66	73	70	273	US$18,000
Gustavo Rojas	71	69	69	65	274	11,400
Mauricio Molina	70	72	70	67	279	8,000
Alan Fort	70	72	70	68	280	6,400

	SCORES				TOTAL	MONEY
Ruberlei Felizardo	67	76	70	68	281	4,700
Tim Hegna	69	72	71	69	281	4,700
Jeff Schmid	70	73	69	70	282	3,100
Adam Spring	70	70	71	71	282	3,100
Rafael Gomez	72	71	71	71	285	2,400
Philip Jonas	75	68	69	73	285	2,400
J. Cardenas	68	72	72	73	285	2,400
Allen MacDonald	73	71	72	70	286	1,900
Angel Romero	72	72	72	70	286	1,900
Peter Hansson	75	69	70	72	286	1,900
Miguel Guzman	71	75	71	70	287	1,650
Rigoberto Velasquez	71	71	72	73	287	1,650
George Goich	73	76	71	68	288	1,253.33
Guillherme Antunes	73	73	73	69	288	1,253.33
Roberto Coceres	73	70	73	72	288	1,253.33
Eduardo Caballero	72	71	73	72	288	1,253.33
Omar Solis	74	71	71	72	288	1,253.33
Renaud Guillard	69	73	72	74	288	1,253.33
Mark Monroe	73	71	72	73	289	960
Scott Ford	74	72	74	70	290	920
A. Zamora	73	75	72	71	291	804
Wesley Burton	73	75	70	73	291	804
Luis Graf	73	72	72	74	291	804
Rafael Barcellos	71	71	74	75	291	804
Maury Beasley	71	75	69	76	291	804
Willie Huaman	74	72	74	72	292	710
Brad Wilson	70	76	73	73	292	710

Torneo de Maestros Telefonica

Olivos Golf Club, Buenos Aires, Argentina
Par 71; 6,692 yards

November 25-28
purse, US$170,000

	SCORES				TOTAL	MONEY
Angel Cabrera	66	66	70	69	271	US$30,600
Scott Dunlap	70	71	67	67	275	14,620
Fabian Montovia	68	72	68	67	275	14,620
Costantino Rocca	71	65	69	70	275	14,620
Vicente Fernandez	67	70	72	67	276	8,840
Frederik Mansson	65	72	68	72	277	7,140
Rodolfo Gonzalez	67	73	68	70	278	5,780
Esteban Isasi	68	71	69	71	279	4,420
Angel Franco	66	68	70	75	279	4,420
Bernardo Gonzalez	67	67	70	75	279	4,420
Jeff Schmid	68	70	68	74	280	3,740
Eduardo Romero	70	71	71	69	281	3,230
Miguel Fernandez	72	70	67	72	281	3,230
Allan MacDonald	68	71	68	74	281	3,230
Rafael Gomez	69	67	74	72	282	2,890
Nick Price	76	68	72	67	283	2,465
Angel Romero	70	73	70	70	283	2,465
Jorge Berendt	69	70	74	70	283	2,465
Peter Hansson	66	76	67	74	283	2,465
Carlos Larrain	71	73	76	64	284	1,768
Carlos Franco	73	71	70	70	284	1,768
Ricardo Gonzalez	69	68	74	73	284	1,768
Gustavo Piovano	71	68	71	74	284	1,768

	SCORES				TOTAL	MONEY
Brad Wilson	67	70	73	74	284	1,768
Adam Sowa	72	69	72	72	285	1,428
Claudio Muskus	67	76	69	73	285	1,428
Marco Ruiz	72	69	71	73	285	1,428
Juan Abbate	72	71	73	70	286	1,275
Ruben Alvarez	69	74	66	77	286	1,275
Andreas Ljundggren	72	72	74	69	287	1,224

Litoral Open

Rosario Golf Club, Rosario, Argentina
Par 36-36–72; 6,427 yards

December 2-5
purse, US$100,000

	SCORES				TOTAL	MONEY
Cesar Monasterio	70	65	72	68	275	US$18,000
Omar Solis	76	68	68	66	278	9,700
Rigoberto Velasquez	66	70	72	70	278	9,700
Rodolfo Gonzalez	69	67	71	72	279	6,400
Miguel Rodriguez	74	68	71	68	281	4,266.67
Jeff Schmid	71	71	71	68	281	4,266.67
Gustavo Rojas	74	69	69	69	281	4,266.67
Scott Dunlap	75	69	69	69	282	2,700
Ruben Alvarez	69	75	67	71	282	2,700
Daniel Vancsik	74	73	67	69	283	2,060
Roberto Coceres	69	73	70	71	283	2,060
Ricardo Gonzalez	75	65	72	71	283	2,060
Claudio Muskus	73	71	66	73	283	2,060
Miguel Fernandez	68	69	71	75	283	2,060
Sebastian Fernandez	68	71	75	70	284	1,600
Miguel Guzman	70	68	73	73	284	1,600
Michael Boyd	70	69	71	74	284	1,600
Rafael Gomez	73	71	72	69	285	1,097.50
Adam Spring	77	71	67	70	285	1,097.50
Rodolfo Rodriguez	72	70	73	70	285	1,097.50
Juan Abbate	73	71	70	71	285	1,097.50
Pedro Benenati	73	69	72	71	285	1,097.50
Marcos Hong	70	74	69	72	285	1,097.50
Gustavo Mendoza	68	73	70	74	285	1,097.50
Gustavo Acosta	73	68	69	75	285	1,097.50
Rafael Eyraud	70	72	80	65	287	820
Luis Carbonetti	66	70	75	76	287	820
Gustavo Piovano	73	71	77	67	288	730
Ernesto Rivas	72	76	72	68	288	730
Jimmy Stobs	72	71	72	73	288	730
Danny Mijovic	73	68	73	74	288	730

Argentina Open

Jockey Club, Buenos Aires, Argentina
Par 35-35–70; 6,668 yards

December 9-12
purse, US$370,000

	SCORES				TOTAL	MONEY
Scott Dunlap	72	66	66	68	272	US$60,000
Ian Woosnam	68	68	69	68	273	30,175
Jose Coceres	67	69	67	70	273	30,175

	SCORES				TOTAL	MONEY
Eduardo Romero	71	70	70	66	277	17,650
Carlos Franco	71	71	67	68	277	17,650
Joe Ogilvie	71	68	70	70	279	12,600
Craig Stadler	71	66	74	69	280	10,800
Mike Nicolette	71	70	73	69	283	7,515
Alex Balicki	75	69	68	71	283	7,515
Rodolfo Gonzalez	69	77	70	68	284	
Padraig Harrington	72	73	71	68	284	
Cesar Monasterio	73	69	70	72	284	
Daniel Vancsik	69	73	76	67	285	
Vicente Fernandez	70	78	68	70	286	
Miguel Fernandez	73	69	72	72	286	
Marco Ruiz	71	67	74	74	286	
Gustavo Rojas	72	73	74	68	287	
Sebastian Fernandez	72	74	72	69	287	
Adam Spring	73	71	73	70	287	
Brad Wilson	67	75	74	71	287	
Mauricio Molina	77	68	73	70	288	
Miguel Guzman	71	77	70	70	288	
Fabian Montovia	72	71	73	72	288	
Felizardo Ruberlei	71	72	72	73	288	
Alberto Gianonne	72	70	73	73	288	
Marten Olander	74	68	73	73	288	
Philip Jonas	73	70	76	70	289	
Pablo Ponce	68	79	72	70	289	
Richard Barcelo	73	70	72	74	289	
Ariel Canete	75	73	73	69	290	
Frederik Mansson	71	75	74	70	290	
Tim Hegna	75	71	74	70	290	
Ernesto Rivas	73	69	77	71	290	
Allen MacDonald	75	68	74	73	290	
Horacio Carbonetti	71	72	74	73	290	
Angel Cabrera	66	77	73	74	290	
Esteban Isasi	68	72	75	75	290	

European Tours

Alfred Dunhill South African PGA
See African Tours chapter.

Mercedes-Benz - Vodacom South African Open
See African Tours chapter.

Heineken Classic
See Australasian Tour chapter.

Benson and Hedges Malaysian Open
See Asia/Japan Tours chapter.

Dubai Desert Classic

Dubai Creek Golf & Yacht Club, Dubai, United Arab Emirates
Par 36-36–72; 6,843 yards

February 11-14
purse, €1,190,000

	SCORES				TOTAL	MONEY
David Howell	69	68	71	67	275	€198,324
Lee Westwood	72	71	69	67	279	132,216
Paul McGinley	67	71	75	67	280	66,997
Mark James	73	69	69	69	280	66,997
Wayne Riley	68	70	70	74	282	42,583.33
Colin Montgomerie	70	70	72	70	282	42,583.33
Edward Fryatt	70	70	70	72	282	42,583.33
Miguel Angel Jimenez	73	67	70	73	283	26,702.67
Jyoti Randhawa	73	69	70	71	283	26,702.67
Anthony Wall	70	70	72	71	283	26,702.67
Michael Jonzon	71	68	76	69	284	19,929
Phil Price	67	73	73	71	284	19,929
Alex Cejka	68	73	75	68	284	19,929
Michael Campbell	71	71	71	71	284	19,929
Warren Bennett	69	70	71	75	285	15,517
Steen Tinning	69	71	72	73	285	15,517
Dean Robertson	71	73	72	69	285	15,517
Jarmo Sandelin	69	70	75	71	285	15,517
John Bickerton	73	73	71	68	285	15,517
Gary Evans	72	70	75	68	285	15,517
Paul Affleck	69	72	74	70	285	15,517
Bob May	69	74	71	72	286	13,209
Steve Webster	70	70	74	72	286	13,209
Pierre Fulke	73	72	74	67	286	13,209
Angel Cabrera	73	71	76	67	287	11,602.50
Per Nyman	71	72	72	72	287	11,602.50
Per-Ulrik Johansson	72	74	70	71	287	11,602.50
Jose Maria Olazabal	69	73	73	72	287	11,602.50
Mark O'Meara	72	67	77	71	287	11,602.50
Francisco Cea	69	73	72	73	287	11,602.50
Jamie Spence	70	69	73	76	288	9,906.75
Russell Claydon	75	71	73	69	288	9,906.75

	SCORES				TOTAL	MONEY
Thomas Levet	69	73	72	74	288	9,906.75
Jose Rivero	72	71	73	72	288	9,906.75
*Sergio Garcia	68	73	75	72	288	
Jonathan Lomas	74	66	77	72	289	8,687
Gary Orr	72	70	73	74	289	8,687
Peter Baker	73	73	71	72	289	8,687
Eduardo Romero	70	75	72	72	289	8,687
Ricardo Gonzalez	74	72	74	69	289	8,687
Shaun Micheel	71	75	71	72	289	8,687
Andrew Oldcorn	76	69	72	73	290	7,378
Ross McFarlane	72	72	75	71	290	7,378
Andrew Sherborne	75	68	75	72	290	7,378
Andrew Coltart	71	70	74	75	290	7,378
Raymond Russell	70	73	77	70	290	7,378
*Trevor Immelman	70	72	72	76	290	
Peter Downie	69	69	75	78	291	6,069
Mark Mouland	71	74	71	75	291	6,069
Richard Green	72	67	75	77	291	6,069
Costantino Rocca	72	74	69	76	291	6,069
Sven Struver	70	71	77	73	291	6,069
Jean Van de Velde	77	69	76	69	291	6,069
Barry Lane	69	74	72	77	292	5,236
Thomas Bjorn	72	73	74	74	293	4,879
Domingo Hospital	75	71	73	74	293	4,879
Joakim Haeggman	72	69	77	76	294	4,165
Ian Garbutt	73	72	75	74	294	4,165
Eamonn Darcy	71	74	74	75	294	4,165
Fredrik Lindgren	70	70	77	77	294	4,165
Santiago Luna	75	70	81	69	295	3,570
David Gilford	71	75	76	73	295	3,570
Van Phillips	72	72	80	71	295	3,570
Derrick Cooper	73	72	79	73	297	3,213
Darren Clarke	70	73	77	77	297	3,213
Jim Payne	73	73	76	75	297	3,213
Mark Pilkington	73	71	79	75	298	2,380
Soren Kjeldsen	72	74	78	74	298	2,380

Qatar Masters

Doha Golf Club, Doha, Qatar
Par 36-36–72; 7,268 yards

February 17-20
purse, €870,000

	SCORES				TOTAL	MONEY
Paul Lawrie	68	65	67	68	268	€143,196.27
Phil Price	70	68	69	68	275	74,622.56
Soren Kjeldsen	70	65	72	68	275	74,622.56
John Bickerton	68	67	71	71	277	42,960.60
Christopher Hanell	71	67	70	70	278	30,759.79
Jean Van de Velde	69	66	70	73	278	30,759.79
Raymond Russell	66	70	70	72	278	30,759.79
Ian Woosnam	68	70	70	71	279	19,274.99
Bob May	67	70	72	70	279	19,274.99
Jamie Spence	71	67	72	69	279	19,274.99
Alex Cejka	69	69	69	73	280	14,378.91
Mathias Gronberg	72	67	71	70	280	14,378.91
Patrik Sjoland	74	69	72	65	280	14,378.91
Kang Wook-soon	71	67	69	73	280	14,378.91

	SCORES				TOTAL	MONEY
Stephen Gallacher	69	68	69	76	282	12,630.42
Katsuyoshi Tomori	69	70	72	72	283	11,363.08
Paul McGinley	72	69	72	70	283	11,363.08
Anders Hansen	72	70	70	71	283	11,363.08
Fredrik Lindgren	72	68	74	69	283	11,363.08
Retief Goosen	70	71	72	71	284	9,923.90
Mark James	67	71	72	74	284	9,923.90
Wayne Riley	69	70	71	74	284	9,923.90
Peter Mitchell	75	67	69	73	284	9,923.90
Padraig Harrington	71	70	72	72	285	8,892.85
Michael Jonzon	71	71	73	70	285	8,892.85
Andrew McLardy	73	69	69	74	285	8,892.85
Jose Rivero	72	70	71	72	285	8,892.85
Iain Pyman	74	70	70	72	286	7,312.85
David Howell	72	72	70	72	286	7,312.85
Miguel Angel Martin	70	72	68	76	286	7,312.85
Andrew Coltart	71	69	74	72	286	7,312.85
Gerry Norquist	74	67	72	73	286	7,312.85
Steve Webster	75	67	71	73	286	7,312.85
Mark Roe	72	68	72	74	286	7,312.85
Paul Broadhurst	72	72	72	70	286	7,312.85
Gary Evans	69	70	71	76	286	7,312.85
Van Phillips	70	72	72	73	287	6,186.33
Fabrice Tarnaud	72	71	72	72	287	6,186.33
Ian Garbutt	71	71	73	72	287	6,186.33
Per Nyman	68	70	74	76	288	5,241.19
Marc Farry	66	75	71	76	288	5,241.19
Mark Mouland	72	70	71	75	288	5,241.19
Paolo Quirici	72	72	72	72	288	5,241.19
Eduardo Romero	69	71	72	76	288	5,241.19
Zhang Lian-wei	71	73	72	72	288	5,241.19
Angel Cabrera	74	69	70	75	288	5,241.19
Costantino Rocca	73	69	73	73	288	5,241.19
Mats Lanner	75	69	70	75	289	4,124.22
Per-Ulrik Johansson	72	72	69	76	289	4,124.22
Warren Bennett	71	69	78	71	289	4,124.22
Henrik Nystrom	75	69	73	72	289	4,124.22
Ricardo Gonzalez	72	72	75	70	289	4,124.22
Paul Affleck	70	74	67	79	290	3,179.09
Jim Payne	75	68	74	73	290	3,179.09
Malcolm Mackenzie	72	70	74	74	290	3,179.09
Soren Hansen	74	69	75	72	290	3,179.09
Richard Green	72	71	73	74	290	3,179.09
Brian Davis	73	71	75	71	290	3,179.09
Philip Walton	72	71	76	72	291	2,534.68
Miles Tunnicliff	71	72	74	74	291	2,534.68
Andrew Oldcorn	73	71	68	79	291	2,534.68
Thomas Gogele	73	70	76	72	291	2,534.68
Robert Jan Derksen	71	72	77	72	292	1,639.61
Santiago Luna	72	72	72	76	292	1,639.61
Roger Chapman	72	68	77	75	292	1,639.61
Paul Eales	71	72	77	72	292	1,639.61
Gordon Brand, Jr.	72	72	75	73	292	1,639.61
Greg Owen	73	71	74	74	292	1,639.61
Marcello Santi	74	70	75	73	292	1,639.61
Stephen Field	71	73	75	73	292	1,639.61
*Trevor Immelman	75	69	78	70	292	
Ross McFarlane	68	75	79	71	293	1,271
Barry Lane	75	68	78	72	293	1,271

	SCORES				TOTAL	MONEY
Steen Tinning	72	68	75	78	293	1,271
Massimo Florioli	73	70	78	77	298	1,265

Algarve Portuguese Open

Le Meridien, Penina, Portugal
Par 35-37–72; 6,875 yards

March 4-7
purse, €560,000

	SCORES				TOTAL	MONEY
Van Phillips	72	68	68	68	276	€93,320
John Bickerton	71	73	64	68	276	62,210
(Phillips defeated Bickerton on first extra hole.)						
Robert Karlsson	69	72	71	67	279	28,916.67
Alex Cejka	71	70	70	68	279	28,916.67
Santiago Luna	68	72	70	69	279	28,916.67
Anthony Wall	71	69	71	69	280	19,600
Daren Lee	75	70	69	67	281	15,400
Craig Hainline	71	73	69	68	281	15,400
Paul Broadhurst	76	68	71	67	282	9,924.57
Ricardo Gonzalez	72	74	68	68	282	9,924.57
Mark Roe	72	69	70	71	282	9,924.57
Bob May	70	69	71	72	282	9,924.57
Fredrik Jacobson	68	71	71	72	282	9,924.57
Paul Lawrie	71	69	69	73	282	9,924.57
Massimo Scarpa	69	71	68	74	282	9,924.57
Ian Garbutt	70	71	72	70	283	7,560
Gerry Norquist	74	73	66	70	283	7,560
Angel Cabrera	72	70	69	72	283	7,560
Iain Pyman	72	70	72	70	284	6,650
David Howell	74	72	68	70	284	6,650
Peter Mitchell	71	71	71	71	284	6,650
Richard Boxall	71	70	71	72	284	6,650
Roger Winchester	70	76	72	67	285	6,132
Roger Wessels	71	75	66	73	285	6,132
Marc Farry	76	67	72	71	286	5,376
Jeev Milkha Singh	73	69	73	71	286	5,376
Raphael Jacquelin	72	70	75	69	286	5,376
Des Smyth	66	72	76	72	286	5,376
Andrew Oldcorn	71	74	69	72	286	5,376
Francis Valera	69	72	71	74	286	5,376
Wayne Riley	72	71	66	77	286	5,376
Peter Baker	73	72	71	71	287	4,424
Barry Lane	72	75	70	70	287	4,424
Miles Tunnicliff	72	69	76	70	287	4,424
Gary Evans	72	69	73	73	287	4,424
Jean Van de Velde	68	73	72	74	287	4,424
Miguel Angel Jimenez	68	73	70	76	287	4,424
Tony Johnstone	71	71	75	71	288	3,752
Thomas Levet	73	70	72	73	288	3,752
Jose Rivero	70	74	71	73	288	3,752
Anders Hansen	73	72	70	73	288	3,752
Gary Orr	73	73	69	73	288	3,752
Katsuyoshi Tomori	68	79	68	73	288	3,752
Jose Coceres	74	72	70	73	289	3,136
David Gilford	69	76	72	72	289	3,136
John Mellor	72	73	73	71	289	3,136
Stephen Gallacher	73	72	70	74	289	3,136

	SCORES				TOTAL	MONEY
Warren Bennett	75	69	70	75	289	3,136
Pedro Linhart	71	69	75	75	290	2,520
Steve Webster	70	77	70	73	290	2,520
Soren Hansen	74	73	70	73	290	2,520
Robert Jan Derksen	73	74	71	72	290	2,520
Andrew Coltart	71	75	72	72	290	2,520
Henrik Nystrom	73	73	75	69	290	2,520
Emanuele Canonica	72	70	73	76	291	1,806
Stephen Bennett	72	70	73	76	291	1,806
Philip Walton	76	68	72	75	291	1,806
Jesus Maria Arruti	72	71	74	74	291	1,806
Eamonn Darcy	76	70	72	73	291	1,806
Peter Hedblom	72	75	74	70	291	1,806
Diego Borrego	72	71	71	77	291	1,806
Domingo Hospital	73	73	68	77	291	1,806
Fabrice Tarnaud	74	72	71	75	292	1,484
Max Anglert	74	71	74	73	292	1,484
Francisco Cea	71	72	75	75	293	1,400
Jamie Spence	74	73	71	76	294	838.50
Retief Goosen	68	78	73	75	294	838.50
Paul Eales	73	72	71	79	295	829.50
Scott Henderson	72	74	73	76	295	829.50
Roger Chapman	78	65	76	76	295	829.50
Thomas Gogele	74	71	75	75	295	829.50
Pierre Fulke	71	76	74	75	296	822
Jorge Berendt	73	74	77	73	297	819
Padraig Harrington	74	73	77	75	299	816
Paul Affleck	71	76	76	77	300	813
Tomas Jesus Munoz	73	74	77	78	302	810
Tom Gillis	73	73	78	79	303	807
*Nuno Campino	73	72	76	85	306	

Turespana Masters - Open Andalucia

Parador Malaga del Golf, Spain
Par 35-37–72; 6,743 yards

March 11-14
purse, €500,000

	SCORES				TOTAL	MONEY
Miguel Angel Jimenez	69	66	62	67	264	€83,330
Steve Webster	69	66	67	66	268	55,550
Raphael Jacquelin	71	67	66	65	269	31,300
Marc Farry	69	67	66	69	271	25,000
Alex Cejka	71	65	67	69	272	17,900
Per-Ulrik Johansson	67	67	68	70	272	17,900
Fredrik Lindgren	67	66	75	64	272	17,900
Thomas Gogele	68	69	68	68	273	11,825
Gary Orr	67	67	69	70	273	11,825
Bob May	73	65	68	68	274	8,694
Roger Winchester	67	67	70	70	274	8,694
John Bickerton	68	68	69	69	274	8,694
Ian Garbutt	67	67	69	71	274	8,694
Richard Boxall	70	69	67	68	274	8,694
Christopher Hanell	67	72	71	65	275	6,760
Rolf Muntz	70	70	68	67	275	6,760
Ignacio Garrido	73	63	66	73	275	6,760
Ricardo Gonzalez	67	68	68	72	275	6,760
Roger Chapman	70	69	65	71	275	6,760

		SCORES			TOTAL	MONEY
Barry Lane	72	68	69	67	276	5,775
Jeev Milkha Singh	70	68	71	67	276	5,775
Greg Owen	68	68	68	72	276	5,775
Anthony Wall	70	70	68	68	276	5,775
Miguel Angel Martin	69	72	69	67	277	5,100
Katsuyoshi Tomori	68	68	70	71	277	5,100
Miles Tunnicliff	68	71	71	67	277	5,100
Soren Hansen	71	68	69	69	277	5,100
Massimo Florioli	69	69	70	69	277	5,100
Angel Cabrera	67	72	69	70	278	4,360
Derrick Cooper	69	71	69	69	278	4,360
Fredrik Jacobson	67	74	71	66	278	4,360
Jorge Berendt	71	69	69	69	278	4,360
Craig Hainline	70	69	71	68	278	4,360
Paolo Quirici	65	72	71	71	279	3,900
Massimo Scarpa	69	71	69	70	279	3,900
Andrew Raitt	70	71	69	69	279	3,900
David Gilford	69	72	70	69	280	3,600
Costantino Rocca	70	71	70	69	280	3,600
Jamie Spence	72	68	70	70	280	3,600
Diego Borrego	67	73	69	72	281	3,300
Per Nyman	72	66	68	75	281	3,300
Francisco Cea	71	69	68	73	281	3,300
Alberto Binaghi	70	71	73	68	282	2,850
Emanuele Canonica	71	69	71	71	282	2,850
John Mellor	70	71	71	70	282	2,850
Carlos Rodiles	70	71	72	69	282	2,850
Robert Karlsson	70	71	70	71	282	2,850
John Senden	72	67	72	71	282	2,850
*Raul Quiros	71	70	68	73	282	
Gary Evans	71	70	71	71	283	2,300
Mark James	67	73	70	73	283	2,300
Padraig Harrington	71	69	71	72	283	2,300
Anders Hansen	68	73	73	69	283	2,300
Jose Manuel Lara	74	67	71	71	283	2,300
Pierre Fulke	69	71	72	72	284	1,900
Paul Affleck	72	69	73	70	284	1,900
Stephen Field	70	69	77	68	284	1,900
Yago Beamonte	71	70	71	73	285	1,700
Peter Mitchell	73	68	71	74	286	1,600
Jesus Maria Arruti	72	69	74	72	287	1,525
Sam Torrance	69	72	72	74	287	1,525
Des Smyth	69	71	76	72	288	1,425
Mark Pilkington	69	70	75	74	288	1,425
Juan Carlos Aguero	72	69	74	75	290	1,350
Jose Sota	70	71	74	78	293	1,300
Manuel Pinero	69	72	78	79	298	1,250

Madeira Island Open

Santo da Serra Golf Club, Madeira, Portugal
Par 36-36–72; 6,606 yards

March 25-28
purse, €490,000

		SCORES			TOTAL	MONEY
Pedro Linhart	70	64	71	71	276	€81,660
Mark James	70	71	69	67	277	54,430
David Howell	68	72	70	69	279	30,670

	SCORES				TOTAL	MONEY
John Bickerton	69	71	72	69	281	16,719.67
Retief Goosen	71	69	71	70	281	16,719.67
Alberto Binaghi	71	73	66	71	281	16,719.67
Padraig Harrington	73	71	66	71	281	16,719.67
Andrew Coltart	72	70	68	71	281	16,719.67
Diego Borrego	71	67	68	75	281	16,719.67
Fredrik Jacobson	71	73	71	67	282	9,081.33
Ross Drummond	68	71	73	70	282	9,081.33
Andrew McLardy	69	73	69	71	282	9,081.33
Dean Robertson	72	70	75	66	283	7,367.50
Niclas Fasth	70	71	72	70	283	7,367.50
Peter Baker	70	72	69	72	283	7,367.50
Santiago Luna	74	70	67	72	283	7,367.50
Nick O'Hern	75	72	72	65	284	5,867.75
Anders Hansen	73	72	70	69	284	5,867.75
Paul Affleck	73	69	72	70	284	5,867.75
Richard Boxall	71	71	72	70	284	5,867.75
Ian Garbutt	71	72	71	70	284	5,867.75
Wayne Riley	72	74	68	70	284	5,867.75
Gary Emerson	72	70	71	71	284	5,867.75
Roger Chapman	75	70	68	71	284	5,867.75
Paul Lawrie	72	73	70	70	285	4,924.50
Miles Tunnicliff	71	75	68	71	285	4,924.50
Fredrik Lindgren	69	73	71	72	285	4,924.50
Lucas Parsons	74	67	70	74	285	4,924.50
David Carter	74	72	72	68	286	4,272.80
Raimo Sjoberg	76	68	71	71	286	4,272.80
Jose Manuel Lara	74	68	72	72	286	4,272.80
Roger Winchester	69	71	73	73	286	4,272.80
Stephen Field	70	68	72	76	286	4,272.80
Steen Tinning	71	72	74	70	287	3,724
Van Phillips	68	77	74	68	287	3,724
Paul Eales	69	75	71	72	287	3,724
Johan Rystrom	71	73	70	73	287	3,724
Thomas Levet	71	71	71	74	287	3,724
Carlos Larrain	74	71	71	72	288	3,087
Costantino Rocca	73	74	70	71	288	3,087
Stephen Bennett	71	75	72	70	288	3,087
Raymond Russell	74	73	71	70	288	3,087
Mark Mouland	75	66	77	70	288	3,087
Massimo Scarpa	74	71	74	69	288	3,087
Daren Lee	73	74	72	69	288	3,087
Raphael Jacquelin	71	67	76	74	288	3,087
Antonio Sobrinho	73	74	71	71	289	2,401
Stephen Gallacher	72	69	77	71	289	2,401
John Senden	73	72	74	70	289	2,401
Kalle Brink	72	75	72	70	289	2,401
Jesus Maria Arruti	71	74	70	74	289	2,401
Thomas Gogele	69	75	68	77	289	2,401
Gordon J. Brand	71	74	73	72	290	1,813
Alex Cejka	73	72	74	71	290	1,813
Des Smyth	72	75	72	71	290	1,813
Dennis Edlund	72	72	71	75	290	1,813
Christopher Hanell	68	71	74	77	290	1,813
Geoff Ogilvy	71	71	70	78	290	1,813
Andrew Sherborne	73	74	70	74	291	1,470
Francisco De Pablo	75	72	71	73	291	1,470
Gary Orr	72	75	73	71	291	1,470
Max Anglert	73	74	69	76	292	1,298.50
Tom Gillis	73	74	71	74	292	1,298.50

		SCORES			TOTAL	MONEY
Andrew Sandywell	76	70	75	71	292	1,298.50
Steven Bottomley	70	76	76	70	292	1,298.50
Peter Mitchell	74	67	75	77	293	732
Andrew Clapp	73	72	73	75	293	732
Jorge Berendt	73	73	72	75	293	732
Marcello Santi	72	75	72	75	294	724
Ian Hutchings	72	73	76	73	294	724
Jean Francois Remesy	72	72	74	77	295	718.50
Gary Evans	71	75	73	76	295	718.50
Mark Roe	74	73	73	76	296	709.50
Nigel Preston	72	75	73	76	296	709.50
Soren Kjeldsen	72	75	74	75	296	709.50
Morten Backhausen	75	72	74	75	296	709.50
Clinton Whitelaw	73	74	75	76	298	702
Jean Pierre Cixous	76	71	83	71	301	699

Estoril Open

Penha Longa, Estoril, Portugal
Par 36-36–72; 6,879 yards

April 15-18
purse, €560,000

		SCORES			TOTAL	MONEY
Jean Francois Remesy	72	69	77	68	286	€93,320
Massimo Florioli	72	75	70	71	288	41,753.33
David Carter	70	72	79	67	288	41,753.33
Andrew Coltart	77	72	70	69	288	41,753.33
Geoff Ogilvy	73	75	71	70	289	20,033.33
Van Phillips	69	77	73	70	289	20,033.33
Peter Mitchell	74	71	72	72	289	20,033.33
Gary Emerson	72	72	72	74	290	12,006
Emanuele Canonica	74	71	73	72	290	12,006
Peter Baker	73	74	73	70	290	12,006
Niclas Fasth	73	69	74	74	290	12,006
Daniel Chopra	72	77	70	72	291	7,578.67
Jose Rivero	72	72	70	77	291	7,578.67
Retief Goosen	70	74	76	71	291	7,578.67
Jamie Spence	72	75	71	73	291	7,578.67
Andrew Raitt	72	70	77	72	291	7,578.67
Robert Coles	72	74	73	72	291	7,578.67
Thomas Levet	79	69	70	73	291	7,578.67
Phil Price	69	77	76	69	291	7,578.67
Ignacio Garrido	76	73	73	69	291	7,578.67
Nick O'Hern	73	73	72	73	291	7,578.67
Mark Mouland	73	75	69	74	291	7,578.67
Anthony Wall	72	72	73	74	291	7,578.67
Tom Gillis	71	77	73	71	292	5,297.60
Dennis Edlund	72	75	76	69	292	5,297.60
John Senden	72	75	75	70	292	5,297.60
Paul Eales	76	72	75	69	292	5,297.60
Gary Orr	77	69	73	73	292	5,297.60
Paul Lawrie	72	74	71	75	292	5,297.60
Raphael Jacquelin	76	71	72	73	292	5,297.60
Des Smyth	76	73	75	68	292	5,297.60
Paul Affleck	76	72	70	74	292	5,297.60
Sean Corte-Real	75	72	69	76	292	5,297.60
Soren Kjeldsen	74	69	72	78	293	3,976
John Bickerton	73	75	74	71	293	3,976

	SCORES				TOTAL	MONEY
Paul McGinley	70	75	74	74	293	3,976
Carl Watts	73	75	73	72	293	3,976
Santiago Luna	74	73	71	75	293	3,976
Ian Hutchings	71	78	74	70	293	3,976
Jonathan Lomas	70	73	77	73	293	3,976
Massimo Scarpa	72	77	70	74	293	3,976
Jeremy Robinson	76	73	73	71	293	3,976
Ian Garbutt	75	70	73	75	293	3,976
Stephen Bennett	73	75	74	72	294	2,968
Jesus Maria Arruti	72	71	77	74	294	2,968
Juan Quiros	73	76	75	70	294	2,968
David Howell	78	70	72	74	294	2,968
Francis Valera	77	71	76	70	294	2,968
Francisco Cea	73	74	73	74	294	2,968
Michael Long	75	73	73	73	294	2,968
Scott Henderson	75	70	74	75	294	2,968
Johan Rystrom	71	77	73	74	295	2,296
Mark James	76	73	71	75	295	2,296
Derrick Cooper	72	76	77	70	295	2,296
Jean Van de Velde	73	73	73	76	295	2,296
Roger Chapman	73	75	70	78	296	1,904
Paolo Quirici	71	72	80	73	296	1,904
Christian Cevaer	74	72	73	77	296	1,904
Andrew Oldcorn	71	74	78	74	297	1,680
Anders Hansen	71	73	77	76	297	1,680
Gordon Sherry	76	73	75	73	297	1,680
Costantino Rocca	76	73	74	75	298	1,540
Carl Suneson	75	72	78	73	298	1,540
Warren Bennett	79	70	79	71	299	1,428
Marc Farry	72	75	77	75	299	1,428
Alberto Binaghi	75	71	75	79	300	840
Ivo Giner	78	71	78	74	301	835.50
Pedro Linhart	73	75	78	75	301	835.50
Fabrice Tarnaud	72	75	76	79	302	829.50
Miles Tunnicliff	72	77	77	76	302	829.50
Philip Walton	77	72	77	77	303	825
Eamonn Darcy	73	76	79	78	306	820.50
Ricardo Gonzalez	74	75	81	76	306	820.50

Peugeot Open de Espana

Real Club de Golf "El Prat", Barcelona, Spain　　　　　　April 22-25
Par 35-37–72; 6,639 yards　　　　　　purse, €840,000

	SCORES				TOTAL	MONEY
Jarmo Sandelin	66	66	66	69	267	€140,000
Ignacio Garrido	65	71	67	68	271	62,633.33
Miguel Angel Jimenez	72	68	67	64	271	62,633.33
Paul McGinley	67	68	66	70	271	62,633.33
Juan Carlos Aguero	65	70	67	70	272	32,480
Jamie Spence	65	68	70	69	272	32,480
Anthony Wall	65	72	69	67	273	23,100
Paul Lawrie	66	66	73	68	273	23,100
Alex Cejka	68	69	68	70	275	17,810
Peter O'Malley	71	67	69	68	275	17,810
Paul Affleck	68	74	68	66	276	14,050
Alvaro Salto	73	63	69	71	276	14,050

	SCORES				TOTAL	MONEY
Gary Evans	72	64	69	71	276	14,050
Diego Borrego	68	70	72	66	276	14,050
John Mellor	70	69	73	65	277	12,096
Ian Garbutt	72	67	71	67	277	12,096
Massimo Scarpa	70	69	70	69	278	10,059
Peter Mitchell	71	71	68	68	278	10,059
Van Phillips	69	69	71	69	278	10,059
Santiago Luna	71	67	71	69	278	10,059
Paul Eales	69	67	73	69	278	10,059
Pierre Fulke	70	70	70	68	278	10,059
Michael Jonzon	67	69	71	71	278	10,059
Des Smyth	74	64	69	71	278	10,059
Michael Long	73	69	70	67	279	7,938
Christopher Hanell	71	70	67	71	279	7,938
Michael Campbell	67	71	73	68	279	7,938
Miguel Angel Martin	71	67	71	70	279	7,938
Sergio Garcia	67	73	70	69	279	7,938
Peter Baker	68	73	69	69	279	7,938
David Carter	69	72	70	68	279	7,938
Soren Hansen	71	68	69	71	279	7,938
Jean Van de Velde	67	75	69	69	280	6,384
Dean Robertson	69	73	71	67	280	6,384
Phil Price	70	69	72	69	280	6,384
Gerry Norquist	74	68	71	67	280	6,384
Thomas Levet	69	69	73	69	280	6,384
Jose Rozadilla	73	69	73	65	280	6,384
Emanuele Canonica	72	64	71	73	280	6,384
Max Anglert	65	76	71	69	281	5,292
Gary Orr	68	70	73	70	281	5,292
Alberto Binaghi	66	76	69	70	281	5,292
Joakim Haeggman	68	72	73	68	281	5,292
Robert Karlsson	70	70	72	69	281	5,292
Costantino Rocca	69	70	72	70	281	5,292
Brian Davis	69	72	70	71	282	4,116
Andrew Oldcorn	71	71	69	71	282	4,116
Ivo Giner	68	74	71	69	282	4,116
Mark McNulty	68	73	73	68	282	4,116
David Howell	68	74	68	72	282	4,116
Retief Goosen	71	70	74	67	282	4,116
Angel Cabrera	70	72	74	66	282	4,116
Soren Kjeldsen	69	71	71	71	282	4,116
Gary Emerson	68	74	71	70	283	3,108
Domingo Hospital	67	73	74	69	283	3,108
Padraig Harrington	71	68	75	69	283	3,108
Andrew Beal	71	68	74	70	283	3,108
Mathias Gronberg	72	70	74	68	284	2,604
Mark Roe	73	64	76	71	284	2,604
Warren Bennett	70	70	74	70	284	2,604
Jose Rivero	67	72	75	71	285	2,394
Roger Winchester	71	67	73	74	285	2,394
Scott Henderson	70	70	73	73	286	2,184
Jose Manuel Carriles	68	72	71	75	286	2,184
Seve Ballesteros	73	69	73	71	286	2,184
Steve Webster	68	72	74	73	287	1,260
Per Haugsrud	69	71	77	73	290	1,257
Jose Manuel Lara	71	71	75	75	292	1,254

Fiat and Fila Italian Open

Circolo Golf, Torino, Italy
Par 36-36–72; 6,954 yards

April 29-May 2
purse, €1,000,000

	SCORES				TOTAL	MONEY
Dean Robertson	70	65	68	68	271	€166,660
Padraig Harrington	68	66	68	70	272	111,100
Russell Claydon	66	68	73	66	273	51,666.67
Phil Price	71	71	68	63	273	51,666.67
Gary Evans	65	72	68	68	273	51,666.67
Miguel Angel Jimenez	68	68	70	68	274	28,075
Ricardo Gonzalez	71	65	68	70	274	28,075
Retief Goosen	69	68	72	66	274	28,075
Francisco Cea	67	65	71	71	274	28,075
John Senden	71	66	71	67	275	18,520
Costantino Rocca	71	68	68	68	275	18,520
Gary Orr	70	65	72	68	275	18,520
Peter Mitchell	67	71	70	68	276	15,045
Mark McNulty	69	71	70	66	276	15,045
Jose Maria Olazabal	71	69	70	66	276	15,045
David Carter	68	68	72	68	276	15,045
Seve Ballesteros	70	71	69	67	277	13,500
Craig Hainline	71	67	69	71	278	12,650
Rodger Davis	69	68	72	69	278	12,650
Patrik Sjoland	67	69	73	70	279	11,700
Emanuele Canonica	71	68	70	70	279	11,700
Olle Karlsson	71	69	69	70	279	11,700
Michael Campbell	69	70	70	71	280	10,050
Raphael Jacquelin	70	72	68	70	280	10,050
Mathias Gronberg	72	70	69	69	280	10,050
Jeev Milkha Singh	71	69	68	72	280	10,050
Roger Wessels	70	66	72	72	280	10,050
Peter Baker	72	69	69	70	280	10,050
Joakim Haeggman	71	71	68	70	280	10,050
Paul Eales	72	68	71	69	280	10,050
Derrick Cooper	66	73	74	68	281	8,014.29
Francis Valera	68	74	69	70	281	8,014.29
Eduardo Romero	69	70	70	72	281	8,014.29
Jarmo Sandelin	71	67	71	72	281	8,014.29
Soren Kjeldsen	71	69	68	73	281	8,014.29
Massimo Scarpa	71	71	65	74	281	8,014.29
Roger Winchester	72	70	68	71	281	8,014.29
Andrew Oldcorn	69	73	69	71	282	6,400
Bernhard Langer	70	68	73	71	282	6,400
Greg Turner	68	72	74	68	282	6,400
Jorge Berendt	69	71	70	72	282	6,400
Massimo Florioli	71	71	67	73	282	6,400
Alex Cejka	71	71	68	72	282	6,400
Mark Roe	73	67	71	71	282	6,400
Marc Farry	71	68	70	73	282	6,400
David Gilford	71	71	68	72	282	6,400
Steen Tinning	72	70	70	71	283	4,800
Marcello Santi	71	68	75	69	283	4,800
Andrew Coltart	69	71	74	69	283	4,800
Jarrod Moseley	69	67	75	72	283	4,800
Mats Lanner	62	77	67	77	283	4,800
Thomas Levet	70	70	72	71	283	4,800
Soren Hansen	69	70	74	70	283	4,800
Barry Lane	69	73	71	71	284	3,600

	SCORES				TOTAL	MONEY
Per Nyman	65	74	74	71	284	3,600
Anthony Wall	71	71	73	69	284	3,600
Antonio Sobrinho	69	72	73	70	284	3,600
Pierre Fulke	71	68	75	70	284	3,600
Robert Jan Derksen	71	71	72	71	285	3,000
Stephen Dodd	72	70	73	70	285	3,000
Daren Lee	72	68	74	71	285	3,000
Miles Tunnicliff	72	66	75	73	286	2,650
Max Anglert	69	71	75	71	286	2,650
Jean Van de Velde	68	72	74	72	286	2,650
Thomas Gogele	72	70	73	71	286	2,650
Andrew Sherborne	71	67	76	73	287	1,492.50
Anders Hansen	75	67	76	69	287	1,492.50
Stephen Gallacher	67	75	74	71	287	1,492.50
Robert Karlsson	71	70	73	73	287	1,492.50
Lee Janzen	72	68	73	74	287	1,492.50
Paolo Quirici	74	68	72	73	287	1,492.50
Steve Webster	70	70	76	72	288	1,479
Clinton Whitelaw	73	69	74	72	288	1,479
Diego Borrego	73	68	74	73	288	1,479
Scott Henderson	72	70	77	70	289	1,468.50
Pedro Linhart	72	69	73	75	289	1,468.50
Jim Payne	70	72	74	73	289	1,468.50
Alberto Binaghi	72	70	75	72	289	1,468.50
Tom Gillis	70	72	79	69	290	1,461
John McHenry	70	72	76	74	292	1,458

Novotel Perrier Open de France

Golf de Medoc, Bordeaux, France
Par 35-36–71; 6,909 yards

May 6-9
purse, €850,000

	SCORES				TOTAL	MONEY
Retief Goosen	69	65	68	70	272	€141,660
Greg Turner	67	65	70	70	272	94,440
(Goosen defeated Turner on second extra hole.)						
Santiago Luna	67	72	67	69	275	47,855
Jose Coceres	69	69	66	71	275	47,855
Ian Woosnam	71	68	66	71	276	30,416.67
Eamonn Darcy	66	70	72	68	276	30,416.67
Jorge Berendt	69	67	68	72	276	30,416.67
Marc Farry	70	63	69	75	277	18,215
Marc Pendaries	67	72	68	70	277	18,215
Andrew Sherborne	66	67	70	74	277	18,215
Emanuele Canonica	73	69	66	69	277	18,215
Massimo Scarpa	68	74	67	70	279	13,152
Diego Borrego	71	70	67	71	279	13,152
Jamie Spence	68	72	66	73	279	13,152
Eduardo Romero	68	70	72	69	279	13,152
Ross McFarlane	71	68	67	73	279	13,152
Des Smyth	70	69	71	70	280	10,625
Jean Francois Remesy	66	68	75	71	280	10,625
Wayne Riley	75	66	72	67	280	10,625
Anders Hansen	70	68	70	72	280	10,625
Anders Forsbrand	68	74	70	68	280	10,625
Jarmo Sandelin	72	68	71	70	281	9,307.50
Tomas Jesus Munoz	69	71	69	72	281	9,307.50

	SCORES				TOTAL	MONEY
Peter Mitchell	68	71	69	73	281	9,307.50
Christian Cevaer	68	70	69	74	281	9,307.50
Alexandre Balicki	69	72	68	73	282	7,788.13
Angel Cabrera	70	66	70	76	282	7,788.13
Jeremy Robinson	67	68	71	76	282	7,788.13
Gustavo Rojas	68	72	73	69	282	7,788.13
Costantino Rocca	69	73	71	69	282	7,788.13
Mark Roe	69	69	70	74	282	7,788.13
Bob May	66	72	71	73	282	7,788.13
Daren Lee	66	73	69	74	282	7,788.13
Roger Chapman	68	74	69	72	283	6,630
Richard Green	72	68	73	70	283	6,630
Roger Wessels	68	69	71	75	283	6,630
Stephen Gallacher	71	70	69	74	284	5,440
Nick O'Hern	69	68	75	72	284	5,440
Jorgen Aker	73	69	70	72	284	5,440
*Gregory Havret	70	68	77	69	284	
Simon Wakefield	69	68	72	75	284	5,440
Jeev Milkha Singh	68	69	73	74	284	5,440
Nicolas Joakimides	70	69	71	74	284	5,440
Kalle Brink	71	71	70	72	284	5,440
Johan Rystrom	70	70	72	72	284	5,440
Lucas Parsons	78	64	70	72	284	5,440
Michele Reale	72	68	70	74	284	5,440
Brian Nelson	69	73	71	71	284	5,440
Carl Suneson	68	74	69	74	285	4,080
Clinton Whitelaw	74	68	70	73	285	4,080
Sebastien Delagrange	69	69	74	73	285	4,080
Howard Clark	73	68	73	71	285	4,080
Carl Watts	71	67	72	75	285	4,080
Fernando Roca	71	69	70	76	286	3,006.88
Henrik Nystrom	69	71	70	76	286	3,006.88
Jesus Maria Arruti	68	74	74	70	286	3,006.88
Andrew Sandywell	68	70	74	74	286	3,006.88
Morten Backhausen	71	68	71	76	286	3,006.88
Frederic Cupillard	72	69	75	70	286	3,006.88
Andrew Raitt	70	69	74	73	286	3,006.88
Richard Boxall	70	72	70	74	286	3,006.88
Stephen Bennett	67	71	74	75	287	2,380
Pascal Edmond	70	72	69	76	287	2,380
Ian Hutchings	67	75	72	73	287	2,380
Jonathan Lomas	71	70	73	74	288	1,630.20
Andrew Beal	69	72	72	75	288	1,630.20
Brian Davis	73	69	71	75	288	1,630.20
Stephen Dodd	65	76	71	76	288	1,630.20
Domingo Hospital	70	69	74	75	288	1,630.20
Steven Alker	71	71	72	75	289	1,264.50
Jim Payne	70	72	73	74	289	1,264.50
John McHenry	67	70	75	78	290	1,254
Benoit Teilleria	70	70	69	81	290	1,254
Nick Ludwell	76	66	75	73	290	1,254
Olle Karlsson	71	68	72	79	290	1,254
Carlos Larrain	71	71	75	73	290	1,254
Scott Henderson	69	72	76	74	291	1,245
*Oliver David	71	70	74	77	292	
Robert Lee	70	68	76	81	295	1,242

Benson and Hedges International Open

The Oxfordshire Golf Club, Thame, England
Par 36-36–72; 7,205 yards

May 13-16
purse, €1,120,000

	SCORES				TOTAL	MONEY
Colin Montgomerie	68	66	71	68	273	€186,670
Angel Cabrera	69	67	71	69	276	97,200
Per-Ulrik Johansson	68	65	74	69	276	97,200
Miguel Angel Jimenez	65	72	72	68	277	51,800
Diego Borrego	74	67	66	70	277	51,800
Jeremy Robinson	73	67	74	64	278	39,200
Jean Van de Velde	71	70	68	70	279	22,276.89
Eamonn Darcy	72	68	68	71	279	22,276.89
Bob May	71	70	68	70	279	22,276.89
Per Nyman	74	66	73	66	279	22,276.89
Nick Faldo	68	69	73	69	279	22,276.89
Eduardo Romero	71	68	73	67	279	22,276.89
Bernhard Langer	68	72	68	71	279	22,276.89
Patrik Sjoland	69	70	71	69	279	22,276.89
Richard Green	72	69	70	68	279	22,276.89
Jonathan Lomas	71	67	71	71	280	14,797.50
Ian Woosnam	71	70	71	68	280	14,797.50
Padraig Harrington	70	71	71	68	280	14,797.50
Jose Maria Olazabal	70	67	69	74	280	14,797.50
Paul McGinley	72	67	70	72	281	12,096
Phil Price	65	70	72	74	281	12,096
Emanuele Canonica	71	70	71	69	281	12,096
Darren Clarke	70	71	71	69	281	12,096
Dean Robertson	72	69	72	68	281	12,096
Gary Evans	72	67	71	71	281	12,096
Rodger Davis	72	69	72	68	281	12,096
Mathias Gronberg	72	69	68	72	281	12,096
Anders Forsbrand	70	70	69	72	281	12,096
Peter O'Malley	71	69	70	72	282	9,912
Paul Affleck	71	69	69	73	282	9,912
Stephen Leaney	70	71	72	69	282	9,912
Soren Hansen	69	68	71	74	282	9,912
Andrew Sherborne	69	72	66	76	283	8,624
Roger Winchester	71	71	71	70	283	8,624
Gary Orr	70	70	72	71	283	8,624
Seve Ballesteros	70	71	69	73	283	8,624
Marc Farry	68	72	74	69	283	8,624
Barry Lane	68	70	73	72	283	8,624
Peter Mitchell	69	71	67	77	284	7,056
John Senden	72	68	75	69	284	7,056
Fredrik Lindgren	70	69	69	76	284	7,056
Sandy Lyle	69	70	72	73	284	7,056
Andrew Raitt	73	68	70	73	284	7,056
Andrew Coltart	72	66	72	74	284	7,056
Santiago Luna	71	70	71	72	284	7,056
Stephen Allan	70	71	72	71	284	7,056
Andrew Beal	70	70	68	77	285	5,712
Stephen Field	70	71	72	72	285	5,712
Richard Boxall	71	71	76	67	285	5,712
Miguel Angel Martin	70	70	71	74	285	5,712
Andrew Oldcorn	70	72	70	74	286	4,592
Soren Kjeldsen	71	70	74	71	286	4,592
Ignacio Garrido	70	72	71	73	286	4,592
Robert Karlsson	70	69	72	75	286	4,592

	SCORES				TOTAL	MONEY
Russell Claydon	69	73	73	71	286	4,592
Christopher Hanell	74	65	75	72	286	4,592
*Adam Frayne	72	69	74	71	286	
Olle Karlsson	72	69	77	69	287	3,556
Greg Turner	71	69	73	74	287	3,556
Olivier Edmond	74	67	72	74	287	3,556
Roger Wessels	67	71	75	74	287	3,556
Tony Johnstone	69	72	72	75	288	3,248
Greg Owen	74	68	75	72	289	3,136
Francis Valera	69	70	73	78	290	3,024
Van Phillips	70	71	74	76	291	2,912
Roger Chapman	71	71	77	78	297	2,800

Deutsche Bank-SAP Open TPC of Europe

St. Leon Rot, Heidelberg, Germany
Par 36-36–72; 7,236 yards

May 21-24
purse, €1,680,000

	SCORES				TOTAL	MONEY
Tiger Woods	69	68	68	68	273	€280,000
Retief Goosen	73	69	68	66	276	186,650
Nick Price	71	76	65	65	277	105,160
Peter Baker	69	73	66	71	279	84,000
Ernie Els	66	73	70	71	280	64,980
Brian Davis	69	73	66	72	280	64,980
Miguel Angel Jimenez	71	72	70	68	281	40,875
Jarmo Sandelin	70	69	73	69	281	40,875
Darren Clarke	70	73	69	69	281	40,875
Barry Lane	73	68	70	70	281	40,875
Peter Senior	72	72	72	66	282	27,440.60
Bernhard Langer	71	74	70	67	282	27,440.60
Bob May	70	71	71	70	282	27,440.60
Jesper Parnevik	71	68	71	72	282	27,440.60
Robert Karlsson	72	71	67	72	282	27,440.60
Gary Orr	66	74	71	72	283	23,671
John Mellor	73	68	76	67	284	21,728
John Senden	72	69	74	69	284	21,728
Jean Van de Velde	68	73	70	73	284	21,728
Marc Farry	69	73	73	70	285	19,656
Colin Montgomerie	71	70	71	73	285	19,656
Sergio Garcia	70	70	71	74	285	19,656
David Gilford	70	75	72	69	286	16,884
Stephen Allan	71	75	72	68	286	16,884
Jeev Milkha Singh	74	73	73	66	286	16,884
Peter O'Malley	70	72	74	70	286	16,884
Roger Winchester	72	70	74	70	286	16,884
Stephen Leaney	71	73	72	70	286	16,884
Diego Borrego	74	68	73	71	286	16,884
Ian Garbutt	73	70	72	71	286	16,884
Steve Webster	72	70	74	71	287	14,364
David Carter	73	72	68	74	287	14,364
Soren Hansen	72	74	71	71	288	13,104
Jose Coceres	73	70	74	71	288	13,104
Jamie Spence	75	72	71	70	288	13,104
Anthony Wall	74	72	72	70	288	13,104
Roger Chapman	70	74	70	74	288	13,104
Greg Turner	73	74	70	72	289	11,592

	SCORES				TOTAL	MONEY
Raphael Jacquelin	73	70	74	72	289	11,592
Padraig Harrington	73	73	70	73	289	11,592
Roger Wessels	77	70	69	73	289	11,592
David Howell	72	70	74	74	290	9,912
Patrik Sjoland	69	73	74	74	290	9,912
Jeremy Robinson	70	73	73	74	290	9,912
Alex Cejka	69	75	72	74	290	9,912
Gary Evans	74	72	70	74	290	9,912
Ian Woosnam	73	71	71	75	290	9,912
Stephen Field	76	71	70	74	291	8,232
Derrick Cooper	71	74	74	72	291	8,232
Mark Roe	73	72	76	70	291	8,232
Silvio Grappasonni	74	69	72	76	291	8,232
Eduardo Romero	72	74	73	73	292	7,056
Heinz Peter Thul	74	73	73	72	292	7,056
Mark O'Meara	71	73	76	72	292	7,056
Christopher Hanell	71	75	72	75	293	6,048
Warren Bennett	72	74	74	73	293	6,048
Per Haugsrud	73	72	75	73	293	6,048
Van Phillips	72	73	74	75	294	5,040
Andrew Oldcorn	72	73	74	75	294	5,040
Domingo Hospital	73	74	73	74	294	5,040
Ricardo Gonzalez	75	72	74	73	294	5,040
Thomas Gogele	70	77	69	78	294	5,040
Dean Robertson	71	76	72	76	295	3,906
Paul McGinley	70	74	76	75	295	3,906
Jorge Berendt	71	75	76	73	295	3,906
Mark Mouland	74	73	79	69	295	3,906
Angel Cabrera	73	73	73	77	296	2,512.50
Des Smyth	74	69	77	76	296	2,512.50
Thomas Levet	73	73	77	73	296	2,512.50
Massimo Scarpa	71	76	77	72	296	2,512.50
Eamonn Darcy	73	74	75	75	297	2,503.50
Clinton Whitelaw	71	75	77	74	297	2,503.50
Nick Faldo	71	75	73	79	298	2,497.50
Michael Jonzon	71	74	77	76	298	2,497.50
Max Anglert	69	76	78	76	299	2,491.50
Steven Richardson	70	75	81	73	299	2,491.50
Olle Karlsson	70	77	75	78	300	2,485.50
Fredrik Lindgren	70	74	80	76	300	2,485.50

Volvo PGA Championship

Wentworth Club, Surrey, England
Par 35-37–72; 7,006 yards

May 28-31
purse, €1,820,000

	SCORES				TOTAL	MONEY
Colin Montgomerie	69	70	67	64	270	€303,350
Mark James	67	70	72	66	275	202,300
Paul Eales	68	70	71	67	276	113,930
Stephen Leaney	73	67	69	68	277	77,233.33
Ernie Els	68	67	74	68	277	77,233.33
Retief Goosen	67	69	70	71	277	77,233.33
Bernhard Langer	65	73	70	70	278	46,900
David Carter	71	70	69	68	278	46,900
Mathias Gronberg	69	73	67	69	278	46,900
Jarmo Sandelin	70	72	71	66	279	33,716.67

	SCORES				TOTAL	MONEY
Sven Struver	75	69	69	66	279	33,716.67
Jose Maria Olazabal	68	70	72	69	279	33,716.67
Darren Clarke	67	67	77	69	280	26,262.33
David Howell	72	72	71	65	280	26,262.33
Robert Karlsson	70	68	71	71	280	26,262.33
Warren Bennett	70	74	69	67	280	26,262.33
Ian Garbutt	74	68	68	70	280	26,262.33
Jean Van de Velde	67	75	70	68	280	26,262.33
Stephen Allan	72	69	71	69	281	20,774
Michael Campbell	68	70	72	71	281	20,774
Eduardo Romero	71	71	67	72	281	20,774
Dean Robertson	68	69	73	71	281	20,774
Jesper Parnevik	70	69	72	70	281	20,774
Sergio Garcia	72	73	70	66	281	20,774
Paul Broadhurst	73	69	72	67	281	20,774
Mark Roe	70	70	73	69	282	18,018
Ian Woosnam	72	73	70	67	282	18,018
Sandy Lyle	70	70	71	71	282	18,018
Roger Wessels	71	73	68	71	283	15,045.33
Costantino Rocca	71	71	72	69	283	15,045.33
Joakim Haeggman	71	72	69	71	283	15,045.33
Thomas Levet	71	71	71	70	283	15,045.33
Jeev Milkha Singh	72	69	71	71	283	15,045.33
Des Smyth	69	72	72	70	283	15,045.33
Peter Lonard	69	70	70	74	283	15,045.33
Gary Orr	71	70	73	69	283	15,045.33
Sam Torrance	70	68	75	70	283	15,045.33
Mark McNulty	71	70	67	76	284	12,922
Rolf Muntz	71	72	73	68	284	12,922
Phil Price	73	69	72	71	285	12,012
Greg Turner	73	67	74	71	285	12,012
Pedro Linhart	67	76	72	70	285	12,012
Raymond Russell	71	72	74	69	286	10,738
Andrew Oldcorn	72	68	73	73	286	10,738
John Bickerton	73	72	74	67	286	10,738
Miguel Angel Jimenez	73	72	75	66	286	10,738
Paul Lawrie	70	71	76	70	287	8,736
Andrew Coltart	72	73	73	69	287	8,736
Michael Long	71	73	71	72	287	8,736
Pierre Fulke	73	68	73	73	287	8,736
Craig Hainline	73	72	72	70	287	8,736
Barry Lane	70	74	71	72	287	8,736
Santiago Luna	71	71	75	70	287	8,736
Francisco Cea	72	73	72	71	288	7,098
David Gilford	70	70	75	73	288	7,098
Lee Westwood	69	73	75	72	289	6,188
Ignacio Garrido	74	70	73	72	289	6,188
Padraig Harrington	74	70	72	73	289	6,188
Nick Faldo	74	71	74	71	290	5,460
Jose Rivero	67	76	71	76	290	5,460
Zhang Lian-wei	74	71	73	72	290	5,460
Patrik Sjoland	73	71	73	74	291	5,096
Derrick Cooper	67	76	74	75	292	4,732
Per Nyman	74	70	78	70	292	4,732
Paul Curry	70	74	71	77	292	4,732
Philip Walton	73	72	74	75	294	2,730

Compass Group English Open

Marriott Hanbury Manor, Ware, England
Par 36-36–72; 7,016 yards

June 3-6
purse, €1,000,000

	SCORES				TOTAL	MONEY
Darren Clarke	68	65	67	68	268	€166,660
John Bickerton	64	73	68	65	270	111,100
David Carter	67	71	67	69	274	56,300
Stephen Leaney	68	70	67	69	274	56,300
Andrew Coltart	68	73	64	70	275	38,700
Colin Montgomerie	70	70	65	70	275	38,700
Dean Robertson	69	70	70	67	276	22,143.33
Fredrik Lindgren	71	71	67	67	276	22,143.33
Gary Orr	68	71	66	71	276	22,143.33
Mark Roe	71	72	68	65	276	22,143.33
Olle Karlsson	67	72	70	67	276	22,143.33
Peter Senior	69	68	69	70	276	22,143.33
Emanuele Canonica	71	67	70	69	277	15,690
Robert Karlsson	71	72	63	71	277	15,690
John Senden	69	72	69	68	278	14,400
Thomas Gogele	67	69	70	72	278	14,400
Costantino Rocca	69	69	68	73	279	12,316.67
Jeev Milkha Singh	68	73	67	71	279	12,316.67
Zhang Lian-wei	70	71	71	67	279	12,316.67
Paul Broadhurst	69	73	67	70	279	12,316.67
Paul Lawrie	69	70	71	69	279	12,316.67
Peter Mitchell	68	69	70	72	279	12,316.67
Geoff Ogilvy	64	71	72	73	280	10,950
Paul Curry	68	71	72	69	280	10,950
Ian Garbutt	70	72	67	72	281	10,200
Peter Lonard	75	67	68	71	281	10,200
Wayne Westner	70	73	69	69	281	10,200
Pedro Linhart	72	70	70	70	282	9,000
Retief Goosen	70	71	68	73	282	9,000
Robert Coles	70	70	73	69	282	9,000
Sam Torrance	67	73	71	71	282	9,000
Stephen Gallacher	72	71	68	71	282	9,000
Andrew Raitt	70	70	72	71	283	7,700
Bob May	72	68	69	74	283	7,700
Gary Emerson	72	71	66	74	283	7,700
Jamie Spence	69	73	69	72	283	7,700
Mark McNulty	67	77	71	68	283	7,700
Mats Hallberg	71	72	72	68	283	7,700
Alberto Binaghi	70	68	69	77	284	5,900
Anders Hansen	73	71	69	71	284	5,900
Daniel Chopra	71	70	72	71	284	5,900
Ignacio Garrido	69	74	71	70	284	5,900
Jim Payne	74	67	71	72	284	5,900
Mark James	71	72	69	72	284	5,900
Mats Lanner	70	72	71	71	284	5,900
Michael Campbell	70	72	74	68	284	5,900
Miles Tunnicliff	71	71	68	74	284	5,900
Roger Winchester	68	70	72	74	284	5,900
Soren Kjeldsen	73	69	70	72	284	5,900
Thomas Levet	71	71	71	71	284	5,900
Gary Evans	72	71	70	72	285	4,400
Jean Van de Velde	70	73	71	71	285	4,400
Nick Faldo	70	74	73	68	285	4,400
Christian Cevaer	72	72	70	72	286	3,600

	SCORES				TOTAL	MONEY
Malcolm Mackenzie	72	72	70	72	286	3,600
Marc Farry	72	72	71	71	286	3,600
Mathias Gronberg	66	74	73	73	286	3,600
Roger Wessels	72	71	72	71	286	3,600
Anthony Wall	73	70	74	70	287	3,000
Paul Eales	70	69	73	75	287	3,000
Ross McFarlane	73	69	73	72	287	3,000
Eamonn Darcy	72	72	72	72	288	2,750
Tom Gillis	68	75	71	74	288	2,750
Joakim Haeggman	75	69	70	75	289	1,918.20
Anders Forsbrand	69	72	74	74	289	1,918.20
Christopher Hanell	73	71	73	72	289	1,918.20
Raphael Jacquelin	70	72	73	74	289	1,918.20
Stephen Dodd	70	70	73	76	289	1,918.20
Massimo Florioli	70	73	72	75	290	1,488
Andrew Bonhomme	70	73	70	77	290	1,488
Steve Webster	69	72	73	76	290	1,488
Stuart Cage	74	70	75	74	293	1,482
Carlos Rodiles	75	69	72	81	297	1,477.50
Francisco Cea	71	71	81	74	297	1,477.50
Jeremy Robinson	70	73	81	75	299	1,473

German Open

Sporting Club Berlin, Berlin, Germany
Par 36-36–72; 7,082 yards

June 10-13
purse, €1,000,000

	SCORES				TOTAL	MONEY
Jarmo Sandelin	69	64	73	68	274	€166,660
Retief Goosen	67	71	68	68	274	111,100
(Sandelin defeated Goosen on first extra hole.)						
Pierre Fulke	69	69	71	67	276	62,600
Roger Wessels	67	67	75	68	277	46,200
Thomas Gogele	71	71	70	65	277	46,200
Padraig Harrington	69	70	69	70	278	30,000
Alex Cejka	66	71	73	68	278	30,000
Santiago Luna	71	70	69	68	278	30,000
David Carter	69	68	73	69	279	20,226.67
Raymond Russell	74	70	63	72	279	20,226.67
Gary Evans	62	75	70	72	279	20,226.67
Geoff Ogilvy	70	66	73	71	280	15,815
Robert Karlsson	72	68	69	71	280	15,815
Steve Webster	70	70	71	69	280	15,815
Jorge Berendt	66	71	72	71	280	15,815
Jean Van de Velde	72	68	72	69	281	13,500
Fabrice Tarnaud	71	72	68	70	281	13,500
Paolo Quirici	72	72	67	70	281	13,500
Soren Hansen	70	71	73	68	282	11,720
Ian Hutchings	71	69	72	70	282	11,720
Peter Mitchell	69	73	74	66	282	11,720
Ricardo Gonzalez	70	73	71	68	282	11,720
Peter O'Malley	69	70	73	70	282	11,720
Raphael Jacquelin	71	72	68	72	283	9,750
Christopher Hanell	70	72	67	74	283	9,750
Per Nyman	70	73	69	71	283	9,750
Soren Kjeldsen	67	72	75	69	283	9,750
Paul Broadhurst	71	70	71	71	283	9,750

		SCORES			TOTAL	MONEY
Jean Francois Remesy	68	71	72	72	283	9,750
Costantino Rocca	69	72	70	72	283	9,750
Mark Roe	71	69	74	69	283	9,750
Bernhard Langer	72	69	72	71	284	8,100
Mark McNulty	70	72	72	70	284	8,100
Gary Orr	70	71	70	73	284	8,100
Andrew Oldcorn	73	67	75	69	284	8,100
Michael Campbell	69	72	73	71	285	6,600
Fredrik Jacobson	72	70	74	69	285	6,600
Paul McGinley	70	69	75	71	285	6,600
Sven Struver	72	71	74	68	285	6,600
John Bickerton	72	71	70	72	285	6,600
Joakim Haeggman	68	75	70	72	285	6,600
Ian Garbutt	68	71	73	73	285	6,600
Roger Winchester	72	72	72	69	285	6,600
Alberto Binaghi	69	72	74	70	285	6,600
Malcolm Mackenzie	71	71	72	71	285	6,600
Robert Jan Derksen	67	69	72	77	285	6,600
John Senden	70	70	75	71	286	5,100
Greg Turner	66	74	72	74	286	5,100
Peter Lonard	72	69	73	72	286	5,100
Andrew Raitt	69	74	73	70	286	5,100
Carl Watts	69	72	72	74	287	4,600
Erol Simsek	68	73	72	75	288	3,900
Peter Baker	71	72	73	72	288	3,900
Johan Rystrom	71	70	72	75	288	3,900
Andrew McLardy	72	72	74	70	288	3,900
Anthony Wall	71	73	72	72	288	3,900
John Mellor	69	70	77	72	288	3,900
Greg Owen	74	69	72	74	289	3,200
*Marcel Siem	73	71	72	73	289	
*Michael Thannhauser	73	69	74	73	289	
Russell Claydon	73	71	73	73	290	3,100
Tom Gillis	72	68	77	74	291	2,950
Daren Lee	71	69	76	75	291	2,950
Silvio Grappasonni	73	71	74	74	292	2,800
Miles Tunnicliff	76	67	74	76	293	2,325
Max Anglert	73	71	75	74	293	2,325
Carlos Rodiles	72	69	80	72	293	2,325
Paul Eales	72	72	73	76	293	2,325
Barry Lane	70	74	74	76	294	1,495.50
Jim Payne	72	72	76	74	294	1,495.50
Craig Ronald	71	73	76	76	296	1,491

Moroccan Open

Royal Golf D'Agadir, Agadir, Morocco
Par 36-36–72; 6,657 yards

June 17-20
purse, €490,000

		SCORES			TOTAL	MONEY
Miguel Angel Martin	67	71	70	68	276	€81,660
David Park	67	69	68	72	276	54,430
(Martin defeated Park on sixth extra hole.)						
Klas Eriksson	75	67	69	68	279	30,670
Jorge Berendt	68	71	72	69	280	22,635
Eric Carlberg	67	72	66	75	280	22,635
Nick O'Hern	70	70	70	71	281	17,150

	SCORES				TOTAL	MONEY
Andrew Raitt	73	68	72	70	283	12,632.67
Daren Lee	68	74	69	72	283	12,632.67
Carlos Larrain	68	70	70	75	283	12,632.67
Stephen Scahill	71	71	70	72	284	9,800
Scott Watson	71	74	72	68	285	8,722
Jesus Maria Arruti	73	71	71	70	285	8,722
David Lynn	73	72	71	70	286	7,882
Marcello Santi	71	74	73	69	287	6,640
Scott Downton	74	71	71	71	287	6,640
Carl Suneson	72	69	74	72	287	6,640
Geoff Ogilvy	72	73	70	72	287	6,640
Johan Selberg	71	72	70	74	287	6,640
Alex Cejka	74	68	69	76	287	6,640
Simon Wakefield	71	72	64	80	287	6,640
Brian Nelson	77	68	72	71	288	5,586
Van Phillips	72	74	71	71	288	5,586
Fabrice Tarnaud	77	67	71	73	288	5,586
Clinton Whitelaw	72	73	72	72	289	5,071.50
Henrik Nystrom	74	71	73	71	289	5,071.50
Mikael Lundberg	73	70	76	70	289	5,071.50
David Howell	74	71	69	75	289	5,071.50
Anders Hansen	74	71	73	72	290	4,284
Alexandre Balicki	73	73	72	72	290	4,284
Simon Hurley	68	74	76	72	290	4,284
Charles Challen	71	72	73	74	290	4,284
Ignacio Garrido	74	70	72	74	290	4,284
Lucas Parsons	73	67	75	75	290	4,284
Costantino Rocca	73	72	69	76	290	4,284
Alvaro Salto	78	68	71	74	291	3,430
Heinz Peter Thul	69	74	74	74	291	3,430
John Wade	70	73	74	74	291	3,430
Ola Eliasson	74	71	74	72	291	3,430
Matthew Blackey	73	72	74	72	291	3,430
Hennie Otto	70	71	75	75	291	3,430
Gordon Sherry	73	69	73	76	291	3,430
Philip Walton	72	70	73	76	291	3,430
Robert Coles	73	66	73	79	291	3,430
Erol Simsek	76	67	74	75	292	2,744
Benoit Teilleria	70	71	77	74	292	2,744
Martin Erlandsson	73	72	76	71	292	2,744
Knud Storegaard	73	73	75	71	292	2,744
Ian Hutchings	73	69	73	77	292	2,744
Ashley Roestoff	73	72	73	75	293	2,254
Wayne Riley	72	69	78	74	293	2,254
Pedro Linhart	74	71	78	70	293	2,254
Ross Drummond	73	73	70	77	293	2,254
Morten Backhausen	74	68	72	79	293	2,254
Andrew McLardy	70	74	75	75	294	1,911
Jean Pierre Cixous	67	73	80	74	294	1,911
Daniel Westermark	71	71	76	77	295	1,666
Rafael Benitez	71	74	75	75	295	1,666
Carlos Rodiles	71	73	71	80	295	1,666
Steven Alker	72	72	73	79	296	1,494.50
Philip Golding	74	71	75	76	296	1,494.50
Tony Johnstone	74	70	80	73	297	1,396.50
Juan Nutt	77	66	71	83	297	1,396.50
Elliot Boult	73	70	78	77	298	1,323
Michele Reale	75	71	77	76	299	1,249.50
John Hawksworth	73	70	82	74	299	1,249.50
Mohamed Makroune	71	72	79	83	305	735

Compaq European Grand Prix

De Vere Slaley Hall, Northumberland, England
Par 36-36–72; 7,088 yards

June 24-27
purse, €910,000

	SCORES				TOTAL	MONEY
David Park	67	65	70	72	274	€151,660
David Carter	65	69	68	73	275	79,030
Retief Goosen	70	68	71	66	275	79,030
Peter O'Malley	66	71	71	70	278	45,500
Lee Westwood	72	70	67	70	279	38,540
Ricardo Gonzalez	70	70	71	71	282	29,575
Dean Robertson	72	70	72	68	282	29,575
Stephen Leaney	71	72	69	71	283	20,423.33
Warren Bennett	73	70	73	67	283	20,423.33
Jose Coceres	69	68	73	73	283	20,423.33
Sven Struver	69	67	74	74	284	14,864.80
Padraig Harrington	71	71	71	71	284	14,864.80
Jamie Spence	68	71	71	74	284	14,864.80
Darren Clarke	71	69	76	68	284	14,864.80
Emanuele Canonica	72	69	69	74	284	14,864.80
Johan Rystrom	69	72	71	73	285	11,810.40
Massimo Scarpa	72	67	74	72	285	11,810.40
Stephen Scahill	73	69	73	70	285	11,810.40
Peter Mitchell	72	65	75	73	285	11,810.40
Andrew Coltart	73	69	71	72	285	11,810.40
Geoff Ogilvy	71	72	73	70	286	10,374
Robert Lee	70	70	77	69	286	10,374
Stephen Gallacher	72	71	72	71	286	10,374
John McHenry	72	71	72	72	287	9,009
Paul Affleck	72	69	73	73	287	9,009
Ian Garbutt	70	68	73	76	287	9,009
Russell Claydon	71	69	74	73	287	9,009
Ross McFarlane	70	71	73	73	287	9,009
Thomas Gogele	70	74	73	70	287	9,009
Alex Cejka	71	71	76	69	287	9,009
Gary Emerson	68	75	75	70	288	7,200.38
Greg Turner	72	70	73	73	288	7,200.38
David Howell	71	69	75	73	288	7,200.38
Thomas Levet	71	73	71	73	288	7,200.38
Jeev Milkha Singh	68	69	72	79	288	7,200.38
Miles Tunnicliff	69	68	73	78	288	7,200.38
Massimo Florioli	74	67	74	73	288	7,200.38
Diego Borrego	70	70	71	77	288	7,200.38
Daren Lee	68	70	76	75	289	5,369
Robert Jan Derksen	69	73	76	71	289	5,369
Michael Campbell	69	70	76	74	289	5,369
Jonathan Lomas	69	73	76	71	289	5,369
Richard Boxall	75	69	74	71	289	5,369
Ian Hutchings	71	73	75	70	289	5,369
Seve Ballesteros	73	69	74	73	289	5,369
Fabrice Tarnaud	71	71	75	72	289	5,369
Brian Davis	70	73	71	75	289	5,369
Stephen Bennett	68	70	75	76	289	5,369
Paul McGinley	67	73	74	75	289	5,369
David Gilford	74	65	71	79	289	5,369
David Lynn	67	72	78	73	290	4,095
Van Phillips	70	73	73	74	290	4,095
Barry Lane	70	74	72	75	291	3,219.13
Anders Forsbrand	71	73	74	73	291	3,219.13

	SCORES				TOTAL	MONEY
Roger Wessels	71	73	74	73	291	3,219.13
Gary Orr	71	70	74	76	291	3,219.13
Jarrod Moseley	70	73	75	73	291	3,219.13
Eric Carlberg	73	70	75	73	291	3,219.13
Carlos Larrain	72	72	74	73	291	3,219.13
John Senden	70	69	76	76	291	3,219.13
Andrew Raitt	74	70	73	76	293	2,502.50
Carlos Rodiles	73	66	78	76	293	2,502.50
Richard Green	72	72	73	76	293	2,502.50
Henrik Bjornstad	74	69	76	74	293	2,502.50
Anders Hansen	69	73	79	73	294	1,167.33
Ignacio Garrido	68	73	75	78	294	1,167.33
Paul Eales	75	69	78	72	294	1,167.33
Philip Walton	72	71	77	75	295	1,356
Peter Baker	72	70	77	76	295	1,356
Andrew Beal	73	68	74	80	295	1,356
Stuart Cage	73	71	76	76	296	1,348.50
Stephen Dodd	74	70	73	79	296	1,348.50
*Kenneth Ferrie	73	70	78	76	297	
Nick O'Hern	72	71	80	75	298	1,344
Jorge Berendt	72	72	82	73	299	1,339.50
Justin Rose	75	69	82	73	299	1,339.50

Murphy's Irish Open

Druids Glen Golf Club, Dublin, Ireland
Par 35-36–71; 7,012 yards

July 1-4
purse, €1,400,000

	SCORES				TOTAL	MONEY
Sergio Garcia	69	68	67	64	268	€233,320
Angel Cabrera	70	66	66	69	271	155,540
Jarrod Moseley	66	69	69	69	273	87,640
Miguel Angel Martin	71	71	72	62	276	59,453.33
Thomas Bjorn	70	66	71	69	276	59,453.33
Eamonn Darcy	68	67	71	70	276	59,453.33
Malcolm Mackenzie	72	70	67	68	277	34,055
Lee Westwood	70	68	71	68	277	34,055
Colin Montgomerie	68	67	71	71	277	34,055
Sven Struver	69	70	70	68	277	34,055
Gary Orr	68	71	72	67	278	24,890
Phil Price	67	65	75	71	278	24,890
Craig Hainline	65	72	72	70	279	21,970
Emanuele Canonica	68	72	72	67	279	21,970
Russell Claydon	69	69	71	71	280	18,573.33
Stephen Leaney	70	71	67	72	280	18,573.33
Ricardo Gonzalez	71	69	68	72	280	18,573.33
John Mellor	68	71	73	68	280	18,573.33
Alex Cejka	67	68	72	73	280	18,573.33
David Howell	69	73	67	71	280	18,573.33
Paul Lawrie	72	69	70	70	281	15,750
Miguel Angel Jimenez	68	72	75	66	281	15,750
David Carter	70	70	70	71	281	15,750
Peter O'Malley	70	66	72	73	281	15,750
Roger Wessels	67	73	71	71	282	14,070
Des Smyth	73	69	67	73	282	14,070
Andrew McLardy	69	67	72	74	282	14,070
Soren Hansen	69	63	76	74	282	14,070

	SCORES				TOTAL	MONEY
Paul Affleck	69	73	69	72	283	12,390
Michael Campbell	68	69	68	78	283	12,390
Jeev Milkha Singh	66	69	75	73	283	12,390
Jim Payne	68	73	70	72	283	12,390
Bernhard Langer	71	67	76	70	284	11,200
Ignacio Garrido	70	71	71	72	284	11,200
Soren Kjeldsen	70	70	75	69	284	11,200
Steve Webster	72	68	70	75	285	10,080
Ian Garbutt	72	68	69	76	285	10,080
Paolo Quirici	69	72	69	75	285	10,080
Michael Jonzon	66	75	69	75	285	10,080
Massimo Scarpa	67	72	77	69	285	10,080
Silvio Grappasonni	69	71	75	71	286	8,400
Jean Francois Remesy	69	72	71	74	286	8,400
David Gilford	69	71	76	70	286	8,400
Costantino Rocca	72	70	74	70	286	8,400
Paul Broadhurst	70	71	74	71	286	8,400
Greg Turner	69	68	72	77	286	8,400
Paul Eales	71	68	75	72	286	8,400
Fabrice Tarnaud	72	70	71	74	287	6,860
Wayne Riley	71	69	74	73	287	6,860
Anders Hansen	67	73	75	72	287	6,860
Peter Baker	70	68	78	71	287	6,860
Derrick Cooper	66	74	73	75	288	5,600
Jonathan Lomas	72	70	73	73	288	5,600
Joakim Haeggman	69	73	76	70	288	5,600
Barry Lane	74	67	74	73	288	5,600
Brian Davis	70	70	75	73	288	5,600
Peter Lonard	71	67	75	76	289	4,760
Stephen Gallacher	72	70	78	71	291	4,340
David Park	70	72	71	78	291	4,340
Marc Farry	70	71	74	76	291	4,340
Ross McFarlane	70	69	79	74	292	3,850
Thomas Levet	71	71	71	79	292	3,850
Alberto Binaghi	68	73	77	74	292	3,850
Patrik Sjoland	69	70	79	74	292	3,850
Anthony Wall	72	68	78	75	293	3,500
Mathias Gronberg	72	69	77	77	295	2,100
John Daly	69	72	81	74	296	2,097
Richard Coughlan	71	71	76	79	297	2,094

Standard Life Loch Lomond

Loch Lomond Golf Club, Glasgow, Scotland
Par 36-35–71; 7,050 yards

July 7-10
purse, €1,400,000

	SCORES				TOTAL	MONEY
Colin Montgomerie	69	65	70	64	268	€233,320
Michael Jonzon	69	66	70	66	271	104,393.33
Sergio Garcia	62	70	71	68	271	104,393.33
Mats Lanner	65	71	66	69	271	104,393.33
Lee Westwood	66	68	67	71	272	54,180
Jesper Parnevik	64	67	71	70	272	54,180
Bob May	71	68	68	67	274	36,073.33
Eduardo Romero	69	67	70	68	274	36,073.33
Michael Campbell	66	68	70	70	274	36,073.33
Roger Winchester	65	69	70	71	275	25,075

	SCORES				TOTAL	MONEY
David Park	69	65	68	73	275	25,075
Patrik Sjoland	65	73	69	68	275	25,075
Retief Goosen	71	65	68	71	275	25,075
Robert Allenby	72	67	69	68	276	21,420
Ian Garbutt	68	68	69	72	277	18,928
Phil Price	68	71	69	69	277	18,928
Angel Cabrera	69	70	69	69	277	18,928
Russell Claydon	71	68	68	70	277	18,928
Max Anglert	71	71	67	68	277	18,928
Jean Van de Velde	69	68	69	72	278	16,380
Thomas Bjorn	70	66	66	76	278	16,380
Fredrik Lindgren	71	69	68	70	278	16,380
Jamie Spence	72	70	71	66	279	14,490
Mark Roe	69	71	69	70	279	14,490
David Carter	72	66	70	71	279	14,490
Darren Clarke	69	70	74	66	279	14,490
Thomas Levet	69	70	70	70	279	14,490
David Howell	67	70	70	72	279	14,490
Greg Owen	71	71	71	67	280	12,040
Miguel Angel Jimenez	72	69	67	72	280	12,040
Bradley Hughes	69	74	68	69	280	12,040
Andrew Coltart	68	70	69	73	280	12,040
Nick Faldo	68	70	68	74	280	12,040
David Gilford	72	66	69	73	280	12,040
Craig Hainline	67	76	70	68	281	10,780
Clinton Whitelaw	69	73	67	72	281	10,780
Jean Francois Remesy	70	68	72	72	282	9,660
Billy Mayfair	70	69	71	72	282	9,660
Stephen Allan	71	69	69	73	282	9,660
Stephen Leaney	73	66	72	71	282	9,660
John Senden	71	67	69	75	282	9,660
Des Smyth	74	64	72	72	282	9,660
Miguel Angel Martin	71	69	72	71	283	8,400
Marc Farry	72	69	74	68	283	8,400
Jarmo Sandelin	72	70	70	71	283	8,400
Mark James	70	70	71	73	284	6,860
Peter Senior	69	73	74	68	284	6,860
Francisco Cea	70	73	73	68	284	6,860
Peter O'Malley	71	66	74	73	284	6,860
Anthony Wall	75	68	73	68	284	6,860
Steve Webster	71	69	71	73	284	6,860
Glen Day	71	72	71	70	284	6,860
Gary Orr	70	72	70	72	284	6,860
Sam Torrance	68	74	72	71	285	5,320
Craig Spence	74	68	69	74	285	5,320
Malcolm Mackenzie	69	73	70	73	285	5,320
Raymond Russell	72	69	73	72	286	4,620
Per-Ulrik Johansson	70	67	77	72	286	4,620
Ignacio Garrido	73	69	72	73	287	4,130
Domingo Hospital	71	71	72	73	287	4,130
Paul Lawrie	67	73	73	74	287	4,130
Ricardo Gonzalez	70	70	72	75	287	4,130
Thomas Gogele	70	69	74	75	288	3,640
Alex Cejka	74	69	72	73	288	3,640
Paolo Quirici	74	68	72	74	288	3,640
Greg Turner	68	75	74	72	289	2,100
Tom Gillis	70	73	72	75	290	2,097
*Matt Kuchar	74	69	71	76	290	
Brian Davis	69	72	71	79	291	2,092.50
Andrew Oldcorn	68	74	74	75	291	2,092.50

	SCORES				TOTAL	MONEY
Barry Lane	74	68	72	79	293	2,088
Daniel Chopra	72	71	78	73	294	2,085
Richard Boxall	71	72	75	77	295	2,082

British Open Championship

Carnoustie, Angus, Scotland
Par 36-35–71; 7,361 yards

July 15-18
purse, €2,841,930

	SCORES				TOTAL	MONEY
Paul Lawrie	73	74	76	67	290	€490,000
Justin Leonard	73	74	71	72	290	259,000
Jean Van de Velde	75	68	70	77	290	259,000
(Lawrie won four-hole playoff.)						
Craig Parry	76	75	67	73	291	140,000
Angel Cabrera	75	69	77	70	291	140,000
Greg Norman	76	70	75	72	293	98,000
David Frost	80	69	71	74	294	70,000
Davis Love III	74	74	77	69	294	70,000
Tiger Woods	74	72	74	74	294	70,000
Jesper Parnevik	74	71	78	72	295	48,720
Scott Dunlap	72	77	76	70	295	48,720
Retief Goosen	76	75	73	71	295	48,720
Hal Sutton	73	78	72	72	295	48,720
Jim Furyk	78	71	76	70	295	48,720
Tsuyoshi Yoneyama	77	74	73	72	296	36,400
Colin Montgomerie	74	76	72	74	296	36,400
Scott Verplank	80	74	73	69	296	36,400
Bernhard Langer	72	77	73	75	297	28,700
Andrew Coltart	74	74	72	77	297	28,700
Frank Nobilo	76	76	70	75	297	28,700
Patrik Sjoland	74	72	77	74	297	28,700
Lee Westwood	76	75	74	72	297	28,700
Costantino Rocca	81	69	74	73	297	28,700
Peter O'Malley	76	75	74	73	298	21,420
Ernie Els	74	76	76	72	298	21,420
Brian Watts	74	73	77	74	298	21,420
Ian Woosnam	76	74	74	74	298	21,420
Miguel Angel Martin	74	76	72	76	298	21,420
Padraig Harrington	77	74	74	74	299	18,900
Jeff Maggert	75	77	75	73	300	16,180
Darren Clarke	76	75	76	73	300	16,180
Payne Stewart	79	73	74	74	300	16,180
Pierre Fulke	75	75	77	73	300	16,180
Thomas Bjorn	79	73	75	73	300	16,180
Tim Herron	81	70	74	75	300	16,180
Len Mattiace	73	74	75	78	300	16,180
Mark McNulty	73	77	76	75	301	13,300
Dudley Hart	73	79	75	74	301	13,300
Peter Baker	77	74	78	72	301	13,300
Nick Price	77	74	73	77	301	13,300
Mike Weir	83	71	72	75	301	13,300
Paul Affleck	79	75	74	73	301	13,300
Duffy Waldorf	80	72	76	74	302	12,180
Mark James	76	74	74	78	302	12,180
Steve Pate	73	76	80	74	303	11,357.50
Naomichi Ozaki	74	78	75	76	303	11,357.50

	SCORES				TOTAL	MONEY
Jeff Sluman	80	74	77	72	303	11,357.50
David Howell	76	78	79	70	303	11,357.50
Neil Price	79	74	76	75	304	10,103.33
Thomas Levet	78	76	76	74	304	10,103.33
Katsuyoshi Tomori	74	75	79	76	304	10,103.33
Choi Kyung-ju	76	72	81	75	304	10,103.33
Bradley Hughes	76	71	78	79	304	10,103.33
Dean Robertson	76	75	78	75	304	10,103.33
Bob Estes	75	76	77	76	304	10,103.33
Stephen Allan	79	73	83	69	304	10,103.33
Peter Lonard	76	78	74	76	304	10,103.33
Dennis Paulson	74	78	79	74	305	9,187.50
Jeremy Robinson	77	76	77	75	305	9,187.50
Santiago Luna	78	74	80	73	305	9,187.50
Phil Price	77	76	77	75	305	9,187.50
Johan Rystrom	78	75	76	77	306	8,890
David Duval	79	75	76	76	306	8,890
Mark Brooks	82	70	76	78	306	8,890
Jarmo Sandelin	75	78	77	77	307	8,750
Sven Struver	77	73	79	79	308	8,680
Lee Thompson	75	78	76	80	309	8,610
Brian Davis	80	71	82	77	310	8,505
John Huston	80	71	77	82	310	8,505
Lee Janzen	80	74	79	78	311	8,400
Shingo Katayama	76	75	78	83	312	8,330
Martyn Thompson	76	78	78	81	313	8,225
Derrick Cooper	75	77	76	85	313	8,225

Out of Final 36 Holes

	SCORES		TOTAL	MONEY
Tom Watson	82	73	155	1,540
Miguel Angel Jimenez	81	74	155	1,540
Rocco Mediate	79	76	155	1,540
Jean Hugo	78	77	155	1,540
Scott Watson	74	81	155	1,540
Phil Mickelson	79	76	155	1,540
Pedro Linhart	80	75	155	1,540
Craig Hainline	75	80	155	1,540
Ross McFarlane	77	78	155	1,540
Paul Eales	78	78	156	1,540
Carlos Franco	80	76	156	1,540
Tom Lehman	76	80	156	1,540
Brandt Jobe	77	79	156	1,540
Stephen Leaney	79	77	156	1,540
Justin Rose	79	77	156	1,540
Michael Long	78	78	156	1,540
Gilberto Morales	80	76	156	1,540
Per Nyman	81	75	156	1,540
Andrew Magee	77	79	156	1,540
Hidemichi Tanaka	82	74	156	1,540
Bob Tway	75	81	156	1,540
Greg Turner	78	78	156	1,540
Corey Pavin	80	76	156	1,540
Michael Campbell	79	77	156	1,540
Andrew Raitt	78	78	156	1,540
*Luke Donald	80	76	156	
Gabriel Hjertstedt	79	78	157	1,260
Rodney Pampling	71	86	157	1,260
Steve Stricker	80	77	157	1,260
Steve Elkington	79	78	157	1,260

	SCORES		TOTAL	MONEY
Mark O'Meara	83	74	157	1,260
Nick Faldo	78	79	157	1,260
Des Smyth	75	82	157	1,260
Jose Maria Olazabal	78	79	157	1,260
Christopher Hanell	81	76	157	1,260
Warren Bennett	77	80	157	1,260
David Park	77	81	158	1,260
Shigeki Maruyama	78	80	158	1,260
Glen Day	79	79	158	1,260
Robert Karlsson	76	82	158	1,260
Richard Green	81	77	158	1,260
Mathias Gronberg	79	79	158	1,260
Mark Calcavecchia	78	81	159	1,260
Stuart Appleby	78	81	159	1,260
David Carter	79	80	159	1,260
Billy Andrade	75	84	159	1,260
Geoff Ogilvy	81	78	159	1,260
Fabrice Tarnaud	80	79	159	1,260
Scott Gump	85	74	159	1,260
Kim Jong-duk	83	76	159	1,260
Jarrod Moseley	85	74	159	1,260
Greg Owen	78	81	159	1,260
Paul McGinley	83	77	160	1,120
Per-Ulrik Johansson	79	81	160	1,120
Craig Spence	81	79	160	1,120
Raymond Russell	82	78	160	1,120
*Paddy Gribben	75	85	160	
Billy Mayfair	81	80	161	1,120
Vijay Singh	77	84	161	1,120
Rich Beem	80	81	161	1,120
Stephen Gallacher	82	79	161	1,120
Marc Farry	82	79	161	1,120
Jon Bevan	81	80	161	1,120
*Graeme Storm	82	79	161	
Ted Tryba	80	82	162	1,120
Stewart Cink	82	80	162	1,120
*Zane Scotland	82	81	163	
Gary Player	81	83	164	1,120
Bob Charles	83	81	164	1,120
Kazuhiko Hosokawa	83	82	165	1,120
Allan MacDonald	80	85	165	1,120
Sandy Lyle	85	81	166	1,120
Seve Ballesteros	80	86	166	1,120
Mark Allen	80	86	166	1,120
Anders Hansen	82	84	166	1,120
Eduardo Herrera	81	86	167	980
Tony Jacklin	85	82	167	980
Andrew Sherborne	87	80	167	980
Prayad Marksaeng	91	79	170	980
Simon McCarthy	82	89	171	980
Sergio Garcia	89	83	172	980
Fred Funk	83		WD	980
Tom Gillis	90		WD	980

TNT Dutch Open

Hilversumsche Golf Club, Hilversum, Amsterdam
Par 36-35–71; 6,636 yards

July 22-25
purse, €1,120,000

	SCORES				TOTAL	MONEY
Lee Westwood	72	68	66	63	269	€186,660
Gary Orr	69	67	65	69	270	124,430
Eduardo Romero	67	68	72	64	271	63,050
Jarrod Moseley	68	70	67	66	271	63,050
Maarten Lafeber	73	68	64	69	274	40,076.67
Darren Clarke	72	65	67	70	274	40,076.67
Craig Spence	73	67	66	68	274	40,076.67
John Huston	69	72	65	69	275	21,488.57
Angel Cabrera	67	71	67	70	275	21,488.57
Rolf Muntz	67	70	66	72	275	21,488.57
Ian Garbutt	70	72	68	65	275	21,488.57
Nick Price	73	66	67	69	275	21,488.57
Andrew Oldcorn	76	66	67	66	275	21,488.57
Jonathan Lomas	70	66	68	71	275	21,488.57
Paul McGinley	68	69	71	68	276	15,142.40
Eamonn Darcy	71	67	69	69	276	15,142.40
Bernhard Langer	70	69	68	69	276	15,142.40
Stephen Leaney	71	69	65	71	276	15,142.40
Dean Robertson	73	68	70	65	276	15,142.40
Andrew Coltart	72	67	68	70	277	12,768
Ricardo Gonzalez	69	69	68	71	277	12,768
David Gilford	68	70	70	69	277	12,768
Anders Hansen	75	68	64	70	277	12,768
Katsuyoshi Tomori	67	72	70	68	277	12,768
Roger Winchester	74	68	65	71	278	11,088
Jim Payne	71	71	67	69	278	11,088
Roger Chapman	69	70	65	74	278	11,088
Mark McNulty	71	68	67	72	278	11,088
Jeremy Robinson	74	68	66	70	278	11,088
Paolo Quirici	73	66	66	74	279	9,232
Paul Eales	68	70	71	70	279	9,232
Massimo Scarpa	74	69	66	70	279	9,232
Peter Lonard	74	65	70	70	279	9,232
Geoff Ogilvy	71	67	70	71	279	9,232
John Bickerton	69	67	72	71	279	9,232
Jean Francois Remesy	71	72	68	68	279	9,232
Ignacio Garrido	67	71	74	68	280	7,840
Robert Jan Derksen	71	68	72	69	280	7,840
Christopher Hanell	72	69	69	70	280	7,840
Mats Lanner	72	68	71	69	280	7,840
Alex Cejka	71	72	70	67	280	7,840
Michael Long	69	70	70	72	281	6,496
Henrik Nystrom	73	70	72	66	281	6,496
Stephen Field	69	71	71	70	281	6,496
Henrik Bjornstad	73	68	67	73	281	6,496
Jeev Milkha Singh	72	70	70	69	281	6,496
Massimo Florioli	69	68	73	71	281	6,496
Pedro Linhart	72	68	71	70	281	6,496
Santiago Luna	72	68	69	73	282	5,152
Diego Borrego	71	72	72	67	282	5,152
Andrew McLardy	70	72	66	74	282	5,152
Jose Rivero	74	69	70	69	282	5,152
Stephen Gallacher	70	72	69	71	282	5,152
Ian Hutchings	70	72	75	66	283	4,256

	SCORES	TOTAL	MONEY
John Mellor	71 71 70 71	283	4,256
Michael Jonzon	70 72 71 70	283	4,256
Francisco Cea	69 72 75 68	284	3,621.33
Stephen McAllister	73 70 75 66	284	3,621.33
Jorge Berendt	71 70 73 70	284	3,621.33
Steen Tinning	70 70 73 72	285	3,192
Fredrik Jacobson	75 67 71 72	285	3,192
Tom Gillis	73 69 74 69	285	3,192
Philip Walton	69 66 75 75	285	3,192
Pierre Fulke	70 72 70 74	286	2,856
Joakim Haeggman	71 72 72 71	286	2,856
Daren Lee	75 68 70 74	287	1,680
Stephen Dodd	69 73 71 76	289	1,677
Stephen Bennett	72 71 74 74	291	1,671
Greg Owen	69 71 73 78	291	1,671
Emanuele Canonica	67 72 72 80	291	1,671
*Maarten Van Den Berg	73 70 76 73	292	
Olle Karlsson	71 72 75 74	292	1,665

Smurfit European Open

The K Club, Dublin, Ireland
Par 36-36–72; 7,179 yards

July 30-August 2
purse, €1,900,000

	SCORES	TOTAL	MONEY
Lee Westwood	69 67 70 65	271	€316,660
Darren Clarke	73 60 66 75	274	165,020
Peter O'Malley	68 69 68 69	274	165,020
Costantino Rocca	69 73 70 65	277	87,760
Robert Karlsson	70 72 69 66	277	87,760
John Senden	67 73 69 69	278	53,350
Angel Cabrera	69 69 70 70	278	53,350
Jose Coceres	67 70 70 71	278	53,350
Gary Emerson	70 69 70 69	278	53,350
Richard Green	71 69 69 70	279	33,044
Peter Lonard	72 67 72 68	279	33,044
Andrew Coltart	71 67 71 70	279	33,044
Per-Ulrik Johansson	73 66 72 68	279	33,044
Russell Claydon	72 69 68 70	279	33,044
Paul Lawrie	67 71 72 70	280	26,776.67
Colin Montgomerie	67 71 69 73	280	26,776.67
Katsuyoshi Tomori	66 69 73 72	280	26,776.67
Jarrod Moseley	70 71 71 69	281	22,641.67
Jamie Spence	71 67 74 69	281	22,641.67
Padraig Harrington	69 73 71 68	281	22,641.67
Mark McNulty	72 69 70 70	281	22,641.67
Michael Campbell	66 74 72 69	281	22,641.67
Brian Davis	69 73 68 71	281	22,641.67
Silvio Grappasonni	68 72 70 72	282	18,810
Steen Tinning	69 73 69 71	282	18,810
Retief Goosen	70 68 73 71	282	18,810
Stephen Allan	68 75 68 71	282	18,810
Craig Spence	68 73 70 71	282	18,810
Nick O'Hern	70 72 70 70	282	18,810
Paul Eales	72 68 70 72	282	18,810
Greg Turner	71 71 71 70	283	15,817.50
Nick Faldo	70 73 70 70	283	15,817.50

	SCORES				TOTAL	MONEY
Andrew Sherborne	73	69	73	68	283	15,817.50
Francisco Cea	71	68	70	74	283	15,817.50
Craig Hainline	69	70	69	76	284	13,110
Stephen Gallacher	68	72	73	71	284	13,110
Domingo Hospital	71	70	75	68	284	13,110
Paul Broadhurst	73	70	72	69	284	13,110
Jean Van de Velde	70	71	70	73	284	13,110
Gary Orr	69	71	73	71	284	13,110
Ian Woosnam	67	72	72	73	284	13,110
Eduardo Romero	71	72	72	69	284	13,110
Peter Baker	70	71	74	69	284	13,110
Ricardo Gonzalez	68	75	72	69	284	13,110
Roger Chapman	68	73	74	70	285	10,450
Jorge Berendt	68	73	68	76	285	10,450
Barry Lane	70	71	73	71	285	10,450
Des Smyth	72	70	72	71	285	10,450
Alex Cejka	69	73	70	74	286	8,550
Soren Kjeldsen	71	71	70	74	286	8,550
Malcolm Mackenzie	67	72	76	71	286	8,550
Soren Hansen	73	70	73	70	286	8,550
Sergio Garcia	71	69	73	73	286	8,550
Anthony Wall	73	70	71	72	286	8,550
Stephen Leaney	70	71	74	72	287	6,127.50
Pedro Linhart	75	68	76	68	287	6,127.50
Diego Borrego	73	70	73	71	287	6,127.50
Damian McGrane	72	70	72	73	287	6,127.50
David Gilford	68	68	79	72	287	6,127.50
Daniel Chopra	72	71	73	71	287	6,127.50
Andrew Raitt	72	71	69	75	287	6,127.50
Paolo Quirici	73	66	71	77	287	6,127.50
Ignacio Garrido	70	72	71	75	288	4,417.50
Roger Wessels	73	70	73	72	288	4,417.50
Raymond Russell	70	71	74	73	288	4,417.50
Bob May	69	72	72	75	288	4,417.50
Clinton Whitelaw	69	69	77	74	289	2,844
Dean Robertson	69	73	75	72	289	2,844
Peter Mitchell	67	70	72	80	289	2,844
David Carter	74	69	75	74	292	2,836.50
Miguel Angel Jimenez	67	75	81	69	292	2,836.50
Philip Walton	72	71	76	78	297	2,832

Volvo Scandinavian Masters

Barseback Golf & Country Club, Malmo, Sweden — August 5-8
Par 35-37–72; 7,318 yards — purse, €1,400,000

	SCORES				TOTAL	MONEY
Colin Montgomerie	67	67	65	69	268	€233,320
Jesper Parnevik	69	68	69	71	277	155,540
Bob May	71	71	67	69	278	78,820
Geoff Ogilvy	74	62	71	71	278	78,820
Francisco Cea	68	72	67	72	279	46,340
Andrew McLardy	70	71	66	72	279	46,340
Robert Karlsson	71	69	71	68	279	46,340
Katsuyoshi Tomori	72	69	69	69	279	46,340
Russell Claydon	72	70	67	71	280	26,304
Brian Davis	73	70	70	67	280	26,304

	SCORES				TOTAL	MONEY
Jarrod Moseley	68	70	73	69	280	26,304
Paul Broadhurst	65	72	68	75	280	26,304
Greg Turner	70	68	70	72	280	26,304
Michael Campbell	70	67	72	72	281	20,160
Gary Orr	69	72	71	69	281	20,160
Steen Tinning	71	66	72	72	281	20,160
David Carter	70	68	68	75	281	20,160
Richard Boxall	72	70	70	70	282	17,406.67
Per Nyman	70	70	67	75	282	17,406.67
Mathias Gronberg	76	68	68	70	282	17,406.67
Peter O'Malley	73	71	69	70	283	14,700
David Park	74	70	68	71	283	14,700
Padraig Harrington	73	69	69	72	283	14,700
Dean Robertson	67	70	73	73	283	14,700
Gary Emerson	72	72	67	72	283	14,700
Wayne Westner	69	72	71	71	283	14,700
Jamie Spence	73	69	70	71	283	14,700
Paolo Quirici	70	68	75	70	283	14,700
Gary Evans	69	69	72	73	283	14,700
Jonathan Lomas	72	72	67	73	284	11,540
Henrik Stenson	69	71	72	72	284	11,540
Adam Mednick	72	70	73	69	284	11,540
Jarmo Sandelin	74	70	68	72	284	11,540
Tony Johnstone	74	70	68	72	284	11,540
Stephen Allan	73	67	68	76	284	11,540
Soren Kjeldsen	70	71	72	71	284	11,540
Michael Long	69	71	74	71	285	9,380
Ignacio Garrido	70	73	71	71	285	9,380
Johan Rystrom	71	73	72	69	285	9,380
Jean Van de Velde	70	70	72	73	285	9,380
Per-Ulrik Johansson	71	68	68	78	285	9,380
Ian Garbutt	70	70	72	73	285	9,380
Rodger Davis	71	72	71	71	285	9,380
Fredrik Jacobson	71	69	75	70	285	9,380
Henrik Nystrom	72	72	68	74	286	7,280
Raphael Jacquelin	69	74	71	72	286	7,280
Malcolm Mackenzie	72	71	74	69	286	7,280
Andrew Coltart	69	70	75	72	286	7,280
Rolf Muntz	74	69	69	74	286	7,280
Miguel Angel Martin	72	70	70	74	286	7,280
Paul McGinley	72	71	68	75	286	7,280
Paul Eales	73	71	71	72	287	5,320
John Mellor	68	72	70	77	287	5,320
Richard Green	71	70	70	76	287	5,320
Jose Rivero	69	69	72	77	287	5,320
Thomas Bjorn	77	66	72	72	287	5,320
Emanuele Canonica	77	64	69	77	287	5,320
Greg Owen	73	69	73	72	287	5,320
Barry Lane	71	69	74	74	288	3,990
Sven Struver	71	69	73	75	288	3,990
Retief Goosen	73	71	71	73	288	3,990
Costantino Rocca	68	73	74	73	288	3,990
Alex Cejka	72	69	71	76	288	3,990
Craig Stadler	72	71	71	74	288	3,990
Ian Hutchings	71	73	70	75	289	2,293.57
Miles Tunnicliff	75	68	74	72	289	2,293.57
Phil Price	72	69	72	76	289	2,293.57
Richard Johnson	70	73	72	74	289	2,293.57
Christopher Hanell	72	70	71	76	289	2,293.57
Stephen Field	76	68	68	77	289	2,293.57

	SCORES				TOTAL	MONEY
Jorge Berendt	73	69	73	74	289	2,293.57
Anders Hansen	72	69	73	76	290	2,076
Stephen Gallacher	72	72	73	73	290	2,076
Mats Lanner	74	70	72	74	290	2,076
Andrew Sherborne	72	70	73	75	290	2,076
Silvio Grappasonni	70	73	71	76	290	2,076
Mikael Lundberg	70	73	75	74	292	2,064
Anders Forsbrand	72	70	72	78	292	2,064
Ross McFarlane	71	73	77	71	292	2,064
Paul Affleck	68	76	73	76	293	2,058
Peter Hansson	70	74	75	77	296	2,055
Niclas Fasth	75	69	75	82	301	2,052

West of Ireland Golf Classic

Galway Bay Golf & Country Club, Galway, Ireland   August 12-15
Par 36-36–72; 7,148 yards   purse, €350,000

	SCORES				TOTAL	MONEY
Costantino Rocca	70	68	68	70	276	€58,330
Padraig Harrington	69	69	68	72	278	38,380
Paul Broadhurst	73	66	72	68	279	18,080
Gary Evans	70	66	71	72	279	18,080
Des Smyth	71	68	69	71	279	18,080
Anders Hansen	67	74	71	68	280	10,500
Paul McGinley	68	69	74	69	280	10,500
Michael Long	69	72	73	66	280	10,500
Eric Carlberg	68	67	74	72	281	7,410
Mats Hallberg	70	71	71	69	281	7,410
Gary Emerson	68	71	72	71	282	6,440
Soren Hansen	67	72	72	72	283	5,666.67
Knud Storegaard	68	71	74	70	283	5,666.67
Elliot Boult	66	75	71	71	283	5,666.67
Maarten Lafeber	71	68	73	72	284	4,931.67
Andrew Raitt	68	75	66	75	284	4,931.67
Benoit Teilleria	70	72	72	70	284	4,931.67
Peter Lawrie	70	76	72	67	285	4,287.50
Andrew Oldcorn	68	76	71	70	285	4,287.50
Bradley Dredge	69	71	76	69	285	4,287.50
Andrew Butterfield	71	70	72	72	285	4,287.50
Ian Hutchings	69	74	71	72	286	3,727.50
Christian Cevaer	72	72	71	71	286	3,727.50
Raimo Sjoberg	74	68	74	70	286	3,727.50
Carl Suneson	71	73	68	74	286	3,727.50
Leif Westerberg	74	72	70	70	286	3,727.50
Fredrik Henge	70	70	71	75	286	3,727.50
Scott Henderson	69	73	74	71	287	3,055.71
Matthew Blackey	70	73	71	73	287	3,055.71
Dominique Nouailhac	70	72	76	69	287	3,055.71
Marcus Wheelhouse	74	72	70	71	287	3,055.71
Andrew Clapp	74	71	71	71	287	3,055.71
Philip Golding	70	72	75	70	287	3,055.71
Nils Rorbaek	67	70	78	72	287	3,055.71
Stephen Gallacher	68	69	77	74	288	2,520
Gary Murphy	72	72	73	71	288	2,520
Jon Robson	70	73	72	73	288	2,520
Johan Skold	71	72	75	70	288	2,520

	SCORES				TOTAL	MONEY
Daniel Westermark	70	73	73	72	288	2,520
Carlos Larrain	72	73	75	68	288	2,520
Adam Mednick	72	74	71	71	288	2,520
Nick O'Hern	71	73	74	71	289	1,995
Martin Erlandsson	70	75	73	71	289	1,995
Gary Clark	70	71	75	73	289	1,995
Justin Rose	71	73	70	75	289	1,995
Simon Hurley	69	71	77	72	289	1,995
Stephen Dodd	68	74	76	71	289	1,995
Henrik Nystrom	74	71	74	70	289	1,995
Klas Eriksson	72	74	70	73	289	1,995
Lee James	69	75	72	74	290	1,505
Gordon Sherry	72	71	73	74	290	1,505
Stephen Scahill	71	75	74	70	290	1,505
Eamonn Darcy	71	75	72	72	290	1,505
Anssi Kankkonen	71	73	73	73	290	1,505
Mark Booth	73	71	76	70	290	1,505
David Lynn	74	72	71	74	291	1,190
Jesus Maria Arruti	68	76	76	71	291	1,190
Greig Hutcheon	72	74	72	73	291	1,190
Brian Nelson	69	76	74	73	292	1,015
Juan Nutt	70	76	76	70	292	1,015
Mike Miller	72	74	73	73	292	1,015
Philip Walton	75	70	75	72	292	1,015
Wayne Westner	70	74	77	71	292	1,015
Daniel Chopra	70	73	72	78	293	781.67
Rudi Sailer	71	74	78	70	293	781.67
Magnus Persson	68	74	78	73	293	781.67
Jose Manuel Carriles	75	70	76	73	294	552.50
Lucas Parsons	72	71	76	75	294	552.50
Euan Little	71	74	75	74	294	552.50
Jose Sota	72	74	74	74	294	552.50
Robert Lee	70	74	76	75	295	545
Marc Pendaries	69	76	78	73	296	540.50
Gianluca Baruffaldi	72	73	74	77	296	540.50
Steven Richardson	70	76	77	74	297	534.50
Alvaro Salto	68	76	80	73	297	534.50
Damian Mooney	73	71	77	77	298	528.50
Paul Dwyer	77	69	76	76	298	528.50
Gustavo Rojas	72	74	80	74	300	524

BMW International Open

Golfclub Munchen Nord-Eichenreid, Munich, Germany
Par 36-36–72; 6,914 yards

August 19-22
purse, €1,190,000

	SCORES				TOTAL	MONEY
Colin Montgomerie	69	64	65	70	268	€198,320
Padraig Harrington	66	67	66	72	271	132,210
Jarrod Moseley	67	68	71	66	272	74,500
John Bickerton	67	69	69	69	274	59,500
Mark James	70	69	66	70	275	39,375
Gary Orr	70	68	69	68	275	39,375
David Howell	67	70	72	66	275	39,375
Andrew Coltart	70	68	71	66	275	39,375
Mathias Gronberg	72	68	67	69	276	22,375
Robert Karlsson	70	71	70	65	276	22,375

	SCORES				TOTAL	MONEY
Jean Francois Remesy	69	69	66	72	276	22,375
Paul Broadhurst	69	73	66	68	276	22,375
Peter Baker	67	71	71	67	276	22,375
Dean Robertson	70	71	71	65	277	18,200
Domingo Hospital	66	71	67	74	278	15,782.67
Bernhard Langer	69	68	72	69	278	15,782.67
Ian Woosnam	70	66	68	74	278	15,782.67
Phil Price	67	69	68	74	278	15,782.67
Stephen Field	67	73	69	69	278	15,782.67
Andrew McLardy	70	72	68	68	278	15,782.67
Dennis Edlund	66	71	72	70	279	13,030.50
Andrew Beal	71	69	69	70	279	13,030.50
Nick Faldo	67	73	72	67	279	13,030.50
Tony Johnstone	68	69	73	69	279	13,030.50
Santiago Luna	71	69	71	68	279	13,030.50
Soren Kjeldsen	73	69	68	69	279	13,030.50
Mark Mouland	69	70	68	73	280	10,727
Wayne Riley	72	63	73	72	280	10,727
Miles Tunnicliff	67	73	71	69	280	10,727
Greg Owen	72	71	67	70	280	10,727
Sven Struver	73	69	69	69	280	10,727
Francisco Cea	70	68	70	72	280	10,727
Paul Lawrie	69	73	70	68	280	10,727
Rodger Davis	73	70	64	74	281	8,806
Michael Long	73	69	70	69	281	8,806
Peter O'Malley	73	70	70	68	281	8,806
Thomas Bjorn	70	70	70	71	281	8,806
David Carter	74	67	71	69	281	8,806
Barry Lane	74	68	71	68	281	8,806
Henrik Bjornstad	73	70	69	69	281	8,806
Andrew Raitt	70	70	71	71	282	7,378
David Gilford	73	69	71	69	282	7,378
Jamie Spence	72	65	72	73	282	7,378
Thomas Gogele	70	69	71	72	282	7,378
Van Phillips	70	73	69	70	282	7,378
John Mellor	71	69	70	73	283	6,307
Peter Fowler	71	70	67	75	283	6,307
Mark McNulty	69	68	74	72	283	6,307
Roger Wessels	73	70	68	72	283	6,307
Emanuele Canonica	70	69	74	71	284	5,236
Ignacio Garrido	73	65	76	70	284	5,236
Jonathan Lomas	70	69	72	73	284	5,236
Paolo Quirici	70	68	73	73	284	5,236
Carlos Rodiles	72	71	72	69	284	5,236
Trevor Immelman	70	72	74	69	285	3,910
Peter Mitchell	69	70	70	76	285	3,910
Retief Goosen	70	69	74	72	285	3,910
Silvio Grappasonni	70	71	73	71	285	3,910
Per-Ulrik Johansson	71	72	71	71	285	3,910
Jeremy Robinson	72	69	70	74	285	3,910
Nick O'Hern	67	74	70	74	285	3,910
Jean Van de Velde	68	73	73	72	286	3,272.50
Warren Bennett	73	67	73	73	286	3,272.50
David Park	62	72	73	80	287	2,283
Derrick Cooper	71	70	71	75	287	2,283
Per Haugsrud	68	74	73	72	287	2,283
Fabrice Tarnaud	74	69	73	71	287	2,283
Soren Hansen	72	69	72	74	287	2,283
Paul McGinley	69	72	74	73	288	1,771.50
Andrew Sherborne	72	71	71	74	288	1,771.50

	SCORES				TOTAL	MONEY
Katsuyoshi Tomori	70	72	73	73	288	1,771.50
Scott Henderson	70	71	75	72	288	1,771.50
Russell Claydon	74	68	73	74	289	1,764
Marc Farry	69	73	78	71	291	1,759.50
Philip Walton	73	70	71	77	291	1,759.50
Alberto Binaghi	72	71	70	82	295	1,755
Stephen Dodd	69	74	75	80	298	1,752

Scottish PGA Championship

Gleneagles Hotel, Perth, Scotland
Par 36-36–72; 7,053 yards

August 27-30
purse, €350,000

	SCORES				TOTAL	MONEY
Warren Bennett	70	69	74	69	282	€58,330
Rolf Muntz	66	71	73	72	282	38,880
(Bennett defeated Muntz on first extra hole.)						
Klas Eriksson	68	70	71	74	283	19,705
Roger Winchester	71	68	72	72	283	19,705
Per Nyman	72	69	72	73	286	14,830
Ian Hutchings	70	74	70	73	287	11,375
Andrew McLardy	73	71	69	74	287	11,375
Greig Hutcheon	69	73	73	73	288	8,750
Roger Chapman	71	72	74	72	289	7,410
Fredrik Jacobson	70	71	77	71	289	7,410
Stuart Cage	70	75	75	70	290	5,860
Raymond Russell	70	75	71	74	290	5,860
Grant Hamerton	71	73	73	73	290	5,860
Gary Evans	68	75	73	74	290	5,860
Stephen Dodd	72	75	70	74	291	4,563.57
Brian Nelson	72	72	74	73	291	4,563.57
Russell Weir	68	75	76	72	291	4,563.57
Daren Lee	71	72	75	73	291	4,563.57
Daniel Chopra	71	75	72	73	291	4,563.57
Justin Rose	68	71	82	70	291	4,563.57
Henrik Bjornstad	72	69	82	68	291	4,563.57
Paul Nilbrink	67	73	77	75	292	3,780
Andrew Clapp	68	72	76	76	292	3,780
Ross Drummond	72	73	72	75	292	3,780
Katsuyoshi Tomori	71	75	71	75	292	3,780
Juan Nutt	74	69	73	76	292	3,780
Elliot Boult	74	71	78	70	293	3,360
Wayne Riley	73	74	75	71	293	3,360
David Howell	72	75	75	71	293	3,360
Murray Urquhart	72	73	74	75	294	2,885
Andrew Bonhomme	70	73	78	73	294	2,885
Massimo Florioli	76	71	75	72	294	2,885
Jeev Milkha Singh	72	72	76	74	294	2,885
Peter Fowler	72	73	77	72	294	2,885
David J. Russell	72	69	76	77	294	2,885
Kalle Brink	71	72	74	77	294	2,885
Peter Smith	71	71	77	76	295	2,520
Sam Torrance	75	68	75	77	295	2,520
Andrew Barnett	78	68	71	78	295	2,520
Greg Owen	69	74	80	73	296	2,310
Lee Vannet	72	75	72	77	296	2,310
Nigel Preston	72	74	76	74	296	2,310

	SCORES	TOTAL	MONEY
Richard Boxall	75 69 75 78	297	1,960
Johan Rystrom	70 73 80 74	297	1,960
Colin Gillies	75 71 77 74	297	1,960
Mathias Gronberg	78 69 74 76	297	1,960
Brian Marchbank	69 75 77 76	297	1,960
Neil Roderick	73 72 75 77	297	1,960
John Greaves	75 68 74 80	297	1,960
Gordon Sherry	70 75 77 76	298	1,610
Scott Henderson	71 70 76 81	298	1,610
Marcello Santi	77 69 76 76	298	1,610
Jean Pierre Cixous	70 75 75 79	299	1,295
Stephen Field	73 74 79 73	299	1,295
Robert Coles	73 73 76 77	299	1,295
Henrik Nystrom	72 74 77 76	299	1,295
John Chillas	76 71 77 75	299	1,295
Kevin Stables	75 72 76 76	299	1,295
Jorgen Aker	71 75 74 80	300	1,050
Mark King	74 73 80 73	300	1,050
Steven Thompson	69 72 81 78	300	1,050
Alan Reid	71 76 76 78	301	980
Andrew Oldcorn	68 75 83 77	303	910
Grant Dodd	73 74 76 80	303	910
Fabrice Tarnaud	74 72 79 78	303	910
Colin Brooks	75 68 83 78	304	560

Canon European Masters

Crans-sur-Sierre Golf Club, Crans-sur-Sierre, Switzerland
Par 36-35–71; 6,848 yards

September 2-5
purse, €1,260,000

	SCORES	TOTAL	MONEY
Lee Westwood	69 69 67 65	270	€210,000
Thomas Bjorn	72 66 68 66	272	140,000
Alex Cejka	70 70 70 66	276	78,860
Marc Farry	70 70 68 70	278	58,200
Sam Torrance	75 71 65 67	278	58,200
Sven Struver	70 70 69 71	280	37,800
Miguel Angel Jimenez	70 73 72 65	280	37,800
Ignacio Garrido	70 76 66 68	280	37,800
Nick O'Hern	71 71 71 68	281	24,527.50
Eduardo Romero	70 73 68 70	281	24,527.50
Stephen Field	68 74 68 71	281	24,527.50
Patrik Sjoland	72 71 71 67	281	24,527.50
Bob May	69 73 69 71	282	19,775
Domingo Hospital	72 72 69 69	282	19,775
Peter O'Malley	73 72 69 69	283	17,388
Michael Campbell	72 66 71 74	283	17,388
Dean Robertson	72 72 71 68	283	17,388
Diego Borrego	73 70 70 70	283	17,388
Roger Wessels	70 72 69 73	284	15,624
Eamonn Darcy	74 73 71 67	285	14,364
Geoff Ogilvy	71 73 69 72	285	14,364
Miles Tunnicliff	72 70 66 77	285	14,364
John Bickerton	70 74 72 69	285	14,364
Ross Drummond	73 72 68 72	285	14,364
Ricardo Gonzalez	71 75 72 68	286	12,852
Tom Gillis	66 80 69 71	286	12,852

		SCORES			TOTAL	MONEY
Ian Garbutt	77	69	70	70	286	12,852
Mats Hallberg	73	74	72	68	287	10,584
Mark Mouland	74	71	70	72	287	10,584
Peter Fowler	73	74	71	69	287	10,584
Steen Tinning	73	72	69	73	287	10,584
Angel Cabrera	68	75	72	72	287	10,584
Massimo Scarpa	72	75	71	69	287	10,584
Per-Ulrik Johansson	76	70	70	71	287	10,584
Darren Clarke	70	70	72	75	287	10,584
Francisco Cea	68	72	75	72	287	10,584
Barry Lane	72	74	70	71	287	10,584
Roger Chapman	71	74	71	72	288	8,694
Nick Faldo	71	73	73	71	288	8,694
Jarrod Moseley	74	71	72	71	288	8,694
Richard Boxall	71	75	71	71	288	8,694
Peter Senior	71	71	77	70	289	7,686
Andrew Sherborne	70	72	75	72	289	7,686
Phil Price	72	73	71	73	289	7,686
Christopher Hanell	75	72	70	72	289	7,686
Daren Lee	71	74	73	72	290	6,678
Jean Francois Remesy	69	78	71	72	290	6,678
Andrew Beal	72	75	73	70	290	6,678
Gary Orr	72	72	70	76	290	6,678
Ian Hutchings	71	76	74	70	291	5,418
Mathias Gronberg	69	78	75	69	291	5,418
David Park	73	73	73	72	291	5,418
Anthony Wall	70	76	72	73	291	5,418
David Carter	73	71	72	75	291	5,418
Pierre Fulke	69	74	70	78	291	5,418
Craig Hainline	74	73	70	75	292	4,284
Malcolm Mackenzie	70	76	73	73	292	4,284
Massimo Florioli	73	74	75	70	292	4,284
Thomas Gogele	73	74	68	78	293	3,843
Gilberto Morales	75	72	75	71	293	3,843
Olle Karlsson	76	69	74	75	294	3,528
Warren Bennett	70	74	74	76	294	3,528
Kim Felton	71	76	73	74	294	3,528
Stuart Cage	73	70	76	76	295	3,213
Wayne Riley	75	71	76	73	295	3,213
David Howell	72	75	75	74	296	1,890
Steve Rey	73	74	71	79	297	1,887
Per Nyman	74	73	78	73	298	1,882.50
Mats Lanner	72	75	75	76	298	1,882.50
Van Phillips	73	70	82	75	300	1,878

Victor Chandler British Masters

Woburn Golf & Country Club, Buckinghamshire, England
Par 34-38–72; 6,973 yards

September 9-12
purse, €1,000,000

		SCORES			TOTAL	MONEY
Bob May	69	67	66	67	269	€166,666
Colin Montgomerie	67	64	68	71	270	111,100
Christopher Hanell	70	69	66	67	272	62,600
Lee Westwood	68	66	72	68	274	46,200
Greg Owen	68	70	70	66	274	46,200
Steve Webster	67	70	70	68	275	35,000

		SCORES			TOTAL	MONEY
Sam Torrance	72	67	69	68	276	27,500
Paul Broadhurst	68	71	72	65	276	27,500
Stephen Leaney	67	70	70	70	277	22,300
Michael Campbell	70	71	67	70	278	16,155
Raymond Russell	71	65	70	72	278	16,155
Tony Johnstone	71	69	68	70	278	16,155
John Bickerton	68	68	71	71	278	16,155
Steen Tinning	69	72	70	67	278	16,155
Paul McGinley	71	71	70	66	278	16,155
Retief Goosen	69	71	68	70	278	16,155
Darren Clarke	71	66	74	67	278	16,155
Mathias Gronberg	72	67	67	73	279	11,600
Ian Woosnam	68	69	69	73	279	11,600
Mark McNulty	73	69	68	69	279	11,600
Eduardo Romero	70	68	66	75	279	11,600
Daren Lee	70	71	71	67	279	11,600
Per Nyman	72	67	73	67	279	11,600
Peter Mitchell	68	74	70	67	279	11,600
Robert Jan Derksen	74	68	68	69	279	11,600
Marc Farry	72	68	70	70	280	9,450
Jamie Spence	70	69	71	70	280	9,450
Santiago Luna	73	68	74	65	280	9,450
Patrik Sjoland	70	73	70	67	280	9,450
Sven Struver	73	69	72	66	280	9,450
Jeev Milkha Singh	68	72	71	69	280	9,450
Paolo Quirici	69	69	72	71	281	7,900
Jonathan Lomas	73	70	70	68	281	7,900
David Carter	71	71	70	69	281	7,900
Thomas Bjorn	70	70	72	69	281	7,900
Derrick Cooper	68	75	68	70	281	7,900
Des Smyth	70	71	69	71	281	7,900
Anthony Wall	71	69	72	70	282	6,400
Pierre Fulke	70	72	71	69	282	6,400
Miguel Angel Martin	74	65	73	70	282	6,400
Soren Kjeldsen	67	72	72	71	282	6,400
Jarmo Sandelin	70	73	66	73	282	6,400
Angel Cabrera	71	68	70	73	282	6,400
Andrew McLardy	70	72	71	69	282	6,400
Richard Boxall	70	69	72	71	282	6,400
Gary Orr	70	69	73	70	282	6,400
Greg Turner	73	70	70	70	283	5,000
Stephen Allan	65	72	75	71	283	5,000
Jesus Maria Arruti	69	70	70	74	283	5,000
Emanuele Canonica	71	70	75	67	283	5,000
Richard Green	73	70	68	72	283	5,000
David Gilford	71	70	72	71	284	4,200
Raphael Jacquelin	70	71	73	70	284	4,200
Nick O'Hern	69	73	68	74	284	4,200
Stephen Gallacher	72	68	73	72	285	3,420
Jose Coceres	70	69	72	74	285	3,420
Silvio Grappasonni	67	68	75	75	285	3,420
Peter Baker	70	73	71	71	285	3,420
John Mellor	70	73	72	70	285	3,420
Eamonn Darcy	69	73	72	73	287	2,800
Anders Hansen	71	72	70	74	287	2,800
Andrew Raitt	70	73	73	71	287	2,800
Richard Coughlan	72	71	71	73	287	2,800
Soren Hansen	68	70	73	76	287	2,800
Mark Mouland	72	70	77	69	288	2,009
Massimo Scarpa	70	70	74	74	288	2,009

	SCORES				TOTAL	MONEY
Carlos Rodiles	72	69	74	74	289	1,515
Olle Karlsson	68	75	77	70	290	1,512
Bernhard Langer	68	75	74	74	291	1,507.50
Marcello Santi	71	71	80	69	291	1,507.50
Andrew Oldcorn	69	74	76	73	292	1,501.50
John McHenry	72	71	73	76	292	1,501.50
Peter Senior	71	70	79	74	294	1,497

Trophee Lancome

Saint-Nom-La-Breteche, Paris, France
Par 36-35–71; 6,903 yards

September 16-19
purse, €1,120,000

	SCORES				TOTAL	MONEY
Pierre Fulke	69	69	65	67	270	€186,660
Ignacio Garrido	67	70	68	66	271	124,430
Santiago Luna	70	66	70	66	272	57,843.33
Colin Montgomerie	66	70	68	68	272	57,843.33
Greg Owen	73	66	67	66	272	57,843.33
Jarmo Sandelin	70	66	69	69	274	36,400
Gary Evans	71	64	73	66	274	36,400
Steve Webster	69	71	68	67	275	26,490
Marc Farry	75	68	66	66	275	26,490
Peter Senior	66	72	70	68	276	19,488
Miguel Angel Jimenez	68	64	70	74	276	19,488
Angel Cabrera	71	69	67	69	276	19,488
Mark McNulty	71	69	68	68	276	19,488
Alex Cejka	64	73	73	66	276	19,488
Tom Gillis	69	74	66	68	277	15,792
Retief Goosen	78	65	69	65	277	15,792
Jose Coceres	66	71	71	69	277	15,792
Ricardo Gonzalez	67	72	71	68	278	13,346.67
Michael Campbell	68	68	70	72	278	13,346.67
Paul Lawrie	72	68	70	68	278	13,346.67
Costantino Rocca	68	72	67	71	278	13,346.67
Dennis Edlund	68	71	72	67	278	13,346.67
Jeev Milkha Singh	72	67	70	69	278	13,346.67
John Mellor	69	71	71	68	279	11,088
Bob May	73	68	68	70	279	11,088
Thomas Bjorn	72	70	67	70	279	11,088
Paul McGinley	72	69	68	70	279	11,088
Russell Claydon	67	73	70	69	279	11,088
Domingo Hospital	72	71	68	68	279	11,088
Roger Wessels	72	70	73	64	279	11,088
Emanuele Canonica	71	69	70	70	280	8,748.44
Rolf Muntz	68	71	72	69	280	8,748.44
Soren Kjeldsen	73	69	68	70	280	8,748.44
Jean Van de Velde	68	70	71	71	280	8,748.44
Stephen Field	71	67	73	69	280	8,748.44
Mark James	70	70	72	68	280	8,748.44
Stephen Leaney	68	70	73	69	280	8,748.44
Steen Tinning	67	72	73	68	280	8,748.44
Brian Davis	68	72	71	69	280	8,748.44
Paolo Quirici	69	72	70	70	281	7,392
Miles Tunnicliff	67	73	69	72	281	7,392
Peter O'Malley	71	71	68	71	281	7,392
Barry Lane	72	71	72	67	282	6,384

	SCORES				TOTAL	MONEY
Fredrik Jacobson	72	69	70	71	282	6,384
Jose Maria Olazabal	68	70	71	73	282	6,384
Ian Woosnam	70	70	75	67	282	6,384
Anthony Wall	72	71	72	67	282	6,384
Klas Eriksson	69	73	68	72	282	6,384
Fredrik Lindgren	71	72	71	69	283	5,488
Mats Lanner	73	68	73	69	283	5,488
Jean Francois Remesy	69	69	74	72	284	4,592
Paul Broadhurst	72	71	71	70	284	4,592
Silvio Grappasonni	74	68	71	71	284	4,592
Peter Mitchell	71	71	74	68	284	4,592
Jose Rivero	67	72	76	69	284	4,592
Stuart Little	72	70	70	72	284	4,592
Miguel Angel Martin	72	69	71	73	285	3,376
Andrew Oldcorn	71	69	74	71	285	3,376
Sven Struver	75	68	72	70	285	3,376
Sam Torrance	68	71	72	74	285	3,376
Christopher Hanell	71	69	75	70	285	3,376
Didier De Vooght	70	70	75	70	285	3,376
Des Smyth	69	70	73	73	285	3,376
David Gilford	72	71	71	72	286	2,267.25
Andrew Beal	72	71	73	70	286	2,267.25
Mathias Gronberg	72	68	78	68	286	2,267.25
Tony Johnstone	70	73	73	70	286	2,267.25
Massimo Florioli	68	71	73	75	287	1,674
Ross McFarlane	70	73	76	69	288	1,668
Francisco Cea	71	72	74	71	288	1,668
Ernie Els	72	69	76	71	288	1,668
John Senden	73	70	75	71	289	1,660.50
Raphael Jacquelin	72	71	71	75	289	1,660.50
Jarrod Moseley	75	68	72	75	290	1,653
Mark Davis	71	72	76	71	290	1,653
Thomas Levet	71	69	76	74	290	1,653
Per-Ulrik Johansson	70	72	76	73	291	1,645.50
Stephen Gallacher	69	73	75	74	291	1,645.50
Andrew Sherborne	74	69	73	76	292	1,641
Massimo Scarpa	70	72	71	80	293	1,638
Phil Price	73	70	77	74	294	1,635

Linde German Masters

Gut Larchenhof, Cologne, Germany
Par 36-36–72; 7,289 yards

September 30-October 3
purse, €1,750,000

	SCORES				TOTAL	MONEY
Sergio Garcia	68	69	72	68	277	€291,700
Padraig Harrington	70	70	70	67	277	151,975
Ian Woosnam	68	74	66	69	277	151,975
(Garcia defeated Woosnam on first and Harrington on second extra hole.)						
Jose Rivero	68	66	75	69	278	80,815
Peter Baker	70	68	69	71	278	80,815
Alex Cejka	66	73	69	71	279	61,250
Carlos Franco	69	75	68	68	280	48,125
Retief Goosen	67	69	74	70	280	48,125
Bernhard Langer	70	71	71	69	281	35,420
Peter Mitchell	72	70	70	69	281	35,420
Colin Montgomerie	70	67	72	72	281	35,420

	SCORES				TOTAL	MONEY
David Gilford	69	76	72	65	282	27,676.50
Joakim Haeggman	71	70	72	69	282	27,676.50
Miguel Angel Jimenez	66	73	72	71	282	27,676.50
Vijay Singh	68	70	70	74	282	27,676.50
Thomas Bjorn	72	69	70	72	283	24,654
Richard Green	72	73	71	68	284	21,875
Paul McGinley	72	74	70	68	284	21,875
Steen Tinning	69	72	74	69	284	21,875
Marc Farry	68	73	74	69	284	21,875
Greg Turner	67	74	71	72	284	21,875
Fred Couples	68	71	73	73	285	19,950
Jean Van de Velde	71	71	76	68	286	18,900
Paul Broadhurst	70	71	73	72	286	18,900
Mark Mouland	69	69	75	73	286	18,900
*Kariem Baraka	71	71	77	67	286	
Andrew Coltart	74	72	72	69	287	17,062.50
Thomas Levet	67	76	72	72	287	17,062.50
Miguel Angel Martin	72	72	71	72	287	17,062.50
Jose Maria Olazabal	67	71	75	74	287	17,062.50
Pierre Fulke	72	69	77	70	288	15,006.25
Michael Campbell	70	75	75	68	288	15,006.25
Gary Evans	73	73	71	71	288	15,006.25
Mark McNulty	72	73	70	73	288	15,006.25
Russell Claydon	74	71	75	69	289	13,650
Anthony Wall	71	72	78	68	289	13,650
Daniel Chopra	71	76	70	72	289	13,650
Tony Johnstone	74	67	75	74	290	12,775
Craig Hainline	72	71	73	74	290	12,775
Miles Tunnicliff	72	75	71	73	291	11,900
Ignacio Garrido	70	73	75	73	291	11,900
Thomas Gogele	74	72	75	70	291	11,900
Phil Price	72	74	73	73	292	10,325
Gary Orr	75	71	73	73	292	10,325
Fredrik Jacobson	73	73	73	73	292	10,325
Jean Francois Remesy	75	70	75	72	292	10,325
David Howell	74	72	74	72	292	10,325
Mats Lanner	73	70	77	72	292	10,325
Andrew Beal	71	76	74	72	293	8,750
Raphael Jacquelin	72	73	77	71	293	8,750
Scott Henderson	75	70	72	76	293	8,750
Stuart Cage	72	69	77	76	294	7,175
Greg Owen	70	70	79	75	294	7,175
Costantino Rocca	72	75	74	73	294	7,175
Malcolm Mackenzie	72	71	78	73	294	7,175
Raymond Russell	74	71	77	72	294	7,175
Steve Webster	72	72	73	77	294	7,175
Rolf Muntz	75	70	75	75	295	5,556.25
Paolo Quirici	70	77	73	75	295	5,556.25
Paul Eales	76	70	76	73	295	5,556.25
Van Phillips	76	71	76	72	295	5,556.25
Gerry Norquist	76	70	76	75	297	4,987.50
Derrick Cooper	71	75	79	72	297	4,987.50
Jarrod Moseley	71	73	78	76	298	4,550
Patrick Platz	74	70	81	73	298	4,550
Ross McFarlane	74	73	79	72	298	4,550
Steven Richardson	76	71	77	75	299	2,625
Philip Walton	73	73	77	78	301	2,620.50
Stephen Leaney	74	72	78	77	301	2,620.50
Jarmo Sandelin	74	72	78	78	302	2,616

Alfred Dunhill Cup

Old Course, St. Andrews, Scotland
Par 36-36–72; 7,094 yards

October 7-10
purse, €1,400,000

FIRST ROUND

UNITED STATES DEFEATED NEW ZEALAND, 2-1
Mark O'Meara (US) defeated Greg Turner, 73-74; Michael Long (NZ) defeated Payne
Stewart, 72-76; Tom Lehman (US) defeated Michael Campbell, 71-74.

SWEDEN DEFEATED ITALY, 3-0
Gabriel Hjertstedt (Swe) defeated Costantino Rocca, 71-75; Jarmo Sandelin (Swe)
defeated Massimo Scarpa, 72-79; Patrik Sjoland (Swe) defeated Emanuele Canonica,
68-74.

AUSTRALIA DEFEATED JAPAN, 2-1
Craig Parry (Aus) defeated Tsuyoshi Yoneyama, 69-70; Isao Aoki (J) defeated Peter
O'Malley, 72-74; Stephen Leaney (Aus) defeated Katsuyoshi Tomori, 69-70.

SCOTLAND DEFEATED PARAGUAY, 2-1
Sam Torrance (Sco) defeated Raul Fretes, 75-77; Carlos Franco (P) defeated Gary Orr,
65-73; Paul Lawrie (Sco) defeated Angel Franco, 71-73.

SOUTH AFRICA DEFEATED CHINA, 2-1
Ernie Els (SA) defeated Zhang Lian-wei, 72-74; David Frost (SA) defeated Cheng Jun,
69-72; Wu Xiang-bing (C) defeated Retief Goosen, 72-73.

ENGLAND DEFEATED INDIA, 2-1
Jeev Milkha Singh (Ind) defeated Lee Westwood, 70-73; Mark James (E) defeated
Jyoti Randhawa, 72-73; David Howell (E) defeated Vijay Kumar, 71-72.

IRELAND DEFEATED ZIMBABWE, 3-0
Paul McGinley (Ire) defeated Tony Johnstone, 70-75; Darren Clarke (Ire) defeated
Mark McNulty, 69-74; Padraig Harrington (Ire) defeated Nick Price, 71-72.

SPAIN DEFEATED FRANCE, 2-1
Marc Farry (F) defeated Miguel Angel Jimenez, 68-73; Sergio Garcia (Sp) defeated
Jean Francois Remesy, 67-70; Jose Maria Olazabal (Sp) tied Jean Van de Velde, 74-74,
Olazabal won at first extra hole.

SECOND ROUND

ITALY DEFEATED UNITED STATES, 3-0
Costantino Rocca (It) defeated Mark O'Meara, 70-72; Emanuele Canonica (It) defeated
Tom Lehman, 72-74; Massimo Scarpa (It) defeated Payne Stewart, 71-72.

NEW ZEALAND DEFEATED SWEDEN, 2-1
Michael Campbell (NZ) defeated Gabriel Hjertstedt, 71-72; Michael Long (NZ)
defeated Patrik Sjoland, 73-74; Jarmo Sandelin (Swe) defeated Greg Turner, 69-70.

PARAGUAY DEFEATED AUSTRALIA, 2-1
Peter O'Malley (Aus) defeated Raul Fretes, 73-76; Angel Franco (P) defeated Stephen
Leaney, 73-74; Carlos Franco (P) tied Craig Parry, 70-70, Franco won on second extra
hole.

JAPAN DEFEATED SCOTLAND, 2-1
Isao Aoki (J) defeated Sam Torrance, 71-76; Katsuyoshi Tomori (J) tied Paul Lawrie,
71-71, Tomori won on first extra hole; Gary Orr (Sco) defeated Tsuyoshi Yoneyama,
69-71.

SOUTH AFRICA DEFEATED INDIA, 3-0
Ernie Els (SA) defeated Jeev Milkha Singh, 69-72; Retief Goosen (SA) defeated Vijay
Kumar, 67-75; David Frost (SA) defeated Jyoti Randhawa, 68-74.

ENGLAND DEFEATED CHINA, 2-1
Lee Westwood (E) defeated Zhang Lian-wei, 69-72; Cheng Jun (C) defeated David
Howell, 70-75; Mark James (E) defeated Wu Xiang-bing, 72-74.

SPAIN DEFEATED ZIMBABWE, 2-1
Sergio Garcia (Sp) defeated Nick Price, 67-70; Jose Maria Olazabal (Sp) defeated
Tony Johnstone, 67-73; Mark McNulty (Z) defeated Miguel Angel Jimenez, 68-73.

IRELAND DEFEATED FRANCE, 2-1
Darren Clarke (Ire) defeated Marc Farry, 67-75; Jean Van de Velde (F) defeated Paul
McGinley, 70-74; Padraig Harrington (Ire) defeated Jean Francois Remesy, 73-74.

THIRD ROUND

NEW ZEALAND DEFEATED ITALY, 2-1
Greg Turner (NZ) defeated Emanuele Canonica, 70-72; Massimo Scarpa (It) defeated
Michael Long, 71-72; Michael Campbell (NZ) defeated Costantino Rocca, 70-74.

SWEDEN DEFEATED UNITED STATES, 2-1
Mark O'Meara (US) defeated Patrik Sjoland, 69-73; Gabriel Hjertstedt (Swe) defeated
Payne Stewart, 69-74; Jarmo Sandelin (Swe) defeated Tom Lehman, 71-74.

JAPAN DEFEATED PARAGUAY, 2-1
Katsuyoshi Tomori (J) defeated Angel Franco, 68-72; Tsuyoshi Yoneyama (J) defeated
Raul Fretes, 68-69; Carlos Franco (P) defeated Isao Aoki, 65-77.

AUSTRALIA DEFEATED SCOTLAND, 2-1
Paul Lawrie (Sco) defeated Peter O'Malley, 71-73; Craig Parry (Aus) defeated Sam
Torrance, 70-71; Stephen Leaney (Aus) defeated Gary Orr, 67-70.

SOUTH AFRICA DEFEATED ENGLAND, 3-0
Ernie Els (SA) defeated David Howell, 67-69; David Frost (SA) defeated Mark James,
71-72; Retief Goosen (SA) defeated Lee Westwood, 66-70.

INDIA DEFEATED CHINA, 3-0
Jyoti Randhawa (Ind) defeated Zhang Lian-wei, 73-74; Jeev Milkha Singh (Ind)
defeated Cheng Jun, 72-74; Vijay Kumar (Ind) defeated Wu Xiang-bing, 73-77.

ZIMBABWE DEFEATED FRANCE, 2-0
Mark McNulty (Z) defeated Marc Farry, 69-73; Tony Johnstone (Z) tied Jean Francois
Remesy, 68-68; Nick Price (Z) tied Jean Van de Velde, 68-68, Price won on third extra
hole.

SPAIN DEFEATED IRELAND, 2-1
Sergio Garcia (Sp) defeated Darren Clarke, 67-68; Paul McGinley (Ire) defeated Jose
Maria Olazabal, 68-70; Miguel Angel Jimenez (Sp) tied Padraig Harrington, 69-69,
Jimenez won on first extra hole.

SEMI-FINALS

AUSTRALIA DEFEATED SWEDEN, 2-1
Craig Parry (Aus) defeated Gabriel Hjertstedt, 72-75; Patrik Sjoland (Swe) defeated
Peter O'Malley, 76-78; Stephen Leaney (Aus) tied Jarmo Sandelin, 80-80, Leaney won
on first extra hole.

SPAIN DEFEATED SOUTH AFRICA, 2-1
Ernie Els (SA) defeated Sergio Garcia, 70-72; Miguel Angel Jimenez (Sp) defeated

David Frost, 73-77; Jose Maria Olazabal (Sp) defeated Retief Goosen, 75-76.

FINAL

SPAIN DEFEATED AUSTRALIA, 2-1
Craig Parry (Aus) tied Sergio Garcia, 69-69, Parry won on first extra hole; Jose Maria
Olazabal (Sp) defeated Stephen Leaney, 72-78; Miguel Angel Jimenez (Sp) defeated
Peter O'Malley, 73-75.

	MATCHES WON	INDIVIDUAL GAMES WON (After Round 3)	PRIZE MONEY TEAM	PLAYER
GROUP 1				
Sweden	3	6	€133,000	€44,332
New Zealand	2	5	63,000	21,000
Italy	1	4	35,700	11,900
United States	1	3	27,300	9,100
GROUP 2				
Australia	2	5	210,000	70,000
Japan	2	5	63,000	21,000
Scotland	1	4	35,700	11,900
Paraguay	1	4	27,300	9,100
GROUP 3				
South Africa	3	8	133,000	44,332
England	2	4	63,000	21,000
India	1	4	35,700	11,900
China	0	2	27,300	9,100
GROUP 4				
Spain	3	6	420,000	140,000
Ireland	2	6	63,000	21,000
Zimbabwe	1	3	35,700	11,900
France	0	2	27,300	9,100

Cisco World Match Play

Wentworth Club, West Course, Surrey, England
Par 434 534 444–35; 345 434 455–37–72; 7,006 yards

October 14-17
purse, €896,000

FIRST ROUND

Craig Parry defeated Paul Lawrie, 4 and 3

Parry	4 3 4	4 3 4	4 3 4	3 3	3 4 4	4 3 4	4 4 5	35	68
Lawrie	4 3 4	5 2 4	3 4 4	3 3	3 4 5	4 3 5	4 4 5	37	70

Parry leads, 2 up

Parry	4 3 4	4 3 3	4 4 4	3 3	4 3 4	4 3 4
Lawrie	5 3 3	6 3 3	4 4 3	3 4	2 4 5	4 3 5

Retief Goosen defeated Sergio Garcia, 2 and 1

Garcia	3 2 4	5 3 4	4 4 4	3 3	3 4 4	5 4 3	4 5 5	37	70
Goosen	4 3 4	4 3 4	4 4 4	3 4	3 4 3	4 4 4	4 4 5	35	69

Goosen leads, 1 up

Garcia	4 3 3	3 2 3	5 4 3	3 0	3 5 4	3 3 5	3 5
Goosen	3 2 3	4 3 4	3 3 4	2 9	3 4 4	3 3 4	4 5

Padraig Harrington defeated Carlos Franco, 7 and 6

Franco	4 3 4	3 3 4	4 4 3	32	3 4 4	4 3 4	4 5 4	35 67
Harrington	3 4 4	4 2 4	4 3 4	32	3 4 5	3 3 3	4 4 4	33 65

Harrington leads, 2 up

Franco	4 4 4	4 3 3	5 4 5	36	3 4 5			
Harrington	4 3 4	4 2 4	4 3 4	32	4 3 4			

Notah Begay III defeated Jose Maria Olazabal, 4 and 3

Olazabal	4 2 5	6 3 4	4 4 4	36	3 4 4	4 2 4	4 5 4	34 70
Begay	4 2 4	4 3 5	4 4 3	33	5 3 4	4 3 4	3 5 4	35 68

Begay leads, 2 up

Olazabal	4 3 4	5 3 4	4 4 4	35	3 4 4	4 2 5		
Begay	4 3 3	5 2 4	4 3 4	32	3 4 5	4 3 4		

SECOND ROUND

Mark O'Meara defeated Craig Parry, 39th hole

O'Meara	3 2 5	3 4 4	3 4 4	32	2 3 4	4 3 4	3 4 4	31 63
Parry	3 2 4	4 3 4	4 3 4	31	3 4 5	4 3 4	3 4 5	35 66

O'Meara leads, 3 up

O'Meara	4 3 4	4 3 5	3 4 4	34	3 3 5	4 3 3	5 5 5	36 70
Parry	3 3 4	4 3 4	4 3 4	32	2 4 4	4 3 4	4 5 5	35 67

Match all-square

O'Meara	4 3		4
Parry	4 3		5

Nick Price defeated Retief Goosen, 6 and 5

Price	4 3 4	4 2 4	3 4 3	31	3 3 4	4 3 4	4 4 4	33 64
Goosen	3 3 4	4 3 4	4 4 4	33	3 4 4	4 4 4	4 5 4	36 69

Price leads, 5 up

Price	3 3 3	4 3 4	3 3 4	30	4 3 5	4
Goosen	3 2 4	4 3 4	4 4 3	31	4 4 3	4

Padraig Harrington defeated Ernie Els, 38th hole

Els	5 3 4	5 3 3	4 4 4	35	2 4 5	5 3 4	4 5 5	37 72
Harrington	4 3 4	4 3 3	4 4 4	33	3 5 4	5 3 3	4 5 4	36 69

Harrington leads, 3 up

Els	4 3 3	4 3 4	3 3 4	31	4 3 5	4 3 4	4 5 4	36 67
Harrington	4 3 5	4 4 4	4 4 4	36	3 4 5	4 3 4	3 5 4	35 71

Match all-square

Els	4 3
Harrington	4 2

Colin Montgomerie defeated Notah Begay III, 2 and 1

Montgomerie	4 3 4	4 3 4	4 3 4	33	3 4 4	3 3 4	3 4 4	32 65
Begay	4 2 4	4 3 3	3 4 4	31	4 4 4	4 3 4	4 4 4	35 66

Montgomerie leads, 1 up

Montgomerie	4 2 4	3 3 4	4 4 4	32	3 4 4	5 3 4	4 4
Begay	5 2 4	4 3 4	4 3 5	34	3 4 4	5 2 3	4 5

SEMI-FINALS

Mark O'Meara defeated Nick Price, 1 up

O'Meara	5 3 4	4 4 4	5 4 4	37	3 3 4	3 3 4	4 5 4	33 70
Price	5 3 3	4 3 4	3 5 4	34	2 3 4	4 2 4	4 4 5	32 66

Price leads, 3 up

O'Meara	3 3 5	4 3 4	4 3 4	33	3 4 4	4 3 5	5 5 3	36 69
Price	3 4 5	5 3 4	4 4 4	36	3 4 4	4 4 5	4 5 4	37 73

Colin Montgomerie defeated Padraig Harrington, 7 and 6

Harrington	4 3 4	5 3 5	4 4 4	36	3 4 3	4 3 C	4 6 5	X	X
Montgomerie	4 3 4	4 2 5	4 4 4	36	3 3 4	4 3 3	4 4 4	32	66

Montgomerie leads, 5 up

Harrington	4 2 4	4 3 4	4 4 4	33	4 4 4	
Montgomerie	4 3 4	4 3 3	4 4 4	33	3 3 4	

FINAL

Colin Montgomerie defeated Mark O'Meara, 3 and 2

O'Meara	5 3 4	4 3 4	4 4 4	35	4 4 4	4 3 4	4 4 3	34	69
Montgomerie	3 2 4	4 3 3	5 4 4	32	3 3 4	3 3 4	4 5 5	34	66

Montgomerie leads, 3 up

O'Meara	4 2 4	5 4 3	5 4 4	35	3 3 4	4 3 4	4
Montgomerie	4 3 4	4 3 4	4 5 4	35	3 4 4	4 3 3	4

PRIZE MONEY: Montgomerie £170,000; O'Meara £90,000; Price, Harrington £50,000 each; Parry, Goosen, Els, Begay £40,000 each; Lawrie, Garcia, Franco, Olazabal £30,000 each.

LEGEND: C—conceded hole to opponent; W—won hole by concession without holing out; X—no total score.

Sarazen World Open

PGA Golf de Catalunya, Barcelona, Spain
Par 36-36–72; 7,204 yards

October 14-17
purse, €560,000

	SCORES				TOTAL	MONEY
Thomas Bjorn	66	69	70	68	273	€93,320
Paolo Quirici	70	68	69	68	275	48,630
Katsuyoshi Tomori	72	67	66	70	275	48,630
Francisco Cea	66	73	69	69	277	28,000
Stephen Dodd	72	71	67	68	278	20,033.33
Emanuele Canonica	68	66	75	69	278	20,033.33
Peter Mitchell	67	70	70	71	278	20,033.33
Jose Coceres	72	71	68	68	279	13,260
Domingo Hospital	69	70	67	73	279	13,260
Steen Tinning	69	67	74	70	280	10,038
Stephen Gallacher	68	69	73	70	280	10,038
Thomas Levet	68	68	72	72	280	10,038
Carlos Rodiles	67	71	71	71	280	10,038
Gary Orr	74	71	69	67	281	8,232
Justin Hobday	73	69	70	69	281	8,232
Fredrik Jacobson	71	72	67	71	281	8,232
Jose Rivero	74	70	71	67	282	7,560
Gary Evans	74	69	73	67	283	6,584
Ignacio Garrido	71	73	70	69	283	6,584
Peter Baker	75	67	71	70	283	6,584
Daren Lee	68	72	72	71	283	6,584
Miguel Angel Martin	69	71	72	71	283	6,584
Diego Borrego	73	69	68	73	283	6,584
Miles Tunnicliff	68	69	72	74	283	6,584
Fernando Roca	73	68	73	70	284	5,460
Andrew Oldcorn	71	70	73	70	284	5,460
Roger Winchester	66	76	71	71	284	5,460
Massimo Scarpa	68	72	72	72	284	5,460
Silvio Grappasonni	75	68	68	73	284	5,460

	SCORES				TOTAL	MONEY
David Park	71	68	71	74	284	5,460
Desvonde Botes	74	69	72	70	285	4,662
Fredrik Lindgren	76	69	70	70	285	4,662
Anders Hansen	77	67	73	68	285	4,662
Anthony Wall	69	69	73	74	285	4,662
Malcolm Mackenzie	69	75	70	72	286	4,088
Jesus Maria Arruti	70	75	69	72	286	4,088
Alberto Binaghi	74	69	72	71	286	4,088
Andrew Sherborne	71	73	71	71	286	4,088
Robert Coles	66	70	79	71	286	4,088
Johan Rystrom	69	74	73	70	286	4,088
John Bickerton	75	69	71	72	287	3,360
Soren Hansen	71	73	73	70	287	3,360
Thomas Gogele	69	74	71	73	287	3,360
Henrik Bjornstad	69	71	73	74	287	3,360
Van Phillips	68	74	71	74	287	3,360
Ross Drummond	70	71	70	76	287	3,360
Soren Kjeldsen	70	72	69	76	287	3,360
Mark Pilkington	72	71	72	73	288	2,632
Costantino Rocca	72	73	70	73	288	2,632
Ross McFarlane	70	72	74	72	288	2,632
Dean Robertson	72	72	74	70	288	2,632
Raymond Russell	70	75	73	70	288	2,632
Per Nyman	74	70	76	68	288	2,632
Christian Cevaer	67	75	74	73	289	2,184
John Mellor	70	72	68	79	289	2,184
Andrew Raitt	68	73	75	74	290	2,016
Andrew McLardy	71	70	73	78	292	1,778
Juan Quiros	71	72	75	74	292	1,778
Mark Davis	73	72	74	73	292	1,778
Carlos Larrain	71	74	77	70	292	1,778
Jonathan Lomas	70	73	77	73	293	1,596
Jamie Spence	73	71	77	72	293	1,596
Daniel Chopra	73	70	77	74	294	1,484
Ian Woosnam	71	72	77	74	294	1,484
Massimo Florioli	70	73	79	73	295	1,400
Scott Henderson	73	71	78	76	298	840
Wayne Riley	72	73	81	74	300	837

Belgacom Open

Royal Zoute, Knokke, Belgium
Par 34-37–71; 6,907 yards

October 21-24
purse, €750,000

	SCORES				TOTAL	MONEY
Robert Karlsson	69	68	69	66	272	€125,000
Jamie Spence	70	68	68	67	273	65,130
Retief Goosen	65	71	67	70	273	65,130
Greg Turner	70	68	69	68	275	34,635
Per-Ulrik Johansson	69	66	70	70	275	34,635
Mats Lanner	72	68	70	66	276	21,060
Thomas Bjorn	73	68	69	66	276	21,060
Paul Broadhurst	73	69	68	66	276	21,060
Stephen Gallacher	72	70	66	68	276	21,060
Des Smyth	70	70	68	69	277	15,000
Steen Tinning	70	69	69	70	278	13,350
Ian Woosnam	70	70	68	70	278	13,350

	SCORES				TOTAL	MONEY
Anthony Wall	72	71	66	70	279	12,070
Jose Rivero	67	71	72	70	280	9,991.88
Jean Francois Remesy	72	68	68	72	280	9,991.88
Paul Lawrie	73	69	68	70	280	9,991.88
Lee Westwood	73	66	67	74	280	9,991.88
Soren Kjeldsen	69	71	69	71	280	9,991.88
John Bickerton	69	71	69	71	280	9,991.88
Bernhard Langer	72	70	71	67	280	9,991.88
Jean Van de Velde	72	69	69	70	280	9,991.88
Roger Winchester	75	66	71	69	281	7,762.50
Greg Owen	74	67	74	66	281	7,762.50
Thomas Levet	71	72	69	69	281	7,762.50
Seve Ballesteros	69	74	69	69	281	7,762.50
Peter Baker	72	72	66	71	281	7,762.50
Nicolas Vanhootegem	69	74	67	71	281	7,762.50
Miguel Angel Martin	72	70	66	73	281	7,762.50
Mark Mouland	70	68	69	74	281	7,762.50
Brian Davis	74	70	68	70	282	6,262.50
Jose Coceres	71	71	70	70	282	6,262.50
Tony Johnstone	67	69	74	72	282	6,262.50
Dean Robertson	67	70	73	72	282	6,262.50
Paul McGinley	71	70	68	73	282	6,262.50
Raphael Jacquelin	72	69	67	74	282	6,262.50
Alex Cejka	68	73	71	72	284	5,400
Andrew Oldcorn	73	69	71	71	284	5,400
Paul Eales	73	69	71	71	284	5,400
Mark James	68	71	72	73	284	5,400
Phil Price	69	70	72	73	284	5,400
Dennis Edlund	71	70	71	73	285	4,650
Van Phillips	70	72	72	71	285	4,650
Marc Farry	76	69	69	71	285	4,650
Philip Walton	73	67	74	71	285	4,650
Joakim Haeggman	68	71	77	69	285	4,650
Darren Clarke	73	67	72	74	286	3,900
Russell Claydon	71	71	71	73	286	3,900
Steve Webster	71	74	70	71	286	3,900
Andrew Beal	73	72	71	70	286	3,900
Peter Mitchell	75	70	72	69	286	3,900
Francisco Cea	69	73	72	73	287	3,225
Silvio Grappasonni	75	69	71	72	287	3,225
Malcolm Mackenzie	72	72	71	72	287	3,225
Tom Gillis	71	72	69	75	287	3,225
Gary Evans	73	70	70	75	288	2,850
Arnaud Langenaeken	74	70	71	74	289	2,493.75
Barry Lane	72	68	75	74	289	2,493.75
Michael Campbell	72	70	75	72	289	2,493.75
Derrick Cooper	74	70	73	72	289	2,493.75
Jonathan Lomas	69	72	75	74	290	2,212.50
Olle Karlsson	72	70	75	73	290	2,212.50
Sven Struver	76	69	71	75	291	2,062.50
Trevor Immelman	72	73	76	70	291	2,062.50
Thomas Gogele	70	73	72	77	292	1,518
David Gilford	76	69	71	76	292	1,518
Rolf Muntz	73	71	73	75	292	1,518
Miles Tunnicliff	75	69	73	75	292	1,518
David Howell	68	74	75	76	293	1,119
Ove Sellberg	71	74	73	78	296	1,116

Volvo Masters

Montecastillo Hotel & Golf Resort, Jerez, Spain
Par 36-36–72; 7,058 yards

October 28-31
purse, €1,400,000

		SCORES			TOTAL	MONEY
Miguel Angel Jimenez	68	67	69	65	269	€232,400
Bernhard Langer	66	70	69	66	271	104,346.67
Padraig Harrington	66	65	73	67	271	104,346.67
Retief Goosen	62	68	70	71	271	104,346.67
Darren Clarke	67	70	70	66	273	54,530
Sergio Garcia	69	68	67	69	273	54,530
Thomas Bjorn	66	71	71	66	274	35,933.33
Miguel Angel Martin	69	68	67	70	274	35,933.33
Michael Campbell	70	65	67	72	274	35,933.33
Peter O'Malley	73	69	69	64	275	23,286.67
Ian Woosnam	71	68	69	67	275	23,286.67
Jean Van de Velde	71	69	68	67	275	23,286.67
Jarmo Sandelin	68	73	67	67	275	23,286.67
Paul Lawrie	69	68	69	69	275	23,286.67
Jose Coceres	71	64	68	72	275	23,286.67
Peter Mitchell	70	71	67	68	276	19,180
Ian Garbutt	68	69	70	69	276	19,180
Colin Montgomerie	70	65	71	70	276	19,180
Anthony Wall	70	65	71	70	276	19,180
Paul Broadhurst	73	68	69	67	277	17,500
Per-Ulrik Johansson	69	70	67	71	277	17,500
Bob May	70	71	69	68	278	15,855
Zhang Lian-wei	67	72	70	69	278	15,855
Robert Karlsson	73	67	69	69	278	15,855
Mark McNulty	69	68	71	70	278	15,855
Andrew Coltart	69	69	70	71	279	14,070
Greg Turner	75	67	66	71	279	14,070
Jamie Spence	66	75	66	72	279	14,070
Patrik Sjoland	69	69	68	73	279	14,070
Ignacio Garrido	71	74	69	66	280	12,810
Lee Westwood	72	68	70	70	280	12,810
Costantino Rocca	67	69	74	71	281	11,550
Soren Kjeldsen	71	70	71	69	281	11,550
Paul McGinley	72	71	70	68	281	11,550
Stephen Leaney	79	67	69	66	281	11,550
David Carter	72	67	73	70	282	9,450
David Howell	72	68	73	69	282	9,450
David Park	70	70	70	72	282	9,450
Alex Cejka	75	69	66	72	282	9,450
Kyi Hla Han	71	65	73	73	282	9,450
Russell Claydon	66	70	71	75	282	9,450
Dean Robertson	69	73	69	72	283	7,560
Seve Ballesteros	68	75	69	71	283	7,560
Angel Cabrera	71	71	71	70	283	7,560
Paul Eales	71	70	72	70	283	7,560
Jarrod Moseley	71	73	70	69	283	7,560
John Bickerton	73	71	69	71	284	6,580
Gary Evans	71	73	70	70	284	6,580
Phil Price	65	74	72	74	285	5,845
Eduardo Romero	68	74	71	72	285	5,845
Jean Francois Remesy	67	72	75	71	285	5,845
Tony Johnstone	70	76	69	70	285	5,845
Steve Webster	66	72	76	72	286	5,460
Nico van Rensburg	67	75	69	76	287	5,040

	SCORES				TOTAL	MONEY
Van Phillips	75	67	71	74	287	5,040
Santiago Luna	74	69	71	73	287	5,040
Gary Orr	75	70	70	72	287	5,040
Pierre Fulke	71	72	78	66	287	5,040
Francisco Cea	71	68	71	78	288	4,550
Mark James	73	73	68	74	288	4,550
Peter Baker	69	73	70	77	289	4,270
Marc Farry	69	72	77	71	289	4,270
Sven Struver	72	72	72	74	290	4,060
Ricardo Gonzalez	72	68	77	75	292	3,850
Christopher Hanell	69	78	72	73	292	3,850
Jose Maria Olazabal	72	70	71		WD	3,640

WGC American Express Championship

Valderrama Golf Club, Sotogrande, Spain
Par 35-36–71; 6,830 yards

November 4-7
purse, $5,000,000

	SCORES				TOTAL	MONEY
Tiger Woods	71	69	70	68	278	$1,000,000
Miguel Angel Jimenez	72	68	69	69	278	400,000
(Woods defeated Jimenez on first extra hole.)						
Dudley Hart	75	68	70	70	283	300,000
Nick Price	69	71	70	74	284	176,666.67
Lee Westwood	73	67	71	73	284	176,666.67
Stewart Cink	75	65	71	73	284	176,666.66
Fred Funk	71	68	74	72	285	135,000
Sergio Garcia	74	69	69	73	285	135,000
Scott Hoch	69	70	72	74	285	135,000
Chris Perry	70	67	72	76	285	135,000
Bob Estes	69	72	72	73	286	93,000
Jim Furyk	68	73	71	74	286	93,000
Justin Leonard	71	67	72	76	286	93,000
Jose Maria Olazabal	73	69	69	75	286	93,000
David Toms	72	68	71	75	286	93,000
Tim Herron	71	66	75	75	287	70,000
Davis Love III	74	70	73	70	287	70,000
Vijay Singh	67	71	75	74	287	70,000
Hal Sutton	75	66	69	78	288	62,000
Bob May	77	69	74	69	289	52,800
Colin Montgomerie	70	72	72	75	289	52,800
Craig Parry	72	73	71	73	289	52,800
Dennis Paulson	76	71	68	74	289	52,800
Jarmo Sandelin	70	74	75	70	289	52,800
Angel Cabrera	74	74	70	72	290	41,750
Retief Goosen	75	69	74	72	290	41,750
Mark James	69	70	74	77	290	41,750
Tom Lehman	72	67	71	80	290	41,750
Jarrod Moseley	76	69	72	73	290	41,750
Stuart Appleby	76	66	74	75	291	37,750
Padraig Harrington	76	74	70	71	291	37,750
Jean Van de Velde	72	73	70	76	291	37,750
Mike Weir	73	68	72	78	291	37,750
Steve Elkington	74	72	71	75	292	36,000
John Huston	72	74	72	74	292	36,000
Jeff Sluman	77	70	69	76	292	36,000
Paul Lawrie	76	68	76	73	293	34,500

	SCORES				TOTAL	MONEY
Rodney Pampling	71	74	69	79	293	34,500
Bob Tway	75	72	71	75	293	34,500
Darren Clarke	79	67	71	78	295	32,250
Ernie Els	74	75	71	75	295	32,250
Phil Mickelson	69	71	77	78	295	32,250
Naomichi Ozaki	76	71	69	79	295	32,250
Loren Roberts	72	72	71	80	295	32,250
Duffy Waldorf	74	77	73	71	295	32,250
Notah Begay III	77	71	73	75	296	30,250
Steve Pate	72	74	72	78	296	30,250
Scott Dunlap	74	71	75	77	297	28,500
Carlos Franco	75	73	74	75	297	28,500
Bernhard Langer	71	70	80	76	297	28,500
Jeff Maggert	70	74	79	74	297	28,500
Ted Tryba	77	71	70	79	297	28,500
Kazuhiko Hosokawa	73	73	72	80	298	27,125
Robert Karlsson	74	68	74	82	298	27,125
Alex Cejka	79	76	72	72	299	26,500
Brent Geiberger	75	71	68	85	299	26,500
Brian Watts	75	74	79	71	299	26,500
Craig Spence	72	73	75	80	300	26,000
Thomas Bjorn	72	81	74	77	304	25,625
David Frost	76	73	74	81	304	25,625
Richard Kaplan	78	75	73	80	306	25,250
Glen Day	78	67	81		DQ	

Johnnie Walker Classic

See Asia/Japan Tours chapter.

Challenge Tour

Tusker Kenya Open

Muthaiga Golf Club, Nairobi, Kenya
Par 35-36–71; 6,825 yards

March 11-14
purse, €91,000

	SCORES				TOTAL	MONEY
Maarten Lafeber	66	66	69	64	265	€14,781.59
Erik Andersson	68	67	65	68	268	9,848.48
Sammy Daniels	68	72	69	61	270	5,554.19
Hennie Otto	70	65	68	68	271	4,099.10
Jorgen Aker	65	72	64	70	271	4,099.10
Richard Bland	75	66	66	65	272	3,451.41
Iain Pyman	65	69	68	71	273	2,933.84
David Jones	71	68	65	69	273	2,933.84
David Park	74	66	67	66	273	2,933.84
Frederic Cupillard	70	71	66	67	274	2,193.73

	SCORES				TOTAL	MONEY
John Hawksworth	68	64	70	72	274	2,193.73
Scott Watson	70	69	68	67	274	2,193.73
Johan Skold	67	70	71	66	274	2,193.73
Mattias Eliasson	68	70	67	70	275	1,475.05
Gustavo Rojas	71	68	67	69	275	1,475.05
Gianluca Pietrobono	69	66	71	69	275	1,475.05
Simon Hurd	69	69	69	68	275	1,475.05
Greig Hutcheon	67	72	70	67	276	1,055.82
Jeremy Robinson	70	69	67	70	276	1,055.82
Ross Bain	68	65	70	73	276	1,055.82
Gary Murphy	71	66	73	66	276	1,055.82
Brett Liddle	70	67	69	70	276	1,055.82
Knud Storegaard	69	70	71	67	277	899.08
Carlos Larrain	66	74	72	65	277	899.08
*Ajay Shah	71	67	69	70	277	
Jacob Okello	68	68	69	72	277	899.08
Andrew Clapp	70	69	70	69	278	789.66
Martin Erlandsson	70	68	67	73	278	789.66
Chris Van Der Velde	67	70	68	73	278	789.66
Simon Wakefield	72	69	72	65	278	789.66
Arnaud Langenaeken	72	68	70	68	278	789.66

OKI Telepizza Challenge

Golf del Guardiana, Badajoz, Spain
Par 36-36–72; 6,978 yards

March 24-27
purse, €63,000

	SCORES				TOTAL	MONEY
David Park	66	69	72	70	277	€10,223.41
Ola Eliasson	67	73	68	70	278	6,818.18
Sammy Daniels	72	74	69	71	286	3,458.22
Euan Little	73	71	71	71	286	3,458.22
Jose Manuel Carriles	70	73	75	69	287	2,304.97
Greig Hutcheon	67	72	72	76	287	2,304.97
Eric Carlberg	69	70	73	75	287	2,304.97
Patxi Amatriain	74	73	69	71	287	2,304.97
Juan Quiros	70	72	73	73	288	1,588.45
Johan Skold	71	75	67	75	288	1,588.45
Dominique Nouailhac	70	72	74	72	288	1,588.45
Gustavo Rojas	74	72	69	73	288	1,588.45
Mattias Eliasson	66	71	75	76	288	1,588.45
Ignacio Garrido	70	70	74	75	289	1,021.19
Jose Rozadilla	73	72	71	73	289	1,021.19
Erik Andersson	71	73	72	73	289	1,021.19
Bradley Dredge	71	72	73	73	289	1,021.19
Nicolas Vanhootegem	71	70	74	75	290	746.31
Mikael Piltz	70	73	74	73	290	746.31
Markus Brier	73	71	76	70	290	746.31
Gianluca Pietrobono	70	75	73	72	290	746.31
Matthew Blackey	73	73	73	72	291	644.97
Victor Casado	73	74	71	73	291	644.97
Ian Poulter	73	74	72	72	291	644.97
David Lynn	71	73	72	76	292	583.53
Luis Navarro	72	71	75	74	292	583.53
Andrew Barnett	73	72	77	70	292	583.53
Leif Westerberg	71	74	74	74	293	528.25
Nils Rorbaek	75	71	75	72	293	528.25
Hennie Otto	72	69	73	79	293	528.25

Open de Cote D'Ivoire

Ivoire Golf Club, Abidjan, Ivory Coast
Par 36-36–72; 6,635 yards

April 15-18
purse, €70,000

	SCORES				TOTAL	MONEY
Ian Poulter	69	72	70	73	284	€11,370.45
Marc Pendaries	71	71	71	73	286	5,086.90
David Park	71	71	75	69	286	5,086.90
Sebastian Delagrange	73	68	72	73	286	5,086.90
Maarten Lafeber	71	71	73	72	287	2,893.80
Simon Wakefield	73	69	72	74	288	2,654.93
Eric Giraud	74	74	70	71	289	2,347.80
Markus Brier	75	67	75	72	289	2,347.80
Simon Hurd	71	73	74	72	290	2,074.80
Warren Bladon	73	72	78	69	292	1,687.48
Phil Golding	72	73	73	74	292	1,687.48
Scott Watson	71	76	74	71	292	1,687.48
Andrew Butterfield	79	71	69	73	292	1,687.48
Eric Carlberg	75	72	75	71	293	1,134.66
Chris Benians	74	70	73	76	293	1,134.66
Didier De Vooght	74	74	71	74	293	1,134.66
Charles Challen	72	76	73	72	293	1,134.66
Michael Dieu	75	76	70	73	294	829.24
Felix Lubenau	74	73	73	74	294	829.24
Ilya Goroneskoul	76	73	72	73	294	829.24
Dominique Nouailhac	73	72	72	77	294	829.24
Christophe Pottier	74	74	74	73	295	743.93
Lionel Alexandre	78	73	76	70	297	670.22
Jean Marc De Polo	75	74	76	72	297	670.22
David R. Jones	71	72	76	78	297	670.22
Johan Skold	74	74	75	74	297	670.22
Maxime Demory	74	74	73	76	297	670.22
Bill Longmuir	74	75	76	73	298	563.07
Jacob Okello	76	74	73	75	298	563.07
Siaka Kone	73	73	76	76	298	563.07
Martin Pettigrew	73	71	75	79	298	563.07
David Higgins	75	76	76	71	298	563.07
Jorgen Aker	74	72	75	77	298	563.07

Comunidad Valenciana Challenge de Espana

Campo de Golf El Saler, Valencia, Spain
Par 36-36–72; 6,950 yards

April 29-May 2
purse, €90,151

	SCORES				TOTAL	MONEY
Carl Suneson	73	68	71	68	280	€14,643.52
Manuel Moreno	75	67	67	73	282	9,756.48
Tomas Jesus Munoz	67	71	71	74	283	5,502.31
Martin Erlandsson	70	69	77	68	284	3,846.92
Didier De Vooght	69	71	73	71	284	3,846.92
Nick Ludwell	75	69	70	70	284	3,846.92
Gustavo Rojas	72	75	68	70	285	3,146.69
Andrew Butterfield	72	72	72	70	286	2,900.58
Eric Carlberg	77	68	71	71	287	2,179.83
Philip Golding	72	74	71	70	287	2,179.83
Grant Hamerton	73	72	71	71	287	2,179.83
David Park	75	70	72	70	287	2,179.83

	SCORES				TOTAL	MONEY
Juan Angel Rosillo	68	78	71	70	287	2,179.83
Mikael Lundberg	74	71	71	71	287	2,179.83
Jose Manuel Lara	72	70	77	69	288	1,274.49
Daniel Westermark	72	73	72	71	288	1,274.49
Jose Manuel Carriles	72	71	73	72	288	1,274.49
Fredrik Henge	72	71	76	69	288	1,274.49
Markus Brier	74	68	73	73	288	1,274.49
Klas Eriksson	73	71	73	72	289	977.85
Ruben Gonzalez	70	74	74	71	289	977.85
Nick O'Hern	75	71	73	70	289	977.85
Andrew Clapp	73	71	77	68	289	977.85
Maarten Lafeber	74	71	74	71	290	821.83
Jeremy Robinson	76	70	73	71	290	821.83
Scott Watson	73	73	73	71	290	821.83
Brian Nelson	76	71	74	69	290	821.83
Dominique Nouailhac	73	71	74	72	290	821.83
Ivo Giner	75	71	73	71	290	821.83
Rudi Sailer	74	71	75	71	291	685.59
Jose Rozadilla	74	72	73	72	291	685.59
Tony Edlund	71	75	73	72	291	685.59
Simon Hurd	71	74	70	76	291	685.59
Ricardo Jimenez	75	72	69	75	291	685.59
Lucas Parsons	72	73	72	74	291	685.59

BIL Luxembourg Open

Kikuoka Golf & Country Club, Chant Val, Luxembourg
Par 36-36–72; 7,066 yards

May 13-16
purse, €63,000

	SCORES				TOTAL	MONEY
Kevin Carissimi	67	70	65	68	270	€10,233.41
Stephen Scahill	72	69	63	67	271	6,818.18
Carl Suneson	68	71	67	69	275	3,845.21
Jose Manuel Lara	70	68	69	69	276	2,688.37
Didier De Vooght	69	66	71	70	276	2,688.37
Gustavo Rojas	67	68	71	70	276	2,688.37
Patrick Platz	70	67	69	71	277	2,031.12
Marcello Santi	72	67	70	68	277	2,031.12
Francesco Guermani	71	67	67	72	277	2,031.12
John Wade	67	68	72	71	278	1,518.74
Maarten Lafeber	71	66	69	72	278	1,518.74
Erol Simsek	70	69	69	70	278	1,518.74
Lucas Parsons	68	69	69	72	278	1,518.74
Bradley Dredge	72	67	70	70	279	1,021.19
Joakim Rask	71	69	65	74	279	1,021.19
Matthew Blackey	70	70	68	71	279	1,021.19
Leif Westerberg	70	69	67	73	279	1,021.19
Johan Skold	71	68	67	74	280	763.72
Sebastien Delagrange	68	73	69	70	280	763.72
Benoit Teilleria	68	69	69	74	280	763.72
David Park	72	70	70	69	281	681.82
Markus Brier	68	72	72	69	281	681.82
Alvaro Salto	70	70	71	71	282	593.77
Patrik Gottfridson	68	71	68	75	282	593.77
Knud Storegaard	69	69	70	74	282	593.77
Fredrik Andersson	67	72	69	74	282	593.77
Frederic Cupillard	72	67	68	75	282	593.77

	SCORES				TOTAL	MONEY
Mikael Lundberg	71	70	69	72	282	593.77
Ian Poulter	69	70	72	72	283	511.87
Andrew Barnett	72	70	70	71	283	511.87
Robert Coles	72	68	70	73	283	511.87

Open dei Tessali

Riva dei Tessali, Tessali, Italy
Par 35-36–71; 6,509 yards

May 20-23
purse, €63,000

	SCORES				TOTAL	MONEY
Gustavo Rojas	69	68	67	68	272	€10,233.41
Didier De Vooght	71	70	66	67	274	6,818.18
Iain Pyman	68	71	67	70	276	3,845.21
David Park	72	66	68	71	277	2,688.37
Marc Pendaries	70	71	67	69	277	2,688.37
Simon Wakefield	69	70	68	70	277	2,688.37
Francesco Guermani	68	70	70	70	278	2,031.12
Johan Skold	68	72	69	69	278	2,031.12
Mattias Eliasson	72	70	69	67	278	2,031.12
Donald Gammon	73	68	69	69	279	1,584.77
Jose Manuel Carriles	70	69	70	70	279	1,584.77
Matthew Blackey	70	73	65	71	279	1,584.77
Markus Brier	71	70	71	68	280	1,320.64
Gianluca Baruffaldi	67	75	70	69	281	1,136.37
Sean Corte-Real	72	67	72	70	281	1,136.37
Brian Nelson	72	73	66	71	282	844.60
Eric Carlberg	74	68	70	70	282	844.60
Raimo Sjoberg	73	69	69	71	282	844.60
Stephen Scahill	74	70	67	71	282	844.60
Alessandro Napoleoni	75	69	71	68	283	659.29
Eric Giraud	71	69	68	75	283	659.29
Fredrik Andersson	71	72	66	74	283	659.29
Juan Nutt	75	69	67	72	283	659.29
Marcello Santi	70	74	69	70	283	659.29
Paul Nilbrink	71	73	69	70	283	659.29
Alessandro Tadini	74	71	70	69	284	509.83
Arnaud Langenaeken	71	73	72	68	284	509.83
Dominique Nouailhac	69	73	70	72	284	509.83
Emmanuele Lattanzi	76	67	71	70	284	509.83
Gianluca Pietrobono	70	70	74	70	284	509.83
Mikael Lundberg	74	70	70	70	284	509.83
Pauli Hughes	73	69	70	72	284	509.83
Rudi Sailer	73	69	75	67	284	509.83
Timothy Maxwell	72	68	74	70	284	509.83
Uli Weinhandl	73	69	72	70	284	509.83

Challenge de Sable

Sable Solesmes, France
Par 36-36–72; 6,760 yards

May 27-30
purse, €70,000

	SCORES				TOTAL	MONEY
Lucas Parsons	67	67	73	63	270	€11,370.45
Kalle Brink	71	66	67	70	274	7,575.75

	SCORES			TOTAL	MONEY
Markus Brier	71	67	68	69	275	4,272.45
Carl Suneson	69	71	66	70	276	2,851.15
Johan Skold	68	69	74	65	276	2,851.15
Marcus Wheelhouse	69	71	68	68	276	2,851.15
Stephen Scahill	68	69	72	67	276	2,851.15
Euan Little	72	68	67	70	277	2,163.53
Klas Eriksson	70	70	70	67	277	2,163.53
Gustavo Rojas	68	69	71	70	278	1,687.48
Heinz Peter Thul	71	72	67	68	278	1,687.48
Nils Rorbaek	71	69	69	69	278	1,687.48
Peter Hedblom	71	67	70	70	278	1,687.48
Donald Gammon	72	68	69	70	279	1,086.54
Ilya Goroneskoul	72	71	70	66	279	1,086.54
Marten Olander	71	71	71	66	279	1,086.54
Scott Watson	70	68	71	70	279	1,086.54
Sebastien Delagrange	70	70	70	69	279	1,086.54
Adam Mednick	68	72	71	69	280	825.83
Mattias Eliasson	74	68	71	67	280	825.83
Andrew Sandywell	71	68	71	71	281	706.39
David Park	70	70	69	72	281	706.39
*Julien Van Hauwe	70	70	67	74	281	
Knud Storegaard	70	71	70	70	281	706.39
Mark Litton	72	70	67	72	281	706.39
Pascal Edmond	69	69	69	74	281	706.39
Simon Wakefield	74	69	70	68	281	706.39
Andrew Clapp	75	68	67	72	282	597.19
Jose Manuel Lara	72	70	69	71	282	597.19
Nick O'Hern	71	68	70	73	282	597.19
Richard Gillot	68	72	73	69	282	597.19

NCC Open

Soderasens Golf Club, Stockholm, Sweden
Par 35-36–71; 6,605 yards

June 10-13
purse, €63,560

	SCORES			TOTAL	MONEY
Per Nyman	72	68	71	70	281	€10,324.37
Klas Eriksson	67	76	69	69	281	5,379.09
Thomas Norret	69	72	72	68	281	5,379.09
(Nyman defeated Eriksson and Norret on second extra hole.)						
Marten Olander	72	68	73	69	282	3,098.55
Knud Storegaard	70	70	73	70	283	2,627.58
David Tapping	66	73	75	70	284	2,224.77
Mattias Eliasson	71	72	70	71	284	2,224.77
Mikael Lundberg	74	68	69	73	284	2,224.77
Henrik Stenson	68	73	71	74	286	1,809.56
Richard Johnson	70	76	67	73	286	1,809.56
Claes Hovstadius	73	73	70	71	287	1,464.58
Fredrik Larsson	76	72	70	69	287	1,464.58
Jesper Kjaerbye	72	74	67	74	287	1,464.58
Joakim Gronhagen	72	70	74	72	288	1,146.47
Kim Wilk	71	76	70	71	288	1,146.47
Bjorn Pettersson	72	75	71	71	289	852.11
Charles Challen	72	74	70	73	289	852.11
Fredrik Andersson	72	71	71	75	289	852.11
Pauli Hughes	71	68	76	74	289	852.11
Don Bell	74	68	78	70	290	689.43

	SCORES				TOTAL	MONEY
Johan Selberg	75	72	70	73	290	689.43
Jose Manuel Carriles	73	72	73	72	290	689.43
Viktor Gustavsson	74	71	71	74	290	689.43
Adam Mednick	75	73	70	73	291	553.62
Anders Gillner	74	74	70	73	291	553.62
Chris Van Der Velde	72	75	69	75	291	553.62
Jimmy Kawalec	72	67	75	77	291	553.62
Johan Edfors	76	72	72	71	291	553.62
Johan Forsman	69	77	73	72	291	553.62
Nils Rorbaek	76	72	71	72	291	553.62
Ove Sellberg	72	74	74	71	291	553.62
*Pontus Ericsson	74	70	73	74	291	
Ulrik Gustafsson	72	71	73	75	291	553.62

Diners Club Austrian Open

Millstater See Golf Club, Austria
Par 35-35–70; 6,066 yards

June 10-13
purse, €77,000

	SCORES				TOTAL	MONEY
Juan Ciola	66	66	67	64	263	€12,507.50
Elliot Boult	68	64	65	66	263	8,333.33
(Ciola defeated Boult on second extra hole.)						
Markus Brier	67	65	67	66	265	4,699.70
Justin Rose	64	71	67	65	267	3,753.75
Didier de Vooght	70	69	64	66	269	3,183.18
Carl Suneson	66	69	68	67	270	2,804.06
David Lynn	70	69	65	66	270	2,804.06
Bradley Dredge	65	67	70	69	271	2,287.29
Marcus Wheelhouse	66	67	68	70	271	2,287.29
Pascal Edmond	64	71	69	67	217	2,287.29
David Park	67	68	69	68	272	1,854.36
Philip Golding	70	69	66	67	272	1,854.36
Arnaud Langenaeken	72	66	66	69	273	1,463.96
Jean Marie Kula	66	70	70	67	273	1,463.96
Shaun Webster	73	66	65	69	273	1,463.96
Benoit Teilleria	72	66	67	69	274	1,032.28
Gary Marks	69	69	73	63	274	1,032.28
Marc Pendaries	65	69	70	70	274	1,032.28
Simon Wakefield	67	68	70	69	274	1,032.28
Frederic Cupillard	67	69	72	67	275	835.21
Maarten Lafeber	70	68	71	66	275	835.21
Marco Bernardini	71	67	72	65	275	835.21
Stephen Scahill	68	68	72	67	275	835.21
Gary Clark	65	68	71	72	276	724.48
Gordon Sherry	67	71	67	71	276	724.48
Simon Hurd	69	70	70	67	276	724.48
Stefano Soffietti	65	71	70	70	276	724.48
Daniel Westermark	69	67	72	69	277	636.26
Duncan Muscroft	68	70	72	67	277	636.26
Eddy Rawlings	67	70	69	71	277	636.26
Michael Welch	67	72	69	69	277	636.26

Is Molas Challenge

Is Molas Golf Club, Sardinia, Italy
Par 35-37–72; 6,980 yards

June 24-27
purse, €63,000

	SCORES				TOTAL	MONEY
Bradley Dredge	69	68	68	65	270	€10,233.41
Markus Brier	67	69	70	66	272	6,818.18
David Higgins	67	67	74	66	274	3,173.63
Grant Hamerton	67	67	72	68	274	3,173.63
Juan Nutt	71	70	68	65	274	3,173.63
Gary Murphy	65	70	68	72	275	2,389.43
Brian Nelson	65	73	70	69	277	1,738.33
Fredrik Henge	71	70	67	69	277	1,738.33
Ian Poulter	68	68	70	71	277	1,738.33
Jose Manuel Lara	69	70	68	70	277	1,738.33
Knud Storegaard	65	73	70	69	277	1,738.33
Roberto Zappa	70	69	67	71	277	1,738.33
Sam Little	70	71	68	68	277	1,738.33
Didier De Vooght	71	70	66	71	278	977.89
Ivo Giner	68	72	67	71	278	977.89
Matthew Blackey	71	71	66	70	278	977.89
Peter Malmgren	72	70	69	67	278	977.89
Ross Bain	70	66	68	74	278	977.89
David Tapping	71	67	70	71	279	726.86
Federico Bisazza	72	71	70	66	279	726.86
Uli Weinhandl	69	73	72	65	279	726.86
Dominique Nouailhac	72	70	71	67	280	624.08
Grant Dodd	72	70	69	69	280	624.08
Niclas Johnsson	73	67	70	70	280	624.08
Thomas Norret	74	69	69	68	280	624.08
Ulrik Gustafsson	70	68	71	71	280	624.08
Baldovino Dassu	70	69	71	71	281	522.11
Fredrik Orest	74	67	73	67	281	522.11
Jean Marc De Polo	72	68	67	74	281	522.11
Luca Fracassi	70	72	72	67	281	522.11
Pascal Edmond	74	69	71	67	281	522.11
Simon Wakefield	71	69	72	69	281	522.11

Open des Volcans

Golf des Volcans, Volcans d'Auvergne National Park, France
Par 36-36–72; 6,701 yards

July 1-4
purse, €70,000

	SCORES				TOTAL	MONEY
Philip Golding	67	68	69	66	270	€11,370.45
Stephen Scahill	70	67	69	66	272	7,575.75
Marc Pendaries	67	73	69	65	274	3,842.48
Peter Hedblom	67	69	69	69	274	3,842.48
David Lynn	69	70	67	70	276	2,774.37
Mattias Eliasson	68	70	69	69	276	2,774.37
Mikael Lundberg	68	68	72	69	277	2,347.80
Victor Casado	71	71	70	65	277	2,347.80
Andrew Barnett	73	67	65	73	278	1,692.60
Andrew Sandywell	70	71	68	69	278	1,692.60
Carl Suneson	69	68	70	71	278	1,692.60

		SCORES			TOTAL	MONEY
Francis Howley	69	65	72	72	278	1,692.60
Jean-Francois Lucquin	69	67	72	70	278	1,692.60
Jose Manuel Carriles	70	66	74	68	278	1,692.60
Benoit Teilleria	73	69	71	66	279	989.63
Iain Pyman	74	68	68	69	279	989.63
Nils Rorbaek	71	68	71	69	279	989.63
Pascal Edmond	70	70	70	69	279	989.63
Sean Corte-Real	67	70	72	70	279	989.63
Brian Nelson	70	71	67	72	280	788.29
Ola Eliasson	75	68	67	70	280	788.29
Jose Manuel Lara	69	72	69	71	281	693.42
Matthew Blackey	68	72	70	71	281	693.42
Raimo Sjoberg	73	68	70	70	281	693.42
Simon Little	69	71	74	67	281	693.42
Sebastien Delagrange	70	70	70	71	281	693.42
Klas Eriksson	71	71	69	71	282	597.19
Knud Storegaard	70	72	65	75	282	597.19
Morten Backhausen	69	70	70	73	282	597.19
Simon Hurd	70	69	72	71	282	597.19

Neuchatel Open Golf Trophy

Neuchatel Golf & Country Club, Switzerland
Par 35-36–71; 6,493 yards

July 2-4
purse, €63,000

		SCORES		TOTAL	MONEY
Richard Johnson	68	69	64	201	€10,233.41
Erol Simsek	66	68	68	202	6,818.18
Gary Marks	66	69	68	203	2,977.58
Marcello Santi	69	68	66	203	2,977.58
Peter Malmgren	71	66	66	203	2,977.58
Simon Hurley	70	68	65	203	2,977.58
Eric Carlberg	69	68	67	204	2,113.03
Pehr Magnebrant	68	70	66	204	2,113.03
Fredrik Larsson	69	70	66	205	1,724
Gustavo Rojas	73	66	66	205	1,724
Luis Claverie	69	70	66	205	1,724
Dimitri Bieri	64	69	73	206	1,322.69
Joakim Rask	73	66	67	206	1,322.69
Marcus Knight	68	69	69	206	1,322.69
Nicolas Joakimides	72	68	67	207	922.91
Niki Zitny	71	69	67	207	922.91
Thomas Norret	69	71	67	207	922.91
Uli Weinhandl	71	70	66	207	922.91
Andrew Clapp	72	69	67	208	712.53
Leif Westerberg	73	66	69	208	712.53
Markus Brier	70	69	69	208	712.53
Nicolas Kalouguine	72	68	68	208	712.53
John Wade	73	67	69	209	622.44
Mattias Nilsson	69	69	71	209	622.44
Rudi Sailer	73	68	68	209	622.44
Didier De Vooght	70	71	69	210	574.33
Tony Edlund	73	69	68	210	574.33
Federico Bisazza	73	66	72	211	528.25
Jacques Blatti	73	70	68	211	528.25
Shaun Webster	67	72	72	211	528.25

Volvo Finnish Open

Espoo Golf Club, Espoo, Finland
Par 36-36–72; 6,734 yards

July 8-11
purse, €70,000

		SCORES			TOTAL	MONEY
Paul Nilbrink	69	72	68	72	281	€11,370.45
Gustavo Rojas	72	72	72	65	281	7,575.75
(Nilbrink defeated Rojas on third extra hole.)						
Daniel Westermark	70	68	72	72	282	3,842.48
Fredrik Larsson	68	72	68	74	282	3,842.48
Klas Eriksson	73	68	72	70	283	2,774.37
Per Nyman	70	69	72	72	283	2,774.37
Antoine Lebouc	72	69	72	71	284	2,088.45
Michele Reale	74	70	68	72	284	2,088.45
Morten Backhausen	70	72	73	69	284	2,088.45
Morten Hagen	70	74	70	70	284	2,088.45
Ulrik Gustafsson	70	69	74	71	284	2,088.45
Urs Kaltenberger	71	74	71	69	285	1,610.70
David Higgins	72	68	72	74	286	1,262.63
Didier De Vooght	76	68	68	74	286	1,262.63
Knud Storegaard	68	71	71	76	286	1,262.63
Mikko Rantanen	72	72	72	70	286	1,262.63
Martin Erlandsson	72	73	72	70	287	955.50
Benoit Teilleria	69	69	71	79	288	753.79
Bjorn Pettersson	70	72	73	73	288	753.79
Elliot Boult	73	70	71	74	288	753.79
Fredrik Orest	74	70	76	68	288	753.79
Jens Nilsson	73	69	71	75	288	753.79
Joakim Rask	74	70	70	74	288	753.79
Jose Manuel Lara	69	74	77	68	288	753.79
Patrik Gottfridson	70	70	78	70	288	753.79
Stefano Soffietti	73	70	71	74	288	753.79
Euan Little	70	70	73	76	289	627.90
Nicolas Vanhootegem	69	74	74	73	290	578.42
Philip Golding	74	70	72	74	290	578.42
Robert Coles	69	73	74	74	290	578.42
Thomas Nielsen	68	73	71	78	290	578.42

BTC Slovenian Open

Bled Golf & Country Club, Bled, Slovenia
Par 36-37–73; 6,941 yards

July 15-18
purse, €70,000

		SCORES			TOTAL	MONEY
Grant Dodd	72	68	66	68	274	€11,370.45
Markus Brier	70	71	69	66	276	5,924.10
Nils Rorbaek	72	71	64	69	276	5,924.10
Bradley Dredge	68	67	71	71	277	3,153.15
Dominique Nouailhac	67	70	71	69	277	3,153.15
Thomas Norret	69	68	67	74	278	2,654.93
David Higgins	68	68	72	71	279	2,443.35
Mikael Lundberg	70	69	71	70	280	1,999.73
Neil Turley	71	71	70	68	280	1,999.73
Sean Quinlivan	69	70	71	70	280	1,999.73
Raimo Sjoberg	70	69	69	72	280	1,999.73
Johan Skold	70	70	68	73	281	1,469.65
Morten Backhausen	69	71	72	69	281	1,469.65

		SCORES			TOTAL	MONEY
Sam Little	74	70	70	67	281	1,469.65
Andrew Bonhomme	70	71	70	71	282	1,126.13
Francis Howley	71	71	70	70	282	1,126.13
Alexandre Balicki	73	68	70	72	283	836.07
Andreas Lindberg	69	72	71	71	283	836.07
Duncan Muscroft	73	71	71	68	283	836.07
Kaweh Alexander Chirband	69	73	73	68	283	836.07
Lionel Alexandre	72	69	72	70	283	836.07
Mattias Eliasson	66	72	73	72	283	836.07
Gary Murphy	71	73	68	73	284	649.35
Hayo Bensdorp	73	71	69	71	284	649.35
Marco Bernardini	69	69	72	74	284	649.35
Pascal Edmond	72	72	71	69	284	649.35
Robert Coles	70	72	69	73	284	649.35
Shaun Webster	73	70	70	71	284	649.35
Stuart McGregor	70	67	74	73	284	649.35
Chris Benians	70	72	73	70	285	559.65
Marco Soffietti	75	69	71	70	285	559.65

Rolex Trophy

Golf Club de Geneve, Geneva, Switzerland
Par 36-36–72; 6,873 yards

July 15-18
purse, €70,000

		SCORES			TOTAL	MONEY
Carl Suneson	68	68	67	65	268	€9,451.79
Adam Mednick	68	68	68	70	274	5,986.13
Brian Nelson	67	71	66	71	275	4,257.51
Stephen Scahill	70	68	69	68	275	4,257.51
David Lynn	68	71	70	67	276	3,056.07
Jose Manuel Lara	74	70	66	66	276	3,056.07
Sebastien Delagrange	68	64	73	72	277	2,331.45
Simon Hurd	72	69	70	66	277	2,331.45
Ian Poulter	71	70	70	68	279	1,952.43
Peter Hedblom	69	72	66	72	279	1,952.43
Simon Wakefield	69	69	70	71	279	1,952.43
Andrew Sandywell	70	70	69	71	280	1,575.29
Matthew Blackey	68	71	71	70	280	1,575.29
Ola Eliasson	71	68	72	69	280	1,575.29
Jean Marie Kula	67	73	71	71	282	1,323.25
Klas Eriksson	74	67	70	71	282	1,323.25
Philip Golding	68	70	74	70	282	1,323.25
Nick Ludwell	66	70	76	72	284	1,197.22
Francesco Guermani	66	73	72	75	286	1,134.21

Finnish Masters

Master Golf Club, Finland
Par 36-36–72; 6,638 yards

July 29-August 1
purse, €112,000

		SCORES			TOTAL	MONEY
Lucas Parsons	68	67	71	66	272	€18,192.72
Thomas Norret	68	68	69	68	273	12,121.20
Erol Simsek	67	71	70	68	276	6,835.92
Leif Westerberg	75	66	67	69	277	5,045.04

	SCORES				TOTAL	MONEY
Mikael Piltz	70	73	67	67	277	5,045.04
Fredrik Henge	70	69	69	71	279	3,770.13
Knud Storegaard	68	72	72	67	279	3,770.13
Luis Claverie	71	73	70	65	279	3,770.13
Simon Hurd	72	70	68	69	279	3,770.13
Bjorn Pettersson	73	70	67	70	280	2,165.80
Eric Carlberg	69	73	71	67	280	2,165.80
Iain Pyman	69	69	73	69	280	2,165.80
Ivo Giner	68	72	72	68	280	2,165.80
Johan Skold	70	71	74	65	280	2,165.80
Kevin Carissimi	72	70	68	70	280	2,165.80
Mark Litton	67	73	71	69	280	2,165.80
Mattias Eliasson	71	73	66	70	280	2,165.80
Victor Casado	70	72	69	69	280	2,165.80
Carl Suneson	72	70	69	71	282	1,292.20
Ian Poulter	74	70	69	69	282	1,292.20
Ola Eliasson	74	67	69	72	282	1,292.20
Frederic Cupillard	75	69	69	70	283	1,109.47
Jose Manuel Carriles	72	71	70	70	283	1,109.47
Jose Manuel Lara	68	76	72	67	283	1,109.47
Marcello Santi	70	72	71	70	283	1,109.47
Martin Erlandsson	71	67	72	73	283	1,109.47
Adam Le Vesconte	69	73	69	73	284	941.30
Andrew Clapp	70	68	76	70	284	941.30
Richard Bland	71	72	70	71	284	941.30
Simon Hurley	70	74	69	71	284	941.30
Stephan Wittkop	74	70	67	73	284	941.30

Beazer Homes Challenge Tour Championship

Bowood Golf & Country Club, Wiltshire, England
Par 36-36–72; 7,317 yards

August 5-8
purse, €112,000

	SCORES				TOTAL	MONEY
Carl Suneson	68	68	70	66	272	€18,192.72
Benoit Teilleria	66	73	70	71	280	8,139.04
Bradley Dredge	73	68	70	69	280	8,139.04
Maarten Lafeber	77	63	66	74	280	8,139.04
Carl Watts	68	71	70	72	281	4,262.44
Lee James	71	70	68	72	281	4,262.44
Nils Rorbaek	75	67	70	69	281	4,262.44
Johan Skold	73	69	71	69	282	3,603.60
Fredrik Henge	73	71	68	71	283	3,188.64
Paul Dwyer	70	73	68	72	283	3,188.64
Justin Rose	72	69	70	73	284	2,356.54
Marc Pendaries	72	69	67	76	284	2,356.54
Matthew McGuire	72	71	70	71	284	2,356.54
Robert Coles	69	73	69	73	284	2,356.54
Rudi Sailer	74	67	72	71	284	2,356.54
Alvaro Salto	71	72	70	72	285	1,501.50
Martin Erlandsson	72	70	72	71	285	1,501.50
Paul Curry	73	70	73	69	285	1,501.50
Victor Casado	70	68	73	74	285	1,501.50
Marco Bernardini	72	69	71	74	286	1,261.26
Peter Lawrie	70	71	72	73	286	1,261.26
Andrew Marshall	73	71	72	71	287	1,127.49
Knud Storegaard	75	68	71	73	287	1,127.49

	SCORES				TOTAL	MONEY
Michael Welch	74	65	73	75	287	1,127.49
Simon Hurd	70	70	74	73	287	1,127.49
Carlos Rodiles	74	70	68	76	288	943.80
Frederic Cupillard	70	74	70	74	288	943.80
Grant Dodd	70	73	71	74	288	943.80
Gustavo Rojas	71	67	76	74	288	943.80
Markus Brier	70	74	72	72	288	943.80
Michael Watson	75	69	72	72	288	943.80
Simon Hurley	71	71	74	72	288	943.80

West of Ireland Golf Classic

See PGA European Tour section.

BMW Russian Open

Moscow Golf & Country Club, Moscow, Russia
Par 36-36–72; 7,006 yards

August 19-22
purse, €126,000

	SCORES				TOTAL	MONEY
Iain Pyman	64	70	68	71	273	€20,466.81
Hennie Otto	68	68	69	69	274	13,636.35
Benoit Teilleria	69	72	70	65	276	6,916.46
Greig Hutcheon	63	68	73	72	276	6,916.46
Carl Suneson	70	68	70	69	277	4,609.95
Johan Skold	67	72	68	70	277	4,609.95
Markus Brier	71	69	70	67	277	4,609.95
Niels Kraay	70	71	69	67	277	4,609.95
Brian Nelson	68	71	72	67	278	2,918.57
David Higgins	68	70	69	71	278	2,918.57
Elliot Boult	69	69	72	68	278	2,918.57
Eric Carlberg	68	74	69	67	278	2,918.57
Gary Murphy	71	69	69	69	278	2,918.57
Maarten Lafeber	70	70	68	70	278	2,918.57
Mattias Eliasson	72	66	70	70	278	2,918.57
Adam Mednick	71	71	67	70	279	1,744.47
Scott Watson	69	72	70	68	279	1,744.47
Steven Alker	70	70	68	71	279	1,744.47
Andrew Barnett	72	70	71	67	280	1,425.06
Fredrik Andersson	71	69	66	74	280	1,425.06
Gary Marks	74	68	71	67	280	1,425.06
Peter Hansson	71	70	73	66	280	1,425.06
Bradley Dredge	67	73	70	71	281	1,187.55
Eric Giraud	69	70	70	72	281	1,187.55
Ivo Giner	71	69	71	70	281	1,187.55
Jean Marie Kula	67	72	70	72	281	1,187.55
Niclas Fasth	69	70	71	71	281	1,187.55
Stephen Scahill	69	72	69	71	281	1,187.55
Carl Watts	70	72	69	71	282	997.55
Justin Rose	73	69	69	71	282	997.55
Kevin Carissimi	70	71	69	72	282	997.55
Marc Cayeux	69	68	74	71	282	997.55
Morten Backhausen	71	69	72	70	282	997.55

Norwegian Open

Sorknes Golf Club, Sorknes, Norway
Par 36-36–72; 6,676 yards

August 19-22
purse, €63,000

	SCORES				TOTAL	MONEY
Pehr Magnebrant	68	77	69	67	281	€10,233.41
Patrik Gottfridson	71	73	69	71	284	6,818.18
Mika Lehtinen	70	74	70	71	285	3,845.21
Jean Hugo	69	70	74	73	286	3,071.25
Fredrik Örest	73	74	67	73	287	2,604.42
Bjorn Pettersson	70	72	71	75	288	2,040.54
Darren Parker	69	75	71	73	288	2,040.54
Fredrik Widmark	75	71	70	72	288	2,040.54
Henrik Stenson	76	73	71	68	288	2,040.54
Lars Tingvall	72	75	69	72	288	2,040.54
Jesper Kjaerbye	75	74	69	71	289	1,451.68
Peter Gustavsson	73	73	72	71	289	1,451.68
Sam Little	71	70	71	77	289	1,451.68
Andreas Lindberg	73	76	69	72	290	1,074.94
Graham Maly	73	70	75	72	290	1,074.94
Ulrik Marcher	70	75	72	73	290	1,074.94
Richard Gillot	70	70	76	75	291	859.95
Fredrik Eskelid	72	73	75	72	292	730.96
John Lawson	73	77	71	71	292	730.96
Martin Wikstrom	72	74	73	73	292	730.96
Oyvind Rojahn	72	71	72	77	292	730.96
Ulrik Gustafsson	72	73	74	73	292	730.96
David Tapping	74	76	73	70	293	622.44
Joakim Rask	69	70	75	79	293	622.44
Paul Nilbrink	74	75	75	69	293	622.44
Fredrik Forsvall	80	70	71	73	294	583.54
Derek Crawford	74	74	71	76	295	546.68
Pauli Hughes	71	71	78	75	295	546.68
Per Larsson	74	73	72	76	295	546.68

Formby Hall Challenge

Formby Hall Golf Club, England
Par 36-36–72; 6,878 yards

August 31-September 3
purse, €70,000

	SCORES				TOTAL	MONEY
Greig Hutcheon	66	70	65	67	268	€11,370.45
Alastair Forsyth	66	68	68	66	268	7,575.75
(Hutcheon defeated Forsyth on second extra hole of playoff held September 21.)						
Paul Curry	65	68	68	70	271	3,842.48
Iain Pyman	72	67	65	67	271	3,842.48
Simon Hurley	69	70	73	71	273	2,893.80
Marc Pendaries	67	67	71	69	274	2,654.93
Dominique Nouailhac	67	72	66	70	275	2,443.35
Elliot Boult	67	70	69	70	276	2,079.35
Pascal Edmond	73	67	69	67	276	2,079.35
Frederic Cupillard	68	71	68	69	276	2,079.35
Gary Murphy	71	70	66	70	277	1,542.45
Ian Harrison	69	70	69	69	277	1,542.45
Didier de Vooght	71	66	68	72	277	1,542.45
Gary Clark	72	66	69	70	277	1,542.45
Simon Khan	67	71	71	69	278	1,025.46

	SCORES			TOTAL	MONEY
Robert Coles	65	69	70	74	278	1,025.46
Lee James	71	69	69	69	278	1,025.46
Benoit Teilleria	66	69	72	71	278	1,025.46
Andrew Clapp	73	68	69	69	279	776.69
Carl Suneson	68	72	67	72	279	776.69
Bradley Dredge	68	69	70	72	279	776.69
Charles Challen	72	67	68	72	279	776.69
Matthew Ellis	69	67	74	69	279	776.69
Robert McGuirk	71	69	71	69	280	679.09
Craig Hislop	67	69	70	74	280	679.09
Nigel Preston	72	69	68	72	281	607.43
Paul Streeter	70	70	74	67	281	607.43
Eddy Rawlings	70	71	72	68	281	607.43
Birgir Hafthorsson	70	69	72	70	281	607.43
Simon Wakefield	67	69	74	71	281	607.43

Ohrlings Swedish Match Play

Kristianstads Golf Club, Sweden   September 2-5
Par 36-36–72; 6,613 yards   purse,€63,560

SEMI-FINALS

Kalle Brink defeated Andrew Butterfield, 2 and 1.
Henrik Stenson defeated Mikael Piltz, 3 and 1.

(Butterfield and Piltz both received €3,488.97.)

FINAL

Brink defeated Stenson, 1 up, 19th hole.

(Brink received €10,324.37; Stenson received €6,878.78.)

Daewoo Warsaw Golf Open

Warsaw Golf International, Warsaw, Poland   September 8-11
Par 36-35–71; 6,601 yards   purse, €102,564

	SCORES			TOTAL	MONEY
Niclas Fasth	73	73	67	67	280	€16,659.98
Hennie Otto	65	74	70	72	281	11,099.99
Knud Storegaard	72	70	71	69	282	5,166.66
Carl Suneson	72	67	70	73	282	5,166.66
Adam Mednick	75	70	72	65	282	5,166.66
Jose Manuel Lara	73	72	68	70	283	3,735
Richard Bland	68	71	70	74	283	3,735
Didier De Vooght	70	70	70	74	284	2,816
Fredrik Larsson	71	72	71	70	284	2,816
Fredrik Andersson	71	71	73	69	284	2,816
Iain Pyman	66	72	73	73	284	2,816
Benoit Teilleria	71	68	71	74	284	2,816
Eric Carlberg	71	73	71	70	285	1,760
Per Nyman	70	73	72	70	285	1,760
Greig Hutcheon	66	77	74	68	285	1,760
Philip Golding	74	68	74	69	285	1,760

	SCORES			TOTAL	MONEY
Robert Coles	70 71 68	76		285	1,760
Johan Selberg	73 70 71	72		286	1,310
Patrik Gottfridson	72 73 70	72		287	1,044
Steven Alker	73 72 74	68		287	1,044
Paul Nilbrink	74 70 71	72		287	1,044
Justin Rose	72 74 73	68		287	1,044
Peter Hedblom	74 71 71	71		287	1,044
Pehr Magnebrant	68 71 74	74		287	1,044
Stephen Scahill	70 75 69	73		287	1,044
Markus Brier	72 71 74	70		287	1,044
Federico Bisazza	72 73 72	70		287	1,044
Ola Eliasson	72 74 66	75		287	1,044
Uli Weinhandl	74 68 74	72		288	812
Richard Johnson	69 75 72	72		288	812
Mark Litton	73 70 72	73		288	812
David Lynn	71 74 68	75		288	812
David Higgins	74 72 72	70		288	812

Gula Sidorna Grand Prix

Ljunghusens Golf Club, Sweden
Par 35-36–71; 6,616 yards
(Third round cancelled — wind.)

September 30-October 3
purse, €120,564

	SCORES		TOTAL	MONEY
Raimo Sjoberg	69 72 67		208	€19,579.10
Klas Eriksson	67 72 71		210	13,044.91
Patrik Gottfridsson	70 72 69		211	7,356.86
Nils Rorbaek	73 70 69		212	4,339.90
Morten Hagen	71 72 69		212	4,339.90
Simon Hurley	73 70 69		212	4,339.90
Andrew Butterfield	67 72 73		212	4,339.90
Mikael Piltz	73 71 68		212	4,339.90
Marcus Brier	69 75 68		212	4,339.90
Matthew Blackey	72 72 68		212	4,339.90
Christophe Pottier	70 69 74		213	3,032.06
Mark Litton	67 76 71		214	2,530.64
Adam Mednick	72 72 70		214	2,530.64
Benoit Teilleria	72 73 69		214	2,530.64
John Wade	73 69 73		215	1,605.02
Eric Carlberg	69 76 70		215	1,605.02
Mattias Eliasson	66 71 78		215	1,605.02
Martin Erlandsson	72 71 72		215	1,605.02
Henrik Stenson	72 70 73		215	1,605.02
Lars Tingvall	70 72 73		215	1,605.02
Fredrik Widmark	71 73 71		215	1,605.02
Jens Nilsson	72 70 74		216	1,156.75
Jesper Kjaerbye	71 72 73		216	1,156.75
Ulrik Gustafsson	70 74 72		216	1,156.75
Pehr Magnebrant	68 71 77		216	1,156.75
Gustavo Rojas	70 72 74		216	1,156.75
David Lynn	74 71 74		216	1,156.75
Lucas Parsons	67 77 72		216	1,156.75
Jose Manuel Carriles	72 73 72		217	930.10
Johan Annerfelt	69 75 73		217	930.10
Jimmy Kawalec	72 68 77		217	930.10
Nicolas Vanhootegem	72 72 73		217	930.10
Joakim Rask	73 72 72		217	930.10

	SCORES	TOTAL	MONEY
Max Anglert	74 70 73	217	930.10
David Higgins	70 73 74	217	930.10

San Paolo Vita Open

Margara Golf Club, Margara, Italy
Par 36-36–72; 6,768 yards

October 6-9
purse, €70,755

	SCORES				TOTAL	MONEY
Alberto Binaghi	69	71	69	69	278	€11,493.09
Mattias Eliasson	71	71	69	68	279	7,657.46
*Roberto Paolillo	73	70	67	69	279	
Niki Zitny	72	70	71	67	280	3,883.92
Elliot Boult	68	72	74	66	280	3,883.92
Erol Simsek	74	71	71	65	281	2,925.01
Henrik Stenson	70	70	72	70	282	2,576.63
Philip Golding	73	72	66	71	282	2,576.63
Federico Bisazza	71	73	68	71	283	2,276.54
Gary Murphy	71	71	68	74	284	1,936.21
Marc Pendaries	70	72	70	72	284	1,936.21
Mario Tadini	73	71	66	74	284	1,936.21
John Wade	71	74	71	69	285	1,228.94
Eric Carlberg	72	74	67	72	285	1,228.94
Pauli Hughes	68	72	71	74	285	1,228.94
Stefano Soffietti	73	71	72	69	285	1,228.94
Gianluca Baruffaldi	72	67	75	71	285	1,228.94
Raimo Sjoberg	73	72	70	70	285	1,228.94
Markus Brier	74	72	69	70	285	1,228.94
Fredrik Orest	71	71	73	71	286	785.06
Peter Malmgren	68	73	73	72	286	785.06
Fredrik Henge	73	69	72	72	286	785.06
Eric Giraud	69	76	71	70	286	785.06
Francesco Guermani	70	71	70	75	286	785.06
Peter Lawrie	70	73	71	73	287	655.37
Andrea Canessa	74	71	72	70	287	655.37
Andrew Clapp	74	69	71	73	287	655.37
Niclas Fasth	75	70	71	71	287	655.37
Bjorn Pettersson	77	69	67	74	287	655.37
Niclas Johnsson	73	69	73	73	288	545.98
Alessandro Tadini	74	70	71	73	288	545.98
Mikko Rantanen	69	71	73	75	288	545.98
Simon Hurley	74	72	72	70	288	545.98
Michele Reale	70	75	71	72	288	545.98
Christophe Pottier	76	66	76	70	288	545.98
Stephen Scahill	72	69	71	76	288	545.98

Philips Challenge Xacobeo 99

Club de Golf La Coruna, Galicia, Spain
Par 36-36–72; 6,664 yards

October 7-10
purse, €80,000

	SCORES				TOTAL	MONEY
Hennie Otto	74	69	66	69	278	€12,994
Pello Iguaran	70	75	66	67	278	8,658

(Otto defeated Iguaran on first extra hole.)

	SCORES			TOTAL	MONEY
Knud Storgaard	70	71	67	71	279	4,882.80
Francisco Cea	76	71	67	66	280	3,900
Martin Erlandsson	68	70	71	72	281	2,815.80
Greig Hutcheon	71	70	68	72	281	2,815.80
Ulrik Gustafsson	74	70	66	71	281	2,815.80
Jean Marie Kula	70	70	73	68	281	2,815.80
Ola Eliasson	65	71	72	73	281	2,815.80
Carlos Rodiles	70	73	73	66	282	2,184
Benoit Teilleria	66	72	74	71	283	2,012.40
David Higgins	76	71	68	69	284	1,840.80
Jose Manuel Lara	70	71	68	77	286	1,677
Daniel Westermark	72	74	71	70	287	1,196
Johan Annerfelt	71	69	73	74	287	1,196
Joaquin Millan	72	68	75	72	287	1,196
Jesus Maria Arruti	74	70	68	75	287	1,196
Murray Urquhart	74	73	70	70	287	1,196
Claes Hovstadius	72	70	71	74	287	1,196
Jesper Kjaerbye	69	78	74	67	288	823.46
Fernando Roca	74	72	70	72	288	823.46
Didier De Vooght	70	74	71	73	288	823.46
Johan Skold	74	72	71	71	288	823.46
Fredrik Andersson	76	70	70	72	288	823.46
Matthew Blackey	72	71	76	69	288	823.46
Charles Challen	72	72	72	72	288	823.46
Justin Rose	73	72	73	71	289	663
Nils Rorbaek	74	73	69	73	289	663
Sebastian Miguel	73	72	71	73	289	663
Richard Gillot	70	72	74	73	289	663
Tony Edlund	73	72	74	70	289	663
Angel Matallana	74	71	74	70	289	663

Challenge de France Bayer

Golf Disneyland, Paris, France
Par 36-36–72; 6,541 yards

October 14-17
purse, €114,336

	SCORES			TOTAL	MONEY
Iain Pyman	76	67	65	67	275	€18,517.59
Gustavo Rojas	71	67	66	71	275	12,337.65
(Pyman defeated Rojas on sixth extra hole.)					
Marten Olander	68	70	68	72	278	5,106.23
Sebastien Branger	69	68	68	73	278	5,106.23
Didier De Vooght	70	67	71	70	278	5,106.23
Simon Hurd	70	66	69	73	278	5,106.23
Markus Brier	67	71	69	71	278	5,106.23
Philip Golding	71	70	68	70	279	3,667.95
Mikael Piltz	67	71	74	68	280	3,378.96
Eric Carlberg	68	74	71	68	281	2,989.94
Henrik Stenson	73	68	70	70	281	2,989.94
Gianluca Baruffaldi	74	70	65	73	282	2,506.44
Nicolas Vanhootegem	67	75	70	70	282	2,506.44
Greig Hutcheon	72	72	71	68	283	2,056.28
Matthew Blackey	71	72	72	68	283	2,056.28
Marc Pendaries	71	73	68	72	284	1,484.97
Francesco Guermani	72	71	69	72	284	1,484.97
Tony Edlund	75	68	72	69	284	1,484.97
Bradley Dredge	68	72	70	74	284	1,484.97

	SCORES				TOTAL	MONEY
Mikael Lundberg	72	67	72	73	284	1,484.97
Peter Lawrie	73	68	71	73	285	1,150.41
Lionel Alexandre	69	72	72	72	285	1,150.41
Ian Poulter	66	69	70	80	285	1,150.41
Pehr Magnebrant	71	70	72	72	285	1,150.41
Johan Skold	70	71	70	74	285	1,150.41
Ola Eliasson	72	68	75	70	285	1,150.41
Martin Erlandsson	69	72	72	73	286	958.12
Euan Little	71	70	70	75	286	958.12
Fredrik Henge	73	69	71	73	286	958.12
Simon Hurley	71	73	71	71	286	958.12
Jean-Damien Yvet	70	71	70	75	286	958.12

First Cuba Grand Final

Varadero Golf Club, Cuba
Par 36-36–72; 6,856 yards

October 28-31
purse, €105,000

	SCORES				TOTAL	MONEY
Stephen Scahill	67	69	71	70	277	€18,081
Jose Manuel Lara	67	71	69	72	279	9,456
Henrik Stenson	70	70	69	70	279	9,456
Patrik Gottfridson	76	67	68	69	280	5,066
Per Nyman	70	71	72	67	280	5,066
Knud Storgaard	71	74	68	68	281	4,113.50
Markus Brier	67	70	71	73	281	4,113.50
Johan Skold	70	74	72	66	282	3,643
Pehr Magnebrant	69	75	66	73	283	2,871.60
Gustavo Rojas	67	71	74	71	283	2,871.60
Niclas Fasth	69	72	70	72	283	2,871.60
Matthew Blackey	69	71	71	72	283	2,871.60
David Higgins	70	70	70	73	283	2,871.60
Kalle Brink	70	70	70	74	284	2,185
Andrew Butterfield	71	72	72	70	285	1,968
Adam Mednick	71	69	72	74	286	1,673.29
Benoit Teilleria	71	74	70	71	286	1,673.29
Marc Pendaries	71	73	72	71	287	1,457.59
Elliot Boult	74	74	71	68	287	1,457.59
Ian Poulter	75	69	70	74	288	1,328.06
Didier De Vooght	74	72	71	71	288	1,328.06
Eric Carlberg	71	73	74	71	289	1,195.77
Greig Hutcheon	75	70	74	70	289	1,195.77
Nils Rorbaek	73	73	72	71	289	1,195.77
Simon Hurd	74	76	71	68	289	1,195.77
Klas Eriksson	71	73	76	70	290	1,106.72
Bradley Dredge	72	74	72	73	291	1,058.11
Erol Simsek	73	73	73	72	291	1,058.11
Ola Eliasson	72	77	73	71	293	1,009.49
Mattias Eliasson	76	72	72	74	294	944.73
Maarten Lafeber	70	80	75	69	294	944.73
Martin Erlandsson	72	79	70	73	294	944.73
Simon Hurley	75	76	69	74	294	944.73

Asia/Japan Tours

Asian PGA Davidoff Tour

London Myanmar Open

Yangon City Golf Resort, Myanmar
Par 36-36–72; 6,638 yards

January 28-31
purse, US$200,000

	SCORES				TOTAL	MONEY
Wang Ter-chang	69	69	65	68	271	US$32,300
Frankie Minoza	68	67	69	70	274	17,330
Koichi Nogami	66	71	66	71	274	17,330
Scott Rowe	70	68	69	68	275	10,000
Carlos Espinosa	72	67	69	68	276	7,500
Thongchai Jaidee	71	66	70	69	276	7,500
Derek Fung	65	69	70	73	277	5,153.33
Boonchu Ruangkit	70	70	68	69	277	5,153.33
Jim Rutledge	67	71	70	69	277	5,153.33
Kyi Hla Han	73	71	68	66	278	3,835
Periasamy Gunasegaran	66	69	69	74	278	3,835
Gerry Norquist	71	69	71	68	279	3,236.66
Lin Wen-tang	73	68	69	69	279	3,236.66
Kotaro Asahara	73	69	69	68	279	3,236.66
Mike Cunning	70	71	72	67	280	2,760
Jee Tae-hwa	74	68	69	69	280	2,760
Danny Zarate	69	69	70	72	280	2,760
Gilberto Morales	67	70	72	71	280	2,760
Cho Chul-sang	71	68	74	68	281	2,344
Hwang Sung-ha	70	69	72	70	281	2,344
Chung Joon	67	71	74	69	281	2,344
Charlie Wi	68	71	75	67	281	2,344
Peter Lawrie	67	72	70	72	281	2,344
Brad Andrews	71	74	69	68	282	2,010
Aaron Meeks	72	69	69	72	282	2,010
Jyoti Randhawa	67	75	70	70	282	2,010
Dominique Boulet	71	74	67	70	282	2,010
Eric Rustand	74	69	66	73	282	2,010
Udorn Duangdecha	73	70	68	71	282	2,010
Lin Chih-chen	69	71	69	74	283	1,648.57
Zaw Moe	70	65	77	71	283	1,648.57
Ramon Brobio	71	71	66	75	283	1,648.57
Tsai Chi-huang	71	72	70	70	283	1,648.57
Ross Bain	72	73	64	74	283	1,648.57
Win Naing Tun	73	70	67	73	283	1,648.57
Yasushi Taki	71	72	69	71	283	1,648.57

Benson and Hedges Malaysian Open

Saujana Golf & Country Club, Kuala Lumpur, Malaysia
Par 36-36–72; 6,947 yards

February 4-7
purse, US$750,000

	SCORES				TOTAL	MONEY
Gerry Norquist	67	67	75	71	280	US$121,125
Alex Cejka	70	73	69	71	283	64,987.50

	SCORES				TOTAL	MONEY
Bob May	72	69	70	72	283	64,987.50
Chang Tse-peng	77	64	73	70	284	27,000
Chawalit Plaphol	76	71	69	68	284	27,000
Shaun Micheel	69	71	70	74	284	27,000
Andrew Coltart	70	71	73	70	284	27,000
Padraig Harrington	70	73	70	71	284	27,000
Prayad Marksaeng	72	72	72	69	285	15,862.50
Edward Fryatt	70	69	71	75	285	15,862.50
Andrew Bonhomme	70	74	70	72	286	10,987.50
Wang Ter-chang	69	72	71	74	286	10,987.50
Kim Jong-duk	73	71	71	71	286	10,987.50
Frankie Minoza	67	74	73	72	286	10,987.50
Christian Chernock	70	71	70	75	286	10,987.50
Scott Rowe	74	70	72	70	286	10,987.50
Christopher Hanell	75	67	72	72	286	10,987.50
Nick O'Hern	74	71	70	71	286	10,987.50
Craig Hainline	70	71	72	73	286	10,987.50
Choi Kyung-ju	68	71	73	74	286	10,987.50
Jim Rutledge	70	74	74	69	287	8,212.50
Gary Evans	75	67	72	73	287	8,212.50
Thomas Levet	72	73	70	72	287	8,212.50
Paul McGinley	74	71	68	74	287	8,212.50
Jarmo Sandelin	74	71	68	74	287	8,212.50
Anders Hansen	70	71	73	73	287	8,212.50
Simon Yates	77	69	68	74	288	6,862.50
Dean Wilson	71	68	75	74	288	6,862.50
Robert Karlsson	74	70	74	70	288	6,862.50
David Howell	70	75	74	69	288	6,862.50
John Bickerton	73	72	73	70	288	6,862.50
Geoff Ogilvy	74	73	68	73	288	6,862.50
Zhang Lian-wei	66	75	75	73	289	5,475
Katsuyoshi Tomori	72	73	71	73	289	5,475
Daniel Chopra	71	74	71	73	289	5,475
Chris Williams	73	71	74	71	289	5,475
Eric Meeks	71	73	73	72	289	5,475
Gilberto Morales	71	72	74	72	289	5,475
Pierre Fulke	73	69	72	75	289	5,475
Andrew McLardy	78	67	73	71	289	5,475
Per Haugsrud	74	70	74	71	289	5,475
John Mellor	72	73	72	72	289	5,475
Brad Andrews	73	74	73	70	290	4,425
Ali Kadir	75	71	70	74	290	4,425
Angel Cabrera	76	70	71	73	290	4,425
Greg Owen	71	72	70	77	290	4,425
Christian Pena	66	75	74	76	291	3,900
Jyoti Randhawa	71	72	70	78	291	3,900
Jose Coceres	75	69	76	71	291	3,900
Lin Keng-chi	72	72	70	78	292	3,525
Rolf Muntz	73	74	74	71	292	3,525
Eric Rustand	70	76	73	74	293	3,075
Robert Huxtable	75	70	75	73	293	3,075
Tomas Jesus Munoz	68	71	80	74	293	3,075
Marcello Santi	70	71	74	78	293	3,075
Jerry Smith	71	73	75	75	294	2,625
S. Murthy	76	70	74	74	294	2,625
Choi Gwang-soo	73	72	73	78	296	2,287.50
Kyi Hla Han	72	73	73	78	296	2,287.50
Jonathan Lomas	73	74	77	72	296	2,287.50
Stephen Bennett	71	76	73	76	296	2,287.50
Robin Byrd	75	72	75	75	297	2,100

	SCORES				TOTAL	MONEY
Robert Jan Derksen	74	71	73	80	298	2,025
Charlie Wi	73	71	80	75	299	1,950
Marimuthu Ramayah	73	74	72	82	301	1,875

Wills Indian Open

Royal Calcutta Golf Club, Calcutta, India   March 11-14
Par 36-36–72; 7,165 yards   purse, US$300,000

	SCORES				TOTAL	MONEY
Arjun Atwal	72	68	66	70	276	US$50,010
Kang Wook-soon	69	70	70	71	280	22,200
Prayad Marksaeng	72	74	66	68	280	22,200
S.S.P. Chowrasia	71	72	68	69	280	22,200
Scott Laycock	73	74	63	71	281	11,400
Scott Rowe	71	71	68	71	281	11,400
Thammanoon Sriroj	71	73	67	71	282	8,400
Eric Meeks	71	71	72	70	284	6,780
David Gleeson	71	68	71	75	285	5,520
Andrew Pitts	74	68	71	72	285	5,520
James Kingston	72	69	73	71	285	5,520
Rodrigo Cuello	75	69	69	73	286	4,890
Stephen Lindskog	70	72	71	73	286	4,890
Kyi Hla Han	70	70	73	74	287	4,560
Dean Wilson	74	72	71	70	287	4,560
Mike Tschetter	76	73	67	71	287	4,560
Scott Taylor	69	73	70	76	288	4,140
Thaworn Wiratchant	74	72	71	71	288	4,140
Basad Ali	72	73	71	72	288	4,140
Rick Todd	75	72	71	70	288	4,140
Aaron Meeks	69	74	76	70	289	3,660
Christian Pena	72	76	72	69	289	3,660
Kazuyoshi Yonekura	70	76	70	73	289	3,660
Choi Kyung-ju	70	73	77	69	289	3,660
Jyoti Randhawa	70	75	76	69	290	3,240
Taimur Hussain	74	72	69	75	290	3,240
Cameron Percey	73	71	70	76	290	3,240
Craig Kamps	74	73	69	75	291	2,700
Boonchu Ruangkit	73	71	73	74	291	2,700
Anthony Kang	72	73	71	75	291	2,700
Mark Murless	71	71	73	76	291	2,700
Chawalit Plaphol	73	75	72	71	291	2,700
Justin Hobday	75	72	74	70	291	2,700

Macau Open

Macau Golf & Country Club, Macau   April 15-18
Par 71; 6,557 yards   purse, US$200,000

	SCORES				TOTAL	MONEY
Lee Westwood	66	69	70	70	275	US$32,300
Andrew Pitts	67	71	68	69	275	22,260
(Westwood defeated Pitts on second extra hole.)						
James Kingston	71	70	69	67	277	11,200
Satoshi Oide	70	69	68	70	277	11,200

		SCORES			TOTAL	MONEY
Zhang Lian-wei	68	72	68	71	279	6,500
Boonchu Ruangkit	71	66	70	72	279	6,500
Hsieh Chin-sheng	68	69	69	73	279	6,500
Kang Wook-soon	66	69	71	73	279	6,500
Nico van Rensburg	71	68	70	71	280	4,230
Marimuthu Ramayah	71	68	70	71	280	4,230
Christian Chernock	70	74	69	68	281	3,670
Lai Hung-lin	70	73	72	67	282	3,236.67
Vivek Bhandari	69	69	74	70	282	3,236.67
Chang Tse-peng	69	65	76	72	282	3,236.67
Des Terblanche	70	75	71	68	284	2,880
Tatsuhiko Ichihara	69	71	69	75	284	2,880
Jeev Milkha Singh	73	69	76	67	285	2,428.57
Thongchai Jaidee	71	69	76	69	285	2,428.57
Clay Devers	70	71	73	71	285	2,428.57
Prayad Marksaeng	67	72	73	73	285	2,428.57
Chris Williams	67	72	73	73	285	2,428.57
Yurio Akitomi	70	70	72	73	285	2,428.57
Yeh Wei-tze	73	69	69	74	285	2,428.57
Park Nam-sin	73	71	71	71	286	2,100
Rafael Ponce	71	72	70	73	286	2,100
Choi Kyung-ju	67	72	74	73	286	2,100
Simon Yates	72	71	74	70	287	1,890
Jim Rutledge	72	69	75	71	287	1,890
Dean Wilson	70	73	70	74	287	1,890
Hsieh Yu-shu	70	70	72	75	287	1,890

Maekyung Daks Open

Lakeside Country Club, Seoul, Korea
Par 36-36–72; 7,325 yards

April 29-May 2
purse, US$275,000

		SCORES			TOTAL	MONEY
James Kingston	67	66	74	70	277	US$41,675
Kyi Hla Han	70	70	69	68	277	27,500
(Kingston defeated Han on fourth extra hole.)						
Dean Wilson	68	72	71	69	280	15,500
Kang Wook-soon	72	72	69	68	281	11,500
Lee Boo-young	68	72	69	72	281	11,500
Derek Fung	71	70	70	71	282	8,500
Christian Pena	72	69	74	68	283	7,000
Choi Gwang-soo	69	74	71	70	284	5,300
Lin Chie-hsiang	68	71	74	71	284	5,300
Taimur Hussain	72	70	72	71	285	4,425
Choi Kyung-ju	73	72	69	71	285	4,425
Eric Meeks	69	72	74	71	286	4,075
Scott Rowe	72	68	73	73	286	4,075
Wang Ter-chang	68	70	77	72	287	3,850
Shin Yong-jin	69	73	72	73	287	3,850
Choi Sang-ho	72	73	73	70	288	3,600
Park Nam-sin	74	68	73	73	288	3,600
Chung Joon	71	73	73	71	288	3,600
Arjun Atwal	74	72	73	70	289	3,050
Aaron Meeks	71	72	76	70	289	3,050
Park No-seok	70	77	72	70	289	3,050
Simon Yates	71	73	76	69	289	3,050
Kim Young-il	70	72	74	73	289	3,050

	SCORES				TOTAL	MONEY
Jim Rutledge	69	74	73	73	289	3,050
Andrew Pitts	71	71	75	72	289	3,050
Adrian Percey	75	71	78	65	289	3,050
Kim Wan-tae	74	67	74	75	290	2,450
Lee Hae-woo	70	73	75	72	290	2,450
Christian Chernock	68	72	77	73	290	2,450
Chris Williams	71	71	72	76	290	2,450

Volvo China Open

Shanghai Silport Golf Club, Shanghai, China
Par 36-36–72; 6,724 yards

May 20-23
purse, US$400,000

	SCORES				TOTAL	MONEY
Kyi Hla Han	68	70	67	68	273	US$72,000
Christian Pena	68	72	70	70	280	44,520
Dean Wilson	70	71	68	72	281	24,600
Jyoti Randhawa	70	71	76	65	282	15,666.66
Taimur Hussain	67	74	73	68	282	15,666.66
*Liang Wen-chong	73	70	68	71	282	
Scott Rowe	67	72	70	73	282	15,666.66
Felix Casas	70	70	72	71	283	8,865
Thammanoon Sriroj	67	68	75	73	283	8,865
Des Terblanche	69	67	73	74	283	8,865
Gilberto Morales	69	69	76	69	283	8,865
Simon Yates	68	72	73	71	284	6,633.33
Scott Laycock	71	72	75	66	284	6,633.33
Tatsuhiko Ichihara	71	67	73	73	284	6,633.33
Rodrigo Cuello	70	71	72	72	285	5,600
Greg Hanrahan	72	74	68	71	285	5,600
Lee Boo-young	73	70	71	71	285	5,600
James Kingston	72	71	72	70	285	5,600
Peter Lawrie	71	70	72	72	285	5,600
Hendrik Buhrmann	71	70	73	72	286	4,688
Wang Ter-chang	74	70	72	70	286	4,688
Gaurav Ghei	69	70	71	76	286	4,688
Zhang Lian-wei	70	74	71	71	286	4,688
Kenny Druce	68	74	73	71	286	4,688
Mike Cunning	72	71	77	67	287	4,140
Amandeep Johl	71	68	71	77	287	4,140
Stuart Holmes	70	73	73	71	287	4,140
Lin Wen-tang	74	68	75	70	287	4,140
Craig Kamps	70	71	70	77	288	3,660
Kim Wan-tae	71	67	76	74	288	3,660
Danny Zarate	68	70	76	74	288	3,660
Darren Cole	73	73	70	72	288	3,660

Casino Filipino Philippine Open

Manila Southwoods Golf & Country Club, Manila, Philippines
Par 36-36–72; 7,188 yards

May 27-30
purse, US$200,000

	SCORES				TOTAL	MONEY
Anthony Kang	68	72	67	66	273	US$32,300
James Kingston	67	68	70	69	274	17,330

	SCORES				TOTAL	MONEY
Kazuyoshi Yonekura	69	67	69	69	274	17,330
Prayad Marksaeng	72	65	69	69	275	10,000
Felix Casas	67	65	72	73	277	8,000
Robert Pactolerin	68	70	71	69	278	5,021.66
Lin Chian-bing	71	69	67	71	278	5,021.66
Thongchai Jaidee	71	66	70	71	278	5,021.66
Scott Laycock	71	70	68	69	278	5,021.66
Dean Wilson	70	71	68	69	278	5,021.66
Gilberto Morales	66	69	75	68	278	5,021.66
Mike Cunning	73	66	71	69	279	3,434
Kyi Hla Han	71	69	69	71	280	3,009
Amandeep Johl	70	73	69	68	280	3,009
Christian Pena	70	72	70	68	280	3,009
Eric Meeks	73	67	70	70	280	3,009
Frankie Minoza	69	72	71	69	281	2,700
Mardan Mamat	69	71	71	71	282	2,416
Thammanoon Sriroj	70	72	69	71	282	2,416
Scott Taylor	73	69	69	71	282	2,416
Andrew Pitts	67	70	73	72	282	2,416
Scott Rowe	72	69	68	73	282	2,416
Arjun Atwal	71	68	75	69	283	2,100
Craig Kamps	75	71	67	70	283	2,100
Ross Bain	71	73	68	71	283	2,100
Stuart Holmes	73	71	70	69	283	2,100
Ahmad Bateman	73	72	66	72	283	2,100
Aaron Meeks	72	66	74	72	284	1,830
Jyoti Randhawa	69	70	76	69	284	1,830
Lee Boo-young	71	70	69	74	284	1,830
Adrian Percey	72	66	70	76	284	1,830

Tianjin Teda Open

Tianjin Warner International Golf Club, China August 19-22
Par 35-35–70; 6,510 yards purse, US$200,000

	SCORES				TOTAL	MONEY
Thammanoon Sriroj	65	70	65	67	267	US$32,300
Park No-seok	67	64	69	68	268	22,260
Yeh Wei-tze	68	68	65	68	269	12,400
Taimur Hussain	65	68	68	69	270	10,000
Kazuyoshi Yonekura	66	67	69	69	271	8,000
Chris Williams	66	68	71	67	272	6,500
Simon Yates	67	70	69	66	272	6,500
Rodrigo Cuello	67	66	65	75	273	4,730
Eric Meeks	72	70	65	66	273	4,730
Boonchu Ruangkit	67	62	71	74	274	3,701.33
Des Terblanche	69	69	68	68	274	3,701.33
Felix Casas	65	70	68	71	274	3,701.33
Rafael Ponce	67	65	74	69	275	3,072
Christian Pena	67	66	72	70	275	3,072
Lu Chien-soon	69	69	71	66	275	3,072
Anthony Kang	67	70	68	71	276	2,760
Cameron Percy	66	74	70	66	276	2,760
Scott Laycock	69	68	69	71	277	2,486.67
Kenny Druce	68	73	66	70	277	2,486.67
Greg Hanrahan	67	73	64	73	277	2,486.67
Lu Wen-teh	69	68	70	71	278	2,280

	SCORES				TOTAL	MONEY
Zhang Lian-wei	73	72	65	68	278	2,280
David Gleeson	70	74	65	69	278	2,280
Jyoti Randhawa	68	70	71	70	279	2,100
Amritinder Singh	69	70	70	70	279	2,100
Adrian Percey	70	75	68	66	279	2,100
Scott Rowe	69	72	70	69	280	1,980
Thaworn Wiratchant	70	70	70	71	281	1,830
Soe Kyaw Naing	73	71	66	71	281	1,830
Wayne Bradley	71	72	69	69	281	1,830
Lai Hung-lin	69	72	70	70	281	1,830

Volvo Masters of Malaysia

Kota Permai Golf and Country Club,
Kuala Lumpur, Malaysia
Par 36-36–72; 6,962 yards

August 26-29
purse, US$200,000

	SCORES				TOTAL	MONEY
Nico van Rensburg	69	69	64	68	270	US$32,300
Simon Yates	70	71	63	70	274	22,260
Toshikazu Sugihara	67	70	68	73	278	11,200
Poh Eing Chong	72	71	68	67	278	11,200
Kyi Hla Han	73	70	68	68	279	7,000
Zhang Lian-wei	71	71	70	67	279	7,000
Greg Hanrahan	67	73	71	68	279	7,000
Jim Rutledge	69	71	71	69	280	4,486.67
Gary Rusnak	69	72	70	69	280	4,486.67
Stephen Lindskog	70	73	67	70	280	4,486.67
Peter Lawrie	74	67	67	73	281	3,264
Eric Meeks	73	70	69	69	281	3,264
Cameron Percy	70	71	68	72	281	3,264
Des Terblanche	72	72	70	67	281	3,264
Toshikazu Fukuda	71	73	65	72	281	3,264
Kenny Druce	68	73	73	68	282	2,760
Richard Kaplan	68	74	70	70	282	2,760
Glenn Joyner	69	65	74	75	283	2,416
Cheng Jun	70	70	72	71	283	2,416
Prayad Marksaeng	69	71	72	71	283	2,416
Danny Zarate	68	72	76	67	283	2,416
Will Yanagisawa	68	72	74	69	283	2,416
Scott Rowe	71	69	71	73	284	2,160
Thammanoon Sriroj	72	73	71	68	284	2,160
Darren Cole	71	75	69	69	284	2,160
Thaworn Wiratchant	72	70	71	72	285	2,040
James Kingston	74	68	70	74	286	1,802.86
Chris Williams	70	69	73	74	286	1,802.86
Anthony Kang	75	70	69	72	286	1,802.86
Mardan Mamat	72	70	71	73	286	1,802.86
Gilberto Morales	73	71	71	71	286	1,802.86
Felix Casas	73	72	71	70	286	1,802.86
Wayne Smith	71	73	71	71	286	1,802.86

ERA Taiwan Open

Sunrise Golf & Country Club, Taiwan
Par 36-36–72; 7,057 yards

September 2-5
purse, US$300,000

		SCORES			TOTAL	MONEY
Kang Wook-soon	68	70	67	69	274	US$50,000
Kyi Hla Han	70	69	68	68	275	33,390
Eric Meeks	74	69	68	67	278	18,600
Arjun Singh	73	67	69	70	279	13,500
Thammanoon Sriroj	73	69	69	68	279	13,500
Lu Wen-teh	73	70	69	69	281	9,000
Craig Parry	75	75	68	63	281	9,000
Bobby Lincoln	68	75	69	69	281	9,000
Mike Tschetter	71	72	71	68	282	6,065
Chen Tze-chung	72	75	67	68	282	6,065
Nico van Rensburg	72	78	68	64	282	6,065
Gary Rusnak	71	69	70	74	284	4,987.50
Scott Rowe	70	71	72	71	284	4,987.50
Olle Nordberg	69	71	74	71	285	4,320
Andre Cruse	72	73	70	70	285	4,320
Wayne Smith	77	74	66	68	285	4,320
Christian Pena	69	75	70	71	285	4,320
Chung Chun-hsing	67	71	74	74	286	3,624
Wang Ter-chang	73	73	69	71	286	3,624
Amandeep Johl	64	74	78	70	286	3,624
Jim Rutledge	72	76	70	68	286	3,624
James Kingston	71	76	70	69	286	3,624
Des Terblanche	75	71	69	72	287	3,240
Tsai Chi-huang	70	73	71	73	287	3,240
Hendrik Buhrmann	72	75	70	70	287	3,240
Robert Huxtable	77	69	72	70	288	2,835
Peter Teravainen	73	71	69	75	288	2,835
Lai Hung-lin	74	73	70	71	288	2,835
Hsu Mong-nan	71	75	70	72	288	2,835
Chen Liang-hsi	70	76	73	69	288	2,835
Yeh Wei-tze	72	78	73	65	288	2,835

Kolon Korean Open

Seoul Country Club, Seoul, Korea
Par 36-36–72

September 16-19
purse, US$300,000

		SCORES			TOTAL	MONEY
Choi Kyung-ju	71	71	67	69	278	US$52,931
Kyi Hla Han	68	71	71	69	279	31,758
*Kim Sung-yoon	72	70	71	68	281	
Shin Yong-jin	66	72	71	72	281	17,752
Choi Gwang-soo	68	69	70	75	282	13,843
Shigenobu Hideto	69	74	73	66	282	13,843
Chung Joon	71	71	71	71	284	9,120
Eric Meeks	71	75	69	69	284	9,120
Kim Wan-tae	71	69	75	70	285	7,166
Periasamy Gunasegaran	68	69	74	75	286	6,351
Yang Yong-eun	78	67	71	71	287	4,717
Yoo Jae-chul	71	69	76	71	287	4,717
Nam Young-woo	74	72	71	70	287	4,717
Kang Wook-soon	71	72	70	74	287	4,717

	SCORES				TOTAL	MONEY
Greg Hanrahan	70	73	73	71	287	4,717
Kim Jong-duk	71	73	70	73	287	4,717
Yoo Jong-ky	70	74	73	70	287	4,717
Hwang Sung-ha	76	68	72	72	288	3,603
Kim Tae-hoon	70	70	78	70	288	3,603
Kwon Myung-ho	70	71	72	75	288	3,603
Anthony Kang	73	73	69	73	288	3,603
Park Nam-sin	69	74	73	72	288	3,603
Chung Do-man	75	69	72	73	289	3,216
Richard Lee	74	72	74	69	289	3,216
Choi Yoon-soo	69	73	74	73	289	3,216
Gerry Norquist	70	74	76	69	289	3,216
Choi Sang-ho	73	69	76	72	290	2,972
*Kim Do-hoon	72	72	71	75	290	2,972
Kim Jin-young	70	74	73	73	290	2,972
Kong John-joon	69	69	77	76	291	2,768

Lexus International

Windmill Park Country Club, Bangkok, Thailand   October 14-17
Par 36-36–72; 6,867 yards   purse, US$220,000

	SCORES				TOTAL	MONEY
Jeev Milkha Singh	69	69	65	72	275	US$35,530
Taimur Hussain	68	67	72	68	275	19,063
Zaw Moe	70	67	65	73	275	19,063
(Singh defeated Hussain on first and Moe on third extra hole.)
Wayne Smith	70	72	66	68	276	11,000
Thongchai Jaidee	72	68	68	69	277	8,250
John Kernohan	69	69	72	67	277	8,250
Jyoti Randhawa	72	68	70	68	278	6,050
Soe Kyaw Naing	70	69	68	71	278	6,050
Boonchu Ruangkit	72	67	70	70	279	4,653
Prayad Marksaeng	70	68	68	73	279	4,653
Rodrigo Cuello	70	69	71	70	280	3,784
Hendrik Buhrmann	66	70	70	74	280	3,784
Tatsuhiko Ichihara	70	71	68	71	280	3,784
Wang Ter-chang	74	68	68	71	281	3,300
Chawalit Plaphol	74	69	68	70	281	3,300
Kyi Hla Han	69	68	72	73	282	2,855.60
Mardan Mamat	67	69	70	76	282	2,855.60
Kenny Druce	70	71	73	68	282	2,855.60
Lin Chien-bing	71	71	74	66	282	2,855.60
Clay Devers	70	72	70	70	282	2,855.60
Gerry Norquist	73	69	69	72	283	2,508
Gilberto Morales	75	69	74	65	283	2,508
Aaron Meeks	70	72	67	74	283	2,508
Arjun Singh	73	69	72	70	284	2,310
Lin Chih-chen	71	71	72	70	284	2,310
Udorn Duangdecha	73	71	68	72	284	2,310
Scott Laycock	72	66	72	75	285	1,955.25
Ahmad Bateman	71	68	76	70	285	1,955.25
Thammanoon Sriroj	70	68	72	75	285	1,955.25
Yeh Wei-tze	77	69	69	70	285	1,955.25
Greg Hanrahan	70	69	73	73	285	1,955.25
Will Yanagisawa	71	71	71	72	285	1,955.25
Lu Wen-teh	70	72	70	73	285	1,955.25
Craig Kamps	70	73	70	72	285	1,955.25

Nokia Singapore Open

Orchid Country Club, Singapore
Par 36-36–72; 6,863 yards

October 21-24
purse, US$400,000

		SCORES			TOTAL	MONEY
Kenny Druce	64	68	70	74	276	US$64,600
Desvonde Botes	67	70	68	71	276	44,520
(Druce defeated Botes on second extra hole.)						
Jyoti Randhawa	70	67	73	68	278	20,266.67
Robert Huxtable	66	69	71	72	278	20,266.67
Sammy Daniels	70	69	67	72	278	20,266.67
Ahmad Bateman	71	71	69	68	279	13,000
Stephen Lindskog	67	71	70	71	279	13,000
Ashley Roestoff	68	67	76	69	280	8,973.33
Thongchai Jaidee	70	70	67	73	280	8,973.33
Mardan Mamat	68	71	70	71	280	8,973.33
Scott Laycock	72	69	71	69	281	7,104
Chris Williams	69	70	72	70	281	7,104
Marcus Cain	75	66	71	70	282	5,656
Boonchu Ruangkit	72	66	71	73	282	5,656
Jarrod Moseley	71	66	72	73	282	5,656
Wayne Smith	73	69	70	70	282	5,656
Danny Zarate	69	69	70	74	282	5,656
*Gerald Rosales	73	71	70	68	282	
Eric Rustand	72	73	68	69	282	5,656
Lucas Parsons	69	73	69	71	283	4,620
Gilberto Morales	74	66	69	74	283	4,620
Prayad Marksaeng	72	68	67	76	283	4,620
Peter Senior	70	70	72	71	283	4,620
Tatsuhiko Ichihara	72	71	73	67	283	4,620
Park Nam-sin	69	69	75	71	284	4,140
Jim Rutledge	70	70	73	71	284	4,140
Rodney Pampling	73	71	71	69	284	4,140
Nico van Rensburg	71	73	71	69	285	3,546.67
Peter Teravainen	74	68	72	71	285	3,546.67
Kang Wook-soon	77	68	69	71	285	3,546.67
Lai Hung-lin	69	69	72	75	285	3,546.67
Clay Devers	70	72	70	73	285	3,546.67
Gaurav Ghei	71	73	71	70	285	3,546.67
Yeh Wei-tze	71	74	70	70	285	3,546.67

Hero Honda Masters

Delhi Golf Club, Delhi, India
Par 36-36–72; 6,888 yards

October 28-31
purse, US$200,000

		SCORES			TOTAL	MONEY
Jyoti Randhawa	69	69	69	70	277	US$32,300
Sammy Daniels	70	69	71	68	278	22,260
Rafael Ponce	69	70	76	68	283	11,200
Christopher Williams	68	70	74	71	283	11,200
Arjun Atwal	70	72	68	74	284	8,000
Jeev Milkha Singh	74	76	69	66	285	6,000
Arjun Singh	71	69	72	73	285	6,000
Mukesh Kumar	69	72	74	70	285	6,000
John Kernohan	72	71	69	74	286	4,230
Scott Taylor	68	72	75	71	286	4,230

	SCORES				TOTAL	MONEY
Hendrik Buhrmann	72	75	69	71	287	3,190
Rodrigo Cuello	70	73	71	73	287	3,190
Greg Hanrahan	74	68	69	76	287	3,190
Gerry Norquist	71	75	71	70	287	3,190
Harmeet Kahlon	72	71	72	72	287	3,190
Shiv Prakash	74	71	72	70	287	3,190
Ali Sher	74	69	70	75	288	2,700
Amritinder Singh	73	76	68	72	289	2,486.66
Basad Ali	72	71	74	72	289	2,486.66
*Ashok Kumar	72	70	68	79	289	
Firoz Ali	68	72	76	73	289	2,486.66
Gaurav Ghei	74	67	74	75	290	2,190
Vijay Kumar	77	73	70	70	290	2,190
Anthony Kang	68	72	72	78	290	2,190
Robert Huxtable	72	74	71	73	290	2,190
S.S.P. Chowrasia	69	77	68	76	290	2,190
Jumman	71	73	74	72	290	2,190
Davender Patel	74	71	73	73	291	1,980
Aaron Meeks	72	71	78	72	293	1,860
Wayne Bradley	73	74	73	73	293	1,860
Pappan	75	71	72	75	293	1,860

Sabah Masters

Sutera Harbour Golf & Country Club,
Kota Kinabalu, Malaysia
Par 36-36–72; 6,889 yards

November 4-7
purse, US$150,000

	SCORES				TOTAL	MONEY
Robert Huxtable	63	65	67	72	267	US$24,225
Thongchai Jaidee	67	69	65	72	273	16,695
Lin Wen-tang	67	68	70	69	274	7,600
Arjun Atwal	63	72	70	69	274	7,600
Greg Hanrahan	64	72	69	69	274	7,600
Taku Yamanaka	69	67	69	70	275	4,875
Simon Yates	64	67	73	71	275	4,875
Mardan Mamat	69	70	67	71	277	3,750
Anthony Kang	73	69	69	67	278	3,032.33
Wayne Bradley	70	69	68	71	278	3,032.33
Adrian Percey	70	70	69	69	278	3,032.33
Soe Kyaw Naing	69	69	71	70	279	2,493.50
Derek Fung	70	71	68	70	279	2,493.50
Yoshiyuki Ohashi	70	70	72	69	281	2,115
Stephen Lindskog	64	70	74	73	281	2,115
Amandeep Johl	66	71	72	72	281	2,115
Scott Taylor	67	71	71	72	281	2,115
Aaron Meeks	73	73	67	68	281	2,115
Danny Zarate	68	71	71	72	282	1,860
Su Chin-jung	73	71	70	69	283	1,710
Rafael Ponce	73	71	66	73	283	1,710
Thaworn Wiratchant	68	73	71	71	283	1,710
Lee Kwang-ju	69	74	70	70	283	1,710
Ross Bain	67	74	70	72	283	1,710
R. Nachimuthu	72	71	69	72	284	1,530
Marciano Pucay	70	71	69	74	284	1,530
Yoshito Nishimoto	69	74	72	69	284	1,530
Cameron Percy	69	69	73	74	285	1,395

	SCORES	TOTAL	MONEY
Tatsuya Kihara	73 70 70 72	285	1,395
Danny Chia	70 75 71 69	285	1,395

Johnnie Walker Classic

Westin Resort, Ta Shee, Taiwan
Par 36-36–72; 7,150 yards

November 11-14
purse, US$1,280,000

	SCORES	TOTAL	MONEY
Michael Campbell	66 71 69 70	276	US$215,328
Geoff Ogilvy	70 71 68 68	277	142,208
Ernie Els	70 67 73 68	278	80,112
Vijay Singh	71 72 68 68	279	64,000
Peter Senior	67 72 74 67	280	54,208
Tiger Woods	68 72 70 71	281	44,800
Frank Nobilo	72 71 70 69	282	35,200
Phil Price	68 72 75 67	282	35,200
Richard Backwell	72 70 73 68	283	25,899
Steen Tinning	69 71 72 71	283	25,899
Angel Cabrera	70 71 69 73	283	25,899
Prayad Marksaeng	71 70 73 70	284	20,736
Peter O'Malley	72 70 70 72	284	20,736
Nick Faldo	72 72 69 71	284	20,736
Roger Wessels	69 73 72 71	285	18,432
Kenny Druce	75 70 70 70	285	18,432
Koichi Nogami	72 68 76 70	286	15,536
Peter Lonard	69 73 70 74	286	15,536
Kyi Hla Han	74 71 69 72	286	15,536
Felix Casas	71 74 70 71	286	15,536
Jeev Milkha Singh	71 74 71 70	286	15,536
Andrew Pitts	69 72 73 72	286	15,536
Chawalit Plaphol	74 72 70 70	286	15,536
Jim Furyk	67 73 78 69	287	13,440
Bradley King	70 71 75 71	287	13,440
Nick O'Hern	67 71 77 72	287	13,440
Simon Yates	72 74 73 69	288	11,904
Jeremy Robinson	66 78 73 71	288	11,904
Robert Allenby	70 72 76 70	288	11,904
Marten Olander	68 70 76 74	288	11,904
Kang Wook-soon	73 72 72 71	288	11,904

Hong Kong Open

Hong Kong Golf Club, Fanling, Hong Kong
Par 35-35–70; 6,648 yards

November 25-28
purse, US$300,000

	SCORES	TOTAL	MONEY
Patrik Sjoland	70 65 62 72	269	US$50,010
Ian Woosnam	66 69 66 69	270	33,000
Gary Rusnak	66 68 69 69	272	18,600
Mark McNulty	70 68 69 66	273	13,800
Felix Casas	71 66 65 71	273	13,800
Ahmad Bateman	72 66 66 70	274	10,200
Peter Baker	67 70 69 69	275	8,400
Scott Rowe	69 71 68 68	276	5,835

	SCORES				TOTAL	MONEY
David Jones	67	71	69	69	276	5,835
Kang Wook-soon	67	68	69	72	276	5,835
Simon Yates	69	68	67	72	276	5,835
Robert Huxtable	70	70	69	68	277	4,980
Mardan Mamat	70	73	67	68	278	4,680
David Frost	72	66	71	69	278	4,680
Olle Nordberg	69	68	67	74	278	4,680
Yeh Wei-tze	72	69	70	68	279	4,140
Lu Wen-teh	71	69	70	69	279	4,140
Richard Kaplan	71	72	67	69	279	4,140
Craig Kamps	69	70	70	70	279	4,140
Pedro Martinez	70	72	67	70	279	4,140
Mike Cunning	65	70	72	72	279	4,140
Andrew Pitts	67	71	72	70	280	3,300
Christian Chernock	73	70	67	70	280	3,300
Hendrik Buhrmann	70	66	73	71	280	3,300
Wang Ter-chang	67	72	70	71	280	3,300
Arden Knoll	73	71	65	71	280	3,300
Chang Tse-peng	72	67	69	72	280	3,300
Chen Yuan-chi	68	71	68	73	280	3,300
Hsieh Yu-shu	67	72	67	74	280	3,300
Gilberto Morales	69	71	73	68	281	2,490
Kazuyoshi Yonekura	66	70	75	70	281	2,490
Jim Rutledge	69	71	71	70	281	2,490
Lu Chien-soon	74	69	68	70	281	2,490
Andrew McLardy	73	71	67	70	281	2,490
Lin Wen-tang	69	73	68	71	281	2,490

Mittweida Thailand Open

Navatanee Golf Course, Bangkok, Thailand
Par 36-36–72; 6,902 yards

December 1-4
purse, US$200,000

	SCORES				TOTAL	MONEY
Fran Quinn	71	66	67	71	275	US$32,300
Simon Yates	71	65	69	71	276	13,165
Scott Rowe	69	70	70	67	276	13,165
Jim Rutledge	67	71	70	68	276	13,165
Christian Pena	69	72	66	69	276	13,165
Yeh Wei-tze	70	66	71	70	277	6,000
Alex Cejka	72	69	68	68	277	6,000
Ahmad Bateman	68	71	68	70	277	6,000
Andrew Pitts	71	67	67	73	278	3,640
Kyi Hla Han	69	69	71	69	278	3,640
Lin Keng-chi	69	69	65	75	278	3,640
Jeev Milkha Singh	69	70	68	71	278	3,640
Robert Huxtable	67	71	68	72	278	3,640
Gaurav Ghei	66	72	69	71	278	3,640
Gerald Rosales	71	68	71	69	279	2,820
Kang Wook-soon	70	69	69	71	279	2,820
Nam Young-woo	70	69	69	71	279	2,820
Nico van Rensburg	71	68	73	68	280	2,416
Stephen Lindskog	72	68	71	69	280	2,416
Mardan Mamat	71	68	69	72	280	2,416
Lin Wen-tang	70	70	69	71	280	2,416
Hajime Tanaka	68	71	72	69	280	2,416
Toshikazu Sugihara	70	69	71	71	281	2,070

	SCORES				TOTAL	MONEY
Thongchai Jaidee	73	69	66	73	281	2,070
Eric Meeks	70	71	70	70	281	2,070
Anthony Kang	66	71	72	72	281	2,070
Mike Cunning	68	72	73	68	281	2,070
Aaron Meeks	67	73	67	74	281	2,070
Felix Casas	71	66	70	75	282	1,720
Uttam Singh Mundy	72	69	71	70	282	1,720
Boonchu Ruangkit	69	70	71	72	282	1,720
Hsieh Yu-shu	71	70	70	71	282	1,720
Lu Wen-teh	70	72	70	70	282	1,720
Bunlue Maneerat	68	72	69	73	282	1,720

Omega PGA Championship

Mission Hills Golf Club, Shenzhen, China
Par 36-36–72; 6,970 yards

December 9-12
purse, US$500,000

	SCORES				TOTAL	MONEY
Fran Quinn	69	67	69	65	270	US$80,750
Simon Yates	68	72	65	68	273	55,650
Eric Meeks	70	65	70	69	274	28,000
Nico van Rensburg	67	68	69	70	274	28,000
Felix Casas	67	66	71	71	275	20,000
Taku Yamanaka	69	73	68	66	276	17,500
Thammanoon Sriroj	70	71	68	69	278	13,750
James Kingston	69	73	66	70	278	13,750
Scott Rowe	73	67	68	71	279	10,575
Anthony Kang	69	67	71	72	279	10,575
Eric Rustand	70	68	74	68	280	8,600
John Kernohan	71	68	71	70	280	8,600
Jim Rutledge	71	71	69	69	280	8,600
Kyi Hla Han	70	69	71	71	281	7,650
Jeev Milkha Singh	74	67	71	70	282	7,050
Thongchai Jaidee	72	68	72	70	282	7,050
Wayne Smith	71	69	71	71	282	7,050
Yeh Wei-tze	72	67	75	69	283	5,958.33
Thaworn Wiratchant	74	70	70	69	283	5,958.33
Zhang Lian-wei	70	70	69	74	283	5,958.33
Kenny Druce	68	71	73	71	283	5,958.33
Kang Wook-soon	70	72	71	70	283	5,958.33
Robert Huxtable	70	72	69	72	283	5,958.33
Jyoti Randhawa	73	67	70	74	284	5,175
Chung Joon	70	70	71	73	284	5,175
Yurio Akitoma	70	70	70	74	284	5,175
Peter Teravainen	71	71	70	72	284	5,175
Danny Zarate	75	67	71	72	285	4,575
Chang Tse-peng	73	69	73	70	285	4,575
Yang Yong-eun	71	71	73	70	285	4,575
Scott Taylor	71	73	70	71	285	4,575

Japan Tour

Token Corporation Cup

Kedoin Golf Club, Kagoshima
Par 36-36–72; 7,100 yards

March 11-14
purse, ¥100,000,000

	SCORES				TOTAL	MONEY
Masashi Ozaki	72	65	69	67	273	¥20,000,000
Toru Taniguchi	67	67	67	73	274	10,000,000
Shinichi Yokota	71	69	66	70	276	4,800,000
Hidemichi Tanaka	74	64	68	70	276	4,800,000
Ryoken Kawagishi	68	70	70	68	276	4,800,000
Takashi Kanemoto	68	73	66	69	276	4,800,000
Hirofumi Miyase	72	65	67	73	277	3,056,666
Shigeki Maruyama	70	68	73	66	277	3,056,666
Tsuneyuni Nakajima	68	66	67	76	277	3,056,666
Taichi Teshima	71	67	69	71	278	2,420,000
Seiki Okuda	69	68	69	72	278	2,420,000
Tadashi Ezure	75	65	69	69	278	2,420,000
Toru Suzuki	70	71	66	72	279	2,020,000
Peter McWhinney	69	68	68	75	280	1,820,000
Daisuke Serizawa	71	68	70	72	281	1,620,000
Tateo Ozaki	72	66	71	72	281	1,620,000
Nobuo Serizawa	72	70	69	70	281	1,620,000
Nozomi Kawahara	72	69	69	72	282	1,084,000
David Ishii	72	69	72	69	282	1,084,000
Yoshinori Kaneko	67	73	69	73	282	1,084,000
Kim Jong-duk	74	67	70	71	282	1,084,000
Hajime Meshiai	69	71	71	71	282	1,084,000
Katsunari Takahashi	71	71	69	71	282	1,084,000
Toshimitsu Izawa	74	68	69	71	282	1,084,000
Kazuhiko Hosokawa	71	69	70	72	282	1,084,000
Yeh Chang-ting	73	69	68	72	282	1,084,000
Tsukasa Watanabe	68	68	69	77	282	1,084,000
Kaname Yokoo	71	65	72	75	283	656,250
Naotoshi Nakamura	72	70	71	70	283	656,250
Kiyoshi Murota	71	68	73	71	283	656,250
Takeshi Sakiyama	69	71	70	73	283	656,250
Yoshitaka Yamamoto	72	69	72	70	283	656,250
Shingo Katayama	70	73	68	72	283	656,250
Todd Hamilton	71	69	70	73	283	656,250
Mitsuo Harada	74	68	70	71	283	656,250

Daido Drinko Shizuoka Open

Shizuoka Country Club, Hamaoka Course, Shizuoka
Par 36-36–72; 6,897 yards

March 18-21
purse, ¥100,000,000

	SCORES				TOTAL	MONEY
Kim Jong-duk	65	68	72	72	277	¥20,000,000
Shusaku Sugimoto	71	66	77	64	278	10,000,000
David Ishii	67	69	71	72	279	6,800,000

	SCORES				TOTAL	MONEY
Mitsuo Harada	71	70	69	70	280	4,800,000
Seiki Okuda	66	69	75	71	281	3,800,000
Yoshinori Kaneko	70	70	69	72	281	3,800,000
Tsukasa Watanabe	70	74	72	66	282	2,443,000
Nobuhito Sato	71	71	72	68	282	2,443,000
Steve Conran	71	68	75	68	282	2,443,000
Shingo Katayama	72	68	73	69	282	2,443,000
Richard Backwell	66	73	72	71	282	2,443,000
Toshiaki Odate	71	68	72	71	282	2,443,000
Kumihiro Matsunaga	72	71	68	71	282	2,443,000
Hidemichi Tanaka	66	73	71	72	282	2,443,000
Yeh Chang-ting	71	69	69	73	282	2,443,000
Masayuki Kawamura	70	72	72	69	283	1,520,000
Yasunori Ida	68	76	70	69	283	1,520,000
Katsunori Kuwabara	70	72	72	69	283	1,520,000
Lin Keng-chi	71	72	72	69	284	1,260,000
Tetsuji Hiratsuka	71	70	73	70	284	1,260,000
Toru Taniguchi	68	70	73	73	284	1,260,000
Toshimitsu Izawa	70	72	74	69	285	990,000
Hideki Kase	71	69	75	70	285	990,000
Peter McWhinney	70	73	71	71	285	990,000
Zaw Moe	69	75	69	72	285	990,000
Tsuyoshi Yoneyama	68	73	77	68	286	800,000
Akihito Yokoyama	72	70	75	69	286	800,000
Mo Joong-kyung	70	72	74	70	286	800,000
Anthony Gilligan	72	71	70	73	286	800,000
Hiroo Kawai	74	69	76	68	287	598,000
Masahiro Kuramoto	68	75	74	70	287	598,000
Akinori Tani	71	72	74	70	287	598,000
Katsunari Takahashi	71	72	73	71	287	598,000
Masanobu Kimura	72	71	73	71	287	598,000
Peter Teravainen	70	73	72	72	287	598,000
Kiyoshi Murota	72	71	70	74	287	598,000
Kaname Yokoo	68	72	73	74	287	598,000

Georgia KSB Open

Tojigaoka Marine Hills Golf Club, Tamano City, Okayama
Par 36-36–72; 6,947 yards

March 25-28
purse, ¥70,000,000

	SCORES				TOTAL	MONEY
Yoshinori Kaneko	65	67	71	72	275	¥14,000,000
Frankie Minoza	68	70	68	70	276	7,000,000
Masahiro Kuramoto	70	68	71	68	277	4,760,000
Satoshi Higashi	68	72	71	67	278	3,080,000
Eduardo Herrera	72	66	70	70	278	3,080,000
Kazuhiro Takami	68	68	75	69	280	2,415,000
Hideki Kase	67	71	70	72	280	2,415,000
Hidemichi Tanaka	71	69	73	68	281	2,135,000
Shigemasa Higaki	72	66	74	70	282	1,904,000
Masayuki Kawamura	67	73	70	72	282	1,904,000
Toshimitsu Izawa	73	70	71	69	283	1,428,000
Kaname Yokoo	69	71	74	69	283	1,428,000
Mitsuo Harada	72	66	75	70	283	1,428,000
Noboru Fujiike	68	72	72	71	283	1,428,000
Hiroyuki Fujita	71	69	72	71	283	1,428,000
Tsuyoshi Yoneyama	72	71	71	70	284	1,064,000

	SCORES			TOTAL	MONEY
Akinori Tani	69	71	73	71	284	1,064,000
Yeh Chang-ting	69	73	70	72	284	1,064,000
Kim Jong-duk	69	74	73	69	285	798,000
Yasunori Ida	72	70	73	70	285	798,000
Lin Keng-chi	68	72	73	72	285	798,000
Shusaku Sugimoto	69	71	72	73	285	798,000
Kazuhiro Fukunaga	69	71	72	73	285	798,000
Nozomi Kawahara	67	67	73	78	285	798,000
Toru Suzuki	68	72	79	67	286	546,000
Mo Joong-kyung	68	75	75	68	286	546,000
Dinesh Chand	70	71	75	70	286	546,000
Kazuhiko Hosokawa	74	69	72	71	286	546,000
Hsieh Chin-sheng	66	68	78	74	286	546,000
Katsunori Kuwabara	72	69	70	75	286	546,000
Eiji Mizoguchi	71	69	71	75	286	546,000

Descente Classic Munsingwear Cup

Taiheiyou Club, Ichihara Course, Chiba   April 1-4
Par 36-36–72; 6,796 yards   purse, ¥67,500,000
(Second round cancelled — wind.)

	SCORES			TOTAL	MONEY
Masayuki Kawamura	69	69	67	205	¥13,500,000
Tsuyoshi Yoneyama	71	67	67	205	5,670,000
Kazuhiko Hosokawa	71	66	68	205	5,670,000
(Kawamura defeated Yoneyama on first and Hosokawa on second extra hole.)					
Eiji Mizoguchi	70	69	67	206	2,790,000
Satoshi Higashi	70	68	68	206	2,790,000
Yasuharu Imano	71	65	70	206	2,790,000
Frankie Minoza	72	70	65	207	2,227,000
Peter Teravainen	69	74	65	208	1,772,000
Kazuhiro Fukunaga	72	69	67	208	1,772,000
Hidemichi Tanaka	68	72	68	208	1,772,000
Terry Price	68	69	71	208	1,772,000
Yasunori Ida	67	68	73	208	1,772,000
David Ishii	72	69	68	209	1,211,000
Lin Keng-chi	68	73	68	209	1,211,000
Seiki Okuda	70	70	69	209	1,211,000
Hiroshi Ueda	71	67	71	209	1,211,000
Masahiro Kuramoto	75	67	68	210	907,000
Mitsutaka Kusakabe	68	74	68	210	907,000
Takashi Umiyama	70	71	69	210	907,000
Yoshinori Mizumaki	74	67	69	210	907,000
Masanobu Kimura	68	70	72	210	907,000
Shigenori Mori	75	68	68	211	650,000
Kaname Yokoo	71	70	70	211	650,000
Noboru Fujiike	71	70	70	211	650,000
Taisuke Kitajima	71	70	70	211	650,000
Teruo Sugihara	71	67	73	211	650,000
Eduardo Herrera	73	71	68	212	455,000
Shusaku Sugimoto	74	68	70	212	455,000
Hiroyuki Fujita	71	71	70	212	455,000
Yoshitaka Yamamoto	73	69	70	212	455,000
Takao Nogomi	70	72	70	212	455,000
Takashi Kanemoto	71	70	71	212	455,000
Ryoken Kawagishi	73	66	73	212	455,000

	SCORES			TOTAL	MONEY
Kimpachi Yoshimura	67	72	73	212	455,000
Yeh Chang-ting	68	70	74	212	455,000

Tsuruya Open

Sports Shinko Country Club, Yamanohara Course, April 15-18
Kawanishi, Hyogo purse, ¥100,000,000
Par 36-36–72; 6,827 yards

	SCORES				TOTAL	MONEY
Naomichi Ozaki	65	70	66	72	273	¥20,000,000
Toru Suzuki	66	70	72	67	275	10,000,000
Taichi Teshima	67	69	71	69	276	6,800,000
Katsumasa Miyamoto	69	72	66	70	277	4,400,000
David Ishii	68	71	67	71	277	4,400,000
Masanobu Kimura	69	72	70	69	280	3,450,000
Toshiaki Odate	70	68	67	75	280	3,450,000
Kimpachi Yoshimura	70	70	71	70	281	2,830,000
Kaname Yokoo	67	73	69	72	281	2,830,000
Todd Hamilton	71	69	74	67	281	2,830,000
Hideki Kase	74	70	64	74	282	2,320,000
Nobuhito Sato	67	72	73	70	282	2,320,000
Mitsuo Harada	70	72	72	69	283	1,795,000
Mitsutaka Kusakabe	72	71	66	74	283	1,795,000
Hiroyuki Fujita	72	68	68	75	283	1,795,000
Kazuhiko Hosokawa	71	70	70	72	283	1,795,000
Yoshitaka Yamamoto	70	74	69	71	284	1,426,666
Toshimitsu Izawa	68	75	67	74	284	1,426,666
Tetsuya Haraguchi	71	72	71	70	284	1,426,666
Tateo Ozaki	73	73	68	71	285	1,100,000
Masayuki Kawamura	70	71	72	72	285	1,100,000
Hisayuki Sasaki	69	72	72	72	285	1,100,000
Richard Backwell	70	69	75	71	285	1,100,000
Mamoru Osanai	70	73	74	68	285	1,100,000
Terry Price	72	73	70	71	286	880,000
Yasuharu Inamo	72	71	71	72	286	880,000
Katsunari Takahashi	73	71	69	74	287	740,000
Kiyoshi Murota	70	71	73	73	287	740,000
Yasunori Ida	70	70	75	72	287	740,000
Anthony Gilligan	68	75	72	72	287	740,000
Shingo Katayama	71	73	73	70	287	740,000

Kirin Open

Ibaragi Golf Club, West Course, Ina, Ibaraki April 22-25
Par 36-35–71; 6,975 yards purse, ¥75,000,000
(Third round cancelled — rain.)

	SCORES			TOTAL	MONEY
Choi Kyung-ju	65	68	71	204	¥15,000,000
Jeev Milkha Singh	70	67	67	204	7,500,000
(Choi defeated Singh on first extra hole.)					
Naomichi Ozaki	67	71	68	206	3,900,000
Kazuhiro Takami	70	69	67	206	3,900,000
Tsuyoshi Yoneyama	69	68	69	206	3,900,000

	SCORES			TOTAL	MONEY
Tsukasa Watanabe	69	72	67	208	2,493,750
Terry Price	69	70	69	208	2,493,750
Yasuharu Imano	66	71	71	208	2,493,750
Peter Teravainen	70	69	70	209	2,100,000
Masashi Ozaki	69	69	72	210	1,650,000
Tateo Ozaki	72	68	70	210	1,650,000
Toshimitsu Izawa	74	69	67	210	1,650,000
Brandt Jobe	71	71	68	210	1,650,000
Dean Wilson	72	71	67	210	1,650,000
Satoshi Higashi	70	70	71	211	1,050,000
Toru Taniguchi	71	70	70	211	1,050,000
Wang Ter-chang	70	70	71	211	1,050,000
Shingo Katayama	69	70	72	211	1,050,000
Kaname Yokoo	70	71	70	211	1,050,000
Hideki Kase	68	69	75	212	700,000
Kazuhiko Hosokawa	68	74	72	212	700,000
Kenichi Kuboya	71	72	69	212	700,000
David Smail	74	69	69	212	700,000
Zhang Lian-wei	70	67	75	212	700,000
Peter Senior	70	71	71	212	700,000
Ryoken Kawagishi	74	71	68	213	504,075
Kyi Hla Han	71	71	71	213	504,075
Mamoru Osanai	70	73	70	213	504,075
Chen Tze-chung	73	72	68	213	504,075
Jim Rutledge	72	73	68	213	504,075
Mike Tschetter	71	67	75	213	504,075
Ian Leggatt	74	70	69	213	504,075
Chawalit Plaphol	70	69	74	213	504,075

Chunichi Crowns

Nagoya Golf Club, Wago Course, Togo, Aichi
Par 35-35–70; 6,502 yards

April 29-May 2
purse, ¥110,000,000

	SCORES				TOTAL	MONEY
Yasuharu Imano	73	68	65	65	271	¥22,000,000
Naomichi Ozaki	70	66	68	68	272	11,000,000
Tateo Ozaki	69	70	68	68	275	7,430,000
Tsukasa Watanabe	80	66	66	64	276	4,840,000
Mitsuo Harada	71	73	66	66	276	4,840,000
Frankie Minoza	74	71	66	66	277	3,960,000
Keiichiro Fukabori	72	68	70	68	278	3,630,000
Nobuo Serizawa	75	69	68	68	280	2,777,500
Toru Suzuki	75	70	68	67	280	2,777,500
Katsunori Kuwabara	75	67	69	69	280	2,777,500
Taichi Teshima	75	68	70	67	280	2,777,500
Shinichi Yokota	74	71	70	65	280	2,777,500
David Smail	73	73	69	65	280	2,777,500
*Tomohiro Kondo	76	69	65	70	280	
Kiyoshi Murota	75	70	66	70	281	1,342,000
Toru Nakamura	74	70	69	68	281	1,342,000
Eduardo Herrera	72	72	69	68	281	1,342,000
Hirofumi Miyase	78	67	71	65	281	1,342,000
Toshiaki Odate	72	74	67	68	281	1,342,000
Mitsutaka Kusakabe	71	73	71	66	281	1,342,000
Hidemichi Tanaka	75	70	65	71	281	1,342,000
Hiroyuki Fujita	71	73	67	70	281	1,342,000

	SCORES				TOTAL	MONEY
Kazuhiko Hosokawa	72	68	68	73	281	1,342,000
Kenichi Kuboya	70	68	73	70	281	1,342,000
Kaname Yokoo	72	68	71	70	281	1,342,000
Mamoru Osanai	72	73	67	69	281	1,342,000
Tetsuya Haraguchi	74	68	69	70	281	1,342,000
Peter Senior	78	68	68	67	281	1,342,000
Todd Hamilton	74	73	65	69	281	1,342,000
Masashi Ozaki	73	73	67	69	282	770,000
Kiyoshi Maita	74	69	71	68	282	770,000
Toshimitsu Izawa	75	71	66	70	282	770,000

Fuji Sankei Classic

Kawana Hotel Golf Club, Fuji Course, Ito, Shizuoka
Par 35-36–71; 6,694 yards

May 6-9
purse, ¥110,000,000

	SCORES				TOTAL	MONEY
Shigemasa Higaki	67	70	65	71	273	¥22,000,000
Steve Conran	66	71	68	70	275	11,000,000
Brandt Jobe	70	71	68	67	276	7,480,000
Masashi Ozaki	71	72	68	66	277	4,840,000
Tateo Ozaki	70	70	66	71	277	4,840,000
Tsukasa Watanabe	71	69	66	72	278	3,960,000
Richard Backwell	68	70	73	68	279	3,630,000
Kazuhiko Hosokawa	67	72	69	72	280	3,355,000
Katsuyoshi Tomori	70	72	67	72	281	2,882,000
Mitsuo Harada	68	66	75	72	281	2,882,000
Taichi Teshima	68	73	69	71	281	2,882,000
Toshimitsu Izawa	71	65	77	69	282	2,139,500
Shigeki Maruyama	68	71	74	69	282	2,139,500
Yasuharu Imano	71	71	69	71	282	2,139,500
Mo Joong-kyung	70	70	69	73	282	2,139,500
Yoshitaka Yamamoto	70	70	74	69	283	1,622,500
Eiji Mizoguchi	67	72	72	72	283	1,622,500
Nobuhito Sato	71	73	68	71	283	1,622,500
Yeh Chang-ting	69	72	71	71	283	1,622,500
Yoshinori Mizumaki	71	71	72	70	284	1,140,857
Akihito Yokoyama	71	64	76	73	284	1,140,857
Seiki Okuda	71	68	70	75	284	1,140,857
Hisayuki Sasaki	65	71	75	73	284	1,140,857
Hirofumi Miyase	72	71	70	71	284	1,140,857
Lin Keng-chi	69	72	72	71	284	1,140,857
Hiroo Kawai	72	70	73	69	284	1,140,857
Shigenori Mori	70	72	69	74	285	814,000
Eduardo Herrera	72	69	70	74	285	814,000
Keiichiro Fukabori	67	72	70	76	285	814,000
Chen Tze-chung	72	70	70	73	285	814,000
Chen Tze-ming	68	66	71	80	285	814,000

Japan PGA Championship

Golf Club Twinfields, Komatsu, Ishikawa
Par 36-36–72; 7,136 yards

May 13-16
purse, ¥110,000,000

	SCORES				TOTAL	MONEY
Naomichi Ozaki	70	71	73	69	283	¥22,000,000
Masashi Ozaki	76	69	70	70	285	11,000,000
Tateo Ozaki	72	72	66	76	286	7,480,000
Kazuhiko Hosokawa	70	73	71	74	288	5,280,000
Katsunari Takahashi	71	72	71	75	289	3,836,250
Toru Suzuki	74	74	69	72	289	3,836,250
Katsunori Kuwabara	73	71	76	69	289	3,836,250
Todd Hamilton	73	71	74	71	289	3,836,250
Nobuo Serizawa	73	73	71	73	290	2,992,000
Kim Jong-duk	74	69	76	71	290	2,992,000
Masayuki Kawamura	73	70	73	75	291	2,332,000
Shigeki Maruyama	76	69	75	71	291	2,332,000
Shigemasa Higaki	72	73	71	75	291	2,332,000
Brandt Jobe	76	71	74	70	291	2,332,000
Shigenori Mori	71	75	70	76	292	1,782,000
Seiki Okuda	73	74	72	73	292	1,782,000
Ryoken Kawagishi	77	72	71	72	292	1,782,000
Hideki Kase	71	76	71	75	293	1,386,000
Katsuyoshi Tomori	74	73	71	75	293	1,386,000
Toshimitsu Izawa	70	71	74	78	293	1,386,000
Hidemichi Tanaka	69	72	79	73	293	1,386,000
Hiroyuki Fujita	70	74	73	76	293	1,386,000
Yasunori Ida	76	70	72	76	294	975,333
Stewart Ginn	78	69	75	72	294	975,333
Hideki Haraguchi	76	73	78	67	294	975,333
Shingo Katayama	77	69	72	76	294	975,333
Hiroo Kawai	74	74	73	73	294	975,333
Frankie Minoza	74	74	73	73	294	975,333
Taichi Teshima	72	75	72	76	295	792,000
David Ishii	75	75	72	73	295	792,000

Ube Kosan Open

Ube Country Club, Mannenike East Course,
Ajisu, Yamaguchi
Par 36-36–72; 6,940 yards

May 20-23
purse, ¥100,000,000

	SCORES				TOTAL	MONEY
Choi Kyung-ju	69	65	66	72	272	¥20,000,000
Kazuhiko Hosokawa	71	66	67	71	275	10,000,000
Satoshi Higashi	69	67	70	70	276	6,800,000
Toshimitsu Izawa	73	70	68	68	279	4,400,000
Chen Tze-chung	73	68	71	67	279	4,400,000
Kim Jong-duk	69	70	68	73	280	3,600,000
Mitsuo Harada	73	69	66	73	281	3,300,000
Takenori Hiraishi	70	70	71	71	282	2,830,000
Takuya Ogawa	70	69	69	74	282	2,830,000
Brandt Jobe	76	69	64	73	282	2,830,000
Ikuo Shirahama	73	71	69	70	283	2,120,000
Anthony Gilligan	71	70	69	73	283	2,120,000
Hideki Haraguchi	71	73	65	74	283	2,120,000
Peter Teravainen	73	70	70	70	283	2,120,000

	SCORES				TOTAL	MONEY
Hsieh Chin-sheng	72	68	70	74	284	1,670,000
Stewart Ginn	72	72	70	70	284	1,670,000
Yoshinori Mizumaki	72	66	72	75	285	1,344,000
Toshimitsu Fukuzawa	73	71	69	72	285	1,344,000
Taichi Teshima	72	69	71	73	285	1,344,000
Shingo Katayama	69	66	74	76	285	1,344,000
Ryuichi Tayasu	71	70	71	73	285	1,344,000
Tsuyoshi Yoneyama	71	69	70	76	286	1,020,000
Yasunori Ida	70	71	71	74	286	1,020,000
Shigemasa Higaki	71	69	70	76	286	1,020,000
Hideki Kase	74	67	71	75	287	800,000
Yuzo Oyama	70	71	72	74	287	800,000
Osamu Yamaguchi	72	72	71	72	287	800,000
Yuji Igarashi	72	73	71	71	287	800,000
Brad Andrews	73	72	74	68	287	800,000
Jun Kikuchi	74	71	70	72	287	800,000

Mitsubishi Motors Tournament

Lake Green Golf Club, Mitake, Gifu
Par 36-35–71; 7,044 yards

May 27-30
purse, ¥100,000,000

	SCORES				TOTAL	MONEY
Tsuyoshi Yoneyama	69	69	66	64	268	¥20,000,000
Kazuhiko Hosokawa	72	68	64	64	268	10,000,000
(Yoneyama defeated Hosokawa on fifth extra hole.)						
Mitsuo Harada	69	66	70	65	270	6,800,000
Hsieh Chin-sheng	69	66	69	69	273	4,800,000
Masashi Ozaki	66	69	68	71	274	3,800,000
Toshimitsu Izawa	67	68	69	70	274	3,800,000
Hideki Kase	72	65	69	69	275	3,056,666
Satoshi Higashi	66	71	68	70	275	3,056,666
Richard Backwell	71	63	73	68	275	3,056,666
Nobuhito Sato	70	69	67	70	276	2,520,000
David Ishii	65	70	69	72	276	2,520,000
Gohei Sato	71	71	68	67	277	2,120,000
Keiichiro Fukabori	68	67	71	71	277	2,120,000
Tsutomu Higa	72	68	71	67	278	1,573,333
Toru Taniguchi	72	66	69	71	278	1,573,333
Shingo Katayama	68	67	71	72	278	1,573,333
Jun Kikuchi	68	68	71	71	278	1,573,333
David Smail	70	71	67	70	278	1,573,333
Tetsuya Haraguchi	68	70	67	73	278	1,573,333
Stewart Ginn	72	64	70	73	279	1,140,000
Yasuharu Imano	71	71	67	70	279	1,140,000
Go Higaki	69	67	75	68	279	1,140,000
Choi Kyung-ju	70	72	68	69	279	1,140,000
Kazunari Matsunaga	70	68	69	73	280	900,000
Taichi Teshima	70	70	70	70	280	900,000
Yeh Chang-ting	72	70	69	69	280	900,000
Tateo Ozaki	69	71	71	70	281	740,000
Toru Suzuki	68	71	74	68	281	740,000
Yoshimitsu Fukuzawa	69	69	74	69	281	740,000
Yasunobu Kuramoto	67	71	68	75	281	740,000
Shoichi Kuwabara	67	71	72	71	281	740,000

JCB Classic Sendai

Omotezao Kokusai Golf Club, Shibata, Miyagi
Par 36-35–71; 6,659 yards

June 3-6
purse, ¥100,000,000

	SCORES				TOTAL	MONEY
Shingo Katayama	69	63	69	67	268	¥20,000,000
Shigemasa Higaki	68	66	65	69	268	10,000,000
(Katayama defeated Higaki on third extra hole.)						
Hideki Kase	68	70	64	68	270	5,800,000
Taichi Teshima	68	65	65	72	270	5,800,000
Hajime Meshiai	70	66	70	67	273	4,000,000
Tsuyoshi Yoneyama	69	68	69	68	274	3,078,000
Daisuke Serizawa	67	66	71	70	274	3,078,000
Katsunori Kuwabara	68	73	62	71	274	3,078,000
Toru Taniguchi	74	63	68	69	274	3,078,000
David Ishii	68	69	67	70	274	3,078,000
Satoshi Higashi	69	70	69	67	275	2,040,000
Mitsuo Harada	67	65	73	70	275	2,040,000
Stewart Ginn	68	68	72	67	275	2,040,000
Keiichiro Fukabori	71	65	74	65	275	2,040,000
Kazuhiko Hosokawa	67	69	69	70	275	2,040,000
Masashi Ozaki	70	64	69	73	276	1,475,000
Kiyoshi Maita	69	71	66	70	276	1,475,000
Masanobu Kimura	71	67	68	70	276	1,475,000
Osamu Yamaguchi	70	71	65	70	276	1,475,000
Tsuneyuki Nakajima	68	69	69	71	277	1,140,000
Toshimitsu Izawa	69	69	70	69	277	1,140,000
Eiji Mizoguchi	66	72	72	67	277	1,140,000
Kim Jong-duk	67	68	72	70	277	1,140,000
Masayuki Kawamura	66	71	70	71	278	800,000
Tsutomu Higa	68	68	71	71	278	800,000
Yasunobu Kuramoto	69	67	70	72	278	800,000
Yasuharu Imano	70	66	71	71	278	800,000
Kazumasa Sakaitani	64	69	72	73	278	800,000
David Smail	72	68	79	79	278	800,000
Hiroo Kawai	70	69	70	69	278	800,000
Takao Nogami	70	71	64	73	278	800,000

Super Mario Yomiuri Open

Yomiuri Country Club, Nishinomiya, Hyogo
Par 36-36–72; 7,035 yards

June 17-20
purse, ¥90,000,000

	SCORES				TOTAL	MONEY
Kim Jong-duk	69	65	68	68	270	¥18,000,000
Hajime Meshiai	69	67	70	67	273	7,560,000
Hidemichi Tanaka	71	70	70	62	273	7,560,000
Choi Kyung-ju	71	70	66	68	275	4,320,000
Satoshi Higashi	68	70	69	69	276	3,138,750
Stewart Ginn	66	68	73	69	276	3,138,750
Toru Taniguchi	71	65	69	71	276	3,138,750
Shingo Katayama	71	67	72	66	276	3,138,750
Seiki Okuda	67	69	69	72	277	2,538,000
Tsuyoshi Yoneyama	72	69	71	66	278	2,178,000
Toru Suzuki	71	66	70	71	278	2,178,000
Taichi Teshima	72	68	68	70	278	2,178,000
Eduardo Herrera	71	70	68	70	279	1,615,500

		SCORES			TOTAL	MONEY
Keiichiro Fukabori	70	69	70	70	279	1,615,500
Tetsuji Hiratsuka	72	68	67	72	279	1,615,500
Lin Keng-chi	65	72	73	69	279	1,615,500
Yasunori Ida	71	69	70	70	280	1,368,000
Naomichi Ozaki	70	70	69	72	281	1,206,000
Hiroyuki Fujita	69	73	71	68	281	1,206,000
Yeh Chang-ting	73	69	71	68	281	1,206,000
Kiyoshi Murota	71	71	69	71	282	990,000
Akihito Yokoyama	74	68	72	68	282	990,000
Yoshitaka Yamamoto	73	69	69	71	282	990,000
Shoichi Kuwabara	70	71	73	69	283	810,000
Nozomi Kawahara	70	72	70	71	283	810,000
David Ishii	72	69	69	73	283	810,000
Tateo Ozaki	71	67	74	72	284	684,000
Kazuo Kanayama	72	70	71	71	284	684,000
Toshimitsu Izawa	71	67	75	71	284	684,000
Shigemasa Higaki	75	67	70	72	284	684,000

Mizuno Open

Setonaikai Golf Club, Kasaoka, Okayama
Par 36-36–72; 7,118 yards

June 24-27
purse, ¥90,000,000

		SCORES			TOTAL	MONEY
Eduardo Herrera	66	69	69	70	274	¥18,000,000
Tsukasa Watanabe	65	71	69	71	276	9,000,000
Tsuyoshi Yoneyama	70	69	68	70	277	6,120,000
Toru Suzuki	71	69	67	71	278	3,960,000
Kaname Yokoo	69	71	66	72	278	3,960,000
Hirofumi Miyase	73	68	68	70	279	2,873,250
Keiichiro Fukabori	70	66	74	69	279	2,873,250
Hiroyuki Fujita	69	73	69	68	279	2,873,250
Chen Tze-chung	71	66	69	73	279	2,873,250
Seiki Okuda	75	68	69	68	280	2,088,000
Stewart Ginn	73	65	69	73	280	2,088,000
Toru Taniguchi	69	73	66	72	280	2,088,000
Nobuhito Sato	68	71	73	68	280	2,088,000
Naomichi Ozaki	71	69	68	73	281	1,503,000
Hsieh Chin-sheng	71	72	68	70	281	1,503,000
Kazuhiko Hosokawa	77	67	70	67	281	1,503,000
David Ishii	73	69	68	71	281	1,503,000
Toshiaki Odate	69	71	70	72	282	1,134,000
Peter McWhinney	71	68	75	67	282	1,134,000
Kosaku Makisaka	70	70	68	74	282	1,134,000
Takao Nogami	76	66	68	72	282	1,134,000
Choi Kyung-ju	72	66	71	73	282	1,134,000
Hiroo Kawai	70	70	71	72	283	858,000
Brian Watts	71	71	68	73	283	858,000
Kim Jong-duk	72	73	67	71	283	858,000
Saburo Fujiki	68	73	72	71	284	667,285
Takenori Hiraishi	71	71	71	71	284	667,285
Taisuke Kitajima	74	69	69	72	284	667,285
Yeh Chang-ting	74	67	71	72	284	667,285
Nozomi Kawahara	69	70	71	74	284	667,285
David Smail	72	72	70	70	284	667,285
Hiroo Okamo	73	71	72	68	284	667,285

Yonex Open Hiroshima

Hiroshima Country Club, Higashi, Hiroshima
Par 36-36–72; 6,950 yards

July 8-11
purse, ¥90,000,000

		SCORES			TOTAL	MONEY
Masashi Ozaki	73	69	67	64	273	¥18,000,000
Shigemasa Higaki	71	65	67	70	273	9,000,000
(Ozaki defeated Higaki on first extra hole.)						
Taichi Teshima	69	70	64	72	275	6,120,000
Satoru Hirota	69	74	68	66	277	3,960,000
David Ishii	70	68	72	67	277	3,960,000
Kaname Yokoo	73	66	70	69	278	3,240,000
Hisayuki Sasaki	75	70	68	68	281	2,652,750
Mitsuo Harada	74	71	71	65	281	2,652,750
Toshimitsu Izawa	69	69	72	71	281	2,652,750
Zaw Moe	73	72	65	71	281	2,652,750
Katsunori Kuwabara	70	68	73	71	282	2,088,000
Yeh Chang-ting	72	71	69	70	282	2,088,000
Kiyoshi Murota	72	72	67	72	283	1,728,000
Eiji Mizoguchi	70	70	72	71	283	1,728,000
Nobumitsu Yuhara	72	71	70	71	284	1,413,000
Nobuhiro Yoshino	71	72	71	70	284	1,413,000
Toshiaki Odate	74	70	69	71	284	1,413,000
Dinesh Chand	72	68	73	71	284	1,413,000
Tatsuaki Nakamura	71	70	74	70	285	1,062,000
Kazunari Matsunaga	67	72	74	72	285	1,062,000
Satoshi Oide	72	72	71	70	285	1,062,000
Yasunobu Kuramoto	73	69	70	73	285	1,062,000
Taisuke Kitajima	67	74	72	72	285	1,062,000
Yoshinori Kaneko	73	72	72	69	286	756,000
Kazuhiro Takami	71	70	73	72	286	756,000
Hajime Meshiai	73	71	71	71	286	756,000
Hidezumi Shirakata	72	71	75	68	286	756,000
Nobuhito Sato	70	73	75	68	286	756,000
Chen Tze-chung	71	72	67	76	286	756,000
Gohei Sato	70	74	72	71	287	582,750
Tsukasa Watanabe	70	72	75	70	287	582,750
Osamu Yamaguchi	73	71	69	74	287	582,750
Jun Kikuchi	70	70	72	75	287	582,750

Aiful Cup

Ajigasawa Kogen Golf Club, Aomori, Kyodo
Par 37-35–72; 7,103 yards

July 22-25
purse, ¥90,000,000

		SCORES			TOTAL	MONEY
Toshimitsu Izawa	67	72	68	67	274	¥18,000,000
Toru Taniguchi	68	67	71	69	275	9,000,000
Hidemichi Tanaka	69	71	67	70	277	5,220,000
Katsunori Kuwabara	69	71	66	71	277	5,220,000
Gohei Sato	73	67	67	72	279	3,420,000
Todd Hamilton	69	66	71	73	279	3,420,000
Ikuo Shirahama	67	69	71	73	280	2,857,500
Dinesh Chand	72	69	69	70	280	2,857,500
Shoichi Kuwabara	69	68	71	73	281	2,538,000
Tsukasa Watanabe	69	69	73	71	282	1,998,000
Seiki Okuda	71	71	73	67	282	1,998,000

		SCORES			TOTAL	MONEY
Hisayuki Sasaki	71	69	70	72	282	1,998,000
Takeshi Sakiyama	69	72	71	70	282	1,998,000
Zaw Moe	69	71	71	71	282	1,998,000
*Hidemasa Hoshino	70	69	70	73	282	
Katsunari Takahashi	72	68	74	69	283	1,293,428
Nobumitsu Yuhara	70	68	74	71	283	1,293,428
Anthony Gilligan	71	69	70	73	283	1,293,428
Keiichiro Fukabori	69	71	73	70	283	1,293,428
Yeh Chang-ting	70	68	73	72	283	1,293,428
Yasuharu Imano	68	71	73	71	283	1,293,428
Chen Tze-chung	71	71	71	70	283	1,293,428
Hiroshi Goda	69	71	73	71	284	891,000
Hiroshi Tominaga	70	71	71	72	284	891,000
Hsieh Chin-sheng	68	73	70	73	284	891,000
Mo Joong-kyung	71	68	72	73	284	891,000
Takenori Hiraishi	69	72	72	72	285	637,000
Shoichi Yamamoto	72	70	69	74	285	637,000
Takanori Hano	71	69	75	70	285	637,000
Kumihiro Matsunaga	72	69	71	73	285	637,000
Taisuke Kitajima	72	68	73	72	285	637,000
Hiroyuki Fujita	70	67	75	73	285	637,000
Nobuhito Sato	70	69	68	78	285	637,000
Kaname Yokoo	70	69	71	75	285	637,000
David Smail	71	70	71	73	285	637,000

NST Niigata Open

Forest Golf Club, East Course, Toyoura, Niigata
Par 36-36—72; 7,065 yards

July 29-August 1
purse, ¥50,000,000

		SCORES			TOTAL	MONEY
Toshimitsu Izawa	64	67	68	70	269	¥10,000,000
Kazuhiko Hosokawa	72	68	69	66	275	5,000,000
Ikuo Shirahama	72	68	68	69	277	2,600,000
Dinesh Chand	73	70	65	69	277	2,600,000
Masanori Kobayashi	65	72	71	69	277	2,600,000
Satoshi Higashi	67	69	69	74	279	1,725,000
Tatsuo Takasaki	70	73	67	69	279	1,725,000
Tatsuaki Nakamura	74	69	67	70	280	1,467,500
Yeh Chang-ting	71	67	71	71	280	1,467,500
Kenichi Kuboya	70	74	64	73	281	1,310,000
Kazuo Kanayama	74	69	70	69	282	952,857
Masayuki Kawamura	71	68	70	73	282	952,857
Takanori Hano	71	68	70	73	282	952,857
Anthony Gilligan	71	71	68	72	282	952,857
Katsunori Kuwabara	72	71	70	69	282	952,857
Nobuhito Sato	68	69	71	74	282	952,857
Takao Nogami	69	69	71	73	282	952,857
Kiyoshi Maita	69	74	72	68	283	630,000
Toru Suzuki	69	74	75	65	283	630,000
Hsieh Chin-sheng	68	72	73	70	283	630,000
Hiroyuki Fujita	70	69	72	72	283	630,000
Lin Keng-chi	75	70	67	71	283	630,000
Hirofumi Miyase	69	71	73	71	284	490,000
Nozomi Kawahara	69	71	72	72	284	490,000
Taisuke Kitajima	71	73	72	69	285	430,000
Masashi Shimada	72	73	66	74	285	430,000
Todd Hamilton	70	69	70	76	285	430,000

	SCORES			TOTAL	MONEY
Masanobu Kimura	69	72	74	71	286	370,000
Hidezumi Shirakata	71	71	75	69	286	370,000
David Smail	70	73	70	73	286	370,000

Hisamitsu-KBC Augusta

Keya Golf Club, Shima, Fukuoka
Par 36-36–72; 7,154 yards
(Fourth round cancelled — rain.)

August 26-29
purse, ¥90,000,000

	SCORES			TOTAL	MONEY
Tsuyoshi Yoneyama	70	66	69	205	¥13,500,000
Takao Nogami	71	64	71	206	6,750,000
Richard Backwell	71	67	69	207	4,590,000
Hajime Meshiai	72	71	65	208	2,790,000
Nobumitsu Yuhara	69	72	67	208	2,790,000
Keiichiro Fukabori	70	69	69	208	2,790,000
Satoshi Higashi	70	73	66	209	2,227,500
Toru Taniguchi	69	68	73	210	1,910,250
Kazuhiko Hosokawa	72	68	70	210	1,910,250
Nozomi Kawahara	70	71	69	210	1,910,250
David Ishii	72	71	68	211	1,633,500
Masashi Ozaki	71	68	73	212	1,189,928
Seiki Okuda	73	71	68	212	1,189,928
Hisayuki Sasaki	70	71	71	212	1,189,928
Toshimitsu Izawa	72	69	71	212	1,189,928
Eiji Mizoguchi	73	71	68	212	1,189,928
Hidezumi Shirakata	72	70	70	212	1,189,928
Frankie Minoza	69	71	72	212	1,189,928
Tateo Ozaki	68	69	76	213	746,357
Yoshinori Kaneko	75	69	69	213	746,357
Naonori Nakamura	73	71	69	213	746,357
Kenichi Kuboya	69	73	71	213	746,357
Yasuharu Imano	75	67	71	213	746,357
Steve Conran	74	71	68	213	746,357
Dinesh Chand	73	72	68	213	746,357
Osamu Yamaguchi	69	74	71	214	526,500
Shigeru Nonaka	74	66	74	214	526,500
Shinichi Akiba	71	73	70	214	526,500
Shigemasa Higaki	74	71	69	214	526,500
Tetsuji Hiratsuka	71	70	73	214	526,500

Japan PGA Match Play

Nidom Classic Course, Tomakomai, Hokkaido
Par 36-36–72; 6,941 yards

September 2-5
purse, ¥80,000,000

FIRST ROUND

Naomichi Ozaki defeated Mitsutaka Kusakabe, 2 and 1.
David Ishii defeated Taichi Teshima, 3 and 2.
Tateo Ozaki defeated Hajime Meshiai, 1 up, 19 holes.
Shigeki Maruyama defeated Kim Jong-duk, 4 and 3.
Tsuyoshi Yoneyama defeated Hideki Kase, 6 and 5.
Toru Taniguchi defeated Satoshi Higashi, 1 up.
Nobumitsu Yuhara defeated Katsunori Kuwabara, 2 and 1.

Todd Hamilton defeated Mitsuo Harada, 1 up, 19 holes.
Toshimitsu Izawa defeated Seiki Okuda, 3 and 2.
Yasuharu Imano defeated Toru Suzuki, 1 up, 19 holes.
Mamoru Osanai defeated Shigemasa Higaki, 4 and 3.
Eduardo Herrera defeated Choi Kyung-ju, 3 and 2.
Shusaku Sugimoto defeated Kazuhiko Hosokawa, 3 and 2.
Keiichiro Fukabori defeated Shingo Katayama, 1 up.
Tsukasa Watanabe defeated Kaname Yokoo, 3 and 1.
Nobuhito Sato defeated Frankie Minoza, Philippines, 2 and 1.

(Each losing player received ¥400,000.)

SECOND ROUND

Ishii defeated Naomichi Ozaki, 3 and 2.
Maruyama defeated Tateo Ozaki, 3 and 2.
Taniguchi defeated Yoneyama, 2 and 1.
Yuhara defeated Hamilton, 3 and 2.
Imano defeated Izawa, 4 and 3.
Osanai defeated Herrera, 1 up.
Sugimoto defeated Fukabori, 4 and 3.
Watanabe defeated Sato, 3 and 2.

(Each losing player received ¥800,000.)

QUARTER-FINALS

Ishii defeated Maruyama, 1 up.
Taniguchi defeated Yuhara, 1 up.
Osanai defeated Imano, 3 and 2.
Watanabe defeated Sugimoto, 6 and 4.

(Each losing player received ¥1,800,000.)

SEMI-FINALS

Taniguchi defeated Ishii, 2 up.
Osanai defeated Watanabe, 1 up.

THIRD-FOURTH PLACE PLAYOFF

Ishii defeated Watanabe, 1 up, 24th hole.

(Ishii received ¥9,000,000; Watanabe received ¥6,000,000.)

FINAL

Osanai defeated Taniguchi, 4 and 3.

(Osanai received ¥30,000,000; Taniguchi received ¥15,000,000.)

Suntory Open

Sobu Country Club, Inzai, Chiba
Par 35-36–71; 7,163 yards

September 9-12
purse, ¥90,000,000

		SCORES			TOTAL	MONEY
Nick Price	67	71	70	68	276	¥18,000,000
Shigeki Maruyama	70	67	69	71	277	9,000,000

	SCORES				TOTAL	MONEY
Eiji Mizoguchi	67	70	73	68	278	6,120,000
Hisayuki Sasaki	69	74	68	69	280	4,320,000
Lin Keng-chi	66	72	77	68	283	3,420,000
Craig Spence	70	70	71	72	283	3,420,000
Nobumitsu Yuhara	72	70	73	69	284	2,751,000
Katsunori Kuwabara	70	72	70	72	284	2,751,000
Akinori Tani	67	71	72	74	284	2,751,000
Kiyoshi Maita	71	73	70	71	285	2,088,000
Stewart Ginn	72	73	67	73	285	2,088,000
Mamoru Osanai	69	70	76	70	285	2,088,000
David Smail	68	70	78	69	285	2,088,000
Hideki Kase	72	72	70	72	286	1,336,500
Koki Idoki	70	71	74	71	286	1,336,500
Keiichiro Fukabori	71	72	74	69	286	1,336,500
Toru Taniguchi	70	69	74	73	286	1,336,500
Kazuhiko Hosokawa	71	68	69	78	286	1,336,500
Shigemasa Higaki	69	76	72	69	286	1,336,500
Kaname Yokoo	68	66	81	71	286	1,336,500
David Ishii	72	72	70	72	286	1,336,500
Hajime Meshiai	72	71	75	69	287	891,000
Akihito Yokoyama	71	72	76	68	287	891,000
Takenori Hiraishi	69	73	74	71	287	891,000
Takanori Hano	70	73	75	69	287	891,000
Hiroshi Goda	69	73	76	70	288	702,000
Yasunori Ida	71	67	78	72	288	702,000
Tsutomu Higa	71	70	74	73	288	702,000
Taisuke Kitajima	70	72	72	74	288	702,000
Steve Conran	71	69	77	71	288	702,000

ANA Open

Sapporo Golf Club, Wattsu Course,
Kitahiroshima, Hokkaido
Par 36-36–72; 7,063 yards

September 16-19
purse, ¥100,000,000

	SCORES				TOTAL	MONEY
Kazuhiko Hosokawa	66	70	69	72	277	¥20,000,000
Naomichi Ozaki	70	68	70	70	278	8,400,000
Katsuyoshi Tomori	72	73	67	66	278	8,400,000
Keiichiro Fukabori	70	68	68	73	279	4,400,000
Lin Keng-chi	70	69	69	71	279	4,400,000
Tsuyoshi Yoneyama	71	70	74	65	280	3,450,000
Todd Hamilton	68	67	75	70	280	3,450,000
Masayuki Kawamura	70	69	71	71	281	2,935,000
Ryoken Kawagishi	72	72	71	66	281	2,935,000
Seiki Okuda	70	74	72	66	282	2,520,000
Katsunori Kuwabara	70	68	70	74	282	2,520,000
Satoshi Higashi	69	70	73	71	283	1,880,000
Hajime Meshiai	69	70	72	72	283	1,880,000
Yoshitaka Yamamoto	73	68	74	68	283	1,880,000
David Smail	72	72	70	69	283	1,880,000
Chen Tze-ming	71	71	74	67	283	1,880,000
Hideki Kase	71	69	72	72	284	1,262,857
Tsukasa Watanabe	69	72	73	70	284	1,262,857
Yasunori Ida	74	71	68	71	284	1,262,857
Stewart Ginn	72	71	72	69	284	1,262,857
Nengah Darma	74	72	68	70	284	1,262,857

		SCORES			TOTAL	MONEY
Kaname Yokoo	72	73	69	70	284	1,262,857
Hiroo Kawai	75	68	71	70	284	1,262,857
Tateo Ozaki	75	70	69	71	285	860,000
Masakazu Noritake	72	68	69	76	285	860,000
Toru Taniguchi	73	73	73	66	285	860,000
Yeh Chang-ting	72	73	73	67	285	860,000
Rick Gibson	72	70	71	72	285	860,000
Kenichi Kuboya	73	73	68	72	286	720,000
Kazumasa Sakaitani	73	66	71	76	286	720,000

Gene Sarazen Jun Classic

Jun Classic Country Club, Ogawa, Tochigi September 23-26
Par 36-36–72; 7,355 yards purse, ¥100,000,000

		SCORES			TOTAL	MONEY
Hajime Meshiai	71	66	70	70	277	¥20,000,000
Hirofumi Miyase	68	70	71	68	277	10,000,000
(Meshiai defeated Miyase on first extra hole.)						
Masashi Ozaki	70	65	72	71	278	5,800,000
Yeh Chang-ting	70	68	71	69	278	5,800,000
Shigemasa Higaki	71	68	70	70	279	4,000,000
Yoshimitsu Fukuzawa	71	69	71	69	280	3,600,000
Eiji Mizoguchi	73	69	72	68	282	3,175,000
Chen Tze-chung	76	68	71	67	282	3,175,000
Tateo Ozaki	69	68	73	73	283	2,320,000
Kazuhiro Takami	74	68	71	70	283	2,320,000
Seiki Okuda	72	69	72	70	283	2,320,000
Toshimitsu Izawa	74	68	72	69	283	2,320,000
Keiichiro Fukabori	72	70	71	70	283	2,320,000
Kaname Yokoo	71	71	71	70	283	2,320,000
Nobuo Serizawa	70	71	72	71	284	1,620,000
Toshiaki Odate	73	72	68	71	284	1,620,000
Mamoru Osanai	69	73	70	72	284	1,620,000
Ikuo Shirahama	72	70	72	71	285	1,260,000
Saburo Fujiki	72	73	69	71	285	1,260,000
Eduardo Herrera	70	73	72	70	285	1,260,000
Yasunobu Kuramoto	71	69	73	72	285	1,260,000
Katsunori Kuwabara	71	70	72	72	285	1,260,000
Masahiro Kuramoto	72	67	74	73	286	865,714
Tatsuo Takasaki	75	69	71	71	286	865,714
Ryoken Kawagishi	73	68	71	74	286	865,714
Nobuhito Sato	73	69	71	73	286	865,714
Kazuhiko Hosokawa	75	70	71	70	286	865,714
Zaw Moe	73	71	71	71	286	865,714
Shingo Katayama	70	72	73	71	286	865,714
Kiyoshi Maita	72	72	70	73	287	634,000
Shigeki Maruyama	72	69	74	72	287	634,000
Richard Backwell	73	72	72	70	287	634,000
Taichi Teshima	75	68	71	73	287	634,000
Steve Conran	73	69	74	71	287	634,000

Japan Open

Otaru Country Club, Hokkaido, Otaru
Par 36-36–72; 7,200 yards

September 30-October 3
purse, ¥120,000,000

	SCORES				TOTAL	MONEY
Naomichi Ozaki	68	76	76	78	298	¥24,000,000
Nobumitsu Yuhara	74	73	75	78	300	11,250,000
Kazuhiko Hosokawa	76	75	73	76	300	11,250,000
Masashi Ozaki	79	76	69	77	301	5,580,000
Kazuhiro Takami	74	75	77	75	301	5,580,000
Kaname Yokoo	75	75	76	76	302	3,762,000
Tateo Ozaki	76	73	74	79	302	3,762,000
Choi Kyung-ju	78	75	73	78	304	3,132,000
Eduardo Herrera	74	76	77	78	305	2,370,000
Yasuharu Imano	73	77	76	79	305	2,370,000
David Ishii	75	78	74	78	305	2,370,000
Kiyoshi Murota	75	75	77	79	306	1,720,000
Toru Taniguchi	77	77	73	79	306	1,720,000
Lin Keng-chi	77	80	73	76	306	1,720,000
Satoshi Higashi	74	75	81	77	307	1,314,000
Hajime Meshiai	78	76	79	74	307	1,314,000
Toshimitsu Izawa	76	76	75	80	307	1,314,000
Toshiaki Odate	77	76	74	80	307	1,314,000
Hsieh Chin-sheng	79	76	76	76	307	1,314,000
Shigeki Maruyama	73	78	78	78	307	1,314,000
Hiroyuki Fujita	76	77	77	78	308	1,140,000
Ryoken Kawagishi	75	78	78	78	309	1,072,500
Keiichiro Fukabori	75	78	74	82	309	1,072,500
Shusaku Sugimoto	72	79	77	81	309	1,072,500
Chen Tze-chung	74	77	81	77	309	1,072,500
Hideki Kase	75	78	80	77	310	948,000
Toru Suzuki	72	76	82	80	310	948,000
Hirofumi Miyase	76	77	82	75	310	948,000
Peter McWhinney	76	80	78	76	310	948,000
Taichi Teshima	78	78	79	75	310	948,000
Mamoru Osanai	82	70	77	81	310	948,000
Dinesh Chand	78	76	78	78	310	948,000

Tokai Classic

Miyoshi Country Club, Miyoshi, Aichi
Par 36-36–72; 7,050 yards

October 7-10
purse, ¥100,000,000

	SCORES				TOTAL	MONEY
Kaname Yokoo	66	67	72	69	274	¥20,000,000
Vijay Singh	68	70	69	68	275	10,000,000
Toshimitsu Izawa	67	68	70	71	276	5,200,000
Shingo Katayama	65	67	71	73	276	5,200,000
Stewart Cink	70	66	68	72	276	5,200,000
Hirofumi Miyase	69	69	71	69	278	3,600,000
Naomichi Ozaki	67	70	74	68	279	3,056,666
Stewart Ginn	70	70	70	69	279	3,056,666
Shigeki Maruyama	71	68	70	70	279	3,056,666
Nobumitsu Yuhara	70	69	70	71	280	2,420,000
Masayuki Kawamura	68	68	72	72	280	2,420,000
Katsunori Kuwabara	71	70	69	70	280	2,420,000
Ikuo Shirahama	71	67	71	72	281	2,020,000

	SCORES				TOTAL	MONEY
Kazuhiro Takami	75	66	69	72	282	1,670,000
Mitsuo Harada	70	70	72	70	282	1,670,000
Taichi Teshima	71	70	73	68	282	1,670,000
David Smail	68	72	74	68	282	1,670,000
Hideki Kase	72	69	68	74	283	1,340,000
Shigemasa Higaki	70	70	74	69	283	1,340,000
Masanori Kobayashi	65	74	73	71	283	1,340,000
Kiyoshi Murota	67	73	72	72	284	1,060,000
Masahiro Kuramoto	65	70	75	74	284	1,060,000
Richard Backwell	72	71	73	68	284	1,060,000
Takashi Kanemoto	70	68	74	72	284	1,060,000
Akihito Yokoyama	69	74	73	69	285	860,000
Jun Kikuchi	71	70	73	71	285	860,000
Chen Tze-ming	74	69	72	70	285	860,000
Tsuneyuki Nakajima	74	70	74	68	286	670,000
Kiyoshi Maita	70	69	70	77	286	670,000
Eiji Mizoguchi	68	73	72	73	286	670,000
Ryoken Kawagishi	69	73	72	72	286	670,000
Naoki Hattori	72	72	70	72	286	670,000
Kenichi Kuboya	67	74	71	74	286	670,000
Kazumasa Sakaitani	73	69	73	71	286	670,000

Bridgestone Open

Sodegaura Country Club, Sodegaura, Chiba
Par 36-36–72; 7,178 yards

October 21-24
purse, ¥110,000,000

	SCORES				TOTAL	MONEY
Shigeki Maruyama	66	68	66	68	269	¥22,000,000
Toshimitsu Izawa	67	67	69	70	273	11,000,000
Craig Spence	69	69	67	70	275	7,480,000
Masashi Ozaki	66	69	70	71	276	4,840,000
Toru Taniguchi	68	68	69	71	276	4,840,000
Hajime Meshiai	68	72	66	71	277	3,648,333
Koki Idoki	69	70	67	71	277	3,648,333
Hirofumi Miyase	68	69	69	71	277	3,648,333
Yoshinori Kaneko	71	67	72	68	278	2,882,000
Seiki Okuda	68	72	70	68	278	2,882,000
Shingo Katayama	71	68	68	71	278	2,882,000
Richard Backwell	73	67	68	71	279	2,442,000
Tsukasa Watanabe	71	69	68	72	280	2,036,666
Stewart Ginn	70	67	72	71	280	2,036,666
Jimmy Green	67	76	69	68	280	2,036,666
Ikuo Shirahama	66	72	71	72	281	1,622,500
Kiyoshi Maita	67	72	69	73	281	1,622,500
Nobumitsu Yuhara	70	70	67	74	281	1,622,500
Yasuharu Imano	71	72	70	68	281	1,622,500
Hisayuki Sasaki	74	66	69	73	282	1,210,000
Hidemichi Tanaka	72	71	67	72	282	1,210,000
Takashi Kanemoto	73	66	71	72	282	1,210,000
Kaname Yokoo	70	68	70	74	282	1,210,000
Akinori Tani	68	73	66	75	282	1,210,000
*Kim Sung-yoon	70	72	69	71	282	
Naomichi Ozaki	71	69	69	74	283	902,000
Hideki Kase	72	69	71	71	283	902,000
Ryoken Kawagishi	71	70	69	73	283	902,000
Shigemasa Higaki	71	72	68	72	283	902,000
David Smail	69	72	72	70	283	902,000

Philip Morris Championship

ABC Golf Club, Tojo, Hyogo
Par 36-36–72; 7,176 yards

October 28-31
purse, ¥200,000,000

	SCORES				TOTAL	MONEY
Ryoken Kawagishi	71	65	66	68	270	¥40,000,000
Katsunori Kuwabara	68	66	69	68	271	20,000,000
Shingo Katayama	72	69	67	68	276	13,600,000
Toshimitsu Izawa	68	72	71	66	277	7,850,000
Zaw Moe	69	65	71	72	277	7,850,000
Shinichi Yokota	69	68	72	68	277	7,850,000
Kaname Yokoo	69	69	67	72	277	7,850,000
Masahiro Kuramoto	69	68	71	70	278	6,700,000
Hidemichi Tanaka	69	69	72	69	279	5,440,000
Shigeki Maruyama	69	68	73	69	279	5,440,000
Naomichi Ozaki	73	68	67	72	280	4,640,000
Satoshi Higashi	78	64	67	71	280	4,640,000
Kazuhiro Takami	70	68	70	73	281	3,480,000
Hirofumi Miyase	70	68	70	73	281	3,480,000
Nobuhito Sato	72	67	73	69	281	3,480,000
Kazuhiko Hosokawa	73	65	72	71	281	3,480,000
David Smail	71	70	71	69	281	3,480,000
Eduardo Herrera	68	70	71	73	282	2,520,000
Toru Taniguchi	70	71	69	72	282	2,520,000
Taichi Teshima	68	71	73	70	282	2,520,000
Mamoru Osanai	71	71	70	70	282	2,520,000
Dinesh Chand	67	68	74	73	282	2,520,000
Nobumitsu Yuhara	67	73	71	72	283	1,816,000
Tsukasa Watanabe	73	71	72	67	283	1,816,000
Yoshitaka Yamamoto	71	74	71	67	283	1,816,000
Stewart Ginn	71	68	71	73	283	1,816,000
Hiroyuki Fujita	73	70	69	71	283	1,816,000
Shigemasa Higaki	73	69	71	71	284	1,480,000
Yasuharu Imano	70	74	70	70	284	1,480,000
Kim Jong-duk	73	70	71	70	284	1,480,000

Acom International

Ishioka Golf Club, Ogawa
Par 36-36–72; 7,051 yards

November 4-7
purse, ¥110,000,000

	SCORES				TOTAL	MONEY
Hidemichi Tanaka	66	69	66	68	269	¥22,000,000
Keiichiro Fukabori	66	71	67	70	274	11,000,000
Hideki Kase	70	72	66	67	275	7,480,000
Seiki Okuda	71	69	68	69	277	5,280,000
Satoshi Higashi	69	68	72	69	278	4,180,000
Toru Suzuki	65	73	72	68	278	4,180,000
Tsuyoshi Yoneyama	66	75	71	67	279	3,242,250
Toshiaki Odate	69	70	66	74	279	3,242,250
Hiroyuki Fujita	69	73	66	71	279	3,242,250
Nozomi Kawahara	71	66	68	74	279	3,242,250
Shingo Katayama	71	71	69	69	280	2,442,000
Kaname Yokoo	72	70	70	68	280	2,442,000
David Smail	71	67	70	72	280	2,442,000
Koki Idoki	67	71	71	72	281	1,730,666
Hisayuki Sasaki	73	70	71	67	281	1,730,666

	SCORES				TOTAL	MONEY
Nobuhito Sato	68	70	68	75	281	1,730,666
Taichi Teshima	70	67	71	73	281	1,730,666
Shusaku Sugimoto	68	70	71	72	281	1,730,666
Go Higaki	72	67	72	70	281	1,730,666
Ikuo Shirahama	69	73	70	70	282	1,030,000
Kiyoshi Murota	73	67	72	70	282	1,030,000
Mitsuo Harada	72	68	72	70	282	1,030,000
Shinichi Yokota	72	68	70	72	282	1,030,000
Lin Keng-chi	71	69	71	71	282	1,030,000
Jun Kikuchi	72	66	72	72	282	1,030,000
Yasuharu Imano	72	70	69	71	282	1,030,000
Hiroo Kawai	71	69	69	73	282	1,030,000
Masanori Kobayashi	68	70	71	73	282	1,030,000
Chen Tze-ming	70	70	72	70	282	1,030,000
Jeev Milkha Singh	73	70	68	71	282	1,030,000

Sumitomo Visa Taiheiyo Masters

Taiheiyo Club, Gotemba, Shizuoka
Par 36-36–72; 7,072 yards

November 11-14
purse, ¥140,000,000

	SCORES				TOTAL	MONEY
Hirofumi Miyase	66	70	69	69	274	¥28,000,000
Ryoken Kawagishi	67	70	66	71	274	11,760,000
Darren Clarke	66	71	71	66	274	11,760,000
(Miyase defeated Kawagishi on first and Clarke on second extra hole.)						
Brandt Jobe	69	74	67	65	275	6,720,000
Naomichi Ozaki	66	70	72	68	276	5,600,000
Taichi Teshima	69	72	68	68	277	4,830,000
Lee Westwood	67	70	70	70	277	4,830,000
Kazuhiko Hosokawa	72	68	70	68	278	4,109,000
Frankie Minoza	68	72	68	70	278	4,109,000
Hajime Meshiai	66	72	69	72	279	3,528,000
Masayuki Kawamura	70	72	68	69	279	3,528,000
Eiji Mizoguchi	71	68	71	70	280	2,632,000
Shigeki Maruyama	68	72	66	74	280	2,632,000
Shusaku Sugimoto	70	69	72	69	280	2,632,000
Chen Tze-chung	72	69	68	71	280	2,632,000
Mark O'Meara	72	70	69	69	280	2,632,000
Yeh Chang-ting	69	77	65	70	281	2,058,000
David Smail	69	75	71	66	281	2,058,000
Hideki Kase	66	73	71	72	282	1,548,000
Katsuyoshi Tomori	69	66	75	72	282	1,548,000
Hisayuki Sasaki	72	71	71	68	282	1,548,000
Mitsuo Harada	71	71	72	68	282	1,548,000
Toru Suzuki	67	73	73	69	282	1,548,000
Mitsutaka Kusakabe	75	68	67	72	282	1,548,000
Hiroyuki Fujita	68	73	71	70	282	1,548,000
Tateo Ozaki	67	73	72	71	283	1,092,000
Toshiaki Odate	71	69	70	73	283	1,092,000
Peter McWhinney	69	70	71	73	283	1,092,000
Kaname Yokoo	68	72	72	71	283	1,092,000
Retief Goosen	71	69	70	73	283	1,092,000

Dunlop Phoenix Tournament

Phoenix Country Club, Miyazaki
Par 36-35–71; 6,856 yards

November 18-21
purse, ¥200,000,000

		SCORES			TOTAL	MONEY
Thomas Bjorn	69	66	68	67	270	¥40,000,000
Sergio Garcia	68	67	68	67	270	20,000,000
(Bjorn defeated Garcia on fourth extra hole.)						
Shigeki Maruyama	71	74	61	65	271	13,600,000
Greg Norman	67	73	73	63	276	8,266,666
Lee Westwood	71	67	74	64	276	8,266,666
Naomichi Ozaki	70	72	65	69	276	8,266,666
Toshimitsu Izawa	71	69	68	69	277	6,350,000
Kaname Yokoo	65	72	70	70	277	6,350,000
Tsukasa Watanabe	70	68	71	69	278	5,440,000
Hidemichi Tanaka	67	72	67	72	278	5,440,000
Retief Goosen	74	67	69	69	279	4,640,000
Hiroyuki Fujita	67	72	68	72	279	4,640,000
Nobumitsu Yuhara	70	70	72	68	280	4,040,000
Katsunori Kuwabara	72	72	70	67	281	3,640,000
Kazuhiko Hosokawa	71	73	70	68	282	3,140,000
Darren Clarke	70	70	72	70	282	3,140,000
Mathew Goggin	67	75	69	71	282	3,140,000
Shusaku Sugimoto	71	66	69	76	282	3,140,000
Tsuyoshi Yoneyama	72	71	72	68	283	2,440,000
Andrew Coltart	74	71	69	69	283	2,440,000
Satoshi Higashi	76	71	66	70	283	2,440,000
Todd Hamilton	71	70	71	71	283	2,440,000
Hisayuki Sasaki	68	70	74	72	284	1,960,000
Masahiro Kuramoto	72	71	67	74	284	1,960,000
Tsuneyuki Nakajima	71	70	73	71	285	1,800,000
David Howell	75	73	70	68	286	1,520,000
Jeev Milkha Singh	74	70	73	69	286	1,520,000
Shingo Katayama	74	71	71	70	286	1,520,000
Hajime Meshiai	71	73	70	72	286	1,520,000
Yasuharu Imano	77	69	68	72	286	1,520,000
Chen Tze-chung	72	70	70	74	286	1,520,000

Casio World Open

Ibusuki Golf Club, Kaimon, Kagoshima
Par 36-36–72; 7,105 yards

November 25-28
purse, ¥140,000,000

		SCORES			TOTAL	MONEY
Tsuyoshi Yoneyama	70	71	68	65	274	¥28,000,000
Taichi Teshima	67	72	70	66	275	14,000,000
Toshimitsu Izawa	68	70	70	68	276	9,520,000
Shingo Katayama	72	67	68	71	278	6,720,000
Naomichi Ozaki	71	64	73	71	279	5,320,000
Hidemichi Tanaka	68	71	68	72	279	5,320,000
Toru Taniguchi	76	70	68	67	281	4,620,000
Tatsuhiko Takahashi	69	66	78	69	282	4,109,000
Takao Nogami	74	68	67	73	282	4,109,000
Hisayuki Sasaki	69	73	71	70	283	3,368,000
Mamoru Osanai	70	71	72	70	283	3,368,000
Brandt Jobe	72	70	70	71	283	3,368,000
Satoshi Higashi	69	73	71	71	284	2,436,000

	SCORES			TOTAL	MONEY
Saburo Fujiki	70	70 72	72	284	2,436,000
Seiki Okuda	69	69 74	72	284	2,436,000
Takashi Kanemoto	70	73 70	71	284	2,436,000
Zaw Moe	69	74 71	70	284	2,436,000
Nobumitsu Yuhara	71	72 72	70	285	1,876,000
Katsunori Kuwabara	69	73 71	72	285	1,876,000
Chen Tze-ming	72	70 70	73	285	1,876,000
Kaname Yokoo	70	73 70	73	286	1,596,000
David Smail	73	72 69	72	286	1,596,000
Masashi Ozaki	72	71 70	74	287	1,334,666
Hideki Kase	70	74 71	72	287	1,334,666
Mitsutaka Kusakabe	74	70 77	66	287	1,334,666
Nobuo Serizawa	69	76 69	74	288	1,092,000
Tsukasa Watanabe	69	72 75	72	288	1,092,000
Katsuyoshi Tomori	69	75 71	73	288	1,092,000
Ryoken Kawagishi	71	72 74	71	288	1,092,000
Jeev Milkha Singh	71	74 72	71	288	1,092,000

Japan Series JT Cup

Tokyo Yomiuri Country Club, Tokyo
Par 35-35–70; 6,958 yards

December 2-5
purse, ¥90,000,000

	SCORES			TOTAL	MONEY
Kazuhiko Hosokawa	63	74 69	64	270	¥30,000,000
Toshimitsu Izawa	65	70 67	70	272	13,000,000
Shingo Katayama	67	74 70	63	274	7,000,000
Kaname Yokoo	66	73 69	68	276	5,200,000
Naomichi Ozaki	67	73 69	68	277	4,200,000
Hajime Meshiai	68	71 69	70	278	3,420,000
Shigeki Maruyama	69	74 67	69	279	3,000,000
Taichi Teshima	69	74 68	69	280	2,600,000
Eduardo Herrera	68	72 70	71	281	2,000,000
Hirofumi Miyase	72	74 67	68	281	2,000,000
Kim Jong-duk	67	75 67	72	281	2,000,000
Hidemichi Tanaka	72	77 67	66	282	1,650,000
Choi Kyung-ju	70	72 73	68	283	1,550,000
Toru Taniguchi	72	75 67	71	285	1,450,000
Masashi Ozaki	74	71 68	73	286	1,300,000
Tsukasa Watanabe	75	75 70	66	286	1,300,000
Tsuyoshi Yoneyama	68	76 69	74	287	1,150,000
Masayuki Kawamura	72	72 71	73	288	1,060,000
Shigemasa Higaki	72	76 70	71	289	960,000
Yasuharu Imano	72	79 70	68	289	960,000
Mamoru Osanai	71	80 70	68	289	960,000
Katsumasa Miyamoto	72	75 73	70	290	870,000
Katsunori Kuwabara	74	78 71	71	294	830,000
Ryoken Kawagishi	71	78 76	71	296	790,000
Yoshinori Kaneko	71	73 78	75	297	750,000

Fancl Okinawa Open

Daikyo Country Club, Onna, Okinawa
Par 36-35–71; 6,359 yards

December 9-12
purse, ¥70,000,000

	SCORES				TOTAL	MONEY
Taichi Teshima	68	69	68	66	271	¥18,000,000
Seiki Okuda	69	68	67	67	271	9,000,000
(Teshima defeated Kobayashi on first extra hole.)						
Masanori Kobayashi	72	66	68	67	273	6,120,000
Katsuyoshi Tomori	69	69	68	68	274	4,320,000
Frankie Minoza	70	67	68	70	275	3,600,000
Hideki Kase	70	70	63	73	276	2,480,625
Kiyoshi Maita	70	65	70	71	276	2,480,625
Yoshinori Mizumaki	70	71	67	68	276	2,480,625
Masahiro Kuramoto	69	72	70	65	276	2,480,625
Mitsuo Harada	68	70	69	69	276	2,480,625
Ryoken Kawagishi	72	66	70	68	276	2,480,625
Shigeki Maruyama	74	68	64	70	276	2,480,625
Toru Taniguchi	67	69	72	68	276	2,480,625
Nobuo Serizawa	70	70	69	68	277	1,416,000
Eiji Mizoguchi	66	69	71	71	277	1,416,000
Taisuke Kitajima	71	68	69	69	277	1,416,000
Keiichiro Fukabori	67	70	72	68	277	1,416,000
Richard Backwell	69	69	71	68	277	1,416,000
Kazumasa Sakaitani	68	68	71	70	277	1,416,000
Ikuo Shirahama	69	70	67	72	278	1,026,000
Anthony Gilligan	69	67	71	71	278	1,026,000
Mamoru Osanai	69	69	71	69	278	1,026,000
Chen Tze-ming	71	65	71	71	278	1,026,000
Satoshi Higashi	68	62	72	77	279	774,000
Toru Suzuki	69	71	67	72	279	774,000
Masakazu Noritake	69	66	73	71	279	774,000
Katsunori Kuwabara	76	65	70	68	279	774,000
Kazuhiro Kinjo	71	68	69	71	279	774,000
Hisayuki Sasaki	67	70	73	70	280	630,000
Masahiro Takahashi	71	69	74	66	280	630,000
Dinesh Chand	70	68	69	73	280	630,000

Australasian Tour

Victorian Open

Victoria Golf Club, Melbourne, Victoria
Par 36-36–72; 6,801 yards

January 7-10
purse, A\$225,000

		SCORES			TOTAL	MONEY
Kenny Druce	67	68	66	74	275	A\$36,000
Lucas Parsons	72	72	66	68	278	20,400
Tony Carolan	70	72	71	66	279	13,500
Robert Allenby	71	68	68	73	280	9,600
*Andrew Webster	71	69	70	70	280	
Shane Tait	72	68	71	70	281	7,600
Andre Stolz	68	67	75	71	281	7,600
Peter Lonard	69	71	69	73	282	5,866.66
Adrian Percey	71	72	68	71	282	5,866.66
Choi Kyung-ju	73	69	70	70	282	5,866.66
Tim Elliott	73	69	70	71	283	4,080
Paul Gow	71	75	66	71	283	4,080
Terry Price	67	75	68	73	283	4,080
Jeff Wagner	70	72	72	69	283	4,080
*Aaron Baddeley	71	75	66	71	283	
Marcus Cain	73	70	71	69	283	4,080
Grant Dodd	69	72	73	70	284	2,451.25
Don Fardon	71	73	72	68	284	2,451.25
Anthony Painter	68	70	71	75	284	2,451.25
Robert Stephens	68	74	68	74	284	2,451.25
Jason Norris	68	77	68	71	284	2,451.25
David Hill	69	74	70	71	284	2,451.25
Adam Le Vesconte	66	73	74	71	284	2,451.25
Brett Partridge	78	68	68	70	284	2,451.25
Wayne Grady	72	74	69	70	285	1,697.14
Paul Moloney	69	70	70	76	285	1,697.14
John Senden	69	72	70	74	285	1,697.14
Leith Wastle	72	73	66	74	285	1,697.14
*Brad Lamb	71	75	67	72	285	
Jamie McCallum	71	72	74	68	285	1,697.14
David Armstrong	70	75	68	72	285	1,697.14
Craig Spence	72	70	73	70	285	1,697.14

Heineken Classic

The Vines Resort, Perth, Western Australia
Par 36-36–72; 7,101 yards

January 28-31
purse, A\$1,500,000

		SCORES			TOTAL	MONEY
Jarrod Moseley	68	68	69	69	274	A\$270,000
Peter Lonard	68	67	72	68	275	108,750
Bernhard Langer	70	68	68	69	275	108,750
Ernie Els	65	66	69	75	275	108,750
Bob May	71	69	70	67	277	60,000
Craig Parry	72	71	68	67	278	54,000

	SCORES				TOTAL	MONEY
Pierre Fulke	69	70	69	71	279	44,000
Paul Devenport	69	70	68	72	279	44,000
Jarmo Sandelin	64	71	68	76	279	44,000
Tim Elliott	70	71	70	69	280	33,500
John Senden	69	69	71	71	280	33,500
Jean Louis Guepy	70	70	68	72	280	33,500
Henrik Bjornstad	68	73	71	69	281	22,600
Andrew Coltart	66	76	68	71	281	22,600
Alex Cejka	71	70	68	72	281	22,600
Per Haugsrud	72	69	68	72	281	22,600
Christopher Hanell	70	71	68	72	281	22,600
Craig Hainline	67	69	72	73	281	22,600
Choi Kyung-ju	69	74	70	69	282	15,267.65
Roger Winchester	65	74	73	70	282	15,267.65
Wayne Smith	68	72	72	70	282	15,267.65
Raymond Russell	70	69	72	71	282	15,267.65
Gary Orr	70	71	70	71	282	15,267.65
Peter O'Malley	71	71	69	71	282	15,267.65
Robert Jan Derksen	70	70	70	72	282	15,267.65
Scott Laycock	69	71	74	69	283	11,550
Thomas Bjorn	73	66	74	70	283	11,550
Lucas Parsons	71	73	69	70	283	11,550
Bradley King	71	70	71	71	283	11,550
Jeremy Robinson	72	71	74	67	284	9,225
Matthew Lane	71	73	73	67	284	9,225
Peter Fowler	72	70	74	68	284	9,225
Daniel Chopra	72	72	70	70	284	9,225
Gavin Coles	69	72	71	72	284	9,225
Wayne Riley	70	71	70	73	284	9,225
Peter Senior	72	70	77	66	285	6,900
Andrew Raitt	69	74	74	68	285	6,900
Anders Hansen	69	71	74	71	285	6,900
Van Phillips	71	73	70	71	285	6,900
Eiji Mizoguchi	69	74	70	72	285	6,900
Ian Garbutt	71	72	70	72	285	6,900
Steve Conran	68	74	70	73	285	6,900
Nick O'Hern	69	70	72	74	285	6,900
Sven Struver	70	68	69	78	285	6,900
John Bickerton	73	71	73	69	286	4,650
Andrew McLardy	68	72	75	71	286	4,650
David Smail	69	74	71	72	286	4,650
Craig Spence	67	73	73	73	286	4,650
Mats Lanner	71	69	72	74	286	4,650
Andrew Sherborne	72	70	70	74	286	4,650
Padraig Harrington	71	73	74	69	287	3,600
Thomas Levet	71	72	72	72	287	3,600
Chris Gray	72	71	74	71	288	3,296.25
Neil Kerry	66	76	73	73	288	3,296.25
Wayne Grady	75	68	71	74	288	3,296.25
Anthony Painter	72	72	69	75	288	3,296.25
Stephen Allan	73	69	75	72	289	3,135
Gary Emerson	74	70	72	73	289	3,135
Anthony Wall	74	70	72	73	289	3,135
Mike Clayton	73	68	74	74	289	3,135
Grant Kenny	72	71	72	74	289	3,135
Craig Jones	71	71	72	75	289	3,135
Gary Evans	70	72	75	73	290	3,030
Justin Cooper	72	70	75	75	292	2,985
Anthony Edwards	73	70	73	76	292	2,985

	SCORES				TOTAL	MONEY
Paul Gow	71	72	72	79	294	2,940
Robert Stephens	68	74	77	76	295	2,910
Fredrik Jacobsen	72	70	76	79	297	2,880

Greg Norman Holden International

The Lakes Golf Club, Sydney, New South Wales
Par 36-37–73; 6,904 yards

February 4-7
purse, A$1,000,000

	SCORES				TOTAL	MONEY
Michael Long	73	72	66	72	283	A$180,000
Michael Campbell	67	72	71	74	284	102,000
Bernhard Langer	71	65	69	80	285	67,500
Rodney Pampling	70	74	70	72	286	41,333.33
Peter O'Malley	70	70	72	74	286	41,333.33
Anthony Painter	66	68	72	80	286	41,333.33
Peter Senior	67	74	71	75	287	32,000
Peter Lonard	79	69	68	72	288	29,000
Shigeki Maruyama	69	78	75	67	289	26,000
Jean Louis Guepy	71	74	70	74	289	26,000
*Aaron Baddeley	72	71	71	75	289	
Peter McWhinney	74	73	73	70	290	20,000
Craig Parry	75	71	71	73	290	20,000
Raymond Russell	70	73	71	76	290	20,000
Lucas Parsons	74	72	72	74	292	15,800
Craig Spence	74	72	71	75	292	15,800
*Kim Felton	72	70	74	76	292	
Grant Moorhead	72	76	68	76	292	15,800
Craig Jones	73	75	75	70	293	11,490
Chris Gray	75	72	73	73	293	11,490
Stephen Allan	76	72	69	76	293	11,490
Wayne Riley	71	77	68	77	293	11,490
Justin Cooper	70	72	68	83	293	11,490
Rodger Davis	74	72	77	71	294	8,290
Steve Conran	76	72	74	72	294	8,290
Steven Alker	72	73	74	75	294	8,290
Matthew Lane	75	72	72	75	294	8,290
Ian Leggatt	72	71	75	76	294	8,290
Paul Gow	69	72	76	77	294	8,290
Jarrod Moseley	68	74	75	77	294	8,290
Scott Laycock	73	73	71	77	294	8,290
John Senden	72	70	74	78	294	8,290
Tim Elliott	69	75	71	79	294	8,290

Ericsson Masters

Huntingdale Golf Club, Melbourne, Victoria
Par 36-37–73; 6,994 yards

February 11-14
purse, A$750,000

	SCORES				TOTAL	MONEY
Craig Spence	64	73	69	70	276	A$144,000
Greg Norman	74	68	66	69	277	81,600
*Kim Felton	69	71	72	67	279	
Craig Parry	70	69	72	68	279	46,200
Greg Turner	69	70	70	70	279	46,200

	SCORES				TOTAL	MONEY
Robin Byrd	67	70	75	69	281	30,400
David Smail	68	72	71	70	281	30,400
Peter Lonard	70	75	68	69	282	24,400
Terry Price	73	70	67	72	282	24,400
Stephen Scahill	74	67	72	70	283	20,800
Ian Leggatt	72	69	71	71	283	20,800
Scott Wearne	72	74	70	68	284	14,320
Paul Gow	71	71	72	70	284	14,320
Peter O'Malley	72	74	67	71	284	14,320
Bradley King	77	66	69	72	284	14,320
Peter Senior	70	74	67	73	284	14,320
Peter McWhinney	67	73	69	75	284	14,320
Wayne Grady	74	65	78	68	285	9,410
Rick Gibson	70	74	73	68	285	9,410
Grant Dodd	73	71	71	70	285	9,410
Chris Gaunt	69	72	71	73	285	9,410
Shane Robinson	71	73	74	68	286	7,872
Tony Carolan	73	74	71	68	286	7,872
David Bransdon	75	73	68	70	286	7,872
Wayne Smith	73	71	71	71	286	7,872
Jarrod Moseley	72	68	73	73	286	7,872
Rodney Pampling	69	73	74	71	287	6,320
Robert Willis	72	73	68	74	287	6,320
David McKenzie	68	73	71	75	287	6,320
Dinesh Chand	77	69	77	65	288	5,216
Gary Player	70	72	76	70	288	5,216
Richard Backwell	73	69	75	71	288	5,216
Chris Williams	72	71	74	71	288	5,216
Stephen Leaney	75	69	72	72	288	5,216

Canon Challenge

Terrey Hills Golf & Country Club,
Sydney, New South Wales
Par 36-36–72; 7,019 yards

February 18-21
purse, A$550,000

	SCORES				TOTAL	MONEY
Rodney Pampling	67	66	68	69	270	A$99,000
Geoff Ogilvy	71	69	66	67	273	56,100
Craig Spence	76	67	67	64	274	37,125
Marcus Cain	68	72	68	69	277	26,400
Anthony Painter	70	72	68	68	278	20,900
Brett Partridge	72	75	64	67	278	20,900
David Smail	72	70	65	73	280	15,537.50
Kenny Druce	70	70	69	71	280	15,537.50
Terry Price	73	69	71	67	280	15,537.50
Paul Gow	75	73	66	66	280	15,537.50
Peter McWhinney	72	70	68	71	281	10,230
Peter Senior	72	71	68	70	281	10,230
Jarrod Moseley	71	70	71	69	281	10,230
Peter Lonard	74	74	65	68	281	10,230
Michael Long	70	70	73	68	281	10,230
David Armstrong	76	72	66	69	283	6,964.50
Tony Carolan	76	71	68	68	283	6,964.50
Nick O'Hern	75	70	71	67	283	6,964.50
Nathan Green	74	71	72	66	283	6,964.50
Steve Conran	70	67	74	73	284	5,940

	SCORES				TOTAL	MONEY
Adam Crawford	69	68	74	74	285	5,011.88
Euan Walters	70	72	71	72	285	5,011.88
Bradley King	72	74	67	72	285	5,011.88
Andre Stolz	74	69	70	72	285	5,011.88
Ian Leggatt	74	69	71	71	285	5,011.88
Anthony Gilligan	72	71	72	70	285	5,011.88
Gary Simpson	74	73	70	68	285	5,011.88
Peter O'Malley	75	71	71	68	285	5,011.88
Matthew Lane	75	72	68	71	286	3,657.50
Stephen Scahill	73	71	72	70	286	3,657.50
Richard Backwell	75	72	70	69	286	3,657.50
Hiroyuki Fujita	73	73	71	69	286	3,657.50

Australasian Tour Championship

Royal Canberra Golf Club, Canberra
Par 36-36–72; 5,769 yards

March 4-7
purse, A$500,000

	SCORES				TOTAL	MONEY
Marcus Cain	68	70	73	65	276	A$90,000
Paul Gow	73	71	68	68	280	51,000
Robin Byrd	70	75	68	68	281	22,350
Rodney Pampling	71	69	72	69	281	22,350
Peter Senior	70	69	73	69	281	22,350
Scott Laycock	68	69	73	71	281	22,350
Stephen Leaney	69	71	69	72	281	22,350
Ian Leggatt	72	69	72	69	282	14,500
Andrew Bonhomme	75	71	70	67	283	13,000
Craig Spence	68	72	72	71	283	13,000
Gary Simpson	72	73	70	69	284	9,300
Neale Smith	70	66	76	72	284	9,300
Euan Walters	68	75	68	73	284	9,300
Jarrod Moseley	70	69	71	74	284	9,300
Peter O'Malley	65	69	72	78	284	9,300
Tony Carolan	71	70	71	73	285	7,200
George Serhan	73	71	74	68	286	5,637.50
David Armstrong	76	69	72	69	286	5,637.50
Peter Fowler	73	71	73	69	286	5,637.50
Tony Christie	68	72	76	70	286	5,637.50
Adrian Percey	71	72	72	71	286	5,637.50
Scott Wearne	70	66	77	73	286	5,637.50
Grant Dodd	78	69	72	68	287	4,490
Anthony Gilligan	71	72	74	70	287	4,490
Justin Cooper	71	75	70	71	287	4,490
Mark Allen	72	72	72	71	287	4,490
David McKenzie	70	68	75	74	287	4,490
Jim Benepe	70	71	77	70	288	3,475
Jamie McCallum	73	74	70	71	288	3,475
Adam Le Vesconte	66	76	74	72	288	3,475
Steve Conran	69	69	78	72	288	3,475

Ford Open Championship

Kooyonga Golf Club, Adelaide, South Australia
Par 37-35–72; 6,648 yards

November 18-21
purse, A$600,000

	SCORES				TOTAL	MONEY
Craig Parry	70	70	70	64	274	A$108,000
Raymond Russell	68	72	69	70	279	61,200
Peter O'Malley	70	71	72	67	280	40,500
Wayne Riley	71	74	70	68	283	26,400
Peter Senior	73	72	68	70	283	26,400
Steve Webster	72	72	72	68	284	20,400
Adrian Percey	74	72	69	69	284	20,400
Tony Mills	71	68	76	70	285	15,450
Nick O'Hern	72	74	69	70	285	15,450
Greg Chalmers	73	71	70	71	285	15,450
Marcus Norgren	74	71	68	72	285	15,450
Gary Simpson	72	73	73	68	286	10,650
Matthew Ecob	71	73	72	70	286	10,650
Tim Elliott	71	75	70	70	286	10,650
*Aaron Baddeley	69	71	74	72	286	
Scott Wearne	70	72	72	72	286	10,650
Scott Hend	72	72	74	69	287	6,903
Cameron Percy	71	75	72	69	287	6,903
Anthony Wall	70	73	74	70	287	6,903
Tobias Dier	74	68	73	72	287	6,903
Martyn Roberts	70	73	72	72	287	6,903
Robert Allenby	72	71	70	74	287	6,903
Steve Collins	72	71	69	75	287	6,903
David McKenzie	64	72	74	77	287	6,903
Scott Laycock	72	73	71	72	288	5,420
Tony Christie	70	77	68	73	288	5,420
Craig Jones	70	75	67	76	288	5,420
Lucas Parsons	69	74	75	71	289	4,180
Shane Robinson	71	73	74	71	289	4,180
Stuart Bouvier	77	70	71	71	289	4,180
Stephen Leaney	70	74	72	73	289	4,180
Kim Felton	75	70	71	73	289	4,180
Shane Tait	70	72	72	75	289	4,180

Holden Australian Open Championship

Royal Sydney Golf Club, Sydney, New South Wales
Par 36-36–72; 6,832 yards

November 25-28
purse, A$1,000,000

	SCORES				TOTAL	MONEY
*Aaron Baddeley	67	68	70	69	274	
Greg Norman	70	73	64	69	276	A$141,000
Nick O'Hern	68	68	70	70	276	141,000
Paul McGinley	67	70	69	71	277	51,833
Michael Long	70	68	68	71	277	51,833
Colin Montgomerie	72	67	67	71	277	51,833
Michael Campbell	69	65	74	70	278	36,000
Peter Lonard	73	66	70	70	279	32,000
Steve Webster	73	72	72	63	280	29,000
Geoff Ogilvy	70	69	69	73	281	27,000
*Scott Gardiner	68	73	72	69	282	
Peter O'Malley	71	67	70	74	282	23,500

	SCORES				TOTAL	MONEY
Paul Gow	64	72	70	76	282	23,500
Craig Spence	69	70	73	71	283	19,000
Jarrod Moseley	66	72	73	72	283	19,000
Nick Faldo	68	74	73	69	284	15,100
Mathew Goggin	68	74	73	69	284	15,100
Stuart Appleby	72	70	71	71	284	15,100
Greg Chalmers	74	65	72	73	284	15,100
*Brett Rumford	70	73	70	72	285	
Brendan Jones	66	70	76	73	285	11,625
Robert Allenby	67	77	68	73	285	11,625
Scott Wearne	74	69	72	72	287	10,800
Craig Warren	73	69	76	69	287	10,800
David Howell	69	72	76	70	287	10,800
Adrian Percey	73	72	72	70	287	10,800
Justin Cooper	71	74	71	71	287	10,800
Grant Dodd	74	67	74	72	287	10,800
Euan Walters	74	71	70	72	287	10,800
Lucas Parsons	69	72	72	74	287	10,800
Anthony Wall	69	68	72	78	287	10,800

Australasian Players Championship

Royal Queensland Golf Club, Brisbane, Queensland
Par 36-37–73; 7,110 yards

December 2-5
purse, A$800,000

	SCORES				TOTAL	MONEY
*Brett Rumford	68	73	71	68	280	
Craig Spence	74	71	68	67	280	A$144,000
(Rumford defeated Spence on fourth extra hole.)						
Craig Parry	70	69	73	69	281	51,500
Raymond Russell	70	71	71	69	281	51,500
Brett Partridge	73	69	69	70	281	51,500
Bradley King	73	69	66	73	281	51,500
Nick O'Hern	73	67	74	68	282	27,200
Rodney Pampling	71	70	70	71	282	27,200
Greg Chalmers	72	65	73	73	283	23,200
Paul Gow	69	71	74	70	284	15,940
Craig Jones	73	72	69	70	284	15,940
Richard Backwell	71	72	70	71	284	15,940
Des Terblanche	71	73	69	71	284	15,940
Marcus Cain	71	75	67	71	284	15,940
Grant Dodd	67	73	71	73	284	15,940
David McKenzie	72	69	70	73	284	15,940
Jarrod Moseley	70	69	71	74	284	15,940
Lucas Parsons	69	67	72	77	285	10,400
*Aaron Baddeley	74	71	74	67	286	
Stuart Bouvier	71	71	74	70	286	8,890
Bradley Hughes	75	71	68	72	286	8,890
Adrian Percey	74	68	71	73	286	8,890
Wayne Smith	72	70	69	75	286	8,890
John Senden	71	73	74	69	287	7,142
Chris McCourt	70	74	72	71	287	7,142
Nathan Green	72	69	74	72	287	7,142
Martyn Roberts	71	74	70	72	287	7,142
Scott Laycock	69	70	74	74	287	7,142
David Bransdon	71	70	72	74	287	7,142
Geoff Ogilvy	73	70	68	76	287	7,142

Australian PGA Championship

Victoria Golf Club, Melbourne, Victoria
Par 36-36–72; 6,830 yards

December 9-12
purse, A$300,000

	SCORES				TOTAL	MONEY
Greg Turner	68	68	70	72	278	A$54,000
Shane Tait	69	71	71	69	280	30,600
Robert Allenby	70	71	71	69	281	15,550
Nick O'Hern	71	66	72	72	281	15,550
Craig Parry	71	70	68	72	281	15,550
Anthony Wall	73	66	73	70	282	10,800
Geoff Ogilvy	71	67	77	68	283	8,475
Brett Partridge	69	70	76	68	283	8,475
David Smail	71	69	73	70	283	8,475
Gavin Coles	70	73	67	73	283	8,475
Peter Fowler	71	73	75	65	284	6,300
Tony Christie	70	70	71	73	284	6,300
Mark Hensby	72	73	70	70	285	5,250
Tony Mills	69	69	75	72	285	5,250
Nathan Gatehouse	73	69	76	68	286	4,560
Matthew King	70	69	78	69	286	4,560
John Senden	69	74	75	69	287	3,528
Stephen Allan	73	72	70	72	287	3,528
Michael Long	73	69	71	74	287	3,528
Rodney Pampling	72	72	68	75	287	3,528
Adrian Percey	73	71	74	70	288	3,015
Bradley Hughes	71	71	74	72	288	3,015
Martin Doyle	69	73	74	72	288	3,015
Paul Moloney	69	72	73	74	288	3,015
Darren Cole	73	73	72	71	289	2,625
Brett Ogle	72	69	76	72	289	2,625
Stephen Scahill	73	73	76	68	290	2,010
David Hill	67	75	78	70	290	2,010
Craig Carmichael	71	73	76	70	290	2,010
Paul Gow	75	70	74	71	290	2,010
Mathew Goggin	71	70	77	72	290	2,010
Kim Felton	68	74	75	73	290	2,010
Matthew Ecob	70	71	75	74	290	2,010
Byron Clarkson	75	71	70	74	290	2,010

Schweppes Coolum Classic

Hyatt Coolum Resort, Coolum, Queensland
Par 36-36–72; 6,918 yards
(Fourth round cancelled — rain.)

December 16-19
purse, A$300,000

	SCORES			TOTAL	MONEY
Nick O'Hern	71	66	69	206	A$54,000
Wayne Smith	72	66	70	208	30,600
David Grenfell	70	71	68	209	13,410
Rob Willis	70	71	68	209	13,410
John Senden	67	71	71	209	13,410
Adrian Percey	71	67	71	209	13,410
Craig Parry	69	68	72	209	13,410
John Wade	70	68	72	210	8,400
Paul Devenport	68	69	73	210	8,400
Michael Campbell	68	71	72	211	7,500

	SCORES			TOTAL	MONEY
Jim Benepe	69	74	69	212	5,775
Craig Jones	68	73	71	212	5,775
Grant Dodd	67	72	73	212	5,775
Paul Gow	69	69	74	212	5,775
Peter Fowler	68	73	72	213	4,800
Andre Stolz	70	73	71	214	3,798.75
Mark Allen	72	70	72	214	3,798.75
Brett Partridge	67	73	74	214	3,798.75
Chad Wright	68	71	75	214	3,798.75
Matthew Ecob	71	72	72	215	2,861.25
Brett Ogle	71	71	73	215	2,861.25
Chris Gaunt	73	71	71	215	2,861.25
Euan Walters	69	72	74	215	2,861.25
Bob Shearer	71	74	70	215	2,861.25
Peter Senior	70	75	70	215	2,861.25
David Podlich	75	71	69	215	2,861.25
Des Terblanche	72	67	76	215	2,861.25
Jamie McCallum	68	76	72	216	2,040
Andrew Bonhomme	71	72	73	216	2,040
Robin Byrd	71	73	72	216	2,040
Lucas Parsons	69	72	75	216	2,040
Scott Hend	70	70	76	216	2,040

African Tours

Alfred Dunhill South African PGA

Houghton Golf Club, Johannesburg, South Africa
Par 36-36–72; 7,309 yards

January 14-17
purse, R3,816,000

		SCORES			TOTAL	MONEY
Ernie Els	67	69	69	68	273	R603,691.20
Richard Kaplan	68	70	69	70	277	439,603.20
David Frost	70	73	71	66	280	186,411.60
Stephen Leaney	73	68	70	69	280	186,411.60
Steve Webster	69	73	68	70	280	186,411.60
Jeev Milkha Singh	73	69	68	70	280	186,411.60
Fran Quinn	69	72	72	68	281	103,604.40
Mark McNulty	69	70	72	70	281	103,604.40
Peter Baker	69	72	71	70	282	82,807.20
Nico van Rensburg	65	74	76	68	283	67,066.20
Patrik Sjoland	72	74	68	69	283	67,066.20
Justin Hobday	71	75	67	70	283	67,066.20
Peter Lonard	73	70	66	74	283	67,066.20
Nic Henning	71	74	72	67	284	54,950.40
Desvonde Botes	74	72	68	70	284	54,950.40
Marc Cayeux	73	68	71	72	284	54,950.40
Steve van Vuuren	72	73	71	69	285	50,562
Andrew McLardy	73	70	69	73	285	50,562
Steen Tinning	72	71	74	69	286	45,919.20
Marco Gortana	74	70	71	71	286	45,919.20
Tjaart van der Walt	72	75	68	71	286	45,919.20
Massimo Scarpa	72	71	74	70	287	41,308.20
John Mellor	71	73	72	71	287	41,308.20
Sven Struver	74	71	70	72	287	41,308.20
Mathias Gronberg	70	75	70	72	287	41,308.20
Gary Orr	71	75	72	70	288	36,824.40
Paul Broadhurst	70	75	71	72	288	36,824.40
Ignacio Garrido	69	75	71	73	288	36,824.40
Roger Wessels	71	76	68	73	288	36,824.40
Anders Hansen	75	72	71	71	289	33,199.20
Chris Williams	72	75	69	73	289	33,199.20
Wimpie Botha	78	69	67	75	289	33,199.20
Darren Fichardt	76	71	73	70	290	30,146.40
Francisco Valera	73	69	75	73	290	30,146.40
Massimo Florioli	73	73	70	74	290	30,146.40
Christopher Hanell	72	74	70	74	290	30,146.40
Mark Mouland	71	70	73	76	290	30,146.40
Per Haugsrud	72	72	74	73	291	25,948.80
Hennie Walters	74	72	72	73	291	25,948.80
Ian Garbutt	76	69	71	75	291	25,948.80
Ashley Roestoff	74	70	71	76	291	25,948.80
Paul McGinley	77	69	69	76	291	25,948.80
Bruce Vaughan	71	69	74	77	291	25,948.80
Andrew Sherborne	73	74	75	70	292	22,896
Rolf Muntz	68	75	73	76	292	22,896
Clinton Whitelaw	69	75	76	73	293	20,224.80
Jamie Spence	73	72	75	73	293	20,224.80
John Bickerton	74	73	73	73	293	20,224.80

	SCORES				TOTAL	MONEY
Gavin Levenson	71	76	73	73	293	20,224.80
Chris Davison	76	71	71	75	293	20,224.80
Bob May	80	67	74	73	294	16,408.80
Warren Abery	70	75	75	74	294	16,408.80
Ian Hutchings	73	72	75	74	294	16,408.80
Marc Farry	72	72	74	76	294	16,408.80
David Carter	70	74	73	77	294	16,408.80
Andrew Beal	73	73	75	74	295	13,737.60
Olivier Edmond	72	71	76	76	295	13,737.60
Paolo Quirici	73	74	76	73	296	12,402
Scott Dunlap	71	75	73	77	296	12,402
Michael Archer	76	71	76	74	297	11,829.60
Anthony Wall	71	74	76	78	299	11,448
Fredrik Lindgren	70	75	79	76	300	11,066.40
Bafana Hlophe	69	76	81	76	302	10,494
Patrick O'Brien	72	72	78	80	302	10,494

Mercedes-Benz - Vodacom South African Open

Stellenbosch Golf Club, Cape Province, South Africa
Par 35-36–71; 7,112 yards

January 21-24
purse, R5,500,000

	SCORES				TOTAL	MONEY
David Frost	69	69	73	68	279	R900,600
Jeev Milkha Singh	71	71	68	70	280	524,970
Scott Dunlap	73	65	71	71	280	524,970
Sven Struver	67	67	73	74	281	279,870
Hennie Otto	72	67	72	71	282	235,410
Thomas Bjorn	72	73	68	70	283	170,050
Ernie Els	71	70	70	72	283	170,050
Bob May	70	70	70	73	283	170,050
*Jean Hugo	74	69	71	70	284	
John Bickerton	71	66	74	73	284	123,120
Wallie Coetsee	71	73	74	67	285	99,607.50
Francisco Cea	74	70	73	68	285	99,607.50
Jonathan Lomas	73	73	68	71	285	99,607.50
Alex Cejka	68	71	74	72	285	99,607.50
Sammy Daniels	71	69	76	70	286	76,665
Steve Webster	73	68	75	70	286	76,665
Nico van Rensburg	73	71	70	72	286	76,665
Ashley Roestoff	69	72	72	73	286	76,665
Peter Baker	72	71	69	74	286	76,665
Mark Roe	71	67	72	76	286	76,665
Van Phillips	74	68	75	70	287	62,510
Chris Davison	74	72	71	70	287	62,510
James Kingston	68	72	76	71	287	62,510
Phil Price	73	70	71	73	287	62,510
Stephen Allan	71	73	70	73	287	62,510
Paul McGinley	69	69	73	76	287	62,510
Patrik Sjoland	71	72	76	69	288	50,872.50
Greg Owen	71	71	75	71	288	50,872.50
Jarmo Sandelin	72	73	71	72	288	50,872.50
Bernhard Langer	72	71	71	74	288	50,872.50
Miguel Angel Martin	71	73	70	74	288	50,872.50
Michael Jonzon	72	71	70	75	288	50,872.50
Gordon Brand, Jr.	77	67	69	75	288	50,872.50
Michael Long	73	72	68	75	288	50,872.50

	SCORES				TOTAL	MONEY
Ian Hutchings	71	71	76	71	289	40,470
Desvonde Botes	71	74	73	71	289	40,470
Dean van Staden	73	73	72	71	289	40,470
Ricardo Gonzalez	71	75	72	71	289	40,470
Mark McNulty	71	73	73	72	289	40,470
Jamie Spence	75	70	72	72	289	40,470
Ian Garbutt	67	72	75	75	289	40,470
Don Gammon	71	71	69	78	289	40,470
Ignacio Garrido	70	69	69	81	289	40,470
Ronnie McCann	67	75	76	72	290	31,350
Soren Kjeldsen	73	69	75	73	290	31,350
Marco Gortana	70	71	75	74	290	31,350
Nick Faldo	70	71	75	74	290	31,350
Alan McLean	75	70	70	75	290	31,350
Derrick Cooper	75	70	69	76	290	31,350
Clinton Whitelaw	70	68	71	81	290	31,350
Pierre Fulke	75	67	77	72	291	23,370
Andrew Beal	72	71	75	73	291	23,370
Andrew Pitts	71	73	73	74	291	23,370
Kevin Stone	74	72	71	74	291	23,370
Ian Woosnam	72	70	74	75	291	23,370
Justin Hobday	70	72	74	75	291	23,370
Massimo Florioli	75	70	69	77	291	23,370
Paul Broadhurst	72	74	79	67	292	18,240
David Carter	74	70	77	71	292	18,240
Mark Mouland	69	70	78	75	292	18,240
Robbie Stewart	72	74	77	70	293	15,675
Thomas Gogele	77	69	73	74	293	15,675
Craig Hainline	70	74	74	75	293	15,675
Steen Tinning	71	73	73	76	293	15,675
David Faught	69	77	71	76	293	15,675
Richard Kaplan	69	72	73	79	293	15,675
Brenden Pappas	71	73	79	71	294	12,540
Wayne Westner	73	73	76	72	294	12,540
Ronald Whittacker	71	74	75	74	294	12,540
Michael Archer	73	73	73	75	294	12,540
Per Nyman	71	75	71	77	294	12,540
Greg Petersen	75	71	77	72	295	11,400
Mark Wiltshire	72	74	71	78	295	11,400
Anthony Wall	73	69	74	79	295	11,400
*Henk Alberts	69	74	78	75	296	
Sean Pappas	69	75	81	83	308	11,400

Vodacom Players Championship

Royal Durban Golf Club, Durban, South Africa
Par 36-36–72; 6,627 yards

January 28-31
purse, R1,000,000

	SCORES				TOTAL	MONEY
Chris Davison	71	68	67	69	275	R158,000
Nic Henning	69	71	70	68	278	115,000
Andre Cruse	70	72	65	72	279	69,200
Mark McNulty	70	74	67	69	280	49,100
Brenden Pappas	71	71	71	68	281	32,700
Bradley Davison	70	69	72	70	281	32,700
Clinton Whitelaw	69	73	67	72	281	32,700
Wayne Bradley	69	68	70	74	281	32,700

	SCORES				TOTAL	MONEY
Darren Fichardt	70	71	73	68	282	19,700
Scott Dunlap	69	69	74	70	282	19,700
Richard Kaplan	69	73	70	70	282	19,700
Sean Ludgater	72	74	70	67	283	16,200
Nico van Rensburg	70	70	72	71	283	16,200
Adilson da Silva	72	73	71	68	284	14,200
Fran Quinn	70	75	69	70	284	14,200
Bruce Vaughan	73	70	68	73	284	14,200
Philip Talbot	72	76	68	69	285	12,950
David Frost	71	72	71	71	285	12,950
Roger Wessels	72	69	75	70	286	11,460
Schalk van der Merwe	72	75	69	70	286	11,460
Desvonde Botes	69	74	72	71	286	11,460
Tjaart van der Walt	73	71	70	72	286	11,460
James Kingston	72	72	68	74	286	11,460
Titch Moore	71	70	70	76	287	10,500
Philip Jonas	72	74	73	69	288	9,600
Warren Abery	69	74	75	70	288	9,600
Michael Archer	74	74	70	70	288	9,600
Marco Gortana	74	72	71	71	288	9,600
Callie Swart	74	71	70	73	288	9,600
Don Gammon	70	76	71	72	289	8,500
Wayne de Haas	73	74	70	72	289	8,500
Doug McGuigan	73	72	68	76	289	8,500

Dimension Data Pro-Am

Gary Player Country Club, Sun City, South Africa
Gary Player Course: Par 36-36–72; 7,526 yards
Lost City Course: Par 36-36–72; 7,637 yards

February 4-7
purse, R2,000,000

	SCORES				TOTAL	MONEY
Scott Dunlap	66	65	70	72	273	R316,000
Steve van Vuuren	67	73	71	67	278	230,000
Bradford Vaughan	71	72	71	65	279	89,800
James Kingston	72	66	70	71	279	89,800
David Frost	74	66	69	70	279	89,800
Desvonde Botes	70	67	71	71	279	89,800
Bruce Vaughan	70	64	68	77	279	89,800
Marco Gortana	72	68	69	71	280	46,200
Nick Price	67	73	68	72	280	46,200
Don Gammon	66	72	74	69	281	37,500
Derek Crawford	67	71	70	73	281	37,500
Lewis Chitengwa	69	73	70	70	282	31,400
Ashley Roestoff	70	71	71	70	282	31,400
Mark McNulty	74	66	71	71	282	31,400
Roger Wessels	68	75	72	68	283	27,400
Kevin Stone	71	72	70	70	283	27,400
Tjaart van der Walt	74	68	70	71	283	27,400
Andre Cruse	75	70	70	69	284	24,900
Warren Abery	65	70	74	75	284	24,900
Michael Archer	71	68	70	76	285	23,600
James Loughnane	73	67	77	69	286	22,200
Brenden Pappas	70	69	75	72	286	22,200
Ulrich Van Den Berg	70	74	70	72	286	22,200
Sean Ludgater	70	73	74	70	287	20,700
Nic Henning	75	70	70	72	287	20,700

	SCORES				TOTAL	MONEY
Andre van Staden	74	68	75	71	288	18,900
Adilson da Silva	72	73	72	71	288	18,900
David Faught	71	71	73	73	288	18,900
Brett Liddle	70	72	72	74	288	18,900
Clinton Whitelaw	70	73	77	69	289	16,000
Fran Quinn	68	73	77	71	289	16,000
Gary Thain	70	73	74	72	289	16,000
Ron Whittaker	70	73	73	73	289	16,000
Ronnie McCann	72	71	73	73	289	16,000
Bobby Lincoln	69	72	75	73	289	16,000
Sammy Daniels	71	70	72	76	289	16,000
Emanuele Canonica	63	72	77	77	289	16,000

South African Masters

Oppenheimer Golf Course, Welkom, South Africa
Par 36-36–72; 7,105 yards

February 11-14
purse, R600,000

	SCORES				TOTAL	MONEY
Desvonde Botes	65	68	72	64	269	R158,000
Dean van Staden	69	69	66	66	270	115,000
Warren Abery	71	66	66	68	271	69,200
Marco Gortana	69	68	71	64	272	49,100
Andrew McLardy	70	69	68	66	273	35,400
Robert Bilbo	66	69	71	67	273	35,400
Ashley Roestoff	70	65	68	70	273	35,400
Andre Cruse	69	72	66	67	274	23,100
Sammy Daniels	72	64	69	69	274	23,100
Jeff Hawkes	74	68	68	65	275	18,066.66
James Kingston	69	72	68	66	275	18,066.66
James Loughnane	70	73	65	67	275	18,066.66
Justin Hobday	61	72	71	72	276	15,700
Bruce Vaughan	72	68	69	68	277	14,450
Tjaart van der Walt	70	69	68	70	277	14,450
Alan Michell	70	73	69	66	278	12,720
Scott Dunlap	73	69	69	67	278	12,720
Ulrich Van Den Berg	71	73	66	68	278	12,720
Des Terblanche	66	69	74	69	278	12,720
Michael Archer	68	69	72	69	278	12,720
Adilson da Silva	68	73	71	67	279	10,950
Brett Liddle	66	72	70	71	279	10,950
Nico van Rensburg	69	69	69	72	279	10,950
Marc Cayeux	69	70	68	72	279	10,950
Ian Palmer	71	72	71	66	280	9,600
Lyall McNeill	67	73	71	69	280	9,600
Wayne de Haas	70	71	70	69	280	9,600
Ian Hutchings	71	68	71	70	280	9,600
Brenden Pappas	69	71	66	74	280	9,600
Tony Johnstone	65	72	75	69	281	8,100
Mark McNulty	68	74	70	69	281	8,100
David Faught	69	70	71	71	281	8,100
Derek Crawford	69	72	69	71	281	8,100
Steve van Vuuren	71	70	69	71	281	8,100
Bobby Lincoln	69	69	70	73	281	8,100
Kevin Stone	69	75	64	73	281	8,100

Stenham Royal Swazi Sun Open

Royal Swazi Sun Golf Club, Mbabane, Swaziland
Par 36-36–72; 6,680 yards

February 18-21
purse, R1,000,000

	SCORES				TOTAL	MONEY
Marc Cayeux	67	68	65	66	266	R158,000
Mark McNulty	68	67	68	66	269	115,000
Nic Henning	67	70	66	67	270	69,200
Ashley Roestoff	66	69	69	67	271	41,933.33
Grant Muller	68	67	66	70	271	41,933.33
Andre Cruse	66	66	68	71	271	41,933.33
Justin Hobday	65	71	69	67	272	27,050
Hennie Otto	67	71	66	68	272	27,050
John Mashego	70	70	65	68	273	21,600
Mark Murless	72	68	68	66	274	18,066.66
Lyall McNeill	67	67	73	67	274	18,066.66
Jeff Hawkes	70	71	65	68	274	18,066.66
Michiel Bothma	68	72	68	67	275	13,525
Ian Kennedy	66	67	73	69	275	13,525
Des Terblanche	69	67	70	69	275	13,525
Ryan Dreyer	68	69	69	69	275	13,525
Lewis Chitengwa	72	67	67	69	275	13,525
Sean Ludgater	67	69	69	70	275	13,525
Michael Green	68	68	69	70	275	13,525
Kevin Stone	67	67	70	71	275	13,525
Bobby Lincoln	69	71	68	68	276	11,250
Richard Kaplan	69	70	67	70	276	11,250
Marco Gortana	71	66	73	67	277	10,350
Tjaart van der Walt	69	69	71	68	277	10,350
Craig Kamps	68	70	70	69	277	10,350
James Kingston	72	67	67	71	277	10,350
Bruce Vaughan	70	69	71	68	278	8,785.71
James Loughnane	72	70	67	69	278	8,785.71
Darren Fichardt	67	70	72	69	278	8,785.71
Brett Liddle	73	66	70	69	278	8,785.71
Adilson da Silva	68	69	70	71	278	8,785.71
Wayne de Haas	70	68	69	71	278	8,785.71
Robbie Stewart	69	67	70	72	278	8,785.71

Lombard Tyres Classic

Krugersdorp Golf Club, Johannesburg, South Africa
Par 36-36–72; 7,030 yards

April 14-17
purse, R125,000

	SCORES				TOTAL	MONEY
Brett Liddle	67	69	64	69	269	R19,625
Hennie Otto	69	67	67	67	270	14,375
Roger Wessels	71	69	64	71	275	10,000
Ashley Roestoff	68	67	70	71	276	7,875
Don Gammon	69	69	68	71	277	5,875
Colin Sorour	71	73	66	68	278	4,750
Dion Fourie	72	71	66	72	280	3,687.50
Warrick Druian	67	70	70	73	280	3,687.50
Vaughn Groenewald	73	71	68	69	281	2,937.50
Ulrich Van Den Berg	72	68	69	72	281	2,937.50
Justin Hobday	71	72	70	69	282	2,562.50
Michael du Toit	74	69	67	72	282	2,562.50

	SCORES				TOTAL	MONEY
Alan Michell	73	69	72	69	283	2,150
Andre Cruse	72	71	71	69	283	2,150
Titch Moore	75	70	69	69	283	2,150
Marc Cayeux	70	74	78	71	283	2,150
Bobby Lincoln	69	71	71	72	283	2,150
Andre van Staden	71	69	74	70	284	1,740
Clinton Whitelaw	72	70	72	70	284	1,740
Hennie Walters	70	73	71	70	284	1,740
Adilson da Silva	70	71	72	71	284	1,740
Darren Fichardt	69	74	70	71	284	1,740
Ryan Dreyer	73	72	71	69	285	1,550
Nic Henning	70	74	70	72	286	1,387.50
Warren Abery	71	74	69	72	286	1,387.50
Brenden Pappas	71	70	72	73	286	1,387.50
Steve van Vuuren	73	71	69	73	286	1,387.50
Bradford Vaughan	66	75	69	76	286	1,387.50
Michiel Bothma	76	71	69	71	287	1,162.50
Ian Palmer	74	66	74	73	287	1,162.50
Schalk van der Merwe	73	71	70	73	287	1,162.50
Bryan Prytz	69	76	69	73	287	1,162.50
Andrew Richter	68	74	70	75	287	1,162.50

Vodacom Series: Gauteng

Zwartkop Country Club, Centurion, South Africa
Par 36-36–72; 7,158 yards

April 21-23
purse, R200,000

	SCORES			TOTAL	MONEY
Nico van Rensburg	71	65	65	201	R31,400
Don Gammon	62	70	71	203	23,000
Darren Fichardt	69	69	68	206	12,266.66
Hennie Otto	66	71	69	206	12,266.66
Dion Fourie	67	70	69	206	12,266.66
Ashley Roestoff	67	71	69	207	7,000
Warren Abery	70	68	70	208	5,266.66
Brett Liddle	68	69	71	208	5,266.66
Bradford Vaughan	65	70	73	208	5,266.66
Andre Cruse	71	70	68	209	4,070
Justin Hobday	66	74	69	209	4,070
Sean Pappas	69	72	69	210	3,650
Damian Dunford	67	70	73	210	3,650
Richard Fulford	70	74	67	211	3,205
Ulrich Van Den Berg	73	70	68	211	3,205
Marc Cayeux	73	68	70	211	3,205
Des Terblanche	67	72	72	211	3,205
Neil Homann	74	68	70	212	2,700
Vaughn Groenewald	69	73	70	212	2,700
Steve van Vuuren	68	72	72	212	2,700
Andre van Staden	64	73	75	212	2,700
Adilson da Silva	69	67	76	212	2,700
Brenden Pappas	71	73	69	213	2,240
Bafana Hlophe	73	70	70	213	2,240
Warrick Druian	68	74	71	213	2,240
Desvonde Botes	69	72	72	213	2,240
Michiel Bothma	69	71	73	213	2,240
De Wet Basson	73	70	72	215	1,970
Brandon Pieters	68	71	76	215	1,970

	SCORES			TOTAL	MONEY
Lyall McNeill	70	75	71	216	1,790
Sammy Daniels	70	73	73	216	1,790
Schalk van der Merwe	72	69	75	216	1,790
Robbie Stewart	69	72	75	216	1,790

Pietersburg Classic

Pietersburg Golf Club, Phalaborwa, South Africa
Par 36-36–72; 7,025 yards

May 6-8
purse, R100,000

	SCORES			TOTAL	MONEY
Hennie Otto	65	65	69	199	R15,700
Des Terblanche	65	71	67	203	9,750
Ashley Roestoff	68	67	68	203	9,750
Don Gammon	71	70	63	204	4,933.33
Mark Murless	72	67	65	204	4,933.33
Ulrich Van Den Berg	70	66	68	204	4,933.33
Titch Moore	71	68	66	205	2,950
Andre van Staden	69	68	68	205	2,950
Marc Cayeux	73	64	69	206	2,350
Sammy Daniels	68	67	71	206	2,350
Brenden Pappas	69	72	66	207	2,100
Sean Pappas	67	69	72	208	2,000
Nico van Rensburg	69	72	68	209	1,900
Nic Henning	74	68	68	210	1,755
Warren Abery	70	71	69	210	1,755
Ian Palmer	73	71	67	211	1,532.50
Richard Kaplan	70	72	69	211	1,532.50
Michael du Toit	69	72	70	211	1,532.50
Lyall McNeill	69	69	73	211	1,532.50
Josef Fourie	71	71	70	212	1,315
Noel Maart	70	71	71	212	1,315
Wallie Coetsee	75	67	71	213	1,130
Wayne Bradley	71	71	71	213	1,130
Darran Warner	74	67	72	213	1,130
Alan McLean	71	70	72	213	1,130
Alan Michell	72	72	70	214	977.50
Bradley Davison	68	74	72	214	977.50
Gregory Jacobs	69	71	74	214	977.50
Justin Hobday	70	70	74	214	977.50

Vodacom Series: Eastern Cape

Humewood Golf Club, Port Elizabeth, South Africa
Par 36-36–72; 6,732 yards

May 13-15
purse, R200,000

	SCORES			TOTAL	MONEY
Ashley Roestoff	68	68	69	205	R31,400
Alan McLean	71	69	66	206	19,500
Justin Hobday	69	67	70	206	19,500
Steve van Vuuren	68	70	70	208	10,400
Ulrich Van Den Berg	68	69	71	208	10,400
Andre Cruse	69	71	69	209	6,500
Bradford Vaughan	68	70	71	209	6,500
Richard Fulford	74	68	68	210	5,200

	SCORES			TOTAL	MONEY
Sammy Daniels	69	72	70	211	4,400
Michael du Toit	68	72	71	211	4,400
Michiel Bothma	70	72	70	212	3,506.66
Bradley Davison	71	70	71	212	3,506.66
Chris Williams	71	70	71	212	3,506.66
John Mashego	70	68	74	212	3,506.66
Hennie Walters	70	68	74	212	3,506.66
Algy Kietzmann	70	72	71	213	2,960
James Loughnane	69	71	73	213	2,960
Bobby Lincoln	73	74	67	214	2,700
Lyall McNeill	72	72	70	214	2,700
Richard Kaplan	73	67	74	214	2,700
Nic Henning	70	72	73	215	2,500
Adilson da Silva	68	75	73	216	2,240
Alan Michell	70	72	74	216	2,240
Wayne Bradley	72	68	76	216	2,240
Sean Ludgater	71	69	76	216	2,240
Ian Palmer	67	71	78	216	2,240
Neil Homann	73	73	71	217	1,940
Noel Maart	73	71	73	217	1,940
Warren Abery	72	68	77	217	1,940

Vodacom Series: KwaZulu-Natal

Selborne Country Club, Pennington, South Africa
Par 36-36–72; 6,707 yards

June 10-12
purse, R200,000

	SCORES			TOTAL	MONEY
Hennie Otto	69	64	69	202	R31,400
Ashley Roestoff	64	74	68	206	23,000
Marc Cayeux	72	66	69	207	13,900
Nico van Rensburg	69	68	70	207	13,900
Sean Pappas	67	73	68	208	7,333.33
Ian Palmer	70	66	72	208	7,333.33
Neil Homann	67	66	75	208	7,333.33
Chris Williams	71	72	67	210	4,900
Mike Michell	67	69	74	210	4,900
Bradford Vaughan	71	70	70	211	4,200
Bryan Prytz	72	72	68	212	3,746.66
Ulrich van den Berg	71	70	71	212	3,746.66
Justin Hobday	70	71	71	212	3,746.66
Mark Murless	73	70	70	213	3,400
Schalk van der Merwe	69	70	75	214	3,260
Richard Kaplan	70	78	67	215	2,965
Des Terblanche	71	70	74	215	2,965
Bafana Hlophe	76	69	71	216	2,504
Andre Cruse	71	73	72	216	2,504
Steve van Vuuren	69	75	72	216	2,504
Andre van Staden	73	71	72	216	2,504
Bradley Davison	72	71	73	216	2,504
Sean Ludgater	71	75	71	217	2,120
Nic Henning	74	71	72	217	2,120
Gregory Jacobs	73	70	74	217	2,120
James Loughnane	73	70	74	217	2,120
Ben Fouchee	69	77	72	218	1,910
Callie Swart	76	69	73	218	1,910

Vodacom Series: Mpumalanga

Hans Merensky Golf Club, Phalaborwa, South Africa
Par 36-36–72; 6,638 yards

August 12-15
purse, R200,000

	SCORES			TOTAL	MONEY
Andre Cruse	72	68	62	202	R31,400
Nico van Rensburg	70	67	68	205	23,000
Brett Liddle	71	69	67	207	12,266.66
Richard Kaplan	69	71	67	207	12,266.66
Justin Hobday	70	65	72	207	12,266.66
Wallie Coetsee	69	69	71	209	7,000
Keith Horne	72	70	68	210	5,266.66
Don Gammon	72	69	69	210	5,266.66
Des Terblanche	67	70	73	210	5,266.66
Bobby Lincoln	70	73	68	211	3,768
Sammy Daniels	69	73	69	211	3,768
Desvonde Botes	70	72	69	211	3,768
Grant Muller	70	70	71	211	3,768
Ashley Roestoff	69	69	73	211	3,768
Lyall McNeill	72	71	69	212	3,140
Ulrich van den Berg	71	71	70	212	3,140
Ian Palmer	70	71	71	212	3,140
Chris Davison	70	74	69	213	2,650
Michiel Bothma	72	70	71	213	2,650
James Loughnane	70	71	72	213	2,650
Gary Thain	72	69	72	213	2,650
Sean Ludgater	69	69	75	213	2,650
Sean Farrell	68	69	76	213	2,650
Bradley Davison	71	74	69	214	2,123.33
Pelop Panagopoulos	71	73	70	214	2,123.33
Mike Lamb	76	67	71	214	2,123.33
Nic Henning	68	74	72	214	2,123.33
Adilson da Silva	69	71	74	214	2,123.33
Warren Abery	68	71	75	214	2,123.33
Steve van Vuuren	71	71	73	215	1,760
Michael Green	74	67	74	215	1,760
Marc Cayeux	71	70	74	215	1,760
Stephen Wilson	72	69	74	215	1,760
Noel Maart	68	71	76	215	1,760

Bearing Man Highveld Classic

Witbank Golf Club, Witbank, South Africa
Par 36-36–72; 6,702 yards

September 10-12
purse, R100,000

	SCORES			TOTAL	MONEY
Bobby Lincoln	67	73	69	209	R15,700
Darren Fichardt	68	72	69	209	9,750
Lyall McNeill	66	73	70	209	9,750
(Lincoln defeated Fichardt and McNeill on first extra hole.)					
Sammy Daniels	69	73	69	211	3,858.33
John Nelson	70	72	69	211	3,858.33
Bradford Vaughan	69	71	71	211	3,858.33
Sean Ludgater	70	69	72	211	3,858.33
Steve van Vuuren	66	73	72	211	3,858.33
Wallie Coetsee	65	73	73	211	3,858.33
Ryan Dreyer	69	74	71	214	2,116.66

	SCORES			TOTAL	MONEY
Marc Cayeux	71	71	72	214	2,116.66
Michael du Toit	68	73	73	214	2,116.66
Chris Davison	71	75	69	215	1,803.33
Patrick O'Brien	69	75	71	215	1,803.33
Dion Fourie	71	72	72	215	1,803.33
Schalk van der Merwe	72	76	68	216	1,595
Rudy Whitfield	74	71	71	216	1,595
Ashley Roestoff	70	73	74	217	1,470
Justin Hobday	68	75	74	217	1,470
Mike Lamb	70	76	72	218	1,290
Russell Fletcher	71	74	73	218	1,290
Pelop Panagopoulos	71	74	73	218	1,290
Travis Fraser	67	75	76	218	1,290
Des Terblanche	67	74	77	218	1,290
Andre Cruse	72	76	71	219	1,051.66
Desvonde Botes	70	76	73	219	1,051.66
Bradley Davison	71	75	73	219	1,051.66
Bryan Prytz	75	71	73	219	1,051.66
Omar Sandys	69	75	75	219	1,051.66
Titch Moore	70	72	77	219	1,051.66

Vodacom Series: Free State

Bloemfontein Golf Club, Bloemfontein, South Africa
Par 36-36–72; 6,648 yards

September 23-25
purse, R200,000

	SCORES			TOTAL	MONEY
Desvonde Botes	68	67	71	206	R31,400
Titch Moore	72	69	66	207	23,000
Hennie Otto	69	70	69	208	16,000
Darren Fichardt	69	70	71	210	10,400
Callie Swart	68	70	72	210	10,400
Michael du Toit	70	74	67	211	6,066.66
Brett Liddle	72	69	70	211	6,066.66
Steve Basson	73	68	70	211	6,066.66
Bradford Vaughan	69	75	68	212	4,600
Adilson da Silva	76	69	68	213	3,768
Sammy Daniels	71	73	69	213	3,768
Patrick O'Brien	68	75	70	213	3,768
Justin Hobday	68	73	72	213	3,768
Chris Davison	74	65	74	213	3,768
Colin Sorour	71	69	74	214	3,260
Nico van Rensburg	77	71	67	215	2,912
Dion Fourie	73	74	68	215	2,912
Steve van Vuuren	75	71	69	215	2,912
Grant Muller	72	71	72	215	2,912
Sean Ludgater	74	67	74	215	2,912
Wayne de Haas	70	73	73	216	2,600
Robbie Stewart	73	75	69	217	2,283.33
Hendrik Buhrmann	74	73	70	217	2,283.33
Mike Lamb	77	69	71	217	2,283.33
Neil Homann	71	73	73	217	2,283.33
Lyall McNeill	75	68	74	217	2,283.33
Phillip Sanderson	71	70	76	217	2,283.33
Bobby Lincoln	72	76	70	218	1,850
Omar Sandys	76	71	71	218	1,850
Rudy Whitfield	73	74	71	218	1,850

	SCORES			TOTAL	MONEY
Damian Dunford	73	73	72	218	1,850
Bradley Davison	71	74	73	218	1,850
Travis Fraser	68	76	74	218	1,850

Royal Swazi Sun Classic

Royal Swazi Sun Golf Club, Mbabane, Swaziland
Par 36-36–72; 6,680 yards

September 28-30
purse, R200,000

	SCORES			TOTAL	MONEY
Bradford Vaughan	68	65	67	200	R32,185
Nic Henning	66	70	67	203	23,575
Patrick O'Brien	72	64	69	205	12,573.33
Justin Hobday	68	68	69	205	12,573.33
Ulrich van den Berg	68	67	70	205	12,573.33
Neil Homann	72	68	66	206	6,662.50
Damian Dunford	71	68	67	206	6,662.50
Keith Horne	68	72	67	207	4,597.12
Mark Murless	66	73	68	207	4,597.12
Andre Cruse	67	69	71	207	4,597.12
Brett Liddle	63	72	72	207	4,597.12
Desvonde Botes	74	67	67	208	3,577.25
Sean Ludgater	68	71	69	208	3,577.25
Phillip Sanderson	68	71	69	208	3,577.25
Steve van Vuuren	70	68	70	208	3,577.25
Michael du Toit	73	68	68	209	3,218.50
Colin Sorour	69	70	71	210	2,979.33
Barry Painting	70	68	72	210	2,979.33
Vaughn Groenewald	71	66	73	210	2,979.33
Schalk van der Merwe	73	71	67	211	2,613.75
John Mashego	70	72	69	211	2,613.75
Sammy Daniels	69	70	72	211	2,613.75
Marc Cayeux	68	70	73	211	2,613.75
Ivano Ficalbi	74	71	67	212	2,214
Andre van Staden	74	70	68	212	2,214
Steve Basson	71	71	70	212	2,214
Callie Swart	73	67	72	212	2,214
Dean van Staden	71	68	73	212	2,214
Ryan Dreyer	70	73	70	213	1,927
Grant Muller	73	67	73	213	1,927
James Kingston	72	67	74	213	1,927

Vodacom Series: Western Cape

Rondebosch Golf Club, Cape Town, South Africa
Par 36-36–72; 6,633 yards

October 8-10
purse, R200,000

	SCORES			TOTAL	MONEY
Sean Ludgater	65	68	71	204	R31,400
Des Terblanche	67	69	70	206	23,000
Bradley Davison	69	70	69	208	12,266.66
Robbie Stewart	70	69	69	208	12,266.66
Hennie Walters	66	71	71	208	12,266.66
Nic Henning	70	71	68	209	7,000
Nico van Rensburg	69	75	66	210	4,788

	SCORES			TOTAL	MONEY
Callie Swart	68	74	68	210	4,788
Adilson da Silva	71	70	69	210	4,788
Phillip Sanderson	72	69	69	210	4,788
Ashley Roestoff	64	71	75	210	4,788
Sammy Daniels	74	68	69	211	3,353.33
Bradford Vaughan	71	70	70	211	3,353.33
Dean van Staden	68	72	71	211	3,353.33
Ulrich van den Berg	69	71	71	211	3,353.33
Damian Dunford	73	66	72	211	3,353.33
Darren Fichardt	71	65	75	211	3,353.33
Warren Abery	71	71	70	212	2,850
Brett Liddle	69	71	72	212	2,850
De Wet Basson	71	73	69	213	2,650
James Loughnane	69	69	75	213	2,650
Patrick O'Brien	74	69	71	214	2,406.66
Don Gammon	70	72	72	214	2,406.66
Steve van Vuuren	67	73	74	214	2,406.66
Noel Maart	71	71	73	215	1,985
Desvonde Botes	74	68	73	215	1,985
Titch Moore	71	71	73	215	1,985
Ivano Ficalbi	70	72	73	215	1,985
Grant Muller	72	68	75	215	1,985
Clinton Whitelaw	70	70	75	215	1,985
Lindani Ndwandwe	66	73	76	215	1,985
John Bele	67	72	76	215	1,985

Platinum Classic

Mooi Nooi Golf Club, Windhoek, Namibia
Par 36-36–72; 6,735 yards

October 29-31
purse, R200,000

	SCORES			TOTAL	MONEY
Bobby Lincoln	69	63	69	201	R47,400
Callie Swart	68	68	65	201	34,500
(Lincoln defeated Swart on second extra hole.)					
Roger Wessels	71	65	66	202	17,745
Neil Homann	69	64	69	202	17,745
Colin Sorour	66	71	66	203	12,390
Ian Hutchings	68	72	64	204	9,735
Hennie Otto	66	70	68	204	9,735
Dion Fourie	64	69	72	205	7,380
Robbie Stewart	71	70	65	206	5,910
Vaughn Groenewald	70	69	67	206	5,910
Andre Cruse	71	67	68	206	5,910
Bafana Hlophe	70	70	67	207	4,500
Bradford Vaughan	69	70	68	207	4,500
Mark Murless	69	70	68	207	4,500
Sean Farrell	69	69	69	207	4,500
Sean Ludgater	69	68	70	207	4,500
Kevin Stone	73	68	67	208	3,678
Trevor Case	72	68	68	208	3,678
Keith Horne	67	71	70	208	3,678
Dean van Staden	69	69	70	208	3,678
James Kingston	68	67	73	208	3,678
Richard Kaplan	72	69	68	209	3,150
Desvonde Botes	71	70	68	209	3,150
Darren Fichardt	70	70	69	209	3,150

	SCORES			TOTAL	MONEY
Travis Fraser	72	68	69	209	3,150
Adilson da Silva	67	70	72	209	3,150
Philip van den Berg	69	72	69	210	2,745
Chris Davison	73	68	69	210	2,745
Stephen Wilson	68	71	71	210	2,745
Andrew McLardy	67	71	72	210	2,745

Hassan II Trophy

Royal Golf Dar-es-Salam, Red Course, Rabat, Morocco
Par 36-37–73; 7,362 yards

November 11-14
purse, US$438,000

	SCORES				TOTAL	MONEY
David Toms	68	70	68	69	275	US$100,000
Chris Perry	69	71	70	65	275	50,000
(Toms defeated Perry on first extra hole.)						
Miguel Angel Martin	71	66	67	73	277	30,000
Tim Herron	69	71	70	69	279	22,000
John Huston	71	71	70	67	279	22,000
Kenny Perry	72	68	72	71	283	15,000
Santiago Luna	68	73	71	71	283	15,000
Shaun Michael	75	71	68	69	283	15,000
Paolo Quirici	73	75	71	67	286	12,000
Henrik Nystrom	72	73	73	69	287	10,500
Ignacio Garrido	71	75	72	69	287	10,500
Raphael Jacquelin	75	72	71	71	289	8,650
Seve Ballesteros	73	74	72	70	289	8,650
Pedro Linhart	70	69	74	77	290	7,233.33
Didier De Vooght	73	72	73	72	290	7,233.33
Roger Chapman	73	73	73	71	290	7,233.33
Francisco Cea	67	73	77	74	291	6,500
Ronan Rafferty	74	77	69	72	292	6,300
Steve Jones	69	72	74	78	293	5,900
Emanuel Canonica	74	73	69	77	293	5,900
Gary Player	76	74	73	70	293	5,900
Younes El Hassani	75	73	72	74	294	5,500
Peter Dawson	77	71	76	71	295	5,400
Richard Boxall	73	77	71	75	296	5,250
Costantino Rocca	77	71	74	74	296	5,250
Bobby Casper	74	75	75	74	298	5,100
Mark Mouland	79	71	72	77	299	5,000
Wayne Westner	78	73	72	77	300	5,000
Rafael Alarcon	79	72	71	79	301	5,000
Mohamed Makroune	72	77	76	75	301	5,000

Zimbabwe Open

Chapman Golf Club, Harare, Zimbabwe
Par 36-36–72; 7,064 yards

November 25-28
purse, R400,000

	SCORES				TOTAL	MONEY
Jean Hugo	72	66	65	68	271	R75,477.71
Ulrich van den Berg	70	65	68	70	273	54,936.31
Hennie Otto	68	69	70	67	274	33,057.32

	SCORES				TOTAL	MONEY
Nasho Kamungeremu	69	70	70	66	275	21,592.35
Nic Henning	67	70	68	70	275	21,592.35
Roger Wessels	73	67	66	70	276	16,910.83
Andre Cruse	67	68	73	69	277	12,921.97
Warrick Druian	70	72	66	69	277	12,921.97
Ashley Roestoff	70	71	70	67	278	9,410.83
Marc Cayeux	73	71	67	67	278	9,410.83
David Faught	73	68	69	68	278	9,410.83
Ian Hutchings	72	70	70	67	279	7,738.85
Sean Pappas	67	70	69	73	279	7,738.85
Bradford Vaughan	72	70	70	68	280	6,573.24
Omar Sandys	71	71	70	68	280	6,573.24
Sean Ludgater	70	68	73	69	280	6,573.24
Sean Farrell	69	71	71	69	280	6,573.24
Michiel Bothma	70	71	66	73	280	6,573.24
Warren Abery	73	70	70	68	281	5,756.37
Chris Davison	69	67	72	73	281	5,756.37
Dion Fourie	71	72	71	68	282	5,302.55
Grant Muller	72	70	69	71	282	5,302.55
Michael Green	70	69	71	72	282	5,302.55
Bradley Davison	68	75	74	66	283	4,800.95
Steve van Vuuren	74	70	71	68	283	4,800.95
Ryan Dreyer	73	67	74	69	283	4,800.95
Bobby Lincoln	69	69	73	72	283	4,800.95
Grant White	68	77	73	66	284	4,239.65
James Loughnane	75	68	72	69	284	4,239.65
Leonard Loxton	74	71	68	71	284	4,239.65
Hal Meier	75	66	69	74	284	4,239.65
Ivano Ficalbi	72	69	69	74	284	4,239.65

Nedbank Million Dollar Challenge

Gary Player Country Club, Sun City, South Africa
Par 36-36–72; 7,669 yards

December 2-5
purse, US$2,570,000

	SCORES				TOTAL	MONEY
Ernie Els	67	66	64	66	263	$1,000,000
Colin Montgomerie	67	69	69	65	268	250,000
Darren Clarke	72	69	64	65	270	200,000
Lee Westwood	68	70	70	66	274	175,000
Jim Furyk	70	71	65	69	275	150,000
Carlos Franco	70	72	68	67	277	135,000
Nick Price	68	72	68	72	280	110,000
John Huston	67	76	68	70	281	110,000
Sergio Garcia	71	67	70	75	283	110,000
Jose Maria Olazabal	69	74	73	68	284	110,000
Miguel Angel Jimenez	76	72	69	69	286	110,000
Paul Lawrie	65	76	71	74	286	110,000

Vodacom Players Championship

Royal Cape Golf Club, Cape Town, South Africa
Par 36-36–72; 6,121 yards

December 9-12
purse, R1,999,999

	SCORES				TOTAL	MONEY
Nic Henning	67	67	72	70	276	R316,000
Darren Clarke	70	68	70	68	276	230,000
(Henning defeated Clarke on second extra hole.)						
Alan McLean	72	66	70	69	277	138,400
Tony Johnstone	68	71	71	68	278	77,650
Justin Hobday	68	71	70	69	278	77,650
David Frost	67	72	69	70	278	77,650
Ernie Els	68	69	70	71	278	77,650
Retief Goosen	67	71	71	71	280	49,200
Dean van Staden	68	67	75	71	281	37,900
Rudi Sailer	68	69	73	71	281	37,900
Hennie Otto	65	70	74	72	281	37,900
Trevor Dodds	70	67	71	73	281	37,900
Deane Pappas	70	74	71	67	282	28,166.66
Andrew McLardy	69	70	75	68	282	28,166.66
Warrick Druian	70	71	73	68	282	28,166.66
Trevor Immelman	75	65	73	69	282	28,166.66
Tim Clark	69	70	72	71	282	28,166.66
Jean Hugo	68	71	71	72	282	28,166.66
Ian Hutchings	74	68	74	67	283	21,072.72
Titch Moore	72	71	73	67	283	21,072.72
Callie Swart	69	71	75	68	283	21,072.72
Marco Gortana	71	70	74	68	283	21,072.72
Chris Davison	71	68	75	69	283	21,072.72
David Faught	68	72	73	70	283	21,072.72
Jean Van de Velde	73	67	73	70	283	21,072.72
John Bele	69	73	71	70	283	21,072.72
Michael Green	69	70	71	73	283	21,072.72
Derek Crawford	68	73	68	74	283	21,072.72
Roger Wessels	67	72	68	76	283	21,072.72
Ian Kennedy	75	67	75	67	284	16,200
Wallie Coetsee	68	72	75	69	284	16,200
Adilson da Silva	70	68	76	70	284	16,200
Ryan Dreyer	68	73	73	70	284	16,200
Andre Bossert	70	68	74	72	284	16,200
Tjaart van der Walt	72	69	71	72	284	16,200
Mark Murless	70	72	70	72	284	16,200

Senior Tours

MasterCard Championship

Hualalai Golf Club, Kaupulehu-Kona, Hawaii

January 22-24

Par 36-36–72; 7,053 yards

purse, $1,100,000

	SCORES			TOTAL	MONEY
John Jacobs	64	69	70	203	$185,000
Jim Colbert	71	68	67	206	98,375
Raymond Floyd	67	69	70	206	98,375
Bob Dickson	68	70	69	207	67,000
Dana Quigley	70	68	69	207	67,000
Gil Morgan	69	73	66	208	46,750
Brian Barnes	73	68	67	208	46,750
Isao Aoki	67	72	70	209	37,000
J.C. Snead	68	71	70	209	37,000
Gary Player	70	68	72	210	32,000
Hugh Baiocchi	71	71	69	211	24,683.34
Larry Nelson	75	67	69	211	24,683.34
Bud Allin	69	71	71	211	24,683.33
George Archer	68	72	71	211	24,683.33
Dave Stockton	72	67	72	211	24,683.33
Larry Ziegler	74	67	70	211	24,683.33
Simon Hobday	69	72	71	212	19,125
Tom Weiskopf	71	73	68	212	19,125
Jim Dent	71	73	69	213	16,000
Vicente Fernandez	74	74	65	213	16,000
Bob Murphy	72	71	70	213	16,000
Bruce Summerhays	71	70	72	213	16,000
David Graham	73	72	69	214	12,687.50
Joe Inman	68	80	66	214	12,687.50
Hale Irwin	68	75	71	214	12,687.50
Lee Trevino	71	73	70	214	12,687.50
Jay Sigel	70	73	72	215	11,000
Leonard Thompson	71	74	70	215	11,000
Bruce Crampton	71	73	72	216	10,000
Bob Eastwood	75	71	70	216	10,000
Graham Marsh	74	74	69	217	9,250
Dave Eichelberger	70	75	73	218	8,750
Jim Albus	74	75	72	221	8,250
Gibby Gilbert	74	76	72	222	7,700
Hubert Green	76	72	74	222	7,700

Royal Caribbean Classic

Crandon Park Golf Club, Key Biscayne, Florida

February 5-7

Par 35-36–71; 6,725 yards

purse, $1,000,000

	SCORES			TOTAL	MONEY
Bruce Fleisher	66	69	70	205	$150,000
Isao Aoki	69	68	70	207	88,000
Dana Quigley	69	71	68	208	66,000

	SCORES			TOTAL	MONEY
Leonard Thompson	70	72	66	208	66,000
Bob Duval	67	71	71	209	44,000
Jim Thorpe	72	69	68	209	44,000
Jose Maria Canizares	69	68	73	210	30,500
Allen Doyle	70	72	68	210	30,500
Raymond Floyd	69	74	67	210	30,500
Lee Trevino	69	71	70	210	30,500
Vicente Fernandez	69	70	72	211	20,600
Joe Inman	78	68	65	211	20,600
Larry Nelson	71	72	68	211	20,600
J.C. Snead	71	70	70	211	20,600
Bobby Stroble	69	74	68	211	20,600
Jim Albus	70	71	71	212	16,000
Bob Dickson	71	73	68	212	16,000
Gil Morgan	72	67	73	212	16,000
Bob Charles	70	73	70	213	11,537.50
Jim Colbert	68	72	73	213	11,537.50
Jim Dent	70	70	73	213	11,537.50
Ed Dougherty	73	70	70	213	11,537.50
Jim Ferree	69	71	73	213	11,537.50
Walter Hall	71	71	71	213	11,537.50
Walter Morgan	67	72	74	213	11,537.50
Larry Ziegler	74	70	69	213	11,537.50
John Bland	69	72	73	214	8,500
Hubert Green	71	70	73	214	8,500
John Jacobs	68	75	71	214	8,500
Bobby Nichols	73	70	71	214	8,500
Brian Barnes	76	68	71	215	6,600
Frank Conner	74	69	72	215	6,600
Al Geiberger	73	73	69	215	6,600
Simon Hobday	72	73	70	215	6,600
John Mahaffey	74	69	72	215	6,600
Tom McGinnis	76	68	71	215	6,600
Bob Murphy	68	76	71	215	6,600
George Archer	73	73	70	216	5,000
Hugh Baiocchi	73	72	71	216	5,000
Dale Douglass	71	70	75	216	5,000
David Graham	69	69	78	216	5,000
Mike Hill	71	74	71	216	5,000
Orville Moody	72	71	73	216	5,000

American Express Invitational

TPC at Prestancia, Sarasota, Florida
Par 36-36–72; 6,933 yards

February 12-14
purse, $1,200,000

	SCORES			TOTAL	MONEY
Bruce Fleisher	67	67	69	203	$180,000
Larry Nelson	69	70	67	206	105,600
Walter Hall	68	73	66	207	86,400
Tom Wargo	68	69	72	209	72,000
Bob Charles	72	69	69	210	57,600
Bob Murphy	68	72	72	212	43,200
Bruce Summerhays	65	75	72	212	43,200
Jim Thorpe	68	70	74	212	43,200
Bob Dickson	69	73	71	213	32,400
Dana Quigley	69	70	74	213	32,400

	SCORES			TOTAL	MONEY
Hugh Baiocchi	67	73	74	214	26,400
Mike Hill	68	74	72	214	26,400
Gil Morgan	75	71	68	214	26,400
John Bland	71	73	71	215	20,400
Vicente Fernandez	69	73	73	215	20,400
Gibby Gilbert	73	71	71	215	20,400
Lee Trevino	71	74	70	215	20,400
Tom Weiskopf	76	71	68	215	20,400
Jim Albus	67	74	75	216	13,845
Jose Maria Canizares	72	69	75	216	13,845
Jim Colbert	69	75	72	216	13,845
David Graham	71	70	75	216	13,845
Hale Irwin	69	74	73	216	13,845
John Jacobs	71	75	70	216	13,845
Walter Morgan	75	73	68	216	13,845
J.C. Snead	71	74	71	216	13,845
Jim Dent	74	73	70	217	10,200
Dale Douglass	71	70	76	217	10,200
Hubert Green	70	72	75	217	10,200
Tom McGinnis	68	75	74	217	10,200
Brian Barnes	70	76	72	218	8,280
Ed Dougherty	72	75	71	218	8,280
John Mahaffey	73	73	72	218	8,280
Bobby Nichols	70	76	72	218	8,280
Chi Chi Rodriguez	70	76	72	218	8,280
Tommy Aaron	74	77	68	219	6,624
Allen Doyle	74	72	73	219	6,624
Dave Eichelberger	72	75	72	219	6,624
Jay Sigel	73	75	71	219	6,624
Howard Twitty	72	75	72	219	6,624

GTE Classic

TPC of Tampa Bay, Lutz, Florida
Par 35-36–71; 6,638 yards

February 19-21
purse, $1,200,000

	SCORES			TOTAL	MONEY
Larry Nelson	70	68	67	205	$180,000
Bruce Fleisher	70	70	67	207	105,600
Graham Marsh	73	69	66	208	86,400
Jim Dent	72	67	70	209	64,800
Hale Irwin	70	69	70	209	64,800
John Bland	71	69	70	210	45,600
J.C. Snead	73	71	66	210	45,600
David Graham	74	69	68	211	36,000
Lee Trevino	71	70	70	211	36,000
Hugh Baiocchi	71	72	69	212	30,000
Bob Murphy	72	69	71	212	30,000
Allen Doyle	73	72	68	213	26,400
Gibby Gilbert	69	71	74	214	22,800
Hubert Green	73	71	70	214	22,800
Leonard Thompson	70	73	71	214	22,800
Jose Maria Canizares	77	72	66	215	17,022.86
Bob Dickson	76	71	68	215	17,022.86
Terry Dill	73	73	69	215	17,022.86
Mike Hill	70	74	71	215	17,022.86
Walter Morgan	70	73	72	215	17,022.86

	SCORES			TOTAL	MONEY
George Archer	69	74	72	215	17,022.85
Walter Hall	72	68	75	215	17,022.85
Jim Albus	71	75	70	216	12,600
Dave Eichelberger	71	75	70	216	12,600
Gary Player	71	73	72	216	12,600
Brian Barnes	76	72	69	217	10,200
Dale Douglass	76	71	70	217	10,200
Vicente Fernandez	73	74	70	217	10,200
Raymond Floyd	74	72	71	217	10,200
Al Geiberger	70	74	73	217	10,200
Jim Thorpe	72	75	70	217	10,200
Butch Baird	73	70	75	218	8,100
John Mahaffey	75	71	72	218	8,100
Orville Moody	77	72	69	218	8,100
Larry Ziegler	73	74	71	218	8,100
Simon Hobday	73	72	74	219	6,750
Jim Holtgrieve	74	71	74	219	6,750
Jay Sigel	75	72	72	219	6,750
Kermit Zarley	75	69	75	219	6,750
Frank Conner	72	73	75	220	5,280
Joe Inman	72	75	73	220	5,280
John Jacobs	71	73	76	220	5,280
Gil Morgan	72	72	76	220	5,280
Barney Thompson	71	77	72	220	5,280
Tom Wargo	77	71	72	220	5,280
Tom Weiskopf	74	72	74	220	5,280
Walter Zembriski	76	73	71	220	5,280

ACE Group Classic

Bay Colony Golf Club, Naples, Florida
Par 36-36–72; 6,915 yards

February 26-28
purse, $1,200,000

	SCORES			TOTAL	MONEY
Allen Doyle	64	70	69	203	$180,000
Vicente Fernandez	65	71	72	208	105,600
George Archer	69	69	71	209	66,000
Graham Marsh	67	69	73	209	66,000
Larry Nelson	67	71	71	209	66,000
Bruce Summerhays	70	73	66	209	66,000
Isao Aoki	73	68	69	210	36,600
Jose Maria Canizares	69	73	68	210	36,600
Walter Hall	70	70	70	210	36,600
John Mahaffey	74	69	67	210	36,600
Jim Albus	72	68	71	211	25,500
Tom Jenkins	69	73	69	211	25,500
Mike McCullough	68	73	70	211	25,500
J.C. Snead	71	72	68	211	25,500
Hugh Baiocchi	67	69	76	212	19,800
Dave Eichelberger	73	72	67	212	19,800
Gibby Gilbert	68	73	71	212	19,800
David Lundstrom	73	67	72	212	19,800
Brian Barnes	73	69	71	213	14,560
Al Geiberger	71	71	71	213	14,560
Orville Moody	72	72	69	213	14,560
Dave Stockton	70	74	69	213	14,560
Leonard Thompson	69	73	71	213	14,560

	SCORES			TOTAL	MONEY
Jim Thorpe	73	73	67	213	14,560
Bud Allin	72	73	69	214	11,190
Hubert Green	74	69	71	214	11,190
Walter Morgan	71	71	72	214	11,190
Bobby Stroble	70	72	72	214	11,190
Bob Dickson	74	72	69	215	8,691.43
Bob Duval	71	72	72	215	8,691.43
Bob Murphy	69	74	72	215	8,691.43
Dana Quigley	73	72	70	215	8,691.43
Rocky Thompson	73	70	72	215	8,691.43
Larry Ziegler	73	71	71	215	8,691.43
John Bland	71	71	73	215	8,691.42
Frank Conner	70	75	71	216	6,750
Raymond Floyd	71	73	72	216	6,750
Joe Inman	70	75	71	216	6,750
Gil Morgan	71	72	73	216	6,750
John Calabria	71	74	72	217	5,520
Jim Dent	73	72	72	217	5,520
Fred Gibson	72	76	69	217	5,520
Simon Hobday	75	73	69	217	5,520
Jim Holtgrieve	71	77	69	217	5,520
John Jacobs	71	77	69	217	5,520

Senior Slam

Cabo Real Golf Club, Cabo San Lucas, Mexico
Par 36-36–72; 6,945 yards

March 6-7
purse, $600,000

	SCORES		TOTAL	MONEY
Gil Morgan	67	65	132	$300,000
Hale Irwin	65	69	134	150,000
Larry Nelson	68	71	139	75,000
Jay Sigel	73	66	139	75,000

Toshiba Senior Classic

Newport Beach Country Club,
Newport Beach, California
Par 35-35–70; 6,307 yards

March 12-14
purse, $1,200,000

	SCORES			TOTAL	MONEY
Gary McCord	67	68	69	204	$180,000
Allen Doyle	68	68	68	204	88,000
Al Geiberger	69	66	69	204	88,000
John Jacobs	67	67	70	204	88,000
(McCord won on fifth extra hole.)					
David Lundstrom	70	68	67	205	52,800
Dana Quigley	68	67	70	205	52,800
George Archer	71	67	68	206	43,200
Bob Duval	68	70	69	207	30,400
Walter Hall	69	68	70	207	30,400
Tom Jenkins	67	70	70	207	30,400
John Mahaffey	71	69	67	207	30,400
Tom McGinnis	69	69	69	207	30,400
Chi Chi Rodriguez	73	67	67	207	30,400

	SCORES			TOTAL	MONEY
John Bland	70	71	67	208	21,600
Hale Irwin	68	69	71	208	21,600
Bruce Summerhays	67	72	69	208	21,600
Butch Baird	69	70	70	209	16,460
Bob Dickson	73	69	67	209	16,460
Gil Morgan	68	70	71	209	16,460
Gary Player	71	69	69	209	16,460
Jay Sigel	70	68	71	209	16,460
Dave Stockton	74	66	69	209	16,460
Jim Albus	68	72	70	210	12,600
J.C. Snead	73	70	67	210	12,600
Howard Twitty	68	73	69	210	12,600
Bob Murphy	70	72	69	211	9,977.15
Rocky Thompson	73	69	69	211	9,977.15
Charles Coody	73	67	71	211	9,977.14
Terry Dill	69	72	70	211	9,977.14
Hubert Green	71	68	72	211	9,977.14
Mike McCullough	72	68	71	211	9,977.14
DeWitt Weaver	73	69	69	211	9,977.14
Gay Brewer	71	72	69	212	7,740
Dale Douglass	74	71	67	212	7,740
Lee Trevino	72	69	71	212	7,740
Tom Wargo	68	69	75	212	7,740
Ray Carrasco	72	72	69	213	6,720
Jim Thorpe	71	71	71	213	6,720
Frank Conner	69	75	70	214	6,000
Bill Hall	70	73	71	214	6,000
Joe Inman	70	72	72	214	6,000
Graham Marsh	70	68	76	214	6,000

Liberty Mutual Legends of Golf

The Slammer & the Squire, St. Augustine, Florida
Par 36-36–72; 6,911 yards

March 19-21
purse, $1,610,000

	SCORES			TOTAL	MONEY (Each)
Hubert Green/Gil Morgan	61	67	66	194	$158,000
John Mahaffey/Tom Wargo	63	70	64	197	91,000
Gibby Gilbert/J.C. Snead	68	67	65	200	53,500
David Graham/Jay Sigel	62	69	69	200	53,500
Butch Baird/Homero Blancas	68	66	68	202	30,500
Mike Hill/Lee Trevino	67	68	67	202	30,500
John Bland/Graham Marsh	66	68	69	203	19,500
George Archer/Simon Hobday	65	67	71	203	19,500
Charles Coody/Dale Douglass	68	68	68	204	16,000
Al Geiberger/Tom Shaw	65	69	70	204	16,000
Dave Hill/Bobby Nichols	67	70	68	205	13,500
Harold Henning/Chi Chi Rodriguez	69	67	69	205	13,500
Tony Jacklin/Larry Ziegler	66	67	72	205	13,500
Jim Dent/Calvin Peete	69	66	71	206	10,666.67
Don January/Gene Littler	67	67	72	206	10,666.67
Bud Allin/Jerry Heard	67	67	72	206	10,666.66
Larry Mowry/Ken Still	69	72	66	207	8,500
Bruce Devlin/Don Massengale	68	69	70	207	8,500
Jim Albus/Larry Laoretti	68	68	71	207	8,500
Tommy Aaron/Don Bies	67	69	71	207	8,500
Orville Moody/Jimmy Powell	65	69	73	207	8,500

	SCORES			TOTAL	MONEY (Each)
Tommy Jacobs/Bob Toski	70	68	70	208	7,000
Miller Barber/Jim Ferree	71	68	71	210	6,500
Gay Brewer/Billy Casper	69	74	70	213	6,000
Billy Maxwell/Mason Rudolph	74	74	78	226	5,500
Lee Elder/Lou Graham	79	72	76	227	4,750
Dow Finsterwald/Doug Sanders	75	74	78	227	4,750

Emerald Coast Classic

The Moors Golf Club, Milton, Florida
Par 36-36–72; 6,843 yards

March 26-28
purse, $1,100,000

	SCORES			TOTAL	MONEY
Bob Duval	61	68	71	200	$165,000
Bruce Fleisher	68	67	67	202	96,800
Buzz Thomas	65	67	72	204	79,200
Walter Hall	70	68	69	207	66,000
George Archer	71	69	68	208	45,466.67
John Bland	74	66	68	208	45,466.67
John Mahaffey	68	68	72	208	45,466.66
John Jacobs	72	68	69	209	33,000
Tom Jenkins	73	65	71	209	33,000
J.C. Snead	71	68	71	210	26,400
Bruce Summerhays	72	69	69	210	26,400
Kermit Zarley	68	69	73	210	26,400
Terry Dill	72	69	70	211	22,000
Jim Albus	75	73	64	212	18,700
Brian Barnes	73	69	70	212	18,700
Allen Doyle	70	70	72	212	18,700
David Graham	72	69	71	212	18,700
Tom McGinnis	70	69	73	212	18,700
Jim Dent	73	70	70	213	12,691.25
Gary McCord	71	71	71	213	12,691.25
Walter Morgan	70	66	77	213	12,691.25
Dana Quigley	70	69	74	213	12,691.25
Dave Stockton	72	69	72	213	12,691.25
Jim Thorpe	73	69	71	213	12,691.25
Howard Twitty	74	69	70	213	12,691.25
Tom Wargo	73	68	72	213	12,691.25
Bob Murphy	76	70	68	214	8,928.34
Leonard Thompson	76	72	66	214	8,928.34
Bob Eastwood	72	69	73	214	8,928.33
Al Geiberger	72	69	73	214	8,928.33
Fred Gibson	71	71	72	214	8,928.33
Bobby Stroble	73	73	68	214	8,928.33
Hugh Baiocchi	74	73	68	215	7,095
Bob Dickson	72	73	70	215	7,095
Dale Douglass	74	70	71	215	7,095
Vicente Fernandez	72	70	73	215	7,095
Jose Maria Canizares	73	70	73	216	5,500
Dave Eichelberger	77	70	69	216	5,500
Jim Ferree	72	76	68	216	5,500
Jim Holtgrieve	72	69	75	216	5,500
Graham Marsh	73	73	70	216	5,500
Paul Reed	77	66	73	216	5,500
Tom Shaw	77	67	72	216	5,500
Rocky Thompson	71	72	73	216	5,500

The Tradition

Golf Club at Desert Mountain, Cochise Course,
Scottsdale, Arizona
Par 36-36–72; 6,998 yards
(Shortened to 36 holes — snow.)

April 1-4
purse, $1,500,000

	SCORES		TOTAL	MONEY
Graham Marsh	69	67	136	$225,000
Larry Nelson	73	66	139	132,000
Vicente Fernandez	70	70	140	99,000
Leonard Thompson	70	70	140	99,000
Bob Duval	73	68	141	66,000
Gary McCord	73	68	141	66,000
John Morgan	71	71	142	51,000
Jim Thorpe	73	69	142	51,000
Brian Barnes	74	69	143	37,500
John Bland	71	72	143	37,500
Terry Dill	72	71	143	37,500
Howard Twitty	69	74	143	37,500
Tom Jenkins	73	71	144	30,000
George Archer	71	74	145	24,775
Mike McCullough	70	75	145	24,775
Walter Morgan	74	71	145	24,775
Bob Murphy	76	69	145	24,775
J.C. Snead	74	71	145	24,775
Bruce Summerhays	72	73	145	24,775
Raymond Floyd	76	70	146	16,757.15
Fred Gibson	76	70	146	16,757.15
Jose Maria Canizares	76	70	146	16,757.14
Al Geiberger	75	71	146	16,757.14
Hale Irwin	72	74	146	16,757.14
David Lundstrom	74	72	146	16,757.14
Dave Stockton	73	73	146	16,757.14
Bruce Fleisher	76	71	147	13,650
Isao Aoki	75	73	148	11,137.50
Frank Conner	76	72	148	11,137.50
Bob Dickson	75	73	148	11,137.50
Dale Douglass	71	77	148	11,137.50
John Mahaffey	77	71	148	11,137.50
Noel Ratcliffe	73	75	148	11,137.50
Jay Sigel	74	74	148	11,137.50
Tom Wargo	74	74	148	11,137.50
Dave Eichelberger	77	72	149	8,437.50
Alberto Giannone	78	71	149	8,437.50
John Jacobs	75	74	149	8,437.50
Dana Quigley	71	78	149	8,437.50
Butch Baird	80	70	150	7,050
Walter Hall	77	73	150	7,050
Simon Hobday	72	78	150	7,050
Mike Malone	73	77	150	7,050
Rocky Thompson	78	72	150	7,050

PGA Seniors' Championship

PGA National Golf Club, Champion Course,
Palm Beach Gardens, Florida
Par 36-36–72; 6,869 yards

April 15-18
purse, $1,750,000

	SCORES				TOTAL	MONEY
Allen Doyle	71	71	68	64	274	$315,000
Vicente Fernandez	70	65	71	70	276	189,000
Jose Maria Canizares	68	71	68	72	279	101,500
Bruce Fleisher	70	70	66	73	279	101,500
Dana Quigley	71	68	71	70	280	61,000
Bruce Summerhays	66	70	74	70	280	61,000
Hugh Baiocchi	72	74	66	69	281	54,000
John Jacobs	69	70	72	71	282	47,000
J.C. Snead	72	68	71	71	282	47,000
Larry Ziegler	70	70	72	70	282	47,000
Ed Dougherty	72	72	69	70	283	36,500
Joe Inman	76	67	69	71	283	36,500
Hale Irwin	75	69	70	69	283	36,500
Gil Morgan	72	71	72	68	283	36,500
Isao Aoki	73	73	69	70	285	28,000
Bob Dickson	69	72	72	72	285	28,000
Lee Trevino	71	74	72	68	285	28,000
Gibby Gilbert	73	67	70	76	286	21,250
John Mahaffey	72	73	70	71	286	21,250
Graham Marsh	71	75	70	70	286	21,250
Tom Weiskopf	71	74	69	72	286	21,250
George Archer	75	70	72	70	287	17,500
Jay Sigel	75	72	70	70	287	17,500
Terry Dill	69	74	71	74	288	14,000
Raymond Floyd	74	70	69	75	288	14,000
Tom Jenkins	71	71	73	73	288	14,000
Mike McCullough	71	71	73	73	288	14,000
Orville Moody	70	73	72	73	288	14,000
Frank Conner	72	71	73	73	289	11,250
John Morgan	71	76	69	73	289	11,250
Jim Colbert	73	70	73	74	290	10,500
Bob Charles	76	67	75	73	291	9,750
Dave Stockton	73	72	70	76	291	9,750
Jim Dent	73	74	71	74	292	8,220
Bob Duval	77	71	69	75	292	8,220
Tommy Horton	74	71	74	73	292	8,220
Toru Nakayama	78	68	72	74	292	8,220
Jim Thorpe	74	70	74	74	292	8,220
Jim Albus	75	73	71	74	293	6,750
Hubert Green	75	71	74	73	293	6,750
Bob Murphy	78	70	71	74	293	6,750
Tom Wargo	76	72	76	69	293	6,750

Home Depot Invitational

TPC at Piper Glen, Charlotte, North Carolina
Par 36-36–72; 6,883 yards

April 23-25
purse, $1,200,000

	SCORES			TOTAL	MONEY
Bruce Fleisher	69	67	69	205	$180,000
Terry Dill	68	68	70	206	96,000

	SCORES			TOTAL	MONEY
Jim Holtgrieve	70	67	69	206	96,000
Allen Doyle	68	68	71	207	59,200
Christy O'Connor, Jr.	72	70	65	207	59,200
DeWitt Weaver	73	65	69	207	59,200
Vicente Fernandez	70	71	67	208	40,800
Kermit Zarley	67	73	68	208	40,800
Tom Jenkins	70	72	67	209	31,200
Walter Morgan	69	73	67	209	31,200
Jay Sigel	67	73	69	209	31,200
Hubert Green	70	72	68	210	24,400
Mike Hill	70	69	71	210	24,400
Howard Twitty	73	67	70	210	24,400
Bob Duval	72	69	70	211	21,600
Frank Conner	69	71	72	212	17,022.86
Joe Inman	71	71	70	212	17,022.86
Bruce Summerhays	68	72	72	212	17,022.86
Leonard Thompson	73	70	69	212	17,022.86
Jim Thorpe	71	71	70	212	17,022.86
Isao Aoki	69	70	73	212	17,022.85
Bob Dickson	67	72	73	212	17,022.85
Graham Marsh	70	71	72	213	12,900
Dana Quigley	70	70	73	213	12,900
Fred Gibson	74	68	72	214	11,440
David Graham	74	68	72	214	11,440
John Jacobs	72	71	71	214	11,440
John Bland	71	72	72	215	9,102.86
Jose Maria Canizares	73	72	70	215	9,102.86
John Mahaffey	74	71	70	215	9,102.86
Mike McCullough	71	72	72	215	9,102.86
J.C. Snead	68	74	73	215	9,102.86
Mike Malone	70	72	73	215	9,102.85
Lee Trevino	74	68	73	215	9,102.85
Bob Charles	73	72	71	216	7,380
Larry Nelson	72	70	74	216	7,380
Tommy Aaron	75	69	73	217	6,720
John Schroeder	74	70	73	217	6,720
Hugh Baiocchi	74	72	72	218	5,640
Jim Dent	74	70	74	218	5,640
Walter Hall	70	71	77	218	5,640
Simon Hobday	74	72	72	218	5,640
Larry Mowry	74	70	74	218	5,640
Tom Shaw	73	69	76	218	5,640
Walter Zembriski	73	71	74	218	5,640

Bruno's Memorial Classic

Greystone Golf Club, Hoover, Alabama
Par 36-36–72; 6,896 yards

April 30-May 2
purse, $1,200,000

	SCORES			TOTAL	MONEY
Larry Nelson	70	67	68	205	$180,000
Dana Quigley	72	68	66	206	105,600
Gil Morgan	71	68	68	207	86,400
Joe Inman	69	68	71	208	72,000
J.C. Snead	73	69	69	211	52,800
Leonard Thompson	72	68	71	211	52,800
Bob Duval	67	73	72	212	40,800

	SCORES			TOTAL	MONEY
John Mahaffey	74	69	69	212	40,800
George Archer	73	75	65	213	27,800
Bob Charles	73	65	75	213	27,800
Al Geiberger	73	68	72	213	27,800
Mike Hill	69	69	75	213	27,800
Jay Sigel	70	71	72	213	27,800
Bruce Summerhays	71	71	71	213	27,800
Graham Marsh	70	71	73	214	20,400
Mike McCullough	73	70	71	214	20,400
Tom Shaw	71	78	65	214	20,400
Brian Barnes	72	71	72	215	14,670
John Bland	72	73	70	215	14,670
Bruce Fleisher	75	67	73	215	14,670
Walter Hall	69	73	73	215	14,670
Simon Hobday	71	69	75	215	14,670
Hale Irwin	72	71	72	215	14,670
John Jacobs	74	70	71	215	14,670
Jimmy Powell	74	71	70	215	14,670
Tommy Aaron	69	71	76	216	9,360
Jim Ahern	71	73	72	216	9,360
Jim Albus	72	72	72	216	9,360
Bill Brask	75	73	68	216	9,360
Bob Dickson	74	69	73	216	9,360
Bob Eastwood	74	73	69	216	9,360
Vicente Fernandez	70	74	72	216	9,360
David Graham	73	71	72	216	9,360
Hubert Green	74	70	72	216	9,360
Bob Murphy	71	70	75	216	9,360
Barney Thompson	75	73	69	217	6,377.15
Larry Ziegler	69	78	70	217	6,377.15
Jose Maria Canizares	71	74	72	217	6,377.14
Jim Colbert	72	75	70	217	6,377.14
Frank Conner	73	70	74	217	6,377.14
Dave Eichelberger	71	72	74	217	6,377.14
Jim Thorpe	72	73	72	217	6,377.14

Nationwide Championship

Golf Club of Georgia, Lakeside Course, Alpharetta, Georgia
Par 36-36–72; 6,885 yards

May 7-9
purse, $1,400,000

	SCORES			TOTAL	MONEY
Hale Irwin	69	68	69	206	$210,000
Bob Murphy	70	70	68	208	123,200
Jose Maria Canizares	70	69	70	209	92,400
Christy O'Connor, Jr.	72	69	68	209	92,400
Mike McCullough	72	71	68	211	67,200
Tom Jenkins	74	70	68	212	56,000
Joe Inman	73	70	70	213	44,800
Gary McCord	71	69	73	213	44,800
Leonard Thompson	69	77	67	213	44,800
Allen Doyle	70	69	75	214	33,600
Bruce Summerhays	72	69	73	214	33,600
Kermit Zarley	69	75	70	214	33,600
George Archer	68	74	73	215	21,882
Hugh Baiocchi	73	70	72	215	21,882
Jim Dent	72	71	72	215	21,882

	SCORES			TOTAL	MONEY
Bob Eastwood	71	75	69	215	21,882
Dave Eichelberger	72	70	73	215	21,882
Bruce Fleisher	72	74	69	215	21,882
Gibby Gilbert	72	70	73	215	21,882
Simon Hobday	69	75	71	215	21,882
Graham Marsh	68	72	75	215	21,882
Walter Morgan	71	72	72	215	21,882
Raymond Floyd	76	69	71	216	14,700
John Mahaffey	71	75	70	216	14,700
J.C. Snead	77	73	66	216	14,700
Isao Aoki	74	75	68	217	12,180
Don Bies	74	70	73	217	12,180
Alberto Giannone	73	72	72	217	12,180
Jim Holtgrieve	70	71	76	217	12,180
Larry Mowry	73	71	73	217	12,180
Butch Baird	74	73	71	218	9,660
John Bland	74	75	69	218	9,660
Orville Moody	74	73	71	218	9,660
Larry Nelson	73	73	72	218	9,660
Larry Ziegler	76	75	67	218	9,660
Frank Conner	71	78	70	219	7,583.34
Mike Hill	73	76	70	219	7,583.34
Brian Barnes	70	72	77	219	7,583.33
Bob Charles	72	76	71	219	7,583.33
Sid Corliss	74	72	73	219	7,583.33
Vicente Fernandez	70	75	74	219	7,583.33

Las Vegas Senior Classic

Las Vegas, Nevada
TPC at Summerlin: Par 36-36–72; 6,909 yards
TPC at The Canyons: Par 36-35–71; 6,839 yards

May 13-16
purse, $1,400,000

	SCORES				TOTAL	MONEY
Vicente Fernandez	69	71	67	67	274	$210,000
Dave Eichelberger	69	71	68	68	276	123,200
John Mahaffey	72	72	66	67	277	100,800
Frank Conner	70	69	69	70	278	75,600
Tom Wargo	73	70	66	69	278	75,600
Hale Irwin	70	72	68	69	279	56,000
John Jacobs	71	72	66	71	280	50,400
Fred Gibson	69	71	66	75	281	44,800
Ed Dougherty	72	71	70	69	282	36,400
Walter Hall	77	67	69	69	282	36,400
Larry Nelson	72	73	66	71	282	36,400
Leonard Thompson	68	73	71	71	283	29,400
Lee Trevino	71	67	71	74	283	29,400
Isao Aoki	65	75	68	76	284	26,600
Allen Doyle	69	75	72	69	285	25,200
Jim Albus	78	64	71	73	286	22,400
Jose Maria Canizares	71	71	69	75	286	22,400
Jim Thorpe	70	74	71	71	286	22,400
Bob Duval	70	72	71	74	287	18,526.67
Barney Thompson	72	74	72	69	287	18,526.67
Rocky Thompson	72	74	66	75	287	18,526.66
Bud Allin	73	73	68	74	288	15,085
Miller Barber	73	71	72	72	288	15,085

	SCORES				TOTAL	MONEY
Tom Jenkins	73	69	71	75	288	15,085
Bob Murphy	78	67	70	73	288	15,085
Butch Baird	74	72	73	70	289	12,460
Terry Dill	72	76	68	73	289	12,460
Alberto Giannone	76	74	70	69	289	12,460
David Graham	70	77	70	72	289	12,460
David Lundstrom	70	79	69	72	290	10,546.67
DeWitt Weaver	68	75	75	72	290	10,546.67
George Archer	76	72	69	73	290	10,546.66
Bob Eastwood	75	74	70	72	291	8,633.34
Howard Twitty	77	73	72	69	291	8,633.34
Hubert Green	74	70	71	76	291	8,633.33
John Schroeder	70	73	75	73	291	8,633.33
Bruce Summerhays	70	72	73	76	291	8,633.33
Kermit Zarley	71	75	70	75	291	8,633.33
Bob Charles	74	70	75	73	292	6,860
Raymond Floyd	78	71	71	72	292	6,860
Mike McCullough	67	79	71	75	292	6,860
Jay Sigel	73	77	70	72	292	6,860
Dave Stockton	66	74	75	77	292	6,860

Bell Atlantic Classic

Hartefeld National Golf Club, Avondale, Pennsylvania   May 21-23
Par 36-36–72; 6,911 yards   purse, $1,100,000

	SCORES			TOTAL	MONEY
Tom Jenkins	70	67	69	206	$165,000
Jim Thorpe	68	73	65	206	96,800
(Jenkins defeated Thorpe on first extra hole.)					
Gil Morgan	71	67	69	207	72,600
Rocky Thompson	68	70	69	207	72,600
Jim Colbert	71	68	69	208	48,400
John Mahaffey	69	71	68	208	48,400
Jesse Patino	70	68	71	209	39,600
Jose Maria Canizares	70	73	67	210	30,250
Bob Charles	69	70	71	210	30,250
Ed Dougherty	70	71	69	210	30,250
Dana Quigley	74	70	66	210	30,250
David Graham	72	72	67	211	24,200
Joe Inman	73	69	70	212	20,900
Jay Sigel	70	73	69	212	20,900
Buzz Thomas	72	73	67	212	20,900
Frank Conner	66	75	72	213	18,150
Jim Holtgrieve	68	72	73	213	18,150
Jack Nicklaus	74	70	70	214	16,500
Jim Albus	70	75	70	215	14,107.50
Bob Eastwood	75	68	72	215	14,107.50
John Grace	72	72	71	215	14,107.50
Mike McCullough	70	75	70	215	14,107.50
Walter Morgan	70	76	70	216	11,825
Noel Ratcliffe	71	74	71	216	11,825
Dave Eichelberger	76	71	70	217	9,808.34
John Morgan	72	74	71	217	9,808.34
Hugh Baiocchi	73	72	72	217	9,808.33
Terry Dill	71	73	73	217	9,808.33
David Lundstrom	70	74	73	217	9,808.33

	SCORES			TOTAL	MONEY
Bobby Stroble	74	72	71	217	9,808.33
Rik Massengale	78	71	69	218	8,085
Barney Thompson	70	73	75	218	8,085
Bud Allin	73	72	74	219	7,260
Charles Coody	76	73	70	219	7,260
Dan Wood	70	75	74	219	7,260
Walter Hall	72	76	72	220	5,845.72
Tom McGinnis	72	76	72	220	5,845.72
John Schroeder	71	77	72	220	5,845.72
Tommy Aaron	71	76	73	220	5,845.71
Don Bies	75	72	73	220	5,845.71
Bobby Cole	74	71	75	220	5,845.71
Bob Wynn	75	71	74	220	5,845.71

Boone Valley Classic

Boone Valley Golf Club, Augusta, Missouri
Par 36-36–72; 6,731 yards

May 28-30
purse, $1,400,000

	SCORES			TOTAL	MONEY
Hale Irwin	68	69	66	203	$210,000
Al Geiberger	67	70	68	205	123,200
Kermit Zarley	70	66	70	206	100,800
Allen Doyle	67	71	69	207	84,000
Jose Maria Canizares	71	69	68	208	54,600
Jim Dent	66	70	72	208	54,600
Dana Quigley	69	69	70	208	54,600
Bruce Summerhays	67	68	73	208	54,600
John Jacobs	67	74	68	209	37,800
Tom Jenkins	69	68	72	209	37,800
David Lundstrom	66	72	72	210	29,750
Mike McCullough	69	70	71	210	29,750
Larry Nelson	71	67	72	210	29,750
Rocky Thompson	67	72	71	210	29,750
Frank Conner	73	63	75	211	21,140
Bob Duval	69	72	70	211	21,140
Bruce Fleisher	70	72	69	211	21,140
Walter Hall	71	69	71	211	21,140
Joe Inman	69	71	71	211	21,140
Chi Chi Rodriguez	72	72	67	211	21,140
Dave Stockton	74	69	68	211	21,140
Terry Dill	71	72	69	212	14,396.67
Graham Marsh	71	72	69	212	14,396.67
Gary Player	72	72	68	212	14,396.67
Tom Wargo	69	72	71	212	14,396.67
Christy O'Connor, Jr.	67	73	72	212	14,396.66
Tom Shaw	70	66	76	212	14,396.66
Tommy Aaron	66	75	72	213	11,620
George Archer	69	71	73	213	11,620
John Bland	73	73	67	213	11,620
Brian Barnes	65	74	75	214	9,870
Walter Morgan	70	71	73	214	9,870
Leonard Thompson	71	69	74	214	9,870
Jim Thorpe	73	71	70	214	9,870
Ed Dougherty	71	70	74	215	7,910
Mike Malone	70	74	71	215	7,910
John Morgan	72	72	71	215	7,910

	SCORES			TOTAL	MONEY
Larry Mowry	72	70	73	215	7,910
Jesse Patino	70	74	71	215	7,910
Barney Thompson	67	76	72	215	7,910

Cadillac NFL Classic

Upper Montclair Country Club, Clifton, New Jersey
Par 36-36–72; 6,816 yards

June 4-6
purse, $1,100,000

	SCORES			TOTAL	MONEY
Allen Doyle	67	66	71	204	$165,000
Joe Inman	67	71	66	204	96,800
(Doyle defeated Inman on fourth extra hole.)					
Lee Trevino	67	70	69	206	79,200
Raymond Floyd	72	69	67	208	59,400
Mike McCullough	71	68	69	208	59,400
Bob Charles	67	71	71	209	44,000
Tom Jenkins	71	71	68	210	37,400
Dana Quigley	74	65	71	210	37,400
Walter Hall	73	69	69	211	27,500
Jay Sigel	70	69	72	211	27,500
J.C. Snead	71	71	69	211	27,500
Tom Wargo	72	68	71	211	27,500
Ed Dougherty	70	72	70	212	18,715.72
Graham Marsh	73	72	67	212	18,715.72
Tom Shaw	72	71	69	212	18,715.72
Hubert Green	70	70	72	212	18,715.71
Jesse Patino	73	67	72	212	18,715.71
Bruce Summerhays	72	70	70	212	18,715.71
Howard Twitty	73	69	70	212	18,715.71
John Bland	70	68	75	213	13,640
John Mahaffey	73	69	71	213	13,640
Dave Stockton	72	72	69	213	13,640
Dave Eichelberger	73	70	71	214	11,275
Jim Holtgrieve	69	75	70	214	11,275
Leonard Thompson	73	71	70	214	11,275
Jim Thorpe	73	69	72	214	11,275
Jim Albus	74	73	69	216	9,350
Bud Allin	72	70	74	216	9,350
Bruce Fleisher	71	72	73	216	9,350
John Schroeder	72	70	74	216	9,350
Bob Dickson	70	74	73	217	7,425
Tom McGinnis	67	72	78	217	7,425
Chi Chi Rodriguez	71	72	74	217	7,425
Barney Thompson	74	72	71	217	7,425
Evan Williams	75	72	70	217	7,425
Kermit Zarley	70	73	74	217	7,425
Alberto Giannone	72	73	73	218	5,940
Hiro Kazami	71	76	71	218	5,940
Mike Malone	70	75	73	218	5,940
Noel Ratcliffe	76	66	76	218	5,940

BellSouth Senior Classic

Springhouse Golf Club, Nashville, Tennessee
Par 36-36–72; 6,783 yards

June 11-13
purse, $1,400,000

	SCORES			TOTAL	MONEY
Bruce Fleisher	71	63	66	200	$210,000
Al Geiberger	67	68	66	201	123,200
Tom Jenkins	69	69	64	202	84,000
Gil Morgan	67	68	67	202	84,000
Bruce Summerhays	71	66	65	202	84,000
Jim Albus	65	70	68	203	53,200
Gary McCord	70	68	65	203	53,200
Kermit Zarley	68	71	66	205	40,133.34
Dana Quigley	71	67	67	205	40,133.33
Jim Thorpe	68	67	70	205	40,133.33
Hugh Baiocchi	68	68	70	206	29,750
Vicente Fernandez	69	67	70	206	29,750
David Lundstrom	66	68	72	206	29,750
John Mahaffey	67	71	68	206	29,750
Larry Nelson	72	70	65	207	25,200
Bob Eastwood	69	72	67	208	23,100
Howard Twitty	66	75	67	208	23,100
Jim Ahern	69	70	70	209	19,740
Jose Maria Canizares	69	72	68	209	19,740
Lee Trevino	71	70	68	209	19,740
Frank Conner	72	72	66	210	15,540
Bob Dickson	69	71	70	210	15,540
Terry Dill	69	72	69	210	15,540
Jay Sigel	68	70	72	210	15,540
DeWitt Weaver	71	65	74	210	15,540
Dale Douglass	73	69	69	211	11,392.50
Dave Eichelberger	69	72	70	211	11,392.50
Gibby Gilbert	72	69	70	211	11,392.50
Hale Irwin	68	70	73	211	11,392.50
Barry Jaeckel	71	70	70	211	11,392.50
Mike McCullough	72	68	71	211	11,392.50
Gary Player	71	70	70	211	11,392.50
Tom Shaw	71	70	70	211	11,392.50
Tommy Aaron	70	72	70	212	8,260
Bob Charles	70	70	72	212	8,260
Joe Inman	67	76	69	212	8,260
Tom McGinnis	70	72	70	212	8,260
Larry Mowry	71	71	70	212	8,260
Leonard Thompson	75	70	67	212	8,260
George Archer	71	72	70	213	6,020
Butch Baird	68	73	72	213	6,020
Don Bies	74	68	71	213	6,020
Harold Henning	67	76	70	213	6,020
Mike Hill	73	71	69	213	6,020
Graham Marsh	74	70	69	213	6,020
Walter Morgan	75	69	69	213	6,020
Jimmy Powell	71	72	70	213	6,020
Larry Ziegler	69	72	72	213	6,020

Southwestern Bell Dominion

Dominion Country Club, San Antonio, Texas
Par 36-36–72; 6,814 yards

June 18-20
purse, $1,100,000

	SCORES			TOTAL	MONEY
John Mahaffey	67	67	70	204	$165,000
Jose Maria Canizares	70	67	67	204	88,000
Bruce Fleisher	67	68	69	204	88,000
(Mahaffey defeated Fleisher on first and Canizares on second extra hole.)					
Larry Nelson	71	67	67	205	66,000
Tom Jenkins	67	70	69	206	48,400
Gil Morgan	70	65	71	206	48,400
Vicente Fernandez	67	70	70	207	37,400
Walter Hall	66	71	70	207	37,400
Fred Gibson	68	68	72	208	29,700
Tom McGinnis	68	72	68	208	29,700
Frank Conner	71	71	67	209	25,300
Dana Quigley	67	73	69	209	25,300
Hugh Baiocchi	67	68	75	210	19,800
Gibby Gilbert	67	69	74	210	19,800
David Graham	66	75	69	210	19,800
Graham Marsh	68	71	71	210	19,800
Jim Thorpe	71	68	71	210	19,800
Brian Barnes	71	70	70	211	14,171.67
Terry Dill	74	70	67	211	14,171.67
Raymond Floyd	74	70	67	211	14,171.67
Steven Veriato	69	72	70	211	14,171.67
Howard Twitty	68	71	72	211	14,171.66
Tom Wargo	68	72	71	211	14,171.66
Jim Colbert	68	73	71	212	10,057.15
David Lundstrom	73	69	70	212	10,057.15
Bob Dickson	69	69	74	212	10,057.14
Mike McCullough	70	69	73	212	10,057.14
Chi Chi Rodriguez	70	70	72	212	10,057.14
Tom Shaw	67	71	74	212	10,057.14
Rocky Thompson	71	69	72	212	10,057.14
John Grace	69	72	72	213	8,085
Leonard Thompson	69	71	73	213	8,085
Bob Eastwood	74	70	70	214	7,425
Gary McCord	72	70	72	214	7,425
Ed Dougherty	73	72	70	215	6,336
Hubert Green	73	73	69	215	6,336
Simon Hobday	70	73	72	215	6,336
Joe Inman	72	68	75	215	6,336
John Morgan	72	72	71	215	6,336
John Bland	74	72	70	216	4,950
Charles Coody	71	75	70	216	4,950
Jim Ferree	72	71	73	216	4,950
John Jacobs	73	74	69	216	4,950
Orville Moody	74	72	70	216	4,950
Bruce Summerhays	77	68	71	216	4,950
Lee Trevino	74	71	71	216	4,950

Ford Senior Players Championship

TPC of Michigan, Dearborn, Michigan
Par 36-36–72; 6,876 yards

June 24-27
purse, $2,000,000

	SCORES				TOTAL	MONEY
Hale Irwin	67	71	64	65	267	$300,000
Graham Marsh	66	70	70	68	274	176,000
John Jacobs	71	69	68	67	275	144,000
Larry Nelson	66	72	69	69	276	120,000
Jose Maria Canizares	69	70	68	70	277	88,000
Hubert Green	70	72	69	66	277	88,000
Bruce Fleisher	72	68	68	70	278	68,000
Gil Morgan	74	72	67	65	278	68,000
Bob Eastwood	71	69	71	68	279	52,000
Raymond Floyd	73	69	70	67	279	52,000
Kermit Zarley	68	72	69	70	279	52,000
Gary McCord	74	67	68	71	280	42,000
Lee Trevino	71	68	71	70	280	42,000
Isao Aoki	71	67	70	73	281	34,000
Hugh Baiocchi	69	73	68	71	281	34,000
Brian Barnes	68	73	68	72	281	34,000
Bob Charles	71	70	70	70	281	34,000
Jim Colbert	71	76	66	68	281	34,000
Allen Doyle	70	73	69	70	282	26,466.67
Leonard Thompson	71	72	70	69	282	26,466.67
Bruce Summerhays	73	69	70	70	282	26,466.66
Ed Dougherty	70	72	72	69	283	20,114.29
David Lundstrom	73	70	70	70	283	20,114.29
John Mahaffey	74	72	70	67	283	20,114.29
Jim Thorpe	68	73	72	70	283	20,114.29
John Bland	68	70	73	72	283	20,114.28
Joe Inman	72	73	72	66	283	20,114.28
Dave Stockton	70	73	68	72	283	20,114.28
Vicente Fernandez	68	70	71	75	284	15,450
Tom Jenkins	70	72	73	69	284	15,450
Gary Player	76	73	70	65	284	15,450
John Schroeder	74	70	71	69	284	15,450
George Archer	68	74	72	71	285	12,900
Walter Hall	76	72	68	69	285	12,900
Tom McGinnis	75	71	69	70	285	12,900
Chi Chi Rodriguez	71	70	70	74	285	12,900
Jim Albus	69	74	73	70	286	10,200
Frank Conner	70	71	72	73	286	10,200
Bob Dickson	73	73	68	72	286	10,200
Dana Quigley	73	69	73	71	286	10,200
Jay Sigel	72	75	69	70	286	10,200
Rocky Thompson	72	72	71	71	286	10,200
Steven Veriato	74	71	68	73	286	10,200

State Farm Senior Classic

Hobbit's Glen Golf Club, Columbia, Maryland
Par 36-36–72; 6,983 yards

July 2-4
purse, $1,300,000

	SCORES			TOTAL	MONEY
Christy O'Connor, Jr.	65	66	67	198	$195,000
Bruce Fleisher	67	67	65	199	114,400

	SCORES			TOTAL	MONEY
Dana Quigley	69	70	68	207	93,600
Terry Dill	71	68	69	208	70,200
Hubert Green	67	69	72	208	70,200
Hugh Baiocchi	68	70	71	209	44,200
Jim Dent	71	71	67	209	44,200
Fred Gibson	68	70	71	209	44,200
John Jacobs	68	71	70	209	44,200
Jim Albus	70	68	72	210	31,200
Jose Maria Canizares	75	69	66	210	31,200
Walter Hall	68	71	71	210	31,200
Allen Doyle	67	71	73	211	24,700
David Lundstrom	71	70	70	211	24,700
Buzz Thomas	68	71	72	211	24,700
Isao Aoki	67	72	73	212	17,923.75
Jim Colbert	71	69	72	212	17,923.75
Ed Dougherty	69	70	73	212	17,923.75
Harold Henning	73	69	70	212	17,923.75
John Morgan	72	69	71	212	17,923.75
Bobby Stroble	69	70	73	212	17,923.75
Tom Wargo	71	70	71	212	17,923.75
Kermit Zarley	69	73	70	212	17,923.75
Brian Barnes	74	71	68	213	11,128
Frank Conner	68	72	73	213	11,128
Charles Coody	74	71	68	213	11,128
Vicente Fernandez	72	71	70	213	11,128
Joe Inman	71	70	72	213	11,128
Tom McGinnis	69	71	73	213	11,128
Orville Moody	70	70	73	213	11,128
Noel Ratcliffe	75	69	69	213	11,128
John Schroeder	72	71	70	213	11,128
Jim Thorpe	72	67	74	213	11,128
Jim Barker	72	74	68	214	7,670
Bob Dickson	70	69	75	214	7,670
Tom Jenkins	71	70	73	214	7,670
Walter Morgan	69	72	73	214	7,670
Howard Twitty	70	70	74	214	7,670
Evan Williams	75	69	70	214	7,670
Bob Charles	74	70	71	215	5,980
Bob Duval	67	73	75	215	5,980
Bob Eastwood	74	68	73	215	5,980
Rocky Thompson	76	69	70	215	5,980
Lee Trevino	74	67	74	215	5,980
Steven Veriato	72	69	74	215	5,980

U.S. Senior Open

Des Moines Golf & Country Club, West Des Moines, Iowa
Par 36-36–72; 6,888 yards

July 8-11
purse, $1,750,000

	SCORES				TOTAL	MONEY
Dave Eichelberger	71	69	73	68	281	$315,000
Ed Dougherty	68	69	75	72	284	185,000
Joe Inman	72	71	72	71	286	89,903
Hale Irwin	71	72	70	73	286	89,903
Gil Morgan	70	71	73	72	286	89,903
Tom Wargo	73	70	75	69	287	59,680
Bruce Summerhays	70	73	70	75	288	53,602

	SCORES				TOTAL	MONEY
Hugh Baiocchi	74	75	69	71	289	45,644
Frank Conner	79	71	67	72	289	45,644
Jim Dent	73	73	73	70	289	45,644
Raymond Floyd	75	74	70	72	291	38,000
Dana Quigley	76	72	73	70	291	38,000
Jim Albus	73	72	74	73	292	30,978
Allen Doyle	75	71	73	73	292	30,978
Bob Duval	73	68	75	76	292	30,978
John Jacobs	71	73	72	76	292	30,978
J.C. Snead	73	70	75	74	292	30,978
Jim Ahern	73	75	71	74	293	23,350
Jim Colbert	80	68	68	77	293	23,350
Bob Dickson	73	75	75	70	293	23,350
Tom Jenkins	75	72	77	69	293	23,350
Christy O'Connor, Jr.	77	73	71	72	293	23,350
Larry Nelson	75	71	73	75	294	17,790
Larry Ringer	72	77	74	71	294	17,790
Leonard Thompson	73	68	76	77	294	17,790
DeWitt Weaver	80	69	71	74	294	17,790
Jose Maria Canizares	71	72	75	77	295	14,545
Jim Thorpe	76	71	74	74	295	14,545
John Mahaffey	73	75	78	70	296	12,485
Dave Stockton	71	74	75	76	296	12,485
Steven Veriato	78	70	73	75	296	12,485
Charles Coody	73	75	75	74	297	11,035
Terry Dill	73	75	73	76	297	11,035
Walter Hall	70	75	75	77	297	11,035
Pete Oakley	75	73	75	74	297	11,035
John Schroeder	76	71	76	74	297	11,035
Tommy Horton	74	75	75	74	298	9,995
Steve Benson	77	73	74	75	299	9,133
Bob Lendzion	74	73	77	75	299	9,133
Graham Marsh	71	77	73	78	299	9,133
Michael Zinni	76	73	77	73	299	9,133

Ameritech Senior Open

Kemper Lakes Golf Club, Long Grove, Illinois
Par 36-36–72; 6,947 yards

July 16-18
purse, $1,300,000

	SCORES			TOTAL	MONEY
Hale Irwin	73	66	67	206	$195,000
Gary McCord	73	69	65	207	95,333.34
Bruce Fleisher	68	72	67	207	95,333.33
Raymond Floyd	70	67	70	207	95,333.33
Jose Maria Canizares	67	72	69	208	62,400
Allen Doyle	70	71	69	210	46,800
Larry Nelson	70	70	70	210	46,800
DeWitt Weaver	67	73	70	210	46,800
Hugh Baiocchi	73	70	68	211	32,500
Fred Gibson	70	67	74	211	32,500
John Mahaffey	68	71	72	211	32,500
Tom McGinnis	71	69	71	211	32,500
Jim Dent	75	67	70	212	21,498.75
Dale Douglass	68	75	69	212	21,498.75
Al Geiberger	74	71	67	212	21,498.75
David Graham	67	76	69	212	21,498.75

	SCORES			TOTAL	MONEY
Graham Marsh	73	69	70	212	21,498.75
Gil Morgan	73	72	67	212	21,498.75
Tom Wargo	72	72	68	212	21,498.75
Kermit Zarley	71	70	71	212	21,498.75
Walter Hall	74	72	67	213	15,600
Bob Murphy	73	69	71	213	15,600
Bob Eastwood	72	70	72	214	13,650
David Lundstrom	69	77	68	214	13,650
Leonard Thompson	75	72	67	214	13,650
Jim Albus	75	71	69	215	10,356.67
Terry Dill	70	73	72	215	10,356.67
Bob Duval	76	71	68	215	10,356.67
Gibby Gilbert	75	68	72	215	10,356.67
Joe Inman	75	70	70	215	10,356.67
Gene Littler	73	71	71	215	10,356.67
Bud Allin	69	71	75	215	10,356.66
Simon Hobday	72	69	74	215	10,356.66
Tom Shaw	74	68	73	215	10,356.66
Dave Eichelberger	72	73	71	216	8,190
Tommy Aaron	70	74	73	217	7,800
Dana Quigley	71	76	71	218	7,020
Jay Sigel	74	71	73	218	7,020
Jim Thorpe	73	73	72	218	7,020
Larry Ziegler	72	74	72	218	7,020

Coldwell Banker Burnet Classic

Bunker Hills Golf Club, Coon Rapids, Minnesota
Par 36-36–72; 6,909 yards

August 23-25
purse, $1,500,000

	SCORES			TOTAL	MONEY
Hale Irwin	64	68	69	201	$225,000
Jim Dent	66	70	67	203	120,000
Dale Douglass	70	68	65	203	120,000
Gil Morgan	71	65	68	204	90,000
Jim Colbert	65	71	69	205	66,000
Allen Doyle	71	66	68	205	66,000
David Graham	65	68	73	206	51,000
Larry Nelson	68	70	68	206	51,000
Vicente Fernandez	69	70	68	207	42,000
Hugh Baiocchi	69	69	70	208	28,665
Frank Conner	69	67	72	208	28,665
Walter Hall	69	72	67	208	28,665
Tom Jenkins	69	70	69	208	28,665
John Mahaffey	70	69	69	208	28,665
Mike McCullough	71	68	69	208	28,665
Dana Quigley	68	72	68	208	28,665
Jay Sigel	73	70	65	208	28,665
J.C. Snead	69	70	69	208	28,665
Bruce Summerhays	69	71	68	208	28,665
Tommy Aaron	70	70	69	209	18,075
Bob Eastwood	71	65	73	209	18,075
Bruce Fleisher	70	69	70	209	18,075
Barney Thompson	70	71	68	209	18,075
George Archer	70	71	69	210	15,000
Bob Dickson	68	71	71	210	15,000
Mark Hayes	73	71	66	210	15,000

	SCORES			TOTAL	MONEY
Jose Maria Canizares	68	70	73	211	12,450
Bob Duval	69	69	73	211	12,450
Hubert Green	70	70	71	211	12,450
John Jacobs	71	71	69	211	12,450
Dave Stockton	72	71	68	211	12,450
Butch Baird	69	70	73	212	9,281.25
Ed Dougherty	70	71	71	212	9,281.25
Gibby Gilbert	71	70	71	212	9,281.25
Joe Inman	72	69	71	212	9,281.25
David Lundstrom	69	69	74	212	9,281.25
Jesse Patino	70	70	72	212	9,281.25
Tom Wargo	76	69	67	212	9,281.25
Kermit Zarley	72	71	69	212	9,281.25
Jim Albus	72	70	71	213	6,900
Dave Eichelberger	70	73	70	213	6,900
Harold Henning	70	72	71	213	6,900
Graham Marsh	68	75	70	213	6,900
Chi Chi Rodriguez	70	72	71	213	6,900
Jim Thorpe	72	69	72	213	6,900

Novell Utah Showdown

Park Meadows Golf Club, Park City, Utah
Par 36-36–72; 7,167 yards

July 30-August 1
purse, $1,350,000

	SCORES			TOTAL	MONEY
Dave Eichelberger	66	63	68	197	$202,500
Dana Quigley	71	62	64	197	118,800
(Eichelberger defeated Quigley on first extra hole.)					
David Graham	68	68	63	199	89,100
Hale Irwin	67	65	67	199	89,100
Gil Morgan	65	67	68	200	64,800
Simon Hobday	67	67	67	201	51,300
Graham Marsh	70	64	67	201	51,300
John Mahaffey	68	64	70	202	38,700
Bobby Stroble	71	67	64	202	38,700
Rocky Thompson	69	67	66	202	38,700
Jose Maria Canizares	68	67	68	203	31,050
Terry Dill	66	70	67	203	31,050
Hugh Baiocchi	71	65	68	204	25,650
Tom Jenkins	70	68	66	204	25,650
Kermit Zarley	69	69	66	204	25,650
Dale Douglass	73	67	65	205	20,958.75
Fred Gibson	67	68	70	205	20,958.75
David Lundstrom	68	67	70	205	20,958.75
Tom Shaw	65	69	71	205	20,958.75
Alberto Giannone	67	71	68	206	15,081.43
John Jacobs	65	71	70	206	15,081.43
Walter Morgan	69	67	70	206	15,081.43
Jesse Patino	72	67	67	206	15,081.43
Bruce Summerhays	70	73	63	206	15,081.43
Buzz Thomas	68	71	67	206	15,081.43
Jim Colbert	71	63	72	206	15,081.42
Vicente Fernandez	74	68	65	207	11,745
Mike Malone	71	69	67	207	11,745
Dave Stockton	67	70	70	207	11,745
Don Bies	68	69	71	208	9,747

	SCORES			TOTAL	MONEY
Walter Hall	71	70	67	208	9,747
Harold Henning	69	72	67	208	9,747
Joe Inman	67	72	69	208	9,747
Mike McCullough	70	68	70	208	9,747
Bobby Cole	69	72	68	209	8,302.50
Howard Twitty	71	69	69	209	8,302.50
George Archer	72	71	67	210	7,425
Ed Dougherty	69	70	71	210	7,425
Leonard Thompson	65	74	71	210	7,425
Al Geiberger	71	69	71	211	6,480
Jimmy Powell	71	69	71	211	6,480
J.C. Snead	70	68	73	211	6,480
Tom Wargo	76	64	71	211	6,480

Lightpath Long Island Classic

Meadow Brook Club, Jericho, New York   August 6-8
Par 36-36–72; 6,842 yards   purse, $1,200,000

	SCORES			TOTAL	MONEY
Bruce Fleisher	64	69	73	206	$180,000
Allen Doyle	68	73	67	208	105,600
Jose Maria Canizares	73	66	70	209	61,440
Raymond Floyd	70	70	69	209	61,440
Joe Inman	72	69	68	209	61,440
Tom Shaw	71	67	71	209	61,440
Jim Thorpe	72	67	70	209	61,440
Hugh Baiocchi	70	69	71	210	31,680
John Jacobs	71	71	68	210	31,680
David Lundstrom	73	65	72	210	31,680
Gil Morgan	71	68	71	210	31,680
Dana Quigley	71	71	68	210	31,680
Mark Hayes	65	71	75	211	24,000
John Bland	70	72	70	212	19,820
Ed Dougherty	72	69	71	212	19,820
Vicente Fernandez	73	68	71	212	19,820
Walter Hall	69	71	72	212	19,820
Walter Morgan	70	70	72	212	19,820
Tom Wargo	69	69	74	212	19,820
Jim Albus	71	72	70	213	13,095
Bud Allin	71	70	72	213	13,095
Jim Colbert	72	67	74	213	13,095
Bob Duval	70	72	71	213	13,095
Dave Eichelberger	69	72	72	213	13,095
Simon Hobday	71	71	71	213	13,095
Mike McCullough	71	68	74	213	13,095
Buzz Thomas	72	66	75	213	13,095
George Burns	71	75	68	214	9,102.86
Frank Conner	72	71	71	214	9,102.86
Bob Dickson	73	69	72	214	9,102.86
Fred Gibson	71	71	72	214	9,102.86
Rocky Thompson	72	73	69	214	9,102.86
Gary Player	72	69	73	214	9,102.85
Leonard Thompson	68	73	73	214	9,102.85
Hubert Green	72	73	70	215	7,200
John Mahaffey	73	74	68	215	7,200
Mike Malone	71	74	70	215	7,200

	SCORES			TOTAL	MONEY
Terry Dill	72	74	70	216	6,000
Gibby Gilbert	71	72	73	216	6,000
Ed Sabo	71	72	73	216	6,000
Bobby Stroble	72	73	71	216	6,000
Howard Twitty	72	73	71	216	6,000
Larry Ziegler	72	72	72	216	6,000

Foremost Insurance Championship

Egypt Valley Country Club, Ada, Michigan
Par 36-36–72; 6,995 yards

August 13-15
purse, $1,000,000

	SCORES			TOTAL	MONEY
Christy O'Connor, Jr.	69	68	68	205	$150,000
Jim Thorpe	69	72	68	209	73,333.34
George Archer	69	70	70	209	73,333.33
John Jacobs	70	69	70	209	73,333.33
J.C. Snead	69	72	70	211	48,000
Bruce Fleisher	68	70	74	212	38,000
Gary Player	70	73	69	212	38,000
John Bland	70	67	76	213	26,400
Jim Dent	71	73	69	213	26,400
Alberto Giannone	74	69	70	213	26,400
Jim Holtgrieve	72	68	73	213	26,400
Noel Ratcliffe	68	72	73	213	26,400
Ed Dougherty	71	70	73	214	18,000
John Grace	72	71	71	214	18,000
Mike McCullough	72	74	68	214	18,000
Bruce Summerhays	71	73	70	214	18,000
Tom Wargo	67	74	73	214	18,000
Tom Jenkins	74	74	67	215	13,675
Dick Lotz	67	72	76	215	13,675
Dave Stockton	70	71	74	215	13,675
Kermit Zarley	68	76	71	215	13,675
David Graham	70	71	75	216	10,775
Tom McGinnis	72	72	72	216	10,775
Dana Quigley	73	71	72	216	10,775
Lee Trevino	68	75	73	216	10,775
Hugh Baiocchi	72	75	70	217	9,100
George Burns	71	71	75	217	9,100
David Lundstrom	75	69	73	217	9,100
Jim Colbert	71	73	74	218	7,087.50
Frank Conner	71	76	71	218	7,087.50
Al Geiberger	76	69	73	218	7,087.50
Harold Henning	70	74	74	218	7,087.50
Mike Hill	73	69	76	218	7,087.50
John Morgan	73	71	74	218	7,087.50
Jesse Patino	74	71	73	218	7,087.50
DeWitt Weaver	72	74	72	218	7,087.50
Jim Albus	76	72	71	219	5,300
Butch Baird	75	72	72	219	5,300
Miller Barber	78	69	72	219	5,300
Barney Thompson	73	73	73	219	5,300
Larry Ziegler	75	72	72	219	5,300

BankBoston Classic

Nashawtuc Country Club, Concord, Massachusetts

August 20-22

Par 36-36–72; 6,787 yards

purse, $1,200,000

	SCORES			TOTAL	MONEY
Tom McGinnis	69	69	67	205	$180,000
Hale Irwin	69	68	68	205	105,600
(McGinnis defeated Irwin on second extra hole.)					
David Graham	71	69	66	206	79,200
Jay Sigel	67	70	69	206	79,200
Jim Dent	71	71	65	207	49,600
Hubert Green	69	72	66	207	49,600
Tom Jenkins	74	66	67	207	49,600
George Archer	71	66	71	208	36,000
Hugh Baiocchi	71	67	70	208	36,000
Gibby Gilbert	72	67	70	209	31,200
Bob Charles	69	72	69	210	24,720
Terry Dill	71	72	67	210	24,720
John Mahaffey	71	69	70	210	24,720
Graham Marsh	71	70	69	210	24,720
Lee Trevino	71	70	69	210	24,720
Fred Gibson	71	73	67	211	19,200
Christy O'Connor, Jr.	69	72	70	211	19,200
Dave Stockton	73	68	70	211	19,200
John Bland	69	69	74	212	15,390
Walter Morgan	73	71	68	212	15,390
Jimmy Powell	73	68	71	212	15,390
Jim Thorpe	73	69	70	212	15,390
Bruce Fleisher	73	72	68	213	11,760
Harold Henning	71	70	72	213	11,760
Mike McCullough	75	69	69	213	11,760
Dana Quigley	70	71	72	213	11,760
Tom Shaw	70	73	70	213	11,760
DeWitt Weaver	70	73	70	213	11,760
Tommy Aaron	71	73	70	214	9,072
Walter Hall	73	68	73	214	9,072
John Jacobs	75	71	68	214	9,072
David Lundstrom	70	72	72	214	9,072
Howard Twitty	73	71	70	214	9,072
Jim Ahern	75	72	68	215	7,080
Don Bies	73	70	72	215	7,080
Mark Hayes	74	69	72	215	7,080
Larry Nelson	75	69	71	215	7,080
Bruce Summerhays	69	74	72	215	7,080
Rocky Thompson	76	71	68	215	7,080
Jim Albus	72	69	75	216	5,400
Dale Douglass	73	72	71	216	5,400
Allen Doyle	73	72	71	216	5,400
Jesse Patino	71	75	70	216	5,400
Gary Player	75	70	71	216	5,400
J.C. Snead	71	73	72	216	5,400
Steven Veriato	74	75	67	216	5,400

AT&T Canada Senior Open

Richelieu Valley Golf Club, Rouville Course, August 26-29
Sainte-Julie, Quebec, Canada purse, $1,350,000
Par 36-36–72; 6,735 yards

		SCORES			TOTAL	MONEY
Jim Ahern	67	68	69	68	272	$202,500
Hale Irwin	67	65	71	69	272	118,800
(Ahern defeated Irwin on second extra hole.)						
Ed Dougherty	68	70	68	67	273	97,200
Tom Jenkins	68	69	71	67	275	81,000
David Lundstrom	70	66	72	69	277	64,800
Hugh Baiocchi	69	67	69	73	278	54,000
Larry Nelson	63	70	73	73	279	48,600
Bruce Fleisher	69	69	70	72	280	38,700
Joe Inman	72	68	70	70	280	38,700
Tom McGinnis	68	68	72	72	280	38,700
Jim Dent	68	72	72	69	281	29,700
Gil Morgan	69	68	68	76	281	29,700
Jim Thorpe	70	69	71	71	281	29,700
Jose Maria Canizares	69	72	71	70	282	22,297.50
Bob Charles	69	70	73	70	282	22,297.50
Graham Marsh	72	70	70	70	282	22,297.50
Dana Quigley	72	68	73	69	282	22,297.50
Jay Sigel	74	67	67	74	282	22,297.50
Leonard Thompson	71	64	74	73	282	22,297.50
Jim Colbert	68	71	72	72	283	16,740
Bob Duval	69	70	75	69	283	16,740
Fred Gibson	72	73	69	69	283	16,740
John Bland	72	67	75	70	284	13,837.50
David Graham	69	73	71	71	284	13,837.50
Walter Morgan	69	73	71	71	284	13,837.50
Howard Twitty	72	72	68	72	284	13,837.50
George Archer	73	70	69	73	285	10,957.50
Bob Dickson	69	69	74	73	285	10,957.50
Terry Dill	68	73	73	71	285	10,957.50
Allen Doyle	71	76	66	72	285	10,957.50
John Jacobs	70	72	71	72	285	10,957.50
Rocky Thompson	68	73	71	73	285	10,957.50
Jim Albus	69	73	70	74	286	8,325
Isao Aoki	71	71	73	71	286	8,325
Frank Conner	75	73	68	70	286	8,325
Dick Lotz	75	69	71	71	286	8,325
Bob Murphy	69	73	73	71	286	8,325
Kermit Zarley	67	72	72	75	286	8,325
Mike McCullough	69	69	76	73	287	6,885
Bruce Summerhays	71	69	73	74	287	6,885
Tom Wargo	69	69	75	74	287	6,885

TD Waterhouse Championship

Tiffany Greens Golf Club, Kansas City, Missouri September 3-5
Par 36-36–72; 6,830 yards

		SCORES		TOTAL	MONEY
Allen Doyle	63	70	65	198	$180,000
Ed Dougherty	66	66	68	200	105,600

	SCORES			TOTAL	MONEY
Gil Morgan	64	69	68	201	86,400
Larry Nelson	68	70	66	204	72,000
Jim Colbert	70	68	67	205	46,800
David Lundstrom	69	67	69	205	46,800
Graham Marsh	68	69	68	205	46,800
Jim Thorpe	66	71	68	205	46,800
Vicente Fernandez	68	69	69	206	32,400
Jim Holtgrieve	71	68	67	206	32,400
Bruce Fleisher	72	67	68	207	28,800
Jim Ahern	68	70	70	208	25,200
Gary McCord	73	69	66	208	25,200
Jose Maria Canizares	69	71	69	209	19,820
Bob Dickson	67	71	71	209	19,820
Bob Duval	70	68	71	209	19,820
Al Geiberger	69	71	69	209	19,820
Fred Gibson	67	69	73	209	19,820
Joe Inman	72	67	70	209	19,820
John Bland	70	69	71	210	14,880
Dave Eichelberger	70	70	70	210	14,880
Mike McCullough	69	72	69	210	14,880
Don Bies	70	68	73	211	12,024
Simon Hobday	70	70	71	211	12,024
John Mahaffey	68	72	71	211	12,024
Jay Sigel	72	71	68	211	12,024
Barney Thompson	70	74	67	211	12,024
Hugh Baiocchi	67	75	70	212	8,720
Brian Barnes	66	75	71	212	8,720
Bob Charles	72	73	67	212	8,720
Bob Murphy	69	70	73	212	8,720
Jimmy Powell	71	71	70	212	8,720
Dana Quigley	68	75	69	212	8,720
J.C. Snead	72	69	71	212	8,720
Bobby Stroble	72	68	72	212	8,720
Bruce Summerhays	70	72	70	212	8,720
Jim Albus	71	72	70	213	6,360
Butch Baird	73	74	66	213	6,360
Gibby Gilbert	69	71	73	213	6,360
David Graham	71	70	72	213	6,360
Larry Mowry	70	72	71	213	6,360

Comfort Classic

Brickyard Crossing, Indianapolis, Indiana
Par 36-36–72; 6,721 yards

September 10-12
purse, $1,200,000

	SCORES			TOTAL	MONEY
Gil Morgan	67	65	69	201	$180,000
Ed Dougherty	68	66	69	203	105,600
Tom Jenkins	67	66	71	204	86,400
Walter Hall	71	66	68	205	59,200
Mike McCullough	69	62	74	205	59,200
J.C. Snead	69	69	67	205	59,200
Jim Ahern	68	67	71	206	36,600
Joe Inman	73	66	67	206	36,600
John Mahaffey	69	66	71	206	36,600
Kermit Zarley	69	69	68	206	36,600
Vicente Fernandez	70	65	72	207	26,400

	SCORES			TOTAL	MONEY
Leonard Thompson	68	70	69	207	26,400
Jim Thorpe	72	66	69	207	26,400
Jim Dent	66	72	70	208	20,400
Terry Dill	67	69	72	208	20,400
Hubert Green	69	66	73	208	20,400
David Lundstrom	68	70	70	208	20,400
Gary McCord	66	69	73	208	20,400
Bob Eastwood	66	72	71	209	15,880
Dave Stockton	67	69	73	209	15,880
Tom Wargo	72	67	70	209	15,880
John Bland	70	67	73	210	13,240
Tony Peterson	72	70	68	210	13,240
Tom Watson	66	69	75	210	13,240
Hugh Baiocchi	70	71	70	211	10,944
Jose Maria Canizares	73	69	69	211	10,944
Frank Conner	72	68	71	211	10,944
Fred Gibson	67	68	76	211	10,944
Graham Marsh	69	71	71	211	10,944
Bud Allin	69	71	72	212	9,040
David Graham	72	70	70	212	9,040
Bobby Stroble	66	73	73	212	9,040
Chi Chi Rodriguez	68	71	74	213	8,280
George Archer	68	72	74	214	7,380
Jesse Patino	68	72	74	214	7,380
Tom Shaw	73	70	71	214	7,380
Barney Thompson	75	69	70	214	7,380
Bobby Cole	73	71	71	215	6,240
Bob Duval	70	68	77	215	6,240
Alberto Giannone	74	69	72	215	6,240
Larry Ziegler	70	70	75	215	6,240

Bank One Championship

Bent Tree Country Club, Dallas, Texas
Par 36-36–72; 7,113 yards

September 17-19
purse, $1,300,000

	SCORES			TOTAL	MONEY
Tom Watson	67	67	62	196	$195,000
Bruce Summerhays	68	67	66	201	114,400
Gil Morgan	70	64	68	202	93,600
Jim Colbert	66	68	69	203	59,800
David Graham	67	67	69	203	59,800
J.C. Snead	71	67	65	203	59,800
Dave Stockton	69	68	66	203	59,800
Jim Albus	72	67	66	205	34,320
Jose Maria Canizares	68	68	69	205	34,320
Alberto Giannone	64	70	71	205	34,320
Joe Inman	67	70	68	205	34,320
Hale Irwin	71	63	71	205	34,320
Allen Doyle	71	65	70	206	26,000
Dale Douglass	66	72	69	207	22,100
Bruce Fleisher	69	71	67	207	22,100
Hubert Green	67	71	69	207	22,100
Larry Nelson	72	67	68	207	22,100
Lee Trevino	69	71	67	207	22,100
Mike McCullough	70	70	68	208	18,330
Hugh Baiocchi	71	68	70	209	15,262

	SCORES			TOTAL	MONEY
Fred Gibson	70	70	69	209	15,262
Gary McCord	70	69	70	209	15,262
Bob Murphy	71	67	71	209	15,262
Bobby Stroble	72	68	69	209	15,262
Ed Dougherty	75	70	65	210	12,393.34
Jesse Patino	69	70	71	210	12,393.33
Dana Quigley	66	72	72	210	12,393.33
Bob Charles	68	71	72	211	10,530
Vicente Fernandez	69	71	71	211	10,530
Tom Jenkins	70	70	71	211	10,530
John Morgan	71	69	71	211	10,530
Charles Coody	71	65	76	212	8,775
John Grace	72	73	67	212	8,775
John Mahaffey	72	69	71	212	8,775
Bud Allin	65	70	78	213	8,775
Jim Ahern	69	70	74	213	7,041.67
Walter Hall	69	74	70	213	7,041.67
David Lundstrom	73	71	69	213	7,041.67
Jay Sigel	70	72	71	213	7,041.67
George Archer	71	68	74	213	7,041.66
Jim Thorpe	70	68	75	213	7,041.66

Kroger Senior Classic

Golf Center at Kings Island, Grizzly Course, Mason, Ohio
Par 35-36–71; 6,639 yards

September 24-26
purse, $1,400,000

	SCORES			TOTAL	MONEY
Gil Morgan	67	68	63	198	$210,000
Ed Dougherty	68	65	67	200	123,200
Dana Quigley	68	66	67	201	100,800
Hale Irwin	67	69	66	202	69,066.67
Graham Marsh	68	67	67	202	69,066.67
Joe Inman	72	63	67	202	69,066.66
John Mahaffey	69	69	65	203	47,600
Lee Trevino	68	67	68	203	47,600
Jim Dent	70	64	70	204	36,400
David Graham	67	72	65	204	36,400
Jimmy Powell	66	68	70	204	36,400
Allen Doyle	70	66	69	205	27,650
Vicente Fernandez	68	68	69	205	27,650
Tom Shaw	70	69	66	205	27,650
Leonard Thompson	71	71	63	205	27,650
Larry Nelson	73	68	65	206	20,463.34
Jay Sigel	69	70	67	206	20,463.34
Jim Ahern	69	68	69	206	20,463.33
Terry Dill	70	69	67	206	20,463.33
Walter Hall	70	65	71	206	20,463.33
Bruce Summerhays	70	68	68	206	20,463.33
Alberto Giannone	71	67	69	207	15,446.67
Mike McCullough	67	70	70	207	15,446.67
Hubert Green	68	68	71	207	15,446.66
John Bland	67	68	73	208	12,768
Jose Maria Canizares	71	68	69	208	12,768
Jim Colbert	66	70	72	208	12,768
Fred Gibson	73	68	67	208	12,768
Tom Jenkins	72	69	67	208	12,768

	SCORES			TOTAL	MONEY
Bob Eastwood	68	71	70	209	10,780
Tom McGinnis	70	72	67	209	10,780
Hugh Baiocchi	69	69	72	210	9,870
Bruce Fleisher	69	69	72	210	9,870
Tommy Aaron	73	70	68	211	7,945
Bud Allin	71	70	70	211	7,945
Bob Charles	69	70	72	211	7,945
Bob Duval	75	65	71	211	7,945
Simon Hobday	71	66	74	211	7,945
David Lundstrom	72	69	70	211	7,945
Ed Sabo	70	72	69	211	7,945
Tom Wargo	75	66	70	211	7,945

Vantage Championship

Tanglewood Park Golf Club, Clemmons, North Carolina
Par 35-35–70; 6,600 yards

October 1-3
purse, $1,500,000

	SCORES			TOTAL	MONEY
Fred Gibson	69	62	64	195	$225,000
Bruce Fleisher	65	68	65	198	132,000
Jay Sigel	71	65	63	199	108,000
Bob Duval	65	66	69	200	81,000
David Graham	66	66	68	200	81,000
Vicente Fernandez	67	68	66	201	57,000
Tom Jenkins	65	65	71	201	57,000
Hubert Green	71	67	64	202	45,000
Christy O'Connor, Jr.	69	65	68	202	45,000
Jim Colbert	70	69	64	203	36,000
Jim Dent	63	70	70	203	36,000
Raymond Floyd	70	68	65	203	36,000
Ed Dougherty	70	69	65	204	29,250
Gibby Gilbert	71	65	68	204	29,250
Gil Morgan	67	69	69	205	25,500
Larry Nelson	68	70	67	205	25,500
Doug Tewell	73	66	66	205	25,500
Jim Ahern	68	70	68	206	19,890
George Archer	67	72	67	206	19,890
Simon Hobday	69	70	67	206	19,890
Hale Irwin	70	71	65	206	19,890
John Morgan	67	69	70	206	19,890
Walter Hall	70	70	67	207	15,375
Joe Inman	72	71	64	207	15,375
Gary McCord	65	72	70	207	15,375
Bruce Summerhays	68	69	70	207	15,375
Hugh Baiocchi	71	73	64	208	12,450
Mike Hill	69	70	69	208	12,450
David Lundstrom	67	70	71	208	12,450
Bobby Stroble	72	69	67	208	12,450
Howard Twitty	70	67	71	208	12,450
John Bland	67	71	71	209	9,471.43
Jose Maria Canizares	70	68	71	209	9,471.43
Dale Douglass	74	67	68	209	9,471.43
Allen Doyle	66	70	73	209	9,471.43
Jim Holtgrieve	72	69	68	209	9,471.43
Tom McGinnis	69	70	70	209	9,471.43
Brian Barnes	68	68	73	209	9,471.42

	SCORES			TOTAL	MONEY
Jim Albus	68	69	73	210	6,900
Terry Dill	68	69	73	210	6,900
Alberto Giannone	72	69	69	210	6,900
Mike Malone	73	72	65	210	6,900
Graham Marsh	71	71	68	210	6,900
Walter Morgan	69	72	69	210	6,900
Dana Quigley	68	71	71	210	6,900
Rocky Thompson	70	70	70	210	6,900

The Transamerica

Silverado Country Club, South Course, Napa, California   October 8-10
Par 36-36–72; 6,632 yards   purse, $1,100,000

	SCORES			TOTAL	MONEY
Bruce Fleisher	66	66	67	199	$165,000
Allen Doyle	69	65	66	200	96,800
Walter Hall	67	68	67	202	79,200
Hubert Green	66	71	66	203	66,000
Al Geiberger	68	69	68	205	45,466.67
Gary McCord	70	69	66	205	45,466.67
Mike McCullough	69	68	68	205	45,466.66
Jose Maria Canizares	69	69	68	206	31,533.34
Tom Jenkins	69	68	69	206	31,533.33
Dana Quigley	70	67	69	206	31,533.33
Jim Colbert	69	69	69	207	23,375
Bob Eastwood	68	70	69	207	23,375
Bob Murphy	73	69	65	207	23,375
Bruce Summerhays	69	67	71	207	23,375
George Archer	68	71	69	208	18,700
David Graham	69	69	70	208	18,700
Barry Jaeckel	70	69	69	208	18,700
Jim Ahern	71	71	67	209	16,005
Jay Sigel	71	70	68	209	16,005
Howard Twitty	67	74	69	210	13,640
DeWitt Weaver	74	68	68	210	13,640
Kermit Zarley	71	72	67	210	13,640
John Bland	71	70	70	211	11,275
John Jacobs	70	73	68	211	11,275
John Morgan	71	70	70	211	11,275
Barney Thompson	73	69	69	211	11,275
Brian Barnes	69	74	69	212	9,350
Dale Douglass	67	74	71	212	9,350
David Lundstrom	69	73	70	212	9,350
Christy O'Connor, Jr.	72	70	70	212	9,350
Bob Charles	70	72	71	213	7,260
Joe Inman	72	71	70	213	7,260
Graham Marsh	69	74	70	213	7,260
Gary Player	76	70	67	213	7,260
Dave Stockton	72	68	73	213	7,260
Rocky Thompson	70	76	67	213	7,260
Larry Ziegler	74	71	68	213	7,260
Jim Albus	71	73	70	214	5,830
Charles Coody	75	65	74	214	5,830
Bob Duval	70	74	70	214	5,830

Raley's Gold Rush Classic

Serrano Country Club, El Dorado Hills, California
Par 36-36–72; 6,776 yards

October 15-17
purse, $1,100,000

	SCORES			TOTAL	MONEY
David Graham	63	71	65	199	$165,000
Larry Mowry	67	69	67	203	96,800
George Archer	70	68	66	204	60,500
Terry Dill	68	69	67	204	60,500
Allen Doyle	66	66	72	204	60,500
J.C. Snead	66	73	65	204	60,500
Tom Jenkins	69	69	67	205	39,600
John Bland	68	71	67	206	33,000
Dana Quigley	71	71	64	206	33,000
Tom Wargo	68	70	69	207	28,600
Bruce Fleisher	70	68	70	208	23,375
Raymond Floyd	70	67	71	208	23,375
Christy O'Connor, Jr.	70	69	69	208	23,375
Howard Twitty	70	69	69	208	23,375
Joe Inman	71	68	70	209	18,150
Bob Murphy	71	68	70	209	18,150
Doug Tewell	69	74	66	209	18,150
Leonard Thompson	67	71	71	209	18,150
Bob Duval	73	68	69	210	14,107.50
Simon Hobday	69	70	71	210	14,107.50
John Mahaffey	71	69	70	210	14,107.50
Jerry McGee	70	70	70	210	14,107.50
Jim Ahern	73	67	71	211	10,312.50
Hugh Baiocchi	70	71	70	211	10,312.50
Jose Maria Canizares	70	73	68	211	10,312.50
Fred Gibson	71	73	67	211	10,312.50
Gary McCord	69	70	72	211	10,312.50
Mike McCullough	71	70	70	211	10,312.50
Bruce Summerhays	68	76	67	211	10,312.50
Lee Trevino	71	70	70	211	10,312.50
Jim Albus	72	68	72	212	7,108.75
Bob Charles	69	70	73	212	7,108.75
Jim Colbert	67	71	74	212	7,108.75
Dave Eichelberger	72	69	71	212	7,108.75
Walter Hall	74	68	70	212	7,108.75
Dick Lotz	72	67	73	212	7,108.75
Gary Player	72	69	71	212	7,108.75
Larry Ziegler	69	72	71	212	7,108.75
Brian Barnes	70	70	73	213	5,390
Jim Dent	70	68	75	213	5,390
Al Geiberger	74	69	70	213	5,390
Tom McGinnis	71	71	71	213	5,390
John Morgan	72	72	69	213	5,390

EMC² Kaanapali Classic

Kaanapali Golf Club, Lahaina, Maui, Hawaii
Par 35-36–71; 6,590 yards

October 22-24
purse, $1,000,000

	SCORES			TOTAL	MONEY
Bruce Fleisher	65	67	67	199	$150,000
Allen Doyle	70	64	66	200	88,000

	SCORES			TOTAL	MONEY
Jim Ahern	66	72	65	203	55,000
Hale Irwin	66	71	66	203	55,000
Tom Jenkins	67	66	70	203	55,000
Steven Veriato	68	71	64	203	55,000
Brian Barnes	67	68	69	204	32,000
Hubert Green	74	66	64	204	32,000
John Jacobs	73	63	68	204	32,000
Bob Duval	69	68	68	205	24,000
Raymond Floyd	71	68	66	205	24,000
Kermit Zarley	75	67	63	205	24,000
Jim Colbert	68	69	69	206	19,000
Frank Conner	70	70	66	206	19,000
Walter Hall	76	68	62	206	19,000
George Archer	71	70	66	207	16,000
Dave Eichelberger	67	71	69	207	16,000
Christy O'Connor, Jr.	70	71	66	207	16,000
Ed Dougherty	70	70	68	208	12,460
Fred Gibson	67	72	69	208	12,460
John Mahaffey	71	69	68	208	12,460
Gary Player	69	70	69	208	12,460
Dave Stockton	69	69	70	208	12,460
Jim Barker	70	70	69	209	8,937.50
Jose Maria Canizares	70	71	68	209	8,937.50
Terry Dill	73	68	68	209	8,937.50
Babe Hiskey	69	72	68	209	8,937.50
Dick Lotz	71	72	66	209	8,937.50
Bob Murphy	67	69	73	209	8,937.50
Jay Sigel	72	70	67	209	8,937.50
Bruce Summerhays	70	70	69	209	8,937.50
Jim Albus	72	70	68	210	6,900
Bob Dickson	70	69	71	210	6,900
Dana Quigley	72	70	68	210	6,900
Bob Eastwood	72	69	70	211	5,875
Mark Hayes	70	71	70	211	5,875
Jim Thorpe	76	70	65	211	5,875
DeWitt Weaver	67	72	72	211	5,875
Hugh Baiocchi	76	68	68	212	5,100
Noel Ratcliffe	72	70	70	212	5,100
Ed Sneed	71	73	68	212	5,100

Pacific Bell Senior Classic

Wilshire Country Club, Los Angeles, California
Par 35-36–71; 6,575 yards

October 29-31
purse, $1,200,000

	SCORES			TOTAL	MONEY
Joe Inman	68	66	65	199	$180,000
Dave Stockton	67	64	70	201	96,000
Bruce Summerhays	66	69	66	201	96,000
John Bland	70	68	64	202	64,800
John Mahaffey	65	68	69	202	64,800
Bruce Fleisher	68	67	68	203	43,200
Bob Murphy	68	66	69	203	43,200
Lee Trevino	67	68	68	203	43,200
Jose Maria Canizares	69	69	66	204	33,600
Gil Morgan	68	71	66	205	31,200
Hubert Green	71	67	68	206	27,600

	SCORES			TOTAL	MONEY
Gary Player	67	67	72	206	27,600
Jim Thorpe	67	68	72	207	24,000
Walter Hall	72	67	69	208	22,200
Dana Quigley	69	73	66	208	22,200
Jim Ahern	70	69	70	209	20,400
Noel Ratcliffe	69	76	65	210	19,200
George Archer	73	66	72	211	16,410
Hale Irwin	68	75	68	211	16,410
John Jacobs	65	71	75	211	16,410
Chi Chi Rodriguez	69	72	70	211	16,410
Charles Coody	72	71	69	212	12,624
Bob Dickson	73	72	67	212	12,624
Terry Dill	72	71	69	212	12,624
Al Geiberger	69	69	74	212	12,624
John Morgan	72	70	70	212	12,624
Butch Baird	72	67	74	213	10,200
Mike McCullough	68	72	73	213	10,200
Tom McGinnis	72	69	72	213	10,200
Jay Sigel	73	68	72	213	10,200
Hugh Baiocchi	71	72	71	214	7,452
Brian Barnes	68	74	72	214	7,452
Allen Doyle	73	70	71	214	7,452
Bob Eastwood	71	71	72	214	7,452
Raymond Floyd	72	73	69	214	7,452
Gary McCord	73	74	67	214	7,452
Larry Nelson	71	72	71	214	7,452
Doug Tewell	72	73	69	214	7,452
DeWitt Weaver	68	71	75	214	7,452
Walter Zembriski	73	72	69	214	7,452

Ingersoll-Rand Senior Tour Championship

Dunes Golf & Beach Club, Myrtle Beach, South Carolina November 4-7
Par 36-36–72; 6,815 yards purse, $2,000,000

	SCORES				TOTAL	MONEY
Gary McCord	71	74	64	67	276	$347,000
Bruce Fleisher	67	73	66	71	277	184,500
Larry Nelson	70	74	68	65	277	184,500
Bruce Summerhays	67	71	68	74	280	139,000
George Archer	68	67	73	73	281	101,500
Dana Quigley	69	73	68	71	281	101,500
Jim Thorpe	74	70	68	70	282	83,000
Raymond Floyd	70	70	70	74	284	74,000
Hugh Baiocchi	69	71	74	71	285	62,500
Allen Doyle	69	73	72	71	285	62,500
Jose Maria Canizares	73	65	72	76	286	47,600
Vicente Fernandez	73	69	71	73	286	47,600
Graham Marsh	71	70	72	73	286	47,600
Christy O'Connor, Jr.	71	67	72	76	286	47,600
J.C. Snead	75	71	69	71	286	47,600
Jim Dent	72	72	71	72	287	38,000
John Mahaffey	73	71	69	74	287	38,000
David Graham	73	71	73	72	289	32,000
Joe Inman	69	77	72	71	289	32,000
Hale Irwin	73	67	74	75	289	32,000
Leonard Thompson	73	76	69	71	289	32,000

	SCORES				TOTAL	MONEY
Ed Dougherty	69	74	73	74	290	26,250
John Jacobs	74	71	72	73	290	26,250
Bob Duval	75	72	72	72	291	23,500
Walter Hall	70	72	78	71	291	23,500
Hubert Green	75	73	69	75	292	21,500
Tom Jenkins	76	72	68	76	292	21,500
Gil Morgan	71	79	71	72	293	20,000
Jim Colbert	74	67	74	79	294	18,750
Fred Gibson	74	75	74	71	294	18,750
Dave Eichelberger	71	76	71	77	295	18,000

Chrysler Senior Match Play Challenge

Hyatt Dorado Beach Golf Club, Dorado, Puerto Rico
Par 36-36–72; 6,885 yards

November 12-14
purse, $720,000

FIRST ROUND

Bruce Fleisher defeated David Graham, 1 up
Vicente Fernandez defeated Jose Maria Canizares, 1 up
Larry Nelson defeated Raymond Floyd, 1 up, 19th hole
Dana Quigley defeated John Mahaffey, 2 and 1
Hale Irwin defeated Al Geiberger, 4 and 3
Bruce Summerhays defeated Joe Inman, 2 and 1
Allen Doyle defeated Jack Nicklaus, 4 and 2
Tom Jenkins defeated John Jacobs, 3 and 2

(Each losing player received $15,000.)

SECOND ROUND

Nelson defeated Quigley, 3 and 2
Fleisher defeated Fernandez, 1 up, 21st hole
Jenkins defeated Doyle, 2 up
Summerhays defeated Irwin, 1 up, 20th hole

(Each losing player received $30,000.)

SEMI-FINALS

Nelson defeated Fleisher, 1 up
Jenkins defeated Summerhays, 1 up

(Fleisher and Summerhays received $60,000 each.)

FINAL

Nelson defeated Jenkins, 3 and 2

(Nelson received $240,000; Jenkins received $120,000.)

Diners Club Matches

Pelican Hill Golf Club, Corona del Mar, California
Par 35-36–71; 6,713 yards

December 11-12
purse, $1,200,000

FIRST-ROUND MATCHES

Jack Nicklaus and Tom Watson defeated Allan Doyle and Dana Quigley, 5 and 4
Bruce Fleisher and David Graham defeated Gil Morgan and Jay Sigel, 3 and 2

THIRD-PLACE MATCH

Morgan and Sigel defeated Doyle and Quigley, 1 up, 19th hole
(Morgan and Sigel received $30,000 each; Doyle and Quigley received $20,000 each.)

CHAMPIONSHIP MATCH

Nicklaus and Watson defeated Fleisher and Graham, 1 up
(Nicklaus and Watson received $100,000 each; Fleisher and Graham received $50,000 each.)

European Seniors Tour

Beko Classic

Klassis Golf & Country Club, Istanbul, Turkey
Par 36-36–72; 6,575 yards

May 7-9
purse, €250,000

	SCORES			TOTAL	MONEY
Tommy Horton	72	70	69	211	€43,125
Alan Tapie	69	74	69	212	28,780
Ray Carrasco	73	76	65	214	16,320
Bernard Gallacher	78	65	72	215	12,800
Malcolm Gregson	73	72	71	216	10,817.50
Norman Wood	69	74	73	216	10,817.50
Brian Waites	77	69	72	218	7,455.36
Brian Huggett	74	76	68	218	7,455.36
Bob Shearer	72	74	72	218	7,455.36
Eddie Polland	73	74	71	218	7,455.36
Joe McDermott	77	72	69	218	7,455.36
Alberto Croce	75	73	70	218	7,455.36
Bob Lendzion	70	76	72	218	7,455.36
Noel Ratcliffe	73	71	75	219	4,482.68
Ian Stanley	77	73	69	219	4,482.68
Bobby Verwey	79	72	68	219	4,482.68
Antonio Garrido	76	74	70	220	3,355.54
Bill Brask	76	74	70	220	3,355.54
Geoff Parslow	75	74	71	220	3,355.54

	SCORES			TOTAL	MONEY
Jim Rhodes	75	75	70	220	3,355.54
Gordon MacDonald	76	73	72	221	2,694.79
Jay Horton	77	71	73	221	2,694.79
Doug Robb	73	76	72	221	2,694.79
John Fourie	78	72	71	221	2,694.79
Craig Defoy	76	75	71	222	2,264.66
David Jones	75	73	74	222	2,264.66
Jerry Bruner	76	72	74	222	2,264.66
Tommy Price	77	73	72	222	2,264.66
Trevor Downing	77	74	71	222	2,264.66
Graham Burroughs	73	75	75	223	1,938.18
Sid Denham	76	77	70	223	1,938.18
Michael Slater	80	70	73	223	1,938.18
Deray Simon	76	70	77	223	1,938.18
Jay Dolan III	77	73	73	223	1,938.18

AIB Irish Seniors Open

Mount Juliet, Kilkenny, Ireland
Par 36-36–72; 6,731 yards

May 14-16
purse, €250,000

	SCORES			TOTAL	MONEY
John Morgan	70	67	72	209	€39,116.50
Brian Barnes	71	69	70	210	20,714.26
Noel Ratcliffe	71	67	72	210	20,714.26
Craig Defoy	68	69	74	211	11,689.18
J.R. Delich	72	68	72	212	9,502.35
Eddie Polland	69	72	71	212	9,502.35
Jim Rhodes	67	75	70	212	9,502.35
Christy O'Connor, Jr.	68	71	74	213	7,816.26
Ray Carrasco	71	70	73	214	6,865.64
Joe Carr	70	74	70	214	6,865.64
Neil Coles	68	70	77	215	5,246.05
David Oakley	74	74	67	215	5,246.05
Bob Lendzion	73	73	69	215	5,246.05
Denis O'Sullivan	71	68	76	215	5,246.05
Terry Gale	73	72	71	216	4,072.44
Jerry Bruner	72	73	71	216	4,072.44
Bob Shearer	73	72	72	217	3,030.27
Geoff Parslow	74	71	72	217	3,030.27
Ian Stanley	74	70	73	217	3,030.27
Barry Sandry	69	75	73	217	3,030.27
Bob Menne	73	72	72	217	3,030.27
Bernard Gallacher	71	74	73	218	2,347.22
Tony Jacklin	77	70	71	218	2,347.22
Alan Tapie	71	77	70	218	2,347.22
Antonio Garrido	70	75	74	219	1,965.80
Arnold O'Connor	71	73	75	219	1,965.80
Bill Brask	68	74	77	219	1,965.80
Agim Bardha	74	71	74	219	1,965.80
Guy Hunt	75	74	70	219	1,965.80
Michael Slater	72	74	73	219	1,965.80

MDIS & Partners Festival of Golf

Mill Ride Golf Club, Ascot, England
Par 36-36–72; 6,567 yards

May 21-23
purse, €110,000

	SCORES			TOTAL	MONEY
David Oakley	68	71	69	208	€15,950
David Huish	73	71	70	214	8,052
Jerry Bruner	70	71	73	214	8,052
Eddie Polland	71	70	75	216	4,950
Ray Carrasco	75	71	71	217	4,455
Neil Coles	77	69	72	218	3,877.50
Tommy Horton	68	73	77	218	3,877.50
Bob Shearer	73	76	70	219	2,887.50
Malcolm Gregson	72	71	76	219	2,887.50
Michael Slater	73	71	75	219	2,887.50
Tony Jacklin	75	73	71	219	2,887.50
Arnold O'Connor	73	72	75	220	1,760
Bill Brask	76	71	73	220	1,760
Bob Menne	72	75	73	220	1,760
Brian Waites	76	70	74	220	1,760
Doug Robb	71	73	76	220	1,760
Jim Rhodes	75	74	71	220	1,760
Alan Tapie	76	73	72	221	1,265
David Creamer	78	70	73	221	1,265
T.R. Jones	75	75	71	221	1,265
Agim Bardha	75	72	75	222	1,080.75
Bernard Gallacher	72	75	75	222	1,080.75
Fritz Gambetta	78	72	72	222	1,080.75
Trevor Downing	76	76	70	222	1,080.75
Gordon Gray	71	73	79	223	968
Liam Higgins	76	74	73	223	968
Norman Wood	79	71	73	223	968
Thomas Persson	76	75	72	223	968
Antonio Garrido	79	70	75	224	880
Bobby Verwey	79	74	71	224	880
Iain Clark	79	71	74	224	880
Vincent Tshabalala	76	72	76	224	880

Philips PFA Golf Classic

Marriott Meon Valley Hotel & Country Club,
Southampton, England
Par 36-36–72; 6,441 yards

May 29-31
purse, €150,000

	SCORES			TOTAL	MONEY
Bob Shearer	70	67	67	204	€23,250
J.R. Delich	69	68	68	205	12,450
Terry Gale	67	73	65	205	12,450
Antonio Garrido	68	68	70	206	6,400
David Huish	71	66	69	206	6,400
Tommy Horton	70	70	66	206	6,400
Bob Lendzion	70	67	70	207	5,300
David Jones	69	66	73	208	4,850
Paul Leonard	69	69	71	209	4,396
Ian Stanley	67	72	71	210	4,000
Arnold O'Connor	70	74	67	211	3,142.50
Bill Brask	72	73	66	211	3,142.50

	SCORES			TOTAL	MONEY
Brian Waites	68	74	69	211	3,142.50
David Oakley	71	71	69	211	3,142.50
Alan Tapie	72	72	68	212	2,127.50
Brian Huggett	69	72	71	212	2,127.50
Eddie Polland	74	69	69	212	2,127.50
Norman Wood	70	72	70	212	2,127.50
Denis O'Sullivan	72	73	68	213	1,810
Barry Sandry	74	73	67	214	1,590
Bobby Verwey	72	70	72	214	1,590
David Creamer	71	70	73	214	1,590
Liam Higgins	73	72	69	214	1,590
Michael Slater	67	76	71	214	1,590
Craig Defoy	72	71	72	215	1,242.86
Geoff Parslow	72	73	70	215	1,242.86
Gordon Parkhill	71	73	71	215	1,242.86
Jerry Bruner	73	69	73	215	1,242.86
Joe McDermott	70	75	70	215	1,242.86
Peter Butler	70	72	73	215	1,242.86
Trevor Downing	71	71	73	215	1,242.86

Jersey Seniors Open

La Moye Golf Club, Jersey
Par 36-36–72; 6,581 yards

June 11-13
purse, €140,000

	SCORES			TOTAL	MONEY
David Jones	69	70	69	208	€19,850
Jim Rhodes	70	71	69	210	10,025
Paul Leonard	69	68	73	210	10,025
Bernard Gallacher	72	69	71	212	5,850
Bob Lendzion	67	73	72	212	5,850
Alan Tapie	72	73	69	214	4,825
Brian Waites	75	69	70	214	4,825
Liam Higgins	68	70	77	215	4,110
David Oakley	73	74	69	216	3,597.50
Neil Coles	72	71	73	216	3,597.50
Antonio Garrido	74	72	71	217	2,630
David Huish	70	72	75	217	2,630
Malcolm Gregson	75	71	71	217	2,630
Maurice Bembridge	75	72	70	217	2,630
Ian Stanley	80	70	68	218	2,055
Agim Bardha	70	76	73	219	1,685.10
Bob Shearer	72	75	72	219	1,685.10
David Creamer	73	73	73	219	1,685.10
Fritz Gambetta	73	73	73	219	1,685.10
Jerry Bruner	71	73	75	219	1,685.10
Arnold O'Connor	72	70	78	220	1,308.35
Bill Hardwick	76	73	71	220	1,308.35
Gordon Parkhill	73	72	75	220	1,308.35
John Fourie	77	74	69	220	1,308.35
Michael Slater	77	72	71	220	1,308.35
Norman Wood	77	72	71	220	1,308.35
Bobby Verwey	72	77	72	221	1,164.50
Brian Huggett	75	72	74	221	1,164.50
Joe McDermott	77	72	72	221	1,164.50
Deray Simon	73	78	71	222	1,041.20
Geoff Parslow	75	74	73	222	1,041.20

	SCORES			TOTAL	MONEY
Hugh Inggs	72	74	76	222	1,041.20
J.R. Delich	73	74	75	222	1,041.20
Joe Carr	73	73	76	222	1,041.20
Ray Carrasco	75	74	73	222	1,041.20

Lawrence Batley Seniors

Huddersfield Golf Club, West Yorkshire, England
Par 36-35–71; 6,447 yards

June 24-26
purse, €140,000

	SCORES			TOTAL	MONEY
Eddie Polland	66	66	72	204	€22,500
Antonio Garrido	71	67	68	206	14,650
David Jones	68	70	70	208	8,600
Jerry Bruner	69	69	72	210	5,916.67
Michael Slater	68	69	73	210	5,916.67
Tommy Horton	69	69	72	210	5,916.67
Bernard Gallacher	71	69	71	211	4,750
Fritz Gambetta	75	66	71	212	3,862.50
Ian Stanley	72	68	72	212	3,862.50
Jim Rhodes	70	70	72	212	3,862.50
Malcolm Gregson	71	71	70	212	3,862.50
Denis O'Sullivan	73	70	70	213	3,100
Neil Coles	73	68	72	213	3,100
Brian Huggett	72	68	74	214	2,525
Brian Waites	71	70	73	214	2,525
David Huish	68	69	77	214	2,525
Liam Higgins	71	73	70	214	2,525
Alberto Croce	72	72	71	215	2,150
Maurice Bembridge	71	72	72	215	2,150
David Creamer	71	77	68	216	1,850
Paul Leonard	69	74	73	216	1,850
Peter Butler	69	73	74	216	1,850
Ray Carrasco	69	73	74	216	1,850
Bill Hardwick	71	73	73	217	1,550
John McTear	72	70	75	217	1,550
Deray Simon	74	74	70	218	1,400
Alan Tapie	76	69	74	219	1,350
Bobby Verwey	72	71	76	219	1,350
Kenny Stevenson	72	73	74	219	1,350
Renato Campagnoli	73	72	74	219	1,350

Elf Seniors Open

Golf de Chantaco, France
Par 35-35–70; 6,262 yards

July 8-10
purse, €150,000

	SCORES			TOTAL	MONEY
Alan Tapie	64	66	70	200	€25,000
John McTear	64	68	71	203	12,995
Liam Higgins	72	65	66	203	12,995
Eddie Polland	68	69	67	204	6,606.67
Jerry Bruner	67	64	73	204	6,606.67
Neil Coles	69	69	66	204	6,606.67
Craig Defoy	72	65	68	205	5,340

	SCORES			TOTAL	MONEY
Jean Garaialde	67	72	66	205	5,340
Brian Waites	65	70	71	206	4,266.67
David Creamer	66	74	66	206	4,266.67
Ian Stanley	67	66	73	206	4,266.67
Christian Bonardi	68	71	68	207	3,050
Gordon Parkhill	68	69	70	207	3,050
Stewart Ginn	69	68	70	207	3,050
Tony Jacklin	72	66	69	207	3,050
Antonio Garrido	72	66	70	208	2,085
Fritz Gambetta	69	68	71	208	2,085
Jeff Van Wagenen	72	66	70	208	2,085
Ray Carrasco	70	69	69	208	2,085
David Jones	70	65	74	209	1,600
Jim Rhodes	69	70	70	209	1,600
Malcolm Gregson	68	71	70	209	1,600
Manuel Ballesteros	72	67	70	209	1,600
Michel Damiano	72	69	68	209	1,600
Alberto Croce	70	69	71	210	1,360
Bill Hardwick	73	69	68	210	1,360
Brian Huggett	70	69	71	210	1,360
Gordon MacDonald	72	69	70	211	1,180
Guy Hunt	68	73	70	211	1,180
Jose Roca	68	72	71	211	1,180
Maurice Bembridge	73	66	72	211	1,180
Randall Vines	68	73	70	211	1,180
Renato Campagnoli	73	69	69	211	1,180

Senior British Open

Royal Portrush Golf Club, Portrush, Northern Ireland
Par 36-36–72; 6,692 yards

July 22-25
purse, €560,000

	SCORES				TOTAL	MONEY
Christy O'Connor, Jr.	76	69	68	69	282	€88,620
John Bland	73	71	71	70	285	56,420
Gary Player	74	74	66	72	286	32,788
John Morgan	71	74	70	72	287	26,600
Bob Charles	72	73	67	77	289	20,720
Stewart Ginn	72	71	76	70	289	20,720
David Oakley	70	71	73	77	291	18,200
Antonio Garrido	71	77	71	73	292	16,800
David Jones	80	70	72	71	293	14,046.67
Jerry Bruner	75	76	72	70	293	14,046.67
Tommy Horton	78	73	71	71	293	14,046.67
John Grace	77	75	71	71	294	10,850
Norman Wood	73	73	75	73	294	10,850
Alan Tapie	76	72	74	73	295	7,840
Eddie Polland	77	75	76	67	295	7,840
Fritz Gambetta	76	70	74	75	295	7,840
John Garner	74	71	76	74	295	7,840
Bernard Gallacher	76	76	72	72	296	6,258
Bill Brask	73	75	75	73	296	6,258
Bob Shearer	73	74	74	76	297	5,194
Brian Huggett	74	73	71	79	297	5,194
Brian Waites	72	77	75	73	297	5,194
Denis O'Sullivan	73	75	76	73	297	5,194
Joe McDermott	76	74	71	76	297	5,194

	SCORES				TOTAL	MONEY
Malcolm Gregson	78	72	72	75	297	5,194
Seiji Ebihara	76	78	71	73	298	4,620
Brian Barnes	77	76	72	74	299	4,358.67
Jim Rhodes	76	73	73	77	299	4,358.67
Neil Coles	74	79	72	74	299	4,358.67
Bob Lendzion	76	74	76	74	300	3,962
Ed Sabo	73	80	72	75	300	3,962
Geoff Parslow	81	74	72	73	300	3,962
Helmuth Schumacher	77	77	73	73	300	3,962
John Fourie	77	74	73	76	300	3,962
Ray Carrasco	70	77	77	76	300	3,962
*Roy Smethurst	80	74	77	69	300	

Energis Senior Masters

Wentworth Club, Edinburgh Course, Surrey, England
Par 36-36–72; 6,598 yards

July 30-August 1
purse, €210,000

	SCORES			TOTAL	MONEY
Neil Coles	68	69	68	205	€35,000
David Huish	72	66	68	206	23,400
Alberto Croce	67	67	74	208	13,500
Ian Stanley	70	70	69	209	9,830
Tony Jacklin	68	70	71	209	9,830
Brian Huggett	69	69	72	210	8,400
Bernard Gallacher	72	72	67	211	7,033.33
John Grace	68	72	71	211	7,033.33
Norman Wood	70	72	69	211	7,033.33
Bill Brask	72	70	70	212	5,400
Christy O'Connor, Jr.	74	69	69	212	5,400
Maurice Bembridge	74	72	66	212	5,400
David Oakley	73	72	68	213	4,250
Denis O'Sullivan	72	73	68	213	4,250
Agim Bardha	69	72	73	214	3,533.33
Bob Shearer	74	70	70	214	3,533.33
Eddie Polland	73	72	69	214	3,533.33
John Morgan	73	74	68	215	2,850
Ray Carrasco	72	75	68	215	2,850
Jim Rhodes	74	70	72	216	2,350
Michael Slater	72	74	70	216	2,350
Alan Tapie	70	74	73	217	1,993.33
David Creamer	69	77	71	217	1,993.33
Jerry Bruner	70	74	73	217	1,993.33
Malcolm Gregson	72	73	72	217	1,993.33
Stewart Ginn	72	73	72	217	1,993.33
Tommy Horton	76	68	73	217	1,993.33
Craig Defoy	72	73	73	218	1,645
Noel Ratcliffe	75	73	70	218	1,645
Randall Vines	70	75	73	218	1,645
Tommy Price	71	72	75	218	1,645

Bad Ragaz PGA Seniors Open

Bad Ragaz Golf Club, Zurich, Switzerland
Par 35-35–70; 6,289 yards

August 6-8
purse, €140,000

	SCORES			TOTAL	MONEY
Bob Shearer	67	63	68	198	€23,450
David Oakley	70	65	66	201	15,650
Bob Menne	68	65	69	202	9,000
Bernard Gallacher	71	68	65	204	5,724
Craig Defoy	72	64	68	204	5,724
Jerry Bruner	70	70	64	204	5,724
Maurice Bembridge	68	70	66	204	5,724
Ray Carrasco	69	67	68	204	5,724
Bobby Verwey	69	65	71	205	3,757.50
Paul Leonard	64	71	70	205	3,757.50
Tomas Persson	69	67	69	205	3,757.50
Tommy Horton	69	66	70	205	3,757.50
Agim Bardha	67	69	70	206	2,835
Michael Slater	67	72	67	206	2,835
Geoff Parslow	69	70	68	207	2,055
John Fourie	68	70	69	207	2,055
John Hudson	71	68	68	207	2,055
Jose Cabo	73	69	65	207	2,055
Lloyd Monroe	68	69	70	207	2,055
Sid Denham	65	72	70	207	2,055
Eddie Polland	67	71	70	208	1,495
Jim Rhodes	69	72	67	208	1,495
Norman Wood	68	70	71	209	1,400
Barry Sandry	69	72	69	210	1,200
Bill Brask	73	66	71	210	1,200
David Huish	74	68	68	210	1,200
Jay Dolan III	67	73	70	210	1,200
Malcolm Gregson	73	70	67	210	1,200
Terry Gale	71	69	70	210	1,200
Ian Stanley	71	69	71	211	1,030
Joe McDermott	72	69	70	211	1,030
Ross Metherell	70	67	74	211	1,030
Tommy Price	73	66	72	211	1,030

De Vere Hotels Seniors Classic

Ferndown Golf Club, England
Par 35-36–71; 6,479 yards

August 13-15
purse, €140,000

	SCORES			TOTAL	MONEY
Ross Metherell	66	65	69	200	€23,450
Bill Brask	67	66	68	201	15,650
Michael Slater	70	69	64	203	9,000
Tommy Horton	66	68	70	204	6,970
David Huish	65	68	72	205	5,935
Terry Gale	65	68	72	205	5,935
Alan Tapie	68	69	69	206	4,683.33
Craig Defoy	68	69	69	206	4,683.33
Jerry Bruner	66	68	72	206	4,683.33
Bobby Verwey	68	69	70	207	3,750
Brian Huggett	66	70	71	207	3,750
Eddie Polland	72	67	69	208	3,260

	SCORES			TOTAL	MONEY
Antonio Garrido	69	69	71	209	2,436.67
Bob Shearer	69	75	65	209	2,436.67
David Jones	71	70	68	209	2,436.67
Fritz Gambetta	67	73	69	209	2,436.67
Guy Hunt	68	71	70	209	2,436.67
J.R. Delich	68	73	68	209	2,436.67
Bob Menne	69	70	71	210	1,554
David Creamer	72	67	71	210	1,554
David Oakley	73	69	68	210	1,554
Ian Stanley	67	72	71	210	1,554
Tomas Persson	70	74	66	210	1,554
Agim Bardha	69	71	71	211	1,250
John Fourie	68	70	73	211	1,250
Malcolm Gregson	69	68	74	211	1,250
Tommy Price	71	70	70	211	1,250
Denis O'Sullivan	70	71	71	212	1,064
Doug Robb	69	70	73	212	1,064
Jim Rhodes	69	74	69	212	1,064
John McTear	70	67	75	212	1,064
Norman Wood	72	68	72	212	1,064

The Dalmahoy Scottish Seniors Open

Marriott Dalmahoy Hotel & Country Club,
Edinburgh, Scotland
Par 36-36–72; 6,511 yards

August 20-22
purse, €140,000

	SCORES			TOTAL	MONEY
Neil Coles	69	68	69	206	€23,100
Jay Dolan III	68	68	71	207	12,061
Jerry Bruner	70	69	68	207	12,061
Agim Bardha	72	66	70	208	6,846
David Creamer	72	69	68	209	5,355
David Jones	71	67	71	209	5,355
Ian Stanley	70	69	70	209	5,355
John McTear	69	70	70	209	5,355
Antonio Garrido	68	71	71	210	4,116
David Oakley	69	68	73	210	4,116
Bernard Gallacher	72	68	71	211	3,420.20
Ray Carrasco	68	70	73	211	3,420.20
Joe Carr	69	69	74	212	2,966.04
Bob Menne	71	70	72	213	2,209.45
Bobby Verwey	72	70	71	213	2,209.45
David Vaughan	73	74	66	213	2,209.45
John Garner	71	72	70	213	2,209.45
Michael Hooper	69	68	76	213	2,209.45
Geoff Parslow	71	70	73	214	1,546.78
Gordon MacDonald	72	70	72	214	1,546.78
Jim Rhodes	68	74	72	214	1,546.78
Jose Cabo	67	71	76	214	1,546.78
Tommy Horton	74	71	69	214	1,546.78
John Fourie	77	67	71	215	1,258.49
Liam Higgins	72	73	70	215	1,258.49
Michael Slater	71	71	73	215	1,258.49
Ross Metherell	70	69	76	215	1,258.49
Tommy Price	73	72	70	215	1,258.49
Bill Brask	74	69	73	216	1,061.68

	SCORES			TOTAL	MONEY
Bob Lendzion	74	73	69	216	1,061.68
J.R. Delich	71	73	72	216	1,061.68
Joe McDermott	73	71	72	216	1,061.68
Manuel Ballesteros	68	75	73	216	1,061.68

The Belfry PGA Seniors Championship

PGA National, The Belfry, Birmingham, England
Par 36-36–72; 6,626 yards

August 27-30
purse, €252,000

	SCORES				TOTAL	MONEY
Ross Metherell	71	68	66	71	276	€42,000
Bill Brask	70	72	66	69	277	28,000
Terry Gale	68	70	68	72	278	15,876
Jim Rhodes	70	72	68	70	280	12,460
Michael Slater	72	65	69	75	281	10,962
Agim Bardha	68	72	74	69	283	8,953
David Huish	68	72	71	72	283	8,953
David Jones	73	71	71	68	283	8,953
Jerry Bruner	69	72	72	70	283	8,953
Jeff Van Wagenen	70	70	73	71	284	7,098
Liam Higgins	75	68	71	71	285	6,542
Craig Defoy	68	74	71	73	286	5,393.73
Renato Campagnoli	70	74	70	72	286	5,393.73
Tommy Price	74	72	71	69	286	5,393.73
Bill Hardwick	70	70	73	74	287	3,544.80
Joe McDermott	74	71	71	71	287	3,544.80
John Grace	70	74	72	71	287	3,544.80
Ray Carrasco	73	70	72	72	287	3,544.80
Tommy Horton	74	71	70	72	287	3,544.80
T.R. Jones	71	71	71	74	287	3,544.80
Bernard Gallacher	74	72	73	69	288	2,570.40
Chick Evans	71	72	75	70	288	2,570.40
Eddie Polland	73	73	71	71	288	2,570.40
Geoff Parslow	66	75	75	72	288	2,570.40
Ian Stanley	71	73	73	71	288	2,570.40
Maurice Bembridge	73	73	73	70	289	2,242.80
Tomas Persson	74	68	78	69	289	2,242.80
J.R. Delich	76	71	74	69	290	2,079
Jose Cabo	73	72	68	77	290	2,079
Alan Tapie	73	74	73	71	291	1,884.96
Bob Lendzion	72	73	73	73	291	1,884.96
Gordon MacDonald	68	73	73	77	291	1,884.96
Ian Richardson	75	72	71	73	291	1,884.96
Norman Wood	71	75	72	73	291	1,884.96

Monte Carlo Invitational

Monte Carlo Golf Club, Monte Carlo, Monaco
Par 34-35–69; 6,179 yards

September 9-11
purse, €175,000

	SCORES			TOTAL	MONEY
Tommy Horton	69	70	68	207	€28,000
Ray Carrasco	70	69	69	208	12,766.67
Bill Brask	70	67	71	208	12,766.67

		SCORES		TOTAL	MONEY
Jerry Bruner	69	69	70	208	12,766.67
Terry Gale	70	69	70	209	6,975
David Jones	69	69	71	209	6,975
Neil Coles	69	74	67	210	5,132
David Oakley	70	65	75	210	5,132
Eddie Polland	72	68	70	210	5,132
Jim Rhodes	68	69	73	210	5,132
Bobby Verwey	71	70	69	210	5,132
Alan Tapie	69	74	68	211	4,050
Gary Player	74	71	67	212	3,390
Agim Bardha	73	68	71	212	3,390
Joe McDermott	70	73	69	212	3,390
Ian Stanley	69	72	71	212	3,390
David Creamer	70	66	76	212	3,390
Manuel Ballesteros	73	73	67	213	2,675
Brian Waites	71	72	70	213	2,675
Denis O'Sullivan	67	75	71	213	2,675
Fritz Gambetta	70	69	74	213	2,675
Paul Leonard	74	69	71	214	2,300
Maurice Bembridge	73	70	72	215	2,016.67
John Garner	76	67	72	215	2,016.67
Bob Lendzion	69	72	74	215	2,016.67
Renato Campagnoli	74	69	75	218	1,692
Malcolm Gregson	71	72	75	218	1,692
Bill Hardwick	72	71	75	218	1,692
Gordon MacDonald	73	71	74	218	1,692
Ross Metherell	73	70	75	218	1,692

Ordina Legends in Golf

Prise d'Eau Golf Club, Tilburg, Netherlands
Par 36-36–72; 6,610 yards

September 17-19
purse, €112,000

		SCORES		TOTAL	MONEY
Michael Slater	66	68	69	203	€16,450
David Huish	71	72	64	207	8,700
Jerry Bruner	67	66	74	207	8,700
Liam Higgins	70	70	69	209	4,745
Gordon MacDonald	70	70	69	209	4,745
Antonio Garrido	70	68	72	210	3,058.75
Renato Campagnoli	69	70	71	210	3,058.75
Arnold O'Connor	66	74	70	210	3,058.75
Jim Rhodes	68	68	74	210	3,058.75
Barry Sandry	73	70	67	210	3,058.75
Jeff Van Wagenen	72	68	70	210	3,058.75
Fritz Gambetta	69	71	70	210	3,058.75
Trevor Downing	70	71	69	210	3,058.75
Maurice Bembridge	70	69	72	211	1,559.26
Neil Coles	71	70	70	211	1,559.26
Paul Leonard	71	67	73	211	1,559.26
Bill Brask	73	71	67	211	1,559.26
Ian Stanley	68	71	72	211	1,559.26
Denis O'Sullivan	71	71	69	211	1,559.26
Terry Gale	66	75	71	212	1,169.06
Norman Wood	71	72	69	212	1,169.06
Alberto Croce	71	71	70	212	1,169.06
Vincent Tshabalala	69	73	70	212	1,169.06

	SCORES			TOTAL	MONEY
J.R. Delich	70	70	73	213	1,025.76
Eddie Polland	72	73	68	213	1,025.76
Bernard Gallacher	71	73	70	214	907.79
Agim Bardha	74	71	69	214	907.79
Tomas Persson	69	71	74	214	907.79
Gordon Gray	75	71	68	214	907.79
Tommy Horton	69	75	71	215	834.80
David Oakley	74	71	70	215	834.80

Te Mes Greek Seniors Open

Glyfada Golf Club, Athens, Greece
Par 36-36–72; 6,675 yards

October 8-10
purse, €175,000

	SCORES			TOTAL	MONEY
Alberto Croce	70	73	68	211	€29,000
Antonio Garrido	69	71	71	211	19,300
(Croce defeated Garrido on fourth extra hole.)					
Bernard Gallacher	69	72	71	212	12,000
Bobby Verwey	74	72	67	213	8,610
Joe Carr	73	71	70	214	7,600
Brian Huggett	71	72	72	215	6,212.50
Manuel Sanchez	72	74	69	215	6,212.50
David Huish	72	72	71	215	6,212.50
Barry Sandry	72	70	73	215	6,212.50
Jim Rhodes	72	72	72	216	4,900
Geoff Parslow	68	74	75	217	4,500
Brian Waites	75	74	69	218	3,216.67
Agim Bardha	71	77	70	218	3,216.67
Norman Wood	70	73	75	218	3,216.67
David Jones	71	73	74	218	3,216.67
Joe McDermott	73	74	71	218	3,216.67
Ross Metherell	75	71	72	218	3,216.67
Denis O'Sullivan	75	71	73	219	2,265
Bryan Carter	74	74	71	219	2,265
Tommy Horton	73	72	75	220	1,852
Snell Lancaster	76	73	71	220	1,852
David Oakley	74	72	74	220	1,852
Michael Slater	73	78	69	220	1,852
Bob Lendzion	75	71	74	220	1,852

Senior Tournament of Champions

Buckinghamshire Golf Club, Denham, England
Par 36-36–72; 6,665 yards

October 22-24
purse, €168,000

	SCORES			TOTAL	MONEY
Eddie Polland	69	71	72	212	€28,000
Tommy Horton	65	78	71	214	14,560
Liam Higgins	71	71	72	214	14,560
Antonio Garrido	71	70	74	215	7,513.33
Terry Gale	69	75	71	215	7,513.33
David Creamer	69	74	72	215	7,513.33
Craig Defoy	70	71	76	217	6,090
Ross Metherell	72	71	74	217	6,090

	SCORES			TOTAL	MONEY
Neil Coles	73	74	71	218	4,935
Brian Waites	68	73	77	218	4,935
Norman Wood	72	71	75	218	4,935
Jerry Bruner	69	74	75	218	4,935
Bernard Gallacher	72	74	73	219	3,430
John Morgan	70	73	76	219	3,430
Malcolm Gregson	71	74	74	219	3,430
J.R. Delich	73	71	75	219	3,430
Bill Brask	73	71	75	219	3,430
David Jones	71	73	75	219	3,430
Jim Rhodes	71	73	75	219	3,430
Ray Carrasco	74	73	73	220	2,520
Ian Stanley	71	73	76	220	2,520
Fritz Gambetta	77	74	69	220	2,520
Alberto Croce	71	79	71	221	2,170
David Huish	68	77	76	221	2,170
Bob Lendzion	72	73	76	221	2,170
Alan Tapie	69	78	75	222	1,988
Brian Huggett	75	73	75	223	1,883
John Garner	72	74	77	223	1,883
Bob Shearer	73	78	73	224	1,683.50
David Oakley	75	73	76	224	1,683.50
Michael Slater	74	71	79	224	1,683.50
Bobby Verwey	74	72	78	224	1,683.50

Japan Senior Tour

ANA Ishigaki-jima Senior Pro-Am

Ishigakijima Country Club, Ishigaki, Okinawa
Par 36-36—72; 6,537 yards

January 31-February 1
purse, ¥5,000,000

	SCORES		TOTAL	MONEY
Hiroshi Ishii	66	64	130	¥300,000
Shozo Miyamoto	64	68	132	260,000
Seiji Ogawa	65	68	133	230,000
Shoji Kikuchi	68	65	133	230,000
Teruo Suzumura	69	65	134	200,000
Fujio Kobayashi	69	67	136	180,000
Isao Matsui	66	70	136	180,000
Hitoshi Tomita	66	70	136	180,000
Akira Kawamata	69	68	137	166,666
Tadao Nakamura	68	69	137	166,666
Tetsuhiro Ueda	62	75	137	166,666
Keiichi Kobayashi	73	66	139	160,000
Shoichi Sato	71	69	140	157,500
Hiroshi Kazami	69	71	140	157,500

	SCORES		TOTAL	MONEY
Wataru Horiguchi	69	71	140	157,500
Shigeru Uchida	67	73	140	157,500
Masaru Amano	69	72	141	150,000
Koichi Uehara	71	71	142	150,000
Seiichi Kanai	69	74	143	146,666
Toshiki Matsui	72	71	143	146,666
Yasuhiro Miyamoto	70	73	143	146,666
Namio Takasu	69	75	144	140,000
Minoru Nakamura	75	69	144	140,000
Hisao Inoue	75	69	144	140,000
Ryosuke Ota	73	72	145	140,000
Kesahiko Uchida	72	74	146	130,000
Sadao Ogawa	73	73	146	130,000
Masaji Kusakabe	73	73	146	130,000
Koji Nakajima	73	74	147	130,000
Hideyo Sugimoto	76	73	149	130,000

Asahi Ryokken Cup

The Classic Golf Club, Kurate-gun, Fukuoka
Par 36-36–72; 6,725 yards

March 12-13
purse, ¥10,000,000

	SCORES		TOTAL	MONEY
Hiroshi Ishii	68	70	138	¥1,500,000
Akira Kawamata	67	72	139	750,000
Tadao Nakamura	69	72	141	450,000
Katsuji Hasegawa	68	73	141	450,000
Masaru Amano	70	72	142	264,000
Koichi Uehara	72	70	142	264,000
Hsieh Min-nan	70	72	142	264,000
Hiroshi Kazami	72	70	142	264,000
Fumio Tanaka	73	69	142	264,000
Fujio Kobayashi	69	74	143	230,000
Hisao Inoue	74	69	143	230,000
Seiji Ogawa	69	77	146	230,000
Takaaki Kono	77	69	146	230,000
*Masami Yamamoto	72	74	146	
Yoshiharu Nakase	73	74	147	225,000
Toru Nakayama	75	72	147	225,000
Shigeru Uchida	73	74	147	225,000
Yasuhiro Miyamoto	73	74	147	225,000
Masaji Kusakabe	72	76	148	220,000
Kanae Nobechi	73	76	149	216,666
Tetsuhiro Ueda	73	76	149	216,666
Norihiko Matsumoto	71	78	149	216,666
Mineyuki Yoshimatsu	77	73	150	210,000
*Hirotake Konomi	72	78	150	
*Fumitaka Iwashita	75	75	150	
Mitsutaka Kono	75	76	151	206,000
Hideyo Sugimoto	75	76	151	206,000
Yoshihiro Takata	72	79	151	206,000
Tadayoshi Bandoh	74	77	151	206,000
Shozo Miyamoto	78	73	151	206,000
*Takehisa Shinozuka	73	78	151	
*Katsushige Matsuo	76	75	151	
*Seiichi Obata	76	75	151	

Castle Hill Open

Castle Hill County Club, Hoi-gun, Aichi   April 23-25
Par 36-36–72; 6,694 yards   purse, ¥30,000,000

	SCORES			TOTAL	MONEY
Fujio Kobayashi	71	74	72	217	¥4,500,000
Seiji Ebihara	74	72	72	218	1,875,000
Mitoshi Tomita	74	76	68	218	1,875,000
Koichi Uehara	72	76	71	219	1,125,000
Norihiko Matsumoto	74	72	73	219	1,125,000
Hsieh Min-nan	73	74	75	222	855,000
Ichiro Teramoto	76	77	70	223	690,000
Seiichi Kanai	77	74	73	224	577,500
Tadami Ueno	73	73	78	224	577,500
Wataru Horiguchi	79	76	70	225	495,000
Katsuji Hasegawa	81	72	73	226	489,000
Seiji Ogawa	78	76	73	227	471,000
Yoshiharu Nakase	73	77	78	228	435,600
Tadao Nakamura	76	75	77	228	435,600
Hiroshi Ishii	73	78	77	228	435,600
Hisao Inoue	73	77	78	228	435,600
Shigeru Uchida	77	77	74	228	435,600
Kesahiko Uchida	77	78	74	229	390,000
Masaji Kusakabe	75	77	77	229	390,000
Tooru Kurihara	77	77	75	229	390,000
Tetsuhiro Ueda	78	74	77	229	390,000
Osamu Watanabe	76	79	74	229	390,000
Akira Azuma	82	76	72	230	358,500
Kuo Chie-hsiung	81	75	74	230	358,500
Kikuo Arai	80	74	77	231	339,000
Toshiki Matsui	80	74	77	231	339,000
Yoshikazu Izumi	76	82	73	231	339,000
Hiroshi Kazami	77	74	81	232	309,000
Tatsuo Fujima	79	76	77	232	309,000
Akira Yabe	80	75	77	232	309,000
Yutaka Suzuki	78	73	81	232	309,000
Yasuhiro Daio	85	74	73	232	309,000
Yasuhiro Miyamoto	83	75	74	232	309,000
Terry Gale	80	75	77	232	309,000

Old Man Par Senior Open

Minakami Kogen Golf Club, Tone-gun, Gunma   August 27-28
Par 36-36–72; 6,636 yards   purse, ¥5,840,000

	SCORES		TOTAL	MONEY
Masaji Kusakabe	66	70	136	¥1,200,000
Kikuo Arai	67	69	136	500,000
Koji Nakajima	69	67	136	500,000
(Kusakabe won on second extra hole.)				
Tadao Nakamura	70	68	138	300,000
Koichi Uehara	71	68	139	201,666
Toru Nakayama	68	71	139	201,666
Hisao Inoue	69	70	139	201,666
Seiji Ogawa	72	69	141	143,125
Fujio Kobayashi	70	71	141	143,125

	SCORES		TOTAL	MONEY
Haruo Yasuda	68	73	141	143,125
Kenichi Tsurumoto	71	70	141	143,125
Shigeru Kawamata	74	68	142	133,750
Mamoru Kondo	74	68	142	133,750
Seiji Ebihara	73	71	144	127,500
Mitoshi Tomita	70	74	144	127,500
Toshiki Matsui	73	71	144	127,500
Masao Kikuchi	75	70	145	116,250
Hisao Kinoshita	74	71	145	116,250
Kanae Nobechi	73	72	145	116,250
Isao Matsui	77	68	145	116,250
Masaharu Ohshima	74	71	145	116,250
Norihiko Matsumoto	72	73	145	116,250
Ichiro Ino	73	73	146	106,250
Tooru Kurihara	72	74	146	106,250
*Haruo Hashimoto	74	72	146	
Hiroshi Kaihata	72	75	147	100,833
Kiyokuri Kimoto	74	73	147	100,833
Minoru Nakamura	74	73	147	100,833
*Ebine Sigemasa	79	68	147	
Yuji Ogawa	76	72	148	100,000

HTB Senior Classic

Mitsui Kanko Iris Golf Club, Hokkaido
Par 36-36–72; 6,442 yards

September 11-12
purse, ¥8,000,000

	SCORES		TOTAL	MONEY
Fujio Kobayashi	70	68	138	¥2,000,000
Koichi Uehara	69	69	138	950,000
(Kobayashi defeated Uehara on second extra hole.)				
Seiichi Kanai	70	72	142	400,000
Tadao Nakamura	72	70	142	400,000
Toru Nakayama	72	70	142	400,000
Hiroshi Ishii	70	73	143	182,500
Hisao Inoue	72	71	143	182,500
Shigeru Uchida	73	71	144	170,000
Katsuji Hasegawa	71	74	145	161,333
Wataru Horiguchi	74	71	145	161,333
Isao Matsui	73	72	145	161,333
Masaru Amano	69	77	146	156,500
Kesahiko Uchida	72	74	146	156,500
Mamoru Unodera	71	75	146	156,500
Koji Nakajima	71	75	146	156,500
*Hisao Saito	76	70	146	
Kikuo Arai	77	71	148	154,000
*Katsuyuki Sakura	79	69	148	
Hisao Kinoshita	77	72	149	152,500
Jun Nobechi	74	75	149	152,500
Namio Takasu	76	74	150	150,500
Hiroshi Yuhara	79	71	150	150,500
*Hideshi Doi	75	75	150	
Takaaki Kono	76	75	151	148,500
Ichiro Yugawa	75	76	151	148,500
Hideyo Sugimoto	79	73	152	147,000
Kanae Nobechi	79	74	153	146,000
Shozo Miyamoto	77	77	154	145,000

	SCORES	TOTAL	MONEY
*Hayashi Tadahiko	78 76	154	
*Shigeki Kameda	75 79	154	

Japan PGA Senior Championship

Shimoakima Country Club, Annaka, Gunma
Par 36-36–72; 6,776 yards

October 7-10
purse, ¥50,000,000

	SCORES				TOTAL	MONEY
Tadami Ueno	77	66	73	71	287	¥7,500,000
Mitsuo Iwata	73	69	73	72	287	3,500,000
(Ueno defeated Iwata on first extra hole.)						
Seiichi Kanai	70	71	73	74	288	2,375,000
Katsuji Hasegawa	70	71	73	74	288	2,375,000
Hisao Inoue	71	74	72	73	290	1,750,000
Toru Nakayama	78	69	74	71	292	1,191,666
Ichiro Teramoto	70	71	74	77	292	1,191,666
Mitoshi Tomita	73	72	74	73	292	1,191,666
Yasuhiro Miyamoto	70	73	71	79	293	850,000
Tadao Suruichi	77	69	69	78	293	850,000
Seiji Ogawa	73	74	71	76	294	740,000
Toshiake Hameki	72	70	75	77	294	740,000
Koichi Hirabayashi	71	71	74	78	294	740,000
Hanuo Yasuda	72	77	72	73	294	740,000
Terry Gale	78	72	70	74	294	740,000
Seiji Ebihara	73	70	78	74	295	677,500
Shigeru Kawamata	69	76	76	74	295	677,500
Shichiro Enomoto	74	73	75	75	297	625,000
Shoji Kikuchi	74	73	73	77	297	625,000
Takashi Kurihara	73	78	73	73	297	625,000
Takayoshi Hishikawa	75	74	76	72	297	625,000
Katsumi Hara	75	75	72	75	297	625,000
Kikuo Arai	73	72	77	76	298	547,500
Hiroshi Kazami	74	75	74	75	298	547,500
Koji Nakajima	73	68	76	81	298	547,500
Toshihiko Kikuichi	77	75	72	74	298	547,500
Toshiki Matsui	78	73	74	73	298	547,500
Norihiko Matsumoto	72	76	74	76	298	547,500
Yoshiharu Nakase	75	76	72	76	299	500,000
Akira Azuma	73	77	75	74	299	500,000
Hisashi Kaji	75	76	73	75	299	500,000

Japan Senior Open

Rokkou Kokusai Golf Club, Kobe
Par 36-36–72; 6,811 yards

October 14-17
purse, ¥50,000,000

	SCORES				TOTAL	MONEY
Graham Marsh	66	69	67	70	272	¥10,000,000
Seiji Ebihara	71	68	70	72	281	4,687,500
Mitoshi Tomita	70	72	68	71	281	4,687,500
Haruo Yasuda	68	71	75	70	284	2,550,000
Masaru Amano	68	72	72	73	285	1,635,000
Mamoru Kondo	71	68	73	73	285	1,635,000
Yoshiaki Namiki	74	68	75	68	285	1,635,000

	SCORES			TOTAL	MONEY
Hisao Inoue	69	71	72	73	285	1,635,000
Kikuo Arai	70	74	74	68	286	1,123,000
Wataru Horiguchi	73	71	75	68	287	990,000
Tadao Nakamura	72	74	70	72	288	815,000
Teruo Sugihara	72	72	72	72	288	815,000
Seiichi Kanai	70	71	73	76	290	660,000
Toru Nakayama	76	69	73	72	290	660,000
Katsuji Hasegawa	72	73	73	74	290	660,000
Toshihiko Kikuichi	74	74	68	75	291	585,000
Shigeru Kawamata	75	73	70	74	292	547,500
Sukree Ohchan	75	72	71	74	292	547,500
Seiji Ogawa	73	72	73	75	293	497,500
Yoshikazu Izumi	72	73	78	70	293	497,500
Akira Kawamata	72	74	72	76	294	456,250
Yoshiharu Nakase	72	77	68	77	294	456,250
Tatsuo Fujima	75	73	75	71	294	456,250
Yasuhiro Miyamoto	70	73	77	74	294	456,250
Fujio Kobayashi	74	68	78	75	295	425,666
Fumio Tanaka	77	68	73	77	295	425,666
Hisashi Suzumura	70	75	77	73	295	425,666
Koichi Uehara	76	74	74	72	296	395,000
Hsieh Min-nan	72	72	79	73	296	395,000
Katsumasa Iwao	73	73	74	76	296	395,000

Tokyo Tower Senior Open

Japan PGA Golf Club, Chiba
Par 36-36–72; 6,623 yards

October 29-30
purse, ¥10,110,000

	SCORES		TOTAL	MONEY
Mitoshi Tomita	70	65	135	¥1,000,000
Katsuji Hasegawa	65	71	136	600,000
Fujio Kobayashi	67	70	137	500,000
Seiji Ogawa	68	70	138	450,000
Tatsuo Fujima	69	71	140	375,000
Yasuhiro Miyamoto	71	69	140	375,000
Seiji Ebihara	70	71	141	272,000
Seiichi Kanai	72	69	141	272,000
Masaji Kusakabe	72	69	141	272,000
Hiroshi Kazami	72	69	141	272,000
Toru Nakayama	67	74	141	272,000
Isao Matsui	71	71	142	250,000
Haruo Yasuda	70	72	142	250,000
Koji Nakajima	72	71	143	240,000
Tetsuhiro Ueda	70	73	143	240,000
Ryosuke Ota	70	73	143	240,000
Teruo Suzumura	69	74	143	240,000
Fumio Tanaka	70	74	144	230,000
Hiroshi Tahara	70	75	145	230,000
Norihiko Matsumoto	72	74	146	230,000
Ichiro Ino	73	74	147	220,000
Masaru Amano	76	72	148	220,000
Shoji Kikuchi	74	74	148	220,000
Takaaki Kono	75	73	148	220,000
Tadao Nakamura	73	77	150	210,000
Masaharu Ohshima	73	77	150	210,000
Ichio Sato	79	72	151	200,000

	SCORES		TOTAL	MONEY
Chen Ching-po	77	75	152	200,000
Isao Katsumata	78	76	154	200,000
Toshiyuki Tsuchiyama	78	76	154	200,000
Hiroshi Yorikawa	77	77	154	200,000

TPC Senior

Karasuyamajo Country Club, Nasu-gun, Tochigi
Par 36-36–72; 6,820 yards

November 16-17
purse, ¥5,000,000

	SCORES		TOTAL	MONEY
Koichi Uehara	74	74	148	¥500,000
Seiji Ebihara	73	75	148	300,000
(Uehara defeated Ebihara on fourth extra hole.)				
Takao Kage	75	74	149	180,000
Koji Nakajima	73	76	149	180,000
Toshiaki Namiki	77	72	149	180,000
Tatsuo Fujima	71	78	149	180,000
Wataru Horiguchi	76	73	149	180,000
Tamotsu Ito	74	76	150	135,000
Fujio Kobayashi	75	75	150	135,000
Yoshimi Watanabe	76	74	150	135,000
Mitoshi Tomita	76	74	150	135,000
Masaru Amano	75	76	151	100,800
Mamoru Kondo	72	79	151	100,800
Masaru Sato	76	75	151	100,800
Michihito Sekiya	74	77	151	100,800
Toshihiko Kikuichi	74	77	151	100,800
Keiichi Hoshino	76	76	152	96,000
Hiro Sakai	78	75	153	93,500
Hsieh Min-nan	79	74	153	93,500
Renkyoku Sugiyama	79	74	153	93,500
Takeshi Tizumi	75	78	153	93,500
Seiji Ogawa	79	75	154	85,142
Shoji Kikuchi	73	81	154	85,142
Masao Kikuchi	74	80	154	85,142
Kanae Nobechi	77	77	154	85,142
Kazuo Yoshikawa	78	76	154	85,142
Masao Harashima	81	73	154	85,142
Tadao Furuichi	77	77	154	85,142
Takahiro Takeyasu	80	75	155	77,500
Mitsuru Ichikura	76	79	155	77,500

Women's Tours

HealthSouth Inaugural

Grand Cypress Resort, Orlando, Florida
Par 36-36–72; 6,220 yards

January 15-17
purse, $550,000

	SCORES			TOTAL	MONEY
Kelly Robbins	70	71	64	205	$82,500
Karrie Webb	68	68	70	206	44,282
Tina Barrett	67	68	71	206	44,282
Cindy Figg-Currier	72	67	68	207	29,060
Jean Bartholomew	70	68	70	208	21,448
Catriona Matthew	66	69	73	208	21,448
Catrin Nilsmark	74	68	67	209	16,328
Helen Alfredsson	74	71	65	210	14,391
Cathy Johnston-Forbes	72	70	69	211	10,457
Janice Moodie	71	71	69	211	10,457
Jenny Lidback	68	74	69	211	10,457
Lorie Kane	70	70	71	211	10,457
Akiko Fukushima	67	73	71	211	10,457
Jane Crafter	67	72	72	211	10,457
Liselotte Neumann	71	71	70	212	7,008
Denise Killeen	71	70	71	212	7,008
Kris Tschetter	70	71	71	212	7,008
Gail Graham	70	71	71	212	7,008
Mardi Lunn	68	73	71	212	7,008
Nancy Lopez	66	74	72	212	7,008
Susie Redman	72	67	73	212	7,008
Pat Bradley	73	71	69	213	5,630
Annika Sorenstam	69	72	72	213	5,630
Patty Sheehan	70	66	77	213	5,630
Michelle McGann	72	73	69	214	4,920
Pearl Sinn	72	72	70	214	4,920
Donna Andrews	71	73	70	214	4,920
Kristi Albers	76	66	72	214	4,920
Cristie Kerr	75	66	73	214	4,920
Jane Geddes	74	71	70	215	4,194
Laura Davies	79	65	71	215	4,194
Amy Alcott	71	73	71	215	4,194
Judy Dickinson	73	69	73	215	4,194

Naples LPGA Memorial

The Club at Pelican Strand, Naples, Florida
Par 36-36–72; 6,328 yards

January 21-24
purse, $750,000

	SCORES				TOTAL	MONEY
Meg Mallon	69	67	69	67	272	$112,500
Kelly Robbins	69	68	68	68	273	60,384
Helen Alfredsson	69	68	68	68	273	60,384
Annika Sorenstam	70	72	67	66	275	32,708
Liselotte Neumann	65	70	71	69	275	32,708
Hollis Stacy	65	71	69	70	275	32,708

	SCORES				TOTAL	MONEY
Laura Davies	67	73	68	69	277	17,964
Lorie Kane	68	72	67	70	277	17,964
Michelle Estill	65	72	70	70	277	17,964
Juli Inkster	66	73	65	73	277	17,964
Karrie Webb	63	69	72	73	277	17,964
Pat Hurst	70	70	69	69	278	12,454
Jane Geddes	68	71	70	69	278	12,454
Helen Dobson	68	73	67	70	278	12,454
Kelli Kuehne	70	74	68	68	280	10,095
A.J. Eathorne	70	72	69	69	280	10,095
Leta Lindley	69	71	69	71	280	10,095
Tracy Hanson	68	69	68	75	280	10,095
Maria Hjorth	75	70	69	67	281	8,310
Mi Hyun Kim	70	71	72	68	281	8,310
Mardi Lunn	67	72	71	71	281	8,310
Cindy Flom	71	70	68	72	281	8,310
Janice Moodie	68	70	71	72	281	8,310
Vicki Fergon	70	70	74	68	282	7,094
Jenny Lidback	69	71	72	70	282	7,094
Susie Redman	69	72	68	73	282	7,094
Joanne Morley	72	70	73	68	283	6,189
Beth Daniel	65	75	72	71	283	6,189
Rachel Hetherington	74	67	69	73	283	6,189
Catrin Nilsmark	71	68	70	74	283	6,189
Becky Iverson	68	73	67	75	283	6,189

Office Depot

Ibis Golf & Country Club, Legend Course,
West Palm Beach, Florida
Par 36-36–72; 6,323 yards

January 27-30
purse, $675,000

	SCORES				TOTAL	MONEY
Karrie Webb	67	69	72	70	278	$101,250
Kris Tschetter	69	73	71	66	279	54,345
Dottie Pepper	70	70	68	71	279	54,345
Gail Graham	74	66	73	67	280	29,437
Kelly Robbins	68	69	72	71	280	29,437
Juli Inkster	67	70	71	72	280	29,437
Michele Redman	68	70	73	71	282	20,040
Helen Alfredsson	71	72	70	70	283	17,662
Leta Lindley	70	71	72	71	284	15,115
Betsy King	70	66	77	71	284	15,115
Mayumi Hirase	71	70	74	70	285	11,633
Se Ri Pak	71	71	71	72	285	11,633
Lisa Hackney	73	67	72	73	285	11,633
Nancy Scranton	71	66	75	73	285	11,633
Charlotta Sorenstam	72	70	74	70	286	9,085
Maria Hjorth	73	71	71	71	286	9,085
Liselotte Neumann	69	69	72	76	286	9,085
Patty Sheehan	70	68	71	77	286	9,085
Lorie Kane	70	73	70	74	287	7,981
Cristie Kerr	71	71	71	74	287	7,981
Catriona Matthew	72	71	75	70	288	7,004
Jane Crafter	69	71	78	70	288	7,004
Janice Moodie	74	71	72	71	288	7,004
Donna Andrews	72	70	71	75	288	7,004

	SCORES			TOTAL	MONEY
Moira Dunn	71	73	77	68	289	5,875
Tina Barrett	73	73	72	71	289	5,875
Catrin Nilsmark	70	73	75	71	289	5,875
Cindy McCurdy	70	72	75	72	289	5,875
Dale Eggeling	71	71	74	73	289	5,875
Tammie Green	68	72	72	77	289	5,875

Valley of the Stars Championship

Oakmont Country Club, Glendale, California
Par 36-36–72; 6,276 yards

February 12-14
purse, $650,000

	SCORES			TOTAL	MONEY
Catrin Nilsmark	68	65	71	204	$97,500
Annika Sorenstam	67	70	67	204	60,510
(Nilsmark defeated Sorenstam on first extra hole.)					
Liselotte Neumann	71	70	67	208	44,156
Jane Geddes	69	70	72	211	31,072
Stephanie Lowe	68	67	76	211	31,072
Helen Alfredsson	70	71	72	213	21,096
Dale Eggeling	70	70	73	213	21,096
Hollis Stacy	72	74	68	214	17,008
Meg Mallon	71	72	72	215	13,861
Leta Lindley	70	73	72	215	13,861
Dottie Pepper	69	72	74	215	13,861
Michele Redman	71	75	70	216	9,912
Pat Hurst	73	72	71	216	9,912
Wendy Doolan	73	72	71	216	9,912
Sherri Turner	69	76	71	216	9,912
Cindy Figg-Currier	70	73	73	216	9,912
Cindy Flom	71	69	76	216	9,912
Emilee Klein	73	72	72	217	8,059
Kris Tschetter	74	68	75	217	8,059
Pearl Sinn	73	75	70	218	7,086
A.J. Eathorne	72	74	72	218	7,086
Lorie Kane	70	76	72	218	7,086
Cristie Kerr	76	69	73	218	7,086
Hiromi Kobayashi	76	72	71	219	5,998
Charlotta Sorenstam	74	73	72	219	5,998
Tracy Hanson	73	74	72	219	5,998
Patty Sheehan	73	72	74	219	5,998
Martha Nause	71	72	76	219	5,998
Juli Inkster	73	74	73	220	4,952
Susie Redman	72	74	74	220	4,952
Elaine Crosby	72	74	74	220	4,952
Rachel Hetherington	70	76	74	220	4,952
Laurie Rinker-Graham	72	73	75	220	4,952
Amy Alcott	73	71	76	220	4,952

Sunrise Hawaiian Ladies Open

Kapolei Golf Course, Kapolei, Oahu, Hawaii
Par 36-36–72; 6,100 yards

February 18-20
purse, $650,000

	SCORES			TOTAL	MONEY
Alison Nicholas	70	66	73	209	$97,500
Moira Dunn	70	72	68	210	52,333
Annette DeLuca	69	71	70	210	52,333
Jan Stephenson	71	69	71	211	34,344
Helen Dobson	71	70	71	212	21,750
Pat Hurst	69	71	72	212	21,750
Maria Hjorth	68	72	72	212	21,750
Cindy McCurdy	68	70	74	212	21,750
Kris Tschetter	72	72	69	213	11,914
Charlotta Sorenstam	71	73	69	213	11,914
Kelly Robbins	71	72	70	213	11,914
Deb Richard	71	69	73	213	11,914
Michele Redman	68	71	74	213	11,914
Vickie Odegard	68	71	74	213	11,914
Mardi Lunn	66	72	75	213	11,914
Cathy Johnston-Forbes	73	71	70	214	8,503
Sherri Steinhauer	71	72	71	214	8,503
Huang Yu-Chen	71	71	72	214	8,503
Dale Eggeling	74	70	71	215	6,807
Kate Golden	69	75	71	215	6,807
Kim Saiki	71	72	72	215	6,807
Hee-Won Han	73	69	73	215	6,807
Tina Barrett	69	73	73	215	6,807
Kristi Albers	72	69	74	215	6,807
Lorie Kane	72	69	74	215	6,807
Catriona Matthew	70	71	74	215	6,807
Hollis Stacy	72	72	72	216	5,181
Leigh Ann Mills	71	73	72	216	5,181
Nanci Bowen	70	73	73	216	5,181
Nancy Ramsbottom	69	73	74	216	5,181
Meg Mallon	70	70	76	216	5,181
Tracy Hanson	70	70	76	216	5,181
Michelle Estill	69	71	76	216	5,181

Australian Ladies Masters

Royal Pines Resort, Ashmore,
Gold Coast, Queensland
Par 37-35–72; 6,300 yards

February 25-28
purse, $750,000

	SCORES				TOTAL	MONEY
Karrie Webb	63	67	64	68	262	$112,500
Janice Moodie	67	67	67	71	272	71,154
Becky Iverson	69	68	71	66	274	51,923
Lorie Kane	68	67	71	69	275	40,385
Jane Crafter	68	66	70	73	277	32,692
Kris Tschetter	68	75	69	66	278	20,769
Eva Dahllof	69	70	70	69	278	20,769
Nicole Lowien	67	72	70	69	278	20,769
Akiko Fukushima	69	68	69	72	278	20,769
Michelle Estill	67	68	70	73	278	20,769
Chikayo Yamazaki	68	69	72	70	279	13,642

	SCORES				TOTAL	MONEY
Jane Geddes	66	69	72	72	279	13,642
Alison Nicholas	68	70	64	77	279	13,642
Jenny Lidback	69	70	71	70	280	11,976
Marnie McGuire	71	72	68	70	281	10,341
Tina Barrett	69	71	69	72	281	10,341
Nanci Bowen	69	70	70	72	281	10,341
A.J. Eathorne	65	70	70	76	281	10,341
Yuri Fudoh	72	72	68	70	282	8,899
Helen Dobson	72	69	70	71	282	8,899
Karen Weiss	67	72	70	73	282	8,899
Rachel Hetherington	71	72	71	69	283	7,809
Wendy Doolan	72	70	72	69	283	7,809
Nancy Harvey	75	68	69	71	283	7,809
Cindy McCurdy	73	70	71	70	284	7,053
Kelly Robbins	69	71	74	70	284	7,053
Luciana Bemvenuti	71	70	69	74	284	7,053
Charlotta Sorenstam	72	72	72	69	285	6,245
Carin Koch	72	67	72	74	285	6,245
Alison Munt	71	71	68	75	285	6,245
Catriona Matthew	70	71	69	75	285	6,245

Welch's/Circle K Championship

Randolf North Golf Course, Tucson, Arizona
Par 35-37–72; 6,222 yards

March 11-14
purse, $625,000

	SCORES				TOTAL	MONEY
Juli Inkster	68	71	69	65	273	$93,750
Dottie Pepper	67	69	69	69	274	58,183
Catriona Matthew	73	69	65	68	275	42,458
Ashli Price-Bunch	67	71	72	66	276	25,081
Tammie Green	68	73	67	68	276	25,081
Hollis Stacy	72	68	66	70	276	25,081
Nancy Scranton	70	65	71	70	276	25,081
Karrie Webb	74	69	66	68	277	15,567
Helen Alfredsson	69	67	73	68	277	15,567
Michele Redman	71	69	65	73	278	12,580
Dale Eggeling	68	67	69	74	278	12,580
Annette DeLuca	68	74	69	68	279	10,692
Charlotta Sorenstam	72	70	68	69	279	10,692
Meg Mallon	70	73	68	69	280	8,884
Moira Dunn	73	69	69	69	280	8,884
Kelly Robbins	72	67	70	71	280	8,884
Tracy Hanson	71	67	71	71	280	8,884
Maria Hjorth	72	72	69	68	281	7,233
Jean Bartholomew	72	71	69	69	281	7,233
Deb Richard	72	70	68	71	281	7,233
Laura Philo	71	70	69	71	281	7,233
Se Ri Pak	67	72	69	73	281	7,233
Mhairi McKay	73	71	70	68	282	6,014
Lorie Kane	70	72	70	70	282	6,014
Akiko Fukushima	68	70	73	71	282	6,014
Leta Lindley	72	71	67	72	282	6,014
Liselotte Neumann	72	72	70	69	283	4,898
Elaine Crosby	72	72	70	69	283	4,898
A.J. Eathorne	72	71	70	70	283	4,898
Gail Graham	71	69	72	71	283	4,898

	SCORES				TOTAL	MONEY
Carin Koch	70	69	72	72	283	4,898
Denise Killeen	68	71	72	72	283	4,898
Vicki Fergon	70	69	71	73	283	4,898
Kristi Albers	72	67	70	74	283	4,898

Standard Register Ping

Moon Valley Country Club, Phoenix, Arizona
Par 36-37–73; 6,435 yards

March 18-21
purse, $850,000

	SCORES				TOTAL	MONEY
Karrie Webb	68	68	69	69	274	$127,500
Lorie Kane	66	70	71	71	278	79,129
Janice Moodie	73	73	69	65	280	51,327
Jane Geddes	75	69	71	65	280	51,327
Wendy Ward	70	71	68	72	281	36,356
Eva Dahllof	75	70	70	67	282	25,805
Kelly Robbins	72	71	71	68	282	25,805
Juli Inkster	68	75	70	69	282	25,805
Leta Lindley	72	69	72	70	283	18,132
Patti Rizzo	73	70	69	71	283	18,132
Kristi Albers	71	73	66	73	283	18,132
Nancy Lopez	72	73	70	69	284	14,191
Catriona Matthew	74	69	70	71	284	14,191
Annika Sorenstam	72	69	71	72	284	14,191
Jill McGill	72	73	72	68	285	11,283
Dottie Pepper	73	71	72	69	285	11,283
Laura Davies	68	72	72	73	285	11,283
Helen Alfredsson	69	69	74	73	285	11,283
Tina Barrett	69	70	70	76	285	11,283
Kim Saiki	70	70	72	74	286	9,914
Diane Barnard	73	70	75	69	287	8,453
Michele Redman	73	72	72	70	287	8,453
Meg Mallon	72	73	71	71	287	8,453
Tracy Hanson	66	69	81	71	287	8,453
Hollis Stacy	72	70	73	72	287	8,453
Cathy Johnston-Forbes	67	76	70	74	287	8,453
Martha Nause	68	73	70	76	287	8,453
*Grace Park	73	72	72	70	287	
Carin Koch	73	72	73	70	288	7,219
Emilee Klein	72	72	70	74	288	7,219

Nabisco Dinah Shore

Mission Hills Country Club, Rancho Mirage, California
Par 36-36–72; 6,460 yards

March 25-28
purse, $1,000,000

	SCORES				TOTAL	MONEY
Dottie Pepper	70	66	67	66	269	$150,000
Meg Mallon	66	69	71	69	275	93,093
Karrie Webb	73	71	70	66	280	67,933
Kelly Robbins	69	73	67	72	281	52,837
Charlotta Sorenstam	72	68	76	66	282	42,772
Juli Inkster	72	66	71	74	283	35,224
Catriona Matthew	72	73	69	70	284	26,502

	SCORES				TOTAL	MONEY
Annika Sorenstam	70	73	71	70	284	26,502
Janice Moodie	69	68	75	72	284	26,502
Sherri Steinhauer	70	72	72	71	285	19,289
Maria Hjorth	77	68	68	72	285	19,289
Helen Alfredsson	69	71	73	72	285	19,289
Rosie Jones	73	70	73	70	286	13,712
Maggie Will	72	71	73	70	286	13,712
Michele Redman	71	74	69	72	286	13,712
Pat Bradley	73	69	72	72	286	13,712
Cindy McCurdy	70	74	69	73	286	13,712
Se Ri Pak	73	69	69	75	286	13,712
Mayumi Hirase	70	72	69	75	286	13,712
Kris Tschetter	68	70	73	75	286	13,712
Muffin Spencer-Devlin	72	69	77	69	287	9,692
Hollis Stacy	74	74	69	70	287	9,692
Michelle Estill	70	76	71	70	287	9,692
Rachel Hetherington	70	74	71	72	287	9,692
Nancy Lopez	72	73	69	73	287	9,692
Dale Eggeling	73	70	70	74	287	9,692
Hiromi Kobayashi	70	69	74	74	287	9,692
Donna Andrews	70	69	74	74	287	9,692
Helen Dobson	74	72	74	68	288	7,812
Dana Dormann	74	73	71	70	288	7,812
Lorie Kane	73	74	71	70	288	7,812
Joan Pitcock	77	68	73	70	288	7,812

Longs Drugs Challenge

Twelve Bridges Golf Club, Lincoln, California
Par 36-36–72; 6,388 yards

April 1-4
purse, $600,000

	SCORES				TOTAL	MONEY
Juli Inkster	69	67	74	70	280	$90,000
Sherri Steinhauer	70	74	69	71	284	55,855
Annika Sorenstam	71	71	73	70	285	32,708
A.J. Eathorne	72	68	75	70	285	32,708
Wendy Doolan	72	68	74	71	285	32,708
Pearl Sinn	72	72	74	68	286	18,215
Susie Redman	75	71	71	69	286	18,215
Jill McGill	73	70	72	71	286	18,215
Hiromi Kobayashi	68	72	75	72	287	13,435
Cindy Figg-Currier	68	72	75	72	287	13,435
Karen Weiss	70	76	74	68	288	11,020
Suzanne Strudwick	75	68	73	72	288	11,020
Akiko Fukushima	73	72	75	70	290	9,661
Sally Little	70	77	72	71	290	9,661
Chris Johnson	72	77	75	67	291	7,749
Jan Stephenson	75	75	71	70	291	7,749
Liselotte Neumann	75	74	72	70	291	7,749
Rachel Hetherington	72	69	75	75	291	7,749
Mhairi McKay	69	72	75	75	291	7,749
Cristie Kerr	74	70	70	77	291	7,749
Laura Philo	75	73	75	69	292	6,012
Cindy Flom	70	71	79	72	292	6,012
Dana Dormann	70	76	73	73	292	6,012
Maria Hjorth	73	70	76	73	292	6,012
Colleen Walker	71	70	76	75	292	6,012

	SCORES				TOTAL	MONEY
Maggie Will	72	73	70	77	292	6,012
Karen Davies	78	70	78	67	293	5,041
Kelli Kuehne	71	71	78	73	293	5,041
Mi Hyun Kim	72	72	75	74	293	5,041
Cindy McCurdy	75	71	71	76	293	5,041

Chick-fil-A Charity Championship

Eagle's Landing Country Club, Stockbridge, Georgia
Par 36-36–72; 6,187 yards

April 23-25
purse, $800,000

	SCORES			TOTAL	MONEY
Rachel Hetherington	67	67	70	204	$120,000
Lorie Kane	67	68	69	204	74,474
(Hetherington defeated Kane on first extra hole.)					
Annika Sorenstam	70	69	66	205	43,610
Jean Bartholomew	74	63	68	205	43,610
Karrie Webb	70	67	68	205	43,610
Kelly Robbins	66	73	67	206	24,287
Rosie Jones	69	69	68	206	24,287
Barb Mucha	72	62	72	206	24,287
Mi Hyun Kim	69	65	73	207	17,914
Leslie Spalding	66	68	73	207	17,914
Denise Killeen	70	66	72	208	13,860
Cindy Figg-Currier	69	67	72	208	13,860
Sherri Steinhauer	68	67	73	208	13,860
Maria Hjorth	65	69	74	208	13,860
Helen Dobson	68	71	70	209	11,344
Cindy Flom	69	68	72	209	11,344
Jane Geddes	71	70	69	210	9,734
Maggie Will	72	68	70	210	9,734
Akiko Fukushima	72	67	71	210	9,734
Charlotta Sorenstam	73	65	72	210	9,734
Juli Inkster	69	68	73	210	9,734
Hiromi Kobayashi	73	71	67	211	8,053
Beth Daniel	74	66	71	211	8,053
Jane Crafter	67	73	71	211	8,053
Se Ri Pak	69	69	73	211	8,053
Michele Redman	71	71	70	212	7,278
Nancy Scranton	70	71	71	212	7,278
Donna Andrews	76	67	70	213	6,017
Hollis Stacy	72	71	70	213	6,017
Mayumi Hirase	74	68	71	213	6,017
Sara Sanders	73	69	71	213	6,017
Kristi Albers	72	70	71	213	6,017
Kelli Kuehne	72	70	71	213	6,017
Cindy McCurdy	70	69	74	213	6,017
Dana Dormann	72	66	75	213	6,017
A.J. Eathorne	70	68	75	213	6,017

City of Hope Myrtle Beach Classic

Wachesaw East Golf Club, Murrells Inlet, South Carolina
Par 36-36–72; 6,231 yards
(Third and fourth rounds cancelled — rain.)

April 29-May 2
purse, $675,000

	SCORES		TOTAL	MONEY
Rachel Hetherington	69	68	137	$101,250
Leta Lindley	70	68	138	48,118
Helen Alfredsson	70	68	138	48,118
Karrie Webb	69	69	138	48,118
Nancy Scranton	71	68	139	22,587
Akiko Fukushima	71	68	139	22,587
Cristie Kerr	69	70	139	22,587
Juli Inkster	68	71	139	22,587
Janice Moodie	73	67	140	14,386
Emilee Klein	71	69	140	14,386
Mayumi Hirase	70	70	140	14,386
Liselotte Neumann	73	68	141	9,571
Susan Ginter	72	69	141	9,571
Karen Weiss	72	69	141	9,571
Laura Philo	72	69	141	9,571
Jenny Lidback	71	70	141	9,571
Donna Andrews	71	70	141	9,571
Kim Saiki	71	70	141	9,571
Catriona Matthew	71	70	141	9,571
Wendy Doolan	70	71	141	9,571
Sherri Steinhauer	73	69	142	6,244
Helen Dobson	73	69	142	6,244
Jan Stephenson	72	70	142	6,244
Deb Richard	72	70	142	6,244
Laura Davies	71	71	142	6,244
Se Ri Pak	71	71	142	6,244
Maggie Will	70	72	142	6,244
Dottie Pepper	70	72	142	6,244
Tina Barrett	70	72	142	6,244
Hiromi Kobayashi	69	73	142	6,244
Jill McGill	69	73	142	6,244

Mercury Titleholders Championship

LPGA International, Daytona Beach, Florida
Par 36-36–72; 6,393 yards

May 6-9
purse, $900,000

	SCORES				TOTAL	MONEY
Karrie Webb	69	66	70	66	271	$135,000
Annika Sorenstam	68	68	68	70	274	83,783
Laura Davies	72	69	66	69	276	44,721
Meg Mallon	69	70	67	70	276	44,721
Chris Johnson	75	63	67	71	276	44,721
Becky Iverson	68	66	66	76	276	44,721
Sherri Steinhauer	74	67	68	68	277	25,135
Kris Tschetter	68	67	73	69	277	25,135
Val Skinner	73	65	70	70	278	20,153
Rosie Jones	71	68	66	73	278	20,153
Tina Barrett	67	73	69	70	279	17,209
Maria Hjorth	68	69	76	67	280	13,327
Cristie Kerr	69	69	73	69	280	13,327

	SCORES				TOTAL	MONEY
Joan Pitcock	74	67	68	71	280	13,327
Trish Johnson	69	69	71	71	280	13,327
Annette DeLuca	71	66	72	71	280	13,327
Helen Alfredsson	68	72	67	73	280	13,327
Dale Eggeling	70	68	69	73	280	13,327
Michele Redman	72	68	74	67	281	9,263
Donna Andrews	69	71	72	69	281	9,263
Jane Geddes	72	70	69	70	281	9,263
Missie McGeorge	69	73	69	70	281	9,263
Kristi Albers	69	72	70	70	281	9,263
Sara Sanders	71	70	69	71	281	9,263
Judy Dickinson	71	69	70	71	281	9,263
Mi Hyun Kim	70	70	69	72	281	9,263
Wendy Doolan	71	70	67	73	281	9,263
Lori Atsedes	70	72	69	71	282	6,922
Stefania Croce	69	71	72	70	282	6,922
Elaine Crosby	70	68	76	68	282	6,922
Lorie Kane	68	70	69	75	282	6,922
Dottie Pepper	71	70	69	72	282	6,922
Julie Piers	74	67	71	70	282	6,922
Pearl Sinn	71	72	71	68	282	6,922

Sara Lee Classic

Hermitage Golf Course, Old Hickory, Tennessee
Par 36-36–72; 6,312 yards

May 14-16
purse, $750,000

	SCORES			TOTAL	MONEY
Meg Mallon	66	65	68	199	$112,500
Kris Tschetter	66	64	70	200	60,384
Annika Sorenstam	61	68	71	200	60,384
Michelle McGann	63	65	73	201	39,627
Mi Hyun Kim	68	66	68	202	32,079
Karrie Webb	72	66	65	203	24,342
Sherri Steinhauer	68	68	67	203	24,342
Nancy Scranton	68	70	66	204	18,681
Erika Wicoff	69	67	68	204	18,681
Dottie Pepper	70	68	67	205	15,096
Kathryn Marshall	69	66	70	205	15,096
Maria Hjorth	70	71	65	206	11,384
Tammie Green	67	71	68	206	11,384
Joanne Morley	69	67	70	206	11,384
Jane Crafter	68	68	70	206	11,384
Cathy Johnston-Forbes	66	69	71	206	11,384
Michele Redman	66	68	72	206	11,384
Joan Pitcock	72	68	67	207	8,680
Patti Rizzo	70	69	68	207	8,680
Dale Eggeling	65	74	68	207	8,680
Kim Saiki	70	66	71	207	8,680
Nancy Lopez	68	68	71	207	8,680
Laurie Rinker-Graham	70	71	67	208	6,987
Kristi Coats	70	71	67	208	6,987
Becky Iverson	72	68	68	208	6,987
Maggie Will	70	69	69	208	6,987
Susie Redman	68	70	70	208	6,987
Melissa McNamara	67	71	70	208	6,987
Cindy Figg-Currier	71	70	68	209	5,563

	SCORES			TOTAL	MONEY
Helen Dobson	72	68	69	209	5,563
Emilee Klein	70	70	69	209	5,563
Mardi Lunn	70	69	70	209	5,563
Lisa Kiggens	70	68	71	209	5,563
Stefania Croce	72	65	72	209	5,563
Laura Philo	70	66	73	209	5,563

Philips Invitational Honoring Harvey Penick

Onion Creek Club, Austin, Texas
Par 35-35–70; 6,101 yards

May 20-23
purse, $800,000

	SCORES				TOTAL	MONEY
Akiko Fukushima	64	67	65	71	267	$120,000
Charlotta Sorenstam	69	65	68	67	269	74,474
Mi Hyun Kim	69	66	65	71	271	48,307
Beth Daniel	70	62	68	71	271	48,307
Janice Moodie	67	69	69	67	272	34,217
Juli Inkster	68	70	65	70	273	28,179
Kelli Kuehne	70	72	67	66	275	22,342
Cindy Flom	67	71	68	69	275	22,342
Kristi Albers	69	72	68	67	276	15,699
Marnie McGuire	74	67	67	68	276	15,699
Deb Richard	72	71	64	69	276	15,699
Jenny Lidback	67	71	69	69	276	15,699
Silvia Cavalleri	73	67	65	71	276	15,699
Heather Daly-Donofrio	69	72	69	67	277	10,868
Annette DeLuca	68	69	70	70	277	10,868
Jennifer Feldott	72	67	67	71	277	10,868
Jane Crafter	68	70	68	71	277	10,868
Meg Mallon	66	71	69	71	277	10,868
Vicki Fergon	69	69	65	74	277	10,868
Cindy Figg-Currier	70	71	72	65	278	8,493
Mayumi Hirase	71	68	71	68	278	8,493
Chris Johnson	74	68	67	69	278	8,493
Ashli Price-Bunch	71	71	66	70	278	8,493
Eva Dahllof	69	66	72	71	278	8,493
Loraine Lambert	70	69	72	68	279	7,447
Susie Redman	66	70	70	73	279	7,447
Michele Redman	69	75	65	71	280	6,163
Jackie Gallagher-Smith	74	69	66	71	280	6,163
Missie McGeorge	73	68	68	71	280	6,163
Melissa McNamara	69	69	71	71	280	6,163
Nancy Scranton	67	69	73	71	280	6,163
Susan Ginter	71	67	70	72	280	6,163
Laura Davies	66	74	67	73	280	6,163
Pearl Sinn	66	66	74	74	280	6,163
Leta Lindley	69	70	66	75	280	6,163

Corning Classic

Corning Country Club, Corning, New York
Par 36-36–72; 6,062 yards

May 27-30
purse, $750,000

	SCORES				TOTAL	MONEY
Kelli Kuehne	69	69	70	70	278	$112,500
Rosie Jones	71	68	68	72	279	69,819
Joan Pitcock	72	69	73	67	281	40,885
Cindy McCurdy	72	69	73	67	281	40,885
Tammie Green	74	71	68	68	281	40,885
Kris Tschetter	72	71	71	68	282	21,511
Stefania Croce	72	68	71	71	282	21,511
Hiromi Kobayashi	68	72	70	72	282	21,511
Kathryn Marshall	67	72	70	73	282	21,511
Betsy King	70	70	77	66	283	13,510
Caroline Blaylock	75	71	69	68	283	13,510
Cathy Johnston-Forbes	68	71	76	68	283	13,510
Dottie Pepper	71	75	68	69	283	13,510
A.J. Eathorne	75	72	65	71	283	13,510
Mardi Lunn	72	73	73	66	284	8,925
Lorie Kane	75	72	69	68	284	8,925
Sherri Steinhauer	71	72	73	68	284	8,925
Mi Hyun Kim	69	76	70	69	284	8,925
Jane Geddes	71	73	71	69	284	8,925
Catriona Matthew	75	71	68	70	284	8,925
Kim Saiki	73	71	69	71	284	8,925
Jamie Hullett	72	66	75	71	284	8,925
Nancy Lopez	73	71	68	72	284	8,925
Jean Bartholomew	73	64	74	73	284	8,925
Mitzi Edge	68	75	74	68	285	6,755
Tina Fischer	77	70	67	71	285	6,755
Becky Iverson	77	66	69	73	285	6,755
Sherri Turner	67	72	71	75	285	6,755
Liz Earley	76	70	70	70	286	5,758
Lori West	72	75	68	71	286	5,758
Catrin Nilsmark	72	74	68	72	286	5,758
Pearl Sinn	72	72	70	72	286	5,758
Silvia Cavalleri	73	71	69	73	286	5,758

U.S. Women's Open

Old Waverly Golf Club, West Point, Mississippi
Par 36-36–72; 6,421 yards

June 3-6
purse, $1,750,000

	SCORES				TOTAL	MONEY
Juli Inkster	65	69	67	71	272	$315,000
Sherri Turner	69	69	68	71	277	185,000
Kelli Kuehne	64	71	70	74	279	118,227
Lorie Kane	70	64	71	75	280	82,399
Carin Koch	72	69	68	72	281	62,938
Meg Mallon	70	70	69	72	281	62,938
Karrie Webb	70	70	68	74	282	53,132
Helen Dobson	71	70	73	69	283	45,244
Maria Hjorth	73	69	70	71	283	45,244
Catriona Matthew	69	68	74	72	283	45,244
*Grace Park	70	67	73	73	283	
Helen Alfredsson	72	68	70	74	284	37,666

	SCORES				TOTAL	MONEY
Becky Iverson	72	64	73	75	284	37,666
Michele Redman	72	71	75	67	285	32,389
Se Ri Pak	68	70	74	73	285	32,389
Dottie Pepper	68	69	72	76	285	32,389
Liselotte Neumann	73	71	69	73	286	27,422
A.J. Eathorne	69	71	71	75	286	27,422
Catrin Nilsmark	69	71	70	76	286	27,422
Cindy McCurdy	72	72	74	69	287	21,832
Leta Lindley	72	72	73	70	287	21,832
Sophie Gustafson	72	72	70	73	287	21,832
Donna Andrews	69	71	72	75	287	21,832
Akiko Fukushima	69	70	71	77	287	21,832
Kim Saiki	70	71	73	74	288	16,006
Stefania Croce	71	71	71	75	288	16,006
Rosie Jones	71	70	72	75	288	16,006
Lisa Kiggens	71	67	73	77	288	16,006
Sherri Steinhauer	68	69	73	78	288	16,006
Mardi Lunn	72	71	74	72	289	11,652
Jean Zedlitz	75	67	75	72	289	11,652
Mhairi McKay	73	68	76	72	289	11,652
Nancy Scranton	69	72	75	73	289	11,652
Dawn Coe-Jones	73	71	71	74	289	11,652
Anna Acker-Macosko	73	71	71	74	289	11,652
Kelly Robbins	70	70	74	75	289	11,652

Wegmans Rochester International

Locust Hill Country Club, Pittsford, New York   June 10-13
Par 35-37–72; 6,162 yards   purse, $1,000,000

	SCORES				TOTAL	MONEY
Karrie Webb	75	67	68	70	280	$150,000
Cindy McCurdy	71	70	72	68	281	93,093
Kristi Albers	74	68	72	69	283	67,933
Se Ri Pak	77	66	73	68	284	47,804
Beth Daniel	70	73	73	68	284	47,804
Gail Graham	70	72	71	72	285	32,456
Rosie Jones	75	69	68	73	285	32,456
Cristie Kerr	72	71	73	70	286	23,651
Becky Iverson	70	73	70	73	286	23,651
Leigh Ann Mills	70	71	71	74	286	23,651
Susie Redman	74	74	71	68	287	16,706
Lisa Kiggens	73	70	75	69	287	16,706
Leslie Spalding	71	72	74	70	287	16,706
Emilee Klein	71	71	73	72	287	16,706
Kim Saiki	71	71	72	73	287	16,706
Lorie Kane	71	77	71	69	288	12,328
Cindy Flom	77	70	72	69	288	12,328
Rachel Hetherington	79	68	70	71	288	12,328
Penny Hammel	73	71	73	71	288	12,328
Meg Mallon	70	76	70	72	288	12,328
Tina Barrett	71	73	71	73	288	12,328
Nancy Lopez	74	72	74	69	289	9,975
Liselotte Neumann	71	71	72	75	289	9,975
Tammie Green	71	71	72	75	289	9,975
Nancy Scranton	75	71	66	77	289	9,975
Shelley Wendels	72	73	76	69	290	8,554
Denise Killeen	71	71	78	70	290	8,554

	SCORES				TOTAL	MONEY
Leta Lindley	73	71	75	71	290	8,554
Deb Richard	72	71	74	73	290	8,554
Jean Zedlitz	68	71	75	76	290	8,554

ShopRite Classic

Seaview Marriott Resort, Bay Course,
Atlantic City, New Jersey
Par 36-35–71; 6,051 yards

June 18-20
purse, $1,000,000

	SCORES			TOTAL	MONEY
Se Ri Pak	63	69	66	198	$150,000
Trish Johnson	64	71	65	200	93,093
Juli Inkster	66	68	69	203	67,933
Rosie Jones	71	68	65	204	52,837
Emilee Klein	70	67	68	205	42,772
Annika Sorenstam	72	65	69	206	28,682
Suzanne Strudwick	69	68	69	206	28,682
Betsy King	68	68	70	206	28,682
Wendy Doolan	69	66	71	206	28,682
Catriona Matthew	71	68	68	207	18,618
Dottie Pepper	69	70	68	207	18,618
Dawn Coe-Jones	69	70	68	207	18,618
Jane Crafter	68	69	70	207	18,618
Sara Sanders	70	68	70	208	15,096
Leta Lindley	67	68	73	208	15,096
Lisa Kiggens	73	68	68	209	12,580
Val Skinner	70	71	68	209	12,580
Mi Hyun Kim	70	69	70	209	12,580
Meg Mallon	68	71	70	209	12,580
Mayumi Hirase	71	66	72	209	12,580
Maria Hjorth	71	71	68	210	10,022
Pearl Sinn	70	70	70	210	10,022
Kristi Albers	70	69	71	210	10,022
Anna Acker-Macosko	68	71	71	210	10,022
Sherri Steinhauer	67	71	72	210	10,022
Stephanie Lowe	70	66	74	210	10,022
Hiromi Kobayashi	75	67	69	211	7,704
Catrin Nilsmark	74	68	69	211	7,704
Marnie McGuire	72	69	70	211	7,704
Cathy Johnston-Forbes	70	71	70	211	7,704
Elizabeth Makings	72	68	71	211	7,704
Mardi Lunn	70	70	71	211	7,704
Tammie Green	69	71	71	211	7,704
Marianne Morris	71	68	72	211	7,704
Kim Saiki	67	71	73	211	7,704

McDonald's LPGA Championship

DuPont Country Club, Wilmington, Delaware
Par 35-36–71; 6,376 yards

June 24-27
purse, $1,400,000

	SCORES				TOTAL	MONEY
Juli Inkster	68	66	69	65	268	$210,000
Liselotte Neumann	67	67	70	68	272	130,330

	SCORES			TOTAL	MONEY
Mardi Lunn	68	74	65	66	273	84,538
Nancy Scranton	69	68	66	70	273	84,538
Rosie Jones	64	72	68	70	274	54,596
Cristie Kerr	70	64	69	71	274	54,596
Emilee Klein	72	68	67	68	275	35,224
Jill McGill	70	69	68	68	275	35,224
Laura Davies	65	71	71	68	275	35,224
Se Ri Pak	68	69	67	71	275	35,224
Mayumi Hirase	70	73	68	65	276	23,487
Sara Sanders	70	68	68	70	276	23,487
Tammie Green	68	70	68	70	276	23,487
Jenny Lidback	67	67	72	70	276	23,487
Meg Mallon	70	71	63	72	276	23,487
Annika Sorenstam	73	68	68	68	277	18,415
Susie Redman	70	68	70	69	277	18,415
Jan Stephenson	69	69	69	70	277	18,415
Dottie Pepper	71	72	68	67	278	16,301
Sherri Steinhauer	74	69	65	70	278	16,301
Hiromi Kobayashi	70	67	71	70	278	16,301
Lisa Kiggens	68	74	69	68	279	14,063
Akiko Fukushima	70	70	69	70	279	14,063
Vickie Odegard	69	70	70	70	279	14,063
Allison Finney	67	69	71	72	279	14,063
Pearl Sinn	71	71	70	68	280	11,087
Mi Hyun Kim	70	70	71	69	280	11,087
Vicki Fergon	67	73	70	70	280	11,087
Jane Crafter	70	69	71	70	280	11,087
Leta Lindley	70	72	67	71	280	11,087
Barb Mucha	70	70	69	71	280	11,087
Kelli Kuehne	68	67	72	73	280	11,087
Alison Nicholas	67	73	66	74	280	11,087
Trish Johnson	67	70	69	74	280	11,087
Lorie Kane	70	66	70	74	280	11,087

Jamie Farr Kroger Classic

Highland Meadows Golf Club, Sylvania, Ohio
Par 34-37–71; 6,319 yards

July 1-4
purse, $900,000

	SCORES			TOTAL	MONEY
Se Ri Pak	68	69	68	71	276	$135,000
Kelli Kuehne	73	66	71	66	276	52,534
Carin Koch	69	67	71	69	276	52,534
Sherri Steinhauer	70	67	69	70	276	52,534
Karrie Webb	70	66	70	70	276	52,534
Mardi Lunn	65	67	74	70	276	52,534
(Pak won on first extra hole.)						
Dina Ammaccapane	69	71	68	69	277	23,851
Mi Hyun Kim	71	71	65	70	277	23,851
Jenny Lidback	67	68	70	72	277	23,851
Cindy McCurdy	69	67	70	72	278	19,021
Laura Philo	71	67	74	67	279	15,525
Eva Dahllof	67	72	72	68	279	15,525
Emilee Klein	70	69	69	71	279	15,525
Luciana Bemvenuti	68	71	69	71	279	15,525
*Kellee Booth	70	70	71	68	279	
Jennifer Feldott	73	66	75	66	280	11,880

	SCORES				TOTAL	MONEY
Chris Johnson	71	69	72	68	280	11,880
Meg Mallon	69	70	71	70	280	11,880
Dale Eggeling	71	73	65	71	280	11,880
Kelly Robbins	69	68	71	72	280	11,880
Beth Daniel	73	70	71	67	281	8,777
Cindy Figg-Currier	72	69	72	68	281	8,777
Missie McGeorge	70	69	74	68	281	8,777
Dana Dormann	67	71	75	68	281	8,777
Charlotta Sorenstam	68	72	70	71	281	8,777
Denise Killeen	71	73	65	72	281	8,777
Julie Piers	73	68	68	72	281	8,777
Susan Ginter	71	67	71	72	281	8,777
Marisa Baena	67	69	70	75	281	8,777
Shani Waugh	69	68	68	76	281	8,777

Michelob Light Classic

Forest Hills Country Club, St. Louis, Missouri
Par 36-36–72; 6,337 yards

July 8-11
purse, $800,000

	SCORES				TOTAL	MONEY
Annika Sorenstam	68	72	68	70	278	$120,000
Tina Barrett	64	72	70	72	278	74,474
(Sorenstam defeated Barrett on third extra hole.)						
Lisa Kiggens	69	66	73	74	282	48,307
Lorie Kane	67	72	68	75	282	48,307
Susan Ginter	70	72	69	72	283	34,217
Wendy Doolan	70	71	72	71	284	22,945
Laura Philo	71	70	71	72	284	22,945
Juli Inkster	71	69	72	72	284	22,945
Nancy Scranton	67	69	71	77	284	22,945
Pearl Sinn	71	74	72	68	285	16,102
Dale Eggeling	72	70	69	74	285	16,102
Eva Dahllof	72	73	74	68	287	13,284
Joanne Morley	68	79	69	71	287	13,284
Kelli Kuehne	70	75	69	73	287	13,284
Connie Masterson	73	73	72	70	288	10,768
Heather Daly-Donofrio	74	72	71	71	288	10,768
Leta Lindley	70	73	73	72	288	10,768
Martha Nause	69	74	72	73	288	10,768
Jane Crafter	70	74	73	72	289	9,460
Stephanie Lowe	71	69	75	74	289	9,460
Kristi Albers	70	76	75	69	290	8,017
Liz Earley	72	74	74	70	290	8,017
Jennifer Feldott	71	75	74	70	290	8,017
Hiromi Kobayashi	70	75	75	70	290	8,017
Chris Johnson	78	71	70	71	290	8,017
Kristal Parker-Gregory	69	70	75	76	290	8,017
Ellie Gibson	72	74	75	70	291	6,487
Pamela Kometani	75	70	75	71	291	6,487
Denise Killeen	74	72	72	73	291	6,487
Rachel Hetherington	68	74	76	73	291	6,487
Muffin Spencer-Devlin	72	72	73	74	291	6,487
Kim Bauer	77	71	67	76	291	6,487

JAL Big Apple Classic

Wykagyl Country Club, New Rochelle, New York
Par 35-36–71; 6,161 yards

July 15-18
purse, $850,000

	SCORES				TOTAL	MONEY
Sherri Steinhauer	68	68	66	71	273	$127,500
Lorie Kane	68	68	68	69	273	79,129
(Steinhauer defeated Kane on fifth extra hole.)						
Juli Inkster	71	67	68	70	276	57,743
Tina Barrett	67	72	68	70	277	44,911
Pearl Sinn	67	71	70	71	279	36,356
Rachel Hetherington	67	72	75	66	280	25,805
Laura Davies	70	70	72	68	280	25,805
Karrie Webb	69	67	71	73	280	25,805
Jenny Lidback	68	72	73	68	281	20,103
Nanci Bowen	71	72	70	69	282	15,373
Se Ri Pak	66	69	77	70	282	15,373
Vicki Goetze-Ackerman	72	71	68	71	282	15,373
Vickie Odegard	72	71	66	73	282	15,373
Barb Mucha	75	67	67	73	282	15,373
Hollis Stacy	74	72	69	68	283	11,767
Emilee Klein	70	70	73	70	283	11,767
Jan Stephenson	72	70	70	71	283	11,767
Cristie Kerr	73	73	70	68	284	10,342
Hiromi Kobayashi	73	70	70	71	284	10,342
Cindy Figg-Currier	73	69	70	72	284	10,342
Mayumi Hirase	75	70	71	69	285	9,072
Pamela Kometani	71	74	71	69	285	9,072
Susan Ginter	70	70	71	74	285	9,072
Allison Finney	73	73	71	69	286	8,246
Cindy Flom	72	74	69	71	286	8,246
Annika Sorenstam	72	73	71	71	287	7,476
Liz Earley	74	72	69	72	287	7,476
Helen Dobson	70	69	75	73	287	7,476
Meg Mallon	70	66	77	74	287	7,476
Siew-Ai Lim	73	72	72	71	288	6,264
Jackie Gallagher-Smith	72	73	72	71	288	6,264
Beth Daniel	71	73	72	72	288	6,264
Michele Redman	69	75	72	72	288	6,264
Caroline Blaylock	76	71	68	73	288	6,264
Kristi Albers	75	69	69	75	288	6,264

Giant Eagle Classic

Avalon Lakes Golf Course, Warren, Ohio
Par 36-36–72; 6,308 yards

July 23-25
purse, $1,000,000

	SCORES			TOTAL	MONEY
Jackie Gallagher-Smith	66	68	65	199	$150,000
Marnie McGuire	68	65	69	202	93,093
Karrie Webb	71	66	67	204	54,514
Leigh Ann Mills	69	68	67	204	54,514
Lorie Kane	67	70	67	204	54,514
Amy Benz	69	69	67	205	25,831
Kim Saiki	69	69	67	205	25,831
Janice Moodie	71	66	68	205	25,831
Se Ri Pak	69	68	68	205	25,831

	SCORES			TOTAL	MONEY
Jan Stephenson	67	69	69	205	25,831
Missie McGeorge	67	67	71	205	25,831
Jill McGill	71	67	68	206	14,808
Emilee Klein	71	67	68	206	14,808
Liselotte Neumann	70	68	68	206	14,808
Sally Dee	72	65	69	206	14,808
Rosie Jones	69	68	69	206	14,808
Gail Graham	71	65	70	206	14,808
Helen Dobson	71	65	70	206	14,808
Val Skinner	69	69	69	207	10,660
Nancy Scranton	69	69	69	207	10,660
Shani Waugh	69	69	69	207	10,660
Kristi Albers	70	66	71	207	10,660
Suzy Green	69	67	71	207	10,660
Cindy Figg-Currier	67	69	71	207	10,660
Michele Redman	67	67	73	207	10,660
Mi Hyun Kim	71	70	67	208	8,259
Maria Hjorth	72	68	68	208	8,259
Charlotta Sorenstam	72	66	70	208	8,259
Muffin Spencer-Devlin	71	67	70	208	8,259
Sara Sanders	69	69	70	208	8,259
Dana Dormann	73	64	71	208	8,259
Mary Beth Zimmerman	68	68	72	208	8,259

du Maurier Classic

Priddis Greens Golf & Country Club, Priddis,
Alberta, Canada
Par 36-36–72; 6,415 yards

July 29-August 1
purse, $1,200,000

	SCORES				TOTAL	MONEY
Karrie Webb	73	72	66	66	277	$180,000
Laura Davies	72	66	69	72	279	111,711
Juli Inkster	68	69	74	69	280	81,519
Dawn Coe-Jones	72	65	72	74	283	63,404
Catriona Matthew	68	70	72	74	284	51,326
Maggie Will	74	69	74	68	285	36,431
Mi Hyun Kim	78	69	69	69	285	36,431
Lorie Kane	70	72	73	70	285	36,431
Carin Koch	71	71	73	71	286	24,486
Sherri Turner	72	72	70	72	286	24,486
Jill McGill	72	71	71	72	286	24,486
Rosie Jones	67	74	72	73	286	24,486
Dina Ammaccapane	73	70	73	71	287	18,177
Se Ri Pak	75	71	68	73	287	18,177
Beth Daniel	72	70	72	73	287	18,177
Michele Redman	70	72	72	73	287	18,177
Maria Hjorth	72	72	73	71	288	15,157
Mhairi McKay	73	69	74	72	288	15,157
Cristie Kerr	71	71	70	76	288	15,157
Helen Dobson	75	74	72	68	289	13,346
Wendy Ward	73	72	75	69	289	13,346
Tammie Green	73	74	71	71	289	13,346
Mardi Lunn	75	74	71	70	290	11,796
Marta Figueras-Dotti	74	69	77	70	290	11,796
Janice Moodie	72	74	72	72	290	11,796
Tracy Hanson	74	74	70	73	291	10,326

	SCORES				TOTAL	MONEY
Kristi Albers	73	74	71	73	291	10,326
Charlotta Sorenstam	72	70	75	74	291	10,326
Nancy Scranton	75	71	70	75	291	10,326
Becky Iverson	73	73	70	75	291	10,326

areaWEB.COM Challenge

Pleasant Valley Country Club, Sutton, Massachusetts   August 5-8
Par 36-36–72; 6,334 yards   purse, $800,000

	SCORES				TOTAL	MONEY
Mardi Lunn	66	71	71	67	275	$120,000
Jan Stephenson	68	70	71	67	276	74,474
Rachel Hetherington	71	66	73	67	277	54,346
Dottie Pepper	67	71	71	69	278	42,269
Jane Crafter	72	67	70	70	279	28,715
Beth Daniel	70	69	69	71	279	28,715
Lorie Kane	69	67	71	72	279	28,715
Sherri Steinhauer	68	68	69	75	280	20,933
Sara Sanders	73	70	69	69	281	17,914
Michele Redman	70	68	72	71	281	17,914
Cindy Figg-Currier	68	74	69	71	282	13,877
Cindy McCurdy	72	69	70	71	282	13,877
Danielle Ammaccapane	71	68	72	71	282	13,877
Caroline Blaylock	67	72	71	72	282	13,877
Jennifer Feldott	68	74	72	69	283	11,093
Lisa Kiggens	71	74	68	70	283	11,093
Denise Killeen	69	71	70	73	283	11,093
Susie Redman	69	76	69	70	284	9,348
Michelle McGann	69	73	71	71	284	9,348
Kelli Kuehne	69	72	72	71	284	9,348
Mi Hyun Kim	69	72	71	72	284	9,348
Karen Davies	69	70	73	72	284	9,348
Dawn Coe-Jones	70	74	73	68	285	7,665
Tina Barrett	73	71	72	69	285	7,665
Heather Daly-Donofrio	69	73	71	72	285	7,665
Marilyn Lovander	66	75	71	73	285	7,665
Hollis Stacy	73	69	69	74	285	7,665
Kristal Parker-Gregory	71	70	77	68	286	6,571
Val Skinner	71	75	70	70	286	6,571
Tracy Hanson	71	71	72	72	286	6,571
Moira Dunn	70	71	70	75	286	6,571

Firstar Classic

Country Club of the North, Beavercreek, Ohio   August 20-22
Par 36-36–72; 6,331 yards   purse, $650,000

	SCORES			TOTAL	MONEY
Rosie Jones	72	67	68	207	$97,500
Becky Iverson	74	66	67	207	52,333
Jan Stephenson	68	71	68	207	52,333
(Jones defeated Stephenson on first and Iverson on fourth extra hole.)					
Mi Hyun Kim	73	70	65	208	24,269
Jill McGill	76	66	66	208	24,269

	SCORES			TOTAL	MONEY
Leta Lindley	72	69	67	208	24,269
Hollis Stacy	69	70	69	208	24,269
Nancy Scranton	67	70	71	208	24,269
Kris Monaghan	68	70	71	209	15,373
Michele Redman	70	73	67	210	12,136
Pat Bradley	71	71	68	210	12,136
Se Ri Pak	70	69	71	210	12,136
Hiromi Kobayashi	68	70	72	210	12,136
Karen Weiss	70	74	67	211	8,876
Pearl Sinn	73	69	69	211	8,876
Kristal Parker-Gregory	70	72	69	211	8,876
Dina Ammaccapane	71	70	70	211	8,876
Beth Daniel	73	67	71	211	8,876
Chris Johnson	71	68	72	211	8,876
Jane Geddes	72	72	68	212	6,481
Maggie Will	71	73	68	212	6,481
Liselotte Neumann	70	73	69	212	6,481
Laurie Rinker-Graham	71	71	70	212	6,481
Jean Bartholomew	70	72	70	212	6,481
Dottie Pepper	72	69	71	212	6,481
Julie Piers	70	71	71	212	6,481
Meg Mallon	70	69	73	212	6,481
Akiko Fukushima	67	70	75	212	6,481
Caroline Keggi	71	73	69	213	4,952
Nancy Harvey	73	70	70	213	4,952
Nicole Jeray	69	74	70	213	4,952
Michelle McGann	71	71	71	213	4,952
Tracy Hanson	67	75	71	213	4,952
Wendy Ward	68	73	72	213	4,952

Oldsmobile Classic

Walnut Hills Country Club, East Lansing, Michigan
Par 36-36–72; 6,191 yards

August 26-29
purse, $700,000

	SCORES				TOTAL	MONEY
Dottie Pepper	67	63	70	70	270	$105,000
Kelli Kuehne	68	70	67	67	272	65,165
Rosie Jones	67	69	69	70	275	42,269
Karrie Webb	66	70	69	70	275	42,269
Beth Daniel	71	65	69	71	276	29,940
Donna Andrews	71	65	69	72	277	24,656
Vickie Odegard	72	70	67	69	278	18,551
Eva Dahllof	67	69	72	70	278	18,551
Helen Alfredsson	69	69	69	71	278	18,551
Mi Hyun Kim	69	71	67	72	279	14,794
Emilee Klein	68	72	71	69	280	12,128
Liselotte Neumann	70	67	72	71	280	12,128
Jenny Lidback	71	69	68	72	280	12,128
Tammie Green	71	69	67	73	280	12,128
Mhairi McKay	71	71	70	69	281	8,920
Lisa Kiggens	71	69	70	71	281	8,920
Tina Barrett	73	65	72	71	281	8,920
Wendy Doolan	70	70	69	72	281	8,920
Dawn Coe-Jones	70	67	72	72	281	8,920
Meg Mallon	71	69	68	73	281	8,920
Betsy King	74	68	65	74	281	8,920

	SCORES			TOTAL	MONEY
Danielle Ammaccapane	70	70 72	70	282	7,460
Cindy McCurdy	68	70 73	72	283	6,692
Julie Piers	69	69 72	73	283	6,692
Gail Graham	70	71 68	74	283	6,692
Dale Eggeling	71	70 67	75	283	6,692
Anne-Marie Knight	68	69 70	76	283	6,692
Kim Saiki	70	72 72	70	284	5,734
Nancy Scranton	69	71 73	71	284	5,734
Kristal Parker-Gregory	70	71 71	72	284	5,734
Amy Fruhwirth	71	69 72	72	284	5,734

State Farm Rail Classic

Rail Golf Course, Springfield, Illinois
Par 36-36–72; 6,403 yards

September 4-6
purse, $775,000

	SCORES			TOTAL	MONEY
Mi Hyun Kim	66	68	70	204	$116,250
Pearl Sinn	69	68	68	205	62,397
Janice Moodie	65	67	73	205	62,397
Lori West	68	68	70	206	37,048
Marisa Baena	67	67	72	206	37,048
Eva Dahllof	72	68	67	207	25,153
Emilee Klein	67	68	72	207	25,153
Tina Barrett	64	70	74	208	19,304
Karen Stupples	64	70	74	208	19,304
Jill McGill	68	74	67	209	13,961
Nancy Scranton	67	71	71	209	13,961
Sally Dee	69	68	72	209	13,961
Jenny Lidback	69	67	73	209	13,961
Betsy King	68	68	73	209	13,961
Donna Andrews	73	68	69	210	10,009
Vickie Odegard	67	73	70	210	10,009
Dottie Pepper	67	72	71	210	10,009
Ashli Price-Bunch	69	69	72	210	10,009
Marnie McGuire	72	64	74	210	10,009
Barb Mucha	67	68	75	210	10,009
Denise Killeen	73	69	69	211	7,900
Marilyn Lovander	68	73	70	211	7,900
Cindy Flom	73	66	72	211	7,900
Cindy McCurdy	69	69	73	211	7,900
Jan Stephenson	67	68	76	211	7,900
Christy Erb	71	72	69	212	5,980
Jane Crafter	67	75	70	212	5,980
Susie Redman	73	68	71	212	5,980
Kris Tschetter	71	69	72	212	5,980
Leslie Spalding	70	70	72	212	5,980
Ellie Gibson	69	71	72	212	5,980
Becky Iverson	69	71	72	212	5,980
Jennifer Feldott	69	71	72	212	5,980
Muffin Spencer-Devlin	68	72	72	212	5,980
Susan Ginter	68	69	75	212	5,980
Amy Benz	68	68	76	212	5,980
*Beth Bauer	71	68	73	212	

Samsung World Championship

Rush Creek Golf Club, Maple Grove, Minnesota
Par 36-36–72; 6,493 yards

September 9-12
purse, $700,000

	SCORES				TOTAL	MONEY
Se Ri Pak	67	71	70	72	280	$150,000
Karrie Webb	72	70	65	74	281	90,000
Rachel Hetherington	73	69	67	74	283	65,000
Rosie Jones	76	68	69	71	284	44,500
Laura Davies	69	71	68	76	284	44,500
Meg Mallon	70	74	69	72	285	30,000
Kelli Kuehne	75	68	70	73	286	27,000
Lorie Kane	70	75	69	74	288	24,000
Juli Inkster	74	72	71	73	290	21,000
Cindy McCurdy	73	74	74	70	291	18,639
Kelly Robbins	75	73	71	72	291	18,639
Helen Alfredsson	73	71	72	77	293	17,278
Janice Moodie	72	74	76	72	294	15,528
Sherri Steinhauer	76	75	68	75	294	15,528
Liselotte Neumann	74	69	75	76	294	15,528
Akiko Fukushima	74	71	72	77	294	15,528
Annika Sorenstam	71	79	74	71	295	14,278
Mardi Lunn	77	75	74	72	298	13,778
Catrin Nilsmark	78	70	75	76	299	13,278

Safeco Classic

Meridian Valley Country Club, Kent, Washington
Par 36-36–72; 6,198 yards

September 16-19
purse, $650,000

	SCORES				TOTAL	MONEY
Maria Hjorth	69	68	70	64	271	$97,500
Catriona Matthew	67	69	68	69	273	60,510
Tina Barrett	69	69	70	67	275	35,433
Annika Sorenstam	71	70	66	68	275	35,433
Rachel Hetherington	70	68	65	72	275	35,433
Chris Johnson	64	75	66	72	277	22,895
Akiko Fukushima	67	73	68	70	278	18,152
A.J. Eathorne	69	71	66	72	278	18,152
Donna Andrews	72	70	68	69	279	13,846
Emilee Klein	70	70	69	70	279	13,846
Carin Koch	70	69	69	71	279	13,846
Karen Weiss	72	71	68	69	280	10,466
Leslie Spalding	67	70	74	69	280	10,466
Michelle McGann	67	70	70	73	280	10,466
Helen Alfredsson	69	65	73	73	280	10,466
Susie Redman	71	71	70	69	281	8,503
Kim Saiki	70	70	71	70	281	8,503
Luciana Bemvenuti	68	70	69	74	281	8,503
Se Ri Pak	69	73	70	70	282	7,359
Amy Benz	70	71	69	72	282	7,359
Jenny Lidback	69	69	71	73	282	7,359
Wendy Ward	68	70	70	74	282	7,359
Lisa Kiggens	71	68	74	70	283	6,155
Sophie Gustafson	74	67	71	71	283	6,155
Marta Figueras-Dotti	71	70	71	71	283	6,155
Amy Fruhwirth	70	70	71	72	283	6,155

	SCORES			TOTAL	MONEY
Jennifer Feldott	73	68	68	74	283	6,155
Tracy Hanson	71	73	72	68	284	4,914
Jean Bartholomew	72	68	74	70	284	4,914
Danielle Ammaccapane	68	72	74	70	284	4,914
Lorie Kane	70	70	73	71	284	4,914
Ashli Price-Bunch	67	71	75	71	284	4,914
Dale Eggeling	72	71	69	72	284	4,914
Becky Iverson	69	74	68	73	284	4,914
Wendy Doolan	66	71	73	74	284	4,914

Safeway LPGA Championship

Columbia Edgewater Country Club, Portland, Oregon
Par 36-36–72; 6,307 yards

September 24-26
purse, $800,000

	SCORES			TOTAL	MONEY
Juli Inkster	67	70	70	207	$120,000
Tina Barrett	68	77	68	213	64,410
Grace Park	74	68	71	213	64,410
Nanci Bowen	70	75	69	214	34,888
Janice Moodie	72	72	70	214	34,888
Se Ri Pak	75	67	72	214	34,888
Moira Dunn	76	70	69	215	22,342
Michele Redman	70	70	75	215	22,342
Rosie Jones	67	80	69	216	15,190
Maggie Will	73	72	71	216	15,190
Mi Hyun Kim	73	72	71	216	15,190
Laura Philo	69	75	72	216	15,190
Beth Daniel	71	72	73	216	15,190
Carin Koch	70	71	75	216	15,190
Cindy McCurdy	74	73	70	217	10,587
Anne Marie Palli	76	69	72	217	10,587
Lorie Kane	74	71	72	217	10,587
Sophie Gustafson	72	72	73	217	10,587
Jenny Lidback	74	68	75	217	10,587
Dale Eggeling	76	73	69	218	8,096
Hollis Stacy	75	74	69	218	8,096
Kelly Robbins	73	76	69	218	8,096
Catriona Matthew	70	78	70	218	8,096
Jackie Gallagher-Smith	76	71	71	218	8,096
Meg Mallon	75	72	71	218	8,096
Sherri Turner	71	75	72	218	8,096
Tracy Hanson	68	78	72	218	8,096
Michelle McGann	74	74	71	219	6,522
Helen Alfredsson	70	78	71	219	6,522
Emilee Klein	73	74	72	219	6,522
Barb Mucha	74	71	74	219	6,522

New Albany Classic

New Albany Country Club, New Albany, Ohio
Par 36-36–72; 6,279 yards

September 30-October 3
purse, $1,000,000

	SCORES				TOTAL	MONEY
Annika Sorenstam	68	66	69	66	269	$150,000
Mardi Lunn	67	71	67	67	272	93,093
Emilee Klein	72	69	68	67	276	67,933
Meg Mallon	70	68	70	69	277	52,837
Maria Hjorth	71	71	70	67	279	42,772
Karrie Webb	69	70	74	67	280	35,224
Beth Daniel	68	75	69	69	281	29,689
Mi Hyun Kim	75	71	69	67	282	23,651
Sherri Steinhauer	71	72	70	69	282	23,651
Cindy Figg-Currier	71	74	67	70	282	23,651
Jill McGill	75	72	67	69	283	17,780
Dina Ammaccapane	70	70	73	70	283	17,780
Rachel Hetherington	70	68	72	73	283	17,780
Allison Finney	71	73	73	67	284	13,888
Denise Killeen	70	73	72	69	284	13,888
Mhairi McKay	72	70	73	69	284	13,888
Nancy Harvey	68	74	72	70	284	13,888
Janice Moodie	73	73	66	72	284	13,888
Liselotte Neumann	69	67	71	78	285	12,077
Kelli Kuehne	73	70	70	73	286	11,322
Deb Richard	69	70	74	73	286	11,322
Pat Hurst	73	71	76	67	287	9,186
Tracy Hanson	74	73	72	68	287	9,186
Lorie Kane	72	69	77	69	287	9,186
Michele Redman	72	75	69	71	287	9,186
Akiko Fukushima	73	69	74	71	287	9,186
Gail Graham	72	73	70	72	287	9,186
Erika Wicoff	69	72	74	72	287	9,186
Sherri Turner	70	71	73	73	287	9,186
Kristal Parker-Gregory	64	77	70	76	287	9,186

First Union Betsy King Classic

Berkleigh Country Club, Kutztown, Pennsylvania
Par 35-37–72; 6,197 yards

October 7-10
purse, $725,000

	SCORES				TOTAL	MONEY
Mi Hyun Kim	68	72	70	70	280	$108,750
Jenny Lidback	69	69	74	69	281	51,683
Helen Dobson	73	68	69	71	281	51,683
Beth Daniel	70	69	70	72	281	51,683
Marisa Baena	70	68	74	70	282	28,273
Jill McGill	72	72	67	71	282	28,273
Lisa Kiggens	67	76	69	72	284	18,240
Susie Redman	73	68	71	72	284	18,240
Joanne Morley	70	74	67	73	284	18,240
Betsy King	69	75	67	73	284	18,240
Lorie Kane	70	74	69	72	285	13,366
Wendy Doolan	74	71	65	75	285	13,366
Stefania Croce	73	73	72	68	286	9,992
Melissa McNamara	74	71	72	69	286	9,992
Maria Hjorth	72	70	74	70	286	9,992

	SCORES				TOTAL	MONEY
Meg Mallon	72	75	68	71	286	9,992
Chris Johnson	76	69	69	72	286	9,992
Kathryn Marshall	76	69	69	72	286	9,992
Amy Benz	67	77	70	72	286	9,992
Kristal Parker-Gregory	74	71	68	73	286	9,992
Katie Peterson	75	71	71	70	287	7,575
Eva Dahllof	75	71	71	70	287	7,575
Muffin Spencer-Devlin	69	78	69	71	287	7,575
Mhairi McKay	73	70	72	72	287	7,575
Jan Stephenson	74	70	76	68	288	6,147
Nancy Scranton	72	74	71	71	288	6,147
Diane Barnard	73	72	71	72	288	6,147
Catriona Matthew	71	74	71	72	288	6,147
Suzanne Strudwick	75	71	69	73	288	6,147
Hiromi Kobayashi	74	70	71	73	288	6,147
Sophie Gustafson	71	73	71	73	288	6,147
Karen Stupples	72	69	73	74	288	6,147

AFLAC Tournament of Champions

Magnolia Grove, Crossing Course, Semmes, Alabama
Par 36-36–72; 6,231 yards

October 14-17
purse, $750,000

	SCORES				TOTAL	MONEY
Akiko Fukushima	71	71	69	68	279	$122,000
Karrie Webb	66	74	70	70	280	64,875
Maria Hjorth	71	64	72	73	280	64,875
Chris Johnson	70	71	69	71	281	42,050
Kelly Robbins	74	75	66	67	282	30,550
Juli Inkster	72	71	71	68	282	30,550
Cindy Figg-Currier	67	71	72	73	283	22,900
Laura Davies	72	68	70	74	284	19,550
Tammie Green	73	69	74	69	285	16,170
Helen Alfredsson	72	72	67	74	285	16,170
Pat Bradley	70	71	70	74	285	16,170
Nancy Lopez	79	70	66	72	287	13,285
Pat Hurst	75	67	71	74	287	13,285
Se Ri Pak	70	73	73	72	288	11,560
Mardi Lunn	74	70	71	73	288	11,560
Rosie Jones	72	71	71	74	288	11,560
Meg Mallon	72	75	70	72	289	10,017
Betsy King	70	74	73	72	289	10,017
Sherri Steinhauer	71	71	75	72	289	10,017
Michele Redman	73	68	70	78	289	10,017
Hiromi Kobayashi	75	70	75	72	292	9,065
Rachel Hetherington	78	68	70	76	292	9,065
Donna Andrews	74	79	70	70	293	8,010
Barb Mucha	74	75	73	71	293	8,010
Gail Graham	72	73	77	71	293	8,010
Kelli Kuehne	72	76	71	74	293	8,010
Pearl Sinn	75	70	72	76	293	8,010
Deb Richard	76	72	75	71	294	7,160
Annika Sorenstam	75	75	72	72	294	7,160
Catrin Nilsmark	75	77	72	71	295	6,705
Amy Fruhwirth	73	74	71	77	295	6,705

PageNet Tour Championship

Desert Inn Golf Club, Las Vegas, Nevada

November 11-14

Par 36-36–72; 6,373 yards

purse, $1,000,000

	SCORES				TOTAL	MONEY
Se Ri Pak	66	66	74	70	276	$215,000
Karrie Webb	68	70	70	68	276	100,500
Laura Davies	71	66	71	68	276	100,500
(Pak defeated Webb and Davies on first extra hole.)						
Akiko Fukushima	72	71	67	69	279	57,000
Lorie Kane	68	70	68	74	280	50,000
Juli Inkster	70	68	69	74	281	43,000
Helen Alfredsson	74	72	68	68	282	30,833
Kelly Robbins	68	72	73	69	282	30,833
Janice Moodie	67	74	71	70	282	30,833
Mi Hyun Kim	73	70	72	68	283	21,500
Liselotte Neumann	76	70	67	70	283	21,500
Rosie Jones	73	71	67	72	283	21,500
Beth Daniel	73	69	72	70	284	16,250
Nancy Scranton	69	69	75	71	284	16,250
Annika Sorenstam	73	69	70	72	284	16,250
Maria Hjorth	71	74	71	69	285	14,250
Becky Iverson	71	73	73	70	287	13,250
Jan Stephenson	71	76	69	71	287	13,250
Mardi Lunn	74	72	71	71	288	11,875
Catriona Matthew	72	70	72	74	288	11,875
Cindy McCurdy	73	69	76	71	289	11,125
Rachel Hetherington	70	75	71	73	289	11,125
Sherri Turner	77	69	73	71	290	10,316
Emilee Klein	74	73	71	72	290	10,316
Sherri Steinhauer	72	71	74	73	290	10,316
Helen Dobson	76	70	71	74	291	9,700
Meg Mallon	75	74	73	70	292	9,300
Jenny Lidback	73	72	76	74	295	9,000
Tina Barrett	74	75	77	72	298	8,775
Kelli Kuehne	72	74	75	77	298	8,775

Diners Club Matches

Pelican Hill Golf Club, Corona del Mar, California

December 11-12

Par 35-36–71; 6,347 yards

purse, $1,200,000

FIRST-ROUND MATCHES

Juli Inkster and Dottie Pepper defeated Kelli Kuehne and Laura Davies, 1 up
Karrie Webb and Kelly Robbins defeated Annika Sorenstam and Lorie Kane, 3 and 1

THIRD-PLACE MATCH

Sorenstam and Kane defeated Kuehne and Davies, 4 and 3
(Sorenstam and Kane received $30,000 each; Kuehne and Davies received $20,000 each.)

CHAMPIONSHIP MATCH

Inkster and Pepper defeated Webb and Robbins, 4 and 3
(Inkster and Pepper received $100,000 each; Webb and Robbins received $50,000 each.)

Ladies European Tour

Royal Marie-Claire Open

Royal Evian Golf Club, Evians-les-Bains, France
Par 36-36–72; 5,975 yards

May 5-7
purse, £50,000

	SCORES			TOTAL	MONEY
Silvia Cavalleri	71	73	71	215	£7,500
Federica Dassu	73	73	70	216	4,287.50
Ana Belen Sanchez	71	72	73	216	4,287.50
Kirsty Taylor	72	69	76	217	2,700
Virginie Roques	71	72	75	218	2,120
Regine Lautens	72	72	75	219	1,750
Laura Navarro	73	74	73	220	1,290
Valerie Michaud	76	70	74	220	1,290
Johanna Head	76	70	74	220	1,290
Marina Arruti	70	79	72	221	960
Claire Duffy	71	76	74	221	960
Mette Hageman	79	72	71	222	797.50
Catherine Schmitt	73	76	73	222	797.50
Myra Murray	72	75	75	222	797.50
Natascha Fink	75	71	76	222	797.50
Stephanie Dallongeville	75	76	73	224	680.83
Marjan De Boer	77	74	73	224	680.83
Joanne Mills	74	75	75	224	680.83
Esther Poburski	70	79	75	224	680.83
Anna Berg	74	73	77	224	680.83
Nicola Moult	74	73	77	224	680.83
Elaine Ratcliffe	76	75	74	225	605
Xonia Wunsch-Ruiz	76	76	73	225	605
Raquel Carriedo	73	73	79	225	605
Elisabeth Quelhas	76	76	74	226	552.50
Barbara Hackett	73	78	75	226	552.50
Helen Hopkins	79	74	73	226	552.50
Alison Munt	73	74	79	226	552.50
Sara Forster	77	75	75	227	492.50
Nina Karlsson	75	78	74	227	492.50
Marlene Hedblom	78	78	71	227	492.50
Iben Tinning	74	72	81	227	492.50

Evian Masters

Royal Evian Golf Club, Evians-les-Bains, France
Par 36-36–72; 5,975 yards

June 9-12
purse, €1,021,408

	SCORES				TOTAL	MONEY
Catrin Nilsmark	69	70	72	68	279	€150,494.40
Laura Davies	69	72	68	72	281	101,583.72
Alison Nicholas	75	68	72	67	282	70,230.72
Lora Fairclough	74	67	72	70	283	53,977.32
Janice Moodie	73	73	69	70	285	42,389.26
Fumiko Muraguchi	72	73	72	70	287	32,607.12

	SCORES				TOTAL	MONEY
Lynnette Brooky	74	71	70	72	287	32,607.12
Hiromi Kobayashi	75	71	73	69	288	20,647.83
Carin Koch	72	73	73	70	288	20,647.83
Kathryn Marshall	73	73	72	70	288	20,647.83
Charlotta Sorenstam	70	71	75	72	288	20,647.83
Laura Philo	72	70	73	73	288	20,647.83
Patricia Meunier Lebouc	76	73	72	68	289	15,375.51
Tina Fischer	72	77	72	68	289	15,375.51
Elisabeth Esterl	69	76	75	69	289	15,375.51
Trish Johnson	69	74	76	70	289	15,375.51
Jane Geddes	74	73	71	71	289	15,375.51
Lisa Hackney	75	77	69	69	290	13,682.45
Maria Hjorth	71	80	68	71	290	13,682.45
Ludivine Kreutz	72	71	74	73	290	13,682.45
Helen Alfredsson	73	72	72	73	290	13,682.45
Catriona Matthew	78	73	73	67	291	12,064.63
Caroline Hall	72	74	74	71	291	12,064.63
Loraine Lambert	73	77	69	72	291	12,064.63
Federica Dassu	73	72	72	74	291	12,064.63
Joanne Morley	72	71	73	75	291	12,064.63
Karen Pearce	76	74	73	69	292	10,490.71
Shani Waugh	77	72	72	71	292	10,490.71
Kirsty Taylor	73	77	70	72	292	10,490.71
Silvia Cavalleri	72	71	74	75	292	10,490.71

Chrysler Open

Halmstad Golfklubb, Halmstad, Sweden
Par 36-36–72; 6,131 yards

July 1-4
purse, €223,950

	SCORES				TOTAL	MONEY
Laura Davies	71	69	66	67	273	€33,592.50
Alison Nicholas	71	72	70	68	281	22,730.93
Catrin Nilsmark	73	70	68	72	283	15,676.50
Ana Belen Sanchez	70	72	70	72	284	10,794.39
Helen Alfredsson	74	71	67	72	284	10,794.39
Liselotte Neumann	74	70	70	72	286	7,838.25
Mette Hageman	70	79	72	66	287	6,158.63
Caryn Louw	72	72	71	72	287	6,158.63
Loraine Lambert	70	74	73	71	288	4,214.74
Maria Hjorth	69	74	73	72	288	4,214.74
Joanne Mills	72	77	67	72	288	4,214.74
Johanna Head	75	69	70	74	288	4,214.74
Asa Gottmo	72	72	67	77	288	4,214.74
Kirsty Taylor	75	72	74	68	289	3,471.23
Raquel Carriedo	76	75	70	69	290	3,269.67
Sofia Gronberg Whitmore	73	70	76	71	290	3,269.67
Lora Fairclough	74	73	72	71	290	3,269.67
Valerie Van Ryckeghem	74	74	69	74	291	3,090.51
Karen Pearce	76	73	72	71	292	2,918.82
Joanne Morley	75	74	71	72	292	2,918.82
Elisabeth Esterl	75	74	71	72	292	2,918.82
Federica Dassu	78	71	72	72	293	2,709.80
Marjan De Boer	77	73	70	73	293	2,709.80
Corinne Dibnah	75	71	72	75	293	2,709.80
Elaine Ratcliffe	75	75	71	73	294	2,508.24
Marlene Hedblom	73	74	73	74	294	2,508.24

	SCORES				TOTAL	MONEY
Lynnette Brooky	76	70	70	78	294	2,508.24
Lisa Educate	76	75	73	71	295	2,273.09
Patricia Meunier Lebouc	76	72	75	72	295	2,273.09
Marina Arruti	78	73	70	74	295	2,273.09
Virginie Roques	74	76	70	75	295	2,273.09

Ladies' French Open

Paris International Golf Club, Baillet-en-France, France
Par 36-36–72; 5,990 yards

July 8-11
purse, €149,300

	SCORES				TOTAL	MONEY
Trish Johnson	70	70	75	67	282	€22,395
Alison Nicholas	73	72	71	67	283	15,153.95
Fiona Pike	72	72	73	68	285	8,281.16
Anne-Marie Knight	71	73	73	68	285	8,281.16
Mette Hageman	71	73	69	72	285	8,281.16
Patricia Meunier Lebouc	72	68	73	73	286	5,225.50
Sofia Gronberg Whitmore	70	72	72	73	287	4,479
Estefania Knuth	76	72	73	67	288	3,354.26
Elaine Ratcliffe	71	75	72	70	288	3,354.26
Loraine Lambert	74	72	69	73	288	3,354.26
Johanna Head	71	72	81	65	289	2,572.93
Sara Eklund	75	75	68	71	289	2,572.93
Vibeke Stensrud	73	72	71	73	289	2,572.93
Catherine Schmitt	79	71	71	69	290	2,276.83
Ana Belen Sanchez	77	71	71	71	290	2,276.83
Caroline Hall	73	71	73	74	291	2,149.92
Lynnette Brooky	74	74	69	74	291	2,149.92
Joanne Mills	76	72	74	70	292	1,949.86
Lara Tadiotto	71	77	73	71	292	1,949.86
Asa Gottmo	74	75	72	71	292	1,949.86
Raquel Carriedo	72	78	70	72	292	1,949.86
Corinne Dibnah	74	73	70	75	292	1,949.86
Natascha Fink	76	74	73	70	293	1,739.35
Ludivine Kreutz	73	77	73	70	293	1,739.35
Nina Karlsson	70	74	78	71	293	1,739.35
Julie Forbes	72	74	75	72	293	1,739.35
Alison Munt	73	72	77	72	294	1,604.98
Barbara Pestana	73	76	73	72	294	1,604.98
Karen Pearce	73	76	76	70	295	1,493
Esther Poburski	79	70	75	71	295	1,493
Laurette Maritz	72	73	72	78	295	1,493

Ladies' Austrian Open

Steiermarkischer Golf Club Murhof, Frohnleiten, Austria
Par 36-36–72; 6,148 yards

July 15-17
purse, €149,300

	SCORES			TOTAL	MONEY
Marina Arruti	68	68	67	203	€22,395
Dale Reid	70	65	70	205	12,802.48
Elisabeth Esterl	65	68	72	205	12,802.48
Johanna Head	70	67	69	206	8,062.20
Silvia Cavalleri	71	66	70	207	6,330.32

	SCORES			TOTAL	MONEY
Trish Johnson	72	69	67	208	4,852.25
Sophie Gustafson	71	70	67	208	4,852.25
Joanne Mills	73	69	67	209	3,354.26
Raquel Carriedo	68	73	68	209	3,354.26
Samantha Head	69	71	69	209	3,354.26
Corinne Dibnah	71	70	69	210	2,572.93
Catherine Schmitt	70	71	69	210	2,572.93
Patricia Meunier Lebouc	70	67	73	210	2,572.93
Federica Dassu	74	68	69	211	2,276.83
Lora Fairclough	67	74	70	211	2,276.83
Barbara Pestana	71	73	68	212	2,090.20
Laurette Maritz	70	73	69	212	2,090.20
Lisa Dermott	70	71	71	212	2,090.20
Caryn Louw	71	68	73	212	2,090.20
Kathi Poppmeier	72	73	68	213	1,828.93
Iben Tinning	76	68	69	213	1,828.93
*Lilian Mensi-Klarbach	73	71	69	213	
Cecilie Lundgreen	73	70	70	213	1,828.93
Nina Karlsson	73	69	71	213	1,828.93
Lisa Educate	71	70	72	213	1,828.93
Jane Leary	67	72	74	213	1,828.93
Gillian Stewart	73	74	67	214	1,604.98
Fiona Pike	71	73	70	214	1,604.98
Julie Forbes	72	70	72	214	1,604.98
Christina Kuld	73	66	75	214	1,604.98

stilwerk Ladies' German Open

Marriott Hotel Treudelberg Golf & Country Club,
Hamburg, Germany
Par 36-36–72; 5,975 yards

July 22-25
purse, €149,300

	SCORES				TOTAL	MONEY
Anne-Marie Knight	74	69	71	64	278	€22,395
Sophie Gustafson	69	73	72	65	279	12,802.48
Laura Davies	75	70	69	65	279	12,802.48
Valerie Van Ryckeghem	71	70	70	70	281	7,196.26
Jane Leary	73	68	69	71	281	7,196.26
Johanna Head	69	72	73	69	283	5,225.50
Alison Nicholas	76	74	66	68	284	4,105.75
Anna Berg	71	72	67	74	284	4,105.75
Ana Belen Sanchez	72	72	71	70	285	3,344.32
Ludivine Kreutz	71	73	73	69	286	2,676.20
Lisa Educate	72	75	70	69	286	2,676.20
Kirsty Taylor	74	72	70	70	286	2,676.20
Sofia Gronberg Whitmore	71	70	74	71	286	2,676.20
Elisabeth Esterl	76	73	71	68	288	2,244.47
Laura Navarro	74	76	69	69	288	2,244.47
Silvia Cavalleri	71	70	73	74	288	2,244.47
Lynnette Brooky	72	76	73	68	289	2,030.48
Corinne Dibnah	74	73	72	70	289	2,030.48
Sara Eklund	74	68	75	72	289	2,030.48
Natascha Fink	75	70	71	73	289	2,030.48
Samantha Head	76	73	74	67	290	1,828.93
Vibeke Stensrud	77	75	69	69	290	1,828.93
Asa Gottmo	74	72	73	71	290	1,828.93
Barbara Pestana	72	74	71	73	290	1,828.93

	SCORES				TOTAL	MONEY
Catrin Nilsmark	75	76	73	67	291	1,649.77
Nicola Moult	76	73	71	71	291	1,649.77
Christina Kuld	72	72	75	72	291	1,649.77
Susan Moon	77	71	71	72	291	1,649.77
Julie Forbes	75	74	74	69	292	1,448.21
Dale Reid	75	74	72	71	292	1,448.21
Fiona Pike	75	74	72	71	292	1,448.21
Karolina Andersson	78	74	69	71	292	1,448.21
Rachel Kirkwood	73	75	71	73	292	1,448.21

McDonald's WPGA Championship of Europe

The Gleneagles Hotel, King's Course, Perthshire, Scotland
Par 37-35–72; 6,049 yards

August 5-8
purse, €447,900

	SCORES				TOTAL	MONEY
Laura Davies	70	69	69	72	280	€67,185
Maria Hjorth	69	70	72	69	280	45,461.85
(Davies defeated Hjorth on second extra hole.)						
Janice Moodie	69	68	73	71	281	27,769.80
Alison Nicholas	70	76	64	71	281	27,769.80
Trish Johnson	70	70	73	69	282	18,990.96
Catrin Nilsmark	68	68	67	80	283	15,676.50
Valerie Van Ryckeghem	74	67	71	73	285	12,317.25
Mhairi McKay	70	67	74	74	285	12,317.25
Caroline Hall	72	70	72	72	286	9,077.44
Raquel Carriedo	70	72	72	72	286	9,077.44
Julie Forbes	73	71	70	72	286	9,077.44
Catriona Matthew	71	74	68	74	287	7,457.54
Sofia Gronberg Whitmore	74	69	68	76	287	7,457.54
Helen Dobson	69	71	76	72	288	6,457.23
Dale Reid	73	71	72	72	288	6,457.23
Iben Tinning	75	70	70	73	288	6,457.23
Karen Pearce	71	71	72	74	288	6,457.23
Suzanne Strudwick	72	71	70	75	288	6,457.23
Tina Fischer	69	68	73	78	288	6,457.23
Shani Waugh	73	70	74	72	289	5,621.15
Caryn Louw	74	71	70	74	289	5,621.15
Marnie McGuire	72	67	74	76	289	5,621.15
Charlotta Sorenstam	71	69	72	77	289	5,621.15
Fiona Pike	73	70	75	72	290	5,218.04
Anne-Marie Knight	73	71	68	78	290	5,218.04
Judith Van Hagen	70	76	73	73	292	4,949.30
Diane Barnard	70	73	73	76	292	4,949.30
Kirsty Taylor	71	73	74	75	293	4,546.19
Barbara Pestana	71	73	73	76	293	4,546.19
Joanne Morley	70	72	73	78	293	4,546.19
Sara Eklund	68	70	76	79	293	4,546.19

Weetabix Women's British Open

Woburn Golf & Country Club, Duke's Course,
Milton Keynes, England
Par 35-38–73; 6,463 yards

August 12-15
purse, €858,475

	SCORES				TOTAL	MONEY
Sherri Steinhauer	71	71	68	73	283	€149,300
Annika Sorenstam	69	71	72	72	284	89,580
Helen Dobson	71	72	72	70	285	47,278.32
Cindy Flom	71	74	69	71	285	47,278.32
Fiona Pike	70	70	71	74	285	47,278.32
Emilee Klein	72	70	73	71	286	23,888
Sophie Gustafson	73	69	72	72	286	23,888
Mardi Lunn	71	72	70	73	286	23,888
Iben Tinning	68	69	75	74	286	23,888
Cindy McCurdy	73	70	68	75	286	23,888
Smriti Mehra	70	70	76	71	287	16,423
Carin Koch	74	72	72	70	288	14,370.13
Suzanne Strudwick	71	70	76	71	288	14,370.13
Rosie Jones	73	71	73	72	289	11,993.76
Laura Philo	69	71	75	74	289	11,993.76
Liselotte Neumann	72	70	72	75	289	11,993.76
Deb Richard	72	73	73	72	290	9,875.12
Laura Navarro	70	70	77	73	290	9,875.12
Melissa McNamara	72	70	75	73	290	9,875.12
Toshimi Kimura	69	74	74	73	290	9,875.12
Cindy Figg-Currier	69	76	72	73	290	9,875.12
Valerie Van Ryckeghem	72	75	70	73	290	9,875.12
Kirsty Taylor	73	71	72	74	290	9,875.12
*Giulia Sergas	71	73	74	73	291	
Joanne Morley	70	75	73	73	291	7,912.90
Alison Nicholas	73	71	73	74	291	7,912.90
Maria Hjorth	71	68	77	75	291	7,912.90
Stephanie Lowe	72	74	70	75	291	7,912.90
Patricia Meunier Lebouc	73	70	72	76	291	7,912.90
Midori Yoneyama	73	70	72	76	291	7,912.90

Compaq Open

Osterakers Golf Club, Stockholm, Sweden
Par 36-37–73; 6,055 yards

August 19-22
purse, €447,900

	SCORES				TOTAL	MONEY
Laura Davies	67	69	71	70	277	€67,185
Helen Alfredsson	67	72	72	70	281	45,461.85
Alison Nicholas	73	70	68	71	282	31,353
Trish Johnson	70	68	71	76	285	24,186.60
Raquel Carriedo	72	73	70	72	287	17,333.73
Sherri Steinhauer	72	70	71	74	287	17,333.73
Mardi Lunn	70	71	76	71	288	12,317.25
Shani Waugh	75	71	70	72	288	12,317.25
Kirsty Taylor	73	70	72	74	289	10,032.96
Joanne Mills	73	71	70	76	290	8,958
Charlotta Sorenstam	75	70	73	73	291	7,718.81
Vibeke Stensrud	76	69	73	73	291	7,718.81
Marie-Josee Rouleau	73	75	70	73	291	7,718.81
Esther Poburski	77	73	70	72	292	6,733.43

	SCORES				TOTAL	MONEY
Catrin Nilsmark	70	77	69	76	292	6,733.43
Annika Sorenstam	70	69	73	80	292	6,733.43
Sofia Gronberg Whitmore	74	73	75	71	293	6,181.02
Maria Hjorth	75	71	72	75	293	6,181.02
Carin Koch	73	72	70	78	293	6,181.02
Joanne Morley	73	73	74	74	294	5,688.33
Claire Duffy	71	71	77	75	294	5,688.33
Catherine Schmitt	74	74	69	77	294	5,688.33
*Maria Boden	71	77	74	73	295	
Lora Fairclough	72	79	73	72	295	5,218.04
Patricia Meunier Lebouc	73	73	77	73	295	5,218.04
Marie-Laure de Lorenzi	75	69	77	75	295	5,218.04
Mia Lojdahl	76	73	72	75	295	5,218.04
Suzanne Strudwick	74	72	79	72	297	4,747.74
Dale Reid	75	73	76	73	297	4,747.74
Silvia Cavalleri	75	75	74	73	297	4,747.74

Cantor Fitzgerald Laura Davies' Invitational

Brocket Hall Golf Club, Hertfordshire, England
Par 35-37–72; 6,186 yards

August 27-30
purse, €447,900

	SCORES				TOTAL	MONEY
Sofia Gronberg Whitmore	67	70	69	69	275	€67,185
Trish Johnson	72	68	70	65	275	45,461.85
(Gronberg defeated Johnson on second extra hole.)						
Raquel Carriedo	66	70	71	74	281	31,353
Kathryn Marshall	70	73	73	67	283	21,588.78
Sophie Gustafson	71	72	69	71	283	21,588.78
Sofie Eriksson	72	70	74	68	284	15,676.50
Lora Fairclough	75	72	67	71	285	13,437
Joanne Mills	74	73	70	69	286	9,226.74
Karen Pearce	71	69	75	71	286	9,226.74
Janice Moodie	72	71	72	71	286	9,226.74
Helen Dobson	72	68	73	73	286	9,226.74
Patricia Meunier Lebouc	71	72	69	74	286	9,226.74
Valerie Van Ryckeghem	73	68	75	71	287	7,076.82
Laura Davies	69	76	68	74	287	7,076.82
Kirsty Taylor	69	73	77	69	288	6,539.34
Wendy Dicks	70	75	70	73	288	6,539.34
Elisabeth Esterl	69	69	72	78	288	6,539.34
Silvia Cavalleri	76	71	72	70	289	5,849.57
Julie Forbes	72	72	73	72	289	5,849.57
Alison Nicholas	72	73	72	72	289	5,849.57
Mardi Lunn	70	70	76	73	289	5,849.57
Lynnette Brooky	72	73	69	75	289	5,849.57
Linda Ericsson	74	72	72	72	290	5,218.04
Shani Waugh	74	67	76	73	290	5,218.04
Laurette Maritz	74	69	73	74	290	5,218.04
Sandrine Mendiburu	68	70	77	75	290	5,218.04
Federica Dassu	73	74	74	70	291	4,546.19
Iben Tinning	75	71	74	71	291	4,546.19
Joanne Morley	72	75	73	71	291	4,546.19
Laura Navarro	71	73	75	72	291	4,546.19
Vibeke Stensrud	72	73	74	72	291	4,546.19
Wen-Lin Li	75	74	68	74	291	4,546.19

globalgolf.com Donegal Irish Ladies' Open

Letterkenny Golf Club, County Donegal, Ireland
Par 36-35–71; 5,955 yards

September 2-5
purse, €149,300

	SCORES				TOTAL	MONEY
Sandrine Mendiburu	71	72	71	72	286	€22,395
Raquel Carriedo	76	72	71	67	286	11,222.37
Laura Davies	77	70	70	69	286	11,222.37
Elisabeth Esterl	75	68	71	72	286	11,222.37
(Mendiburu defeated Esterl on first and Carriedo and Davies on second extra hole.)						
Alison Nicholas	72	70	73	72	287	6,330.32
Trish Johnson	75	75	69	69	288	4,195.33
Marlene Hedblom	72	72	74	70	288	4,195.33
Nina Karlsson	76	66	72	74	288	4,195.33
Dale Reid	74	71	68	75	288	4,195.33
Joanne Morley	77	72	71	69	289	2,866.56
Wendy Dicks	70	72	71	76	289	2,866.56
Ludivine Kreutz	76	74	70	70	290	2,428.60
Riikka Hakkarainen	75	67	77	71	290	2,428.60
Kirsty Taylor	71	73	73	73	290	2,428.60
Erica Steen	75	71	76	69	291	2,120.06
Alison Munt	77	74	70	70	291	2,120.06
Natascha Fink	71	75	72	73	291	2,120.06
Joanne Mills	76	70	72	73	291	2,120.06
Mette Hageman	71	74	70	76	291	2,120.06
Corinne Dibnah	77	72	72	71	292	1,896.11
Catherine Schmitt	73	70	76	73	292	1,896.11
Ana Larraneta	74	74	71	73	292	1,896.11
Marina Arruti	76	76	72	69	293	1,672.16
Wen-Lin Li	77	73	73	70	293	1,672.16
Samantha Head	79	75	69	70	293	1,672.16
Laurette Maritz	73	76	73	71	293	1,672.16
Mia Lojdahl	74	72	75	72	293	1,672.16
Marine Monnet	79	70	72	72	293	1,672.16
Elaine Ratcliffe	72	73	74	74	293	1,672.16
Lora Fairclough	75	73	69	77	294	1,493

Ladies' Hannover Expo 2000 Open

Rethmar Golf Links, Hannover, Germany
Par 36-36–72; 5,852 yards

September 17-19
purse, €149,300

	SCORES			TOTAL	MONEY
Sandrine Mendiburu	73	64	71	208	€22,395
Lora Fairclough	72	71	67	210	15,153.95
Claire Duffy	70	68	73	211	10,451
Raquel Carriedo	71	72	69	212	8,062.20
Elaine Ratcliffe	74	70	69	213	6,330.32
Anna Berg	67	71	76	214	5,225.50
Patricia Meunier Lebouc	70	74	71	215	4,105.75
Catherine Schmitt	71	71	73	215	4,105.75
Kirsty Taylor	70	75	71	216	3,165.16
Trish Johnson	73	72	71	216	3,165.16
Mette Hageman	69	76	73	218	2,454.49
Mia Lojdahl	72	72	74	218	2,454.49
Laura Navarro	73	71	74	218	2,454.49
Lara Tadiotto	70	73	75	218	2,454.49

	SCORES			TOTAL	MONEY
Sara Eklund	72	69	77	218	2,454.49
Ana Belen Sanchez	74	76	69	219	2,032.96
Nicola Moult	74	73	72	219	2,032.96
Valerie Van Ryckeghem	71	74	74	219	2,032.96
Tina Fischer	70	73	76	219	2,032.96
Vibeke Stensrud	70	73	76	219	2,032.96
Judith Van Hagen	72	69	78	219	2,032.96
*Niloufar Azam	76	71	73	220	
*Rikke Rasmussen	72	74	74	220	
Alison Munt	71	73	76	220	1,828.93
Barbara Pestana	72	72	76	220	1,828.93
Deni Booker	74	75	72	221	1,739.35
Ludivine Kreutz	71	75	75	221	1,739.35
Rachel Kirkwood	76	75	71	222	1,627.37
Asa Gottmo	72	76	74	222	1,627.37
Erica Steen	70	77	75	222	1,627.37

Ladies' Italian Open

Poggio dei Medici Golf Club, Tuscany, Italy
Par 37-36–73; 6,296 yards

September 24-26
purse, €149,300

	SCORES			TOTAL	MONEY
Samantha Head	71	72	71	214	€22,395
Marina Arruti	74	71	70	215	9,044.59
Patricia Meunier Lebouc	73	71	71	215	9,044.59
Mette Hageman	70	73	72	215	9,044.59
Riikka Hakkarainen	72	70	73	215	9,044.59
Trish Johnson	70	71	74	215	9,044.59
Vibeke Stensrud	75	71	70	216	4,479
Tina Fischer	73	72	72	217	3,202.49
Lynnette Brooky	70	74	73	217	3,202.49
Sandrine Mendiburu	73	71	73	217	3,202.49
Claire Duffy	68	73	76	217	3,202.49
Johanna Head	74	70	74	218	2,485.85
Laurette Maritz	70	73	75	218	2,485.85
Sofia Gronberg Whitmore	75	75	69	219	2,314.15
Iben Tinning	73	77	70	220	2,090.20
Laura Navarro	72	76	72	220	2,090.20
Raquel Carriedo	71	76	73	220	2,090.20
Joanne Mills	73	73	74	220	2,090.20
Alison Munt	72	73	75	220	2,090.20
Mia Lojdahl	74	71	75	220	2,090.20
Rachel Kirkwood	74	74	73	221	1,896.11
*Giulia Sergas	75	71	75	221	
Ana Belen Sanchez	80	73	69	222	1,716.95
*Sofia Sandolo	74	75	73	222	
Marie-Laure de Lorenzi	73	75	74	222	1,716.95
Kirsty Thomas	78	69	75	222	1,716.95
Kirsty Taylor	73	74	75	222	1,716.95
Valerie Van Ryckeghem	72	73	77	222	1,716.95
Esther Poburski	67	78	77	222	1,716.95
Amaia Arruti	69	74	79	222	1,716.95

Air France Madame Biarritz Open

Golf de Biarritz-Le Phare, Biarritz, France
Par 35-35–70; 5,688 yards

October 7-9
purse, €149,300

	SCORES			TOTAL	MONEY
Sofia Gronberg Whitmore	66	66	68	200	€22,395
Sandrine Mendiburu	66	66	71	203	15,153.95
Alison Munt	70	69	65	204	10,451
Pernilla Sterner	66	71	68	205	7,196.26
Marie-Laure de Lorenzi	68	68	69	205	7,196.26
Samantha Head	68	68	70	206	4,479
Joanne Mills	68	68	70	206	4,479
Patricia Meunier Lebouc	67	67	72	206	4,479
Valerie Van Ryckeghem	70	69	68	207	2,809.83
Kirsty Taylor	68	69	70	207	2,809.83
Marie-Josee Rouleau	68	69	70	207	2,809.83
Trish Johnson	69	67	71	207	2,809.83
Susan Elliott	66	64	77	207	2,809.83
Riikka Hakkarainen	71	69	68	208	2,314.15
*Virginie Auffret	68	66	74	208	
Nicola Moult	65	71	73	209	2,239.50
Vibeke Stensrud	70	72	68	210	2,060.34
Claire Duffy	70	70	70	210	2,060.34
Stephanie Arricau	72	67	71	210	2,060.34
Mette Hageman	65	71	74	210	2,060.34
Laurette Maritz	68	67	75	210	2,060.34
Elisabeth Esterl	72	71	68	211	1,828.93
Laura Navarro	71	69	71	211	1,828.93
Jane Leary	68	72	71	211	1,828.93
Regine Lautens	66	73	72	211	1,828.93
Julie Forbes	69	74	69	212	1,537.79
Ludivine Kreutz	73	70	69	212	1,537.79
Dale Reid	69	74	69	212	1,537.79
Johanna Head	70	72	70	212	1,537.79
Barbara Pestana	72	70	70	212	1,537.79
Caroline Hall	71	70	71	212	1,537.79
Karolina Andersson	70	70	72	212	1,537.79
Anna Berg	72	68	72	212	1,537.79
Corinne Dibnah	69	71	72	212	1,537.79

Marrakesh Palmeraie Open

Palmeraie Golf Palace, Marrakesh, Morocco
Par 36-36–72; 6,237 yards

October 22-24
purse, €149,300

	SCORES			TOTAL	MONEY
Trish Johnson	70	67	67	204	€22,395
Valerie Van Ryckeghem	71	72	66	209	15,153.95
Raquel Carriedo	69	69	72	210	10,451
Catherine Schmitt	69	74	68	211	8,062.20
Marlene Hedblom	71	71	70	212	5,777.91
Joanne Morley	70	70	72	212	5,777.91
Sandrine Mendiburu	75	71	68	214	3,635.46
Laurette Maritz	72	73	69	214	3,635.46
Deni Booker	75	69	70	214	3,635.46
Amaia Arruti	72	71	71	214	3,635.46
Isabella Maconi	73	74	68	215	2,454.49

	SCORES			TOTAL	MONEY
Suzanne Strudwick	75	71	69	215	2,454.49
Regine Lautens	74	71	70	215	2,454.49
Kirsty Taylor	69	73	73	215	2,454.49
Vibeke Stensrud	70	71	74	215	2,454.49
Pernilla Sterner	74	73	69	216	2,007.01
Lora Fairclough	72	73	71	216	2,007.01
Samantha Head	69	75	72	216	2,007.01
Sophie Gustafson	71	73	72	216	2,007.01
Elaine Ratcliffe	72	71	73	216	2,007.01
Wendy Dicks	72	70	74	216	2,007.01
Karina Orum	70	68	78	216	2,007.01
Sofia Gronberg Whitmore	73	71	73	217	1,694.56
Stephanie Arricau	68	76	73	217	1,694.56
Suzanne Dickens	71	72	74	217	1,694.56
Nina Karlsson	71	71	75	217	1,694.56
Marjan De Boer	72	70	75	217	1,694.56
Erica Steen	72	69	76	217	1,694.56
Julie Forbes	75	73	70	218	1,381.03
Lara Tadiotto	75	70	73	218	1,381.03
Christina Kuld	74	71	73	218	1,381.03
Aideen Rogers	74	70	74	218	1,381.03
Ana Larraneta	71	72	75	218	1,381.03
Joanne Mills	68	75	75	218	1,381.03
Esther Poburski	67	76	75	218	1,381.03
Jane Leary	69	73	76	218	1,381.03

Princess Lalla Meriem Cup

Royal Golf Dar-es-Salam, Red Course, Rabat, Morocco
Par 36-37–73; 6,400 yards

November 12-14
purse, US$70,000

	SCORES			TOTAL	MONEY
Lora Fairclough	72	72	73	217	US$13,000
Samantha Head	73	72	74	219	9,000
Sofia Gronberg	69	75	77	221	5,500
Amaia Arruti	74	72	77	223	4,000
Johanna Head	75	72	76	223	4,000
Joanne Morley	76	72	77	225	3,000
Elisabeth Esterl	74	77	75	226	2,750
Raquel Carriedo	74	78	74	226	2,750
Federica Dassu	74	76	78	228	2,600
Karina Orum	75	77	76	228	2,600
Anne-Marie Palli	74	75	80	229	2,600
Marina Arruti	72	79	78	229	2,600
Valerie Van Ryckeghem	76	75	79	230	2,600
Patricia Meunier Lebouc	76	76	78	230	2,600
Diane Barnard	78	76	76	230	2,600
Regine Lautens	73	84	77	234	2,600
Xonia Wunsch-Ruiz	77	80	78	235	2,600
Veronique Palli	82	85	81	248	2,600

Praia D'el Rey Rover European Cup

Praia D'el Rey Golf & Country Club, Obidos, Portugal
Par 36-36–72; 6,652 yards

November 19-21
purse, €210,000

FIRST DAY
Foursomes

Laura Davies and Alison Nicholas defeated Alan Tapie and Bill Brask, 2 up
John Morgan and Eddie Polland defeated Trish Johnson and Sandrine Mendiburu, 4 and 2
Marie-Laure de Lorenzi and Raquel Carriedo halved with Antonio Garrido and David Jones
Sofia Gronberg-Whitmore and Sophie Gustafson halved with Jerry Bruner and Ross Metherell
Neil Coles and Tommy Horton defeated Lora Fairclough and Maria Hjorth, 1 up

POINTS: Ladies European Tour 2, European Seniors Tour 3

SECOND DAY
Fourball

Horton and Morgan defeated Davies and Johnson, 1 up
Gronberg-Whitmore and Carriedo defeated Polland and Jones, 2 and 1
Gustafson and Mendiburu halved with Garrido and Bruner
Fairclough and Hjorth defeated Coles and Metherell, 4 and 3
Nicholas and de Lorenzi halved with Tapie and Brask

POINTS: Ladies European Tour 3, European Seniors Tour 2

THIRD DAY
Singles

Johnson defeated Metherell, 1 up
Davies defeated Bruner, 1 up
Morgan defeated Nicholas, 2 and 1
Hjorth halved with Brask
Tapie defeated Carriedo, 1 up
Jones defeated Mendiburu, 2 up
Fairclough defeated Garrido, 1 up
Gustafson defeated Coles, 5 and 3
Gronberg-Whitmore halved with Horton
De Lorenzi defeated Polland, 4 and 3

POINTS: Ladies European Tour 6, European Seniors Tour 4

TOTAL POINTS: Ladies European Tour 11, European Seniors Tour 9

(Each member of Ladies European team received €14,000; each member of European Seniors team received €7,000.)

Japan LPGA Tour

Daikin Orchid Ladies

Ryukyu Golf Club, Okinawa
Par 36-36–72; 6,260 yards

March 5-7
purse, ¥60,000,000

	SCORES			TOTAL	MONEY
Yoko Inoue	69	64	73	206	¥10,800,000
Ok-Hee Ku	68	68	73	209	4,740,000
Kasumi Fujii	69	68	72	209	4,740,000
Aki Nakano	72	70	69	211	3,000,000
Yukiyo Haga	68	73	70	211	3,000,000
Michiko Hattori	68	70	73	211	3,000,000
Woo-Soon Ko	72	70	70	212	1,546,800
Michie Ohba	70	71	71	212	1,546,800
Yuri Fudoh	69	72	71	212	1,546,800
Fumiko Muraguchi	69	70	73	212	1,546,800
Midori Yoneyama	64	73	75	212	1,546,800
Mayumi Murai	67	72	74	213	1,074,000
Lee Oh-Soon	72	71	71	214	834,000
Hee-Won Han	71	71	72	214	834,000
Kaori Harada	74	69	71	214	834,000
Akane Ohshiro	70	73	71	214	834,000
Tatsuko Morimoto	70	74	70	214	834,000
Natsuko Noro	70	74	70	214	834,000
Man-Soo Kim	69	69	76	214	834,000
Huang Yu-Chen	73	69	73	215	570,000
Kyoko Ono	68	72	75	215	570,000
Chikayo Yamazaki	73	68	74	215	570,000
Kaori Higo	70	69	76	215	570,000
Harumi Sakagami	68	70	77	215	570,000
Akemi Yamaoka	73	70	73	216	498,000
Hiroe Tani	70	72	74	216	498,000
Mikino Kubo	72	70	74	216	498,000
Jae-Sook Won	71	73	72	216	498,000
Nayoko Yoshikawa	71	70	75	216	498,000
Young-Me Lee	71	70	75	216	498,000
Hiromi Takamura	70	71	75	216	498,000

Saishunkan Ladies

Kumamoto Kuukou Country Club, Kumamoto
Par 36-36–72; 6,432 yards

March 19-21
purse, ¥60,000,000

	SCORES			TOTAL	MONEY
Nahoko Hirao	66	75	74	215	¥10,800,000
Michie Ohba	75	71	69	215	5,280,000
(Hirao defeated Ohba on first extra hole.)					
Harumi Sakagami	74	74	68	216	3,900,000
Hee-Won Han	74	72	70	216	3,900,000
Jae-Sook Won	75	71	72	218	2,700,000

	SCORES			TOTAL	MONEY
Nayoko Yoshikawa	74	72	72	218	2,700,000
Toshimi Kimura	75	74	71	220	1,950,000
Junko Yasui	72	75	73	220	1,950,000
Misayo Fujisawa	73	78	70	221	1,188,000
Kumiko Hiyoshi	73	77	71	221	1,188,000
Hiromi Takamura	72	77	72	221	1,188,000
Mieko Nomura	75	75	71	221	1,188,000
Kaori Harada	70	76	75	221	1,188,000
Young-Me Lee	70	80	72	222	930,000
Lee Oh-Soon	70	77	75	222	930,000
Ikuyo Shiotani	74	77	72	223	698,000
Michiko Hattori	73	77	73	223	698,000
Midori Yoneyama	75	77	71	223	698,000
Natsuko Noro	71	77	75	223	698,000
Tomo Sakakibara	74	71	78	223	698,000
Aki Takamura	70	75	78	223	698,000
Chieko Nishida	75	76	73	224	534,000
Kyoko Odo	74	77	73	224	534,000
Miyuki Shimabukuro	73	78	73	224	534,000
Yueh-Chyn Huang	75	77	72	224	534,000
Ok-Hee Ku	76	74	74	224	534,000
Akemi Yamaoka	74	76	74	224	534,000
Yuko Moriguchi	74	74	76	224	534,000
Yuri Kawanami	72	74	78	224	534,000
Aiko Takasu	74	76	75	225	468,000
Masako Ishihara	75	77	73	225	468,000
Fumiko Muraguchi	74	73	78	225	468,000

Nasu Ogawa Ladies

Nasu Ogawa Golf Club, Ogawa, Tochigi
Par 36-36—72; 6,166 yards
(Second round cancelled — rain.)

April 23-25
purse, ¥37,500,000

	SCORES		TOTAL	MONEY
Ok-Hee Ku	70	73	143	¥5,750,000
Hee-Won Han	69	75	144	2,962,500
Yukiko Ishiguro	70	74	144	2,962,500
Lee Oh-Soon	71	74	145	2,250,000
Natsuko Noro	71	75	146	1,687,500
Fumiko Muraguchi	70	76	146	1,687,500
Kumiko Hiyoshi	72	75	147	1,312,500
Ikuyo Shiotani	75	73	148	1,031,250
Huang Yu-Chen	74	74	148	1,031,250
Mieko Nomura	75	74	149	666,000
Miyuki Shimabukuro	74	75	149	666,000
Nayoko Yoshikawa	73	76	149	666,000
Michiko Hattori	71	78	149	666,000
Nahoko Hirao	70	79	149	666,000
Yuri Fudoh	77	73	150	532,500
Hisako Ohgane	71	79	150	532,500
Yuko Motoyama	75	76	151	407,250
Mayumi Ishii	75	76	151	407,250
Etsuko Kawakami	76	75	151	407,250
Harumi Sakagami	77	74	151	407,250
Yu-Chuan Tai	71	80	151	407,250
Akane Ohshiro	75	77	152	311,250

	SCORES		TOTAL	MONEY
Mika Adaniya	76	76	152	311,250
Nobuko Kizawa	74	78	152	311,250
Michie Ohba	76	76	152	311,250
Fukumi Tani	73	79	152	311,250
Kaori Higo	73	79	152	311,250
Akemi Yamaoka	73	79	152	311,250
Rie Mitsuhashi	77	75	152	311,250
Wen-Lin Li	77	75	152	311,250
Man-Soo Kim	71	81	152	311,250
Kayo Yamada	71	81	152	311,250

Katokichi Queens

Sakaide Country Club, Sakaide, Kagawa
Par 36-36–72; 6,312 yards

April 30-May 2
purse, ¥50,000,000

	SCORES			TOTAL	MONEY
Ayako Okamoto	73	70	69	212	¥9,000,000
Fumiko Muraguchi	71	72	70	213	3,950,000
Aki Takamura	73	67	73	213	3,950,000
Junko Yoshida	71	74	70	215	2,500,000
Yuri Kawanami	71	73	71	215	2,500,000
Miyuki Shimabukuro	72	72	71	215	2,500,000
Hee-Won Han	72	74	70	216	1,625,000
Akemi Kuwashima	72	70	74	216	1,625,000
Tomiko Ikebuchi	72	76	69	217	1,063,333
Hisako Ohgane	70	76	71	217	1,063,333
Megumi Matsuo	72	72	73	217	1,063,333
Michiko Okada	74	74	70	218	669,000
Nayoko Yoshikawa	77	71	70	218	669,000
Yu-Chuan Tai	72	75	71	218	669,000
Chikayo Yamazaki	73	74	71	218	669,000
Kyoko Ono	70	76	72	218	669,000
Huang Yu-Chen	73	72	73	218	669,000
Michiko Hattori	74	72	72	218	669,000
Kaori Higo	75	70	73	218	669,000
Ok-Hee Ku	75	69	74	218	669,000
Yueh-Chyn Huang	74	68	76	218	669,000
Toshimi Kimura	77	72	70	219	445,000
Hiromi Takamura	74	74	71	219	445,000
Junko Yasui	77	70	72	219	445,000
Fuki Kido	78	69	72	219	445,000
Jae-Sook Won	74	71	74	219	445,000
Ayako Shibata	72	72	75	219	445,000
Yumi Akagi	72	77	71	220	395,000
Aki Nakano	76	72	72	220	395,000
Midori Yoneyama	74	72	74	220	395,000
Yuko Motoyama	71	73	76	220	395,000

Gunze Cup World Ladies

Yomiuri Golf Club, Tokyo
Par 36-36–72; 6,414 yards

May 6-9
purse, ¥60,000,000

		SCORES			TOTAL	MONEY
Yoko Inoue	73	69	69	71	282	¥10,800,000
Yuri Fudoh	71	68	74	70	283	5,280,000
Yuka Irie	73	75	71	69	288	3,900,000
Megumi Matsuo	71	74	71	72	288	3,900,000
Natsuko Noro	71	72	73	73	289	3,000,000
Michie Ohba	75	71	74	70	290	1,800,000
Kaori Higo	73	73	73	71	290	1,800,000
Se Ri Pak	70	76	72	72	290	1,800,000
Marnie McGuire	73	75	70	72	290	1,800,000
*Shiho Ohyama	74	72	71	73	290	
Midori Yoneyama	69	72	74	75	290	1,800,000
Harumi Sakagami	74	73	71	73	291	1,140,000
Junko Yasui	71	75	76	70	292	1,080,000
Nayoko Yoshikawa	73	74	73	73	293	930,000
Michiko Okada	75	71	72	75	293	930,000
Jae-Sook Won	72	72	74	75	293	930,000
Mayumi Ishii	72	72	73	76	293	930,000
Yuka Shiroto	71	75	76	72	294	720,000
Takayo Bandoh	73	77	70	74	294	720,000
Man-Soo Kim	73	71	74	76	294	720,000
Aki Nakano	75	75	70	75	295	594,000
Michiko Hattori	73	72	74	76	295	594,000
Aki Takamura	75	72	76	73	296	558,000
Fuki Kido	73	74	77	72	296	558,000
Hiromi Takamura	74	73	75	74	296	558,000
Akane Ohshiro	76	72	72	76	296	558,000
Miyuki Shimabukuro	73	73	77	74	297	516,000
Toshimi Kimura	75	73	77	72	297	516,000
Kumiko Hiyoshi	74	73	78	72	297	516,000
Yuko Motoyama	71	76	77	74	298	492,000

Yakult Ladies

Kokusai Country Club, Munakata, Fukuoka
Par 36-36–72; 6,276 yards

May 14-16
purse, ¥60,000,000

		SCORES		TOTAL	MONEY
Fumiko Muraguchi	68	69	68	205	¥10,800,000
Yuri Fudoh	73	65	69	207	4,740,000
Akemi Yamaoka	68	69	70	207	4,740,000
Yuka Irie	71	69	68	208	3,600,000
Yueh-Chyn Huang	72	71	66	209	2,700,000
Aki Takamura	70	68	71	209	2,700,000
Kasumi Adachi	69	73	68	210	1,540,800
Chikayo Yamazaki	73	67	70	210	1,540,800
Huang Yu-Chen	69	70	71	210	1,540,800
Michie Ohba	70	68	72	210	1,540,800
Ok-Hee Ku	68	69	73	210	1,540,800
Mikino Kubo	72	70	69	211	1,044,000
Chieko Nishida	72	72	68	212	804,000
Lee Oh-Soon	67	76	69	212	804,000
Harumi Sakagami	72	70	70	212	804,000

	SCORES			TOTAL	MONEY
Hiroe Tani	70	70	72	212	804,000
Akemi Kuwashima	73	67	72	212	804,000
Masaki Maeda	70	69	73	212	804,000
Junko Yasui	70	68	74	212	804,000
Fuki Kido	73	71	69	213	546,000
Man-Soo Kim	71	72	70	213	546,000
Mitsuko Kawasaki	72	70	71	213	546,000
Yuri Kawanami	73	67	73	213	546,000
Kaori Higo	72	73	69	214	504,000
Mieko Nomura	73	71	70	214	504,000
Hisako Ohgane	72	70	72	214	504,000
Nobuko Kizawa	74	72	69	215	450,000
Yu-Chuan Tai	73	72	70	215	450,000
Aiko Takasu	70	71	74	215	450,000
Hisako Takeda	73	69	73	215	450,000
Shoko Asano	70	70	75	215	450,000
Bie-Shyun Huang	69	71	75	215	450,000

Chukyo TV Bridgestone Ladies

Kasugai Country Club, Kasugai, Aichi
Par 36-36–72; 6,261 yards

May 21-23
purse, ¥50,000,000

	SCORES			TOTAL	MONEY
Fumiko Muraguchi	70	70	67	207	¥9,000,000
Kaori Higo	69	73	68	210	4,400,000
Shin Sora	71	72	68	211	3,500,000
Yuri Fudoh	73	74	65	212	3,000,000
Michiko Hattori	73	73	67	213	2,083,333
Toshimi Kimura	72	71	70	213	2,083,333
Young-Me Lee	68	73	72	213	2,083,333
Ming-Yeh Wu	71	72	71	214	1,375,000
Hee-Won Han	68	72	74	214	1,375,000
Huang Yu-Chen	73	74	68	215	925,000
Mayumi Murai	75	72	68	215	925,000
Yuko Moriguchi	74	71	70	215	925,000
Ok-Hee Ku	76	67	72	215	925,000
Aki Takamura	74	73	69	216	750,000
Mizue Igarashi	76	70	70	216	750,000
Riyuko Ogura	75	70	71	216	750,000
Yuko Motoyama	73	75	69	217	575,000
Hisako Takeda	72	75	70	217	575,000
Chieko Nishida	75	71	71	217	575,000
Kumiko Hiyoshi	74	69	74	217	575,000
Michie Ohba	72	76	70	218	475,000
Maki Hasegawa	75	73	70	218	475,000
Miyuki Shimabukuro	73	72	73	218	475,000
Aki Nakano	73	70	75	218	475,000
Hsiu-Feng Tseng	77	70	72	219	425,000
Junko Yasui	71	75	73	219	425,000
Man-Soo Kim	78	68	73	219	425,000
Ae-Sook Kim	72	74	73	219	425,000
Tatsuko Morimoto	76	68	75	219	425,000
Mineko Nasu	72	70	77	219	425,000

Kosaido Ladies Golf Cup

Chiba Kosaido Country Club, Ichihara, Chiba
Par 36-36–72; 6,246 yards

May 28-30
purse, ¥60,000,000

	SCORES			TOTAL	MONEY
Junko Yasui	73	70	72	215	¥10,800,000
Miyuki Shimabukuro	71	72	72	215	5,280,000
(Yasui defeated Shimabukuro on fourth extra hole.)					
Ok-Hee Ku	73	74	69	216	3,600,000
Kyoko Ono	71	75	70	216	3,600,000
Mayumi Murai	73	70	73	216	3,600,000
Midori Yoneyama	69	73	75	217	2,400,000
Fumiko Muraguchi	72	73	73	218	1,950,000
Toshimi Kimura	73	71	74	218	1,950,000
Yuri Fudoh	75	75	69	219	1,218,000
Aki Takamura	74	74	71	219	1,218,000
Yu-Chuan Tai	74	73	72	219	1,218,000
Ae-Sook Kim	71	72	76	219	1,218,000
Bie-Shyun Huang	72	76	72	220	846,000
Yuka Irie	75	72	73	220	846,000
Akemi Kuwashima	74	72	74	220	846,000
Man-Soo Kim	73	73	74	220	846,000
Shiho Katano	74	71	75	220	846,000
Mineko Nasu	70	71	79	220	846,000
Mikiyo Nishizuka	73	77	71	221	592,000
Kaori Higo	79	70	72	221	592,000
Jae-Sook Won	70	77	74	221	592,000
Kasumi Adachi	74	75	73	222	510,000
Huang Yu-Chen	75	74	73	222	510,000
Yuki Sekine	75	73	74	222	510,000
Aiko Takasu	75	72	75	222	510,000
Fuki Kido	74	73	75	222	510,000
Masaki Maeda	71	75	76	222	510,000
Mika Tajiri	76	71	75	222	510,000
Orie Fujino	73	69	80	222	510,000
Hisako Ohgane	74	76	73	223	414,000
Seiko Watanabe	76	74	73	223	414,000
Michiko Okada	76	74	73	223	414,000
Misayo Fujisawa	75	74	74	223	414,000
Yuri Kawanami	71	76	76	223	414,000
Kotomi Akiyama	73	74	76	223	414,000
Akemi Yamaoka	74	73	76	223	414,000
Kumiko Hiyoshi	75	71	77	223	414,000

Resort Trust Ladies

St. Creek Golf Club, Asuke, Aichi
Par 36-36–72; 6,408 yards

June 4-6
purse, ¥50,000,000

	SCORES			TOTAL	MONEY
Hiromi Takamura	65	71	72	208	¥9,000,000
Young-Me Lee	70	71	71	212	4,400,000
Orie Fujino	73	71	71	215	3,250,000
Hee-Won Han	71	72	72	215	3,250,000
Megumi Matsuo	72	76	68	216	2,500,000
Kaori Higo	72	74	71	217	1,750,000
Yuko Moriguchi	71	73	73	217	1,750,000

	SCORES			TOTAL	MONEY
Kasumi Adachi	69	72	76	217	1,750,000
Tatsuko Morimoto	71	73	74	218	1,010,000
Midori Yoneyama	68	74	76	218	1,010,000
Harumi Sakagami	68	73	77	218	1,010,000
Mikino Kubo	71	70	77	218	1,010,000
Rie Mitsuhashi	73	76	70	219	770,000
Junko Yasui	73	74	72	219	770,000
Chie Yoshida	73	70	76	219	770,000
Yuri Kawanami	76	73	71	220	496,363
Huang Yu-Chen	72	76	72	220	496,363
Yoko Inoue	73	75	72	220	496,363
Aiko Hashimoto	71	76	73	220	496,363
Michiko Okada	69	77	74	220	496,363
Fumiko Muraguchi	75	71	74	220	496,363
Natsuko Noro	68	77	75	220	496,363
Mayumi Murai	70	75	75	220	496,363
Ikuyo Shiotani	72	72	76	220	496,363
Michie Ohba	74	69	77	220	496,363
Kayo Yamada	72	70	78	220	496,363
Aki Takamura	70	79	72	221	390,000
Ae-Sook Kim	74	75	72	221	390,000
Woo-Soon Ko	73	74	74	221	390,000
Fuki Kido	74	73	75	222	365,000
Yuriko Ohtsuka	73	73	76	222	365,000

Suntory Ladies Open

Japan Memorial Golf Club, Yokawa, Hyogo
Par 36-36–72; 6,389 yards

June 11-13
purse, ¥50,000,000

	SCORES			TOTAL	MONEY
Kaori Higo	65	69	72	206	¥9,000,000
Yuka Irie	69	67	70	206	4,400,000
(Higo defeated Irie on fourth extra hole.)					
Ikuyo Shiotani	68	72	67	207	3,000,000
Fuki Kido	68	68	71	207	3,000,000
Shin Sora	67	67	73	207	3,000,000
Hisako Takeda	68	72	71	211	2,000,000
Michie Ohba	68	73	71	212	1,625,000
Hee-Won Han	67	69	76	212	1,625,000
Nahoko Hirao	70	74	69	213	1,125,000
Young-Me Lee	74	70	69	213	1,125,000
Harumi Sakagami	71	70	73	214	895,000
Ok-Hee Ku	71	68	75	214	895,000
Mineko Nasu	71	77	67	215	720,000
Orie Fujino	71	73	71	215	720,000
Mikino Kubo	67	74	74	215	720,000
Natsuko Noro	68	72	75	215	720,000
Man-Soo Kim	70	68	77	215	720,000
Nayoko Yoshikawa	71	73	72	216	505,000
*Miho Koga	75	69	72	216	
Kasumi Adachi	73	71	72	216	505,000
Hisako Ohgane	72	70	74	216	505,000
Kozue Azuma	72	70	74	216	505,000
Mina Nishikawa	73	71	73	217	445,000
Mikiyo Nishizuka	71	72	74	217	445,000
Keiko Arai	76	71	71	218	415,000

	SCORES			TOTAL	MONEY
Yuko Motoyama	71	75	72	218	415,000
Toshimi Kimura	70	73	75	218	415,000
Chieko Nishida	75	68	75	218	415,000
Jae-Sook Won	76	72	71	219	385,000
Kumiko Hiyoshi	71	74	74	219	385,000

Apita Circle K Sankus Ladies

New Green Golf Club, Nakatsugawa, Gifu
Par 36-36–72; 6,334 yards

June 18-20
purse, ¥50,000,000

	SCORES			TOTAL	MONEY
Kaori Higo	68	73	71	212	¥9,000,000
Huang Yu-Chen	74	72	68	214	3,633,333
Mei-Chi Cheng	71	72	71	214	3,633,333
Ok-Hee Ku	73	69	72	214	3,633,333
Kumiko Hiyoshi	71	74	71	216	1,937,500
Ayako Okamoto	70	74	72	216	1,937,500
Kasumi Adachi	72	72	72	216	1,937,500
Hisako Takeda	71	72	73	216	1,937,500
Aki Nakano	74	71	72	217	1,017,500
Yuko Moriguchi	72	72	73	217	1,017,500
Mieko Nishida	73	71	73	217	1,017,500
Fuki Kido	71	69	77	217	1,017,500
Chihiro Furukawa	72	72	74	218	785,000
Yukiko Ishiguro	73	71	74	218	785,000
Yuko Motoyama	71	70	77	218	785,000
Miyuki Shimabukuro	71	76	72	219	585,000
Hee-Won Han	72	74	73	219	585,000
Rie Mitsuhashi	73	73	73	219	585,000
Toshimi Kimura	73	71	75	219	585,000
Young-Me Lee	72	71	76	219	585,000
Mayumi Murai	70	77	73	220	455,000
Masaki Maeda	75	72	73	220	455,000
Maki Sasayama	74	72	74	220	455,000
Akemi Yamaoka	70	75	75	220	455,000
Ae-Sook Kim	71	73	76	220	455,000
Akemi Kuwashima	74	72	75	221	405,000
Natsuko Noro	73	76	72	221	405,000
Mayumi Inoue	70	75	76	221	405,000
Keiko Arai	75	74	72	221	405,000
Michie Ohba	72	77	72	221	405,000

Japan Women's Open

Kasumigaseki Country Club, Kawagoe, Saitama
Par 36-36–72; 6,347 yards

June 24-27
purse, ¥70,000,000

	SCORES				TOTAL	MONEY
Mayumi Murai	66	71	72	72	281	¥14,000,000
Huang Yu-Chen	72	73	69	68	282	7,700,000
Hee-Won Han	72	72	72	71	287	5,425,000
Aki Takamura	75	70	70	73	288	3,255,000
Kaori Higo	72	74	69	73	288	3,255,000
Mikino Kubo	71	72	72	75	290	2,227,000

	SCORES				TOTAL	MONEY
Harumi Sakagami	73	71	71	75	290	2,227,000
Ae-Sook Kim	72	79	69	71	291	1,640,666
Hiromi Takamura	71	72	76	72	291	1,640,666
Michie Ohba	72	73	72	74	291	1,640,666
Shin Sora	72	77	72	71	292	1,150,666
Chieko Nishida	71	73	72	76	292	1,150,666
Ok-Hee Ku	73	74	68	77	292	1,150,666
Fumiko Muraguchi	73	76	73	71	293	892,333
Fuki Kido	73	73	74	73	293	892,333
Akemi Yamaoka	72	74	71	76	293	892,333
Kyoko Ono	72	75	76	71	294	692,000
Yukiko Ishiguro	75	75	73	71	294	692,000
Natsuko Noro	70	74	76	74	294	692,000
Chikako Matsuzawa	73	75	72	74	294	692,000
Yuri Kawanami	70	77	70	77	294	692,000
Midori Yoneyama	72	72	69	81	294	692,000
Hsiu-Feng Tseng	74	73	73	75	295	600,000
Yuri Fudoh	73	74	71	77	295	600,000
Yuko Motoyama	74	71	77	74	296	561,500
Chihiro Furukawa	74	76	71	75	296	561,500
Michiko Okada	72	73	74	77	296	561,500
Kasumi Adachi	72	74	73	77	296	561,500
*Yun-Jye Wei	77	73	76	71	297	
Michiko Hattori	73	74	76	75	298	519,000
Mitsuko Kawasaki	77	72	73	76	298	519,000
Kiyo Yamamura	77	74	71	76	298	519,000

Toyo Suisan Ladies Hokkaido

Kosaido Sapporo Country Club, Kita-hiroshima, Hokkaido   July 9-11
Par 36-36–72; 6,424 yards   purse, ¥50,000,000

	SCORES			TOTAL	MONEY
Toshimi Kimura	71	70	69	210	¥9,000,000
Huang Yu-Chen	70	68	73	211	4,400,000
Midori Yoneyama	72	73	67	212	3,250,000
Yuko Moriguchi	72	70	70	212	3,250,000
Aki Nakano	71	74	69	214	2,250,000
Mieko Nomura	75	67	72	214	2,250,000
Bie-Shyun Huang	75	71	69	215	1,285,000
Junko Yasui	74	71	70	215	1,285,000
Fumiko Muraguchi	72	72	71	215	1,285,000
Woo-Soon Ko	72	72	71	215	1,285,000
Jae-Sook Won	71	71	73	215	1,285,000
Harumi Sakagami	74	72	70	216	800,000
Ok-Hee Ku	72	72	72	216	800,000
Kasumi Adachi	74	69	73	216	800,000
Hsiu-Feng Tseng	70	73	73	216	800,000
Aki Takamura	76	71	70	217	625,000
Kumiko Hiyoshi	73	73	71	217	625,000
Mikino Kubo	74	72	71	217	625,000
Yuri Kawanami	74	73	71	218	466,666
Aiko Hashimoto	73	72	73	218	466,666
Ayumi Sobue	73	72	73	218	466,666
Rie Fujiwara	73	71	74	218	466,666
Ai-Yu Tu	73	70	75	218	466,666
Yukiko Ishiguro	74	67	77	218	466,666

	SCORES			TOTAL	MONEY
Mineko Nasu	77	72	70	219	390,000
Yuka Irie	74	75	70	219	390,000
Yoko Inoue	77	71	71	219	390,000
Kaori Harada	77	71	71	219	390,000
Ayako Shibata	76	71	72	219	390,000
Hisako Ohgane	78	68	73	219	390,000
Mayumi Murai	75	71	73	219	390,000
Rie Mitsuhashi	74	71	74	219	390,000

Sumitomo Visa Taiheiyo Club Ladies

La Vista Golf Resort, Chonan, Chiba   July 23-25
Par 36-36–72; 6,390 yards   purse, ¥60,000,000

	SCORES			TOTAL	MONEY
Junko Yasui	70	72	68	210	¥10,800,000
Aki Takamura	67	74	71	212	5,280,000
Michiko Hattori	71	74	68	213	3,600,000
Michie Ohba	69	74	70	213	3,600,000
Fumiko Muraguchi	71	71	71	213	3,600,000
Midori Yoneyama	74	69	71	214	2,250,000
Hisako Takeda	68	74	72	214	2,250,000
Ai-Yu Tu	72	74	69	215	1,278,000
Huang Yu-Chen	71	74	70	215	1,278,000
Man-Soo Kim	73	72	70	215	1,278,000
Ok-Hee Ku	72	71	72	215	1,278,000
Carin Koch	70	73	72	215	1,278,000
Annika Sorenstam	71	70	74	215	1,278,000
Kasumi Fujii	75	72	69	216	876,000
Yuri Fudoh	75	70	71	216	876,000
Chieko Nishida	68	73	75	216	876,000
Misayo Fujisawa	72	75	70	217	696,000
Chihiro Furukawa	74	72	71	217	696,000
Ayako Shibata	68	73	76	217	696,000
Shoko Asano	72	75	71	218	540,000
Toshimi Kimura	75	72	71	218	540,000
Young-Me Lee	74	73	71	218	540,000
Kaori Higo	73	73	72	218	540,000
Mieko Nomura	69	76	73	218	540,000
Hsiu-Feng Tseng	71	74	73	218	540,000
Vicki Goetze-Ackerman	69	73	76	218	540,000
Orie Fujino	70	77	72	219	456,000
Woo-Soon Ko	74	72	73	219	456,000
Kayoko Ikoma	74	72	73	219	456,000
Yukiko Ishiguro	72	73	74	219	456,000
Rie Murata	69	75	75	219	456,000
Shin Sora	69	75	75	219	456,000
Keiko Arakaki	70	74	75	219	456,000

Golf 5 Ladies

Mizunami Country Club, Gifu
Par 36-36–72; 6,449 yards

July 30-August 1
purse, ¥50,000,000

	SCORES			TOTAL	MONEY
Aki Nakano	72	69	72	213	¥9,000,000
Kasumi Fujii	72	72	71	215	4,400,000
Michiko Hattori	70	73	73	216	3,250,000
Ok-Hee Ku	74	69	73	216	3,250,000
Yuka Irie	71	75	71	217	2,083,333
Masaki Maeda	73	70	74	217	2,083,333
Aiko Hashimoto	72	71	74	217	2,083,333
Huang Yu-Chen	76	71	71	218	1,021,428
Akane Ohshiro	71	75	72	218	1,021,428
Yuri Fudoh	76	71	71	218	1,021,428
Kaori Higo	72	74	72	218	1,021,428
Kumiko Hiyoshi	70	72	76	218	1,021,428
Mikiyo Nishizuka	73	69	76	218	1,021,428
Yuko Moriguchi	71	71	76	218	1,021,428
Hee-Won Han	75	73	71	219	700,000
Toshimi Kimura	73	71	75	219	700,000
Chieko Nishida	73	73	74	220	575,000
Young-Me Lee	75	71	74	220	575,000
Mayumi Murai	75	69	76	220	575,000
Ikuyo Shiotani	75	75	71	221	470,000
Miyuki Shimabukuro	71	75	75	221	470,000
Hiromi Takamura	78	69	75	222	450,000
Yuriko Ohtsuka	76	74	72	222	450,000
Chieko Amanuma	71	76	76	223	395,000
Junko Yasui	75	73	75	223	395,000
Kyoko Ono	73	74	76	223	395,000
Nayoko Yoshikawa	75	72	76	223	395,000
Jae-Sook Won	72	77	74	223	395,000
Akemi Yamaoka	73	73	77	223	395,000
Chikayo Yamazaki	74	76	73	223	395,000
Hsiu-Feng Tseng	73	77	73	223	395,000
Hisako Ohgane	74	71	78	223	395,000

NEC Karuizawa 72

Karuizawa 72 Golf Club, Nagano
Par 36-36–72; 6,465 yards
(Second round cancelled — rain.)

August 13-15
purse, ¥45,000,000

	SCORES		TOTAL	MONEY
Hee-Won Han	68	67	135	¥8,100,000
Keiko Arai	66	71	137	3,960,000
Ikuyo Shiotani	70	68	138	2,700,000
Yuri Fudoh	69	69	138	2,700,000
Harumi Sakagami	68	70	138	2,700,000
Chieko Amanuma	71	68	139	1,800,000
Wen-Lin Li	71	69	140	1,350,000
Megumi Matsuo	69	71	140	1,350,000
Ok-Hee Ku	68	72	140	1,350,000
Akiko Fukushima	72	69	141	815,625
Kozue Azuma	72	69	141	815,625
Kaori Harada	69	72	141	815,625

	SCORES			TOTAL	MONEY
Man-Soo Kim	69	72		141	815,625
Hisako Takeda	72	70		142	652,500
Aki Nakano	74	68		142	652,500
Rie Murata	68	74		142	652,500
Tomiko Ikebuchi	72	71		143	417,115
Kasumi Fujii	72	71		143	417,115
Michiko Hattori	72	71		143	417,115
Jeanne Kei	72	71		143	417,115
Mitsuko Kawasaki	71	72		143	417,115
Ayako Okamoto	73	70		143	417,115
Junko Ishii	71	72		143	417,115
Yuri Kawanami	71	72		143	417,115
Young-Me Lee	71	72		143	417,115
Shoko Asano	73	70		143	417,115
Mineko Nasu	70	73		143	417,115
Fumiko Muraguchi	70	73		143	417,115
Mayumi Ishii	70	73		143	417,115
Fumiko Omata	71	73		144	301,500
Mayumi Yamada	71	73		144	301,500
Michie Ohba	73	71		144	301,500
Kyoko Ono	71	73		144	301,500
Chae-Eun Song	73	71		144	301,500
Junko Yasui	70	74		144	301,500
Misayo Fujisawa	70	74		144	301,500
Natsuko Noro	70	74		144	301,500
Shin Sora	69	75		144	301,500

Shin Caterpillar Mitsubishi Ladies

Daihakone Country Club, Hakone, Kanagawa
Par 36-37–73; 6,668 yards

August 20-22
purse, ¥60,000,000

	SCORES			TOTAL	MONEY
Fumiko Muraguchi	74	72	70	216	¥10,800,000
Keiko Arai	73	70	74	217	5,280,000
Hee-Won Han	74	74	71	219	2,850,000
Aki Takamura	76	72	71	219	2,850,000
Toshimi Kimura	74	73	72	219	2,850,000
Yuri Fudoh	72	73	74	219	2,850,000
Michiko Hattori	71	74	74	219	2,850,000
Ikuyo Shiotani	73	71	75	219	2,850,000
Aki Nakano	73	78	69	220	1,350,000
Ok-Hee Ku	71	77	72	220	1,350,000
Akane Ohshiro	73	73	75	221	1,104,000
Ae-Sook Kim	70	78	74	222	924,000
Kasumi Fujii	73	75	74	222	924,000
Mineko Nasu	72	76	74	222	924,000
Ai-Yu Tu	74	73	75	222	924,000
Junko Omote	75	71	76	222	924,000
Man-Soo Kim	72	78	73	223	618,000
Junko Yasui	77	73	73	223	618,000
Yu-Chuan Tai	75	75	73	223	618,000
Hiroe Tani	73	76	74	223	618,000
Woo-Soon Ko	73	74	76	223	618,000
Rie Mitsuhashi	71	76	76	223	618,000
Yumi Akagi	72	76	76	224	510,000
Kumiko Hiyoshi	75	72	77	224	510,000

	SCORES			TOTAL	MONEY
Megumi Yamanaka	74	72	78	224	510,000
Yuka Irie	72	71	81	224	510,000
Yoko Inoue	77	75	73	225	468,000
Mayumi Murai	77	73	75	225	468,000
Lee Oh-Soon	72	76	77	225	468,000
Miyuki Shimabukuro	73	79	74	226	396,000
Michie Ohba	72	80	74	226	396,000
Nahoko Hirao	77	75	74	226	396,000
Mitsuko Kawasaki	74	78	74	226	396,000
Kozue Azuma	75	77	74	226	396,000
Shoko Asano	74	77	75	226	396,000
Mieko Nomura	73	77	76	226	396,000
Kyoko Ono	76	74	76	226	396,000
Yoko Tsuchiya	73	74	79	226	396,000

Yonex Ladies

Yonex Country Club, Teradomari, Niigata
Par 36-36–72; 6,375 yards

August 27-29
purse, ¥50,000,000

	SCORES			TOTAL	MONEY
Natsuko Noro	73	72	65	210	¥9,000,000
Michiko Hattori	74	70	67	211	4,400,000
Yoko Inoue	71	70	72	213	3,500,000
Fumiko Muraguchi	70	74	70	214	3,000,000
Man-Soo Kim	72	75	68	215	2,250,000
Chae-Eun Song	73	71	71	215	2,250,000
Aiko Takasu	70	74	72	216	1,750,000
Rie Mitsuhashi	74	73	70	217	1,250,000
Mineko Nasu	71	75	71	217	1,250,000
Aki Takamura	74	71	72	217	1,250,000
Takayo Bandoh	74	73	71	218	920,000
Kozue Azuma	75	72	71	218	920,000
Kumiko Hiyoshi	78	70	71	219	770,000
Aki Nakano	78	70	71	219	770,000
Yuka Shiroto	73	72	74	219	770,000
Ikuyo Shiotani	73	71	75	219	770,000
Mayumi Ishii	77	74	69	220	620,000
Mayumi Murai	74	70	76	220	620,000
Ayako Okamoto	74	76	71	221	469,444
Fuki Kido	78	71	72	221	469,444
Nahoko Hirao	74	76	71	221	469,444
Toshimi Kimura	73	77	71	221	469,444
Midori Yoneyama	75	73	73	221	469,444
Yueh-Chyn Huang	74	74	73	221	469,444
Ai-Yu Tu	77	74	70	221	469,444
Kaori Harada	79	72	70	221	469,444
Junko Yasui	73	73	75	221	469,444
Junko Ishii	76	74	72	222	385,000
Hisako Ohgane	75	75	72	222	385,000
Kaori Higo	74	75	73	222	385,000
Miyuki Shimabukuro	74	74	74	222	385,000
Hisako Takeda	75	73	74	222	385,000
Akane Ohshiro	79	72	71	222	385,000
Kaori Suzuki	70	75	77	222	385,000

Fujisankei Ladies Classic

Fujizakura Country Club, Kawaguchiko, Yamanashi
Par 35-36–71; 6,304 yards

September 3-5
purse, ¥60,000,000

	SCORES			TOTAL	MONEY
Midori Yoneyama	69	70	68	207	¥10,800,000
Takayo Bandoh	70	71	69	210	4,740,000
Aki Takamura	74	68	68	210	4,740,000
Ayako Okamoto	71	74	66	211	3,600,000
Orie Fujino	72	71	69	212	2,500,000
Chieko Nishida	71	71	70	212	2,500,000
Michie Ohba	71	70	71	212	2,500,000
Nobuko Kizawa	70	71	72	213	1,800,000
Aki Nakano	70	74	70	214	1,274,000
Mineko Nasu	74	70	70	214	1,274,000
Yuri Fudoh	73	70	71	214	1,274,000
Hee-Won Han	75	70	70	215	1,002,000
Fumiko Muraguchi	68	75	72	215	1,002,000
Ok-Hee Ku	70	72	73	215	1,002,000
Chihiro Furukawa	74	73	69	216	882,000
Man-Soo Kim	71	74	72	217	680,000
Mayumi Murai	74	71	72	217	680,000
Kaori Higo	73	72	72	217	680,000
Rie Mitsuhashi	69	75	73	217	680,000
Hsiu-Feng Tseng	73	71	73	217	680,000
Nayoko Yoshikawa	74	70	73	217	680,000
Ae-Sook Kim	73	76	69	218	540,000
Fumiko Omata	72	74	72	218	540,000
Michiko Okada	74	72	72	218	540,000
Kyoko Ono	75	70	73	218	540,000
Nahoko Hirao	75	74	70	219	480,000
Kumiko Hiyoshi	75	73	71	219	480,000
Kotomi Akiyama	72	75	72	219	480,000
Chae-Eun Song	75	72	72	219	480,000
*Mayumi Nakajima	73	73	73	219	
Akane Ohshiro	71	75	73	219	480,000
Atsuko Ueno	70	74	75	219	480,000

Japan LPGA Championship Konika Cup

Biwako Country Club, Ritto, Shiga
Par 36-36–72; 6,500 yards

September 9-12
purse, ¥70,000,000

	SCORES				TOTAL	MONEY
Fuki Kido	71	69	71	70	281	¥12,600,000
Midori Yoneyama	71	74	72	70	287	6,160,000
Yukiyo Haga	74	72	71	72	289	4,900,000
Yuko Moriguchi	75	71	73	71	290	4,200,000
Aki Nakano	69	73	74	75	291	2,916,666
Mayumi Hirase	76	73	69	73	291	2,916,666
Yuri Kawanami	72	71	76	72	291	2,916,666
Ayako Okamoto	72	73	73	74	292	1,750,000
Yuri Fudoh	72	76	70	74	292	1,750,000
Hee-Won Han	71	74	75	72	292	1,750,000
Toshimi Kimura	73	74	75	71	293	1,169,000
Fumiko Muraguchi	72	76	73	72	293	1,169,000
Yueh-Chyn Huang	73	76	72	73	294	959,000

	SCORES				TOTAL	MONEY
Chihiro Furukawa	73	72	75	74	294	959,000
Michie Ohba	70	76	73	75	294	959,000
Takayo Bandoh	76	72	73	73	294	959,000
Lee Oh-Soon	77	74	72	72	295	749,000
Mitsuko Kawasaki	75	71	72	77	295	749,000
Miyuki Shimabukuro	74	75	75	72	296	644,000
Ok-Hee Ku	75	73	74	75	297	567,000
Man-Soon Kim	78	70	72	77	297	567,000
Hiromi Takamura	73	79	72	74	298	476,000
Ai-Yu Tu	78	73	70	77	298	476,000
Ikuyo Shiotani	70	75	78	75	298	476,000
Hiromi Kobayashi	76	74	73	75	298	476,000
Bie-Shyun Huang	73	78	72	75	298	476,000
Mei-Chi Cheng	72	71	81	74	298	476,000
Michiko Hattori	76	76	71	75	298	476,000
Aki Takamura	76	76	72	74	298	476,000
Shoko Asano	75	73	73	77	298	476,000
Tomoko Ueda	75	77	75	71	298	476,000
Kyoko Ono	75	74	75	74	298	476,000

Yukijirushi Ladies Tokai Classic

Ryosen Golf Club, Inabe, Mie
Par 36-36–72; 6,388 yards

September 17-19
purse, ¥60,000,000

	SCORES			TOTAL	MONEY
Young-Me Lee	70	68	67	205	¥10,800,000
Yuri Fudoh	70	67	71	208	4,740,000
Hsiu-Feng Tseng	67	70	71	208	4,740,000
Michie Ohba	69	70	70	209	3,300,000
Harumi Sakagami	67	67	75	209	3,300,000
Fuki Kido	67	71	72	210	2,400,000
Huang Yu-Chen	73	69	69	211	1,650,000
Junko Yasui	69	71	71	211	1,650,000
Kaori Higo	70	70	71	211	1,650,000
Kyoko Ono	72	68	71	211	1,650,000
Fumiko Muraguchi	69	73	70	212	948,000
Ok-Hee Ku	74	68	70	212	948,000
Yueh-Chyn Huang	74	67	71	212	948,000
Mikiyo Nishizuka	70	70	72	212	948,000
Chieko Nishida	71	69	72	212	948,000
Kotomi Akiyama	72	68	72	212	948,000
Midori Yoneyama	70	69	73	212	948,000
Jae-Sook Won	69	72	72	213	616,800
Yuko Moriguchi	71	69	73	213	616,800
Masaki Maeda	67	72	74	213	616,800
Michiko Hattori	67	72	74	213	616,800
Tatsuko Morimoto	69	69	75	213	616,800
Aki Nakano	69	72	73	214	528,000
Yoko Yamagishi	70	71	73	214	528,000
Miyuki Shimabukuro	70	71	73	214	528,000
Yuri Kawanami	70	70	74	214	528,000
Yoko Inoue	70	70	74	214	528,000
Kayo Yamada	70	75	70	215	474,000
Hisako Takeda	71	74	70	215	474,000
Hee-Won Han	71	73	71	215	474,000
Ikuyo Shiotani	69	73	73	215	474,000

Miyagi TV Cup Dunlop Ladies Open

Rainbow Hills Golf Club, Tomiya, Miyagi
Par 36-36–72; 6,476 yards

September 24-26
purse, ¥60,000,000

	SCORES			TOTAL	MONEY
Ok-Hee Ku	71	69	72	212	¥10,800,000
Harumi Sakagami	70	71	73	214	5,280,000
Yuri Fudoh	71	72	72	215	4,200,000
Hsiu-Feng Tseng	72	72	72	216	3,300,000
Kayo Yamada	69	70	77	216	3,300,000
Miyuki Shimabukuro	71	74	72	217	2,100,000
Midori Yoneyama	72	71	74	217	2,100,000
Aki Nakano	71	67	79	217	2,100,000
Kyoko Ono	71	75	72	218	1,264,000
Fumiko Muraguchi	73	70	75	218	1,264,000
Hee-Won Han	72	69	77	218	1,264,000
Mitsuko Kawasaki	76	72	71	219	912,000
Michiko Hattori	69	76	74	219	912,000
Yuko Moriguchi	73	71	75	219	912,000
Toshimi Kimura	70	72	77	219	912,000
Kaori Higo	72	70	77	219	912,000
Yu-Chuan Tai	73	72	75	220	672,000
Yuri Kawanami	73	72	75	220	672,000
Huang Yu-Chen	70	72	78	220	672,000
Rie Fujiwara	73	76	72	221	516,000
Fuki Kido	78	70	73	221	516,000
Aki Takamura	78	70	73	221	516,000
Woo-Soon Ko	75	73	73	221	516,000
Akemi Yamaoka	73	74	74	221	516,000
Hisako Takeda	72	74	75	221	516,000
Man-Soo Kim	72	72	77	221	516,000
Ming-Yeh Wu	76	71	75	222	432,000
Ayako Okamoto	75	71	76	222	432,000
Mikino Kubo	71	74	77	222	432,000
Junko Yasui	71	73	78	222	432,000
Kumiko Hiyoshi	76	69	77	222	432,000
Yoko Yamagishi	76	69	77	222	432,000
Chikayo Yamazaki	68	75	79	222	432,000

Osaka Ladies Open

Hanna Country Club, Daito, Osaka
Par 36-36–72; 6,345 yards

October 1-3
purse, ¥60,000,000

	SCORES			TOTAL	MONEY
Hee-Won Han	70	68	73	211	¥10,800,000
Woo-Soon Ko	71	75	66	212	5,280,000
Jae-Sook Won	70	76	69	215	3,060,000
Chae-Eun Song	71	75	69	215	3,060,000
Akane Ohshiro	76	70	69	215	3,060,000
Hsiu-Feng Tseng	73	70	72	215	3,060,000
Young-Me Lee	73	68	74	215	3,060,000
Man-Soo Kim	69	73	74	216	1,800,000
Yuka Irie	74	73	70	217	1,215,000
Huang Yu-Chen	73	71	73	217	1,215,000
Aki Nakano	70	72	75	217	1,215,000
Ae-Sook Kim	68	72	77	217	1,215,000

	SCORES			TOTAL	MONEY
Aki Takamura	71	75	72	218	960,000
Shiho Katano	71	69	78	218	960,000
Mikino Kubo	73	72	74	219	780,000
Midori Yoneyama	74	69	76	219	780,000
Kuniko Sameshima	70	73	76	219	780,000
Chihiro Furukawa	71	71	77	219	780,000
Mika Tajiri	73	77	70	220	567,600
Tatsuko Morimoto	72	76	72	220	567,600
Mizue Igarashi	75	74	71	220	567,600
Mikako Kanamori	71	74	75	220	567,600
Michiko Okada	69	73	78	220	567,600
Kozue Azuma	74	75	72	221	486,000
Yumi Akagi	69	78	74	221	486,000
Aiko Hashimoto	71	75	75	221	486,000
Yuka Shiroto	75	71	75	221	486,000
Junko Yasui	76	69	76	221	486,000
Hisako Takeda	73	72	76	221	486,000
Yuri Kawanami	74	71	76	221	486,000

TaKaRa World Invitational

Caledonian Golf Club, Yokoshiba, Chiba
Par 36-36–72; 6,226 yards

October 7-10
purse, ¥80,000,000

	SCORES				TOTAL	MONEY
Laura Davies	68	69	76	72	285	¥14,400,000
Janice Moodie	72	71	73	73	289	7,040,000
Aki Takamura	73	70	74	73	290	4,800,000
Man-Soo Kim	72	70	74	74	290	4,800,000
Fuki Kido	68	74	74	74	290	4,800,000
Toshimi Kimura	73	73	72	73	291	3,200,000
Bie-Shyun Huang	72	72	74	74	292	2,400,000
Liselotte Neumann	70	72	75	75	292	2,400,000
Midori Yoneyama	71	68	77	76	292	2,400,000
Yuri Fudoh	71	77	74	71	293	1,509,333
Hee-Won Han	73	72	75	73	293	1,509,333
Nobuko Kizawa	70	74	73	76	293	1,509,333
Harumi Sakagami	73	74	76	71	294	1,224,000
Huang Yu-Chen	71	70	78	75	294	1,224,000
Kaori Higo	74	72	73	74	294	1,224,000
Mitsuko Kawasaki	73	72	71	78	294	1,224,000
Kyoko Ono	75	72	75	73	295	904,000
Mei-Chi Cheng	71	72	75	77	295	904,000
Akane Ohshiro	68	76	74	77	295	904,000
Aki Nakano	72	74	72	77	295	904,000
Chieko Nishida	75	71	74	76	296	752,000
Hisako Ohgane	72	77	71	76	296	752,000
Woo-Soon Ko	71	70	76	79	296	752,000
Michiko Hattori	77	71	76	73	297	688,000
Riyo Fukuroi	75	74	74	74	297	688,000
Yueh-Chyn Huang	69	71	81	76	297	688,000
Hsiu-Feng Tseng	71	74	74	78	297	688,000
Akemi Yamaoka	73	74	72	78	297	688,000
Keiko Arai	75	72	79	72	298	624,000
Fumiko Muraguchi	76	73	76	73	298	624,000
Mika Adaniya	73	72	78	75	298	624,000

Fujitsu Ladies

Tokyu Seven Hundred Club, Chiba
Par 36-36–72; 6,490 yards

October 15-17
purse, ¥60,000,000

	SCORES			TOTAL	MONEY
Michiko Hattori	68	67	69	204	¥10,800,000
Ok-Hee Ku	70	71	70	211	4,740,000
Chieko Nishida	68	72	71	211	4,740,000
Harumi Sakagami	73	70	70	213	3,600,000
Fuki Kido	71	76	67	214	2,160,000
Junko Yasui	73	74	67	214	2,160,000
Michie Ohba	72	71	71	214	2,160,000
Toshimi Kimura	72	70	72	214	2,160,000
Yuri Fudoh	72	70	72	214	2,160,000
Akane Ohshiro	69	76	70	215	1,050,000
Fumiko Muraguchi	73	72	70	215	1,050,000
Yuri Kawanami	72	72	71	215	1,050,000
Aki Nakano	70	72	73	215	1,050,000
Kumiko Hiyoshi	72	69	74	215	1,050,000
Kayo Yamada	71	70	74	215	1,050,000
Yueh-Chyn Huang	74	69	73	216	810,000
Mineko Nasu	75	68	73	216	810,000
Yuka Shirato	71	76	70	217	608,571
Shin Sora	78	69	70	217	608,571
Keiko Arai	72	73	72	217	608,571
Nayoko Yoshikawa	72	72	73	217	608,571
Huang Yu-Chen	73	71	73	217	608,571
Kozue Azuma	75	69	73	217	608,571
Kaori Higo	72	70	75	217	608,571
Mei-Chi Cheng	77	68	73	218	516,000
Mika Ishijima	73	72	73	218	516,000
Lee Oh-Soon	72	72	74	218	516,000
Yoko Inoue	71	71	76	218	516,000
Yukiko Ishiguro	73	68	77	218	516,000
Shoko Asano	74	72	73	219	456,000
Takayo Bandoh	72	73	74	219	456,000
Hsiu-Feng Tseng	73	72	74	219	456,000
Junko Omote	74	71	74	219	456,000
Man-Soo Kim	74	71	74	219	456,000

Hisako Higuchi Kibun Classic

Kinojo Golf Club, Soja, Okayama
Par 36-36–72; 6,380 yards

October 22-24
purse, ¥70,000,000

	SCORES			TOTAL	MONEY
Kumiko Hiyoshi	68	70	73	211	¥12,600,000
Michiko Hattori	68	72	72	212	6,160,000
Miyuki Shimabukuro	72	72	69	213	4,900,000
Man-Soo Kim	77	70	67	214	4,200,000
Mikiko Tani	74	71	70	215	2,916,666
Ikuyo Shiotani	72	72	71	215	2,916,666
Fuki Kido	67	73	75	215	2,916,666
Aiko Hashimoto	71	74	71	216	1,750,000
Orie Fujino	71	74	71	216	1,750,000
Ae-Sook Kim	70	70	76	216	1,750,000
Kasumi Fujii	74	74	69	217	1,190,000

	SCORES			TOTAL	MONEY
Midori Yoneyama	73	73	71	217	1,190,000
Yoko Inoue	69	75	73	217	1,190,000
Ok-Hee Ku	71	73	73	217	1,190,000
Norimi Terasawa	70	73	74	217	1,190,000
Kaori Harada	71	76	71	218	875,000
Michie Ohba	75	72	71	218	875,000
Keiko Arakaki	72	73	73	218	875,000
Nobuko Kizawa	72	73	73	218	875,000
Aki Takamura	72	77	70	219	672,000
Fumiko Muraguchi	72	76	71	219	672,000
Takayo Bandoh	73	74	72	219	672,000
Mineko Nasu	75	71	73	219	672,000
Chikayo Yamazaki	71	71	77	219	672,000
Yuko Moriguchi	73	74	73	220	623,000
Rie Murata	70	74	76	220	623,000
Chie Yoshida	71	78	72	221	574,000
Masaki Maeda	73	76	72	221	574,000
Toshimi Kimura	73	75	73	221	574,000
*Miho Koga	75	73	73	221	
Young-Me Lee	74	73	74	221	574,000
Keiko Arai	75	71	75	221	574,000

Nichirei International

Sose Country Club, Chiba
Par 36-36–72; 6,404 yards

October 29-31
purse, US$702,000

FIRST DAY
Better Ball

Laura Davies and Mardi Lunn (USA) tied with Aki Nakano and Kaori Higo, 67-67.
Tina Barrett and Cindy McCurdy (USA) defeated Fuki Kido and Junko Yasui, 66-70.
Lorie Kane and Janice Moodie (USA) tied with Hee-Won Han and Midori Yoneyama, 68-68.
Nancy Scranton and Rachel Hetherington (USA) defeated Ok-Hee Ku and Yuri Fudoh, 67-68.
Rosie Jones and Sherri Steinhauer (USA) defeated Fumiko Muraguchi and Hiromi Kobayashi, 67-69.
Akiko Fukushima and Aki Takamura (Japan) defeated Liselotte Neumann and Mi Hyun Kim, 64-67.

POINTS: United States 4, Japan 2

SECOND DAY
Better Ball

Kane and Moodie (USA) defeated Nakano and Higo, 63-65.
Barrett and McCurdy (USA) defeated Kido and Yasui, 67-68.
Neumann and Kim (USA) defeated Han and Yoneyama, 66-72.
Scranton and Hetherington (USA) defeated Ku and Fudoh, 66-67.
Muraguchi and Kobayashi (Japan) defeated Jones and Steinhauer, 68-71.
Davies and Lunn (USA) defeated Fukushima and Takamura, 63-70.

POINTS: United States 5, Japan 1

THIRD DAY
Singles

Davies (USA) tied with Higo, 71-71.
Nakano (Japan) defeated Lunn, 74-79.
Neumann (USA) defeated Muraguchi, 69-72.
Barrett (USA) defeated Yasui, 70-74.
Kido (Japan) defeated Kane, 69-75.
Jones (USA) defeated Fudoh, 72-73.
Steinhauer (USA) defeated Han, 73-74.
Takamura (Japan) defeated Moodie, 73-76.
Yoneyama (Japan) defeated Scranton, 74-77.
Kim (USA) defeated Ku, 69-74.
Hetherington (USA) defeated Fukushima, 74-75.
Kobayashi (Japan) defeated McCurdy, 68-76.

POINTS: United States 6½, Japan 5½

TOTAL POINTS: United States 15½, Japan 8½

(Each member of USA team received $37,500; each member of Japanese team received $21,000.)

Mizuno Classic

Seta Golf Course, Otsu, Shiga
Par 36-36–72; 6,423 yards

November 5-7
purse, ¥84,960,000

	SCORES			TOTAL	MONEY
Maria Hjorth	70	64	67	201	¥12,744,000
Laura Davies	70	70	66	206	5,450,821
Ok-Hee Ku	69	70	67	206	5,450,821
Fumiko Muraguchi	70	66	70	206	5,450,821
Aki Nakano	70	66	70	206	5,450,821
Carin Koch	68	71	68	207	2,579,279
Helen Dobson	72	66	69	207	2,579,279
Jenny Lidback	71	67	69	207	2,579,279
Sherri Turner	69	72	67	208	1,732,865
Woo-Soon Ko	67	71	70	208	1,732,865
Sherri Steinhauer	71	66	71	208	1,732,865
Rachel Hetherington	67	70	71	208	1,732,865
Charlotta Sorenstam	69	70	70	209	1,370,829
Lorie Kane	71	67	71	209	1,370,829
Catriona Matthew	70	71	69	210	1,100,125
Tina Barrett	70	71	69	210	1,100,125
Midori Yoneyama	70	73	67	210	1,100,125
Denise Killeen	69	71	70	210	1,100,125
Rosie Jones	69	71	70	210	1,100,125
Hisako Takeda	72	68	70	210	1,100,125
Jill McGill	70	72	69	211	840,042
Kim Saiki	72	70	69	211	840,042
Akiko Fukushima	72	71	68	211	840,042
Toshimi Kimura	69	71	71	211	840,042
Jan Stephenson	70	69	72	211	840,042
Hiromi Kobayashi	72	67	72	211	840,042
Michele Redman	71	68	72	211	840,042
Yuri Fudoh	71	72	69	212	645,165
Mayumi Hirase	68	72	72	212	645,165
Cindy Flom	74	67	71	212	645,165

	SCORES			TOTAL	MONEY
Akane Ohshiro	75	69	68	212	645,165
Mi Hyun Kim	72	72	68	212	645,165
Gail Graham	70	70	72	212	645,165
Wendy Doolan	71	69	72	212	645,165
Cindy McCurdy	65	72	75	212	645,165

Itoen Ladies

Great Island Club, Chonan, Chiba
Par 36-36–72; 6,376 yards

November 12-14
purse, ¥60,000,000

	SCORES			TOTAL	MONEY
Yuri Fudoh	68	71	68	207	¥10,800,000
Aki Nakano	68	69	71	208	5,280,000
Mitsuko Kawasaki	73	70	68	211	3,900,000
Kumiko Hiyoshi	73	68	70	211	3,900,000
Michiko Okada	71	72	69	212	3,000,000
Kaori Higo	73	73	67	213	2,400,000
Shin Sora	71	75	68	214	1,800,000
Michiko Hattori	71	72	71	214	1,800,000
Mineko Nasu	69	72	73	214	1,800,000
Nahoko Hirao	71	73	71	215	1,155,000
Fumiko Muraguchi	70	72	73	215	1,155,000
Hee-Won Han	72	74	70	216	900,000
Junko Omote	76	68	72	216	900,000
Nayoko Yoshikawa	73	71	72	216	900,000
Hsiu-Feng Tseng	74	69	73	216	900,000
Young-Me Lee	72	70	74	216	900,000
Woo-Soon Ko	71	69	76	216	900,000
Junko Yasui	73	74	70	217	630,000
Fuki Kido	72	73	72	217	630,000
Jae-Sook Won	68	76	73	217	630,000
Shoko Asano	72	76	70	218	546,000
Harumi Sakagami	71	75	72	218	546,000
Kyoko Ono	76	69	73	218	546,000
Ai-Yu Tu	74	73	72	219	468,000
Aiko Hashimoto	70	76	73	219	468,000
Ritsu Imahori	71	75	73	219	468,000
Kozue Azuma	71	75	73	219	468,000
Mayumi Murai	74	72	73	219	468,000
Yuko Moriguchi	73	73	73	219	468,000
Mayumi Hirase	74	70	75	219	468,000
Keiko Arai	69	74	76	219	468,000
Midori Yoneyama	74	69	76	219	468,000
Aki Takamura	70	70	79	219	468,000

Daio Seishi Elleair Ladies Open

Elleair Golf Club, Matsuyama, Ehime
Par 36-36–72; 6,352 yards

November 19-21
purse, ¥75,000,000

	SCORES			TOTAL	MONEY
Mayumi Hirase	69	68	69	206	¥13,500,000
Michie Ohba	69	68	70	207	6,600,000
Kaori Higo	71	67	70	208	4,500,000

	SCORES			TOTAL	MONEY
Aki Nakano	68	72	68	208	4,500,000
Chikako Matsuzawa	68	69	71	208	4,500,000
Aki Takamura	71	70	69	210	3,000,000
Rie Murata	72	71	69	212	2,250,000
Harumi Sakagami	71	70	71	212	2,250,000
Mikino Kubo	72	69	71	212	2,250,000
Yuka Irie	72	72	69	213	1,500,000
Kumiko Hiyoshi	71	73	70	214	1,275,000
Fumiko Muraguchi	71	73	70	214	1,275,000
Yuri Fudoh	70	71	73	214	1,275,000
Ok-Hee Ku	69	71	74	214	1,275,000
Toshimi Kimura	70	74	71	215	937,500
Miyuki Shimabukuro	71	72	72	215	937,500
Mayumi Murai	72	71	72	215	937,500
Yuri Kawanami	69	73	73	215	937,500
Junko Yasui	71	70	74	215	937,500
Ai-Yu Tu	72	72	72	216	667,500
Masaki Maeda	73	71	72	216	667,500
Ayako Okamoto	70	73	73	216	667,500
Hiromi Takamura	74	70	72	216	667,500
Hsiu-Feng Tseng	71	72	73	216	667,500
Lee Oh-Soon	74	69	73	216	667,500
Takayo Bandoh	73	69	74	216	667,500
Orie Fujino	74	70	73	217	585,000
Ae-Sook Kim	71	72	74	217	585,000
Michiko Hattori	70	76	71	217	585,000
Jae-Sook Won	73	74	70	217	585,000

Japan LPGA Meiji Nyugyo Cup

Hibiscus Golf Club, Miyazaki
Par 36-36–72; 6,466 yards

November 25-28
purse, ¥60,000,000

	SCORES				TOTAL	MONEY
Kaori Higo	70	67	68	70	275	¥10,800,000
Ok-Hee Ku	72	70	69	68	279	5,400,000
Mineko Nasu	69	68	74	71	282	3,600,000
Mayumi Hirase	71	72	71	69	283	3,000,000
Man-Soo Kim	72	72	69	71	284	2,100,000
Mayumi Murai	72	72	72	69	285	1,980,000
Kyoko Ono	71	70	72	73	286	1,740,000
Jae-Sook Won	70	72	71	73	286	1,740,000
Aki Takamura	72	72	69	73	286	1,740,000
Yuri Fudoh	70	74	75	68	287	1,440,000
Fuki Kido	72	73	69	73	287	1,440,000
Yukiyo Haga	71	70	72	74	287	1,440,000
Kasumi Fujii	66	75	76	72	289	1,290,000
Aki Nakano	74	69	71	75	289	1,290,000
Lee Oh-Soon	73	73	77	67	290	1,170,000
Kasumi Adachi	70	75	71	74	290	1,170,000
Yuko Moriguchi	76	71	72	72	291	966,000
Michiko Okada	69	73	75	74	291	966,000
Hsiu-Feng Tseng	72	73	72	74	291	966,000
Ayako Okamoto	76	72	69	74	291	966,000
Michiko Hattori	71	70	72	78	291	966,000
Harumi Sakagami	74	73	73	72	292	825,000
Akane Ohshiro	77	71	71	73	292	825,000

	SCORES				TOTAL	MONEY
Fumiko Muraguchi	76	69	76	72	293	735,000
Ae-Sook Kim	74	73	73	73	293	735,000
Huang Yu-Chen	75	70	74	74	293	735,000
Yuri Kawanami	77	71	71	74	293	735,000
Yuka Irie	73	70	76	75	294	645,000
Young-Me Lee	75	72	71	76	294	645,000
Megumi Matsuo	70	77	71	77	295	570,000